All the
MEN
of the Bible

Books in This Series

All the Apostles of the Bible

All the Divine Names and Titles in the Bible

All the Doctrines of the Bible

All the Men of the Bible

All the Messianic Prophecies of the Bible

All the Miracles of the Bible

All the Parables of the Bible

All the Prayers of the Bible

All the Promises of the Bible

All the Women of the Bible

All the

MEN

of the Bible

ZONDERVAN®

ZONDERVAN

All the Men/All the Women Compilation SC
Copyright © 2005 by Herbert Lockyer

All the Men of the Bible
Copyright © 1958 by Herbert Lockyer

All the Women of the Bible
Copyright © 1967 by The Zondervan Corporation
Formerly published as *The Women of the Bible*

Requests for information should be addressed to:
Zondervan, 3900 *Sparks Dr. SE, Grand Rapids, Michigan 49546*

ISBN 978-0-310-60588-1

Printed in the United States of America

15 16 17 18 19 20 /DCI/ 30 29 28 27 26 25 24 23 22 21 20 19 18 17 16

ABOUT THE AUTHOR

DEDICATED TO
BERT AND JEFF DUVALL, OF TEXAS,
WHOSE GENEROSITY KNOWS NO BOUNDS

ABOUT THE AUTHOR

Dr. Herbert Lockyer was born in London in 1886 and held pastorates in Scotland and England for twenty-five years before coming to the United States in 1935.

In 1937 he received the honorary Doctor of Divinity degree from Northwestern Evangelical Seminary.

In 1955 he returned to England where he lived for many years. He then returned to the United States where he continued to devote time to the writing ministry until his death in November of 1984.

All poetry is but a giving of names.
Biography is the only true history:
History is the garb of biography.
Thomas Carlyle

The beginning of all instruction is the study of names.
—*Antisthenes,* c. 400 B.C.

Contents

Below is a partial list of the major and familiar male characters of the Bible covered in this book, alphabetically arranged for easy reference:

The Romantic History
of Bible Names

I

The Romantic History
of Bible Names

Many readers of the Bible treat its genealogical lists as despised regions, and wonder why they form part of a divine revelation such as the Bible is. At first glance, there seems to be no point or profit in the bare enumeration of the names of men who died thousands of years ago.

Yet because the Bible is the inspired Word of God, even these uninteresting lists of names were written for our learning, and if properly studied they yield remarkable results. Many of these names describe nations, as well as men, and have therefore a priceless historical value. Consulting them, we find they often show the course taken by men in their settlement over the earth. Ancient Hebrew names, which at first sight might appear unattractive, and are passed over as unworthy of serious thought, have something about them which compels our prayerful consideration. In many cases Bible names are fragments of ancient history, revelations of divine purposes, expressions of hopes and prophecies of the future.

Every Jew kept a record of his lineage and was proud if he could claim royal or priestly descent. Joseph, for example, could boast of himself as "a son of David." The genealogical lists of Chronicles, Ezra, Nehemiah, Matthew and Luke, containing the majority of named men, prove how meticulous the Jews were in the preservation of their pedigree. It was common in almost every Jewish family to transcribe a family tree.

Josephus, the Jewish historian who lived in the time of our Lord, tells us that he could trace his ancestry back to the Maccabeans, or priest-rulers, from public registers. He also states that wherever Jews settled such registers were kept of births and marriages of the priesthood, and that registers went back some two thousand years. That the Israelites were most interested in the preservation of their pedigree can be proven by I Chronicles 9:1. The forfeit of those tribes who had lost their pedigree is seen in Ezra 2:59 and Nehemiah 7:63.

Truth taught by names is another important aspect to observe. The significance of names opens up a field of pleasant and profitable investigation to all true lovers of Scripture. While many of the names may not have been designed to be typical, they are certainly suggestive of spiritual truth, as can be seen in the names Jacob gave his sons.

11

In ancient Israel the name of a person was supposed to indicate some characteristic of that person, or be linked to circumstances, however trivial or monotonous, connected with his birth. Names and nature, as well as names and facts, were made to correspond, as can be found in the name Moses gave his son (Ex. 2:22), and the naming of Ichabod (I Sam. 4:21). As we review the suggested meanings given to the names alphabetically set forth in the following chapter, we will find that they cover many associations.

Names denote natural or personal qualities. A classic illustration of this is Abigail's plea to David for her worthless husband: "...as his name is, so is he: Nabal is his name and folly is with him" (I Sam. 25:25). Nabal means "fool." In effect then, Abigail said, "Pay no attention to my husband. He's a fool by name, and a fool by nature."

Names point to an occupation. There are many instances of these occupational names: Archippus, "governor of horses"; Asa, "physician"; Carmi, "vine-dresser."

Names bear a symbolic or prophetic feature. An instance of this is seen in the name Shear-jashub, "a remnant shall return" (Isa. 7:3). Maher-shalal-hash-baz, one of the longest names in the Bible, means "Haste ye, haste ye, to the spoil" (Isa. 8:1).

Names are fixed immediately after birth. In the choice of a name for a child, the mother usually exercised such a privilege (Gen. 19:37; 29:32). Sometimes, however, the father chose the name (Gen. 4:26; 16:15). Occasionally other interested persons came forward with a name (Ruth 4:17; Luke 1:57-63).

John the Baptist and Christ had names divinely given *before* their birth (Luke 1:13; Matt. 1:21).

Names are bestowed indifferently on men and women. Now and again a man and a woman bear the same name, for example, Abihail (Esther 2:15; I Chron. 2:29). Then persons and places have the same name. Did you know that Eden is the name of a man as well as the garden where Adam first lived, and that Bethlehem is the name of a person as well as the town where Jesus was born?

Names are connected with family relationships. A few names are taken from relatives (Luke 1:59). Ahab means "father's brother"; Ahban, "brother is son"; Ahiam, "maternal uncle." Ab means "father," so we have many names beginning with these letters, such as Abimelech ("whose father is king").

Names carry a religious relationship or significance. Sometimes a name expressed some hope or aspiration on the part of parents, as in John, meaning, "gracious gift of God." Other names (such as Samuel, meaning "God hath heard") were conceived in the spirit of prayer because they expressed religious expectation on behalf of the child. This name marks the fact that the child was born in answer to prayer.

Ancient peoples fashioned names out of the names of their gods, proved in Pan-Bel-adagal, meaning "I look to Bel," and in other heathen names in which gods are invoked. This also characterizes many Hebrew names into which the idea of God enters freely. The divine name *El*, meaning "God," is incorporated within many proper names of persons, as in Israel or Eliakim. The same is true of names containing *Jah*, or *Jeho*, as in Jahaziah and Jehoiakim. Other names extol divine sovereignty, as in Adonijah, meaning, "Jehovah is Lord."

Names are changed by God's direct intervention. Many names were not only given by God but changed by His direction: Abram to Abraham; Sarai to Sarah; Jacob to Israel; Oshea to Joshua.

Names deemed important had an acute consciousness of meaning. This fact is borne out in such names as Reuben, "see, a son"; Judah, "praise"; Joseph, "he adds." At times, given names reflect the characteristics of the parents, which the children inherited. Weak, indecisive parents were likely to coin weak, indecisive names for their children who manifested character in keeping with their names.

Names are from the vegetable world. We have many instances of names of this order: Adam, "red earth"; Elah, "oak"; Asnah, "bramble"; Shamar, "thorn."

Names are associated with natural objects in the world: Geshem, "rain"; Barak, "lightning"; Boanerges, "sons of thunder"; Adoni-Bezek, "lightning of the Lord."

Names are taken from the animal creation: Caleb, "dog"; Dan, "lion's whelp"; Shaphan, "rock-badger"; Achbor, "mouse"; Parosh, "flea."

Names, separate or double, of the same person are frequent. Some examples are: "Saul who is called Paul," "Simon Barjonas," "Simon Zelotes," "Judas Iscariot." Alongside of these double names we have those men who carry a distinguished and honorable surname.

By "surname" is meant an additional name — a name to be distinguished from the "Christian" name, the name over and above, a *sur-*, or *super-*name. As surnames, as we presently know them, were unknown among the Hebrews, the word as used in the Bible simply means the bestowal of a flattering or honorable title. Foreigners, envious of the privileges of the Jews, were eager to surname themselves by the name of Israel, that is, be enrolled as members of the Jewish nation (Isa. 44:5). God surnamed Cyrus, meaning that He gave him the honored title of "my shepherd," thereby appointing him to be His instrument for the restoration of His people (Isa. 44:28).

In the New Testament the custom of bestowing this kind of surname was becoming more widespread, for example, Simon surnamed Peter (Acts 10:5, 32); James and John surnamed Boanerges (Mark 3:17); Judas surnamed Iscariot (Luke 22:3).

Then we have names to which labels are attached indicating work or worth such as Elijah the Tishbite, Nehemiah the king's cupbearer, John the Baptist, James the Lord's brother and Luke the beloved physician.

When some of these persons experienced a changed life, why permit them to carry an appendage so suggestive of the old, worthless life? If Mary Magdalene was no longer demon-possessed, why continue to write of her, "out of whom went seven devils"? It may be that the wearers of some of these labels carried them so as not to forget the past. They were not to forget the pit from whence they had been digged (Isa. 51:1). Perhaps they were retained that those who bore them might maintain a fitting humility.

We conclude this first section of our study with two features suggested by Elsdon C. Smith, in his most enlightening book, *Story of Our Names*.

1. *The Treasure of a Name.* How true it was when Solomon declared that "a good name is rather to be chosen than great riches" (Prov. 22:1). A name is not only a person's most prominent feature to others, but his greatest treasure. The old Roman proverb states, "without a name a man is nothing." Because "a good name is better than precious ointment" (Eccl. 7:1), all who bear good names should pray for grace to live in harmony with them.

2. *The Abiding Influence of Bible Names.* Do we realize the tremendous influence of the Bible on our surnames and Christian names? It is reckoned that more than half the people of the civilized world have names originating from the Bible's vast collection.

With the publication of the Genevan Bible in 1560, the adoption of Bible names became popular. The common people, now interested in Biblical characters, had a long list of names from which to choose, and baptismal registers became records of Bible names. Elsdon C. Smith tells us that about the only Old Testament names used with any frequency before the Protestant Reformation were Adam, Elias, Samson, David, Solomon, Daniel, Joseph and Benjamin. After the Reformation the type of name changed. Because of the Puritan hatred of Roman Catholicism saints' names were avoided. Names like Elijah, Moses, Aaron, Joshua and Nathaniel became popular. English names not in the Bible were rejected as pagan. Even the longest name in the Bible, Maher-shalal-hash-baz, was often used.

Today many of our most frequently used Christian names and surnames are traceable directly to the Bible, particularly to the New Testament. Over a century ago Old Testament names were more prominent. Now *John* for a boy and *Mary* for a girl hold the lead.

The Alphabetical Order of
All Men Named in the Bible

II

The Alphabetical Order of All Men Named in The Bible

The Bible revolves around personalities and, as Augustine expressed it, "The sacred record, like a faithful mirror has no flattery in its portrait." The biographies of men outside the Bible sometimes leave us cold. The characters portrayed seem to be too ideal. Nothing is said about their faults, weaknesses and sins. But as we pursue our journey through the Scriptures, we are greatly encouraged, for here are those of like passions as ourselves.

In his arresting chapter on "Composite Portraits," in *The Joy of Bible Study*, Harrington Lees reminds us that

> ...the lives of men and women who speak to us from the pages of Scripture may be a veritable gold-mine of experience to us if we can remember the fact that they lived similar lives and triumphed—by faith, as the writer to the Hebrews reminds us—or, if they entered not into their land of promise, failed through disobedience or unbelief. All good biography is fruitful, but Scripture biography is singularly so.

The Bible is the most faithful book in the world. It tells the truth about its men and women. We have the tendency to eulogize our heroes, omitting altogether their faults. But the Bible gives us a true picture; light or shade, good or evil are depicted without apology or excuse. It is a wonderful canvas of human life. Every phase of human nature is exhibited in the portraits of the Bible gallery.

Because of the limitations of space we were not able to give a full synopsis of the Bible men biographically treated. For those who desire to follow this line of study the following suggestions may be of service.

Begin with a person whose story is briefly told. Enoch, for example, only occupies six or seven verses, yet what a story they unfold. Mastering a character like Enoch whets the appetite for the study of another who fills a larger niche in the Bible's gallery of saints.

Collect all relevant Bible passages. It is essential, with the aid of a concordance, to gather into a group all references to the person to be studied.

Analyze the character of the person. Read and reread gathered Bible material with a pencil in hand, noting particular or peculiar traits.

Set down the elements of power and success. Show how heredity or personal ability produce these elements.

17

Describe evidences of weakness and failure. Indicate the circumstances responsible for these.

Elaborate on victory over difficulties. There is rich material along this line in characters like Joseph, David and Paul.

Suggest various helps to success. In some Bible lives there were many paths to fame and honor.

Mark out any privileges abused. When dealing with a person such as Esau, it is easy to sketch his loss.

Depict opportunities for good neglected, or how the opportunities could have been improved.

Fill in details of the life. Recorded facts of birth, parentage, death, etc., should be mentioned.

Summarize the lessons to be learned from the life. The lives of great men remind us that we too can make our lives sublime!

Note any relation the person may have had to God or to Jesus Christ. Divine relationship shapes character and determines destiny.

Study the authors who have written on Biblical characters. Once you have undertaken personal study, there is a wide field of literature to choose from, such as the books listed in the bibliography.

It has been a painstaking yet profitable task to acquaint oneself with the thousands of named and unnamed men of the Bible. With the majority of them, it has been a mere handshake and the simple questions: "Who are you? Where were you born? What is your background?"

For the most part we have nothing but the monotony of their names. Their human history was not written for our learning. We know nothing of the facts of their families, their sorrows or songs, their tears or triumphs, their vices or virtues. In the company of others, however, we lingered longer, seeing that the Divine Artist sketched their profiles in fuller detail.

Nowhere in all the world have we such an album of human life. The Bible's portrait gallery is superb. What a mixture of character it presents! Here you will find kings and knaves, princes and paupers, the tenderhearted and the traitorous, saints and sinners, the courageous and the cowardly. Here we have men of like passions as ourselves. No wonder the Bible speaks of itself as a *mirror.* As we look at the lives of its men, pure and profane, we see ourselves.

The formidable assignment of alphabetically arranging *all* the men of the Bible appeared when it was discovered that there are well over three thousand specifically named.

How rich in biographical material the Bible is! A distinguishing feature of Holy Writ is its faithfulness in recording human life and character. What a perfect biography of humanity it is! Think of what we can learn from —

The lowly life of Mephibosheth
The tried friendship of Ittai

The holy fidelity of Nathan
The lofty courage of Benaiah
The patriarchal kindness of Barzillai
The princely courtesy of Araunah.

Then there are those men who stand out as beacons, lights, warning us of dangerous vices, such as —

Joab's deeds of blood
Ammon's intemperate passion
Absalom's base ambition
Shimei's violence and meanness
David's fatal lapses.

There are also saints at hand to encourage and guide heavenly pilgrims of every age. Think of the variety covered by the men of the Bible! We have —

Abraham for explorers
Job for merchant princes
Moses for patriots
Samuel for rulers
Elijah for reformers
Joseph for men of distinction
Daniel for the forlorn
Jeremiah for the persecuted
Caleb for the soldier
Boaz for the farmer
Amos for the lay-preacher.

Well, all the men of the Bible, from A to Z are lined up for us, so let us go out and make their acquaintance, shall we? And as we meet each one of them, may help be ours to emulate their graces but shun their failures.

A

AARON [Aâr' on]—A MOUNTAIN OF STRENGTH or ENLIGHTENED. *The son of Amran and of Jochebed* his wife, and of the family of Kohath, who was the second son of Levi, who was the third son of Jacob. Miriam was Aaron's elder sister and Moses was his junior brother by some three years. Aaron married Elisheba, daughter of Amminadab and sister of Naashon, and by her had four sons — Nadab and Abihu, Eleazar and Ithamar (Ex. 6:16–23).

The Man Who Was an Excellent Speaker

It is somewhat fitting that Aaron should not only begin the list of men under the letter A—one of the longest lists of all—but also of all the men listed alphabetically in the Bible.

The first glimpse we have of this great Bible saint is that of an eloquent speaker, and because of this fact he was chosen by God to be the prophet and spokesman of his brother Moses in his encounters with Pharaoh. The fame of his oratory was known in heaven, and recognized by God. A great orator has been defined as a good man well-skilled in speaking, and of such capacities was Aaron. When Moses protested against appearing before Pharaoh, pleading that he was not eloquent, but slow of speech and of a slow tongue (Ex. 3:10; 4:11, 12) did he refer to a defect of speech he suffered from? "Not eloquent" means, *not a man of words* and "slow of speech, and of a slow tongue" means *heavy of speech and heavy of tongue.*

There are those authorities who suggest that Moses had a stammer or lisp, a physical impediment of speech necessitating a spokesman of Aaron's ability. It would seem as if God's promise that He would be with his mouth and was able to help him overcome any disability as a speaker, bears out the thought of an actual defect of speech. This we do know, Aaron must have spoken with great power when he addressed Pharaoh on the signs and plagues of Exodus four through eleven.

Aaron plays an important part in the inauguration and development of priestly functions, all of which are prescribed in Leviticus. Among the mature males of Israel there were three classes:

From the tribes of Israel came the *warriors.*

From the tribe of Levi came the *workers.*

From the family of Aaron came the *worshipers.*

Aaron became the first high priest of Israel, and in Aaron and his sons we have a fitting type of Christ and His Church. The ministry of Aaron in connection with the Tabernacle with all of its services is referred to by the writer of the Hebrews as a figure of the true ministry of the High Priest who is Jesus.

Yet in spite of his high and holy calling, Aaron suffered from the murmurings of the people (Ex. 16:2; Num. 14:2). He was persuaded by the people to make a golden calf and was reproved by Moses for his action (Ex. 32). Aaron's penitence, however, was complete, and his service faithful. Perhaps Aaron could be placed at the head of all Old Testament penitents, for his own sins as well as for the sins of others. While Aaron was Jesus Christ in type and by imputation, he yet remains Aaron all the time, Aaron of the molten image and of many untold transgressions besides. With Moses, Aaron was excluded from the Promised Land (Num. 20:12). He died at the age of 123 years on Mount Hor, in the land of Edom, and was buried there (Num. 20).

A profitable meditation on "The Priestly Calling" could be developed along the line of the following suggestions.

I. Aaron was a type of Christ, the Great High Priest.

    A. Both were chosen of God. Christ is the only mediator between God and man.

    B. Both had to be clean, seeing they bore the vessels of the Lord. Aaron was a sinner and needed cleansing—Christ was sinless.

    C. Both are clothed—Aaron with his coat, robe and ephod; Christ robed in garments of glory and beauty.

D. Both are crowned—Aaron with his mitre, or holy crown, Christ with His many diadems.

E. Both are consecrated or set apart—Aaron was blood sprinkled and had his hands filled for the Lord (Lev. 8:24–27); Christ is sanctified forever (John 17:16, 17).

F. Both feed on the bread of consecration (cf. Lev. 22:21, 22 with John 4:32).

G. Both are blameless. No man with a blemish could come nigh to offer a sacrifice unto the Lord. Christ was holy, harmless, undefiled.

II. Aaron's sons were types of the Christian. What a precious truth the priesthood of all true believers is.

A. They had names closely associated. "Aaron and his sons" appears ten times. Aaron's sons were called *in* him. We were chosen *in* Christ from the eternal past. *Priests* because *sons*, is true in both cases.

B. They had the same calling. Aaron and his sons were priests. Christ and ourselves are priests unto God.

C. They had the same anointing. Aaron and his sons were accepted by the same blood and anointed with the same oil. Christ entered the veil by His own blood, and we enter by the same blood. Head and members alike are anointed with the same blessed Spirit.

D. They had their hands filled with the same offering, ate the same food, were under the same authority. How these aspects are likewise applicable to Christ and His own!

ABAGTHA [Ă băg′ thă]—HAPPY, PROSPEROUS. *One of the seven chamberlains* or eunuchs sent by king Ahasuerus to fetch his queen, Vashti, to the banquet (Esther 1:10, 11).

ABDA [Ăb′ dă]—SERVANT OT WORSHIPER.
1. *Father of Adoniram,* Solomon's officer in charge of forced levy (I Kings 4:6).
2. *A chief Levite* after the exile, the son of Shemaiah or Shammua (Neh. 11:17). He is called Obadiah in I Chronicles 9:16.

ABDEEL [Ăb′ de el]—SERVANT OF GOD. *The father of Shelemiah,* and one of those ordered by king Jehoiakim to arrest Jeremiah and Baruch (Jer. 36:26).

ABDI [Ăb′ dĭ]—SERVANT OF JEHOVAH.
1. *Grandfather of Ethan,* a Merarite, and one of those set over the service of song by David (I Chron. 6:44).
2. *A son of Elam,* who had married a foreign wife (Ezra 10:26).

ABDIEL [Ăb′ dĭ el]—SERVANT OF GOD. *The son of Guni,* a Gadite of Gilead (I Chron. 5:15).

ABDON [Ăb' dŏn]—SERVILE, SERVICE or CLOUD OF JUDGMENT.
1. *A son of Hillel,* the Pirathonite, Abdon judged Israel for eight years, and because of a plurality of wives, had forty sons and thirty nephews, who rode seventy ass colts (Judg. 12:13–15). Perhaps the same as Bedan in I Samuel 12:11.
2. *A Benjamite* in Jerusalem (I Chron. 8:23).
3. *The first-born of Jehiel* from Maachah (I Chron. 8:30; 9:36).
4. *A son of Micah* sent with others by king Josiah to Huldah the prophetess to enquire of Jehovah regarding the Book of the Law found in the Temple (II Chron. 34:20). Called Achbor in II Kings 22:12. Also the name of a Levitical city in Asher (Josh. 21:30; I Chron. 6:74).

ABEDNEGO (Ă bĕd'–ne gō]—SERVANT OF NEBO or SERVANT OF LIGHT. The name given by the prince of the eunuchs of King Nebuchadnezzar to Azariah, one of the four young princes of Judah who were carried away into Babylon. He was one of the three faithful Jews delivered from the fiery furnace (Dan. 1:7; 2:49; 3). How God honored the faith and courage of these Hebrew youths!

The Man Who Defied a King

There are at least four lessons to be learned from the dauntless, defiant witness of Abed-nego and his two companions:
I. God's dearest servants are sometimes called to pass through heavy trials.
II. God is able to deliver when help seems farthest off. He does not promise to keep us free *from* trouble, but that He will be with us *in* trouble.
III. God's permitted furnace purifies, but never destroys us. As we pass through the fire, He is with us and we cannot be burned.
IV. God's children must never be ashamed of Him. No matter how adverse the situation, we must be bold and unshaken in our witness.

ABEL [Ā' bĕl]—MEADOW, VANITY or VAPOR. *The second son of Adam and Eve* slain by his brother Cain (Gen. 4:1–15; Matt. 23:35; Heb. 11:4; 12:24).

The Man Who Was First to Die

Abel's name, meaning breath or vapor, is associated with the shortness of his life. What was his life but a vapor? (Ps. 90 : 6; Jas. 4:14) Abel was a shepherd and a possessor of flocks and herds; Cain was a tiller of the ground. It was not occupation, however, that parted these first two brothers in the world, but their conception of what was pleasing and acceptable to God. Abel feared God and because he did, he offered to God the best of his flock. His was a sacrifice of blood and represented the surrender of a heart to God. Cain brought what he had gathered from the earth, an offering representing his own effort. Because God accepted Abel's offering and not Cain's, the angry brother slew Abel in the field. But Abel's blood cried from the ground for punishment. Abel's blood is placed alongside Christ's shed blood

(Heb. 12:24), which is better than Abel's in that his blood cried out for vengeance but the blood of Christ cries out for mercy. Abel's blood, although the blood of a righteous man (Matt. 23:35), cannot atone, but Christ's blood is ever efficacious (I John 1:7). Abel is unique among Bible men in a fourfold direction:

He was the first one of the human race to die.

He was the first person on the earth to be murdered.

He was the first man to be associated with Christ.

He was the first saint to present an offering acceptable to God.

Abel is also the name given to geographical locations (I Sam. 6:18; II Sam. 20:14).

ABIA, ABIAH [Ă bĭ' ă, Ă bĭ' ah]—JEHOVAH IS FATHER.

1. *The second son of Samuel* the prophet and judge of Israel, Abia, with his brother Joel or Vashni, judged so unworthily as to force Israel to desire a king (I Sam. 8:2; I Chron. 6:28).

2. *A son of Rehoboam* (I Chron. 3:10; Matt. 1:7). Called Abijam in I Kings 14:31; 15:6–8.

3. *The seventh son of Becher* the son of Benjamin (I Chron 7:8).

4. *A priest* in the days of David, appointed to service in the Tabernacle (Luke 1:5). Also the name of the wife of Hezron, grandson of Judah by Pharez (I Chron. 2:24). Our study of Bible men will bring out the fact that the same name is often borne by both men and women.

ABIALBON [Ă' bĭ–ăl' bŏn]—FATHER OF STRENGTH. *One of David's heroes* who came from Beth-arabah (II Sam. 23:31). He is called Abiel in I Chronicles 11:32.

ABIASAPH [Ă bĭ' a săph]—REMOVER OF REPROACH or FATHER OF GATHERING. *The third son of Korah,* first-born of Izhar, second son of Kohath (Ex. 6:24).

ABIATHAR [Ă bĭ' a thär]—FATHER OF SUPERFLUITY or EXCELLENT FATHER. *Son of Ahimelech* and the eleventh high priest in succession from Aaron (I Sam. 22:20–22; 23:6, 9).

Abiathar escaped and fled to David in the cave of Adullam when Doeg the Edomite slew his father and eighty-five priests. He went back to Jerusalem with the Ark when David fled from Absalom. He was joint high-priest with Zadok and conspired to make Adonijah king. He rebelled against David in his old age, was spared by Solomon for the sake of his first love, but dismissed from office for his treachery at the last.

ABIDA, ABIDAH [Ă bĭ' dă, Ă bĭ' dah]—FATHER OF KNOWLEDGE. *The fourth son of Midian,* the fourth son of Keturah and Abraham (Gen. 25:4; I Chron. 1:33).

ABIDAN [Ăb′ i dăn]—THE FATHER JUDGETH. *A Benjamite chieftain,* the son of Gideoni and representative prince in the taking of the census (Num. 1:11; 2:22; 7:60, 65; 10:24).

ABIEL [Ă bī′ el]—FATHER OF STRENGTH.

1. *Son of Zeror* and father of Ner and of Kish and grandfather of Saul, Israel's first king (I Sam. 9:1; 14:51).

2. *One of David's* heroes from Beth-arabah (I Chron. 11:32). Called Abi-albon in II Sam. 23:31.

ABIEZER [Ă bī ẽ′ zûr]—FATHER OF HELP or IN HELP.

1. *The son of Hammoleketh,* who was the sister of Machir and daughter of Manasseh. Gideon belonged to this family (Josh. 17:2; Judg. 6:11; I Chron. 7:18). Perhaps the same as Jeezer (Num. 26:30).

2. *An Anethothite,* one of David's thirty-seven chief heroes, who had command of the army during the ninth month (II Sam. 23:27; I Chron. 11:28; 27:12). Also the name of a district (Judg. 6:34).

ABIGIBEON [Ă bī gĭb′ e on]—FATHER OF GIBEON. *A descendant of Benjamin* who dwelt at Gibeon, whose family afterwards settled in Jerusalem (I Chron. 8:29).

ABIHAIL [Ăb i hā′ il]—FATHER OF MIGHT.

1. *A Levite,* father of Zuriel, the chief of the Merarites in the time of Moses (Num. 3:35).

2. *The head of a family* of the tribe of Gad (I Chron. 5:14).

3. *The father of Esther,* the niece of Mordecai who became Queen of Persia in the place of Vashti (Esther 2:15; 9:29).

Abihail occurs as a woman's name two times in the Bible (I Chron. 2:29; II Chron. 11:18).

ABIHU [Ă bī′ hū]—HE IS MY FATHER. *The second son of Aaron,* who was destroyed with his brother Nadab for offering strange, or unauthorized fire upon the altar (Ex. 6:23; 24:1, 9; 28:1; Lev. 10:1, 2).

ABIHUD [Ă bī′ hud]—FATHER OF HONOR or OF MAJESTY. *A son of Bela,* son of Benjamin (I Chron. 8:3).

ABIJAH, ABIAH, ABIA [Ă bī′ jah, Ă bī′ ah, Ă bī′ ă]—JEHOVAH IS MY FATHER or FATHER OF THE SEA.

1. *A son of Jeroboam* who died in his youth (I Kings 14:1).

2. *A priest in David's time* who was head of the eighth course in Temple service (I Chron. 24:10). See Abiah.

3. *Son and successor of Rehoboam* whose mother was Maachah, Absalom's daughter (II Chron. 11:20, 22; 12:16; 13; 14:1). Called Abijam in I Kings 14:31. See Abia.

4. *A priest* who sealed the covenant made by Nehemiah and the

people to serve the Lord. As further references are encountered to this act, it will be borne in mind that it represented the re-dedication of the people to the worship and work of God after their return from the Babylonian captivity.

5. *Another priest* who returned from exile. Perhaps the same person as the preceding Abijah (Neh. 12:1–4, 12–17). Also the name of the mother of Hezekiah, king of Judah (II Chron. 29:1; she is also called Abi, II Kings 18:2).

ABIJAM [Ă bī′ jăm]—FATHER OF LIGHT. *Rehoboam's son* (I Kings 14:31; 15:1–8). Called Abijah in II Chronicles.

ABIMAEL [Ă bĭm′ a el]—MY FATHER IS GOD. *A son of Joktan of the family of Shem* (Gen. 10:26–28; I Chron. 1:20–22).

ABIMELECH [Ă bĭm′ e lĕch]—FATHER OF THE KING.
1. *A king of Gerar* in the time of Abraham (Gen. 20; 21:22–32; 26:1–16, 26–31).

The Man Who Rebuked Another for Lying

Abimelech would have taken Sarah, Abraham's wife, into his harem, but learning that she was the wife of another, returned her uninjured. Abraham appears here in a bad light. He deceived Abimelech, but when found out was justly rebuked by the God-restrained Abimelech. Certainly the righteous should rebuke the ungodly (I Tim. 5:20), but how sad it is when the ungodly have just reason for rebuking the righteous. What a degradation it was for Abraham, then, to be rebuked by a heathen king!

Abraham sought to palliate his deception by claiming that Sarah was actually his half sister, daughter of the same father but not the same mother (Gen. 20:12, 16).

A lie if half a truth
Is ever the worst of lies.

Abraham was the more blameworthy because he had done the same thing before (Gen. 12) and had suffered much in the same way as upon this occasion. How grateful Abimelech was for the dream warning him of his danger! The covenant made with Abraham is somewhat significant —

I. It was proposed by Abimelech who, although knowing how Abraham had failed God, yet saw how favored he was of God (Gen. 21:22).

II. It revealed certain distrust of Abraham. Abimelech requested Abraham not to be tempted to sin in such a direction again (Gen. 21:23).

III. It was meant to secure Abraham's good will. The king desired the favor of the wandering pilgrim who had failed to act kingly. Abraham consented to the king's request (Gen. 21:24).

IV. It gave Abraham the opportunity of rebuking Abimelech. The matter of the stolen well had to be put right. Wrong had to be repudiated before a covenant could be agreed upon (Gen. 20:9; 21:23, 26).

V.   It secured for Abraham the inheritance of Beer-sheba, "the well of oath," which possession the patriarch sanctified (Gen. 21:27–33).

2.   *The son of Gideon* by a concubine in Shechem who belonged to a leading Canaanite family (Judg. 8:30, 31; 9; 10:1).

The Man Who Was Bramble King

This Abimelech, who made the first attempt to set up a monarchy in Israel, is known as "The Bramble King." But his violent and ill-fated reign over Israel only lasted for three years. After the death of Gideon his father, Abimelech took seventy pieces of silver from his mother's people with which he hired vain and light persons to follow him. He slew seventy persons of his father's house. Jotham, the youngest son of Gideon, who is also called Jerubbaal, hid himself and when Abimelech was proclaimed king by the men of Shechem, he revealed himself and warned the Shechemites against Abimelech in a parable about trees, from whence he received his nickname as "Bramble King." What a tragic death this would-be king of Israel suffered (Judg. 9: 53, 54)! A fitting end, surely, for one who sowed a Biblical city with salt (Judg. 9:45).

3.   *Son of Abiathar,* the high priest in David's time (I Chron. 18:16). Also known as Ahimlech.

4.   *A name given to Achish,* King of Gath (according to Ellicott), to whom David fled (I Sam. 21:10).

ABINADAB [Ă bĭn' a dăb]—FATHER or SOURCE OF LIBERALITY.

1.   *An Israelite* of the tribe of Judah in whose house the Ark rested after its return by the Philistines (I Sam. 7:1; II Sam. 6:3, 4; I Chron. 13:7).

2.   *The second son of Jesse,* the father of David (I Sam. 16:8; 17:13; I Chron. 2:13).

3.   *A son of King Saul* (I Sam. 31:2; I Chron. 8:33; 9:39; 10:2). He was slain along with his father and his brother Jonathan at Gilboa.

4.   *The father of one of Solomon's officers* (I Kings 4:11).

ABINOAM [Ă bĭn' o ăm]—FATHER OF PLEASANTNESS, OF BEAUTY or OF GRACE. *The father of Barak* (Judg. 4:6, 12; 5:11, 12).

ABIRAM [Ă bī' ram]—FATHER IS THE EXALTED ONE.

1.   *A son of Eliab, a Reubenite* who with others conspired against Moses and Aaron in the wilderness, and who perished with his fellow-conspirators (Num. 16:1–27; 26:9).

2.   *The first-born son of Hiel* the Bethelite, who began to rebuild Jericho, but who came under the curse foretold by Joshua (Josh. 6:26; I Kings 16:34).

ABISHAI, ABSHAI [Ă bĭsh' ă ī]—POSSESSOR OF ALL THAT IS DESIRABLE. *A son of. David's sister Zeruiah,* and a brother of Joab and Asahel. After his numerous victories against the Philistines, he became one of David's thirty heroes (I Sam. 26:6–9;.II Sam. 2:18, 24; 3:30; 10:10, 14). He is also called Abshai (I Chron. 18:12).

ABISHALOM [Ă bĭsh' a lom]—FATHER OF PEACE. *Father of Maachah,* who was the wife of Jeroboam (I Kings 15:2, 10). Called Absalom in II Chronicles 11:20, 21.

ABISHUA [Ă bĭsh' u ă]—FATHER OF SAFETY or OF SALVATION.
1. *A son of Phinehas,* who was the grandson of Aaron (I Chron. 6:5, 50; Ezra 7:5).
2. *A son of Bela,* the son of Benjamin (I Chron. 8:4).

ABISHUR [Ăb' i shur]—FATHER OF OXEN or OF A WALL. *A son of Shaminai,* who was the grandson of Jerahmeel, a Judahite (I Chron. 2:28, 29).

ABITUB [Ăb' ĭ tŭb]—FATHER or SOURCE OF GOODNESS. *A Benjamite,* son of Shahariam (I Chron. 8:11). Called Ahitub in the Common Version.

ABIUD [Ă bī' ud]—FATHER OF HONOR or OF TRUSTWORTHINESS. *A son of Zerubbabel,* and a member of the royal tribe from which Christ sprang (Matt. 1:13).

ABNER, ABINER [Ăb' nûr]—FATHER OF LIGHT. *The son of Ner,* cousin of Saul and captain of his army. Because of his relationship to the king and his force of character he exercised great influence during Saul's reign and afterwards (I Sam. 14:50, 51; 17:55, 57).

The Man Who Was Destitute of Lofty Ideals

Although Abner was the only capable person on the side of Saul and his family, he had little time for the lofty ideas of morality or religion (II Sam. 3:8, 16).

As Saul's commander-in-chief, he greatly helped his cousin to maintain his military prowess. After Saul's death, he set Ish-bosheth, Saul's son, on the throne.

As an enemy of Joab, David's general, he fought long and bravely against him, and after a severe defeat, killed Asahel in self-defense (II Sam. 2).

As a proud man, he resented most bitterly the remonstrance of Ish-bosheth, over the matter of Saul's concubines, and negotiated with David to make him king of Israel (II Sam. 3:7–22).

As an unprincipled man, he reaped what he sowed. Joab, dreading the loss of his own position, and thirsting for revenge, murdered Abner at Hebron. David gave him a public funeral, and afterwards charged Solomon to avenge Abner's murder (II Sam. 3:26–37; I Kings 2:5, 6).

ABRAM, ABRAHAM [Ā' brăm, Ā' bră hăm]—THE FATHER OF A MULTITUDE. The original name of the youngest son of Terah was Abram, meaning "father of height." Abraham was given to him when the promise of a numerous progeny was renewed to him by God (Gen. 11:26; 17:5, 9).

The Man Who Was God's Friend

Abraham's place in the Bible's portrait gallery is altogether unique and unapproachable. He stands out as a landmark in the spiritual history of the world. Chosen of God to become the father of a new spiritual race, the file leader of a mighty host, the revelation of God found in him one of its most important epochs. In himself, there was not much to make him worthy of such a distinction. His choice was all of grace.

Abraham's life is given us in detail, and we know him as we know few men of the Bible. He was from the great and populous city of Ur, and therefore a Gentile although he became the first Hebrew. He was a rough, simple, venerable Bedouin-like sheep master. He uttered no prophecy, wrote no book, sang no song, gave no laws. Yet in the long list of Bible saints he alone is spoken of as "the father of the faithful" and as "the friend of God" (Isa. 41:8). Let us briefly sketch his story and character.

I. He was born in Ur of the Chaldees, of parents who were heathen. Little is known of him until he was seventy years old, a striking proof that he had yielded himself to God before he left his heathen home for the far-off land of Canaan.

II. He received a distinct revelation from God, and of God, but we are not told how and when. This, however, we do know: He gave up a certainty for an uncertainty and went out not knowing whither he went. Willingly he surrendered the seen for the unseen.

III. He was taught the lesson of patience, of waiting upon the Eternal God. It was many years before the promise of God was fulfilled to him—promises three in number—of a *country*, Canaan; of *posterity*, as the stars of heaven; of a *spiritual seed*, through whom all the families of the earth would be blessed.

IV. He believed as he waited. His soul fed upon the promises of God. He believed God in the face of long delay and also amid difficulties that seemed insuperable. This is why he is called "the father of all them that believe."

V. He was renowned for his active, working, living faith (Gen. 15:6). Abraham believed in God and it was counted to him for righteousness.

VI. He was subject to failures. His character, like the sun, had its spots. Abraham's conduct to Hagar on two occasions, in sending her away, is painful to remember. Then his departure from Canaan into Egypt when the famine was on was surely not an act of faith. The falsehood which on two occasions he told with regard to Sarah his wife gives us a glimpse into a natural character somewhat cowardly, deceitful and distrustful (Gen. 12:19; 20:2).

VII. He was called to offer up special sacrifices. The first is fully described in Genesis fifteen, where the five victims offered in sacrifice to God were symbolic and typical of the whole Mosaic economy to come. Then we have the offering up of Isaac, an act of faith on Abraham's part and yet a trial of faith (Gen. 22). What a demand God made! But Abraham did not withhold his only son of promise. What God wanted was Abraham's heart, not Isaac's life. So when the knife was raised to slay Isaac, a provided substitute appeared. After this sacrifice Abraham received the testimony that he had pleased God.

The Bible offers us many types of Christ, Isaac being one of the chiefest, but Abraham is *the only type in Scripture of God the Father.* Abraham so loved God as to give up his only son, and centuries before Christ was born entered into the inner heart of John 3:16. After serving God faithfully, Abraham died when 175 years of age.

There are many profitable lessons to be gleaned from the biography of this notable man of God:

Faith has always trials. Being a Christian does not mean that trial is impossible or unnecessary. The greater the faith, the greater the trial.

Faith shines through the cloud. How the patience and meekness of Jesus are manifest through His trials! Take away Abraham's trials and where is his faith? Faith must be tried, in order that faith may live.

Faith in spite of trial glorifies God. Abraham's story is written in tears and blood, but how God was glorified by his trials of faith! Abraham's obedience of faith earned him the honor, "Abraham My friend!" Truly, there is no greater rank or greater honor than to be described thus. Yet such is our privilege if ours is the obedience of faith, for did not Jesus say, "I have called you friends"? He also said, "Ye are my friends *if* ye do whatsoever I command you."

ABSALOM [Ăb' sa lŏm]—FATHER OF PEACE. *The third son of David* by his wife Maacah, daughter of Talmai, king of Geshur. He was born of a polygamous marriage (II Sam. 3:2, 13, 14).

The Man Whose Lovely Hair Meant His Death

What a singular fascination there is in the story of Absalom who, lacking capacity, certainly made up for it in charm! As to the story of his rebellion against David his father, such a heartless deed carries with it one of the most solemn lessons in the whole of the Bible. Let us briefly touch on some aspects of Absalom's character and conduct.

I. He was of royal descent on both sides, for his mother was a king's daughter. Undoubtedly he was heir to the throne, and the favorite, the idol of his father.

II. He was gifted with remarkable physical beauty—"no blemish in him" (II Sam. 14:25). A commanding presence, natural dignity, extraordinary graces of person made him a conspicuous figure.

III. He also possessed a charm of eloquence and persuasiveness which won him the hearts of all Israel, who felt that in him they had a God-sent champion.

IV. He had a traitorous nature. Absalom murdered his own brother (II Sam. 13:29), was guilty of designing politeness (II Sam. 15:2, 3), and conspired against his own father (II Sam. 15:13, 14).

V. He came to an untimely end (II Sam. 18:9). Having everything in his favor—a throne ready made for him, and fortune bowing at his feet to load him with favors, his life ended in tragedy. Brilliant in its beginnings, he was buried like a dog in a pit in a lonely wood, leaving a name that was execrated. What brought Absalom to his *Paradise Lost?*

A. His all-absorbing egotism. Self-aggrandizement was Absalom's sin. He had no thought, no feeling, no pity for anyone else but himself. Those around him were only of use to him as they helped him to secure his own desires and build up his own grandeur. Filial affection and generous sentiment were sacrificed on the altar of his inordinate ambition. But in trying to save his life, he lost it.

B. His was a practical godlessness. Those around Absalom recognized God, and had a religious faith giving some restraint and principle to their conduct. But the handsome, selfish, scheming Absalom had none of this feeling. He was his own master. His own will was his only law. He was destitute of principle and destitute of faith. Love, tenderness, pity, were not his traits because he had no reverence for God.

C. His glory brought about his final tragedy. Adding to the beauty of Absalom was his flowing hair forming a crown to his person which made him the delight of Israel's daughters. Being proud of his chief ornament he must have carefully attended to it. But as Absalom was pursued by Joab's men his beautiful hair was caught fast in the thick and tangled boughs of an oak tree and he could not free himself. Thus his graceful personal endowment left him a target for those who hated him and sought his death.

May such a lesson not be lost upon us! Our chief glory can become the cause of our greatest shame. Our choicest endowments and most cherished gifts can become our greatest temptations. Our gifts, like ourselves, need to be rewashed every day in the fountain of God's truth, and guarded and sanctified by prayer, if they are to be fit for the highest service.

ACHAICUS [Ă chā' i cŭs]—BELONGING TO ACHAIA. As slaves were often named from the country of their birth, it seems probable that this member of the Church at Corinth was a slave born in Achaia

(I Cor. 16:17). Along with Stephanas and Fortunatus this Corinthian visited Paul at Philippi and refreshed his spirit.

ACHAN, ACHAR, ACHOR [Ā′ chăn, Ā′ chär, Ā′ chôr]—TROUBLE.
The son of Carmi of the tribe of Judah (Josh. 7; I Chron. 2:7).

The Man Who Brought Trouble to a Nation

It did not take Joshua long to discover that his defeat at Ai, after a succession of victories, was due to some transgression of the divine covenant (Josh. 7:8–12). Thus, as the result of an inquiry, Achan was exposed as the transgressor, and confessing his sin in stealing and hiding part of the spoil taken at the destruction of Jericho, was put to death in consequence. In keeping with the custom of those days, Achan was probably stoned with his immediate relatives, and their dead bodies burned—the latter making punishment more terrible in the eyes of the Israelites.

Achan was put to death in "the valley of Achor" meaning "the valley of trouble"—the valley being called atter Achan who had been the troubler of Israel (Josh. 7:25, 26). Thus in I Chronicles 2:7 Achan is spelled as Achar. But "the valley of trouble" became a "door of hope" all of which is spiritually suggestive (Isa. 65:10; Hos. 2:15).

I. Covetousness means defeat. God had forbidden anyone taking to himself the spoils of Jericho, but one man, *only one* amongst all the hosts of Israel, disobeyed and brought failure upon all. Achan's sin teaches us the oneness of the people of God. "*Israel* hath sinned" (Josh. 7:11). The whole cause of Christ can be delayed by the sin, neglect or lack of spirituality of one person (I Cor. 5:1–7; 12:12, 14, 26).

II. The whole process of sin. Along with Eve and David in their respective sins, Achan also saw, coveted and took. James expresses the rise, progress and end of sin when he says that man is "drawn away of his own lust, and enticed. Then when lust hath conceived, it bringeth forth sin: and sin, when it is finished, bringeth forth death" (Jas. 1:14, 15). The inward corruption of Achan's heart was first drawn forth by enticing objects—desire of gratification was then formed —ultimately determination to attain was fixed.

III. Prayer was rejected for action. When the most unexpected defeat of Ai came about, Joshua fell on his face before the Lord, and earnestly asked for an explanation of the reverse. But God said, "Get thee up; wherefore liest thou thus upon thy face? ...Take away the accursed thing" (Josh. 7:10, 13). God cannot hear and bless if there is sin in the camp. For often we acknowledge the greatness of our *national* sins, but fail to drag out our *personal* sins testifying against us. Once Achan was discovered and judged, Israel went forward to victory.

IV. The richness of divine mercy. When the accursed thing was removed and chastisement exercised, triumph quickly followed trouble. The valley of Achor became a door of hope. The locust-eaten years are restored. Confession and forgiveness open closed lips, quicken dormant energies and liberate power in the service of the Lord.

ACHBOR [Ăch' bôr]—A MOUSE.

1. *Father of Baal-hanan* and king of Edom (Gen. 36:38, 39; I Chron. 1:49).

2. *Son of Michaiah* and one of Josiah's messengers (II Kings 22: 12, 14). Called Abdon in II Chronicles 34:20.

3. *A Jew*, whose son *Elnathan* was sent by Jehoiakim to bring back Urijah the prophet from Egypt (Jer. 26:22; 36:12).

ACHIM [Ā' chim]—JEHOVAH WILL ESTABLISH. *An ancestor of Joseph*, husband of Mary, our Lord's mother (Matt. 1:14).

ACHISH [Ā' chish]—SERPENT CHARMER.

1. *Son of Maoch* and the king of Gath to whom David fled (I Sam. 21:10–14; 27:2–12).

2. *A king of Gath*, who reigned about forty years later than No. 1, in Solomon's time (I Kings 2:39, 40).

ADAIAH [Ăd-a ī' ah]—JEHOVAH HATH ADORNED or PLEASING TO JEHOVAH.

1. *A man of Boscath* and father of Josiah's mother (II Kings 22:1).

2. *A Levite* descended from Gershom (I Chron. 6:41–43).

3. *A son of Shimhi* the Benjamite (I Chron. 8:12–21).

4. *A Levite* of the family of Aaron, and head of a family living in Jerusalem (I Chron. 9:10–12).

5. *The father of Captain Masseiah* who helped Jehoiada put Joash on the throne of Judah (II Chron. 23:1).

6. *A son of Bani* who married a foreign wife during the exile (Ezra 10:29).

7. *Another of a different Bani family* who did the same thing (Ezra 10:34, 39).

8. *A descendant of Judah* by Perez (Neh. 11:5).

9. *A Levite* of the family of Aaron. Most likely the same person as No. 4 (Neh. 11:12).

ADALIA [Ăd a lī' ă]—THE HONOR OF IZED. *The fifth of Haman's ten sons* all of whom were hanged with their father (Esther 9:8).

ADAM [Ăd'ăm]—OF THE GROUND or TAKEN OUT OF THE RED EARTH. *The first human son of God* (Luke 3:38), and God's masterpiece and crowning work of creation.

The Man God Made

All men should be interested in the history of the first man who ever breathed, man's great ancestor, the head of the human family, the first being who trod the earth. What a beautiful world Adam found himself in with everything to make him happy, a world without sin and without sorrow! God first made, as it were, the great house of the world, then brought His tenant to occupy it. And it was not an empty house, but furnished with everything needed to make life content. There was not a single need God had not satisfied.

The Bible does not tell us how long Adam's state of blessedness and innocence lasted. But Paradise was lost through listening to the voice of the tempter. Relieved of his occupation as a gardener, Adam was condemned to make his livelihood by tilling the stubborn ground, and to eat his bread in the sweat of his face.

I. Adam was a necessary complement to the divine plan. "There was not a man to till the ground" (Gen. 2:5). The accomplishment of God's plan required human instrumentality. God made the earth for man, and then the man for the earth.

II. Adam was fashioned a creature of God, bearing the image of God and possessing God-like faculties (Gen. 1:27; Ps. 8:6; Eccles. 7:29).

III. Adam was created a tripartite being, having a spirit, soul and body (Gen. 2:7; I Thess. 5:23).

IV. Adam was alone and needed companionship to satisfy his created instincts (Gen. 2:18), thus Eve was formed.

Society, friendship and love
Gifts divinely bestowed upon man.

V. Adam was enticed and sinned (Gen. 3:6). After the satanic tempter there came the human tempter, and the act of taking the forbidden fruit offered by Eve ruined Adam and made him our federal head in sin and death. "In Adam we die."

VI. Adam received the promise of the Saviour. The first promise and prophecy of One, able to deal with Satan and sin was given, not to Adam, but to the one responsible for Adam's trangression (Gen. 3:15), and in the coats of skins God provided to cover the discovered nakedness of Adam and Eve we have a type of the sacrifice of the Cross. In Adam we die, but in Christ we can be made alive. The first man Adam was of the earth earthy, but the Second Man, the last Adam, was from heaven and kept His first estate of sinless perfection.

Adam was not only the name of earth's first man and the joint name of both Adam and Eve (Gen. 5:2), but also the name of a town on the east of Jordan (Josh. 3:16).

ADAR, ADDAR [Ā' där, Ăd' där]—FIRE GOD or HEIGHT. Son of Bela and grandson of Benjamin (I Chron. 8:3). Also the name of the twelfth month of the Jewish sacred year (Ezra 6:15), and of a city south of Judah (Josh. 15:3).

ADBEEL [Ăd' bē al]—LANGUISHING FOR GOD. Third son of Ishmael and grandson of Abraham (Gen. 25:13; I Chron. 1:29).

ADDI [Ăd'dī]—MY WITNESS or ADORNED. An ancestor of Joseph, the husband of Mary, our Lord's mother (Luke 3:28).

ADER [Ā' dûr]—A FLOCK. *A son of Beriah*, grandson of Shaharaim, a Benjamite (I Chron. 8:15). See Eder.

ADIEL [Ā'dĭ el]—ORNAMENT OF GOD.
1. *A descendant of Simeon* (I Chron. 4:36).
2. *A priest*, son of Jahzerah (I Chron. 9:12).
3. *Father of Azmaveth*, who was supervisor of David's treasuries. Perhaps the same as No. 2 (I Chron. 27:25).

ADIN [Ā' dĭn]—DELICATE or ORNAMENT.
1. *One whose family returned from exile with Zerubbabel* (Ezra 2:15; Neh. 7:20).
2. *One whose posterity came back with Ezra* (Ezra 8:6).
3. *The name of a family* sealing the Covenant (Neh. 10:14–16).

ADINA [Ăd' ĭ nă]—ORNAMENT. *A Reubenite and one of David's military officers* (I Chron. 11:42).

ADINO [Ăd' ĭ nō]—DELICATE or ORNAMENT. *An Eznite.* One of David's thirty heroes (II Sam. 23:8).

ADLAI [Ăd' la ĭ]—JUSTICE OF JEHOVAH or WEARY. *Father of Shaphat*, who was overseer of David's cattle in the lowlands (I Chron. 27:29).

ADMATHA [Ăd' ma thă]—GOD-GIVEN. *One of the seven princes* of Persia and Media in the reign of King Ahasuerus (Esther 1:14).

ADNA [Ăd'nă]—PLEASURE.
1. *A son of Pahath-moab* who had married a foreign wife during the exile (Ezra 10:30).
2. *A priest*, head of his father's house in the days of Joiakim (Neh. 12:12–15).

ADNAH [Ăd' nah]—PLEASURE.
1. *A Manassite* who joined David at Ziklag (I Chron. 12:20).
2. *A man of Judah* who held high military rank under Jehoshaphat (II Chron. 17:14).

ADONI-BEZEK [Ā dō' nĭ-bĕ' zek]—LORD OF LIGHTNING or OF BEZEK. *A king of Bezek*, captured by the men of Judah and Simeon and taken to Jerusalem where he was mutilated. The cutting off of his thumbs and great toes not only rendered him harmless but reminded him that man reaps what he sows (Judg. 1:5–7; Gal. 6:3).

ADONIJAH [Ăd o nĭ' jah]—JEHOVAH IS LORD.
1. *The fourth son of David and Haggith*, born in Hebron (II Sam 3:4). Adonijah was the victim of Oriental intrigue. After the death

of Absalom, he became the rightful heir to the throne (I Kings 2:15), but Bathsheba had other designs for her son Solomon who, when secure on the throne interpreted Adonijah's desire for Abishag as an effort to secure the kingdom. Self-preservation compelled Solomon to order Adonijah's death, a sentence carried out by Benaiah.

2. *A Levite* sent by Jehoshaphat to teach the Law (II Chron. 17:8).

3. *A chieftain* who with Nehemiah sealed the covenant (Neh. 10:14–16).

ADONIKAM [Ă dŏn' Ĭ kăm]—MY LORD HAS RISEN or HAS RAISED ME.

1. *An Israelite* whose descendants returned from exile (Ezra 2:13; Neh. 7:18).

2. *Another Israelite,* whose family returned from exile with Ezra (Ezra 8:13).

ADONIRAM, ADORAM [Ăd o nī' ram, Ă dō' ram]—MY LORD IS HIGH or THE LORD OF MIGHT. *A son of Abda* and an officer over tribute during the reigns of David and Solomon (I Kings 4:6; 5:14). See also *Hadoram.*

ADONI-ZEDEK, ADONI-ZEDEC [Ă dō' nĭ zē' dĕc]—LORD OF JUSTICE. *A king of the Canaanites,* who was slain by Joshua (Josh. 10:1, 3). Sometimes identified as Adoni-bezek.

ADORAM [Ă dō' ram]—HIGH HONOR or STRENGTH.

1. *An officer* set over the tribute in David's time (II Sam 20:24). Perhaps the same as Adoniram.

2. *An officer* under Solomon then under Rehoboam (I Kings 12:18).

ADRAMMELECH [Ă drăm' me lĕch]—ADAR IS KING or HONOR OF THE KING. *A son of Sennacherib,* king of Assyria, who, with his brother Sharezer, slew their father in the temple of Nisroch (II Kings 19:37; Isa. 37:38). Also the name of the heathen god, Adar (II Kings 17:31).

ADRIEL [Ă' drĭ el]—HONOR OF FLOCK OF GOD. *A man of Issachar* to whom Saul gave his daughter Merab in marriage (I Sam. 18:19; II Sam. 21:8).

AENEAS [Ae' ne ăs]—PRAISE. *This name of a Trojan hero* was also the name of the paralytic healed by Peter (Acts 9:33, 34).

AGABUS [Ăg' a bŭs]—A LOCUST. *A Christian prophet* in Jerusalem who foretold a widespread famine, and also Paul's imprisonment and shackles (Acts 11:28; 21:10, 11). Some scholars see two persons of the same name in these references.

AGAG [Ă' găg]—FLAMING or WARLIKE. *The poetic name of Amalek,* slain by Samuel as a religious act (Num. 24:7; I Sam. 15:8–23). Agagite is the name given to Haman, the Jews' enemy (Esther 3:1, 10).

AGEE [Ăg′ e ē]—FUGITIVE. *The father of Shammah,* one of David's valiant men (II Sam. 23:11).

AGRIPPA [Ă grĭp′ pá]—ONE WHO AT HIS BIRTH CAUSES PAIN. *Great-grandson of Herod the Great.* Agrippa's father was eaten by worms. See *Herod* (Acts 25:13–26; 26). Was Agrippa almost persuaded by Paul's eloquent witness to become a Christian? Bible scholars disagree on the point. There are those who affirm that the original language indicates clearly that Agrippa interrupted Paul to warn him that he was going too far in presuming that he was admitting his argument. "Too eagerly art thou persuading thyself that thou canst make me a Christian." The R.V. of 1881 has it, "With but little persuasion thou wouldest fain make me a Christian." However, the words of Agrippa as they stand in the A.V. have formed the basis of many an earnest and powerful gospel appeal.

AGUR [Ā′ gûr]—GATHERER. *The son of Jakeh* and author of the maxims in Proverbs thirty. Many writers feel that this name is symbolical of Solomon himself.

AHAB [Ā′ hăb]—FATHER'S BROTHER.
1. *The son of Omri,* and his successor as the seventh king of Israel (I Kings 16:28–33).

The Man Who Wanted Another's Vineyard

Ahab was an able and energetic warrior. His victories over the Syrians pushed the borders of his kingdom to the border of Damascus. Great renown became his, also great wealth indicated by the ivory palace he built for himself (I Kings 21:1; 22:39). Success, however, made him greedy for still more. Not since Solomon's time had a king been so victorious as Ahab, and what was a little matter like Naboth's vineyard to one who had grasped so much? With his wealth, Ahab bought all he wanted. One tenant, however, could not be bought out. Sentiment, affection and tender memories were more to Naboth than all the king's money.

Ahab could not say "All is mine" until the vineyard on his estate was his. First of all, there was no flaw in Ahab's advances. A fair price and richer land were offered Naboth. The sin came after Naboth's refusal to sell, because of a thousand sacred ties. Ahab sinned in not entering into a poorer man's feelings. Naboth was not obstinate. His vineyard was a sacred heritage, a precious tradition. If we are to be Christlike we must be considerate of others.

Ahab's next fault was that of making an awful grievance of his disappointment. He acted like a spoiled child and in a sulky fit told of failure to secure the vineyard to Jezebel, his strong-minded wife. Ahab and Jezebel are the Macbeth and Lady Macbeth of this inspired story. Ahab played into his wife's hands, and those hands were eager to shed blood.

Points for possible expansion are:

I. Ahab established idolatry. He was a dangerous innovator and a patron of foreign gods (I Kings 16:31–33; 21:26).

II. He was a weak-minded man, lacking moral fiber and righteousness (I Kings 21:4).

III. He was the tool of his cruel, avaricious wife (I Kings 21:7, 25).

IV. His doom, along with that of Jezebel, was foretold by Elijah (I Kings 21:22) and by Micaiah (I Kings 22:28).

2. *The name of the false prophet* who was in Babylon during the exile, and was roasted in the fire by Nebuchadnezzar (Jer. 29:21–23).

AHARAH [Ă här' ah]—BROTHER OF RACH. *Third son of Benjamin* (I Chron. 8:1). See also Ahiram and Aher (Num. 26:38).

AHARHEL [Ă här' hel]—BROTHER OF RACHEL or AFTER MIGHT. *A son of Harum,* and a founder of a family included in the tribe of Judah (I Chron. 4:8).

AHASAI, AHZAI [Ă hăs' a ĭ]—MY HOLDER or PROTECTOR; CLEAR-SIGHTED. *A priest* of the family of Immer (Neh. 11:13).

AHASBAI [Ă hăs' ba ĭ)—SHINING. *Father of one of David's heroes* (II Sam. 23:34).

AHASUERUS [Ă hăs ū ē' rŭs]—KING or MIGHTY MAN.

1. *A Persian monarch,* to whom accusations against the Jews were brought, bore this name (Ezra 4:6).

2. *It was also the name of a Median king,* father of Darius (Dan. 9:1).

3. *A Persian king* who became the husband of Esther (Esther 1: 2, 19).

The Man Whose Sleeplessness Saved a Nation

Two years after Queen Vashti was deposed, Esther the Jewess, and the ward of Mordecai, became the wife of Ahasuerus, and queen in Vashti's place. Two years after Esther's enthronement, wicked Haman prevailed upon the king to order the destruction of all the Jews in his empire, but the plan backfired. The king had a sleepless night, and robbed of slumber called for records carefully preserved in the royal archives. Reading of the plot to end his life, and of how Mordecai had informed the king, Ahasuerus felt that Mordecai was worthy of honor and reward. That sleepless night resulted in Mordecai's promotion to high office, the exposure of Haman's dark and devilish plot, the preservation of the Jewish nation and the hanging of Haman and his sons on the gallows Haman had prepared for Mordecai.

A character study on Ahasuerus could be worked out on his sensuality, fickleness, lack of forethought, despotism and cruelty.

AHAZ [Ā' hăz]—JEHOVAH HATH SEIZED or SUSTAINS.

1. *A Benjamite* of the family of Saul (I Chron. 8:35, 36; 9:41, 42).

2. *The son of Jotham,* king of Judah and father of Hezekiah, Ahaz became the eleventh king of Judah and reigned for sixteen years (II Kings 16). He is called Achaz in Matthew 1:9. An Assyrian inscription gives the name of the king as Jehoahaz. But the abbreviation Ahaz was commonly used and was found on the seal ring of one of his courtiers. Perhaps the consistent omission of the first part of the name Jeho, meaning "Jehovah" was deliberate because of the abhorrent apostasy of Ahaz.

The Man Who Rejected a Message of Hope

Let it not be forgotten that it was to king Ahaz that Isaiah's first evangelistic announcement was made in the promise of Emmanuel. The prophet sent a message to terrified Ahaz, but he would not turn to God and trust His deliverance. In order to help restore the faith of the wavering king, Isaiah urged Ahaz to ask for a sign from Jehovah, but he refused and in rejecting the message of hope, forfeited his soul.

It is interesting to observe that Ahaz came between two good men — between his father, Jotham, and his son, Hezekiah.

Summarizing the chief aspects of the reign of Ahaz we note his:

I. Pursuit of the religious policy of Jehoram (II Kings 8:18); of Ahaziah (II Kings 8:27); of Joash (II Chron. 24:18). The religious vices of Ahaz were possible because of a corrupt church and a corrupt state (Isa. 1:4, 13).

II. Rejection of David's way to tread Jeroboam's way. This bad ruler exceeded the idolatry of his time by burning his children in the fire (II Chron. 28:3). Ahaz did honor to the gods of Assyria who were reckoned to be more powerful than Jehovah. The terrible slaughter of one hundred twenty thousand valiant men of Judah had no salutary effect upon Ahaz (II Chron. 28:6).

AHAZIAH [Ā ha zī' ah]—JEHOVAH HOLDS or POSSESSES.

1. *A son of Ahab,* the Ahaziah of Israel—its eighth king who reigned for only two years. He followed the religious policy of his idolatrous father. He died as the result of a fall from the palace window (I Kings 22:49, 51; II Kings 1:2; I Chron. 3:11; II Chron. 20:35, 37).

2. *A son of Jehoram* or Joram, the Ahaziah of Judah who was Judah's fifth king, and who reigned for only one year. He is also known as Jehoahaz and Azariah. Since his wife was a daughter of Ahab and Jezebel, it is not to be wondered at that he was a Baal worshiper (II Kings 8:24–29; 9:16–29; 10:13; 12:18; 13:1; 14:13; II Chron. 22).

AHBAN [Äh' băn]—BROTHER OF INTELLIGENCE. *Son of Abishur,* a Judahite of the house of Jerahmeel (I Chron. 2:29).

AHER [Ā′ hûr]—ONE THAT IS BEHIND or ANOTHER. *A Benjamite,* perhaps the same as Ahiram (I Chron. 7:12).

AHI [Ā′ hĭ]—MY BROTHER or BROTHER OF JEHOVAH.
1. *Chief of the Gadites* in Gilead (I Chron. 5:15).
2. *Son of Shamer,* an Israelite of the tribe of Asher (I Chron. 7:34).

AHIAH [Ā hĭ′ ah]—JEHOVAH IS MY BROTHER.
1. *The son of Ahitub* and grandson of Phinehas, son of Eli (I Sam. 14:3).
2. *One of Solomon's scribes* (I Kings 4:3).
3. *A descendant of Benjamin* (I Chron. 8:7). See also Ahijah.

AHIAM [Ā hĭ′ am]—A MOTHER'S BROTHER. *The son of Sharar* the Hararite (the Sacar of I Chron. 11:35), and one of David's heroes (II Sam. 23:33; I Chron. 11:35).

AHIAN [Ā hĭ′ an]—FRATERNAL, BROTHER OF DAY, or BROTHERLY. *Son of Shemidah,* a Manassachite (I Chron. 7:19).

AHIEZER [Ā hĭ ē′ zûr]—BROTHER OF HELP.
1. *The son of Ammishaddai,* and head of the tribe of Dan, in the wilderness (Num. 1:12; 2:25; 7:66–71; 10:25).
2. *A son of Shemaah* and a Danite chief who joined David at Ziklag (I Chron. 12:3).

AHIHUD [Ā hĭ′ hud]—BROTHER OF HONOR, OF MAJESTY, or OF MYSTERY.
1. *A prince of Asher,* who was appointed to help in the division of the land (Num. 34:27).
2. *A Benjamite* of the family of Ehud (I Chron. 8:7).

AHIJAH (Ā hĭ′ jah]—A BROTHER IN JEHOVAH.
1. *A prophet* belonging to Shiloh, who foretold to Jeroboam the revolt of the ten tribes. This Ahijah was the champion of the rights of the people in the face of the oppression of Solomon and Rehoboam and led the revolt that rent the kingdom of David asunder (I Kings 11:26–12:20).
2. *Father of Baasha,* king of Israel who conspired against Nadab son of Jeroboam and reigned in his stead (I Kings 15:27, 33; 21:22; II Kings 9:9).
3. *Son of Jerahmeel,* a Judahite (I Chron. 2:25).
4. *A Pelonite,* and one of David's thirty heroes (I Chron. 11:36).
5. *A Levite* who had charge of the Tabernacle treasures (I Chron. 26:20).
6. *A Levite* who, with Nehemiah, sealed the covenant (Neh. 10:26).

AHIKAM [Ā hĭ′ kam]—MY BROTHER HATH RISEN or APPEARED. *Son*

of Shaphan, and a prince of Judah and an officer in Josiah's court (II Kings 22:12, 14; 25:22; Jer. 26:24).

AHILUD [Ă hī' lud]—A BROTHER OF ONE BORN.

1. *The father of Jehoshaphat,* the recorder under David and Solomon (II Sam. 8:16; 20:24; I Kings 4:3; I Chron. 18:15).

2. *Father of Baana,* one of Solomon's twelve purveyors (I Kings 4:12).

AHIMAAZ [Ă hĭm' a ăz]—A RASCAL, POWERFUL BROTHER or MY BROTHER IS COUNSELOR.

1. *Father of Ahinoam,* Saul's wife (I Sam. 14:50).

2. *A son of Zadok* the priest, who kept David informed of Absalom's revolt (II Sam. 15:27, 36; 17:17, 20).

3. *One of Solomon's officers,* responsible for the monthly supply of victuals for the royal household (I Kings 4:15).

AHIMAN [Ă hī' man]—BROTHER OF MAN or BROTHER OF A GIFT.

1. *A son of Anak,* who lived in Hebron and who was destroyed by Judah (Num. 13:22; Josh. 15:14; Judg. 1:10).

2. *A Levite porter* who had charge of the gate of the Temple through which the king passed (I Chron. 9:17).

AHIMELECH [Ă hĭm' e lĕch]—BROTHER OF THE KING or MY BROTHER IS KING.

1. *A son of Ahitub* and chief at Nob, who was slain for assisting David when he fled from Saul (I Sam. 21:1–8; 22:9–20; 23:6; 30:7).

2. *A Hittite officer* and follower of David (I Sam. 26:6).

3. *The son of Abiathar* the priest who escaped slaughter at Nob (II Sam. 8:17; I Chron. 18:16; 24:6). Some writers feel that the names of Abiathar and Ahimelech in these verses have been transposed.

AHIMOTH [Ă hī' mŏth]—BROTHER OF DEATH. *Son of Elkanah,* descended from Kohath son of Levi (I Chron. 6:25).

AHINADAB [Ă hĭn' a dăb]—BROTHER OF LIBERALITY. *Son of Iddo* and one of Solomon's purveyors in Mahanaim (I Kings 4:14).

AHIO [Ă hī' ō]—FRATERNAL or HIS BROTHER.

1. *A son of Abinadab* and brother of Uzzah. It was in Abinadab's house that the Ark of God rested for twenty years after its return by the Philistines (II Sam. 6:3, 4; I Chron. 13:7).

2. *A son of Elpaal,* a Benjamite (I Chron. 8:14).

3. *A son of Jehiel* by his wife Maachah and an ancestor of Saul (I Chron. 8:31; 9:37).

AHIRA [Ă hī' ră]—BROTHER OF EVIL. *A son of Enan* and head of the tribe of Naphtali during the wilderness journey (Num. 1:15; 2:29; 7:78, 83; 10:27).

AHIRAM [Ă hī' ram]—EXALTED BROTHER. *A Benjamite* of the Ahiramites (Num. 26:38). Called Ehi in Genesis 46:21, and supposed to be the Aher of I Chronicles 7:12.

AHISAMACH [Ă hĭs' a măch]—BROTHER OF SUPPORT. *Father of Aholiab* the craftsman, a Danite (Ex. 31:6; 35:34; 38:23).

AHISHAHAR [Ă hĭsh' a här]—BROTHER OF THE DAWN. *Son of Bilhan* and grandson of Jediael (I Chron. 7:10).

AHISHAR [Ă hī' shär]—BROTHER OF SONG or OF A SINGER. *An official* over Solomon's household (I Kings 4:6).

AHITHOPHEL [Ă hĭth' o phĕl]—BROTHER OF FOLLY. *One of David's privy counselors* and father of one of David's heroes, a Gilonite (II Sam. 15:12–34; 16:15–23; 17).

The Man Who Was Noted for His Advice

There was no one who could hold a candle to Ahithophel in his day as an able and famous politician. His counsel "was as if a man had inquired at the oracle of God" (II Sam. 16:23). Such counsel was a proverb in Israel in David's time. Matthew Henry speaks of him as "a politic, thinking man and one that had a clear head, and a great compass of thought." Perhaps David and Ahithophel had been friends from their boyhood up and are before us in Psalms such as 41:9; 55:13, 14.

Ahithophel, the wise and trusted counselor, however, was found unfaithful because he also thought of himself, and not of David. Ahithophel joined Absalom and advised the prince to take his father's harem (II Sam. 15:12; 16:21). He advised pursuit of the fugitive monarch, but Hushai, another counselor, thwarted this move (II Sam. 17:11)). Ahithophel was so disgusted over the collapse of his influence, for he could foresee that the insurrection against David was doomed to failure, that he went home a crestfallen man and set his affairs in order and hanged himself (II Sam. 17:23).

AHITUB (Ă hī' tub]—BROTHER OF BENEVOLENCE or FATHER OF GOODNESS.

1. *A son of Phinehas* and grandson of Eli (I Sam. 14:3; 22:9, 11, 12, 20).

2. *A son of Amariah* and father of Zadok the priest (II Sam. 8:17; I Chron. 6:11, 12). Perhaps the same as No. 1.

3. *A priest* and ruler of the House of God in Nehemiah's time (I Chron. 9:11; Neh. 11:11).

AHLAI [Äh′ lai]—JEHOVAH IS STAYING. *Father of one of David's thirty heroes* (I Chron. 11:41). Also the name of *a daughter of Sheshan* (I Chron. 2:31).

AHOAH [Ă hō ah]—A BROTHER'S NEED. *Son of Bela*, a Benjamite, and founder of a family (I Chron. 8:4).

AHOLIAB [Ă hŏ′ li ăb], AHOLAH [Ă ho′ lah], AHOLIBAH [Ă hŏl-I bah], AHOLIBAMAH [Ă hŏl i bā′ mah]—A TENT. These names in the A.V. are also given in the R.V. as Oholah - her own tent; Oholiab - a father's tent; Oholibah - my tent is in her; Oholibamah - tent of high place.
1. *A Danite*, appointed by God to work with Bezaleel in the erection of the Tabernacle (Ex. 31:6; 35:34; 36:1, 2; 38:23).
2. *A chief* who sprang from Esau (Gen. 36:41; I Chron. 1:52).

AHUMAI [Ă hŭ′ ma ĭ]—BROTHER OF WATER. *Son of Jahath* and a descendant of Judah (I Chron. 4:2).

AHUZAM [Ă hŭ′ zam]—POSSESSION or A HOLDING FAST. *A son of Ashur*, of the family of Hezron (I Chron. 4:5, 6).

AHUZZATH [Ă hŭz′ zath]—POSSESSION or HOLDING FAST. *A friend of Abimelech*, king of the Philistines in Isaac's time (Gen. 26:26).

AIAH, AJAH [Ă ĭ′ ah, Ā′ jah]—A VULTURE or BIRD OF PREY.
1. *A son of Zebeon*, the Horite (Gen. 36:24; I Chron. 1:40).
2. *The father of Rizpah*, Saul's concubine (II Sam. 3:7; 21:8, 10, 11).

AKAN [Ā′kăn]—ACUTE OR TWISTED. *Son of Ezer*, grandson of Seir the Horite (Gen. 36:27; I Chron. 1:42). Also called Jakan.

AKKUB [Ăk′kŭb]—CUNNING, ARTFUL or LAIN IN WAIT.
1. *A son of Elioenai*, of the family of David (I Chron. 3:24).
2. *A porter* in the second temple (I Chron. 9:17; Neh. 11:19; 12:25), and founder of family of hereditary porters (Ezra 2:42; Neh. 7:45).
3. *The chief of a family* of the Nethinims who came to Jerusalem after the exile (Ezra 2:45).
4. *A priest* employed by Ezra to expound the Law to the people (Neh. 8:7).

ALAMETH [Ăl′ a mĕth]—YOUTHFUL VIGOR. *Son of Becher* and grandson of Benjamin (I Chron. 7:8).

ALEMETH [Ăl′ e mĕth]—HIDING PLACE or COVERING. *A descendant of Jonathan*, son of Saul (I Chron. 8:36; 9:42). Also the name of a Levitical city (I Chron. 6:60).

ALEXANDER [Ăl ĕx ăn' dûr]—DEFENDER, HELPER OF MEN or ONE WHO TURNS AWAY EVIL.

1. *The son of Simon the Cyrenian* who was compelled to carry the cross of Christ (Mark 15:21).

2. *A leading man in Jerusalem* when Peter and John were tried there (Acts 4:6).

3. *A convert of Paul's* who was present at the Ephesian tumult. Perhaps the same as No. 1 (Acts 19:33).

4. *A convert to Christianity* who became an apostate (I Tim. 1:20). Perhaps the same as No. 6.

5. *Alexander the Great,* king of Macedonia, who followed his father Philip and who also brought the Jews into contact with Greek literature and life. He is described though not named in Daniel 2:39 and 6:6.

6. *The coppersmith* who opposed Paul (II Tim. 4:14). This Ephesian Jew was likely the same as the one who corrupted the faith, not from ignorance but deliberately in opposition to his judgment. Dr. Alexander Whyte deals with No. 4 and No. 6 as the same person.

ALIAH [Ă lĭ' ah]—SUBLIMITY. *A duke of Edom,* descended from Esau, who is called Alvah in the Vulgate (Gen. 36:40; I Chron. 1:51). See Alvah.

ALIAN [Ă lĭ' an]—SUBLIME. *A son of Shobal* and descendant of Seir (Gen. 36:23; I Chron. 1:40). Called Alvan in Genesis 36:23.

ALLON [Ăl' lŏn]—AN OAK. *A Simeonite* descended from Shemaiah (I Chron. 4:37). Also the name of a city near Kadesh (Josh. 19:33).

ALMODAD [Ăl mō' dăd]—THE AGITATOR. *The oldest son of Joktan,* of the family of Shem (Gen. 10:26; I Chron. 1:20).

ALPHAEUS [Ăl phē' us]—TRANSIENT, CHIEF OR A THOUSAND.

1. *The father of Levi* or Matthew the Apostle (Mark 2:14).

2. *The father of James,* one of the twelve apostles (Matt. 10:3; Mark 3:18; Luke 6:15; Acts 1:13). Sometimes identified as the same person in No. 1 and also as Cleophas.

ALVAH [Ăl' vah]—SUBLIMITY or HIGH. *A duke of Edom* descended from Esau (Gen. 36:40; I Chron. 1:51). See Aliah.

ALVAN [Ăl' van]—SUBLIME. *Son of Shobal,* a Horite (Gen. 36:23; I Chron. 1:40). Called Alian in I Chronicles 1:40; Alvah in Genesis 36:40; Aliah in I Chronicles 1:51.

AMAL [Ă' măl]—LABOR or SORROW. *Son of Helem,* an Asherite (I Chron. 7:35).

AMALEK [Ăm' a lĕk]—WARLIKE or DWELLER IN THE VALE. *Son of*

Eliphaz and grandson of Esau and founder of a tribal family known as the Amalekites (Gen. 36:12, 16; Ex. 17; I Chron. 1:36). Amalek appears to have separated from his brethren and true to his name, became the head of a warlike tribe. Balaam described him as "the first of the nations" (Num. 24:20).

AMARIAH [Ăm a rī′ ah]—JEHOVAH HATH SAID or PROMISED.
1. *A son of Meraioth,* a priest descended from Phinehas (I Chron. 6:7, 52).
2. *The son of Azariah,* a high priest in Solomon's time (I Chron. 6:11).
3. *A descendant of Kohath,* son of Levi (I Chron. 23:19; 24:23).
4. *Chief priest* of Jehoshaphat's time (II Chron. 19:11).
5. *A Levite* appointed by Hezekiah to distribute tithes and offerings (II Chron. 31:15).
6. *A man of the family of Bani* who married a foreign wife (Ezra 10:42).
7. *A priest* who signed the covenant (Neh. 10:3; 12:2, 13).
8. *A descendant of Judah* by Perez (Neh. 11:4).
9. *An ancestor of Zephaniah* the prophet in Josiah's time (Zeph. 1:1).

AMASA [Ăm′ a să]—BURDEN-BEARER.
1. *The son of David's half-sister Abigail* whom Absalom made captain of his rebel army (II Sam. 17:25; 19:13; 20). Amasa was completely defeated by his cousin Joab in the forest of Ephraim (II Sam. 18:6–8). David not only forgave Amasa but gave him Joab's place (II Sam. 19:13). Joab treacherously slew him (II Sam. 20:9–12).
2. *The name of an Ephraimite* who with others resisted the bringing into Samaria the Jews Ahaz had made prisoners (II Chron. 28:12).

AMASAI [Ă măs′ a ī]—BURDENSOME.
1. *A descendant of Kohath,* son of Levi (I Chron. 6:25; II Chron. 29:12).
2. *A chieftain* who joined David at Ziklag and became one of his captains (I Chron. 12:18). Perhaps the same as Amasa, No. 1.
3. *A Levite* who helped in the return of the Ark from the house of Obed-edom (I Chron. 15:24).

AMASHAI [Ă măsh′ a ī]—CARRYING SPOIL or BURDEN-BEARER. *A priest,* son of Azareel who lived in Jerusalem at Nehemiah's request (Neh. 11:13). Also called Amashsai.

AMASIAH [Ăm a sī′ ah]—JEHOVAH IS STRONG. *A son of Zichri,* one of Jehoshaphat's commanders (II Chron. 17:16).

AMAZIAH [Ăm a zī′ ah]—JEHOVAH HAS STRENGTH.

1. *Son of Joash or Jehoash,* king of Judah. Amaziah came to the throne after the assassination of his father. The writer of II Kings gives him unqualified praise for his religious acts (II Kings 14), but in Chronicles he is accused of gross apostasy (II Chron. 25:14).

2. *The priest at Bethel* who opposed the prophet Amos in the matter of idol-worship (Amos 7:10).

3. *A man of the tribe of Simeon* (I Chron. 4:34).

4. *A Levite* descended from Merari (I Chron. 6:45).

AMI [Ā' mī]—THE BEGINNING. *The head of a family* of Solomon's servants, whose descendants returned with Zerubbabel from exile (Ezra 2:57). He is called Amon, meaning "steadfast" in Nehemiah 7:59.

AMINADAB [Ă mĭn' a dăb]—THE KINSMAN IS GENEROUS. *Son of Aram* (or Ram), who was the son of Esrom, ancestor of our Lord (Matt. 1:4; Luke 3:33).

AMITTAI [Ă mĭt' ta ī]—TRUE or TRUTHFUL. *The father of the prophet Jonah* (II Kings 14:25; Jonah 1:1).

AMMIEL [Ăm' mĭ el]—A DEVOTED ALLY or KINSMAN OF GOD.

1. *The son of Gemalli* and spy of the tribe of Dan sent out by Moses (Num. 13:12).

2. *The father of Machir,* of Lo-debar (II Sam. 9:4, 5; 17:27).

3. *The father of Bath-sheba,* one of David's wives (I Chron. 3:5).

4. *The sixth son of Obed-edom* who, with his family, was associated with the Tabernacle porters (I Chron. 26:5).

AMMIHUD [Ăm mī' hŭd]—MAN OF PRAISEWORTHINESS or MY PEOPLE IS HONORABLE.

1. *The father of Elishama,* chief of Ephraim (Num. 1:10; 2:18; 7:48).

2. *A man of Simeon* and father of Shemuel (Num. 34:20).

3. *A Naphtalite* whose son, Pedahel, also assisted in the division of the land (Num. 34:28).

4. *Father of Talmai* and king of Geshur. Absalom fled to Talmai after he slew his brother Ammon (II Sam. 13:37).

5. *Son of Omri,* father of Uthai (I Chron. 9:4).

AMMIHUR [Ăm mī' hŭr]—MY PEOPLE IS NOBLE. *Father of Talmai* (II Sam. 13:37). Same as (4) above. "R" is found in Hebrew text, though pronounced traditionally as "Ammihud."

AMMINADAB [Ăm mĭn' a dăb]—MY PEOPLE IS WILLING or MY KINS-MAN IS GENEROUS.

1. *A Levite,* Aaron's father-in-law (Ex. 6:23).

2. *A prince* of Judah (Num. 1:7; 2:3; 7:12, 17; 10:14; Ruth 4:19, 20).

3. *A son of Kohath,* son of Levi (I Chron. 6:22). Perhaps the same as No. 1.

4. *A Kohathite* who assisted in the return of the Ark from the house of Obed-edom (I Chron. 15:10, 11).

AMMINADIB [Ăm' mi nă' dib]—MY PEOPLE IS LIBERAL OT PRINCELY. Someone famous for the chariots provided for King Solomon (S. of Sol. 6:12). Perhaps it is not a proper name.

AMMISHADDAI [Ăm mĭ shăd' da ī]—AN ALLY IS THE ALMIGHTY. *Father of Ahiezer,* captain of the tribe of Dan in Moses' time (Num. 1:12; 2:25; 7:66, 71; 10:25).

AMMIZABAD [Ăm mĭz' a băd]—THE KINSMAN HATH ENDOWED. *Son of Benaiah,* third of David's captains (I Chron. 27:6).

AMMON [Ăm' mŏn]—PERTAINING TO THE NATION. *The younger son of Lot* by his younger daughter, born in a cave near Zoar, and ancestor of the Ammonites (Gen. 19:38; Num. 21:24). See Ben-amni.

AMNON [Ăm' nŏn]—FAITHFUL OT TUTELAGE.
1. *The eldest son of David* by Ahinoam the Jezreelitess, he was slain by Absalom (II Sam. 3:2; 13).
2. *The son of Shimon,* of the tribe of Judah (I Chron. 4:20).

AMOK [Ā' mok]—DEEP. *A chief of priests* who returned with Zerubbabel from exile (Neh. 12:7, 20).

AMON [Ā' mon]—SECURITY OT A WORKMAN.
1. *Governor* of the city of Samaria under Ahab (I Kings 22: 26; II Chron. 18:25).
2. *Son of Manasseh,* and fifteenth king of Judah, who reigned for two years (II Kings 21:18–25).
3. *One of the clan* known as "Solomon's servants" (Neh. 7:59). Called Ami in Ezra 2:57.
4. *A son of Manasses,* and an ancestor of Christ (Matt. 1:10). Amon is also the name of an Egyptian sun-god.

AMOS [Ā' mos]—BURDEN-BEARER OT ONE WITH A BURDEN.
1. *This prophet of "judgment,"* which is the key word of the book he wrote, was a citizen of Tekoa, west of the Dead Sea (Amos 1:1; 7:8–16; 8:2).

The Man Who Was a Dresser of Sycamore Trees

Although he was one of the oldest of the prophets, we know little about Amos save what he himself tells us. He does not appear to have belonged to any rank or influence. The opposite is the case, seeing he styles himself a herdsman (Amos 7:14). He was no "professional prophet, speaking for a living." Amos did not belong to the order of the prophets, nor had he been educated in the school of the prophets. The prophetic office was thrust upon him (Amos 7:14, 15). When the call came he exchanged the life of a shepherd and cultivator of sycamore trees for that of a prophet.

The desert life of Amos exercised great formative influences upon him. With time to think and pray, he was qualified to form clear judgments. The art of the seer is not cultivated in crowds.

Contemporary with Hosea, Amos prophesied in the days of Uzziah, king of Judah and in the time of Jeroboam. Most of the prophets confined their message in the main to Israel, but to Amos, Israel was only one of the nations. He took in a whole range of various nationalities and indicted them for their sins and proclaimed the judgment of God alike upon nations and individuals.

Amos pronounced judgment upon the oppression of the poor, commercial dishonesty, selfish indulgence and idolatrous worship, and was the first prophet to predict the captivity of Israel, and to announce God's rejection of His chosen people. The great lessons of the Book of Amos are:

I. Sin is sin in all its blackness, against the bright background of God's grace.

II. Mere ritual is not pleasing to God. The very worship of Israel was sin (Amos 4:4, 5; 5:21–24). Israel thought of God as a vain monarch, pleased with gifts and empty phrases. Amos had nothing but utter contempt for forms of religion that did not disturb one's conscience or change one's life.

III. The greatest perils, both of nations and men, lie not in poverty, but in prosperity.

IV. God's dealings with men are for their discipline, not their doom. Discipline, however, if unheeded, only hastens doom and determines destiny. Thus Amos is rightly called "the prophet of divine law."

2. *An ancestor of Joseph,* husband of Mary, our Lord's mother (Luke 3:25).

AMOZ [Ă' mŏz]—STRONG or BRASS. *The father of the prophet Isaiah,* a Judahite, who must be carefully distinguished from Amos (II Kings 19:2, 20; Isa. 1:1).

AMPLIATUS, AMPLIAS [Ăm' plĭ as]—ENLARGED. *A convert of Paul's* who lived in Rome and to whom the apostle sent a greeting (Rom. 16:8). This name, a common slave designation, is found inscribed in the catacombs.

AMRAM [Ăm' răm]—EXALTED PEOPLE or INEXPERIENCE.

1. *A grandson of Levi,* son of Kohath and father of Aaron, Moses and Miriam. Amram died at 137 years of age (Ex. 6:18, 20).

2. *A son of Bani*, who married a foreign wife during the exile (Ezra 10:34).

3. *A son of Dishon* and grandson of Anah (I Chron. 1:41). This name should be Hamram or Hamran.

AMRAPHEL [Ăm′ ra phĕl]—POWERFUL PEOPLE. *The king of Shinar*, ally of Chedorlaomer, in Abraham's time (Gen. 14:1, 9).

AMZI [Ăm′ zĭ]—ROBUST or MY STRENGTH.

1. *A descendant of Merari*, who was a son of Levi, and progenitor of Ethan, whom David set over the service of song (I Chron. 6:46).

2. *Ancestor of Adaiah*, a priest of the course in the second Temple (Neh. 11:12).

ANAH [Ā′ nah]—FRUITFUL IN GRAPES or ANSWERING.

1. *A son of Seir* the Horite, and one of the chiefs of the land (Gen. 36:20, 29; I Chron. 1:38).

2. *A son of Zibeon*, son of Seir (Gen. 36: 24; I Chron. 1:40, 41). Also the name of a daughter of Zibeon (Gen. 36: 2, 14).

ANAIAH [Ăn a ĭ′ ah]—JEHOVAH HATH ANSWERED.

1. *A prince or priest* who assisted in the reading of the law to the people (Neh. 8:4).

2. *A Jew* who, with Nehemiah, sealed the covenant (Neh. 10:22).

ANAK [Ā′ năk]—GIANT, OR LONG-NECKED OR ORNAMENT. *Son of Arba*, and ancestor of the Anakims (Num. 13:22, 28, 33). See also Anakim (Deut. 1:28).

ANAN [Ā′ nan]—HE BECLOUDS or COVERS. *A returned exile* who acted with Nehemiah in the sealing of the covenant (Neh. 10:26).

ANANI [Ăn ă′ nĭ]—COVERED WITH GOD. *A son of Elioenai*, of the family of David (I Chron. 3:24).

ANANIAH [Ăn a nĭ′ ah]—JEHOVAH IS A PROTECTOR. *The father of Maaseiah* and grandfather of Azariah (Neh. 3:23).

ANANIAS [Ăn a nĭ′ as]—JEHOVAH IS GRACIOUS. This name is the Greek form of Hananiah, meaning, "Jehovah hath been gracious" from the Aramaic, meaning, "beautiful."

1. *The disciple* who conspired with his wife to deceive the apostles in regard to the value obtained for their property (Acts 5:1–6).

The Man Who Kept Back Part of the Price

How opposite Aquila and Priscilla are Ananias and Sapphira, both of whom agreed to a dishonest transaction! They were not compelled to sell their property but because of a recognized custom among the early Christian fraternity of having one common fund to draw upon, these two disciples wanted to maintain the appearance of self-denying liberality. There was no harm in keeping back part of the price—they might have kept back *all*. Their evil consisted in pretending to give *all*. Their lying was combined with hypocrisy. A *certain* part was retained, likely the greater part which would look more like the whole.

Peter, supernaturally endowed to detect and expose the fraud of Ananias and Sapphira, was their instrument of sudden death. Punishment was:

I. Prompt — it followed immediately the committal of sin.

II. Decisive — it marked the magnitude of sin.

III. Conspicuous — it was before many witnesses.

IV. Divine — it was not an act of Peter who simply reproved the two who, united in crime, were not separated in death (Ps. 19:13). It was God who punished them.

2. *A godly disciple of Damascus* to whom was made known the conversion of Saul of Tarsus (Acts 9:10–17; 22:12), and who baptized Saul.

3. *The high priest* anointed by Herod (Acts 23:2; 24:1).

ANATH [Ā' năth]—ANSWER OR A GRANTING. *Father of Shamgar,* third judge after Joshua (Judg. 3: 31; 5:6).

ANATHOTH [Ăn' a thŏth]—ANSWERED PRAYERS.

1. *The eighth of the nine sons of Becher,* son of Benjamin (I Chron. 7:8).

2. *Head and representative* of the men of Anathoth who added his seal to the covenant (Neh. 10:19). Also name of a Levitical city, now known as Anata (Josh. 21:18).

ANDREW [Ăn' drew]—MANLINESS. *Brother of Simon Peter,* and one of the twelve apostles (Matt. 4:18; 10:2).

The Man Who was the First Missionary

Because he brought his own brother to the newly found Messiah, Andrew earned the distinction of being the first missionary of the cause of Christ (John 1:41). Andrew belonged to Bethsaida of Galilee —was a disciple of John the Baptist—attached himself to Christ with whom he enjoyed a special friendship (Mark 13:3; John 1:35–37). He was ever prompt to help (John 6:8, 9; 12:21, 22). After Christ's ascension, Andrew preached in Jerusalem. Tradition has it that he was crucified because of his rebuke of Aegeas for obstinate adherence to idolatry. He was nailed to a cross in the form of an X, hence the name *St. Andrew's Cross.* Lessons to be learned from Andrew are:

I. It is only in true discipleship that rest can be found.

II. If we cannot perform more conspicuous service we can yet serve the Lord. Although Peter was the spiritual father of the Pentecost converts, Andrew was their spiritual grandfather.

III. We must discover our own gift and the gift in others and guide such into right channels of service.

IV. If we are Christ's ours will be the passion to lead others to Him.

ANDRONICUS [Ăn drō nī′ cus]—CONQUERER or CONQUERING MEN. *A Jewish believer,* once a fellow-prisoner of Paul to whom the apostle sent a greeting (Rom. 16:7).

ANER [Ā′ nûr]—WATERFALL or AFFLICTION. *A brother of Mamre,* the Amorite, Abraham's ally in battle (Gen. 14:13, 24). Also the name of a Levitical city in Manasseh (I Chron. 6:70), now known as Anim.

ANIAM [Ā′ ni ăm]—SIGHING OF THE PEOPLE. *A son of Shemidah,* a Manassehite (I Chron. 7:19).

ANNAS [Ăn′ nas]—GRACE OF JEHOVAH. *A Jewish high priest,* the son of Seth, appointed to office in his thirty-seventh year by Quirinus, and who was in office when John the Baptist began his ministry (Luke 3:2; John 18:13, 24; Acts 4:6). Annas was an astute and powerful ecclesiastical statesman, who took part not only in the trial of Jesus, but also in those of Peter and John.

ANTIPAS [Ăn′ tĭ păs]—LIKENESS OF HIS FATHER.
1. See *Herod,* No. 3. Name is an abbreviation of Antipater.
2. *The believer at Pergamos* in Asia Minor who sealed his witness with his blood (Rev. 2:12, 13).

ANTOTHIJAH [Ăn to thī′ jah]—ANSWER OF JEHOVAH. *A son of Shashak,* a Benjamite (I Chron. 8:24).

ANUB [Ā′ nub]—STRONG or HIGH. *A son of Coz,* descendant of Caleb and Hur (I Chron. 4:8).

APELLES [Ă pĕl′ lēs]—I SEPARATE or EXCLUDE. *An approved Christian* at Rome to whom Paul sent a greeting (Rom. 16:10). A typical Jewish name. Apelles is yet found among the dependants of the Emperor. "Approved" means that this disciple's fidelity to Christ had been tried and had stood the test. Apelles had proved his faith. Weymouth translates it—"Greetings to Apelles—that veteran believer."

APHIAH [Ă phī′ ah]—REVIVIFIED or STRIVING. *One of Saul's ancestors* (I Sam. 9:1).

APHSES [Ăph′ sēs]—THE DISPERSED. *A Levite chief* of the eighteenth of the twenty-four courses in the service of the Temple (I Chron. 24:15).

APOLLOS [Ă pŏl′ los]—A DESTROYER or YOUTHFUL GOD OF MUSIC. *An eloquent and learned Jew* born at Alexandria and deeply versed in Old Testament Scriptures (Acts 18:24; 19:1; I Cor. 1:12; 3:4–6, 22; 4:6; 16:12; Titus 3:13).

The Man Whose Influence Was Enriched

This educated, cultured Alexandrian Jew was an orator and an efficient worker in the Church who knew only the baptism of John (Acts 18:24, 25). The influence of Apollos was ample and varied and, under Aquila and Priscilla, was heightened and enriched.

I. His was the influence of eloquence (Acts 18:24). Apollos wielded an ever powerful instrument of blessing—a consecrated eloquence.

II. His was the influence of exposition. Apollos was mighty in the Scriptures (Acts 18:26). What a tribute it is to be mighty in the mightiest of books!

III. His was the influence of spiritual knowledge. Apollos taught by word of mouth the things of the Lord.

IV. His was the influence of fervency. Apollos was also "fervent in spirit" (Acts 18:25). "A lively, affectionate preacher," as Matthew Henry calls him.

V. His was the influence of accuracy. Apollos taught "carefully" or "accurately" the truth of Christ (Acts 18:25 RV). Incorrectness in teaching is detrimental to all concerned.

VI. His was the influence of courage. Apollos spoke "boldly." He had no hesitation in his tone. Courage flashed in his eyes (Acts 18:26).

Yet with all his excellent gifts and goodly influence, Apollos had a distinct limitation. He knew that Christ was coming, but his was only a partial Christianity. Yet what he knew and taught profoundly impressed many in the synagogue. Under the tuition of Aquila and Priscilla, two deeply taught believers, Apollos was led into a deeper understanding of the truth. Instructed in the way of the Lord, Apollos went out to expound the truth more fully and accurately and thereafter became an unashamed herald of the Christian faith especially among the Jews (Acts 18:28).

Later on, Apollos became an apostle and one of Paul's trusted friends and companions, and remained active in his ministry during Paul's life (I Cor. 16:12; Titus 3:13). So effective a preacher did he become that some of the Corinthians put him before both Peter and Paul. Martin Luther hazarded the guess that Apollos was the writer of the Epistle to the Hebrews.

APPAIM [Ăp′ pa ĭm]—FACE or PRESENCE. *Son of Nadah,* of the family of Hezron (I Chron. 2:30, 31).

AQUILA [Ăq′ uĭ lă]—EAGLE. *A Jew whom Paul found at Corinth* on his arrival from Athens (Acts 18:2, 18, 26; Rom. 16:3; I Cor. 16:19; II Tim. 4:19).

The Man Who Is Always Linked with His Wife

A characteristic feature of Aquila and Priscilla is that their names are always mentioned together. In the truest sense they were "no more twain but one." They were one in their common interest in Christ, and all they accomplished together in the name of the Lord was the result of that perfect unity of spiritual nature, of purpose and of aim.

I.   By occupation they were tent-makers. Perhaps it was because Paul followed the same trade that he was attracted to them when he went to Corinth from Athens.

II.   By their oneness in spiritual things they were hospitable. Being in full sympathy with Paul's message they willingly received him unto their house, and he remained with them for a year and a half. What blessed times of fellowship the three of them must have had!

III.   By their faithfulness they encouraged the saints. Paul tells us that these two devoted people were willing to "lay down their own necks" for the apostle. What they did for Paul earned the gratitude of all the churches.

IV.   By their spiritual insight, Apollos and many other saints were helped. They had a "church in their house" and because of their spiritual quality and knowledge of Scripture many were blessed.

A fact that cannot escape our notice is that Priscilla is usually named first in the references to Aquila and herself. Perhaps this most "noble Roman lady" became a Christian before her husband. Maybe she was a more active worker than her husband! Chrysostom says that it was Priscilla's careful expositions of the way of God that proved so helpful to Apollos. Together, Aquila and Priscilla are a pertinent example for Christian husbands and wives.

ARA [Ā' rä]—STRONG. *Son of Jether,* of the tribe of Asher (I Chron. 7:38).

ARAD [Ā' răd]—FUGITIVE.
1.   *The Canaanite king* who attacked the Israelites near Mount Hor and was defeated (Num. 21:1; 33:40).
2.   *Son of Beriah,* a Benjamite and one of the principal men of Aijalon (I Chron. 8:15). Also the name of a town south of Judah (Josh. 12:14).

ARAH [Ā' rah]—WAYFARER.
1.   *A son of Ulla,* an Asherite (I Chron. 7:39).
2.   *The father of a family* that returned from exile (Ezra 2:5; Neh. 7:10). Perhaps the same person as No. 1.
3.   *A Jew* whose granddaughter became the wife of Tobiah the Ammonite (Neh. 6:18).

ARAM [Ā' răm]—EXALTED.
1.   *A son of Shem* (Gen. 10:22, 23; I Chron. 1:17).
2.   *Son of Kemuel,* Abraham's nephew (Gen. 22:21).
3.   *Son of Shamer,* of the tribe of Asher (I Chron. 7:34; Matt. 1:3, 4,

Luke 3:33). Also the name used of the whole country of Syria (Num. 23:7), and of the hill country north of Canaan (I Chron. 2:23).

ARAN [Ă' răn]—A WILD GOAT or FIRMNESS. *Son of Dishan,* the Horite, a descendant of Esau (Gen. 36:28; I Chron. 1:42).

ARAUNAH [Ă rau' nah]—JEHOVAH IS FIRM. *The Jebusite* who owned a threshing floor on Mount Moriah, which David purchased in order to erect an altar. Because of his sin in numbering the people, the land was smitten with a plague. When the plague was stayed, David presented a costly offering to the Lord (II Sam. 24:16–24). Called Ornan in I Chronicles 21:15.

ARBA [Ăr' ba]—THE CROUCHER or STRENGTH OF BAAL. *The father of Anak,* so named because he was the father of the city which bore his name. Kirjath-arba, later Hebron, was a chief seat of the Anakims (Josh. 14:15; 15:13; 21:11).

ARCHELAUS [Ăr chĕ lā' us]—PEOPLE'S CHIEF. *A son of Herod the Great* (Matt. 2:22). See Herod.

ARCHIPPUS [Ăr chĭp' pus]—MASTER OF THE HORSE. *A Christian at Colosse* conspicuous as a champion of the Gospel — a close friend of Philemon — an office-bearer in the Church (Col. 4:17; Philem. 2). Because of the spiritual atmosphere of Colosse (Rev. 3:14–19), it is not surprising to find Paul exhorting his fellow-soldiers to maintain his zeal and fidelity.

ARD [Ărd]—DESCENT.
1. *A son of Benjamin,* and founder of the Ardites (Gen. 46:21).
2. *A son of Bela,* son of Benjamin (Num. 26:40). Called Addar in I Chronicles 8:3.

ARDON [Ăr' dŏn]—DESCENDANT. *A son of Caleb,* son of Hezron, a Judahite (I Chron. 2:18).

ARELI [Ă rē' lī]—VALIANT or HEROIC. *A son of Gad* and founder of the tribal family, the Arelites (Gen. 46:16; Num. 26:17).

ARETAS [Ăr' e tăs]—PLEASING or VIRTUOUS. *Father-in-law of Herod the Tetrarch,* whose deputy sought to apprehend Paul at Damascus (II Cor. 11:32).

ARGOB [Ăr' gŏb]—HEAP OF STONES or STRONG. *A man assassinated* along with Pekahiah, king of Israel, by Pekah who aspired to the throne (II Kings 15:25). Also the name of the kingdom of Og in Bashan (Deut. 3:4, 13, 14).

ARIDAI [Ă rĭd' a ī] probably GIFT OF THE PLOUGH or THE BULL. *The ninth of Haman's sons*, hanged along with his father and brothers (Esther 9:9).

ARIDATHA [Ă rĭd' a thă]—GREAT BIRTH. *The sixth son of Haman* who suffered the death of hanging at the hands of the Jews (Esther 9:8).

ARIEH [Ă rī' eh]—LION OF JEHOVAH. *A companion of Argob,* and assassinated along with him by Pekah, son of Remaliah (II Kings 15:25).

ARIEL [Ă' rĭ el]—LION OF GOD or GOD'S ALTAR-HEARTH.
1. *A chief of the Jews* whom Ezra sent with others to Iddo at Casiphia (Ezra 8:16, 17).
2. *The name of a Moabite* whose two sons were slain by Benaiah (II Sam. 23:20; I Chron. 11:22). Also the symbolic name of Jerusalem (Isa. 29:1–7).

ARIOCH [Ă' rĭ och]—LION-LIKE or SERVANT OF THE MOON-GOD.
1. *The king of Ellasar* in Syria and confederate with Chedorlaomer (Gen. 14:1, 4).
2. *Captain of the king's guard* at Babylon under Nebuchadnezzar (Dan. 2:14–25).

ARISAI [Ă rĭs' a ī]—MEANING OBSCURE. *The eighth son of Haman* the Agagite who was hanged with the rest of the male members of the family (Esther 9:9).

ARISTARCHUS [Ăr ĭs tär' chus]—THE BEST RULER. *A Macedonian of Thessalonica* and one of Paul's travel-companions. This convert from Judaism is spoken of as Paul's "fellow-prisoner," implying imprisonment for the Gospel's sake (Acts 19:29; 20:4; 27:2; Col. 4:10; Philem. 24).

ARISTOBULUS [Ăr ĭs to bū lus]—THE BEST COUNSELOR. *A Christian in Rome,* whose household Paul greeted. Tradition says that he was one of the seventy disciples and that he preached in Britain (Rom. 16:10).

ARMONI [Ăr mŏ' nī]—PERTAINING TO THE PALACE. *A son of Saul* by the concubine Rizpah. He was slain by the Gibeonites to satisfy justice (II Sam. 21:8–11).

ARNAN [Ăr' nan]—STRONG or AGILE. *A descendant of David* and founder of a tribal family (I Chron. 3:21).

ARNI [Ăr' nī]—REJOICING. *An ancestor of Jesus Christ* (Luke 3:33). This spelling is given in the R.V. Called Aram and Ram. (See Ruth 4:19; I Chron. 2:9, 10; Matt. 1:3, 4).

AROD [Ā' rŏd]—POSTERITY. *A son of Gad* and founder of the Arodi or Arodites (Gen. 46:16; Num. 26:17).

ARPHAXAD, ARPACHSHAD [Är phăx' ad]—ONE THAT RELEASES. *The third son of Shem,* and a remote ancestor of Abraham (Gen. 10: 22, 24; 11:10–13; I Chron. 1:17, 24; Luke 3:36).

ARTAXERXES [Är tăx ûrx' ēs]—POSSESSOR OF AN EXALTED KINGDOM. In his concordance, Young distinguishes three of the Persian kings bearing this name.

1. *The Longimanus of secular history.* It was during the seventh year of the reign of this Persian king that Ezra went up to Jerusalem (Ezra 7:1–21; 8:1; Neh. 2:1; 5:14; 13:6).

2. *The Cambyses of secular history,* another Persian king who reigned in Ezra's time (Ezra 4:7–23).

3. *The king of Persia* who reigned around the time of Darius (Ezra 6:14).

ARTEMAS [Är' te mäs]—WHOLE or SOUND. Another meaning of this name is "gift of Artemas," Artemas being the Greek goddess of hunting. Paul's companion at Nicopolis, whom the apostle used to send a message to Titus (Titus 3:12).

ARZA [Är'ză]—FIRM or DELIGHT. *The steward of king Elah's house* in Tirzah (I Kings 16:9).

ASA [Ā' sä]—PHYSICIAN.

1. *The third king of Judah* who succeeded Abijah. He was the great-grandson of Solomon (I Kings 15; II Chron. 14–16). He was an ancestor of Jesus Christ (Matt. 1:7, 8).

The Man Who Was Good and Right

Asa is a marvel. In spite of the fact that his father was a sinful man and his mother a heathen woman, he yet shines forth as one of Judah's most godly kings. He is praised for his religious zeal which led him to reform the worship of the people. Because of his devotion to God he deposed his idolatrous mother—an astonishing act for an oriental.

Asa's heart toward God was like David's and such was the secret of his godliness in a foul environment. He is spoken of as doing "that which was good and right in the eyes of the Lord, his God." Some people are presumptuous enough to settle what is good and right in their own eyes. Asa, however, did not invent a goodness or righteousness he could adapt to his own convenience and ambition. He only wanted what was good and right in God's sight.

I. Asa prayed before battle. He did not shrink from war with the Ethiopians. Before meeting the foe he met God. "Lord, it is nothing with Thee to help."

II. Asa began upon a good foundation. It took courage and Asa "took courage, and put away the abominable idols." Our idols of fortune, fashion, popularity, self-indulgence, must be severely dealt with if we desire God's best. We can only be right with God and with one another when we are right about our little gods, and man-made idols.

III. Asa was victorious. Being right with God, Asa was honored of Him. His foes surrendered for they saw that his God was with him.

IV. Asa was impartial. The grandeur of this good king is seen in that he would not even allow his mother to keep an idol. So he ruthlessly destroyed the little royal shrine. What was wrong for the subject was also wrong for the queen. Thus horrible abominations had to be abolished. No wonder when Asa died, his people sorely missed and mourned him!

2. *A Levite,* son of Elkanah and head of a family of Netophathites (I Chron. 9:16).

ASAHEL [Ā' sa hĕl]—GOD HATH MADE or GOD IS DOER.

1. *A Levite* sent by Jehoshaphat to teach the law to the people in Judah (II Chron. 17:8).

2. *A Levite* Hezekiah employed as an officer of the offerings, tithes and dedicated things (II Chron. 31:13).

3. *Father of a certain Jonathan,* appointed by Ezra to take a census of those Jews who had married foreign wives while in exile (Ezra 10:15).

4. *The youngest son of Zeruiah,* David's sister, and the brother of Joab and Abishai. He was slain by Abner unwillingly (II Sam. 2:18–32; 3:27, 30; 23:24; I Chron. 2:16; 11:26; 27:7).

The Man Who Died in His Boots

Conspicuous among those of David's brethren and those of his father's house who came to him while hiding in the cave of Adullam were the three sons of Zeruiah his sister, Joab, Abishai and Asahel. Asahel was the favorite among the three. Little is recorded of him beyond his activity and the manner of his death.

I. He was famous for his swiftness of foot. Speed was a much valued gift in ancient times.

II. He was near the top of David's thirty heroes. Courage made him a conspicuous fighter.

III. He was a commander of a division in David's army. He had proved himself worthy of position.

IV. He believed in persistence. He persisted in following Abner, the captain of Saul's host in the battle that began by the pool of Gibeon. Abner was unwilling to slay him, knowing how he was beloved. He seems to have struck Asahel at last only in self-defense.

V. He dies for his ambition. Asahel would aim at nothing less than the glory of slaying Saul's general, and he was slain himself instead. Thus he died in harness or as we have put it, in his boots.

ASAHIAH [Ā sa hĭ' ah]—JEHOVAH HATH MADE. *An officer of king Josiah's* sent with others to enquire about the Law found by Shaphan (II Kings 22:12, 14; II Chron. 34:20).

ASAIAH [Ā sa ī' ah]—JEHOVAH IS DOER.
1. *A descendant of Simeon,* a Simeonite prince (I Chron. 4:36).
2. *Of the family of Haggiah* and Merari (I Chron. 6:30).
3. *Son of a Shilonite* living in Jerusalem (I Chron. 9:5).
4. *A descendant of Merari* who helped in the return of the Ark from the house of Obed-edom (I Chron. 15:6, 11). Perhaps the same person as No. 2.

ASAPH [Ā' saph]—HE THAT GATHERED or REMOVED REPROACH.
1. *Father of Joah* who was the recorder to Hezekiah (II Kings 18:18, 37; II Chron. 29:13; Isa. 36:3, 22).
2. *Son of Berechiah* of the Gershonite family appointed by David over the service of song and by Solomon in the Temple services (I Chron. 6:39; 15:17, 19). David called this Asaph "the seer" (II Chron. 29:30).
3. *A Levite,* whose posterity lived in Jerusalem after the exile (I Chron. 9:15).
4. *A descendant of Kohath,* son of Levi, whose descendants were tabernacle porters in David's time (I Chron. 26:1).
5. *The keeper of the king's park* in Palestine under the king of Persia (Neh. 2:8).

ASAREEL, ASAREL [Ā sā' re el]—GOD IS JOINED. *A son of Jehallelel,* a descendant of Judah through Caleb the spy (I Chron. 4:16).

ASARELAH, ASHARELAH—[Ăs a rē' lah]—UPRIGHT TOWARD GOD. *A son of Asaph*—No. 2 above (I Chron. 25:2). Perhaps the Azareel of I Chronicles 25:18. Also known as Jesharelah in I Chronicles 25:14.

ASHBEA [Ăsh bē' ă]—MAN OF BAAL or LET ME CALL AS WITNESS. *A descendant of Shelah,* a Judahite who wrought in fine linen (I Chron. 4:21).

ASHBEL [Ăsh' bĕl]—MAN OF BAAL. *The second son of Benjamin* and father of a tribal family known as the Ashbelites (Gen. 46:21; Num. 26:38; I Chron. 8:1).

ASHCHENAZ, ASHKENAZ [Ăsh' che năz, Ăsh' ke năz]—A FIRE THAT SPREADS. *Eldest son of Gomer* (Gen. 10:3; I Chron. 1:6; see Jer. 51:27).

ASHER [Ăsh' ûr]—HAPPY. *The eighth son of Jacob* and second of Zilpah, Leah's maid and progenitor of a tribe (Gen 30:13. 35:26; 49:20; Deut. 33:24, 25). The New Testament form is Aser (Luke 2:36;

Rev. 7:6). Asher was the founder of the Asherites (Num. 1:13; Judg. 1:32). Also the name of a town east of Shechem (Josh. 17:7).

The Man with Shoes of Iron and Brass

In the blessings of Jacob and Moses, Asher is described as being not only acceptable to his brethren, but as one blessed of God with royal dainties or bountiful supplies. Of all the tribes of Israel the tribe of Asher has the least eventful history. It never produced a great warrior, judge, king or counselor. The land of Asher was as uneventful as the tribe itself. No great battles were fought there in Israel's time.

I. Asher and his bounties. Asher was the tribe of rich pastures. Asher dwelt in the midst of plenty and being willing to share what he had, was most acceptable to his brethren. Dipping the foot in oil may refer to the olive-trees, so plentiful in that thickly wooded part of Palestine. Acre, the port and town given to Asher, has been regarded as the key of Palestine, and as oil has been recently discovered near by, perhaps the fatness of the prophecies of Jacob and Moses is about to be realized to the full.

II. Asher and his female representative. No other tribe of Israel is represented in Scripture by a woman. One member of the tribe, a widow, represents the individual history of the tribe. "One Anna, a prophetess, the daughter of Phanuel, of the tribe of Asher" (Luke 2: 36–38). It was Anna who confessed Christ, at His birth, on the part of Israel.

III. Asher and his love of ease. The chief defect in the character of Asher was his unwillingness to drive out the Canaanites. He was content to dwell among them. The command was to utterly drive them out and make no terms with them. "Live and let live," seems to have been Asher's policy. Asher's rich bounties had an enervating effect upon the tribe. The people were conspicuous by their absence during the war with Sisera (Judg. 5:17). Apart from Anna, none of the tribe appear to have been eminent for prowess or piety. Prosperity resulted in ease and declension.

IV. Asher and the promise of endurance. Completing the blessing of Moses was a wonderful promise of endurance for the days of pilgrimage. "Thy shoes shall be iron and brass, and as thy days so shall thy strength be." The words for shoes and strength are peculiar to this verse, and are found nowhere else in the Bible. Many guesses have been made as to the true meaning of these words. Such a promise was well understood by those who, as they journeyed through the great and terrible wilderness had raiment that waxed not old upon them and feet that did not swell. Anna is a fitting illustration of the promised endurance, seeing that she was long past eighty years of age when she saw the Saviour.

ASHPENAZ [Ăsh' pe năz]—HORSE'S NOSE. *The prince of the eunuchs* at Babylon during the reign of Nebuchadnezzar (Dan. 1:3).

ASHUR [Ash' ŭr]—FREEMAN. *A son of Hezron,* son of Pharez (I Chron. 2:24; 4:5), and founder of the tribe of Ashurites (II Sam. 2:9).

ASHVATH [Ash' văth]—WROUGHT. *A son of Japhlet,* an Asherite (I Chron. 7:33).

ASIEL [A' sĭ el]—GOD HATH MADE. *Great-grandfather of Jehu* a Simeonite (I Chron. 4:35).

ASNAH [As' nah]—A BRAMBLE or DWELLER IN THE THORNBUSH. *A Nethinim,* whose descendants returned from the Babylonian captivity with Zerubbabel (Ezra 2:50).

ASNAPPER [As năp' pŭr]—ASNAP THE GREAT. *High Assyrian dignitary* called "great and noble" who settled various foreign tribes in Samaria (Ezra 4:10). See Esar-haddon.

ASPATHA [As' pa thă]—HORSE-GIVEN. *The third son of Haman,* the Jews' enemy who was hanged with his father and brothers (Esther 9:7).

ASRIEL, ASHRIEL [As' rĭ el, Ash' rĭ el]—VOW OF GOD or GOD IS JOINED.
1. *A son of Gilead* (Num. 26:31; Josh. 17:1, 2).
2. *A son of Manasseh* (I Chron. 7:14).

ASSHUR, ASSUR [As' shur]—LEVEL PLAIN.
1. *Likely a descendant of Ham,* the builder of Nineveh, or of Assyria itself (Gen. 10:11).
2. *A son of Shem* and brother of Elam (Gen. 10:22; I Chron. 1:17).

ASSHURIM [As shu' rim]—MIGHTY ONES. *A son of Dedan,* or his descendants (Gen. 25:3).

ASSIR [As' sĭr]—CAPTIVE.
1. *A son of Korah* who was the grandson of Kohath (Ex. 6:24; I Chron. 6:22).
2. *A son of Ebiasaph* and grandson of Elkanah (I Chron. 6:23, 37).
3. *A son of Jeconiah,* son of Jehoiakim (I Chron. 3:17).

ASYNCRITUS [A sўn' cri-tŭs]—INCOMPARABLE. *A Christian in Rome* to whom Paul sends a salutation (Rom. 16:14).

ATER [A' tûr]—BOUND or SHUT.
1. *The ancestor of an exiled family* (Ezra 2:16; Neh. 7:21).
2. *Ancestor of a family of gatekeepers* who returned from exile with Zerubbabel (Ezra 2:42; Neh. 7:45).
3. *The chief of the people* who, with Nehemiah, sealed the covenant (Neh. 10:17).

ATHAIAH [Ăth a ĭ' ah]—JEHOVAH IS HELPER. *The son of Uzziah* a Judahite in Nehemiah's time (Neh. 11:4).

ATHALIAH [Ăth a lĭ' ah]—JEHOVAH IS STRONG or HATH AFFLICTED.
1. *A son of Jeroham*, a Benjamite (I Chron. 8:26).
2. *The father of Jeshiah*, a returned exile (Ezra 8:7). Also the name of the wife of Jehoram, king of Judah (II Kings 8:26).

ATHLAI [Ăth' laī]—JEHOVAH IS STRONG. *A son of Bebai* who put away his foreign wife (Ezra 10:28).

ATTAI [Ăt' taī]—SEASONABLE or OPPORTUNE.
1. *Grandson of Sheshan*, a Jerahmeelite (I Chron. 2:35, 36).
2. *A Gadite* who joined David at Ziklag (I Chron. 12:11).
3. *A son of Rehoboam*, son of Solomon (II Chron. 11:20).

AUGUSTUS [Ŏu gŭs' tus]—SACRED OR KINGLY. *Name of the Caesar* who became Emperor of Rome after the death of his uncle, Julius Caesar (Luke 2:1; Acts 25:21, 25; 27:1).

AZALIAH [Ăz a lĭ' ah]—JEHOVAH IS NOBLE or HATH SPARED. *Father of Shapham* the scribe (II Kings 22:3; II Chron. 34:8).

AZANIAH [Ăz a nĭ' ah]—JEHOVAH IS HEARER or HATH GIVEN EAR. *A Levite*, father of Jeshua, whose son signed the covenant (Neh. 10:9).

AZARAEL, AZAREEL [Ă zăr' a el, Ă zăr' e el]—GOD IS A HELPER.
1. *An Aaronite* who joined David at Ziklag (I Chron. 12:6).
2. *A priest*, responsible for the service of his sons in David's time (I Chron. 25:18). Perhaps the Asarelah the son of Asaph.
3. *A Danite prince* in David's time (I Chron. 27:22).
4. *A son of Bani* who married a foreign wife during the exile (Ezra 10:41).
5. *A priest of the family of Immer* (Neh. 11:13; 12:36).

AZARIAH [Ăz a rĭ' ah]—JEHOVAH IS KEEPER or HATH HELPED. The fact that there are almost thirty men bearing the name of Azariah is proof that it was a common name in Hebrew, especially in the family of Eleazar, whose name has a similar meaning, and is almost identical with Ezra, Zerahiah and Seraiah. See also Azariahu and Zacharias.
1. *The son of Zadok* and a descendant of David's high priest (I Kings 4:2).
2. *The son of Nathan*, ruler of Solomon's officers (I Kings 4:5).
3. *The son of Amaziah*, who was made king of Judah after his father (II Kings 14:21; 15:1–27; I Chron. 3:12).
4. *A man of Judah*, of the family of Zerah and of the house of Ethan (I Chron. 2:8).

5. *The son of Jehu* and grandson of Obed, a Judahite (I Chron. 2:38,39).

6. *A son of Ahimaz* and grandson of Zadok (I Chron. 6:9).

7. *A son of Johanan* and grandson of No. 6 who served in Solomon's time (I Chron. 6:10, 11).

8. *A son of Hilkiah,* and father of Seraiah the high priest in Josiah's reign (I Chron. 6:13, 14; 9:11; Ezra 7:1).

9. *A Levite of the family of Kohath* and an ancestor of Samuel the prophet (I Chron. 6:36).

10. *A prophet,* son of Obed, he encouraged Asa to persevere in his national religious revival (II Chron. 15:1).

11. *A son of king Jehoshaphat* (II Chron. 21:2).

12. *Another son of the above* (II Chron. 21:2).

13. *Son of Jehoram* (II Chron. 22:6).

14. *The son of Jehoram* and a captain who assisted in the overthrow of Athaliah and the elevation of Joash to the throne of Judah (II Chron. 23:1).

15. *The son of Obed* who also assisted in the above task (II Chron. 23:1).

16. *The high priest* who hindered Uzziah from burning incense on the altar (II Chron. 26:17, 20).

17. *The son of Johanan* and a chief of the tribe of Ephraim (II Chron. 28:12).

18. *The father of Joel* and a Kohathite (II Chron. 29:12). He assisted in the purification of the Temple in Hezekiah's time.

19. *The son of Jehalelel,* a Merarite who also assisted in Hezekiah's revival (II Chron. 29:12).

20. *The chief priest* of the house of Zadok in King Hezekiah's time (II Chron. 31:10, 13).

21. *The son of Meraioth,* and an ancestor of Ezra (Ezra 7:3).

22. *The son of Maaseiah,* of the family of Ananiah, who repaired a portion of the wall of Jerusalem (Neh. 3:23, 24).

23. *An Israelite who returned with Zerubbabel* (Neh. 7:7). Name also given as Seraiah.

24. *One of the priests* who explained the Law to the people as Ezra read it. Perhaps the same person as No. 22 (Neh. 8:7).

25. *Another priest* who sealed the covenant (Neh. 10:2).

26. *A prince of Judah* who joined in the procession with Nehemiah (Neh. 12:33).

27. *A son of Hoshaiah* and an opponent of Jeremiah whom he charged with false prophecies (Jer. 43:2).

28. *The Hebrew and original name of Abed-nego,* who with Daniel and others was carried away captive to Babylon (Dan. 1:6, 7, 11, 19; 2:17).

AZAZ [Ā′ zăz]—STRONG. *Father of a Reubenite chief* in Jeroboam's time (I Chron. 5:8).

AZAZIAH [Ăz a zī′ ah]—JEHOVAH IS STRONG.
1. *A Levite harpist* who assisted in the musical service when the Ark returned from the house of Obed-edom (I Chron. 15:21).
2. *Father of Hoshea* the prince of Ephraim in David's time (I Chron. 27:20).
3. *A Levite overseer* of dedicated things in the Temple in Hezekiah's reign (II Chron. 31:13).

AZBUK [Ăz′ bŭk]—PARDON. *The father of Nehemiah*—not the governor of the same name—who repaired a portion of the wall (Neh. 3:16).

AZEL, AZAL [Ā′ zĕl, Ā′zăl]—NOBLE. *A Benjamite* and a descendant of Jonathan, Saul's son (I Chron. 8:37, 38; 9:43, 44). Also the name of a hamlet (Zech. 14:5).

AZGAD [Ăz′ găd]—WORSHIP, SUPPLICATION or STRONG OF FORTUNE.
1. *Founder of a family* that returned with Ezra and Zerubbabel (Ezra 2:12; Neh. 7:17).
2. *One who returned from exile with Ezra* (8:12).
3. *A chief of a family of Jews* who sealed the covenant (Neh. 10:15).

AZIEL [Ā′ zī′ el]—GOD IS MIGHT. *A Levite* who assisted in the choral service of the Tabernacle (I Chron. 15:20). Called Jaaziel in I Chronicles 15:18.

AZIZA [Ă zī′ ză]—ROBUST or STRONG. *A son of Zattu* who married a foreign wife while in exile (Ezra 10:27).

AZMAVETH [Ăz′ ma vĕth]—DEATH IS STRONG or COUNSEL.
1. *One of David's thirty heroes* (II Sam. 23:31; I Chron. 11:33).
2. *A son of Jehoada* (also called Jarah), and descendant of Saul (I Chron. 8:36; 9:42).
3. *A Benjamite* whose two sons joined David at Ziklag (I Chron. 12:3).
4. *One of David's treasury officers* (I Chron. 27:25). Also the name of a village (Neh. 12:29). Now called Hizmeh.

AZOR [Ā′ zôr]—HELPER. *Great-grandson of Zorobabel* and an ancestor of Jesus Christ (Matt. 1:13, 14).

AZRIEL [Ăz′ rǐ el]—HELP OF GOD or GOD IS HELPER.
1. *A chief man of the half tribe of Manasseh* (I Chron. 5:24).

2. *Father of Jerimoth*, ruler of Naphtali in David's time (I Chron. 27:19).

3. *Father of Seraiah* of Jeremiah's time (Jer. 36:26).

AZRIKAM [Ăz' rĭ kăm]—MY HELP HATH RISEN.
1. *A son of Neariah* of the family of David (I Chron. 3:23).
2. *A son of Azel*, of the family of Saul (I Chron. 8:38; 9:44).
3. *A Levite*, and a descendant of Merari (I Chron. 9:14; Neh. 11:15).
4. *The governor of the palace* under King Ahaz (II Chron. 28:7).

AZUR, AZZUR [Ā' zur, Ăz' zŭr]—HELPER.
1. *Father of Jaazaniah*, a prince seen in vision (Ezek. 11:1).
2. *One of those* who sealed the covenant (Neh. 10:17).
3. *Father of Hananiah* who withstood Jeremiah (Jer. 28:1).

AZZAN [Ăz' zan]—STRONG OR SHARP. *The father of Paltiel*, a prince of Issachar, who assisted in the portion of the land (Num. 34:26).

B

BAAL [Bā' al]—POSSESSOR OR CONTROLLER.
1. *A Reubenite* of the house of Joel who lived before the captivity of the tribes (I Chron. 5:5, 6).
2. *A Benjamite*, son of King Saul's ancestor Jehiel (I Chron. 8:30; 9:35, 36, 39). Also the name of the male deity of the Phoenicians and Canaanites, as Ashtoreth was their chief female deity. Baal is likewise the name of a village of Simeon (Num. 22:41; I Chron. 4:33).

BAAL-HANAN [Bā' al-hā' nan]—THE LORD IS GRACIOUS.
1. *Son of Achbor* and the seventh of the Edomite kings (Gen. 36:38, 39; I Chron. 1:49, 50).
2. *A custodian* of the olive and sycamore trees in David's time (I Chron. 27:28).

BAALIS [Bā' al Ĭs]—LORD OF JOY OR RULES. *The king of the Ammonites* who reigned after Nebuchadnezzar's capture of Jerusalem (Jer. 40:14).

BAANA, BAANAH [Bā' a nă, Bā' a nah]—SON OF GRIEF OR AFFLICTION.
1. *The son of Ahilud* and one of Solomon's purveyors in Jezreel (I Kings 4:12).
2. *The son of Hushai* and another of Solomon's purveyors responsible for Asher (I Kings 4:16).

3. *The father of Zadok,* who returned from exile with Zerubbabel and who helped to repair the wall (Neh. 3:4).

BAANAH [Bä′ a nah]—SON OF GRIEF.
1. *The father of Heleb,* one of David's thirty heroes (II Sam. 23:29; I Chron. 11:30).
2. *A captain of Ish-bosheth's army* and one of his murderers (II Sam. 4:5–12).
3. *One who returned from exile with Zerubbabel* (Ezra 2:2; Neh. 7:7; 10:27).

BAASEIAH [Bä′ a sě′ iah]—JEHOVAH IS BOLD. *A Levite,* descendant of Gershom and ancestor of Asaph the musician (I Chron. 6:40).

BAASHA [Bä′ a shǎ]—BOLDNESS, OFFENSIVE or HE WHO LAYS WASTE. *The son of Ahijah,* of the tribe of Issachar who obtained the throne of Israel by usurpation. He conspired against Nadab the son of Jeroboam I, and slew all his heirs. Baasha died in his bed after reigning for twenty-four years, and his dynasty was extinguished two years after his death (I Kings 15:27–16:13; II Chron. 16:1–6; Jer. 41:9).

BAKBAKKAR [Bǎk bǎk′ kar]—DILIGENT SEARCHER. *A Levite* who returned from exile (I Chron. 9:15).

BAKBUK [Bǎk′ buk]—A FLAGON or HOLLOW. *One of the Nethinims* who returned from exile (Ezra 2:51; Neh. 7:53).

BAKBUKIAH [Bǎk bŭk ĭ′ ah]—WASTED BY JEHOVAH or EFFUSION OF JEHOVAH.
1. *A Levite of Asaph's family,* resident of Jerusalem who held high office after the exile (Neh. 11:17; 12:9).
2. *One of the Temple porters* (Neh. 12:25). Perhaps these are the same person.

BALAAM [Bä′ laam]—A PILGRIM, DEVOURING or LORD OF THE PEOPLE. *A diviner,* son of Beor and resident of the town of Pethor (Num. 22; 23; 24; Deut. 23:4).

The Man Who Heard an Ass Speak

Peter, Jude and John deal with Balaam as a historical presence (II Pet. 2:15; Jude 11; Rev. 2:14).

In Balaam we have a fitting yet tragic illustration of our Lord's teaching about the light in us being darkness. Balaam had a *head* full of light but a *heart* that was dark—and great was the darkness! This man of Mesopotamia, counted a prophet, yet followed the unholy practice of Eastern soothsayers.

Balak the king, greatly alarmed because of the Israelites swarming the Plains of Moab, sent for Balaam to pronounce a curse upon the people of God so that he would have nothing more to fear. Balaam refused and declared that all who blessed Israel would be blessed. Balak sent for Balaam again and again, tempting him with bribes but Balaam remained firm. In a further approach of Balak, Balaam was more cautious in his refusal. Instead of saying with Daniel, "Thy gifts be to thyself and give thy rewards to another," Balaam caught the bait held out and proved that he loved the wages of unrighteousness.

Balak's messengers were not immediately dismissed. Balaam asked for time to consult God as to what he should do. The line of duty, however, was perfectly clear. There was no need to pray. God allowed Balaam to go, but he did not carry divine approval with him. Sometimes God punishes us by allowing us to have our own way. Thus Balaam started to Balak but did not reach him. Suddenly the ass he was riding stopped and could not be induced to proceed. God's angel was before him although Balaam could not see him standing in the way with his drawn sword. Then the ass, the most stupid of all beasts, was made to speak and reprove one of the wisest of men. Awestruck at what had happened and trembling with fear, Balaam confessed, "I have sinned." Balaam must have known that his whole conduct was displeasing to God and that he had been wilfully blind.

Back Balaam went and with a great parade built seven altars and offered bullocks and rams on every altar. But God was not pleased with such offerings. Yet God employed Balaam for His own purposes, for He put into his mouth some of the most blessed and glorious words spoken concerning His people Israel. With his heart turned towards the eternal world Balaam wanted to die the death of a righteous man, but his end was far from righteous. He died in a general massacre and we have no record of his repentance. He died in his sins.

Clearly evident are the lessons to be learned from this renowned man who was self-willed (Num. 22:5-22); saved from death by a beast (Num. 22:33); double-minded in that he was eloquent in prophecy but presumptuous in seeking to alter the divine plan (Num. 23; 24); a failure in his mission (Num. 24:10); an evil counselor (Num. 31:16); overcome by the besetting sin of avarice (II Pet. 2:13):

The clearest knowledge without grace is worthless.

The presence of any sin is ruinous, especially covetousness.

The most pious wishes are sometimes vain. The road to hell can be paved with good resolutions.

To die well one must live well.

BALADAN [Băl' a dăn]—HAVING POWER, or A SON HE HATH GIVEN. *The father of Berodach-baladan, king of Babylon in Hezekiah's time (II Kings 20:12; Isa. 39:1).*

BALAK, BALAC [Bă' lăk, Bă' lăc]—WASTER, EMPTYING or DESTROYS. *The King of Moab, and son of Zipper who hired Balaam to curse Israel when, toward the end of their wilderness journeyings they were in*

Balak's territory (Num. 22; 23; 24; Judg. 11:25; Micah 6:5). Like Balaam, Balak also lives to the end of the Bible. *Balac* is the Greek form of Balak (Rev. 2:14). Revealing the superstition of the human mind, Balak had recourse to supernatural help and sought out Balaam, the soothsayer of Pethor—a man of divination with power to bless and curse, the Simon Magus of his day. How deceived Balak was when he thought he could sow the air with curses which would work where his sword could not reach!

BANI [Bā′ nī]—BUILT or POSTERITY.

1. *The Gadite,* and one of David's thirty heroes (II Sam. 23:36).
2. *The son of Shamer,* an Aaronite (I Chron. 6:46).
3. *The father of Imri,* a Judahite through Pharez (I Chron. 9:4).
4. *Father of a family* that returned with other captives from Babylon (Ezra 2:10; 10:29). Called Binnui in Nehemiah 7:15).
5. *One whose descendants had married foreign wives* during the exile (Ezra 10:34).
6. *A descendant of No. 5* who also had married a foreign wife (Ezra 10:38).
7. *A Levite,* father of Rehum who repaired part of the city wall (Neh. 3:17; 8:7).
8. *A Levite* who regulated the devotions of the people after Ezra read and expounded the Law (Neh. 9:4, 5; 10:13).
9. *A chieftain* who sealed the covenant (Neh. 10:14).
10. *A Levite* whose son was overseer of the Levites after the exile. Perhaps the same person as No. 7 or No. 8 (Neh. 11:22).

BARABBAS [Bā răb′ bas]—SON OF A FATHER or SON OF RETURN. *The notable prisoner,* committed to prison for robbery and murder, but preferred to Christ (Matt. 27:16–26).

The Man Who Had a Substitute

Barabbas should have died for his crimes but Jesus occupied his cross, along with the two other thieves. What a night Barabbas must have spent before Christ was selected in his place! The thief and murderer had visions of a terrible death. All the torture of crucifixion came up before him. Then as the light of morning looked in through the bars of his prison he hears the march of soldiers coming to take him out to his horrible death.

Can we not imagine how stupefied he must have been when he heard the officer of the guard say, "Barabbas you are free. Another is to die in your stead"? When Barabbas came to himself and realized how true the news was, out he went, grateful to the One condemned to die as his substitute. A just and holy Man to die in the place of a thief and murderer? Yes, Barabbas was saved at such a cost. What a picture of divine grace this substitutionary death presents! Thereafter, whenever Barabbas thought of Christ, he could say, "He died for me."

BARACHEL [Băr′ a chĕl]—GOD HAS BLESSED. *Father of Elihu,* one of Job's friends (Job 32:2, 6).

BARAK [Bā′ răk]—LIGHTNING or THUNDER. *The son of Abinoam,* a Naphtalite, who, with Deborah, defeated Sisera the leader of the Canaanites (Judg. 4:6; Heb. 11:32).

The Man Whose Bravery a Woman Inspired

In the deliverance of Israel, Deborah, and not Barak, is placed first. It is not Barak and Deborah. Barak said to Deborah, "If thou wilt go with me," and she answered, "I will go with thee." Thus at the word of Deborah, Barak led his men to battle and completely routed the enemy. Pursuing Sisera, Barak discovered he had been slain by a woman. The glory of victory that day did not go to Barak but to Deborah, his guiding spirit, and to Jael, who slew the enemy's leader.

Do we have here a hint beforehand of how the seed of the woman should bruise the serpent's head? It was by the nails and the workman's hammer that our salvation was actually wrought. The nail that pierced the feet of the Saviour pierced the serpent's head.

BARIAH [Bā rī′ ah]—FUGITIVE. *A son of Shemaiah,* of the family of David (I Chron. 3:22).

BAR-JESUS [Bär-jē′ zus]—SON OF JOSHUA. *The name of the false prophet,* a Jew, otherwise known as Elymas, who opposed Paul and Barnabas at Paphos (Acts 13:6). In Paul's judgment upon this false prophet there is a play upon words. Elymas was full of deceit and not of wisdom: Bar-jesus meaning, "son of Jesus" had become "a son of the devil" (Acts 13:6; Phil. 3:2).

BAR-JONA [Bär-jō′ nă]—SON OF JOHANAN or JOHN. *The surname of Simon Peter* (Matt. 16:17).

BARKOS [Bär′ kŏs]—PARTLY-COLORED. *One of the Nethinims,* whose descendants returned from exile (Ezra 2:53; Neh. 7:55).

BARNABAS [Bär′ na băs]—SON OF PROPHECY or CONSOLATION. *Surname of Joses,* Paul's companion in several of his missionary journeys (Acts 4:36; 9:27).

The Man Renowned for His Winsomeness

The features of this lovable man stand out in bold relief.

I.   His magnificent generosity. The first recorded deed of this Levite of Cyprus was the selling of his property and the grateful sacrifice of the money secured to the common fund of the first Christian community (Acts. 4:36). The Church has many on her ancient roll who knew what it was to be baptized with the baptism of Barnabas. His exuberant generosity inspired them to surrender their all.

II. His impressive personality. The Lycaonians named Barnabas

Jupiter, the name of the emperor of gods in Grecian mythology (Acts 14:12). Evidently this "son of comfort" had a commanding, dignified, venerable appearance and his physical nobility added to his influence. The culture and consecration of a commendable physical personality is not to be despised. Also mentally and morally, Barnabas was a man among men.

III. His innate goodness. What triple grace this man possessed! "A good man and full of the Holy Ghost and of faith" (Acts 11:24). God-possessed, Barnabas was full of love, sympathy and faith. Vision and allegiance were his. Spirit-filled, he exuded the comfort of the Spirit. Dean Church says that Barnabas was "an earthly reflection of the Paraclete."

IV. His notable ministry. Barnabas had an inspiring influence (Acts 11:25, 26), was trustworthy (Acts 11:29, 30), was adapted to missionary work (Acts 13:2), encouraged converts (Acts 11:23), was a son of Christian prophecy in that he uttered God's messages, was a devoted toiler and self-supporting (I Cor. 9:6).

V. His lamentable contention. It is sad to realize that such a captivating man as Barnabas was a party to a quarrel. How true it is that there are "surprises of sin in holiest histories." The doleful story of the sharp contention between Paul and Barnabas is told in Acts 15: 36–39. Perhaps both good men were wrong. Paul proposed to Barnabas that they should visit the brethren in every city where they had labored. Barnabas agreed and wanted to take Mark, his nephew, with them. Paul felt that Mark, having left them once, was not fit to accompany them, so they parted. Had Paul been too resentful against Mark? Had Barnabas been too eager to urge the claims of his relative? Was one too stern, the other too easy? It is good to know that they were afterwards reconciled.

There are also hints of a certain lack of firmness in Barnabas' otherwise strong character. Writing of dissembling Jews, Paul had to say that even "Barnabas was carried away with their dissimulation" (Gal. 2:13). Barnabas, like the rest of us, had some defective qualities. There has only been one perfect Man on earth — the Saviour Barnabas loved and rejoiced to preach about.

BARSABAS, BARSABBAS [Bär′ sa băs]—SON OF SABA or A SON THAT SUSPENDS THE WATER.

1. *The surname* of the Joseph nominated with Matthias to succeed Judas in the apostolic band (Acts 1:23).

2. *The surname* of the disciple sent with Silas to Antioch (Acts 15:22).

BARTHOLOMEW [Bär thŏl′ o mew]—SON OF TOLMAI. *One of the twelve,* mentioned only in the lists of the apostles (Matt. 10:3; Mark 3:18; Luke 6:14; Acts 1:13). Bartholomew is really not a name but a patronymic. This apostle is identified as Nathanael.

BARTIMAEUS [Bär ti mae′ us]—SON OF TIMAEUS or HONORABLE. *The blind beggar* Jesus healed at the gate of Jericho (Mark 10:46; Luke 18:35).

BARUCH [Bā′ rōōch]—BLESSED.

1. *The son of Zabbai* who helped to rebuild the wall (Neh. 3:20; 10:6).

2. *The son of Neriah*, the son of Maaseian (Jer. 32:12–16). Jeremiah owed much to this loyal secretary who acted as his amanuensis while he was in prison: Baruch made a heavy sacrifice when he threw in his lot with Jeremiah and became his scribe.

3. *A descendant of Perez*, a returned exile (Neh. 11:5).

BARZILLAI [Bär zĭl′ la ī]—MADE OF IRON or STRONG.

1. *A wealthy Gileadite of Rogelim*, numbered among the friends of David (II Sam. 17:27–29; 19:31–40; I Kings 2:7).

The Man of Invincible Charm

Barzillai the Gileadite and his family are remembered for many generations, the habitation of his son Chimham is found by Bethlehem, the city of David in the days of the captivity of the land (Jer. 41:17). What an invincible charm there is about this lovable old man! In his warm commendation of Barzillai, Alexander Whyte speaks of him as an aged, venerable, hospitable highland chief and then goes on to apply the highland characteristics of loyalty, courtesy, hospitality and passionate love of hills and valleys to this ripe old saint. This old testament character displays virtues worthy of emulation.

I. His courageous loyalty. When David sorely needed support at the time of Absalom's rebellion, Barzillai rallied to his side. Like a true man of iron, he offered David indomitable loyalty (II Sam. 17:27–29). With a hero's scorn of consequences Barzillai brought necessary provisions to the hungry, thirsty followers of David. Are we as loyal to our heavenly Monarch as Barzillai was to King David?

II. His reverence of character. Barzillai was drawn to David because of the virtues he manifested. Although David was unpopular, Barzillai knew the soul of David and that he was a man after God's own heart and that therefore he was a man after his own heart. D. L. Moody once said that "Character is what a man is in the dark." To Barzillai, David was *still* godly although a fugitive, and his great, loving heart bled for the king as, like a poor panting beast, he hid from his pursuers. Bountifully he provided David with necessary sustenance as he lay at Mahanaim (II Sam. 19:32).

III. His wide influence. Barzillai is described as a great man, with a noble seat at Rogelim, and whose noble possessions were carried with a noble humility (II Sam. 19:32). He did not squander his wealth on idle pleasures nor hoard it for selfish ends. His position, prestige and purse were beneficially used for others. David wanted to reward

Barzillai but as Professor Eadie says, "The dialogue on this occasion is one of the most lovely to be on the page of history."

Barzillai felt his services were trivial and unworthy of any recompense from David. Barzillai's son received of the king's bounty and had an inheritance with David in Jerusalem (II Sam. 19:40). When David lay on his deathbed one of his charges to Solomon was, "Show kindness to the son of Barzillai the Gileadite" (I Kings 2:7). As for Barzillai himself he felt that at his time of life there were some things not worth doing. He was dead to the delights of sense, as Matthew Henry expresses it.

IV. His beautiful old age. Although not spared the infirmities of old age (II Sam. 19:35), he retained his charm. At eighty years of age his heart of love was deep and broad. Old John Trapp says of Barzillai as he reached an honored age, "He had lost his colour but kept his sweet savour with the rose." May grace be ours to grow old gracefully and beautifully!

V. His death was contemplated. Barzillai was not afraid to face the crossing of the bar. The pathetic desire expressed to David can be rendered, "The grave is ready for me; let me go out and get ready for it" (II Sam. 19:37). At eighty, Barzillai was still the loving child of the parents with whom he desired to be buried, and his love of his kindred is to be praised. Thus as Alexander Whyte puts it, "Barzillai having shown us how to live, shows us also how to die. Barzillai dies the same devout and noble and magnanimous man he has all his days lived." If ours is grace to live well, grace will be given to die well.

2. *Father of Adriel*, husband of Merab, Saul's eldest daughter (II Sam. 21:8).

3. *A priest* whose genealogy was lost, and who married a daughter of Barzillai, David's friend (Ezra 2:61; Neh. 7:63).

BASHAN-HAVOTH-JAIR [Bā' shăn-hā' voth-jā' ûr]—FRUITFUL VILLAGE OF JAIR. *A name of Jair* which he gave to Argob after its capture (Deut. 3:14).

BAVAI, BAVVAI [Băv' a ī]—WISHES. *A son or descendant of Henadad* who helped in the repair of the wall [Neh. 3:18).

BAZLITH, BAZLUTH [Băz' lith, Băz' lŭth]—ASKING. *One of the Nethinims* whose descendants returned from exile (Ezra 2:52; Neh. 7:54)

BEALIAH [Bē a lī' ah]—JEHOVAH IS LORD. *A Benjamite warrior* who joined David at Ziklag (I Chron. 12:5).

BEBAI [Bĕb' a ī]—FATHERLY.

1. *A man whose descendants returned from exile with Zerubbabel* (Ezra 2:11; Neh. 7:16).

2. *Another whose posterity came back with Ezra.* Perhaps the same man as No. 1 (Ezra 8:11; 10:28).
3. *A chieftain* who sealed the covenant (Neh. 10:15).

BECHER [Bĕ′ chûr]—YOUNG CAMEL or FIRST BORN.
1. *A son of Benjamin* (Gen. 46:21; I Chron. 7:6, 8).
2. *A son of Ephraim* (Num. 26:35). Called Bered in I Chronicles 7:20.

BECHORATH [Bĕ chŏ′ rath]—FIRST BIRTH. *Son of Aphiah or Abiah,* and grandson of Becher, son of Benjamin (I Sam. 9:1).

BEDAD [Bĕ′ dăd]—SON OF ADAD or SEPARATION. *Father of Hadad,* king of Edom (Gen. 36:35; I Chron. 1:46).

BEDAN [Bĕ′ dăn]—SON OF JUDGMENT.
1. *A Hebrew judge* who ruled between Gideon and Jephthah (I Sam. 12:11). Some versions give the name as Barak.
2. *Descendant of Machir,* who was the son of Manasseh (I Chron. 7:17).

BEDEIAH [Bĕ dĕ′ iah]—SERVANT OF JEHOVAH. *A son of Bani* who married a foreign wife in exile (Ezra 10:35).

BEELIADA [Bĕ ĕl ĭ′ a dä]—THE LORD KNOWS. *A son of David* born in Jerusalem (I Chron. 14:7). Also called Eliada in II Samuel 5:16 and I Chronicles 3:8.

BEERA [Bĕ ĕ′ rä]—EXPOUNDER or A WELL. *Son of Zophah,* an Asherite of the family of Heber (I Chron. 7:37).

BEERAH [Bĕ ĕ′ rah]—EXPOUNDER. *A prince of the Reubenites* who became a captive of Tilgath-pilneser (I Chron. 5:6).

BEERI [Bĕ ĕ′ rī]—EXPOUNDER or MAN OF THE WELL.
1. *A Hittite,* father of Judith wife of Esau (Gen. 26:34).
2. *The father of Hosea* the prophet (Hosea 1:1).

BELA, BELAH [Bĕ′ lä, Bĕ′ lah]—DEVOURING or CONSUMPTION.
1. *The first king of Edom* the Bible mentions. His father's name was Beor (Gen. 36:32, 33; I Chron. 1:43, 44).
2. *The eldest son of Benjamin,* and founder of the family of Belaites (Gen. 46:21; Num. 26:38, 40).
3. *A son of Azaz* of the tribe of Reuben (I Chron. 5:8). Also the name of a city (Gen. 14:2, 8).

BELSHAZZAR [Bĕl shăz′ zar]—BEL PROTECT THE KING or THE LORD'S

LEADER. *The son of Nebuchadnezzar* and last of the kings of Babylon (Dan. 5; 7:1; 8:1).

The Man Whose Sacrilege Brought Judgment

The story of King Belshazzar is a short one. He bursts upon the stage, then disappears. All we know about him is told in one brief chapter. What we do know about Belshazzar is that he made a great feast to which a thousand of his lords were invited and that they drank out of the vessels of gold and silver taken from the house of God as they toasted their heathen gods. Drunkenness was a prevailing vice in all ranks of the Babylonians. Belshazzar, who feared neither God nor man, manifested his vanity, profaneness and pride in the sacrilegious use of the holy vessels, and in the midst of the drunken orgy, a hidden hand writing out mysterious words interrupted their godless mirth.

Although he could not decipher the writing on the wall, Belshazzar's conscience somehow interpreted the words over against the candlestick. Terror gripped him because he felt the message spelled his doom. His own wise men failed to read the writing, so Daniel was brought in and informed the king of its significance, and that night Belshazzar, king of Babylon, was slain. The army of Darius ransacked the palace and quickly mingled the king's blood with the wine in the banqueting hall.

BELTESHAZZAR [Bĕl te shaz' zar]—BEL PROTECT HIS LIFE OT THE LORD'S LEADER. *The name given to youthful Daniel* by the prince of Nebuchadnezzar's eunuchs (Dan. 1:7; 2:26; 4; 10:1).

BENAIAH [Bĕ nā' iah]—JEHOVAH HATH BUILT OT IS INTELLIGENT.

1. *A Levite,* son of Jehoiada of Kabzeel in Judah, whose father was a priest, and one of David's heroes (II Sam. 8:18; 20:23; 23:20, 23; I Kings 1).

The Man of Dauntless Courage

I. Benaiah was inspired by a noble ambition. He came of a noble ancestry, whose forefathers had left their impress upon the history of the nation. *Born* well, Benaiah sought to *live* well. Absalom became a traitor to his godly father and broke his heart. The sons of priestly Eli lived in sin and died in disgrace. Benaiah, privileged with the example of godly parentage, looked upon life as a challenge to personal and individual responsibility.

II. He was fearless in his destruction of Israel's foes. Born in an age of warfare, when youths were valiant in fight and middle-aged men were veterans, Benaiah had been valiant in many a campaign against hostile nations. This grandson of a valiant man of Kabzeel had many mighty deeds to his credit (I Chron. 11:22–25 RV). Three glimpses are given of Benaiah's bravery. He confronted two lionhearted men of Moab—giants among their fellows—either of whom would have been more than a match for any ordinary soldier; but Benaiah took them both on and was the victor. Then he attacked the Egyptian of "great stature" but although this dark-skinned giant carried a spear "like a weaver's beam" Benaiah met him with an ordinary staff and left the field victorious.

Benaiah's next exploit finds him attacking not "lionhearted men" but an actual lion that had alarmed the people. A pit was dug to trap the marauding lion, and snow fell and hid the trap in a most effective way. The lion fell into the pit and vainly tried to extricate itself. Benaiah, the hero who had vanquished a giant and conquered two lion-hearted Moabites, descended the pit on a snowy day and single-handed slew the lion. No wonder David, who also had slain a lion, gave Benaiah the chief place among the favored three. A greater than Benaiah dealt a death blow at our three great foes — the world, the flesh, the devil.

2. *Another of David's valiant men* from Pirathon (II Sam. 23:30; I Chron. 11:31; 27:14).

3. *The head of a Simeonite family* (I Chron. 4:36).

4. *One of David's priests* in Jerusalem (I Chron. 15:18, 24; 16:5, 6).

5. *The father of one of David's counselors* (I Chron. 27:34).

6. *The grandfather of Jahaziel* (II Chron. 20:14).

7. *A Levite overseer* of Temple offerings in Hezekiah's time (II Chron. 31:13).

8. *One of the family of Parosh* (Ezra 10:25).

9. *A son of Pahath-moab* (Ezra 10:30).

10. *A son of Bani* (Ezra 10:35).

11. *A son of Nebo* (Ezra 10:43).

12. *Father of Pelatiah,* a Judahite prince (Ezek. 11:1, 13).

BEN-AMMI [Bĕn-Ăm' mĭ]—SON OF MY PEOPLE. *The son whom Lot's youngest daughter bore* to him and from whom the Ammonite tribe sprang (Gen. 19:38).

BEN-DEKAR [Bĕn dē' kär]—SON OF DEKAR. *Solomon's purveyor* in Bethshemesh (I Kings 4:9).

BEN-GEBER [Bĕn gē' bûr]—SON OF GEBER. *Solomon's purveyor in Ramoth-gilead* (I Kings 4:13).

BEN-HADAD [Bĕn hā' dăd]—SON OF THE GOD HADAH.

1. *Benhadad I,* son of Tabrimon of Damascus. This king of Syria made a league with Asa, king of Judah, to invade Israel (I Kings 15:18, 20; II Chron. 16:2, 4).

2. *Benhadad II,* the son of No. 1 who was an able general and statesman and who reigned in the time of Ahab king of Israel. He was assassinated by the usurper Hazael (I Kings 20; II Kings 6:24; 8:7, 9).

3. *Benhadad III,* the son of Hazael who suffered heavy defeats from the Assyrians (II Kings 13:2, 24, 25; Amos 1:4). The name is also the general title of the kings of Damascus (Jer. 49:27).

BEN-HAIL [Bĕn hā' il]–SON OF MIGHT OR VALIANT. *A prince of Judah* sent by Jehoshaphat to teach the cities (II Chron. 17:7).

BEN-HANAN [Bĕn hā' nan]–SON OF KIND ONE or VERY GRACIOUS. *A son of Shimon,* registered with the tribe of Judah (I Chron. 4:20).

BEN-HESED [Bĕn hĕ' sed]–SON OF BENEVOLENCE. *Solomon's purveyor* in Aruboth (I Kings 4:10).

BEN-HUR [Bĕn hûr']–SON OF HUR. *Another of Solomon's purveyors* in Mount Ephraim (I Kings 4:8).

BENINU [Bĕn' ĭ nū]–OUR SON or POSTERITY. *A Levite* who, with Nehemiah, sealed the covenant (Neh. 10:13).

BENJAMIN [Bĕn' ja mĭn]–SON OF THE RIGHT HAND.
1. *The youngest son of Jacob* and the only one born in Canaan; founder of a tribal family. His mother, Rachel, who died in giving birth to Benjamin, named him with her last breath Benoni "son of sorrow." Jacob changed the name to Benjamin (Gen. 35:18, 24).

The Man Beloved of Jehovah

The prophecy of Jacob regarding Benjamin is short and easily verified. Personal courage and martial temperament, a characteristic of the Benjamites throughout history, are before us in Benjamin as a ravening wolf devouring the prey and dividing the spoil. Benjamin was the last, the bravest and the best-beloved tribe of all the tribes of Israel, the center of the affections of the whole family, and the dwelling place of the beloved of the Lord (Deut. 33:12).

Some Benjamites of the Bible are the second of the Judges, Ehud, Saul, the first of Israel's kings and Saul of Tarsus, who was "not a whit behind the chiefest of the apostles." Although "the smallest of the tribes" (I Sam. 9:21), Benjamin was not to be despised. Christ came from a small village. In the division of the land, as Joshua records it, Jerusalem was assigned to Benjamin (Josh. 18:28)— a fact referred to by the psalmist, "There is little Benjamin their ruler." Between the shoulders of Benjamin, the God of Israel caused His name to dwell. In Benjamin He "covered Israel all the day long."

The tribe of Benjamin, as the seat of God's love, ought to be the meeting place for all Israel; Jerusalem is so, in a figure. It has open gates for all the tribes of Israel.

2. *A son or descendant of Harim* who put away his foreign wife (Ezra 10:32).

3. *A son of Bilhan* and a great-grandson of Benjamin (I Chron. 7:10).

4. *One who took part in the repair of the wall* (Neh. 3:23).

5. *Another who did the same* (Neh. 12:34). Also the name of one of the gates of Jerusalem (Jer. 20:2; 37:13; 38:7; Zech. 14:10).

BENO [Bĕ′ nō]—HIS SON. *A descendant of Merari through Jaaziah* (I Chron. 24:26, 27).

BEN-ONI [Bĕn ō′ nī]—SON OF MY SORROW. *The name Rachel gave to her second son.* See Benjamin (Gen. 35:18).

BEN-ZOHETH [Bĕn-Zō′ hĕth]—CORPULENT or STRONG. *A son of Ishi,* a Judahite (I Chron. 4:20).

BEOR [Bĕ′ ôr]—SHEPHERD, A TORCH or BURNING.
1. *The father of Bela* the first king of Edom (Gen. 36:32; I Chron. 1:43).
2. *The father of Balaam* the prophet (Num. 22:5). Also known as Bosor (II Pet. 2:15).

BERA [Bĕ′ rǎ]—GIFT or EXCELLENCE. *A King of Sodom* defeated by Chedorlaomer (Gen. 14:2).

BERACHAH [Bĕr′ a chah]—BLESSING. *One of Saul's brethren* who joined David at Ziklag (I Chron. 12:3). Also the name of "the valley of blessing" (II Chron. 20:26). The modern name is Bereikut.

BERAIAH [Bĕr a ī′ ah]—JEHOVAH HATH CREATED. *A son of Shimhi,* a Benjamite (I Chron. 8:13, 21).

BERECHIAH, BERACHIAH [Bĕr e chī′ ah, Bĕr a chī′ ah]—JEHOVAH IS BLESSING or BENDING THE KNEE.
1. *The father of Asaph* the chief singer, descendant of Gershon (I Chron. 6:39; 15:17).
2. *A son of Zerubbabel* (I Chron. 3:20).
3. *The son of Asa* who lived near Jerusalem (I Chron. 9:16).
4. *A Levite doorkeeper* of the Tabernacle (I Chron. 15:23).
5. *An Ephraimite* in Pekah's time (II Chron. 28:12).
6. *Father of Mershullam* who assisted in the repair of the wall of Jerusalem (Neh. 3:4, 30; 6:18).
7. *Father of the prophet Zechariah* (Zech. 1:1, 7). Called Barachias in Matthew 23:35, meaning, "who bends the knee to God."

BERED [Bĕ′ red]—SEED, PLACE or HAIL. *An Ephraimite,* perhaps the same as Becher (I Chron. 7:20). Also name of place in South Canaan (Gen. 16:14).

BERI [Bĕ′ rī]—EXPOUNDER or MAN OF THE WELL. *A son of Zophah,* an Asherite (I Chron. 7:36).

BERIAH [Bĕ rī′ ah]—UNFORTUNATE or IN EVIL.
1. *A son of Asher* (Gen. 46:17; Num. 26:44, 45; I Chron. 7:31).
2. *A son of Ephraim* (I Chron. 7:23).

3. *A son of Elpaal,* a Benjamite (I Chron. 8:13, 16).
4. *Son of the Levite Shimei* (I Chron. 23:10, 11).

BERODACH-BALADAN [Bē rō′ dăch-băl′ a dăn]—BOLD. *A king of Babylon* (II Kings 20:12; Isa. 39:1). See Merodach-baladan.

BESAI [Bē′ saī]—TREADING DOWN. *One of the Nethinims* who returned from exile (Ezra 2:49; Neh. 7:52).

BESODEIAH (Bĕs o dē′ iah] FAMILIAR WITH JEHOVAH. *Father of Meshullam* who helped to repair the old gate (Neh. 3:6).

BETH-GADER [Bĕth-gā′ dur]—WALLED PLACE. *A descendant of Caleb,* son of Hur (I Chron. 2:51).

BETHLEHEM [Bĕth′ lĕ hĕm]—HOUSE OF BREAD. *A descendant of Caleb,* son of Hur (I Chron. 2:51, 54; 4:4). Also the name of two towns (Gen. 35:19; Josh. 19:15).

BETH RAPHA [Bĕth-rā′ phå]—HOUSE OF A GIANT or PLACE OF FEAR. *The son of Eshton,* grandson of Chelub (I Chron. 4:12).

BETHUEL [Bĕth ōō′ el]—ABODE OF GOD or DWELLER IN GOD. *A son of Nahor* by his wife Milcah (Gen. 22:22). Also the name of a town (I Chron. 4:30).

BETH-ZUR [Bĕth′-zûr]—PLACE OF ROCK. *The son of Maon* (I Chron. 2:45). Also the name of a city (Josh. 15:58).

BEZAI [Bē′ zaī]—SHINING or HIGH.
1. *One of those who sealed the covenant* (Neh. 10:18).
2. *One whose posterity* to the number of 323 returned from exile with Zerubbabel (Ezra 2:17; Neh. 7:23).

BEZALEEL [Bē zăl′ e el]—UNDER GOD'S SHADOW.
1. *The chief architect of the Tabernacle* to whom was assigned the design and execution of its works of art (Ex. 31:2; 35:30; 36: 1, 2; 38:22).

The Man Who Was a Spirit-filled Workman

Bezaleel was chiefly responsible for works of metal, wood and stone. Aholiab had charge of the textile fabric. Bezaleel, however, was chief in both departments and was the principal workman and for the accomplishment of a divinely commissioned task he received divine empowerment. Whom the Lord calls, He qualifies (I Thess. 5:24).

I. His character. Bezaleel meaning, "in the shadow of God," is suggestive of this artificer's character. Although he doubtless received the name from godly parents who knew what it was to dwell beneath the shadow of the Almighty, Bezaleel himself must have lived a life in the will of God, and was therefore responsive when the call came.

II. His commission. Bezaleel alone had the right to devise. He was the principal workman in the erection of the Tabernacle, the pattern of which came direct from God (Ex. 25:40). The choice of Bezaleel proves that the Holy Spirit is sovereign in His work. We cannot understand why He chooses certain people for great tasks. As the wind, He blows where He listeth. His gifts are distributed severally as He *wills*.

III. His cunning. This English word as used in the Bible simply represents *skill, ability*. Thus Bezaleel was filled with all wisdom and understanding in *all manner of* workmanship. All he needed to accomplish the mind and will of God was divinely bestowed. God's commands are His enablings. "Give what Thou commandest," prayed Augustine, "then command that Thou wilt." So the Great Overseer, the Holy Spirit, possessed Bezaleel and inspired him to prepare the temporary habitation of God. In our time, the same empowering Spirit gives to "every man his work," and only that which is accomplished under the guidance of the Spirit can be pleasing to God and fit for a place in His great Temple.

2. *One of the sons of Pahath-moab* who had married a foreign wife (Ezra 10:30).

BEZER [Bē′ zûr]—STRONG or GOLD ONE. *A son of Zophah*, an Asherite (I Chron. 7:37).

BICHRI [Bĭch′ rī]—YOUTHFUL, FIRST-BORN or FIRST-FRUITS. *The father of the rebellious Sheba* who rose against David, descendant of Becher (II Sam. 20).

BIDKAR [Bĭd′ kär]—SERVANT OF KAR or IN SHARP PAIN. *A captain of Jehu*, who executed the sentence on Jehoram, son of Ahab (II Kings 9:25).

BIGTHA [Bĭg′ thă]—GIVEN BY FORTUNE. *One of the eunuchs or chamberlains* who served in the presence of Ahasuerus (Esther 1:10).

BIGTHAN, BIGTHANA [Bĭg′ thăn, Bĭg′ tha nă]—GIFT OF FORTUNE or GIVING MEAT. *One of the two chamberlains*, keepers of the palace door, whose plot against the king was discovered and defeated by Mordecai (Esther 2:21; 6:2).

BIGVAI [Bĭg′ va ī]—HAPPY or OF THE PEOPLE.
1. *One of the leaders* of the exiles who returned from Babylon with Zerubbabel (Ezra 2:2; Neh. 7:7).
2. *Founder of a family* of two thousand who returned from exile (Ezra 2:14; Neh. 7:19).
3. *One whose descendants returned* from exile with Ezra (Ezra 8:14).
4. *The head of a family* that with Nehemiah sealed the covenant (Neh. 10:16).

BILDAD [Bĭl′ dăd]—SON OF CONTENTION, LORD ADAD or OLD FRIENDSHIP. *One of Job's three friends,* a Shuhite, descended from Shuah, Abraham's son by Keturah (Job 2:11; 8:1; 18:1; 25:1; 42:9).

The Man Who Made a Speech

Bildad's name is an interesting study. One meaning of it is "Lord of Hadad" and "Hadad" means *to shout.* Studying the speeches of this second speaker who came to comfort Job, one can see how apt the name is, for Bildad was inclined to be loud, insistent and boisterous in his declarations.

This Shuhite, in a vehement fashion, implied as he continued the discussion opened by Eliphaz, that all the extraordinary misfortune overtaking Job were the certain proof of hidden and exceptional crimes of which Job must have been guilty. Doubtless Bildad thought his speech was rich in ideas. But he is before us as the religious dogmatist whose dogmatism vested upon human tradition. With proverbial wisdom and pious phrases, abounding throughout his discourses, Bildad sought to illustrate the principle that Job suffered because of his sin.

With philosophy, wisdom and tradition gathered from the fathers (Job 8:8), Bildad sought to convince Job of his wrongs. But the mystery of Job's sufferings was not to be unraveled in that way. The wisdom of man and tradition has its limits. What has been handed down and accepted by each succeeding generation as truth, is not necessarily so. Every man must be fully persuaded in his own mind. The mysterious dealings of God can only be revealed by God Himself. He is His own Interpreter.

BILGAH [Bĭl′ gah]—CHEERFUL or BURSTING FORTH.
1. *A descendant of Aaron,* head of the fifteenth course of Tabernacle priests in David's time (I Chron. 24:14).
2. *A chief of priests* who returned from exile with Zerubbabel (Neh. 12:5, 18).

BILGAI [Bĭl′ ga ī]—BURSTING FORTH or FIRST BORN. Perhaps the same person as No. 2 under Bilgah (Neh. 10:8).

BILHAN [Bĭl′ han]—TENDER or BASHFUL. From the same root of Bilhah, handmaid of Laban's youngest daughter Rachel.
1. *A son of Ezer,* son of Seir the Horite (Gen. 36:27; I Chron. 1:42).
2. *A son of Jediael,* son of Benjamin (I Chron. 7:10).

BILSHAN [Bĭl′-shăn]—SEARCHER or INQUIRER. *A prince of the Jews* and companion of Zerubbabel (Ezra 2:2; Neh. 7:7).

BIMHAL [Bĭm′ hăl]—SON OF CIRCUMCISION. *A son of Japhlet,* an Asherite (I Chron. 7:33).

BINEA [Bĭn′ e ă]—WANDERER. *A son of Moza* and a descendant of Jonathan, Saul's son (I Chron. 8:37; 9:43).

BINNUI [Bĭn′ nụ ī]—A BUILDING or FAMILYSHIP.
1. *Father of a Levite* who had charge of the gold and silver vessels Ezra brought back from Babylon (Ezra 8:33).
2. *A son of Pahath-moab* (Ezra 10:30).
3. *A son of Bani* (Ezra 10:38).
4. *A son of Henadad* (Neh. 3:24; 10:9).
5. *One whose descendants returned* from exile with Zerubbabel (Neh. 7:15). Called Bani in Ezra 2:10).
6. *A Levite* who returned from exile (Neh. 12:8).

BIRSHA [Bûr′ shă]—THICK or STRONG. *A king of Gomorrah* at the time of Chedorlaomer's invasion (Gen. 14:2).

BIRZAVITH [Bûr′ za vĭth]—OLIVE WELL or WOUNDS. *A grandson of Beriah* who was a son of Asher (I Chron. 7:31). Also given as Birgaith.

BISHLAM [Bĭsh′ lăm]—PEACEFUL. *An officer of Artaxerxes* in Canaan in the time of Zerubbabel's return from Babylon, who was adverse to the rebuilding of the Temple (Ezra 4:7).

BIZTHA [Bĭz′ thă]—EUNUCH. *One of the seven chamberlains* at the court of Ahasuerus (Esther 1:10).

BLASTUS [Blăs′ tus]—A SUCKER or A BUD. *A palace chamberlain* who had charge of Herod Agrippa's bedchamber (Acts 12:20).

BOANERGES [Bō a nûr′ jēs]—SONS OF RAGE or OF THUNDER. *The name given by Christ* to James and John on account of their impetuosity (Mark 3:17; Luke 9:54, 55).

BOAZ, BOOZ [Bō′ ăz, Bō′ ŏz]—STRENGTH or FLEETNESS. *The wealthy and honorable Bethlehemite,* or Judahite, who became the second husband of Ruth the Moabitess, and ancestor of David and of Christ (Ruth 2, 3, 4; Matt. 1:5). *The name of the left pillar of Solomon's* Temple was Boaz, for "in it is strength" (I Kings 7:21). Boaz was true to his name and comes before us strong in grace, integrity and purpose. As the lord of the harvest, master of servants, redeemer, bridegroom and life-giver, he is a fitting type of Christ.

BOCHERU [Bŏch′ e rōō]—YOUTH or FIRST-BORN. *Son of Azel,* a Benjamite of the family of king Saul (I Chron. 8:38; 9:44).

BOHAN [Bō′ hăn]—THUMB or STUMPY. *A son of Reuben,* after whom a stone was named as a mark of division between Judah and Benjamin (Josh. 15:6; 18:17).

BUKKI [Bŭk' kĭ]—MOUTH OF JEHOVAH or DEVASTATION SENT BY JEHOVAH.

1. *Son of Abishua* and father of Uzzi, fifth in descent from Aaron in the line of high priests through Phinehas (I Chron. 6:5, 51).

2. *A son of Jogli*, a prince of the tribe of Dan, entrusted with the task of dividing Canaan among the tribes of Israel (Num. 34:22).

BUKKIAH [Bŭk kĭ' ah]—MOUTH OF JEHOVAH. *A Levite* of the sons of Heman, and leader of the sixth band or course in the Temple service (I Chron. 25:4, 13).

BUNAH [Bŭ' nah]—UNDERSTANDING or PRUDENCE. *Son of Jerahmeel*, a Judahite (I Chron. 2:25).

BUNNI [Bŭn' nĭ]—MY UNDERSTANDING or BUILT.

1. *A Levite* who assisted in the teaching of the Law of Moses (Neh. 9:4).

2. *The father of Hashabiah*, another Levite (Neh. 11:15).

3. *The representative of a family* that sealed the covenant (Neh. 10:15).

BUZ [Bŭz]—CONTEMPT or DESPISED.

1. *The second son of Milcah and Nahor* the brother of Abraham and founder of a tribal family (Gen. 22:21; Job 32:2, 6).

2. *The father of Jahdo*, a Gadite (I Chron. 5:14).

BUZI [Bŭ' zĭ]—CONTEMNED OF JEHOVAH or MY CONTEMPT. *An Aaronite* and father of Ezekiel, the prophet and priest (Ezek. 1:3).

C

CAESAR [Cae' zar]—ONE CUT OUT. *The surname always used in the New Testament for all Roman emperors.* See Augustus, Tiberius and Claudius (Matt. 22:17, etc.). To Caesar the Jews paid tribute and it was also to him that those Jews who were Roman citizens (for example, Paul, Acts 25:10–21), had the right of appeal.

CAIAPHAS [Cā' ia phăs]—A SEARCHER or HE THAT SEEKS WITH DILI-GENCE. *Joseph Caiaphas, the son-in-law of Annas,* was high priest of the Jews for eighteen years (Matt. 26:3, 57).

The Man with Sadducaean Insolence

Dr. David Smith refers to this wicked man whom the Spirit of God used to declare divine purposes as, "a man of masterful temper, with his full share of the insolence which was a Sadducaean characteristic." The Sadducees were a sect among the Jews, so called from their founder Sadoc who lived about 260 years before Christ. Their principal tenets were:

I. There is no angel, spirit or resurrection; the soul finishes with the body (Matt. 22:23; Acts 23:8).

II. There is no fate or providence—all men enjoy the most ample freedom of action—absolute power to do good or evil.

III. There is no need to follow tradition. Scripture, particularly the first five books of the Bible, must be strictly adhered to. Caiaphas, as an ardent Sadducee, figures three times in the New Testament.

A. At the raising of Lazarus. After the miracle at Bethany, the rulers were alarmed at the popularity of Jesus which the resurrection of Lazarus brought Him, and convened a meeting of the Sanhedrin to decide what should be done with Jesus. Caiaphas presided and with a high hand forced a resolution that Jesus should be put to death (John 11:49, 53).

B. At the trial of Jesus. At a further meeting of the Sanhedrin when Jesus appeared before its members and was tried and condemned, Caiaphas again displayed his character by his open determination to find Jesus guilty. Since he was the high priest, his announcements were clothed with authority, but his shameless disregard of the forms of law to bring about the death of Jesus, revealed his warped conscience (Matt. 26:57, 58; John 18:24). Yet Caiaphas used language somewhat prophetic when he said that it was expedient for one man to die for the people, and Christ did die for Jew and Gentile alike. By His death He broke down the middle wall (Eph. 2:14–18).

C. At the trial of Peter and John. Caiaphas also took part in the examination of Peter and John when called in question over the marvels of the healing of the lame man. The manifestation of God's power was so evident that Annas and Caiaphas could do nothing about the apostles (Acts 4).

CAIN [Cāin]—ACQUISITION, FABRICATION or POSSESSED. *Eldest son of Adam and Eve*, the first man to be born naturally, and founder of the family of Kenites (Kenite is called Kain in the Hebrew) (Gen. 4; Num. 24:22; Heb. 11:4; I John 3:12; Jude 11). Also the name of a town (Josh. 15:57).

The Man Who Was Earth's First Murderer

The terrible story of Cain proves how quickly man's fallen nature developed. It did not take long for his heart to become desperately wicked, and the line of Cain continued in sin. It was in such the foul sin of polygamy was first experienced.

By calling Cain was an agriculturist, but he was not happy in his calling since he did not fear God. His heart became jealous as he witnessed the happiness of his brother Abel and his favor with God.

Ultimately he yielded to his jealous feelings and slew Abel, just as the Jews for envy sought Christ's death.

Because Cain's heart was destitute of love, his sacrifice had no heart in it and was therefore miserable, worthless and unacceptable to God. "The sacrifice of the wicked is an abomination to the Lord, but the prayer of the upright is His delight." Cain was right in his *desire* to bring an offering but wrong in his *doing* (Gen. 4:3). He sought to draw near to God with the product of his own labor. Abel brought the first-born of the flock—a blood-offering—the divine acceptance of which provoked Cain's evil temper for he "was wroth." An angry look resulted in an angry deed because in a moment of ungoverned passion Cain lifted up his hand and murdered his brother, and buried his body. But although Cain tried to conceal his dastardly crime the Lord marked the spot and brought home to the murderer his foul deed.

God set a mark on Cain, but what it was Scripture does not say. Evidently it was sufficient to make him feel the wrath of God and the abhorrence of his fellowmen. Yet the punishment of Cain reveals a judgment mingled with mercy. His brand, perhaps some kind of stigma, made Cain realize the awfulness fo the sin of fratricide, but acted as a protection against the violence of the avenger of blood. The narrative seems to affirm that Cain's mark was not consigning him to perpetual punishment, but was a token of God's redemptive compassion.

CAINAN, KENAN [Cā ï' nan, Kē' nan]—ACQUISITION.
1. *A son of Enos,* son of Seth (Gen. 5:9–14; I Chron. 1:2; Luke 3:38).
2. *A son of Arphaxad* and father of Sala (Luke 3:36).

CALEB [Cā' leb]—BOLD, IMPETUOUS (also an animal name, meaning "dog").
1. *A son of Jephunneh,* usually so designated to distinguish him from other persons bearing the same name (Num. 13:6, 30).

The Man Who Desired a Mountain

Although Caleb was not an Israelite by birth, he was "an Israelite indeed." He was one of the chief spies sent out by Moses. He was courageous and persevered when the other spies became discouraged. He was invincible in driving out giants, completely devoted to God and vigorous in old age. Six times it is recorded of Caleb, "he hath fully followed the Lord."

His consecration was thorough. What magnificent adverbs are used to describe Caleb. He followed faithfully, wholly, fully. He never lowered his standards, but was perpetually wholehearted.

His courage was unfaltering. Giants did not disturb Caleb nor did those dastards who were ready to stone him.

His request was answered. To Caleb, whose life was woven of one piece throughout, reward crowned his faith and faithfulness. Through autumn winds and premonitions of snow, he brought forth fruit in his old age. When we come to the record of Caleb's personal inheritance in the land of Canaan we find him at eighty years of age asking of Joshua, "Now therefore give me this mountain." Caleb was a man of altitudes. He was not content with the average or the commonplace. He never thought in terms of fences or walled cities. It was the heights for Caleb, and although the mountain he wanted was filled with hostile Anakims, he refused defeat and claimed his inheritance. At long last a worthy recompense came to this noble man for "to patient faith the prize is sure."

2. The son of Hezron, a Judahite and father of Hur and grandfather of Caleb No. 1. There is some confusion about this Caleb (I Chron. 2:18, 19, 42).

3. The son of Hur the son of Caleb No. 2 (I Chron. 2:50).

CANAAN, CHÁNAAN [Cä' năan]—LOWLAND or TRADER. A son of Ham and grandson of Noah (Gen. 9:18–27; I Chron. 1:8, 13), and founder of the family of Canaanites (Gen. 10:18). It is also the name of the country in which they dwelt (Gen. 11:31).

CARCAS [Cär' cas]—SEVERE or AN EAGLE. One of seven chamberlains who served in the presence of king Ahasuerus (Esther 1:10).

CAREAH [Cä rē' ah]—BALD HEAD. Father of Johanan, governor of Judah in the time of Gedaliah (II Kings 25:23). Also spelled Kareah.

CARMI [Cär' mī]—VINEDRESSER, NOBLE or MY VINEYARD.

1. Father of Achan "who troubled Israel," a Judahite (Josh. 7:1, 18; I Chron. 2:7). Perhaps the Carmi of I Chronicles 4:1 should be Chelubai.

2. One of the sons of Reuben and father of the tribal family of Carmites (Gen. 46:9; Ex. 6:14; Num. 26:6; I Chron. 5:3).

CARPUS [Cär' pus]—FRUIT or THE WRIST. A resident of Troas with whom Paul stayed, and with whom he left the cloak he urged Timothy to bring him (II Tim. 4:13).

CARSHENA [Cär shē' nă]—SPOILER or SLENDER. A prince of Persia at the court of Ahasuerus (Esther 1:14).

CEPHAS [Cē' phas]—ROCK. A surname given to Simon Peter (John 1:42).

CHALCOL, CALCOL, [Chăl' cŏl, Căl' cŏl]—SUSTAINING or WHO NOURISHES. A son of Zerah (called Mahol) whose offspring were noted for their wisdom (I Kings 4:31; I Chron. 2:6).

CHEDORLAOMER [Chĕd or lā′ o mûr]—SHEAF BAND or SERVANTS OF THE GOD LAGAMAR. *A king of Elam* in Abraham's time who held sovereignty of Babylon (Gen. 14).

CHELAL [Chĕ′ lăl]—COMPLETION or COMPLETENESS. *A son of Palath-moab* who put away his foreign wife (Ezra 10:30).

CHELLUH [Chĕl′ lŭh]—UNION. *One of the sons of Bani* who married a foreign wife (Ezra 10:35).

CHELUB [Chĕ′ lŭb]—WICKER BASKET, BIRD'S CAGE or BOLDNESS.
1. *A brother of Shuah,* a Judahite (I Chron. 4:11).
2. *Father of Ezri,* and superintendent of the tillers of the ground in David's time (I Chron. 27:26).

CHELUBAI [Chĕ′ lŭ′ baī]—BINDING TOGETHER OF THE LORD. *Son of Hezron,* elsewhere called Caleb (I Chron. 2:9).

CHENAANAH [Chĕ nā′ a nah]—SUBDUER or FLAT.
1. *The father of the false prophet Zedekiah* who smote Micaiah (I Kings 22:11, 20; II Chron. 18:10, 23).
2. *The brother of Ehud,* son of Bilhan, a Benjamite (I Chron. 7:10).

CHENANI [Chĕn′ a nī]—FIRM or CREATOR. *A Levite* who helped bring the returned exiles into agreement about the covenant worship of God (Neh. 9:4).

CHENANIAH [Chĕn a nī′ ah]—JEHOVAH IS FIRM or PREPARATION.
1. *A chief Levite* when David brought up the Ark from the house of Obed-edom (I Chron. 15:22, 27).
2. *An Izharite,* an officer of David's (I Chron. 26:29).

CHERAN [Chĕ′ ran]—UNION or LUTE. *Son of Dishon,* the son of Seir the Horite (Gen. 36:26; I Chron. 1:41).

CHESED [Chĕ′ sed]—A DEVIL or INCREASE. *The fourth son of Nahor,* and nephew of Abraham (Gen. 22:22).

CHILEAB [Chĭl′ e ăb]—PERFECTION OF THE FATHER. *The second son of David* by Abigail (II Sam. 3:3). Called Daniel in I Chronicles 3:1.

CHILION [Chĭl′ ĭ on]—WASTING AWAY or COMPLETE. *One of the two sons of Elimelech and Naomi* who married Orpah in Moab and died there (Ruth 1:2; 4:9).

CHIMHAM [Chĭm′ hăm]—LONGING or PINING. *Perhaps the son of Barzillai,* the Gileadite (II Sam. 19:37-40; Jer. 41:17).

CHISLON [Chĭs′ lon]—TRUST or STRONG. *The father of Elidad,* the prince of Benjamin in Moses' time who assisted in the division of the land (Num. 34:21).

CHUSHAN-RISHATHAIM [Chŭ′ shan rĭsh a thā′ im]—BLACKNESS OF INIQUITIES. *A king of Mesopotamia,* defeated by Othniel (Judg. 3:8–10).

CHUZA [Chŭ′ zȧ]—MODEST. *A steward of Herod Antipas,* son of Herod the Great whose wife ministered to Christ and His disciples (Luke 8:3).

CIS [Cĭs]—SNARING. *The father of king Saul.* Cis is the Greek form of Kish (Acts 13:21).

CLAUDIUS [Clôu′ dĭ ŭs]— (meaning uncertain).
1. *The successor of Caligula* as emperor (Acts 11:28; 18:2).
2. *A Roman officer,* Claudius Lysias, chief captain in Jerusalem in Paul's time (Acts 23:26).

CLEMENT [Clĕm′ ĕnt]—KIND or MERCIFUL. *A Christian of Philippi* who labored with Paul (Phil. 4:3). Possibly the apostolic father with the same name (Clement of Rome).

CLEOPAS, CLOPAS [Clē′ o păs]—THE WHOLE GLORY. *One of the two disciples* returning to Emmaus after the death of Christ, and to whom He appeared (Luke 24:18). Same as Cleophas.

CLEOPHAS [Clē′ o phăs]—THE WHOLE GLORY. *The husband of one of the Marys* who was the halfsister of the Virgin Mary (John 19:25). Same person as Clopas.

COLHOZEH [Cŏl hŏ′ zeh]—ALL-SEEING ONE or WHOLLY A SEER. *Father of Shallun* who helped repair the wall (Neh. 3:15). The Colhozeh of Nehemiah 11:5 may be the same person.

CONANIAH, CONONIAH [Cŏn a nī′ ah, Cŏn o nī′ ah]—JEHOVAH HATH ESTABLISHED or STABILITY OF THE LORD.
1. *A chief Levite* of high station in Josiah's time (II Chron. 35:9).
2. *A Levite* who had charge of tithes and offerings in Hezekiah's time (II Chron. 31:12, 13).

CORE [Cŏ′ rē]—ICE or HARD. *The Greek form* of Korah (Jude 11).

CORNELIUS [Cŏr nē′ lĭ ŭs]—THE BEAM OF THE SUN. *A converted Roman* centurion at Caesarea, a devout man (Acts 10). He was the first Gentile convert and through his conversion the door of faith was opened unto the Gentiles. Disgusted with the Gentile paganism of his day he turned to God but did not have a full understanding of the Gospel of Grace. Through Peter's ministry, Cornelius became a believer and was received into the fellowship of the Church. From this point there is no difference between Jew and Gentile. In Christ they become one (Eph. 2:18). Benevolence, prayerfulness, obedience and spiritual receptivity characterize this godly Roman centurion.

COSAM [Cŏ' sam]—MOST ABUNDANT. *A son of Elmodam,* and an ancestor of Jesus in the line of Joseph, husband of Mary (Luke 3:28).

COZ [Cŏz]—NIMBLE. *A descendant of Caleb* (I Chron. 4:8).

CRESCENS [Crĕs' cens]—INCREASE. *A companion of Paul* in his final imprisonment, sent by the apostle to Galatia (II Tim. 4:10). Legend has it that he was one of the seventy disciples sent fourth by Christ and that he became a bishop of Chalcedon.

CRISPUS [Crĭs' pus]—CURLED. *Ruler of the Jewish synagogue* at Corinth, and one of the few personally baptized by Paul (Acts 18:8; I Cor. 1:14).

CUSH [Cŭsh]—BLACK or ETHIOPIA.
1. *Eldest son of Ham* and grandson of Noah and founder of a tribal family (Gen. 10:6–8; I Chron. 1:8–10). Also the name of the land where the Cushites dwelt (Isa. 11:11; 18:1). Cushite is translated Ethiopian.
2. *A Benjamite,* and enemy of David. (See Fausset's dictionary).

CUSHI [Cŭ' shī]—BLACK or AN ETHIOPIAN.
1. *The messenger* who brought news to David concerning Absalom's defeat (II Sam. 18:21–32).
2. *An ancestor of Jehudi* who lived in Jeremiah's time (Jer. 36:14).
3. *The father of Zephaniah* the prophet who lived in the time of Josiah, king of Judah (Zeph. 1:1).

CYRENIUS [Cy rĕ' nĭ ŭs]—ONE WHO GOVERNS. *Governor of Syria* whose full name was Pablius Sulpiciua Quirnus (Luke 2:2).

CYRUS [Cy' rus]—AS MISERABLE or AN HEIR. *Cyrus, the founder of the Persian Empire,* conquered Babylon and was anointed by God to free the Jews from captivity. The prophets frequently foretold the coming of Cyrus. Isaiah, for example, mentioned him by name two hundred years before he was born (II Chron. 36:22, 23; Ezra 1:1–8; 3:7; 4:3–5; 5:13–17; 6:3–14; Isa. 44:28; 45; Dan. 1:21; 6:28; 10:1). Classical writers adorn the life and labors of Cyrus with a variety of legendary incidents for which no confirmation can be produced.

D

DALAIAH [Dăl a ï' ah]—JEHOVAH IS DELIVERER. *A descendant of Shechaniah* (I Chron. 3:24). Delaiah is the same name as the original.

DALPHON [Dăl' phon]—DROPPING. *The second of the ten sons of Haman,* all of whom were put to death by the Jews (Esther 9:7).

DAN [Dăn]—HE THAT JUDGES. *The fifth son of Jacob,* and first of Bilhah, Rachel's handmaid. Dan was the full brother of Naphtali and founder of a tribal family (Gen. 30:6; Ex. 31:6). The name Dan also describes the most northern city of Canaan. "Dan even to Beersheba" (II Sam. 24:15).

The Man Whose Name is Blotted Out

With our finite minds there is a mystery about Dan we cannot solve. The history of the tribe of Dan is darker than the history of any other of the twelve tribes of Israel. When we come to the sealing of the twelve tribes (Rev. 7), Dan's name is left out. The omission is absolute — the tribe is cut off from its brethren and its name blotted out. Yet we cannot be absolutely certain that the tribe of Dan is finally cut off, for in Ezekiel's glowing prophecy there is a portion for Dan (Ezek. 48:1).

The prophecy of Jacob concerning Dan carries a twofold character —"Dan shall judge his people as one of the *sceptres* of Israel." *Tribe* also means *sceptre* (Gen. 49:10). No man among the Judges did so much for Israel single-handed as Samson the great Danite.

A further thought is associated with Jacob's prophecy of Dan. "*I have waited* for thy salvation, O Lord." This is the first mention of *salvation* in Scripture. But Dan's history is adverse to the salvation predicted of him. His birth arose out of jealousy and inordinate desire. *Dan* became the Ishmael of Jacob's family. Persistent idolatry clung to the Danites from first to last. It was because Dan was likened unto a *serpent* that some of the early fathers predicted that Antichrist would come from him. "*They* are not *all Israel* which are of Israel." As there was one among the Twelve Apostles, so there was one among the Twelve Tribes who had not the seal of God. This we do know, Dan's glory as one of the sceptres of Israel with courage as a lion's whelp, is of no avail without the seal of God upon his forehead.

DANIEL [Dăn' iel]—GOD IS MY JUDGE.
1. *The second son of David,* also called Chileol (I Chron. 3:1).
2. *A son or descendant of Ithamar* who, after the return from exile, sealed the covenant (Ezra 8:2; Neh. 10:6).
3. *The celebrated Jewish prophet,* fourth of the so-called Major Prophets, of royal or noble descent. Daniel was taken to Babylon and

trained with others for the king's service (Ezek. 14:14, 20; 28:3; Dan. 1:6, 21).

The Man Who Kept His Window Open

Nothing is known of the ancestry and early life of this celebrated Jewish prophet who exercised tremendous influence in the Babylonian court, and whose name can mean: "Who in the name of God does Justice." Daniel was not a priest like Jeremiah or Ezekiel but like Isaiah he was descended from the time of Judah and was probably of royal blood (Dan. 1:3–6). A comparison of II Kings 20:17, 18 with Isaiah 29: 6, 7 seems to indicate that Daniel was descended from king Hezekiah.

As a youth of the age of fifteen or thereabouts, Daniel was carried captive to Babylon (Dan. 1:1–4) in the third year of Jehoiakim. From then on his whole life was spent in exile. What Daniel was like we are not expressly told but the details given in the first chapter of his book suggest he must have been a handsome youth. There is a tradition to the effect that "he had a spare, dry, tall figure with a beautiful expression." Dr. Alexander Whyte says of Daniel: "There is always a singular lustre and nobility and stately distinction about him. There is a note of birth and breeding and aristocracy about his whole name and character." As we study his character we cannot but be impressed with his refinement, his reserve and the high sculpture of his life.

Daniel comes before us as an interpreter of dreams and of signs, a conspicuous seer, an official of kings. He lived a long and active life in the courts and councils of some of the greatest monarchs the world has known, like Nebuchadnezzar, Cyrus and Darius. Close intimacy with heaven made Daniel the courtier, statesman, man of business and prophet he was. Bishop Ken reminds us that "Daniel was one that kept his station in the greatest of revolutions, reconciling politics and religion, business and devotion, magnanimity with humility, authority with affability, conversation with retirement, Heaven and the Court, the favour of God and of the King."

The significant meaning of Daniel's name accords with the character and contents of the Book of Daniel, written by the prophet himself — the first six chapters in the *third* person, the last six in the *first* person.

As the distinguished historian of some of the most important dispensational teaching given in the Bible, Daniel's book sets forth:

A statement of God's judgment on history.

The purpose of God until the final consummation.

The vindication of righteousness.

It would take a whole book to deal with Daniel's prophetic visions of Gentile dominion and defeat. Profitable homiletical material can be used showing Daniel's self-control (Dan. 1:8; 10:3), undaunted courage (5:22, 23), constant integrity (6:4), unceasing prayerfulness (2:17, 18; 6:16), native humility (10:17) and spiritual vision (7:9, 12; 10:5, 6).

DARA [Dä′ rǎ]—BEARER. *Son of Zerah* son of Judah by Tamar (I Chron. 2:6). Sometimes identified with Darda.

DARDA [Där' dä]—A PEARL OF WISDOM. *A son of Mahol,* a Judahite celebrated for his wisdom (I Kings 4:31).

DARIUS (Då rī' us]—HE THAT INFORMS HIMSELF OF A KING.
1. *The son of Hystaspes,* and king of Persia B.C. (521–485). He allowed the Jews to rebuild the Temple (Ezra 4:5, 24).
2. *Darius the Persian,* Darius Nothus and probably the last king of Persia (Neh. 12:22).
3. *Darius the Mede,* the son of Ahasuerus of the seed of the Medes. He succeeded Belshazzar as king of Babylon at sixty-two years of age (Dan. 5:31; 6:9, 25; 9:1; 11:1).

DARKON [Där' kon]—BEARER OF SCATTERING. *A servant of Solomon,* whose sons were among those who returned from exile with Zerubbabel (Ezra 2:56; Neh. 7:58).

DATHAN [Dä' than]—BELONGING TO LAW OF FOUNT. *A son of Eliab* the Reubenite, who with Korah a Levite, and Abiram and On, two other Reubenites, conspired against Moses and Aaron in the wilderness and were destroyed for their rebellion (Num. 16; 26:9; Deut. 11:6; Ps. 106:17).

DAVID [Dä' vid]—BELOVED. *The youngest son of the eight sons of Jesse the Bethlehemite, the second and greatest of Israel's kings, the eloquent poet and one of the most prominent figures in the history of the world* (Ruth 4:17, 22; I Sam. 16: 13).

The Man After God's Own Heart

Volumes have been written on the trials and triumphs of David, a mountain peak among Bible characters, who was carefully chosen as Israel's second king by God Himself. David's father, Jesse, was a man of no great rank who lived in the little town of Bethlehem. In his youth David was trained to tend his father's sheep. Being the youngest of the family he was not brought into public notice, yet it pleased God to raise him from a low estate and set him upon the throne. He was overlooked by the prophet Samuel, but the prophet obeyed when God said, "Arise anoint him, this is he." All we can do in this study is to offer a brief sketch of David's eventful life. We view him as:

I. A Warrior. David was courageous as a champion and a great soldier (I Sam. 17:40; II Sam. 5:7). His fight with Goliath the giant made him a marked man. He had not the training of a soldier. As yet he had not reached the years of manhood. Dressed like a poor country shepherd lad, he had no weapons save his sling. Never were two warriors more unequally matched, but when David was victorious over Goliath there was no empty boasting, no reliance upon his own powers. God gave the victory and David gave Him all the glory. He became a man of war and because of that was not allowed to build the Temple (I Chron. 28:3).

II.   As a Musician. Because he was a skilful player on the harp he found himself in the presence of the wretched king, Saul, who could only be soothed by David's music. Poetic genius made him the sweet psalmist of Israel, and no poet has been so constantly used and quoted through the ages. His majestic psalms are the masterpiece of spiritual literature.

III.   As a Saint. David was accepted as a child of God. The general trend of his life was spiritual (I Sam. 13:14; I Kings 15: 5). What other man has had the reputation of being known as a man after God's own heart? Such an expression does not refer to any remarkable goodness in David, but to him as one whom God had chosen to be the ruler of His people. He was the man according to God's special choice. His psalms of praise, worship and meditation indicate the God-ward direction of his life.

IV.   As a Sinner. David violated a divine law (Deut. 17:17; II Sam. 5:13), yielded to his gross sin in a period of ease (II Sam. 11) and was rebuked by the prophet Nathan (II Sam. 12). David stained his character by his sin against Uriah and by the deceitful way he gained this gallant soldier's wife as his own. Such a grievous sin brought the bitterest anguish of heart. David's confession was not a cold, formal acknowledgment of guilt, but a true and heartfelt humbling of himself before God and a deep cry for pardon and restoration to divine favor as psalms thirty-two and fifty-one clearly prove.

V.   As a Prophet. David had a prophetic gift given to few. He was one of those holy men of old moved by the Holy Spirit to set forth many glorious truths related to Christ as Saviour and Messiah. When we come to the New Testament we find the Psalms quoted from more often than any other part of the Old Testament.

VI.   As a Type. Not only did David prophesy about Christ, he resembled Him in many ways. For example:

Both were born in the humble town of Bethlehem.

Both were of low estate on earth, having no rank to boast of, no wealth to recommend them to the world.

Both were shepherds—the one caring for sheep, the other for souls.

Both were sorely oppressed and persecuted but opened not their mouths.

Both came to kingship. David subdued his foes and had a kingdom stretching from shore to shore. Jesus was born a King, and is to have an everlasting Kingdom.

VII.   As a Star. Does not the children's hymn urge us to be "a star in someone's sky?" David has lighted many a spiritual traveler on the way to heaven. Glory alone will reveal what his psalms meant to Christ and to His followers in all ages. Yet he is nothing compared to the Sun of Righteousness Himself. None can compare to David's greater son, the Lord Jesus Christ, who died and rose again to become our Saviour, Friend and King.

DEBIR [Dĕ' bûr]—SPEAKER. *The king of Eglon*, ally of Adoni-zedec, who joined four other kings against Joshua, but was defeated and executed by Joshua (Josh. 10:3). Also the name of a city near Hebron (Josh. 10:38).

DEDAN [Dĕ' dan]—LOW or THEIR FRIENDSHIP.
1. *A grandson of Cush* son of Ham (Gen. 10:7; I Chron. 1:9).
2. *A son of Abraham* by Keturah (Gen. 25:3; I Chron. 1:32). Also the name of a district near Edom (Jer. 25:23).

DEKAR [Dĕ' kär]—LANCE BEARER or PERFORATION. *Father of one of Solomon's purveyors* at Mahaz (I Kings 4:9).

DELAIAH [Dĕl a ĭ' ah]—JEHOVAH IS DELIVERER.
1. *A descendant of Aaron*, and one of David's priests (I Chron. 24:18).
2. *One of the Nethinims*, founder of a family whose genealogy had been lost (Ezra 2:60; Neh. 7:62).
3. *One who tried to dishearten Nehemiah* (Neh. 6:10).
4. *A Judahite prince*, son of Shemaiah who urged king Jehoiakim not to burn the sacred roll (Jer. 36:12, 25).
5. *A son of Elioenai* (I Chron. 3:24).

DEMAS [Dĕ' mas]—POPULAR or RULER OF PEOPLE. *A companion of Paul* during his first Roman imprisonment (Col. 4:14; Philem. 24).

The Man Who Forsook His Friend

This seems to be an indication that this native of Thessalonica was not fully trusted even when he was near to Paul (Phil. 2:20). Scripture has this against him, that he forsook Paul for this present world (II Tim. 4:10). It is amazing how a student of Comparative Anatomy can build up a whole unknown structure from one or two known bones. In the same way we can sketch the character of Demas from the few references to him in the Bible's portrait gallery.

Before he met Paul we can picture him as an agreeable young man with no particular vice. The material of his character had no rent in it. It was only shoddy throughout. Under the strong influence of Paul's personality, Demas was like a piece of soft iron, temporarily magnetized by the presence of a magnet. Becoming a disciple, he was carried away by the enthusiasm of sacrifice. He wanted to live with Paul and die with him, and have a throne and a halo among the martyred saints.

But when Demas came up to the great capital of the then known world in company with the Lord's prisoners, Paul and Epaphras, it was a different story. He was not a prisoner, and gradually the contrast between the cell and the outer world became intolerable to him. He saw the magnificent halls of the Caesars, the gorgeous homes of the rich and the glitter of a world of music, venal loves, jest and wine. Such a gay world cast its glamor over Demas, and he yielded to its charms. The prison where his friends were languishing seemed wretched alongside the music-haunted, scented, dazzling halls of Rome. Thus Paul had to write one of the most heartbreaking lines in his letters:

"Demas hath forsaken me, having loved this present world." This man of wavering impulse who surrendered the passion of sacrifice and sank in the swirling waters of the world, is a true reflection of the thought that where our love is, there we finally are.

DEMETRIUS [Dĕ mĕ′ trĭ ŭs]—BELONGING TO DEMETER. Demeter was the goddess of agriculture and rural life.

1. *The silversmith at Ephesus* who made silver models of the celebrated Temple of Diana, and who opposed Paul and incited the mob against him (Acts 19:24, 38).

2. *A believer,* well-commended by the Apostle John (III John 12). This man of God had the testimony of all men of the truth and of John also. It is one of the finest recommendations of the Gospel when a Christian impresses and attracts those around him by the reality of his or her life.

DEUEL [Deŭ′ el]—INVOCATION OF GOD or GOD IS KNOWING. *The father of Eliasaph,* a Gadite prince (Num. 1:14; 2:14; 7:42, 47). Called Reuel (friend of God) in Numbers 2:14.

DIBLAIM [Dĭb′ la ĭm]—DOUBLE EMBRACE or TWIN BALLS. *Father of Gomer wife* of Hosea the prophet (Hos. 1:3).

DIBRI [Dĭb′ rĭ]—ON THE PASTURE BORN or PROMISE OF THE LORD. *A Danite* whose daughter married an Egyptian and whose son was stoned for blasphemy (Lev. 24:11).

DIDYMUS [Dĭd′ ў mŭs]—A TWIN. *The surname of the apostle Thomas* (John 11:16; 20:24; 21:2).

DIKLAH [Dĭk′ lah]—PALM GROVE. *A son of Joktan* of the family of Shem (Gen. 10:27; I Chron. 1:21).

DIONYSIUS [Dĭ o nўs′ ĭ ŭs]—DIVINELY TOUCHED or THE GOD OF WINE. *A member of the Athenian supreme court* at Athens who became a convert to Christianity (Acts 17:34).

DIOTREPHES [Di ŏt′ re phēs]—NOURISHED BY JUPITER. *The professed disciple* who refused to recognize the authority of John as an apostle, and who loved to have the pre-eminence (III John 9). Diotrephes tried to act like a little Caesar. Pride and self-pleasing led to the dethronement of Christ. The word "pre-eminence" occurs twice in the New Testament. Paul speaks of Christ having the "pre-eminence" (Col. 1:18). Diotrephes substituted self for Christ.

DISHAN [Dĭ' shan]—LEAPING. *The youngest son of Seir* the Horite (Gen. 36:21-30; I Chron. 1:38, 42).

DISHON [Dĭ' shon]—LEAPING.
1. *The fifth son of Seir* the Horite (Gen. 36:21, 26, 30; I Chron. 1:38).
2. *The son of Anah* and grandson of Seir (Gen. 36:25; I Chron. 1:41).

DODAI [Dŏ' da ī]—BELOVED OF JEHOVAH. *An Ahohite,* one of David's captains (I Chron. 27:4).

DODANIM [Dŏ' da nĭm]—A LEADER. *A descendant or race descended from Javan* the son of Japhet (Gen. 10:4; I Chron. 1:7).

DODAVAH [Dŏ' da vah]—JEHOVAH IS LOVING. *Father of the Eliezer* who prophesied about the ships (II Chron. 20:37). Also called Dodwaha.

DODO [Dŏ' dō]—LOVING.
1. *Grandfather of the judge Tolah* of the tribe of Issachar (Judg. 10:1).
2. *Father of the second of David's thirty heroes* (II Sam. 23:9; I Chron. 11:12).
3. *A man of Bethlehem,* father of Elhanan and another of David's heroes (II Sam. 23:24; I Chron. 11:26).

DOEG [Dŏ' eg]—TIMID or FEARFUL. *Chief of Saul's herdsmen,* an Edomite, who informed Saul of Ahimelech's help for David. Because of Doeg's report Ahimelech and his companions were slain (I Sam. 22:7-22).

DUMAH [Dŭ' mah]—SILENCE or RESEMBLANCE. *A son of Ishmael* son of Abraham by Hagar (Gen. 25:14; I Chron. 1:30). Also the name of two cities (Josh. 15:52; Isa. 21:11).

E

EBAL [Ē' bal]—BARE.
1. *Son of Shobal,* son of Seir the Horite (Gen. 36:23; I Chron. 1:40).
2. *A Son of Joktan,* son of Eber, grandson of Shem (I Chron. 1:22). Also the name of a mountain in Ephraim (Deut. 11:29).

EBED [Ě′ bed]—SERVANT or SLAVE.

1. *The father of Gaal,* an Ephraimite who rebelled against Abimelech when he reigned in Shechem (Judg. 9:26–35).

2. *A chief of the father's house of Adin* who returned from Babylon with fifty males under the leadership of Ezra (Ezra 8:6).

EBED-MELECH [Ě′ bed-mē ′lěch]—SERVANT or SLAVE OF THE KING. *An Ethiopian eunuch* of the palace in Zedekiah's time who assisted Jeremiah in his release from prison (Jer. 38:7–12; 39:16).

The Man Who Was a Credit to His Class

It is said of Ebed-melech that he was an *Ethiopian* which means that he was a heathen and one of a despicable type at that time. "Can the Ethiopian change his skin?" No! But this Ethiopian had a transformed moral character, and was a triumph of grace in the clan to which he belonged. The Eastern eunuchs were a pitilessly cruel race, whose delight was to wound and vex. No clan had a worse reputation for cruelty, but here again Ebed-melech was different. He was as kind as the rest of his clan was cruel. Kitto calls him, "The benevolent Eunuch." Then he is likewise described as a *servant of the king.* Royal servants were usually a godless company. But Ebed-melech was as faithful a servant to God as he was to king Zedekiah. He loved the prophet Jeremiah and risked his own life to save the man of God.

Among the lessons to be gleaned from the record of this eunuch who was greater than his fellows are:

He was superior to his surroundings.

He put more pretentious people to shame.

He had the courage of his convictions.

He had a kind way of doing kindness.

He achieved a great service with poor instruments.

Old rags and cords! How God can use weak things for the accomplishment of His plan!

His faith in God was the secret of his noble life.

He was divinely rewarded. God is a grand Paymaster.

EBER [Ě′ bûr]—A SHOOT.

1. *A descendant of Shem* through Arphaxad, and the progenitor of various peoples (Gen. 10:21–25; 11:14–17; I Chron. 1:18–25).

2. *The head of a family in Gad* (I Chron. 5:13).

3. *A son of Elpaal* a Benjamite (I Chron. 8:12).

4. *A son of Shashak* a Benjamite (I Chron. 8:22).

5. *A priest,* head of the father's house of Amok in the days of the high priest, Joiakim (Neh. 12:20). Name is also used of the descendants of Eber (Num. 24:24) (No. 1). Heber is another spelling.

EBIASAPH [Ě bĭ′ a sǎph]—THE FATHER OF GATHERING. *A son of Elkanah* and a great-grandson of Korah (I Chron. 6:23, 37; 9:19). Also given as Abiasaph.

EDEN [E' děn]—DELIGHT.

1. *The son of Joah,* a Gershomite (II Chron. 29:13).
2. *A Levite* in Hezekiah's time appointed to distribute oblations (II Chron. 31:15). Also the name of man's first abode (Gen. 2:8).

EDER, EDAR [E' dûr, E' där]—A FLOCK.

1. *A son of Elpaal,* a Benjamite (I Chron. 8:15). See Ader.
2. *A son of Mushi,* a Levite of the family of Merari (I Chron. 23:23; 24:30). Also the name of two places (Gen. 35:21; Josh. 15:21).

EDOM [E' dom]—RED EARTH. *The elder son of Isaac,* and so named in memory of the red color of the lentil pottage for which he sold his birthright to his twin brother Jacob (Gen. 25:30; 36:1, 8, 19). See Esau. Name is also used to describe those descended from Esau, the Edomites (Gen. 36:9).

EGLON [Ěg' lŏn]—CIRCLE or CHARIOT. *A king of Moab* who captured Jericho and who, after his long oppression of the Israelites, was slain by Ehud, son of Gera (Judg. 3:12–17). Also the name of a city near Judah (Josh. 10:3).

EHI [E' hī]—UNITY. *Son of Benjamin* (Gen. 46:21). Same as Ehud in I Chronicles 8:6.

EHUD [E' hŭd]—STRONG or UNION.

1. *The son of Bilhan,* great-grandson of Benjamin (I Chron. 7:10; 8:6).
2. *The son of Gera,* the second judge of Israel (Judg. 3:15–26; 4:1).

The Man Who Was Left-Handed

This left-handed man was a ruler in Israel, and the peculiar thing about the tribe of Benjamin to which Ehud belonged was that in it were seven hundred left-handed men. So skillful had they all become in the use of the left hand that they could sling stones at a hair's breadth and never miss.

Eglon, king of Moab, oppressor of Israel, imposed an outrageous tax upon the people, and Ehud received a divine commission to destroy the oppressor. Meeting the king in his summerhouse and saying that he had a secret message for him, Ehud, the left-handed man, put his left hand to his right side, pulled out a dagger and Eglon died. Thus for the salvation of Israel the left-handed weapon did its work. Wonderful is it not, that God can use all kinds for the fulfilment of His purpose?

EKER [E' kŭr]—ONE TRANSPLANTED. *Son of Ram,* a Judahite and of the household of Jerahmeel (I Chron. 2:27).

ELADAH [Ĕl′ a dah]—GOD HATH ADORNED. *A descendant of Ephraim* (I Chron. 7:20). Also given as Eleadah.

ELAH, ELA [Ē′ lah]—AN OAK or LIKE A TREE.
1. *A duke of Edom,* named from his habitation (Gen. 36:41; I Chron. 1:52).
2. *The father of one of Solomon's purveyors* (I Kings 4:18).
3. *The son and successor of Baasha,* king of Israel, who only reigned for about a year and who was killed while drunk by Zimri (I Kings 16:6–14).
4. *The father of Hoshea,* last king of Israel (II Kings 15:30; 17:1; 18:1, 9.)
5. *A son of Caleb,* son of Jephunneh (I Chron. 4:15).
6. *One of the tribe,* a Benjamite (I Chron. 9:8). Also the name of the valley where David slew Goliath (I Sam. 17:2, 19).

ELAM [Ē′ lăm]—YOUTH or HIGH.
1. *A son of Shem* and founder of the Elamites (Gen. 10:22; I Chron. 1:17; Ezra 4:9; Acts 2:9).
2. *Son of Shashak,* a Benjamite (I Chron. 8:24).
3. *Son of Meshelemiah,* a Kohathite (I Chron. 26:3).
4. *The head of a family* of 1,254 that returned from exile with Zerubbabel (Ezra 2:7; Neh. 7:12).
5. Another whose posterity returned from exile (Ezra 2:31; Neh. 7:34). Perhaps same person as No. 4.
6. *One whose descendants came back with Ezra* (Ezra 8:7).
7. *The father of Jehiel,* ancestor of Shechaniah, who confessed the trespass of marrying foreign wives (Ezra 10:2, 26).
8. *A chieftain who,* with Nehemiah, sealed the covenant (Neh. 10:14).
9. *A priest* who assisted in the dedication of the rebuilt wall (Neh. 12:42). Elam is also the name of the country inhabited by his descendants (Gen. 14:1, 9).

ELASAH, ELEASAH [Ĕl′ a sah]—GOD HATH MADE.
1. *A priest* who married a foreign wife (Ezra 10:22).
2. *The ambassador* Zedekiah sent to Nebuchadnezzar (Jer. 29:3).

ELDAAH [Ĕl′ da ah]—WHOM GOD CALLED. *A son of Midian* and descendant of Abraham (Gen. 25:4; I Chron. 1:33).

ELDAD [Ĕl′ dăd]—GOD IS A FRIEND or GOD HATH LOVED. *One of the two elders* who assisted Moses in the government of Israel (Num. 11:26, 27).

ELEAD [Ē′ le-ăd]—GOD IS WITNESS or GOD CONTINUETH. Perhaps a *son of Ephraim* who, with his brother, was killed by invaders (I Chron. 7:21).

ELEASAH, ELASAH [E' lĕ' a sah]—GOD HATH MADE or IS DOER.

1. *A son of Helez,* a Judahite with Egyptian blood in his veins (I Chron. 2:39, 40).

2. *A son of Rapha or Raphaiah,* a descendant of Saul and Jonathan (I Chron. 8:37; 9:43).

ELEAZAR [E le ā'zar]—GOD IS HELPER.

1. *The third son of Aaron* by Elisheba and father of Phinehas (Ex. 6:23, 25). He was consecrated a priest (Ex. 28:1) and was chief of the Levites (Num. 3:32).

2. *A son of Amminadab,* set apart to care for the Ark after its return (I Sam. 7:1).

3. *A son of Dodo,* the Ahohite, one of the three chief captains of David's army (II Sam. 23:9; I Chron. 11:12).

4. *A son of Mahli,* a Merarite, who had daughters only, who married their cousins (I Chron. 23:21, 22; 24:28).

5. *A priest* who participated in the dedication of the rebuilt wall (Neh. 12:42).

6. *A son of Phinehas,* a Levite (Ezra 8:33).

7. *A son of Eliud* and an ancestor of Christ (Matt. 1:15).

ELHANAN [El hā' nan]—GOD HATH BEEN GENEROUS or MERCY OF GOD.

1. *A son of Jair,* who slew Lahmi the brother of Goliath (II Sam. 21:19; I Chron. 20:5).

2. *A son of Dodo* the Bethlehemite, and one of David's thirty heroes (II Sam. 23:24; I Chron. 11:26).

ELI [E' lī]—JEHOVAH IS HIGH or MY GOD. *The high priest and judge of Israel* of the family of Ithamar (I Sam. 1–4; 14:3).

The Man Who Lacked Parental Authority

There are few Bible men in whose character we cannot find some great and glaring fault. There is usually a dead fly in the ointment, a rent in the garment, a spot on the whitest sheet. Eli was a good man whose life was pure. He loved and delighted in God's service, but was faulty in one point. He failed to exercise the proper authority of a parent over his children.

Eli belonged to the tribe of Levi, and for years acted as a judge and as High Priest in Israel. He lived at Shiloh in a dwelling adjoining the Temple for the greater portion of his life. We know little about him until he was well advanced in age. The first mention of him is when Hannah came to pour out her heart.

Eli's fault which brought sorrow upon his declining years was the conduct of his own two sons, Phinehas and Hophni, who, although lacking their father's character and qualities, were yet put into the priest's office. Their conduct disgraced their high calling and shocked the people so much that they "abhorred the offering of the Lord." While Eli warned them of their shameful ways, he did not rebuke them with the severity their evil deeds merited. He should have exercised the stern authority of a father and rebuked them as a judge. Instead Eli only mildly reasoned with his sons saying: "Why do ye such things?" But the sons disregarded such a weak and useless protest for their hearts were cold and callous and so they no longer heeded their father's feelings.

Although Eli had no power to change the hearts of his sons, he could have prevented their ministry before the Lord, but he "restrained them not." He wanted to be kind to them but it was a false and mistaken kindness. A seasonable correction would have saved them from ruin. Eli had no need to be harsh and severe, only firm and decided in the matter of obedience. Eli was twice warned that judgment would overtake him and his sons, but such warning was lost upon him. He dearly loved his sons and could not take action against them.

What a pitiable spectacle Eli presents! An old man of ninety, almost blind, waited to hear the result of the grim battle between the Israelites and the Philistines. How he trembled for his nation, his sons and also for the Ark of God which would be dishonored if it fell into enemy hands! Then the messenger came with news of the slaughter of his sinful sons and of the taking of the Ark. As Eli heard mention of the latter he fell off his seat by the side of a gate and died of a broken neck, yes, and of a broken heart! As is often the case, children bring down their father's gray hairs with sorrow to the grave.

ELIAB [Ĕ lĭ' ăb]—GOD IS A FATHER.

1. *A son of Helon* and leader of the tribe of Zebulun when the census was taken in the wilderness (Num. 1:9; 2:7; 7:24, 29).

2. *A son of Pallu or Phallu,* a Reubenite, and father of Dathan and Abiram (Num. 16:1, 12; 26:8, 9; Deut. 11:6).

3. *The eldest son of Jesse* and brother of David (I Sam. 16:6; 17:13, 28). Called Elihu in I Chronicles 27:18.

4. *A Levite* in David's time who was a Tabernacle porter and musician (I Chron. 15:18, 20; 16:5).

5. *A Gadite* warrior who with others came over to David when a fugitive in the wilderness (I Chron. 12:9).

6. *An ancestor of Samuel* the prophet; a Kohathite Levite (I Chron. 6:27). Called Elihu in I Samuel 1:1 and Eliel in I Chronicles 6:34.

ELIADA [Ĕ lĭ' a dă]—GOD IS KNOWING or GOD KINDLY REGARDED.

1. *One of David's sons* (II Sam. 5:16; I Chron. 3:8).

2. *A Benjamite,* a mighty warrior who led two hundred thousand of his tribe to the army of Jehoshaphat (II Chron. 17:17).

ELIADAH [Ĕ, lĭ' a dah]—GOD IS KNOWING. *The father of Rezon,* the captain of a roving band that annoyed Solomon (I Kings 11:23).

ELIAH [Ē lī ah]—GOD IS JEHOVAH.

1. *A son of Jeroham*, the Benjamite who was head of his tribe (I Chron. 8:27).

2. *One of the sons of Elam* who married a foreign wife (Ezra 10:26).

ELIAHBA [Ē lī' ah bă]—GOD DOTH HIDE. *A Shaalbonite*, and one of David's famous guard (II Sam. 23:32; I Chron. 11:33).

ELIAKIM [Ē lī' ā kĭm]—GOD IS SETTING UP or DOTH ESTABLISH.

1. *A son of Hilkiah*, successor of Shebna as master of Hezekiah's household (II Kings 18:18, 26, 37; 19:2).

2. *The original name of king Jehoiakim* (II Kings 23:34; II Chron. 36:4).

3. *A priest* who helped at the dedication of the rebuilt wall in Nehemiah's time (Neh. 12:41).

4. *The eldest son of Abiud* or Judah and father of Azor in Christ's genealogy (Matt. 1:13; Luke 3:30).

ELIAM [Ē lī' am]—GOD IS ONE OF THE FAMILY or GOD'S FOUNDER OF THE PEOPLE. *The father of Bath-sheba*, wife of David (II Sam. 11:3). Called also Ammiel.

ELIAS, ELIJAH [Ē lī' as, Ē lī' jah]—GOD IS JEHOVAH or GOD HIMSELF.

1. *Elias is the Greek form of Elijah* (Matt. 11:14). Elijah the Tishbite is the grandest and most romantic character Israel ever produced (I Kings 17; 18; 19).

The Man Who Had No Fear of Man

No career in the Old Testament is more vividly portrayed, or has as much fascination as that of the unique character of Elijah. The New Testament attests to his greatness and reveals what an indelible impression he made upon the mind of his nation. All we know of him before his dramatic appearance can be summed up in the words: "Elijah the Tishbite, who was of the inhabitants of Gilead" (I Kings 17:1). Scripture is silent about his past history. Suddenly and with abrupt impetuosity the figure of the prophet bursts upon the scene to rebuke the godless and to reawaken and restore the nation of which he was a part. This man of iron is presented in many ways:

As a fearless, bold and dauntless reformer (I Kings 18:17-46).

As a rebuker of kings (I Kings 21:20; II Kings 1:16).

As a mighty intercessor, praying with faith and intensity (I Kings 17:20, 22; 18:36-38; Jas. 5:17).

As a man prone to discouragement (I Kings 19:4).

As one capable of fallible judgment (I Kings 19:4, 18).

As a prophet divinely honored (II Kings 2:11; Matt. 17:3).

As a performer of miracles (I Kings 19:8).

As a God-inspired prophet ready to obey and trust God (I Kings 17:1; 21:9-24; II Kings 1:2-17).

As a saint whose end was glorious (II Kings 2:1).

Both mystery and majesty are associated with Elijah, the mightiest of the prophets. His history in I Kings can be appropriately studied under five prepositions:

Before Ahab (I Kings 17:1). When God commands us to speak, no thought of peril need make us dumb.

By Cherith (I Kings 17:2–7). Faith moves on, trusting that when the first step is taken the next will be revealed.

At Zarephath (I Kings 17:10, 24). Elijah was miraculously fed on three occasions—by ravens (I Kings 17:6); by a widow (I Kings 17:9); by an angel (I Kings 19:5–8).

On Carmel (I Kings 18). Here we see the power of a fully surrendered man.

In the wilderness (I Kings 19). The overwrought prophet suffered a lapse of confidence, but was quickly restored.

Elijah, the rugged prophet, suggests John the Baptist, who came in the same spirit and power of the prophet.

Note these points of correspondence:

Their familiarity with the deserts and solitude.

Their austere manner and dress.

Their strong reproof of prevailing evils.

Their intrepid fidelity in calling all classes to repentance.

Their exposure of the wrath of a wicked king.

Their continued influence after death through disciples.

Their fruitful labors. "Many of the children of Israel did they turn to the Lord their God."

2. *A son of Harim* who married a foreign wife during the exile (Ezra 10:21).

3. *A Benjamite* and son of Jeroham, resident at Jerusalem (I Chron. 8:27 R.V.).

4. *An Israelite* induced to put away his foreign wife. (Ezra 10:26).

ELIASAPH [Ė lĭ' a săph]—GOD HATH ADDED or GOD IS GATHERED.

1. *The son of Deuel* and head of the Gadites at the census in the wilderness (Num. 1:14; 2:14; 7:42, 47; 10:20).

2. *A son of Lael,* a Levite and prince of the Gershonites during the wilderness wanderings (Num. 3:24).

ELIASHIB [Ė lĭ' a shĭb]—GOD IS REQUITER or GOD HATH RESTORED.

1. *A priest* in David's time from whom the eleventh priestly course took its name (Chron. 24:12).

2. *A son of Elioenai,* descendant of Zerubbabel, a Judahite (I Chron. 3:24).

3. *The high priest* at the time of the rebuilding of the city wall (Neh. 3:1, 20, 21; 13:4, 7, 28).

4. *A Levite and singer* who put away his foreign wife (Ezra 10: 24).

5. *A son of Zattu* who married a foreign wife (Ezra 10:27).

6. *A son of Bani* who also married a foreign wife (Ezra 10:26).

7. *An ancestor of Johanan* who helped Ezra in the assembly of foreign wives (Ezra 10:6; Neh. 12:10, 22, 23).

ELIATHAH [Ě lǐ' a thah]—GOD HATH COME. *A son of Heman* and a musician in David's reign (I Chron. 25:4, 27).

ELIDAD [Ě lǐ' dăd]—GOD IS A FRIEND OR GOD HATH LOVED. *A prince* of the tribe of Benjamin and a member of the commission in the division of Canaan (Num. 34:21).

ELIEL [Ě lǐ el]—GOD IS GOD.
1. *A Levite* of the family of Kohath and an ancestor of Samuel the prophet (I Chron. 6:34).
2. *A chief man of the half tribe of Manasseh* in Bashan (I Chron. 5:24).
3. *A son of Shimhi* the Benjamite (I Chron. 8:20).
4. *A son of Shashak,* A Benjamite (I Chron. 8:22).
5. *A Mahavite* and a captain in David's army (I Chron. 11:46).
6. *Another of David's heroes* (I Chron. 11:47).
7. *A Gadite* who joined David at Ziklag (I Chron. 12:11). Perhaps the same person as No. 5 or 6.
8. *A chief of Judah* in David's reign (I Chron. 15:9). Perhaps the same man as No. 5.
9. *A chief Levite* who helped in the return of the Ark from the house of Obed-edom (I Chron. 15:11).
10. *A Levite overseer* of tithes and offerings in Hezekiah's time (II Chron. 31:13).

ELIENAI [Ě lǐ ě' na ǐ]—UNTO GOD ARE MINE EYES. *A son of Shimhi,* a Benjamite (I Chron. 8:20).

ELIEZER [Ě lǐ ē zûr]—GOD IS MY HELP.
1. *The second son of Moses* and Zipporah to whom his father gave this name as a memento of his gratitude to God (Ex. 18:4; I Chron. 23:15, 17; 26:25).
2. *A son of Becher* and grandson of Benjamin (I Chron. 7:8).
3. *A priest* who assisted in the return of the Ark to Jerusalem (I Chron. 15:24).
4. *A Reubenite* ruler in David's time (I Chron. 27:16).
5. *The prophet who rebuked Jehoshaphat* for his alliance with king Ahaziah in the Ophir expedition (II Chron. 20:37).
6. *A chieftain* sent with others to induce many of the Israelites to return with Ezra to Jerusalem (Ezra 8:16).
7. *A priest* who put away his foreign wife (Ezra 10:18).
8. *A Levite* who had done the same (Ezra 10:23).
9. *One of the sons of Harim* who had done likewise (Ezra 10:31).
10. *An ancestor of Joseph,* husband of Mary (Luke 3:29).

11. *Abraham's chief servant,* and "son of his house," that is, one of his large household. He is named "Eliezer of Damascus" probably to distinguish him from others of the same name (Gen. 15:2; 24).

The Man Who Found a Wife for His Master

There can be little doubt that the Damascus Eliezer is the nameless servant Abraham sent to his own country and kindred to secure a bride for Isaac, his son of promise. Of the search of Eliezer, Dr. C. I. Scofield says that the entire chapter (Genesis 24) is highly typical, and then he gives us this most helpful outline:

I. Abraham—type of a certain king who would make a marriage for his son (Matt. 22:2; John 6:44).

II. The unnamed servant—type of the Holy Spirit who does not speak of or from himself, but takes of the things of the bridegroom with which to win the bride (John 16:13, 14).

III. The servant—type of the Spirit as enriching the bride with the bridegroom's gifts (I Cor. 12:7–11; Gal. 5:22).

IV. The servant—type of the Spirit as bringing the bride to the meeting with the bridegroom (Acts 13: 4; 16:6, 7; Rom. 8:11; I Thess. 4:14–17).

V. Rebekah—type of the Church, the *ecclesia,* the "called out" virgin bride of Christ (Gen. 24:16; II Cor. 11:2; Eph. 5:25–32).

VI. Isaac—type of the bridegroom "whom not having seen" the bride loves through the testimony of the unnamed servant (I Pet. 1:8).

VII. Isaac—type of the bridegroom who goes out to meet and receive His bride (Gen. 24:63; I Thess. 4:16, 17).

Points to emphasize as we peruse this beautiful chapter twenty-four with its love-quest are clearly evident:

Prayer should precede our pursuits (v. 12).

Leading depends upon living (v. 27).

The Lord is before us and with us (v. 40).

The place of privilege (v. 43 with John 4:14).

The importance of a personal decision (v. 58).

The right attitude for the reception of God's gifts (v. 63).

ELIHOENAI, ELIOENAI [Ĕ lĭ ho ē′ na ĭ, Ĕ lĭ o ē′ na ĭ]—TO JEHOVAH ARE MINE EYES.

1. *A son of Neariah* of the family of David (I Chron. 3:23, 24).

2. *The head of a family of Simeon* (I Chron. 4:36).

3. *The head of one of the families of the sons of Becher,* son of Benjamin (I Chron. 7:8).

4. *A son of Pashur,* a priest who put away his foreign wife (Ezra 10:22). Perhaps the same person as the one mentioned in Nehemiah 12:41.

5. *A son of Zattu* who married a foreign wife (Ezra 10:27).

6. *A priest,* perhaps the same person as No. 4 (Neh. 12:41).

7. *The seventh son of Meshelemiah,* the son of Kore (I Chron. 26:3). Also given as Elihoenai.

8. *A descendant of Pahath Moab* who returned with Ezra in Artaxerxes' time (Ezra 8:4).

ELIHOREPH [Ĕl ĭ hō′ reph]—GOD OF HARVEST RAIN or GOD IS A REWARD. *One of king Solomon's scribes* (I Kings 4:3).

ELIHU [Ĕ lī′ hū]—HE IS GOD HIMSELF.
1. *The father of Jeroham* and great-grandfather of Samuel the prophet, who also has the name of Eliel (I Sam. 1:1; I Chron. 6:34).
2. *A man of Manasseh* who joined David at Ziklag (I Chron. 12:20).
3. *A Kohathite* of the family of Korah, and a Tabernacle porter in David's time (I Chron. 26:7).
4. *A brother of David,* who became ruler over Judah (I Chron. 27:18). Also known as Eliab.
5. *The youngest of Job's friends,* the son of Barachel, a Buzite (Job 32:2–6; 34:1; 35:1; 36:1).

The Man Who Was a Self-Assertive Dogmatist

The lineage of Elihu, the fourth speaker in Job's dialogue, is given in fuller detail. He was the son of Barachel the Buzite, the kindred of Ram (Job 32:2). Buz was the brother of Uz and son of Nahor (Gen. 22:21). Buz is also mentioned along with Tema and the Arab tribes (Jer. 25:23).

Elihu's name, "God is Lord," suggests his desire to exalt the Almighty. One writer has described him as "the forerunner of Jehovah." This youthful, somewhat self-assertive speaker reaches a high level and has "a far juster and more spiritual conception" in dealing with the problem that has confronted Eliphaz, Bildad and Zophar. But he gives only half the truth, and his appeal, although so lofty and eloquent, is marred by a self-assertiveness evident from his sayings, "Great men are not always wise: neither do the aged understand judgment" (Job 32:9) and, "My words shall be the uprightness of my heart" (Job 33:3).

It is interesting to observe that Job did not reply to Elihu as he did to the other three, "Who is this that darkeneth counsel by words without knowledge?" This was Jehovah's word to Elihu, in which He lays the very charge at his feet which he had sought to bring against His servant Job (Job 34:35; 35:16).

Elihu's vindication appears to be along three lines:
I. He first of all condemns Job for his self-justification (Job 32:2; 33:8, 9).
II. He sets out to modify the doctrine of the three friends by affirming that affliction is as much a judgment upon sin as a warning of judgment to come (Job 34:10, 11).
III. He then unveils in a way completely overmastering the mind, the majesty and glory of God, the climax of which is in Job 37:5.

Elihu claimed inspiration for his presence and message (Job 32:8). Eagerness was his to speak before he did, but youth and modesty kept him back (Job 32:4–8, 18, 19). What Elihu seemed to forget was, trial can overtake the saintliest of men (I Pet. 1:7).

ELIKA [Ĕl' i kă]—GOD IS REJECTOR or HATH SPEWED OUT. *A Harodite,* one of David's mighty men (II Sam. 23:25).

ELIMELECH [Ē lĭm' e lĕch]—GOD IS KING. *The husband of Naomi* and father of Mahlon and Chilion, Ephrathites of Bethlehem-judah (Ruth 1:2, 3; 2:1, 3; 4:3–9; I Sam. 17:12).

The Man Whose Ways Contradicted His Name

It is one thing to have a good name, but a different matter altogether to have a life corresponding to that name. Elimelech's name implies that God is King, an expressive name given him by godly parents when the nation followed the Lord. But Elimelech belied the name he bore, for had he truly believed that God was King, he would have stayed in Bethlehem in spite of the prevailing famine.

But one might argue that it was a wise thing to do to leave a famine-stricken land for another land where there was plenty of food for his family. Surely that was a journey any father would undertake to save his dear ones from starvation. But Elimelech was a Jew and as such had the promise, "In the days of famine ye shall be satisfied." Had he firmly believed in the sovereignty of God, Elimelech would have remained in Bethlehem, knowing that need can never throttle God. Had he not declared that bread and water for His own would be sure? Alas, however, Elimelech did not live up to his wonderful name! In going down to Moab, he stepped out of the will of God, who had forbidden His people to have any association with the Moabites. In Moab, Elimelech and his two sons found graves. Yet such a wrong move was overruled by God, for as the result of it, Ruth the Moabitess returned to Bethlehem with Naomi, who was to become the ancestress of our blessed Lord.

ELIPHAL [Ĕl' I phăl] GOD IS JUDGE or HATH JUDGED. *The son of Ur,* and one of David's heroes (I Chron. 11:35).

ELIPHALET, ELIPHELET [Ē lĭph' a lĕt, Ē lĭph' e lĕt]—THE GOD OF DELIVERANCES or GOD IS ESCAPE.

1. *The last of David's sons* (II Sam. 5:16; I Chron. 3:8; 14:7). The names of Elphalet and Phaltiel are the same as Eliphalet.

2. *Another son of David* born after he made Jerusalem his home and center (I Chron. 3:6). Called Elpalet in I Chronicles 14:5.

3. *A son of Ahasbai,* and one of David's heroes (II Sam. 23:34).

4. *A son of Eshek* and descendant of Saul, a Benjamite (I Chron. 8:39).

5. *A leader of the sons of Adonikam* who returned from exile with Ezra (Ezra 8:13).

6. *A son of Hashum* who put away his foreign wife (Ezra 10:33).

ELIPHAZ [Ĕl' i phăz]—GOD IS FINE GOLD or GOD IS DISPENSER.

1. *A son of Esau* by Adah daughter of Elon (Gen. 36:4–16; I Chron. 1:35, 36).

2. *The chief of Job's three friends*, a descendant of Teman, son of Eliphaz from whom a part of Arabia took its name (Gen. 36:11; Job 2:11; 4:1; 15:1; 22:1; 42:7, 9; Jer. 49:20).

The Man Who Was a Religious Dogmatist

Teman was noted for its wisdom and this Temanite descendant was a law unto himself. His name means "refined gold" but his fine gold was that of self-glory and of self-opinion from which he would not budge. As a wise man he gloried in his wisdom, and represented the orthodox wisdom of his day. This wise man from the East declared that God was just and did not dispense happiness or misery in a despot fashion, committing people to what He deemed best.

Eliphaz was a religious dogmatist, basing all his deductions upon a solitary remarkable experience he had had, namely that of a spirit passing before his face, causing his hair to stand up (Job 4:12–16). As the result of this weird occasion he felt he had a message of divine justice to declare (Job 4:17–21). Thus his speeches, delivered with a sacerdotal pathos are hard, cruel and rigidly dogmatic. His folly was that he tried to press Job into the mold of his own experience.

In his first speech (Job 4, 5), Eliphaz begins by informing Job of all his affliction, namely, sin. Approaching Job in a courteous yet cold manner, Eliphaz seeks to prove that all calamity is judgment upon sin. The crux of his argument is: "Remember, I pray thee, who ever perished being innocent? or where were the righteous cut off?" (Job 4:7).

In his second speech Eliphaz reveals a spirit wounded by Job's sarcastic remarks (Job 15:2). He then proceeds to maintain his argument that Job is suffering because of his sin (Job 15:16).

In his third speech, Eliphaz definitely charges Job with sin (Job 22:5) and seeks to point out to him the pathway of restoration (Job 22:21).

ELIPHELEH [Ĕ lĭph' e leh]—JEHOVAH IS DISTINCTION or DISTINGUISHED. *A Levite singer and harpist* who had charge of the choral service when the Ark was returned (I Chron. 15:15–21). Also given as Eliphelehu.

ELISEUS Ĕl ĭ sĕ' us]—GOD IS SALVATION. *The Greek form of the name of Elisha* (Luke 4:27).

ELISHA [Ĕ lī' shă]—GOD IS SAVIOUR. *The son of Shaphat* of Abelmeholah, of the tribe of Issachar, the companion and successor of Elijah (I Kings 19:16–19; II Kings 2–13).

The Man Who Was a Model Leader

There is a striking difference between Elijah and Elisha, both of whom labored in the Northern Kingdom. Elijah's name means, *Jehovah my God* and suggests the *Law* while Elisha's name speaks of *grace—Jehovah my Saviour.*

Elisha left a peaceful occupation to become a model spiritual leader. Elijah prepared Elisha for his commission (II Kings 2:1–14), and the two became devoted to each other. Elisha's character is marked by mercy (II Kings 2:21), disinterestedness (II Kings 5) and toleration (II Kings 5:19). He earned a wonderful posthumous influence (II Kings 13:20, 21). What a victorious death was his (II Kings 13:14–19)! Summarizing the life of this prophet who spoke with the authority of an oracle of God (II Kings 3:16, 17), we see him etched as:

A man of indomitable faith (I Kings 19:20, 21; II Kings 1–18).
A man of swift action (II Kings 2:12–18).
A man of spiritual power (II Kings 2:19–22).
A man of dauntless courage (II Kings 3).
A man of deep sympathy (II Kings 4:1–7).
A man of God (II Kings 4:8–37).
A man of willing help (II Kings 4:38–41).
A man who merited blessing (II Kings 4:42–44).
A man of clear understanding (II Kings 5:1–19).
A man of force and might (II Kings 6:1–7).
A man who knew secrets (II Kings 6:8–23).
A man of remarkable foresight (II Kings 6:24–33; 7).
A man of unerring counsel (II Kings 8:1–6).
A man of tears and sorrow (II Kings 8:7–15).

Elisha suggests the ministry of Christ. On the whole, Elijah's work was destructive — he was the prophet of fire. Elisha's task was more merciful and beneficial. He had double the power of Elijah (II Kings 2:8, 9, 15), and consequently performed twice as many miracles as his former master. The following contrasts between these two prophets can be noted:

Elijah was a prophet of the wilderness;
    Elisha was a prince of the court.
Elijah had no settled home;
    Elisha enjoyed the peace of a home.
Elijah was known by his long hair and shaggy mantle;
    Elisha by his staff and bald head.
Elijah was mainly prophetical;
    Elisha's work was mainly miraculous.
Elijah's ministry was one of stern denunciation;
    Elisha's task was that of teaching and winning.
Elijah was a rebuker of kings;
    Elisha was a friend and admirer.
Elijah was a messenger of vengeance;
    Elisha was a messenger of mercy.
Elijah represented exclusiveness;
    Elisha stood for comprehension.
Elijah was fierce, fiery, energetic;

Elisha was gentle, sympathetic, simple.
Elijah was a solitary figure;
Elisha was more social.
Elijah had an extraordinary disappearance from earth;
Elisha's death was ordinary.

ELISHAH [Ĕ lī' shah]—*The eldest son of Javan*, grandson of Noah and founder of a tribal family (Gen. 10:4; I Chron. 1:7; Ezek. 27:7).

ELISHAMA [Ĕ lĭsh' a mä]—GOD IS HEARER or GOD HAS HEARD.
1. *The son of Ammihud* and prince of the Ephraimites at the outset of the wilderness sojourn (Num. 1:10; 2:18; 7:48, 53; 10:22; I Chron. 7:26).
2. *A son of David* born in Jerusalem (II Sam. 5:16; I Chron. 3:8).
3. *Another son of David,* who is also called Elishua (I Chron. 3:6).
4. *A son of Jekamiah,* a Judahite (I Chron. 2:41).
5. *Father of Nethaniah* and grandfather of Ishmael "of the seed royal" who lived at the time of the exile (II Kings 25:25; Jer. 41:1). Perhaps the same person as No. 4.
6. *A scribe or secretary to Jehoiakim* (Jer. 36:12, 20, 21).
7. *A priest* sent by Jehoshaphat to teach the people the Law (II Chron. 17:8).

ELISHAPHAT [Ĕ lĭsh' a phăt]—GOD IS JUDGE or HATH JUDGED. *One of the "captains of hundreds"* who supported Jehoiada in the revolt against Athaliah (II Chron. 23:1).

ELISHUA [Ĕl Ĭ shu' ă]—GOD IS RICH or GOD IS SALVATION. *A son of David* born in Jerusalem (II Sam. 5:15; I Chron. 14:5). Likewise called Elishama in I Chronicles 3:6.

ELIUD [Ĕ lī' ud]—GOD IS MAJESTY OR GOD IS MY PRAISE. *The son of Achim* and father of Eleazar and ancestor of Christ (Matt. 1:14, 15).

ELIZAPHAN, ELZAPHAN [Ĕ lĭz' a phăn]—GOD IS PROTECTOR or HATH CONCEALED.
1. *The son of Uzziel,* chief ruler of the Kohathites when the census was taken at Sinai (Num. 3:30; I Chron. 15:8).
2. *The son of Parnach,* prince of the tribe of Zebulun in the wilderness (Num. 34:25).
3. *Ancestor of certain Levites* assisting in the revival under Hezekiah (II Chron. 29:13).

ELIZUR [Ĕ lī' zur]—GOD IS A ROCK. *The son of Shedeur,* and prince of the Reubenites who helped in the census Moses took (Num. 1:5; 2:10; 7:30, 35; 10:18).

ELKANAH [Ĕl' kă nah]—GOD HATH CREATED or IS JEALOUS, POS-
SESSING.

1. *A Levite* of the family of Kohath and brother of Assir and Abiasaph (Ex. 6:24; I Chron. 6:23).

2. *The father of the prophet Samuel,* and a descendant of No. 1
in the fifth generation (I Sam. 1:1-23; 2:11, 20; I Chron. 6:27, 34).

3. *A descendant of Levi* through Kohath (I Chron. 6:25, 36).

4. *A descendant of Kohath* (I Chron. 6:26, 35). Perhaps the same
person as No. 3.

5. *An ancestor of Netophathite villagers* (I Chron. 9:16).

6. *A Korhite* who joined David at Ziklag (I Chron. 12:6).

7. *A Levite, doorkeeper* of the Ark (I Chron. 15:23). Perhaps the
same as No. 6.

8. *An officer in king Ahaz' household* and second only to the king,
who was slain when Pekah invaded Judah (II Chron. 28: 7).

ELMODAM, ELMADAN [Ĕl mŏ' dam]—THE GOD OF MEASURE. *The
son of Er,* and ancestor of Joseph, Mary's husband (Luke 3:28).

ELNAAM [Ĕl' na ăm]—GOD IS PLEASANT or PLEASANTNESS. *The father
of David's guard,* Jeribai and Joshaviah (I Chron. 11:46).

ELNATHAN [Ĕl' na thăn]—GOD HATH GIVEN OR IS GIVING.

1. *The father of Nehushta,* Jehoiakim's queen (II Kings 24:8; Jer.
26:22; 36:12, 25).

2. *Name of three Levites in Ezra's time* (Ezra 8:16).

ELON [Ĕ' lŏn]—AN OAK or STRONG.

1. *The father of Esau's wife* (Gen. 26:34; 36:2).

2. *The second of Zebulun's three sons* (Gen. 46:14; Num. 26:26).

3. *The Zebulonite who judged Israel* for ten years (Judg. 12:11,
12). Elon is also the name of a town (Josh. 19:43; I Kings 4:9).

ELPAAL [Ĕl' pă al]—GOD IS A REWARD or IS WORKING. *The son of
Shaharaim,* a Benjamite and head of his father's house (I Chron. 8:11,
12, 18).

ELPALET [Ĕl' pa lĕt]—GOD IS ESCAPE. *A son of David* (I Chron.
14:5). See Eliphalet (I Chron. 3:6).

ELUZAI [Ĕ lū' za ī]—GOD IS MY STRENGTH. *A Benjamite* who joined
David at Ziklag (I Chron. 12:5).

ELYMAS [Ĕl' ў măs]—A MAGICIAN or A SORCERER. *The false prophet
or Jewish impostor,* Bar-jesus, meaning son of Jesus or Joshua, who
withstood Paul and Barnabas at Paphos in Cyprus (Acts 13:8).

ELZABAD [Ĕl' za băd]—GOD HATH ENDOWED or BESTOWED.
1. *A Gadite* who joined David at Ziklag (I Chron. 12:12).
2. *The Son of Shemaiah* and a Korhite Levite (I Chron. 26:7).

ELZAPHAN [Ĕl' za phăn]—GOD HAS CONCEALED or PROTECTED.
1. *The second son of Uzziel* and grandson of Levi (Ex. 6:22; Lev. 10:4). Called also Elizaphan.
2. *A prince of Zebulun,* who assisted in the division of Canaan (Num. 34:25).

EMMOR [Ĕm' môr]—AN ASS. *The father of Sychem* (Acts 7:16). Same as Hamor.

ENAN [Ē' nan]—HAVING EYES or A FOUNTAIN. *The father of Ahira,* of the tribe of Naphtali, who assisted in the Sinai census (Num. 1:15; 2:29; 7:78, 83; 10:27).

ENEAS [Ē' ne ăs]—I PRAISE or PRAISE OF JEHOVAH. *A man of Lydia,* healed by Peter (Acts 9:33, 34).

ENOCH, HENOCH [Ē' nŏch, Hē' nŏch]—TEACHER, INITIATED, DEDICATED.
1. *The eldest son of Cain,* who had a city called after him (Gen. 4:17, 18; I Chron. 1:3).
2. *A son of Jared,* a descendant of Seth and father of Methuselah (Gen. 5:18–23; Luke 3:37; Heb. 11:5; Jude 14).

The Man Who Was Missed

In some six verses the Bible sets forth the brief biography of this Old Testament saint—but what a biography! We know nothing of the rank or profession of Enoch. Two things of great interest characterize him, namely, his holy life on earth and his glorious exit from earth.

Enoch walked with God. Twice over we are reminded of this evident fact. The wicked are "without God." Enoch was at peace with God. Although born a child of wrath, he became a child of grace. He must have been at peace with God; two cannot walk together unless they be agreed (Amos 3:3).

Enoch enjoyed close communion with God. What a real union of hearts the repeated phrase, "walked with God" implies! What sweet hours of holy and happy intercourse God and Enoch must have had as they communed with each other. There was never a cloud between their fellowship. God was a pleasure to Enoch, and Enoch pleased God.

Enoch was separated from the world. This seventh man from Adam did not walk in the way of the sinners of his corrupt age. His character and conduct were a distinct rebuke to the godless around. Jude tells us that Enoch functioned as a prophet, declaring God's just judgment upon the unrighteousness of his time.

Enoch's life was one of progress. Walking with God implies a steady progress in his course. He did not walk for awhile and then stand still. Each day found him nearer the divine goal. In unbroken companionship with his Friend, he found himself more weaned from the world and more ripe for heaven. He did not attempt to walk alone to heaven. He walked *with* God, and as he took each step his eyes were fixed on his heavenly Companion.

Enoch had an unusually glorious end. He is the only one of the line of whom it is not said that "he died." He was not—God took him. "He was not" suggests that his friends sought for him. He was a missing person they could not trace. "God took him," which means he was translated that he should not taste death. Among the millions upon millions of men who have lived, only two out of the vast number never died—Enoch and Elijah! Andrew Bonar has the sweet suggestion that God and Enoch were in the habit of taking a long walk together every day and that one day God said to his companion, "Why go home? Come all the way with Me." Thus at 365 years of age—a year for every day of our year—God took His servant directly to heaven.

ENOS, ENOSH [Ē′ nos, Ē′ nosh]—MAN IS HIS FRAILTY. *The son of Seth* and father of Cainan, he lived for 905 years (Gen. 4:26; 5:6-10; I Chron. 1:1). He was also an ancestor of Christ (Luke 3:38). It is mentioned in connection with the birth of Enos that it was then that man began to call upon the name of the Lord. This first mention of recourse to prayer is suggestive. Men were somehow driven by sickness, frailty and dependence to cry for health and help to the invisible Creator.

EPAENETUS [Ē päen′ e tŭs]—LAUDABLE, WORTHY OF PRAISE. *A native of Asia or Achaia,* greeted by Paul as "my well-beloved" (Rom. 16:5).

EPAPHRAS [Ēp′ a phrăs]—CHARMING or FOAMY. *A fellow laborer* of Paul and in some sense his fellow-prisoner (Col. 1:7; 4:12; Philem. 23.

The Man Who Was a Giant in Prayer

This Colossian is described in many ways. He was Paul's "fellow-servant" and "servant," his "fellow-prisoner," and a "faithful minister." He was also Paul's representative at Colossae where he had founded the church (Col. 1:7), and sought under Paul's advice to combat prevalent heresies there. The apostle had affection for Epaphras, who ministered unto his need and the need of others.

It is in his prayer-ministry, however, that Epaphras is conspicuous. This giant in prayer knew how to lay all before the Lord, and laboring in secret, made the saints to be perfect and complete in their *standing* through his *kneeling.* He "strove earnestly in his prayers" for the Colossians. He wrestled in prayer that they might be perfect in the perfection of Christ, and "fully assured in all the will of God."

Paul also testified to the perseverance as well as the prayers of Epaphras. He knew how to *toil* on behalf of the saints of God. He was practical as well as prayerful.

His prayers for the stability and maturity of others were numerous, continuous and strenuous. Epaphras brought to Paul at Rome a report of the Colossian Church where he had ministered in Paul's stead, an account that cheered his heart and resulted in the writing of the Colossian Epistle which Epaphras took back with him to his flock. Can we say that we are true successors of the devoted servant of God? Like him, do we know how to wrestle in agony of prayer? (Rom. 15:30). Epaphras also manifested great *zeal* or properly "great labour of anxiety" for those under his care. Too few of us are concerned about the spiritual welfare of others.

EPAPHRODITUS [Ě păph ro dī' tus]—LOVELY, HANDSOME, CHARMING. *A trusted messenger between Paul and the churches* (Phil. 2:25; 4:18). Epaphras is a shortened form of this common name.

The Man with a Kind Heart

How fully and fittingly Paul describes the commendable character of this kindly man who went as Paul's representative to the Philippian Church!

He was a *brother*—a term implying a spiritual relationship.

He was a *companion in labor*—their hearts beat as one in the cause they both loved.

He was a *fellow soldier*—together they endured all the hardness and discipline of daring and suffering which discipleship involves (II Tim. 3:14).

He was a *messenger* — or "apostle" as the word really is; and he was ever the Lord's messenger in the Lord's message.

He was a *sacrificial witness*. What a brief but blessed biography Paul gives us of his dear companion. He "ministered to my wants" — "longed after you all" — caused much "heaviness" because of his fatal sickness — was mercifully spared lest his death should have brought "sorrow upon sorrow" to Paul.

He *regarded not his life*. Literally he gambled his life to assist and bless the Philippians. How rich was the Early Church in leaders who were entirely abandoned to God, that through their consecrated lives their fellow-saints might be filled with all the "fulness of God"!

EPHAH [Ě' phah]—OBSCURITY or DARKNESS.

1. *A son of Jahdai,* a Judahite (I Chron. 2:47).

2. *A son of Midian,* son of Abraham by Keturah and father of a tribal family (Gen. 25:4; I Chron. 1:33; Isa. 60:6). Also the name of Caleb's concubine (I Chron. 2:46); and description of a measure (Ex. 16:36).

EPHAI [Ē' phāi]—FATIGUED or OBSCURED. *A Netophathite*, who was promised protection but was subsequently massacred by Ishmael (Jer. 40:8, 13; 41:3).

EPHER [Ē' phûr]—MULE or YOUNG CALF.
1. *The second son of Midian*, son of Abraham (Gen. 25:4; I Chron. 1:33).
2. *A son of Ezra*, a Judahite (I Chron. 4:17).
3. *A chief of the half-tribe of Manasseh* (I Chron. 5:24).

EPHLAL [Ēph' lăl]—JUDICIOUS or JUDGING. *A descendant of Pharez*. through Jerahmeel (I Chron. 2:37).

EPHOD [Ē' phŏd]—COVERING. *The father of Hanniel*, prince of Manasseh, who assisted Joshua in the division of Canaan (Num. 34:23). Also the name of a priestly garment (Ex. 25:7).

EPHRAIM [Ē' phră ĭm]—DOUBLY FRUITFUL. *The second son of Joseph* by Asenath and founder of a tribal family (Gen. 41:52; Num. 1:10). Also the name of a town (II Sam. 13:23), a city (John 11:54), a gate of Jerusalem (II kings 14:13), and a wood (II Sam. 18:6).

The Man Who Represented Fruitful Pruning

In Jacob's prophetic blessing of his sons the prominent feature of Joseph's portion was that of *fruitfulness*, a prophecy receiving its fulfilment in the double tribe springing from Joseph, namely, Ephraim and Manasseh, like two branches out of the parent stem. Joseph himself was "a fruitful bough" because he had been so well pruned. The sharp knife of adversity led to the sweet fruit, and the fruitful bough ran over the wall. Ephraim and Manasseh were the heads of most fruitful tribes. The Book of Hosea, however, reveals how the blessings showered upon these tribes were ill requited.

Joseph named his second son Ephraim because as he said "God hath caused me to be fruitful in *the land of my affliction*." Here Joseph, although a Hebrew, speaks as a Gentile. Ephraim was the fruitfulness of his father in the land of Egypt as a Gentile prince, and Jacob rightly calls his seed "the fulness of the Gentiles," when he adopts him on his dying bed.

The representative man of the tribe of Ephraim is Joshua. No other like him arose afterwards in this tribe. Jeroboam, the son of Nebat, founder of the kingdom of Ephraim, was the exact opposite to Joshua in faith and conduct.

The significance of Ephraim's name must not be lost upon us. What Joseph said of him indicated that God had brought good out of evil, privilege out of pain, triumph out of tragedy. In spite of any affliction that may be ours, do we remain fruitful in every good work? To Joseph the birth of Ephraim came as luscious fruit after the severe pruning of ill-treatment, slavery and prison. See John 15:1–8.

EPHRON [Ē' phron]—STRONG or FAWN. *A son of Zohar a Hittite,* from whom Abraham purchased a field with the cave in which he buried Sarah (Gen. 23:8). Also the name of a mountain (Josh. 15:9).

ER [Ûr]—AWAKE or ON THE WATCH.
1. *The eldest son of Judah* by the daughter of Shuah the Canaanite, whose wickedness, which is not described, merited death (Gen. 38:3–7; 46:12; Num. 26:19; I Chron. 2:3).
2. *A son of Shelah,* youngest son of Judah by the above Shuah (I Chron. 4:21).
3. *An Ancestor of Christ* who lived between David and Zerubbabel (Luke 3:28).

ERAN [Ē' răn]—WATCHFUL. *A son of Ephraim's* eldest son Shuthelah and founder of a tribal family (Num. 26:36).

ERASTUS [Ē răs ' tus]—BELOVED.
1. *A Christian who assisted Paul* and whom he sent into Macedonia (Acts 19:22; II Tim. 4:20).
2. *A high official of Corinth,* a convert of Paul's (Rom. 16:23). Several authorities suggest that these two men are the same person.

ERI [Ē' rī]—MY WATCHER. *A son of Gad* and founder of a tribal family (Gen. 46:16; Num. 26:16).

ESAIAS [Ē sā' ias]—JEHOVAH HAS SAVED. *The Greek form of Isaiah* (Matt. 3:3).

ESAR-HADDON [Ē' sar-hăd' don]—VICTORIOUS or ASHUR HATH GIVEN BROTHERS. *The favorite son of Sennacherib* and one of the greatest kings of Assyria, equally eminent as a military leader and a political ruler (II Kings 19:37; Ezra 4:2; Isa. 37:38).

ESAU [Ē' sôu]—HAIRY. *The eldest son of Isaac* and twin brother of Jacob by Rebekah. His name is associated with his appearance at birth (Gen. 25:25).

The Man Who Bartered His Birthright

This cunning hunter and man of the field (Gen. 25:27) supplies us with one of the tragic biographies among the men of the Bible. He is prominent in God's portrait gallery as the man rejected of God because he had sold his birthright. Let us briefly sketch what Scripture records of "Esau, who is Edom." Had he retained his birthright we might have read "Esau, who is Israel." The wrong act, however, left a black mark upon his future history.

He was a profane person. What a terrible epitome! It is like a label fastened to Esau as he disappears from Bible history (Heb. 12:16). The work "profane" does not mean that he delighted in profanity, but that he was a man of the earth who lived for worldly things and nothing else. With many good qualities, Esau was of the earth, earthy.

He sold his birthright. As the elder son of his father, even although he came from the womb only a half-hour before his twin brother, Jacob, he was entitled by law and custom to receive twice as much as a younger son's portion, and to be regarded in due time as the head of the family. But we all know the story of how, for a mess of pottage, he bartered away his spiritual and temporal rights. The record says that Esau sold his birthright because he "despised" it. How easily some men part with the rich blessings they are heirs to!

His was a fruitless repentance. Esau lifted up his voice and cried, "Bless me, even me also, O my father!" But his repentant prayer was directed, not to God, but to Isaac. In the whole of Genesis Esau does not mention the name of God. Had Esau's repentance been Godward, what a different story we would have had! Esau only repented of *his bargain,* not of *his sin.* Such a bargain turned out to be a bad one, and he was sorry for it. Further, all Esau sought was *restitution,* not *pardon.* He had lost one blessing, and sought another.

Under grace the penitent sinner who has wasted his substance has a Saviour to turn to, and repenting of his sin, finds mercy. Esau, even with his tears, found no mercy. God was not in his thoughts, and he had therefore to abide by the consequences of what he had brought upon himself. Yet he learned his lesson, for Esau called his firstborn Eliphaz, "strength of God," and his second son Reuel, "joy of God."

ESHBAAL [Esh-bā′ al]—A MAN OF BAAL. *The fourth son of Saul,* the same as Ishbosheth, meaning "a man of shame" (I Chron. 8:33; 9:39).

ESHBAN [Esh′ ban]—INTELLIGENCE or MAN OF UNDERSTANDING. *A son of Dishon,* son of Seir the Horite (Gen. 36:26; I Chron. 1:41).

ESHCOL [Esh′ col]—CLUSTER OF GRAPES. *One of the three Amorite brothers* who helped Abraham in his pursuit of the four kings who captured Lot (Gen. 14:13, 24). Also the name of the valley or brook of Eshcol, famous for its grapes (Num. 13:23, 24; 32:9; Deut. 1:24).

ESHEK [E′ shek]—STRIFE or VIOLENCE. *A descendant of Saul* through Jonathan, a Benjamite (I Chron. 8:39).

ESHTEMOA, ESHTEMOH [Esh te mō′ ă, Esh′ te mōh]—OBEDIENCE. *A son of Hodiah,* a descendant of Ezra, a Maachathite. (I Chron. 4:17, 19). Also the name of a town (Josh. 15:50).

ESHTON [Esh′ ton]—REST. *A grandson of Chelab* through Mehir, a Judahite (I Chron. 4:11, 12).

ESLI [Ĕs' lĭ]—GOD AT MY SIDE or JEHOVAH HATH RESERVED. *An ancestor of Christ* who lived after the captivity and likely the same person named Azaliah in the genealogy (Luke 3:25).

ESROM [Ĕs' rom]—ENCLOSURE. *Son of Phares in Christ's genealogy* (Matt. 1:3; Luke 3:32). Possibly the same person as Hezron.

ETAM [Ē' tăm]—WILD BEASTS' LAIR. *A name found in the list of Judah's descendants* but likely the name of a place rather than a person (I Chron. 4:3, 32; II Chron. 11:6; Judg. 15:8).

ETHAN [Ē' than]—ANCIENT, FIRMNESS or PERPLEXITY.
1. *The Ezrahite* renowned for his wisdom in Solomon's time (I Kings 4:31).
2. *A son of Zerah,* son of Judah (I Chron. 2:6, 8).
3. *A descendant of Gershon,* son of Levi (I Chron. 6:42).
4. *A descendant of Merari,* son of Levi (I Chron. 6:44; 15:17, 19).

ETHBAAL [Ĕth bā' al]—WITH HIM IS BAAL or BAAL'S MAN. *A king of Sidon,* father-in-law of Ahab, who held the throne of Tyre for thirty-two years (I Kings 16:31).

ETHNAN [Ĕth' nan]—GIFT or HIRE. *A son of Helah,* of the family of Ashur, of the family of Hezron (I Chron. 4:7).

ETHNI [Ĕth' nĭ]—BOUNTIFUL or MY GIFT. *A Gershonite Levite* and an ancestor of Asaph whom David set over the service of song (I Chron. 6:41). Likely the same person named Jeaterai in I Chronicles 6:21.

EUBULUS [Eū bŭ lus]—WELL-ADVISED or PRUDENT. *A disciple* at Rome who, with others, saluted Timothy. [II Tim. 4:21].

EUTYCHUS [Eū' tў chŭs]—HAPPY or FORTUNATE. *A young man of Troas* who fell asleep during Paul's long sermon, fell off his window seat, broke his neck and was taken up as dead. Paul, however, revived him (Acts 20:7–12). Dr. Alexander Whyte speaks of Eutychus as "the father of all such as fall asleep under sermons."

EVI [Ē'vĭ]—DESIRE. *One of the five kings of Midian,* slain in the war waged by Moses against the Midianites because they seduced the Israelites to licentious idolatry (Num. 31:8; Josh. 13:21).

EVIL-MERODACH [Ē' vĭl-mē rŏ' dach]—MAN OF GOD MERODACH or MARDUK. *The son and successor of Nebuchadnezzar* who reigned for some eight years. He it was who released Jehoiachin whom his father had kept imprisoned for thirty-seven years (II kings 25:27; Jer. 52:31).

EZBAI [Ĕz' ba ĭ]—BEAUTIFUL. *The father of one of David's thirty heroes* (I Chron. 11:37). Referred to as Paarai the Arbite in II Samuel 23:35.

EZBON [Ĕz' bŏn]—SPLENDOR.

1. *The son of Gad* and founder of a Gadite family (Gen. 46:16). Also spoken of as Ozni in Numbers 26:16.

2. *The son of Bela,* son of Benjamin, and head of his father's house (I Chron. 7:7).

EZEKIAS [Ĕz e kĭ' as]—JEHOVAH IS STRENGTH. *The Greek form of Hezekiah* (Matt. 1:9, 10).

EZEKIEL [Ĕ zē kĭ el]—GOD IS STRONG or THE MAN GOD STRENGTHENS. *The son of Buzi, a priest* who prophesied to the exiles by the river Chebar, and fourth of "The Greater Prophets" (Ezek. 1:3; 24:24).

The Man Who Was Every Inch a Churchman

Little is known of this man of a priestly family (Ezek. 1:3; 30:1). His father's name, Buzi, was a Gentile one (Gen. 22:21; Job 32:2, 6). Referring to himself as "a priest," Ezekiel was akin to Jeremiah who was also a prophet and a priest. Because of his priestly lineage, levitical tendencies appear in his book (Ezek. 40–46), as well as foregleams of the high priestly character of the Messiah (Ezek. 21:25; 45:22). Ezekiel is every inch a churchman, and his strong ecclesiastical characteristics pervade and give tone to his prophecies.

Ezekiel's call came in his thirtieth year (Ezek. 1:1), in the fifth year and on the fifth day of the month of king Jehoiachin's captivity (Ezek. 1, 2). With the call to service there came the impartation of the prophetic gift (Ezek. 3:22). The theme of the prophetic message he was commissioned to proclaim was the same as that of Jeremiah, namely, the downfall of Judah and Jerusalem with judgment upon foreign nations. The keynote of his book is: through tribulation into rest. Residing with a company of captives by the river Chebar (Ezek. 1:1; 8:1) he labored as "a prophet of the iron harp."

With divine authority Ezekiel dispelled illusions, denounced false prophets, declared repentance, restoration and renewal. He was a true shepherd of souls. Dr. Donald Fraser wrote of him: "Like a giant, he wrestled against Jewish degeneracy and Babylonish pride. Remote as we are from his times, we are stirred by his vivid imagination and his power of fervid denunciation and strenuous appeal. Even when the understanding is puzzled, the heart burns inwardly at the recital of Ezekiel's visions and those burdens which the Lord laid upon his spirit."

Ezekiel was happy in his home life (Ezek. 8:1). God, however, revealed to him that the desire of his eyes would die of a sudden sickness, which his wife did during the siege of Jerusalem. Although her death was a heavy blow, yet Ezekiel was not allowed to publicly weep or lament her passing. His anguish was to serve as a sign that Jerusalem would be destroyed without wailing or lamentation (Ezek. 24:15–27). After a prophetic ministry lasting for at least twenty-two years, tradition has it that Ezekiel was put to death by his fellow exiles because of his faithfulness and boldness in denouncing them for their idolatry.

Several aspects of the prophet's life can be applied with profit to ourselves:

I.   He was an exile (Ezek. 1:1); so are we (Heb. 11:13; I Pet. 2:11).

II. He was an ambassador (Ezek 1:1; 2:1–6; 3:1–3); so are we (Eph. 6:20).

III. He was a watchman (Ezek. 3:17–20); so are we (Heb. 13:17).

IV. He was a sign (12:1–7); so are we (I Tim. 1:10).

EZER, EZAR [Ē′ zŭr, E′ zar]—TREASURE or HELP.

1. *A son of Ephraim* slain by the inhabitants of Gath while stealing their cattle (I Chron. 7:21).

2. *A priest of Nehemiah's time* (Neh. 12:42).

3. *A man of Judah* and descendant of Hur (I Chron. 4:4). Perhaps the Ezra of I Chronicles 4:17.

4. *A valiant Gadite* who joined David at Ziklag (I Chron. 12:9).

5. *A Levite* who shared in the repair of the wall (Neh. 3:19).

6. *A son of Seir* the Horite (Gen. 36:21, 27, 30; I Chron. 1:38,42).

EZRA, EZRAH [Ĕz′ rä]—HELP or MY HELPER.

1. *The head of one of the twenty-two courses of priests* that came up from exile with Zerubbabel and Jeshua (Neh. 10:2–8; 12:1, 13). Probably the Azariah of Ezra 7:1.

2. *A descendant of Judah* through Caleb (I Chron. 4:17).

3. *The famous scribe and priest* descended from Hilkiah the high priest (Ezra 7:1–25).

The Man Who Honored Scripture

Ezra or I Esdras, as he is called in the Vulgate, was the son or grandson of Seraiah, the high priest who was slain after the taking of Jerusalem (II Kings 25:18, 21). As a priest, he was descended from Zadok and from Phinehas (Ezra 7:1–6). He was also a ready scribe (Ezra 7:6, 11, 12, 20), which occupation implied three things:

He was a student and as such had a duty to himself to study the will of God as revealed in His Word, that he might hide it in his own heart (Ezra 7:10).

He was an interpreter with a duty to his own generation in teaching his fellow exiles what he had learned. In this way he gave the "sense" of the Word (Neh. 8:2–8).

He was a copyist, which meant that this learned man had a duty to his own race in multiplying and preserving intact the very words of God (Ezra 7:10, 11).

Ezra was also an able administrator. He conducted the Jewish exiles back to Jerusalem in peace and safety, and establishing himself as their leader, reformed them with a vigorous hand. Summarizing his life and labors, we can say that this Old Testament reformer was:

    I. A man of deep humility and self-denial (Ezra 7:10–15; 10:6).

    II. A man of great learning with a fervent zeal for God's honor (Ezra 7:10; 8:21–23).

    III. A man of great trustworthiness (Ezra 7:13, 26).

    IV. A man anxious to commend his cause to others (Ezra 8:2–20).

    V. A man who knew how to pray (Ezra 8:21; 10:1).

    VI. A man deeply grieved over the sins of the people (Ezra 9:3; 10:6).

    VII. A man who spared no pains to bring the people to repentance.

Traditional history says that it was Ezra who instituted the Great Synagogue, became its first President, settled the Canon of Jewish Scripture and began the building of synagogues in Jewish provincial towns. Ezra lived to a good old age, dying like Moses at the age of 120 years.

Ezra was a studious, prayerful ecclesiastic who set his heart to realize definite ideals:

To know the Law of Jehovah. What a passion was his to ascertain, explain and administer that Law!

To will to do the Law. Ezra not only taught the Law but urged the people to serve the Lord with heart, mouth and mind.

The key words of the Book of Ezra are Restoration, Reorganization, Reformation. The emphasis is upon the preservation of the national and religious life of the people. The leading ideas of the book are:

The Purity of Worship
The Sanctity of the Sabbath
The Power of Prayer
The Faithfulness of God
Order in Religion and Delight in Praise
Mutual help in Service
The Purity of Common life.

EZRI [Ez' rī]—GOD IS A HELP. *Overseer of laborers* who tilled David's fields (I Chron. 27:26).

F

FELIX [Fē' lĭx]—HAPPY, PROSPEROUS. *A cruel Roman governor of Judea,* appointed by the Emperor Claudius, whose freedman he was (Acts 23:24, 26; 24:2–27; 25:14). Felix is described by Tacitus as a bad and cruel governor, even though the title of "most excellent" was given to him.

The Man Who Procrastinated

As a true preacher, Paul pressed home the truth until it pricked the conscience of Felix so much so that he "trembled." He did not resent Paul's plain speaking but postponed the interview "till a more convenient season." Such a "convenient season," however, did not come, and Felix became a type of many whose consciences are stirred by the preached Word, but whose hopes of eternal security are ruined by a like procrastination. The two sworn enemies of the soul are "Yesterday" and "Tomorrow."

Yesterday slays its thousands. Past sins plunge many into darkness and despair. Priceless opportunities were trampled upon, and the harvest is past. But God says there is mercy still and free forgiveness through repentance.

Tomorrow slays its tens of thousands. Vows, promises, resolutions are never fulfilled. "Some other time," many say, when urged to repent and believe. They fail to realize that *now* is the acceptable time. How pitiful it is that the *convenient season* never dawns for them! The pathway to their hell is strewn with good resolutions, and as they cross "The Great Divide," the mocking voice cries out: "Too late! Too late!"

FESTUS [Fĕs' tus]—JOYFUL, FESTAL, PROSPEROUS. *Porcius Festus was a Roman governor of Judea* in the reign of Nero (Acts 24:27; 25; 26: 24, 32).

The Man Who Called Paul Mad

Felix, seeking to court the favor of the Jews, left Paul in prison, thinking that the Jews would compensate him for such a favor. This act was an investment in iniquity. But the Jewish complaints against Felix led to his recall by Nero, so Paul passed into the hands of Festus, Felix' successor. Festus, not knowing much about Jewish matters, brought the question of Paul's imprisonment before Agrippa who was conversant with many aspects of the Jewish religion. It perplexed Festus to know that Paul, a Jew with the utmost reverence for the Law and the worship of the Temple, was yet hated by his compatriots.

Agrippa agreed to hear Paul for himself, so we come to the apostle's masterly defense before the king and Bernice. With a wonderful vividness Paul gave a retrospective analysis of his former life and then a sketch of his present sacrificial witness to Christ as the risen, glorified Son of God. Such was the impact of Paul's remarkable appeal that Festus, the Roman governor, forgot the usual dignity of his office and burst out into a loud laugh of scorn saying: "Paul, thou art beside thyself; much learning doth make thee mad."

With characteristic calmness and with a firm control of his natural impulses so that no unguarded utterance might escape his lips, Paul answered Festus in all courtesy: "I am not mad, most noble Festus; but speak forth the words of truth and soberness." In his incomparable *Bible Characters,* Alexander Whyte says that a single word will sometimes immortalize a man. "What will you give me?" was all Judas said. So with one word Festus is as well known to us as if a whole chapter had been written about him. He said Paul was *mad.*

But the uncontrolled and unbecoming outburst of Festus did not stagger Paul. Did they not say of his Master, for whom he had suffered much "He is beside Himself"? The apostle counted it a privilege to share his Master's madness. Later on, he wrote about being a fool for His sake. He knew that no man is a true Christian who is not the world's fool (I Cor. 3:18; 4:10; II Cor. 11:23). All around us are those who have never been borne along by the enthusiasm of God, who deem the spiritual man to be mad (Hos. 9:7).

FORTUNATUS [Fôr tū nā' tus]—PROSPEROUS. *A believer from Corinth* who, with Stephanus and Achaicus, visited Paul and refreshed his spirit by their coming [I Cor. 16:17). A. J. Maclean comments that Fortunatus was probably baptized by Paul (I Cor. 1:16), and that Lightfoot felt that he may well have been alive forty years later and could therefore have been the Fortunatus mentioned by Clement in his *Epistle.* Evidently he was among the more spiritual believers in the Corinthian Church.

G

GAAL [Gā' al]—REJECTION or CONTEMPT. *A son of Ebed,* who aided the Shechemites when he organized the rising against Abimelech (Judg. 9:26–41). Gaal was defeated and driven out of Shechem, and terrible vengeance overtook the city.

GABBAI [Găb' ba ī]—INGATHERER or TAXGATHERER. *A Benjamite* who consented to live in Jerusalem after the captivity (Neh. 11:8).

GAD [Găd]—GOOD FORTUNE, A TROOP or A SEER.

1. *The seventh son of Jacob,* first-born of Zilpah, Leah's maid, and full brother of Asher. A tribe also sprang from Gad (Gen. 30:11; 35:26; 46:16; 49:19; Ex. 1:4; I Chron. 5:11; 12:14).

The Man of Enlargement

No name in all the twelve tribes of Israel is so much played upon in Jacob's blessing as the name of Gad, meaning "a troop." Invaders and robbers might try to plunder Gad but victory would be his with resultant enlargement. Jacob predicted for the tribe of Gad a time of sore conflict, yet of final conquest. "He shall overcome at last." God enabled Gad to discomfit and defeat his foes (I Chron. 5:18–22).

The men of Gad had faces like "the faces of lions," and when David needed help, the Gadites of lion-like character befriended the fugitive king. "They put to flight all them of the valleys, both of the east and of the west." These Gadite helpers of David "executed the justice of the Lord, and His judgments with Israel." Jephthah the Gileadite, of the tribe of Gad, judged Israel six years after delivering the nation from Ammonite oppression.

How fortunate Gad was to have God to enlarge him! "The place where we dwell... is too strait for us." Such an energetic, aggressive tribe could not remain static, so their inheritance was extended beyond its original limits until it covered the whole of Gilead. How loathe we are to possess our spiritual possessions! May ours be the enlargements of heart David prayed for (Ps. 119:32)! May ours also be the constant victorious Christian experience!

2. The prophet who joined David when in "the hold," and through whose advice he left it for the forest of Hareth (I Sam. 22:5; II Sam. 24:11-19; I Chron. 21:9-19; II Chron. 29:25). Gad, "the king's seer," announced God's judgment upon David for numbering the people. "The arm of flesh will fail us, we dare not trust our own." Gad the prophet advised the erection of the altar, and is also before us as an associate of the prophet Nathan.

GADDI [Găd' dī]—BELONGING TO FORTUNE or FORTUNATE. *A son of Susi,* and a chief of Manasseh who was sent out to explore Canaan (Num. 13:11).

GADDIEL [Găd' dĭ el]—GOD IS FORTUNE BRINGER or GOD HATH GIVEN FORTUNE. *The son of Sodi,* and a chief of Zebulun, the tribe's representative in the exploration of Canaan (Num. 13:10).

GADI [Gă' dī]—FORTUNATE or A GADITE. *The father of king Menahem,* who killed Shallum and succeeded him as king of Israel (II Kings 15:14, 17).

GAHAM [Gă' hăm]—BLACKNESS or FLAMING. *A son of Nahor* and his concubine Reumah (Gen. 22:24).

GAHAR [Gă' här]—HIDING PLACE or PROSTRATION. *Head of the family of Nethinims* whose posterity returned with Zerubbabel from captivity (Ezra 2:47; Neh. 7:49).

GAIUS [Gă' ius]—I AM GLAD. This common Roman name is shared by four men, and some writers find it difficult to differentiate between them.

1. *A companion of Paul* and native of Macedonia. He was seized in the riot at Ephesus (Acts 19:29).

2. *A man of Derbe* in Lycaonia and likewise a companion of Paul. This Gaius of Derbe (Acts 20:4) is sometimes identified as Gaius at Corinth — see next Gaius.

3. *The Corinthian converted and baptized by Paul,* and who was the apostle's host while he was in Corinth (Rom. 16:23; I Cor. 1:14).

4. *The godly man to whom John sent his third epistle* (III John 1). It is evident that the Apostle of Love had a deep affection for this saint he called "the wellbeloved." It would seem as if John had at sometime led him to Christ (III John 4). John desired the material, physical and spiritual prosperity of Gaius (III John 2, 3). The apostle also commended him for his faithful care of ministering brethren — a responsibility some seem to neglect these days (III John 5–8).

GALAL [Gā' lăl]—ROLLING OF ONE'S DAY UPON THE LORD.
1. *The name of a Levite* who returned from exile (I Chron. 9:15).
2. *Another Levite*, the son of Jeduthun who came up from exile (I Chron. 9:16; Neh. 11:17).

GALLIO [Găl' lĭ ō]—HE THAT SUCKS. *The Roman proconsul of Achia,* the elder brother of Seneca, described by Seneca as a man of extreme amiability of character (Acts 18:12, 14, 17).

The Man with a Righteous Carelessness

The antagonistic Jews of Corinth brought Paul before Gallio, charging the apostle with having persuaded men to "worship God contrary to the law" (v. 13). But when Gallio realized that Paul was not guilty of "villainy," but only of questions which the Jews as a self-administering community were competent to decide for themselves, he dismissed them, saying he "cared for none of those things," meaning questions concerning Jewish law. Because of his statement, Gallio has been crowned with a condemnation he does not deserve. His apparent carelessness proves:

I.   There are more important concerns in life than the settlement of frivolous and petty disputes.

II.   There should be that determination not to meddle needlessly in other men's affairs. It is folly to judge questions we do not understand.

III.   There should be patience, leaving trifling wrongs to arrange and compose themselves. Blessed are the peacemakers.

IV.   There should be the firm resolve to be just and impartial rather than to curry favor and win thereby a little passing popularity. Righteousness should always be placed above policy. Thus we can learn from Gallio's attitude lessons both profitable and wise.

GAMALIEL [Gȧ mā' lĭ el]—GOD IS RECOMPENSER OT THE GIFT OR REWARD OF GOD.
1. *A chief of Manasseh* chosen to aid in taking the census in the wilderness (Num. 1:10; 2:20; 7:54, 59; 10:23).
2. *The renowned Doctor of Jewish law* (Acts 5:34), and instructor of the apostle Paul (Acts 22:3). It may be that Paul's instruction in the Law began when he was about the age of twelve (Luke 2:42). Like his Master, Paul, as Saul of Tarsus, sat in the midst of the doctors, hearing and asking questions. These learned men sat in a high chair,

and the scholars on the floor and were thus literally at their masters' feet (see Deut. 33:3).

The Man Who Was Tolerant

Ellicott speaks of Gamaliel as one of the heroes of rabbinical history. His dramatic speech before the Council on Peter's behalf, and the part he played in the instruction of Paul mark him out a man worthy of note. Gamaliel was the son of Simeon, perhaps of Luke 2:25, and the grandson of the great Hillel, the representative of the best school of Pharisaism, the tolerant and largehearted rival of the narrow and fanatic Shammai. Through the weight of years and authority Gamaliel rose to eminence and counseled with moderation.

Being of the house and lineage of David, this cultured teacher had full sympathy with the claims of Christ, who was welcomed as the Son of David. Perhaps he was influenced to a decision for Christ through contact with a brother-teacher like Nicodemus (John 3:1, 2; 7:50, 51) and can therefore be included among the many chief rulers who secretly believed in Christ (John 12:42, 43).

Digging beneath Gamaliel's able and successful performance before the Council at Jerusalem, Alexander Whyte feels that he was only a "fluent and applauded opportunist" and warns young men against his presentation. "He was a politician, but he was not a true churchman or statesman. He was held in repute by the people; but the people were blind, and they loved to be led by blind leaders, and Gamaliel was one of them." With all his insight and lawyerlike ability, Gamaliel turned all things completely upsidedown when he sat in judgment, and gave his carefully balanced caution concerning the Son of God, comments Dr. Whyte.

Perhaps the renowned author of *Bible Characters* is right when he suggests that Gamaliel made the tremendous and irreparable mistake of approaching Jesus Christ and His cause on the side of policy, handling Him as a matter open to argument and debate. But Christ is an Ambassador of Reconciliation, and we are not permitted to sit in judgment on God, and on His message of mercy to us. Without apology Dr. Whyte pronounces Gamaliel as "a liberal long before his time. He was all for toleration, and for a free church in a free state, in an intolerant and persecuting day."

GAMUL [Gā′ mŭl]—MATURED or RECOMPENSED. *A priest*, descendant of Aaron, and leader of the twenty-second course in the sanctuary service in David's time (I Chron. 24:17).

GAREB (Gā′ rĕb]—REVILER or ROUGH. *One of David's worthies* (II Sam. 23:38; I Chron. 11:40). Also the name of a hill near Jerusalem (Jer. 31:39).

GASHMU [Găsh′ mū]—CORPOREALNESS. *An influential Samaritan in Nehemiah's time* (Neh. 6:6). Perhaps the same as Geshem.

GATAM [Gā' tam]—PUNY or BURNT VALLEY. *The fourth son of Eliphaz,* son of Esau, and one of the dukes of an Edomite clan (Gen. 36:11, 16; I Chron. 1:36).

GAZEZ [Gā' zĕz]—SHEARER.
1. *A son of Caleb* by Ephah his concubine (I Chron. 2:46).
2. *A son of Haram,* who was another of Ephah's sons (I Chron. 2:46).

GAZZAM [Găz' zam]—SWAGGERER or DEVOURER. *A founder of a family of Nethinims* who returned from exile with Zerubbabel (Ezra 2:48; Neh. 7:51).

GEBER [Gĕ' bûr]—A HERO or STRONG.
1. *One of Solomon's twelve purveyors* for Southern Gilead (I Kings 4:13).
2. *The son of Uri,* who was over great pasture lands east of Jordan (I Kings 4:19). The two Gebers are sometimes identified as the same person.

GEDALIAH [Gĕd a li' ah]—JEHOVAH IS GREAT.
1. *A son of Ahikam* and grandson of Shaphan, king Josiah's secretary and Governor of Mizpah (II Kings 25:22–25; Jer. 39:14; 40:5–16; 41; 43:6). This Judean of high birth was the one who protected Jeremiah, whose views he shared, from the anti-Chaldeans. Nebuchadnezzar made him governor over "the poor people left in the land." He only ruled however, for two months. The anniversary of his treacherous murder is observed as one of the four Jewish feasts (Zech. 7:5; 8:19).
2. *A priest,* of the sons of Jeshua, who had taken a strange wife during the exile (Ezra 10:18).
3. *Grandfather of the prophet Zephaniah* (Zeph. 1:1).
4. *One of the six sons of Jeduthun,* a harper and head of the second of twenty-four companies or twelve musicians (I Chron. 25:3, 9).
5. *A son of Pashur and the prince* who caused Jeremiah to be imprisoned (Jer. 38:1, 4).

GEDOR [Gĕ' dôr]—A FORTRESS.
1. *The son of Jehiel* and brother of Ner and an ancestor of king Saul (I Chron. 8:31; 9:37).
2. This name occurs in connection with two Judahite families. Penuel is called the father of Gedor, and Jered is in the same relation. The *Targum* gives both these names to Moses as coming from Jehudijah, identified as Pharaoh's daughter (I Chron. 4:4, 18). Gedor is also the name of a town or village in the tribe of Simeon (I Chron. 4:39).

GEHAZI [Gĕ' hā' zī]—DENIER or VALLEY OF VISION. *The servant of the prophet Elisha* who likely stood in the same relationship to Elisha as Elisha had done to Elijah (II Kings 4:12–36; 5:20–27; 8:4, 5).

The Man Who Was Unholy Amid Holiness

Gehazi's name, "valley of vision," is appropriate enough if we think of what he saw as to the nature of wicked men when the prophet opened his eyes. As the servant of Elisha, the man of God, Gehazi should have been a good man. But a holy man had an unholy servant. Gehazi was near, yet far distant from all that was pure and beautiful. It is possible in our time for a man to build churches, yet be a destroyer of Christian doctrine generally.

What a contrast exists between one man and another: Elisha — living a vibrant spiritual life, the grand prayer-life and faith-life; Gehazi — grubbing in the earth and seeking contentment in the dust. And these contrasts still exist.

Dinsdale T. Young enlarges upon the following features of Gehazi, the avaricious servant in this telling fashion:

I.   He was familiar with sacred things, yet a stranger to their power. Gehazi was irreligious amid religion. He lived with good men and had a knowledge of God, yet succumbed to the hardening influence of spiritual things.

II.   He had the incapacity to understand a saint. Gehazi failed to understand or appreciate both the character and conduct of Elisha.

III.   He was enslaved in his youth. Gehazi's early manhood was marred by evil thoughts, greed, deliberate lying and revolting hypocrisy. How his wrecked youth should warn the young today to remember their Creator!

IV.   He prostituted a strong and imaginative mind. The story Gehazi concocted and told to Naaman was skilfully constructed. His invention was a lie, and the cleverness in telling it revealed his depravity. How tragic when genius and gifts sell their birthright for a mess of pottage.

V.   He was successful at a fearful cost. He gained the social splendor he desired in the gold and garments Naaman gave him. But think of the price Gehazi paid. He lost his health, for he became a leper, a judgment Gehazi himself felt to be just. Gehazi also brought a blight upon his family. Instead of leaving his ill-gotten gains to his descendants, his judgment likewise fell upon his seed.

VI.   He was likely restored to Divine favor. The incident of Gehazi recounting to King Joram the great deeds of Elisha seems to suggest that he had been restored to health and usefulness. For the Gehazi of modern society there is forgiveness. Christ's blood can make the vilest clean.

GEMALLI [Gē măl′ lĭ]—CAMEL OWNER or RIDER OF A CAMEL. *The father of Ammiel,* ruler of his tribe and one of the twelve spies sent out to explore the land (Num. 13:12).

GEMARIAH [Gĕm a rī′ ah]—JEHOVAH HATH FULFILLED or ACCOMPLISHMENT OF THE LORD.

1.   *A prince,* son of Shaphan the scribe and brother of Ahikam

(Jer. 36:10–25). This scribe sought in vain to keep King Jehoiakim from burning the roll.

2. *A son of Hilkiah*, sent by King Zedekiah as ambassador to Nebuchadnezzar. He also carried a letter from Jeremiah to the captive Jews (Jer. 29:3).

GENUBATH [Ge̅-nŭ' băth]—THEFT. *A son of Hadad* the Edomite, the fugitive prince, by the sister of Queen Tahpenes, the wife of Pharaoh, who governed Egypt toward the end of David's reign [I Kings 11:20).

GERA [Ge̅' ră]—ENMITY or PILGRIMAGE. *A son or grandson of Benjamin*. The four different Geras named may be reduced to this one Gera: The Gera of Judges 3:15 indicated as the ancestor of Ehud; and the Gera of II Samuel 16:5 as the ancestor of Shimei. (See also Gen. 46:21; II Sam. 19:16, 18; I Kings 2:8; I Chron. 8:3–7).

GERSHOM [Gûr' shŏm]—A STRANGER THERE.
1. *The first-born son of Moses* and Zipporah. He was born in Midian (Ex. 2:22; 18:3; I Chron. 23:15, 16).
2. *The eldest son of Levi*, and referred to as Gershon (Gen. 46:11; Josh. 21:6).
3. *One of the family of Phinehas*, and one of the "heads of houses" who returned with Ezra from Babylon (Ezra 8:2).
4. *Father of Jonathan*, the Levite who became priest to the Danites who settled at Laish (Judg. 18:30). The Danite tribe was guilty of the evil of setting up a graven image.

GESHAM, GESHAN [Ge̅' shăm]—FIRM, STRONG. *A son of Jahdai* and descendant of Caleb (I Chron. 2:47).

GESHEM [Ge̅' shem]—RAIN. *The Arabian* who along with Sanballat and Tobiah, sought to oppose the building of the wall by Nehemiah (Neh. 2:19; 6:1, 2). See Gashmu (6:6).

GETHER [Ge̅' thûr]—VALE OF TRIAL. *Third of Aram's sons* (Gen. 10:23; I Chron. 1:17). The latter reference reckons him among the sons of Shem.

GEUEL [Ge̅ ŭ' el]—SALVATION OF GOD or MAJESTY OF GOD. *A son of Machi*, a prince of Gad and the representative of the Gadite tribe sent out to explore Canaan (Num. 13:15).

GIBBAR [Gĭb' bar]—MIGHTY MAN. *A man whose children returned from captivity* with Zerubbabel (Ezra 2:20). Perhaps the Gibeon of Nehemiah 7:25.

GIBEA [Gĭb' e ă]—HIGHLANDER. *A son of Sheva,* and grandson of Caleb (I Chron. 2:49). Perhaps this reference is more geographical than genealogical, Gibeah in Judah being meant.

GIDDALTI [Gĭd dăl' tĭ]—I HAVE MAGNIFIED or I MAGNIFY GOD. *A son of Heman,* and one of the heads of music (I Chron. 25:4, 29).

GIDDEL [Gĭd' del]—VERY GREAT or HE HATH MAGNIFIED.
1. *A member of the family of Nethinims* who returned from exile with Zerubbabel (Ezra 2:47; Neh. 7:49).
2. *Sons of Giddel,* Solomon's servants who also came up to Jerusalem from exile (Ezra 2:56; Neh. 7:58).

GIDEON, GEDEON [Gĭd' e on, Gĕd' e on]—A CUTTING DOWN, HE THAT BRUISES or GREAT WARRIOR. *A son of Joash* of the family of Abiezer, a Manassite, who lived in Ophrah and delivered Israel from Midian. He is also called Jerubbaal, and judged Israel forty years as the fifth judge (Judg. 6; 7; 8).

The Man of Might and Valor

Without doubt Gideon is among the brightest luminaries of Old Testament history. His character and call are presented in a series of tableaux. We see:

I. Gideon at the flail. The tall, powerful young man was threshing wheat for his farmer-father when the call came to him to rise and become the deliverer of his nation. History teaches that obscurity of birth is no obstacle to noble service. It was no dishonor for Gideon to say, "My family is poor."

II. Gideon at the altar. Although humble and industrious, Gideon was God-fearing. His own father had become an idolator but idols had to go, and Gideon vowed to remove them. No wonder they called him Jerubbaal, meaning "Discomfiter of Baal."

III. Gideon and the fleece. Facing the great mission of his life, he had to have an assuring token that God was with him. The method he adopted was peculiar, but found favor with heaven, God condescending to grant Gideon the double sign. With the complete revelation before us in the Bible, we are not to seek supernatural signs, but take God at his Word.

IV. Gideon at the well. How fascinating is the incident of the reduction of Gideon's army from thirty-two thousand to ten thousand, then to only three hundred. Three hundred men against the countless swarms of Midian! Yes, but the few choice, brave, active men *and God* were in the majority. God is not always on the side of big battalions.

V. Gideon with the whip. Rough times often need and warrant rough measures. The men of Succoth and Penuel made themselves obnoxious, but with a whip fashioned out of the thorny branches off the trees, Gideon meted out to them the punishment they deserved.

VI. Gideon in the gallery of worthies. It was no small honor to have a niche, as Gideon has, in the illustrious roll named in the eleventh chapter of Hebrews, where every name is an inspiration, and every character a miracle of grace.

Preachers desiring to continue the character-study of Gideon still further might note his humility (Judg. 6:15); caution (Judg. 6:17); spirituality (Judg. 6:24); obedience (Judg. 6:27); divine inspiration (Judg. 6:34); divine fellowship (Judg. 6:36; 7:4, 7–9); strategy (Judg. 7:16–18); tact (Judg. 8:1–3); loyalty to God (Judg. 8:23); the fact that he was weakened by his very prosperity (Judg. 8:24–31).

GIDEONI [Gĭd e ŏ' nī]—A CUTTING OF or HE THAT BRUISES. *The father of Abidan*, a prince of Benjamin. He was one of the census-takers at Sinai in the time of Moses (Num. 1:11; 2:22; 7:60, 65; 10:24).

GILALAI [Gĭl' a laī]—WEIGHTY. *A Levitical musician* who took part in the consecration of the wall of Jerusalem (Neh. 12:36).

GILEAD [Gĭl' e ăd]—MASS OF TESTIMONY or STRONG.
1. *Father of Jephthah*, judge of Israel, and grandson of Zelophedad (Judg. 11:1, 2).
2. *Son of Machir*, and grandson of Manasseh (Num. 26:29, 30; 27:1; 36:1; Josh. 17:1–3).
3. *A chief of the family of Gad* (I Chron. 5:14). Also the name of a mountainous area in Jordan (Gen. 37:25; Judg. 7:3).

GINATH [Gĭ' năth]—PROTECTION. *The father of Tibni*, who tried to dethrone Omri after the death of Zimri (I Kings 16:21, 22).

GINNETHO, GINNETHON [Gĭn'ne thō, Gĭn' ne thŏn]—GREAT PROTECTION. *A prince or a priest* who, with Nehemiah, sealed the covenant (Neh. 12:4, 16).

GISPA, GISHPA [Gĭs' pă]—BLANDISHMENT or ATTENTIVE. *An overseer of the Nethinims* in Nehemiah's time (Neh. 11:21).

GOG [Gŏg]—A ROOF or A MOUNTAIN.
1. *A Reubenite, and grandson of Joel* (I Chron. 5:4).
2. *A prince of Rosh, Meshech and Tubal*, and not the mystic character of Revelation 20:8–15. Who is this dominant figure Ezekiel pictures as leading a great host of Northern nations against Israel? Ezekiel 38:2, 3, 14, 16, 18; 39:1, 11 are passages to be closely studied.

The Man of the Future

Gog is mentioned as the son of Shemaiah, in the line of Reuben, as above. Here in Ezekiel Gog appears as the chief prince of Meshech and Tubal, and is foretold as being defeated and five-sixths of his army destroyed as he comes up from "the north parts" and invades "the mountains of Israel."

There are those who affirm that Gog merely represents a title of royal dignity, similar to the Egyptian word Pharaoh. It has also been suggested that as Ezekiel represents Gog as being accompanied in his invasion of the land of Israel by the Persians, Ethiopians, Libyans and others, that the term may be a general designation for all the enemies of Israel. Those who hold this theory find confirmation for it in Revelation 20:8–10 where Gog and Magog are linked together as if they were persons who seem to symbolize all the future foes of Israel. This may be the reason why various writers in the seventh century identified Gog with the Antichrist.

Historically, Gog may have been an actual ruler of a non-Semitic nation over against the north of Palestine and Asia Minor, Armenia, Syria or Scythia.

Prophetically, Gog is to be the chief prince, the fearsome force in the great Northern Confederacy in which Russia will play a prominent part.

GOLIATH [Gŏ lǐ′ ath]—THE EXILE or SOOTHSAYER. The famous giant of Gath, who defied the armies of Israel (I Sam. 17:4, 23; 21:9; 22:10; II Sam. 21:19).

The Man a Pebble Killed

The story of David and Goliath has thrilled our hearts from childhood days. How spectacular it must have been to see a stripling like David slay a massive man some ten feet high with only a pebble from the stream. Saul's proffered armor was of no use against Goliath. David had to meet the giant with the weapon he was used to. A ready-made suit was of no avail for the son of Jesse.

The religious character of the duel between Goliath and David should not be lost sight of. The giant cursed David by his gods. David went out to meet Goliath "in the name of the Lord of Hosts." But why did David take *five* stones, if his God was able to direct a single one into the forehead? Did he want to make sure that if one pebble failed, he would have four more to swing? Going over the passages we discover that Goliath had four sons, all of whom were giants, and five pebbles were needed to slay the lot of them. Thus the choice of five was an act of faith. Through God, only one pebble was needed. David went forth to meet Goliath with five pebbles and he came back with five—four in his hand and the other in Goliath's massive forehead. How God delights to use the insignificant things of life to accomplish His purpose!

GOMER [Gŏ′ mûr]—COMPLETION or HEAT. *The first born of Japheth* and father of Ashkenaz, Riphath, and Togarmah. Also the head of many families (Gen. 10:2, 3; I Chron. 1:5, 6; Ezek. 38:6). The eldest son of Japheth is the father of the ancient Cimmerians or as the Assyrians called them, Gimirra, who settled on the northern shores of the Baltic Sea. The modern and familiar name in English history,

Crimea, and the Cimbri of old times are derived from the Cimmerians, the immediate descendants of Gomer. Their original home appears to have been north of the Euxine, but by the seventh century they had completely conquered Cappadocia and settled there.

The Man Who Became a Nation

The Gauls and Celts of ancient times, and of more modern date, the Germans, French and British are descendants of Gomer. In the *Talmud*, Gomer is spoken of as Germani, that is, Germany. The present divided land of Germany was first called "The Land of Gomer" or *Gomerland*, and many old maps bear the name of Ashkenaz, one of the sons of Gomer. Other maps carry the name Gomer.

The major portion of Germany was never connected with the old Roman Empire. Although presently divided, with communists controlling the East, and the western powers eager to keep West Germany free from communist control, prophecy declares that "Gomer and all his bands," will be found allied to the Northern Confederacy. Owing to Germany's divided condition, European stability is endangered. With West Germany under intense Soviet pressure to refuse any military alliance with western nations, one wonders how long they can resist the determination of Russia to reunite all Germany under the "Hammer and the Sickle."

Gomer is also the name of Hosea's wife, the daughter of Diblaim, and affords another instance of the same name being used by a man and a woman (Hos. 1:3).

GUNI [Gū' nī]—PROTECTED or PAINTED WITH COLORS.
1. *A son of Naphtali* and founder of a tribal family called the Gunites (Gen. 46:24; Num. 26:48; I Chron. 7:13).
2. *Father of Abdiel* and a Gadite chief (I Chron. 5:15).

H

HAAHASHTARI [Hā a hǎsh' ta rī]—THE COURIER. *A descendant of Judah* from Ashur, father of Tekoa, by his second wife Naarah (I Chron. 4:6).

HABAIAH, HOBIAH [Hā bā' iah]—JEHOVAH HATH HIDDEN or IS PROTECTION. *The head of a priestly family* who returned from Babylonian captivity with Zerubbabel. Although claiming sacerdotal descent, the members of this priestly family failed to trace their genealogy and were therefore not allowed to serve (Ezra 2:61; Neh. 7:63).

HABAKKUK [Hā bǎk' kuk]—LOVE'S EMBRACE or HE THAT EMBRACES. *The eighth of the Minor Prophets* whose parentage, birthplace and era are unrecorded (Hab. 1:1; 3:1).

The Man Who Caressed the People

Although he is not much more than a mere name to us, we know that Habakkuk was a prophet of Judah and of the tribe of Levi and of the temple singers (Hab. 3:19). He is also referred to as a prophet and the last prophet before the destruction of Jerusalem (Hab. 3:11). Rabbinical tradition makes him the son of the Shunammite woman whom Elisha restored to life (II Kings 4:16). Habakkuk prophesied the coming of the Babylonians upon Judah. This invasion took place in 606 B.C. and also in 597 B.C. and 586 B.C. "In your days" (Hab. 1:5), would indicate that he prophesied scarcely a generation before the first invasion.

In his prophecy Habakkuk was true to his name, which means "strong embrace of God," for he caressed and comforted the people as one would embrace a weeping child until its tears are dried. A modern writer suggests that his name may have contributed somewhat to the unpopularity of the prophet. "His name is against him; its coarse gutterals, falling upon the modern ears with a forbidden ring, and creating a prejudice from the beginning."

From the book Habakkuk wrote, we gather that he was the questioning prophet. He wants to know "Why?" and "How?" Answers were granted him. Why does God permit the destruction of His own people by a hand so cruel and unclean? The prophet waited patiently for an answer, and it came. The ungodly shall pass; the just shall live by faith.

Then we have a chant of derision against the Chaldeans raised by their victims — a fivefold *woe:*

I.   Their insatiable greed.

II. Their overreaching ambition.

III. Their cruel tyranny.

IV. Their shameful treatment of conquered people.

V.   Their brutal idolatry.

Then there is Habakkuk's great message of faith which gave Paul a hint of the most precious truth of the Gospel (Rom. 1:17; Gal. 3:11; Heb. 10:38) and aided the Reformation under Martin Luther, the charter of evangelical liberty.

HABAZZINIAH, HABAZINIAH [Hăb a zĭ nī′ ah]—MEANING UNCERTAIN. *The head of a family of Rechabites* and grandfather of Jaazariah the chief Rechabite in Jeremiah's time (Jer. 35:3).

HACHALIAH [Hăch a lī′ ah]—JEHOVAH IS HIDDEN. *The father of Nehemiah* the Tirshatha (Neh. 1:1; 10:1). Also the name of a hill in Judah (I Sam. 23:19; 26:3).

HACHMONI [Hăch′ mō nī]—THE WISE. *The father of Jehiel* who was a companion of the sons of David, and also founder of a tribal family (I Chron. 11:11; 27:32).

HADAD [Hă' dăd]—MIGHTY or FIERCENESS.

1. *A son of Bedad,* king of Edom and of the city of Avith (Gen. 36:35, 36; I Chron. 1:46, 47).

2. *An Edomite prince* of Solomon's time (I Kings 11:4–25).

3. *Eighth son of Ishmael,* and grandson of Abraham (Gen. 25:15; I Chron. 1:30). Also called Hadar.

4. *The last of the early kings* of Edom (I Chron. 1:50, 51). This is the Hadar of Genesis 36:39 who, as a child, escaped massacre under Joab, David's general.

HADADEZER, HADAREZER [Hăd ăd ĕ' zûr, Hăd är ĕ' zûr]—MIGHTY IS THE HELP, HADAR IS A HELP or BEAUTY OF ASSISTANCE. *The son of Rehob,* and king of Zobah in Syria who was defeated by David and driven across the Euphrates (II Sam. 8:3–12; I Kings 11:23). Called Hadarezer in I Chronicles 18:8 and 19:16, 19).

HADLAI [Hăd' la ī]—FRAIL or LAX. *A man of Ephraim,* father of Amasa, one of the chiefs of the tribe in the reign of Pekah (II Chron. 28:12).

HADORAM [Hă dō' ram]—HADAR IS HIGH.

1. *A son of Joktan* of the family of Shem (Gen. 10:27; I Chron. 1:21).

2. *A son of Tou,* king of Hamath in David's time (I Chron. 18:10).

3. *An officer over Rehoboam's taxes,* who was killed at the revolt of Shechem (II Chron. 10:18). Adoniram is the longer form (I Kings 4:6). See also Adoram of II Samuel 20:24.

HAGAB [Hă' găb]—A LOCUST or BENT. *Founder of a family of Nethinims* who returned with Zerubbabel to Jerusalem [Ezra 2:46). Nehemiah omits the name in his list.

HAGABAH, HAGABA [Hăg' a bah, Hăg' a bă]—A LOCUST. *Another Nethinim* who returned from captivity (Ezra 2:45; Neh. 7:48).

HAGGAI [Hăg' ga ī]—FESTAL or BORN OF A FESTIVAL DAY. *The tenth of the Minor Prophets,* and the first of those to prophesy after the captivity (Ezra 5:1; 6:14).

The Man Who Was a Messenger

All we know of Haggai is told us in the first verse of his book, where we have a description of himself and his message, which gives us a key to the whole of his ministry. Haggai was "The Lord's messenger in the Lord's message." We reject the legend that he was an angel incarnate.

His name is suggestive and may imply that he was born on a Feast Day. Another meaning is "Jehovah hath quieted." As a prophet, he was contemporary with Zechariah (Hag. 1:1; 2:1, 20; Zech. 1:1). He prophesied in the second year of the reign of Darius Hystaspes, King of Persia, sixteen years after Cyrus' decree permitting the rebuilding of the Temple. Compare Zechariah 1:1–11 with Ezra 4:24 and 5:1.

As a prophet, he preached righteousness and predicted the future. As a man, he was simple, strong in faith and bold in hope. He urged the people to work and be strong (Hag. 2:4), assuring them that when they began to build the Temple, God would begin to bless them.

The *first message* was one of stern rebuke (Hag. 1:1–11).

The *second message* was one of comfort and commendation (Hag. 1:12–15).

The *third message* was a cheering one of encouragement (Hag. 2:1–9).

The *fourth message* was an assuring one concerning cleansing and blessing (Hag. 2:10–19).

The *fifth message* was a steadying one associated with safety (Hag. 2:20–23).

Dr. Stuart Holden suggests that these five lessons can be gathered from Haggai:

I. *Danger of lapsing* into self-content, even after honest and sincere beginnings in the work of Christ.

II. That *the time for blessing is always at hand*. The people said: "The time has not come." God said: "My time is an eternal NOW." The only hindrance to blessing lies in His people.

III. In the will of God for His people — particularly in respect to the great work of building His Temple — *there is always a conjunction of precept and power, of duty and dynamic*. The promises of God are "Yea and Amen" to those who are in Christ Jesus, *walking* in Him, and *living* in Him.

IV. *The greatest of all mistakes is to leave God out in His own work.* To live in the light of His presence is to build for eternity.

V. In the work to which we pledge ourselves as God's children, *the greatest need of all is for patience*. We shall be opposed if our work is worth opposing; but the opposition of the Evil One is the opportunity to express our faith and loyalty toward God. "Our God is marching on. The best is yet to be; and we may reckon upon God."

HAGGERI [Hăg′ gē rī]—WANDERER. *The father of Mibhar*, one of David's brave men (I Chron. 11:38).

HAGGI [Hăg′ ḡī]—FESTIVE or BORN ON A FESTIVAL. *The second son of Gad* and founder of the tribal family of Haggites (Gen. 46:16; Num. 26:15).

HAGGIAH [Hăg ḡī′ ah]—FEAST OF JEHOVAH. *A descendant of Merari*, the son of Levi (I Chron. 6:30).

HAKKATAN [Hăk′ ka tăn]—THE YOUNGER or THE LITTLE ONE. *The father of Johanan* and head of a family of returning exiles with Ezra

(Ezra 8:12). The name, says Young, is simply Katan, meaning "little," with the definite article prefixed.

HAKKOZ, KOZ, COZ [Hăk' kŏz, Kŏz, Cŏz]—THE THORN or THE NIMBLE.

1. *A descendant of Aaron* and chief of the seventh course in the sanctuary service appointed by David (I Chron. 24:10; see Koz in Ezra 2:61; Neh. 3:4, 21). This family of priests failed to prove their identity.

2. *A man of Judah* (I Chron. 4:8).

HAKUPHA [Hă kŭ' phă]—INCITEMENT or BENT, CURVED. *Founder of a family of Nethinims* who returned from Babylon with Zerubbabel (Ezra 2:51; Neh. 7:53).

HALOHESH, HALLOHESH [Hă lŏ' hesh, Hăl lŏ' hesh]—THE WHISPERER or THE ENCHANTER.

1. *The father of Shallum* who ruled over a portion and helped to rebuild the wall (Neh. 3:12).

2. *One of the number sealing the covenant with Nehemiah* (Neh. 10:24). Some writers identify these two men as the same person.

HAM [Hăm]—HOT or DARK, COLORED, SWARTHY. *The youngest son of Noah* and father of Canaan and founder of many peoples (Gen. 5:32; 6:10; 7:13; 9:18, 22; Ps. 78:51).

The Man Whose Sin Brought a Curse

In consequence of the improper conduct of Ham when Noah was drunk, the heart of his father was set against him. Without doubt, Ham's act was the manifestation of an impure heart. Perhaps he had always been a filthy dreamer.

Because every imagination of our heart is defiled (Gen. 8:21), we are all the sons of Ham in this respect. There is none clean, no not one (Rom. 3:10, 12).

The indignation of Noah found expression in the thrice repeated curse upon Canaan, one of Ham's sons (Gen. 9:25-27). Ham himself suffered in failing to receive the blessing pronounced on his brothers, Shem and Japheth. The peoples polluted by Ham's sin (Gen. 10:15-19) inhabited the land later promised to Abraham's seed; thus the curse of servitude was fulfilled in Joshua's conquest of the Canaanites, when he made them hewers of wood and drawers of water (Josh. 9:23, 27).

The Hebrew word for Ham means "hot" and is surely prophetic of the climates that have created the blackness of the skin of the Negro, and the dark complexions of other peoples from the same stock. Egypt is called "the land of Ham" (Ps. 105:23) and the Egyptian word for "Ham" is *Kem*, meaning black and warm. From Ham we have the Egyptians, Africans, Babylonians, Philistines and Canaanites.

HAMAN [Hā′ man]—WELL DISPOSED. *The son of Hammedatha*, the chief minister of king Ahasuerus, who is called the Agagite because of his Amalekitish descent (Esther 3:1–5).

The Man Who Hated Jews

Haman, an oriental despot's favorite, had an innate passion for elevation. He never considered principle when seeking the king's honor. But Mordecai pricked Haman's bubble and would not bow to him. How could he honor an Amalekite whom God had cursed (Ex. 17: 14–16)! All of Haman's tragedy is condensed in the arrestive designation—he was the Jews' enemy. As the first great anti-semite, he came to prove that they who curse the Jews are cursed of God.

Haman, the vain and fussy courtier, the vulgar and unwise upstart, the cruel enemy of the Jews, the villain of the plot, is a name still hated by the Jews. Long ago at *The Feast of Purim*, it was customary to hang an effigy of Haman; but as the gibbet was sometimes made in the form of a cross, riots between Jews and Christians were the result, and a warning against insults to the Christian faith was issued by the Emporer Theodosius II. The Jews, however, in *The Feast of Purim* still celebrate their victory from annihilation by Haman.

HAMMATH, HEMATH [Hăm′ math, Hē′ math]—WARMTH OR HOT SPRING. *The founder or father of the house of Rechab* (I Chron. 2:55). Also the name of a city near Tiberius famous for its hot baths (Josh. 19:35).

HAMMEDATHA [Hăm mĕd′ a thả]—GIVEN BY HOM—MOON GOD OR HE THAT TROUBLETH THE LAW. *The Persian name of the father of Haman* the Agagite we have just considered (Esther 3:1, 10; 8:5; 9:10, 24).

HAMMELECH [Hăm′ me lĕch]—THE KING. *The father of Jerahmeel*, and of royal blood (Jer. 36:26; 38:6). Although given as a proper name, perhaps it should have been translated "the king" as stated in the R.V.

HAMOR, EMMOR [Hā′ mor]—AN ASS. *The prince of Shechem*, a Hivite (Gen. 33:19; 34:1–26).

HAMUEL, HAMMUEL [Hă mū′ el]—GOD IS A SUN OR WARMTH OF GOD. *A son of Mishma*, a Simeonite, of the family of Shuah (I Chron. 4:26).

HAMUL [Hā′ mŭl]—PITY OR PITIED. *The younger son of Pharez*, son of Judah by Tamar, and founder of the Hamulites (Gen. 46:12; Num. 26:21; I Chron. 2:5).

HANAMEEL, HANAMEL [Hă năm' e el]—GOD HATH PITIED, GIFT or
GRACE OF GOD. *The son of Shallum* and cousin of the prophet Jeremiah
(Jer. 32:7–12). See this portion on advice concerning a good investment.

HANAN [Hā' nan]—GRACIOUS or MERCIFUL.
1. *A son of Shashak* and a Benjamite chief (I Chron. 8:23).
2. *A son of Azel,* descendant of Jonathan and Saul (1 Chron. 8:38;
9:44).
3. *A son of Maachah,* one of David's heroes (I Chron. 11:43).
4. *A Nethinim* who returned from exile (Ezra 2:46; Neh. 7:49).
5. *A Levite who assisted Ezra* when he read and explained the Law
(Neh. 8:7).
6. *A Levite who sealed the covenant* with Nehemiah. Perhaps the
same person as No. 5 (Neh. 10:10; 13:13).
7. *A chief of the people* or a family who also sealed the covenant
(Neh. 10:22).
8. *Another chief* who likewise signed the covenant (Neh. 10:26).
9. *The son of Igdaliah,* an officer in the Temple whose sons had
a chamber therein (Jer. 35:4).

HANANEEL [Hă năn' e el]—GOD IS GRACIOUS or THE MERCY OF GOD.
The builder of the tower bearing his name near the sheepgate of
Jerusalem (Neh. 3:1; 12:39; Jer. 31:38; Zech. 14:10).

HANANI [Hā nă' nĭ]—GRACIOUS or HE HATH SHEWED ME MERCY.
1. *One of the sons of Heman* and a head musician (I Chron. 25:
4, 25).
2. *The seer* who rebuked Asa for buying off Ben-hadad, king of
Syria (II Chron. 16:7).
3. *The father of Jehu,* the seer who testified against Baasha and
Jehoshaphat (I Kings 16:1, 7; II Chron. 19:2; 20:34).
4. *A priest* who had taken a foreign wife while in exile (Ezra 10:20).
5. *A brother of Nehemiah* who brought news of Jerusalem and became its governor (Neh. 1:2; 7:2).
6. *A musical priest* who assisted in the purification and dedication
of the walls (Neh. 12:36).

HANANIAH [Hăn a nĭ' ah]—JEHOVAH IS GRACIOUS or GIFT OF THE
LORD.
1. *A son of Heman,* and one of many musicians. Heman's sons
were especially employed to blow horns (I Chron. 25:4, 23).
2. *A chief captain* in the army of king Uzziah (II Chron. 26:11).
3. *The father of Zedekiah,* and one of the princes during the reign
of king Jehoiakim (Jer. 36:12).
4. *The son of Azur* of Gibeon whose false prophecy was withstood
by the prophet Jeremiah (Jer. 28).
5. *Grandfather of Irijah,* who arrested Jeremiah on a charge of
deserting to the Chaldeans (Jer. 37:13).

6. *Son of Shashak* and head of a Benjamite family (I Chron. 8:24).

7. *The Hebrew name of Shadrach*, who was of the house of David (Dan. 1:6, 7, 11, 19; 2:17).

8. *A son of Zerubbabel* and an ancestor of Christ (I Chron. 3:19, 21; Luke 3:27 R.V.).

9. *A son of Bebai* who returned from exile and put away his foreign wife (Ezra 10:28).

10. *An apothecary and priest* who helped to rebuild the wall of Jerusalem (Neh. 3:8).

11. *One associated with Hanun* in the repair of the wall (Neh. 3:30).

12. *The governor of the castle* and joint ruler with Nehemiah's brother over Jerusalem (Neh. 7:2).

13. *An individual who added his signature to the covenant* (Neh. 10:23).

14. *A priest* in the time of Jehoiakim (Neh. 12:12, 41).

HANNIEL, HANIEL [Hän' nĭ el, Hän' ĭ el]—FAVOR or GRACE OF GOD.

1. *A son of Ephod and prince of the Manassites*, who assisted in the division of the land (Num. 34:23).

2. *A son of Ulla*, a prince and hero of Asher (I Chron. 7:39).

HANOCH, HENOCH [Hä' nŏch, Hē nŏch]—DEDICATED.

1. *A son of Midian* and a descendant of Abraham by Keturah (Gen. 25:4; I Chron. 1:33). Also called Henoch.

2. *The eldest son of Reuben* and founder of the family of the Hanochites (Gen. 46:9; Ex. 6:14; Num. 26:5; I Chron. 5:3).

3. *The son of Jared*, a descendant of Seth (I Chron. 1:3). Called Enoch in Genesis 5:18.

HANUN [Hä' nŭn]—ENJOYING FAVOR, GRACIOUS or HE THAT RESTS.

1. *The son of Nahash*, king of the Ammonites, who resented David's message of condolence which resulted in a most disastrous war (II Sam. 10:1–4; I Chron. 19:2–6).

2. *A son of Zalaph* who assisted in the repair of a portion of the wall (Neh. 3:30).

3. *Another Jew* who, with the people of Zanoah, repaired one of the gates of the wall of Jerusalem (Neh. 3:13).

HAPPIZZEZ, APHSES [Ăph' sēs]—THE DISPERSION. *The head of the eighteenth course of priests* (I Chron. 24:15).

HARAN [Hä' ran]—ENLIGHTENED or STRONG.

1. *The third son of Terah*, younger brother of Abraham and father of Lot (Gen. 11:26–31).

2. *A Gershonite Levite* in David's time, and one of the family of Shimei (I Chron. 23:9).

3. *A son of Caleb* the spy, by his concubine, Ephah, and called Charun. His son was named Gazez (I Chron. 2: 46). Haran or its New

Testament equivalent Charrun, is also the name of the place Abram and his family emigrated to from Ur (Gen. 11:31, 32).

HARBONA, HARBONAH [Här bō′ nă, Här bō′ nah]—ASS DRIVER or THE ANGER OF HIM WHO BUILDS. *Third of the seven eunuchs* or chamberlains who served Ahasuerus, king of Persia (Esther 1:10; 7:9).

HAREPH [Hä′ reph]—EARLY BORN or PLUCKING OF. *A son of Caleb,* son of Hur and father of Beth-gader, and a Judahite chief (I Chron. 2:51). Called Hariph in Nehemiah 7:24.

HARHAIAH [Här ha ī′ ah]—JEHOVAH IS PROTECTING. *Father of the goldsmith Uzziel,* who repaired a part of the wall (Neh. 3:8).

HARHAS [Här′ has]—GLITTER or SPLENDOR. *The grandfather of Shallum,* the husband of Huldah the prophetess of king Josiah's time (II Kings 22:14).

HARHUR [Här′ hûr]—NOBILITY or DISTINCTION. *A member of the Nethinim family* who returned from exile with Zerubbabel (Ezra 2:51; Neh. 7:53).

HARIM [Hä′ rim]—CONSECRATED or SNUB-NOSED.
1. *A priest* who was in charge of the third division in the work of the sanctuary (I Chron. 24:8; Ezra 2:39; 10:21; Neh. 3:11; 7:42).
2. *A returned exile* who had married a foreign wife (Ezra 10:31).
3. *One who had signed the covenant* with Nehemiah (Neh. 10:5).
4. *Another who had signed the covenant* with Nehemiah (Neh. 10:27).
5. *Head of a priestly family* (Neh. 12:15). Perhaps the same as No. 3.

HARIPH [Hä′ riph]—EARLY BORN or AUTUMNAL RAIN. *Founder of a Jewish family* who sealed the covenant (Neh. 10:19). Called Jorah in Ezra 2:18. Some old versions have Jodah.

HARNEPHER [Här′ ne phûr]—PANTING. *A son of Zophah,* an Asherite (I Chron. 7:36).

HAROEH [Här′ o eh]—THE SEER. *A son of Shobal,* father of Kirjath-jearim, of the tribe of Judah (I Chron. 2:52). Perhaps the Reaiah of I Chronicles 4:2.

HARUM [Hä′ rum]—EXALTED or ELEVATED. *The father of Aharhel* a descendant of Coz, from Caleb son of Hur. A man of Judah (I Chron. 4:8).

HARUMAPH [Hā rụ' maph]—FLAT OF NOSE. *The father of Jedaiah,* who helped in the repair of the gate (Neh. 3:10).

HARUZ [Hā' ruz]—INDUSTRIOUS. *Father of Meshullemeth,* Manasseh's queen and mother of Amon, king of Judah (II Kings 21:19).

HASADIAH [Hăs a dī' ah]—JEHOVAH IS KIND or HATH SHEWN KIND-NESS. *A son of Zerubbabel* and descendant of king Jehoiakim (I Chron. 3:20).

HASENUAH [Hăs e nū' ah]—THE VIOLATED. *A Benjamite chief* whose name is actually Senuah (I Chron. 9:7).

HASHABIAH [Hăsh a bī' ah]—JEHOVAH IS ASSOCIATED or HATH DEVISED.
1. *A Merarite Levite* descended through Amaziah and an ancestor of Jeduthun (I Chron. 6:45).
2. *Another Merarite Levite* and co-musician (I Chron. 9:14).
3. *The fourth of the sons of Jeduthun,* likewise a sanctuary musician (I Chron. 25:3).
4. *A descendant of Hebron,* son of Kohath, and an inspector of the country (I Chron. 26:30).
5. *A son of Kemuel,* prince of the Levites in David's time (I Chron. 27:17).
6. *A chief of the Levites,* who assisted king Josiah at his great passover feast (II Chron. 35:9).
7. *A Merarite Levite* who joined Ezra at the river of Ahava (Ezra 8:19; Neh. 10:11).
8. *A chief of the priests of the family of Kohath* (Ezra 8:24).
9. *A ruler of half of Keilah,* who helped in the repair of the wall (Neh. 3:17).
10. *A Levite* who sealed the covenant with Nehemiah. Perhaps the same person as in Nehemiah 12:24.
11. *The son of Bunni,* a Levite (Neh. 11:15).
12. *Another Levite,* the son of Mattaniah and a temple attendant (Neh. 11:22). See No. 14.
13. *A priest of the family of Hilkiah* in Joiakim's days (Neh. 12:21).
14. *A chief Levite* appointed for thanksgiving when the people returned from exile (Neh. 12:24). Perhaps the same person as No. 12.

HASHABNAH [Hā shăb' nah]—JEHOVAH IS A FRIEND. *A chief who sealed the covenant with Nehemiah* (Neh. 10:25).

HASHABNIAH, HASHABIAH [Hăsh ab nī' ah]—JEHOVAH IS A FRIEND.
1. *His son Hattush* helped to repair the wall (Neh. 3:10).

2. *One of the Levites* who by exhortation prepared the exiles for the sealing of the covenant (Neh. 9:5).

HASHBADANA, HASHBADDNA [Hăsh băd' a nă]—REASON or THOUGHT. *One of those who stood on the left hand of Ezra* as he read the law (Neh. 8:4).

HASHEM [Hă' shem]—ASTONISHED or SHINING. *The father of several of David's mighty men* (I Chron. 11:34).

HASHUB, HASSHUB [Hă' shub, Hăs' shub]—ASSOCIATED or THOUGHTFUL.
1. *Father of Shemaiah*, a descendant of Merari (I Chron. 9:14).
2. *A son of Pahath-moab* who joined others in the repair of the wall (Neh. 3:11).
3. *A Jew who repaired the wall* over against his own house (Neh. 3:23). A good place for reformation to begin.
4. *The head of a family*, joining Nehemiah in the sealing of the covenant (Neh. 10:23).

HASHUBAH [Hă shōō' bah]—ESTEEMED or ASSOCIATION. *A son of Zerubbabel* and descendant of King Jehoiakim (I Chron. 3:20).

HASHUM [Hă' shum]—WEALTHY or SHINING.
1. *Founder of a family* whose descendants returned with Zerubbabel (Ezra 2:19; 10:33; Neh. 7:22).
2. *A priest who stood at Ezra's side* as he read the Law to the people (Neh. 8:4).
3. *The head of a family* that sealed the covenant (Neh. 10:18).

HASRAH [Hăs' rah]—SPLENDOR. *Same as Harhas* in II Kings 22:14 (II Chron. 34:22).

HASSENAAH, SENAAH [Hăs se nă' ah, Sĕ nă' ah]—THORNY or THE THORN HEDGE. *His sons built the Fish Gate* (Neh. 3:3). Identical with Senaah of Ezra 2:35 and Nehemiah 7:38.

HASUPHA, HASHUPHA [Hă sũ' phă, Hă shōō' phă]—NAKEDNESS or MADE BARE. *Head of a Nethinim family* that returned from exile (Ezra 2:43; Neh. 7:46). Inaccurately stated as Hashupha.

HATACH, HATHACH [Hă' tăch]—A GIFT. *A chamberlain eunuch* appointed by King Ahasuerus to attend Queen Esther. It was through him that Esther learned the details of Haman's plot against the Jews. He thus had his part in their deliverance (Esther 4:5-10).

HATHATH [Hă' thăth]—BRUISED or TERROR. *A son of Othniel the Kenite and judge of Israel*, through Caleb, son of Hur (I Chron. 4:13).

HATIPHA [Hăt′ Ĭ phă]—CAPTIVE. *Founder of a family of Nethinims* that returned from exile with Zerubbabel (Ezra 2:54; Neh. 7:56).

HATITA [Hăt′ Ĭ tă]—EXPLORATION. *A member of the guild of porters or gatekeepers* that returned from exile (Ezra 2:42; Neh. 7:45).

HATTIL [Hăt′ til]—DECAYING or VACILLATING. *One of Solomon's servants or slaves* (Ezra 2:57; Neh. 7:59).

HATTUSH [Hăt′ tush]—CONTENDER or GATHERED TOGETHER.
1. *A man of Judah,* son of Shemiah and family of Shecaniah (I Chron. 3:22).
2. *A descendant of David* who returned with Ezra from Babylon (Ezra 8:2; Neh. 3:10; 10:4).
3. *A priest* who returned from captivity (Neh. 12:2).

HAVILAH [Hăv′ i lah]—CIRCLE.
1. *A son of Cush,* and descendant of Ham (Gen. 10:7; I Chron. 1:9).
2. *A son of Joktan* and descendant of Shem (Gen. 10:29; I Chron. 1:23). Also name of two places (Gen. 2:11; 25:18; I Sam. 15:7).

HAZAEL [Hăz′ a el]—GOD SEES or HATH SEEN. *A Syrian courtier,* anointed by Elijah as king over Syria. Hazael murdered his master and usurped the throne (I Kings 19:15, 17).

HAZAIAH [Hă ză′ iah]—JEHOVAH IS SEEING or HATH SEEN. *A man of Judah* and of the family of Shelah (Neh. 11:5).

HAZARMAVETH [Hă′ zar mă′ veth]—COURT OF DEATH. *A son of Joktan,* fifth in order from Shem (Gen. 10:26; I Chron. 1:20).

HAZIEL [Hă′ zĬ el]—VISION OF GOD or GOD IS SEEING. *A Gershonite Levite,* son of Shimei or Shimi in David's time (I Chron. 23:9).

HAZO [Hă′ zō]—VISION OR SEER. *A son of Nahor* by Milcah his wife (Gen. 22:22).

HEBER, EBER [Hĕ′ bûr]—FELLOWSHIP, PRODUCTION or ONE THAT PASSES.
1. *The head of a tribe of Gadites* (I Chron. 5:13).
2. *A son of Shashak,* a Benjamite (I Chron. 8:22).
3. *A son of Beriah* the son of Asher (Gen. 46:17; Num. 26:45; I Chron. 7:31, 32), and ancestor of Christ (Luke 3:35).
4. *The husband of Jael* who killed Sisera—a Kenite and descendant of Moses (Judg. 4:11, 17, 21; 5:24).
5. *A son of Ezra,* of the family of Caleb, son of Jephunneh (I Chron. 4:18).

6. *A son of Elpaal,* a Benjamite (I Chron. 8:17). For others see Eber.

HEBRON [Hĕ' bron]—UNION or COMPANY.

1. *The third son of Kohath* and founder of a tribal family (Ex. 6:18; Num. 3:19; I Chron. 6:2, 18; 23:12, 19; 26:23).

2. *A son of Mareshah* and father of Korah (I Chron. 2:42, 43; 15:9).

HEGE, HEGAI [Hĕ' gē, Hĕg' a ī]—VENERABLE. *Chief chamberlain of king Ahasuerus,* and keeper of women (Esther 2:3, 8, 15).

HELDAI, HELEM, HELED [Hĕl' da ī, Hĕ' lem, Hĕ' led]—ENDURING or DURABLE.

1. *A Netophathite,* descendant of Othniel and one of David's captains for monthly service (I Chron. 27:15).

2. *An Israelite exile* to whom special honor was given (Zech. 6:10). In verse fourteen his name appears as Helem.

HELEB, HELED [Hĕ' lĕb, Hĕ' led]—ENDURANCE or FAT. *The son of Baanah,* and one of David's valiant men (II Sam. 23:29). See I Chronicles 11:30 for Heled.

HELEK [Hĕ' lĕk]—SMOOTHNESS or PORTION. *The second son of Gilead* and founder of the tribal family of Helekites (Num. 26:30; Josh. 17:2).

HELEM [Hĕ' lem]—MANLY VIGOR or STRENGTH.

1. *An Asherite,* brother of Shamer (I Chron. 7:35). May be the Hotham of I Chronicles 7:32.

2. *Apparently the same as Heldai of Zechariah* 6:10, 14.

HELEZ [Hĕ' lĕz]—STRENGTH or ALERTNESS.

1. *A Paltite or Pelonite,* and one of David's guard (II Sam. 23:23, 26; I Chron. 11:27; 27:10).

2. *A man of Judah* and son of Azariah and a descendant of the great family of Hezron (I Chron. 2:39).

HELI [Hĕ' lī]—ELEVATION or ASCENDING. *The father of Joseph* the husband of Mary, mother of Christ (Luke 3:23). The Hebrew name is the same as Eli the high priest.

HELKAI (Hĕl' ka ī]—JEHOVAH IS A PORTION. *A priest and head of his father's house* of Meraioth (Neh. 12:15). See Hilkiah.

HELON [Hĕ' lon]—STRONG. *The father of Eliab* and chief of the tribe of Zebulon at the time the census was taken at Sinai (Num. 1:9; 2:7; 7:24, 29; 10:16).

HEMAM [Hē′ mam]—FAITHFUL or RAGING.

1. *A son of Lotan* the eldest son of Seir (Gen. 36:22). Given in I Chronicles 1:39 as Homam.

2. *A son of Zerah,* the son of Jacob (I Kings 4:31; I Chron. 2:6). A sage whose reputation for wisdom was high in Solomon's reign.

3. *The son of Joel* and grandson of Samuel, and of the Levite family of Korah (I Chron. 6:33; 15:17). Heman is called "the singer" or "the musician," and was the first of the three chief Levites appointed to conduct the vocal and instrumental music of the Tabernacle in David's time. Evidently Heman played the cymbal (I Chron. 25: 1–6; II Chron. 5:12; 35:15). Heman was also the writer of the most melancholy of all the Psalms (Ps. 88). It has been suggested that Heman composed it to console David during some inconsolable season. Heman is also referred to as David's "seer in the matters of God." What a responsible position that must have been!

HEMATH [Hē′ math]—WARMTH. *A person or place* (I Chron. 2:55; Amos 6:14). Variations of name are Hamath and Hammath.

HEMDAN [Hēm′ dan]—PLEASANT or DESIRABLE. *The eldest son of Dishon,* son of Anah (Gen. 36:26). In I Chronicles 1:41 the name is given as Amram.

HEN [Hĕn]—GRACE or FAVOR. *A son of Zephaniah,* one of those whose memory was to be perpetuated by crowns laid up in the Temple (Zech. 6:14). Also called Josiah in Zechariah 6:10.

HENADAD [Hĕn′ a dăd]—FAVOR OF HADAD or HADAD IS GRACIOUS. *The head of a Levite family* who supported Zerubbabel when the foundation of the Temple was laid and who assisted in its re-building (Ezra 3:9; Neh. 3:18, 24; 10:9).

HEPHER [Hē′ phûr]—A DIGGING or A WELL.

1. *The youngest son of Gilead* and founder of the tribe of Hepherites. This Hepher was the father of Zelophedad whose daughters secured rights to their father's property (Num. 26:32; 27:1; Josh. 17:2, 3)

2. *The second son of Narah,* one of Asher's two wives (I Chron. 4:6).

3. *A Mecherathite,* one of the thirty heroes of David (I Chron. 11:36). (See Josh. 12:17; I Kings 4:10 for "the land of Hepher.")

HERESH [Hē′ resh]—WORK or SILENCE. *The head of a Levite family* and attached to the Tabernacle staff (I Chron. 9:15).

HERMAS [Hûr′ mas]—INTERPRETER or MERCURY. *A Christian in Rome* to whom Paul sent a greeting (Rom. 16:14). Hermas, a common name among slaves, was the name of the Greek god corresponding to the Roman Mercury.

HERMES [Hûr′ mēs]—GAIN or MEANING AS AT HERMAS. *A Christian Greek in Rome,* possibly a slave in Caesar's household, to whom Paul sent a salutation. Lightfoot tells us that Hermes was a common slave's name (Rome 16:14).

HERMOGENES [Hûr mŏğ′ e nēs]—BEGOTTEN OF MERCURY or GENERATION OF LUCRE. *A companion of Paul* who, with Phygelus, deserted the apostle in a time of trial. Many of the so-called friends of Paul caused him great sorrow of heart (II Tim. 1:15).

HEROD [Hûr′ od]—SON OF THE HERO or THE GLORY OF THE SKIN. Space forbids a detailed account of the genealogical table of the family of Herod. From Antipater, Governor of Idumaea, there were many branches. Elaborating on the history of the Herods, Henry S. Nash in his *Hastings Dictionary* article says that they brought into history a considerable amount of vigor and ability, and that the main interest attaching to the Herods is not concerned with their characters as individual rulers.

"They acquire dignity when they are viewed as parts of a supremely dramatic situation in universal history. The fundamental elements in the situation are two.

"The course of world-power in antiquity, and the relation between it and the political principle in the constitution of the Chosen People.

"The religious genius of Judaism, and its relation to the political elements in the experience of the Jews."

Among the many of the Herodian house, mention can be made of three, prominent in New Testament history.

1. Herod the Great. This son of Antipater had shown himself before his father's death both masterful and merciless. Because of his rule he earned the tile "Herod the Great." He is remembered for his massacre of the innocents, the murder of several of his sons and for his own appalling death. Stewart Perowne in his recent monumental study, *The Life and Times of Herod the Great,* tells us that Herod's life was as "eventful as his buildings were magnificent... His charm made him a close personal friend, first of Mark Antony, later of Augustus and Agrippa . . . Herod's greatest achievement was the building of the Temple in Jerusalem" (Matt. 2:1–22; Luke 1:5).

2. Herod Antipas, son of Herod the Great by his Samaritan wife, Matthaec. He became tetrarch of Galilee and Pernea. A man of craft, his cunning served him well. "The corroding immorality of his race shows itself in his marriage with Herodias, his brother's wife." His lust proved his undoing and also cost John the Baptist his head. Ultimately he was banished (Matt. 14:1–6; Mark 6:14–22; 8:15; Luke 3:1, 19; 8:3; 9:7, 9; 13:31; 23:7–15; Acts 4:27; 13:1).

3. The grandson of Herod the Great, and the son of Aristobulus and Bernice. He became Herod Agrippa I. Caligula gave him the governments of the tetrarchs Philip and Lysanias with other marks of royal favor. Parading as a little tin god, he was smitten with a foul disease and died in great agony (Acts 12; 23:35).

HERODION [Hē rō dǐ ŏn]—CONQUEROR OF HEROES. *A Jewish Christian in Rome,* whom Paul called a kinsman and to whom he sent a greeting. Perhaps he was a freedman of the Herods (Rom. 16:11).

HESED [Hē′ sed]—KINDNESS or PITY. *The father of one of Solomon's purveyors* in Aruboth, in Judah (I Kings 4:10).

HETH [Hĕth]—TERRIBLE. *The second son of Canaan,* ancestor of the Hittites. The wives of Esau are called "daughters of Heth" (Gen. 10:15; 23:3–20; 27:46; 49:32; I Chron. 1:13).

HEZEKI [Hĕz′ e kī]—JEHOVAH IS STRENGTH. *A son of Elpaal,* a descendant of Benjamin (I Chron. 8:17).

HEZEKIAH [Hĕz e kī′ ah]—JEHOVAH IS STRENGTH or A STRONG SUPPORT IS JEHOVAH. Also given as Hizkiah, Hizkijah, Ezekias.
1. *Son and successor of Ahaz* as king of Judah (II Kings 16: 20). He is referred to in well over one hundred references in II Kings, I and II Chronicles, Jeremiah, Hosea and Micah.

The Man Who Asked for Added Years

Hezekiah was one of the best kings who ever sat upon the throne of Judah, and is distinguished as the greatest in faith of all Judah's kings (II Kings 18:5). Sincere and devout, he was not a perfect man by any means, nor outstanding because of any brilliant gifts he possessed. This good king, however, is to be admired when one remembers his family background. Having such a wicked, apostate father as Ahaz, the wonder is that his son became the noble king he did. He had no pious training, but only a heritage of weakness in his moral fibre, for which God graciously made all fair allowance.

With Hezekiah's ascent to the throne at the age of twenty-five there began a period of religious revival in which he was encouraged by the noblest and most eloquent of the Hebrew prophets, Isaiah, who knew how to carry his religion into his politics.

I. Hezekiah was a man who prayed about the difficulties and dangers overtaking him. What faith and confidence in God he revealed when he spread Sennacherib's insolent letter before the Lord. Both Hezekiah and Isaiah defied mighty Assyria, God using one angel to slay one hundred and eighty-five thousand in the Assyrian camp.

The king knew how to pray about personal matters as well as military dangers. When smitten with a fatal illness, he turned his face to the wall and prayed. Isaiah, his friend and counselor, came to him with a message from God that he would not die but live. "I will add unto thy days fifteen years." Hezekiah asked with all his heart that he might live, and God continued his life.

But the question arises, why did Hezekiah desire the removal of his illness and the continuation of his life? What object did he have in mind? Was the king anxious to live in order to promote the glory of God, or was he actuated by some personal motive? It is apparent that Hezekiah was afraid of death and loved life in itself. Death was not the same to Hezekiah as it was to Paul, who had a desire to depart, seeing death was far better than life.

At the time of his sickness, Hezekiah had no son, and this fact possibly added to his desire to live. Three years after his recovery Manasseh was born, who became a curse upon the earth and an abomination in the sight of the Lord. Here, then, was one of the results of Hezekiah's answered prayer. It might have been better for Judah if Hezekiah had died without such an heir. Many prayers we offer are mistakes. God graciously grants our requests but "brings leanness to our souls" (Ps. 106:15). Perhaps Hezekiah's sin began in his unwillingness to go to heaven when God sent for him (II Kings 20:1-3).

II. Hezekiah's simple faith in God was the source and secret of his strength. He believed God ruled among the armies of heaven and of earth. His faith was the intuitive perception that God was near— a real Personality and not a mere tendency making for righteousness. The loss of faith is ultimately the loss of moral power. One of the main lessons of Hezekiah's life is, *Have faith in God*.

III. Hezekiah lost favor with God because of pride. After all the divine blessings showered upon him, he allowed his heart to be lifted up with pride. Vanity and self-sufficiency led the king astray. His heart became obsessed with his household treasures. He turned from God to goods. "Hezekiah rendered not again according to the benefit done unto him; for his heart was lifted up: therefore there was wrath upon him, and upon Judah and Jerusalem" (II Chron. 32:24, 25). Sin never ends with the person committing it.

The four crises Hezekiah faced were:

The crisis of choice, and he chose to forsake the idols of his father and purge the kingdom of idolatry (II Chron. 28:23, 25; II Kings 18:22).

The crisis of invasion (II Chron. 32:1-19). Prayer brought deliverance (II Chron. 32:20, 21).

The crisis of sickness. Obedience furnished the foundation of the king's prayer for healing (Isa. 38:1-5).

The crisis of prosperity. Alas, Hezekiah manifested pride when he displayed his treasures to the ungodly (Isa. 39).

2. *A son of Neariah* and a descendant of the royal house of Judah (I Chron. 3:23).

3. *An ancestor of the prophet Zephaniah* (Zeph. 1:1). Given in Common Version as Hizkiah.

4. *An exile,* descendant of Ater who returned from exile in Babylon (Ezra 2:16; Neh. 7:21).

HEZION [Hē′ zĭ on]—VISION. *The father of Tabrimon and grand-father of Benhadad,* king of Syria in Asa's time (I Kings 15:18). Perhaps the same as Rezon of I Kings 11:23.

HEZIR [Hē′ zûr]—RETURNING HOME or A SWINE.
1. *A descendant of Aaron* whose family grew and became leaders of the seventeenth monthly course in David's day (I Chron. 24:15).
2. *A chief of the people who sealed the covenant* (Neh. 10:20).

HEZRAI, HEZRO [Hĕz′ ra ī, Hĕz′ rō]—ENCLOSED or BEAUTIFUL. *A Carmelite,* one of David's mighty men (II Sam. 23:35; I Chron. 11:37).

HEZRON, ESRON [Hĕz′ rŏn]—SHUT IN, BLOOMING or DART OF JOY.
1. *A son of Pharez or Perez* and grandson of Judah and founder of a tribal family (Gen. 46:12; Num. 26:6, 21; Ruth 4:18, 19; I Chron. 2:9; 4:1).
2. *A son of Reuben* and founder of the Hezronite family (Gen. 46:9; Ex. 6:14; Num. 26:6; I Chron. 5:3). Also name of a town called Hazor (Josh. 15:23).

HIDDAI [Hĭd′ da ī]—JOYFUL or MIGHTY. *A man from Gaash,* one of David's heroes (II Sam. 23:30).

HIEL [Hī′ el]—GOD LIVETH or THE LIFE OF GOD. *A native of Bethel* who rebuilt Jericho and who experienced the curse pronounced upon the rebuilding of it by Joshua (I Kings 16:34).

HILKIAH [Hĭl kī′ ah]—PORTION OF JEHOVAH or JEHOVAH IS PRO-TECTION.
1. *The father of Eliakim* who was over Hezekiah's household (II Kings 18:18, 26, 37; Isa. 22:20; 36:3, 22).
2. *High priest* in king Josiah's reign (II Kings 22:4–14; 23:4, 24).
3. *A descendant of Merari,* son of Levi (I Chron. 6:45).
4. *A son of Hosah,* descendant of Merari, and a gatekeeper at the Tabernacle (I Chron. 26:11).
5. *A priest* who stood with Ezra as he read the law to the people (Neh. 8:4; 11:11; 12:7, 21).
6. *A priest of Anathoth* and father of the prophet Jeremiah and contemporary of Gemariah (Jer. 1:1).

HILLEL [Hĭl′ lel]—PRAISED GREATLY. *Father of Abdon,* of the judges of Israel. He lived in Mount Ephraim (Judg. 12:13, 15).

HINNOM [Hĭn′ nom]—GRATIS. *A person of whom nothing is known* save that he had a son whose name is not given. The valley of Hinnom was the place where human sacrifice and filth were burned (Josh. 15:8; 18:16).

HIRAH [Hī′ rah]—DESTINATION or NOBILITY. *An Adullamite,* and friend of Judah, with whom he shared a partnership in the matter of flocks (Gen. 38:1, 12).

HIRAM [Hī′ ram]—CONSECRATION.
1. *The king of Tyre,* and friend of both David and Solomon (II Sam. 5:11; I Kings 5:1, 8; II Chron. 2:11, 13).
2. *A man of eminence* and the principal architect sent by king Hiram to Solomon (I Kings 7:13, 40, 45). Also called Huram.

HIZKIAH, HEZEKIAH [Hĭz kī′ ah,   Hĕz e kī′ ah]—JEHOVAH IS STRONG. *An ancestor of Zephaniah the prophet.* In the Hebrew the name is the same as Hizkijah and Hezekiah (Zeph. 1:1).

HIZKIJAH [Hĭz kī′ jah]—JEHOVAH IS STRONG. Perhaps Ater-hizkijah given in lists of returned exiles (Neh. 10:17).

HOBAB [Hō′ băb]—BELOVED, LOVER or FAVORED. *Either the father-in-law of Moses or the father-in-law's son.* In Numbers 10:29 he is called the son of Raguel or Reuel, who is also identified with Jethro (Num. 10:29; Judg. 4:11).

HOD [Hŏd]—GLORY or MAJESTY. *A son of Zophah,* a descendant of Asher (I Chron. 7:37).

HODAIAH [Hŏd a ī′ ah]—HONORER OF JEHOVAH. *The Hodaviah, son of Elioenai,* a descendant of the royal line of Judah from which Jesus sprang (I Chron. 3:24).

HODAVIAH [Hŏd a vī′ ah]—JEHOVAH IS HIS PRAISE.
1. *A chief of the half tribe of Manasseh,* east of Jordan (I Chron. 5:24).
2. *The son of Hasenuah,* a Benjamite (I Chron. 9:7).
3. *A Levite* and founder of the family of the Ben-hodaviah (Ezra 2:40). Called Hodevah in Nehemiah 7:43.

HODEVAH [Hō dĕ′ vah]—JEHOVAH IS HONOR. *A Levite family that* returned from captivity (Neh. 7:43).

HODIAH, HODIJAH [Hō dī′ ah, Hō dī′ jah]—SPLENDOR OF JEHOVAH.
1. *A Levite* of the time of Ezra and Nehemiah (Neh. 8:7; 9:5; 10:10, 13).
2. *A chief of the people under Nehemiah* (Neh. 10:18). Also name of wife of one Ezra, also called Jehudijah (I Chron. 4:19).

HOHAM [Hŏ′ ham]—JEHOVAH PROTECTS THE MULTITUDE. *An Amorite king of Hebron,* who entered into league with other kings against Joshua. One of the five kings captured in the cave of Makkedah and put to death (Josh. 10:3).

HOMAM, HEMAM [Hŏ′ mam, Hĕ′ mam]—RAGING or DESTROYER. *Son of Lotan* and grandson of Seir (I Chron. 1:39). See Genesis 36:22 for Hemam.

HOPHNI [Hŏph′ nī]—STRONG. *A son of Eli,* the high priest and judge who proved unworthy of his sacred offices (I Sam. 1:3; 2:34; 4:4, 11, 17). Hophni is always associated with his brother Phinehas. The two were partners in evil practices and brought a twice-pronounced curse upon their heads (I Sam. 2:34; 3). Both were slain at the battle of Aphek, and this coupled with the loss of the Ark, caused the death of Eli. Both sons disgraced their priestly office in a twofold way:
I. In claiming and appropriating more than their due of the sacrifices (I Sam. 2:13–17).
II. In their immoral actions in the Tabernacle (2:22; Amos 2:7, 8).

HORAM [Hŏ′ ram]—ELEVATED. *A king of Gezer,* defeated and slain by Joshua (Josh. 10:33).

HORI [Hŏ′ rī]—FREE or NOBLE.
1. *A son of Seir,* a Horite, and founder of the "Horites" (Gen. 36:22, 29, 30).
2. *A Simeonite* whose son Shaphat was one of the spies (Num. 13:5).

HOSAH [Hŏ′ sah]—FLEEING FOR REFUGE. *A Levite porter* selected by David to be one of the first doorkeepers to the Ark after its return (I Chron. 16: 38; 26:10, 11, 16). Also name of a city of the tribe of Asher (Josh. 19:29).

HOSEA, OSHEA, OSEE, HOSHEA—[Hō zĕ′ ă, Ō shĕ′ ă, Hō shĕ′ ă]—JEHOVAH IS HELP or SALVATION.
1. *The son of Beeri* and first of the so-called Minor Prophets (Hosea 1:1).

The Man with a Sorrowful Heart

Little is known of Hosea's history beyond what we find in his writings. He has been called the first prophet of Grace and Israel's earliest evangelist. He was a native of the Northern Kingdom, the iniquities and idolatries of which weighed heavily on his heart. He bore the same name as that of the last king of Israel (II Kings 15:30). In Jewish tradition, he is identified with Beerah of Reuben (I Chron. 5:6). Christian tradition, however, relates him to the Hosea of the tribe of Isaachar.

The home tragedy overtaking him earned him the title of "The

Prophet of a Sorrowful Heart." Through the wrongs he suffered he came to realize the sins committed by Israel against God, and the long history of unfaithfulness to Him. The accounts of Hosea's marriage, the birth of his children and his wife's unfaithfulness and restoration make sad reading. Hosea was called to express God's message and to manifest His character.

Gomer, his wife, was immoral; hence the word of the Lord came to him amid much personal anguish; his home life was destroyed. Society was corrupt and God's law spurned, and Hosea came to see in his own suffering a reflection of what the sorrow of God must be, when Israel proved utterly unfaithful.

Three children were born to Hosea and Gomer:

I.   Jezreel, recalling the deed of blood (II Kings 10), and by it a knell was rung in the ears of Jeroboam. The name of this child was an omen of coming judgment.

II.   Lo-ruhamah, meaning, "one who never knew a father's love." This expressive name pointed to a time when, no more pitied by Jehovah, Israel would be given over to her enemies.

III.   Lo-ammi, signifying "one not belonging to me." Israel had turned from a father's love and deserved not to belong to God. Thus this third child's name prophesied the driving out of the children of Israel from their land to exile.

Gomer, the erring wife, is received back (Hos. 3:1, 2), the price of her redemption being paid by Hosea. So the prophet was not only God's messenger of grace — he reflected God's character and foreshadowed ultimate redemption through the Messiah and Israel's reestablishment as a nation.

The four lessons we learn from the broken heart and the Book of Hosea have been fully expounded by Dr. Stuart Holden:

Anguish quickens apprehension.

Iniquity inspires moral indignation.

Suffering begets sympathy.

The divine character sanctifies human conduct.

2.   Joshua's earlier name — changed by Moses (Num. 13:8, 16). Deuteronomy 32:44 gives Hoshea.

3.   *The son of Azaziah* and prince of Ephraim in David's reign (I Chron. 27:20).

4.   *A son of Elah,* the last king of the Northern Kingdom (II Kings 15:30).

5.   *A chief under Nehemiah* who with others signed the covenant (Neh. 10:23).

Hosea is called Osee in the New Testament copy from the LXX.

HOSHAIAH [Hŏsh a ī' ah]—GOD HATH SAVED.

1.   *The man who led the princes of Judah* and walked behind the chorus at the dedication of the wall (Neh. 12:32).

2. *The father of Jezaniah* or Azariah, and a man of influence in Nebuchadnezzar's time (Jer. 42:1, 2).

HOSHAMA [Hŏsh' a mă]—JEHOVAH HATH HEARD. *A son of Jeconiah or Jehoiachin*, king of Judah (I Chron. 3:18).

HOTHAM, HOTHAN [Hŏ' tham, Hŏ' than]—SIGNET RING or DETERMINATION.
1. *A son of Heber* of the family of Beriah. An Asherite (I Chron. 7:32).
2. *An Aroerite*, whose two sons Shama and Jehiel were among David's heroes (I Chron. 11:44).

HOTHIR [Hŏ' thûr]—ABUNDANCE. *The thirteenth son of Heman*, David's seer and singer. A Kohathite (I Chron. 25:4, 28).

HOZAI— JEHOVAH IS SEEING. *The writer of the history of King Manasseh* (II Chron. 33:19 A.V.; also in footnote, R.V.).

HUL [Hŭl]—CIRCLE. *The second son of Aram* and grandson of Shem. A descendant of Noah (Gen. 10:23; I Chron. 1:17). Called son of Shem.

HUPHAM [Hŭ' pham]—PROTECTED or A COVERING. *A son of Benjamin* and founder of a tribal family known as the Huphamites (Num. 26:39). Name is given as Huppim in Genesis 46:21 and I Chronicles 7:12. Also expressed as Huram (I Chron. 8:5).

HUPPAH [Hŭp' pah]—A COVERING or PROTECTION. *A priest* of the thirteenth course in David's time. Either a son of Bela or of Ir or Iri, one of Bela's five sons (I Chron. 24:13). This name is given as Huppim in Genesis 46:21 and I Chronicles 7:12, 15.

HUR [Hûr]—NOBLE or SPLENDOR.
1. *The man who, with Aaron, held up the hands of Moses,* so that by the continual uplifting of the sacred staff Israel might prevail over Amalek. Jewish tradition has it that Hur was the husband of Miriam and the grandfather of Bezaleel (Ex. 17:10, 12; 24:14).
2. *A son of Caleb* the son of Hezron (Ex. 31:2; 35:30; I Chron. 2: 19, 20; II Chron. 1:5).
3. *The fourth of the five kings* of Midian slain with Balaam (Num. 31:8; Josh. 13:21).
4. *The father of one of Solomon's purveyors* in Mount Ephraim (I Kings 4:8).
5. *The father of Caleb* and eldest son of Ephratah (I Chron. 2: 50; 4:4).
6. *A son of Judah* (I Chron. 4:1).
7. *The father of Rephaiah,* who was ruler of half of Jerusalem and who assisted in the repair of the walls (Neh. 3:9).

HURAI [Hŭ' raī]—A LINEN WEAVER or NOBLE. *One of David's heroes* from the brooks of Gaash (I Chron. 11:32). Also called Hiddai (II Sam. 23:30).

HURAM [Hŭ' ram]—NOBLE or INGENIOUS.
1. *A Benjamite,* son of Bela (I Chron. 8:5).
2. *The king of Tyre,* called Hiram in II Samuel 5:11 and Huram in II Chronicles 2:3, 12.
3. *A Tyrian artificer* employed by Solomon (II Chron. 4:11, 16).

HURI [Hŭ' rī]—LINEN WEAVER. *The father of Abihail,* a Gadite (I Chron. 5:14).

HUSHAH [Hŭ' shah]—HASTE or PASSION. *A son of Ezer,* the son of Hur, a Judahite (I Chron. 4:4).

HUSHAI [Hŭ' shaī]—QUICK or HASTENING. *One of David's two leading men,* an Archite (II Sam. 15:32, 37; 16:16–18; 17:5–15; I Chron. 27:33). This native of Erech was the friend and counselor of David who overthrew the counsels of Ahithophel.

HUSHAM [Hŭ' sham]—HASTE or PASSION. *A king of Edom,* who succeeded Jobab. He came from the land of Teman (Gen. 36:34, 35; I Chron. 1:45, 46).

HUSHIM [Hŭ'shim]—OPULENT or HASTING.
1. *A son of Dan* (Gen. 46:23). Called Shusham in Numbers 26:42.
2. *The son of Aher,* a Benjamite (I Chron. 7:12). Also the name of one of the two wives of Shaharaim (I Chron. 8:8, 11).

HUZ [Hŭz]—FIRM. Also given as Uz, the *eldest son of Nahor and Milcah* (Genesis 22:21).

HYMENAEUS [Hȳ me nae' us]—NUPTIAL or FROM HYMEN, THE GOD OF MARRIAGE. *A professed Christian* who had fallen into heresies, who tried to shipwreck the faith of true believers and who was excommunicated by Paul (I Tim. 1:20; II Tim. 2:17).

I

IBHAR [Ĭb' här]—CHOOSER or GOD DOTH CHOOSE. *One of David's sons,* born at Jerusalem (II Sam. 5:15; I Chron. 3:6; 14:5).

IBNEIAH [Ĭb nē' iah]—JEHOVAH DOTH BUILD. *The Benjamite son of Jeroham* and head of his father's house in Jerusalem (I Chron. 9:8).

IBNIJAH [Ĭb nī' jah]—JEHOVAH IS BUILDER. *A Benjamite, father of Reuel,* whose family dwelt in Jerusalem (I Chron. 9:8).

IBRI [Ĭb'rī]—PASSER OVER or A HEBREW. *A son of Jaaziah,* a Merarite Levite in David's time (I Chron. 24:27).

IBSAM, JIBSAM [Ĭb'sam, Jĭb' sam]—FRAGRANT. *A man of Issachar,* of the family of Tola (I Chron. 7:2).

IBZAN [Ĭb' zăn]—SPLENDID or ACTIVE. *One of the minor judges* who succeeded Jephthah, and who judged Israel seven years and was buried at Bethlehem. He had thirty sons and thirty daughters whose marriages he arranged. His sixty children testified to his plurality of wives and his social importance. Jewish tradition identifies Ibzan as Boaz (Judg. 12:8, 10).

ICHABOD [Ĭ' cha bŏd]—THE GLORY IS NOT, WHERE IS THE GLORY or INGLORIOUS. *The posthumous son of Phinehas and grandson of Eli.* His name commemorated a tragic crisis in Israel's history, namely, the great slaughter of the people, including Hophni and Phinehas, and the capture of the Ark by the Philistines. Such terrible calamity resulted in Eli's death at ninety-eight. The wife of Phinehas was so shocked over the dread news that when her child was born she called him Ichabod saying, "The glory is departed from Israel: for the ark of God is taken" (I Sam. 4:21, 22).

IDBASH [Ĭd' băsh]—HONEY SWEET or CORPULENT. *One of the three sons of Abi-etam,* a man of Judah (I Chron. 4:3).

IDDO [Ĭd' dō]—AFFECTIONATE, FESTAL, FAVORITE or HIS POWER.
1. *Father of Ahinadab,* and one of Solomon's purveyors at Mahanaim (I Kings 4:14).
2. *A descendant of Gershom,* son of Levi (I Chron. 6:21). Called Adaiah, and ancestor of Asaph the seer (I Chron. 6:41).
3. *A son of Zechariah* and a chief in David's time of the half tribe of Manasseh east of Jordan (I Chron. 27:21).
4. *A seer* who denounced the wrath of God against Jeroboam, the son of Nebat, and who wrote a book of visions (II Chron. 9:29; 12:15; 13:22).
5. *Grandfather of the prophet Zechariah* (Ezra 5:1; 6:14; Zech 1:1).
6. *A priest* who returned from Babylon (Neh. 12:4, 16).
7. *The chief at Casiphia* through whom Ezra obtained help. He was a Nethinim (Ezra 8:17).
8. *A man who put away his foreign wife* (Ezra 10:43). Jadau is a corruption of Iddo.

IGAL [Ĭ'găl]—DELIVERER or HE WILL VINDICATE.

1. *Son of Joseph* of the tribe of Issachar, and one of the spies sent from Kadesh to search Canaan (Num. 13:7).

2. *The son of Nathan of Zobah*, and one of David's guard (II Sam. 23:36). Called Joel, the brother of Nathan, in I Chronicles 11:38, and identical with Igeal in I Chronicles 3:22.

IGDALIAH [Ĭg da lī' ah]—GREAT IS JEHOVAH or GREATNESS OF THE LORD. *"A man of God," father of Hanan,* who had a chamber in the Temple and is mentioned in connection with Jeremiah's interview with the Rechabites (Jer. 35:4).

IGEAL [Ĭğ' e ăl]—DELIVERER. *A son of Shemaiah* and descendant of king Jeconiah (I Chron. 3:22). Originally the same as Igal.

IKKESH [Ĭk' kĕsh]—PERVERSE or SUBTLE. *Father of Ira the Tekoite,* and one of David's heroes (II Sam. 23:26; I Chron. 11:28; 27:9).

ILAI [Ĭ' laī]—ELEVATED or SUPREME. *An Ahohite* and another of David's heroes (I Chron. 11:29). Called Zalmon in II Samuel 23:28.

IMLA, IMLAH [Ĭm' lă, Ĭm' lah]—GOD DOTH FILL, FULFILLING, or PLENTITUDE.—*The Father of Michaiah,* a prophet in the days of Ahab who, along with Jehoshaphat, consulted Imla before the Ramoth-gilead expedition (I Kings 22:8, 9; II Chron. 18:7, 8).

IMMER [Ĭm' mŭr)—TALKATIVE or PROMINENT.

1. *A descendant of Aaron* and head of a family of priests (I Chron. 9:12; Ezra 2:37; 10:20; Neh. 7:40; 11:13).

2. *A priest* of the sanctuary in David's time (I Chron. 24:14).

3. *One who returned from Babylon* without a genealogy (Ezra 2:59; Neh. 7:61). Perhaps the name of a place rather than that of a person.

4. *The father of Zadok* (Neh. 3:29).

5. *A priest in Jeremiah's time* (Jer. 20:1).

IMNA [Ĭm' nă]—GOD DOTH RESTRAIN or WITHDRAWING. *A son of Helem* and an Asherite chief (I Chron. 7:35).

IMNAH [Ĭm' nah]—PROSPERITY or HE ALLOTTETH.

1. *The eldest son of Asher* and founder of a tribal family (Num. 26:44; I Chron. 7:30). Name given as Jimnah or Jimna (Gen. 46:17).

2. *A Levite, father of Kore,* in Hezekiah's reign (II Chron. 31:14).

IMRAH [Ĭm' rah]—STUBBORN or HEIGHT OF JEHOVAH. *An Asherite, son of Zophah* (I Chron. 7:36).

IMRI [Ĭm′ rĭ]—PROJECTING or ELOQUENT.
1. *A Judahite, son of Bani* and descendant of Perez (I Chron. 9:4).
2. *Father of the Zaccur* who helped to rebuild the wall (Neh. 3:2).

IPHEDEIAH [Iph e dē′ iah]—JEHOVAH DOTH DELIVER or REDEMPTION OF THE LORD. *A Benjamite chief,* son of Shashak (I Chron. 8:25).

IR [Ûr]—WATCHER. *A Benjamite,* the father of Shuppim and Huppim (I Chron. 7:12). Perhaps same as Iri of I Chronicles 7:7.

IRA [Ĭ′ rä]—WATCHER, WATCHFUL or CITY WATCH.
1. *A Jairite, and priest* or chief minister to David (II Sam. 20:26).
2. *The Ithrite,* and one of David's guard (II Sam. 23:38).
3. *Son of Ikkesh,* a Tekoite and another of David's guard (I Chron. 11:28, 40; 27:9).

IRAD [Ĭ′ răd]—WILD ASS. *Son of Enoch* and grandson of Cain (Gen. 4:18).

IRAM [Ĭ′ ram]—WATCHFUL. *A chieftain of Edom* (Gen. 36:43; I Chron. 1:54).

IRI [Ĭ′rĭ]—JEHOVAH IS WATCHER. *A son of Bela,* son of Benjamin (I Chron. 7:7). See Ir.

IRIJAH [Ĭ rĭ′ jah]—GOD DOTH SEE, PROVIDE or FEAR OF THE LORD. *A captain of the guard in Jerusalem* who arrested Jeremiah on the charge of intending to desert to the Chaldeans (Jer. 37:13, 14).

IRNAHASH [Ûr nä′ hăsh]—SERPENT or MAGIC CITY. *A descendant of Chelub* from Judah through Caleb son of Hur (I Chron. 4:12). Some writers suggest this may be a city and not a person.

IRU—[Ĭ′ rōō]—WATCH. *Eldest son of the celebrated Caleb,* Joshua's companion (I Chron. 4:15). Correct name may be Ir.

ISAAC [Ĭ′ zaac] HE LAUGHETH or LAUGHING ONE. *The son of Abraham and Sarah,* who was born at Gerar when Abraham was one hundred years of age and Sarah was about ninety years old (Gen. 17:19, 21; 21:3–12; 22:2–9).

The Man Whose Birth Caused a Laugh

Isaac is one of the few cases in the Bible in which God selected a name for a child and announced it before he was born. In the Old Testament we have Isaac, Ishmael, Solomon, Josiah, Cyrus and Isaiah's son; in the New Testament, John the Baptist and Jesus.

Isaac's beautiful and suggestive name, "he laughed," commemorates the two laughings at the promise of God — the laughing of the father's joy and the laughing of Sarah's incredulity which soon passed into penitence and faith (Gen. 21:6). Isaac was the child of the covenant, "I will establish My covenant *with him.*" To three patriarchs in succession was this covenant specifically given: to *Abraham,* as he left Chaldea (Gen. 12:3); to *Isaac,* when in Canaan during the famine (Gen. 26:4); to *Jacob,* at Bethel (Gen. 28:14). Isaac, however, was the first to inherit the covenant, and to him God gave the whole inheritance of Abraham (Gen. 24:35).

We have no record of Isaac's early life apart from the fact that he was circumcised when eight days of age (Gen. 21:4). Doubtless as a lad he became God's child in heart and life, ever mindful of the covenant he was heir to. When, according to Josephus, Isaac was twenty-five years of age, he was taken from Beer-sheba to the land of Moriah, where, as the burnt offering, Abraham presented him to God. While we have Abraham's unquestioning faith in his submission to the divine command to offer up his only son, we must not forget Isaac's supreme confidence in his father and also his willing consent to become the victim (Gen. 22:12; 26:5; Heb. 11:17). Thus in Isaac we have a type of Him who *gave Himself* for our sins. From the day of his surrender to death, Isaac became a dedicated man. "The altar sanctified the gift."

When his mother Sarah died, Isaac was a man of thirty-six, and was deeply grieved over the death of his mother. Comfort was his when he took Rebekah as his wife to help fill the vacant place in his heart. To the credit of Isaac it must be said that he was the only one of the patriarchs who had but one wife. It is also perfectly clear from the ancient idyll, one of the most beautiful in all literature, that Isaac left the choice of his wife to God. When the caravan bearing Rebekah neared home, Isaac was in the fields *meditating* or "praying," as the margin expresses it (Gen. 24:63).

For many years Isaac and Rebekah were childless, but God heard Isaac's prayers and Rebekah gave birth to twins, Jacob and Esau. Isaac seems to have outlived his wife, and died at the age of 180 (Gen. 35:28). For some fifty years Isaac was almost blind, a sad and pitiful lot for God's chosen one.

The character of Isaac, beautiful though it was in many ways, yet carried a few blots. He followed his father, Abraham, in deceitfulness when he called his wife his sister, bringing upon himself the rebuke of Abimelech. He also loved "savoury food," which should have been alien to a man so calm and still, lord of his passion and himself. Then in the matter of Esau and the blessing, Isaac surely rebelled against the Lord's purpose.

Among the commendable features of his character, mention can be made of Isaac's submission (Gen. 22:6, 9); meditation (Gen. 24:63); instinctive trust in God (Gen. 22:7, 8); deep devotion (Gen. 24:67; 25:21); peaceableness (Gen. 26:20–22); prayerfulness (Gen. 26:25); faith (Heb. 11:16, 17). "The fear of Isaac" (Gen. 31:42, 53), means the God tremblingly adored by the patriarch.

ISAIAH, ESAIAS [Ī zā′ iah, Ī za′ ias]—JEHOVAH IS HELPER or SALVA-
TION IS OF THE LORD. The name of the greatest of the Assyrian group
of prophets is synonymous with Joshua or Jesus and symbolic of his
message. Little is known of this gospel prophet, often severe in tone.
He is described as the son of Amoz, not Amos the prophet (Isa. 1:1;
2:1; 6:1; 7:3; 13:1). Some scholars suggest that Amoz was the uncle of
Uzziah which, if true, would make Isaiah the king's cousin. Evidently
Isaiah was of good family and education.

The Man of Many Parts

Isaiah's home and the scene of his labors was Jerusalem. His wife
was a prophetess (Isa. 8:3) and bore the prophet two sons, whose names
were symbolic of those aspects of the nation's history which Isaiah
enforced in his prophecies:

Shear-jashub, meaning, "a remnant shall return" (Isa. 7:3).

Maher-shalal-hash-baz, implying, "Haste ye, speed to the spoil" (Isa.
8:1–4). Often names were given for signs and wonders in Israel.

Isaiah's original call to service is unrecorded, but in chapter six we
have his vision and commission. A prophet of Judah, Isaiah ministered during the reign of Uzziah, Jotham, Ahab and Hezekiah, kings
of Judah. He comes before us as a man of many parts — a man eminently gifted and called of God as the first and chief of Israel's prophets
and poets.

I.   The Writer. Isaiah wrote a history of the reign of Uzziah and
Ahaz (II Chron. 26:22; 32:32). No other Old Testament writer uses
so many beautiful and picturesque illustrations, epigrams and metaphors as Isaiah, who was also a poet of no mean order (Isa. 1:13; 5:18;
12:1–6; 13:3).

The book bearing his name is made up of sixty-six chapters, and
is a miniature Bible with its sixty-six books.

II.   The Statesman. Isaiah was an ardent patriot, loving God and
his nation. He was a bold, true statesman, seeking no court favor.
How strongly he denounced all foreign alliances, (Isa. 7:5; 37:22)!
It is Isaiah who gives us the earliest recorded vision of world-wide
peace (Isa. 2:1–4).

III.   The reformer. Like Noah, Isaiah was also a preacher of
righteousness, and exposed formalism as a bad substitute for spiritual
life and conduct (Isa. 36–39). Yet, like all the greatest contributors
to moral uplift, Isaiah, amid all his rebukes and denunciations of
evil, was truly optimistic.

IV.   The Prophet. In no uncertain language Isaiah foretold the
future of Israel and Judah, and the downfall of Gentile nations. Many
of his predictions in regard to ancient nations have been fulfilled.
Then Isaiah was *The Christ-Harbinger*, prophesying the coming of
the Messianic King and Suffering Saviour. Chapter fifty-three of his
prophecy drips with the ruby blood of the Redeemer. No wonder
Jerome described Isaiah as "The Evangelical Prophet."

V.   The Teacher. To perpetuate his message and influence, Isaiah formed a group of disciples to whose teaching and training he devoted himself when his public ministry seemed useless. He was not only a counselor of kings and princes, but an instructor of those who were eager for his vision. He was an orator without peer — Jerome likened him to Demosthenes. This trait must have made an impact upon those he sought to train.

VI. The Theologian. This dreamer and poet, architect and builder, prophet and statesman was also a theologian able to discourse upon the sovereignty and holiness of God with utmost clarity. What an artist with words Isaiah was! Every word from him stirs and strikes, as he expounds the lordship of Jehovah — the need of all men for cleansing — the forgiving grace of God. The prophet insisted upon reverence for God whose usual title he gave as "The Holy One of Israel." Sometimes stern in tone, he could also be tender and compassionate (Isa. 15:5; 16:9).

The time of his death is unknown. Legend has it that he was placed inside a hollow tree and sawn asunder at the command of Manasseh (Heb. 11:37).

ISCARIOT [Ĭs cặr′ Ĭ ot]—MAN OF KERIOTH or A MAN OF MURDER. *The designation of the traitor* is sometimes associated with *scortea*, a "leathern apron" which applied to Judas as the bearer of the bag, that is, "Judas with the apron." The Hebrew *ascara*, implies strangling (angina), given him after his death (Matt. 10:4; John 6:71 R.V.). See Judas.

ISHBAH [Ĭsh′ bah]—HE PRAISES or APPEASER. *Father of Eshtemoa*, a Judahite. It has been conjectured that he was the son of Mered by his Egyptian wife Bithiah (I Chron. 4:17).

ISHBAK [Ĭsh′ băk]—FREE, EMPTY or EXHAUSTED. *A Son of Abraham* by Keturah and founder of a tribal family in northern Arabia (Gen. 25:2; I Chron. 1:32).

ISHBI-BENOB [Ĭsh′ bĭ-bē′ nŏb]—DWELLER ON THE MOUNT or HE THAT PREDICTS. *A son of Rapha* and one of the four Philistines of the giant stock attacking David in battle, but slain by Abishai (II Sam. 21:16).

ISHBOSHETH [Ĭsh bŏ′ sheth]—A MAN OF SHAME. *One of Saul's younger sons* who was made king over Israel by Abner. He was originally called Eshbaal, "The Lord's man" but his name was changed after Saul's departure (II Sam. 2:8 with I Chron. 8:33; 9:39). Ishbosheth contested the throne of Israel with David for seven years. Ultimately he was deserted by Abner and murdered in his bed by two of his captains.

ISHI [Ĭ′ shī]—MY HELP or SAVING.

1. *A son of Appaim,* a descendant of Pharez son of Judah, and of the house of Jerahmeel (I Chron. 2:31).

2. *A descendant of Judah* through Caleb the spy (I Chron. 4:20).

3. *A Simeonite* whose tribe overcome the Amalekites (I Chron. 4:42).

4. *One of the heads of the half tribe of Manasseh* (I Chron. 5:24). Also the symbolic name given to God's people (Hos. 2:16).

ISHIAH, ISSHIAH, ISHIJAH [I shī′ ah, Is shī′ ah, I shī′ jah]— JEHOVAH EXISTS or FORGIVETH.

1. *The fifth son of Izrahiah,* and one of the tribal heads of Issachar in David's time (I Chron. 7:3).

2. *A descendant of Moses* (I Chron. 24:21).

3. *A descendant of Levi* (I Chron. 24:25).

4. *One of the Bene-Harim* who married a foreign wife (Ezra 10:31).

ISHMA [Ish′ mă′—DESOLATION, DISTINCTION or ELEVATED. *One of the sons of Etam* and a descendant of Caleb the son of Hur (I Chron. 4:3).

ISHMAEL [Ish′ ma el]—GOD HEARETH.

1. *The son of Abraham,* by Hagar, Sarah's Egyptian maid. Ishmael was born when Abraham was eighty-six years of age, and was circumcised when he was thirteen years of age, along with his father and his servants. He received the divine promise that he would beget twelve princes and become a great nation. He died at the age of 137 (Gen. 16:11–16; 17:18–26; 25:9–17; 28:9; 36:3). Ishmael was the founder of the tribal family called Ishmaelites, sometimes referred to as Midianites (Gen. 37:25–28).

The Man Who Became an Outcast

Ishmael, who was some fourteen years older than Isaac, was not his father's heir and did not share his father's property. Abraham was tenderly attached to Ishmael (Gen. 17:18), and the casting out of the boy and his mother by Sarah was a great grief to Abraham. Such a hard transaction was necessary to keep the inheritance unbroken for Isaac's possession. "To thee will I give it" (Gal. 3:16; 4:30). Ishmael's name is a monument of God's goodness in answering prayer. "God shall hear." What did He hear? He heard the moaning of Hagar's broken heart. God said concerning Ishmael: "I will make him a great nation" (Gen. 21:18).

The names of Ishmael's twelve sons have been preserved but there is no record of any good they achieved (Gen. 25:13–16).

Paul tells us that the record of Hagar and Ishmael is an allegory (Gal. 4:24). Hagar and Sarah represent two covenants — Jewish and Christian. Hagar represents the law, and Ishmael, because he was born of the bond woman, typifies those who are under the law. Isaac, because of his super-natural birth, represents those born anew by the Spirit of God.

The casting out of Ishmael has been productive of bitter fruit, surviving in the religion of Mohammed. The wild hearts beat on in the bosoms of those who form the Arab world. Little did Sarah know, when she persuaded Abraham to take Hagar that she was originating a rivalry which has run in the keenest strife through the ages, and which oceans of blood have not stopped.

The Moslem Arabs claim descent from Ishmael. Ishmael's mother and wife were Egyptian, which differentiates them from pure Hebrew. Arabian tribes springing from Ishmael are scattered throughout the Arabian peninsula. When Ishmael received his name, the Lord said that he would be "a wild man," or "a wild-ass man" as the Hebrew expresses it.

2. *An ancestor of Zebadiah* who was one of Jehoshaphat's judicial officers (II Chron. 19:11).

3. *A Son of Azer* and a descendant of Saul through Jonathan (I Chron. 8:38; 9:44).

4. *A son of Jehohanan* and one of the military officers associated with Jehoiada in the revolution to raise Joash to the throne (II Chron. 23:1).

5. *A son of Pashbur* and one of the priests persuaded by Ezra to put away his foreign wife (Ezra 10:22).

6. *A son of Nethaniah,* a member of the royal house of David who took part in the murder of Gedaliah. His vile conduct and character are fully described by Jeremiah (40:8–16; 41).

ISHMAIAH, ISMAIAH [Ish ma ī ' ah, Is ma ī' ah]—JEHOVAH HEARETH.

1. *Son of Obadiah* and head of the Zebulunites in David's reign (I Chron. 27:19).

2. *A Gibeonite* who joined David at Ziklag (I Chron. 12:4).

ISHMERAI [Ish' me raī]—GOD KEEPETH. *Son of Elpaal* and a descendant of Benjamin and chief of his tribe (I Chron. 8:18).

ISHOD [I' shŏd]—MAN OF HONOR or MAN OF SPLENDOR. *Son of Hammoleketh,* of the tribe of Manasseh, and because of his near relationship to Gilead, an influential person (I Chron. 7:18). Proper name is Ish-dod.

ISHPAH, ISPAH [Is 'pah]—BALD. *Son of Beriah,* a Benjamite (I Chron. 8:16).

ISHPAN [Ish' păn]—FIRM or STRONG. *A son of Shashak,* a chief Benjamite (I Chron. 8:22).

ISHUAH, ISUAH [Ish' u ah, Is' u ah]—EQUAL or SELF-SATISFIED. *The second son of Asher*, who perhaps died childless, accounting for no list of heirs (Gen. 46:17; I Chron. 7:30). Called Isuah in I Chronicles 7:30.

ISHUI, ISHUAI, ISUI, JESUI, ISHVI [Ish' u i, Ish' u ai, Is' u i, Jes' u i]—EQUALITY.

1. *The third son of Asher*, and founder of the tribal family of the Jesuites (Gen. 46:17; Num. 26:44; I Chron. 7:30).

2. *The second son of Saul* by his wife Ahinoam (I Sam. 14:49).

ISLIAH, JEZLIAH [Jez li' ah]—DELIVERANCE. *A Benjamite*, son of Elpaal and descended from Shaharaim (I Chron. 8:18).

ISMACHIAH [Is ma chi ah]—JEHOVAH SUPPORTETH. *An overseer* connected with the Temple during Hezekiah's reign (II Chron. 31:13).

ISMAIAH [Is ma i' ah]—JEHOVAH HEARS. *A Gibeonite warrior* who was over David's thirty valiant men (I Chron. 12:4).

ISPAH [Is' pah]—STRONG or HE WILL BE EMINENT. *A son of Beriah*, the Benjamite (I Chron. 8:16).

ISRAEL [Is' ra el]—HE STRIVETH WITH GOD or RULING WITH GOD. *The new name given to Jacob* at Jabbok (Gen. 32:28). The name also stands for the whole body of Jacob's descendants (Gen. 34:7; John 1:47). See Jacob.

ISSACHAR [Is' sa kar]—THERE IS HERE or REWARD.

1. *The ninth son of Jacob* and the fifth by Leah. Of Issachar as an individual not a word is recorded after his birth (Gen. 30:18; 49:14, 15; Deut. 33:18,19).

The Man Who Couched Down

The birth of Issachar was regarded by his mother as a kind of payment from the hand of God, "God hath given me my hire," said Leah, "because I have given my maiden to my husband: and she called his name Issachar" (that is, hire). In Jacob's blessing to Issachar, he is described as a "strong ass couching down between two burdens," or "between the sheep-folds." Two things are here mentioned as a *pair*, meaning they belong to each other; they are on either hand of Issachar, as necessary accompaniments to each other and to him. Between them his lot is cast.

When Israel was at war against Jabin, king of Canaan (Judg. 4), Reuben was at ease among the sheepfolds (Judg. 5:16), but the princes of Issachar fought valiantly, jeopardizing their lives unto death (Judg. 5:18). Then it is said that the children of Issachar had an understanding of the times and knew what Israel ought to do.

The strong-boned ass used with the cart, because of its capacity for bearing heavy burdens, was the apt figure used by Jacob to represent Issachar's great strength, a strength revealed on the field of battle. The love of ease, however, made the people of Issachar unwilling to use their strength at all times in the interests of their country. They *couched down* in luxury and the restfulness of a rural life. The tragedy overtaking many is their *couching down* when they ought to be rising up. Their prosperity induces indolence, and like the rich fool in the parable, they take their ease (Luke 12:19). The voice from heaven still cries, "Woe to them that are at ease in Zion" (Amos 6:1).

2. *A Levite doorkeeper* of the Tabernacle in David's time (I Chron. 26:5).

ITHAI [Ith' a ī]—BEING or EXISTING. *One of David's mighty men* (I Chron. 11:31). Called Ittai in II Samuel 23:29.

ITHAMAR [Ith' a mär]—PALM-COAST or PALM TREE. *The fourth and youngest son of Aaron* and Elisheba (Ex. 6:23; I Chron. 6:3; 24:1). His consecration, along with Aaron's other sons is noted in Exodus twenty-eight. Other historical facts regarding Ithamar are:
He was forbidden to mourn for Nadab and Abihu (Lev. 10:6).
He was forbidden to leave the tent of meeting (Lev. 10:7).
He was entrusted by Moses with priestly duties (Lev. 10:12).
He was rebuked by Moses for neglect (Lev. 10:16).
He was set over the Gershonites and Merarites in sanctuary service (Ex. 38:21; Num. 4:21–23; 7:7).
He was an ancestor of Eli (I Kings 2:27; I Chron. 24:3).
His family, in David's time, was only half the size of Eleazar's (I Chron. 24:4).
His family is represented among the returned exiles (Ezra 8:2).

ITHIEL [Ith' ĭ el]—GOD IS or GOD IS WITH ME.
1. *A Benjamite*, the son of Jesaiah (Neh. 11:7).
2. *One of the two persons to whom Agar addressed* his discourse (Prov. 30:1. See R. V. margin).

ITHMAH [Ith' mah]—PURITY or BEREAVEMENT. *A Moabite*, and one of David's thirty heroes (I Chron. 11:46).

ITHRA [Ith' rä]—EXCELLENCE. *The father of Absalom's captain, Amasa*, and husband of Abigail (II Sam. 17:25).

ITHRAN [Ith' ran]—EXCELLENT or ABUNDANCE.
1. *A Horite*, son of Dishon or Dishan (Gen. 36:26; I Chron. 1:41).
2. *An Asherite*, son of Zophah (I Chron. 7:37) and who is thought to be identical with Jether (I Chron. 7:38).

ITHREAM [Ith' re ăm]—REMNANT or ABUNDANCE OF THE PEOPLE. *The sixth son of David*, born at Hebron. His mother was Eglah (II Sam. 3:5; I Chron. 3:3). Eglah was Michal and died giving birth to Ithream.

ITTAI [It 'ta ī]—PLOWMAN or LIVING.

1. *The Gittite leader* who, with six hundred Philistines, attached himself to David at the outbreak of Absalom's rebellion. This inhabitant of Gath was determined to follow David in all his trials. How admirable was the affirmation of his loyalty to the fugitive king: "As the Lord liveth, and as my lord the king liveth, surely in what place my lord the king shall be, whether in death or life, even there also will thy servant be" (II Sam. 15:21). Although a stranger and not of Israel, Ittai was more faithful than many who were Israelites by birth. His fidelity brought him a position of great trust (II Sam. 18:2).

2. *A Benjamite*, son of Ribai, who was one of David's heroes (II Sam. 23:29). He is called Ithai in I Chronicles 11:31.

IZHAR, IZEHAR [Iz' här, Iz' e här]—BRIGHT ONE or OLIVE OIL. *Son of Kohath,* son of Levi, and founder of a tribal family (Ex. 6:18, 21; Num. 3:19, 27). Also known as Zohar.

IZRAHIAH [Iz ra hī' ah]—JEHOVAH IS APPEARING or DOTH ARISE. *Son of Uzzi* and a grandson of Tola son of Issachar (I Chron. 7:3). See Jezrahiah.

IZRI [Iz' rī]—CREATIVE or FORMER. *A Levite son* of Jeduthun and chief of one of the Temple choirs (I Chron. 25:11). Perhaps the same person called Zeri in I Chronicles 25:3.

IZZIAH, JEZIAH [Jē zī' ah]—JEHOVAH EXALTETH. *A son of Parosh* who had married a foreign wife (Ezra 10:25).

J

When it comes to Bible names, the J's seem to have the longest list. There are over four hundred males listed under this letter; hence this section will be the longest in this study.

JAAKAN, JAKAN, AKAN [Jā' a kăn, Jā' kan, Ā' kăn]—INTELLIGENT. *A descendant of the Horites* of Mount Seir (Deut. 10:6; I Chron. 1:42). In Genesis 36:27 he is called Akan, a son of Ezer, son of Seir.

JAAKOBAH [Jā ăk' o bah]—TO JACOB or SUPPLANTING. *A Simeonite prince* and third son of Jacob (I Chron. 4:36).

JAALA, JAALAH [Jā ă' lă, Jā ă' lah]—DOE or ELEVATION. *A servant of Solomon* and founder of a tribal family. (Ezra 2:56; Neh. 7:58).

JAALAM [Jā ă' lam]—HE WILL BE HID. *A son of Esau by Aholibamah*, daughter of Anah (Gen. 36:5, 14, 18).

JAANAI, JANAI [Jā ă' naī]—JEHOVAH ANSWERS. *A Gadite chief* who dwelt in Bashan (I Chron. 5:12).

JAARE-OREGIM [Jā är e-Ŏr' e ğĭm]—FORESTERS or TAPESTRY OF THE WEAVERS. *The father of Elhanan,* one of David's heroes who killed the brother of the giant, Goliath (II Sam. 21:19). In I Chronicles 20:5 he is called Jair. Young says that Oregim, meaning "weavers," ought not to be a part of the name.

JAARESHIAH, JARESIAH [Jăr e sī' ah]—GOD DOTH NOURISH or PLANT. *A Benjamite, son of Jeroham* (I Chron. 8:27).

JAASAU, JAASU, JASSAI [Jā' a sau]—JEHOVAH MAKETH. *A son of Bani* induced by Ezra to put away his foreign wife (Ezra 10:37).

JAASIEL, JASIEL [Jā a' sĭ el, Jā' sĭ el]—GOD IS MAKER.
1. *One of David's mighty men,* and a Mesobaite (I Chron. 11:47).
2. *A son of Abner,* Saul's cousin (I Chron. 27:21).

JAAZANIAH [Jā ăz a nī' ah]—JEHOVAH DOTH HEARKEN.
1. *A son of a Maachathite* and a Jewish captain who swore allegiance to Gedaliah (II Kings 25:23). See Jezaniah (Jer. 40:8).
2. *A chief Rechabite,* son of a certain Jeremiah — not the prophet of that name (Jer. 35:3).
3. *A son of Shaphan,* a visionary exciting to idolatry in Ezekiel's time (Ezek 8:11).
4. *A son of Azur,* a wicked prince of Judah seen in vision by Ezekiel (Ezek. 11:1). The prophet prophesied against his counsels.

JAAZIAH [Jā a zī' ah]—GOD CONSOLETH or DETERMINES. *A son of Merari,* a Levite registered as head of his father's house in Solomon's time. He called his son Beno (I Chron. 24:26, 27).

JAAZIEL [Jā ă' zĭ el]—GOD IS DETERMINING or CONSOLING. *A Levite of the second rank* skilled in the use of the psaltery. He also had regular duty in the tent in Jerusalem (I Chron. 15:18). Called Aziel in I Chronicles 15:20.

JABAL [Jā' bal]—A RIVER, MOVING or WHICH GLIDES AWAY. *Son of the Canaanite*, Lamech, by his wife Adah. He became the father of those dwelling in tents and possessing cattle (Gen. 4:20).

JABESH [Jā' besh]—A DRY PLACE. *The father of king Shallum* who assassinated king Zechariah in order to reign in his stead (II Kings 15:10–14). Also the abbreviated name of Jabesh-gilead (I Sam. 11:1, 9).

JABEZ [Jā' bĕz]—HE MAKES SORROW or HEIGHT. *A man of Judah* named Jabez by his mother because she bore him in sorrow. He was noted for his honorable character and in his vow there is a play upon the meaning of his name (I Chron. 4:9, 10).

The Man Who Wanted a Blessing

The somewhat dreary genealogy of Judah in the opening chapters of Chronicles is enlivened by the heartfelt prayer of Jabez. Dr. Donald Fraser's beautiful comment on the passage is worthy of note:

> If the names are as rows of hard stones that fatigue us when we walk on them, all the more precious this fragrant shrub, growing among them, and casting a sweet scent around. For some cause untold, a mother bare her son with unusual grief and called him Jabez—Sorrowful; but it was God's good pleasure to turn this Benoni into a Benjamin, the Son of Sorrow into the Son of the Right Hand; and the sad-hearted mother's fear was not fulfilled, for Jabez proved more honorable than his brethren. If we inquire the reason, it was because he prayed.

He asked much and obtained much. The Lord did grant things for him, whereof, surely, Sorrowful was glad.

Jabez is also the name of a city in Judah where a family of scribes dwelt (I Chron. 2:55).

JABIN [Jā' bin]—GOD DISCERNETH or INTELLIGENT.
1. *A Canaanite*, king of Hazor in Galilee, defeated by Joshua near the Waters of Merom (Josh. 11:1–14).
2. *Another king of Canaan* who reigned at Hazor and oppressed Israel for twenty years. His army was defeated by Deborah and Barak. Probably a descendant of the first Hazor (Judg. 4; Ps. 83:9).

JACHAN, JACAN [Jā' chan]—AFFLICTING or TROUBLOUS. *A Gadite chief*, head of a father's house (I Chron. 5:13).

JACHIN [Jā' chin]—HE DOTH ESTABLISH or FOUNDING.
1. *The fourth son of Simeon* and founder of a tribal family (Gen. 46:10; Ex. 6:15; Num. 26:12). Called Jarib in I Chronicles 4:24.
2. *A priest in Jerusalem* after the captivity (I Chron. 9:10; Neh. 11:10.)
3. *A head of one of the families of the sons of Aaron* associated with the courses of the sacerdotal body (I Chron. 24:17).

Jachin is also the name of the right pillar in Solomon's temple (1 Kings 7:21; II Chron. 3:17).

JACOB [Jā' cob]—HE THAT SUPPLANTETH or FOLLOWETH AFTER.

1. *The second son of Isaac and Rebekah,* and a twin brother of Esau. Jacob appeared a short time after Esau and is therefore called the younger brother. Isaac was sixty years old when Jacob and Esau were born.

The Man of Two Natures

Jacob is an outstanding illustration of the presence and conflict of the two natures within a believer. Similar to Dr. Jekyll and Mr. Hyde of Robert Louis Stevenson's story, Jacob is good and bad; he rises and falls, yet in spite of his failures was a chosen instrument.

Jacob's character then, is full of interest and difficulty because of its weakness and strength. His is not a life to be described by a single word as, for example, the *faith* of Abraham or the *purity* of Joseph. Jacob seemed to have a many-sided life. He was a man of *guile*, yet a man of *prayer*. Inconsistencies are everywhere. His life began with a prophetic revelation of God to his mother, but Jacob's early years were a singular mixture of good and bad—the bad being very bad.

I. Jacob was the victim of his mother's partiality. "Rebekah loved Jacob" (Gen. 25:28). This fault must be kept in mind as we judge his character.

II. Jacob was selfish. When his brother came in from the fields faint with hunger, Jacob would not give him food without bargaining over it.

III. Jacob was naturally crafty and deceitful. He violated his conscience when he allowed his mother to draw him away from the path of honor and integrity. He practiced deception upon his blind father with the covering of kid skins. Then he told a deliberate lie in order to obtain a spiritual blessing. He further sinned upon most sacred ground, when he blasphemously used the name of the Lord to further his evil plans.

The thoroughness with which he carried out his mother's plan is one of the worst features in the life of this misguided son. "Had it been me," says Martin Luther, "I would have dropped the dish." It would have been better for Jacob had he dropped that dish of venison. But his proficiency in evil doing is to be despised.

In the life of this sharp trader who mended his ways, for there were two remarkable spiritual experiences in his life—at Bethel and Peniel —the preacher might find the following points suggestive: Jacob cheated (Gen. 25:29–34); deceived (Gen. 27:1–29); was compelled to flee (Gen 27:43; 28:1–5); was brought on to a higher level (Gen 28:10–22); had a romance spoiled, and was paid back in his own coin of deception (Gen. 29:15–30); was affectionate (Gen. 29:18); was industrious (Gen. 31:40); was prayerful (Gen. 32:9–12, 24–30); received a divine call to the promised land (Gen. 31); was disciplined by God through affliction (Gen. 37:28; 42:36); was a man of faith (Heb. 11:21); was blessed with sons who became the foundation of a nation. The Hebrew nation is spoken of as "the sons of Jacob" and "the children of Israel" (Gen. 48; 49; Num. 24:19).

2. *The father of Joseph,* the husband of Mary (Matt. 1:15, 16).

JADA [Jă′ dă]—WISE or KNOWING. *A son of Onam,* and grandson of Jerahmeel (I Chron. 2:28, 32).

JADAU [Jā dă′ u]—FAVORITE or FRIEND. *One of the family of Nebo* who had married a foreign wife. The correct name is Jaddai (Ezra 10:43).

JADDUA [Jăd dū′ ă]—VERY KNOWING or KNOWN.
1. *One of the Levites* who with Nehemiah sealed the covenant (Neh. 10:21).
2. *A son of Jonathan,* descendant of Jeshua the high priest, who returned from exile with Zerubbabel (Neh. 12:11, 22).

JADON [Jā′ dŏn]—HE THAT RULETH or ABIDETH. *A Meronothite* who helped in the repair of the wall of Jerusalem (Neh. 3:7). Josephus says that Jadon was the name of the man of God sent from Judah to Jeroboam (I Kings 13).

JAHATH [Jā′ hăth]—REVIVAL or GRASPING.
1. *A grandson of Judah* descended through Shobal (I Chron. 4:2).
2. *A son of Libni,* a Levite of the family of Gershom (I Chron. 6:20, 43).
3. *A son of Shimei,* a Levite of the family of Gershom (I Chron. 23:10, 11).
4. *A descendant of Kohath,* a son of Levi (I Chron. 24:22).
5. *A Merarite Levite,* an overseer of workmen engaged in the repair of the Temple in Josiah's reign (II Chron. 34:12).

JAHAZIAH [Jā hă zī′ ah]—JEHOVAH REVEALS. *One who was employed to enumerate* those who had married foreign wives during the exile (Ezra 10:15).

JAHAZIEL [Jā hă′ zĭ el]—GOD SEETH or REVEALS.
1. *A Benjamite* who joined David at Ziklag (I Chron. 12:4).
2. *A priest in David's reign* employed to sound the trumpet (I Chron. 16:6).
3. *A son of Hebron* the Kohathite (I Chron. 23:19).
4. *An Asaphite Levite* who encouraged Jehoshaphat and his army against the invading hosts of Moab (II Chron. 20:14).
5. *The ancestor of a family of exiles* who returned with Ezra from Babylon (Ezra 8:5).

JAHDAI [Jäh' da ī]—GUIDE or HE DIRECTETH. *A member of the family of Caleb* the spy (I Chron. 2:47).

JAHDIEL [Jäh' dĭ el]—UNION OF GOD or GOD MAKETH GLAD. *A leading man in the half tribe of Manasseh,* east of Jordan (I Chron. 5:24).

JAHDO [Jäh' dō]—UNION. *A Gadite,* son of Buz, and father of Jeshishai (I Chron. 5:14).

JAHLEEL [Jäh' lĕ el]—GOD WAITS or GOD DOTH GRIEVOUSLY AFFLICT. *The third son of Zebulun* and founder of a tribal family (Gen. 46:14; Num. 26:26).

JAHMAI [Jäh' ma ī]—JEHOVAH PROTECTS or LUSTY. *A son of Tola,* son of Issachar, Jacob's ninth son (I Chron. 7:2).

JAHZEEL, JAHZIEL [Jäh' zĕ el, Jäh' zĭ el]—GOD APPORTIONS or DISTRIBUTETH. *The first-born of Naphtali* the sixth son of Jacob, and his second by Bilhah. Founder of a tribal family (Gen. 46:24; Num. 26:48; I Chron. 7:13).

JAHZEIAH, JAHAZIAH [Jā hä zī' ah]—JEHOVAH SEETH. *A son of Tikvah* who opposed the proposition that the Jews should put away their foreign wives they married in captivity (Ezra 10:15; R.V. margin).

JAHZERAH [Jäh' ze rah]—JEHOVAH PROTECTS or MAY HE LEAD BACK. *A priest of the family of Immer* (I Chron. 9:12). Called Ahasai in Nehemiah 11:13.

JAIR [Jā' ur] JEHOVAH ENLIGHTENS, AROUSETH or WHO DIFFUSES LIGHT.
1. *A son of Segub* and grandson of Hezron, and reckoned with the tribe of Manasseh (Numbers 32:41; Deut. 3:14; I Chron. 2:22). Founder of a tribal family (II Sam. 20:26).
2. *A Gileadite* who judged Israel for twenty-three years, succeeding Tola in office. He may have been related to No. 1 (Judg. 10:3–5).
3. *A Benjamite* whose son, Mordecai, was Esther's cousin (Esther 2:5).
4. *The father of Elhanan,* who slew Lahmi the brother of the giant, Goliath (I Chron. 20:5). He is called Jaare-oregim in II Samuel 21:19.

JAIRUS [Jā ī' rus]—HE WILL ENLIGHTEN or DIFFUSE LIGHT. *A ruler of the synagogue* whose daughter Jesus raised from the dead (Mark 5:22; Luke 8:41).

JAKEH [Jā' keh]—PIOUS or HEARKENING. *The father of Agur,* the author of Proverbs thirty (Prov. 30:1; see R.V. margin).

JAKIM [Jā' kim]—A SETTER UP or HE RAISES UP.
1. *A son of Shimhi,* a Benjamite (I Chron. 8:19).
2. *A descendant of Aaron* and head of a family of Aaronites responsible for the twelfth of twenty-four courses of priests (I Chron. 24:12).

JALAM, JAALAM [Jā a' lām]—HIDDEN. *Chieftain of Edom.* Son of Esau by his wife Aholibamah (Gen. 36:5, 18; I Chron. 1:35).

JALON [Jā' lon]—OBSTINATE or JEHOVAH ABIDES. *A son of Ezra* registered with the tribe of Judah, a Calebite (I Chron. 4:17).

JAMBRES [Jăm' brēz]—OPPOSER or THE SEA WITH POVERTY. *One of the two Egyptian magicians* at the court of Pharaoh who sought to counteract the work of Moses (II Tim. 3:8). Mentioned along with Jannes.

JAMES [Jāmez]—SUPPLANTER.
1. *The son of Zebedee,* and the elder brother of John, and one of the Twelve (Matt. 4:21; 10:2; 17:1; Mark 1:19, 29; 3:17; 5:37; 9:2; 10:35; 41; 13:3; 14:33; Luke 5:10; 6:14; 8:51; 9:28, 54; Acts 1:13; 12:2). From the foregoing references several facts emerge:
James' father Zebedee, was a Galilean fisherman and prosperous, since he employed servants to assist in the management of his boats.
Zebedee had a house in Jerusalem and was known as a friend of the High Priest, Caiaphas, and his household. This would mark Him as a man of social position.
His mother's name was Salome, whom tradition says was a sister of the Virgin Mary, which may help to throw light upon the relation of her sons to the Master. This would also make James a cousin to Jesus after the flesh.
James worked in partnership with his father and brothers and was busy with his boats and nets when the call of Christ reached him.
His name is coupled with his brother John in the lists of the apostles, which could mean that when they were sent forth two by two, James and John would be paired. Evidently they were men of like spirit and disposition and received from Jesus the title "Sons of Thunder."
He was on terms of special intimacy with Christ, although he never attained the distinction of his brother John.
His life came to an untimely end when he was martyred by Herod Agrippa. The cup and the baptism of pain and death were his. Seventeen years passed between his call to service and his death. He was the second of the martyrs and the first of the apostles to give his life for Christ.
We have no word from his pen nor word he spoke unless Acts 4:24–30 be an exception, but James was content to be a disciple. He never sought fame, power, a great name. He had no ambition to be first.

2. *The son of Alphaeus* (Matt. 10:3; Mark 3:18; Luke 6:15; Acts 1:13). We know little of this James apart from his own name and his father's name, coming to us under the double form of Alphaeus and Clopas (John 19:25 R. V.). Evidently he did nothing that needed any record. We do know that this son of Alphaeus was called *the Little* (not *the Less*). Perhaps he was short of stature and to distinguish him from others of the same name he was known as "James the Little."

His mother was one of the devoted women who stood by the cross and visited the tomb.

He had a brother Joses, who was also a believer (Mark 15:40; 16:1; John 19:25).

Tradition says that he had been a tax-gatherer. It may be his father Alphaeus was the same Alphaeus who was the father of Levi the tax-gatherer, who became Matthew the Apostle.

3. *The Lord's brother* (Matt. 13:55; Mark 6:3; Acts 12:17; 15:13; 21:18; I Cor. 15:7; Gal. 1:19; 2:9, 12; Jas. 1:1). Acute controversy has raged around whether this James was an actual brother of Christ and also one of the Twelve.

The Man with Camel's Knees

Because of his relationship to Christ we deem it necessary to devote a little more attention to this honorable James. How exactly was he related to the Lord? There are some writers who affirm that there are only two persons by the name of James in the New Testament and that the one we are presently considering was the son of Alphaeus and Mary the sister of our Lord's mother, that is, the James under No. 2. Various explanations have been given of this third James.

He was a child of Joseph by a former marriage. Those like the Roman Catholics, who argue for the perpetual virginity of Mary, are against our Lord having any natural relatives apart from His mother.

The word "brother" or "kinsman" is used loosely, and means "cousin," according to Jewish usage. If he was a son of the virgin Mary's sister, then he would be our Lord's cousin, or "cousin-brother," as the Indians express it.

He, being the natural son of Joseph and Mary after their marriage, was actually our Lord's half-brother. The language of the passages cited under this James indicates that he had a relationship with Christ *within* rather than *without* the immediate family of Joseph and Mary. In the remonstration with Christ concerning His preaching, the whole circumstance points to James as being one of Mary's sons (Matt. 12:46–50). The facts are these:

I. He is spoken of as being among the sisters and brothers of Christ (Matt. 13:55, 56; John 2:12; 7:3, 10).

II. He was not a believer during our Lord's life. Along with the other children of Joseph and Mary, James did not accept the Messiahship of Jesus (Matt. 13:57; Luke 7:20, 21; John 7:5). There can be no doubt, however, that he did not remain unmoved by the goodness, unselfishness and example of Christ. Living with Him for almost thirty years must have left its impact upon James.

III. He was a witness of Christ's resurrection (I Cor. 15:7). It would seem as if James was won to faith by a special manifestation of the risen Lord. *Seen of James!* Paul would only know of one "James," the one often alluded to in the Acts of the Apostles. The result of that glorious sight and conversation transformed James into a disciple and a believer. It is after this experience that we find "the brethren of the Lord" joined with "the apostles" and "the women" assembled together in the upper chamber (Acts 1:14).

IV. He became a pillar of the Church at Jerusalem, rising to eminence (Acts 12:17; 15:4–34; 21:18, 19; Gal. 2:1–10).

V. He became known for his piety and was named "James the Just." Tradition has it that he was a Nazarite from his mother's womb, abstaining from strong drink and animal food and wearing linen. We are told of his strict adherence to the law (Acts 21:17–26; Gal. 2:12).

VI. He was the writer of the epistle bearing his name, which has always been attributed to "James the Just." But such was his character that he styled himself not as the *brother,* but only the *servant* or "slave" of the Lord Jesus Christ. His epistle gives us an admirable summary of practical duties incumbent upon all believers.

VII. He was a man who believed in the power of prayer, as evidenced by the space he devotes to it in his epistle. Because of his habit of always kneeling in intercession for the saints, his knees became calloused like a camel's; thus he became known as "The Man with Camel's Knees."

VIII. He was cruelly martyred by the Scribes and Pharisees, who cast him from the pinnacle of the Temple. As the fall did not kill him, his enemies stoned him, finally dispatching him with a fuller's club (see Matt. 4:5; Luke 4:9). Across from the Valley of Jehoshaphat, there is a sepulcher called "The Tomb of St. James."

4. *James,* the father of the Apostle Judas (Luke 6:16 R.V.). We have no further record of this James. Hastings states that, "the A.V. 'Judas the *brother* of James' is an impossible identification of the Apostle Judas with the author of the Epistle (Jude 1)."

JAMIN [Jā' min]—THE RIGHT HAND or PROSPERITY.

1. *A son of Simeon* the second son of Jacob and founder of a tribal family (Gen. 46:10; Ex. 6:15; Num. 26:12; I Chron. 4:24).

2. *A man of Judah,* descendant of Hezron (I Chron. 2:27).

3. *A priest* who assisted Ezra in the reading and explanation of the law (Neh. 8:7, 8).

JAMLECH [Jăm' lech]—JEHOVAH RULES or LET HIM CONSTITUTE A KING. *A Simeonite prince* (I Chron. 4:34).

JANNA, JANNAI [Jăn' nă]—HE WILL ANSWER. *The father of Melchi,* and an ancestor of Christ (Luke 3:24).

JANNES [Jăn′ nēs]—FULL OF PLEASURE, FAVOR or IMPOVERISHED. *One of the two Egyptian magicians* who withstood Moses (Ex. 7:11, 12, 22; 8:7, 18, 19; 9:11; II Tim. 3:8). The names of these opponents are not given in the Old Testament. Ancient Jewish writers expressed extravagant views on Jannes and Jambres, some affirming that they were the sons of Balaam, that they were drowned in the Red Sea or put to death for inciting Aaron to make the golden calf.

JAPHETH [Jā′ pheth]—BEAUTY, LET HIM ENLARGE or HE THAT PERSUADES. *The second son of Noah,* born in the patriach's five hundredth year, and founder of those who spread over the north and west regions of the earth (Gen. 5:32; 6:10; 7:13). The Medians, Greeks, Romans, Russian and Gauls are referred to as descendants of Japheth. Most of the nations springing from him reappear in the endtime period under Gog (Ezek. 38; 39). For Greece see Zechariah 9:13.

JAPHIA [Jā phī′ ă]—HIGH, SHINING, GLEAMING or WHICH ENLIGHTENS.
1. *A king of Lachish* captured and executed by Joshua at Gibeon (Josh. 10:3).
2. *A son of David* born at Jerusalem (II Sam. 5:15; I Chron. 3:7; 14:6). Also the name of a town near Carmel (Josh. 19:12).

JAPHLET [Jăph′ let]—JEHOVAH CAUSES TO ESCAPE or MAY HE DELIVER. *An Asherite* of the family of Heber, a grandson of Beriah (I Chron. 7:32).

JARAH [Jā′ rah]—HONEY or UNVEILER. *A son of Ahaz* and a descendant of King Saul (I Chron. 9:42). Called Jehoadah in I Chronicles 8:36.

JAREB [Jā′ reb]—CONTENTIOUS, AVENGER or REVENGER. *A king of Assyria* (Hos. 5:13; 10:6). It is not clear whether this is a proper name or an appellation. Some old versions have "The King Avenger."

JARED, JERED [Jā′ red, Jē′ red]—DESCENDING or HE THAT DESCENDS. *The son of Mahalaleel* and father of Enoch (Gen. 5:15–20; I Chron. 1:2) and ancestor of Christ (Luke 3:37).

JARESIAH [Jăr e sī′ ah]—JEHOVAH GIVES A COUCH. *A son of Jeroham,* a Benjamite (I Chron. 8:27).

JARHA [Jär′ hă]—AN ADVERSARY. *An Egyptian slave* and husband of Ahlai, the daughter of Sheshan (I Chron. 2:34, 35).

JARIB [Jā′ rib]—HE DOTH CONTEND or STRIVING.
1. *A son of Simeon* (I Chron. 4:24). Also known as Jachin (Gen. 46:10; Ex. 6:15).

2. *One of the chief men* who accompanied Ezra to Jerusalem (Ezra 8:16).

3. *A priest* who had married a foreign wife (Ezra 10:18).

JAROAH [Jā rō′ah]—NEW MOON. *A Gadite descendant* through Buz (I Chron. 5:14).

JASHEN [Jā′ shen]—SHINING or SLEEPING. *The father of one of David's heroes* (II Sam. 23:32). Perhaps the Hashem of I Chronicles 11:34.

JASHOBEAM [Jā′ shŏ′ be ăm]—THE PEOPLE RETURN TO GOD.

1. *The son of Zabdiah*, a Hachmonite and one of David's mighty men (I Chron. 11:11; 27:2).

2. *A Korahite descended from Kohath*, who joined David at Ziklag (I Chron. 12:6).

JASHUB [Jăsh′ ŭb]—TURNING BACK or HE RETURNS.

1. *The third of the four sons of Issachar* and founder of a tribal family (Num. 26:24; I Chron. 7:1). Perhaps the Job of Genesis 46:13.

2. *A son of Bani*, who, after his return from exile, put away his foreign wife (Ezra 10:29).

JASHUBI-LEHEM [Jăsh′ u bī lĕ′ hĕm]—BREAD RETURNS or TURNING BACK TO BETHLEHEM. *A member of the family of Shelah*, son of Judah (I Chron. 4:22).

JASON [Jā′ son]—HEALING or HE THAT CARES.

1. *A believer* Paul sends greetings to and whom he called his "kinsman," that is, a fellow Hebrew Christian (Rom. 16:21).

2. *A believer in Thessalonica* who was hospitable to Paul and Silas (Acts 17:5-9). Perhaps the two Jasons are the same person.

JATHNIEL [Jăth′ nĭ el]—GOD BESTOWETH GIFTS or GOD IS GIVING. *A son of Meshelemiah* of the house of Asaph, who was a gatekeeper at the Tabernacle (I Chron. 26:2; see also I Chron. 9:14).

JAVAN [Jā′ văn]—SUPPLE, CLAY or HE THAT DECEIVES. *The fourth son of Japheth*, son of Noah (Gen. 10:2, 4; I Chron. 1:5, 7), and founder of descendants spreading afar (Isa. 66:19). Also the name of a city in South Arabia (Ezek. 27:13, 19). Now Yemen, or the same as Uzal.

JAZIZ [Jā′ zĭz]—SHINING or HE MOVES ABOUT. *A Hagerite and overseer* of David's flocks (I Chron. 27:31).

JEATERAI [Jē ăt'e raī]— STEDFAST. *A descendant of Gershom,* son of Levi (I Chron. 6:21). Called Ethni in verse forty-one.

JEBERECHIAH [Jē bĕr e chī' ah]—JEHOVAH DOTH BLESS or IS BLESSING. *The father of Zechariah* and friend of Isaiah (Isa. 8:2).

JECAMIAH [Jĕc a mī' ah]—MEANING UNCERTAIN. *A son of Jecamiah* (I Chron. 3:18). See Jekamiah.

JECHONIAS, JECHONIAH [Jĕch o nī' as]—ESTABLISHED OF THE LORD. *An ancestor of Christ* (Matt. 1:11, 12). Greek form of King Jeconiah.

JECONIAH [Jĕc o nī' ah]—JEHOVAH DOTH ESTABLISH or PREPARATION OF THE LORD. *The next to last of the kings of Judah* (I Chron. 3:16, 17; Esther 2:6; Jer. 24:1; 27:20; 28:4; 29:2). Altered form of Jehoiachin, and called Jechonias in Matthew 1:11, 12.

JEDAIAH [Jē dā' iah]—JEHOVAH IS PRAISE or JEHOVAH KNOWETH.
1. *A descendant of Simeon* (I Chron. 4:37).
2. *A man of Harumaph* who repaired the part of the wall near his own house (Neh. 3:10).
3. *A descendant of Aaron* whose family came up from Jerusalem (I Chron. 9:10; 24:7; Ezra 2:36; Neh. 7:39).
4. *A chief of the priests* who returned with Zerubbabel (Neh. 11:10; 12:6, 19; Zech. 6:10, 14).
5. Another priest with the same history (Neh. 12:7, 21).

JEDIAEL [Jē dī' a el]—GOD KNOWETH or KNOWN OF GOD.
1. *A son of Benjamin* and founder of a family (I Chron. 7:6, 10, 11). Also called Ashbel (Num. 26:38).
2. *The son of Shimri,* and one of David's valiant men (I Chron. 11:45).
3. *A Manassite* who joined David at Ziklag (I Chron. 12:20).
4. *A son of Meshelemiah,* a descendant of Korah and doorkeeper in David's time (I Chron. 26:2).

JEDIDIAH [Jĕd I dī' ah]—BELOVED OF JEHOVAH or JEHOVAH IS A FRIEND. *The name given to Solomon by Nathan* the prophet as instructed of the Lord (II Sam. 12:25). See Solomon.

JEDUTHUN [Jĕd' u thŭn]—A CHOIR OF PRAISE or ONE WHO GIVES PRAISE. *A Levite chief singer or musician* appointed by David, and also founder of an official musical family (I Chron. 16:41). Also known as Ethan.

JEEZER [Jē e' zûr]—HELP. *A son of Gilead,* grandson of Manasseh (Num. 26:30). See Abiezer.

JEHALELEEL, JEHALELEL [Jē ha lē' le el]—HE PRAISETH GOD.
1. *A descendant of Judah* through Caleb the spy and founder of a family (I Chron. 4:16).
2. *A Merarite Levite* in Hezekiah's time (II Chron. 29:12).

JEHDEIAH [Jeh dē' iah]—UNION OF JEHOVAH or JEHOVAH INSPIRES WITH JOY.
1. *A son of Shubael* of the house of Amram (I Chron. 24:20).
2. *A Meronothite overseer* of David's asses (I Chron. 27:30).

JEHEZEKEL [Jē hĕz' e kĕl]—GOD DOTH STRENGTHEN or GOD IS STRONG. *A descendant of Aaron* who was the head of the twentieth course of priests (I Chron. 24:16). His name is the same as Ezekiel.

JEHIAH [Jē hī' ah]—GOD LIVETH or IS LIVING. *A Levite doorkeeper* of the ark in David's time (I Chron. 15:24).

JEHIEL [Jē hī' el]—GOD LIVETH
1. *A Levite of the second degree* who played the psaltery (1 Chron. 15:18–20; 16:5).
2. *A Levite of the family of Gershom* and chief of the house of Laadan in David's time (I Chron. 23:8; 26:21, 22; 29:8).
3. *A son of Hachmoni* and companion of David's sons (I Chron. 27:32). Perhaps a tutor of the king's sons.
4. *A son of Jehoshaphat,* king of Judah, placed by his father over one of the fenced cities of Judah, but slain with his brother by Jehoram (II Chron. 21:2–4).
5. *A son of Heman the singer,* he aided Hezekiah in his religious reforms (II Chron. 29:14). R.V. has Jehuel.
6. *A Levite* set over the dedicated things by King Hezekiah (II Chron. 31:13).
7. *A chief priest* in Josiah's time who assisted in the reformation (II Chron. 35:8).
8. *The father of Obadiah* who returned from exile with Ezra (Ezra 8:9).
9. *The father of Shechaniah* who was the first to acknowledge the guilt of taking foreign, or non-Jewish wives (Ezra 10:2).
10. *A priest* who had taken a foreign wife (Ezra 10:21).
11. *A man of Elam's family* who had done the same thing (Ezra 10:26). See Jeiel.

JEHIELI [Jē hī' e lī]—HE LIVES BY MERCY. *A son of Laadan* the Gershonite, set over the treasuries of the sanctuary in David's time (I Chron. 26:21, 22).

JEHIZKIAH [Jĕ hĭz kĭ′ ah]—JEHOVAH IS STRONG or DOTH STRENGTHEN. *A son of Shallum,* a head of an Ephraimite tribe in the reign of Pekah who assisted in securing the release of captives (II Chron. 28:12). He was a strong supporter of the prophet Oded.

JEHOADAH, JEHOADDAH [Jĕ hŏ′ a dah]—JEHOVAH UNVEILS or HATH ADORNED. *A son of Ahaz* and great grandson of Jonathan, Saul's son (I Chron. 8:36). Also called Jarah (I Chron. 9:42).

JEHOAHAZ, JOAHAZ [Jĕ hŏ′ a hăz]—JEHOVAH UPHOLDS, HATH LAID HOLD or THE LORD THAT SEES.

1. *A son and successor of Jehu* and father of Joash who reigned for seven years (II Kings 10:35; 13; 14; II Chron. 25:17, 25). We know little of this king of Israel apart from the length of his reign and the low estate of his kingdom owing to Syrian aggression.

2. *The son and successor of King Jehoram* and father of King Joash, of Judah (II Chron. 21:17; 25:23). Called Ahaziah.

3. *A son of Josiah* who was deposed by Pharaoh-nechoh and who only reigned for three months (II Kings 23:30–34; II Chron. 36:1–4). Also called Shallum (I Chron. 3:15).

JEHOASH, JOAHAZ, JOASH [Jĕ hŏ′ ăsh, Jŏ′ ăsh]—JEHOVAH SUPPORTS or HATH LAID HOLD. Here is another example of a name given to a king in each of the two lines, Israel and Judah.

1. Jehoash of Judah, *son of Ahaziah* and father of Amaziah (II Kings 11:21; 12:1–18; 14:13). When but an infant his brothers and cousins were massacred, but he was concealed until he was seven years old and then crowned as king. His preservation meant the continuation of the royal seed. Ultimately he was slain by some of his officers.

2. Jehoash of Israel, *son and successor of Jehoashaz* on the throne of Israel. He was the father of Jeroboam II (II Kings 13:10, 25; 14:8–17). See Joash. It was this king who visited Elisha when he was about to die, and wept over him as a great influence about to be lost to Israel.

JEHOHANAN, JOHANAN [Jĕ hŏ hā′ nan, Jŏ′ hā′ nan]—JEHOVAH IS GRACIOUS.

1. *A Korathite Levite* who had charge of the sixth course of gatekeepers in David's reign (I Chron. 26:3).

2. *The second in honor of Jehoshaphat's captains,* who had two hundred eighty thousand men under him (II Chron. 17:15).

3. *The father of Ishmael,* a captain who aided Jehoiada in the revolt against Athaliah (II Chron. 23:1).

4. *A son of Bebai* who had taken a foreign wife (Ezra 10:28).

5. *A priest* who returned with Zerubbabel (Neh. 12:13).

6. *A priest or singer* who officiated at the dedication of the Jerusalem wall (Neh. 12:42).

7. *The son of Tobiah* the Ammonite (Neh. 6:18 R.V.). See Johanan.

JEHOIACHIN [Jĕ hoi' a chĭn]—JEHOVAH DOTH ESTABLISH. *A son of Jehoiakim,* king of Judah, who was placed on the throne by Nebuchadnezzar, but only reigned for three months. He was carried away to Babylon and remained a captive until freed from prison by Evil-merodach and given palace favors (II Kings 24:8, 12, 15; 25:27; II Chron. 36:8, 9; Jer. 52:31). Also called Coniah (see Jer. 22:24, 28; 37:1).

JEHOIADA [Jĕ hoi' a dă]—JEHOVAH KNOWS or KNOWLEDGE OF THE LORD.

1. *The father of Benaiah* and one of David's officers. Probably the priest and leader of the Aaronites who brought thirty-seven hundred men to David at Ziklag (II Sam. 8:18; 20:23; 23:20, 22; I Kings 1; 2; 4:4; I Chron. 11:22, 24; 12:27; 18:17; 27:5).

2. *The high priest who made Joash king,* and possibly the husband of Jehosheba, whose presence of mind saved the infant Jehoash from massacre (II Kings 11:4–17; 12:2–9; II Chron. 23; 24).

3. *A son of Beniah,* son of Jehoiada, the third of David's counselors (I Chron. 27:34).

4. *A son of Paseah,* who repaired "the old gate" (Neh. 3:6). Called Joiada in the R. V.

5. *A priest in Jerusalem* before the exile, but displaced by Zephaniah (Jer. 29:26).

JEHOIAKIM [Jĕ hoi' a kĭm]—JEHOVAH SETS UP. *The name given by Pharaoh-nechoh* to Eliakim son of Josiah, king of Judah, whom he made king instead of Jehoahaz. His reign of eleven years is not favorably viewed by Jeremiah (II Kings 23:34–36; 24:1–6, 19; I Chron. 3:15, 16; II Chron. 36: 4–8; Jer. 1:3; 22:18, 24).

The Man Who Was a Frivolous Egotist

Jehoiakim lacked moral sense and religious appreciation and was a man after the mold of his grandfather Manasseh. He took no interest in the reforms for which his father had worked. With his approval many heathen practices of Manasseh's reign were resumed.

The burning of the roll containing the sacred Word of God was the most remarkable scene in the history of this evil king who had no regard for God and no respect for the rights of others. He severely oppressed the people of Judah in order to maintain the pomp and extravagance of his court. Such a flagrant rejection of all that was godly and just brought Jeremiah out into the open, and he addressed the king in no uncertain terms. The king's doom was predicted. At last he was put to death by Nebuchadnezzar, and his body was left to decay, unburied, beyond the gates of Jerusalem. When we come to the line of our Saviour's ancestors there is a blank where a name should have been. "Josias," so we read (Matt. 1:11), (not Jehoiakim) begat Jechonias. The name is gone—taken out of the book of generations.

JEHOIARIB [Jĕ hoi' a rĭb]—JEHOVAH DOTH CONTEND.
1. *A priest in Jerusalem* (I Chron. 9:10).
2. *The head of an Aaronite family* who shared in the charges of the sanctuary (I Chron. 24:7). See Joiarib.

JEHONADAB, JONADAB [Jĕ hŏn' a dăb, Jŏn' a dăb]—JEHOVAH IS LIBERAL.
1. *Son of Shimeah,* David's brother, and the friend of Ammon the son of David, who is described as "a very subtil man" (II Sam. 13:3, 32).
2. *Son of Rechab,* a Kenite, who composed the rules imposed upon the Rechabites (II Kings 10:15, 23).

JEHONATHAN [Jĕ hŏn' a than] JEHOVAH HATH GIVEN. In the R. V. the English form of this name is given twice as Jonathan.
1. *Son of Uzziah* and an official appointed by David to have charge over royal treasures (I Chron. 27:25).
2. *A Levite* sent by Jehoshaphat to teach the people (II Chron. 17:8).
3. *A priest* and head of his father's house of Shemaiah in the days of the high priest Joiakim (Neh. 12:18). Called Jonathan in Nehemiah 12:35.

JEHORAM, JORAM [Jĕ hŏ' ram, Jŏ' ram]—JEHOVAH IS HIGH or EXALTED.
1. *A son of Ahab,* who became king of Israel after the brief reign of his brother Ahaziah (II Kings 1:17; 3:1, 6; 9:24; II Chron. 22:5–7). When Jehoram allied himself with Jehoshaphat, he paid tribute to the power of the king of Moab. Dr. Joseph Parker has this to say of the somewhat remarkable character of Jehoram:

> He was not an imitator of the evil of his father as to its precise form, but he had his own method of serving the devil. He superseded the arts of wickedness practiced by Ahab and Jezebel and found a way of his own of living an evil life . . . He re-established the worship of the calf, after the pattern which Jeroboam, its founder, had patronized . . . He made a kind of trick of wickedness, and knew how to give a twist to old forms.

Elisha was active during Jehoram's reign, and rebuked the king ultimately slain by Jehu.
2. *Son of Jehoshaphat,* who succeeded his father on the throne of Judah. He was married to Athaliah, daughter of Ahab and Jezebel. History does not record much of this king's life apart from the fact that he "walked in the ways of the kings of Israel" (I Kings 22:50; II Kings 1:17; 8:16; 25, 29; 12:18; II Chron. 21;16). He gave his

patronage to the worship of the Tyrian Baal. Although he knew the fate of those who had been guilty of idolatrous worship, he yet pursued his evil way. For provoking God by his idolatry, Jehoram was severely punished, and paid for his sin. He departed without any regret on the part of the people. Dishonor followed this king who died in contempt, for his body was not buried in "the sepulchers of kings."

3. *A priest sent by Jehoshaphat* with Elishama to teach the law to Judah (II Chron. 17:8).

JEHOSHAPHAT [Jĕ hŏsh′ a phăt]—JEHOVAH IS JUDGE.
1. *A recorder* during the reigns of David and Solomon (II Sam. 8:16; I Kings 4:3; I Chron. 18:15).
2. *One of Solomon's purveyors* (I Kings 4:17).
3. *A son of Asa*, king of Judah, who succeeded his father (I Kings 15:24; 22).

The Man with a Good Record

Because he carried out the religious reforms of his father, history gives Jehoshaphat a good name. What a beautiful expression that is " . . . he walked in the first ways of his father David"—meaning in the former or earlier ways of David, as contrasted with his later conduct. Because of his godward bent, "the Lord was with Jehoshaphat." Negatively, he "sought not after Baalim."

Here was a man who in every point was equally strong, a man of foresight, a man of reverence, a man of an honest heart, a man who felt that idolatry and true worship could not coexist in the same breast. He did not concern himself with "the doings of Israel." His was a blessed, spiritual singularity. He laid down a clear program for himself, and followed it out with patient and faithful endeavor. He did not seek riches and honor. No wonder the Lord "established the kingdom in his hand"! Points for the preacher to develop are:

I. He was one of the best kings of Judah (I Kings 15:24).
II. He had a godly father whose example he emulated (II Chron. 14:2).
III. He developed a system of religious instruction for the people (II Chron. 17:7–9).
IV. He commanded the judges to be just (II Chron. 19:6–9).
V. He trusted God for victory in a crisis (II Chron. 20).
VI. He manifested weakness in his alliance with wicked kings (I Kings 22:1–36).

4. *Son of Nimshi* and father of Jehu, who conspired against Joram, son of king Ahab (II Kings 9:2, 14).
5. *One of the priests* who assisted in bringing up the Ark from Obed-edom (I Chron. 15:24). Also the name of a valley east of Jerusalem which figures in coming judgment (Joel 3:2, 12). See also Josaphat.

JEHOSHUA [Jĕ hŏsh′ u ah]—JEHOVAH SAVES. *The name sometimes given to Joshua* the son of Nun (Num. 13:16; I Chron. 7:27).

JEHOZABAD [Jē hŏz′ a băd]—JEHOVAH HATH ENDOWED.
1. *The son of Shomer* or Shimrith from Moab. He was among the number who slew Jehoash (II Kings 12:21; II Chron. 24:26).
2. *A Korathite porter,* son of Obed-edom (I Chron. 26:4).
3. *A Benjamite,* a high military officer under king Jehoshaphat (II Chron. 17:18).

JEHOZADAK, JOZADAK [Jē hŏz′ a dăk]—JEHOVAH IS JUST. *The father of Jeshua* the high priest, and grandson of Azariah, the high priest during the exile (I Chron. 6:14, 15).

JEHU [Jĕ′ hū]—JEHOVAH IS HE.
1. *A son of Hanani,* the prophet who denounced Baasha and his house, reproved Jehoshaphat and wrote a book (I Kings 16:1, 7, 12; II Chron. 19:2; 20:34).
2. *A son of Obed* and descendant of Hezron (I Chron. 2:38).
3. *A son of Josibiah* a Simeonite (I Chron. 4:35).
4. *A Benjamite of Anathoth* who joined David at Ziklag (I Chron. 12:3).
5. *The king of Israel,* appointed by Elijah in the place of Ahab. He is often called for brevity's sake, "The son of Nimshi." He reigned twenty-eight years (I Kings 19:16, 17).

The Man of Speed

Under Jehu there was a dynastic revolution, resulting in the overthrowing of the regnant religious establishment. "Jehu took no heed to walk in the law of the Lord" (II Kings 10:31). This king brought about no positive vital godliness, whose boasted "zeal for the Lord" (II Kings 10:16) was really zeal for Jehu.

There is one sentence revealing for us an insight into Jehu's character. "He driveth furiously." He came with all speed not merely because he was on an urgent errand, but because he was urged on by a headlong disposition, which earned him the reputation of a reckless driver among the watchmen. Jehu is thus a type of many who, in worldly and in religious matters, may be called reckless drivers. Without prudence or righteousness they plunge into matters of importance. The prodigal was a son of Nimshi in that he drove furiously when it came to living riotously in the far country.

It was also with lightning speed that Jehu destroyed Baal out of Israel, but he did his extermination in the wrong way, for the weapons of warfare are not carnal. For reasons of state policy Jehu maintained the worship of Bethel and Dan. He tried to serve God and Mammon. To Jehu, religion was only a political instrument. Hosea saw that the blood of Jezreel rested upon the house of Jehu, and that it would be avenged (Hos. 1:4).

JEHUBBAH [Jē hŭb′ bah]—HIDDEN. *An Asherite* and a descendant of Shamer and of the family of Beriah (I Chron. 7:34).

JEHUCAL, JUCAL [Jē hū′ cal, Jū′ cal]—JEHOVAH IS ABLE. *A son of Shelemiah,* the courtier sent by king Zedekiah to entreat for the prayers of Jeremiah (Jer. 37:3; 38:1).

JEHUDI [Jē hū′ dī]—A MAN OF JUDAH, A JEW. *An officer sent by king Jehoiakim* to ask Baruch for the roll of Jeremiah's prophecies and who read it to the princes of Judah (Jer. 36:14–23).

JEHUSH [Jē′ hŭsh]—COLLECTOR. *A Benjamite* of the family of Saul (I Chron. 8:39).

JEIEL, JEHIEL, JEUEL [Jē ĭ′ el, Jē hī′ el]—TREASURE OF GOD, or GOD SNATCHES AWAY.

1. *A chief among the Reubenites* (I Chron. 5:7).
2. *A Benjamite,* the father of Gibeon, progenitor of Saul (I Chron. 9:35–39).
3. *A son of Hotham* and one of David's valiant men. Perhaps another Reubenite chief (I Chron. 11:44). Vulgate has Jeuel.
4. *A Levite gatekeeper and singer* in David's reign (I Chron. 15:18, 20; 16:5).
5. *A Levite* of the sons of Asaph (II Chron. 20:14).
6. *A principal scribe* who recorded the number of soldiers in king Uzziah's army (II Chron. 26:11).
7. *A Levite of the family of Elizaphan* in the time of Hezekiah (II Chron. 29:13).
8. *A Levite in the days of Josiah* of Judah (II Chron. 35:9).
9. *A son of Adonikam* who returned with Ezra. Vulgate has Jeuel (Ezra 8:13).
10. *One of the family of Nebo* who had married a foreign wife (Ezra 10:43).

JEKAMEAM [Jĕk a mē′ am]—HE DOTH ASSEMBLE THE PEOPLE. *A son of Hebron,* grandson of Levi (I Chron. 23:19; 24:23).

JEKAMIAH, JECAMIAH [Jĕk a mī′ ah, Jĕc a mī′ ah]—JEHOVAH IS STANDING or DOTH GATHER.

1. *A man of Judah,* and a descendant through Sheshan through Jerahmeel (I Chron. 2:41).
2. *A son or descendant of king Jeconiah* (I Chron. 3:18).

JEKUTHIEL [Jē kū′ thĭ el]—GOD IS MIGHTY or REVERENCE FOR GOD. *A son of Ezra,* a descendant of Caleb the spy (I Chron. 4:18).

JEMUEL [Jē mū′ el] GOD IS LIGHT or DESIRE OF GOD. *A son of Simeon,* and founder of a tribal family (Gen. 46:10; Ex. 6:15). Called Nemuel in I Chronicles 4:24.

JEPHTHAH, JEPHTHAE [Jĕph' thah, Jĕph' tha ē]—HE DOTH OPEN or SET FREE. *A Gileadite,* illegitimate child expelled by his brother from the paternal abode. He became a Judge in Israel and delivered the people from the Ammonites. He judged Israel for six years (Judg. 11; Heb. 11:32).

The Man Who Made a Vow

While Jephthah is described as a "mighty man of valour" and one upon whom "the Spirit of the Lord" descended, he is conspicuous as a man who in all sincerity made a rash vow. He vowed a vow to be fulfilled if the Lord would deliver the Ammonites to him. As a thanksgiving to God, he said he would offer up whatever came out of his house at his return from battle. Jephthah defeated the Ammonites, and on his return, his daughter, an only child, came out to meet him. He told her of his vow and declared he could not go back upon his word. The daughter begged for two months' respite in order to go away and bewail her virginity. On her return, her father fulfilled the vow.

In those twilight, uncivilized times there was the practice of the sacrifice of human beings at times of special stress, but whether Jephthah offered up his daughter as a human sacrifice or surrendered her to perpetual virginity in fulfillment of his vow may be debatable. We do know that it was the custom for the daughters of Israel to lament the daughter of Jephthah the Gileadite for four days every year. And we can imagine how they would return softened, sobered and sanctified as the result of their act of remembrance.

For the preacher these aspects can be developed: Jephthah was an outcast (Judg. 11:1, 2); rose to leadership (Judg. 11:4–10); was moved by the Spirit (Judg. 11:29); made a rash vow (Judg. 11:30, 31); saved Israel from his foes (Judg. 11:33); kept his vow (Judg. 11:39).

JEPHUNNEH [Jē phŭn' neh]—IT WILL BE PREPARED, APPEARING or HE THAT BEHOLDS.

1. *The father of Caleb,* the representative spy from the tribe of Judah (Num. 13:6; 14:6, 30, 38; 26:65; 32:12; 34:19).

2. *An Asherite,* son of Jether (I Chron. 7:38).

JERAH [Jē' räh]—MOON or SON OF THE MOON. *A son of Joktan* of the family of Shem (Gen. 10:26; I Chron. 1:20).

JERAHMEEL [Jē räh' me el]—GOD HATH COMPASSION or IS MERCIFUL.

1. *A son of Hezron,* grandson of Judah, who had two wives and a numerous progeny (I Sam. 27:10; I Chron. 2:9, 42).

2. *A son of Kish* the Merarite (not Saul's father) (I Chron. 24:29).

3. *An officer of Jehoiakim,* king of Judah, who was sent to arrest Jeremiah and Baruch (Jer. 36:26).

JERED [Jē red]—DESCENT or FLOWING. *A Son of Ezra,* and descendant of Caleb the spy and father of the inhabitants of Gedor (I Chron. 4:18). See Jered (I Chron. 1:2).

JEREMAI [Jĕr′ e maï]—JEHOVAH IS HIGH. *A Hebrew of the family of Hashum* who was persuaded to put away his foreign wife (Ezra 10:33).

JEREMIAH, JEREMY, JEREMIAS [Jĕr e mî′ ah]—JEHOVAH IS HIGH or EXALTED OF GOD.

1. *An inhabitant of Libnah* whose daughter, Hamutal, was the wife of Josiah and mother of Jehoahaz (II Kings 23:31; 24:18; Jer. 52:1).

2. *A Manassehite* and head of a family (I Chron. 5:24).

3. *A Benjamite* who joined David at Ziklag (I Chron. 12:4).

4. *A Gadite* who also joined David (I Chron. 12:10).

5. *Another Gadite* who did the same (I Chron. 12:13).

6. *Son of Hilkiah,* the prophet from Anathoth in the days of Josiah and who was of the line of Abiathar (II Chron. 35:25; 36:12, 21, 22; Jer. 1:1).

The Man of Inconsolable Grief

This man who was *born* a priest but *became* a prophet by the divine call of God comes before us as one of the grandest men of Old Testament history. He was called to the prophetic office through a vision (Jer. 1:1, 4–16) and labored for some forty years. The book Jeremiah wrote gives us more details of his life, methods and work, as an Old Testament prophet, than of any other prophet. He is referred to as a son of Hilkiah, not only to distinguish him from others of the same name, but to prove that he was of priestly origin. He came from the priestly town of Anathoth, a name meaning, "answered prayers."

His call antedated his birth (Jer. 1:5), and he was consecrated to God before his birth. He was distinguished by his humility and native modesty. He felt he was a child and not mature enough to function as a prophet. With Browning he could say:

> I was not born
> Informed and fearless from the first, but shrank
> From aught which marked me out apart from men:
> I would have lived their life, and died their death
> Lost in their ranks, eluding destiny.

But Jeremiah could not elude destiny. So we have:

I. His equipment for a God-appointed task (Jer. 1:7–9).

II. His sufferings. What sorrow and anguish were his (Lam. 1:12; 3:1). He was not permitted to marry (Jer. 16:2). Solitude was at once his penalty and greatness. Then we have his sad antagonisms (Jer. 1:18; 15:16, 17, 20; 20:1–18).

III. His persecutions. These came to him from many quarters (Jer. 11:18–20; 12:6; 20:6; 26; 37; 38:13–28; 43:6). Bitter, however, were his denunciations of his foes (Jer. 11:20; 15:18; 17:18; 18:21–23).

IV. His death. Tradition has it that he was stoned to death in

Egypt by the Jews, and that when Alexander entered Egypt he rescued his bones from obscurity and buried them in Alexandria. See Hebrews 11:37.

Jeremiah's ministry was an intensely sad one and his song is in the minor key. His was a divine melancholy that made his head "waters" and his eyes a fountain of tears. The truths he had to proclaim were unwelcome and brought him enemies, but he carried out his task without fear or favor. In these days of national apostasy and international strife, the preacher could not do better than live near the Book of Jeremiah, which has, as its dominant note, true religion in heart and life, in church and nation.

7. *A priest* who sealed the covenant with Nehemiah (Neh. 10:2; 12:1, 12, 34).

8. *A descendant of Jonadab*, son of Rechab (Jer. 35: 3).

JEREMOTH, JERIMOTH [Jĕr′ e mŏth, Jĕr′ ĭ mŏth]—ELEVATION OF HEIGHTS.

1. *A son of the Benjamite Beriah* (I Chron. 8:14).
2. *One who married a foreign wife* (Ezra 10:26).
3. *Another who did the same* (Ezra 10:27).
4. *Another who did the same* (Ezra 10:36).
5. *A Levite* (I Chron. 25:22). Called Jerimoth in I Chronicles 24:30.
6. *A Naphtalite* (I Chron. 27:19). See Jerimoth.

JERIAH, JERIJAH [Jē rī′ ah]—JEHOVAH HATH FOUNDED. *A descendant of Hebron,* grandson of Levi and the chief of one of the Levitical courses in David's time (I Chron. 23:19; 24:23).

JERIBAI [Jĕr′ ĭ baī]—JEHOVAH CONTENDS or CONTENTIOUS. *A son of Elnaam* and one of David's mighty men (I Chron. 11:46).

JERIEL [Jĕ′ rĭ el]—FOUNDED or FOUNDATION OF GOD. *A son of Tola,* son of Issachar (I Chron. 7:2).

JERIMOTH [Jĕr′ ĭ mŏth]—HEIGHTS.

1. *A son of Bela,* son of Benjamin (I Chron. 7:7).
2. *A son of Becher,* son of Benjamin (I Chron. 7:8).
3. *A valiant man who joined David at Ziklag* (I Chron. 12:5).
4. *A son of Mushi,* grandson of Levi (I Chron. 23:23; 24:30).
5. *A son of Heman,* who assisted in the service of song (I Chron. 25:4). See Jeremoth, I Chronicles 25:22.
6. *A ruler in Naphtali in David's time* (I Chron. 27:19).
7. *A son of David* and father of Rehoboam's wife (II Chron. 11:18). Not mentioned elsewhere.

JEROBOAM [Jĕr o bō′ am]—ENLARGES, STRUGGLER FOR THE PEOPLE or THE PEOPLE HAVE BECOME NUMEROUS.

1. *The son of Nebat* from Zereda in Manasseh, who became the first king of the ten tribes of Israel. This Ephraimite, Jeroboam I, reigned for twenty-two years. His mother's name was Zeruah, who was widowed at the time of his birth. This is the Jeroboam who rebuked the unnamed prophet (I Kings 11:26-40; 12-16).

The Man Who Made Israel Sin

The dreadful description of Jeroboam tied to his name like a label, is that "he made Israel to sin." His sin — the root and fruit of it — are the chief things the Bible records of this widow's son. We are familiar with the incident of Ahijah taking Jeroboam's new garment and tearing it into twelve pieces, giving Jeroboam ten pieces and prophesying the rending of Solomon's kingdom, and the government of ten tribes of that kingdom passing into Jeroboam's hands. No wonder Solomon sought to kill him. But after the king's death and the refusal of Rehoboam to follow good advice, the kingdom split and ten tribes went with Jeroboam.

Solomon had lost his kingdom by idolatry and Jeroboam proposed to keep his ten-tribe kingdom by idolatry. So, abandoning the commandment and promise of God, Jeroboam set up golden bulls, one in Bethel and the other in Dan. People must have religion of some sort, Jeroboam reasoned, as he made the worship of the calves a part of the constitution of his kingdom. How sad it is to read that the Lord gave Israel up because of the sins of Jeroboam! The consequences of national idolatry continued, for eighteen kings sat upon the throne of Judah after his death, but not one of them gave up the golden calves. Of fifteen of them it is said that they departed not from the sin of Jeroboam. As with the kings, so with the people who continued to walk in all the sins of Jeroboam which he did (II Kings 17:22, 23).

There is no need to linger over what befell Jeroboam himself. He was warned by the man of God from Judah, but without avail. His son fell sick and died, and Jeroboam shortly after was defeated by his enemies. Then the Lord struck him and he died. Yet his name lives on with the terrible mark against it. "He made Israel to sin."

2. *A son of Joash or Jehoash the* grandfather of Jehu, who succeeded Joash as king over the ten tribes, and who reigned for forty-one years (II Kings 13:13; 14:16-29; 15:1, 8; I Chron. 5:17; Amos 1:1; 7:9-11). Both Hosea (Hos. 1:1) and Amos describe the temporary prosperity of Israel with the accompaniment of social and moral degeneracy during the reign of Jeroboam II. Under him, Israel regained the territory it lost to its hereditary enemy, Syria. The aspect of commanding interest in Jeroboam's age when materialism was in the saddle was the appearance of a man with a message. Amid the shallow optimism possessing king and people alike was the voice of Amos, the herdsman of Tekoa, saying in effect: "The grass withereth, the flower fadeth, but the word of our God shall stand forever."

Israel's prosperity ended with the death of this Jeroboam. A period of anarchy followed. Then he was succeeded by his son Zachariah, who after a reign of only six months, was murdered by Shallum who, in turn, was assassinated one month later. Think of it, three kings sat on Israel's throne in seven months! Four out of six kings succeeding Jeroboam died violent deaths. In less than fifteen years four of Israel's kings were murdered.

JEROHAM [Jĕr' o hăm]—LOVED or HE FINDETH MERCY.
1. *The father of Elkanah,* and grandfather of Samuel (I Sam. 1:1; I Chron. 6:27, 34).
2. *The head of a Benjamite family* dwelling in Jerusalem (I Chron. 8:27).
3. *A Benjamite and father of Ibneiah.* Perhaps the same as No. 2 (I Chron. 9:8).
4. *A priest, whose son, Adaiah,* lived in Jerusalem after the exile, and who was of the house of Malchijah (I Chron. 9:12; Neh. 11:12).
5. *A Benjamite of Gedor* whose two sons joined David at Ziklag (I Chron. 12:7).
6. *The father of Azareel,* prince of Dan in the reign of David (I Chron. 27:22).
7. *The father of Azariah* who aided Jehoiada in putting Joash on the throne (II Chron. 23:1).

JERUBBAAL [Jĕ rŭb' ba ăl]—BAAL STRIVES, LET BAAL DEFEND HIS CAUSE or CONTENDER WITH BAAL. *The name given to Gideon* by his father Joash (Judg. 6:32). See Gideon and next name.

JERUBBESHETH [Jĕ rŭb' be shĕth]—CONTENDER WITH IDOL or LET THE IDOL OF CONFUSION DEFEND ITSELF. *Another name given to Gideon* by those who wished to avoid pronouncing the name of Baal in the former name (II Sam. 11:21).

JESAIAH, JESHAIAH [Jĕ sā' iah, Jĕ shā' iah]—JEHOVAH IS OPULENT or HATH SAVED.
1. *A son of Hananiah* and grandson of Zerubbabel (I Chron. 3:21).
2. *A son of Jeduthun* and a musician in David's time (I Chron. 25:3, 15).
3. *A Levite,* son of Rehabiah and grandson of Eliezer, son of Moses (I Chron. 26:25).
4. *A son of Athaliah* and head of his father's house at Elam, who with seventy males returned from Babylon with Ezra (Ezra 8:7).
5. *A Merarite* included in the above seventy (Ezra 8:19).
6. *A son of Benjamin,* the father of Ithiel whose descendants dwelt in Jerusalem (Neh. 11:7).

JESHARELAH [Jĕ shăr' e lah]—UPRIGHT TOWARDS GOD. *A Levite* who presided over the service of song (I Chron. 25:14). See Asharelah.

JESHEBEAB [Jĕ shĕb' e ăb]—SEAT or DWELLING OF FATHER. *A descendant of Aaron* and head of the fourteenth course of priests in sanctuary service (I Chron. 24:13).

JESHER [Jĕ'shur]—UPRIGHTNESS. *A son of Caleb,* son of Hezron (I Chron. 2:18).

JESHISHAI [Jĕ shĭsh' a ī]—JEHOVAH IS ANCIENT. *A Gadite* and a descendant of Buz (I Chron. 5:14).

JESHOHAIAH [Jĕsh o hā' iah]—HUMBLED BY JEHOVAH. *A Simeonite prince* (I Chron. 4:36).

JESHUA, JESHUAH [Jĕsh' u ă, Jĕsh' u ah]—JEHOVAH IS SALVATION or HELP.

1. *A descendant of Aaron* and priest of the sanctuary (1 Chron. 24:11; Ezra 2:36; Neh. 7:39).

2. *A Levite in Hezekiah's time* who had to do with the receipt and distribution of Temple offerings (II Chron. 31:15; Ezra 2:40; Neh. 7:43).

3. *A high priest* who returned with Zerubbabel, and the son of Jozadak, who built an altar and is also called Joshua (Ezra 2:2; 3:2–9; 4:3; 5:2; 10:18; Neh. 7:7; Zech. 3; 6:11–13).

4. *The father of Jozabad,* the Levite who was responsible for the sanctuary vessels (Ezra 8:33).

5. *A son of Pahath-moab,* whose descendants returned from exile with Zerubbabel (Ezra 2:6; Neh. 7:11).

6. *The father of Ezer* who helped to repair the wall (Neh. 3:19).

7. *A Levite* who helped Ezra read and explain the Law to the people (Neh. 8:7; 9:4, 5; 12:8, 24).

8. *The name given to Joshua* the son of Nun (Neh. 8:17).

9 *The son of Azariah,* a Levite, who with the others sealed the covenant (Neh. 10:9).

Also the name of a city of Benjamin (Neh. 11:26).

JESIAH [Jĕ sī' ah]—JEHOVAH EXISTS.

1. *One who joined David at Ziklag* (I Chron. 12:6).

2. *A Kohathite,* descendant of Uzziel (I Chron. 23:20). Called also Isshiah.

JESIMIEL [Jĕ sĭm ĭ el]—GOD SETTETH UP. *A prince* of the tribe of Simeon (I Chron. 4:36).

JESSE [Jĕs' se]—JEHOVAH EXISTS or FIRM. *The son of Obed* and father of David, and grandson of Boaz and Ruth, and an ancestor of Christ (Ruth 4:17, 22). Jesse had eight sons and two daughters by different wives (I Sam. 17:12–14, 25). Isaiah speaks of "the stock of Jesse," a phrase indicating that it was from Jesse the Messiah would come. The humble descent of the Messiah is contrasted with the glorious kingdom He is to have (Isa 11:1).

JESUI [Jĕs′ u ī]—JEHOVAH IS SATISFIED. *A descendant of Asher* (Num. 26:44). See Ishui. Founder of the Jesuites.

JESUS [Jē′zus]—JEHOVAH IS SALVATION. Jeshua, Jehoshua and Joshua are forms of the common name of Jesus. In this section we are only indicating those who, apart from Christ, are known by this name.

1. *Joshua, the military leader* (Acts 7:45; Heb. 4:8).

2. *An ancestor of Christ,* who lived about four hundred years after David (Luke 3:29).

3. *Jesus called Justus,* the Jewish Christian associated with the Apostle Paul (Col. 4:11).

4. *The Man Christ Jesus* (I Tim. 2:5). See chapter 4, page 363. See Jeshua.

JETHER, JETHRO [Jē′ thûr, Jĕth′ rō]—ABUNDANCE, EXCELLENCE or PRE-EMINENT.

1. *The first-born son of Gideon* and father of Amasa, Absalom's commander-in-chief (Judg 8:20; I Kings 2:5).

2. *A son of Jerahmeel,* son of Hezron (I Chron. 2:32). He died childless.

3. *An Ishmaelite,* the father of David's nephew, Amasa (I Kings 2:5, 32).

4. *A son of Ezra,* and a descendant of Caleb the spy (I Chron. 4:17).

5. *A descendant of Asher* (I Chron. 7:38).

JETHETH [Jē′ theth]—SUBJECTION. *A chieftain of Edom* of the family of Esau (Gen. 36:40; I Chron. 1:51).

JETHRO [Jĕth′ rō]—PRE-EMINENCE or EXCELLENCE. *The father-in-law of Moses,* and an Arab sheik and priest of Midian (Ex. 3:1, 4:18; 18:1–12). Called Reuel or Raguel meaning "friend of God" in Exodus 2:18 and Numbers 10:29, and Jether in Exodus 4:18.

JETUR [Jē′ tŭr]—DEFENSE or HE THAT KEEPS. *A son of Ishmael,* son of Hagar, Abraham's concubine (Gen. 25:15; I Chron. 1:31). Also the name of a tribe that sprang from Jetur (I Chron. 5:19).

JEUEL, JEIEL [Jē ŭ′ el, Jē ī′ el]—TREASURE OF GOD or SNATCHING AWAY.

1. *A descendant of Zerah,* son of Judah (I Chron. 9:6). His clan of six hundred lived at Jerusalem.

2. *A Levite,* descendant of Elizaphan who assisted in the reform under Hezekiah (II Chron. 20:14). Also known as Jeiel.

3. *A contemporary of Ezra* who returned from Babylon. Likewise known as Jeiel (Ezra 8:13).

JEUSH, JEHUSH [Jĕ' ŭsh, Jĕ' hŭsh]—HE WILL GATHER TOGETHER.

1. *A son of Esau* by his wife Aholibamah (Gen. 36:5, 18; I Chron. 1:35).

2. *A son of Bilhan* and grandson of Jediael, a Benjamite (I Chron. 7:10).

3. *A son of Shimei,* a Gershonite and head of a family (I Chron. 23:10, 11).

4. *A son of Rehoboam,* and grandson of King Solomon (II Chron. 11:19).

5. *A descendant of King Saul* (I Chron. 8:39).

JEUZ [Jĕ' ŭz]—COUNSELOR or COUNSELING. *Son of Shaharaim* by his wife Hodesh (I Chron. 8:10).

JEZANIAH, JAAZENIAH [Jĕz a nĭ' ah]—JEHOVAH DOTH HEARKEN or DETERMINE. *The captain of Jewish forces,* son of Hoshaiah, a Maacathite. Generally called Jaazeniah (Jer. 40:8; 42:1).

JEZER [Jĕ' zûr]—FORMATION. *A son of Naphtali* and founder of a tribal family (Gen. 46:24; Num. 26:49; I Chron. 7:13).

JEZIAH [Jĕ zī' ah]—JEHOVAH UNITES. *One of the Parosh family* who put away his foreign wife (Ezra 10:25).

JEZIEL [Jĕ' zī el]—GOD UNITES or ASSEMBLY OF GOD. *Son of Azmaveth,* a Benjamite who, with his brother Pelet, joined David at Ziklag (I Chron. 12:3).

JEZLIAH [Jĕz lī' ah]—JEHOVAH UNITES. *A son of Elpaal* a Benjamite (I Chron. 8:18).

JEZOAR [Jĕ zō'ar]—MEANING UNCERTAIN. *A son of Helah,* wife of Asher, a descendant of Caleb the son of Hur (I Chron. 4:7).

JEZRAHIAH [Jĕz ra hī' ah]—JEHOVAH IS SHINING or THE LORD ARISES. *An overseer of singers* in Nehemiah's time (Neh. 12:42). See also Izrahiah (I Chron. 7:3).

JEZREEL [Jĕz' re el]—GOD SOWS.

1. *A descendant of the father* of Etam (I Chron. 4:3).

2. *The symbolic name of Hosea* the prophet's eldest son, who was so named seeing God had avenged the blood of Jezreel (Hos. 1:4, 5).

Also symbolic name of Israel (Hos. 1:4, 11), and the name of towns (Josh. 15:56; I Kings 21:23).

JIBSAM [Jĭb' sam]—LOVELY, SWEET. *A son of Tola*, son of Issachar (I Chron. 7:2).

JIDLAPH [Jĭd' laph]—HE WEEPETH, MELTING AWAY or HE THAT DISTILS. *A son of Nahor* and Milcah (Gen. 22:22).

JIMNAH, JIMNA [Jĭm' nah, Jĭm' nă]—PROSPERITY. *The first-born son of Asher* and founder of a tribal family (Gen. 46:17; Num. 26:44). Called Imnah (I Chron. 7:30).

JOAB [Jŏ' ăb]—JEHOVAH IS A GOOD FATHER.
1. *A descendant of Caleb* the son of Hur, a Judahite (I Chron. 2:54).
2. *Son of Seraiah*, grandson of Kenaz, associated with valley craftsmen (I Chron. 4:13, 14).
3. *An Israelite* whose posterity went up from Babylon with Zerubbabel (Ezra 2:6; Neh. 7:11).
4. *One* whose descendants went up from Babylon with Ezra (Ezra 8:9.)
5. *The son of David's half-sister*, Zeruiah. This nephew of David became the most overbearing captain in his uncle's army (I Sam. 26:6; II Sam. 2; 13).

The Man Who Was Overambitious

Joab was the first person to be thought of in Joab's mind. His apparent devotion to David had one objective, namely that he himself should have first place. He loved self. He murdered those who stood in the way of pre-eminence as the leader of Israel's hosts (II Sam. 3:27). Alexander Whyte says, "Had it not been for David, Joab would have climbed up into the throne of Israel. . . Even the king himself was afraid of his commander-in-chief. The sovereign took his orders meekly from his subject." In his own well-read and picturesque way, Dean Stanley describes Joab aptly as the Marlborough of the empire of Israel.

W. O. E. Osterley gives us the following summary of Joab's life and labors:

I. He was a skilled general, proven by the number of victories he gained (II Sam. 2:12–32; 10; 11:1; 12:26–29; 20:4–22; I Chron. 11:6–9).

II. He was loyal to the house of David as his whole life of devoted service illustrates (II Sam. 12:26; 14:1; 18:20; 19:5–7).

III. He was guilty of vindictiveness and ruthless cruelty. The treacherous and bloodthirsty acts of which Joab was guilty constitute a dark blot upon his character (II Sam. 3:22–27; 18:14; 20:9, 10; I Kings 11:16).

The tragedy is that in spite of all his abundant energy, boldness, ability, shrewdness and common sense, he never manifested any real faith in God. The nearest he came to such a faith is to be found in II Samuel 10:12, where his trust was more in "Providence" than a personal resting in the God of Israel. Full of self-confidence, ambition and selfishness, Joab never got far away from his own interests.

JOAH [Jō' ah]—JEHOVAH IS BROTHER.

1. *A son of Asaph* the recorder under King Hezekiah (II Kings 18:18, 26; Isa. 36: 3, 11, 22).

2. *Son of Zimmah* and descendant of Gershom son of Levi (I Chron. 6:21; II Chron. 29:12).

3. *A son of Obed-edom*, a Tabernacle porter (I Chron. 26:4).

4. *A son of Joahaz*, a recorder under King Josiah who helped to repair the house of the Lord (II Chron. 34:8).

JOAHAZ [Jō' a hăz]—JEHOVAH HELPS or HATH LAID HOLD OF. *Father of Joah*, King Josiah's recorder (II Chronicles 34:8). For others see Jehoahaz.

JOANNA, JOANAN [Jō Ăn' nă]—JEHOVAH HATH BEEN GRACIOUS. *The grandson of Zerubbabel*, an ancestor of Joseph, Mary's husband (Luke 3:27). Also the name of a female disciple, the wife of one of Herod's officers (Luke 8:3; 24:10). A further illustration of the same name identifying male and female.

JOASH, JEHOASH [Jō' ash, Jē hō' ăsh]—JEHOVAH SUPPORTS, IS STRONG or HASTENS TO HELP.

1. *A son of Becher*, a Benjamite (I Chron. 7:8).

2. *An officer* who had charge of David's oil-cellars (I Chron. 27:28).

3. *A son of Manasseh* and father of Gideon, of the family of Abiezer (Judg. 6:11–31; 7:14; 8:12, 32).

4. *A son of Ahab*, king of Israel (I Kings 22:26; II Chron. 18:25).

5. *A son of Ahaziah*, king of Judah (II Kings 11:2). Also called Jehoash.

6. *A son of Jehoahaz*, and grandson of Jehu (II Kings 13).

7. *A descendant of Shelah*, son of Judah (I Chron. 4:22).

8. *A Benjamite of Gibeah* who joined David at Ziklag (I Chron. 12:3).

JOATHAM [Jō' a thăm]—THE LORD IS UPRIGHT. *An ancestor of Joseph* as given by Matthew 1:9.

JOB [Jōb]—HATED, ONE EVER RETURNING TO GOD or HE THAT WEEPS.

1. *The third son of Issachar* (Gen. 46:13). Called Jashub in Numbers 26:24 and I Chronicles 7:1.

2. *A descendant of Aram*, son of Shem, dwelling in Uz, and possibly

contemporary with Abraham, and who died at the age of 240 years. References to the patriarch apart from his book are to be found in Ezekiel 14:14 and James 5:11.

The Man of Patience

This renowned Old Testament saint dwelt in the land of Uz on the borders of Idumaea. Job's portrait is clearly defined for us in his dramatic book.

I. As to his character, he was perfect and upright, feared God and eschewed evil (Job 1:1). Here we have the manward, Godward and selfward aspects of his life.

II. As to his family, he had seven sons and three daughters (Job 1:2, 18, 19).

III. As to his possessions, he was a wealthy landowner, having seven thousand sheep, three thousand camels, five hundred yoke of oxen, five hundred she asses and a large household (Job 1:3, 13-19).

IV. As to reputation, Job, who lived long before Israel with its religious, social and political organizations existed, was reckoned as the greatest of all the men of the East (Job 1:3).

V. As to his friends, candid friends, there were Eliphaz, Bildad, Zophar and Elihu (Job 2:11; 36:1).

VI. As to his foes, we have mention of the Sabeans and Chaldeans (Job 1:15, 17).

VII. As to his sufferings, he lost his property, sons and wealth. But his losses were doubly recompensed (Job 42:11-13).

VIII. As to his prayer-life, Job knew how to seek God. Thus we have restrained prayer (Job 15:4), purity of prayer (Job 16:17), empty prayer (Job 21:15), profitable prayer (Job 22:27), blessedness of prayer (Job 33:26), interceding prayer (Job 42:8), emancipating prayer (Job 42:10; see 8:5).

IX. As to his patience, the Bible presents him as our model. Faith was strained but Job emerged victorious (Job 19:1-27; Jas. 5:11).

As to the remarkable book bearing Job's name, the following summary might suffice:

Its purpose. It is not an apologetic vindication of the ways of God to man; not a philosophic proof of the doctrine of immortality; not an argumentative refutation of the so-called Hosaic doctrine of retribution; not a word of exhortation to man not to pry into the deep designs of providence, neither is it the testing and improvement of Job's piety. That is acknowledged by God and admitted by Satan to be perfect. It has been written to prove:

That God can be loved for His own sake; that goodness may be unselfish and disinterested; that the righteous can serve God for nought and trust in Him even when He seems to be an enemy.

That the painful riddle of human life is capable of a blessed solution; that the sufferings of the righteous are not necessarily due to their own sins; that the inequalities of this life are to be redressed in the life to come. Justice will be done somehow, sometime, somewhere.

But the Bible is the Book of Christ, and the great theme of Job is the mystery of the Cross: How can the sufferings of the righteous be reconciled with the justice of God? Job is a type of the righteous man, of the Nation, of the Church and of Christ Himself.

Hence we have in Job the picture of a righteous man suffering because it pleased the Lord, for a wise purpose, to bruise him. God reversed the verdict of the men who rejected him and numbered him among the transgressors.

Key Verse: 13:15. "Though he slay me, yet will I trust in him." This is an Old Testament anticipation of the cry of dereliction that came from Christ upon the Cross: "Why didst Thou forsake me?"

Key Thought: Confidence in God (Job 23:10; 27:2-6). He knoweth. In the depth of his darkness and in the agony of his suffering, Job held on to God. My Redeemer liveth.

JOBAB [Jŏ′ băb]—HOWLING or TRUMPET CALL.
1. *A son of Joktan* the Shemite (Gen. 10:29; I Chron. 1:23).
2. *The second king of Edom* and son of Zerah of Bozrah (Gen. 36:33, 34; I Chron. 1:44, 45).
3. *A King of Madon,* whose city was conquered by Joshua (Josh. 11:1).
4. *A son of Shaharaim,* a Benjamite (I Chron. 8:9).
5. *A son of Elpaal,* another Benjamite (I Chron. 8:18).

JODA [Jŏ′ dă]—HASTE.
1. *A Levite* also called Judah (Ezra 3:9); Hodaviah (Ezra 2:40); Hodevah (Neh. 7:43).
2. *An ancestor of Christ* who lived at the time of the exile (Luke 3:26). Also given as Juda.

JOED [Jŏ′ ed]—JEHOVAH IS WITNESS. *A son of Pedaiah,* descended from Jeshiah, a Benjamite (Neh. 11:7).

JOEL [Jŏ′ el]—JEHOVAH IS GOD or THE LORD IS GOD.
1. *The first-born son of Samuel* the prophet (I Sam. 8:2; I Chron. 6:33; 15:17). Called Vashni in I Chronicles 6:28.
2. *A Simeonite prince* (I Chron. 4:35).
3. *The father of Shemaiah,* a Reubenite (I Chron. 5:4, 8).
4. *A chief Gadite* (I Chron. 5:12).
5. *An ancestor of Samuel* the prophet (I Chron. 6:36).
6. *A chief man of Issachar,* descendant of Tola (I Chron. 7:3).
7. *One of David's heroes* and a brother of Nathan (I Chron. 11:38).
8. *A Gershonite in David's time* (I Chron. 15:7, 11; 23:8).
9. *Another Gershonite,* keeper of the treasures of the Lord's house (I Chron. 26:22).
10. *A prince of Manasseh* in David's reign (I Chron. 27:20).

11. *A Kohathite* who assisted Hezekiah in the cleansing of the Temple (II Chron. 29:12).

12. *One of Nebo's family* who had taken a foreign wife (Ezra 10:43).

13. *A son of Zechri,* and overseer of the Benjamites in Jerusalem (Neh. 11:9).

14. *Son of Pethuel,* and prophet in the days of Uzziah, king of Judah (Joel 1:1; Acts 2:16).

The Man Who Foresaw Pentecost

Because nothing is known of Joel beyond what the opening verse of his book states, he has been styled "The Anonymous Prophet." Scripture is silent as to his birthplace, parentage and rank. All we know is that he was a son of Pethuel, or Bethuel as the LXX expresses it. But who Pethuel is no one knows. Its meaning, however, is significant, "vision of God," and springs from a word implying "to open the eyes."

Joel was a common name among the Hebrews and is still so among the Orientals. The use of his name as "the son of Pethuel" was necessary to distinguish him from the other Joels we have considered. It would seem as if his home was in Jerusalem or its immediate neighborhood. Thus he speaks repeatedly of Zion (Joel 2:1, 15, 23; 3:16, 17, 21), the children of Zion (Joel 2:23), Judah and Jerusalem (Joel 2:32; 3:1–20), the children of Judah and Jerusalem (Joel 3:6, 8, 19).

It may be that Joel was a Jew of Jerusalem, and owing to his peculiar mention of priests, a priest-prophet himself (Joel 1:9, 10). His references to the Temple and its worship are frequent (Joel 1:9–16; 2:14, 17; 3:18). It is also likely that he lived and prophesied in the early days of Joash and Jehoida, 870–865 B.C., while the victory of Jehoshaphat was fresh in the nation's memory. For this reason he is termed "The Pioneer Prophet."

Dr. A. B. Simpson says,

> Amos begins his longer message with a direct quotation from Joel, as a sort of text for his whole book. Isaiah expands the thoughts which Joel uttered into the larger and loftier message of his pen. Peter, on the Day of Pentecost quotes the prophecy of Joel as the very foundation of the out-pouring of the Holy Spirit, which had occurred and which was to continue through the whole New Testament age. And even the great Apocalypse of John is but a larger unfolding of the promise of the Lord's coming which Joel gave in brief outline.

What is God's call to us through the Prophet Joel?

I.   There is the call to repentance (Joel 2:25–27).
II. There is the promise of refreshment (Joel 2:28, 29).
III. There is the message of deliverance (Joel 3:1).
IV. There is the secret of rest (Joel 3:17–21).

JOELAH [Jō′ ĕ′ lah]—GOD IS SNATCHING. *A son of Jeroham of Gedor* who joined David at Ziklag (I Chron. 12:7).

JOEZER [Jō ĕ′ zûr]—JEHOVAH IS HELP. *A Korhite* who joined David in Ziklag (I Chron. 12:6).

JOGLI [Jŏg′ lĭ]—EXILED, or LED INTO EXILE. *Father of Bukki* and a Danish prince who took part in the division of the land (Num. 34:22).

JOHA [Jŏ′ hă]—JEHOVAH IS LIVING.
1. *A son of Beriah*, grandson of Shaharaim, a Benjamite (I Chron. 8:16).
2. *A son of Shimri*, and one of David's heroes (I Chron. 11:45).

JOHANAN [Jō hā′ nan]—JEHOVAH IS GRACIOUS.
1. *A son of Kareah or Careah*, chief of the "captains of the forces" who, after the fall of Jerusalem, joined Gedaliah at Mizpah (II Kings 25:23; Jer. 40:13-16).
2. *The eldest son of Josiah*, king of Judah (I Chron. 3:15).
3. *A son of Elioenai* (I Chron. 3:24).
4. *A grandson of Ahimaaz*, father of Azariah, a Levite (I Chron. 6:9, 10).
5. *A Benjamite* who joined David's valiant men at Ziklag (I Chron. 12:4).
6. *The eighth of the Gadites* who joined forces with David at Ziklag. He was made captain of David's army (I Chron. 12:12).
7. *An Ephraimite* who opposed making slaves of captives, in Ahaz' time (II Chron. 28:12). Hebrew for name here is Jehohanan.
8. *A son of Hakkatan*, of the clan of Azgad (Ezra 8:12).
9. *A priest* who, with Ezra, summoned the exiles to Jerusalem. Called Jehohanan in the Hebrew (Ezra 10:6).
10. *A son of Tobiah* the Ammonite and husband of Meshullam's daughter (Neh. 6:18).
11. *A priest in the days of Joiakim*, the grandson of Jozadak (Neh. 12:22, 23).

JOHN [Jŏhn]—JEHOVAH HATH BEEN GRACIOUS.
1. *A kinsman of Annas* the High Priest (Acts 4: 6).
2. *A son of Mary*, sister of Barnabas, and surnamed Mark (Acts 12:12, 25; 13:5, 13; 15:37). See Mark.
3. *The son of Zacharias and Elisabeth*, who appeared as the forerunner of Christ, and who was beheaded by Herod (Matt. 3:1, 4, 13).

The Man Who Was Plain But Powerful

With the appearance of John the Baptist we have the burial of the Old Dispensation and the emergence of the New. We seem to see his rugged figure standing with arms outstretched, as with one hand he takes the Old Testament, and with the other holds the New, and who, through his ministry, makes the transition from Law to Grace. He was the foreclosure of the old and the forerunner of the new. Perhaps we can helpfully gather the witness of John around these salient features:

I. His parentage. John came as the child of promise and was born in a city of Judah when his parents were old, and his mother long past conception (Luke 1:7, 13, 39). His parents were of priestly descent, his mother being a kinswoman of Mary the mother of our Lord (Luke 1:36).

II. His ascetic affinities. John, as a man of the desert, knew what it was to practice self-denial (Matt. 3:4). A Nazarite from his birth, he developed self-reliance and spiritual strength as he communed with God in the desert solitudes he loved (Luke 1:15). He was a plain man in every way, akin to Elijah whom many took him for.

He was plain of dress. He dressed simply, his raiment consisting of camel's hair, that is, either a robe of camel's skin or cloth woven from camel's hair. What a humble habit compared with the luxurious robes of soft wool worn by the fashionable and great of his time!

He was plain of food. No sumptuous dishes for this Elijah-like prophet. It was on rough food he thrived. Vegetable honey exuding from fig-trees and palms, and edible locusts, classed among the flying, creeping things the Israelites were allowed to eat (Lev. 11:22), formed his diet (Matt. 3:4). John the Baptist could subscribe to the words of a devout Englishman of a past century:

> I shall be spare of sleep, sparer of diet, and sparest of time that, when the days for eating, drinking, clothing, and sleeping shall be no more, I may eat of my Saviour's hidden manna, drink of the new wine in my Father's kingdom, and inherit that rest which remaineth for the people of my God for ever and ever.

He was plain of speech. Living near to nature, he heard God's voice in solitude as well as in Scripture. Familiar with the Old Testament, he made frequent use of its picturesque language (Luke 3:17; Isa. 66:24; with Amos 9:6). After his sojourn in the desert, brooding over the need and peril of his time, he came forth to speak of barren trees fit only for burning—vipers fleeing before the flaming scrub. John saw in his desert surroundings much that symbolized his nation's calamity and which lent color to his solemn warnings of impending doom.

There is a great deal we would like to say about this man sent from God who had the privilege of acting as the forerunner and then as the baptizer of Jesus, who said of him that he was greater than a prophet. Space, however, forbids a full exposition of this mighty character in the Bible's portrait gallery. The preacher might be able to expand the following features: his self-denial (Matt. 3:4); courage (Matt. 3:7; 14:4); powerful preaching (Mark 1:5); humility (Mark 1:7); holiness (Mark 6:20); burning zeal (John 5:35); honor (Matt. 11:11); ministry of witness (John 10:41); preparatory work (Matt. 11:10); testimony (John 1:29-36); results (Matt. 9:14); death (Matt. 14:10), of which Spurgeon said, "John was the first Baptist Minister to lose his head through dancing."

4. *John, the son of Zebedee and Salome,* the fisherman who became the beloved disciple, *The Apostle of Love.*

The Man Whom Jesus Loved

This younger brother of James has the rare distinction of being known as "the disciple whom Jesus loved." The original of his name means, "whom Jehovah loves" and John's experience corresponded to his name. From the many references to this honored disciple we can gather these facts:

He was a native of Bethsaida in Galilee.

His godly parents were probably cousins of Christ, and John was their youngest son.

His mother followed Christ, ministered unto Him, was at the Cross and among those who went to anoint the body of Christ with sweet spices.

His father was a fisherman owning his own vessel and prosperous enough to hire servants.

John himself was also a successful fisherman.

He was called to discipleship while plying his nets.

He was the youngest of the disciples, the *Benjamin* among the Twelve.

He was one of the select triumvirate, Christ's inner cabinet of three, Peter and James being the other two.

He was surnamed by Christ as a son of "Boanerges" because of his prophetic zeal and resolution to witness for Christ.

He was treated by Christ with greater familiarity than the others enjoyed.

He sat next to Christ at the Last Supper.

He was intrusted with the care of the mother of Jesus.

He died when he was almost one hundred years of age.

He wrote the gospel and three epistles bearing his name, and also the Book of Revelation. How true are Wesley's words of John the Beloved:

> A Caesar's title less my envy moves
> Than to be styled the man whom Jesus loves;
> What charms, what beauties in his face did shine
> Reflected ever from the face divine.

From manifold references in the four gospels, the Acts and Revelation, the preacher can develop these traits in John's character: his natural energy (Mark 3:17); his intolerance (Mark 9:38); his vindictiveness (Luke 9:54); his ambition (Mark 10:35–37); his eagerness to learn (John 13:23; I John 2:9); his sympathy (John 19:26); his love (I John 4:7–21).

JOIADA [Joi' a dă]—JEHOVAH SETS UP or HATH KNOWN.

1. *Son of Eliashib*, whose son married the daughter of Sanballat the Horonite (Neh. 13:28). A great-grandson of Jeshua the high priest (Neh. 12:10, 11, 22; 13:28).

2. *A son of Paseah* who helped to repair the gate of Jerusalem (Neh. 3:6). Also called Jehoiada.

JOIAKIM [Joi' a kĭm]—JEHOVAH SETS UP or ESTABLISHES. *A high priest,* son of Jeshua the priest who returned with Zerubbabel (Neh. 12:10, 12, 26).

JOIARIB, JEHOIARIB [Joi′ a rĭb, Jē hoi′ a rĭb]—JEHOVAH DEPENDS or CONTENDS.

1. *A descendant of Aaron,* father of Jedaiah (Neh. 11:10; 12:6, 19). See Jehoiarib.

2. *One whom Ezra sent to Iddo* to ask for ministers for the Temple (Ezra 8:16).

3. *A descendant of Pharez* whose family dwelt in Jerusalem (Neh. 11:5).

JOKIM [Jŏ′ kim]—JEHOVAH SETS UP. *A descendant of Shelah,* son of Judah (I Chron. 4:22).

JOKSHAN [Jŏk′ shan]—FOWLER. *A son of Abraham* by Keturah and father of Sheba (or Saba) and Dedan (Gen. 25:2, 3; I Chron. 1:32).

JOKTAN [Jŏk′ tan]—LITTLE, SMALL or DISPUTE. *A son of Eber* of the family of Shem, from whom thirteen Arab tribes sprang (Gen. 10:26; I Chron. 1:19–23).

JONADAB [Jŏn′ a dăb]—JEHOVAH IS LIBERAL, WHO ACTS AS A PRINCE or BOUNTEOUS.

1. *A son of Shimeah,* David's brother (II Sam. 13:3, 5, 32, 35).

2. *The son of Rechab,* the Kenite, whom Jehu took with him to show him his zeal for the Lord. He became head of a tribe refraining from agriculture and from wine (I Chron. 2:55; Jer. 35:6–19). See Jehonadab.

JONAH, JONA, JONAS [Jō′ nah, Jō′ nă, Jō′ nas]—A DOVE. *The son of Amittai,* and the first Hebrew prophet, or missionary, sent to a heathen nation (II Kings 14:25; Jonah 1:1).

The Man Who Ran Away

The meaning of the prophet's name is suggestive. When first chosen, it doubtless meant to Jonah's mother gentleness and love. This son of Amittai was a citizen of Gath-hepher in Zebulun of Galilee and a subject of the Northern Kingdom. He is thus a proof of the false statement of the Pharisees about no prophet coming out of Galilee (John 7:52).

Jonah lived in the early part of the reign of Jeroboam II, and in a period when the kingdom was in a divided and abject condition. He is without doubt one of the earliest, if not the first, of the prophets whose writings are preserved to us. He is the first of a new order of prophets, appearing that he might declare God's love claims the whole world. By friend and foe Jonah has been ridiculed and tortured and treated as a myth or parable. Our Lord, however, believed him to be

a historic person; so do we! For proof in this direction compare
Jonah 1:7 with Matthew 12:39, 40 and Luke 11:29, 30; Jonah 3:5
with Matthew 12:41.

Jonah's mission was to Nineveh and therefore beyond the bounds of
Israel, which is in perfect harmony; for whenever God brought His
people into any relation with other peoples, He made Himself known
to them as was the case in Egypt through Joseph and Moses; to the
Philistines through the capture of the Ark; to the Assyrians by Elisha;
to Nebuchadnezzar and Belshazzer by Daniel.

Within the Book of Jonah we have the most beautiful story ever
told in so small a compass. In 1,328 words we are given a wealth of
incident and all the dialogue needed to carry on the grand and varied
action. Jonah was an isolationist, believing that salvation was for the
Jews, and the Jews only. Through affliction he came to know of God's
embracing love (John 3:16). Dealing with Jonah as a servant, Dr. C.
I. Scofield gives us these helpful points: disobedient (Jonah 1:1-11);
afflicted (Jonah 1:12-17); praying (Jonah 2:1-9); delivered (Jonah
2:10); recommissioned (Jonah 3:1-3); powerful (Jonah 3:4-10); perplexed, fainting but not forsaken (Jonah 4:1-11).

Another serviceable outline for the worker can be developed around
these thoughts:

Chapter one: A disobedient prophet running *from* God and punished.

Chapter two: A praying prophet running *back* to God and delivered.

Chapter three: A faithful prophet running *with* God and rewarded.

Chapter four: An angry prophet running *ahead* of God and rebuked.

Here are other aspects to deal with: Jonah was sent to a foreign field
(Jonah 1:2); sought to flee from his unwelcome task (Jonah 1:3); was
overtaken in his flight (Jonah 1:4-17); found God in the depth of the
sea (Ps. 139:10; Jonah 2); became a revivalist (Jonah 3); was disappointed with his own work (Jonah 3:5-10; 4:1); reveals bigotry
(Jonah 4:1-3); was taught the breadth of divine mercy (Jonah 4:4-11).
See below Jonas, Jona.

Jona is given as the name of the father of Peter (Matt. 16:17; John
1:42; 21:15).

JONAN, JONAM [Jō' nan]—GOD HATH BEEN GRACIOUS. *An ancestor
of Joseph,* the husband of Mary, the mother of our Lord (Luke 3:30).

JONAS, JONA [Jō' nas, Jō' nă]—A DOVE. *The father of the Apostle
Peter.* Barjona means "son of Jona" (John 1:42; 21:15, 16, 17).

JONATHAN [Jŏn' a than]—THE LORD GAVE.
1. *A Levite* who entered the service of Micah as "father and priest."
The son of Gershom, son of Manasseh (Judg. 17:10; 18:30).
2. *Eldest son of King Saul* and close friend of David. Jonathan
left one son, Mephibosheth (I Sam. 13:2, 3). With his father Jona-

than fell in battle with the Philistines and there is nothing comparable in literature to David's lament and eulogy when he heard of their death (II Sam. 1).

The Man Who Was Content To Be Second

The story of Jonathan is remarkable in that we know so much about him, yet he was never called to office. While he lived, he was known only as the eldest son of Saul. He knew he would never succeed his father as king. With true humility he could say to David, whom he loved, "I shall be next to thee." After his lamentable death he is only mentioned as the father of Mephibosheth. He is not to be found among the worthies in Hebrews eleven. Doubtless he was one not counted worthy by the world.

Jonathan personified all the Christian virtues or graces that Peter wrote about (II Pet. 1:5-7). In battle, his valour was absolutely stainless, and he acted without fear. As to the love-covenant Jonathan made with David, how rare it is to see two men loving one another as these two did. Truly, Jonathan was possessed of a heroic faith (I Sam. 14:6); undaunted courage (I Sam. 14:7-14); self-sacrificing friendship (I Sam. 18:4; 19:2).

3. *A Son of Abiathar,* a high priest in David's time (II Sam. 15:27, 36; 17:17, 20; I Kings 1:42, 43).

4. *A son of Shimea,* David's brother (II Sam. 21:21; I Chron. 20:7).

5. *Son of Jashen* and one of David's heroes (II Sam. 23:32; I Chron. 11:34).

6. *A son of Jada* and grandson of Onam (I Chron. 2:32, 33).

7. *An uncle of David* (I Chron. 27:32), who was a scribe.

8. *The father of Ebed* who returned with Ezra (Ezra 8:6).

9. *The son of Asahel,* who assisted in the matter of foreign wives (Ezra 10:15).

10. *A descendant of Jeshua* the high priest (Neh. 12:11).

11. *A priest descended from Melicu* (Neh. 12:14).

12. *A priest descended from Shemaiah* (Neh 12:35). Called Jehonathan in Nehemiah 12:18.

13. *A scribe* in whose house Jeremiah was imprisoned (Jer. 37:15, 20; 38:26).

14. *A son of Kareah* who went to Gedaliah (Jer. 40:8).

JORAH [Jō' rah, Jō' raī]—RAIN OF AUTUMN. A Gadite chief (I Chron. 5:13; Ezra 2:18).

JORAM [Jō' ram]—JEHOVAH IS HIGH.

1. *A son of Toi,* king of Zobah (II Sam. 8:10). Called Hadoram, meaning "Hadah is exalted" (I Chron. 18:10).

2. *A son of Jehoshaphat,* who reigned for eight years (II Kings 8:16-19; 11:2; I Chron. 3:11; Matt. 1:8). Called also Jehoram.

3. *A son of Ahab,* king of Israel, who reigned for eleven years.

With him the dynasty of Omri ceased (II Kings 8:16–29). Called also Jehoram.

4. *A Levite,* descendant of Eliezer the son of Moses (I Chron. 26:25).

5. *One of the priests sent by Jehoshaphat* to instruct the people (II Chron. 17:8).

JORIM [Jŏ' rim]—HE THAT EXALTS THE LORD. *An ancestor of Jesus Christ* (Luke 3:29).

JORKOAM [Jôr' ko ăm]—SPREADING THE PEOPLE. *A son of Raham,* and descendant of Hebron through Caleb the spy (I Chron. 2:44). Some writers have Jokdeam or Jorkeam. See Joshua 15:56 for the name of a city.

JOSAPHAT [Jŏs' a phăt]—THE LORD JUDGES. *An ancestor of Christ* (Matt. 1:8). See Jehoshaphat.

JOSE [Jŏ' se]—AID. *An ancestor of Christ through Mary* (Luke 3:29).

JOSECH [Jŏ' sĕch]—*An ancestor of Christ* who probably lived after the exile (Luke 3:26). K.J.V. and A.V. call him Joseph.

JOSEDECH [Jŏs' e dĕch]—JEHOVAH IS RIGHTEOUS. *The father of Joshua* the high priest who helped to rebuild the altar and the temple (Hag. 1:1, 12, 14; 2:2, 4; Zech. 6:11.) Also called Jozadak (Ezra 3:2, 8; 5:2).

JOSEPH [Jŏ' zeph]—MAY GOD ADD or INCREASER.

1. *Poetic description of the descendants of Joseph* the son of Jacob (Deut. 33:13).

2. *The Father of Igal,* one of the spies sent by Moses into Canaan (Num. 13:7).

3. *A son of Asaph* (I Chron. 25:2, 9).

4. *A man of the family of Bani* who had taken a foreign wife (Ezra 10:42).

5. *A priest* of the family of Shebaniah in Joaakim's time (Neh. 12:14).

6. *Ancestor of Joseph,* Mary's husband (Luke 3:24).

7. *Another ancestor of Joseph* in the same line (Luke 3:26).

8. *A more remote ancestor of Joseph,* Mary's husband (Luke 3:30).

9. *A disciple* nominated with Matthias to take the place of Judas Iscariot among the disciples. Matthias was chosen (Acts 1:23). This Joseph must have been a commendable Christian since he was nominated as an apostle.

10. *The eleventh son of Jacob* and first of Rachel, and one of the

most outstanding men of the Bible, meriting honorable mention (Gen. 30:24, 25).

The Man Whose Dream Came True

The story of this young man who went from pit to palace and from rags to riches, never loses its charm for young and old alike. It would take a book itself to fully portray all the vicissitudes and virtues of Joseph, who kept his record clean. All that we can do in our treatment of him is to suggest a few aspects of his character for development.

Joseph was a youthful dreamer and his dream came true (Gen. 37:5–9; 41:42–44).

Joseph labored as a slave, but was faithful in hard places (Gen. 39:1–6, 20–23).

Joseph enjoyed the presence of God and won the confidence of his master (Gen. 39:2, 4).

Joseph had physical beauty, but it was never a snare to him (Gen. 39:6).

Joseph resisted temptation. His godless mistress could not seduce him. Grace was his to flee youthful lusts. Thus he did not commit a "great wickedness" (Gen. 39:7–13).

Joseph was silent amid foul accusations and the appearance of guilt and unjust punishment (Gen. 39:14–20).

Joseph was unspoiled by sudden prosperity. When days of honor followed days of humiliation, he did not yield to pride (Gen. 41:14–16).

Joseph the interpreter of dreams proved that "prison walls do not a prison make." He acknowledged his dependence upon God for illumination, proving that he was not a mere dreamer but an interpreter of dreams (Gen. 40).

Joseph manifested great wisdom, brotherly love, filial devotion and utter submission to God (Gen. 43:20; 45:8, 14, 23; 47:7). He knew how to return good for evil (Gen. 50:16–21). If we cannot have all the gifts of Joseph, who is a perfect type of Christ, we can certainly covet all his graces. If we cannot have his greatness, we can certainly emulate his goodness.

R. W. Moss says, "A very high place must be given Joseph among the early founders of his race. In strength of right purpose he was second to none, whilst in graces of reverence and kindness, of insight and assurance, he became the type of a faith that is at once personal and national (Heb. 11:22), and allows neither misery nor a career of triumph to eclipse the sense of Divine destiny."

11. *The husband of Mary,* and foster-father of our Lord (Matt. 1:16–24; 2:13; Luke 1:27; 2:4–43; 3: 23; 4: 22; John 1:45; 6:42).

The Man of Wood and Nails

It is somewhat unique that two Josephs were associated with Christ, one at His birth and the other at His death. Both of these godly men gave Jesus of their best. In this section we think of Joseph the carpenter, who was present at the manger when Jesus was born, even though he was not His father. While Christ came as the Son of Man, He was never *a* son of a man.

Joseph's presence at Christ's birth witnesses to a severe test that had emerged triumphant. Mary was the pure young woman he had fallen in love with, and was about to make his wife. Yet the Child she was about to bear would not be his. Seeing her "great with child," without fanfare Joseph was minded to put her away. He never acted rashly with his espoused, although he was baffled by her condition. This serves for all time as an example of godly wisdom and tender consideration for others.

Bitterly disappointed that Mary had apparently betrayed him, yet believing, he made no haste. As a praying man he waited upon God, and his love for and patience with Mary were rewarded. God understood his mental difficulties and rewarded Joseph's conscientious attitude toward Mary by revealing His redemptive plan. God never fails those who carry their anxieties to Him. Joseph received a direct and distinct revelation from God, and at once his fears were banished, and his line of duty made clear.

Tenderly he cared for his dear one as if the Child she was bearing were his own. Overawed by the mystery of it all, that his beloved Mary had been chosen as the mother of the Lord he as a devout Jew had eagerly anticipated, we can imagine how he would superintend every detail of the Nativity.

What holy thoughts must have filled the mind of Mary's guardian. Where suspicion regarding Mary's purity once lurked, strong faith now reigned as he looked into the lovely face of Mary's Child. At last God's promises had been fulfilled and before him was the Babe through whom God's covenants would be established.

When it became necessary because of Herod's hatred to flee into Egypt, Joseph cared for Mary and her first-born Son with reverent devotion until tidings came that Herod was dead, and that they could safely return to their own land. While a shroud of secrecy covers the thirty years Christ spent at home, we can be sure of this, that between Jesus and Joseph there was an affection strong and deep.

Briefly stated, we have these glimpses of Joseph:

I.   He was "a son of David" and could claim royal or priestly descent (Matt. 1:20).

II.   His family belonged to Bethlehem, David's city.

III.   He followed the trade of carpenter, and doubtless taught Christ how to use wood and nails (Matt. 13:55).

IV.   He was a pious Israelite, faithful in all the ordinances of the Temple (Luke 2:22–24, 41, 42).

V.   He was a kindly, charitable man, treating Mary gently in her time of need (Matt. 1:19; Luke 2:1–7).

VI.   He was faithful in his care of Christ, and deserved to be called His "father" (Luke 2:33. John 1:45; 6:42).

VII.   He never appears in the Gospels after Christ was twelve years of age and became "a son of the Law" (Luke 2:41–51), which may suggest that he died during the interval. This would explain why Jesus at His death asked John to care for His mother.

VIII.   He died, tradition says, at the age of 111 years, when Jesus was but eighteen years of age.

12.   *Joseph of Arimathaea,* a secret disciple of Jesus, whose unused grave was surrendered to Jesus. Thus the One born in a virgin womb was buried in a virgin tomb (Matt. 27:57–60; Mark 15:43; Luke 23:50; John 19:38).

The Man Who Gave His Grave to Jesus

This wealthy and devout Israelite, a member of the Sanhedrin, lived in a city of Jews (Luke 23:51). It is to the provision he made for the body of Christ that Isaiah had reference when he said, "He made His grave with the rich" (Isa. 53:9). Of this renowned Joseph we discover:

I.   He was an honorable counselor (Mark 15:43). Because of his adherence to the Law and integrity of life he was a member of the governing body known as the Sanhedrin.

II.   He looked for the kingdom of God. Immersed in Old Testament Scriptures, he anticipated the reign of the promised Messiah.

III.   He was "a good man and just" (Luke 23:50, 51). As the Bible never uses words unnecessarily, there must be a distinction between "good" and "just." As a "good man" we have his own *internal* disposition — what he was in himself. As a "just man" we have his *external* conduct — what he was towards others. His just dealings were the fruit of the root of his goodness. His was the belief that knew how to behave.

IV.   He was a secret disciple (John 19:38). Joseph of Arimathaea was similar to Nicodemus in his respect for our Lord as a man, admiration for Him as a teacher, belief in Him as the Christ, and yet, till now, his lack of confessing Him before men. Dreading the hostility of his colleagues on the Sanhedrin, he kept his faith secret.

V.   He begged the body of Jesus (Matt. 27:58). As soon as Jesus was dead, Joseph hastened to Pilate for permission to inter His body. David Smith observes that when the condemnation of Jesus was over— a condemnation in which Joseph took no part — he realized how cowardly a part he had played and, stricken with shame and remorse, plucked up courage and went in to Pilate and asked for the body of Jesus. It was common for friends of the crucified to purchase their bodies, which would otherwise have been cast out as refuse, and give them decent burial (Mark 15:45).

VI.   He gave his grave to Christ (Matt. 27:59, 60). With lingering reverence Joseph paid his last respects to the One he admired, and in the hour of sorrow helped the friends and not the foes of the righteous Sufferer. Joseph had a garden close to Calvary, where he had hewn a smoothed and polished tomb in the side of the rock as his own last resting place, in which, aided by Nicodemus, he buried the linen-covered and perfumed body of Christ.

VII.   Joseph, legend tells us, was sent to Britain by Philip the Apostle, and founded the Church of Glastonbury. Medieval chroniclers delighted to tell of the staff Joseph stuck into the ground. The staff supposedly took root, brought forth leaves and flowers and became the parent of all the Glastonbury thorns from that day to this.

JOSES [Jŏ′ sēs]—HE THAT PARDONS.
1. *One of the brethren of our Lord* (Matt. 13:55; Mark 6:3). R.V. gives name as Joseph.
2. *The son of Mary*, probably the same as No. 1 (Matt. 27:56; Mark 15:40–47).
3. *The personal or natal name of Barnabas*, the companion and missionary colleague of Paul (Acts 4:36). The R.V. gives Joseph.

JOSHAH [Jŏ′ shah]—JEHOVAH IS A GIFT or UPRIGHTNESS. *A Simeonite chief*, son of Amaziah (I Chron. 4:34).

JOSHAPHAT [Jŏsh′ a phăt]—JEHOVAH JUDGES.
1. *A Mithnite*, one of David's valiant men (I Chron. 11:43).
2. *A priest*, one of the trumpeters before the Ark during its removal to Jerusalem (I Chron. 15:24). R.V. gives Jehoshaphat.

JOSHAVIAH [Jŏsh a vī′ ah]—JEHOVAH IS EQUALITY or SITTETH UPRIGHT. *One of David's heroes* (I Chron. 11:46).

JOSHBEKASHAH [Jŏsh bĕk′ a shah]—SEAT OF HARDNESS. *A son of Heman*, and David's leader of song (I Chron. 25:4, 24).

JOSHEB-BASSHEBETH, JOSHEB-BASSEBET—Given as a proper name in the R.V. of II Samuel 23:8. Probably Ish-baal, meaning "there is a Lord" or Jashobeam (I Chron. 11:11).

JOSHUA, JEHOSHUA, JEHOSHUAH, JESHUA, JESUS [Jŏsh′ u ă, Jĕ hŏsh′ u ă, Jĕsh′ u ă, Jĕ′ sus]—JEHOVAH IS SALVATION.
1. *The son of Nun* and successor of Moses and author of the book bearing his name. He is also called Hoshea (Num. 13:8, 16; Deut. 32:44).

The Man Who Was a Soldier-Saint

Joshua has been rightly called, "The first soldier consecrated by sacred history." A profitable way of studying his profile is to think of him in the following roles:

As a Son. Joshua was the son of Nun — a name meaning "prosperity, durable" — and of the tribe of Ephraim. Nothing is known of his mother. One usually finds, however, a good and gracious woman in the background of a man who reaches a position of influence and honor. Without doubt, Joshua's parents feared the God of Israel, and he continued their godly influence.

As a Slave. Born during the weary years of bondage his nation suffered in Egypt under Pharaoh, Joshua knew something of the lash of the whip, the almost impossible task in the brick-fields, and the deep sigh of liberty. But little did he realize that although a slave, he would rise to become Israel's supreme leader and commander. He had witnessed the moral and social degradation of his countrymen brought about by the terrible idolatries of that time. Thus, when he came to the position of leadership, his solemn commands were colored by early experience (Josh. 24:15).

As a Soldier. Joshua was pre-eminent as a military leader who knew how to plan campaigns, discipline his forces, use spies, but above all, pray and trust in God. Many a general has closely studied Joshua's conquest of Canaan and followed his strategy. Read how he discomfited Amalek (Ex. 17:9-16)! He never stooped to pilfering and plunder. It was as true of him as of Sir Henry Havelock, of whom it was said, "He was every inch a soldier, and every inch a Christian." Joshua was first of all a good soldier of the Lord whom he encountered and obeyed as Captain of the Lord's host (Josh. 5:13-15).

As a Servant. Joshua's victory over Amalek gave him the open door of further usefulness and responsibility. That he was prepared for the responsibilities of leadership is evidenced by the fact that because of his unswerving loyalty and devotion, he is called "the servant of Moses'" (Num. 11:28; Josh. 1:1).

As a Spy. Joshua, along with eleven others, was chosen to search the land of Canaan (Num. 13:1-16). It was at this time that Moses changed his servant's name from Oshea or Hoshea, meaning "help" to Joshua, meaning "God's help" or "salvation." The changed name indicated the desire of Moses to lift the thoughts of the people Godward, and to lead them from reliance upon leaders to God's help. Along with Caleb, Joshua brought back a faithful report of the land, which the people rejected, and wandered thereby for forty years in the wilderness. But Joshua profited by such an experience (Josh. 2:1, 2).

As a Saviour. Moses, representing the Law, brought the people to the border of the land, but it took a Joshua (God's salvation) to take them into the land. Divinely commissioned for such a task, he was probably about eighty-five years of age when he assumed command at Shittim. What a saviour he was! How marvelously was he helped to roll away Israel's reproach and to lead them to possess their possessions! His conquests and victories are typical of all the Lord has made possible for His own.

As a Statesman. What magnanimity and unselfish statesmanship Joshua revealed! Once the division of the land was completed, he carried through the setting up of the Tabernacle, the appointing of the cities of refuge, the arrangement of the Levitical order and service, with the same precision and thoroughness that characterized his other work as Israel's Premier and leader.

As a Saint. Joshua's saintliness marked him out as Moses' successor (Deut. 34:9). What a soldier-saint he was!

He was filled with the Spirit of God (Deut. 34:9).

He enjoyed the presence of God (Josh. 1:5; 6:27).

He was indwelt by the word of God (Josh. 1:8).

He was ever obedient to the will of God (Num. 32:12; Josh. 5:14).

No wonder his death at 110 years of age was deeply mourned and his eminent service universally acknowledged! The brief but noble epitaph of the historian is eloquent with meaning, "before Joshua, the servant of the Lord." Dead, he could yet speak, for the nation continued to serve the Lord all the days of the elders that outlived Joshua (Josh. 24:3).

2. *A Beth-shemite,* and owner of a field in the days of Eli (I Sam. 6:14, 18).

3. *The Governor of Jerusalem* in the days of Josiah (II Kings 23:8).

4. *The son of Josedech* and high priest at the time of the rebuilding of the Temple (Hag. 1:1; 2:4; Zech. 3; 6:11).

JOSIAH [Jō sī ah]—THE FIRE OF THE LORD or JEHOVAH SUPPORTS. *The king of Judah* who succeeded his father Amon, when only eight years old, and one of Judah's good kings (I Kings 13:2; II Chron. 34:3).

The Man Who Sought After God

The history of Israel's later kings makes dreary reading. Says J. G. Greenhough,

> Four-fifths of them were equally deficient in brains and morals, a combination of wickedness and folly, with nothing of the king about them but the name. But here and there you come upon a man amidst all these royal puppets. It is like finding a garden in a Sahara, or a jewel in a heap of sham trinkets and dirty stage finery. Josiah breaks a long, monotonous series of absolutely worthless monarchs. Before and behind him are moral waste and darkness. He stands out as a figure worth looking at and loving . . . Josiah's good reign was like a burst of brilliant sunset, before the final darkness comes on.

In a life worth studying, let us list a few incidents illustrating the noble character of Josiah.

He was left parentless at eight years of age. Josiah had a sorrowful childhood, and as a king at eight years of age, he was introduced to scenes of violence, outrage and civil war. But God was more than a Father to this fatherless boy.

He had a good and darling mother. We know nothing about the mother who undertook Josiah's training apart from her name, Jedidah, meaning, "God's darling," which she was not called for nought. She sought to make her son what she was called, "God's darling," and her labor had its sweet reward.

He sought after God at the age of sixteen. After sixteen years in the nursing hands of his good mother, Josiah turned from the ways of his father Amon and his grandfather Manasseh, and took his nobler and remoter ancestor, David, as his model. In life's fair morning, Josiah set his heart to seek the Lord.

He purged Judah and Jerusalem when he was twenty. Youth did not deter Josiah from necessary reformation. Out went all forms of idolatry. Borne along by a noble rage, he swept away the groves full of abominations. Would that the fervent zeal and righteous enthusiasm of this earnest, passionate young man might characterize more young men today!

He rebuilt the Temple when he was twenty-six. This consecrated young man saw that it was of no use destroying idols unless he had something better to replace them. Thus when his destroying fever had spent its force, Josiah began to rebuild and repair the house of God. In turning over the rubbish of the Temple, the king made a strange discovery. He came across a buried and forgotten copy of the Law, the reading of which strangely affected him. Profoundly humbled, he laid the axe to his own corruptions, and went forward to grow in wisdom and godliness.

He reigned for thirty-one years and was only thirty-nine when he died. That Josiah was beloved by his people is indicated by their deep and long-continued mourning after his death.

2. *A son of Zephaniah* who dwelt in Jerusalem in Zechariah's time (Zech. 6:10). Perhaps the Hen of verse fourteen.

JOSIBIAH [Jŏs ĭ bī' ah]—JEHOVAH CAUSES TO DWELL. *A Simeonite* (I Chron. 4:35). Also called Joshibiah.

JOSIPHIAH [Jŏs ĭ phī' ah]—JEHOVAH WILL INCREASE. *Head of the house of Shelomith* after the exile (Ezra. 8:10).

JOTHAM, JOATHAM [Jŏ' tham]—JEHOVAH IS UPRIGHT.
1. *The youngest son of Gideon.* He escaped from Abimelech (Judg. 9:5, 7, 21, 57).
2. *A son of Jahdai* (I Chron. 2:47).
3. *A son of Azariah* or Uzziah and king of Judah. He was the father of Ahab, king of Judah (II Kings 15:32). Little is known of this Jotham apart from his rebuilding of the Temple gates.

JOZABAD, JOSABAD [Jŏz' a băd, Jŏs' a băd]—JEHOVAH HATH BE-STOWED or ENDOWED.
1. *A Gederathite of Judah* who joined David at Ziklag (I Chron. 12:4). Also called Josabad.
2. *A man of Manasseh* who did the same (Chron. 12:20).
3. *Another Manassite* who did the same (I Chron. 12:20).
4. *A Levite,* and one of the overseers of tithes in Hezekiah's reign (II Chron. 31:13).
5. *A Levite chief* in Josiah's reign (II Chron. 35:9).
6. *A son of Jeshua,* employed in weighing the sanctuary vessels brought from Babylon (Ezra 8:33).
7. *A priest* who had married a foreign wife (Ezra 10:22).
8. *A Levite* who had also married a foreign wife (Ezra 10:23).
9. *A Levite interpreter* of the Law read by Ezra (Neh. 8:7).
10. *A chief Levite* in Jerusalem after the exile (Neh. 11:16).

JOZACHAR, JOZACAR [Jŏz' a chär]—JEHOVAH REMEMBERS. *The son of the Moabitess, Shimeath.* He slew Joash or Jehoash, king of Judah (II Kings 12:21). Erroneously called Zabad in II Chronicles 24:26.

JOZADAK [Jŏz' a dăk]—JEHOVAH IS GREAT or JUST. *A priest,* the father of Jeshua who returned from exile with Zerubbabel (Ezra 3:2, 8; 5:2; 10:18; Neh. 12:26). Called Josedech in Haggai and Zechariah. See also Jehozadak.

JUBAL [Jū' bal]—PLAYING, RAM'S HORN or A TRUMPET. *The younger son of Adah,* wife of Lamech, and the inventor of musical instruments (Gen. 4:21). Jubilee is from his name, which is used to describe the trumpet employed at the glad time of the Jewish jubilee.

JUCAL, JEHUCAL [Jŭ cal]—ABLE. *A son of Shelemiah* and prince of Judah, a deadly enemy of Jeremiah (Jer. 38:1).

JUDAH, JUDA, JODA [Jū'dah]—OBJECT OF PRAISE or PRAISE OF THE LORD. *The fourth son of Jacob by Leah,* and founder of a tribal family (Gen. 29:35; Num. 26:19–21; 1 Chron. 2:3–6).

The Man Who Was Praised

The character of Judah is revealed in his confession of sin before Joseph (Gen. 44:18–34). This appeal has been described as "One of the noblest pieces of natural eloquence in any literature, sacred or profane." In the last words of Jacob much is said of Judah (Gen. 49:8). We have:

I. His praise. "Thou art he whom thy brethren shall praise." The origin of his name is to be found in the gratitude of his mother at the time of his birth (Gen. 29:35). A still more distinguished mother praised the Lord for a greater Son who came from the tribe of Judah (Luke 1:46, 47).

II. His conquests. "Thy hand shall be in the neck of thine enemies." Here we have the prophecy of a conqueror, the anticipation of the figure of the lion, which was emblazoned on the flag of Judah, and was symbolic of the strength of the tribe in battle. Judah was the first tribe called to fight the Canaanites after Joshua's death (Judg. 1:1, 2) — a battle ending in victory for Judah. See also Psalm 18:40.

III. His pre-eminence. "Thy father's children shall bow down before thee." The superiority of the tribe of Judah continued almost to the end of the Old Testament and passed on to Him who has the pre-eminence in all things. Judah was first in numbers, first in territory, first in marching order, first in prowess, first in war.

IV. His regal dignity. The lion-king of the forest became the symbol of Judah, as the king of the tribes (Num. 2:3, 4). "A lion's whelp," speaks of the first energy of youth, and the early days of Judah were full of vigor and energy. How prophetic all this is of Him who came as the Lion of the tribe of Judah! The old divines said that Christ was a lamb in His death, but a lion in His resurrection. How different is His prowess from the deadly power of him who is a roaring lion!

2. *An ancestor of Kadmiel* who helped to rebuild the Temple (Ezra 3:9).

3. *A Levite* who had taken a strange wife (Ezra 10:23).

4. *A Benjamite,* son of Senuah, second in authority over Jerusalem in Nehemiah's day (Neh. 11:9).

5. *A Levite* who returned from exile with Zerubbabel (Neh. 12:8).

6. *A prince of Judah* (Neh. 12:34).

7. *A priest and musician* (Neh. 12:36).

JUDAS, JUDA, JUDE [Ju' das]—PRAISE OF THE LORD.

1. *The disciple surnamed Iscariot,* who betrayed the Master and then hanged himself. He was the only one of the Twelve who was not a Galilean. He acted as treasurer of the apostolic band (John 6:71; 12:6; 13:26, 29).

The Man Who Was Guilty of a Horrible Crime

The Gospels represent the betrayal of Christ by Judas as a horrible, diabolical crime. And it stands out as the darkest deed in human history. The word "betray" is a remarkable one meaning "to deliver up." This is what Judas did — delivered up Jesus. Yet such a dastardly action was overruled, for Jesus was delivered by the determinate counsel of God.

Judas is a strange character and everything about his choice and conduct is mysterious. Why was he chosen? All we can say in answer is in the declaration, "that the scriptures might be fulfilled" (Matt. 26:56). The greater mystery is, why did Christ choose you and me to be His followers? Think of these features:

I. Judas' terrible crime was predicted (Ps. 109:5-8; Acts 1:16).

II. His cruel bargain was foretold (Zech. 11:12, 13).

III. He became a devil incarnate. "One of you is a devil." As Jesus became God-incarnate, Judas became the devil-incarnate.

IV. He is called "a son of perdition." Because the same designation is used of the Man of Sin, some writers feel that this grim figure will be Judas incarnate (II Thess. 2:3).

V. He was a thief. He kept the bag which represented responsibility. Christ chose Judas as treasurer for the Twelve because of his commercial instinct and business acumen, but he prostituted his gift. His very endowment became a snare. A blessing was turned into a curse.

VI. He betrayed Christ with a kiss. The hatefulness of his crime reached its limit when he gave the enemies of Christ the symbol of affection. How wicked is the human heart—deceitful above all things!

VII. He was the recipient of divine patience. Why he persisted in following Christ we cannot say. All we can do is marvel at the love and patience of Christ as He bore with Judas for three years. He knew all along that this so-called disciple would betray Him, yet He kept the door open. Even when He met Judas after his contract with the foes of Christ, He greeted him as "friend." We would have scorned the traitor and hissed "enemy" or "traitor." Not so Christ, who is patient toward all men.

VIII. He went out to his own place (Acts 1:25). It was in self-excommunication. Christ did not excommunicate Judas — He only ratified the choice. Up to the last He gave Judas a chance to halt and turn from his wickedness. But when the die had been cast, Jesus said, "What thou doest, do quickly."

We leave our glimpse of the despicable man of the Bible with two lessons in mind:

The journey into sin gains momentum. We never know where a wrong path may end. Sin only needs opportunity to carry us to its utmost depths.

It is sadly possible to be associated with Jesus, to hear His gracious words, witness His wonderful works, yet refuse Him our heart's allegiance and be ultimately lost.

2. *Half-brother of Jesus,* brother of James and writer of the epistle known by his name (Matt. 13:55; Mark 6:3; Luke 6:16; Acts 1:13; Jude 1). See Jude.

3. *An apostle* also known as Lebbeus or Thaddeus (John 14:22).

4. *A Galilean* who stirred up sedition shortly after the birth of Christ (Acts 5:37).

5. *One with whom Paul lodged* in the street called Straight (Acts 9:11).

6. *The prophet surnamed Barsabas,* sent with Silas to Antioch (Acts 15:22, 27).

JUDE [Jūde]—PRAISE.—Jude is the English form of the name Judas. The author of the next to last book of the Bible describes himself as *a brother of James* (Jude 1). See James, No. 4. Although he calls himself "the servant of Jesus Christ," he was our Lord's brother, and like the rest of His brethren did not believe in Christ when they lived together under the same roof (Matt. 13:55; John 7:5).

His brief epistle contains an earnest warning appeal to the saints to defend the faith in an age of apostasy. Couched in vivid and picturesque language, Jude's letter was addressed to a church or circle of churches exposed to false teachers. What a message it has for our hearts in these days of modernistic teaching!

JULIUS [Jū' lǐ ŭs]—CURLY HEADED. *A centurion of Augustus' band* who conducted Paul to Rome (Acts 27:1, 3). Evidently he was kind to the apostle and treated him with all deference and respect (Acts 27:3–43; 28:16).

JUNIA, JUNIAS [Jū' niǎ]—BELONGING TO JUNO. *A Jewish Christian of Rome.* This kinsman and fellow prisoner of Paul became a Christian before Paul (Rom. 16:7).

JUSHAB-HESED [Jŭ' shăb-hĕ' sed]—LOVINGKINDNESS IS RETURNED. *A son of Zerubbabel,* of the family of David (I Chron. 3:20).

JUSTUS [Jŭs' tus]—JUST OR RIGHTEOUS.
1. *A surname of Joseph or Barsabas,* the disciple who was the unsuccessful candidate for apostleship (Acts 1:23).
2. *A godly man of Corinth,* whose house was next to the synagogue and with whom Paul lodged (Acts 18:7).
3. *The surname of a Jew* called Jesus from whom Paul sent a salutation to the Colossian Church (Col. 4:11).

K

KADMIEL [Kăd' mĭ el]—GOD IS OF OLD.
1. *A Levite* and head of a tribal family which returned from Babylon with Zerubbabel (Ezra 2:40; Neh. 7:43).
2. *A Judahite* who assisted in the rebuilding of the Temple (Ezra 3:9).
3. *A Levite* who led the devotions of the people (Neh. 9:4, 5; 10:9; 12:8, 24).

KALLAI [Kăl' la ī]—JEHOVAH IS LIGHT or SWIFT. *A priest,* and head of his father's house of Sallai in the line of Joiakim the high priest (Neh. 12:20).

KAREAH, CAREAH [Kā rĕ' ah, Cā rĕ' ah]—BALD. *The father of Johanan,* a captain of the Jews when Gedaliah was governor of Jerusalem II Kings 25:23; Jer. 40:8, 13).

KEDAR [Kĕ'där]—POWERFUL. *One of the sons of Ishmael,* the son of Abraham and Hagar (Gen. 25:13; I Chron. 1:29). Also name of the tribe which sprang from Kedar (Ps. 120:5).

KEDEMAH [Kĕd' e mah]—EASTERN. *Youngest son of Ishmael* and head of a tribal family (Gen. 25:15; I Chron. 1:31).

KEILAH [Kēi' lah]—ENCLOSED. *A descendant of Caleb,* son of Jephunneh (I Chron. 4:19). Also the name of a city in Judah (Josh. 15:44).

KELAIAH—[Kē lă' iah]—JEHOVAH IS LIGHT. *A Levite* who had married a foreign wife (Ezra 10:23). Also called Kelita.

KELITA [Kĕl′ ĭ tă]—DWARF or POVERTY.
1. *Same as Kelaiah* (Ezra 10:23), see above.
2. *A priest* who explained the Law when read by Ezra (Neh. 8:7).
3. *A Levite* who sealed the covenant made by Nehemiah (Neh. 10:10).

KEMUEL [Kē mū′ el]—CONGREGATION OF GOD or GOD STANDS.
1. *The third son of Nahor*, Abraham's brother, and head of a branch of Aramaeans (Gen. 22:21).
2. *A prince of the tribe of Ephraim* and a commissioner for the allotment of Canaan (Num. 34:24)
3. *A Levite*, the father of Hashabiah, ruler of the Levites in David's time (I Chron. 27:17).

KENAN [Kē′ nan]—ONE ACQUIRED or BEGOTTEN. *The son of Enosh*, the grandson of Adam (I Chron. 1:2). Called Cainan in Genesis 5:9.

KENAZ, KENEZ [Kē′ năz]—THIS POSSESSION or HUNTING.
1. *The fourth son of Eliphaz*, the son of Esau (Gen. 36:11, 15; I Chron. 1:36).
2. *A duke of Edom*, chieftain in Mount Seir. Perhaps the same as No. 1 (Gen. 36:42; I Chron. 1:53).
3. *The brother of Caleb* the son of Jephunneh, and father of Othniel, one of Israel's judges (Josh. 15:17; Judg. 1:13; 3:9, 11; I Chron. 4:13).
4. *A grandson of Caleb* the son of Jephunneh (I Chron. 4:15). For Kenezites or Kenizzites see Genesis 15:19 and Joshua 14:6, 14.

KEROS [Kē′ ros]—THE REED OF A WEAVER'S BEAM. *One of the Nethinims* whose descendants returned from exile with Zerubbabel (Ezra 2:44; Neh. 7:47).

KIRJATH-JEARIM [Kûr′ jath-jē′ a rĭm]—CITY OF FORESTS. The name of tribal appellation of a descendant of Caleb, son of Hur (I Chron. 2:50–53). Also name of a city of Judah (Josh. 9:17).

KISH, CIS [Kĭsh, Cĭs]—POWER or STRAW.
1. *A. Benjamite*, a son of Abiel and father of Saul, Israel's first king (I Sam. 9:1, 3; 10:11, 21). Called Cis in Acts 13:21.
2. *Son of Abi-gibeon*, a Benjamite (I Chron. 8:30; 9:36).
3. *A Levite in David's time*, of the family of Merari and the house of Mahli (I Chron. 23:21, 22; 24:29).
4. *A Levite and a Merarite* who assisted in the cleansing of the Temple in Hezekiah's time (II Chron. 29:12).
5. *A Benjamite*, ancestor of Mordecai, the cousin of Queen Esther (Esther 2:5).

KISHI [Kĭsh′ ĭ]—BOW OF JEHOVAH. *A Merarite Levite,* ancestor of Ethan (I Chron. 6:44). Also called Kushaiah.

KITTIM [Kĭt′ tim]—THEY THAT BRUISE. *A son of Javan,* son of Japheth (Gen. 10:4; I Chron. 1:7). His descendants covering Cyprus and the adjacent coasts and islands are called Chittim.

KOHATH [Kō′ hath]—ASSEMBLY. *The second son of Levi* and ancestor of Moses. He died at the age of 133, and was the head of the Kohathites (Gen. 46:11; Num. 3:27, 30). The Kohathites held particular offices in sanctuary service.

KOLAIAH [Kŏl a ĭ′ ah]—THE VOICE OF JEHOVAH.
1. *A Benjamite* who settled in Jerusalem after the captivity (Neh. 11:7).
2. *The father of the false prophet Ahab,* who suffered death for his false prophecies (Jer. 29:21).

KORAH, KORE, CORE [Kō′ rah, Kō′ rē, Cō′ rē]—BALDNESS or ICV.
1. *A son of Esau by Aholibamah,* and founder of a tribe (Gen. 36:5, 18).
2. *A son of Eliphaz* and grandson of Esau (Gen. 36:16).
3. *A son of Hebron,* son of Mareshah, son of Caleb (I Chron. 2:43).
4. *A grandson of Kohath,* son of Levi — ancestor of sanctuary musicians (I Chron. 6:22).
5. *The son of Izhar,* the grandson of Levi, who with Dathan and Abiram conspired against Moses and Aaron (Ex. 6:21, 24; Num. 16). Jude 11 gives Core for Korah.
Korah, along with his two companions, resisted the civil authority of Moses. For refusing to appear before him as commanded, Korah, Dathan and Abiram along with their households and houses were swallowed up by the earth (Num. 16). Then there came the further revolt of Korah against Moses and Aaron, in the interests of the people at large as against the tribe of Levi. The rebels were consumed by fire from the Lord (Num. 17). There followed the opposition of Korah and 250 Levites against the monopoly of the priesthood claimed by Aaron. The "gainsaying," meaning *against the Word,* was Korah's denial of the authority of Moses as God's chosen spokesman, and intrusion into the priest's office (Jude 11).

KORE [Kō′ rē]—A PARTRIDGE or A CRIER.
1. *A Korahite* whose son, Shallum, was a Tabernacle gatekeeper (I Chron. 9:19; 26:1, 19).
2. *A Levite,* son of Immah, set over the free will offerings in Hezekiah's time (II Chron. 31:14).

KOZ [Kŏz]—THE THORN.

1. *A priest* whose descendants returned from exile with Zerubbabel, but lost their position through inability to prove their descent (Ezra 2:61; Neh. 7:63).

2. *Ancestor of Meremoth,* who helped in the repair of the wall (Neh. 3:4, 21).

KUSHAIAH [Kōō shā' iah]—BOW OF JEHOVAH. *A Levite of the family of Merari* (I Chron. 15:17). Called Kishi in I Chronicles 6:44.

L

LAADAH [Lā' a dah]—ORDER or FESTIVAL. *A Judahite, son of Shelah* and father of the inhabitants of Mareshah (I Chron. 4:21).

LAADAN [Lā' a dăn]—WELL ORDERED or FESTIVE-BORN.
1. *A descendant of Ephraim* through his son Beriah (I Chron. 7:26).
2. *A descendant of Gershon,* the son of Levi (I Chron. 23:7, 8, 9; 26:21).

LABAN [Lā' ban] —WHITE or GLORIOUS. *The son of Bethuel and* grandson of Nahor. Laban was the brother of Rebekah and father of Rachel and Leah. He lived in Padan-aram (Gen. 24:29, 50; 27:43; 28:2, 5).

The transactions between Laban and Jacob are well known, and speak of cunning on both sides. After twenty years Laban was reluctant to part with Jacob, whose presence was an assurance of divine blessing. "In character Laban is not pleasing," says T. A. Moxon, "and seems to reflect in an exaggerated form the more repulsive traits in the character of his nephew, Jacob: yet he shows signs of generous impulses on more than one occasion, and especially at the final parting with Jacob."

LAEL [Lā' el]—DEVOTED TO GOD. *A Gershonite,* father of Eliasaph (Num. 3:24).

LAHAD [Lā' hăd]—OPPRESSED or DARK COLORED. *A son of Jahath,* great-grandson of Shobal, the son of Judah (I Chron. 4:2).

LAHMI [Läh' mī]—MY WAR or A WARRIOR. *A brother of Goliath the Gittite.* Lahmi was slain by Elhanan, the son of Jair (I Chron. 20:5).

LAISH [Lā' ish]—A LION. *A man of Gallim,* father of Phalti or Phaltiel. His son became the husband of Michal, David's wife (I Sam. 25:44; II Sam. 3:15.)

LAMECH [Lā' mech]—OVERTHROWER, A STRONG YOUNG MAN or WHO IS STUCK.

1. *A son of Methusael* of the race of Cain, who had two wives, Adah and Zillah. It is not difficult to trace in the moral character of Lamech a close resemblance to Cain. We can detect the same haughty spirit, the same self-confidence, the same disregard of human life, the same absence of reverence for God. His address to his wives is that of one who glories in his self-strength and vigor (Gen. 4:18, 19, 23, 24).

2. *A son of Methuselah,* and father of Noah. This antediluvian was of the race of Seth (Gen. 5:26–31) and an ancestor of Christ (Luke 3:36).

LAPPIDOTH, LAPIDOTH [Lăp' i dŏth]—TORCHES, ENLIGHTENED or LIGHTENING FLASHES. *The husband of Deborah the prophetess* (Judg. 4:4). Deborah herself was "a woman of lightning flashes."

LAZARUS [Lăz' a rŭs]—GOD HATH HELPED or WITHOUT HELP.

1. *The beggar in the parable of the rich man.* This is the only instance where Jesus gives a name to a parabolic character, and there was an idea in early times that it was not a parable but a story from real life (Luke 16:19–31).

2. *The brother of Mary and Martha* of Bethany whom Jesus raised from the dead (John 11; 12:1–17).

The Man Who Lived Again

Alexander Whyte comments,

Lazarus of Bethany comes as near to Jesus of Nazareth, both in his character, and in his services, and in his unparalleled experience, as mortal men ever come. Lazarus' name is never to be read in the new Testament till the appointed time comes when he is to be sick, ...to die, and to be raised from the dead for the glory of God. Nor is his voice heard. Lazarus loved silence. He sought obscurity. He liked to be overlooked. He revelled in neglect...The very Evangelists pass over Lazarus as if he were a worm and no man.

I. He is the subject of the greatest and most startling miracle of the gospel story.

II. He was the friend of Jesus, being loved by Him. Jesus wept at his grave.

III. His resurrection threatened the life of Jesus. The Sanhedrin were determined to put Him to death.

IV. His attendance at Simon's banquet excited the enthusiasm of the people (John 12:9, 17, 18).

After his presence as an honored guest at Simon's house, Lazarus vanishes from the gospel story. Of all men, he should have stood by Jesus at His trial and crucifixion. Doubtless Lazarus was forced to flee, seeing that the infuriated elders determined his death (John 12: 10, 11). With a deep affection for his Friend, Lazarus would withdraw more for His sake than for his own. He felt his presence only increased the Master's danger.

LEBANAH, LEBANA [Lĕb'a nah, Lĕb a nă]—POETIC DESIGNATION FOR THE MOON. *The head of a family of Nethinims* who returned from exile (Ezra 2:45; Neh. 7:48).

LEBBAEUS [Lĕb bae' us]—MAN OF HEART. *An apostle surnamed Thaddeus* (Matt. 10:3). See Thaddaeus.

LECAH [Lĕ' cah]—ADDITION. *Son of Er,* the son of Shelah, the son of Judah (I Chron. 4:21). Lecah may be the name of the place where Er dwelt.

LEHABIM [Lĕ' hā bĭm]—FLAME-COLORED. *The third son of Mizraim,* who is reckoned to be the ancestor of the Egyptian Lybians (Gen. 10:13; I Chron. 1:11).

LEMUEL [Lĕm' u el]—DEVOTED TO GOD or GOD IS BRIGHT. *The royal author of Proverbs* 31:1, 4 who reproduces what his mother taught him. He has been identified as Solomon or Hezekiah. It is also suggested that the name may be a fanciful title to represent any virtuous king, invented for the purpose of conveying certain axioms.

LETUSHIM [Lĕ tŭ' shim]—OPPRESSED or STRUCK. *Son of Dedan,* grandson of Abraham by Keturah (Gen. 25:3).

LEUMMIM [Lĕ ŭm'mim]—PEOPLES or NATIONS. *Another son of Dedan* and founder of a tribe called Beni Lam (Gen. 25:3).

LEVI [Lĕ' vī]—JOINED or ADHESION.
1. *Another name for Matthew,* the one-time Roman tax-gatherer (Mark 2:14; Luke 5:27, 29). See Matthew.
2. *An ancestor of Jesus Christ* (Luke 3:24).
3. *Another ancestor of Jesus Christ* (Luke 3:29).
4. *The third son of Jacob by Leah.* Levi had three sons, and died in Egypt at the age of 137 (Gen. 29:34; 46:11; Ex. 6:16). His descendants, the Levites, had care of the sanctuary. The Book of Leviticus describes their ministry.

The Man of Isolation

Isolation is a feature in the history of Levi, quite as much as it characterizes Simeon, with whom he is paired. *The capacity to stand alone* made Simeon and Levi conspicuous among their brethren in their attack upon the Shechemites, and proved a valuable instrument for the work of the Lord. The tribe of Levi was fitted by the discipline of trial to discharge a most important duty in Israel — a duty which made Levi second in importance to none but Judah, whose *forerunner* and counterpart he was formed to be. Levi stands before Judah in the prophecies of Jacob — Judah before Levi in the blessings of Moses, the man of God.

"The true Levites," says Dr. C. H. Waller, "are the men who have been made lonely among their brethren that they may live alone with Jehovah, and so dwell as the families of others that they may unite them to the family of God."

Levi came under the ban of Jacob, who, in his prophecy set Simeon and Levi under a "curse." To the patriarch they were bad brothers.

Dr. Dinsdale Young has a telling chapter on Simeon and Levi in which he elaborates on these features:

I.   They constituted an unholy brotherhood — they had a common disposition (Gen. 49:5).

II.   They had unhallowed belongings (Gen. 49:5) — sinful homes and perverted instruments.

III.   They drew from their father a heart-felt prayer (Gen. 49:6). Reviewing their sinful courses, the dying father prays for them.

IV.   Their father uttered a righteous imprecation upon their sin. Jacob did not curse *them,* but their sin (Gen. 49:7).

V.   A just judgment was pronounced upon them, "I will divide them" (Gen. 49:7). Though divided and scattered, they were not cut off from the promised land. Theirs was not the abundant entrance of others, yet they were privileged to enter.

LIBNI [Lĭb′nī]—WHITE or DISTINGUISHED.
1.   *Son of Gershon* and grandson of Levi. Also founder of a tribal family (Ex. 6:17; Num. 3:18, 21; I Chron. 6:17, 20).
2.   *Grandson of Merari* the son of Levi (I Chron. 6:29).

LIKHI [Lĭk′ hī]—JEHOVAH IS DOCTRINE or CHARACTERIZED BY KNOWLEDGE. *A son of Shemidah,* a Benjamite (I Chron. 7:19).

LINUS [Lī′ nus]—NETS. *A Christian at Rome* from whom Paul sent greetings. (II Tim. 4:21). Early writers identify him as the first Bishop of Rome, whose episcopate lasted about twelve years.

LO-AMMI [Lŏ′-ăm′ mī]—NOT MY PEOPLE. *A symbolic name given by Hosea to his son* (Hos. 1:9, 10; 2:23). See Hosea.

LOT [Lŏt]—CONCEALED or MYRRH. *The son of Haran,* Abraham's brother, who accompanied Abraham from Mesopotamia to Canaan (Gen. 11:27, 31; 12:4; 13:1).

The Man with a Worldly Mind

We deem it necessary to spend a little time with this character because we believe Lot to be a representative man. Perhaps there is no Bible figure who represents so many men of today as Lot of Sodom. Where you can find one Abraham, one Daniel or one Joshua you will find a thousand Lots.

Lot started out well. But he acquired riches and with his wealth came trouble. He and his uncle, Abraham, came out of Egypt with great possessions. Then came the strife among the herdsmen of both men. Lot could not pick a quarrel with his uncle, so he separated from him and made the greatest mistake of his life in doing so. If determined to have the well-watered plain, Lot should have asked Abraham to choose for him. But no, when he lifted up his eyes and saw the fruitful land, his decision was made.

The moments of solemn, decisive choice reveal the character of the two men involved. Lot's choice was a bad and selfish one, ending in disaster. Abraham's choice was lofty, unworldly, superior to all petty consideration. Although, as elder of the two, he had the undisputable right to precedence in the choice, Abraham behaved like the high-minded, noble-hearted gentleman he was and so left the choice to Lot. The meanness of Lot is seen in that he took the best. The crisis of that moment was decided by the tenor of Lot's life. In spite of his general righteousness, Lot must have had a vein of great selfishness within.

In one of his unique speeches — *The Subject of Salaries* — Benjamin Franklin said, "There are two passions which have a powerful influence in the affairs of men. These are *Ambition* and *Avarice*: the love of power and the love of money. Separately, each of these has great force in prompting man to action; but when united in view of the same object they have in many minds the most violent effects." It was thus that Lot became "a bad lot." In his choice *ambition* and *avarice* became one. Points to ponder are:

I. His wealth (Gen. 13:5). Lot had a house — Abraham was content with a tent (Gen. 18:1; 19:3). Lot was no pilgrim (Heb. 11:13).

II. His choice (Gen. 13:10, 11). Lot was guided by selfishness, and pitching his tent toward Sodom was soon living in it (Gen. 14:12).

III. His righteous soul (II Pet. 2:8). Lot did many things that were inconsistent with his true character and that were dishonoring to God. He sat down with the ungodly. Yet he showed some good qualities. He entertained the angels — believed their message — endeavored to restrain the wicked Sodomites. His good, however, was mixed with evil.

IV. His loss (Gen. 19:17-28). Lot narrowly escaped judgment. He lost everything, his wife was turned into a pillar of salt, he lost his wealth, he sacrificed his influence, for the people of Sodom despised him, his relatives mocked him, his two daughters shamed him. Lot offered no prayer for Sodom and manifested no desire for the salvation of its people. His only concern was for his own safety, and angels delivered him.

LOTAN [Lō′ tan]—A COVERING. Son of Seir the Horite (Gen. 36:20, 22, 29; I Chron. 1:38, 39).

LUCIFER [Lōō′ cĭ fẽr]—THE SHINING ONE. *A name applied to the king of Babylon* by Isaiah to describe his glory and pomp (Isa. 14:12). Prophetically, a name of Satan.

LUCIUS [Loo' cius]—OF THE LIGHT or LUMINOUS.
1. *A Christian from Cyrene,* a teacher at Antioch (Acts 13:1).
2. *A kinsman of Paul.* Perhaps the same as No. 1 (Rom. 16:21).

LUD [Lŭd]—BENDING. *The son of Shem* and founder of descendants found in various parts (Gen. 10:22; I Chron. 1:17; Isa. 66:19; Ezek. 27:10).

LUDIM [Loo' dim]—BENDING. *Son of Mizraim* (Gen. 10:13; I Chron. 1:11).

LUKE, LUCAS [Looke, Loo' cas]—LIGHT-GIVING or LUMINOUS.
The Man Who Wrote the Most Beautiful Book in the World
Less is known of Luke than any other New Testament writer. This we do know, he was a Gentile and probably the brother of Titus (II Cor. 8:16; 12:18). Paul speaks of him as a "beloved physician." Luke must have been a man of some wealth, otherwise he could not have traveled with Paul as his friend and useful companion (Acts 1:1; Col. 4:14; II Tim. 4:11; Philem. 24). Tertullian said of this native of Antioch that he received his illumination from Paul.

Luke was a man of learning and knowledge, an exact observer and faithful recorder. His medical training taught him to be exact. He is in the first rank as a reliable historian, scholarly, skilful and sympathetic (Luke 1:1–3; Acts 1:1–3). His gospel is the most literary of the four. With his Greek mind he had a sense of form, a beautiful style — studied and elaborate. A poet, he was unsurpassed as a word-painter. Luke's gospel has been described as the most wonderful book ever written, the most beautiful book in the world. Above it and within it we hear the rustle of the angels' wings, the music of angels' songs.

Luke's qualifications for his great ministry were manifold. Above and beyond all else, he had the inspiration of the Holy Spirit. Then there was his long and close companionship with Paul, and Luke the follower of Paul set down in a book the Gospel which Paul loved to preach. Luke also had abundant opportunities for personal acquaintance with other apostles. His liberal education also indicated that in him God had a proper vessel for the accomplishment of His plan. The wisdom of the divine choice was justified.

Luke's mission was to proclaim Christ's humanity. His is *The Gentile Gospel,* thus he traces Christ's lineage back to Adam, and gives prominence to the sympathy and sociableness of Jesus as the Man (Luke 15:1) who came to save (Luke 19:10). As the representative of Grecian reason and culture, Luke presented Christ as the true Representative of universal man.

Luke wrote both the gospel bearing his name and the Book of Acts (Luke 1:1; Acts 1). The characteristic features of his gospel are clearly defined.

I. Its gratuitousness. It is *par excellence* the gospel of pardon and redemption (Luke 1:28; 2:40).

II. Its sympathy. Christ is before us as the Healer of broken hearts and the Sharer of our woes. Luke is the gospel of philanthropy.

III. Its joyfulness. How full of praise the Gospel of Luke is! Angelic joy is prominent (Luke 1:14; 2:10, 13; 15:7).

IV. Its thanksgiving. The Church continues the hymns of high praise Luke taught her to sing.

V. Its teaching of the holy spirit. It is profitable to gather out all Luke's references to the special missions of the Spirit (Luke 1:15, 35, 41; 2:23, 26; 3:22; 4:1).

LYSANIAS [Lĭ sā' nĭ as]—ENDING SADNESS or DRIVES AWAY SORROW. *A tetrarch of Abilene* (Luke 3:1).

LYSIAS [Lŷ sĭ as]—HE WHO HAS THE POWER TO SET FREE. *Chief captain of the Roman garrison at Jerusalem,* who rescued Paul from the mob of hostile Jews (Acts 23:26; 24:7, 22).

M

MAACAH, MAACHAH [Mā' a cah, Mā' a chah]—COMPRESSION or OPPRESSION.

1. *Son of Nahor,* Abraham's brother (Gen. 22:24).
2. *A king of Maachah* (II Sam. 10:6).
3. *The father of Achish,* king of Gath in Solomon's time (I Kings 2:39).
4. *The father of Hanan,* one of David's mighty men (I Chron. 11:43).
5. *The father of Shephatiah,* ruler of the Simeonites in David's time (I Chron. 27:16). Also the name of several women (see II Sam. 3:3; I Chron. 2:48; 3:2; 8:29; II Chron. 11:21, 22; 15:16), and the name of a Syrian city (II Sam. 10:8).

MAADAI [Mā ăd' aī]—JEHOVAH IS ORNAMENT or WAVERING. *One of the sons of Bani* who had married a foreign wife (Ezra 10:34).

MAADIAH [Mā a dī' ah]—ORNAMENT OF JEHOVAH. *A chief priest* who returned from captivity (Neh. 12:5).

MAAI [Mā ā' ĭ]—JEHOVAH IS COMPASSIONABLE. *A priest* who blew a trumpet at the dedication of the walls (Neh. 12:36).

MAASAI, MAASIAI [Mā ăs' ĭ' aī]—WORK OF JEHOVAH. *An Aaronite* whose family of Immer dwelt in Jerusalem after the captivity (I Chron. 9:12).

MAASEIAH [Mā a sē′ iah]—WORK OF JEHOVAH or JEHOVAH IS A REFUGE.

1. *A Levite* who acted as a porter and also assisted in the service of praise in David's reign (I Chron. 15:18, 20).

2. *One of the captains* who co-operated with the high priest Jehoiada in placing Joash on the throne of Judah (II Chron. 23:1).

3. *An officer of king Uzziah* (II Chron. 26:11).

4. *Son of Ahaz,* king of Judah (II Chron. 28:7).

5. *The governor of Jerusalem* in Josiah's reign (II Chron. 34:8).

6. *A priest* who had married a foreign wife (Ezra 10:18).

7. *A priest of the family of Harim* who had done the same thing (Ezra 10:21).

8. *A priest of the family of Pashur* who had done the same thing (Ezra 10:22).

9. *Another of the same* (Ezra 10:30).

10. *Father of Azariah* who repaired a part of the wall of Jerusalem beside his own house (Neh. 3:23).

11. *A priest who assisted Ezra* in the reading of the Law (Neh. 8:4).

12. *A priest who explained the Law* read by Ezra (Neh. 8:7).

13. *One who sealed the covenant* (Neh. 10:25).

14. *A man of Judah,* a descendant of Pharez (Neh. 11:5).

15. *A Benjamite* whose descendants lived in Jerusalem after the exile (Neh. 11:7).

16. *A priest* who assisted at the dedication of the wall. Perhaps the same as No. 11 (Neh. 12:41).

17. *Another priest* who took part in the above ceremony (Neh. 12:42).

18. *A priest* whose son was sent by king Zedekiah to inquire of the Lord (Jer. 21:1; 29:25; 37:3).

19. *The father of a false prophet* during the Babylonian captivity (Jer. 29:21).

20. *Son of Shallum.* An officer of the temple in Jehoiakim's reign (Jer. 35:4).

21. *The grandfather of Baruch,* Jeremiah's scribe and messenger (Jer. 32:12; 51:59).

MAASIAI [Mā ăs′ i aī]—WORK OF JEHOVAH. *An Aaronite* whose family came to Jerusalem after the exile (I Chron. 9:12).

MAATH [Mā′ ath]—WIPING AWAY. *An ancestor of Jesus* through Mary. He lived after Zerubbabel (Luke 3:26).

MAAZ [Mā′ ăz]—ANGER or COUNSELOR. *A son of Ram,* the eldest son of Jerahmeel (I Chron. 2:27).

MAAZIAH [Mā a zī′ ah]—STRENGTH or CONSOLATION OF JEHOVAH.

1. *A descendant of Aaron* responsible for sanctuary service in David's time (I Chron. 24:18).

2. *A priest* who on behalf of his father's house sealed the covenant (Neh. 10:8).

MACHBANNAI, MACHBANAI [Măch' ba naī]—CLOTHED WITH A CLOAK. *A Gadite warrior* who joined David at Ziklag (I Chron. 12:13).

MACHI [Mā' chī]—DECREASE. *A Gadite,* the father of Jeuel, one of Moses' spies (Num. 13:15).

MACHIR [Mā' chĭr]—SOLD or SALESMAN.
1. *The only son of Manasseh* and founder of a tribe (Gen. 50:23; Num. 26:29; 27:1).
2. *A son of Ammiel,* who was kind to David (II Sam. 9:4, 5; 17:27).

MACHNADEBAI [Măch na dĕ' baī]—GIFT OF THE NOBLE ONE. *A Jew who had taken a foreign wife* (Ezra 10:40).

MADAI [Măd' a ī]—MIDDLE. *A son of Japheth,* whose descendants lived in Media (Gen. 10:2; I Chron. 1:5).

MADMANNAH [Măd măn' nah]—HEAP. *A son of Caleb,* the son of Jephunneh (I Chron. 2:49). Also the name of a city of Judah (Josh. 15:31).

MAGDIEL [Măg' dĭ el]—RENOWN or HONOR OF GOD. *A duke of Edom* descended from Esau (Gen. 36:43; I Chron. 1:54).

MAGOG [Mā' gŏg]—EXPANSION or INCREASE OF FAMILY. *The second son of Japheth* and founder of descendants occupying Magog, or Scythia (Gen. 10:2; I Chron. 1:5; Ezek. 38:2; 39:6; Rev. 20:8). The grandson of Noah was the father of those Josephus calls the "Magogites," and those the Greeks call "Scythians." When Ezekiel used the terms Gog and Magog, he used them in a historical sense of the future, referring to the Prince of the Northern Confederacy and his scope of rule, and they are thus literally to be understood. Gog is the symbolic designation for the future head of all nations embraced within the Northern Confederacy (Ezek. 38; 39). Magog is the symbolic territory covered. When the Apostle John uses the terms it is to describe the wicked on the earth at the close of Christ's millennial reign, and is thus to be symbolically understood. Gog and Magog in the Book of Revelation are to be thought of in a *moral,* not a *geographical* sense (Rev. 20:8).

MAGOR-MISSABIB [Mā' gôr-mĭs' sa bĭb]—FEAR or TERROR IS ABOUT. *A prophetic name given to Pashur,* a priest and governor of the Temple who ill-treated the prophet Jeremiah (Jer. 20:3).

MAGPIASH, MAGBISH [Măg′ pĭ ăsh]—MOTH SLAYER or CLUSTER OF STARS. *One of the chiefs who with Nehemiah sealed the covenant* (Neh. 10:20).

MAGUS [Mă′ gŭs]—MAGICIAN. See *Simon Magus* (Acts 8:9).

MAHALALEEL, MAHALALEL, MALELEEL [Mā hā′ la lē el]— THE PRAISE OF GOD or GOD IS SPLENDOR.
1. *Son of Cainan*, the grandson of Seth (Gen. 5:12–17; I Chron. 1:2).
2. *One of the tribe of Judah*, of the family of Perez who lived in Jerusalem after the exile (Neh. 11:4).

MAHARAI [Mā hăr′ a ī]—IMPETUOUS or HASTY. *A Netophathite,* one of David's warriors (II Sam. 23:28; I Chron. 11:30; 27:13).

MAHATH [Mā′ hăth]—INSTRUMENT OF SEIZING or DISSOLUTION.
1. *A Kohathite Levite* of the line of Samuel (I Chron. 6:35; II Chron. 29:12).
2. *A Levite,* one of the overseers who cared for the tithes and offerings in Hezekiah's time (II Chron. 31:13).

MAHAZIOTH [Mā hā′ zĭ ŏth]—VISION OF SIGNIFICANCE. *One of the sons of Heman* who was responsible for the service of song in David's reign (I Chron. 25:4, 30).

MAHER-SHALAL-HASHBAZ [Mā′ hûr-shăl′ al-hăsh′ băz]—HASTEN THE SPOIL, RUSH ON THE PREY. *Symbolic name of Isaiah's son* (Isa. 8:1, 3).

MAHLAH, MAHALAH [Măh′ lah, Mā hā′ lah]—DISEASE or MILD-NESS. *A Manassite* whose mother was Hammoleketh (I Chron. 7:18). Also the name of Zelophehad's daughter (Num. 26:33).

MAHLI, MAHALI [Măh′ lī, Mā′ ha lī]—SICK or WEAK.
1. *A son of Merari,* son of Levi and brother of Mushi. Also the founder of a tribal family (Ex. 6:19; Num. 3:20, 33).
2. *A Levite,* son of Mushi (I Chron. 6:47; 23:23; 24:30).

MAHLON [Măh′ lon]—SICKLY or MILD. *Elder son of Naomi,* and Ruth's first husband who died in Moab (Ruth 1:2, 5; 4:9, 10).

MAHOL [Mā′ hŏl]—DANCING or JOY. *The father of three noted wise men* in Solomon's time (I Kings 4:31).

MAHSEIAH, MAASEIAH [Mā a sē′ iah]—JEHOVAH IS A REFUGE. *Grandfather of Baruch and Seraiah* (Jer. 32:12; 51:59).

MALACHI ⌈Măl' a chī]—MESSENGER OF JEHOVAH or MY MESSENGER.

1. *The last of the Old Testament prophets,* and author of the last book of The Minor Prophets.

The Man Who Believed in God's Electing Love

Nothing is known of Malachi save what his prophecy tells us. Ancient writers looked upon him as an angel incarnate, while a great number of Jews believed him to be Ezra the Scribe. It would seem as if he was connected with Nehemiah's work. Perhaps he prepared the way for it, helped in it and followed it up. Compare Malachi 1:8 with Nehemiah 5:15, 18, where it seems clear that he prophesied either during Nehemiah's absence in Persia (Neh. 13:6) or after Nehemiah assumed governorship. As the last of the prophets, he was the seal of all the goodly fellowship of prophets.

While Malachi's prominent message was the rebuke of the remnant and the announcement of future purging and blessing, the keynote of his book appears to be the unchangeableness of God, and His unceasing love (Mal. 1:2; 3:6). The tone of his message is expostulation blended with judgment. Yet gracious promises and assurances are interspersed like pearls gleaming against a dark background.

Features to note are the *whereins* repeated by Malachi's hearers. Against such the prophet amplifies and enforces his original charge (Mal. 1:2, 6, 7; 2:17; 3:7–9). We have:

I. The charge made against God involving an utter disregard of Him (Mal. 1:1, 2).

II. The rejection of the worship of God (Mal. 1:6–14).

III. The intense oration of His law (Mal. 2:1–9).

IV. Social wrongs and disorder in the home (Mal. 2:10, 16).

V. The blatant perversion of judgment (Mal. 2:17).

VI. Gross immorality and degradation (Mal. 3:5).

VII. Robbery in the service of the Temple (Mal. 3:7–9).

Other features to develop are:

Priestly qualifications—holiness, communion with God, usefulness and knowledge (Mal. 2:6, 7).

Ritual may be valuable. Only our capacity limits God's gifts (Mal. 3:10). Give and get (Mal. 3:12).

An ideal picture of the true gospel ministry (Mal. 2:5, 6).

The Lord's care for and interest in His people (Mal. 3:16, 18).

MALCHAM, MALCAM [Măl' cham]—REGNANT or RULE. *Son of Shaharaim,* a Benjamite (I Chron. 8:9). Also the name of an idol of the Ammonites (Zeph. 1:5). Perhaps the same as Molech and Mileom.

MALCHIAH, MALCHIJAH [Măl chī' ah, Măl chī' jah]—JEHOVAH IS KING.

1. *A Gershonite,* ancestor of Asaph, a leader of the singing in David's time (I Chron. 6:40).

2. *A priest,* the father of Pashur whose family lived in Jerusalem after the exile (I Chron. 9:12; Neh. 11:12).

3. *Head of the fifth course of priests.* Perhaps the same person as No. 1 (I Chron. 24:9).

4. *A son of Parosh who had married a foreign wife* (Ezra 10:25).

5. *Another son of Parosh who had done the same* (Ezra 10:25).

6. *Another who had done the same* (Ezra 10:31).

7. *The son of Rechab,* who repaired the dung gate (Neh. 3:14).

8. *One of the sons of Harim* who helped to repair the wall (Neh. 3:11).

9. *One of the guild of goldsmiths* who helped to repair the wall (Neh. 3:31).

10. *A prince or Levite* who stood at Ezra's left hand as he read the law (Neh. 8:4).

11. *A priest* who assisted in the dedication of the wall (Neh. 10:3; 12:42).

12. *Father of Pashur* whom Zedekiah sent to Jerusalem to consult the Lord (Jer. 21:1; 38:1).

MALCHIEL [Măl' chĭ el]—GOD IS A KING. *A son of Beriah,* son of Asher (Gen. 46:17; Num. 26:45; I Chron. 7:31). Founder of a tribal family.

MALCHIRAM [Măl chĭ' ram]—MY KING IS EXALTED or GOD IS EXALTED. *The son of Jeconiah,* son of king Jehoiakim of Judah (I Chron. 3:18).

MALCHI-SHUA, MELCHI-SHUA [Măl' chĭ-shū' ă, Mĕl' chĭ-shōō' ă] —KING OF HELP. *The third son of Saul,* slain by the Philistines at Mount Gilboa (I Sam. 14:49; 31:2; I Chron. 10:2).

MALCHUS [Măl' chus]—KING or COUNSELOR. *The high priest's servant* whose ear Peter cut off. He was healed by Jesus (John 18:10). Luke, the physician, is the only one who mentions the healing of the ear (Luke (22:51).

MALELEEL [Mā lĕ' le el]—PRAISE OF GOD. *An ancestor of Christ* (Luke 3:37). See Mahalaleel.

MALLOTHI [Măl' lo thī]—JEHOVAH IS SPEAKING or IS SPLENDID. *One of Heman's sons* responsible for the service of song (Chron. 25:4, 26).

MALLUCH [Măl' luch]—REIGNING or COUNSELOR.

1. *A Levite* of the family of Merari, of the house of Mushi (I Chron. 6:44).

2. *A son of Bani* who had married a foreign wife (Ezra 10:29).

3. *One of the family of Harim* who had done the same (Ezra 10:32).

4. *A priest and chief of the people* who signed the Covenant (Neh. 10:4; 12:2).

5. *Another chief who had done the same* (Neh. 10:27).

MAMRE [Măm' rē]—FATNESS or VIGOR. *An Amorite chieftain,* confederate with Abraham (Gen. 14:13, 24). Also the name of a place (Gen. 13:18) now known as Rameh or Ramel.

MANAEN [Măn' a ĕn]—CONSOLER COMFORTER. *A Christian prophet or teacher* in the Church at Antioch (Acts 13:1). As an early associate or "foster-brother" of Herod the tetrarch, he is thought by some writers to have befriended Herod.

MANAHATH ([Măn' a hăth]—RESTING PLACE or REST. *A son of Shobal,* son of Seir the Horite, and founder of a tribal family (Gen. 36:23; I Chron. 1:40; 2:52, 54). Also the name of a city in Benjamin (I Chron. 8:6).

MANASSEH, MANASSES [Mā năs' seh, Mā năs' sĕs]—CAUSING FORGETFULNESS.

1. *The elder son of Joseph,* who was born in Egypt and was half Hebrew and half Egyptian. He was the founder of a tribe (Gen. 41:51; Num. 1:10). Manasseh and his brother Ephraim were Jacob's Gentile descendants, since both were children of an Egyptian mother. Ephraim means "the multitude of nations," or "the fulness of the Gentiles," and was prophetic of Christ as the Saviour of the world. The tribe of Manasseh produced two out of the four Old Testament men whose faith has been thought worthy of notice in the New Testament—Gideon and Jephthah (Heb. 11:32).

2. *The grandfather of Jonathan* who. with his sons, became a priest to the tribe of Dan when they set up a graven image in Laish (Judg. 18:30). Perhaps Moses should be read for Manasseh in the verse.

3. *The son of Hezekiah* and father of Amon, king of Judah, who succeeded his father when he was only twelve years of age (II Kings 20:21; 21).

The Man Whose Policy Was Wrong

Manasseh, the prodigal king of the Old Testament, was overwhelmed by Assyrian forces and in the twenty-third year of his reign was taken as a prisoner to Babylon where he lingered for twelve years. During these years he turned to God and was restored to freedom and his kingdom. For the next twenty years left to him, he sought to undo the wrong of the past. His long reign of fifty-five years, the longest in Jewish history, closed not inauspiciously. He died a penitent, and left a son who followed his father in his sins but not in his repentance.

Gathering together what we can of Manasseh's life, it would seem that he was a man of policy:

His policy of idolatry. How he hated the first two commandments of Sinai, and reversed the reforms of his father! How exceedingly bold he was in his idolatry!

His policy of immorality. Idolatry and immorality go together, thus in rejecting God there came the worship of the Syrian Venus. This action let loose a flood of iniquity over the land of Judah.

His policy of persecution. Manasseh allowed nothing to stand in the way of license and open evil. Martyrdom became the cost of service. Idolatry was set up under the pain of death.

His policy of destruction. As far as he could, Manasseh destroyed the Word of God. Every copy found was consigned to the flames. God's truth testified too plainly against the sins of king and people. So complete was this destruction of the Word of God that when Josiah, Manasseh's grandson, came to the throne, a copy of it was found in the Temple.

But Manasseh's eyes were opened to his sinful condition and he sobbed out the misery of his helpless and craven soul. The *occasion* of his repentance was affliction. In the prison-house of Babylon he prayed. As to the *character* of his repentance, he besought the Lord and humbled himself before the God of his fathers and prayed unto Him. Penniless and penitent, his cry for mercy came from a broken heart, and God graciously received this prodigal king. Alas, however, he stopped short of being out-and-out for God! He allowed the high places of idolatry to remain. It will not be possible to doubt God's grace in heaven in the ages to come if we can but catch a glimpse of Manasseh—godly-reared, apostate, idolatrous, devilish, stricken, humbled, repentant Manasseh!

4. *One of the family of Hashum* who had married a foreign wife (Ezra 10:33).

5. *One of the family of Pahath-moab* who had done the same (Ezra 10:30).

MANASSES, MANASSEH [Mă năs′ sĕz, Mă năs′ seh]—MAKING TO FORGET. *A king of Judah* (Deut. 4:43; Matt. 1:10; Rev. 7:6). See Manasseh.

MANOAH [Mă nō′ ah]—REST or QUIET. *A Danite* belonging to Zorah, and father of Samson (Judg. 13; 16:31). Manoah was a godly, hospitable man and was against any alliance with the Philistines. A divine messenger brought him word of Samson's birth. We have four glimpses of this devout worshiper of Jehovah:

His remonstrance with Samson over his Philistine marriage (Judg. 14:2, 3).

His visit with Samson to Timnah (Judg. 14:5, 6).

His presence at his son's marriage (Judg. 14:9, 10).

His death before Samson's tragic death (Judg. 16:31).

MAOCH [Mă′ ŏch]—POOR or OPPRESSION. *Father of Achish*, king of Gath, to whom David fled when persecuted by Saul (I Sam. 27:2).

MAON [Mā′ on]—HABITATION. *Son of Shammai*, of the tribe of Judah

(1 Chron. 2:45). Also the name of a city in Judah now called Main (Josh. 15:55; I Sam. 25:2). Also the name of a tribe (Judg. 10:12).

MARESHAH [Mă rĕ' shah]—AT THE HEAD or POSSESSION.
1. *The father of Hebron* (I Chron. 2:42).
2. *The son of Laadah* (I Chron. 4:21). Also the name of a fortified city of Judah (Josh. 15:44).

MARK, MARCUS [Märk, Mär' cus]—A LARGE HAMMER or POLITE. John Mark was *a Jew and a son of Mary*, who was a leading Christian at Jerusalem.

The Man Who Recovered Himself

Mark was the Roman surname of this young associate of the apostle, while his first name, John, was his Hebrew name. Mark was an apostle but held no official position among the original Twelve. The first time we come across "John, whose surname was Mark," it is in connection with one of the most remarkable prayer meetings ever held. Herod, who had just beheaded James, had Peter under arrest. But the many friends of "The Big Fisherman" gathered in the home of "Mary the mother of John Mark" for prayer, which the Lord wonderfully answered (Acts 12:12).

Mark's mother was a godly, well-to-do widow in Jerusalem and her house was a favorite meeting place for the saints (Acts 12:12; Col. 4:10). Her brother, Barnabas, Mark's uncle, was a wealthy Levite from the island of Cyprus (Acts 13:1-5). In Barnabas, Mark had a staunch and gifted friend and counselor (Acts 11:24). While we are not told how or when Mark became a disciple of Christ, it is evident that he owed his conversion to Peter, since the apostle speaks of him as "Marcus, my son" (I Pet. 5:13). Thereafter he became a close companion of Peter for about twelve years. Doubtless Mark had heard and seen Christ. Tradition identifies Mark as "the certain young man," who followed Christ when all His disciples forsook Him and fled (Mark 14:51).

Mark became an attendant of Paul and Barnabas when they set out on their great mission tour (Acts 13:5), and these two godly men must have had a formative influence upon the character of young Mark. However, our next glimpse of him is disappointing. In the early years of his service, Mark was guilty of vacillating (Acts 13:13; 15:38). The ploughman looked back. So full of promise, Mark failed Paul and Barnabas at a crisis and brought about a severance of friends. The fear of what lay ahead in arduous missionary enterprise moved Mark to retrace his steps (Acts 13:13; 15:38).

But Mark won his spurs again and recovered his place in apostolic esteem. The years the locusts had eaten were restored and he became a valued colleague of Paul (Col. 4:10, 11; Philem. 24). A further impressive testimony to Mark's reinstatement is found in Paul's tribute to Mark's usefulness (II Tim. 4:11). The wound was thoroughly healed.

In the eventide of his life, Peter could write affectionately of Mark (I Pet. 5:13). Tradition says that Mark became a bishop and a martyr and that his body was removed to Venice and buried there. St. Mark's of Venice is dedicated to his fragrant memory. *The Lion,* the emblem of Mark's Roman Gospel, is emblazoned on the standard of the Venetian Republic.

As the ministry of Mark was peculiarly a Gentile one, he is recognized by his Gentile name. Writing specifically for Romans, who stood for power, Mark manifests Christ's power in service. Accustomed as Mark was to the might of Rome's legions, he exhibits the soldier's rapidity of movement and readiness to repel attack, and gives us in his shortest and simplest gospel, a progressive series of victorious conflicts. Vividness, compactness, direction, circumstantial evidence characterize his gospel.

The main lessons to be learned from the life of Mark are apparent:

I.   The blessings of a godly home. The Christian Church owes much to "Mary, the mother of John Mark."

II.   Much depends upon the choice of friends. Mark's life was lived in the company of godly men such as Peter, Paul and Barnabas.

III.   The possibilities of life. A widow's son became an apostle and a great historian, and his name is upon the lips of men the world over.

IV.   The reward for faithful service. We do not read of Mark preaching a single sermon or performing even one miracle. All that is said about him is that he was a *helper of others.* Such service never fails to receive its reward.

MARSENA [Mär′ se nä]—WORTHY. *One of the seven princes of Media* and Persia who had the right of access to the royal presence (Esther 1:14).

MASH [Măsh]—DRAWN OUT. *A son of Aram,* son of Shem (Gen. 10:23). Given as Meshech in I Chronicles 1:17.

MASSA [Măs′ sä]—BURDEN. *A son of Ishmael* and representative of a north Arabian tribe (Gen. 25:14; I Chron. 1:30).

MATHUSALA [Mä thōō′ sa lä]—WHEN HE IS DEAD IT SHALL BE SENT (FLOOD). *An ancestor of our Lord* (Luke 3:37). See Methuselah.

MATRI [Mä′ trī]—JEHOVAH IS WATCHING or RAIN. *The head of a Benjamite family* to which Saul belonged (I Sam. 10:21).

MATTAN [Măt′ tan]—GIFT.

1.   *A priest of Baal* slain before the altar during the revolution which led to the overthrow of Athaliah (II Kings 11:18; II Chron. 23:17).

2.   *The father of Shephatiah,* a prince in Judah in Zedekiah's time (Jer. 38:1).

MATTANIAH [Măt ta nǐ' ah]—GIFT OF JEHOVAH.

1. *A brother of Jehoiakim*, made king instead of his nephew, Jehoiakim, also called Zedekiah (II Kings 24:17).

2. *A Levite*, descendant of Asaph and founder of a tribal family (I Chron. 9:15; II Chron. 20:14; Neh. 11:17, 22; 12:8, 25, 35).

3. *A son of Heman the singer* in David's time (I Chron. 25:4, 16).

4. *A descendant of Asaph* who assisted Hezekiah in the cleansing of the Temple (II Chron. 29:13).

5. *A descendant of Elam* who had married a foreign wife (Ezra 10:26).

6. *A son of Zattu* who had done the same (Ezra 10:27).

7. *One of the family of Pahath-moab* who had done the same (Ezra 10:30).

8. *A son of Bani* guilty of the same act (Ezra 10:37).

9. *A Levite* whose descendant, Hanan, was one of Nehemiah's treasurers (Neh. 13:13).

MATTATAH, MATTATHAH [Măt' ta thah]—GIFT. *A son of Hashum* who put away his foreign wife (Ezra 10:33).

MATTATHA [Măt' ta thă]—A GIFT. *A son of Nathan* and grandson of David (Luke 3:31).

MATTATHIAS, MATTITHIAH [Măt ta thǐ' as, Măt tǐ thǐ' ah]—GIFT OF JEHOVAH.

1. *The son of Amos* and ancestor of Christ (Luke 3:25).

2. *An ancestor of the above*, separated by five generations (I Chron. 9:31; 25:3; Luke 3:26).

MATTENAI [Măt te nă' ī]—BESTOWMENT or GIFT OF JEHOVAH.

1. *A son of Hashum*, probably the same as Mattatah (Ezra 10:33).

2. *A son of Bani* who had married a foreign wife (Ezra 10:37).

3. *A priest of the family of Joiarib* (Neh. 12:19).

MATTHAN [Măt' than]—A GIFT.

1. *Grandfather of Joseph*, Mary's husband (Matt. 1:15; Luke 3:24).

2. *A more remote ancestor*, called Matthat (Luke 3:29).

MATTHEW [Măt' thew]—GIFT OF JEHOVAH.

The Man Who Left All to Follow Christ

This son of Alphaeus was a Hebrew with two names, a common thing in Galilee at that time. Mark and Luke, when recording Matthew's call to discipleship, speak of him as Levi, but Matthew himself uses the name he has been loved by throughout the Christian era. In his despised occupation he was Levi, a name meaning "joined," and joined he was to the world's crooked extortionate ways and mercenary aims.

He was also joined by his vocation to a hated foreign power under whose yoke orthodox Jews chafed.

Thus Levi and his craft were so detested that the very name *publican* or *tax-gatherer* was commonly associated with *sinner* (Luke 15:1). His original name connected him with the tribe of Levi, the priestly house set aside for sanctuary service. But this Levi degraded his holy name. Whether the Lord changed the name to Matthew when He called Levi or whether the new found disciple chose it himself, we do not know. Meaning "the gift of God," Matthew's new name magnified the transforming power of Christ and indicated that Matthew was like the One who called him, a gift to Israel and to the world.

The call to service came when he was sitting at the receipt of custom (Matt. 9:9; Luke 5:27) at Capernaum, the first world center, "the Great West Trunk Road from Damascus and the Far East to the Mediterranean Sea." Matthew was a "publican," which is not to be confused with the modern usage of the term as an English innkeeper. "Publican" is from the Latin word *publicannus,* meaning the collector of Roman taxes, the gathering of which was farmed out to minor officials ready to undertake this odious duty among their countrymen. A publican's reward was that he could extort for his own benefit more than was due, so long as the extortion did not lead to revolt. This was why the publicans, as a class, were spoken of as "leeches." They gorged themselves with money in the process of gathering money for the Caesars and consequently were reckoned to be outside the pale of decent society and of the synagogue.

"Jesus of Nazareth, the carpenter's Son, knew Matthew the publican quite well," says Alexander Whyte. "Perhaps only too well. Jesus and His mother had by this time migrated from Nazareth to Capernaum. He had often been in Matthew's toll-booth with His mother's taxes, with other poor people's taxes." But the outcast was called by Christ to a better occupation, to better wealth than silver and gold, to serve a better King than Caesar. Without hesitation Matthew left all, arose and followed Christ (Luke 5:28).

To celebrate his surrender to Christ, Matthew entertained Christ and others to a feast in his own house (Matt. 9:10; Luke 5:29). This feast was a token of gratitude for his emancipation from a sordid occupation, and revealed a missionary spirit. Such an "At Home" served a threefold purpose:

I.   It was a *Jubilee Feast* to commemorate his translation into a new life. Matthew wanted all and sundry to know that he was now a new creature in Christ Jesus.

II.   It was a *Farewell Dinner* to declare his determination henceforth to follow and serve his new found King. It was his public confession of surrender to the call of Christ.

III.   It was a *Conversazione* to introduce his old associates and friends to his new found Saviour, that they too might have an opportunity of hearing His wonderful words of life. Matthew sought to make a dinner party an evangelistic service. He knew many would come to his house to meet Christ who would not go to the synagogue to hear Him. Doubtless many publicans and sinners learned that day that Christ did not despise them.

Matthew became not only an apostle but also the writer of the first gospel. He left behind an undying image of his Lord. Matthew has given us *The Galilean Gospel*—unique in every way. When he rose and left all to follow Christ, the only things Matthew took out of his old life were his pen and ink. It is well for us that he did, since he took them with him for such a good purpose.

Matthew's gospel is striking in that it alone gives us the Parables of the Kingdom. The theme of his book, known as "the Hebrew Porch of the New Testament" is *The King and His Kingdom*. Some fifty-six times he uses the word "kingdom." In his record of the life and labors of Christ, Matthew has given us the image of Christ as it fell upon his own heart.

Trained to systematic methods and well acquainted with Jewish character and religion, Matthew was fitted to commend Christ to the Jews. He appeals to the student of Old Testament literature. As a writer, he is before us as an eyewitness of the events he describes and as earwitness of the discourses he records. As to his qualifications, Matthew had a love of truth and was sensible of the mercy of God, and the misery of man. In self-effacing humility, he loses sight of himself in adoration of his Hero. It is thus that his book can be divided in this three-fold way:

The early days of the Messiah (Matt. 1–4:16).

The signs and works of the Messiah (Matt. 4:17—16:20).

The passion of the Messiah (Matt. 16:21—28:20).

MATTHIAS [Măt' thĭ' as]—GIFT OF GOD. *A disciple chosen by lot to succeed Judas Iscariot* as an apostle. He had been a follower of Jesus from the beginning of His ministry and was a witness of His resurrection (Acts 1:23, 26). Tradition says Matthias was one of the seventy (Luke 10:1).

David Smith feels that the choice of Matthias was not of God. The disciples prayed for guidance but instead of trusting for divine direction, had recourse to the superstitious practice of casting lots. The election of Matthias was set aside, Paul becoming the true successor to the vacant office. We have no record of him after his election. Tradition says that he went to Ethiopia and labored there where ultimately he was martyred.

MATTITHIAH [Măt tĭ thĭ ah]—GIFT OF JEHOVAH.

1. *A Korhite*, eldest son of Shallum, who had charge of "things made in the pans" (I Chron. 9:31).

2. *A Levite singer* and gate-keeper in David's time (I Chron. 15: 18, 21; 16:5).

3. *Son of the singer Jeduthun,* and a musician who played the harp (I Chron. 25:3, 21).

4. *A son of Nebo* who put away his foreign wife (Ezra 10:43).

5. *A prince*, priest or Levite who supported Ezra when he addressed the exiles about the Law (Neh. 8:4).

MEBUNNAI [Mĕ bun' naī]—BUILT UP. *A Hushathite*, one of David's heroes (II Sam. 23:27). Perhaps the Sibbecai of I Chronicles 11:29.

MEDAD [Mĕ' dăd]—LOVE. *An elder* who, though not present at the Tabernacle when the Spirit came upon the elders, yet received the gift (Num. 11:26, 27). See Eldad.

MEDAN [Mĕ' dan]—JUDGMENT. *A son of Abraham by Keturah* and brother of Midian (Gen. 25:2; I Chron. 1:32).

MEHETABEL, MEHETABEEL [Mĕ hĕt' a bĕl, Mĕ hĕt' a beel]—GOD BLESSES or IS DOING GOOD. *Father of a certain Delaiah* guilty of opposing Nehemiah in his good work (Neh. 6:10). Also the name of the wife of Hadar, eighth king of Edom (Gen. 36:39).

MEHIDA [Mĕ hī' dă, Mĕ hī' dă]—UNION or FAMOUS. *Founder of a family of Nethinims*, members of which returned from exile with Ezra (Ezra 2:52; Neh. 7:54).

MEHIR [Mĕ' hûr]—PRICE or DEXTERITY. *A Judahite*, a son of Chelub through Caleb son of Hur (I Chron. 4:11).

MEHUJAEL [Mĕ hū' ja el]—GOD IS COMBATING. *Son of Irad* and father of Methusael, of the family of Cain (Gen. 4:18).

MEHUMAN [Mĕ hū' man]—FAITHFUL. *One of the seven chamberlains* who served in the presence of Ahasuerus, king of Persia (Esther 1:10).

MEHUNIM, MEUNIM [Mĕ hū' nim, Mĕ ū' nim]—PLACE OF HABITATION. *One of the Nethinims* whose descendants returned from exile with Zerubbabel (Ezra 2:50; Neh. 7:52). Founder of an Arab tribe (II Chron. 26:7).

MELATIAH [Mĕl a tī' ah]—JEHOVAH HATH SET FREE. *A Gibeonite* who helped to repair the wall of the city (Neh. 3:7).

MELCHI [Mĕl' chī]—JEHOVAH IS MY KING.
1. *An ancestor of Christ* through Mary (Luke 3:24).
2. *A previous ancestor of Christ* (Luke 3:28).

MELCHISEDEC, MELCHIZEDEK [Mĕl chĭs' e dĕc, Mĕl chĭz' e dĕk] —KING OF RIGHTEOUSNESS or JUSTICE. *The priest and king of Salem,* who met Abraham and blessed him (Gen. 14:18; Ps. 110:4; Heb. 5: 6, 10; 6:20; 7:1–21). His pedigree is not recorded (Ezra 2:59, 62).

The Man Who Prefigured Christ's Priesthood

Although a mysterious figure, Melchisedec is yet a figure of great importance. His biography is short. He comes before us in history (Gen. 14); in prophecy (Ps. 110); in doctrine (Heb. 7), and prefigures Christ's priesthood. He is King of Righteousness, and King of Peace—cause and effect. Christ alone can bring us peace since He is our righteousness (Isa. 32:17). In a book consisting of genealogies, Melchisedec has no record of father, mother, birth or death. Such silence is part of the divine plan to make him typify more strikingly the mystery of Christ's birth and the eternity of His priesthood.

The priesthood of this mysterious man was not based on what he was, or on any inherited right. Christ was without father on earth as to His humanity, and without mother as to His deity. He was the only-begotten of the Father, and without pedigree as to His priesthood. The greatness of Melchisedec is seen in that Abraham gave him tithes, and was blessed of him. Christ being greater, deserves and demands our all.

In Christ we have an unchallengeable priesthood, for He was made Priest by the solemnity of a divine oath. His is also an uninterrupted priesthood, for death cannot overtake Him. His priesthood is likewise nontransferable—it cannot be delegated to anyone on earth. Christ, like Melchisedec, had in His office as Priest, no ancestor, no associate, no descendant. With the Aaronic priesthood it was different.

Tradition identifies Melchisedec as Shem, the son of Noah (Gen. 11:11), or as Philitis, the builder of the great Pyramid of Egypt.

MELCHISHUA, MALCHISHUA [Měl′ chǐ shōō′ ǎ, Măl′ chǐ shū′ ǎ] —KING OF HELP. *The third son of Saul* (I Sam. 14:49; 31:2; I Chron. 8: 33; 9:39; 10:2).

MELEA [Mē′ le ǎ]—FULNESS. *An ancestor of Christ,* through Mary. He lived shortly after David (Luke 3:31).

MELECH [Mē′ lech]—A KING. *A son of Micah and descendant of Saul and Jonathan* (I Chron. 8:35; 9:41).

MELICU [Měl′ ǐ cū]—COUNSELOR. *A priest in Jerusalem* in the days of Joiakim, grandson of Jozadek—called also Malluch (Neh. 12:14).

MELZAR [Měl′ zar]—THE OVERSEER or STEWARD. *One of the seven princes of Persia and Media* who had the care of Daniel and his companions (Dan. 1:11, 16).

MEMUCAN [Mē mū′ can]—IMPOVERISHED. *One of the princes at the court of Ahasuerus,* whose counsel was adverse to Vashti (Esther 1:14, 16, 21).

MENAHEM [Mĕn' a hĕm]—COMFORTER. *The son of Gadi* who, when news reached Tirzah that Shallum had murdered the king, went to Samaria and slew Shallum and reigned in his stead. He reigned for ten years (II Kings 15:14–23).

MENAN, MENNA [Mĕ' nan]—CONSOLING or COMFORTING. *An ancestor of Christ through Mary.* He lived shortly after David's time (Luke 3:31).

MEONOTHAI [Mĕ ŏn' o thāi]—JEHOVAH'S HABITATIONS. *Father of Ophrah* and descendant of Judah through Caleb, son of Hur (I Chron. 4:14).

MEPHIBOSHETH [Mĕ phĭb' o shĕth]—UTTERANCE OF BAAL or DESTROYING SHAME.
1. *A son of Rizpah,* Saul's concubine and the daughter of Aiah. David gave him up to the Gibeonites (II Sam. 21:8).
2. *The son of Jonathan,* son of Saul. Also called Meribbaal, meaning "a striver against Baal" (II Sam. 4:4; 9:6–13; 16:1, 4; 19:24–30; 21:7; I Chron. 8:34; 9:40).

The Man Who Was Lame in Both Feet

Mephibosheth was only five years old when Jonathan, his father, and Saul, his grandfather, both fell in the same battle on Mount Gilboa, and with their death their family fell from the throne. In the terror of that day of defeat and death, the nurse caught up Jonathan's child and fled with him in her arms. But in her haste she let the little prince fall, and thus Mephibosheth was lame in both feet for the rest of his life.

Preachers can find excellent material in what is said of Mephibosheth —a type of the redeemed sinner.

I.   He belonged to the royal line, but was made a cripple by a fall (II Sam. 4:4).

II.   He lived in exile from the king but was remembered because of a covenant (I Sam. 20:14, 15; II Sam. 9:3, 4).

III.   He was called into the king's presence and exalted because of the merits of another (II Sam. 9:5, 7).

IV.   He was given a glorious heritage (II Sam. 9:9).

V.   He lived a life of self-denial during the king's absence (II Sam. 19:24).

VI.   He was subject to persecution and slander (II Sam. 16:3; 19:27).

VII.   He rejoiced at the return of the king and cared little for material things (II Sam. 19:30).

MERAIAH [Mĕr a ī' ah]—REVELATION OF JEHOVAH or STUBBORNNESS.

A priest, head of his father's house in the days of Joiakim after the exile (Neh. 12:12).

MERAIOTH [Mē rā′ ioth]—REVELATIONS or REBELLION.

1. *A priest, son of Zerahiah,* ancestor of Azariah in Solomon's time (I Chron. 6:6, 7, 52; Ezra 7:3).

2. *A priest, son of Ahitub,* father of younger Zadok of the high priestly line (I Chron. 9:11; Neh. 11:11).

3. *Another priest* at the close of the exile (Neh. 12:15).

MERARI [Mē rā′ rī]—BITTER or UNHAPPY. *The third and youngest son of Levi* and founder of one of the three Levitical families—the Merarites (Gen. 46:11; Ex. 6:16, 19; Num. 26:57).

MERED [Mē′ red]—REBELLIOUS. *A son of Ezra,* descendant of Judah through Caleb, son of Jephunneh (I Chron. 4:17, 18).

MEREMOTH [Mĕr′ e mŏth]—STRONG or ELEVATION.

1. *The son of Uriah the priest,* employed to weigh the gold and silver Ezra brought back from Babylon, and who helped to repair the city wall (Ezra 8:33; Neh. 3:4, 21).

2. *A son of Bani* who put away his foreign wife (Ezra 10:36).

3. *A priest* who, with Nehemiah, signed the covenant (Neh. 10:5; 12:3).

MERES (Mē′ rēz)—WORTHY. *One of the seven princes of Persia and Media* who had access to the king's presence (Esther 1:14).

MERIB-BAAL [Mĕr′ ib-bā′ al]—CONTENDER AGAINST BAAL. *Son of Jonathan.* See Mephibosheth (I Chron. 8:34; 9:40).

MERODACH-BALADAN [Mē rŏ′ dăch-băl′ a dăn]—MERODACH HATH GIVEN A SON or THE SON OF DEATH. (Merodach was *a Babylonian idol*— the god of war). The king of Babylon in Hezekiah's time (Isa. 39:1). See Berodach-baladan and Evil-merodach.

MESHA [Mē′ shă]—FREEDOM or RETREAT.

1. *A king of Moab,* son of Chemosh-malech (II Kings 3:4).

2. *The eldest son of Caleb,* brother of Jerahmeel (I Chron. 2:42).

3. *A Benjamite* and son of Shaharaim (I Chron. 8:8, 9).

MESHACH [Mē′ shach]—AGILE or EXPEDITIOUS. The name given to Mishael, *one of Daniel's friends,* by the chief of Nebuchadnezzar's eunuchs (Dan. 1:7; 2:49; 3). With his other two companions he defied the edict of the king and was miraculously delivered from the fiery furnace.

MESHECH, MESECH [Mĕ' shech, Mĕ' sech]—DRAWING OUT.
1. A son of Japheth (Gen. 10:2; I Chron. 1:5).
2. A son of Shem (I Chron. 1:17). Also the name of a tribe (Ps. 120:5).
The descendants of the son of Japheth are the Mosochi. Meshech usually appears with Tubal (Ezek. 38:2, 3; 39:1). The Mosochi or Moschi were a race inhabiting a part of the country between the Black and Caspian Seas. From Moschi comes Muscovites—the natives of Russia—then Moscow, the large metropolis of European Russia. Meshech along with Tubal is mentioned as trading in slaves (Ezek. 27:13), a traffic Moscow is notoriously famous for today. Moscow is now the hub of the communist universe, and will likely be the center of authority when the Northern Confederacy is finally formed.

MESHELEMIAH [Mĕ' shĕl e mī' ah]—JEHOVAH RECOMPENSES. A Kohathite whose son Zechariah was a gate-keeper of the Tabernacle (I Chron. 9:21; 26:1, 2, 9). Called Shelemiah in I Chronicles 26:14. Perhaps the Meshullam of Nehemiah 12:25.

MESHEZABEEL, MESHEZABEL [Mĕ shĕz' a beel]—GOD SETS FREE.
1. Father of a certain Berechiah who helped to repair the city wall (Neh. 3:4).
2. A person who sealed the covenant (Neh. 10:21; 11:24).

MESHILLEMITH, MESHILLEMOTH [Mĕ shĭl' le mĭth, Mĕ shĭl' le mŏth]—RECOMPENSES.
1. A priest whose descendants lived in Jerusalem (I Chron. 9:12).
2. An Ephraimite, father of that Berechiah who urged the release of the captives brought from Judah by Pekah's army (II Chron. 28:12).
3. A priest of the family of Immer, whose descendant, Amashai, lived in Jerusalem (Neh. 11:13).

MESHOBAB [Mĕ shō' băb]—RESTORED or DELIVERED. One of the Simeonite princes who seized pasture lands near Gedor (I Chron. 4:34).

MESHULLAM [Mĕ shŭl' lam]—ASSOCIATE or A FRIEND.
1. An ancestor of Shaphan, the scribe of King Josiah's time (II Kings 22:3).
2. A son of Zerubbabel and descendant of Jeconiah, son of King Jehoiakim (I Chron. 3:19).
3. A leading man among the Gadites in the reign of Jothan (I Chron. 5:13).
4. A Benjamite, descended from Shaharaim through Elpaal (I Chron. 8:17).
5. A Benjamite, father of Sallu, who dwelt in Jerusalem (I Chron. 9:7; Neh. 11:7).
6. Another Benjamite, son of Shephathiah, also of Jerusalem (I Chron. 9:8).

7. *A priest,* son of Zadok and father of the high priest, Hilkiah, who lived in Josiah's reign (I Chron. 9:11; Neh. 11:11).

8. *A priest,* son of Mishilemith of the house of Immer (I Chron. 9:12).

9. *A Kohathite Levite* who, with others, superintended the repair of the Temple in Josiah's time (II Chron. 34:12).

10. *A chief man* who, with others, returned from exile with Ezra (Ezra 8:16).

11. *One who assisted in the numbering of those who had married foreign wives* (Ezra 10:15).

12. *A son of Bani* who had married a foreign wife (Ezra 10:29).

13. *A son of Berechiah* who helped to repair two portions of the wall (Neh. 3:4, 30; 6:18).

14. *The son of Besodeiah* who also repaired a part of the city wall (Neh. 3:6).

15. *A prince or priest* who stood beside Ezra as he read and explained the Law (Neh. 8:4).

16. *A priest* who, on behalf of his father's house, signed the covenant with Nehemiah (Neh. 10:7).

17. *A chief of the people* who also signed the covenant (Neh. 10:20).

18. *A priest* of the family of Ezra who assisted at the dedication of the wall (Neh. 12:13, 33).

19. *Another priest,* head of his father Ginnethon's house, in the days of Joiakim the priest (Neh. 12:16).

20. *A Levite,* and sanctuary porter after the exile (Neh. 12:25).

METHUSAEL, METHUSHAEL [Mē thōo' sa el]—MAN OF GOD. *Son of Mehujael,* a descendant of Cain, and father of Lamech (Gen. 4:18).

METHUSELAH, MATHUSALA [Mē thōo' se lah]—A MAN OF THE JAVELIN or IT SHALL BE SENT (DELUGE). *The son of Enoch,* and grandfather of Noah, who lived longer than any other man recorded in history (Gen. 5:21–27).

The Man Who Lived the Longest

The Bible represents human life as vastly prolonged before the Flood. Afterwards it grew rapidly briefer. The longevity of the antediluvian races proves that the constitution of man was different from what it is today. With the Flood a change took place so that now the duration of human life is rarely over one hundred years. No strength of constitution, temperance or vegetable diet can add years to such a limit. The instructive register of Genesis five shows that the man who lived for the shortest period lived for 365 years, and the one who lived for the longest period lived for 969 years.

The remarkable longevity served a useful purpose in that it made possible the reception and preservation of ancient traditions. Perhaps Adam lived for about 113 years after the birth of Methuselah, and Methuselah could not have been more than 369 years old when his grandson Noah was born. Thus, Noah conversed with one who had conversed with Adam and Enoch had the privilege of conversing with Adam. God knows how to preserve His truth for the guidance and sanctification of succeeding generations.

Although Methuselah, whose name was fitting for a time when the earth was full of violence, lived for almost a millennium, nothing whatever is recorded of his long life save the birth of his children. What an immense influence he could have exerted through the years if only, like his father Enoch, he had walked with God! It is not the *length* of a life that counts, but the *quality* of it.

Why did Methuselah die thirty-one years short of a millennium? Has God reserved the privilege of living for one thousand years for the millennial saints? During our Lord's millennial reign, life is to be prolonged again, so that one hundred years shall be the duration of childhood, and a grown man's ordinary age shall be in the age of a tree (Isa. 65:20, 22).

MEZAHAB [Měz' a hăb]—OFFSPRING OF THE SHINING ONE. *Grandfather of Mehetabel, wife of Hadar, the eighth king of Edom* (Gen. 36:39; I Chron. 1:50).

MIAMIN [Mǐ' a mǐn]—FORTUNATE.
1. *A son of Parosh* who had married a foreign wife [Ezra 10:25).
2. *A priest* who returned from exile with Zerubbabel (Neh. 12:5).

MIBHAR [Mǐb' här]—YOUTH or CHOICE. *A son of Haggeri* and one of David's heroes (I Chron. 11:38).

MIBSAM [Mǐb' sam]—SWEET ODOR.
1. *A son of Ishmael,* son of Hagar (Gen. 25:13; I Chron. 1:29).
2. *A son of Simeon* descended from No. 1 (I Chron. 4:25).

MIBZAR [Mǐb' zar]—A STRONGHOLD or FORTIFIED. *An Edomite chieftain,* descended from Esau (Gen. 36:42; I Chron. 1:53).

MICAH, MICHAH, MICA, MICHA [Mǐ' cah, Mǐ'chah, Mǐ' că, Mǐ' cha]—WHO IS LIKE JEHOVAH.
1. *An Ephramite* who hired a Levite to be priest to his image (Judg. 17; 18). This unworthy character brought great calamity to Israel. Dr. C. I. Scofield says of Micah's consecration of the Levite that it affords a striking illustration of apostasy. "With his entire departure from the revealed will of God concerning worship and priesthood there is yet an exaltation of false priesthood. Saying, 'Blessed be thou of Jehovah,' Micah's mother makes an idol; and Micah expects the blessing of Jehovah because he has linked the idolatry to the ancient levitical order."
2. *The head of a family of Reuben* (I Chron. 5:5).

3. *A son of Mephibosheth*, grandson of Saul (I Chron. 8:34, 35; 9:40, 41).

4. *A Levite* of the family of Asaph (I Chron. 9:15). See Micha.

5. *A son of Uzziel*, a Kohathite (I Chron. 23:20; 24:24, 25).

6. *Father of Abdon* whom Josiah sent to enquire of the Lord when the Law was found (II Chron. 34:20).

7. *The prophet surnamed the Morasthite*, and called Michaiah in the V.L. (Jer. 26:18; Mic. 1:1).

The Man of Strong Convictions

Micah prophesied during the reign of Jothan, Ahaz and Hezekiah (Mic. 1:1; Jer. 26:18). He was a younger contemporary of Hosea. He is called "the Morasthite" since he came from Moresheth Gath. Micah, unlike Isaiah, was no politician. He did not censure the habit of looking to Egypt or to Assyria for help. He denounces the depravity of the nation, and threatens the vengeance of God. Isaiah prophesied to royalty, Micah ministered to common people, the sort who heard Jesus gladly. Isaiah was a courtier; Micah, a rustic from an obscure town some twenty-five miles southwest of Jerusalem.

Micah was probably a yeoman, farming his own plot of land, and in vivid sympathy with the class to which he belonged. The land hunger of rich men, always to be deprecated, was positively dangerous to a country like Palestine with little foreign trade, relying mainly on the produce of the soil for the support of its citizens. The grasping avarice of large landholders doomed to poverty a considerable part of the population, and so Micah stands out as a preacher to the poor and oppressed. He regarded selfish luxury, joined with oppression of the poor, as the crowning sin of Judah. The people were heavily taxed, the Assyrians demanding large payments in tribute to satisfy their lavishness in their architectural magnificence. Thus Zion was built up with blood and Jerusalem with iniquity (Mic. 3:10). Because of such exaction and idolatry, Micah was called and empowered to declare the judgment of God (Mic. 3:8).

Micah was a man of strong convictions and corresponding courage, and as a true preacher, uncovered sin and pointed to the coming Christ. As a prophet he went against the stream and uttered truths the people did not want. For this he was consequently stoned—the usual lot of a faithful prophet. His cry, in essence, was:

Back to Bethlehem (Mic. 5:2). In other words, back to the Messianic hope. Back to David, who did so much for the nation, and to whom God promised He would raise up the Messiah. Back to David, the constant ideal of the monarchy. The Messiah of Israel's coming golden age would be like David.

Back to ethical righteousness (Mic. 6:8). Micah brushed aside all former ritual in favor of a righteousness given by God, and that had a heart for the need of others. It was a righteousness based upon God's salvation.

Back to the prince of peace (Mic. 4:1-3; 5:2-7). Micah heralded the message that the reign of the Messiah was Israel's only hope of peace. We know it to be the only hope of world peace. The Messianic predictions form the most significant passages in Micah.

The most outstanding incident in Micah's prophetic career was his preaching which led to the reformation under Hezekiah (Jer. 26:18). When king and people sought God and repented, He turned from the fierceness of His anger. The humble crofter of Philistia was chosen as God's messenger to the people, and the secret of his power was the fulness of the Holy Spirit (Mic. 3:8).

The book Micah wrote is characterized by deep spirituality, with a simple, but not rugged style. Sin and corruption, the sighing and agony of the people over the misrule of men in authority, the insistence on return to God, are all dealt with in no uncertain tones (Mic. 1:2; 3:1; 6:1). Broadly speaking, Micah's prophecy can be divided thus:

> Chapters one, two and three — *judgment.*
> Chapters four and five — *comfort.*
> Chapters six and seven — *salvation.*

MICAIAH, MICHAIAH [Mī cā' iah, Mī chā' iah]—WHO IS LIKE JEHOVAH. Here is a name occurring many times in the Old Testament and used of women as well as men. It is spelled in different ways. See Mica and Micah.

1. *A prophet, son of Imlah,* who foretold the fall of Ahab at Ramoth-gilead (I Kings 22:8, 9; II Chron. 18:8). There are no truer hearts to God than his. Carefully compare the three great prophets of I Kings — Ahijah, Elijah and Micaiah.

2. *The father of Achbor,* a chief officer of King Josiah (II Kings 22:12, 14).

3. *A prince of Judah* ordered by Jehoshaphat to teach the people (II Chron. 17:7).

4. *A priest of the family of Asaph* who blew a trumpet at the dedication of the wall [Neh. 12:35, 41).

5. *The son of Gemariah,* a prince of Judah in Jehoiakim's time (Jer. 36:11, 13).

Also the name of the daughter of Uriel of Gibeah. (See I Kings 15:2; II Chron. 11:20; 13:2).

MICHA [Mī' chă]—WHO IS LIKE JEHOVAH.

1. *Son of Mephibosheth* (II Sam. 9:12). See Micah.
2. *A Levite* (Neh. 11:17, 22). See Micah, No. 4.
3. *A Levite* who sealed the covenant (Neh. 10:11).

MICHAEL [Mī' chaël]—WHO IS LIKE GOD.

1. *An Asherite,* father of Sethur, whom Moses sent to spy the land (Num. 13:13).

2. *A Gadite,* descendant of Buz and head of his father's house (I Chron. 5:13).

3. *Another Gadite*, ancestor of the preceding (I Chron. 5:14).

4. *A Levite* of the family of Gershon and ancestor of Asaph (I Chron. 6:40).

5. *A chief man* of the tribe of Issachar of the family of Tola (I Chron. 7:3).

6. *A Benjamite* of the family of Beriah (I Chron. 8:16).

7. *A Manassite captain* who joined David at Ziklag (I Chron. 12:20).

8. *The father of Omri*, prince of Issachar in David's reign (I Chron. 27:18).

9. *A son of Jehoshaphat* (II Chron. 21:2).

10. *The father of Zebadiah* who returned from exile with Ezra (Ezra 8:8).

Also the name of the archangel who came to Daniel and is called by him "Prince of the people of Israel" (Dan. 10:13, 21; 12:1; Jude 9; Rev. 12:7).

Saul's youngest daughter, who became David's wife, was called Michal.

MICHRI [Mĭch' ri]—JEHOVAH POSSESSES or VALUABLE. *A Benjamite* and ancestor of a family in Jerusalem (I Chron. 9:8).

MIDIAN, MADIAN [Mĭd' ĭ an]—STRIFE or CONTENTION. *A son of Abraham by Keturah*, whose descendants covered many parts (Gen. 25: 2, 4; Ex. 2:15, 16; I Chron. 1:32, 33). Occasionally the Midianites are identified with the Ishmaelites (Judg. 6:33; 7:12).

MIJAMIN, MIAMIN [Mĭj' a mĭn, Mĭ' a mĭn]—ON THE RIGHT HAND or FORTUNATE.

1. *A descendant of Aaron*, of the family of the sixth of the twenty-four courses of priests (I Chron. 24:9).

2. *A priest* who, with Nehemiah, sealed the covenant (Neh. 10:7) and perhaps the trumpeter of Nehemiah 12:41. See Miamin and Miniamin.

MIKLOTH [Mĭk' loth]—RODS or STICKS.

1. *A military captain* in David's reign (I Chron. 27:4).

2. *A Benjamite* of the family of Jeiel of Gibeon (I Chron. 8:32; 9:37, 38).

MIKNEIAH [Mĭk nē' iah]—JEHOVAH IS JEALOUS or POSSESSION OF JEHOVAH. *A Levite* of the second degree and gatekeeper of the Ark. He played a harp (I Chron. 15:18, 21).

MILALAI [Mĭl a lā' ĭ]—JEHOVAH IS ELEVATED or ELOQUENT. *A Levite* who played a musical instrument at the dedication of the wall (Neh. 12:36).

MINIAMIN [Mĭn′ ĭ a mĭn]—ON THE RIGHT HAND or FORTUNATE.
1. A Levite in Hezekiah's time who distributed tithes and offerings (II Chron. 31:15).
2. A priest who returned with Zerubbabel. Also called Miamin (Neh. 12:17, 41).

MIRMA, MIRMAH [Mûr′ ma]—DECEIT or HEIGHT. A son of Shaharaim by his wife Hodesh (I Chron. 8:10).

MISHAEL [Mĭsh′ a el]—HIGH PLACE or WHO IS WHAT GOD IS.
1. A son of Uzziel, son of Kohath (Ex. 6:22; Lev. 10:4).
2. One who stood with Ezra when he preached to the people on the Law (Neh. 8:4).
3. A companion of Daniel, who is also called Meshek (Dan. 1:6, 7, 11, 19; 2:17).

MISHAM [Mĭ′ sham]—SWIFTNESS or IMPETUOUS. A Benjamite, a son of Elpaal, who with his brothers built Ono and Lod (I Chron. 8:12).

MISHMA [Mĭsh′ mă]—FAME or HEARING. A son of Ishmael, son of Hagar (Gen. 25:14; I Chron. 1:30; 4:25, 26).

MISHMANNAH [Mĭsh măn′ nah]—FATNESS or VIGOR. A Gadite who joined David at Ziklag (I Chron. 12:10).

MISPERETH, MISPAR, MIZPAR [Mĭs′ pe rĕth, Mĭz′ pär]—WRITING or A NARRATIVE. One of those who returned with Zerubbabel from captivity (Ezra 2:2). Called Mispar. The feminine form of this name is Mispereth (Neh. 7:7).

MITHREDATH [Mĭth′ re dăth]—GIVEN BY MITHRA, ANIMATING SPIRIT OF FIRE.
1. The treasurer of Cyrus, king of Persia, through whom the sacred vessels were restored to the Jews (Ezra 1:8).
2. An enemy of the Jews in the time of King Artaxerxes. He was averse to the rebuilding of the wall (Ezra 4:7).

MIZPAR [Mĭz′ pär]—FEAR or WRITING. The chief of a tribe in the land of Edom, who returned with Zerubbabel (Ezra 2:2).

MIZRAIM [Mĭz′ ra ĭm]—TRIBULATIONS. The second son of Ham and father of Ludim, whose descendants were found in Egypt (Gen. 10:6, 13; I Chron. 1:8, 11).

MIZZAH [Mĭz′ zah]—TERROR or JOY. Son of Reuel, son of Esau, and one of the dukes of Edom (Gen. 36:13, 17; I Chron. 1:37).

MNASON [Mnā' son]—A DILIGENT SEEKER.

The Man Who Was Loyal to the End

Described as "an old disciple," Mnason came into the life of Paul at a needy hour. Friends tried to dissuade him from going up to Jerusalem where bonds awaited him, but like his Master before him, he steadfastly set his face to go to Jerusalem. Thus this early disciple from Cyprus accompanied Paul on his last journey, and Paul lodged at his hospitable home (Acts 21:16). The figure of Mnason is drawn in the slightest possible outline "with a couple of hasty strokes of the pencil." We see him as:

I. *A disciple of old standing*. Can we not picture Paul's bountiful host as a grand old man with hoary head his crown of glory, and a serene face suggesting a kindly Christian heart within? "An honest old gentleman," Matthew Henry calls him. The R.V. speaks of him as "an early disciple," being possibly one of the converts of Peter on the Day of Pentecost. Conybeare and Howson suggest that Mnason was converted during the life of our Lord. There is a tradition that he was one of the twenty Jews sent out.

II. *Old yet still bearing*. The original meaning of "disciple" is *learner*. Thus Mnason had the honorable description of being "an old learner." Too often we associate learning with the young who, when they leave school, speak of their education as "finished." But the old man from Cyprus was not too old to learn. On the tombstone of the historian, John R. Green, is the inscription, "He died learning." Paul had been a believer for some twenty-five years when he wrote, "That I may know Him." The oldest saint, as well as the youngest Christian, needs to obey the exhortation about growing in grace and in the knowledge of our Lord and Saviour Jesus Christ.

III. *Ready for service although aged*. While Mnason was not able to undertake all of the long, arduous and perilous missionary journeys Paul faced, he could help those who were called and qualified to do so. He was content to fill a little space even though it was only to give a night's lodging for God's workers. Mnason felt it a privilege to entertain Paul and his companions. Here was one given to ungrudging hospitality, and who remained until the end of his day an effective witness to God's faithfulness.

MOAB [Mō' ab]—WATER OF A FATHER or DESIRE. *The son of Lot by his eldest daughter* (Gen. 19:37). It is best to draw a veil over such an incestuous union, testifying as it does to the corrupt influence of Sodom over Lot and his daughters. The descendants of the Moabites and Ammonites were closely related, and covered many chief places in Judah, the Salt Sea and Reuben (Gen. 36:35; Ex. 15:15; Judg. 3:28). The Israelites were commanded to have no dealings with the Moabites (Ruth 1:22; 2:2, 6; I Kings 11:1; II Chron. 24:26).

MOADIAH, MAADIAH [Mō a dī' ah, Mā a dī' ah]—FESTIVAL OF JE-

HOVAH. *A priest in Joiakim's time,* grandson of Jozadek (Neh. 12:17). See Maadiah.

MOLID [Mō′ lid]—BEGETTER. *A descendant of Jerahmeel,* grandson of Pharez, son of Judah (I Chron. 2:29).

MORDECAI [Môr′ de caī]—DEDICATED TO MARS, A LITTLE MAN or BITTER BRUISING.

1. *A Jew who returned from Babylon with Zerubbabel* (Ezra 2:2; Neh. 7:7).

2. *A Benjamite,* son or descendant of Jair, son of Shimei, son of Kish. He brought up Esther, his uncle's daughter, and adopted her as his own daughter after the death of her parents (Esther 2:5, 7).

The Man Who Was a Virtuous Patriot

What joy must have filled the heart of this foster-father of Esther, when he saw her elevated to the position of queen, and himself exalted to high office in the court. Exile and poverty were now past. Mordecai sat in the king's gate, and was aware of the plot on the king's life by two chamberlains. Mordecai reported the plot to the king, thus saving his life. According to Persian customs, a record of this act was carefully preserved in the royal archives (Esther 2:21–23; 6:1–3), and during a sleepless night of the king, was read. It resulted in Mordecai's consequent reward.

Mordecai may not appear as the most attractive of men. His message to Esther lacked courtesy and chivalry. Evidently he was insensible to the charms and graces of Esther which made her eligible as Vashti's successor. To the credit of Mordecai, however, it must be said that he refused to extend honor to one whom God had cursed (Ex. 17:14–16). Mordecai was of the tribe of Benjamin, and thus would not bow to Haman, who was an Amalekite and as such a direct descendant of the hereditary enemies of Israel.

Matthew Henry, quoting from the apocryphal chapters of Esther, says that Mordecai appeals to God in this manner:

> Thou knowest, Lord that it was neither in contempt nor pride, nor for any desire for glory, that I did not bow down to proud Haman, for I could have been content with good will for the salvation of Israel to kiss the soles of his feet, but I did this that I might not prefer the glory of man above the glory of God, neither will I worship any but Thee.

We cannot but admire Mordecai standing erect while the crowd of servants lay flat on their faces. While we have no record of his faith in God, yet his action proves him to have been a godly Jew who would not bow to any but God. "So did not I because of the fear of God," has to be our motto whatever fellow servants may say or do.

MOSES [Mō′ zez]—DRAWN FORTH, TAKEN OUT OF THE WATER or A SON. *The youngest son of Amram and Jochebed,* of the family of Kohath (Ex. 2:10–21; Acts 7:20–38; Heb. 11:24, 25).

The Man Who Was God's Friend

The great Hebrew leader and legislator was born at the time the king of Egypt had resolved on the destruction of every newly born male child among the Israelites. The story of his rescue from the water by Pharaoh's daughter, of her adoption of him as her own son and his royal upbringing has charmed our hearts from earliest years.

It would take a volume in itself to fully expound the virtues and vicissitudes of Moses the historian, orator, leader, statesman, legislator and patriot. His greatest honor, however, was the privilege of being known as "the friend of God." What holy intimacy existed between God and this prophet so supernaturally guided and aided in his life and labors! No wonder this mighty leader of Israel was David Livingstone's favorite Bible hero!

Moses lived for 120 years, a period divided into three sections of forty years each:

The first forty years—from his birth until the flight into Midian. As Pharaoh's son, Moses learned how to be SOMEBODY.

The second forty years—from the flight into Midian to the Exodus. In desert places he learned how to become a NOBODY.

The third forty years—from the Exodus to his own exodus. As the leader of God's hosts he learned that GOD WAS EVERYBODY — the One he could speak to face to face as a man speaks to his friends.

The remarkable life of Moses can be viewed under three more aspects:

I.   The moment when he turned fully to God.

II.   The moment when he absolutely broke with the world. The refusal and choice of Hebrews 11:24, 25 must be carefully noted. It is not enough to refuse—we must choose. We must back up a negative with a positive.

III. The moment when between himself and God there was the sprinkled blood, the blood of atonement.

Further, Moses, the Law-giver in Israel, supplies us with a fitting type of Christ. Taken together we have these similarities which pastors can develop:

Both were preserved from the perils of infancy (Ex. 2:2–10 with Matt. 2:14, 15).

Both were tempted but had mastery over evil (Ex. 7:11 with Matt. 4:1).

Both knew what it was to fast for forty days (Ex. 34:28 with Matt. 4:2). Solitude was their strength.

Both had power to control the sea (Ex. 14:21 with Matt. 8:26).

Both fed a multitude (Ex. 16:26 with Matt. 14:20, 21).

Both had a radiant face (Ex. 34:35 with Matt. 17:2).

Both endured murmurings (Ex. 15:24 with Mark 7:2).

Both were discredited at home (Num. 12:1 with John 7:5).

Both were mighty intercessors (Ex. 32:32 with John 17).

Both spoke as the oracles of God (Deut. 18:18 with John 7:46).

Both had seventy helpers (Num. 11:16, 17 with Luke 10:1).

Both established memorials (Ex. 12:14 with Luke 22:19).

Both reappeared after death (Matt. 17:3 with Acts 1:3).

Moses gave us the first five books of the Old Testament, known as *The Pentateuch.* When Jesus said, "Moses wrote of me," He set His seal to the Mosaic authorship of these books. Moses died in the plains of Moab. At the ripe age of 120 years, while yet "his eye was not dim, nor his natural force abated," God called His faithful servant to climb Nebo's lonely mountain, where, upon its summit he was kissed to sleep by the angels and God buried him—the only man in the Bible to have God as his undertaker (Deut. 34:6).

MOZA [Mō′ză]—OFFSPRING or A GOING FORTH.

1. *A son of Caleb,* son of Jephunneh, of the family of Hezron (I Chron. 2:46).

2. *A Benjamite,* descendant of Saul and Jonathan (I Chron. 8:36, 37; 9:42, 43).

MUPPIM [Mŭp′pim]—OBSCURITIES. *A son of Benjamin,* Jacob's youngest son (Gen. 46:21).

MUSHI [Mū′shī]—DRAWN OUT. *A Levite,* son of Merari, son of Levi and founder of a tribal family (Ex. 6:19; Num. 3:20; 26:58).

N

NAAM [Nā′am]—SWEETNESS or PLEASANTNESS. *A son of the cele-brated Caleb,* companion of Joshua (I Chron. 4:15).

NAAMAN [Nā′a man]—DELIGHT, PLEASANT or AGREEABLE.

1. *A son of Benjamin* and founder of a tribal family (Gen. 46:21).

2. *A son of Bela,* son of Benjamin (Num. 26:40; I Chron. 8:4).

3. *A son of Ehud,* or Abihud, grandson of Benjamin (I Chron. 8:7).

4. *A Syrian captain* in the army of Ben-hadad, king of Damascus. This able commander was cured of leprosy by Elisha the prophet (II Kings 5; Luke 4:27).

The Man Who Was Valiant But Leprous

What a blight Naaman's leprosy must have cast on his path! Successful, valiant, noble, yet a leper. His loathesome disease must have haunted him day and night. As there was no physician in Syria who could help him, he had the dread of going to the grave with his foul ailment. But God has a way of using little things to achieve His beneficent purpose. Among the captives brought from Israel to Syria was a girl chosen to act as maid to Naaman's wife. This slave maiden loved the Lord and was not ashamed to own Him. Thus when her mistress bemoaned the disease and despair of her husband, the girl sang the praises of Elisha. We can imagine how she would relate the miracles of the prophet, and, since her life was consistent with her testimony, the captive girl was believed.

With faith in the witness of the maid, Naaman went to Samaria, but felt rebuffed when Elisha would not see him, and instead sent his servant to the captain with the order: "Go wash in Jordan seven times."

How angry Naaman was to be told to wash himself in the muddy Jordan! Away he went in a rage, simply because his pride had been hurt. Elisha was indifferent to Naaman's honor and wealth, and also to the virtue of the better rivers in Damascus. But Naaman's excellent servant wanted his master cured of his dread disease, and influenced by him, Naaman obeyed the word of Elisha and was made whole. For the minister this old-time miracle bristles with forceful application.

NAARAI [Nā' a raī]—PLEASANTNESS OF JEHOVAH. *One of David's heroes* and son of Ezbai (I Chron. 11:37). He is called Paarai the Arbite in II Samuel 23:35.

NAASHON [Nā ăsh' on]—ORACLE or ONE THAT FORETELLS. *Brother of Elisheba,* Aaron's wife (Ex. 6:23). Perhaps Nahshon, the son of Amminadab.

NAASSON [Nā ăs' son]—ENCHANTER or SERPENT OF THE SUN. *An ancestor of Jesus Christ* (Matt. 1:4; Luke 3:32).

NABAL [Nā' bal]—PROMINENCE or FOOLISH. *A wealthy but churlish sheepmaster of Maon* whose business was in Carmel (I Sam. 25; II Sam. 2:2).

The Man Who Was a Fool by Name and Nature

Nabal is a striking illustration of a man with a name indicative of his nature. When David came to Nabal asking food for his hungry men, this churlish man refused. David set out to kill Nabal but Abigail, his beautiful wife, pled for the life of her unworthy husband. What a contrast they afford! Abigail so beautiful and Nabal so bestial — The Beauty and the Beast. Pleading for Nabal's life, Abigail said to David, "As is his name, so is he. Nabal is his name and folly is with him." In effect, she said, "Pay no attention to my churlish husband. He's a fool by name and a fool by nature."

After his drunken orgy, Nabal was told of David's threat to take his life and he died of fright. David afterwards married Abigail, a woman of good understanding and who, as Edith Deen tells us in her most valuable handbook, *All the Women of the Bible,* was "the greatest influence for good and helped David to remember that he was God's anointed into whose keeping the kingdom of Israel had been entrusted."

NABOTH [Nä' bŏth]—PROMINENCE. *A Jezreelite of the tribe of Issa-char,* whom Jezebel, wife of Ahab, caused to be put to death to obtain his vineyard adjoining the palace (I Kings 21; II Kings 9:21–26). For this dastardly act doom was pronounced upon Ahab and his house by Elijah. "The murder of Naboth seems to have deeply impressed the popular mind," comments W. F. Boyd, "and the deaths of Joram and Jezebel near the spot were regarded as Divine retribution on the act."

NACHON [Nä' chôn]—STROKE. *A Benjamite* at whose threshing floor Uzzah was smitten for touching the Ark (II Sam. 6:6). Also called Chidon in I Chronicles 13:9.

NACHOR [Nä' chôr]—NOBLE or BURNING. *An ancestor of Jesus Christ* (Luke 3:34).

NADAB [Nä' dăb]—OF ONE'S FREE WILL or LIBERAL.
1. *Elder son of Aaron,* destroyed by fire for offering strange fire upon the altar (Ex. 6:23; 24:1, 9). If we would worship and serve God acceptably, it must be in the way of His appointing.
2. *Son of Jeroboam I,* king of Israel. He was slain by Baasha (I Kings 14:20; 15:25, 27, 31).
3. *Great-grandson of Jerahmeel,* son of Hezron (I Chron. 2:28, 30).
4. *A Benjamite,* a son of Gibeon and Maachah (I Chron. 8:30; 9:36).

NAGGE, NAGGAI [Năg' ğe]—SPLENDOR OF THE SUN. *An ancestor of Jesus Christ* (Luke 3:25).

NAHAM [Nä' ham]—SOLACE or CONSOLATION. *Brother of Hodiah,* wife of Ezra, and descendant of Caleb, son of Jephunneh (I Chron. 4:19).

NAHAMANI [Nä häm' a nï]—COMFORTER or COMPASSIONATE. *A chief man who returned with Zerubbabel from Babylon* (Neh. 7:7).

NAHARAI, NAHARI [Nä hăr' a ï, Nä' ha rï]—SNORING or SNORTING ONE. *A Beerothite,* Joab's armorbearer (II Sam. 23:37; I Chron. 11:39).

NAHASH [Nä' häsh]—SERPENT or ORACLE.
1. *An Amorite king* who besieged Jabesh-gilead and was defeated by Saul (I Sam. 11:1, 2; 12:12).
2. *The father of Shobi,* and another Ammonite king (II Sam. 10:2; 17:27; I Chron. 19:1, 2). Also the name of the mother of Abigail (II Sam. 17:25).

NAHATH [Nä' häth]—DESCENT, LOWNESS or QUIET.
1. *A son of Reuel,* son of Esau (Gen. 36:13, 17; I Chron. 1:37).

2. *A son of Zophai* (I Chron. 6:26). Perhaps the Toah of I Chronicles 6:34.

3. *A Levite,* overseer of the offerings in the days of Hezekiah (II Chron. 31:13).

NAHBI [Näh' bï]—CONCEALED or JEHOVAH'S PROTECTION. *A prince of Naphtali,* and representative spy sent out by Moses (Num. 13:14).

NAHOR, NACHOR [Nä' hôr]—BREATHING HARD or SLAYER.

1. *A son of Serug* and grandfather of Abraham (Gen. 11:23-25; I Chron. 1:26).

2. *A son of Terah,* brother of Abraham, husband of Milcah, who bore him eight children (Gen. 11:26, 29).

NAHSHON, NAASSON [Näh' shŏn, Nä ăs' son]—ENCHANTING or OMINOUS. *Son of Amminadab* and prince of Judah in the days of Moses (Num. 1:7; 2:3). See Naashon.

NAHUM [Nä' hum]—COMPASSIONATE, COMFORTER or FULL OF COMFORT.

1. *The prophet who was born at Elkosh in Galilee,* and who prophesied against Nineveh (Nah. 1:1).

The Man Who Preached Doom

Nothing is known of this Minor Prophet outside of what we find in the opening of his small yet strong book. He was born at Elkosh, a village of Palestine. But although Nahum is among the notable unknown of the Bible, he was a student of the history of his time and was raised up to comfort God's people. He prophesied against Nineveh about 150 years after Jonah's revival there. At that time the city was still at the height of its glory (Nah. 3:16, 17). The empire was extremely cruel. The people gloated that "space failed for corpses of their enemies." They made "pyramids of human heads." Pillars were covered with the flayed skins of their rivals.

Nahum's mission was to declare the terrible doom of Nineveh and one hundred years later it fell. So great was the destruction of the city of the most ferocious, sensual, diabolically atrocious race of men that ever lived, that Alexander the Great marched by and did not know that a great city was under his feet. Lucian wrote, "Nineveh is perished and there is no trace left where once it was." Nahum, convinced that God was slow to anger but would yet take vengeance on His adversaries, "focusses the light of God's moral government upon wicked Nineveh and chants the death and dirge of the world's greatest oppressor."

The leading lessons to be gleaned from the Book of Nahum are encouraging to faith:

I. The goodness and unchangeableness of Jehovah.

II. The limits of divine forbearance.

III.   Right prevails in the end.

IV.   Darkness comes before the dawn.

V.   The universality of God's government, its gracious purpose: its retributive character.

VI.   Man's extremity is faith's hour and God's opportunity.

2. *Another Nahum.* In the A. V. Naum is mentioned as an ancestor of Jesus Christ (Luke 3:25).

NAPHISH, NEPHISH [Nā' phish, Nĕ' phish]—NUMEROUS or RESPIRATION. *A son of Ishmael,* son of Abraham and Hagar and founder of a clan who settled west of Jordan (Gen. 25:15; I Chron. 1:31; 5:19).

NAPHTALI, NEPHTHALIM [Năph' ta lī, Nĕph' tha lĭm]—OBTAINED BY WRESTLING. *The sixth son of Jacob* and second by Bilhah, Rachel's maid. Rachel gave her son his name because she had wrestled in prayer for God's favor and blessing (Gen. 30:8; 35:25). The tribe that descended from Naphtali bears his name (Num. 1:15, 42).

The Man Who Lacked Self-Control

In the last words of Jacob (Gen. 49:21), the patriarch speaks of Naphtali as "a hind let loose: he giveth goodly words"—a fluent orator but as erratic as the wild gazelle. Henry Thorne wrote of him,

> He is gifted undoubtedly, but he has no self-control. He will scamper through life aimlessly and without a goal. His uncontrolled energy may some day be his ruin. He may possibly leap over a fence, but he may also jump into a ditch. Byron was gifted, but of him it has been said —
>
> > He laid his hand upon the ocean's main,
> > And played familiar with his hoary locks.
>
> He was a man of brilliant talent and magnificent capacity, but he was also "a hind let loose." There was a wild extravagance in his career of wrong-doing that marred his influence and spoiled his life.

Nothing but divine grace can restrain those who are erratic. He who rebuked the rude tempest with a word (Job 38:11; Mark 4:39) and produced a great calm, can rebuke the turbulent and the reckless in any nature, and cause the energy that is wasted by folly to flow into channels of usefulness. God can make the rebel a priest and a king.

NARCISSUS [När' cĭs' sus]—FLOWER CAUSING LETHARGY or ASTONISHMENT. *A Roman* whose household Paul greeted. The apostle's salutation is not addressed to Narcissus himself but to the members of his household. He may have been the favorite freedman of Claudius the emperor (Rom. 16:11).

NATHAN [Nā' than]—HE HATH GIVEN.

1. *The third child of David,* born after he came to reign over Israel (II Sam. 5:14; I Chron. 3:5; 14:4).

2. *The distinguished prophet* during the reigns of David and Solomon, who brought home to David the enormity of his sin. What a piercing arrow from the divine bow that was — *Thou art the man*

(II Sam. 7:2–17; 12; I Kings 1; I Chron. 17). Although the confidential adviser of King David, Nathan was unsparing in his condemnation of his monarch's sin. Nathan also wrote a history (II Chron. 9:29).

3. *The father of Igal,* one of David's heroes (II Sam. 23:36).

4. *Father of Solomon's chief officer* (I Kings 4:5).

5. *Son of Attai* and father of Zabad, of the tribe of Judah (I Chron. 2:36).

6. *Brother of Joel,* one of David's heroes (I Chron. 11:38).

7. *A chief man with Ezra* at the brook of Ahava (Ezra 8:16).

8. *A son of Bani* who put away his foreign wife (Ezra 10:39).

9. *A chief man in Israel* (Zech. 12:12).

10. *An ancestor of Jesus Christ* (Luke 3:31).

NATHANAEL [Nă thăn' a el]—THE GIFT OF GOD. *A native of Cana in Galilee* whom Jesus called an Israelite in whom there was no guile (John 1:45–49; 21:2).

The Man Who Was Guileless

Nathanael is supposed to be the same as Bartholomew the Apostle. The name of Nathanael occurs in John but in none of the other gospels. He is introduced at the beginning and at the close of Christ's ministry. His doubt of Christ's Messiahship vanished when he met Him, and he was one of the seven to whom the risen Lord manifested Himself at the Lake of Galilee.

It may be that he bore a double name and is referred to as Bartholomew, whom John never mentions, just as the other evangelists never mention Nathanael. The name Bartholomew stands in conjunction with that of Philip. If the rule is accepted that Andrew and Simon are put together because the one led the other to Christ, there is a presumption in favor of Bartholomew of the first three gospels being the same as Nathanael of John's gospel, from the fact recorded by John only, that it was Philip who brought Nathanael to the Saviour. We reject the tradition that he was the bridegroom at the Cana marriage, or one of the two disciples on the Emmaus road.

Profitable aspects to be developed are these:

I. Nathanael owed his introduction to Jesus to a friend. Have you introduced others to Him?

II. Nathanael was prepared to listen to conversation about Christ. He readily received the witness of one who had found the Messiah. Have you found Him, and are you telling others the story?

III. Nathanael's hopes were realized in an unexpected way. Often joy and rest come to us from the least expected quarter.

IV. Nathanael accepted the sure test of truth and the sure cure of prejudice. "Come and see," "Taste and see."

V. Nathanael's faith rejoiced the Master, and secured for him the promise of a growing blessing.

NATHAN-MELECH [Nă' than-mĕ' lech]—THE KING IS GIVER. *A*

eunuch or chamberlain who lived in Josiah's time and had a chamber within the precincts of the Temple (II Kings 23:11).

NAUM [Nă um]—COMFORT. *An ancestor of Jesus Christ through Mary.* See Nahum (Luke 3:25).

NEARIAH [Nē a rī' ah]—JEHOVAH HATH SHAKEN or DRIVES AWAY.
1. *Grandson of Shechaniah,* descendant of David (I Chron. 3:22, 23).
2. *A Simeonite captain* who assisted in the war against the Amalekites (I Chron. 4:42).

NEBAI [Něb' a ī]—NARROWING or PROJECTING. *A person who with Nehemiah sealed the covenant* (Neh. 10:19).

NEBAJOTH, NEBAIOTH [Nē bā' joth, Nē bā' ioth]—HUSBANDRY. *The eldest son of Ishmael,* son of Hagar (Gen. 25:13; 28:9; 36:3; I Chron. 1:29), and founder of a tribal family (Isa. 60:7).

NEBAT [Nē' băt]—CULTIVATION. *Father of Jeroboam,* who rebelled against Rehoboam and became the first king of the ten tribes of Israel (I Kings 11:26; 12:2, 15). As Jeroboam I is always referred to as "the son of Nebat," distinguishing him from Jeroboam II, one wonders what influence father had over son.

NEBO [Nē' bō]—HEIGHT. *An ancestor of certain Jews* who had taken foreign wives while in exile (Ezra 10:43). Also the name of the mountain on which Moses died, and the name of a Chaldean idol (Deut. 32:49; 34:1; Isa. 46:1).

NEBUCHADNEZZAR, NEBUCHADREZZAR, REZZAR [Něb u chad něz' zar]—NEBO, DEFEND THE BOUNDARY. *Son of Nabopolassar and king of Babylon,* who figures prominently as an enemy of God's people (II Kings 24:1, 10, 11; Dan. 1–5).

The Man Whose Pride Turned Him Mad

This first Gentile monarch was the one who captured Jerusalem and destroyed both city and temple. The inhabitants were carried into Babylon as slaves. Nebuchadnezzar set up a golden image in Dura, and the three Hebrew youths who refused to bow down to the image were thrown into the fiery furnace but divinely preserved. Drunk with pride, Nebuchadnezzar had dreams Daniel interpreted. Driven out for a time from men, and living among oxen, he became a new man and turned from his humiliation to honor God.

The encyclical letter written by the first head of Gentiles, for Nebuchadnezzar was "a king of kings," reaches far and wide in the lesson it teaches to all Gentile powers, until the times of the Gentiles shall be fulfilled (Dan. 4: 34–37; Rev. 11:15–17). In this letter we **have:**

I.   The dream of a tree reaching in its height to heaven, and seen by all the world. This related to the king himself, who swayed the scepter of a universal empire, and whose power led to pride (Prov. 16:5–18).

II.   The wise advice received from Spirit-anointed Daniel made clear how the king's error could be healed. God has been speaking to the Gentile nations ever since he gave them dominion, but a deaf ear has been turned to divine entreaties. In the face of appalling perils Gentile monarchy is crumbling today.

III.   The patience of God is manifest in that twelve months have elapsed before the threatened judgment overtook the proud monarch. How long-suffering God is!

IV.   Sore punishment led to deep humiliation and to a noble confusion in the presence of the world. God abased Nebuchadnezzar, and the day is coming when He will likewise abase the Gentile nations of earth. When the mightiest of all monarchs returns, He will lay hold of Gentile government and introduce His own world-kingdom and reign as the King of all Gentile kings. The scepter of universal dominion will rest in His pierced hands.

NEBUSHASBAN, NEBUSHAZBAN [Nĕb u shăs′ ban]—NEBO, SAVE ME. *A Babylonian prince* who held the office of Rab-saris under Nebuchadnezzar (Jer. 39:13).

NEBUZAR-ADAN [Nĕb′ u zär-ä′ dan]—NEBO HATH AN OFFSPRING. *The captain of the guard* left behind in Jerusalem after its capture (II Kings 25:8, 11, 20; Jer. 39:9, 10).

NECHO, NECO [Nĕ′ chō]—WHO WAS BEATEN. *The appellation given to the king of Egypt* (II Chron. 35:20, 22; 36:4). See Pharaoh.

NEDABIAH [Nĕd a bī′ ah]—JEHOVAH IS WILLING or BOUNTIFUL. *A son of king Jeconiah*, son of Jehoiakim, king of Judah (I Chron. 3:18).

NEHEMIAH [Nĕ he mī′ ah]—JEHOVAH HATH CONSOLED.
1.   A chief man who returned from exile (Ezra 2:2; Neh. 7:7).
2.   The son of Hachaliah and cup-bearer to king Artaxerxes (Neh. 1:1).

The Man Who Had a Mind to Work

Nehemiah and Hanani were the sons of Hachaliah (Neh. 1:1; 2:5; 7:2), and the references suggest that the family belonged to the capital. Nehemiah, although born in exile, grew up in the faith of Israel's God. Nehemiah's name appears as a prince, not as a priest (Neh. 9:38; 10:1), and he was perhaps the chief man who returned from Babylon with Zerubbabel (Ezra 2:2; Neh. 7:7). As the king's cup-bearer, he held a high place of honor in the palace of Shushan (Neh. 1:11), having confidential access to the king. His Persian name was Sheshbazzar (Ezra 1:8). He was one of the princes who signed the covenant (Neh. 9:38; 10:1). He became Governor of Jerusalem (Neh. 10:1). Josephus says that Nehemiah died of old age and that the repaired walls of the city constituted his best and most enduring monument.

For his patriotic task (Neh. 1:1–4), Nehemiah was well qualified. As a true Israelite, he labored for the purity of public worship, the integrity of family life, the sanctity of the sabbath. Ezra was the student and preacher; Nehemiah, the soldier and statesman. He was courageous and God-fearing, and brought to his labors a noble disinterestedness, and unblemished rectitude, a dauntless spirit and unswerving loyalty to God. Alexander Whyte in his helpful essay of Nehemiah speaks of him:

> As a self-contained man. A man of his own counsel. A man with the counsel of God alone in his mind and in his heart. A reserved and resolute man. A man to take command of other men. A man who will see things with his own eyes, and without all eyes seeing him. A man in no haste or hurry. He will not begin till he has counted the cost. And then he will not stop till he has finished the work.

While we are compelled to pass over a full exposition of the book of this patriotic Jew whose heart was stirred with sorrow over the derelict condition of Jerusalem, we must linger over some of its important aspects.

I.   He illustrates the strength which comes from an inspiring purpose and definite aim. Open opposition and underhanded wiles had to be faced, but undauntedly Nehemiah persisted in his task (Neh. 6:3). Among the hostile methods directed against his noble mission were:

Ridicule (Neh. 2:19; 4:2). But Nehemiah prayed that such reproach might return to the reproachers which it did (Neh. 4:4–6).

Fear (Neh. 4:7–23). Enemies delivered an ultimatum but Nehemiah set a watch. Swords and trowels were united (Neh. 4:18).

Guile (Neh. 6:2–4). Nehemiah knew that conferences were useless, and so shunned them.

False accusation (Neh. 6:5–9). This patriot had no selfish motives behind his endeavors.

Temptation to tempt God (Neh. 6:10–13). Nehemiah refused to hide himself in the Temple as if he was doing wrong.

Corruption of friends and associates (Neh. 6:17–19). This was the meanest act of Nehemiah's foes.

II.   He sets forth the strength that comes from humble dependence upon God. True to God and his principles, Nehemiah surmounted all his enemies and obstacles. His sterling character stood the acid test, for he was a man of dependence upon God (Neh. 1:5–11), singlehearted in his devotion to God and his work, wise in taking proper precautions against surprise attacks, ever encouraging to those who labored with him. Making his prayer to God, Nehemiah knew that God would fight for him (Neh. 4:9, 20).

III. He manifested the strength which comes from the sense of union and of fellowship. All classes of people, even the daughters, were ready to take their place around the damaged walls. High and low worked together for the accomplishment of a God-inspired task (Neh. 3:12). With scorn, Nehemiah rebuked the pride and negligence of the nobles "who put not their necks to the work of their Lord" (Neh. 3:5). Fulfilling their obligation by repairing "every man over against his house," the willing-heart with one mind to work illustrates the chain of living Christian fellowship set forth in Ecclesiastes 4:9. See I Corinthians 12:4–7.

3. *A son of Azbuk* and ruler of half the district of Jerusalem who repaired part of the wall—a common-sense enthusiast even as his illustrious namesake (Neh. 3:16).

NEHUM [Nĕ' hum]—CONSOLATION. *A chief man* who returned from exile with Zerubbabel (Neh. 7:7). Called Rehum in Ezra 2:2.

NEKODA [Nĕ kō' dă]—HERDSMAN or DISTINGUISHED.
1. *One of the Nethinims* whose descendants returned from exile (Ezra 2:48; Neh. 7:50).
2. *Another one of the above* whose descendants also returned from exile, but could not prove their genealogy (Ezra 2:60; Neh. 7:62).

NEMUEL [Nĕ mū' el]—GOD IS SPREADING.
1. *A Reubenite,* son of Eliab and brother of Dathan and Abiram, who strove against Moses (Num. 26:9).
2. *A son of Simeon,* second son of Jacob and Leah (Num. 26:12; I Chron. 4:24). Founder of a tribal family.

NEPHEG [Nĕ' pheg]—AN OFFSHOOT.
1. *A son of Izhar,* son of Kohath (Ex. 6:21).
2. *A son born to David after he became king of Israel* (II Sam. 5:15; I Chron. 3:7; 14:6).

NER [Nûr]—A LAMP or BRIGHTNESS. *A Benjamite,* son of Abiel and father of Abner, Saul's chief captain (I Sam. 14:50, 51).

NEREUS [Nĕ' re ŭs]—NAME OF A SEA GOD, WHO UNDER POSEDON OR NEPTUNE RULED THE MEDITERRANEAN SEA. *A Christian in Rome* to whom Paul sent a greeting (Rom. 16:15). Probably the son of Philologus. The phrase, "all the saints that are with them," indicates a community of believers accustomed to meet together for worship and fellowship.

NERGAL-SHAREZER [Nûr' gal-shā re' zer]—NERGAL, PROTECT THE KING.
1. *A prince of Nebuchadnezzar* (Jer. 39:3).

2. *Another prince* who held office in Jerusalem (Jer. 39:3, 13). Perhaps these two are the same person.

NERI [Nē' rī]—LIGHT OF THE LORD. *An ancestor of Christ* and somehow genealogically the father of Shealtiel (Luke 3:27).

NERIAH [Nē rī' ah]—LAMP OF JEHOVAH. *Son of Masseiah* and father of Baruch and Seraiah, scribe and messenger of Jeremiah (Jer. 32:12, 16).

NETHANEEL, NETHANEL [Nē thăn' e el]—GOD GIVES or HATH GIVEN.

1. *A prince of the tribe of Issachar* in the early period of the wilderness wanderings (Num. 1:8; 2:5; 7:18, 23; 10:15).
2. *One of David's brothers,* fourth son of Jesse (I Chron. 2:14).
3. *A priest who blew a trumpet* when the Ark was brought back to the city of David (I Chron. 15:24).
4. *A Levite* whose son Shemaiah was employed by David for sanctuary service (I Chron. 24:6).
5. *A son of Obed-edom* appointed by David as gatekeeper for the Tabernacle (I Chron. 26:4).
6. *A prince of Judah* whom king Jehoshaphat sent to teach the people (II Chron. 17:7).
7. *A chief Levite* in Josiah's time (II Chron. 35:9).
8. *A son of Pashur* who had married a foreign wife (Ezra 10:22).
9. *A priest of the family of Jediah* who lived in the days of Joiakim (Neh. 12:21).
10. *An Aaronite musician* who assisted in the dedication of the wall (Neh. 12:36).

NETHANIAH [Nĕth a nī' ah]—JEHOVAH HATH GIVEN.

1. *Father of that Ishmael who slew Gedaliah,* whom Nebuchadnezzar had left governor in the land (II Kings 25:23, 25).
2. *A son of Asaph,* and chief singer in David's time (I Chron. 25:2, 12).
3. *A Levite* whom Jehoshaphat sent to teach the cities of Judah (II Chron. 17:8).
4. *The father of Jehudi* whom the princes of Judah sent to bring Baruch (Jer. 36:14).

NEZIAH [Nē zī' ah] —PRE-EMINENT or PURE. *One of the Nethinims,* the sacred official class, whose descendants returned from exile (Ezra 2:54; Neh. 7:56).

NICANOR [Nĭ că' nor] —CONQUEROR, VICTORIOUS or I CONQUER. *One of the seven disciples* chosen by the Church at Jerusalem to look after Greek-speaking widows and the poor in general (Acts 6:5).

NICODEMUS [Nĭc o dē' mus]—INNOCENT BLOOD or VICTOR OVER THE
PEOPLE. *An elderly and somewhat wealthy Pharisee* and a member of
the Sanhedrin (John 3:1-9; 7:50; 19:39).

The Man Who Came to Jesus by Night

Whenever Nicodemus is mentioned it is always with the label,
"the same that came to Jesus by night." Why is this master in Israel
always spoken of in this way? Was he a coward, afraid of what the
fellow-members of the Sanhedrin would say if they saw him seeking
out Jesus? We feel that he came by night because it was the best
time for both Jesus and himself to have a quiet, uninterrupted conversation about spiritual matters. Nicodemus had been occupied all
day with his teaching duties, and Jesus had been active in His out-of-
door ministry. Now both could relax and talk through the night. It
may be that Nicodemus had such a heart hunger that he could not
wait until morning, and so came running to Jesus as soon as he could.

There had been no direct voice from God in Israel for a long time,
and here was One whose message carried the stamp of divine authority.
So Nicodemus, the cautious enquirer, but a man of spiritual perception (John 3:2), sought out Christ, and listened to one of His remarkable conversational sermons. Nicodemus figures three times in John's
gospel:

He came to Christ (John 3:2). This master in Israel confessed
Christ to be a Teacher sent from God and heard that in spite of his
culture, position and religion, he needed to be born anew by the Spirit
of God. His name, meaning "innocent blood," is suggestive. Nicodemus came to realize that his salvation was dependent upon the shedding of innocent blood (John 3:14, 16).

He spoke for Christ (John 7:45-52). As a fair-minded man, Nicodemus, although a disciple at heart and afraid to avow his faith, raised
his voice on behalf of Christ as the Sanhedrin devised measures against
Him. The rulers were His avowed enemies, and Nicodemus raised a
point of order in favor of the One he had learned so much from.
Perhaps he should have been more courageous and outspoken on
Christ's behalf. When the Sanhedrin condemned Jesus to death, there
was no protest from Nicodemus. It is likely that he absented himself
from that fateful meeting.

He honored Christ (John 19:39, 40). After the death of Christ,
ashamed of his cowardice, Nicodemus rendered loving though belated
service to Christ. Openly he joined Joseph of Arimathaea, another
secret disciple, in preparing Christ's body for a kingly burial. But the
dead cannot appreciate our loving attention. Mary gave her spices to
Jesus while He was alive. It is better to give flowers to the living than
reserve them for their burial.

NICOLAS, NICOLAUS [Nĭc' o las]—CONQUEROR OF THE PEOPLE. *A
proselyte of Antioch,* one of the seven disciples selected by the apostles
to care for widows and the poor (Acts 6:5).

NIGER [Nĭ′ gûr]—BLACK. *The Latin surname of Simeon,* one of the prophets and teachers in Antioch. Simeon was the Jewish name, and Niger an assumed Gentile name (Acts 13:1).

NIMROD [Nĭm′ rŏd]—VALIANT, STRONG or HE THAT RULES. *A son of Cush,* son of Ham. Nimrod was a mighty hunter and a potent monarch whose land bore his name (Gen. 10:8, 9; I Chron. 1:10; Micah 5:6).

NIMSHI [Nĭm′ shĭ]—JEHOVAH REVEALS or DRAWN OUT. *An ancestor of Jehu,* and generally designated "son of Nimshi" (I Kings 19:16; II Kings 9:2, 20; II Chron. 22:7).

NOADIAH [Nō a dĭ′ ah]—JEHOVAH HATH MET, ASSEMBLED or ORNA-MENT OF THE LORD. *A son of Binnui,* who had charge of the gold and silver vessels brought back from captivity (Ezra 8:33). Also the name of the so-called prophetess whose evil pronouncements were intended to terrify Nehemiah (Neh. 6:14).

NOAH, NOE [Nō′ ah]—REST.
1. *The son of Lamech* of the posterity of Seth—the tenth from Adam. He died at the age of 950 years (Gen. 5:29, 30, 32; 6:8). The LXX version says that the name is a play on the statement, "This same shall give us rest."

The Man Who Built the Ark

Nothing is known of the early life of Noah, who first appeared on the scene when he was five hundred years old. Evidently his father, Lamech, was a religious man and gave his son a fitting name, meaning *rest.* This much we do know about Noah, he lived in a time when men were universally corrupt, so much so that God said He would destroy the human race (Gen. 6:1–7).

In the midst of an age of moral darkness, Noah was perfect in his generation. He walked with God and had a life radiant with right-eousness. Intimate with God, he learned of His purpose to destroy mankind (Heb. 11:7), and was given the strange and almost impossible task of building a vessel large enough to shelter his family and a pair of all the birds and the beasts of that time.

Noah set about the tremendous work of the Ark's construction. Daily he had to endure the ridicule of the godless. At last the waters of judgment covered the earth, but all within the Ark were safe and saved. What a striking illustration the Ark affords of Christ, who preserves us from the flood of divine judgment. Here is an outline for the pastor to extend:

I.　Noah walked with God in spite of surrounding iniquity (Gen. 6:8–12). There were saints in Caesar's household.

II.　Noah was obedient when appointed to a difficult task (Gen. 6:14–21; 7:5).

III. Noah was remembered by God and delivered from death (Gen. 8:1). Romans 8:1 tells where we rest.

IV. Noah, by faith, worked out his salvation (Heb. 11:7). See Philippians 2:12.

V. Noah warned his neighbors of impending judgment. (II Peter 2:5). See Ezekiel 33:1–20.

VI. Noah built the first recorded altar (Gen. 8:20). See Hebrews 13:10.

VII. Noah was honored by God with an everlasting covenant (Gen. 9:12–17). See Hebrews 9:15.

2. *Also the name of a daughter of Zelophehad*, the grandson of Gilead (Num. 26:33).

NOBAH [Nō' bah]—BARKING. *A Manassite captain of Kenath* who gave the town his own name (Judg. 8:11).

NOBAI, NEBAI [Nĕb' a ī]—FRUIT OF THE LORD. *One of the chiefs* of the people who, with Nehemiah, sealed the covenant (Neh. 10:19). See Nebo.

NOGAH [Nō' gah]—BRILLIANCE or SHINING. *A son of David*, born after he became king of Israel (I Chron. 3:7; 14:6).

NOHAH [Nō' hah]—REST. *Fourth son of Benjamin* (I Chron. 8:2). Perhaps another name for Shephupham (Num. 26:39 R. V.).

NUN [Nŭn]—FISH or CONTINUATION. *An Ephraimite*, father of Joshua, Israel's great military leader (Ex. 33:11; Num. 11: 28). Joshua is always spoken of as "the son of Nun."

NYMPHAS [Nўm' phas]—SACRED TO THE MUSES or BRIDEGROOM. *A believer of Laodicea* or Colosse to whom Paul sent a loving greeting. He was an influential person whose house was used as a meeting place for Christians (Col. 4:15).

O

OBADIAH [Ō ba dī' ah]—SERVANT or WORSHIPER OF JEHOVAH. Among the Semitic peoples many names, such as the one before us, were common, occurring frequently in the Old Testament. Little or nothing is known about the Obadiahs of the Bible, but the name has also been found on an ancient Hebrew seal.

1. *The pious governor of Ahab's palace* who hid one hundred of Jehovah's prophets (I Kings 18:3–16).

2. *The founder of a family of the lineage of David* (I Chron. 3:21).

3. *A man of Issachar* of the family of Tola (I Chron. 7:3).

4. *Son of Azel,* a descendant of king Saul (I Chron. 8:38; 9:44).

5. *Son of Shemaiah,* a Levite of Netophah (I Chron. 9:16).

6. *A Gadite* who joined David at Ziklag (I Chron. 12:9).

7. *Father of Ishmaiah,* prince of Zebulun in David's time (I Chron. 27:19).

8. *A prince of Judah,* sent by Jehoshaphat to teach the people (II Chron. 17:7).

9. *A Levite,* one of the overseers of the workmen who repaired the Temple in Josiah's time (II Chron. 34:12).

10. *Son of Jehiel,* a descendant of Joab who returned from exile with Ezra (Ezra 8:9).

11. *A priest* who, on behalf of his father's house, sealed the covenant (Neh. 10:5).

12. *A Levite,* founder of a family of sanctuary porters (Neh. 12:25).

13. *The prophet of Judah* who lived over 550 years before Christ (Obad. 1).

The Man Who Prophesied Disaster

This Minor Prophet cannot be identified. His book, the briefest in the Old Testament, gives his name, but there the record ends. Pusey says, "The silence of Scripture as to Obadiah stands in remarkable contrast with the anxiety of man to know something about him." His origin, age, life, country, parents and grave are all unknown. His is the voice of a stranger. He has been identified with the Levite of the same name sent by Jehoshaphat to teach in the cities of Judah (See No. 8). He has also been linked with the pious Obadiah of Ahab's house (See No. 1). Of the prophet's personal history not a single incident or even tradition has been preserved. The work is more important than the worker.

It would seem as if the prophet lived and labored between the taking of Jerusalem and the destruction of Idumea, since he speaks of "foreigners" entering Jerusalem and the day of Judah's destruction and distress (Obad. 11–14). Although his book is the shortest in the Hebrew Canon, consisting of only twenty-one verses, yet it demands more of our attention, proportionately, than any other book. Looking at it from the aspect of size, it is little, but weighty. *Multum in parvo.*

Obadiah's prophecy has always been a favorite one with the Jews. It is principally from Obadiah that they learned to apply the name Edom to Rome. "Edom" stands as the typical designation for all the deadliest foes of the House of Israel.

Edom was descended from Esau, the brother of Jacob, and thus the people were akin to the Children of Israel. Since the days of the Exodus there has been frequent conflict between the two races. The Edomites had shown themselves unfriendly to Moses and the Israelites, refusing them passage through their territory when marching towards Canaan, and this bitterness still continues, accounting for the present animosity of the Arab world toward the Jew.

Obadiah's style in writing is full of individuality. It is animated and vigorous, abounding in appeals and having the preponderance of interrogation of great point and vehemence. His language is simple and pure, with utterance often highly poetic.

The lessons to be gathered from Obadiah's description of the character and career, the downfall and doom of Edom; are clearly evident:

    I. The similarity of sin and punishment.

    II. God will not cast off His people forever.

    III. Greed and cruelty are hateful to God.

    IV. Pride goes before a fall.

    V. The ultimate kingdom is the Lord's.

OBAL [O' bal]—BARE or INCONVENIENCE OF OLD AGE. *A son of Joktan* of the family of Shem (Gen. 10:28). Called Ebal in I Chronicles 1:22.

OBED [O' bed]—WORSHIPER or A SERVANT WHO WORSHIPS.

1. *Son of Boaz,* by Ruth, and better than ten sons to her, since through Obed she became an ancestress of Jesus Christ (Ruth 4:17–22; I Chron. 2:12; Matt. 1:5; Luke 3:32).

2. *Son of Ephlal,* descendant of Judah (I Chron. 2:37, 38).

3. *One of David's valiant men* (I Chron. 11:47).

4. *A son of Shemaiah,* a gatekeeper at the Tabernacle in David's time (I Chron. 26:7).

5. *Father of Azariah,* in the time of Athaliah (II Chron. 23:1).

OBED-EDOM [O' bed-ĕ' dom]—SERVANT OF EDOM or LABORER OF THE EARTH.

1. *A Levite,* one of David's bodyguard, in whose house the Ark was hid for three months. Its presence brought blessing to Obed-edom and all his family (II Sam. 6:10–12; I Chron. 13:13, 14; 15:25).

2. *A Levite,* gatekeeper of the Tabernacle, who marched before the Ark during its removal to Jerusalem (I Chron. 15:18–24; 26:4, 8, 15).

3. *A Levite* of the second degree who did regular duty at the tent erected for the Ark (I Chron. 16:5, 38).

4. *A son of Jeduthun,* who also served at the sanctuary. Perhaps Obed-edom the Korathite (I Chron. 16:38; II Chron. 25:24).

OBIL [O' bĭl]—DRIVER, LEADER or ONE WHO WEEPS. *An Ishmaelite camel keeper,* who had charge of David's camels (I Chron. 27:30).

OCRAN [Oc' ran]—TROUBLER. *Father of Pagiel,* chosen by Moses to number the people (Num. 1:13; 2:27; 7:72, 77; 10:26).

ODED [O' ded]—AIDING or HE HATH RESTORED.

1. *The father of the prophet Azariah* who encouraged Asa, king of Judah (II Chron. 15:1, 8).

2. *An Israelite prophet* in the reign of Pekah who successfully protested against the enslavement of the Judahites (II Chron. 28:9).

OG [Ŏg]—LONG-NECKED or BREAD BAKED IN ASHES. *The giant king of Bashan.* This man of huge stature, the last of the Rephaim, was slain at Edrei. The only big things of any note about this massive man, whose conquests lingered long in the imagination of the people (Ps. 135:11; 136:20), were his big body and his big bed (Num. 21:33; 32:33; Deut. 3:1–13).

OHAD [Ŏ′ hăd]—POWERFUL. *The third son of Simeon* (Gen. 46:10; Ex. 6:15).

OHEL [Ŏ′ hel]—BRIGHTNESS or A TENT. *A son of Zerubbabel,* descendant of King Jehoiakim (I Chron. 3:20).

OHOLIAB, AHOLIAB [Ŏ hŏ′ li ăb, Ā hŏ′ li ăb]—TENT OF THE FATHER. *The chief assistant of Bezaleel* (Ex. 31:6; 35:34; 36:1, 2; 38:23).

OLYMPAS [Ŏ lўm′ pas]—HEAVENLY. *A believer at Rome* to whom Paul sent a salutation (Rom. 16:15).

OMAR [Ŏ′ mar]—MOUNTAINEER, ELOQUENT or HE THAT SPEAKS. *A son of Eliphaz* and grandson of Esau. Chieftain of a tribe by the same name (Gen. 36:11, 15; I Chron. 1:36).

OMRI [Ŏm′ rĭ]—A BUNDLE OF CORN, IMPETUOUS or JEHOVAH APPORTIONS.
1. *Father of Ahab,* captain of the host, afterwards made king instead of Zimri who had slain Elah (I Kings 16:16–30; II Kings 8:26; II Chron. 22:2; Micah 6:16). Omri was one of the most important kings of Israel and the founder of a dynasty. He reigned for twelve years.
2. *A son of Becher,* son of Benjamin (I Chron. 7:8).
3. *A Judahite* of the family of Perez (I Chron. 9:4).
4. *Son of Michael* and a prince of the tribe of Issachar in David's time (I Chron. 27:18).

ON [Ŏn]—SUN or STRENGTH. *A Reubenite chief* who took part in the rebellion of Korah (Num. 16:1). Also the name of the capital of Lower Egypt (Gen. 41:45, 50).

ONAM [Ŏ′ nam]—WEALTHY or STRENGTH.
1. *Son of Shobal,* son of Seir (Gen. 36:23; I Chron. 1:40).
2. *A son of Jerahmeel,* a Judahite (I Chron. 2:26, 28).

ONAN [Ŏ' nan]—STRONG or PAIN. *Second son of Judah,* by the daughter of Shua the Canaanite. The method he adopted to evade the object of his marriage with his brother's widow was evil in God's sight, and He slew him (Gen. 38:4, 8, 9; 46:12; Num. 26:19; I Chron. 2:3).

ONESIMUS [Ŏ nĕs' Ĭ mŭs]—PROFITABLE. *The slave of Philemon,* Paul's convert (Col. 4:7–9; Philemon 10–19). Onesimus ran away from his master and came into contact with Paul, who led him to Christ after they met in Rome. Paul urged him to return to his master and entreated Philemon to receive Onesimus, not as a slave, but as a brother in the Lord. How the apostle approached Onesimus provides us with a beautiful exhibition of Christian courtesy.

ONESIPHORUS [Ŏn e sĭph' o rŭs]—BRINGING ADVANTAGE. *A believer in Ephesus* who befriended Paul (II Tim. 1:16; 4:19).

The Man Who Was Kind to His Friend

From the description Paul gives us of Onesiphorus, he must have been a lovely character. In his revealing essay of this rare character, Alexander Whyte speaks of him as "an elder in the Church of Ephesus, and a better elder there never was."

Much controversy has raged around Paul's cameo of Onesiphorus. Was he adorning the brow of a living man with a garland? Or was he placing a wreath upon the tomb of a saint? Some see in Paul's reference to "the house of Onesiphorus" a proof for the lawfulness of prayers for the dead. But Paul's language does not constitute a prayer, but only a wish or exclamation. The dead are beyond the influence of our intercessions.

There are several traits of the admirable life of Onesiphorus we can profitably meditate upon:

I. He was repeatedly kind. "He *oft* refreshed me." In the overwhelming heat of his trials, Paul found himself revived when this dear saint came his way. What a blessed ministry it is to refresh the needy children of God!

II. He associated himself with Paul's suffering. "He was not ashamed of my chain." Some of the apostle's friends did not like to own any connection with a chained man. But not so Onesiphorus. He had a big soul and brought consolation to the manacled prisoner. Many of God's best servants are harassed with chains of sorrow and of affliction. Let us not shrink from helping them.

III. He made it his business to find Paul. "He sought me out." Matthew Henry says, "A good man will seek opportunities of doing good, and will not shun that offer." Is there someone you should hunt up and cheer?

IV. He and his house were blessed for kindness shown. "The Lord give mercy to the house of Onesiphorus." Paul was not able to reward his friend for all his gracious solicitation, but the Lord could, and would. In ministering to Paul, Onesiphorous had ministered to the Lord, and of the Lord would be blessed.

OPHIR [Ŏ′ phûr]—FAT or RICH. *A son of Joktan,* a descendant of Shem (Gen. 10:29; I Chron. 1:23). Also the name of a place in South Arabia famous for gold and other products (I Kings 9.28; Ps. 45:9).

OPHRAH [Ŏph′ rah]—HAMLET or HIND. *A son of Meonothai,* of the tribe of Judah (I Chron. 4:14). Also the name of two different cities (Josh. 18:23; Judg. 6:11).

OREB [Ŏ′ reb]—A RAVEN or CAUTIOUS. *One of the two Midianite princes* defeated and put to death by Gibeon (Judg. 7:25; 8:3; Ps. 83:11). *Also the name of a rock near Beth-bareh,* whereon Oreb and Zeeb were slain (Judg. 7:25; Isa. 10:26).

OREN [Ŏ′ ren]—STRENGTH or FINE TREE. *Third son of Jerahmeel,* a Judahite (I Chron. 2:25).

ORNAN [Ŏr′nan]—STRONG or THAT REJOICES. *The Jebusite prince* whose threshing floor was purchased by David for an altar (I Chron. 21:15–25; II Chron. 3:1). Called Araunah in II Samuel 24:16.

OSEE [Ŏ′ zee]—SALVATION. *The Greek name of the prophet Hosea* (Rom. 9:25).

OSHEA [Ŏ shĕ′ ă]—GOD SAVES. The name of Joshua son of Nun, servant of Moses (Num. 13:8, 16).

OTHNI [Ŏth′ nī]—LION OF GOD or JEHOVAH IS FORCE. *A son of Shemaiah* and porter of the Tabernacle in David's time (I Chron. 26:7).

OTHNIEL [Ŏth′ nĭ el]—POWERFUL ONE or LION OF GOD. *A son of Kenaz,* younger brother of Caleb, who, after the death of Joshua, judged Israel for forty years. He is the first to be mentioned among the "Judges" (Josh. 15:17; Judg. 1:13; 3:9, 11: I Chron. 4:13). The Othniel mentioned in I Chronicles 27:15 is probably the same person.

Little is recorded of this saviour who came from the tribe of Judah. He followed the Lord with all his heart, and, Spirit-empowered, he fought for Israel and prevailed.

OZEM [Ŏ′ zem]—STRENGTH or THAT FASTS.
1. *The sixth son of Jesse,* and David's brother (I Chron. 2:15).
2. *A son of Jerahmeel,* son of Hezron (Chron. 2:25).

OZIAS [Ŏ zī′ as]—STRENGTH FROM THE LORD. *An ancestor of Jesus Christ* (Matt. 1:8, 9). See Uzziah and Uzza (Ezra 2:49; Neh. 7:51).

OZNI [Ŏz′ nī]—ATTENTIVE or JEHOVAH HEARS. *A son of Gad,* the seventh son of Jacob, and founder of the tribal family called Oznites (Num. 26:16). Perhaps the Ezbon of Genesis 46:16.

P

PAARAI [Pā′ a raī]—REVELATION OF JEHOVAH or OPENING. *One of David's heroes,* from Aruboth in Judah (II Sam. 23:35). Called Naarai in I Chronicles 11:37.

PADON [Pā′ don]—DELIVERANCES or REDEMPTION. *One of the family of Nethinims,* members of which returned from exile (Ezra 2:44; Neh. 7:47).

PAGIEL [Pā′ ği el]—GOD MEETS or PREVENTION OF GOD. *A son of Ocran* and chief of the tribe of Issachar, chosen to take a census of the people (Num. 1:13; 2:27; 7:72, 77; 10:26).

PAHATH-MOAB [Pā′ hath-mŏ′ ab]—GOVERNOR OF MOAB.
1. *A person, part of whose clan returned from exile with Zerubbabel* (Ezra 2:6; 10:30; Neh. 3:11; 7:11).
2. *Another of the same clan* who returned from exile (Ezra 8:4). Also the name of a family sealing the covenant (Neh. 10:14).

PALAL [Pā′ lal]—HE HATH JUDGED. *A son of Uzai,* who assisted in the repair of the city wall (Neh. 3:25).

PALLU, PHALLU [Păl′ lū, Phăl′ lū]—DISTINGUISHED or WONDERFUL. *The second son of Reuben* and founder of a tribal family (Gen. 46:9; Ex. 6:14; Num. 26:5, 8; I Chron. 5:3).

PALTI, PHALTI [Păl′ tī, Phăl′ tī]—DELIVERANCE BY GOD or BY RAPHU.
1. *A son of Raphu,* a Benjamite and representative spy (Num. 13:9).
2. *The son of Laish,* to whom Michal, David's wife, was given (I Sam. 25:44). See Paltiel.

PALTIEL, PHALTIEL [Păl′ tī el, Phăl′ tī el]—DELIVERER OF THE LORD.
1. *Son of Azzan* and prince of Issachar (Num. 34:26).

2. *Son of Laish* and the man to whom David's wife, Michal, was given (II Sam. 3:15). The same as Palti, No. 2.

PARMASHTA [Pär' mäsh' tă]—SUPERIOR. *A son of Haman, the* Jews' enemy (Esther 9:9).

PARMENAS [Pär' me năs]—FAITHFUL or I ABIDE. *One of the seven disciples* elected to care for Greek-speaking widows, the poor and the financial affairs generally of the Early Church (Acts 6:5).

PARNACH [Pär' năch]—VERY NIMBLE. *The father of Elizaphan,* a chief of Zebulun (Num. 34:25).

PAROSH, PHAROSH [Pä' rŏsh, Phä' rŏsh]—A FUGITIVE or FRUIT OF THE NORTH.
1. *One whose clan returned from exile with Zerubbabel* (Ezra 2:3; Neh. 7:8).
2. *Another whose descendants returned with Ezra* (Ezra 8:3).
3. *One whose descendants had married foreign wives* (Ezra 10:25).
4. *The father of Pedaiah* who helped to repair the city wall (Neh. 3:25).
Also the name of a family that, with Nehemiah, sealed the covenant (Neh. 10:14).

PARSHANDATHA [Pär shăn' da thă]—GIVEN TO PERSIA or DUNG OF IMPURITY. *A son of Haman the Agagite,* who was hanged with the rest of his brothers (Esther 9:7).

PARUAH [Pär ōō' ah]—FLOURISHING or INCREASE. *The father of Jehoshaphat,* one of Solomon's purveyors (I Kings 4:17).

PASACH [Pä' sach]—A DIVIDER or LIMPING. *A son of Japhlet,* an Asherite of the family of Beriah (I Chron. 7:33).

PASEAH, PHASEAH—[Pä sě' ah, Phä sě' ah]—LAME.
1. *A son of Eshton,* grandson of Chelub, a Judahite (I Chron. 4:12).
2. *One whose clan was reckoned among the Nethinims* (Ezra 2:49; Neh. 7:51).
3. *The father of Jehoiada* who helped rebuild the city wall (Neh. 3:6).

PASHUR, PASHHUR [Păsh' ŭr]—FREE or MULTIPLIES LIBERTY.
1. *A son of Malchijah* and head of a priestly family in Jerusalem (I Chron. 9:12; Ezra 2:38; 10:22; Neh. 7:41; 11:12).
2. *A son of Immer the priest,* who put Jeremiah in stocks because of his discouraging predictions (Jer. 20:1-6; 38:1).

3. *A priest who sealed the covenant* (Neh. 10:3).

4. *Son of Melchiah,* a prince of Judah in Jeremiah's day (Jer. 21:1; 38:1).

PATHRUSIM [Păth rōō' sĭm]—THE SOUTH LAND. *A descendant of the fifth son of Mizraim,* son of Ham (Gen. 10:14; I Chron. 1:12).

PATROBAS [Păt' ro băs]—ONE WHO PURSUES THE STEPS OF HIS FATHER. *A Christian in Rome* to whom Paul sent a greeting (Rom. 16:14).

PAUL [Pôul]—LITTLE. *The great apostle to the Gentiles,* whose original name was Saul, a grander title than that of Paul (Acts 13:9).

The Man Who Founded Churches

How impossible it is to sketch in a page or two the worth and work of the chief missionary of early Christianity! Whole volumes have been written on this expositor of a divine revelation, and the first and most prolific contributor to that marvel of literature, the New Testament. Dr. John Clifford suggests that the making of this remarkable man is revealed to us in six photographs, taken at different times, some by himself, others by the Evangelist Luke. They mark the successive stages of Paul's growth and suggest the formative energies operative at the chief epoch of his career. (See Acts 7:58; 22:3; 26:4, 5; Rom. 7; Gal. 1:13, 15; Phil. 3:5, for these epochs).

Here is a brief summary of this energetic, commanding, masterful man, who is one of the great characters, not only in the Bible, but in all history.

I. He was a native of Tarsus, and his father was a Roman—a fact significant in Paul's labors (Acts 21:39; 22:3, 25; 25:16).

II. He was a Pharisee Jew—a Pharisee by *birth,* son of Pharisees, and a Pharisee by *belief,* the hope and resurrection of the dead (Matt. 22:23; Acts 23:5, 6; Phil 3:5).

III. He was a freeborn citizen of Rome (Acts 22:25, 28).

IV. He had had a strict religious training. Circumcision admitted him to the covenant relation of his fathers (Phil. 3:5). As a Jewish boy, he would memorize Scripture (Deut. 6:4–9) and familiarize himself with Jewish history (Deut. 6:20–25).

V. He was a tent maker by trade (Acts 18:3). A Talmudic writer asks, "What is commanded of a father towards his son? To circumcise him, to teach him the law, to teach him a trade." (See I Cor. 4:12; I Thess. 2:9; II Thess. 3:8).

VI. He had received a good education, finishing up under the great philosopher, Gamaliel (Acts 22:3). As Paul quotes from the Greek poets, he must have been well acquainted with Greek philosophy and literature. Paul, however, studied not only in Jerusalem but also in "The College of Experience." Knowledge comes not only from books, but from the responsibility and experience of life (Phil. 4:11-13).

VII. He had been a persecutor of Christ and of Christians (Acts 8:1-4). Enthusiastically Paul endeavored to stamp out the Christian faith. There is no evidence, however, that he himself killed anyone.

VIII. He became a new creature in Christ Jesus. The persecutor became a believer (Acts 9:3-9; 22:6-11; 26:12-18). Paul never tired of telling the story of his striking conversion on that Damascus road.

IX. He had ten years' training for his remarkable work. In Arabia, Damascus, Jerusalem, Syria and Cilicia, Paul spent much time in the study of Scripture and in prayer, knowing that God had called him to function as a witness and minister of the truth (Gal. 1:15-24).

X. He was a great missionary and church builder. Paul undertook three fruitful missionary journeys, the influence of which cannot be overestimated (Acts 13:1; 28:31). In all his travels, trials and triumphs, Paul was borne along by the one incentive—"To do the will of Him that sent me" (John 6:38; Acts 21:13, 14).

XI. He was a heart-stirring preacher. Three of his sermons are preserved for us in Acts and serve as models for preachers of all time. Paul relied upon Scripture and appealed to historical facts and prophecy. Ponder his sermon to Jews at Antioch (Acts 13:16-41); his sermon to Gentiles at Athens (Acts 17:22-31).

XII. He was a most gifted writer. Of the twenty-seven books forming the New Testament, Paul was the author of fourteen of them, if we include Hebrews. How revealing are his valuable epistles! As Robert Speer puts it, "They show us his character with all its varied elements, his religious intensity, his originality, freshness and depth of thought, and his intellectual boldness and strength, while they reveal to us also his rich moral nature and his human heart enlarged by the grace of Christ."

Paul's bodily size and appearance may have been against him, judging from a second century apocryphal description of him: "He was a man little of stature, partly bald, with crooked legs, of vigorous physique, with eyes set close together and nose somewhat hooked." What he was in his appearance mattered little. Paul lived only to win others to Christ and to make Him known. If legend be true, at the end of his honored life, his foes led him out to the Appian Way where they severed his noble head from his frail body, and he died triumphantly for the Lord he dearly loved. To him life was Christ, and death a gain.

PAULUS [Pôu' lus]—LITTLE. *The surname of Sergius,* Roman deputy at Paphos who believed the Gospel when Elymas the sorcerer was struck blind (Acts 13:7, 12).

PEDAHEL [Pĕd' a hĕl]—GOD DELIVERS or GOD HATH SAVED. *A prince of the tribe of Naphtali,* chosen to divide the land (Num. 34:28).

PEDAHZUR [Pē däh' zur]—THE ROCK DELIVERS or POWERFUL. *Father of Gamaliel*, the chief of Manasseh, chosen to help number the people (Num. 1:10; 2:20; 7:54, 59; 10:23).

PEDAIAH [Pē dā' iah]—JEHOVAH DELIVERS or REDEMPTION OF THE LORD.
1. *Grandfather of King Josiah* (II Kings 23:36).
2. *Son or grandson of Jeconiah* (I Chron. 3:18, 19).
3. *Father of Joel*, ruler of Manasseh in David's reign (I Chron. 27:20).
4. *A son of Parosh* who assisted in the repair of the city wall (Neh. 3:25).
5. *A prince or priest* who stood on Ezra's left hand as he read the Law to the people (Neh. 8:4; 13:13).
6. *A Benjamite of the family of Jeshiah* (Neh. 11:7).

PEKAH [Pē' kah]—OPENING OF THE EYES or WATCHFULNESS. *Son of Remaliah* and a captain under Pekahiah, against whom he conspired in order to reign in his stead. But he reaped as he sowed, for in turn he himself was slain by Hoshea the son of Elah (II Kings 15:25–37; 16:1, 5; II Chron. 28:6; Isa. 7:1).

PEKAHIAH [Pĕk a hī' ah]—JEHOVAH HATH GIVEN SIGHT. *Son and successor of Menahem*, king of Israel, and slain by Pekah, after reigning two years (II Kings 15:22–26).

PELAIAH [Pĕl a ī' ah]—JEHOVAH HATH MADE ILLUSTRIOUS.
1. *A son of Elioenai*, of the family of David (I Chron. 3:24).
2. *A priest* who explained the Law as Ezra read it (Neh. 8:7).
3. *A Levite* who, with others, sealed the covenant (Neh. 10:10).

PELALIAH [Pĕl a lĭ' ah]—JEHOVAH JUDGES. *A priest* descended from Malchiah (Neh. 11:12).

PELATIAH [Pĕl a tī ' ah]—JEHOVAH DELIVERS or SETS FREE.
1. *A son of Hananiah* and grandson of Zerubbabel (I Chron. 3:21).
2. *A Simeonite captain*, successful in the war against Amalek (I Chron. 4:42).
3. *A son of Benaiah*, seen in vision by Ezekiel the prophet (Ezek. 11:1, 13). Also the name of a family sealing the covenant (Neh. 10:22).

PELEG [Pĕ' lĕg]—DIVISION. *A son of Eber*, a Shemite, whose name indicates the time before the earth was divided (Gen. 10:25; 11:16–19; I Chron. 1:19, 25).

PELET [Pĕ' let]—ESCAPE or LIBERATION.

1. *A son of Jahdai* of the family of Caleb, son of Hezron (I Chron. 2:47).

2. *A son of Azmaveth,* one of David's captains (I Chron. 12:3).

PELETH [Pě′ leth]—SWIFTNESS or FLIGHT.

1. *A Reubenite* and father of On, who joined Korah, Dathan and Abiram in their revolt against Moses and Aaron (Num. 16:1).

2. *A son of Jonathan,* descendant of Pharez son of Judah (I Chron. 2:33).

PENUEL, PENIEL [Pě nū′ el, Pě nī′ el]—THE FACE OF GOD.

1. *A man of Judah* and the ancestor of the inhabitants of Gedor (I Chron. 4:4).

2. *A Benjamite of the family of Shashak* (I Chron. 8:25). Also the name of an encampment east of Jordan where Jacob wrestled with the angelic visitor (Gen. 32:30, 31; Judg. 8:8, 9, 17).

PERESH [Pě′ resh]—SEPARATE or DISTINCTION. *A son of Machir* son of Manasseh (I Chron. 7:16).

PEREZ, PHARES, PHAREZ [Pě′ rěz, Phā′ rēz, Phā′ rěz]—BURSTING THROUGH, A BREACH. *A son of Judah* and one of the twins Tamar bore, who became the father of a tribal family and an ancestor of Jesus Christ (Gen. 38:29; Num. 26:20; Ruth 4:12, 18; I Chron. 27:3; Matt. 1:3).

PERIDA [Pě rī′ dă]—SEPARATION. *One of the servants of Solomon* whose descendants returned from exile with Zerubbabel (Neh. 7:57). Called Peruda in Ezra 2:55.

PERSIS [Pûr′ sis]—THAT WHICH DIVIDES. *A saint to whom Paul sent an affectionate greeting.* (Rom. 16:12).

PETER [Pě′ tûr]—A ROCK or STONE. *The Greek form of the Aramaic surname, Cephas.* Peter was the brother of Andrew and the son of Jona, or Johanan (Matt. 4:18; John 1:40; I Cor. 1:12).

The Man Who Fell but Rose Again

Peter is another of those outstanding characters in the Bible gallery of men, requiring a book all his own to fully expound his life and labors. From the many references to this *reed* transformed into a *rock,* we gather these facts and features of "The Big Fisherman."

He was a fisherman of Bethsaida, a name meaning "the house of fish." Afterwards he resided in Capernaum, where Jesus frequently lodged during His Galilean ministry.

His father was Jona, or Jonah, and Andrew was his brother. Both sons were fishermen on the Lake of Galilee and were evidently in partnership with Zebedee and his sons.

He first met Christ at Bethany beyond Jordan, where John the Baptist exercised his ministry. Both Peter and Andrew were disciples of the Baptist. It was Andrew who introduced Peter to Christ.

He received a triple call as friend, disciple and apostle. Through daily contact with Jesus, seeing and hearing His words and works, Peter's character was deepened and strengthened.

He was a man with many facets of character. His life can be approached from many angles. He was naturally impulsive (Matt. 14:28; 17:4; John 21:7); tenderhearted and affectionate (Matt. 26:75; John 13:9; 21:15–17); gifted with spiritual insight (John 6:68), yet sometimes slow to apprehend deeper truths (Matt. 15:15, 16); courageous in his confession of faith in Christ, yet guilty of a most cowardly denial (Matt. 16:16; John 6:69; Mark 14:67–71); self-sacrificing yet inclined towards self-seeking (Matt. 19:27), and presumption (Matt. 16:22; John 13:8; 18:10); immovable in his convictions (Acts 4:19, 20; 5:28, 29, 40, 42).

He became the leader and spokesman of the Apostolic Twelve and of the three privileged to witness the raising of Jairus' daughter, the Transfiguration, our Lord's agony in the Garden. He himself became a miracle worker, especially during the time portrayed in Acts.

He made a confession of Christ's deity which became the foundation of the Church, and was appointed steward with authority of the keys, meaning that his was to be the privilege of opening the door of salvation to the Jews.

He miserably failed his Lord in an hour of crisis, being the only disciple to deny Christ, yet he was restored and recommissioned by Jesus after His resurrection. He became the dauntless leader of the infant Church and was foremost to protest his loyalty to Christ. After Pentecost, Peter's ministry appears in four stages:

I. Jerusalem activities, 29–35 A.D., when James eventually succeeded to leadership of the Church.

II. Palestinean mission, 35–44 A.D., during which he remained for a while at Lydda and Joppa. He received a call to Caesarea, and in the house of Cornelius opened the door of privilege to the Gentiles.

III. Syrian mission with Antioch as a center, 44–61 A.D., during which he was accompanied by his wife, who became the pioneer Zenana missionary.

IV. Rome, 61 A.D. It would seem as if Peter reached here before Paul's release from his first imprisonment, and a few years later suffered martyrdom by crucifixion, as Christ prophesied he would. Legend has it that Peter deemed himself unworthy to die in exactly the same way as his Lord had, and so begged his crucifiers to crucify him upside down.

PETHAHIAH [Pĕth a hĭ' ah]—JEHOVAH HATH SET FREE.

1. A priest whose family was appointed by David to the nineteenth course (I Chron. 24:16).

2. *A Levite* who had married a foreign wife (Ezra 10:23).

3. *Another Levite* who regulated the devotions of the people (Neh. 9:5). Perhaps the same as No. 2.

4. *A son of Meshezabeel,* of the family of Zorah, and an official of the king of Persia for all matters concerning the returned exiles (Neh. 11:24).

PETHUEL [Pē thŭ' el]—GOD DELIVERS or THE NOBLE-MINDEDNESS OF GOD. *Father of Joel the prophet* (Joel 1:1).

PEULTHAI, PEULETHAI [Pē ŭl' thaī]—FULL OF WORK or JEHOVAH WORKS. *A Kohathite,* son of Obed-edom and a doorkeeper of the Tabernacle in David's time (I Chron. 26:5).

PHALEC [Phā' lec]—DIVISION. *The father of Ragau* and an ancestor of Jesus Christ. (Luke 3:35). See also Peleg.

PHALLU [Phăl' lŭ]—ADMIRABLE. *A son of Reuben* (Gen. 46:9).

PHALTI [Phăl' tī]—DELIVERANCE. *A son of Laish,* to whom Michal, David's wife, was given (I Sam. 25:44). See Palti.

PHANUEL [Phā nŭ' el]—VISION OF GOD. Of the tribe of Aser and *father of the prophetess, Anna,* who gave thanks in the Temple at seeing the child Jesus (Luke 2:36, 38).

PHARAOH [Phā' raōh]—SUN, GREAT HOUSE or THE DESTROYER. This was a title used as the general description of the sovereign of Egypt, both with and without the personal name attached. *Pharaoh* is an Egyptian term derived from *Phra,* meaning the sun, to which the Egyptians likened themselves. This is why we often see them represented with a disc or figure of the sun upon their heads. The Pharaohs of Bible times are as follows:

1. *The one who took Sarah from Abraham* (Gen. 12:15-20).

2. *The one who reigned when Joseph was prime minister* (Gen. 37:36; 40-50).

3. *The one who was king of Egypt when Moses was born* and in whose palace Moses was brought up (Ex. 1 and 2).

4. *The one who was king when Moses was fully grown* (Ex. 2:15).

5. *The one who persecuted the Israelites,* and whom Moses and Aaron challenged (Ex. 3:10, 11; 4:21, 22; 5-18).

6. *The one who reigned in the days of Solomon* and whose daughter Solomon married (I Kings 3:1; 7: 8).

7. *The one who was king in the days of Isaiah* (Isa 19:11; 30:2, 3; 36:6).

8. *The one who was father of Bithiah, wife of Mered,* of the tribe of Judah (I Chron. 4:18).

PHARAOH-HOPHRA [Phă' raōh-hŏph' ră]—PRIEST OF THE SUN. *Another king of Egypt* whose overthrow by Nebuchadnezzar was foretold by Jeremiah (Jer. 44:30).

PHARAOH-NECHO or NECHOH [Phă' raōh-ně' chō, Phă' raōh-ně' choh]—PHARAOH THE LAME. *A king of Egypt who fought against Nabopolassar,* king of Assyria, slew King Josiah at Megiddo, bound Jehoahaz at Riblah and made Eliakim his brother king in his stead (II Kings 23:29, 33–35; Jer. 37:5, 7; 46:2).

PHARES—[Phă ' rēz]—BREACH or RUPTURE. *Elder son of Judah by Tamar,* and father of Esrom (Matt. 1:3; Luke 3:33). See Pharez.

PHAREZ, PEREZ [Phă' rěz, Pě' rěz]—BREAK FORTH VIOLENTLY. *Elder son of Judah by Tamar his daughter-in-law,* and father of Hezron and Hamul. See Phares above (Gen. 38:29; 46:12; Num. 26:20, 21; Ruth 4:12, 18). For Pharzites see Numbers 26:20.

PHICHOL [Phī' chol]—GREAT, STRONG or MOUTH OF ALL. *Chief captain of Abimelech,* king of the Philistines in Abraham's time (Gen. 21:22, 32; 26:26).

PHILEMON [Phī lě' mon]—FRIENDLY or AFFECTIONATE. *A believer in Colossi* to whom Paul addressed a beautiful cameo of knightliness (Philemon 1).

The Man Whose Slave Came Back

Philemon, the rich, influential and pious Colossian was doubtless led to Christ by Paul, who therefore had power in his appeal for the return of Onesimus, Philemon's runaway slave, another convert of the apostle. The prayers, love, generosity, and hospitality of Philemon were ever in Paul's mind (Philemon 5, 7, 21, 22). His well-furnished home was the rendezvous of believers. "The church" met in his home, and, as the leader of the Christian congregation in Colosse, Philemon's influence must have been considerable. The close tie between Paul and Philemon is expressed in the phrase, "beloved and fellow worker."

Paul's approach to Philemon contained a sincere appraisal of character. With instinctive kindness and conscious diplomacy, the apostle praises Philemon for his Christian life and labors. From the lips of Onesimus he had heard often of Philemon's love, faith and liberality. The tired hearts of the poor or otherwise distressed and harassed saints had found in Philemon a pillar of comfort and strength, and Paul, without flattery, extols the one whose life was the fruit of a loving heart. Such a commendation of Philemon prepared his mind for the apostle's request on behalf of Onesimus. Purposely, Paul puts Philemon's love first, seeing it was an act of love he was to prompt him to manifest.

Philemon was urged to deal with Onesimus, not as chattel, but as a Christian. The kingly heart of Paul begged for the forgiveness of one who had sinned against his own name, for Onesimus means *profitable.* How could Philemon spurn such a gracious overture? Did he not owe all he was in grace to Paul? As Martin Luther put it, "Paul strips himself of his right and therefore compels Philemon to betake himself to his right."

Paul also urged that Philemon's forgiveness must be warm, full and free, "Receive him, that is, mine own bowels." The apostle's fervent plea did not fall upon deaf ears. Onesimus was met with the desired reception (Col. 4:9). Legend has it that Onesimus became the Bishop of Berea.

There is something touching in Paul's request to Philemon to pray that he might be liberated and then enjoy the loving hospitality of his home. Paul says that he wrote his letter with his own hand, and his signature eased the way for the return of Onesimus to his wronged master. It also shows us how to act in all graciousness to all men.

Of the Epistle to Philemon, "a little idyll of the progress of Christianity," as it has been called, much might be said. Bishop Handley Moule compares it with the admired letter of Pliny to his friend Sabinianus, to ask pardon for a young freedman who had offended Sabinianus. "It's [Pliny's letter] a graceful, kindly letter, written by a man whose character is the ideal of his age and class: the cultured and thoughtful Roman gentleman of the mildest period of the empire. . . . His heart has not the depth of Paul to clasp Onesimus in his arms and to commend him to Philemon as a friend in God for immortality." Nowhere in literature is there a gem so admirably adapted for the purpose on hand.

PHILETUS [Phĭ lē′ tus]—BELOVED, WORTHY OF LOVE or AMIABLE. *A heretic condemned,* along with Hymenaeus, for denials of the resurrection (II Tim. 2:17).

PHILIP [Phĭl′ ĭp]—WARRIOR or A LOVER OF HORSES.

1. *One of the twelve apostles,* a native of Bethsaida in Galilee (Matt. 10:3; Mark 3:18). Tradition has it that he was the one who requested of Jesus that he might first go and bury his father (Matt. 8:21, 22).

The Man of a Timid, Retiring Disposition

Unlike Andrew and John, Philip did not approach Jesus, but waited till He accosted him and invited him to join His company. Andrew and John found Jesus—Jesus found Philip, whose name is a Greek one both by custom and derivation. A Jewish name he must have had, since all the apostles were Jews, but what it was remains unknown.

In three lists Philip is bracketed with Nathanael as companion and fellow worker. Both were Galileans. This Philip must not be confused with Philip the Deacon, considered below. We never read of the later Philip before Pentecost, nor of Philip the Apostle after Pentecost.

The conversion and call of Philip are expressed simply: "Jesus . . . findeth Philip, and saith unto him, Follow me" (John 1:43). The call to faith and to follow came at once, and Philip was ready for both. The impressive feature of his conversion is that as soon as Christ found him, Philip sought to bring others to Christ. The convert became a soul winner. "Come and see," he said to Nathanael, and he won his friend.

When the hungry multitude gathered around Christ at the Sea of Galilee, Philip was tested by Christ (John 6: 5). Philip was singled out for a test of his faith, and for a great opportunity, which he lost, and with it lost a blessing. Instead of telling the Master that He was able to feed the hungry crowd, Philip made a mental calculation of how much food would be necessary to give each person a portion, and how much it would cost, and declared the project to be impossible. The seeking Greeks were led to Philip but although he sympathized with their request to see Christ, he was afraid and almost lost another opportunity (John 12:21). Yet Philip experienced familiar friendship with Jesus, for did He not call him by name? Slow to apprehend truth, he missed much, but Jesus had nothing but kind words for him (John 14:8). Tradition tells us that Philip died as a martyr at Heirapolis.

2. *A son of Herod the Great* and husband of Herodias. This was the royal Philip, who, disinherited by his father, lived a private life (Matt. 14:3; Mark 6:17; Luke 3:19).

3. *Another son of the above Herod* who was tetrarch of Iturea (Luke 3:1).

4. *One of the seven deacons of the Church at Jerusalem* who had four daughters (Acts 6:5; 8; 21:8).

The Man Who Loved to Evangelize

Philip was not content to serve tables, he loved to preach the Word, and was most successful in revival work. He was not a man to act on his own authority. He was a God-sent and Spirit-controlled evangelist (Acts 8:26–30). When the Spirit said, "Go," he obeyed with alacrity.

I. After the martyrdom of Stephen, Philip preached in Samaria with great success (Acts 8:4–8).

II. He led the Ethiopian to Christ and was the means of introducing Christianity to a heathen country (Acts 8:26–39).

III. He preached from city to city until he reached Caesarea (Acts 8:40).

IV. His four daughters were also preachers.

V. He had a godly home (Acts 21:8), in which Paul loved to stay, for he and Philip were like-minded.

PHILOLOGUS [Phĭ lol′ o gŭs]—A LOVER OF WORDS or OF LEARNING. *A believer in Rome* to whom Paul sent a salutation (Rom. 16:15).

PHINEHAS [Phĭn′ ĕ hăs]—FACE OF TRUST or MOUTH OF A SERPENT.
1. *A son of Eleazar*, one of Aaron's sons, who slew Zimri and Cozbi. He manifested great zeal, was the third high priest of the Jews and discharged his office most faithfully for nineteen years (Ex. 6:25; Num. 25:14, 15).
2. *The younger son of Eli*, the priest and judge of Israel. Phinehas, with his brother Hophni, disgraced the sacred office of priesthood and both were slain (I Sam. 1:3; 2:34; 4:4–19; 14:3).
3. *The father of Eleazar*, a priest who returned with Ezra (Ezra 8:33).

PHLEGON [Phlĕ′ gon] BURNING or ZEALOUS. *A believer in Rome* to whom Paul sent a loving greeting (Rom. 16:14).

PHURAH [Phŭ′ rah]—BEAUTY or BEARS FRUIT. *A servant of Gideon* who went down with him to visit the host of Midian (Judg. 7:10, 11). Also called Purah.

PHUT, PUT [Phŭt, Pŭt]—BROW or EXTENSION. *The third son of Ham*, Noah's son (Gen. 10:6; I Chron. 1:8), whose dwelling was in Lybia (Ezek. 27:10) and whose descendants became hired servants of the Syrians (Nah. 3:9).

PHUVAH, PUA, PUAH [Phŭ′ vah, Pŭ′ ă, Pŭ′ ah]—UTTERANCE.
1. *The second son of Issachar* (Gen. 46:13; Num. 26:23; I Chron. 7:1).
2. *The father of Tola* of the tribe of Issachar, who judged Israel after the death of Abimelech (Judg. 10:1).

PHYGELLUS, PHYGELUS [Phȳ jĕl′ lus]—FUGITIVE. *A believer in the province of Asia* who deserted Paul in the latter part of his labors (II Tim.1:15).

PILATE [Pī′ late]—ONE ARMED WITH A DART. *The surname of the fifth Roman procurator of Judea*, who was recalled by Tiberius and banished to Vienna, where tradition says he committed suicide in 41 A.D. (Matt. 27).

The Man Who Sinned Against Conscience

What a different story we would have had if Pilate had obeyed his own conscience and also had followed his wife's intuition and advice. Pilate held office for some twelve years, and by his covetous and cruel government caused himself to be hated both by the Jews and Samaritans. His first name, Pontius, means, "belonging to the sea."

What a man he was for shirking responsibilities! He turned Christ over to the Jewish authorities (John 18:31), and then to Herod (Luke 23:7). When Christ was returned to him, he proposed to inflict a minor penalty (Luke 23:22). When he could not silence the cry of the mob for the blood of Christ, he directed attention to Barabbas (Matt. 27:17), and when the die was cast, engaged in a hypocritical ceremony (Matt. 27:24).

Some authorities affirm that the name Pilate is from "Pilus," a felt cap which was worn by a slave as an emblem of liberty.

PILDASH [Pĭl' dăsh]—FLAME OF FIRE. *Sixth son of Nahor,* Abraham's brother (Gen. 22:22).

PILEHA, PILHA [Pĭl' e hă]—WORSHIP or PLOWING. *One of those who, with Nehemiah, sealed the covenant* (Neh. 10:24).

PILTAI [Pĭl' tai]—JEHOVAH CAUSES TO ESCAPE. *A priest,* head of his father's house of Moadiah in the days of Joiakim Neh. 12:17).

PINON [Pĭ' non]—ORE, FIT or PEARL. *A duke of Edom,* of the family of Esau, who gave his name to a town (Gen. 36:40, 41; I Chron. 1:52).

PIRAM [Pĭ' ram]—A WILD ASS or SWIFT. *A Canaanite,* king of Jarmuth, and one of those slain by Joshua before Gideon (Josh. 10:3).

PISPAH [Pĭz' pah]—EXPANSION. *An Asherite,* a son of Jether (I Chron. 7:38).

PITHON [Pĭ' thon]—HARMLESS or GIFT OF MOUTH. *A son of Micah* and descendant of King Saul (I Chron. 8:35; 9:41).

POCHERETH [Pŏch' e rĕth]—BINDING. *A servant of Solomon* whose descendants returned from exile with Zerubbabel (Ezra 2:57; Neh. 7:59).

PORATHA [Pŏr' a thă]—HAVING MANY CHARIOTS or FRUITFUL. *One of the sons of Haman the Agagite.* He died with his brothers (Esther 9:8).

PORCIUS [Pŏr'cĭ ŭs]—MEANING UNCERTAIN. *The procurator of the Jews who succeeded Felix* and who sent Paul to Rome. See Festus (Acts 24:27).

POTIPHAR [Pŏt' ĭ phar]—WHO IS OF THE SUN or A FAT BULL. *The captain of Pharaoh's guard* to whom Joseph was sold by the Midianites. It was his wife who tried to seduce Joseph (Gen. 37:36; 39:1).

POTI-PHERAH, POTI-PHERA [Pŏt' ĭ-phē' rah]—BELONGING TO THE

SUN. *A priest of On and father of Asenath,* Joseph's wife (Gen. 41:45, 50; 46:20).

PROCHORUS [Prŏch' o rŭs]—LEADING IN A CHORUS, DANCE or LEADER OF SINGERS. *One of the seven disciples chosen to care for widows and the poor* (Acts 6:5).

PUBLIUS [Pŭb' lĭ ŭs]—COMMON. *The chief man and landowner on the island of Melita* when Paul was shipwrecked (Acts 28:7, 8). Now Malta.

PUDENS [Pŭ' denz]—BASHFUL or SHAMEFACED. *A believer in Rome* who united with Paul in sending a greeting to Timothy (II Tim. 4:21).

PUL [Pŭl]—STRONG. *King of Assyria* who invaded Israel in the days of Menahim and was bribed to depart (II Kings 15:19; I Chron. 5:26). Also the name of a tribe or place in Africa (Isa. 66:19).

PUTIEL [Pŭ' tĭ el]—GOD ENLIGHTENS or AFFLICTED BY GOD. *Father-in-law of Eleazar,* son of Aaron (Ex. 6:25).

PYRRHUS [Pўr' rhŭs]—MEANING UNKNOWN. *The father of Sopater of Berea* (Acts 20:4 R.V.).

Q

Among the thousands of persons named in the Bible, there is only one under the letter Q, namely, Quartus, the Corinthian Christian whom Paul calls "a brother" and who joined the apostle in sending a salutation to the Church at Rome. Whether the apostle meant a brother of Erastus or a brother in the Lord is not clear (Rom. 16:23). Probably Quartus was among the seventy Jesus sent forth.

QUARTUS [Quär' tus]—THE FOURTH.
This name is associated with a quarternion of soldiers, that is, a file of four, the usual number for a night watch. Peter was placed under the guard of four quarternions of soldiers, or sixteen soldiers, in order that each might guard him three hours at a time (Acts 12:4).

It may be fitting at this point to discover the significance of the many friends Paul speaks of. Romans and Colossians are unique for their number of personal salutations. Paul himself was such a friendly person that friends gathered around him as moths do around a lighted lamp. In the majority of cases all we have is the mention of a name. Now and again Paul adds a brief, endearing term. But the fact that he mentions many by name, as in the case of Quartus, proves that he must have had some contact with them. Either he had met them on his journeys and they were blessed by his ministry, or they had ministered unto the apostle of their substance. By including their names in his letters, he gave them an imperishable memory.

There were multitudes of others who had labored with Paul in the Gospel, too numerous perhaps to be called by name. The apostle rejoiced, however, that their names, although not mentioned in his lists, were written in the Book of Life, and fully known of the Lord (Phil. 4:3). John also besought Demetrius to greet all his friends by name (III John 14).

R

RAAMAH, RAAMA [Rā′ a mah]—TREMBLING or GREATNESS. *The fourth son of Cush,* eldest son of Ham, and father of Sheba and Dedan (Gen. 10:7; I Chron. 1:9). Also the name of a place on the Persian Gulf and associated with Sheba as trading with Tyre (Ezek. 27:22).

RAAMIAH, REELAIAH [Rā a mī′ ah, Rē el ā′ iah]—JEHOVAH CAUSES TREMBLING. *One of the twelve chiefs* who returned with Zerubbabel (Ezra 2:2; Neh. 7:7).

RABMAG [Răb′ măg]—HEAD OF THE MAGI or CHIEF OF THE MAGICIANS. *The title of Nergal-sharezer, a Babylonian official* of Nebuchadnezzar present at the taking of Jerusalem (Jer. 39:3–13). Mag from magus (magi) might have been applied to a sacred caste in Babylon.

RABSARIS [Răb′ sa rĭs]—GRAND MASTER OF THE EUNUCHS.
1. *An officer under Nebuchadnezzar,* king of Babylon, and possibly the one who ordered the release of Jeremiah (Jer. 39:3–13).
2. *The title of an Assyrian official* sent by Sennacherib, king of Assyria, to Hezekiah to demand the surrender of Jerusalem (II Kings 18:17).

RABSHAKEH [Răb′ sha keh]—HEAD OF THE CUPBEARERS. *The title of the Assyrian military official under King Sennacherib,* who accompanied Rabsaris on the journey to Hezekiah to demand Jerusalem's surrender (II Kings 18:17–37; 19:4–8; Isa. 36:2–22; 37:4–8).

RADDAI [Răd′ da ī]—JEHOVAH SUBDUES or CUTTING UNDER. *The fifth son of Jesse,* the father of David (I Chron. 2:14).

RAGAU [Rā′ gôu]—A FRIEND. *Father of Saruch* and an ancestor of Christ (Luke 3:35). See Reu.

RAGUEL [Rā gū' el]—SHEPHERD, FRIEND OF GOD or JEHOVAH IS A FRIEND. *The father of Hobab* and father-in-law of Moses (Num. 10:29). Also called Jethro and Reuel.

RAHAM [Rā' hăm]—PITY, LOVE or AFFECTION. *The son of Shema,* the son of Hebron, descended from Caleb (I Chron. 2:44).

RAKEM, REKEM [Rā' kem, Rĕ' kem]—FRIENDSHIP or VARIEGATED. *Son of Sheresh,* grandson of Manasseh (I Chron. 7:16).

RAM [Răm]—HIGH or ELEVATED.
1. *Father of Amminadab* and son of Hezron and an ancestor of David and of Christ (Ruth 4:19; I Chron. 2:9, 10; Matt. 1:3, 4). He appears as Arni in Luke 3:33.
2. *Son of Jerahmeel,* brother of Ram, a man of Judah (I Chron. 2:25, 27).
3. *Head of the family to which Elihu belonged.* Also a descendant of Buz (Job 32:2).

RAMIAH [Rā mī' ah]—EXALTED IS JEHOVAH. *A son of Parosh* who had married a foreign wife (Ezra 10:25).

RAMOTH [Rā' moth]—HIGH PLACES or HEIGHTS. *A son of Bani* who put away his foreign wife (Ezra 10:29). Also the name of a Gershonite Levitical city in Issachar (I Chron. 6:73). Perhaps Jarmuth of Joshua 21:29, and Remath of Joshua 19:21. The name is likewise given to a Levitical city in Gilead in Had, and appears as Ramoth-gilead and Ramoth-mizpah (Deut. 4:43; Josh. 20:8; 21:38; I Chron. 6:80). See also south Ramoth (I Sam. 30:27).

RAPHA, RAPHAH [Rā' phă]—HE HAS HEALED, FEARFUL or RELAXATION.
1. *The fifth son of Benjamin* (I Chron. 8:2).
2. *A descendant of Jonathan,* Saul's son (I Chron. 8:37). Called Rephaiah in I Chronicles 9:43.
3. *An ancestor of certain Philistine warriors* slain in David's time and called "the giants" (II Sam. 21:16, 20, 21; I Chron. 20:4–8).

RAPHU [Rā'phu]—FEARED or HEALED. *A Benjamite,* father of Palti, and a spy sent out by Moses to report on Canaan (Num. 13:9).

REAIAH, REAIA [Rĕ a ī' ah, Rĕ a ī' ă]—JEHOVAH HAS SEEN or PROVIDED FOR.
1. *A son of Shobal,* son of Judah (I Chron. 4:2). Perhaps the Haroeh, meaning "the seeing one," of I Chronicles 2:52.
2. *Grandfather of Beerah,* prince of Reuben when Israel was carried away to Assyria (I Chron. 5:5).

3. *One of the family of Nethinims* whose descendants returned from exile with Zerubbabel (Ezra 2:47; Neh. 7:50).

REBA [Rĕ′ bă]—OFFSPRING, FOURTH PART or ONE WHO STOOPS. *One of the five Midianite kings* slain by Israel while they were in the plains of Moab (Num. 31:8; Josh. 13:21).

RECHAB [Rĕ′ chăb]—COMPANIONSHIP, A HORSEMAN or SQUARE.

1. *A son of Rimmon,* a Beerothite, captain of the band who slew Ish-bosheth in his bed, and who was put to death by David (II Sam. 4:2–9).

2. *Father of Jehonadab* and founder of a tribe known as the "Rechabites" (II Kings 10:15, 23).

The Man Who Vowed to Be Separate

This particular order had its rise in the religious revival that took place under Elijah and Elisha. The tenets of the followers of Rechab were a reaction and a protest against the luxury and license which under Jezebel and Ahab threatened to destroy the simplicity of the ancient nomadic life of Israel. Accordingly, the Rechabites vowed to drink no wine, nor build houses, nor sow seed, nor plant vineyards, but dwell in tents all their days. They were to remember they were strangers in the land. For 250 years they adhered faithfully to their rules but were driven from their tents when in 607 B.C. Nebuchadnezzar invaded Judah.

Of these noteworthy people, whose high moral example was specially commended by God, Dr. Dinsdale Young elaborates on these points:

I.   They honored the memory of the good.

II. They were marked by great simplicity of life.

III. They were worshipers of Jehovah.

IV. They maintained their integrity amid surrounding degeneracy.

V.   They had their principles severely tested.

VI. They received special blessing.

May all of us be found among God's true Rechabites!

3. *A descendant of Hemath a Kenite* (I Chron. 2:55).

4. *The father of Malchiah,* a chief man who, after his return from exile, helped to repair the wall of Jerusalem (Neh. 3:14).

REELAIAH [Rĕ el ā′ iah]—TREMBLING CAUSED BY JEHOVAH. *One of the principal men who returned from exile* with Zerubbabel (Ezra 2:2). Called Raamiah in Nehemiah 7:7.

REGEM [Rĕ′ gĕm]—FRIENDSHIP or A FRIEND. *A son of Jahdai* of the family of Caleb, son of Jephunneh (I Chron. 2:47).

REGEM-MELECH [Rĕ′ gem-mĕ′ lech]—FRIEND OF THE KING. *A man sent from Bethel* with a deputation to question the priest and prophets about a day of fasting and humiliation in memory of the Temple's destruction (Zech. 7:2).

REHABIAH [Rē ha bī' ah]—JEHOVAH IS COMPREHENSIVE or GOD IS MY EXTENT. *The eldest son of Eliezer* and grandson of Moses (I Chron. 23:17; 24:21; 26:25).

REHOB [Rē' hŏb]—WIDTH or AN OPEN SPACE.
1. *The father of Hadadezer,* king of Zobah in David's time (II Sam. 8:3, 12).
2. *A Levite* who with Nehemiah sealed the covenant (Neh. 10:11). Also the name of a Levitical town on the boundary line of the territory of Asher (Num. 13:21). Now called Hunin.

REHOBOAM, ROBOAM [Rē hō bō' am, Rō bō' am]—FREER OF THE PEOPLE or THE PEOPLE IS ENLARGED. *The son of Solomon by Naamah,* an Ammonitess (I Kings 11:43; 14:21).
At the revolt he was left with only two tribes.

The Man Who Scorned Good Advice

Although Rehoboam was the son of a wise father, he himself had a small mind. From the fifty references to this man, who scorned wise counsel, we can learn a great many facts. Although named as an ancestor of Christ (Matt. 1:7), he was unworthy of such an honor for three reasons.

I. He was dominated by a false principle. Rehoboam entertained an erroneous idea of the relation between a sovereign and his subjects. He was obsessed with the false premise that the subjects existed for the sovereign and not the sovereign for the subjects. Daily surrounded by unscrupulous flatterers who fed his self-importance, Rehoboam came to accept the nonsensical fiction of "the divine right of kings," that led him to treat his subjects as mere puppets to be manipulated for the benefit of his reigning house.

Whether this outlook was the result of a perverse disposition or wrong training may be hard to decide. Rehoboam had been brought up under the autocratic rule of his father, Solomon, to whom *subjects* were synonymous to *slaves.* When the people appealed, it was more against Solomon than Rehoboam, who had not had the opportunity of proving his quality as a king. So the first appeal to Rehoboam was, "Thy father made our yoke grievous," and the son sought to copy the defect of his father. Lamentable failure, however, overtook this feeble son of an illustrious father.

II. He followed the wrong advice. Alexander Whyte introduces his homily on *Rehoboam* with the sentence: "Just by one insolent and swaggering word, King Rehoboam lost for ever the ten tribes of Israel. And all Rehoboam's insane and suicidal history is written in our Bible for the admonition and instruction of all hot-blooded, ill-natured, and insolent-spoken men among ourselves."

What a different history of the Jews would have been written had Rehoboam not followed the advice of reckless counselors. When he went to Shechem, the rallying center of the northern tribes, to be formally crowned as king in succession to Solomon, the people were willing to accept Rehoboam on one condition, namely that he should lighten the burdens imposed upon them by Solomon. This reasonable request, which should have been acceded to without any hesitation, was met with the cautious reply: "Come again to me after three days." But Rehoboam lost a golden opportunity of healing the sores of fears and of preserving the unity of God's ancient people.

First of all, the king sought the advice of the old men who had been counselors of his father and whose ripe experience qualified them to guide Rehoboam. They urged the king to be kind and considerate. "Speak good words unto them, and they will be thy servants forever." But with his mind already made up, he rejected the counsel of the old men, and consulting the opinion of his young, rash companions who had always fed his vanity, he followed their advice and, assuming a haughty attitude, announced that he would add to the yoke of the people. "My father chastised you with whips, but I will chastise you with scorpions."

The effect was instantaneous, and a long-suffering people, smarting for so long under a sense of wrong, refused to be cowed, like the brave Hungarian people, by empty boastings. Thus the slumbering embers of revolt burst into a flame, and the kingdom was rent in twain and Israel's greatness destroyed.

III. He failed to give God the first place. If Rehoboam had consulted the Supreme King of Nations before seeking the advice of old and young men, how beneficial the monarchy would have been. While at the first he posed as the defender of the faith of his fathers and maintained the Temple services with signal fidelity, he failed to render God an undivided homage. The last years of Solomon's brilliant reign were darkened by the recognition of heathen gods and their degrading cults which, along with the fact that Rehoboam was the son of a heathen woman, helped to explain his apostasy. So attempting the impossible, he sought to please God and worship idols at the same time. But said Rehoboam's perfect Descendant: "No man can serve two masters."

At first pious (II Chron. 12:1) Rehoboam fell into such iniquity that an Egyptian scourge came upon the king and the two tribes he ruled. Brief penitence stayed vengeance, but the rot had set in (II Chron. 12: 5, 8). So we leave Rehoboam, who went astray in a threefold direction, ruining himself and the people he sought to govern. He lost the best part of his kingdom and reduced Israel as a whole to a subordinate rank among nations.

REHOBOTH [Rĕ hō′ both]—WIDE SPACES. *The name of an Edomite king* (Gen. 36:37). Also the name of a well dug by the servants of Isaac (Gen. 26:22).

REHUM [Rē′ hum]—PITY, BELOVED or MERCIFUL.

1. *One of the principal men who returned with Zerubbabel* (Ezra 2:23; Neh. 12:3). Called Nehum in Nehemiah 7:7.

2. *A Persian chancellor* under Artaxerxes (Ezra 4:8, 9, 17, 23).

3. *A Levite,* son of Bani, who helped to repair the wall at Jerusalem (Neh. 3:17).

4. *A member of the priestly family* that with Nehemiah sealed the covenant (Neh. 10:25).

REI [Rē′ ī]—JEHOVAH IS A FRIEND, FRIENDLY or SOCIABLE. *David's friend* when Adonijah attempted to become king. He was likely an officer in the royal guard (I Kings 1:8).

REKEM [Rē′ kem]—FRIENDSHIP or VARIEGATION.

1. *One of the five kings of Midian,* slain by Phinehas in the plains of Moab (Num. 31:8; Josh. 13:21).

2. *A son of Hebron* and father of Shammai (I Chron. 2:43, 44).

Also the name of a city in Benjamin, now called Ain-Karim (Josh. 18:27).

REMALIAH [Rĕm a lī′ ah]—JEHOVAH INCREASES, JEHOVAH HATH ADORNED or EXALTATION OF THE LORD. *The father of Pekah,* who slew Pekahiah and reigned in his stead (II Kings 15:25–37; 16:1, 5; II Chron. 28:6; Isa. 7:1–9; 8:6).

REPHAEL [Rē′ pha el]—GOD IS A HEALER, GOD HATH HEALED or MEDICINE OF GOD. *A Kohathite,* son of Shemaiah, the first-born of Obed-edom, and a member of a family of Tabernacle gatekeepers (I Chron. 26:7).

REPHAH [Rē′ phah]—RICHES or HEALING. *A grandson of Ephraim,* through Beriah, and an ancestor of Joshua (I Chron. 7:25).

REPHAIAH [Rĕph a ī′ ah]—JEHOVAH HEALS.

1. *A head of a family in David's house,* a Judahite (I Chron. 3:21).

2. *A Simeonite captain* who helped to lead the expedition into Edom (I Chron. 4:42).

3. *A son of Tola,* son of Issachar (I Chron. 7:2).

4. *A Benjamite* and descendant of Saul (I Chron. 9:43) and called Rapha in I Chronicles 8:37.

5. *One who helped Nehemiah* repair the wall (Neh. 3:9).

RESHEPH [Rē′ sheph]—HASTE or A FLAME. *A son of Rephah,* grandson of Sarah the daughter of Ephraim (I Chron. 7:25).

REU, RAGAU [Rē′ ū, Rā′ gôu]—FRIEND or FRIENDSHIP. *A son of Peleg,* the fourth from Shem, and father of Shereg. An ancestor of

Abraham (Gen. 11:18–21; I Chron. 1:25). Like other men of that time, Reu was long-lived.

REUBEN [Reōō′ ben]—BEHOLD A SON or VISION OF THE SON. *The first-born of Jacob by Leah* and founder of a tribal family (Gen. 29:32; 30:14).

The Man of Forfeited Privileges

In Jacob's dying blessing (Gen. 49:3, 4) are three circumstances concerning Reuben that seem to summarize his tragic story.

I. The privileges that should have been his. As the eldest son he was entitled to three portions above his brethren, namely, the priesthood, the birthright and the kingdom. But all three were forfeited and given to the others.

By right of birth, elevation to priestly eminence should have been Reuben's, but he proved himself unworthy of this "excellence of dignity." Impetuosity and instability totally unfitted him for the priesthood which went to Levi.

By right of birth, royal dignity should have been his as the first-born of his tribe, but Judah prevailed and the right of the scepter passed from Reuben to Judah.

By right of birth, Reuben should have been the head of the representative tribe. He was the beginning of his father's strength (Deut. 21:17), and though the eldest son, forfeited a double inheritance in the land. This right of the firstborn became Joseph's (Deut. 21:17). Reuben carried little importance in the history of Israel.

II. His irresolute and vacillating nature. Reuben revealed characteristics unbefitting one upon whom high responsibilities should have devolved. He lacked the tenacity and courage one expects to find in the eldest son of the family. He had none of his father's transformed nature after he became Israel.

Jacob described his son as being "unstable as water" (Gen. 49:4). Water is a suggestive symbol of instability. Think of the waterfall, as it splashes against the ledges of a rock! The rock abides; the fickle stream moves on in never-ceasing restlessness. Jacob saw in his first-born son all the evidences of instability. Although a double excellency was within the reach of Reuben his father had to say of him, "Thou shalt not excel." The reward of unreliability and instability is inferiority. "Thou shalt not excel." The tribe of Reuben never rose to prominence and was among the first to be carried into captivity (I Chron. 5:26). In the blessing of Moses, Reuben's doom is sealed. Nothing but a depleted remnant would be his. "Let his men be very few" (Deut. 33:6). No judge, no prophet, no hero sprang from Reuben. By his sin Reuben had permanently impoverished his posterity.

III. His despicable crime. Reuben lost all the honors that should have been his because of his adulterous act with Bilhah, his father's concubine. Jacob, in his blessing, attributes Reuben's forfeited privileges to this heinous sin — a sin which brought a curse upon him.

This evil stream flowed on, for two Reubenites were ringleaders with Korah in assailing God's established order, and perished because of their defiance of God. Deborah, in her patriotic song, Judges 5, rebuked the children of Reuben for characteristic selfishness. Again the innate fickleness appeared.

Can it be that in spite of all his sad failures, there is a ray of hope for Reuben in the prophetic benediction of Moses, "Let Reuben live and not die" (Deut. 33:6)? Is this an evidence of divine grace— life for a sinner whose sin merited death? There is a gate of Reuben in the Golden City, and a tribe of Reuben in the Israel of God (Rev. 7:5). Reuben's name is *not first*, yet through grace it is there. "Let Reuben live and not die." Heaven will be full of Reubens who should have died but who live forevermore to sing the praises of God's redeeming grace.

REUEL [Reōō' el]—FRIEND OF GOD or GOD IS A FRIEND.

1. *A son of Esau* by Bashemath, daughter of Ishmael (Gen. 36:4–17; I Chron. 1:35, 37).

2. *The father-in-law of Moses* (Ex. 2:18). Called Jethro and Raguel (Num. 10:29).

3. *The father of Eliasaph*, and a Gadite (Num. 2:14). Called Deuel in Numbers 1:14.

4. *A Benjamite*, a son of Ibnijah, belonging to Jerusalem (I Chron. 9:8).

REZIA [Rē zĭ' ă]—JEHOVAH IS PLEASING. *An Asherite*, a son of Ulla (I Chron. 7:39). Also spelled Rizia.

REZIN [Rē' zin]—DOMINION or GOOD WILL.

1. *The last king of Damascus*, in the days of Jothan, king of Judah. He was slain by Tiglath-pileser (II Kings 15:37; 16:5–9; Isa. 7:1–8; 8:6; 9:11). Damascus sustained a siege of more than a year's duration, but was eventually taken and its king slain (II Kings 16:9).

2. *A founder of a family of Nethinims* whose descendants returned with Zerubbabel from captivity (Ezra 2:48; Neh. 7:50).

REZON [Rē' zŏn]—PRINCELINESS or NOBLE. *A son of Eliadah* and a subject of Hadadezer, king of Zobah. Although one of the king's military officers, he fled to Damascus, where he founded a kingdom and became a thorn in Solomon's side. His successors were bitter adversaries of Israel (I Kings 11:23).

RHESA [Rhē' să]—WILL or COURSE. *A descendant of Zerubbabel* and ancestor of Christ (Luke 3:27).

RIBAI [Rī' baĭ]—JEHOVAH CONTENDS or CONTENTIOUS. *The father of*

Ittai or Ithai, a Benjamite of Gibeah and one of David's valiant men (I1 Sam. 23:29; I Chron. 11:31).

RIMMON [Rĭm' mon]—A POMEGRANITE. *The father of two captains who served under King Ishbosheth and became his murderers* (II Sam. 4:2-9). Rimmon is also the name of a Syrian god, looked upon "as air-, weather-, and storm-god assimilated by popular etymology to the word for 'pomegranite,' " hence the meaning of the name. The symbol of the beneficent deity was the axe and a bundle of lightning-darts. It was in Rimmon's temple at Damascus that Naaman worshiped.

Rimmon is likewise the name of a city in Simeon now known as Um-er-Rumamin (Josh. 15:32; Zech. 14:10), and of a rock in Benjamin near Gibeah, now called Rummon or Rammun (Judg. 20:45, 47; 21:13), and of two cities, one in Simeon (I Chron. 4:32) and the other in Zebulon, spoken of in Hebrews as Rimmons (I Chron. 6:77).

RINNAH [Rĭn' nah]—A WILD CRY or STRENGTH. *A man of Judah,* a son of Shimon (I Chron. 4:20).

RIPHATH [Rĭ' phăth]—A CRUSHER OF ENEMIES. *One of the sons of Gomer,* son of Japheth (Gen. 10:3; I Chron. 1:6). Another reading is Diphath (I Chron. 1:6).

ROHGAH [Rŏh' gah]—CLAMOR or ALARM. *A son of Shamer,* grandson of Beriah, son of Asher (I Chron. 7:34).

ROMAMTI-EZER [Rŏ măm' tĭ-ĕ' zûr]—HIGHEST HELP or I HAVE EXALTED HELP. *A son of Heman,* a singer in the Tabernacle in David's time, who was among the twenty-fourth course of singers (I Chron. 25:4, 31).

ROSH [Rŏsh]—A CHIEF, PRINCE or THE BEGINNING.
1. *A son of Benjamin* who went down to Egypt with Jacob and his sons (Gen. 46:21; Num. 26:38).
2. *The prince of northern people* mentioned along with Meshech and Tubal (Ezek. 38:1, 2; 39:1, R.V.).

The Man of the Northern Confederacy

It is not very difficult to prove that God, by His Spirit, gave to Ezekiel over twenty-five hundred years ago, a clear picture of the part Russia would play in the development and control of a Northern Confederacy of Nations. The R.V. of Ezekiel 38:2 reads: "Gog the land of Magog, the Prince of Rosh, Meshach and Tubal." Rosh, mentioned as a descendant of Benjamin (Gen. 46:21) means, "a prince over." The Araxes were called "Rhos."

That "the Prince of Rosh" is Asiatic Russia receives confirmation from the *Imperial Dictionary.* "Evidence exists of an ancient people called Rosh, or Rhos, supposed to be the original stem from which

the Russia or modern Russians have derived their race and name."
The saintly scholar, Bishop Lowther says: "Rosh, taken as a proper
name, in Ezekiel, signifies the inhabitants of Scythia, from whom
modern Russians derived their name." The Orientals called the
people who dwelt on the banks of the River Araxes "Rhos" or "Rosh,"
and the Arabic name for that river was also called "Rosh." Russia
was once known as Muscovy. It was Ivan IV, or "Ivan the Terrible,"
as he was called, who was the first to use the title, "Czar of Russia."

The discovery of Russia in Ezekiel's prophecy is not a fundamen-
talist invention of this mid-century. Prophetic students have been
accused of pressing Scripture interpretation beyond what is written
in this connection. But long before Russia became the threat to world
freedom, progress and peace she is today, Biblical scholars recognized
her portrayal in Ezekiel.

We must conclude therefore, that Ezekiel's "episode of Gog's invasion" (A. B. Davidson) points irrefutably and undeniably to the
Russians.

RUFUS [Rōō' fus]—RED.
1. *A son of Simon the Cyrenian* who was compelled to bear the
Cross (Mark 15:21).
2. *A believer in Rome* greeted by Paul as "the chosen in the Lord"
together with "his mother and mine" (Rom. 16:13). Some writers feel
that these two may have been the same persons. "Simon's widow might
have emigrated to Rome with her two sons, where they became
people of eminence in the Church, and that this is the reason why
the brothers are mentioned by Mark (15:21), who probably wrote in
Rome" (*Hastings Dictionary*).

S

SABTA, SABTAH [Săb' tă, Săb' tah]—BREAKING THROUGH. *The third
son of Cush,* son of Ham, whose descendants dwell in the middle of
South Arabia (Gen. 10:7; I Chron. 1:9).

SABTECHA, SABTECHAH [Săb' te chă, Săb' te chah]—SURRENDER.
The youngest son of Cush, whose descendants dwelt on the east side of
the Persian Gulf (Gen. 10:7; I Chron. 1:9).

SACAR [Să' cär]—HIRED or MERCHANDISE.
1. *Father of Ahiham,* one of David's heroes (I Chron. 11:35).
Called Sharar in II Samuel 23:33.
2. *A son of Obed-edom,* a Tabernacle gatekeeper in David's time
(I Chron. 26:4).

SADOC [Sã' dŏc]—RIGHTEOUS, JUST. *Son of Agor* and father ot Achim, and an ancestor of Christ (Matt. 1:14). Called Zadoc in Ezra 7:2.

SALA, SALAH [Sã'lă, Sã' lah]—MEANING UNCERTAIN, PERHAPS FIRM. *Son of Arphaxad,* third son of Shem, and father of Eber (Gen. 10:24; 11:12–15; Luke 3:35).

SALATHIEL, SHEALTIEL [Sã' lã' thĭ el, Shē ăl' tĭ el]—ARK or LOAN OF GOD. *Son or grandson of Jeconiah,* son of Jehoiakim, king of Judah (I Chron. 3:17; Ezra 3:2, 8; 5:2; Hag. 1:2, 12, 14; 2:2, 23). Ancestor of Christ (Matt. 1:12; Luke 3:27).

SALLAI [Săl' la ĭ]—EXALTED or REJECTED.
1. *Son of Meshullam,* a chief of the family of Benjamites living in Jerusalem (Neh. 11:8).
2. *A priest* who returned from exile with Zerubbabel (Neh. 12:20). Also called Sallu in Nehemiah 11:7.

SALMA [Săl' mă]—STRENGTH, FIRMNESS. *A son of Caleb* son of Hur and father of Bethlehem (I Chron. 2:51, 54).

SALMON, SALMA, SALMAH [Săl' mŏn, Săl' mă]—PEACEABLE. *The father of Boaz,* Ruth's husband, and a man of Judah. Also an ancestor of Christ (Ruth 4:20, 21; I Chron. 2:11; Matt. 1:4, 5; Luke 3:32). Salmon is also the name of a mountain (Ps. 68:14).

SALU [Sã' lu]—UNFORTUNATE or EXALTED. *A Simeonite,* father of Zimri whom Phinehas slew (Num. 25:14).

SAMGAR-NEBO [Săm' gär-nĕ' bō]—BE GRACIOUS, NEBO. *A prince of Nebuchadnezzar,* who sat in the gate at Jerusalem (Jer. 39:3).

SAMLAH [Săm' lah]—GARMENT or ASTONISHMENT. *The fifth of the ancient kings of Edom,* a native of Masrekah (Gen. 36:36, 37; I Chron. 1:47, 48).

SAMSON [Săm' son]—DISTINGUISHED, STRONG or SUN-MAN.
The Man of Contrasts
One of the most renowned of the Hebrew judges, Samson was a son of the Danite, Manoah, who judged Israel for twenty years. He was unique in that his birth and manner of life were foretold. Supernaturally endowed, he killed a lion, thirty Philistines and one thousand men. He broke the strongest bands, carried off the gates of Gaza and pulled down the Temple of Dagon (Judg. 13:24–16:30). He is found among the illustrious in Faith's Hall of Fame (Heb. 11:32).

As long as Samson remained a Nazarite he was unconquerable. He only of all the judges of whom we have any history, does everything single-handed and alone. Samson never called the armies of Israel together; he asked no assistance. What he did, he did alone in his own unconquerable strength. We are not told how he managed his court, nor about the wisdom of his judgments, nor about the manner of Israel's life for a whole generation under her gigantic judge.

The complex story of Samson teaches us the evils of mixed or foreign marriages (Judg. 14:3), the laxity of sexual relations and of playing with temptation. C. W. Emmet says that Samson "teaches us that bodily endowments, no less than spiritual, are a gift from God, however different may be our modern conception of the way in which they are bestowed, and that their retention depends on obedience to His laws."

But if Samson stands as an example "of impotence of mind in body strong," he also stands, in Milton's magnificent conception, as an example of patriotism and heroism in death, to all who "from his memory inflame their breast to matchless valour and adventures high."

The deadly results of Samson's self-indulgence after he broke his Nazarite vow, appear in their dark and ominous order:
Self-confidence: "I will go out" (Judg. 16:20).
Self-ignorance: "He wist not" (Judg. 16:20).
Self-weakness: "The Philistines laid hold on him" (Judg. 16:21).
Self-darkness: "They put out his eyes" (Judg. 16:21).
Self-degradation: "They brought him *down* to Gaza" (Judg. 16:1–3, 21).
Self-bondage: "They bound him with fetters" (Judg. 16:21).
Self-drudgery: "He did grind in the prison-house" (Judg. 16:21).
Self-humiliation: "Call for Samson, that he may make us sport" (Judg. 16:25, 27).

Samson stands out as a man of striking contrasts. He had a kind of Dr. Jekell and Mr. Hyde being.

I. He was separated as a Nazarite (Judg. 13:5), yet tampered with evil associations (Judg. 14:1–3).

II. He was occasionally Spirit-possessed (Judg. 13:25; 15:14), yet yielded to carnal appetites (Judg. 16:1–4).

III. He appeared childish in some of his plans (Judg. 15:4), yet was courageous in battle (Judg. 15:1–4).

IV. He was mighty in physical strength (Judg. 16:3, 9, 13, 14), yet weak in resisting temptation (Judg. 16:15–17).

V. He had a noble beginning but a sad end (Judg. 16:30).

SAMUEL [Săm′ u el]—HEARD, ASKED OF GOD, OFFERING OF GOD or APPOINTED BY GOD.

The Man Who Had God's Ear

Samuel was the earliest of the Hebrew prophets after Moses and the last of the Judges. He was the son of Elkanah of Ephraim (I Sam.

1:1), and of Hannah, Elkanah's other wife. Samuel was her first-born and possibly saw the light of day at Ramah (I Sam. 2:11; 7:17). Hannah bore Elkanah five other children (I Sam. 2:21). There are many points of resemblance between Hannah and Mary, the mother of our Lord (I Sam. 2:1–11 with Luke 1:46–56).

Samuel was a Nazarite (I Sam. 1:11), the character of the vow being:

Abstinence from intoxicating drinks; self-denial and separation from sensual indulgence.

Free growth of hair, indicating the complete dedication of all the power of the head to God.

Avoidance of contact with a dead body as a token of absolute purity of life (Num. 6).

Samuel's call to service came when weaned and dedicated to God by his mother (I Sam. 1:24–28; 3:1–18). When Samuel was around twelve years of age he received his first revelation of the Lord, which was a clear message of doom against Eli's guilty house (I Sam. 3:11–14).

Samuel's ministry was of a fourfold nature. We see him:

I.   As a prophet. As a prophet of the Lord (I Sam. 2:27–35; 3:19–21; 8:22), his faithfulness was a rebuke to the unfaithfulness of Eli. To the end of his days Samuel exercised the office of prophet and his ministry was not in vain. Under the impact of his courageous pronouncements Israel renounced her idolatry and shook off the yoke of the Philistines.

II.   As an intercessor. Samuel was born in answer to prayer and his name constantly reminded him of the power of prayer and of the necessity of maintaining holy intimacy with God. Samuel deemed it a sin not to pray for others (I Sam. 7:5–8; 8:6; 12:17, 19, 23; 15:11).

III.   As a priest. Although Samuel was only a Levite and not a priest by descent, the words, "I will raise up," imply an extraordinary office (I Sam. 2:35; 7:9, 10; 13:8–10; Judg. 2:16). The exercises of priestly functions are proved by the following:

By intercession (I Sam. 7:9).

By offering sacrifices (I Sam. 7:9, 10).

By benediction (I Sam. 10:17, 25).

By anointing kings (I Sam. 10:1; 16:13).

IV.   As a judge. Of Samuel it is said that he "judged Israel all the days of his life." Even after the government of Israel had changed from that of a theocracy to a monarchy, Samuel still acted as a circuit judge, going from place to place giving divine judgment upon moral and spiritual questions, and maintaining in the hearts and lives of the people the law and authority of Jehovah (I Sam. 7:15–17). The appointment of his own sons as Judges to succeed him (I Sam. 8:1) was a parental mistake, for their wickedness gave the people reason for demanding a king (I Sam. 8:5).

The universal reverence and love the nation had for Samuel is proven by the grief manifested at his death. "All Israel lamented him" (I Sam. 25:1; 28:3). His passing as one of the great heroes of

Hebrew history makes impressive reading. Faith was the animating principle of his honored life and labors (Heb. 11:32).

SANBALLAT [Săn băl' lat]—THE ENEMY IS SECRET. *A Horonite,* an enemy of the Jews. He opposed Nehemiah in the building of the wall (Neh. 2:10, 19; 4:1, 7; 6:1–14; 13:28). This most inveterate of Nehemiah's opponents derided the efforts of repair, and sought to hinder the work of the builders.

SAPH [Săph]—CONSUMMATION or PRESERVER. *One of the four Philistine giants slain by David's heroes* (II Sam. 21:18; I Chron. 20:4). Also called Sippai.

SARAPH [Sā' raph]—BURNING. *A descendant of Shelah,* son of Judah, who exercised dominion in Moab (I Chron. 4:22).

SARGON [Sär' gon]—THE CONSTITUTED KING or SNARES. *A king of Assyria* who succeeded the last Shalmaneser. He was a predecessor of Sennacherib (Isa. 20:1).

SARSECHIM [Sär sē' chim]—CHIEF OF THE EUNUCHS. *A prince of Babylon* when Nebuchadnezzar took Jerusalem (Jer. 39:3).

SARUCH [Sā' ruch] BRANCH—*Father of Nachor and son of Ragau,* and an ancestor of Christ (Luke 3:35).

SAUL, SHAUL [Sôul]—ASKED FOR or DEMANDED.
1. *The son of Kish,* and first king of Israel (I Sam. 9–11).
A Man Who Lost His Kingdom
No man among Bible men had so many chances thrust upon him to make a success of life, and no man ever so missed them. Saul not only missed great opportunities, he deliberately abused them. His sun rose in splendor, but set in a tragic night. The downgrade of his life is the old familiar story of pride, egotism and the abuse of power leading to moral degradation and ruin. Here are the steps down the ladder:
He was a man anointed and filled with the Spirit. (I Sam. 11:6).
In his early years he was humble and practiced self-control (I Sam. 10:22; 10:27; 11:13).
Self-will restricted his influence (I Sam. 13:12, 13).
He became disobedient and was guilty of rash vows (I Sam. 15:11–23).
Jealousy prompted him to hunt and harm David (I Sam. 18:8; 19:1).
He patronized the superstition he had forbidden (I Sam. 28:7).
Wounded in battle, he ended up a suicide (I Sam. 31:4).
Having already destroyed his moral life, he ultimately destroyed his physical life. Saul's sad story is repeated almost daily.

2. *The sixth of the ancient kings of Edom,* from Rehoboth on the Euphrates (Gen. 36:37, 38).

3. *The original name of Paul,* a native of Tarsus (Acts 7:58). For fuller treatment see Paul.

SCEVA [Scē' vă]—I DISPOSE. *A member of one of the Jewish families* from which high priests were ordinarily chosen. His seven sons were exorcists, that is, they professed to have power over demons by naming over them the name of Jesus (Acts 19:14).

SEBA [Sē' bā]—OLD MAN. *The eldest son of Cush,* son of Ham (Gen. 10:7; I Chron. 1:9). Also the name of his land in northern Ethiopia (Ps. 72:10; Isa. 43:3).

SECUNDUS [Sē cŭn' dus]—SECONDARY or FAVORABLE. *A believer of Thessalonica* who accompanied Paul from Macedonia to Asia Minor (Acts 20:4). Perhaps he carried alms from his city for needy saints.

SEGUB [Sē' gub]—EXALTED, PROTECTION or FORTIFIED.

1. *The youngest son of Hiel the Benjamite* who rebuilt Jericho, and who was possibly sacrificed by his father when the gates were set up in defiance of a curse (I Kings 16:34).

2. *A son of Hezron,* grandson of Judah (I Chron. 2:21, 22).

SEIR [Sē' ûr]—ROUGH or WOODED. *The grandfather of Hori,* ancestor of the Horites (Gen. 36:20, 21; I Chron. 1:38). Also the name of a hilly region south of the Salt Sea (Gen. 14:6).

SELED [Sē' lĕd]—EXULTATION. *A man of Judah* of the family of Jerahmeel and grandson of Pharez, son of Judah (I Chron. 2:30).

SEMACHIAH [Sĕm a chī' ah]—JEHOVAH SUPPORTS or SUSTAINS. *A son of Shemaiah* and a Levite gatekeeper of the Tabernacle in David's time (I Chron. 26:7). Perhaps the same as Ismachiah (II Chron. 31:13).

SEMEI [Sĕm' e ī]—HEAR or OBEY. *An ancestor of Jesus Christ* (Luke 3:26), who lived after the exile. See Shimei.

SENNACHERIB [Sĕn năch' e rĭb]—THE MOON-GOD, SIN (the moon-god) HATH INCREASED THE BROTHERS or DESTRUCTION OF THE SWORD. *A son of Sargon* who succeeded to the throne after the murder of his father (II Kings 18:13; 19:16, 20, 36; II Chron. 32; Isa. 36:1; 37:17, 21, 37).

The Man Who Built Nineveh

This Assyrian king saw his boasted army destroyed in one night. He himself was slain by two of his sons in Nineveh in the Temple of Nisroch (II Kings 19:37). Sennacherib's great achievement in this area was the creation of Nineveh as a metropolis of the empire. It was he who built the wonderful palace of Konyungik and the great wall of Nineveh.

The Assyrian king's invading hosts marching through Judah leaving destruction behind them were vividly described by Byron in *The Destruction of Sennacherib:*

> The Assyrians came down like the wolf on the fold,
> And his cohorts were gleaming in purple and gold;
> And the sheen of their spears was like stars on the sea,
> When the blue wave rolls nightly on deep Galilee.

Fear seized the heart of Hezekiah as he faced the threats of Sennacherib and Rabshakeh, but the courage and faith of Isaiah were a strong tower to the troubled king and the inhabitants of Jerusalem. The prophet reminded Hezekiah that Jehovah, and not the horses, material force and human cleverness, was the hope of Judah. Jerusalem was God's city and He would preserve it (Isa. 37:33, 35). As we know, the city was saved by a remarkable providence. God commissioned one angel to slay one hundred eighty-five thousand Assyrians. If He can do that with one angel, what is He not able to do with a legion of the angelic army?

SENUAH [Sē nū' ah]—THE VIOLATED. *A Benjamite,* father of Judah who was second in charge over Jerusalem in Nehemiah's day (Neh. 11:9).

SEORIM [Sē ŏ' rim]—FEAR, DISTRESS. *A priest of David's time* to whom the fourth charge of the sanctuary was given by lot (I Chron. 24:8).

SERAIAH [Sĕr a ï' ah]—JEHOVAH IS PRINCE, THE LORD IS MY PRINCE, or SOLDIER OF THE LORD.

1. *One of king David's scribes* (II Sam. 8:17; see I Chron. 18:16 for Shavsha).

2. *The son of Azariah* and chief priest at Jerusalem when Nebuchadnezzar took it. This Seraiah, along with other renowned captives, was put to death at Riblah (II Kings 25:18; I Chron. 6:14; Ezra 7:1; Jer. 52:24).

3. *A son of Tanhumeth,* from Netophah, whom Gedaliah advised to submit to the Chaldeans. He was one of "the captains of the forces" (II Kings 25:23; Jer. 40:8).

4. *The second son of Kenez,* brother of Othniel and father of Joab (I Chron. 4:13, 14).

5. *A prince of Simeon,* son of Asiel and grandfather of Jehu, who drove furiously (I Chron. 4:35).

6. *One of the twelve leaders, a priest who returned from exile with Zerubbabel* (Ezra 2:2; Neh. 10:2; 12:1, 12).

7. *A priest, son of Hilkiah*, dwelling in Jerusalem after the exile and called "ruler of the house of God" (Neh. 11:11; 12:1).

8. *A chief man, son of Aziel*, and sent by Jehoiakim to apprehend Jeremiah and Baruch (Jer. 36:26).

9. *A son of Neriah and brother of Baruch*, a prince of Judah who went to Babylon with Zedekiah (Jer. 51:59, 61). For "quiet prince" the R.V. has "chief chamberlain."

SERED [Sē' red]—DELIVERENCE or FEAR. *The eldest son of Zebulun* and founder of a tribal family, the Seredites (Gen. 46:14; Num. 26:22, 26).

SERGIUS PAULUS [Sûr' jĭ ŭs Pa͞o' lus]—SMALL or LITTLE. *Proconsul or Roman deputy of Cyprus* when Paul and Barnabas visited it, and who was converted to God by Elymas or Bar-jesus being struck with blindness (Acts 13:7). It is said of Sergius that he:

Was a prudent man.

Desired to hear the word of God.

When he saw what was done, believed.

Was astonished at the doctrine of the Lord.

SERUG [Sē' rug]—SHOOT, BRANCH or FIRMNESS. *A son of Reu*, father of Nahor, father of Terah, and so an ancestor of Abraham (Gen. 11:20-23; I Chron. 1:26).

SETH, SHETH [Sĕth, Shĕth]—COMPENSATION, APPOINTED or SUBSTITUTED. *The third son of Adam and Eve*, born after the murder of Abel. Seth came as Abel's substitute (Gen. 4:25, 26; 5:3-8; I Chron. 1:1; Luke 3:38). Seth became the father of Enos, and died at the age of 912. When Eve said, "God hath set for me another seed instead of Abel," the word she used for "set" was *shâth* or *shĕth*, meaning "setting."

SETHUR [Sē' thur]—SECRETED, HIDDEN. *The son of Michael*, the representative spy sent from the tribe of Asher (Num. 13:13).

SHAAPH [Shā' ăph]—UNION, FRIENDSHIP.

1. *A son of Jahdai*, son of Caleb, by his concubine Ephah (I Chron. 2:47).

2. *A son of Caleb*, son of Hezron, by his concubine Maachah (I Chron. 2:49).

SHAASHGAZ [Shā ăsh' găz]—SERVANT OF THE BEAUTIFUL. *A chamberlain of King Ahasuerus*, who had charge of the king's concubines (Esther 2:14).

SHABBETHAI [Shăb' be thaī]—SABBATH BORN.

1. *A Levite* who assisted in the matter of those who had taken strange wives (Ezra 10:15).
2. *One who explained the law* read to the people by Ezra (Neh. 8:7).
3. *A chief Levite* in Jerusalem after the exile (Neh. 11:16).

SHACHIA [Shā chǐ' ă]—CAPTIVE OF THE LORD. *A Benjamite,* son of Shaharaim (I Chron. 8:10).

SHADRACH [Shā' drach]—DECREE OF MOON-GOD or SOFT, TENDER. The name given by the prince of the eunuchs at Babylon to *Hananiah, one of the three faithful Hebrew youths* (Dan. 1:7; 3:12–30). With his two companions, Meshach and Abednego, Shadrach was miraculously delivered from the burning fiery furnace.

SHAGE, SHAGEE [Shā' gē]—WANDERING or ERRING. *Father of Jonathan the Hararite,* one of David's mighty men (I Chron. 11:34). Some read Agee instead of Shagee on the authority of II Samuel 23:11.

SHAHARAIM [Shā ha rā' im]—DOUBLE DAWNING. *A Benjamite* who went to Moab and had numerous descendants of his two wives, Harhim and Baara (I Chron. 8:8).

SHALLUM, SHALLUN [Shǎl' lum]—RECOMPENSE, RETRIBUTION or SPOILATION.
1. *A son of Jabesh,* who slew Zechariah, son of Jeroboam II. He became King of Israel for one month just before the near extinction of the nation, and was slain by Menahem, son of Gadi (II Kings 15:10, 13–15).
2. *A son of Tikvah* and husband of Huldah the prophetess in the days of Josiah (II Kings 22:14; II Chron. 34:22).
3. *A son of Sisamai* and father of Jakaniah, also a descendant of Judah (I Chron. 2:40, 41).
4. *The fourth son of king Josiah* (I Chron. 3:15).
5. *Grandson of Simeon,* second son of Jacob and a descendant of Shaul (I Chron. 4:25).
6. *The father of Hilkiah,* a member of the high priestly family of Zadok and an ancestor of Ezra (I Chron. 6:12, 13; Ezra 7:2). Called Meshullam in I Chronicles 9:11.
7. *The fourth son of Naphtali,* the second son of Bilhah, Rachel's handmaid (I Chron. 7:13). Called Shillem in Genesis 46:24.
8. *A son of Kore,* a Korhite and chief porter at the sanctuary (I Chron. 9:17, 19, 31; Ezra 2:42; Neh. 7:45).
9. *The father of Jehizkiah* who opposed the reduction of Jewish captives to slaves (II Chron. 28:12).
10. *A Tabernacle gatekeeper* whose foreign wife was put away (Ezra 10:24).

11. *One of the sons of Bani* who also had taken a foreign wife (Ezra 10:42).

12. *A son of Halohesh*, ruler of the half of Jerusalem, who with his daughters assisted in the repair of the wall (Neh. 3:12).

13. *A son of Col-hozeh*, ruler of part of Mizpah, who repaired the gate of the fountain (Neh. 3:15).

14. *The father of Hanameel*, uncle to the prophet Jeremiah (Jer. 32:7, 8).

15. *The father of Maaseiah*, an officer of the Temple in the time of Jehoiakim (Jer. 35:4).

SHALMAI [Shăl' ma ī]—JEHOVAH IS RECOMPENSER. *One of the Nethinims* whose descendants returned with Zerubbabel from exile (Ezra 2:46; Neh. 7:48).

SHALMAN [Shăl' man]—PEACEABLE. *An Assyrian king* who laid waste Beth-arbel. Sometimes identified with Shalmaneser (Hos. 10:14).

SHALMANESER [Shăl man ē zûr]—THE GOD SHALMANA IS CHIEF or PEACE TAKEN AWAY. *The name of several Assyrian kings.* This was Shalmaneser IV who succeeded Tiglath-pileser and who invaded Israel and carried off Hoshea and the ten tribes to Assyria (II Kings 17:3; 18:9).

SHAMA [Shă' mă]—HEARER or HE HATH HEARD. *A son of Hothan*, the Aroerite, and one of David's mighty men (I Chron. 11:44).

SHAMED [Shă' mĕd]—WATCHER, DESTROYER. *The third son of Elpaal* (I Chron. 8:12).

SHAMER [Shă' mûr]—PRESERVER.
1. *Son of Mahli* and grandson of Merari (I Chron. 6:46).
2. *Son of Heber*, son of Beriah, son of Asher (I Chron. 7:34). Spelled Shomer in I Chronicles 7:32.

SHAMGAR [Shăm' gär]—CUPBEARER or A SURPRISED STRANGER.
The Man Who Was Ready When Need Arose
Shamgar was the son of Anath, and third judge of Israel after the death of Joshua. His spectacular deliverance of Israel from the Philistines is suggestive (Judg. 3:31). Shamgar the son of Anath was ready to serve God in the common working day.

When he drove his oxen out that morning he did not dream that before nightfall he would accomplish a memorable deliverance for his land. But the call came and he was ready.

Another lesson to be learned from Shamgar is that God can be served with unlikely instruments. "What is that in thy hand?" In

Shamgar's hand was an oxgoad with which he slew six hundred Philistines.

We may not have genius, brilliance, gifts of speech or song, but if we are in the hand of Christ, He can take foolish things to confound the wise.

SHAMHUTH [Shăm' hŭth]—FAME, RENOWN or DESOLATION OF INIQUITY. *An Izrahite,* a captain of David's army who served in the fifth month (I Chron. 27:8). Perhaps Shammah.

SHAMIR [Shă' mĭr]—OPPRESSED, A PRISON or A THORN. *A son of Micah,* a Levite and descendant of Uzziel (I Chron. 24:24). Also the name of the hill country of Judah (Josh. 15:48), and of a city on Mount Ephraim, the home and burial place of Tola (Judg. 10:1, 2).

SHAMMA [Shăm' mă]—FAME, RENOWN or DESOLATION. *A son of Zophah* an Asherite (I Chron. 7:37).

SHAMMAH [Shăm' mah]—LOSS.
1. *A son of Reuel* and descendant of Esau and Ishmael, who became a duke of Edom (Gen. 36:13, 17; I Chron. 1:37).
2. *The third son of Jesse* and brother of David (I Sam. 16:9; 17:13).
3. *The son of Agee the Hararite,* and first of David's three mighty men (II Sam. 23:11).
4. *Another Hararite,* and one of David's heroes (II Sam. 23:33). Called Shammoth in I Chronicles 11:27, Shamhuth in I Chronicles 27:8.
5. *A Harodite,* also one of David's valiant men (II Sam. 23:25).

SHAMMAI [Shăm' ma ĭ]—CELEBRATED or WASTE.
1. *A son of Onam,* son of Jerahmeel, grandson of Judah (I Chron. 2:28, 32).
2. *The father of Maon* and son of Rekem of the house of Caleb son of Hezron (I Chron. 2:44, 45).
3. *A son or grandson of Ezra* registered with the tribe of Judah (I Chron. 4:17).

SHAMMOTH [Shăm' moth]—RENOWN. *A Harorite,* one of David's valiant men (I Chron. 11:27). See Shammah.

SHAMMUA, SHAMMUAH [Shăm mŭ' ă, Shăm mŭ' ah]—FAMOUS.
1. *A Reubenite,* son of Zaccur, sent by Moses to spy out the land of Canaan (Num. 13:4).
2. *A son of David by Bath-sheba,* born in Jerusalem (II Sam. 5:14; I Chron. 14:4). He bore his uncle's name (I Chron. 2:13), and is also called Shimea (I Chron. 3:5).
3. *A grandson of Juduthun* and father of Abda or Obadiah, a

Levite who led the Temple worship after the exile (Neh. 11:17). Called Shemaiah in I Chronicles 9:16.

4. *A priest in the family of Bilgah* in the days of Nehemiah, and head of his father's house (Neh. 12:18).

SHAMSHERAI [Shăm she rā' ī]—HEROIC. *A son of Jeroham,* a Benjamite (I Chron. 8:26).

SHAPHAM [Shā' pham]—YOUTHFUL, VIGOROUS. *A chief of Gad,* dwelling in Bashan, second in rank (I Chron. 5:12).

SHAPHAN [Shā' phan]—PRUDENT, SHY, ROCK BADGER or WILD RAT.
1. *A scribe,* son of Azaliah, father of Gemariah. It was this Shaphan who laid before King Josiah the law book discovered by Hilkiah in the temple (II Kings 22:3–14; II Chron. 34:8–20; Jer. 36:10–12) and who was the chief lay leader in the outworking of Josiah's reforms. For two generations his family played a worthy part as servants of Jehovah and as friends of Jeremiah.
2. *Father of Ahikam,* a chief officer in the court of Josiah (II Kings 22:12; 25:22; II Chron. 34:20; Jer. 26:24; 39:14; 40:5; 41:2; 43:6).
3. *A father of Elasah* by whom Jeremiah the prophet sent a letter to the exiles in Babylon (Jer. 29:3).
4. *The father of Jaaganiah* whom Ezekiel saw as enticing people to idolatry and whom he denounced as a ringleader (Ezek. 8:11).

SHAPHAT [Shā' phat]—JUDGE or HE HATH JUDGED.
1. *A Simeonite,* son of Hori, and tribe representative sent as a spy to Canaan (Num. 13:5).
2. *The father of Elisha the prophet* (I Kings 19:16, 19; II Kings 3:11; 6:31).
3. *A son of Shemaiah* included in the royal genealogy of Judah (I Chron. 3:22).
4. *A chief of Gadite in Bashan* (I Chron. 5:12).
5. *A son of Adlai* and David's overseer of cattle in the valley (I Chron. 27:29).

SHARAI [Shăr' a ī]—JEHOVAH IS DELIVERER, FREE or MY SON. *A son of Bani* induced to put away his foreign wife (Ezra 10:40).

SHARAR [Shā' rär]—FIRM or STRONG. *A Hararite,* father of one of David's mighty men (II Sam. 23:33). Called Sacar (I Chron. 11:35).

SHAREZER, SHEREZER [Sha rē'zĕr, She rē' zer]—PROTECT or PRESERVE THE KING.
1. *A son of Sennacherib,* king of Assyria, who with his brother Adrammelech killed their father in the temple of Nisroch at Nineveh (II Kings 19:37; Isa. 37:38).

2. *A man sent from Bethel* to consult the priests and prophets as to a day of humiliation (Zech. 7:2).

SHASHAI [Shăsh' a ī]—WHITE, PALE, NOBLE or FREE. *One of the sons of Bani* who married a foreign wife (Ezra 10:40).

SHASHAK [Shā' shăk]—ASSAULTER, RUNNER. *A son of Elpaal* a Benjamite (I Chron. 8:14, 25).

SHAUL [Shā' ul]—ASKED.
1. *A son of Simeon* by a Canaanitish woman (Gen. 46:10; Ex. 6:15; Num. 26:13; I Chron. 4:24).
2. *A king of Edom* from Rehoboth in the Euphrates (I Chron. 1:48, 49). Called Saul in Genesis 36:37.
3. *A son of Kohath,* son of Levi and founder of a tribal family (Num. 26:13; I Chron. 6:24).

SHAVSHA, SHISHA [Shăv' shă, Shī' shă]—NOBILITY or SPLENDOR. *A scribe in David's, time* and afterwards in Solomon's day (I Chron. 18:16). Perhaps identical with Seraiah the scribe (II Sam. 8:17); Sheva in II Samuel 20:25; Shisha in I Kings 4:3.

SHEAL [Shē' al]—REQUEST or AN ASKING. *A son of Bani* who put away his strange wife (Ezra 10:29).

SHEALTIEL [Shē ăl' tĭ el]—I HAVE ASKED OF GOD. *A son of Jeconiah,* and father of Zerubbabel who led the Jews back from the Babylonian exile (Ezra 3:2, 8; 5:2; Neh. 12:1; Hag. 1:1, 12, 14; 2:2). Also an ancestor of Christ (Matt. 1:12; Luke 3:27). Also called Salathiel.

SHEARIAH [Shē a rī' ah]—JEHOVAH IS DECIDER or HATH ESTEEMED. *A son of Azel,* a Benjamite and descendant of Jonathan of the family of Saul (I Chron. 8:38; 9:44).

SHEAR-JASHUB [Shē' är-jā' shŭb]—A REMNANT RETURNS. *A son of Isaiah the prophet,* whose name was designed to embody a prophecy (Isa. 7:3; 10:21).

SHEBA [Shē' bă]—SEVENTH, AN OATH or CAPTIVITY.
1. *Son of Raamah,* son of Cush, son of Ham (Gen. 10:7; I Chron. 1:9).
2. *Son of Joktan* of the family of Shem (Gen. 10:28; I Chron. 1:22).
3. *Son of Jokshan,* son of Abraham by Keturah (Gen. 25:3; I Chron. 1:32).
4. *A son of Bichri* who rebelled against David after Absalom's death. This worthless adventurer, who snatched at what he thought

was a chance of winning the sovereignty of northern Israel, had his head cut off by the people of Abel (II Sam. 20:1–22).

5. *A chief Gadite,* dwelling in Gibeah in Bashan (I Chron. 5:13, 16). Also the name of the Arabian home of the Queen of Sheba (1 Kings 10:1) and a city in Simeon (Josh. 19:2).

SHEBANIAH [Shĕb a nī' ah]—JEHOVAH IS POWERFUL, JEHOVAH HATH DEALT TENDERLY or THE LORD CONVERTS.

1. *A priest and trumpeter in David's time* who assisted in bringing up the ark from the house of Obed-edom (I Chron. 15:24).

2. *A Levite* who assisted in the services of the Tabernacle and who sealed the covenant on behalf of his family (Neh 9:4, 5; 10:10).

3. *Another priest* who with Nehemiah sealed the covenant (Neh. 10:4; 12:14).

4. *A Levite* who did the same (Neh. 10:12).

SHEBER [Shē' bûr]—BREAKING or FRACTURE. *A son of Caleb,* son of Jephunneh by his concubine (I Chron. 2:48).

SHEBNA, SHEBNAH [Shĕb' nă]—YOUTHFULNESS, TENDERNESS or WHO RESTS HIMSELF.

1. *A scribe* or palace-governor of king Hezekiah (II Kings 18:18, 26, 37; 19:2; Isa. 36:3, 11, 22; 37:2).

2. *The treasurer over the king's house*—a man of great influence who was fond of display (Isa. 22:15–25) and against whom Isaiah directed one of his utterances.

SHEBUEL [Shĕb' u el]—GOD IS RENOWN or RETURN, O GOD.

1. *A son of Gershon,* son of Levi, grandson of Moses (I Chron. 23:16; 26:24).

2. *A son of Heman,* chief singer of the sanctuary in David's time (I Chron. 25:4). Also called Shubael.

SHECHANIAH [Shĕch a nī' ah]—JEHOVAH IS A NEIGHBOUR or JEHOVAH HATH DWELT.

1. *Head of a family of David's house,* but not in succession to the throne (I Chron. 3:21, 22).

2. *A descendant of a family that returned with Ezra from exile* (Ezra 8:3).

3. *Another whose descendants returned from exile* (Ezra 8:5).

4. *A son of Jehiel* who first confessed the trespass of taking strange, or non-Jewish wives (Ezra 10:2).

5. *Father of Shemaiah* who helped to repair the wall (Neh. 3:29).

6. *Father-in-law of Tobiah,* the Ammonite who opposed Nehemiah (Neh. 6:18).

7. *A priest* who returned with Zerubbabel (Neh. 12:3).

SHECHEM, SICHEM, SYCHEM, SYCHAR [Shĕ′ chem]—SHOULDER.

1. *A son of Hamor,* a Hivite prince—"a prince of the country"—that is, of Shechem. It is not certain whether the Levitical city was named after the son of Hamor, or whether he was named after the city (Gen. 33:18, 19, 34; Josh. 24:32; Judg. 9:28).

The Man Who Disgraced His Princely Dignity

Shechem, a neighbor of Jacob, took advantage of his daughter's visit to the daughters of the Hivites. Doubtless Dinah was young and un-accustomed to the ways of the world, and taking advantage of her, Shechem proved himself unworthy of his high office. He was led into sin by what he saw, and while it is said that Shechem came to love the girl he had wronged and wanted to make her his wife, yet such a proposal was not possible, owing to God's command about His people marrying those of Gentile nations. The scheme of Jacob's sons need not be told. Suffice it to say that Simeon and Levi, Dinah's brothers, treacherously slew Shechem for his betrayal of their sister. To the credit of Shechem it is said that "he was more honourable than all the house of his father." As for Simeon and Levi, they earned a sad epitaph (Gen. 49:5–7).

2. *A son of Gilead,* son of Manasseh and founder of a tribal family (Num. 26:31; Josh. 17:2).

3. *A son of Shemidah,* a Manassite (I Chron. 7:19).

Shechem is also a name renowned in history. Jacob rested there (Gen. 33:18). Jesus met the woman of Samaria at the one-time city of refuge and the first residence of the kings of Israel (John 4:12). It is said that Justin Martyr was born here, about A.D. 100.

SHEDEUR [Shĕd′ e ur]—SHEDDING OF LIGHT or ALL MIGHTY. *Father of Elizur,* the Reubenite chief who assisted Moses in the wilderness (Num. 1:5; 2:10; 7:30, 35; 10:18).

SHEHARIAH [Shē ha rī′ ah]—JEHOVAH IS THE DAWN or BROKEN FORTH AS THE DAWN. *A son of Jeroham,* a Benjamite (I Chron. 8:26).

SHELAH, SALAH, SALA [Shĕ′ lah]—PEACE, PRAYER or THAT BREAKS.

1. *Youngest son of Judah,* by the daughter of Shuah the Canaanite, and founder of a tribal family (Gen. 38:5–26; 46:12; Num. 26:20; I Chron. 2:3; 4:21).

2. *A son of Arphaxad*—also called Salah (I Chron. 1:18, 24). Also the name used for the pool at Jerusalem (Neh. 3:15) and translated Siloah.

SHELEMIAH [Shĕl e mī′ ah]—JEHOVAH IS RECOMPENSE, RECOMPENSES or GOD IS MY PERFECTION.

1. *A Levite,* a doorkeeper of the Tabernacle in David's time (I Chron. 26:14).

2. *One of the sons of Bani* who put away his strange wife (Ezra 10:39).

3. *Another of the same family* who had done the same (Ezra 10:41).

4. *The father of the Hananiah* who helped to repair the wall (Neh. 3:30).

5. *A priest who had charge of the treasuries* and distributed money among the Levites (Neh. 13:13).

6. *A son of Cushi* and grandfather of Jehudi who brought Baruch before the princes of Judah (Jer. 36:14).

7. *The son of Abdeel* who was ordered by Jehoiakim to take Baruch the scribe and Jeremiah the prophet (Jer. 36:26).

8. *The father of Jehucal* who was sent by Zedekiah to Jeremiah in order to plead for his prayers (Jer. 37:3; 38:1).

9. *The father of Irijah,* captain of the guard, who arrested Jeremiah when he was about to leave Jerusalem (Jer. 37:13).

SHELEPH [Shě' leph]—DRAWN OUT. *A son of Joktan* of the family of Shem in southern Arabia (Gen. 10:26; I Chron. 1:20).

SHELESH [Shě' lesh]—MIGHT or TRIED. *An Asherite,* son of Helem and grandson of Beriah (I Chron. 7:35).

SHELOMI [Shěl' o mī]—JEHOVAH IS PEACE or PEACEFUL. *Father of Ahihud,* prince of Judah who lived during the latter part of the wilderness journey (Num. 34:27).

SHELOMITH [Shěl' o mĭth]—PEACEFULNESS.
1. *A son of Shimei,* a Gershonite Levite in David's time (1 Chron. 23:9). The R.V. gives the name as Shelomoth.

2. *A son of Izhar,* of the Kohath family (1 Chron. 23:18). Called Shelomoth in I Chronicles 24:22.

3. *A descendant of Moses* through Eliezer, set over David's dedicated treasures (1 Chron. 26:25, 26, 28).

4. *A son or daughter of king Rehoboam* (II Chron. 11:20).

5. *An ancestor of a family that returned with Ezra* (Ezra 8:10).
Shelomith is also the name of the daughter of Dibri (Lev. 24:11) and of the daughter of Zerubbabel (I Chron. 3:19).

SHELUMIEL [Shě lū' mĭ el]—GOD'S PEACE or A FRIEND OF GOD. *The son of Zurishaddai* and a prince of the tribe of Simeon who assisted Moses in numbering the people (Num. 1:6; 2:12; 7:36, 41; 10:19).

SHEM, SEM [Shěm, Sěm]—RENOWN, or NAME. *A son of Noah,* and ancestor of Christ (Gen. 5:32).
From his name, it is to be inferred that Shem was a distinguished person. The men of Babel sought to make themselves a name (Gen. 11:4) and become, thereby, rivals of Shem. The greatness of Shem

arose from the fact that he was a forerunner of Christ. Shem's name meaning "renown" foreshadowed the greater name "above every name" before which every knee shall bow (Luke 3:36). In offering praise to God, Noah said, "Blessed be the Lord God of Shem" (Gen. 9:26).

SHEMA [Shĕ' mă]—REPUTE, FAME or RUMOR.

1. *A son of Hebron* and father of Raham (I Chron. 2:43, 44).
2. *A Reubenite,* a son of Joel and father of Azaz (I Chron. 5:4, 8).
3. *A Benjamite,* head of the inhabitants of Aijalon (I Chron. 8:13). Called Shimhi in verse twenty-one and Shimei in the R.V.
4. *A priest* who assisted Ezra in the public reading of the law (Neh. 8:4). Also the name of a city in Judah (Josh. 15:26).

SHEMAAH [Shĕ mă' ah]—THE FAME. *A Benjamite of Gibeah* and father of two valiant men who joined David at Ziklag (I Chron. 12:3).

SHEMAIAH [Shĕm a ī' ah]—JEHOVAH IS FAME, JEHOVAH HAS HEARD or OBEYS THE LORD.

Evidently this popular name was shared by many Bible men, and at times two of the following may be the same individual. It is not an easy matter to identify them exactly.

1. *A prophet sent by God* to prevent Rehoboam from warring against the house of Israel. His part in the revolution and history are clearly defined (I Kings 12:22; II Chron. 11:2; 12:5, 7, 15).
2. *Son of Shechaniah* and father of Hattush, descendant of Zerubbabel (I Chron. 3:22).
3. *Father of Shimri,* perhaps Shimei, and head of a family of Simeon (I Chron. 4:37). See verses twenty-six and twenty-seven.
4. *A son of Joel,* perhaps Shema of I Chronicles 5:8, and head of a family of Reuben (I Chron. 5:4).
5. *A Merarite Levite* dwelling in Jerusalem (I Chron. 9:14; Neh. 11:15).
6. *A Levite, father of Obadiah* (I Chron. 9:16). Called Shammua in Nehemiah 11:17.
7. *Head of the Levitical Kohath clan* who assisted in bringing the Ark from the house of Obed-edom (I Chron. 15:8, 11).
8. *The son of Nathaneel,* a Levite, who recorded the priestly office in David's time (I Chron. 24:6).
9. *Oldest son of Obed-edom,* a Korhite Levite and a gatekeeper of the Tabernacle in David's reign (I Chron. 26:4, 6, 7).
10. *A Levite,* commissioned by Jehoshaphat, to teach the people in Judah (II Chron. 17:8).
11. *A son of Jeduthun* who helped in the purification of the Temple under Hezekiah (II Chron. 29:14).
12. *A Levite in Hezekiah's time* who was over the freewill offerings of God (II Chron. 31:15).

13. *A chief Levite* in the days of Josiah (II Chron. 35:9).

14. *A son of Adonikam* who returned with Ezra from exile (Ezra 8:13).

15. *A chief man under Ezra* sent to Iddo to ask for ministers. (Ezra 8:16).

16. *A priest of the family of Harim* who married a foreign wife (Ezra 10:21).

17. *A person who helped to repair the wall* (Neh. 3:29).

18. *A son of Delaiah* hired by Sanballat and Tobiah to intimidate Nehemiah (Neh. 6:10).

19. *A priest,* one of the twenty-four courses of priests that with Nehemiah sealed the covenant (Neh. 10:8; 12:6, 18, 34, 35).

20. *A singer* who took part in the dedication of the wall (Neh. 12:36).

21. *Another, or perhaps the same person as the previous one,* who gave thanks at the dedication (Neh. 12:42).

22. *The father of Urijah the prophet* who was slain by Jehoiakim for prophesying against Jerusalem and Judah (Jer. 26:20).

23. *A prophet called "the Nehelamite"* who in captivity was actively engaged in reproving or opposing Jeremiah (Jer. 29:24–32).

24. *The father of Delaiah,* a prince of the Jews to whom Baruch read the roll he had written under Jeremiah's direction (Jer. 36:12).

SHEMARIAH, SHAMARIAH [Shĕm a rī' ah, Shăm a rī' ah]—GOD HATH KEPT or GOD IS MY GUARD.

1. *A mighty man,* a Benjamite who joined David at Ziklag (I Chron. 12:5).

2. *A son of Rehoboam,* son of Solomon (II Chron. 11:19).

3. *One of the family of Harim* who had married a foreign wife (Ezra 10:32).

4. *One of the family of Bani* who had done the same (Ezra 10:4).

SHEMEBER [Shĕm ē' ber]—SPLENDOR OF HEROISM. *The King of Zeboim* who defeated other kings in the cities of the plain (Gen. 14:2, 8, 10).

SHEMER [Shē' mûr]—ONE KEPT BY THE LORD or GUARDIAN. *Owner of a hill purchased by Omri* and on which he built Samaria (I Kings 16:24). Shomer in I Chronicles 7:32.
See others under Shamed and Shamer.

SHEMIDAH, SHEMIDA [Shē mī' dah, Shē mī' dă]—FAME OF KNOWING or SCIENCE OF THE HEAVENS. *A son of Gilead* and grandson of Manasseh (Num. 26:32; Josh. 17:2; I Chron. 7:19). Founder of a tribal family (Num. 26:32).

SHEMIRAMOTH [Shē mĭr' a mŏth]—FAME OF THE HIGHEST or HEIGHT OF THE HEAVENS.

1. *A Levite* responsible for the choral service of the Tabernacle (I Chron. 15:18, 20; 16:5).
2. *Another Levite,* whom Jehoshaphat sent to teach the people in Judah (II Chron. 17:8.)

SHEMUEL [Shĕ mŭ′ el]—HEARD OF GOD.
1. *A Simeonite* appointed to assist in dividing the land west of Jordan (Num. 34:20). Perhaps the name is equivalent to Shelumiel.
2. *The father of Joel* (I Chron. 6:33).
3. *A grandson of Issachar* and head of a family (I Chron. 7:2).

SHENAZAR [Shĕ nā′ zar]—LIGHT or SPLENDOR. *A son or grandson of Jecamiah,* son of Jehoiakim king of Judah (I Chron. 3:18). See Sheshbazzar.

SHEPHATIAH [Shĕph a tī′ ah]—JEHOVAH IS JUDGE.
1. *The fifth son of David* by Abital (II Sam. 3:4; I Chron. 3:3).
2. *A Benjamite,* father of Meshullam whose home was in Jerusalem (I Chron. 9:8).
3. *A valiant man who came to David at Ziklag* (I Chron. 12:5).
4. *A prince of Simeon in David's reign* (I Chron. 27:16).
5. *A son of king Jehoshaphat* (II Chron. 21:2).
6. *A person whose many descendants returned from exile with Zerubbabel* (Ezra 2:4; Neh. 7:9).
7. *One of Solomon's servants* who also returned from exile (Ezra 2:57; Neh. 7:59).
8. *One whose descendant, Zebadiah, returned from exile* with eighty males (Ezra 8:8).
9. *A descendant of Pharez,* who dwelt in Jerusalem (Neh. 11:4).
10. *A son of Mattan,* a prince of Judah in Zedekiah's time (Jer. 38:1).

SHEPHO, SHEPHI [Shĕ′ phō, Shĕ′ phī]—UNCONCERN or SMOOTHNESS. *A son of Shobal* and a Horite chief (Gen. 36:23; I Chron. 1:40).

SHEPHUPHAM, SHEPHUPHAN [Shĕ phŭ′ phan]—AN ADDER. *A son of Bela,* son of Benjamin and father of a tribal family (I Chron. 8:5). Called Muppim in Genesis 46:21 and Shuppim in I Chronicles 7:12, 15; 26:16.

SHEREBIAH [Shĕr e bī′ ah]—JEHOVAH HATH MADE TO TREMBLE or JEHOVAH IS ORIGINATOR.
1. *A priest* with eighteen sons and brethren who returned with Ezra. Evidently a family of singers (Ezra 8:18, 24; Neh. 8:7; 9:4, 5).
2. *A Levite* who with Nehemiah sealed the covenant (Neh. 10:12; 12:8, 24).

SHERESH [Shĕ′resh]—UNION or ROOT. *A son of Machir* of the Manassite clan (I Chron. 7:16).

SHESHAI [Shĕ′shaī]—FREE, NOBLE or WHITISH. *A son of Anak,* who resided at Hebron, having been driven there by Caleb (Num. 13:22; Josh. 15:14; Judg. 1:10).

SHESHAN [Shĕ′shan]—FREE, NOBLE. *A Jerahmeelite,* grandson of Pharez son of Judah whose only daughter was given in marriage to an Egyptian slave (I Chron. 2:31, 34, 35).

SHESHBAZZAR [Shĕsh băz′zar]—O SUN-GOD PROTECT THE SON. *The prince of Judah made governor of Judah by Cyrus* (Ezra 1:8, 11; 5:14, 16). Elsewhere called Zerubbabel (Ezra 3:8).

SHETH [Shĕth]—COMPENSATION.
1. *A Moabite chief.* The Moabites were makers of war and tumult, and are named "sons of tumult" in the R.V. (Num. 24:17).
2. *A son of Adam* (I Chron. 1:1).

SHETHAR [Shĕ′thär]—STAR or COMMANDER. *One of the seven princes of Persia and Media* who had the right of access to the king's presence (Esther 1:14).

SHETHAR-BOZNAI [Shĕ′thär-bŏz′na ī]—STARRY SPLENDOR. *A Persian official* who with others attempted to prevent the returned Jewish exiles from rebuilding the Temple (Ezra 5:3, 6; 6:6, 13).

SHEVA, SHAVSHA [Shĕ′vă]—SELF-SATISFYING or VANITY.
1. *A scribe* or secretary of David (II Sam. 20:25).
2. *The father of Machbenah* and son of Maachah, concubine of Caleb son of Jephunneh (I Chron. 2:49).

SHILHI [Shĭl′hī]—ONE ARMED WITH DARTS. *Father of Azubah,* mother of King Jehoshaphat (I Kings 22:42; II Chron. 20:31).

SHILLEM [Shĭl′lem]—RETRIBUTION or RECOMPENSE. *The fourth son of Naphtali* and founder of a tribal family (Gen. 46:24; Num. 26:49). Called Shallum in I Chronicles 7:13.

SHILONI [Shī lŏ′nī]—SENT ONE. *Father of Zechariah,* of the sons of Parez or Pharez, son of Judah (Neh. 11:5). The R.V. says a Shilonite—see I Kings 11:29.

SHILSHAH [Shĭl′shah]—MIGHT, HEROISM or TRIAD. *The ninth son of Zophah,* an Asherite (I Chron. 7:37).

SHIMEAH, SHIMEA [Shǐm'e ah, Shǐm'e ǎ]—SPLENDOR or SOME-
THING HEARD.

1. *Son of Mikloth,* a Benjamite of the family of Saul (I Chron.
8:32).

2. *One of David's brothers* (II Sam. 13:3; 21:21). Appears as
Shammah (I Sam. 16:9; 17:13). See II Samuel 21:21.

3. *A son of David* (I Chron. 3:5). See Shammuah.

4. *Father of Haggiah,* a Merarite (I Chron. 6:30).

5. *Father of Berachiah,* of the family of Gershon (I Chron. 6: 39).

SHIMEAM [Shǐm'e ǎm]—FAME or RUMOR. *A son of Mikloth,* a
Benjamite resident in Jerusalem (I Chron. 9:38). Same as Shimeah
in I Chronicles 8:32. Founder of a tribal family (I Chron. 2:55).

SHIMEI, SHIMI, SHIMHI [Shǐm'e ī, Shī'mī, Shǐm'hī]—JEHOVAH
IS FAME or FAMOUS.

Shimei, we are told, was a popular name among the Hebrews, being
especially common in Levitical circles. But of the majority of men
bearing it, little is known apart from the name.

1. *The Benjamite of the clan of Saul,* son of Gera who cursed
David when he fled from Absalom (II Sam. 16:5, 7, 13; 19:16, 18, 21,
23). Although we have little knowledge of this most prominent Shimei,
what we do know proves him to be, as Dr. Alexander Whyte expresses
it, "A reptile of the royal house of Saul." This Shimei can be described
as:

The Man Who Hated the Truth He Knew

This man who lived to curse knew only too well that David had
never shed a single drop of Saul's blood, but it was not in his interest
to admit the truth he knew. Because of his tribal and family connections it was natural for Shimei to be David's bitter enemy, and to heap
his curses and insults upon the fugitive monarch.

When, however, David triumphantly returned after Absalom's tragic
death, Shimei met the king with a hypocritical repentance. David
accepted his apology and gave an oath that he would not put him to
death. When further resistance was useless, Shimei feigned obedience
to David, but in his heart was still bitterly opposed to him.

On his deathbed David's last words to Solomon about Shimei's
blood being spilt, cause one to wonder whether David's long-suppressed
revenge upon his enemy found utterance. Solomon would not allow
Shimei to go beyond the walls of Jerusalem. All the time he remained
in his city of refuge he was safe. If he passed without it, he would
die. Shimei kept this arrangement for three years, then broke it on
some trifling occasion and justly forfeited his life. At the command of
Solomon he was executed by Benaiah. This was the last of those acts
of justice on offenders against David which Solomon performed.

How do we act when men say all manner of evil against us falsely?
Do we see the Lord in it all, and that He will work out our salvation

in spite of adverse and sore criticisms and circumstances? Do we rest in the fact that the Lord will look upon our affliction and will requite us good for all evil, if only we wisely and silently and adoringly submit ourselves to it?

2. *A Courtier*, Shimei by name, an officer of David, remained true to the king when Adonijah sought to usurp the throne (I Kings 1:8).

3. *A son of Elah*, one of the twelve purveyors of Solomon, in Benjamin (I Kings 4:18). This Shimei has been identified as the one above in I Kings 1:8.

4. *A son of Gershon*, son of Levi, who founded a subdivision of the tribal family of Gershon (Ex. 6:17).

5. *A grandson of Jeconiah*, son of Jehoiakim king of Judah. A prince of the royal house (I Chron. 3:19).

6. *A son of Zacchur*, the Benjamite with sixteen sons and six daughters (I Chron. 4:26, 27).

7. *A Reubenite*, son of Gog (I Chron. 5:4).

8. *A Merarite*, son of Libni (I Chron. 6:29).

9. *Father of a chief family in Judah* (I Chron. 8:21).

10. *A Levite of the family of Laadan*—grandson of Levi (I Chron. 23:9).

11. *A Levite* to whom the tenth lot fell in the singing service of the Tabernacle during David's time. A son of Jeduthun (I Chron. 25:3, 17).

12. *A Ramathite* who was overseer in David's vineyards (I Chron. 27:27).

13. *A descendant of Heman*, who took part in the cleansing of the Temple in Hezekiah's time (II Chron. 29:14).

14. *A Levite* and brother of Conaniah, who had charge of the tithes (II Chron. 31:12, 13).

15. *A Levite* who had taken a strange wife (Ezra 10:23).

16. *One of the family of Hashum* who put away his wife (Ezra 10:33).

17. *A son of Bani*, who also put away his strange wife (Ezra 10:38).

18. *A Benjamite*, son of Kish and grandfather of Mordecai (Esther 2:5).

19. *A representative*, perhaps of the Gershonites who participated in mourning for national guilt (Zech. 12:13).

SHIMEON [Shĭm' e on]—HEARING or AN ANSWERING OF PRAYER. *A son of Harim* who had married a foreign wife (Ezra 10:31).

SHIMMA [Shĭm' mà]—FAME or RUMOR. *The third son of Jesse* and brother of David (I Chron. 2:13). Also called Shamma.

SHIMON [Shĭ' mon]—TRIED or VALUER. *A descendant of Caleb* son of Jephunneh, registered with the tribes of Judah (I Chron. 4:20).

SHIMRATH [Shĭm' răth]— WATCH or GUARDING. *A son of Shimhi of Aijalon,* and descendant of Benjamin (I Chron. 8:21).

SHIMRI, SIMRI [Shĭm' rĭ, Sĭm' rĭ]—JEHOVAH IS WATCHING.
1. *A Simeonite* and head of a tribal family (I Chron. 4:37).
2. *Father of Jediael,* one of David's heroes (I Chron. 11:45).
3. *A son of Hosah* and Tabernacle gatekeeper (I Chron. 26:10).
4. *A son of Elizaphan* who assisted in Hezekiah's reformation (II Chron. 29:13).

SHIMRON, SHIMROM [Shĭm' rŏn, Shĭm' rŏm]—A GUARD or WATCH. *The fourth son of Issachar* and founder of a family. (Gen. 46:13; Num. 26:24; I Chron. 7:1). Also the name of a city of Zebulun whose kings Jabin called to his assistance (Josh. 11:1; 19:15). Also called Shimron-meron.

SHIMSHAI [Shĭm' shaĭ]—JEHOVAH IS SPLENDOR or SUNNY. *A scribe of Rehum* who complained to Artaxerxes about the Jews rebuilding the temple (Ezra 4:8, 9, 17, 23).

SHINAB [Shĭ' năb]—TOOTH OF THE FATHER. *The king of Admah* in Abraham's time (Gen. 14:2, 8–10), and defeated by Chedorlaomer.

SHIPHI [Shĭ' phĭ]—JEHOVAH IS FULNESS or ABOUNDING. *Father of Ziza,* a Simeonite prince (I Chron. 4:37).

SHIPHTAN [Shĭph' tan]—JUDGE or JUDICIAL. *Father of Kemuel,* an Ephraimite prince appointed to divide the land of Jordan (Num. 34:24).

SHISHA [Shĭ' shă]—DISTINCTION or NOBILITY. *Father of Elihoreph and Ahiah,* two of king Solomon's scribes (I Kings 4:3). See Shavsha.

SHISHAK [Shĭ' shăk]—MEANING OF NAME OBSCURE. *Sesconchis I,* founder of the twenty-second Bubastic dynasty, who reigned for twenty-one years. Jeroboam fled to him and was protected against Solomon. Shishak plundered Jerusalem in the fifth year of Rehoboam (I Kings 14:25; II Chron. 12:2–9). His name has been found on the Egyptian monuments in the form of Sheshnok. He might have been of Ethiopian origin. Tradition has it that with the aid of the military caste, he dethroned the Pharaoh who gave his daughter to Solomon.

SHITRAI [Shĭt' ra ĭ]—JEHOVAH IS DECIDING. *A Sharonite* who cared for David's herds in the plain of Sharon (I Chron. 27:29).

SHIZA [Shĭ' ză]—SPLENDOR or VEHEMENT LOVE. *The father of a Reubenite chief,* one of David's heroes. (I Chron. 11:42).

SHOBAB [Shō' băb]—RETURNING or RESTORED.

1. *A son of David born after he became king of Israel* (II Sam. 5:14; I Chron. 3:5; 14:4).

2. *A son of Caleb,* son of Hezron, whose mother's name was Azubah (I Chron. 2:18).

SHOBACH [Shō' băch]—EXPANSION, ONE WHO POURS OUT or CAPTIVITY. *A commander-in-chief under Hadarezer,* king of Zobal, defeated and slain by Joab (II Sam. 10:16, 18). Called Shophach in I Chronicles 19:16.

SHOBAI [Shō' ba ī]—JEHOVAH IS GLORIOUS or ONE WHO LEADS CAPTIVE. *A Levite and founder of a family of gatekeepers* whose descendants returned from exile with Zerubbabel (Ezra 2:42; Neh. 7:45).

SHOBAL [Shō' bal]—WANDERING or A TRAVELER.

1. *A son of Seir the Horite* and one of the dukes (Gen. 36:20, 23, 29; I Chron. 1:38, 40).

2. *A son of Caleb,* son of Hur (I Chron. 2:50, 52).

3. *A son of Judah* and father of Reaiah (I Chron. 4:1, 2).

SHOBEK [Shō' bek]—FREE OR ONE WHO FORSAKES. *A Jewish chief* who with Nehemiah signed the covenant (Neh. 10:24).

SHOBI [Shō' bī]—JEHOVAH IS GLORIOUS or ONE WHO LEADS CAPTIVE. *A son of Nahash the king of Ammon,* who, with Machir of Lo-debar, showed kindness to David at the time of his flight from Absalom (II Sam. 17:27).

SHOHAM [Shō' hăm]—BERYL or ONYX.—*A Levite,* a son of Jaaziah (I Chron. 24:27).

SHOMER [Shō' mûr]—KEEPER or WATCHMAN. *A son of Heber,* an Asherite (I Chron. 7:32). Also spelled Shamer in verse thirty-four. Shomer is likewise the name of the mother of Jehozabad (II Kings 12:21), and called Shimrith in II Chronicles 24:26.

SHOPHACH [Shō' phăch]—EXTENSION. *The captain of the host of Hadarezer,* king of Zobah in David's time (I Chron. 19:16, 18). Called Shobach in II Samuel 10:16.

SHUA [Shōō' ă]—WEALTH. *The father of Judah's Canaanite wife* (Gen. 38:2, 12). Also the name of a daughter of Heber (I Chron. 7:32).

SHUAH [Shōō' ah]—PROSPERITY or DEPRESSION.

1. *A son of Keturah* by Abraham (Gen. 25:2; I Chron. 1:32). Probably Bildad the Shuhite belonged to this tribe (Job. 2:11).

2. *Brother of Chelub,* a descendant of Caleb son of Hur (I Chron. 4:11).

SHUAL [Shōō' al]—A FOX or A SMALL PET. *The third son of Zophah,* an Asherite (I Chron. 7:36). Also the name of a district in Benjamin (I Sam. 13:17). See Shalim and Hazar-shual.

SHUBAEL [Shōō' ba el]—MEANING OF NAME OBSCURE.
1. *A son or descendant of Amram,* grandson of Levi (I Chron. 24:20).
2. *A singer in the Tabernacle in David's time* (I Chron. 25:20). Perhaps the same as Shebuel in I Chronicles 25:4.

SHUHAM [Shōō' ham]—DEPRESSION. *A son of Dan* and founder of a tribal family (Num. 26:42, 43). Sometimes identified as Hushim in Genesis 46:23.

SHUNI [Shōō' nī]—FORTUNATE, CALM, QUIET. *The third son of Gad* and founder of a tribal family (Gen. 46:16; Num. 26:15).

SHUPHAM, SHUPPIM [Shōō' pham, Shŭp' pim)—SERPENT.
1. *A son of Benjamin* (Num. 26:39). Most likely the Shephuphan son of Bela (I Chron. 8:5).
2. *A Benjamite* (I Chron. 7:12, 15).
3. *A Levite gatekeeper* of the Tabernacle in David's time. (I Chron. 26:16).

SHUTHELAH [Shōō' the lah]—SETTING OF TELAH or A PLANT.
1. *A son of Ephraim* and founder of a tribal family (Num. 26: 35, 36; I Chron. 7:20).
2. *A son of Zabad,* a descendant of Ephraim (I Chron. 7:21).

SIAHA, SIA [Sī' a hà, Sī' ǎ]—CONGREGATION. *One of the Nethinims* who returned with Zerubbabel (Ezra 2:44; Neh. 7:47).

SIBBECHAI, SIBBECAI [Sĭb' be chaī, Sĭb' be caī]—JEHOVAH IS INTERVENING or ENTANGLING. *One of the family of Hushah* who slew Saph or Saffai, a Philistine giant in David's time (II Sam. 21:18; I Chron. 11:29; 20:4; 27:11). Called Mebunnai in II Samuel 23:27.

SIDON, ZIDON [Sī' dŏn]—FORTIFIED. *The eldest son of Canaan, son of Ham,* and founder of the tribal family, Sidonians (Gen. 10:15; Judg. 3:3). Also the name of the city now known as Saida.

SIHON [Sī' hŏn]—GREAT or SWEEPING OUT. *A king of the Amorites* at the time of Canaan's conquest. He refused to allow Israel to pass through his land and was defeated at Jahaz (Num. 21:21–33; Deut. 1:4; 3:2, 6; 4:46).

SILAS, SILVANUS [Sī′ las, Sĭl vā′ nus]—LOVER OF WORDS. *A distinguished member and prophet of the Apostolic Church at Jerusalem* who figures as the companion of Paul in his triumphs and trials. From the Book of Acts we learn that:

I. He was one of the chief men among the brethren and therefore of Jewish birth (Acts 15:32).

II. He was sent as a delegate from the Apostolic Council with Paul and Barnabas to report the Council's decision (Acts 15:22).

III. He was probably a Roman citizen (Acts 16:37).

IV. His double qualification as a leading Jewish Christian and a Roman citizen eminently fitted him to take the place of Barnabas as Paul's companion (Acts 15:40).

V. He suffered with Paul in prison (Acts 16:19, 25, 29), joining in the prayers and praises that midnight hour resulting in the conversion of the keeper of the prison.

VI. He was also associated with Peter, acting as bearer or scribe of Peter's first Epistle (I Pet. 5:12).

VII. He is probably the Silvanus who preached the Apostolic doctrine (II Cor. 1:19; see I Thess. 1:1; II Thess. 1:1).

SIMEON, SYMEON [Sĭm′ e on]—HEARING, HEARS AND OBEYS or HEARING WITH ACCEPTANCE.

1. *The second son of Jacob by Leah* (Gen. 29:33).

The Man Who Was Self-Willed

It is not easy to deal with Simeon alone, since he is always associated with his brother, Levi. "Simeon and Levi are brethren" (Gen. 49:5). Of Simeon's personal history we know little. His name implies hearing with obedience, but Simeon was deaf in the day he should have heard, and disobedient and irresponsive when his lot hung in balance.

The first thing recorded about Simeon is that with Levi his brother, he drew the sword in treachery against the Shechemites and slew all the males. When rebuked by their father, they upheld indignantly their right to act as they did. Both acted "in their selfwill" (Gen. 49:6), which means they took malicious delight in their gross crime.

Simeon next appears in the story of Joseph, who felt it would be better to retain Simeon until Benjamin had been brought to the palace. Joseph felt with his father Jacob that Simeon and Levi would be best apart. In fact, Simeon had no blessing while joined with Levi and no prosperity while he was with Reuben. When separated, Simeon, at first, did not multiply (I Chron. 4:24–27). During the forty years in the wilderness the decrease of Simeon was remarkable. Because of the idolatry of the tribe, thousands were slain.

In the land of Canaan, Simeon joined with Judah, and this association marked a turning point in the history of the tribe. Judah and

Simeon went up together to Canaan (Judg. 1:1–3). Simeon means "obedient hearing," and Judah, "praise." The absorption of Simeon into the inheritance of Judah gave Simeon a place and work in Israel. In the final division of the land, foretold by Ezekiel, between Benjamin and Issachar, there is a portion for Simeon.

Over the gate to the Golden City, Simeon's name is inscribed—"Of the tribe of Simeon were sealed 12,000"—a way for even Simeon to enter the city of God above. From the time the Simeonites became aware of what God had done for them there was no more curse and no more captivity for them. Hitherto instruments of cruelty, they became instruments of warfare against the enemies of the Lord, ultimately earning the right to be included among the number eternally sealed (Rev. 7:7).

Self-will fittingly describes Simeon's career until he was separated from Levi. God hates self-will for He knows how it accounts for uncontrolled passions, and the failure to respond to higher appeals. Because of their self-will God, in His governmental dealings, scattered and impoverished the Simeonites. May we not come nigh their dwelling but ever seek to learn, prove and obey "that good and acceptable and perfect will of God."

2. *A just and devout man in Jerusalem who awaited the coming of Jesus, the Messiah* (Luke 2:25–34).

The Man Who Died Satisfied

The adoration and prophecy of Simeon, who waited for the consolation of Israel and blessed the Consoler when He appeared, is rich in spiritual suggestion. This spectator of the most significant birth of all history, endued with a prophetic spirit, kept the lamp of prophecy burning when religion was at a low ebb in Israel. Simeon means "one who hears and obeys" and this saintly Simeon knew the voice speaking in the prophets of old, and obeyed the light he saw. Coming into the Temple, he took the Babe in his arms and blessed God. What a wonderful benediction his was!

At last faith had been justified and Simeon could die without fear. Have our eyes seen the salvation of the Lord? Can we die in peace? In his swan song, Simeon was not ashamed to declare that the One born in the city of David was the Saviour of the world. This was more than the letter-learned scribes of his times had discerned. These were the men who looked upon Christ as a sign to be spoken against and to whom He would become a stone of stumbling and a rock of offense.

With godly Simeon it was different, for he was Spirit-taught and knew that Mary's Child was the One through whom the world was to be blessed. As he eagerly anticipated Christ's first advent, are we found patiently awaiting His second advent? When He does appear and we see Him as He is, ours will be the thrill Simeon experienced as He gazed upon the Lord's Christ.

3. *An ancestor of Jesus* (Luke 3:30).

4. *A disciple and prophet at Antioch,* surnamed Niger (Acts 13:1).

5. *The original name of a son of Jonas,* or John, and brother of Andrew an apostle of Christ. See Simon (Acts 15:14).

SIMON [Sī' mon]—HEARING.

1. *Simon Peter,* one time Galilean fisherman, an early disciple and apostle of Jesus Christ (Matt. 4:18; 10:2). For a brief outline of his life and labor, see material under Peter.

2. *Another of the Twelve Apostles,* called the "Canaanite," because of his connection with Cana in Galilea.

The Man Who Was Zealous

The Hebrew *canna* means, "zealous," thus the Greek Zelotes (Luke 6:15; Acts 1:13). As a Zealot, Simon belonged to the historical party which bore that name. This communion of noble-hearted men loved their own land and cherished their belief in its rightful independence, which made any foreign interference or dominion hateful. Their zeal for the laws of God which were their national laws, the guardian and source of their independence and liberty, attracted a lover of freedom such as Simon.

What we admire about this apostle is the fact that after he became Christ's follower, he never ceased to be known as the Zealot. What had attracted him as a man, he came to love as a Christian. In Christ's teaching the Zealot found the helper and handmaid of everything that he in his calmer moments could hope or look for. The lesson we gather for our own hearts is that we may carry our true and noblest selves into our following of Christ. Whatever hopes and aspirations we may have apart from Christ can find a true home in Christ. Simon, the Jewish patriot who chafed under the foreign yoke and sighed for emancipation, came to experience a sweeter yoke and a more blessed emancipation. May an increasing number of Christ's disciples strive to earn the honorable title, "zealous of spiritual gifts" (I Cor. 14:12).

3. *One of the brothers of our Lord* (Matt. 13:55; Mark 6:3).

4. *The one-time leper in Bethany,* in whose house the head of Jesus was anointed with oil (Matt. 26:6–13; Mark 14:3–9; John 12:1–8).

5. *A Cyrenian who was compelled to bear the cross* after Jesus and who was the father of Alexander and Rufus (Matt. 27:32). Shortly after, Jesus bore the cross, not only for Simon but for all men.

6. *A Pharisee* in whose house Jesus dined and had His feet washed with tears and anointed with ointment (Luke 7:40–44). This wealthy Simon or Simeon had every reason to be pleased with the banquet he provided, for he saw Jesus signally honored and the Pharisees, including himself, severely rebuked for their lack of forgiving love and grace. The woman's heart was as full of ointment as the box she carried. What sweet perfume filled the atmosphere as she stole to Christ's feet and washed them with her scalding tears, and then wiped those sacred feet with her long black hair! With the light of heaven in

her eyes and the blessed words of Jesus ringing in her ears, "Thy sins are forgiven; go in peace," she left Simeon's house with all her sins blotted out.

7. *The father of Judas Iscariot* (John 6:71; 12:4; 13:2, 26).

8. *A sorcerer* or magician in Samaria who sought to purchase the gifts of the Spirit with money (Acts 8:9–24).

The Man Who Tried to Buy Power

The first glimpse we have of Simon Magus is that he paraded himself as "some great one," and is an exaggerated specimen of popularity seekers among us today. This Samaritan mountebank, who carried on his astounding impositions, was as bad as he was clever. He professed to be converted and was so deceitful that he completely deceived Philip.

In Samaria, Philip was having tremendous success in his evangelistic work, and Simon fell under the influence of his message, so much so that he professed belief in Christ and was baptized. But when Peter and John came on the scene to establish the work begun by Philip, through the laying on of hands, miraculous gifts were imparted to many of those Samaritan believers.

Simon, with his innate love of witchery, offered to buy from the apostles the power of conferring spiritual gifts, and was rebuked in language of such sternness as to lead him to beg of Peter to pray that the severe judgment of God would not fall upon him because of his sin. Peter detected that the thought of Simon's heart had not been changed. Calvin says, "We may conjecture that Simon Magus repented." Scripture, however, is silent about his life after Peter's rebuke. Ignatius, the earliest of the Fathers, calls Simon "the first born of Satan." Irenaeus marks him out as the first of all heretics. Because of his sin, the word simony came into being, a term meaning the effort to procure spiritual office by gifts. Simon Magus loved the praises and adulations of men. How we have to guard against the perils of popularity! Says Alexander Whyte, "Starve the self-seeking quack that is still within you. Beat him black and blue, as Paul tells us he did."

9. *A tanner of Joppa,* with whom Simon Peter lodged when sent for by Cornelius (Acts 9:43; 10:6, 27, 32). What precious fellowship those two Simons must have had during those days! A tanner and a fisherman! How they come to Jesus from every walk of life!

SIPPAI, SAPH [SÏp paī, Săph]—JEHOVAH IS PRESERVER. *A son or a descendant of Rapha,* the gigantic ancestor of the Rephaim, slain by Sibbechai, the Hushathite in David's time (I Chron. 20:4). Called Saph in II Samuel 21:18.

SISAMAI, SISMAI [SÏ săm' a ī]—JEHOVAH IS DISTINGUISHED. *A son of Eleasah* and father of Shallum, a Jerahmeelite (I Chron. 2:40).

SISERA [Sĭs' e rǎ]—MEDITATION, BATTLE ARRAY or SEES A HORSE.

1. *Commander of the Canaanite army* which held northern Israel in subjection. He was killed by Jael (Judg. 4:21, 22; I Sam. 12:9; Ps. 83:9). In his flight after battle with the Israelites under Barak, Sisera, overcome by fatigue, sought shelter in the tent of Jael, who treacherously slew him while asleep—the death prophesied by Deborah (Judg. 4:9). The most tragic aspect of the murder of Sisera is that of his anxious mother awaiting the return of her son. Jael's cruel act broke a mother's heart.

2. *One of the Nethinims* whose descendants returned with Zerubbabel (Ezra 2:53; Neh. 7:55).

SO [Sō]—LIFTED UP. *King of Egypt* of Ethiopian descent whose aid against Syria, Hoshea, the last king of Israel, endeavored to secure (II Kings 17:4).

SOCHO, SHOCO, SHOCHO [Sŏ' chō, Shō' cō, Shō' chō]—LEDGE or FORTIFICATION. *A son of Heber* (I Chron. 4:18). Also the name of a city in Judah rebuilt by Rehoboam (II Chron. 11:7; 28:18). Perhaps Socoh (Josh. 15:35).

SODI [Sō' dī]—JEHOVAH DETERMINES, A FAMILIAR ACQUAINTANCE or MY SECRET. *A Zebulunite,* father of Gaddiel, one of the twelve spies sent out to spy Canaan (Num. 13:10).

SOLOMON [Sŏl' o mon]—PEACE or PEACEABLE. *The tenth son of David,* and second by Bath-sheba, and the third king of Israel who reigned for forty years (II Sam. 5:14; 12:24). Solomon was also known as Jedidiah meaning, "beloved of the Lord."

The Man Who Was Full Yet Failed

We know little of the early life of Solomon. The name given him by Nathan, but not repeated because of its sacredness, implies David's restoration to divine favor (II Sam. 12:25). Loved of the Lord suggests the bestowal of unusual gifts (II Sam. 12:24, 25). It is also evident that young Solomon was greatly influenced both by his mother and Nathan (I Kings 1:11, 12).

With reference to the character and reign of Solomon, we cannot but agree with Alexander Whyte that, "The shipwreck of Solomon is surely the most terrible tragedy in all the world. For if ever there was a shining type of Christ in the Old Testament church, it was Solomon . . . but everyday sensuality made him in the end a castaway." Taking him all in all, Solomon stands out as a disappointing figure of Hebrew history. Think of the advantages he began with! There were the almost undisputed possession of David's throne, immense stores of wealth laid up by his father, exceptional divinely imparted mental abilities, the love and high hopes of the people. Solomon's start like the cloudless dawn of a summer's morning, might have been beautiful all his life through, but it ended in gloom because he wandered into God-forbidden paths. Thus a life beginning magnificently ended miserably. The man who penned and preached a thousand wise things failed to practice the wisdom he taught.

The work of Solomon was the development of his father's ideas of a consolidated kingdom, and what marvelous success crowned his efforts. Exercising the power of an oriental despot, he gave Israel a glory, prestige and splendor unsurpassed in the world's history. On the whole, however, Solomon seemed to rule for his own aggrandizement and not for the welfare of the people. Doubtless Solomon's artistic and literary gifts provided the masses with beneficial instruction, but the glory of Solomon brought the common people tears and groans. The great wealth provided by David for the building of a Temple speedily disappeared under Solomon's lavish spending, and the people had to pay heavily by taxation and poverty for his magnificent whims. Yet Jesus said that the lilies of the field had greater glory than all the gaudy pomp and pride of Solomon.

Solomon's ambition in the morning of his life was most commendable. His dream was a natural expression of this ambition, and his God-imparted wisdom an evidence of it (I Kings 3). Then his sacrifice at Gibeon indicates that Solomon desired religion to be associated with all external magnificence. Solomon's remarkable prayer also breathes the atmosphere of true piety and of his delight in the full recognition of God. Alas, however, Solomon came to the end of his days minus popularity and piety!

This first great naturalist the world ever saw, who wrote one thousand and five songs, three thousand proverbs and who had sagacity beyond compare, took his first step downward when he went to Egypt for his queen. A daughter of Pharaoh, sitting on the throne of David, must have shocked and saddened the godly elect of Israel. With this strange wife came her strange gods.

Then came the harem of outlandish women who caused Solomon to sin (Neh. 13:26). His wives—seven hundred of them and three hundred concubines—whom Solomon clave unto in love, turned him into an idolater (I Kings 11:1-8). Polygamy on such a vast scale and concession for his wives to worship their own heathen gods was bad enough, but to share in such sacrilegious worship in sight of the Temple Solomon himself had built, was nauseating to God.

Thus sensuality and pride of wealth brought about Solomon's deterioration. In the Book of Ecclesiastes which the king wrote, he surely depicted his own dissatisfaction with even life itself. All rivers ran into Solomon's sea: wisdom and knowledge, wine and women, wealth and fame, music and songs; he tried them all, but all was vanity and vexation of spirit simply because God had been left out.

Of Solomon's actual end little is known. He is described as an "old man" at sixty years of age. Whether Solomon repented and returned to God was a question warmly debated by the Early Fathers. There is no record of his repentance. He never wrote a penitential psalm like his father before him (Ps. 51). We have his remorse, discontent, disgust, self-contempt, "bitterer to drink than blood," but no sobs for his sin, no plea for pardon. Thus, with such a tragic failure before us, let us take to heart the fact that Solomon's wisdom did not teach him self-control, and that the only legacy of his violated home life was a son "ample in foolishness and lacking in understanding," as C. W. Emmet expresses it.

SOPATER, SOSIPATER [Sŏp′ a tûr, Sŏ sĭp′ a tûr]—OF GOOD PARENTAGE or DEFENDS HIS FATHER. *A Christian of Berea* who accompanied Paul from Greece to Asia on his way to Syria. Mention of his father's name, Pyrrhus, R.V., unusual in the New Testament, may suggest that he was of noble birth. As a kinsman or fellow countryman of Paul, Sopater joined him in sending salutations to the saints (Acts 20:4; Rom. 16:21).

SOPHERETH [Sŏph′ e rĕth]—LEARNING. *A servant of Solomon,* of a family of Nethinims, whose descendants returned with Zerubbabel (Ezra 2:55; Neh. 7:57).

SOSTHENES [Sŏs′ the nĕs]—OF SOUND STRENGTH or SAVIOUR FROM "I SAVE."
1. *The chief ruler of the synagogue at Corinth* who suffered at the hands of the Hellenistic Greeks when Gallio dismissed the case against Paul (Acts 18:17 R.V.).
2. *The believer or "brother" whom Paul unites with himself in addressing the Corinthian Church* (I Cor. 1:1). Perhaps both references are to the same man, Sosthenes of Acts 18:17 becoming a Christian after the Gallio outburst.

SOTAI [Sŏ′ ta ĭ]—JEHOVAH IS TURNING ASIDE or DEVIATOR. *Another of Solomon's servants* whose descendants returned with Zerubbabel (Ezra 2:55; Neh. 7:57).

STACHYS [Stă′ chўs]—AN EAR OF CORN or YOKE. *A Christian in Rome* to whom Paul sent a greeting (Rom. 16:9).

STEPHANAS [Stĕph′ a năs]—CROWNED. *A believer in Corinth* of some importance, whose household formed the first fruits of Paul's preaching in Achaia. With Fortunatus and Achaicus, Stephanas joined the apostle at Ephesus and was of great assistance to him there (I Cor. 1:16; 16:15, 17).

STEPHEN [Stĕ′ phen]—WREATH or CROWN. *One of the seven primitive disciples chosen to serve tables.* Stephen was the most prominent of these. Although called to supervise benevolences, he overleaped the limitations of his task and became a powerful preacher. He was also the first martyr of the Christian Church, being stoned to death by the Jews (Acts 6:5–9; 7:59; 11:19; 22:20).

The Man with an Angel Face

The remarkable defense of Stephen in which he summarized Old Testament teachings provoked the Jewish leaders so much that they cast him out of the city and brutally stoned him to death. God, however, can make the wrath of man to praise Him, thus the prominent fruit of Stephen's martyrdom was the conviction and conversion of Saul of Tarsus, who witnessed Stephen's illegal murder, unsanctioned by Roman law. Stephen's character is worthy of emulation. He was a man:

Full of Faith—no room for doubt or fear in his heart (Acts 6:5).

Full of Grace—a gift from God proving itself in graciousness (Acts 6:8 R.V.).

Full of Power—the ability of God to do things (Acts 6:8).

Full of Light—the Holy Spirit within gave him the face of an angel (Acts 6:15).

Full of Scripture—Stephen covered history from Abraham to Christ (Acts 7).

Full of Wisdom (Acts 6:3, 10), wisdom from above (Jas. 1:5).

Full of Courage—the face and fear of man did not trouble Stephen (Acts 7:51–56).

Full of Love—the stones broke Stephen's head but not his heart. Grace was his to forgive his murderers (Acts 7:60).

SUAH [Sū' ah]—RICHES, DISTINCTION or SWEEPINGS. *An Asherite,* eldest son of Zophah (I Chron. 7:36).

SUSI [Sū'-sī]—JEHOVAH IS SWIFT, REJOICING or HORSEMAN. *A Manassite,* father of Gaddi, one of the twelve men sent to spy out the land (Num. 13:11).

T

TABBAOTH [Tăb' ba ŏth]—SPOTS. *A member of a family of Nethinims* who returned from exile with Zerubbabel (Ezra 2:43; Neh. 7:46).

TABEAL [Tā' be al]—GOD IS GOOD or NOT SCORNFUL. *Father of one of the allied kings* which Rezin of Damascus and Pekah of Israel attempted to make their puppet king of Judah (Isa. 7:6).

TABEEL [Tā' be el]—GOD IS GOOD. *A Persian official* in Samaria who complained to Artaxerxes about the activity of the Jews (Ezra 4:7).

TABRIMON, TABRIMMON [Tăb' rĭ mon]—RIMMON IS GOD. A son of Hezion and father of Ben-hadad, king of Syria in Asa's time (I Kings 15:18).

TAHAN [Tā' hăn]—PRECIOUSNESS or INCLINATION.
1. A son of Ephraim and founder of a tribal family (Num. 26:35).
2. A descendant of the same family in the fourth generation (I Chron. 7:25).

TAHATH—[Tā' hăth]—DEPRESSION or HUMILITY.
1. A Kohathite Levite, son of Assir and father of Uriel (I Chron. 6:24, 37).
2. Son of Bered, grandson of Shuthelah the son of Ephraim (I Chron. 7:20). Also the name of the twenty-fourth station of Israel from Egypt, and the eleventh from Sinai (Num. 33:26, 27).

TAHREA, TAREA [Täh' re ă, Tā' re ă]—FLIGHT or ADROITNESS. A grandson of Mephibosheth, son of Micah, and so a descendant of Saul through Jonathan (I Chron. 8:35; 9:41).

TALMAI [Tăl' maī]—BOLD, SPIRITED or MY FURROWS.
1. A son of Anak in Hebron and probably the founder of the family of Anakims, driven from Hebron by Caleb (Num. 13:22; Josh. 15:14; Judg. 1:10).
2. A king of Geshur, whose daughter Maacah was one of David's wives and Absalom's mother (II Sam. 3:3; 13:37; I Chron. 3:2).

TALMON [Tăl' mon]—OPPRESSOR or VIOLENT. A Levite porter and founder of a tribal family, members of which returned with Zerubbabel and served as porters in the new Temple (I Chron. 9:17; Ezra 2:42; Neh. 7:45; 11:19; 12:25).

TANHUMETH [Tăn' hu měth]—CONSOLATION. A Netophathite and one of the Hebrew captains who joined Gedaliah at Mizpah (II Kings 25:23; Jer. 40:8).

TAPPUAH [Tăp' pōō ah]—APPLE or HIGH PLACE. A son of Hebron (I Chron. 2:43). Also the name of a city near Hebron (Josh. 12:17; 15:34) and another in Ephraim, now known as Atuf (Josh. 16:8; 17:8).

TARSHISH, THARSHISH [Tär' shish, Thär' shish]—HARD or CONTEMPLATION. This name is frequently mentioned in the Old Testament, principally in connection with a place hard to identify. The navy and ships of Tarshish prove it to have been of maritime importance. Josephus, the Jewish historian, wrongly identified it with Tarsus (I Kings 10:22; II Chron. 9:21; Jonah 1:3; 4:2).

1. *A grandson of Javan,* grandson of Noah (Gen. 10:4, I Chron. 1:7).

2. *A Benjamite,* son of Bilhan, the grandson of Benjamin (I Chron. 7:10).

3. *One of the seven highest princes of Persia* who were privileged to enter the king's presence when they desired (Esther 1:14).

TARTAN [Tär' tan]—GREAT INCREASE. *The commander-in-chief of Sargon* and of Sennacherib, kings of Assyria, sent to Hezekiah (II Kings 18:17; Isa. 20:1).

TATNAI [Tăt' na ī]—OVERSEER OF GIFTS. *A Persian governor* west of the Euphrates river who opposed the rebuilding of the Temple, and wrote to Darius to prevent the same (Ezra 5:3, 6; 6:6, 13).

TEBAH [Tĕ' bah]—SLAUGHTER OF CATTLE, THICK, STRONG. *A son of Nahor* by Reumah his concubine and brother of Abraham. Also head of a tribal family (Gen. 22:24). See Tibhath the town (I Chron. 18:8).

TEBALIAH [Tĕb a lī' ah]—JEHOVAH IS PROTECTOR or JEHOVAH HATH PURIFIED. *A son of Hosah,* a Merarite gatekeeper at the Tabernacle in David's time (I Chron. 26:11).

TEHINNAH [Tĕ hĭn' nah]—ENTREATY or GRACE, SUPPLICATION. *A son of Eshton,* a descendant of Judah and father of Ir-nahash (I Chron. 4:12).

TEKOH, TEKOA [Tĕ kō' ă]—FIRM, SETTLEMENT. The name, not of an individual, but of *a family of Ashur,* a descendant of Hezron grandson of Judah (I Chron. 2:24; 4:5; 11:28).

TELAH [Tĕ' lah]—VIGOR or FRACTURE. *An Ephraimite,* father of Tahan, a descendant of Ephraim through Beriah (I Chron. 7:25).

TELEM [Tĕ' lem]—A LAMB or OPPRESSION. *A gatekeeper* of the sanctuary who, returning from exile, put away his foreign wife (Ezra 10:24). Also the name of a city in Judah (Josh. 15:24). See also Telaim of I Samuel 15:4. Perhaps the same as Talmon of Nehemiah 12:25.

TEMA [Tĕ' mă]—SUN BURNT or ADMIRATION. *A son of Ishmael* and founder of a tribal family that settled around the Persian Gulf (Gen. 25:15; I Chron. 1:30; Job 6:19; Isa. 21:14; Jer. 25:23). The modern Taima.

TEMAN, TEMANI [Tĕ' man]—PERFECT.
1. *A son of Eliphaz,* son of Esau (Gen. 36:11, 15; I Chron. 1:36).

2. *An Edomite chief* (Gen. 36:42; I Chron. 1:53). Also the name of a race and an Edomite city. Eliphaz is referred to as "the Temanite" (I Chron. 1:45; Job 2:11).

TEMENI [Tĕm' e nī]—FORTUNATE. *A descendant of Ashur,* and descendant of Caleb son of Hur (I Chron. 4:6).

TERAH, TARAH, THARA [Tĕ' rah, Tā' ra, Thā' rǎ]—WILD GOAT or TURNING, WANDERING. *A son of Nahor* and father of Abraham and ancestor of Christ (Gen. 11:24–32; Josh. 24:2; I Chron. 1:26; Luke 3:34). See Numbers 33:27, 28.

The Man Who Died Half Way

Along with his three sons, Abraham, Nahor and Haran, Terah migrated from Ur of the Chaldees to Haran, where he died. The reference to him serving other gods led some of the Jewish Fathers to think of Terah as a maker of idols (Josh. 24:2). Why did Terah die at Haran? Was it not his intention to go to Canaan (Gen. 11:31, 32)?

It was God's purpose to separate Abraham from his kindred (Gen. 12:1), but Terah and Lot left with him, an exodus, perhaps, Abraham could not prevent. Lot, although he reached Canaan, was a constant grief to his uncle. The death of Terah seems to suggest that complete separation unto God often means the severance of some of earth's dearest ties. Terah is also a type of many who step out for Christ but whose hopes of discipleship die half way. Beginning in the Spirit they end in the flesh. Halfway converts never make wholehearted saints. Are you at Haran, or is yours the joy of living in Canaan?

TERESH [Tĕ' resh]—REVERENCE or AUSTERE. *A chamberlain* who kept the door of the palace, and who with Bigthana plotted to murder King Ahasuerus. Mordecai discovered the plot and Teresh was executed (Esther 2:21; 6:2).

TERTIUS [Tûr' tius]—from the Latin, meaning, THE THIRD. *Paul's amanuensis,* who wrote at the apostle's dictation the Epistle to the Romans. Paul usually added his own autograph (Rom. 16:22, 25–27). Some writers have identified Tertius as Silas.

TERTULLUS [Tûr tŭl' lus]—derived from Tertius, and meaning, LIAR or IMPOSTOR. *A Roman advocate* employed by the Jewish authorities to prosecute Paul before Felix, the Roman Governor or Procurator (Acts 24:1, 2; 25:8).

The style of his rhetorical address or brief was common to Roman advocates. With his power of glib eloquence as well as knowledge of Roman laws, the orator Tertullus sought to impress the mind of the judge. With the trick of his class, he began with flattery of the judge. All of the flattering epithets of the hired orator, however, stand out in striking contrast with "the righteousness, temperance, and judgment to come," Paul later spoke about to the same ruler.

From flattery of the judge, Tertullus passed to invective against the defendant, charging him with crimes he never committed. Paul in his defense presented a marked difference between his own frank manliness and the advocate's servile flattery. Tertullus could not rouse the conscience of Felix as Paul did. "Felix trembled," as Paul pressed home the truth of the Gospel and sent for him "the oftener," we read. What a tragedy it was that Felix did not follow his Spirit-impressed conscience!

THADDAEUS [Thǎd dae' us]—BREAST, ONE THAT PRAISES or MAN OF HEART. *One of the twelve apostles of Christ* (Matt. 10:3; Mark 3: 18), also called Labbeus, or Lebbeus, and sometimes identified as Jude, who wrote the epistle bearing his name. This apostle then, was known by three names, two of which were terms of endearment used toward him from early days. In this least known among the apostles, we have a man who discovered that love is the secret of obedience and that obedience is the secret of blessedness.

THAHASH [Thā' hǎsh]—KEEP SILENCE or REDDISH. *A son of Reumah,* concubine of Nahor, Abraham's brother (Gen. 22:24).

THAMAH, TAMAH, TEMAH [Thā' mah]—COMBAT, LAUGHTER or SUPPRESSES. *A member of a family of the Nethinims* whose descendants returned from exile with Zerubbabel (Ezra 2:53; Neh. 7:55).

THEOPHILUS—[Thē ŏph' ĭ lŭs]—LOVED BY GOD, LOVER OF GOD, or FRIEND OF GOD. *A Christian of high rank* for whose use Luke wrote his gospel and the Acts of the Apostles (Luke 1:3; Acts 1:1). The term "most excellent," used also of Felix and Festus (Acts 23:26; 24:3; 26:25), indicates that Theophilus was a Roman official to whom Luke paid due deference, even though he was on intimate terms with him. It has been suggested "Theophilus" was the name this Gentile nobleman chose at his conversion to Christianity. Evidently Luke had fully instructed him in the cardinal truths of the Gospel (Luke 1:3).

THEUDAS [Theŭ' das]—FALSE TEACHER. *A Jewish impostor* mentioned by Gamaliel before the Sanhedrin as the leader of an unsuccessful rebellion of four hundred men, who were destroyed with him (Acts 5:36). The identity of Theudas has occupied the attention of scholars since the time of Josephus, who also mentions a leader of this name at the head of an insurrection. The description Gamaliel gives us of Theudas as "boasting himself to be somebody" that is, some great personage, may agree with the account given by Josephus that Theudas was the Simon, previously a slave of Herod's, who proclaimed himself king and burned Herod's palaces. Theudas was his alias to conceal his servile origin.

THOMAS [Thŏm' as]—TWIN. *One of the twelve apostles of Christ,* and called also Didymus (Matt. 10:3; Mark 3:18; Luke 6:15; John 11:16; 14:5; 20:24–29; 21:2; Acts 1:13).

The Man Who Doubted

Thomas, we are told, was not really a name but an epithet, meaning, like its Greek equivalent Didymus, "the twin." David Smith suggests that the apostle's name was Judas, but that he was named "the twin" to distinguish him from Judas, the son of James, and Judas Iscariot. Tradition credits him with the authorship of a gospel which is included in apocryphal literature.

Zealous, inquisitive and incredulous, he earned the title of "Thomas the Doubter." Because of his hesitancy in accepting the disciples' story of the Resurrection of Christ, Thomas has come down through the centuries as a typical pessimist and sceptic. But was he an habitual doubter? Some authorities suppose that the name Didymus alluded to his doubting propensities, since some versions render it as "double-minded."

Had we only the record of the first three gospels, Thomas would be to us simply a name, but John rescued him from oblivion, made him a reality to us and surrounded him with an undying interest. Tradition has it that he died a martyr.

Three traits seem to stand out in John's cameo of Thomas:

I. When he saw what he ought to do, nothing kept him back. When Jesus expressed his intention of going into Judea again, Thomas urged the disciples to accompany Christ even though it might mean death (John 11:16).

II. When he saw what he ought to do, he only wanted to see how he was to do it. At the Last Supper he acknowledged his ignorance of the place the Lord was going to and asked how he could know the way (John 14:5).

III. When he saw what it was he had to believe, he only wanted to see that it was right, and then to him there was no help for it. After our Lord's resurrection Thomas refused to believe in its reality except upon conditions which he himself laid down. How stirring was his confession of faith once convinced of the Resurrection (John 20:28; 21:2).

TIBERIUS [Tī bē' rĭ ŭs]—SON OF TIBER. *The stepson of Augustus* and third Emperor of Rome, A.D. 14–37 (Luke 3:1). His full name was Tiberius Caesar Augustus. A Souter reminds us that Tiberius was "an able general and a competent Emperor, but the unhappy experiences of his early life made him suspicious and timorous, and he put many of his rivals or supposed rivals to death. In his later years he was much under the influence of a villainous schemer, Sejamus."

TIBNI [Tĭb' nī]—INTELLIGENT or STRAW. *A son of Ginath,* who disputed the throne for four years with Zimri or Omri (I Kings 16:21-23).

TIDAL [Tī' dal]—BREAKS THE YOKE or RENOWN. *A king of Goüm or Goyim,* confederate with Chedorlaomer, Amraphel and Arioch, who invaded the cities of the plain in Abraham's time (Gen. 14:1-9). He is identified as Tudhal, king of Gutium.

TIGLATH-PILESER, TILGATH-PILNESER [Tĭg' lath-pĭ lē' zer, Tĭl' gath-pĭl nĕ' zer]—HINDERS, BINDS or MY STRENGTH IS THE GOD NINIB. *An Assyrian king* who reigned 745-727 B.C. Probably the Pul of II Kings 15:19, 29; 16:7, 10; I Chronicles 5:6, 26; II Chronicles 28:20. His reign was an active and important one, and his expeditions were most successful. He probably died when making one of them. The reader should consult both Biblical and secular history for a full account of this Babylonian monarch's exploits.

TIKVAH, TIKVATH [Tĭk' vah, Tĭk' văth]—STRENGTH or EXPEC-TATION.
1. *Father of Shallum,* husband of Huldah the prophetess (II Kings 22:14; II Chron. 34:22). Also called Tokhath.
2. *The father of Jahaziah* who recorded those who had married foreign wives (Ezra 10:15).

TILON [Tī' lon] —SCORN. *A son of Shimon,* whose registry was with the tribe of Judah through Caleb the son of Jephunneh (I Chron. 4:20).

TIMAEUS [Tī mae' us]—HIGHLY PRIZED. *Father of the blind beggar,* Bartimeus, who received his sight from Christ at Jericho (Mark 10:46).

TIMNA, TIMNAH [Tĭm' nä, Tĭm' nah]—RESTRAINING or INACCES-SIBLE.
1. *A chief of Edom* descended from Esau (Gen. 36:40; I Chron. 1:51).
2. *A son of Eliphaz,* son of Esau (I Chron. 1:36). Also the name of a concubine of Eliphaz son of Esau (Gen. 36:12), and also of a daughter of Seir the Horite, and sister of Lotan (Gen. 36:22; I Chron. 1:39). Timnah is likewise the name of a city in Judah, now called Tibneh (Josh. 15:10, 57; II Chron. 28:18).

TIMON [Tī' mon]—HONORABLE or DEEMED WORTHY. *One of the*

seven chosen to relieve the apostles of semi-secular work in the Early Church (Acts 6:5).

TIMOTHEUS, TIMOTHY [Tǐ mǒ' the ŭs, Tǐm' o thy̆]—HONORED OF GOD, WORSHIPING GOD or VALUED OF GOD. *A young man of Lystra,* son of Eunice, a Jewess, by a Greek father who was probably dead when Paul first visited the home (Acts 16:1).

The Man Who Confessed a Good Confession

As Paul contributes a full portrait of his spiritual son, many years his junior, let us string together the salient features of Timothy.

I.   He was the child of godly heritage (II Tim. 1:5). His mother was a Christian Jewess and the daughter of another devout Jewess, Lois. His Greek father's name is unknown. It may be that Eunice became a Christian when Paul visited Lystra, a town not far from Paul's birthplace, Tarsus.

II.   He was a youthful reader of Scripture (II Tim. 3:15). From a "babe" he had had knowledge of the Truth. How blessed children are if cradled in the things of God!

III.   He was Paul's child in the faith (I Cor. 4:17; I Tim. 1:2; II Tim. 1:2). Probably Paul, a visitor of Timothy's house, led the young lad to Christ during his ministry in Iconium and Lystra since he refers to his persecutions there, which Timothy himself knew about (II Tim. 3:10, 11). One writer suggests that when Paul recovered from his stoning at Lystra it was in Timothy's home he found shelter and succor.

IV.   He was ordained as a minister of the Gospel (I Tim. 4:14; II Tim. 1:6, 7). Conscious of Timothy's unique gifts, especially of evangelism (Rom. 16:21; II Tim. 4:5), it was fitting that Paul should choose him as a companion and fellow-worker. Faithfully he served Paul "as a son with his father," in the furtherance of the Gospel (Phil. 2:22). How indispensable he became to the apostle (Acts 17:14, 15; 18:5; 20:4)! Paul had no other companion so "like-minded" as Timothy, who enjoyed Paul's constant instruction (II Tim. 2:3; 3:14).

V.   He was an ambassador charged with difficult tasks. The responsible and delicate mission of restoring a backsliding church required both gift and grace (I Cor. 14:17), as did the comfort of believers in the midst of tribulation (I Thess. 3:2).

VI.   He was co-sufferer with Paul in the afflictions of the Gospel (II Tim. 1:8). Tradition says that Timothy died as a martyr for his faithfulness as a bishop in the reign of Domitian or Nerva. While attempting to stop an indecent heathen procession during the Festival of Diana, this God-honoring minister sealed his testimony with his blood. The two epistles Paul addressed to Timothy are rich in their pastoral counsel.

TIRAS [Tǐ' ras]—DESIRE OF PARENTS. *A son of Japheth* and founder of a tribal family in Thracia (Gen. 10:2; I Chron. 1:5).

TIRHAKAH [Tûr' ha kah]—EXALTED. *A king of Cush,* the third and last king of the twentieth dynasty, and successor of Sevechus. Also known as Tarakos. He was contemporary with king Hezekiah (II Kings 19:9; Isa. 37:9).

TIRHANAH [Tûr' ha nah]—KINDNESS. *A son of Caleb,* brother of Jerahmeel, by Maacah his concubine (I Chron. 2:48).

TIRIA [Tûr' I ă]—FOUNDATION. *A son of Jehaleleel,* a descendant of Judah through Caleb son of Jephunneh (I Chron. 4:16).

TIRSHATHA [Tûr' sha thă]—REVERENCE or BEHOLDING THE TIME. *The Persian title given to Zerubbabel* and Nehemiah as governors of Judah under the king of Persia. The Persian word means "His Excellency" or "His Reverence" (Ezra 2:63; Neh. 7:65, 70; 8:9; 10:1).

TITUS [Tī' tus]—HONORABLE FROM "I HONOR." *Titus was born of Gentile parents, and was a convert from heathenism.* It is more than likely that Paul led him to Christ (Gal. 2:3; Titus 1:4).

The Man Who Refreshed His Master

There seemed to have been a peculiar bond of affection between Paul and his Grecian convert. How Paul loved him and appreciated his trusted companionship (II Cor. 7:6, 13)! What an inspiration he was to Paul on several of his journeys (Gal. 2:1, 3)! In II Corinthians Paul mentions Titus some nine times. Paul sent Titus to Corinth as his delegate. Paul anxiously awaited the return of Titus, and he refreshed the spirit of the apostle both by his presence and the good news he brought from Corinth (II Cor. 2:12, 14).

In the precious epistle Paul sent to Titus, we learn more facts about the loving co-operation between these two noble men. When Paul was released from prison, Titus accompanied him on a visit to Crete, Paul leaving him there to assist the Church in a fourfold way:

I.   Set in order things that were wanting.
II. Ordain elders in every city.
III. Avoid unprofitable discussion.
IV. Duly assert his authority (Titus 1:5; 2:1; 3:9, 15).

It may be that Paul sent his epistle to Titus by the hands of Zenas and Apollos (3:13), to assist him in the difficult task at Crete.

Paul then wanted Titus to join him for the winter in Nicopolis (3:12). Titus was with the apostle during part of his second imprisonment in Rome (II Tim. 4:10). Both men were sustained in their arduous labors by "the blessed hope" (Titus 2:13).

A godly man of Corinth is spoken of as Titus Justus (Acts 18:7, R.V.). Titus himself is not mentioned directly in the Acts. Doubtless he was included in the "certain others" in Acts 15:2.

TOAH [Tŏ' ah]—DEPRESSION or HUMILITY. *A Kohathite Levite,*

father of Eliel and grandfather of Jeroham, who was the grandfather of the prophet Samuel (I Chron. 6:34). Called Tohu in I Samuel 1:1.

TOB-ADONIJAH [Tŏb'-ad o nī' jah]—GOOD IS MY LORD JEHOVAH or MY GOOD GOD. *One of the Levites sent by Jehoshaphat* to teach the law to the people in the cities of Judah (II Chron. 17:8).

TOBIAH, TOBIJAH [Tō bī' ah, Tō bī' jah]—JEHOVAH IS GOOD.
1. *A Levite* sent by Jehoshaphat to instruct the people of Judah (II Chron. 17:8).
2. *A founder* of a tribal family the descendants of which returned from exile but were unable to trace their genealogy (Ezra 2:60; Neh. 7:62).
3. *An Ammonite* who with Sanballat and others ridiculed the efforts of the Jews to rebuild the wall of Jerusalem (Neh. 2:10; 4:3, 7). This enemy of Nehemiah and of the Jews was silenced by the diligence of the people.
4. *A chief man* whose posterity returned from exile (Zech. 6:10, 14). He it was who obtained the gold and silver for Joshua's crown.

TOGARMAH [Tō gär' mah]—ALL BONE or STRONG. *The third son of Gomer,* son of Japheth, his brothers being Ashkenaz and Riphath (Gen. 10:3; I Chron. 1:6; Ezek. 27:14; 38:6).
Perhaps there is prophetic significance attached to Togarmah and "the house of Togarmah of the north quarters, and all his bands" (Ezek. 38:6). Jewish writers of the past usually wrote of the "Turks" as Togarmah, and the Armenians as "The House of Targon." It is not difficult, therefore, to identify Togarmah as Armenia or Turkey, the people of which assert their descendancy from Targon, or the Togarmah of Scripture.
The ultimate alliance of Turkey, according to prophecy, is with the Northern Confederacy Ezekiel defines. Dr. Sale-Harrison observes: "It is interesting to note that in Scripture "The King of the North" is called "The Old Assyrian" and apparently arises out of the present "Turkish territory." In the final alignment of the nations then, Togarmah will be allied with the north.

TOHU [Tō' hu]—HUMILITY, DEPRESSION or THAT LIVES. *A Kohathite,* a son of Zuph, ancestor of Samuel (I Sam. 1:1). Called Nahath in I Chronicles 6:26, and Toah in I Chronicles 6:34.

TOI, TOU [Tō' ī, Tō' ū]—WANDERING or ERROR. *A king of Hamath* on the Orontes in David's time, who congratulated David on his defeat of a common foe, Hadadezer (II Sam. 8:9, 10; I Chron. 18:9, 10).

TOLA [Tō' lä]—SCARLET, FROM THE COLOR OF A WORM.

1. *A son of Issachar* and founder of a tribal family (Gen. 46:13; Num. 26:23; I Chron. 7:1, 2).

2. *The son of Puah* of the tribe of Issachar. This Tola, sometimes identified with the first one, was the first of the five minor Judges, and judged Israel for twenty-three years. He lived and died at Shamar (Judg. 10:1, 2).

TROPHIMUS [Trŏph' Ĭ mŭs]—NOURISHING or WELL EDUCATED. *A believer living in Ephesus,* who with others accompanied Paul to Jerusalem (Acts 20:4; 21:29; II Tim. 4:20). Trophimus was falsely accused by the Jewish leaders who, seeing him with Paul, hastily concluded that he had brought his missionary companion into the inner court of the Temple which non-Jews were not allowed to enter. The last glimpse we have of Trophimus was when Paul left him at Miletus sick. The apostle who had the gift of healing could do nothing for his sick friend—a fact quack faith healers should note.

TUBAL [Tōō' bal]—WORLDLY POSSESSIONS or FLOWING FORTH. *A son of Japheth* (Gen. 10:2; I Chron. 1:5). Also the name of a country in Asia Minor mentioned in connection with Meshech (Isa. 66:19; Ezek. 27:13; 32:26; 38:2, 3; 39:1). This place is now identified as Tobolsk, capital of Asiatic Russia, and is therefore heavy with prophetic significance.

TUBAL-CAIN [Tōō' bal-cāin]—PRODUCTION OF FORGED WORK or FLOWING FORTH OF CAIN. *The son of Zillah,* one of Lamech's wives, of the race of Cain (Gen. 4:22).

The Man Who Invented Metal Tools

Tubal (or the Tibureni, noted for production of bronze articles, Ezek. 27:13) and Cain meaning "smith" marks Tubal-cain as "the father of every forger of copper and iron." In Ezekiel 27:13, Tubal is found bringing brass to the market of Tyre, and in Persian the word means copper. The alloy we call brass was absolutely unknown to the ancients. From the world's first coppersmith we learn that "metals and their use were kept a guarded secret in the possession of a single family, or clan, for many generations."

TYCHICUS [Tĭch' Ĭ cŭs]—FORTUNATE or FORTUITOUS. *A Christian in Asia Minor,* who traveled in advance of Paul as well as with him at times (Acts 20:4). Paul sent him to Ephesus where he delivered, and likely read, the circular letter, the Epistle to the Ephesians, to the Church there (Eph. 6:21). Then he went to Colosse and did the same with Colossians (Col. 4:7). He also had a mission to fulfill in Crete (II Tim. 4:12; Titus 3:12). Paul speaks of him in affectionate terms—"A brother beloved and faithful minister in the Lord," and able to "comfort your hearts."

TYRANNUS [Tǐ răn' nus]—ABSOLUTE, SOVEREIGN or A TYRANT (from Tyrus, meaning strength). *A teacher* in a philosophical school in Ephesus in which Paul disputed daily for two years (Acts 19:9). Instructions in the Law were given in this school by Jewish scribes. Ellicott suggests that "Tyrannus was also a physician, and that, as such, he may have known Luke, or, possibly may have been among the Jews whom the decree of Claudius (Acts 18:2) had driven from Rome. An unconverted teacher of philosophy or rhetoric was not likely to have lent his class-room to a preacher of the new faith."

U

UCAL [Ŭ' cal]—POWER. *An unknown person who is coupled by Agur with Ithiel* (Prov. 30:1).

UEL [Ŭ' el]—WILL OF GOD. *A son of Bani* who married a strange, or foreign wife during the exile, and then put her away (Ezra 10:34).

ULAM [Ŭ' lam]—SOLITARY, FRONT or THEIR FOLLY.
1. *A son of Sheresh,* grandson of Manasseh (I Chron. 7:16, 17).
2. *A son of Eshek,* a Benjamite of the family of Saul (I Chron. 8:39, 40). This Benjamite family was especially noted as archers (II Chron. 14:7, 8).

ULLA [Ŭl' lǎ]—BURDEN, A YOKE or ELEVATION. *An Asherite,* probably descended from Helem (I Chron. 7:39).

UNNI, UNNO [Ŭn' nǐ]—POOR, AFFLICTED or ANSWERING IS WITH JEHOVAH.
1. *A Levite* who was a contemporary of the high priest Jeshua (Neh. 12:9), and who returned with Zerubbabel.
2. *A Levite porter* over the choral services in the Tabernacle in David's time (I Chron. 15:18, 20). This Unni played a psaltery.

UR [Ŭr]—LIGHT, BRIGHTNESS or SETTLEMENT. *The father of Eliphal,* one of David's mighty men (I Chron. 11:35). Ur is also the name of the city where Abraham was born (Gen. 11:28, 31; 15:7; Neh. 9:7).

URBANE, URBANUS [Ŭr' băne]—URBANE or POLITE. *This was a common name among slaves,* often found in inscriptions of the imperial household. Here it is the name of *a Christian to whom Paul* sent a greeting (Rom. 16:9).

URI [Ŭ' rǐ]—LIGHT OF JEHOVAH or ENLIGHTENED. Sometimes this name was used as an abbreviation of Urijah.

1. *The father of Bezaleel,* the craftsman associated with the building of the Tabernacle (Ex. 31:2; 35:30; 38:22; I Chron. 2:20; II Chron. 1:5).

2. *The Father of Geber,* one of Solomon's taxgatherers (I Kings 4:19).

3. *A porter or gatekeeper* who put away his wife (Ezra 10:24).

URIAH, URIJAH, URIAS [Ū rī′ ah, U rī′ jah, U rī′ as]—JEHOVAH IS LIGHT.

1. *A high priest in Jerusalem,* who built an altar according to the pattern provided by King Ahaz (II Kings 16:10–16).

2. *A priest,* father of Meremoth, who helped rebuild the wall of Jerusalem (Ezra 8:33; Neh. 3:4, 21).

3. *A priest* who stood with Ezra as he read the law and addressed the people (Neh. 8:4).

4. *A priest* whom Isaiah deemed worthy to act as a witness. He is described as "a faithful witness" (Isa. 8:2). See Revelation 1:4; 2:13.

5. *A prophet,* the son of Shemaiah of Kirjath-jearim, whom Jehoiakin sent for into Egypt and slew him (Jer. 26:20–23).

6. *Uriah,* or Urias (Matt. 1:6) was also the name of the Hittite, husband of Bath-sheba, and one of David's thirty heroes (II Sam. 11; 12:9–15; 23:39; I Kings 15:5; I Chron. 11:41).

As David's general, Uriah distinguished himself by his loyalty and bravery in the army of the king. Alas, Uriah was barbarously, even murderously treated by the monarch he served! Failing to use Uriah as a shield for his sin against Uriah and Bath-sheba his wife, David had him killed in battle.

Thomas Goodwin points out that it was the "matter of Uriah," even more than the matter of Bath-sheba, that awakened the anger of the Lord against David. That is to say, it was David's sin of deliberation and determination, rather than his sin of sudden and intoxicating passion. But both sins matter and earn the judgment of God. Uriah had every right to disobey David in his deceitful commands. Through Nathan, the adulterer and murderer was brought back to God and wrote his confession in a penitential psalm (Ps. 51).

URIEL [Ū′ rĭ el]—A LIGHT, FLAME OF GOD or GOD IS MY LIGHT OR FIRE.

1. *A Levite of the family of Kohath,* son of Tahath, of the house of Izhar (I Chron. 6:24; 15:5, 11).

2. *A man of Gibeah,* father of Michaiah, one of Rehoboam's wives (II Chron. 13:2).

In the Apocrypha Uriel is one of four archangels responsible for the luminaries of heaven, and the angel with whom Jacob wrestled.

UTHAI [Ū′ tha ĭ]—JEHOVAH IS HELP.

1. *A son of Ammihud,* a man of Judah of the family of Perez or Pharez, who lived in Jerusalem (I Chron. 9:4).

2.   *A son of Bigvai,* who returned with Ezra from exile to Jerusalem (Ezra 8:14).

UZ [Ŭz]—FIRMNESS.
1.   *A son of Aram* and grandson of Shem (Gen. 10:23; I Chron. 1:17).
2.   *A son of Dishan,* a Horite in the land of Edom (Gen. 36:28; I Chron. 1:42). Uz is also the name of the land where Job was born and lived, and was part of the great Arabian desert running into Chaldea (Job 1:1; Jer. 25:20; Lam. 4:21).

UZAI [Ŭ' za ī]—HOPED FOR.   *Father of Palal* who helped to rebuild the damaged wall of Jerusalem (Neh. 3:25).

UZAL [Ŭ' zal]—A WANDERER.   *The sixth son of Joktan,* of the family of Shem, who settled in South Arabia, where the kings of Yemen dwelt (Gen. 10:27; I Chron. 1:21; Ezek. 27:19).

UZZA, UZZAH [Ŭz' zȧ, Ŭz' zah]—STRENGTH.
1.   *A son of Abinadab* who died for touching the Ark (II Sam. 6:3–8; I Chron. 13:7–11).   Perez-uzzah means "the breach of Uzzah."
2.   *A son of Shimei,* a Merarite (I Chron. 6:29).
3.   *A Benjamite,* brother of Ahihud, a son or descendant of Ehud (I Chron. 8:7).
4.   *Founder of a family of Nethinims* who returned from exile with Zerubbabel (Ezra 2:49; Neh. 7:51).
5.   *Owner of the garden in which Manasseh and Amon, kings of Judah,* were buried (II Kings 21:18, 26).

UZZI [Ŭz' zī]—THE MIGHT OF JEHOVAH.
1.   *A son of Bukki* and father of Zerahiah. Also a descendant of Aaron (I Chron. 6:5, 6, 51; Ezra 7:4).
2.   *A grandson of Issachar* and father of Izrahiah, and head of his father's house (I Chron. 7:2, 3).
3.   *A son of Bela,* Benjamin's son, and head of his house (I Chron. 7:7).
4.   *The father of Elah,* a Benjamite (I Chron. 9:8).
5.   *An overseer of the Levites* in Jerusalem after the exile (Neh. 11:22).
6.   *A priest of the family of Jedaiah* in the days of the high priest Joiakim (Neh. 12:19, 42).

UZZIA [Ŭz zī' ȧ]—MIGHT OF JEHOVAH.   *An Asherite,* and one of David's mighty men (I Chron. 11:44).

UZZIAH [Ŭz zī' ah]—STRENGTH OF THE LORD.
1.   *A son of Uriel,* a Kohathite (I Chron. 6:24).

2. *The father of Jehonathan*, keeper of David's storehouses (I Chron. 27:25).

3. *A priest*, son of Harim, who put away his foreign wife (Ezra 10:21).

4. *The father of Athaniah*, who returned with other exiles to Jerusalem (Neh. 11:4).

5. *The son of Amaziah* and father of Jotham, king of Judah.

The Man Who Became a Leper through Pride

This renowned Uzziah, or Azariah, as he is sometimes called, demands more attention (II Kings 15:13, 30–34; II Chron. 26; 27:2; Isa. 1:1; 6:1; 7:1; Hos. 1:1; Amos 1:1; Zech. 14:5). His story can be gathered around three aspects:

I. His prosperity. Uzziah ascended the throne at the age of sixteen years, and it is said that "his mother's name also was Jecoliah of Jerusalem." These words, "his mother's name," are found about thirty times in Kings and Chronicles, and seem to indicate that the mother largely determined the character and conduct of the son. See II Kings 8:26; 12:1; 14:2.

Of Uzziah it is written that "as long as he sought the Lord, God made him to prosper" (see I Chron. 28:9; Ps. 69:32). As a king of Judah, Uzziah is remembered principally for the era of prosperity which prevailed during his reign. He reigned for fifty-two years, and a graphic account of what he accomplished for Judah has been preserved (II Chron. 26). Under Uzziah, Jerusalem was adorned with many and costly improvements, to which her citizens pointed with patriotic pride.

II. His pride. God finds it difficult to entrust prosperity to many of His people. It turns their heads and leads to pride as with Uzziah, of whom it is also said, "When he was strong, his heart was lifted up to his destruction." The king's special sin was a rash intrusion into the priest's office, and in this he was a type of the antichrist of the last days (Ex. 30:7, 8; Dan. 11:36, 37; II Thess. 2:3, 4). The king usurped the function of the chief priest and offered incense. Religiously, Uzziah is classed among the good kings (II Kings 15:1, 3), and had he been content to remain a good king, all would have been well.

III. His punishment. For his intrusion into the sacred duties of the priesthood, Uzziah was smitten with leprosy, and had to withdraw from public affairs, his son Jotham acting as his representative (II Kings 15:5). The leprous condition was an appropriate expression of God's indignation at Uzziah's presumption (see Ex. 4:6; Lev. 13:3, 12, 13, 25; Luke 4:27). Ultimately, he went to a leper's grave, but in the year the leper king died, Isaiah, who had looked upon Uzziah as his hero-king, had a vision that transformed his life and ministry (Isa. 6.).

Thus Uzziah is a blazing warning against the spiritual pride that brings presumption (II Chron. 26:16–21). Such a warning is needed today when the two chief snares of Satan for the servants of God seem to be spiritual pride and fleshly lust.

UZZIEL [Ŭz' zĭ el]—GOD IS STRONG. There are six Bible men bearing this suggestive name.

1. *A son of Kohath*, son of Levi, kinsman of Aaron on his father's side (Ex. 6:18, 22; Lev. 10:4; Num. 3:19, 30; I Chron. 6:2; 15:10; 23:12, 20; 24:24).

2. *A Simeonite* who, in Hezekiah's reign, led a successful expedition against the Amalekites (I Chron. 4:42).

3. *A son of Bela,* son of Benjamin (I Chron. 7:7).

4. *A son of Heman,* an instrumentalist, set by David over the service of song (I Chron. 25:4).

5. *A Levite,* son of Jeduthun, who assisted Hezekiah in his work of reformation (II Chron. 29:14).

6. *The son of Harhaiah,* a goldsmith, who repaired a part of the wall of Jerusalem (Neh. 3:8).

Members of the tribal family of Uzziel are spoken of as Uzzielites (Num. 3:27; I Chron. 26:23).

V

VAJEZATHA, VAIZATHA [Vă jĕz' a thă]—BORN OF IZED, STRONG AS THE WIND or SINCERE. *The tenth son of Haman* of Esther's time, who shared the fate of his brothers (Esther 9:9).

VANIAH [Vă nī' ah]—GOD IS PRAISE or DISTRESS. *One of the sons of Bani* who married a foreign wife (Ezra 10:36).

VASHNI [Văsh' nī]—GOD IS STRONG. *First-born of Samuel* the prophet (I Chron. 6:28). The prophet's oldest son is also named as Joel (I Sam. 8:2).

VOPHSI [Vŏph' sī]—FRAGRANT or RICH. *The father of Nahbi* of the tribe of Judah who, with others, was sent to spy out the land (Num. 13:14).

Z

ZAAVAN, ZAVAN [Zā' a văn, Zā' van]—CONQUEST or CAUSING FEAR. *A son of Ezer,* a descendant of Seir the Horite (Gen. 36:27; I Chron. 1:42).

ZABAD [Zā' băd]—ENDOWER, HE HATH GIVEN or A GIFT. There are many names derived from this root in the Old Testament. It is associated with Zebulun (Gen. 30:20), and is found in fuller form in Zabdiel and Zebadiah (my gift is Jehovah).

1. *A son of Nathan* and grandson of Pharez, son of Judah (I Chron. 2:36, 37).

2. *A son of Tuhath,* father of Shuthelah, of Ephraim (I Chron. 7:21).

3. *A son of Ahlai,* one of David's mighty heroes (I Chron. 11:41).

4. *The son of Shimeath,* who assisted in the slaying of Joash, the king of Judah (II Chron. 24:26).

5. *A son of Zattu* who married a strange wife (Ezra 10:27).

6. *A son of Hashum who also put away his wife* (Ezra 10:33).

7. *A son of Nebo who likewise put away his wife* (Ezra 10:43).

ZABBAI [Zăb' baī]—ROVING ABOUT, HUMMING.

1. *One of the sons of Bebai* who married a foreign wife (Ezra 10:28).

2. *Father of Baruch* who helped to repair the wall of Jerusalem (Neh. 3:20).

ZABBUD [Zăb' bud]—WELL REMEMBERED, ENDOWED. *A son of Bigvai,* who returned with Ezra from exile (Ezra 8:14).

ZABDI [Zăb' dī]—THE GIFT OF JEHOVAH, JEHOVAH IS ENDOWER or DOWRY.

1. *The father of Carmi,* father of Achan. Also called Zimri (Josh. 7:1, 17, 18; I Chron. 2:6).

2. *A Benjamite,* son of Shimshi (I Chron. 8:19).

3. *A Shiphmite* from Shepham in Judah, and a storekeeper in David's time (I Chron. 27:27).

4. *A son of Asaph,* a Levite and father of Micha (Neh 11:17).

ZABDIEL [Zăb' dī el]— MY GIFT IS GOD or GOD IS ENDOWER.

1. *The father of Jashobeam,* one of David's officers, (I Chron. 27:2).

2. *A son of Haggedolim* and an overseer of priests in Jerusalem (Neh. 11:14).

ZABUD [Zā' bud]—ENDOWED or GIVER. *The son of Nathan,* a friend and chief minister of Solomon (I Kings 4:5 R.V.).

ZACCAI [Zăc' ca ī]—PURE, INNOCENT. *Founder of a family,* members of which returned from exile with Zerubbabel (Ezra 2:9; Neh. 7:14).

ZACCHAEUS [Zăc chae' us]—PURE or JUSTIFIED.

The Man Who Overcame Obstacles

Zacchaeus was the wealthy man of Jerusalem who gathered revenue for the Roman government, but who became a disciple of Christ (Luke 19:1–10). A "chief publican," Zacchaeus might have been of a higher grade than Matthew.

Although not one of Christ's expected converts, Zacchaeus had heard much about Christ and was determined to see Him for himself. When ultimately Christ came his way there were two obstacles in his way—the crowd, and his own short stature. But he quickly overcame both hindrances.

I. The crowd. It is strange that those who were enthusiastic about Christ were the very people blocking Zacchaeus' view. What a lesson for our hearts can be gleaned from this fact!

II. The short stature. The other difficulty was Zacchaeus himself. His native hindrance was his small stature, which he quickly overcame. Up the tree he climbed and had the best view of Jesus that day. If we would see Jesus we too must scramble higher than ourselves.

III. The call to discipleship. Our Lord called Zacchaeus down and invited Himself to his house. Zacchaeus was a sinner and Christ saved him. Quickly Zacchaeus revealed the depth of his surrender to his newly found Master. There came an immediate and generous restitution.

ZACCUR, ZACCHUR [Zăc′ cur, Zăc′ chur]—WELL REMEMBERED, PURE.

1. A Reubenite, father of Shammua, one of the spies sent out by Moses (Num. 13:4).

2. A Simeonite, son of Hamuel and father of Shimei (I Chron. 4:26).

3. A Merarite Levite, a son of Jaaziah (I Chron. 24:27).

4. A son of Asaph and father of Michaiah. Also head of a course of musicians set up by David (I Chron. 25:2, 10; Neh. 12:35).

5. A son of Imri, who rebuilt part of the wall after Nehemiah came from Shushan (Neh. 3:2).

6. A Levite who sealed the covenant (Neh. 10:12).

7. A son of Mattaniah and father of Hanan (Neh. 13:13).

ZACHARIAH [Zăch a rī′ ah]—JEHOVAH IS RENOWNED.

1. Son of Jeroboam II, king of Israel (II Kings 14:29; 15:8, 11).

2. Father of Abi or Abijah, wife of Ahaz and mother of Hezekiah (II Kings 18:2; II Chron. 29:1).

ZACHARIAS [Zăch a rī as]—JEHOVAH IS RENOWNED.

1. The son of Barachias, or Jehoiada (II Chron. 24:20–22). This Zacharias is the martyr mentioned by Christ (Matt. 23:35; Luke 11:51) who was the righteous man murdered by the Jews in the court of the Temple, between the sanctuary and the house.

2. The father of John the Baptist (Luke 1:5–67; 3:2).

The Man Who Was Stricken Dumb

The priest of the eighth course of Abia was visited by the angel Gabriel as he was ministering in his turn in the Temple. The revelation came to him about the birth of a son in his old age, and of his name and mission. His disbelief of the divine message was punished by dumbness, an affliction which vanished when John was circumcised and named.

In obedience to Gabriel's command, the babe was named John, and upon his presentation to God, Zacharias, by the Spirit, composed his magnificent Benediction. After this he vanishes from Holy Writ.

3. *The name suggested for John the Baptist* by his friends (Luke 1:59).

ZACHER [Zā' chûr]—FAME. *A son of Jeiel, father of Gibeon,* a Benjamite—also called Zechariah (I Chron. 8:31; 9:37).

ZADOK [Zā' dŏk]—RIGHTEOUS, JUSTIFIED.

The Man Who Remained Loyal

1. *The son of Ahitub and father of Ahimaaz,* a priest in David's time (II Sam. 8:17; 15:24–36; 17:15; 18:19, 27; 19:11; 20:25). Other references may be found in I Kings, I, II Chronicles, Ezra and Ezekiel.

This Zadok was appointed priest by Solomon in the place of Abiathar, because of his own loyalty (I Kings 1:8), and the disloyalty of Abiathar (I Kings 1:7).

Zadok was the founder of an important part of the priesthood and from Solomon's time his descendants constituted the most prominent family among the order of priests.

As a young man, he was mighty of valor (I Chron. 12:27, 28).

As a friend of David, Zadok remained true to him during Absalom's rebellion (II Sam. 15:24–29).

As a priest he remained faithful to David although his colleague deserted the king (I Kings 1:7, 8). For his loyalty he retained his high and holy office till his death (I Kings 2:26, 27).

2. *The father of Jerusha,* wife of Uzziah and mother of Jotham, king of Judah (II Kings 15:33; II Chron. 27:1).

3. *Son of Ahitub,* grandson of Azariah, high priest in Solomon's great Temple (I Chron. 6:12; 9:11).

4. *The son of Baana* who shared in the repair of the wall of Jerusalem (Neh. 3:4).

5. *A priest,* son of Immer (Neh. 3:29).

6. *One of the chiefs of the people* who sealed the covenant (Neh. 10:21).

7. *A son of Meraioth,* of priestly ancestry (Neh. 11:11).

8. *The scribe or priest* appointed by Nehemiah to take charge of the treasuries of the Lord's house (Neh. 13:13). He may have been the same Zadok of Nehemiah 3:29.

ZAHAM [Zā' ham]—FATNESS or LOATHING. *A son of Rehoboam,* Solomon's son (II Chron. 11:19).

ZALAPH [Zā' laph]—PURIFICATION or FRACTURE. *The father of a certain Hanun* who repaired a part of the wall of Jerusalem (Neh. 3:30).

ZALMON, SALMON [Zăl' mŏn, Săl' mŏn]—SHADY or ASCENT. *An Ahohite,* one of David's mighty men (II Sam. 23:28), who is also called Ilai in I Chronicles 11:29. Zalmon is likewise the name of a wooded mountain area near Shechem (Judg. 9:48; Ps. 68:14).

ZALMUNNA [Zăl mŭn' nă]—SHELTER IS DENIED or WITHDRAWN FROM PROTECTION. *One of the two kings of Midian* slain by Gideon (Judg. 8:5–21; Ps. 83:11).

ZANOAH [Zā nō' ah]—BROKEN DISTRICT. *One of the family of Caleb,* son of Jephunneh (I Chron. 4:18). Also the name of two cities (Josh. 15:34, 56; Neh. 3:13; 11:30).

ZAPHNATH-PAANEAH [Zăph' nath-pā a nē' ah]—SAVIOR OF THE WORLD or GIVER OF THE NOURISHMENT OF LIFE. *This common type of an Egyptian name* given to Joseph by Pharaoh came from a root meaning "God hath said he liveth" (Gen. 41:45). From the sound of the name the Jews felt it meant the revealer of secrets, or one discovering hidden things. How typical Joseph is of Jesus, who came as the true Saviour of the world (I John 4:14). See Joseph.

ZARA, ZARAH, ZERAH [Zā' rā, Zā' rah, Zē' rah]—SPROUT or BRIGHTNESS. *The son of Judah* by his daughter-in-law Tamar or Thamar (Gen. 38:30; 46:12; Num. 26:20; Josh. 7:1, 24; 22:20; I Chron. 2:4–6; 9:6; Neh. 11:24; Matt. 1:3).

ZATTU, ZATTHU [Zăt' tu, Zăt' thu]—LOVELY, PLEASANT.
1. *Founder of a family* whose descendants returned with Zerubbabel from captivity (Ezra 2:8; 10:27; Neh. 7:13).
2. *A member of the family* who put away his strange wife and sealed the covenant (Neh. 10:14).

ZAZA [Zā' ză]—ABUNDANCE or PROJECTION. *A son of Jonathan,* a Jerahmeelite (I Chron. 2:33).

ZEBADIAH [Zĕb a dī' ah]—JEHOVAH HATH ENDOWED, or THE LORD IS MY PORTION.
1. *A grandson of Elpaal,* a Benjamite of the house of Beriah (I Chron. 8:15).
2. *A son of Elpaal,* also a Benjamite (I Chron. 8:17, 18).

3. *A son of Jeroham of Geder,* who joined David at Ziklag (I Chron. 12:7).

4. *A son of Meshelemiah,* a Korhite Levite in David's reign (I Chron. 26:1, 2).

5. *A son of Asahel,* son of Zeruiah and Joab's brother (I Chron. 27:7).

6. *One of the Levites sent forth by Jehoshaphat to teach* the people the law (II Chron. 17:8).

7. *The son of Ishmael,* a prince of Judah, who judged cases in the court established by Jehoshaphat (II Chron. 19:11).

8. *The son of Shephatiah* and head of a tribal family (Ezra 8:8).

9. *A priest of the house of Immer* who put away his strange wife (Ezra 10:20).

ZEBAH [Zē' bah]—VICTIM or SACRIFICE. *This Midianite king* defeated and slain by Gideon is always mentioned along with Zalmunna (Judg. 8; Ps. 83:11). The death of these two kings meant a turning point in the struggle of the Israelites against their Midianite oppressors. For this reason their slaughter is graphically described, and was commemorated long after as a crisis in the nation's history (Ps. 83:11; Isa. 9:4; 10:26).

ZEBEDEE [Zĕb' e dee]—JEHOVAH IS GIFT or THE GIFT OF GOD. *The husband of Salome and father of James and John,* two of the apostles. Since he is referred to as having "hired servants," he must have been comparatively rich (Matt. 4:21; 10:2; 20:20; 26:37; 27:56; Mark 1:19, 20; 3:17; 10:35; Luke 5:10; John 21:2). A fisherman by trade, it was only natural that his sons followed the same occupation.

ZEBINA [Ze bī' nă]—ONE WHO IS BOUGHT. *One of the sons of Nebo* who put away his foreign wife (Ezra 10:43).

ZEBUL [Zē' bul]—AN HABITATION. *An officer of Abimelech and* governor of Shechem (Judg. 9:28, 41). Zebul was a strategist. With no forces at his command, he was obliged to use craft, which he did most effectively, in the suppression of the revolt of Gaal.

ZEBULUN, ZABULON [Zĕb' u lŭn, Zăb' u lŏn]—DWELLING or WISHED FOR HABITATION.
The Man of the Open Door
The tenth son of Jacob and the sixth of Leah (Gen. 30:20). He was progenitor of three tribal families through his three sons, Sered, Elon and Jahleel, who went down into Egypt with the other sons and grandsons of Jacob (Gen. 46:14; 49:13; Josh. 19:10; Rev. 7:8). Zebulun became the commercial tribe, and one of the few tribes from which there was an opening by way of the sea to the vast world

beyond. By maintaining this open door, the people were able to bring in the treasures of the deep (Deut. 33:19).

This mercantile tribe had the opportunity of being a missionary tribe. It may be that such an open door for usefulness was in the mind of Moses when he said of Zebulun, and her neighbor Issachar, "They shall call the people unto the mountain; there shall they offer sacrifices of righteousness" (Deut. 33:19). The Bible speaks of other open doors (I Cor. 16:9; Rev. 3:8).

The suggestive name of Zebulun meaning "to dwell," may have come about through Leah saying, "Now will my husband dwell with me." Is not the Lord Himself a place for the saint to dwell (I Kings 8:13)? Zebulun became the earthly habitation for the Lord of Glory as prophesied by Isaiah of old (Isa. 9:1-7). Zebul is used of God's dwelling in the Temple (II Chron. 6:2) and of heaven (Isa. 63:15).

ZECHARIAH, ZECHER [Zĕch a rī'ah]—JEHOVAH REMEMBERS or JEHOVAH IS RENOWNED.

The Man Who Preached Hope and Mercy

1. *The prophet in Judah,* whose Spirit-inspired book is the eleventh among the Minor Prophets (Ezra 5:1; 6:14; Zech. 1:1; 7:1; 7:8).

Among the many bearing the name of Zechariah, the one who wrote the Book of Zechariah, was, like Haggai, a prophet of the Restoration. As a son of the priest named Iddo (Neh. 12:4), Zechariah was of priestly descent, and likely a priest himself. Doubtless he was born in Babylon and exercised his ministry in times of political turbulence and great unrest. His call was one for righteousness in home life, in the political arena and in worship.

Zechariah's mission was of a varied nature. He had to:

I. Arouse the people to activity in rebuilding the Temple.

II. Restore the theocratic spirit or recognition of God-government.

III. Rekindle the nation's faith and hope during the coming desolation.

IV. Reorganize the true worship of God.

V. Remove idolatry from the nation.

As "the prophet of hope and mercy" Zechariah has given us a series of eight night visions which portrayed the final restoration of Israel and the security and blessing which will be their portion when the Lord reigns in their midst. The prophet uses the personal pronoun freely and is always careful to date his oracles. Note:

The scouts of Jehovah; He watches over His own (Zech. 1:7-17).
The four horns; enemies are destroyed (Zech. 1:18-21).
God is surveyor; enlargement and security (Zech. 2:1-8).
Joshua consecrated; righteousness restored (Zech. 3).
The lampstand; the sufficiency of grace (Zech. 4).
The flying roll; sinners judged (Zech. 5:1-4).

The woman; sin removed (Zech. 5–11).

The four chariots; judgment begins (Zech. 6:1–8).

One or two unique features of the Book of Zechariah are worthy of mention. His references to Christ are numerous and detailed. Next to Isaiah, Zechariah carries the most frequent prophecies of the Messiah, especially to Him as the suffering King. The prophet depicts Him as:

The meek King (Zech. 9:9 with Matt. 21:5; John 12:13).

The One sold for thirty pieces of silver (Zech. 11:13 with Matt. 26:15).

The pierced Saviour (Zech. 12:10 with John 19:37).

The smitten Shepherd (Zech. 13:7 with Matt. 26:31; Mark 14:27).

Zechariah is the first of the prophets to mention Satan. He recognized sin as an independent working power and personifies sin in the woman of his vision.

Numerous lessons can be gleaned from this Old Testament prophet who saw Christ's day and rejoiced.

Calamity should not create despondency but inspire wisdom.

A lost vocation can be restored.

All past guilt can be atoned for.

The will of God abides and prevails.

The servant dies but the Master lives and His work continues.

The supplies of divine grace are continuous and abundant.

Fasting and feasting are nothing in themselves.

Faith and faithfulness are everything.

The key to the eastern situation is the Jew.

Many other Zechariahs are to be found in the Bible's vast portrait gallery of men.

2. *A chief Reubenite* when genealogies were prepared (I Chron. 5:7).

3. *A son of Meshelemiah,* a Levite, a gatekeeper of the Tabernacle in David's time (I Chron. 9:21; 26:2, 14).

4. *A brother of Ner* and uncle of Saul (I Chron. 9:37), also called Zacher (I Chron. 8:31).

5. *A Levite musician* in David's reign (I Chron. 15:18, 20; 16:5).

6. *A Tabernacle priest* in David's time (I Chron. 15:24).

7. *A son of Isshiah,* a Levite of the family of Kohath (I Chron. 24:25).

8. *A son of Hosah,* a gatekeeper of the Tabernacle (I Chron. 26:11).

9. *The father of Iddo* and chief of the half tribe of Manasseh (I Chron. 27:21).

10. *A prince of Judah* used by Jehoshaphat to teach the law (II Chron. 17:7).

11. *The father of Jahaziel,* who encouraged the king's army against Moab (II Chron. 20:14).

12. *The third son of Jehoshaphat* (II Chron. 21:2).

13. *Son of Jehoiada the priest*, who was stoned to death for rebuking the people for their idolatry. Announcement of divine judgment was more than the idolaters could stand, so at the bidding of the king in the court of the Lord's house he died a death similar to that of Stephen. His dying words, "The Lord look upon it, and require it," were long remembered (II Chron. 24:20, 21).

14. *A person who understood the visions of God* (II Chron. 26:5).

15. *A son of Asaph,* a Levite who helped to cleanse the Temple (II Chron. 29:13).

16. *A son of Kohath,* a Levite, and overseer of temple repairs (II Chron. 34:12).

17. *A prince of Judah* in the days of Josiah (II Chron. 35:8).

18. *A chief man* who returned with Ezra from exile (Ezra 8:3).

19. *A son of Bebai* who also returned (Ezra 8:11, 16).

20. *A returned captive* who put away his wife (Ezra 10:26).

21. *A prince* who stood beside Ezra (Neh. 8:4).

22. *The son of Amariah,* a descendant of Pharez (Neh. 11:4).

23. *A Shilonite* (Neh. 11:5).

24. *Son of Pashur,* a priest (Neh. 11:12).

25. *A priest of Joiakim's time* (Neh. 12:16).

26. *An Asaphite,* who helped in the purification of the wall of Jerusalem (Neh. 12:35, 41).

27. *A witness Isaiah used.* Perhaps the same Zechariah of II Chronicles 26:5 and Isaiah 8:2.

ZEDEKIAH [Zĕd e kī′ ah]—JEHOVAH IS MIGHT or JEHOVAH IS RIGHTEOUS.

The Man Who Vacillated

1. *The last king of Judah* before its fall at the hands of the Babylonians. Zedekiah is classed among the evil kings. He was the third son of Josiah to become king. Mattaniah was his original name, but upon his succession to Jehoiachin, Nebuchadnezzar named him Zedekiah. What we know of him can be found in II Kings 24, 25; I Chronicles 3:15; II Chronicles 36:10, 11, as well as in almost fifty references in Jeremiah. (See 1:3; 21:1, 3, 7, 8). Jeremiah prophesied during the whole of the reign of Zedekiah.

As a ruler, Zedekiah lacked the three indispensable qualifications for leadership, namely, poise, vision, resolution. He came to a disrupted kingdom, and while he meant well, Zedekiah could not keep his head amid confusion. Vacillating, he lacked the courage to labor on with a resolute heart. He was easily persuaded to rebel against the Chaldeans (II Kings 25), and under Jeremiah's advice surrendered the city to the Chaldeans (Jer. 21:9, 10).

This troubled reign ended tragically. Zedekiah attempted to escape from the disaster Jeremiah had predicted, but was overtaken and brought to Nebuchadnezzar, who slew the captive king's children before his eyes, then blinded the king himself and sent him in chains to Babylon. Zedekiah, however, died on the way.

The Man Who Was Rude

2. *A son of Chenaanah,* a false prophet who encouraged Ahab to attack the Syrians at Ramoth-gilead (I Kings 22:11, 24; II Chron. 18:10, 23). When Micaiah, a true prophet of God, contradicted Zedekiah's prediction, he struck the man of God upon the cheek and insulted him. Micaiah did not retaliate, but warned Zedekiah that he would come to regret his action (I Kings 22:11–25), which he did. Along with other political agitators, Zedekiah brought on himself the cruel punishment of being roasted in the fire by the order of Nebuchadnezzar.

3. *A son or successor of Jeconiah* (I Chron. 3:16).

4. *A son of Maaseiah,* a false and immoral prophet (Jer. 29:21).

5. *The son of Hananiah,* a prince in the reign of Jehoiakim (Jer. 36:12).

ZEEB [Zĕ′ eb]—WOLF. *A prince of Midian* defeated and slain by Gideon at the winepress, and afterwards named Zeeb (Judg 7:25; 8:3; Ps. 83:11).

ZELEK [Zĕ′ lek]—RENT or A SHADOW. *An Ammonite,* one of David's valiant captains (II Sam. 23:37; I Chron. 11:39).

ZELOPHEHAD [Zĕ lŏ′ phe hăd]—THE FIRST-BORN. *The son of Hepher* and grandson of Gilead, who died during the wilderness wanderings, leaving no male issue, but only five daughters. This lack of issue meant the enacting of a law whereby an inheritance could pass to a daughter (Num. 17:1–8: 26:33). Thus the five daughters of Zelophehad successfully asserted their claim to their father's inheritance (Josh. 17:3; I Chron. 7:15).

ZELOTES [Zĕ lŏ′ tēs]—ZEALOUS or FULL OF ZEAL. *The surname of Simon,* one of the Twelve, also called "The Canaanite" from being a native of Cana (Matt. 10:4; Mark 3:18; Luke 6:15; Acts 1:13). By this epithet he is distinguished from Simon Peter. See Simon Zelotes.

ZEMIRA, ZEMIRAH [Ze mĭ′ ră, Ze mĭ′ rah]—A MELODY or A SONG. *A son of Becher,* a Benjamite (I Chron. 7:8).

ZENAS [Zĕ′ nas]—THE GIFT OF ZEUS. *A Christian lawyer,* skilled in Jewish law, whom Paul asks Titus to bring or send to him from Crete, with Apollos (Titus 3:13).

Have you ever thought what occupations are represented by many of the men of the Bible?

ZEPHANIAH [Zĕph a nī′ ah]—JEHOVAH IS DARKNESS or GOD HIDES.

The Man of Moral Earnestness

1. *A son of Cushi,* who prophesied in the days of Josiah (Zeph 1:1). The prophet Zephaniah gives us a most minute account of his genealogy—a rare thing for a prophet! Possibly he pursued this course for two reasons:

To distinguish himself from three others of the same name, mentioned below.

To point out his relation to the great monarch, Hezekiah. The Hizkiah of Zephaniah 1:1 is identical with King Hezekiah. Zephaniah was therefore of royal descent.

The prophecy of Zephaniah, ninth among the Minor Prophets, is one of reproof and judgment. George Adam Smith said of it, "No hotter book lies in all the Old Testament." What a graphic picture of Judah's spiritual pride this prophet of judgment paints! Worshippers of God were found sprawled on their housetops worshiping the moon and stars (Zeph. 1:4, 5). The spirit of practical atheism had possessed the people (Zeph. 1:12), and their religious leaders had lost their moral seriousness (Zeph. 3:4).

Zephaniah sees no way out of such departure from God but judgment, so he announces the day of the Lord, denounces idolaters, waverers and apostates and pronounces doom on wrongdoers (Zeph. 1:7, 8). Much that he predicted has been partially fulfilled, but ultimate fulfillment is still future.

The Lord is "in the midst" for judgment (Zeph. 1–3:8).

The Lord is "in the midst" for salvation (Zeph. 3:9–20).

The present value of the Book of Zephaniah must not be lost sight of. We have:

I. The revelation of social and moral conditions.

II. An earnest moral tone and deep sense of sin.

III. The disciplinary value of suffering (Zeph. 3:7, 11, 13).

IV. The comforting doctrine of Providence.

V. Are we God's Zephaniahs—His sheltered ones (Ps. 17:8; 27:5, 7)?

Other men with the name of Zephaniah are:

2. *A Levite of the family of Kohath* and of the house of Izhar, who is mentioned among the ancestors of Heman the singer (I Chron. 6:36–38).

3. *A priest,* the son of Maaseiah, who ministered in Jerusalem in the reign of King Hezekiah and the prophet Jeremiah. This Zephaniah had the oversight of the Temple and was put to death at Riblah (II Kings 25:18–30; Jer. 21:1; 29:25–29; 37:3; 52:24–29).

4. *The father of one Josiah* who lived in the day of Zerubbabel and the prophet Zechariah, and into whose house in Jerusalem the messenger from the Jews went (Zech. 6:10–14).

ZEPHO, ZEPHI [Ze′ phō, Ze′ phī]—WATCH or THAT SEES. *A son of*

Eliphaz, grandson of Esau and one of the "dukes" of Edom (Gen. 36:11, 15; I Chron. 1:36).

ZEPHON, ZAPHON [Zĕ′phon]—DARK, WINTRY or EXPECTATION. *A son of Gad* who founded a tribal family (Num. 26:15). Called Ziphion in Genesis 46:16. The Zephonites were descendants of Zephon (Num. 26:15).

ZERAH, ZARAH, ZARA [Zĕ′rah, Zā′rah]—SPROUT or SPRINGING UP OF LIGHT.
1. *A son of Reuel,* son of Esau. One of the "dukes" (Gen. 36:13, 17; I Chron. 1:37).
2. *The father of Jobab,* second of the early kings of Edom (Gen. 36:33; I Chron. 1:44).
3. *One of the twins born to Judah* by his daughter-in-law, Tamar (Gen. 38:30; Num. 26:20; Josh. 7:1, 24; I Chron. 2:4).
4. *A son of Simeon,* of a tribal family (Num. 26:13; I Chron. 4:24). Called Zohar, meaning "dazzling whiteness" (Gen. 46:10; Ex. 6:15).
5. *A Levite of the family of Gershon* (I Chron. 6:21).
6. *The father of Ethni,* a Levite (I Chron. 6:41).
7. *The Ethiopian king* who led an army against Asa but suffered a great slaughter at Mareshah (II Chron. 14:9–15).

ZERAHIAH [Zĕr a hī′ ah]—THE LORD IS RISEN or JEHOVAH IS APPEARING.
1. *A priest,* son of Uzzi, an ancestor of Ezra (I Chron. 6:6, 51; Ezra 7:4).
2. *The father of Elihoenai,* a descendant of Pahath-moab (Ezra 8:4).

ZERETH [Zĕ′reth]—BRIGHTNESS, SPLENDOR. *A son of Helah,* descendant of Judah through Caleb, son of Hur (I Chron. 4:7).

ZERI, IZRI [Zĕ′rī]—BALM. *A son of Jeduthun* responsible for the service of song in David's time (I Chron. 25:3).

ZEROR [Zĕ′rôr]—A BUNDLE or THAT STRAITENS. *Father of Abiel,* a Benjamite and an ancestor of Saul (1 Sam. 9:1).

ZERUBBABEL, ZOROBABEL [Zē rŭb′ ba bĕl, Zō rŏb′ a bĕl]—AN OFFSPRING OF BABEL or BEGOTTEN IN BABYLON.

The Man with a Purpose

A son of Shealtiel, related to David and heir to the throne of Judah (I Chron. 3:19). He is also spoken of as a son of Pedaiah, brother of Shealtiel, who doubtless died childless, and made his nephew his legal heir, calling him his son (Ex. 2:10; Ezra 3.2, 8; Neh. 12:1). He represented the Davidic monarchy (Hag. 2:20–23) and was an ancestor of our Lord (Matt. 1:12, 13; Luke 3:27). Sheshbazzar was perhaps the name given to Zerubbabel by the Babylonians (Ezra 1:8, 11; 5:14).

Exiles, returning from captivity, were led by Zerubbabel and others (Ezra 2:1–64; Neh. 7:5–7; 12:1–9). In the ruined city of Jerusalem he acted along with the high priest Jeshua in the restoration of Temple services (Ezra 3:1–9). Ultimately Zerubbabel became Persian governor under Darius, and after much delay succeeded in rebuilding the Temple (Zech. 4:1–14). There were those who looked upon Zerubbabel as the coming Messiah (Zech. 3:1, 8–10). Because of the deep personal interest he took in the Temple it was often called Zerubbabel's Temple.

ZETHAM [Zē' tham]—SHINING or PLACE OF OLIVES. *A son or grandson of Jehieli,* a Gershonite (I Chron. 23:8; 26:22).

ZETHAN [Zē' than]—SHINING or PLACE OF OLIVES. *A son of Bilhan,* grandson of Benjamin (I Chron. 7:10).

ZETHAR [Zē' thär]—SACRIFICE or HE THAT EXAMINES. *A eunuch,* one of the seven chamberlains of King Ahasuerus (Esther 1:10).

ZIA [Zī' ă]—TERROR or TERRIFIED. *A Gadite* and probably head of his father's house (I Chron. 5:13).

ZIBA [Zī' bă]—PLANTATION or STRENGTH. *One of Saul's servants* who served Mephibosheth, but who falsely obtained half of his master's property from David (II Sam. 9:2–12; 16:1–4; 19:17, 29). Mephibosheth cleared himself of Ziba's treachery (II Sam. 19:24–30).

ZIBEON [Zĭb' e on]—WILD ROBBER or SEIZING PREY.
1. *A Hivite,* grandfather of Adah, one of Esau's wives (Gen. 36:2, 14).
2. *A son of Seir the Horite* (Gen. 36:20, 24, 29; I Chron. 1:38, 40).

ZIBIA [Zĭb' ĭ ă]—STRENGTH or A FEMALE GAZELLE. *A Benjamite,* son of Hodesh (I Chron. 8:9).

ZICHRI [Zĭch' rī]—FAMOUS, RENOWNED.
1. *A son of Izhar,* grandson of Levi (Ex. 6:21). Also known as Zithri.
2. *A Benjamite, son of Shimhi* (I Chron. 8:19).
3. *A Benjamite, son of Shashak* (I Chron. 8:23)
4. *A Benjamite, son of Jeroham* (I Chron. 8:27).
5. *A Levite, son of Asaph* (I Chron. 9:15). Likely the same person as Zaccur (I Chron. 25:2, 10; Neh. 12:35).
6. *A descendant of Eliezer,* son of Moses (I Chron. 26:25)

7. *Father of Eliezer,* a chief Reubenite in David's time (I Chron. 27:16).

8. *Father of Amasiah,* a captain of Jehoshaphat (II Chron. 17:16).

9. *Father of Elishaphat* and captain in Jehoshaphat's army who helped to make Joash king of Israel (II Chron. 23:1).

10. *A valiant Ephraimite* who slew the son of Ahaz, king of Judah (II Chron. 28:7).

11. *Father of Joel,* a Benjamite and overseer of the Benjamites after the exile (Neh. 11:9).

12. *A priest of the sons of Abijah* who lived in the days of Nehemiah and the high priest Joiakim (Neh. 12:17).

ZIDKIJAH [Zĭd kĭ′ jah]—JEHOVAH IS MIGHT. *A chief prince of the Jews* who sealed the covenant (Neh. 10:1).

ZIDON, SIDON [Zĭ′ dŏn, Sĭ′ dŏn]—FORTRESS. *Eldest son of Canaan,* son of Ham (Gen. 10:15; I Chron. 1:13).

Also the name of a famous city in Asher, now called Saida (Gen. 10:19).

ZIHA [Zĭ′ hă]—SUNNINESS.

1. *Founder and head of a family of Nethinims* who returned from exile with Zerubbabel (Ezra 2:43; Neh. 7:46). It may be that Ziha is the same person of Nehemiah 11:21.

2. *A ruler of the Nethinims* in Jerusalem (Neh. 11:21).

The Nethinim or Nethinims, meaning "men who are given," were the servants or slaves of the Temple and given for the service of the Levites (Ezra 8:20). Originally they were assigned to lowly duties (Josh. 9:23) but gradually rose to superior positions (Ezra 8:24) becoming, in prestige, equivalent to the Levites.

ZILTHAI, ZILLETHAI [Zĭl′ thaī]—SHADOW OF THE LORD.

1. *A Benjamite,* son of Shimhi (I Chron. 8:20).

2. *A Manassite,* captain of one thousand, who joined David at Ziklag (I Chron. 12:20).

ZIMMAH [Zĭm′ mah]—COUNSEL, CONSIDERATION.

1. *A son of Jahath,* a Gershonite Levite (I Chron. 6:20).

2. *Another Gershonite Levite* of the fourth degree (I Chron. 6:42).

3. *Father of Joah* who assisted in Hezekiah's reform (II Chron. 29:12).

ZIMRAN [Zĭm′ ran]—CELEBRATED OT THE SINGER. *A son of Abraham by Keturah* (Gen. 25:2; I Chron. 1:32).

ZIMRI [Zĭm′ rī]—CELEBRATED OT VINE.

1. *A prince of the tribe of Simeon,* slain by Phinehas (Num. 25:14).

2. *A captain who slew Elah,* and who in turn was slain by Omri (I Kings 16:9–20; II Kings 9:31). He seized the throne of his king, Elah, but only held it for seven days. He encouraged Israel to sin after the ways of Jeroboam (I Kings 16:9–20).

3. *A son of Zerah,* son of Judah (I Chron. 2:6).

4. *A Benjamite,* descendant of Jonathan, Saul's son (I Chron. 8:36; 9:42).

Also the name of an unknown place (Jer. 25:25).

ZINA [Zī' nă]—BORROWED. *A son of Shimei, a Gershonite* (I Chron. 23:10). Also called Zizah in verse eleven.

ZIPH [Zĭph]—REFINING PLACE.

1. *A grandson of Caleb,* son of Hezron (I Chron. 2:42).

2. *A son of Jehaleleel,* son of Caleb, son of Jephunneh (I Chron. 4:16).

ZIPHAH [Zī' phah]—LENT. *A son of Jehaleleel,* a descendant of Caleb (I Chron. 4:16).

ZIPHION [Zĭph' ĭ on]—LOOKING OUT or SERPENT. *A son of Gad,* also called Zephon (Gen. 46:16; Num. 26:15).

ZIPPOR [Zĭp' por]—A SPARROW or EARLY IN THE MORNING. *Father of Balak,* king of Moab, who hired Balaam to curse Israel (Num. 22:2–18; Josh. 24:9; Judg. 11:25).

ZITHRI [Zĭth' rī]—JEHOVAH IS PROTECTION, TO HIDE or OVERTURN. *A son of Uzziel,* son of Kohath (Ex. 6:22).

ZIZA, ZIZAH [Zī' ză, Zī' zah]—FERTILITY or BRIGHTNESS.

1. *A Simeonite,* son of Shiphi, descendant of Shemaiah (I Chron. 4:37).

2. *A Levite* of the family of Gershon (I Chron. 23:11). Spelled Zina in verse ten.

3. *A son of Rehoboam* by his queen Maachah (II Chron. 11:20).

ZOHAR [Zō' här]—WHITE, SHINING or DISTINCTION.

1. *Father of Ephron,* from whom Abraham bought the cave of Machpelah (Gen. 23:8; 25:9).

2. *A son of Simeon,* second son of Judah (Gen. 46:10; Ex. 6:15).

ZOHETH [Zō' heth]—CORPULENT, STRONG. *A son of Ishi,* registered with the tribe of Judah (I Chron. 4:20).

ZOPHAH [Zō' phah]—WATCH or EXPANSE. *A son of Helem,* grandson of Beriah, son of Asher (I Chron. 7:35, 36).

ZOPHAI [Zŏ' phaī]—WATCHER. *A son of Elkanah*, father of the prophet Samuel (I Chron. 6:26). Called Zuph in I Samuel 1:1.

ZOPHAR [Zŏ' phar]—HAIRY, EXPANSE or PLEASANT ABODE.

The Man Who Boasted of His Knowledge of God

A Naamathite, third in order of Job's friends (Job 2:11; 11:1; 20:1; 42:9).

Described in the Septuagint as "King of the Minaeans."

The three friends of Job represent three ways of solving the mysterious problems of divine government in the affairs of men. Eliphaz the Temanite is the symbol of human experience or history. Bildad the Shuhite is the symbol of human tradition or philosophy. Zophar the Naamathite is the symbol of human merit or moral law. Zophar of Naamah (Josh. 15:41) had a name suggestive of his manner. It comes from a root meaning "to twitter," and one of his faults was he dealt with profound things in a more lighthearted, flippant way than his two companions.

Zophar was a religious dogmatist, resorting to rigorous legal and religious methods (Job 11:3-20). His dogmatism, however, rested upon what he thought he knew. He advocated good living. If Job would only turn from his sin and sincerely repent, then God would pardon and restore him. With forcible language, Zophar declared that suffering is judgment warning the sinner to repent and escape heavier punishment.

Zophar himself erred in that he presumed to know all about God and pleaded the worth of human merit in His sight. So he called on poor Job to prepare his heart (Job 11:13). Dr. C. I. Scofield says that "Zophar was a religious dogmatist who assumes to know all about God: what God will do in any given case, why He will do it, and all His thoughts about it. Of all forms of dogmatism this is most irreverent, and least open to reason." Self-effort or human merit can never satisfy God or produce a rightousness pleasing to Him.

ZUAR [Zū' ar]—LITTLE, SMALLNESS. *Father of Nethaneel*, a chief of Issachar (Num. 1:8; 2:5; 7:18, 23; 10:15).

ZUPH [Zŭph]—HONEYCOMB. *A Kohathite*, an ancestor of the prophet Samuel (I Sam. 1:1; I Chron. 6:35). Also the name of a place (I Sam. 9:5). See Zophai (I Chron. 6:26).

ZUR [Zûr]—ROCK.
1. *A prince of Midian* and father of Cozbi (Num. 25:15; 31:8; Josh. 13:21).
2. *A son of Jehiel*, a Benjamite (I Chron. 8:30; 9:36).

ZURIEL [Zū' rĭ el]—GOD IS A ROCK. *A Merarite chief*, son of Abihail (Num. 3:35 R.V.).

ZURISHADDAI [Zū rĭ shăd' da ĭ]—THE ALMIGHTY IS A ROCK. Father *of Shelumiel,* the chief of the tribe of Simeon, chosen to help Moses number the people (Num. 1:6; 2:12; 7:36, 41; 10:19).

The Great Host of Unnamed Bible Men

III

The Great Host of Unnamed Bible Men

Did you know that there are thousands upon thousands of unnamed men in the Bible? Many of them can be called "God's Anonymous Men." Too often we fix our attention exclusively on the greater characters of the Book, yet the vast host of the inconspicuous and unnamed has been preserved by the pen of inspiration as being worthy of our meditation. The unknown saints — unknown, that is, to human fame—must not be passed by. While full consideration must be given to those God called into the limelight, we dare not ignore others who remain in the shadow of obscurity or anonymity. So let us think of many Bible men whose deeds are recorded, but not their names. The following list is by no means complete.

While three of Adam's sons are named, others born of him and Eve are not named (Gen. 5:4). Were they among the many who perished in the Flood?

None of the carpenters who assisted in the building of the Ark are mentioned, neither are several of those who labored in the preparation of the Tabernacle. The same is true of the overseers of the Temple repairs in the reign of Jehoash, whose honesty was such that their superiors had no need to scrutinize their accounts.

Gideon's three hundred men, valiant heroes all, deserve to be named but appear among the unknown servants of the Lord.

The three valiant men who at the risk of life brought water from the well of Bethlehem are not named. These anonymous heroes, however, left behind a stirring example of courage and of love for their leader.

Also among the unnamed of the Bible we have the seven thousand who refused to bow to Baal. God knew them but Elijah was not aware of them. If only the members of this host had openly declared themselves as being on God's side, how they would have cheered the lonely heart of Elijah.

The nameless prophet who has been referred to as, "this great man of God who comes out of a cloud, shines for a splendid moment before all men's eyes, and then dies under a cloud," is another unknown man. Heroic, he was yet human, an unnamed man whose fascinating story lies in its mixture of courage and weakness (I Kings 13:1–3).

The New Testament abounds in its anonymous characters, historical and literary. By the latter, we mean those employed in parabolic form, which our Lord freely used. Those He portrays might have been individuals He had observed. Many of these literary characters are as forceful as many of the historical ones. Think of:

The Hypocrites — (Matt. 6:2, 16; 7:5).
The Wise Men — (Matt. 2:1).
The Sower — (Matt. 13:3, 24).
The Shepherd — (Matt. 18:12).
The Brother — (Matt. 18:15).
The King — (Matt. 18:23).
The Householder — (Matt. 20:1).
The Man with Two Sons — (Matt. 21:28).
The King — (Matt. 22:2, 12).
The Servant — (Matt. 24:46).
The Bridegroom — (Matt. 25:1).
The Traveler — (Matt. 25:14).
The Strong Man — (Mark 3:27).
The Rich Man — (Mark 10:25).
The Man Journeying — (Mark 13:34).
The Creditor — (Luke 7:41).
The Good Samaritan — (Luke 10:36).
The Friend — (Luke 11:5, 11).
The Rich Fool — (Luke 12:16).
The Wise Steward — (Luke 12:42).
The Guest — (Luke 14:7).
The Builder — (Luke 14:28).
The King — (Luke 14:31).
The Loving Father and His Sons — (Luke 15).
The Shrewd Steward — (Luke 16:1–13).
The Snobbish Pharisees — (Luke 18:9–14).

The historical unnamed characters of the New Testament are far more numerous than all the named men of the Bible put together. Here is a galaxy of these anonymous men, famous or infamous as the case may be, although unknown by name:

The Wise Men from the East — (Matt. 2:1, 2).
The Sick and Lunatic Men — (Matt. 4:23, 24).
The Leper — (Matt. 8:2).
The Centurion and His Servant — (Matt. 8:5, 9).
The Certain Scribe — (Matt. 8:19).
The Two Demon-Possessed Men — (Matt. 8:28).
The Palsied Man and His Four Bearers — (Matt. 9:2).
The Two Blind Men — (Matt. 9:27).
The Man with a Withered Arm — (Matt. 12:10).
The Demoniac — (Matt. 12:22).
The Four Thousand Men — (Matt. 15:38).
The Lunatic — (Matt. 17:15).
The Young Child — (Matt. 18:2; 19:13).
The Rich Young Ruler — (Matt. 19:16).
The Blind Men — (Matt. 20:34).
The Man Who Owned an Ass — (Matt. 21:3).

The Lawyer — (Matt. 22:35).
The Man Who had a Chamber — (Matt. 26:18).
The Two False Witnesses — (Matt. 26:60).
The Soldiers Who Stripped Christ — (Matt. 27:27).
The Two Thieves — (Matt. 27:38).
The One Who Offered the Sponge — (Matt. 27:48).
The Saints Who Were Raised — (Matt. 27:52).
The Centurion — (Matt. 27:54).
The Man with an Unclean Spirit — (Mark 1:23).
The Maniac of the Tombs — (Mark 5:2).
The Executioner of John — (Mark 6:27).
The Lad Who Gave His Lunch — (Mark 6:38).
The Five Thousand Men — (Mark 6:44).
The Deaf and Dumb Man — (Mark 7:32).
The One Who Cast Out Devils — (Mark 9:38).
The Young Men — (Mark 14:51; 16:5).
The Shepherds — (Luke 2:8).
The Widow's Son — (Luke 7:12).
The Seventy Disciples — (Luke 10:1).
The Questioners — (Luke 12:13; 13:23).
The Man with Dropsy — (Luke 14:2).
The Ten Lepers — (Luke 17:12).
The Pharisee and the Publican — (Luke 18:10).
The Nobleman — (Luke 19:12).
The Unnamed Disciple — (Luke 24:13).
The Ruler of the Feast — (John 2:9).
The Samaritans — (John 4:40).
The Nobleman — (John 4:46).
The Infirm Man — (John 5:5).
The Man Born Blind — (John 9:1).
The Greeks — (John 12:20).
The Unnamed among the 120 — (Acts 1:15).
The Men Among the Three Thousand — (Acts 2:41).
The Lame Man — (Acts 3:2).
The Five Thousand Men — (Acts 4:4; 5:14).
The Eunuch — (Acts 8:37).
The Cripple — (Acts 14:8).
The Jailer — (Acts 16:27).

Paul in his Epistles sent personal greetings to many of his fellow laborers whom he knew and named. But think of those who are summarized as "the brethren" or referred to as "other fellow labourers, whose names are in the book of life." Glance over the unnamed men referred to in the following passages: Acts 17:34; 19:10, 14; 21:33; 22:25; 23:16, 18; 27:11; 28:8, 16; I Corinthians 5:1; 6:1; II Corinthians 11:32; 12:2; Philippians 4:3; II Thessalonians 3:11, 14; Jude 4.

Many heroes of the faith are named by the sacred writer (Heb. 11), but what about the others equally faithful and sacrificial, about whom the historian did not write (Heb. 11:32, 36)? Space prevents us from enumerating all the men symbolized in the Book of Revelation.

We cannot but wonder why there are so many anonymous servants. Tradition has given names to several of them such as the Wise Men, the Rich Ruler and the Two Thieves, but Scripture is silent as to their identity. Is there a lesson to be learned from such obscurity? We praise famous men, but what can we do about those who pass away with no memorial, who die as though they have never been?

It is comforting to realize that although multitudes of workers are "unknown" they are "yet well known." They are "manifest unto God," who sees that which is hidden from the human eye, and whose approval is the highest reward. Their abiding influence cannot be hid. Of the unknown, who are in the majority, J. I. Hasler says:

> Though such unknown ones may not be lights in the world which "cannot be hid," as are their more famous counterparts, yet they are like salt mingling with the mass to stay corruption, or like the leaven which works obscurely. The "Elijahs" because of their very prominence, cannot escape commemoration; the "anonymous servants" need special commemoration because of the less prominent nature of what they do. Their value lies in the silent witness of sheer goodness, integrity of character, and their faith in GOD. In their ministry in the home circle or in the Church, and in their helpful influence on other lives with which they come into contact they truly serve God. In a Kentish churchyard one such found a resting-place and on his tombstone is this significant inscription, "He encouraged others in doing good."

For ourselves, it is sufficient to know that, whether our names are blazoned abroad or unknown, easy or difficult to pronounce, short or long, full of meaning or unattractive, they are written upon God's palms and in heaven every child of His is to have a new name (Isa. 49:16; Rev. 2:17).

The Greatest of All Bible Men

IV

The Greatest of All Bible Men

Because Christ is the light, lighting every man that cometh into the world (John 1:4, 9), all the men of the Bible, and all men of all ages for that matter, are related to the Man Christ Jesus, either directly or indirectly. In this alphabetical treatment of Bible men, we purposely omitted any specific reference to Him who was found in fashion as a Man so that we could devote an entire chapter to His descent and designations.

It must be understood that it is not our purpose to give a study in *Christology*. Professor Alexander Stewart says, "He who would worthily write the life of Christ must have a pen dipped in the imaginative sympathy of a poet, in the prophet's fire, in the artist's charm and grace and in the reverence and purity of the saint." Our endeavor is to show His relation to men. Thomas Dekker wrote of Christ in 1570:

> The best of man
> That e'er wore earth about Him as a sufferer:
> A soft, meek, patient, humble, tranquil spirit,
> The first true Gentleman that ever breathed.

In the days of His flesh, Christ constantly asserted His own superior greatness among men. No man dared make the same claim. Familiar as He was with the great saints in God's portrait gallery, He could say of Himself, "Behold a greater is here" (Matt. 12; John 4:10–18; 8: 53–58).

He was greater than Abraham in the pre-eminence of His rank. The Jews boasted that Abraham was the head and founder of their race. Christ is the Head of the Church.

He was greater than the Temple in the magnificence of His glory. The Temple was the center and expression of worship. Now we gather in His name whether it be in cabin or cathedral.

He was greater than Solomon in the excellence of His wisdom. Israel's illustrious king was the richest and wisest of the kings, but both his wealth and wisdom were derived from Him who was made unto our *wisdom.*

He was greater than Jonah in the beneficence of His mission. The runaway prophet was against God blessing Gentiles as well as Jews. Christ came not to call the righteous, but sinners to repentance.

He was greater than Jacob in the munificence of His gift. Jacob gave his people a well (John 4:12). Christ provided, for all who are His, rivers of living water (John 7:37–39).

363

Christ came into the world of men as the holiest Man ever born. In human form, He was the same as other Bible men but unique in character. All the men of the Bible, with the sole exception of Adam, were born with inherent evil (Ps. 51:5). Christ was born sinless (Heb. 4:15). He was separate from sinners in that He was without inherent or practiced sin. No man could convince or convict this Man among men of sin.

HIS GENEALOGIES

Both Matthew and Luke set forth the genealogies of Christ. The Old Testament opens with the thought, "Behold, I make all things." The New Testament begins with the promise, "Behold, I make all things new." This is why it introduces us right away to the Second Man, the Lord from Heaven. The inspired historian begins with Christ's historic genealogy, for it must be made clear that He is bone of our bone and flesh of our flesh.

Matthew, especially interested in the Jew, sets forth Christ as "the son of David" and traces His lineage back two thousand years to Abraham. As the rightful Heir to the Kingdom, Matthew proclaims Christ as the King of Israel.

Luke, writing for the Gentiles, gives a careful outline of natural descendants and proves that Christ sprang from the first man, Adam. Step by step, he carries us back to the father of the human race. Prominence is given to Christ in Luke's gospel as the Son of Man. As the Son of God, He became the Son of Man, that He might make the sons of men the sons of God.

As it was common for the Jews to distribute genealogies into divisions containing some mystical number, some generations were repeated or omitted. Three great epochs are covered by these genealogical trees, representing three great stages in the development of Old Testament promises in relation to men.

Abraham to David

To Abraham and his seed were promises made, and in his seed all nations are to be blessed.

David to Captivity in Babylon

Blessings to nations should come through a king of the Davidic line.

The Captivity to Christ

As the result of their bondage, the people were cured of their idolatry. Israel was more spiritual after the Dispersion. Only a small remnant returned to Palestine. The rest remained in Babylon or were scattered abroad (Jas. 1:1).

In the fulness of time Christ came to realize all the promises made to Abraham and David and to the people scattered abroad through the prophets. The heavenly descent of Christ is told with exquisite simplicity and delicacy.

Since the first promise that the Messiah would come as "the seed of the woman" (Gen. 3:15), generation after generation looked forward to the coming of the great Deliverer. Such a Monarch was to come in the direct line of descent from certain ancient sovereigns and saints, and every Jewish mother had hopes of bearing such a Saviour. This was why barrenness produced unutterable sorrow, as the distress of Hannah reveals. Jewish mothers hoped that out of the number of their children, God might raise up one to sit on David's throne. At last, Mary was the one to be favored above all women.

The genealogies of Old and New Testaments alike then are signposts pointing to Christ as the end of the old dispensation and the beginning of the new. Specimens of depravity are dragged from the long-forgotten past to take their places among the lineal ancestors of Jesus to prove that the glory of the line is not in the line itself but in Him in whom the genealogies end.

His Names

We distinguish between the explicit names and the titles of respect, dignity or office used of our Lord. As this volume is taken up with all the men of the Bible and their names, with their meanings, it is our purpose in this chapter to indicate the expressed names of Him who spake as no man spake. The manifold designations and titles used to describe His Person, Power and Position show a fascinating aspect fully dealt with in that most useful handbook, *Titles of The Triune God* by Herbert F. Stevenson.

Jesus

We place this peerless name first because it is the ineffable name of Him who wrapped Himself around with the garment of our humanity. Other names are dear, but His is dearer. *Jesus* was the name divinely given before His birth. "Thou shalt call His name JESUS" (Matt. 1:21). This familiar name, so sweet in a believer's ear, occurs some seven hundred times in the New Testament.

The name *Joshua* is equivalent to *Jesus,* and the Old Testament warrior is a fitting type of our Lord. Joshua saved the people of Israel by leading them through the River Jordan, He fought their battles and was steadfast in his allegiance to God and His people. Jesus is our heavenly Joshua, who fought the grim battle on our behalf at Calvary, providing thereby a blood-bought deliverance for sin-bound souls. He is now our Leader, our Protector, and will never cease in His care of us until He has us safely in the sheepfold on the other side.

Among English-speaking peoples the names of Jehovah and Jesus are considered too sacred for sinful human beings to adopt, but in Spain, Portugal and South America, the people have no qualms about using Jesus as a Christian name. Among the Greeks and Scandinavians, there is no hesitancy about using Christ as a Christian name.

Christ

Pilate asked, "What then shall I do with Jesus who is called Christ?" By divine revelation Peter recognized Jesus as the Christ (Matt. 16:16). Although referred to as a title by many, Christ is a definite name used over three hundred times in the New Testament and means "The Anointed One." Prophets had foretold His coming as the Messiah and now His kingly authority is recorded. Our Lord used the name Jesus of Himself (Acts 9:5), but never the name Christ.

From Christ comes "Christian" and from "Christian," "Christianity." The Gospel we preach to a needy world is the Gospel of Christ (Rom. 1:16). As the Christ-ones we can only honor Christ by having the same power resting upon us as we seek to serve Him.

Both Jesus and Christ are combined and used as "Jesus Christ" some one hundred times in the New Testament (Matt. 16:20; Acts 2:36). Taken together, these two names imply the mystic union existing in Him as the God-Man. His work and worth are one, even as His name and nature are.

Lord

In announcing His birth to the shepherds, the angel spoke of Him as "Christ the Lord" (Luke 2:11). It is somewhat remarkable to observe that the word Lord comes into prominence after the resurrection when God "made that same Jesus...both Lord and Christ." Before His resurrection we read of "the body of Jesus" and afterwards, "the body of the Lord Jesus." Lord is a name expressing His sovereignty and majesty and no man can own Him as Lord but by the Holy Spirit (I Cor. 12:3; I Pet. 3:15 R.V.).

Among the ancients a name not only summed up a man's history but represented his personality with which it was almost identical. Hence "in My name," that is, His full name, "The Lord Jesus Christ," there is the suggestion of actual incorporation with the divine speaker.

Shiloh

The name of a revered city (Josh. 18:1), Shiloh is also a name used prophetically of Christ (Gen. 49:10). Meaning "one who pacifies," this name speaks of Christ as the Peacemaker. Christ not only provided peace by His cross and proclaimed peace, He is peace personified. *He* is our peace. Peace then, is not something but Someone.

A few writers suggest that Shiloh means, "He whose right it is." Such an interpretation, however, is not far removed from the above meaning since the right or prerogative to usher in a reign of peace is Christ's (Ezek. 21:27). During His millennial reign, the name of Christ will be as ointment poured forth.

Emmanuel

The true believer has no difficulty in accepting Isaiah's prophecy of Christ who was virgin-born. "They shall call His name Emmanuel" (Isa. 7:14; Matt. 1:23). This further name meaning "God with us" indicates a progressive revelation of the Lord. In the Old Testament, it is "God *for* us." As the result of the Incarnation it is "God *with* us," for Christ came as God manifest in flesh. He came and dwelt among men (John 1:14). Through the advent of the Holy Spirit it is now "God *in* us." "*Christ in you,* the hope of glory" (Col. 1:27).

The prophet Isaiah also gives us a plurality of names under the singular form, "His *name*" (Isa. 9:6). Actually there are five names mentioned, although Isaiah says, "His name shall be called..." We have another instance of the use of the singular form to describe a plurality of persons in our Lord's commission, in which we are instructed to baptize all believers, "In the *name* of the Father, and of the Son, and of the Holy Spirit" (Matt. 28:19). One name — three Persons. A proof, surely, of the unity of the Godhead. Isaiah's names of Christ emanating from "His name," speak of the unity of His transcendent attributes. They are the various facets of the same brilliant diamond.

Wonderful

That this word is a name can be proved by the reply of the angel of the Lord to Manoah who had asked his name, "Why askest thou thus after my name, seeing it is secret" (Judg. 13:18)? The word for secret is "wonderful," and the same word in the next verse, "wonderously."

Is not Christ wonderful in all His works, ways and words? As we meditate upon His wonderful grace and contemplate His wonderful government we can truly say, "The world has never seen His like — and never will!"

Counselor

Some expositors bring these first two names together and refer to Christ as "The Wonderful Counselor" or "The Wonder of a Counselor." The One who could speak with authority came as the Embodiment of perfect wisdom and knowledge (Prov. 8:14). How tragic it is when men fail to ask counsel at His mouth (Josh. 9:14; II Chron. 25:16)! These are days when godless rulers take counsel together to destroy God's cause (Ps. 2:1; Neh. 6:7), but His counsel ever prevails. The life of a person or of a people is enriched when His name is joyfully and triumphantly accepted as "Counselor."

The Mighty God

Faith and fear can never exist together. If Christ is received and revered as "The Mighty God," doubts disappear. No foe is dreaded when this One, whom the winds and the waves obeyed, is at hand to preserve and bless. How can we yield to worry or unbelieving anxiety if we believe that all the power of the Godhead is at our disposal?

The Everlasting Father

What grief a father's death can cause! How we feel the loss of his transient guidance and provision! But the One born in Bethlehem was named "The Everlasting Father." In His everlasting love, within His everlasting arms, within His Father's heart which pitieth His own, we have safety, rest and comfort.

"The Father of Eternity" is given as the literal meaning of this expressive name. The attribute of everlastingness is His. He is from everlasting to everlasting and He permits us to share in His abiding and undecaying life.

The Prince of Peace

Loyal hearts live on His legacy of peace. "My peace I leave with you." Christ breathes an assured tranquility into our hearts. He makes us the recipients of a peace passing all understanding — and *misunderstanding* as well! Through His finished work at Calvary He provided peace for troubled hearts. We cannot *make* our peace with God. Through the blood of the Cross peace has been made. All the sinner can do is to accept this peace.

The royal day is coming when Christ will return to earth as the Prince of Peace. When He comes to usher in His reign there will be no frontiers to His kingdom of peace and righteousness (Zech. 4:5–9).

The Branch

Zechariah had a vision of the Lord when he wrote of Him, "Behold, the man whose name is The BRANCH" (Zech. 6:12). Just as the branch is the dependent part of a tree, so while on earth Christ thought of Himself as a Branch. "The Son can do nothing of Himself." In true humility He expressed His utter dependence upon the Father.

What are we but branches (John 15:5)? As such we have nothing and can do nothing apart from Christ. The function of the branch is to bear fruit. As the "Branch" Christ brought to fruition all the promises given to prophets and kings of old.

The Last Adam

Christ is not spoken of as "the *second* Adam" but as "the *last* Adam." No further federal Head is to come. Adam was the head of the human race. Christ is the Head of the spiritual race. Mankind is divided into those who are "in Adam" or "in Christ." The first Adam was created out of the dust of the earth. The last Adam was conceived of the Holy Spirit. The first Adam was born innocent and became a sinner. The last Adam was born holy and remained sinless. The first Adam was a man and remained a man, developing human frailties. The last Adam was made a quickening spirit — a life-giving Saviour. The first Adam was of the earth, earthy and natural. The last Adam was from heaven and spiritual (I Cor. 15:45–47).

The Word of God

John alone uses the glorious name. Describing Christ's return in power and glory, he says, "His name is called The Word of God" (Rev. 19:13). It is beyond the mind of men to conceive all that is embodied in this name of His. John elsewhere speaks of Him as being the Word from the dateless past (John 1:1).

As words are the expression of thought, so Christ came as the expression or revealer of the Father. He appeared as the culmination of the revelation of the Father (John 1:18; 14:9).

How one wishes it could have been possible within the scope of this book on Bible men to have dealt with the manifold titles and designations of Christ, as well as His explicit names! One writer has suggested that there are 365 names and titles given to Him, whose name is above every name, that is, an inspiring revelation of Him for each day of the year. If, however, we could bring them all together what else could we do but sing with Charles Wesley?

> Join all the glorious names
>   Of wisdom, love, and power,
> That ever mortals knew,
>   That angels ever bore:
> *All* are too mean to speak His worth,
>   Too mean to set my Saviour forth.

Bibliography

Bibliography

Bible Character Studies

Biblical Character Studies (London: James Nisbet and Co.).

Cumming, Elder, *Spiritual Photography* (Scotland: Drummonds Tract Society).

Mackay, W. Mackintosh, *Bible Types of Modern Men* (New York: George H. Doran Co.).

——, *The Men Whom Jesus Made* (New York: George H. Doran Co.).

Matheson, George, *Representative Men of the Bible* (London: Hodder and Stoughton).

Men of the Old Testament (Manchester: James Robins).

Moody, Talmadge and Parker, *Bible Characters* (Grand Rapids: Zondervan Publishing House).

Sell, Henry T., *Studies of Great Bible Men* (New York: Fleming H. Revell).

Waller, C. H., *The Names on the Gates of Pearl* (Sampson Low, Marston, Searle & Rivington).

White, W. W., *Studies in Old Testament Characters* (New York: International YMCA).

Whyte, Alexander, *Bible Characters* (Grand Rapids: Zondervan Publishing House).

Young, Dinsdale T., *Neglected People of the Bible* (London: Hodder and Stoughton).

Studies on the Twelve Apostles

Cumming, Elder, *He Chose Twelve* (Scotland: Drummonds Tract Society).

Edwards, F., *These Twelve* (London: Alexander and Shepheard).

Greenhough, J. G., *The Apostles of Our Lord* (London: Hodder and Stoughton).

Jones, J. D., *The Glorious Company of the Apostles* (London: James Clarke).

Lord, F. Townley, *The Master and His Men* (London: Carey Press).

M'Lean, Daniel, *Studies of the Apostles* (Edinburgh: John Menzies Co.).

Smith, Elsdon C., *The Study of Our Names* (New York: Harper Brothers).

Stevenson, Herbert F., *Titles of the Triune God* (London: Marshall, Morgan & Scott; New York: Fleming H. Revell).

Concordances and Commentaries

Baxter, J. Sidlow, *Explore the Book* (London: Marshall, Morgan & Scott).

Cruden, Alexander, *Cruden's Complete Concordance* (Grand Rapids: Zondervan Publishing House).

Davis, John, *A Dictionary of the Bible* (Philadelphia: Wilde and Co.).

Ellicott's Commentary of the Whole Bible (Grand Rapids: Zondervan Publishing House).

Fausset's Bible Encyclopaedia and Dictionary (Grand Rapids: Zondervan Publishing House).

Hastings, James, *The Dictionary of the Bible* (London: Hodder and Stoughton).

————, *The Greater Men and Women of the Bible* (London: Hodder and Stoughton).

The Scofield Reference Bible (New York: Oxford Press).

The Student's Bible Companion (London: Pickering and Inglis).

Young's Analytical Concordance (London: Lutterworth Press; New York: Funk & Wagnalls).

Index of Major Characters

Index of Major Characters

This is a partial index of the more familiar male characters in the Bible. Not designed to be complete, it will, nevertheless, serve to guide the reader quickly to the listing of the character in which he is interested.

All the
WOMEN
of the Bible

All the
WOMEN
of the Bible

ZONDERVAN

Contents

ABOUT THE AUTHOR

Dr. Herbert Lockyer was born in London in 1886 and held pastorates in Scotland and England for twenty-five years before coming to the United States in 1935.

In 1937 he received the honorary Doctor of Divinity degree from Northwestern Evangelical Seminary.

In 1955 he returned to England where he lived for many years. He then returned to the United States where he continued to devote time to the writing ministry until his death in November of 1984.

Introduction

In 1956, during one of his business trips to Europe, Pat Zondervan, of the Zondervan Publishing House, and I met in a London hotel to talk over matters of mutual interest. Having been associated with both Pat and Bernie Zondervan from the small beginning of their now large publishing concern, I was always excited over any new venture undertaken. I was not prepared, however, for Pat's surprising proposal that I should author a large volume on *All the Men of the Bible*. But after a full discussion of the project, I consented, somewhat reluctantly, to the commission. At the time I did not realize that the Bible mentions some 3,000 men, but when I did I became frightened at the task of trying to delineate God's portrait gallery of male characters. Well, the volume appeared in 1958, and has gone through many editions.

The most logical companion study to follow would have been *All the Women of the Bible*, but in 1955 there had appeared a book bearing this title by the gifted authoress, Edith Deen. Published by Harper and Brothers, New York, this entrancing and incomparable coverage of the theme is the most comprehensive one extant, and one which no student of the female characters of Scripture should be without. It is superb in its classification and exposition of every known and unknown woman in the Bible, and will remain a classic in its field. Along with multitudes of other Bible lovers I acknowledge with gratitude my debt to Edith Deen for her monumental work.

Having received scores of requests from readers for a further companion on the women of the Bible, the publisher urged me to accede to his desire to author this volume. After much prayerful thought I decided to undertake the assignment in my own particular style, hence this further addition to the *All* series.

A continuous sojourn for over a year in the world of Bible women, caused one to realize how intimately they were associated with the unfolding purpose of God. With the first woman He fashioned there came the first promise and prophecy of His redemptive plan for mankind. Because He is no respector of person or sex, He used — and still uses — women to accomplish His beneficent ministry in a world of need. While it is sadly true that it was a woman who brought sin into God's fair universe, it was likewise a woman who gave the world the Saviour from its sin. Furthermore, the student of Scripture female biography is impressed with the fact that men and nations are influenced by the quality of women; and it is still true that "the hand that rocks the cradle rules the world."

Another impressive fact I discovered was the way in which women in Bible times find an echo in the traits of women today, as Dr. W. Mackintosh Mackay so convincingly proves in his two volumes on *Bible Types of Modern Women,* and as Dr. George Matheson does in *The Representative Women of the Bible.* In the latter work, Dr. Matheson portrays fifteen Bible women as representing different types of female qualities as well as of universal humanity. One of his observations is that, "The women of the Sacred Gallery were much more dependent on environment than were men; the men could seek foreign influence, the women had to wait till foreign influence should seek them." Human nature remains very much the same, as millenniums come and go. As long as history continues, women remain women, in spite of their present effort to become more masculine. Looking into the mirror of Scripture, women of today can see their counterparts both in the women whose names remain and in the lives of those who are anonymous. Unattractive women, like Leah of old, still clutch and strive desperately to hold the man they love. Others, who are beautiful like Rachel, Leah's sister, still feel that life owes them romance and happiness. This is not because of any brains they may have, but simply because of their beauty — which is still, in spite of all artificial aids to enhance it, only skin deep. Hannah illustrates both the despair of being childless and yet the grace of noble motherhood (I Samuel 1–2:11); and in the motherly advice to a son, Solomon pictures the tireless life of a good and faithful wife and mother (Proverbs 31).

Referring to the fact that the women of the Bible form a feminine picture gallery unmatched in the whole of literature, H. V. Morton remarks that, "the change, the inventions, the fashions which are the keynote of our time, are perhaps apt to make us forget that men and women have not changed much since the age of Genesis."

In *God Speaks to Women Today*, Eugenia Price deals with 26 females of Scripture, and in a most stimulating and provocative way provides us not only with vivid character sketches of these women, but also with a summary of their dilemmas so common to women in our century. This popular authoress "whose every new book makes news," also reminds us that we can study Bible women as an isolated group whose lives are lived on an island, remote from other human beings. Studying what the Bible says about them, "we also learn about their husbands, their children, their relatives and friends." How can one read all about Ruth the Moabitess, without a knowledge of her association even with King David, and his greater Son, even our Lord Jesus Christ! Woman is an integral part of humanity, and if humanity is to be purified and Christianized to a far greater extent, it is imperative to have an enlightened, spiritual womanhood. May God increase the number of Christian women through whom He can draw a sin-cursed, war-weary earth nearer to Himself!

All the
WOMEN
of the Bible

1

The Life and Lot of Bible Women

Although Bible women for the most part are shadowy, subordinate figures, particularly in the Old Testament, there were those like Sarah, Rebekah, Rachel, Miriam, Deborah, Ruth and Esther who were outstanding, each having a distinction of her own, as our next chapter shows. 'What is striking is the fact that whether the women were queens or commoners, chaste or bad, their lives are frankly portrayed, proving the Bible to be a faithful biography of humanity.

The sacred record of woman's special creation (Genesis 1:26, 27; 2:18-24), declares not only her full humanity but also her superiority to the lower animal world which God also brought into being. Woman appeared as the counterpart and helper of man, and being part of his inmost being holds an intimate relationship to him. Adam, being a collective term for mankind, includes women. "Let us make *man* . . . and let *them* . . . ." "In the image of God created he *him;* male and female created he *them*" (Genesis 1:26, 27). Woman is the feminine of man. While higher criticism and evolution discredit the Biblical record of woman's formation from the rib of man (Genesis 2: 21-24), the passage emphasizes, most profoundly, the inseparable unity and fellowship of a woman's life with that of man's. She is not only man's helper (Genesis 2:18), but also his complement, and is most essential to the completion of his being. Matthew Henry's comment on the creation of Eve is most expressive —

If man is the head, she [woman] is the crown, a crown to her husband, the crown of the visible creation. The man was dust refined, but the woman was double-refined, one remove further from the earth. . . . The woman was *made of a rib out of the side of Adam;* not made out of his head to rule over him, nor out of his feet to be trampled upon by him, but out of his side to be equal with him, under his arm to be protected, and near his heart to be beloved.

Eve, then, was Adam's second self and differed from him in sex only, not in nature. Priority of creation gave Adam headship but not superiority. Both man and woman were endowed for equality and for mutual interdependence. Often woman excels man in the capacity to endure ill-treatment, sorrow, pain and separation. Throughout history, man, through pride, ignorance or moral perversion has treated woman as being greatly inferior, and has enslaved and degraded her accordingly. Among many heathen tribes today woman is a mere chattel, the burden-bearer, with no rights whatever to equality with man.

While the ancient world was predominantly a man's world, woman enjoyed a status in Israel not generally experienced in the East. The Jews, holding to the revelation given to Moses of woman's endowments, worth and rightful position, were outstanding among other oriental nations in holding woman in high esteem, honor and affection. Christianity, as we are to see, brought full emancipation to womanhood, and wherever Christ is recognized as Saviour and His truth is obeyed, woman is esteemed as man's loved companion, confidant and, in many ways, his better half.

Before dealing with the manifold features of the life of Bible women, it may prove helpful to briefly outline the approach to women in the Scriptures. We take, first of all —

Old Testament Times

The position of women in Israel was in marked contrast with her status in surrounding heathen nations. Israelite law was designed to protect woman's weakness, safeguard her rights, and preserve her freedom (Deuteronomy 21:10-14; 22:13; 22:28). Under divine law her liberties were greater, her tasks more varied and important, and her social standing more respectful and commanding than that of her heathen sister. The Bible has preserved the memory of women whose wisdom, skill and dignity it willingly acknowledged. Numerous names of devout and eminent Hebrew women adorn the pages of the Old Testament. To some extent, a woman was her husband's property (Genesis 12:18; Exodus 20:17; 21:3) and owed him absolute fidelity. While the husband had no formal rights over the person of his wife, nevertheless, he was recognized as lord and master. By her chastity, diligence and love woman created an honorable position for herself within family and community circles.

Any prominence woman attained was obtained by force of character. There were those, like Deborah, who achieved greatness. Others, such as Esther, had greatness thrust upon them. Womanly virtues were foreign to pagan culture under which woman became subject to inferior and degrading conditions. Decline of woman in Israel was always due to the invasion of heathen influences. Morality lapsed as idolatrous customs were countenanced. "The prominence of women in idolatry and in the abominations of foreign religions is indicated in the writings of the prophets (Jeremiah 7:8; Ezekiel 8:14, see Exodus 22:18). The sordid effect of idolatrous women ruined the religious life of Judah and Israel and contributed to their overthrow."

Inter-Testament Times

During the so-called 400 silent years from Malachi to Matthew, the women portrayed in the apocryphal literature of the Jews "reveal all the varied characteristics of their sex so conspicuous in Old Testament history." Anna, Edna (Tobias 1:9; 2:1-14; 7:10, 12), Sarah (Tobias 10:10; 14:13), Judith (16:1-17), Susanna, whose story is told in the LXX Version, all typify the ideal womanly virtues of "devout piety, ardent patriotism, poetic fervor and wifely devotion." Cleopatra (I Maccabees 10:58), influential in the counsel of kings, and conspicuous for political intrigue, is a striking example of the perverted use of a woman's power.

The New Testament Times

It is from the teaching of our Lord, as well as from His example, that we gather the original function of woman and the obligation of purity toward her (Matthew 5:27-32). What an understanding of, and sympathy with, women He manifested (Luke 10:38, 42; Matthew 5:27-32)! The reverence Jesus had for woman and "the new respect for her begotten by His teaching were well-grounded, on their human side, in the qualities of His own mother. The fact that He was born of woman has been cited to her praise in the ecumenical creeds of Christendom." With the coming of Christ a new era dawned for womanhood, and wherever He is exalted woman comes into her own. From the outset of His sojourn on the earth, women were intuitively responsive to His teachings and devoted to His person.

Early Church Times

Through the examples of Jesus in His attitude toward women, and as the result of the truth He taught, women were prominent in the activities of the Early Church. Among the first converts in Europe (Acts 16:13-15), the apostles set high standards for Christian women (I Timothy 3:11; Titus 2:3-5; I Peter 3:1-6) and exalts woman as a type of the Church, the Lamb's Bride (Ephesians 5:21-33). Women ministered unto the apostles of their substance, and came to hold official positions of spiritual influence in the church (Romans 16:1). Later, Tertullian wrote of the spiritual wealth and worthiness of Christian women, and of how their modesty and simplicity was a rebuke to and reaction from the shameless extravagancies of the immoralities of heathen women. That they were among the most conspicuous examples of the transforming power of Christianity is manifest from the admiration and astonishment of the pagan Libanius who exclaimed, "What women these Christians have!"

Present Times

Through the centuries the social and legal status of woman has fluctuated. In times of fierce persecution they suffered much. Where heathenism still reigns the life and lot of women are far from the freedom and joy they experience where Christianity is recognized. From the 18th century on, women in civilized lands have experienced universal education and the right to vote, and through the impact of the Christian faith they are equal with men in the great achievements of education, art, literature, social services and in missionary activities. Christian women, in particular, present to the world morality, home happiness and piety, domestic honesty, and full devotion to Christ. As morals become more lax, and society degenerates, God-fearing wives and mothers are more than ever vital factors in the spiritual elevation of the nation. Two courses confront every woman today. The one consists of pleasure-chasing, sin-loving, divorce-exalting, and sex perversion all springing from a rejection of Christ; the other course is the noblest and most beneficial for our homes, nation and church, namely, that of a God-inspired devotion which centers in the home, husband and children, and in the Scriptures. Moral laxity among girls today, and the ever-increasing divorce rate with its progressive polygamy, constitute a call to continuous intercession that God will raise womanhood to the noble heights He intended for all the daughters of Eve.

As it may prove interesting to learn how Bible women lived, worked, dressed and expressed themselves religiously, we begin, first of all, with the institution, God originally created them for, namely —

MARRIAGE

The indissoluble nature of marriage, Jesus emphasized, is likewise demonstrated in the first man's one wife (Matthew 19:3-11). Originally, God sanctioned monogamy, that is, the marriage of one wife or husband at a time. From the earliest days in ancient Israel marriage symbolized festive joy, whether secular or spiritual, as well as the union and communion between God and His people. "I will greatly rejoice in the LORD, my soul shall be joyful in my God; for he hath clothed me with garments of salvation, he hath covered me with the robe of righteousness, as a *bridegroom* decketh himself with ornaments, and as a *bride* adorneth herself with her jewels" (Isaiah 61:10, see John 3:29). Marriage, the sacrament of human society, was ordained of God for the purpose of a husband and wife to share and perpetuate their happiness in the creation of a family within the sphere of their own love. Marriage was not meant to be an end in itself but the means to ends outside of those who are married. By God's creative will Adam and Eve were made one flesh so that the world could be populated with family units.

The Pictorial Bible Dictionary reminds us that —

> Distinctly Christian marriage is one in which husband and wife covenant together with God and publicly witness their commitment not only to each other but together to Him, to the end that they shall in unity fulfill His purposes throughout life (I Corinthians 7:39; II Corinthians 6:14). Marriage is contracted "in the Lord," received as a divine vocation, acknowledged with humility and thanksgiving, and sanctified by the Word of God and prayer (I Timothy 4:4, 5).

POLYGAMY

As civilization developed, and sin increased, man perverted the divine ideal and purpose in marriage, and became a polygamist, a man with more than one wife. Lamech, of the family of Cain, the world's first murderer, appears to be the first to violate the original ordinance, for he is spoken of as having two wives, Adah and Zillah (Genesis 4:23). By the time of Noah, polygamy had degenerated into interracial marriages of the most incestuous and illicit kind (Genesis 6:1-4). By the time Moses came to write the Law, polygamy had apparently become general, and although accepted as a prevailing custom, was never approved. The Mosaic Law sought to restrict and limit such a departure from God's original purpose by wise and humane regulations. The curse that almost invariably accompanies polygamy is seen in Elkanah's home life with his two wives, Hannah and Peninnah. The Old Testament presents similar indirect exposures of what polygamy can lead to. Failures and calamities in the reigns of David and Solomon are attributed to the numerous wives each had (II Samuel 5:13; I Kings 11:1-3, see Deuteronomy 17:7).

Under polygamy power was transferred from the wives to the queen mother, or chief wife (I Kings 2:9; 15:13). The husband had to house and feed his wives. Sometimes separate establishments were provided for the wives collectively or individually, "The house of the women" (Esther 2:3, 9; I Kings 7:8). Often wives had a separate tent (Genesis 31:33). For meals and social intercourse the wives gathered at one common table. Since the advent of Hollywood, film capital of the world, the command relevant to multiplying wives — and husbands — has been flouted (Deuteronomy 17:17). Movie manners have had most disastrous results, particularly in the matter of disregard for the sanctity of marriage. Hollywood has been described as "a town where marriages are too often tossed aside as casually as last year's Easter bonnet." The quick changing of partners is a vile principle, especially where children are concerned. What a travesty of the divine purpose of marriage it is when a woman has several children by a succession of husbands!

One of the reasons why Hollywood is a matrimonial cesspool is because husbands and wives are continually in the arms of others, making love for the screen. Not only does this unnatural association make for unfaithfulness on the part of those who make love for the movies, but tends to create jealousy and strife in the home life of married actors.

Films out of movie studios produced on TV are certainly tilting the scales against Christian morality, and constitute one of our most serious sinister evils. With such a menace to marriage and morals resulting in the collapse of a divinely ordained home life, how can we expect the nation to be strong? Much of the sexual perversion of our time can be laid at the door of Hollywood, whose terrible defiance of moral values has produced the atmosphere of immorality polluting a nation professing to trust in God.

DIVORCE

While divorce was originally instituted "to protect the sanctity of wedlock by outlawing the offender and his moral offense," and was granted only in case of adultery (Matthew 5:32), it is most ludicrous to see how quickly people can be divorced today for trifling reasons. One has read of a marriage being dissolved because the husband snored too much. The free extension of divorce to include any marital infelicity, in which Hollywood leads the way, is to be deplored. The alarming increase of the divorce rate is having a most disastrous effect upon the characters of the children of broken homes. What presently concerns us, however, is the Biblical aspect of divorce in relation to women.

The public dissolution of the marriage contract was, in some cases, allowed by the Law of Moses. But such an allowance was much abused by the licentious, who sought to put away a wife for the most trivial cause (Deuteronomy 24:1-4). To some degree a woman was the property of her husband and he could repudiate her if he found "indecency in her" (24:1). Divorce was not pronounced by any court of law. A public announcement by the husband was made and a bill of divorcement given to the wife stating the repudiation and freedom of the wife. "She is not my wife, neither am I her husband" (Hosea 2:2). The divorced woman usually returned to her parents' home, and was free to marry again. No priest was allowed to marry such a repudiated woman (Deuteronomy 24:1; Isaiah 50:1; 54:6; Jeremiah 3:8; Leviticus 21:14). The Mosaic Law refused the right of divorce to a man forced to marry a girl whom he had humbled or to a husband who wrongfully accused his wife of misconduct before marriage (Deuteronomy 22:19, 29).

Jesus taught the indissolubility of the marriage union, and affirmed that such was symbolic of the indissoluble union between Himself and His Church, just as the prophets spoke of monogamy as being symbolic of the union of God with Israel (Isaiah 54: 5; Jeremiah 3:14; 31:32; Hosea 2:19; Matthew 9:15). While Jesus recognized the Mosaic bill of divorcement which declared adultery to be the sole reason of separation, He did not make divorce mandatory. Behind His teaching on this subject (Matthew 5:31, 32; 19:3-9; Mark 10:2-12; Luke 16:18) there would seem to be the underlying principle that if a marriage is destroyed by unfaithfulness, it could not be further destroyed by divorce.

The teaching of Paul on the same problem has given rise to much controversy with some affirming that the Apostle allows for the remarriage of the so-called innocent party (I Corinthians 7:12-16, see Romans

7:2). Paul, who is the only other one in the New Testament besides Christ to speak of divorce, in no way modifies what Christ taught. The Apostle does not discuss the causes responsible for the disruption of marriage, but only the question of manners and morals *in* the relation. He nowhere teaches that a Christian partner deserted by an ungodly partner is free to marry someone else. If the husband or wife deserts, the remaining party should remain as he or she is. The Bible nowhere offers an easy road out of marriage such as is provided today. "Nothing could be more beautiful in the morals of the marriage relation than the direction given by Paul for the conduct of all parties in marriage in all trials." It is still widely held in the Christian Church that while severe marital difficulties may warrant a separation, there should never be divorce for any cause whatever.

FAMILY

Many mothers find honorable mention in the Bible. The constant reference to them in the biographies of successive kings indicates their importance as determining factors in the life of their royal sons. "The law of thy mother" (Proverbs 1:8; 6:20) pays tribute to her teaching, authority and example. Contempt for these merited the divine curse (Proverbs 19:26; 20:20; 30:11, 17). Among the Jews, women administered the affairs of the home with a liberty, sagacity and leadership unknown to surrounding Oriental peoples. Her varied domestic duties were more independent and honorable, and she was in no sense the slave or chattel of her husband. "More than elsewhere, perhaps, the family in Israel was the cornerstone of society. In ancient times in particular, the individual counted very little, the family was everything, and the tribe was only the family on a larger scale."

God's Law required children to honor the mother equally with the father (Exodus 20:12), and such joint esteem continued through patriarchal times, and resulted in a happy and prosperous home life (Psalms 127:4, 5; 144:12-15). Dread judgment overtook those who cursed their parents (Leviticus 20:9). Mothers carefully attended to their children in their dependent years, and their love for their offspring is only sur-

passed by God's love for His own (Isaiah 49:15). The Israelites were careful about the morals and religious training of their children, believing that with God's Law written upon their hearts they would be safeguarded when they came to years of responsibility (Deuteronomy 4:4; 11:19; Joshua 4:6, 21; Psalm 78:5, 6; Proverbs 4:3, 4). Discipline, though somewhat stern, was not fruitless (Proverbs 22:15; 23:13; 29:17). Paternal and maternal affection was abundant for children who were worthy of it (Genesis 22:7; 37:3, 35; 43:14; 44:20; I Samuel 1:27; Lamentations 2:11, 19; 4:4, 5; 5:13). Filial devotion was held in high honor among the Jews, and mutual happiness prevailed (Exodus 20:12; Leviticus 19:3; Proverbs 1:8; 17:6; Ephesians 6:1-3). Jesus manifested righteous indignation when the sacredness of childhood was outraged. To Him, little children were models to those who aspired to enter the kingdom of heaven (Matthew 11:25; 18:2-6; Mark 9:36, 37; Luke 9:47, 48, etc.).

WIDOWS

The lot of widows who, from earliest times wore a distinctive garb (Genesis 38:14, 19), was generally precarious and widows were therefore regarded as being under God's special care (Psalms 68:5; 146:9; Proverbs 15:25). Childless widows usually returned to the parental home (Genesis 38:11; Leviticus 22:13). Deprived of husband and protector, a widow was exposed to all sorts of mean actions and extortions, hence laws to protect her and to uphold her cause. Those who ill-treated her were punished (Exodus 22:22; Deuteronomy 14:29; II Samuel 14:4; II Kings 4:1; Isaiah 1:17; Jeremiah 7:6). The Early Church cared for its poor widows, especially if they had been notable for good works (Acts 6:1; I Timothy 5:4, 9, 10, 16; James 1:27). Perhaps the most notable widow in the Bible is the poor one who in casting her two mites or a farthing — the smallest copper coin of Herod Antipas— surrendered her all for the service of the Temple (Mark 12:42; Luke 21:1-4).

DRESS AND ORNAMENTS

Ever since the first woman thought up the use of leaves for clothing (Genesis 3:7), women have become skillful in the provision and variety of their covering garments and ornaments. Animal pelts quickly followed leaves, with God Himself being the originator of such a warm and convenient form of clothing (Genesis 3:21). While none of the textiles the ancients used have survived, the many tools employed to dress the skins and fasten them together have been found. That women had greatly progressed in personal dress and decorations during some three and a half millenniums from Eve's day to the time of Isaiah is evidenced by the long catalog the prophet gives of the extensive wardrobe and jewelry of Hebrew women. There were —

anklets, cauls, crescents, pendants, bracelets, mufflers, headtires, ankle chains, sashes, perfume balm, amulets, rings, nose jewels, festival robes, mantles, shawls, satchels, hand-mirrors, fine linen, turbans and veils.

Modern women, with all their extensive, elaborate and expensive wardrobes, would find it hard to match the feminine attire of over 2,000 years ago. The reproof of Isaiah for female haughtiness and excessive ornamentation was directed against exceptional tendencies to extravagance (Isaiah 3:16). How could the women grind meal and attend to other womanly household duties, if dressed up to kill? (Isaiah 47:2). In the light of the prophet's rebuke we can understand Peter's counsel to Christian women not to be overconcerned about their external adornment such as showy apparel, braiding of hair, and display of jewels of gold. Rather should they seek the inner apparel of a meek and quiet spirit (I Peter 3:3, 4).

While Hebrew women were forbidden to wear the same form of clothing as men (Deuteronomy 22:5), female clothing yet carried a somewhat basic pattern to that worn by men. But "there was always sufficient difference in embossing, embroidery and needlework so that in appearance the line of demarcation between men and women could be readily detected." The headdress of women was of a different quality, kind or color from that worn by men; and garments were longer than those of a man, reaching almost to the ankles. Women of moderate circumstances were able to produce beautiful garments, "the fruit of her

own hands" (Proverbs 31:19). Many articles of female clothing are mentioned in the Bible, some of which cannot be exactly identified. Undergarments were fashioned out of cotton, linen or silk, according to the wealth and position of a woman. Outer robes and skirts were made of fine needlework wrought with multicolored threads. The kerchief Ezekiel mentions was probably a headdress or veil of some sort (13:18, 21), while the mufflers Isaiah refers to were likely two-piece veils, one part covering the face below the eyes, the other, the head, down the neck (3:16-24). In early history, veils did not cover the faces of women, except when they were introduced to the men they were to marry (Genesis 24:16, 65). In the Cairo Museum can be seen the original dress of a royal Egyptian lady. A huge wig of black human hair and sheep's wool covers her plaited natural hair. She has a necklace consisting of three rows of semi-precious stones, and her garment is a single piece of exceedingly fine linen, pleated into a chevron pattern behind. Close fitting, the edge in front is fringed. Wimples, or "shawls," and stomachers — the part of a woman's dress covering the breast and the pit of the stomach, and often highly ornamented — were other parts of female clothing. Saul clothed the daughters of Israel in scarlet (II Samuel 1:24).

The modern craze among women of painting the eyelids, plucking out eyebrows and pencilling false ones supposedly to enhance beauty, is spoken of in the Bible as a device unworthy of God-fearing women. The treacherous Jezebel painted her eyes (II Kings 9:30). In these days when colossal sums are spent on cosmetics, it is interesting to find references in the Bible to make-up. Evacuations at Shechem have unearthed make-up jars as used by Egyptian women, to hold stibium, a compound rubbed out with oil or ointments and used as a powder which was applied with a brush to the eyebrows and lashes, to make the eyeballs seem whiter and the eyes larger. "Thou rentest thy face with painting"; "Thou paintedst thy eyes" (Jeremiah 4:30; Ezekiel 23:40). Describing the dress and ornaments Sarah wore as a citizen of Ur of the Chaldees, Albert E. Bailey in *Daily Life in Bible Times* speaks of her having, "at her girdle a small conical copper box with leather cover that held her toilet kit: tweezers, ear-pick, stiletto and a round-ended paint stick. More than likely at home she kept a bronze razor and used cuttlefish bone as a depilatory. When she was ready for the parade she must have beauty. Though she may have discarded a good deal of this town make-up when her husband, Abraham, became a nomad, she kept it by her for occasions. According to the story in Genesis 12:12-16, when she went back to civilization for a time in Egypt even Pharaoh could not resent her."

Among archaeological discoveries in Ras Shamrah was a necklace made up of beads of gold and silver, amber and pearls, worn in ancient Israel. These are doubtless included in the *tablets, chains about thy neck, ornaments of fine gold, chains of gold,* which the Bible mentions (Exodus 35:22; Proverbs 1:9; 25:12; Song of Solomon 1:10). Sometimes half-moons and small bottles of perfume served as pendants (Isaiah 3:18, 19). The necessary hand mirror was also thought of, and consisted of cast, convex of silver or brass. The laver of brass for the Tabernacle was made out of "the lookingglasses of the women assembling" (Exodus 38:8). Elihu speaks of the sky which is strong as a molten looking glass (Job 37:18).

Jewels were varied and abundant. Wives, and also their sons and daughters, wore golden earrings (Genesis 35:4; Exodus 32:2; Numbers 31:50). There were likewise signet rings, worn by the Israelites around the neck (Genesis 38:18), and by the Egyptians upon the finger, and in later days by the Israelites too (Genesis 41:42; Jeremiah 22:24). Gold bracelets were added to help out female beauty (Genesis 24:22; Ezekiel 16:11, 12). Nose rings or jewels made necessary the piercing of the nostrils, and rings were often worn on the toes and anklets or spangles on the ankles (Isaiah 3:18). It is said that Arabs liked to kiss their wives through the nose ring frequently mentioned in Scripture (Genesis 24:22; Judges 8:24; Proverbs 11:22; Hosea 2:13). Nose rings were also used to drag prisoners to the triumphant procession of their conqueror (II Kings 19:28; Isaiah 37:29, etc.).

TASKS

We have the adage that "men must work, and women must weep." In Bible times women both worked and wept. While not treated as beasts of burden, as they are even today in some dark corners of the earth, women had to shoulder manifold tasks. For instance, they were grinders of grain, two women working a rotating handmill together. Grinding was a woman's job in preparation for baking, and was often done during the night, when sufficient flour would be ground to last the next day (Deuteronomy 24:6; Job 41:24; Proverbs 31:15; Matthew 24:41, see Judges 9:53). It was an insulting humiliation for a man or a youth to be required to do the grinding (Judges 16:21; Lamentations 5:13).

Not only did women grind the grain, churn the butter and prepare the meals (Genesis 18:6; II Samuel 13:8; John 12:2), they had to invite and receive guests (Judges 4:18; I Samuel 25:18; II Kings 4:8-10), and draw water for household use as well as for the guests and camels (Genesis 24:11, 15-20; I Samuel 9:11; John 4:7). Pitchers filled with water were carried on the head. The wives of farmers would carry, on their heads, fuel, in the form of dried, flat cakes of dung and straw. Often these dung and straw slabs constituted a heavy load. Women also spun the wool, and made the family clothes (Exodus 35:26; I Samuel 2:19; Proverbs 31:19). Sometimes her weaving and needlework aided the family income (Proverbs 31:14, 24), and supported charity (Acts 9:39).

In time of war women and children were taken away in bullock carts by the conquerors. Under the Assyrians the treatment of prisoners was very severe and cruel. Unlike the men, women were not chained (Nahum 3:10), but the coarse soldiers escorting them amused themselves by "discovering their skirts and to see the shame of nakedness" (Nahum 3:5). Ancient bas-reliefs of female prisoners depict them as tearing their hair, throwing dust upon their heads, and bewailing their lot. What a baptism of tears, anguish and indignities women have received through the centuries from brutes of men!

RELIGIOUS SERVICE

As we conclude this section dealing with the life and lot of Bible women, reference must be made to their preeminence in the spiritual realm. It is true that woman was the leader in the first transgression (II Corinthians 11:3; I Timothy 2:14), but she redeemed her position to become most influential in the religious life of mankind. The pages of the Old Testament carry the names of women who remain because of their devotion to God. The prayers and piety of Hannah, for example, purified and vitalized the religious life of the entire Jewish nation. Mary, the mother of our Lord, will ever be revered as the most blessed among women because she believed that God would perform the miraculous. In Scripture biography, women are more conspicuous than men in religious devotion. When Jesus entered upon His ministry women intuitively responded to His teachings, sympathized with Him in His darkest hours and found in Him their Benefactor and Friend. Women were the last to leave the cross, first at the tomb on Christ's resurrection day, and first to proclaim the glorious news of His victory o'er the grave.

In the annals of the Early Church, women are likewise notable for their spiritual devotion, fidelity in teaching the Word of God, and sacrificial support of God's servants. Their faith and prayers were mingled with those of the apostles in preparation for Pentecost, and all through the Christian era the church owes more than it realizes to the prayers, loyalty and gifts of its female members. Today, churches would go to pieces if it were not for the presence, perseverance and prayers of women. In church attendance, women far outstrip men; and in Sunday school work, women's meetings and groups, missionary service and in church activities, women hold the field in spiritual endeavor. From the time when women labored with Paul in the Gospel (Philippians 4:3), religious leaders have been dependent upon the ministries of women. The spiritual value of a godly woman's influence is seen in the fact that many rose to a position of eminence as prophetesses (Exodus 15:20; Numbers 12:2; Judges 4:6; II Kings 22:14; Luke 2:36; Acts 21:8; Romans 16:1, 6, 12; I Corinthians 11:5). Gifted and consecrated women figure prominently in the labors of Paul. Owing much to the Redeemer for her emancipation and ennoblement, woman has endeavored to pay her debt in unreserved devotion to Him who was born of a woman. Chaucer, of the 13th century asked —

What is better than wisdom? — Woman.
And what is better than a good woman? — Nothing.

Myriads of women were — and are — good because with Cowper they learned to sing—

> 'Tis joy enough my All in All,
> At Thy dear feet to lie;
> Thou wilt not let me lower fall,
> And none can higher fly.

2

Alphabetical Exposition of Named Bible Women
Abi to Zipporah

Many of the personal names people are known by today go back to the early twilight of human history when man learned to distinguish his fellowmen by names, and a large number of our names, especially surnames, are the simple names of Bible characters. Further, the Jews of old attached special significance to their names, most of which had definite meanings, emphasized by the frequent occurrence of the phrase, "He shall be called." William Camden (1551-1623), the English historian, in *Remains Concerning Britain* wrote —

It seemeth to have been the manner, at the giving of names, to wish the children might perform and discharge their names as when Gunthram, King of the French, named Clotharious at the font, he said, *Crescat puer et Lujus sit nominis executor* — meaning, "Let the boy grow up and he will fulfill his name."

In early English history Bible names associated with personal traits and also dramatic incidents were chosen as font or baptismal names, as the lists of female names in Webster's *Dictionary* reveal. Thus Eve, because of her association with the creation of the world, along with its cognates, Eva and Evelyn, enjoyed widespread popularity as did several poetic names as Sarah, meaning, lady, princess, queen; Susanna, Lily; Hannah, grace; Miriam, bitterness or sorrow; Esther, star; Hagar, flight, etc.

A remarkable feature of the Puritan Age was the choice of names expressing the sense of humiliation and consciousness of sin. There is no other explanation for the mentality of parents choosing names like Delilah, Tamar and Sapphira for their daughters. In these modern days when reason proudly rejects the Puritan faith, it is well to remember what we owe to the men and women whose Bible names bore witness to a consecration of life to what was best and noblest.

As we hope to prove, the women of the Bible form the most remarkable portrait gallery in existence. Many of them are among the immortals, with records imperishably enshrined for us in God's biography of humanity. As H. V. Morton expresses it—

They form a feminine picture gallery unmatched in the whole of literature. Their histories, the diversity of their fate, and the influence which the story of their lives has exerted on the World, make them unique. Why, one may wonder, do these women so far from us in time and so briefly described, live so vividly in the imagination? It is not merely because they happen to occur in Scripture: it is because they are so palpably alive.

George Matheson develops a similar thought in his *Representative Women of the Bible*.

Amid the galleries of the ancient world there is one whose female characters are unique: it is that of the Bible. As I look into this Judaic Gallery that which arrests me most is the beginning of it and the end of it. At its opening and at its close the hand of the artist has been strikingly at work, and in each case on a female portraiture. The hall of entrance and the hall of exit are each occupied by a picture of Woman. The pictures are different in execution and unlike in their expression; but in each the idea is the same — the enfranchisement of the feminine soul. . . . The entrance portrait is that of Eve, a hymn of female conquest expressed in colours. . . . Woman is recognized as the prospective possessor of the Garden of Life — the future mistress of the home. . . . At the other end of the Gallery — the completing end . . . we have an exultant woman proclaiming to all the earth the tidings of her emancipation. "He that is mighty hath done great things for me." We hear womanhood rejoicing in the lifting of her chain . . . the prediction of the morning that the female spirit should bruise the serpent's head. . . . One of the effects of Christianity has been the enfranchisement of Woman. . . . Yet not simply *one* of the effects of Christianity: it is *the* effect of which all other changes are results.

Further, our expositions of Bible women who stand out in their race and time as no

21

women of later generations stand out, will be allied to present-day application — a feature W. Mackintosh Mackay has so admirably developed in his *Bible Types of Modern Women*. We shall see how the best among female characters in Scripture who were trail blazers for larger freedom of thought and action have contributed to the present high status of womanhood; and how the worst Bible women remain as signals marking the dangerous shoals, quicksands and rocks of life. Circumstances wrecking their lives still exist as death traps.

As human nature has not changed much through past millenniums, the whole of womanhood, which is presented to us as the women of the Bible, unchanging, unvarying from age to age, is a feminine portrait gallery drawn with a marvelous stark economy and unsurpassed in its variety in the whole of literature. Eve is the mother of all those mothers who have seen their favorite first-born branded with shame. Among our friends can be found an acquaintance devoted and firm-minded like Sarah; a monument of fierce and doting motherhood such as Rebekah was; a well-favored Rachel, "whose easy charm vanishes into an envious and petulant old age." Within our own families we have opportunities of studying Mary and Martha. As for Potiphar's wife she "moves through the newspapers in a variety of guises, and Delilah is a character known to the police and the legal profession: the female Judas who is always willing to entrap a Samson for silver."

For the sake of convenience we have chosen to list the named women of the Bible alphabetically rather than chronologically. In this way it is easier for those who use the material to identify each character. As truth is the common property of us all, the writer sincerely hopes that the sketches he has drawn will prove to be useful in the ministry of those who have opportunities of winning girls and women for the Master. Eternity alone will reveal the extent of the influence of women whose spirit came to rejoice in God their Saviour, and who, having discovered the Well of Life, left their waterpots.

ABI
THE WOMAN WITH A BAD HUSBAND BUT A GOOD SON

Scripture References — II Kings 18:2; II Chronicles 29:1; 26:5
Name Meaning — My father is Jehovah, *or* The Will of God
Family Connections — Abi was the daughter of Zechariah who had an understanding of the visions of God, and was one of the witnesses used by Isaiah (18:2). She also became the wife of the godless King Ahaz, and was the mother of the godly King Hezekiah. She is also named Abijah, of which Abi is a contraction. Abijah was also the name of several men including the son and successor of the wife of Judah's grandson Hezron, to whom was traced the origin of Tekoa (I Chronicles 2:24).

In spite of the idolatry of her royal husband, Abi or Abijah, true to her name, clung to the Fatherhood of God and sought to do His will. She counteracted any evil influence of Ahaz over their young son, Hezekiah, who, when he came to the throne, did that which was right in the sight of the Lord according to all that King David, his royal ancestor had done. Inspired by God, about whom he had learned a great deal from his noble mother, Hezekiah brought about a mighty, national, religious revival. The name Hezekiah means, "Strong in the Lord," and doubtless his mother Abijah or Abi, had much to say in the choice of such a name reflecting, as it did, her confidence in Jehovah. There are many mothers like Abi in the world who have godless husbands but good, Christian children! The reverse is also true for there are those women who have godly husbands but most ungodly children.

ABIA or ABIAH
THE WOMAN WHO WAS AN ANCESTRESS OF CHRIST

Scripture Reference — I Chronicles 2:24
Name Meaning — God is Father
Family Connections — She was the wife of Hezron, grandson of Judah by Pharez, and mother of Ashur, father of Tekoa. From the genealogies of Jesus (Matthew 1; Luke 3) who came of the tribe of Ju-

dah, Abiah has honor as an ancestress of the Saviour. Some writers identify Abiah with the female Abijah, seeing that Abi and Abiah are variants of her name. Abiah was also the name of the second son of the prophet Samuel (I Samuel 8: 2). We are not informed as to the influence of Abiah's home life. It is to be hoped that she knew and honored God as her heavenly Father.

ABIGAIL
THE WOMAN WITH BEAUTY AND BRAINS

Scripture References — I Samuel 25:1-42; II Samuel 3:3

Name Meaning — Father of Joy, *or* Cause of Joy

Family Connections — Scripture gives us no clue as to Abigail's parentage or genealogy. Ellicott suggests that the name given this famous Jewish beauty who became the good angel of Nabal's household was likely given her by the villagers of her husband's estate. Meaning "Whose father is joy," Abigail was "expressive of her sunny, gladness-bringing presence." Her religious witness and knowledge of Jewish history testify to an early training in a godly home, and acquaintance with the teachings of the prophets in Israel, Her plea before David also reveals her understanding of the events of her own world.

The three conspicuous characters in the story of one of the loveliest females in the Bible are Nabal, Abigail and David. Nabal is described as "the man churlish and evil in his doings" (I Samuel 25:3), and his record proves him to be all that. Churlish means, a bear of man, harsh, rude and brutal. Destitute of the finer qualities his wife possessed, he was likewise avaricious and selfish. Rich and increased with goods and gold, he thought only of his possessions and could be classed among those of whom it has been written —

> The man may breathe but never lives
> Whoe'er receives but nothing gives —
> Creation's blot, creation's blank,
> Whom none can love and none can thank.

Nabal was also a drunken wretch, as well as being unmanageable and stubborn and ill-tempered. Doubtless he was often "very drunken." This wretch of a man was likewise an unbeliever, "a son of Belial," who bowed his knee to the god of this world and not to the God of his fathers. Further, as a follower of Saul he shared the rejected king's jealousy of David. Added to his brutal disposition and evil doings was that of stupidity, as his name suggests. Pleading for his unworthy life, Abigail asked for mercy because of his foolishness. "As his name is, so is he; Nabal is his name, and folly is with him" (verse 25). Nabal means "a fool," and what Abigail actually meant was, "Pay no attention to my wretched husband for he's a fool by name, and a fool by nature." Truly, such a man will always provoke the profoundest perversion in all who read his story.

Abigail is as "a woman of good understanding, and of a beautiful countenance." In her, winsomeness and wisdom were wed. She had brains as well as beauty. Today, many women try to cultivate beauty and neglect their brains. A lovely face hides an empty mind. But with Abigail, loveliness and intelligence went hand in hand, with her intelligence emphasizing her physical attractiveness. A beautiful woman with a beautiful mind as she had is surely one of God's masterpieces.

Added to her charm and wisdom was that of piety. She knew God, and although she lived in such an unhappy home, she remained a saint. Her own soul, like that of David, was "bound in the bundle of life with the Lord God." Writing of Abigail as "A Woman of Tact" W. Mackintosh Mackay says that, "she possessed in harmonious combination these two qualities which are valuable to any one, but which are essential to one who has to manage men — *the tact of a wise wife* and *the religious principle of a good woman.*" Eugenia Price, who writes of Abigail as, *A Woman With God's Own Poise*, says that, "only God can give a woman poise like Abigail possessed, and God can only do it when a woman is willing to cooperate as Abigail cooperated with Him on every point." True to the significance of her own name she experienced that in God her Father there was a source of joy enabling her to be independent of the adverse, trying circumstances of her miserable home life. She must have had implicit confidence in God to speak to David as she did about her divinely predestined future. In harmony with her many attractions was "the ornament of a meek and quiet spirit, which is more lustrous than the diamonds that decorate the delicate fingers of our betters, shone as an ornament of gold about her head, and chains about her neck."

David is the other outstanding character in the record. He it was who fought the battles of the Lord, and evil had not been found in him all his days (25:28). He could match Abigail's beauty, for it was said of him that he was "ruddy . . . of a beautiful countenance, and goodly to look to" (I Samuel 16:12). When Abigail and David became one they must have been a handsome pair to look upon! Then, in addition to being most musical, David was equal with Abigail in wisdom and piety for he was "prudent in matters, . . . and the Lord [was] with him" (I Samuel 16:18).

The sacred historian tells us how these three persons were brought together in a tragic way. David was an outlaw because of Saul's hatred, and lived in the strongholds of the hills with his loyal band of 600 followers. Having often helped Nabal's herdsmen out, being in need of food for his little army, David sent a kind request to Nabal for help. In his churlish fashion, Nabal bluntly refused to give David a crumb for his hungry men, and dismissed David as a marauding hireling. Angered, David threatened to plunder Nabal's possession and kill Nabal and all those who emulated his contempt. Abigail, learning from the servants of David's request and her husband's rude refusal, unknown to Nabal, acted with thought, care and great rapidity. As Ellicott comments —

Having often acted as peace-maker between her intemperate husband and his neighbours, on hearing the story and how imprudently her husband had behaved, saw that no time must be lost, for with a clever woman's wit she saw that grave consequences would surely follow the churlish refusal and the rash words, which betrayed at once the jealous adherent of Saul and the bitter enemy of the powerful outlaw.

Gathering together a quantity of food and wine, sufficient she thought for David's immediate need, Abigail rode out on an ass and at a covert of a hill met David and his men — and what a momentous meeting it turned out to be. With discreet tact Abigail averted David's just anger over Nabal's insult to his messengers, by placing at David's feet food for his hungry men. She also revealed her wisdom in that she fell at the feet of David, as an inferior before a superior, and acquiesced with him in his condemnation of her brutal, foolish husband.

As a Hebrew woman was restricted by the customs of her time to give counsel only in an emergency and in the hour of greatest need, Abigail, who had risked the displeasure of her husband whose life was threatened, did not act impulsively in going to David to plead for mercy. She followed the dictates of her disciplined will, and speaking at the opportune moment her beautiful appeal from beautiful lips, captivated the heart of David. "As his own harp had appeased Saul, the sweet-toned voice of Abigail exorcised the demon of revenge, and woke the angel that was slumbering in David's bosom." We can never gauge the effect of our words and actions upon others. The intervention of Abigail in the nick of time teaches us that when we have wisdom to impart, faith to share, and help to offer, we must not hesitate to take any risk that may be involved.

Abigail had often to make amends for the infuriated outbursts of her husband. Neighbors and friends knew her drunken sot of a husband only too well, but patiently she would pour oil on troubled waters, and when she humbly approached with a large peace offering, her calmness soothed David's anger and gave her the position of advantage. For her peace-making mission she received the king's benediction (25:33). Her wisdom is seen in that she did not attempt to check David's turbulent feelings by argument, but won him by wise, kind words. Possessing heavenly intelligence, self-control, common sense and vision, she exercised boundless influence over a great man, and marked herself out as a truly great woman. After Abigail's successful, persuasive entreaty for the life of her worthless husband, the rest of her story reads like a fairy tale. She returned to her wicked partner to take up her hard and bitter life again.

It is to the credit of this noble woman that she did not leave her godless husband or seek divorce from him, but remained a loyal wife and the protector of her worthless partner. She had taken him for better or for worse, and life for her was worse than the worst. Wretched though her life was, and spurned, insulted and beaten as she may have been during Nabal's drinking bouts, she clung to the man to whom she had sworn to be faithful. Abigail manifested a love stronger than death. But the hour of deliverance came ten days after her return home, when by a divine stroke, Nabal's worthless life ended. When David hearkened to the plea of Abigail and accepted her person, he rejoiced over being kept back by her counsel from taking into his own hands God's prerogative of justice (Romans 12:19).

When David said to Abigail, "Blessed be thy advice," he went on to confess with his usual frank generosity that he had been wrong in giving way to wild, ungovernable passion. If Abigail had not interceded he would have carried out his purpose and destroyed the entire household of Nabal, which massacre would have included Abigail herself. But death came as the great divorcer or arbiter, and Nabal's wonderful wife had no tears of regret, for amid much suffering and disappointment she had fulfilled her marriage vows. In that farmer's house there had been "The Beauty and the Beast." The Beast was dead, and the Beauty was legally free of her terrible bondage.

After Nabal's death, David "communed with Abigail" (25:39) — a technical expression for asking one's hand in marriage (Song of Solomon 8:8) — and took her as his wife. Married to Israel's most illustrious king, Abigail entered upon a happier career. By David, she had a son named Chileab, or Daniel (compare II Samuel 3:3 with I Chronicles 3:1). The latter name means, "God is my Judge," and one has an inkling that the choice of such a name was Abigail's because of her experience of divine vindication. She accompanied David to Gath and Ziklag (I Samuel 27:3; 30:5, 18). Matthew Henry's comment at this point is, "Abigail married David in faith, not questioning but that, though now he had not a house of his own, yet God's promise to him would at length be fulfilled." Abigail brought to David not only "a fortune in herself," but much wealth so useful to David in the meeting of his manifold obligations.

Among the lessons to be learned from the life of Abigail, the first is surely evident, namely, that much heartache follows when a Christian woman marries an unbeliever. Unequal yokes do not promote true and abiding happiness. The tragedy in Abigail's career began when she married Nabal, a young man of Naon. Already we have asked the question, Why did she marry such a man? Why did such a lovely girl throw herself away upon such a brute of a man? According to the custom of those times marriages were man-made, the woman having little to say about the choice of a husband. Marriage was largely a matter of family arrangement. Nabal was of wealthy parentage and rich in his own right with 3,000 sheep and 1,000 goats and thus seemed a good catch for Abigail. But character should be considered before possessions.

Many a woman in the world today made her own choice of a partner. Perhaps she knew of his failures and thought that after marriage she would reform him, but found herself joined to one whose ways became more evil. Then think of those brave, unmurmuring wives who have to live with the fool of a husband whose drunken, crude ways are repellant, yet who, by the grace of God accept and live with their trial; and who, because of a deep belief in divine sufficiency retain their poise. Such living martyrs are among God's heroines. All of us know of those good women chained with the fetters of a wretched married life for whom it would be infinitely better for them —

To lie in their graves where the head, heart and breast,
From care, labour and sorrow forever should rest.

Thinking of modern Abigails the appropriate lines of noble Elizabeth Barrett Browning come to mind —

The sweetest lives are those to duty wed,
Whose deeds, both great and small, and close-knit strands
Of an unbroken thread; where love ennobles all.
The World may sound no trumpets, ring no bells:
The Book of Life the shining record tells.

ABIGAIL No. 2

She was David's half-sister of whom we know nothing apart from the fact she had the same mother as David, but a different father, namely, Zeruiah Nahash, and that she became the wife of Jether also known as Ithra. This Abigail became the mother of Amasa, a leader in David's army (II Samuel 17:25; I Chronicles 2:16, 17). Amasa came to a tragic end at the hands of his cousin, Joab.

ABIHAIL

This name is used of both males and females in Scripture.

Name Meaning — Father, *or* Cause of Strength *or* Father of Splendor

ABIHAIL No. 1

She was the daughter of a son of Merari, of the tribe of Levi the mother of Zuriel, a "prince" among the families of Merari (Numbers 3:35).

ABIHAIL No. 2

She was the wife of Abishur of the tribe of Judah, in the line of Hezron and Jerahmeel (I Chronicles 2:29).

ABIHAIL No. 3

She was the mother of Rehoboam's wife, Nahalath, and daughter of Eliab, David's eldest brother. There was frequent intermarriage in the Davidic house. The LXX Version makes this Abihail the second wife of Rehoboam (II Chronicles 11:18).

ABIHAIL was also the name of Queen Esther's father (2:15; 9:29).

ABIJAH (see Abi)

ABISHAG

The Woman Who Nursed a King

Scripture References — I Kings 1:3, 4; 2:13-25

Name Meaning — My father wanders or errs, *or* My father causes wandering

Family Connections — She was a Shunammitess from Issachar.

Because of the feebleness of King David his physicians recommended a fresh young maiden be found to "cherish" him, a treatment implying that through physical contact she could give David the advantage of her superabundant vitality. Abishag was chosen for the task with great care on account of her virginity, youth, beauty and physical vigor, and as a practical nurse for the aging king. The prescribed method was not successful, for David died soon after Abishag had taken on her duties.

After David's death, Adonijah, the rebellious son of David and Haggith, desired Abishag as his wife, and approached Bathsheba, Solomon's mother, with a seemingly harmless but really insidious request, "Let Abishag be given to me." Seeing nothing wrong with such a request, but thinking it simply an affair of the heart, Bathsheba innocently acted as a matchmaker. Solomon, with due reverence, received his mother, but as soon as the request was presented, the mental acumen of the king saw through the scheme. He construed Adonijah's desire as virtual treason seeing legal rights followed the possession in marriage of a deceased king's wife. Matthew Henry observes, "That Abishag was married to David before she lay with him, and was his secondary wife, appears from its being imputed as a great crime to Adonijah that he desired to marry her after his father's death." Although David had not "known" Abishag (1:3), that is, had no sexual relations with her, nevertheless she was considered an inheritor, and with her could go the rights to the throne. "Having once failed in an abortive attempt to seize the kingdom, Adonijah now sought in a more subtle way to gain his objective." But his scheme cost him his life, and relentless judgment fell upon him for his intrigue. Because of her close association with David, Abishag was present when, through Bathsheba's intercession, Solomon was placed on the throne. "If that act had been questioned she would have been a most important witness. By reason of this and of her personal charms, she might become a strong helper to any rival of Solomon who should intrigue to supplant." With keen insight Solomon saw what was behind Adonijah's wish to marry Abishag, and he was slain by the hand of Benaiah.

ABITAL

Scripture References — II Samuel 3:4; I Chronicles 3:3

Name Meaning — Whose father is as dew

The historian took a mere seven words to tell us all there is to know about this colorless female character. Born in Hebron, she was one of David's many wives. In his most profitable study, *Personal Names in the Bible,* W. F. Wilkinson reminds us that in the figurative language of Scripture poetry, "Dew often represents blessing, beneficence, refreshment, consolation; and in this sense it may be understood in such a name. Or its significance, when thus used, may be found in the early appearance and rapid evanescence of dew (Hosea 6:4; 13:3); and so it may intimate the death of a young husband, perhaps the birth of a child." Perhaps the name Abital was chosen by the parents to whom her birth came as a blessing, as a source of consolation.

ACHSAH
THE WOMAN WHO WANTED MORE

Scripture References — Joshua 15:16, 17; Judges 1:12, 13; I Chronicles 2:4, 9

Name Meaning — Adorned, *or* Bursting the Veil

Family Connections — Achsah was the daughter of Caleb, prince of the tribe of Judah. She was the only girl in the family, and had three brothers (I Chronicles 4:15). She became the wife of Othniel, son of Kenaz, Caleb's younger brother. Othniel became one of Israel's judges and had, through the Spirit of God, the noble faith of his race (Judges 3:8-11).

The story of Achsah is told in charming and picturesque detail in the above Scripture. Her father promised her in marriage to the gallant man who was able to capture Debir, or Keriath-sepher which means, "The City of the Book." The feat was accomplished by Othniel, and Caleb gave to his daughter, as a dowry, a portion of the south land. Not satisfied, she wanted springs of water to irrigate her fields, so Caleb gave her the upper springs and the nether springs. Although, as a Jewess, Achsah looked for great things through faith in God's promise of the land, her request for an addition to the generous dowry already bestowed, reveals an element of covetousness in her disposition. W. Mackintosh Mackay in his character-study of Achsah speaks of her as "The Discontented Bride."

Not content with the noble present her father Caleb had given her, she urged Othniel her husband to make a further request, but reading between the lines of the story it would seem as if he felt it ungracious to ask for more. Thus Achsah, who had not learned to be content with what she had (Hebrews 13:5), approached her father with a significant word, "Give me *also,*" and as Dr. Mackay expresses it, "There is always a something more needed to complete the circle of perfect peace in every earthly lot; the

... little more, and how much it is;
The little less, and what worlds away."

Solomon reminds us that the human heart is like the horseleech whose two daughters never have enough, and bear the names of *Give, Give* (Proverbs 30:15). There is, of course, a divine discontent all of us should foster. Dissatisfied with our growth in sanctity of life we should constantly pray, "More holiness give me," and as the bride's father graciously granted his daughter's request, so our Heavenly Father will answer our yearning for the life more abundant.

Caleb gave Achsah the springs of water she desired, and in the upper and nether springs we have a type of the spiritual and temporal mercies from our Father above. As heirs of the promise, His children can humbly and confidently ask and expect great blessings from His generous hand. Both *upper,* or heavenly provision, and *nether,* or earthly necessities come from Him in whom are all our springs (Psalms 81:10; 84:11; Isaiah 33:16; Luke 11:13; John 4:13, 14; 7:37-39; Ephesians 3:20; I John 3:22). At times it seems as if the "nether springs" dry up, as Job experienced when the Lord took away so many of his earthly possessions and pleasures. But the "upper springs" never run dry for, like those Achsah received, they flow from the everlasting hills. "The river of water of life flowing out of the throne of God and of the Lamb" cannot fail. When the waters of earth fail, we have a reservoir above, never impoverished by drought.

ADAH No. 1
THE WOMAN WHO GAVE THE WORLD ITS FIRST MUSICIAN

Scripture Reference — Genesis 4:19-23

Name Meaning — Adornment, beauty, pleasure. The pure Hebrew name is found in the compounds, Adaiah, "whom Jehovah adorns," and Maadiah, "ornament from Jehovah."

Family Connections — Adah, and the co-wife, Zillah, are the first women to be named after Eve. The names of Cain's wife, and the other daughters of Adam and Eve are not given. Adah was one of the two wives of Lamech who was of the seventh generation from Adam. Adah was the mother of two sons, Jabal and Jubal. Jabal became a famous shepherd, the father of a tent-dwelling people, and nomad tribes. Jubal was the first person to introduce the noble art of music to the world, "the father of all such as handle the harp and the organ." Says Matthew Henry, "When Jabal had set them in a way to be rich, Jubal put them in a way to be merry. Jabal was their Pan, and Jubal their Appollo."

The world certainly owes a great debt to Adah's two sons, particularly to the musical Jubal. In his *Table Talk*, Martin Luther, the great Reformer, wrote —

> Music is a fair and glorious gift of God, and takes its place next to Theology. . . . The fairest and most glorious gift of God is music. Kings and princes and great lords should give their support to music. Music is a discipline; it is an instructress; it makes people milder and gentler, more moral, and more reasonable.

Lamech was not only the father of two sons by Adah, who gave much to the world, but he was also the first polygamist in the Bible, and probably in the world. Lamech's initial polygamous household led the way in so much jealousy, heartache and sorrow. Adah and Zillah, by their agreement to become wives of the same man, yielded to a union that degraded the dignity of womanhood, profaned God's ordinances and brought terrible complications by sin upon the human race. The destruction of true family life and the injection of poison into the veins of children born in a polygamist's household, must be reckoned as Lamech's responsibility.

Further, Lamech's *Poem* in praise of himself, and dedicated to his two wives, is worthy of note. The oldest poetic fragment in the Bible, it was known as *The Song of the Terrible Lamech:*

Adah and Zillah, hear my voice,
You wives of Lamech, give ears to my words;
I kill a man for wounding me.
. . . .
If Cain is to be avenged seven-fold.
Then Lamech seventy and seven-fold.

With the weapons which another son, Tubal-Cain, invented, Lamech exults over the violent revenge he can take over any who attack him, and so with the vigorous poem in praise of armed defense and bloodshed, joined with indications of luxury and a life of pleasure, the historian concludes the record of the race of Cain.

ADAH No. 2
THE WOMAN WHO BECAME A GRIEF OF MIND

Scripture References — Genesis 26:34; 36:2
Family Connections — This second Adah was a daughter of Elon the Hittite. She became one of the wives of Esau, and was the woman who became a "grief of mind" to his parents, Isaac and Rebekah. She became the mother of Eliphaz, Esau's first-born son, and along with Esau's other wives after the settlement in Mount Seir became an ancestress of the Edomites who were treated as brothers by the Israelites.

Scholars are agreed that this Adah is the Bashemath of Genesis 26:34; 36:2. Women received new names when they married. Bullinger suggests that this second name was dropped in Genesis 36:2 to avoid confusion with the daughter of Ishmael. In Genesis 26 we have general history, but in Genesis 36, precise genealogy.

AGAR (see HAGAR)

AHINOAM No. 1

Scripture Reference — I Samuel 14:50
Name Meaning — Brother of pleasantries

Two women are known by this name in the Old Testament. The first Ahinoam was the daughter of Ahimaaz. She was the wife of Saul, Israel's first king, to whom she bore a noble son, Jonathan, who inherited his mother's commendable traits. It was her daughter, Merab, who was first promised to David in marriage, but it was Michal her next daughter who became the young champion's first wife. Saul had two more sons by Ahinoam, namely, Isha and Melchishua.

Her name is most suggestive. As we have seen, it means "brother of pleasantries," in the sense of "pleasing or dear brother." A parallel name is that of Abinoam, father of Barak, one of the heroes of the Book of Judges, whose name means, "brother's delight." Wilkinson suggests as a feasible origin for such a name, "Extreme partiality of affection exhibited by a very young infant for a brother — a domestic phenomenon by no means unusual."

AHINOAM No. 2

Scripture References — I Samuel 25:43; 27: 3; 30:5; II Samuel 2:2; 3:2; I Chronicles 3:1

She was the Jezreelitess who became one of David's eight wives. She became the mother of David's first son, Amnon, who dishonored his half-sister Tamar, and was murdered for this act of seduction by Tamar's brother, Absalom. Did Amnon inherit his evil trait from his Jezreelite mother who probably was bad as she was beautiful? Outward beauty was David's snare, and thus some of his children had more of outward attractiveness than inward grace. Ahinoam, along with Abigail, Nabal's widow, were captured by the Amalekites at Ziklag but David attacked them and recovered both his wives.

AHLAI No. 1

Scripture Reference — I Chronicles 2:31, 34
Name Meaning — O would that!

The first Ahlai was the daughter of Sheshan who had several daughters, and a descendant of Pharez, elder son of Judah by Tamar whose name appears in the royal genealogy of Jesus (Matthew 1). She was given in marriage to an Egyptian servant, Jarba, and became the mother of Attai.

AHLAI No. 2

She was the mother of Zabad, one of David's mighty men (I Chronicles 11:41).

AHOLAH (see SYMBOLIC WOMEN)

AHOLIBAH (see SYMBOLIC WOMEN)

AHOLIBAMAH or OHOLIBAMAH

Scripture Reference — Genesis 36:2-25
Name Meaning — Tent of the high places

This female character was one of Esau's wives, and the mother of Jeush, Jaalam, and Korah, who are spoken of as "Dukes" (Genesis 36:18). There seems to be some confusion about references to her. For instance, she is referred to as a daughter of Elon the Hittite and also as a daughter of Anah (Genesis 26:34; 36:2). Aholibamah is also identified with Judith mentioned in Genesis 26:34. Each of Esau's wives has a name in the genealogy different from that in history. Aholibamah was her personal name, and Judith her second name. Her father, Anah, received a second name also from his discovery of the hot springs, Beeri being from Beer, a well.

Through Aholibamah, Esau's descendants, the Edomites, became the occupants of Mount Seir, and were troublesome to the descendants of Jacob (Numbers 20:14-21). They were the ancestral stock of the Idumeans, from whom Herod the Great came.

ANAH

Scripture Reference — Genesis 36:2, 18, 25

The meaning of this name is uncertain. Cruden suggests that it may signify, "one who answers, or who sings" — "one who is poor, or afflicted." Anah was the daughter of Zibeon and the mother of the foregoing Aholibamah. It is likewise the name of two men (Genesis 36:20, 24, 29; I Chronicles 1: 38, 40, 41). Anah is the only named mother of any of Esau's wives.

Some authorities read *son* instead of *daughter* and suggest that it is quite possible to reduce all the foregoing references to one person.

ANNA

THE WOMAN WHO BECAME THE FIRST CHRISTIAN MISSIONARY

Scripture Reference — Luke 2:36-38
Name Meaning — Favor, *or* Grace. Anna is the same with Hannah of the Old Testament, and was the Phoenician name used by Virgil for the sister of Dido, queen of Carthage.
Family Connection — Anna was the daughter of Phanuel, a name identical with Penuel, and meaning, "The face, or appearance of God." The name of her husband who died young is not given. Like Anna, he, too, doubtlessly waited for the

salvation of God. Her father was of the tribe of Asher — one of the so-called "lost tribes." This is all we know of the ancestry of Anna, who, although her biography is one of the briefest in Bible history, lived a life that is still fragrant. Her name is a popular one for girls. Elsdon C. Smith in *The Story of Our Names* says that there are over half-a-million girls and women in America alone who have the name of Anna.

In our exposition of this most renowned of Bible widows we deem it best to take her record as given by the beloved physician, Luke, who says of her that —

She Was a Prophetess

Jezebel, the self-styled and false prophetess is the only other one in the New Testament (Revelation 2:20) to bear this designation. Philip's four daughters also prophesied (Acts 21:9). The narrative does not tell us why she was known as a prophetess. It may be that her long departed husband had been a prophet, or because under divine inspiration she herself told future events, or spent her time celebrating the praises of God (I Samuel 10:5; I Chronicles 25:1-3). To prophesy simply means to proclaim a divine message, and Anna was one to whom it was given to know events before and after, and one through whom God spoke to others. Anna must be included in that continuous line of prophets and prophetesses who had heralded the coming of the Messiah through succeeding generations. As she gazed upon the face of the Babe of Bethlehem Anna knew that the past predictions of Him were fulfilled. Through her long, godly life her mind had become saturated with Old Testament prophecies concerning the coming of the seed of the woman to bruise the serpent's head. Waiting unceasingly for Christ she believed, along with Simeon, that Mary's first-born Son was indeed the rod out of the stem of Jesse (Isaiah 11:1; Micah 5:2).

She Was of a Great Age

Anna was married for only seven years, and remained a widow for eighty-four years. All of this means that she must have been over one hundred years old when her failing eyes beheld the Saviour she had long-

ingly expected. She had grown old in the service of the sanctuary, and having seen, with Simeon, God's Salvation, was ready to depart in peace. How encouraging it is to meet those who through a long life have remained true to the Lord and whose gray hairs are honorable because of a life lived in the divine will, and who, when they pass away, are ready for glory.

She Was a Widow

Paul exhorted young Timothy to "honour widows who are widows indeed," and Anna, a worthy widow, all should certainly honor. In fact, we wonder if the Apostle had the aged Anna before his mind's eye when he gave Timothy this thought —

She that is a widow indeed, and desolate, trusteth in God, and continueth in supplication and prayers night and day (I Timothy 5: 3, 5).

Anna was desolate, that is, alone, or solitary. A widow can know what it is to face a long, lonely and cheerless life, and a solitude made more acute because of the remembrance of happier days. But it was not so with Anna. When as a young, motherless wife, God withdrew from her the earthly love she rejoiced in, she did not bury her hope in a grave. In the place of what God took, He gave her more of Himself, and she became devoted to Him who had promised to be as a Husband to the widow, and through her long widowhood was unwearying in devotion to Him. She "trusted in God," and her hoary head was a crown of glory (Proverbs 16:31). Repose of soul was hers for eighty-five years because the one thing she desired was to have God's house as her dwelling place all the days of her life.

She Departed Not From the Temple

When death ravaged her own home, Anna turned from all legitimate concerns to join the band of holy women who devoted themselves to continual attendance at the "night and day services of the Temple." She was no occasional attender or dead member, but a constant, devout worshiper. Her seat in the Temple was always occupied. What an inspiration worshipers of this sort are to a faithful pastor who feels he can minister more freely when they are present because of their prayer support! When their seat is empty in the church, he knows there must be something unusual accounting for their absence.

She Served God With Fastings and Prayers

Without doubt, Anna was one of God's own elect, which cry day and night unto Him, and who was heard in that she feared. It was not in some retired nook of the Temple she prayed, or in a corner where females only supplicated God. She would join with others openly in the presence of the congregation and pour out her soul audibly in the Temple. The One to whose birth she witnessed was to say that praying and fasting are necessary requisites in a God-used life, and Anna not only prayed but also fasted. She was willing to miss a meal in order to spend more time before God. Hers was a life of godly self-control. She had learned how to crucify the flesh in order to serve God more acceptably.

She Gave Thanks Likewise Unto the Lord

Anna's prayers were paired with praises. How arrestive is the phrase, "she coming in that instant." This was no mere coincidence. Through her long pilgrimage, day after day, she went to the Temple to pray for the coming of the Messiah, and although He seemed to tarry she waited for Him, believing that He would come. Then one day the miracle happened, for as she entered the Temple she heard sounds of exultation and joy proceeding from the inner court, and then from the lips of the venerable Simeon she heard the words, "Now, Lord, lettest Thou Thy servant depart in peace, for mine eyes have seen Thy salvation." Gazing upon the Holy Child who was none other than her long-looked-for Messiah, Anna, too, was ready to depart in peace and be joined with her husband above.

She Spake of Him to All

Anna not only prayed and praised, but went out to proclaim the glad tidings to those who had shared her hope and faith. Note, again, the glimpse we have of Anna in her brief record. We see her, first of all, as —

A *Daughter* of Phanuel of the tribe of Asher — a somewhat interesting fact seeing that she is the only one of note mentioned in the Bible of the tribe of Asher, even though the name means blessedness.

A *Widow* of a great age.

A *Devout Worshiper* of the living God.

A *Prophetess* proclaiming the prophetic word.

Now she assumes another role. Old though she is, she goes forth to become —

A *Missionary.* Anna was one of the godly remnant in Israel who, through centuries, even in the darkest days before Christ came, looked for the Dayspring from on high. Thus, as she heard Simeon's praise for prophecy fulfilled, she went out to her godly intimates to declare the glad tidings. Faith, through her long years of waiting, was rewarded and she became the first female herald of the Incarnation to all who looked for the Redeemer in Jerusalem. In Anna we have "a sample of an aged female's waiting faith, as Simeon is of an aged man's." Blessed are all those who patiently and prayerfully await Christ's second appearance (Hebrews 9:28).

APPHIA

Scripture Reference — Philemon 2
Name Meaning — That which is fruitful

This believer, belonging to Colossae, the ancient Phrygian city now a part of Turkey, is spoken of as our "dearly beloved" and "our sister" (R.V., margin). It is likely that she lived out the significance of her name by being a fruitful branch of the Vine. Apphia is believed to have been the wife of Philemon and either the mother or sister of Archippus who was evidently a close member of the family. She must have been closely associated with Philemon, otherwise she would not have been mentioned in connection with a domestic matter (Philemon, verse 2). Tradition has it that Philemon, Apphia, Archippus and Onesimus were stoned to death during the reign of Nero. It was Onesimus who went to Colossae with a message for the Philemon household.

ASENATH

THE WOMAN A KING GAVE TO HIS PRIME MINISTER

Scripture References — Genesis 41:45-50; 46:20
Name Meaning — An Egyptian name im-

plying, "one who belongs to Neit the heathen goddess of wisdom, of Sais."

Family Connections—Three times over Asenath is spoken of as "the daughter of Potipherah, priest of On." This priest was associated with the "Great Temple of the Sun" at Heliopolis, near to modern Cairo. She became the wife of Joseph, Egypt's great deliverer, and before famine stalked the land bore two sons, Manasseh, meaning, "God hath removed from me all my troubles and from my father's house"; and Ephraim, implying, "God hath made me fruitful in the land of my affliction."

The marriage Pharaoh arranged between Joseph and Asenath revealed his determination to completely identify Joseph with Egyptian life. Joseph had become a most valuable man in the land of Egypt, and was next to Pharaoh in power. Among the honors he lavished upon Joseph was a marriage into a caste of priests ranking high in Egypt. These were the sages trained in the wisdom of Egypt (Acts 7:22), and by his marriage to the daughter of one of these sages, Joseph became assimilated with the priestly caste — heathen in nature. As Kuyper expresses it in *Women of the Old Testament*—

> Joseph's marriage was a diplomatic arrangement, designated by Pharaoh to place him inside a strictly delineated, aristocratic society, and thus to convert him into a naturalized Egyptian. But by becoming son-in-law to Potipherah, Joseph became involved in Egyptian idolatry and became a member of a caste which borrowed all of its prestige from that idolatry.

Although around the 5th century, A.D., there was an effort to attach Asenath as the heroine of a remarkable Jewish and heathen romance, in which she renounced her false gods before her marriage, the fact remains that as a Hebrew with a pronounced God-consciousness pervading his life Joseph should have refused to marry an idolatress. Had he resisted Pharaoh's arrangement, as he had resisted the tempting allurements of another Egyptian woman, Potiphar's wife, he would have still held his position of power, for as a statesman, Joseph was indispensable to Pharaoh and to Egypt. Future history proved that some of the blood of Asenath coursed through the veins of Ephraim and Manasseh injecting separa-

tion and idolatry into Jacob's generations. The influence and distinction Joseph attained was annihilated, and the glory of Jacob's family passed to Judah alone. If you ask why Joseph's tribe was so swiftly obliterated, the Scriptures point to only a single answer: Joseph married Asenath, daughter of Potipherah, high priest of the Sun worshipers of On. What a treatise this is on Paul's injunction about believers having no agreement with the temple of idols! (II Corinthians 6:11-18).

ATARAH

Scripture Reference — I Chronicles 2:26
Name Meaning — Crown

Atarah was the second wife of Jerahmeel, grandson of Pharez, and mother of Onam. Jerahmeel's first wife by whom he had five children is not mentioned by name (I Chronicles 2:26, 28).

ATHALIAH
The Woman Who Was a Notorious Murderess

Scripture References — II Kings 8:26; 11; II Chronicles 22; 23:13-21; 24:7
Name Meaning — Taken away of the Lord, or Jehovah has afflicted. Athaliah is also the name of two males (I Chronicles 8:26, 27; Ezra 8:7).

Family Connections — She was the daughter of Ahab and Jezebel, and so was half Israelite and half Phoenician, and she personified all the evil of her ill-famed parents and transferred the poison of idolatry into Jerusalem's veins. She was the granddaughter of Omri, 6th king of Israel, "who waded through slaughter to a throne he never inherited." Athaliah married Jehoram, son of Jehoshaphat. After many years of strife between the kingdoms of Judah and Israel political relations were more friendly, and as a mother of political expediency on the part of Jehoshaphat — which remains a blot upon his otherwise good memory — he gave his eldest son, Jehoram, in marriage to Athaliah whose brothers, loyal to the worship of Jehovah were murdered by Jehoram. Of this union Ahaziah was born who, with such a revolting figure as a mother, licentious and the personification of despicable arrogance, never had a chance to develop finer qualities of character. With such a mother as his wicked counselor what else could he do but walk in the ways of godless Ahab (II Chronicles 22:3).

After reigning for eight years Jehoram died, unmourned, of a predicted incurable disease. While he reigned, he was dominated by Athaliah who had the stronger character of the two, and who, having inherited from her evil mother strength of will and fanatical devtion to the worship of Baal, made Judah idolatrous. Ahaziah only reigned for a year. Wounded in battle by Jehu, he fled to Megiddo, where he died, and his wicked mother (II Chronicles 24:7) became envious of the throne. But the sons of Ahaziah stood in her way, and with fanatical ambition she seized the opportunity and massacred all the legal heirs — so she thought. This wholesale, merciless, cruel-hearted murderess sought to exterminate the last vestiges of the House of David through which the promised Messiah was to come. Behind her dastardly crime to destroy "The Seed Royal" we can detect the evil machinations of the devil — a murderer from the beginning — to annihilate the promised seed of the woman predestined to bruise the satanic head. A bad woman bent on destruction is doubly dangerous.

After putting to death her young grandsons, Athaliah reigned for six years, and was the only woman to reign as queen of Judah. The daughter of a king, wife of a king, mother of a king, she is now queen. While her husband reigned she was the power *behind* the throne — now she is the power *on* the throne, and proof of her energy, forcefulness and ability are seen in the length of her reign. A despotic ruler, her every gesture had to be obeyed. During her reign part of the Temple of Jehovah was pulled down and the material used in the building of a temple of Baal. But the God who overrules in the destinies of men and nations, intervened to redeem His promise of a Saviour from the tribe of Judah.

Unknown to Athaliah as she set out to massacre all her grandsons, the youngest was hid from the orgy of destruction. The sister of Ahaziah, Jehosheba, wife of Jehoiada the high priest hid Joash until he

was seven years old (II Kings 11:2; II Chronicles 22:11). Jehoiada had plotted to put Joash (Jehoash) on the throne and waited for the opportune moment to declare the remaining son of Ahaziah the lawful king of Judah. Athaliah came into the Temple as the coronation of Joash took place, and rending her robe, cried: "Treason!" To save the Temple from being defiled with her evil blood she was slain just outside the door where the avenging guards waited to end her infamous life. Thus, as Edith Deen expresses it,

> The horses trampled over her body where she lay dead at the gates. In her miserable end Athaliah bore a singular resemblance to her mother Jezebel, who was abandoned to the dogs. Athaliah was left in a horse-path, to be trampled upon. Like her mother she died a queen, but without a hand to help her or an eye to pity her.

Among the lessons one can gather from the record of the murderess is that we reap what we sow. To Athaliah life was cheap, and thus those who thwarted her purpose must be destroyed. But taking the sword, she perished by it. She breathed out murder, and was in turn murdered. A further lesson we learn from her stained history is that no one can thwart God's purposes of grace. Having promised a sinful world a Saviour, none could make such a promise null and void. Persecution and martyrdom have never been able to destroy the loyal worship of the true God. Idolatry and infidelity cannot possibly annihilate the imperishable Word of God. As we leave the shameful story of Athaliah we find ourselves in full agreement with the summary of her bloody career as given by Dr. Robert G. Lee —

> Her very name is an execration. She put the whole nation under the shadow of a great horror. She trampled on all faith. She violated all obligation. She lived with the shrieks of those she butchered in her ears. She lived with her hands red with the blood of princes and princesses. She died, frantic with rage, with the accusation of Treason on her lips. She died in the barnyard under the battleaxes of an aroused people.

AZUBAH No. 1

Scripture Reference — I Chronicles 2:18, 19
Name Meaning — Deserted desolation

The promise of God not to desert His

people is confirmed in a few symbolical names. For instance, in the phrase, "Thou shalt no more be termed *forsaken* — or — *desolate*" (Isaiah 62:4), we have in the last word, *Azubal*. The first holder of the name was the first wife of Caleb, not Joshua's friend, but one of his descendants. She became the mother of Caleb's three sons, Jesher, Shobab and Ardon.

AZUBAH No. 2

Scripture References — I Kings 22:42; II Chronicles 20:31

The second Azubah was the daughter of Shilhi whose name, signifying "Armed of the Lord," speaks of a man who knew God as His defense. She became the wife of King Asa, third king of Judah, who reigned for 46 years and who is reckoned among the good and noble rulers in Judah. Azubah became the mother of Jehoshaphat, who, in spite of wrong alliances he formed, stands out as another commendable king. There is every evidence that she was one of the God-fearing women of her time, and was a strong religious force in the life of her son. The recurring phrase in the genealogy of some of Israel's rulers, "His mother's name was — and he did that which was right in the sight of the Lord," testifies to the godly influence of the mother in the life of her son.

BAARA

Scripture Reference — I Chronicles 8:8
Name Meaning — The burning one

Baara was a Moabitess whom Shaharaim, a Benjamite, married when he went into the land of Moab. Hushim was his other wife. Her name has an interesting connection and is derived from Beera, "to burn," or "a burning," "a kindling." Some scholars suppose that it designates the same person before called Hodesh, by allusion to the kindling of fires as beacons which was customary among the Israelites in very ancient times to announce the appearance of the new moon.

BASHEMATH, BASEMETH, BASMATH

Name Meaning — Fragrant *or* Perfumed

These variations of the same name all mean the same thing and are from basam, an aromatic plant — the "balsam." The R.V. gives Basmath in all of the following references.

BASHEMATH No. 1

Scripture References — Genesis 26:34; 36:10

She was one of the wives of Esau, who is also called the daughter of Elon the Hittite. Esau married her out of spite because his father was not pleased with his other wives who were among the daughters of Canaan. Bashemath was doubtless the name of praise conferred upon her at marriage (see Adah).

BASHEMATH No. 2

Scripture References — Genesis 28:9; 36:3, 4, 13

She was the daughter of Ishmael, and the last of Esau's three wives according to the Edomites genealogy. From this Bashemath came her son Renel, from whom four Edomite tribes were descended (see Mahalath).

BASHEMATH No. 3

Scripture Reference — I Kings 4:15

Bashemath was a daughter of Solomon who became the wife of Ahimaaz, one of the King's tax collectors at Naphtali.

BATHSHEBA
The Woman Whose Beauty Resulted in Adultery and Murder

Scripture References — II Samuel 11:2, 3; 12:24; I Kings 1:11-31; 2:13-19; I Chronicles 3:5
Name Meaning — The Seventh Daughter, *or* The Daughter of an Oath. "Bath" means "daughter." A kindred name is Bath Shua, a Canaanite name which implies, "the daughter of opulence." The wife of Judah is referred to as "Shua's daughter" (Genesis 38:2; I Chronicles 2: 3). Bath Shua was also the name of the daughter of Ammiel and wife of David (I Chronicles 3:5).
Family Connections — Bathsheba came of a God-fearing family. She was the daughter of Eliam or Ammiah, who was the son of Ahithophel. Eliam, whose name means "God is gracious," was one of David's gallant officers. Bathsheba became the wife of Uriah, the most loyal of David's men. After the murder of Uriah, she be-

came the wife of David, and mother of five sons by him. The first died in infancy. The others were Solomon, Shimea, Shobub and Nathan. She is mentioned in our Lord's genealogy as "her that had been the wife of Uriah" (Matthew 1:6).

The sacred record informs us that David's association with Bathsheba was the only stain upon the escutcheon of David. "David did that which was right in the eyes of the LORD, and turned not aside from any thing that he commanded him all the days of his life, save only in the matter of Uriah" (I Kings 15:5). If this was the only blot on his page, it was a heavily engrained one, and one that could not be erased, as far as the effects of his treatment of Uriah was concerned. While God freely pardons a sinner, often the effects of committed sin remain. The tragic lapse in the life of the man after God's own heart is built up with consummate art, from David's first sight of Bathsheba to the climax of his unutterable remorse when realizing the enormity of his most grievous sin, he flung himself upon the mercy of God.

The sad story begins with the significant phrase, "But David tarried still at Jerusalem" (II Samuel 11:1). The Israelites were at war with the Ammonites, and the king who had shown himself brave and victorious in battle should have been with his army. But now a mature man, and veteran of many wars, and ruler over Israel for some twelve years now David had become somewhat soft and self-indulgent. He had had his day of hard campaigning and war weariness. Now it was time to leave the rigors and risks of battle to his officers, and sit back and take things easy. But no longer fighting the battle of the Lord, David was open to attack and so found himself involved in the triangle drama of passion, intrigue and murder.

Lazing around on the flat roof of his palace, David saw a woman on the roof of a nearby house undressing and bathing herself, and his passions were excited. Bathsheba, the woman exposing herself nudely, was "very beautiful to look upon," and David, ever attracted by lovely women, coveted her, and became guilty of an outrageous disgrace. Although David was to confess that his foul sin was his, and his

alone, one wonders how far Bathsheba was the accomplice in such a sin, as well as its provocation. Had she been a careful, modest woman, surely she would have looked around the easily seen adjacent roofs, and if others had been looking her way, she would have been more appropriately modest in bathing herself.

Further, when sent for by David, had she been a true wife and a woman of principle she should have refused to obey the king's summons. As she saw David feasting his eyes upon her, did she have a presentiment of what would happen? If not, then, when before the king, she should have bravely refused to yield to adultery. Later on in the sacred record, a heathen woman — a queen — brave Vashti, stoutly refused to expose herself before wine-inflamed men, and was expelled from court. Had Bathsheba shown the same determination to preserve her dignity, David, the anointed of Israel, would never have sinned as he did. After the adulterous act in the king's bedchamber, Bathsheba manifested no sense of guilt, but after her husband's murder almost immediately went to the palace to supplement David's many wives.

Bathsheba only added insult to the injury by indulging in her illicit affair with another man, while her lawful husband was risking his life in the service of her seducer. Learning of Bathsheba's pregnant condition, David hurried Uriah home to allay suspicion, but returning, the devoted soldier, a man of highest principle, refused any physical contact with his wife. David's clever plan failed, and the plot thickens. Uriah must be gotten rid of, so he was sent back to the battlefield with a letter to Joab to put Uriah in a foremost place where he was bound to be killed. Godly, gallant Uriah had no ideas that that sealed letter carried his death warrant. Thus, for David lust, adultery, deceit, treachery and murder followed in quick succession.

After the accustomed period of mourning Bathsheba became the wife of David, and their child of an adulterous union was born without disgrace, only to die within a week of his birth. "The Lord struck the child that Uriah's wife bare David." The deep grief of David over the sickness and death of the child, while not relieving the king of his murderous crime, gives us a glimpse of his better nature and of his faith in reunion beyond the grave. Perhaps no other passage of the Bible has been used to comfort sorrowing hearts in the hour of death as that in which David assures us of immortality. Mourning over his dead child he said, "Can I bring him back again?" No, he could not. Then came words binding up the cruel wound death causes, "I shall go to him, but he shall not return to me." Both David and Bathsheba must have had much agony of soul as they became deeply conscious that the death of their son, conceived out of wedlock, was a divine judgment upon their dark sin.

Divinely instructed, Nathan the prophet brought David to a realization of his terrible evil, and sincere in his confession of his iniquity, he received from Nathan the assuring word, "The Lord also hath put away thy sin." Much has been written about David's repentance preserved for us in Psalm 51 — a Psalm saturated with penitential tears — and of Psalm 32, expressing David's gratitude to God for His pardoning grace and mercy. But graciously forgiven, even God could not avert the natural consequences of David's transgression, and he came to prove its inevitable subsequent sorrow. Evil rose up against him in his own house (II Samuel 12:11). David found himself disgraced by one son (13:4), banished by another (15:19), revolted against by a third (I Kings 2), bearded by his servant, betrayed by his friends, deserted by his people, bereaved of his children.

What about Bathsheba? With David, was she made conscious of her share in the iniquitous transaction of the past? Co-responsible in David's sin, did her tears of repentance mingle with those of her husband's? It would seem so, because God blessed them with another son whom they called Solomon, meaning, "Beloved of the Lord." Why was not such a son given to one of David's other wives? Given to David and Bathsheba was not Solomon an evidence and expression of God's pardoning love for both? Then, is not Bathsheba's inclusion in the genealogy of Jesus (Matthew 1) another token that God had put her sins behind His back? Restored to divine favor, and now virtuous and wise as well as

beautiful, Bathsheba brought up her son Solomon in all godly diligence and care. Solomon himself came to write, "Train up a child in the way he should go" (Proverbs 22:6), which counsel reflected his own godly upbringing. Tradition says that it was Bathsheba who composed Proverbs 31, as an admonition to Solomon on his marriage to Pharaoh's daughter. If this be so, we can understand all the warnings against the flatteries of strange women with which Proverbs abounds.

After her lapse, recovery and the birth of Solomon the rest of Bathsheba's life is veiled in silence. We can imagine how noble calmness, gentle dignity and queenly courage became hers. That she retained her influence over David until his death is proven by the way she reminded the king of his promise to make their son, Solomon, his successor. The veil of silence is lifted again when Solomon became king, and Bathsheba, whom Solomon revered, came into his presence to ask that Abishag, who cared for David in his last days, be given in marriage to Adonijah, the son of Haggith, one of David's other wives.

A lesson we can learn from Bathsheba is that being assured of God's forgiveness she did not let her one sin ruin her entire life. Repentant, she used her mistake as a guide to future, better conduct. When we brood over sins God has said He will remember no more against us, we actually doubt His mercy, and rob ourselves of spiritual power and progress. Read again Psalm 51 and then Psalm 32.

BERNICE

The Woman Guilty of Incestuous Conduct

Scripture References—Acts 25:13, 23; 26:30

Name Meaning — Bernice (Greek — *Bernicke*), or Berenice, is a Macedonian corruption of *Pherenice,* and means, "victorious," or "carrying off victory." Wilkinson informs us that the name occurs in previous history, being given "to the wife of Ptolemy, one of Alexander's generals, who became King of Egypt, and founder of an illustrious dynasty." Another compound with *nike,* implying "victory," is found in Eunice (Greek — *Eunicke*) the name of Timothy's mother. ". . . The word is expressive of a good or happy victory, and in its origin doubtless commemorated some such event. It is noticeable that *nike* was a favorite termination of females in the Macedonian age, as for example, *Thessalonice*, the daughter of Philip, King of Macedon, and *Stratonice*, the name of the wife of Antigonus, one of Alexander's generals and successors."

Family Connections — Bernice was the eldest daughter of Herod Agrippa I who ruled, A.D. 38-45, and is described as the one "who vexed the church" (Acts 12:1). Josephus says that she was first married to Marcus. After a while she married her Uncle Herod, king of Chalcis. When he died, she was suspected of evil relations with her own brother Agrippa, with whom she always appeared as his consort. In company with Agrippa, Bernice visited Festus when he became procurator of Judea. Leaving Agrippa, she married Polemon, or Ptolemy, king of Cilicia who for her sake embraced Judaism by the rite of circumcision. She soon left Ptolemy, however, for a future period of intimacy with her brother. Subsequently she became the mistress of Vespasian, then of Titus, son of Vespasian, but when Titus became emperor, he cast her aside.

"If heredity stands for anything, its lessons are forcibly taught in the history of the Herodian family." For instance, Bernice and her sister Drusilla (Acts 24:24, see DRUSILLA), were two of the most corrupt and shameless women of their time in Roman history. As Bernice, a wicked woman who lived an incestuous life, listened to Paul's impassioned appeal as he repeated what God had done for his soul, one wonders what impression it made upon her evil heart. As her brother listened, he said to Paul, "Almost thou persuadest me to be a Christian." What a different record would have been written if Agrippa and Bernice had repented of their sordid sin, and yielded their lives to Him whose blood can make the foulest clean!

BILHAH

Scripture References — Genesis 29:29; 30: 3, 4, 5, 7; 35:22, 25; 37:2; 46:25; I Chronicles 4:29; 7:13

This slave girl was the handmaid of Rachel, Jacob's much loved wife, whom Laban gave his daughter when she married Jacob. Childless for many years, Rachel gave Bilhah to Jacob as a secondary wife, that she might have children by her. Such an act was strictly in accordance with the Code of Hammurabi. In this polygamus system, Bilhah was ranked above a mere concubine but did not have the prestige and position of a free-born mistress. Bilhah bore Jacob two sons, Dan from whom sprang Samson, called a Danite (Judges 13:2), and Naphtali, the founder of a very large tribe.

Reuben, Jacob's first son was guilty of incest with Bilhah and "Israel heard it" (Genesis 35:22). Because he had defiled his father's mistress in this way, Reuben was deprived of his birthright which was given to the sons of Joseph (Genesis 35:22; 49:4; I Chronicles 5:1). A sidelight of the morals of that time is given by Blunt, the commentator who reminds us that so vivid was the desire for the promised Redeemer that —

The wife provoked, instead of resenting, the faithlessness of her husband, the mother taught her own child deceit, daughters deliberately worked their own and their father's shame, and the daughter-in-law courted the incestuous bed, and to be childless was a byeword.

(See Genesis 16:2; 30:3, 9; 25:23; 27:13; 38:14.)

BITHIAH

Scripture Reference — I Chronicles 4:18
Name Meaning — A daughter of Jehovah

Evidently a woman of position, Bithiah is spoken of as a daughter of Pharaoh. Whether Pharaoh as used here was an Egyptian title or a proper Hebrew name is not easy to determine. Says Wilkinson, "This Pharaoh may have been an Israelite, deriving his name from the Hebrew word *pernoth* or *paroth*, from *para* meaning 'to take the lead.' If we suppose him to have been really a king of Egypt, which is not altogether inconceivable, the name of the daughter may be understood to imply her conversion to the Israelitish faith, and admission into the bond of the covenant." Perhaps she was among the Egyptians who became proselytes after the disaster of the Red Sea, and, like Ruth, renounced home, country and the past to take an Israelite husband and to have Israel's God as her God. She married Mered, a descendant of the tribe of Judah, whose other wife was Jehudijah, "the Jewess," to distinguish her from Bithiah of Egyptian extraction.

CANDACE

Scripture Reference — Acts 8:27
Name Meaning — Queen or Ruler of Children

The exact name of this Ethiopian queen is not given by Luke. It was the name of a dynasty, not of an individual, and was used for many years by the queens of Ethiopia, just as Pharaoh was the hereditary title given to ancient Egyptian kings and Caesar to Roman emperors. The fascinating context Luke gives us is taken up with the eunuch, a man of great authority, a potentate in his way, returning through the desert to Meroe, Ethiopia, interested in Old Testament Scripture. Philip the Evangelist found him sitting in his chariot reading Isaiah 53, and from this chapter so full of the truth of the cross, preached unto him Jesus. The eunuch was converted to God, and baptized there in the desert, and returned to his country rejoicing. Tradition has it that he witnessed to the Candace of his newly-found Saviour and that she, too, embraced the Christian faith. Such was the influence of this converted eunuch, that many souls were saved and ultimately he became bishop of the first Christian Church in Ethiopia. It is interesting to note that the present emperor of Ethiopia is a professed believer.

CHLOE

Scripture Reference — I Corinthians 1:10, 11
Name Meaning — Green herb

We are not told anything about the background of this Corinthian matron and head of a Christian household. Evidently she was well-known to the Corinthians by her personal name which means "green herb," and in the Greek represents the first green shoot of plants. Chloe is therefore emblematic of fruitful grace and beauty. It was while he was benefiting from the hospitality of her home that Paul received information of strife among leaders in the Early Church and which he sought to deal with in this first chapter of First Corinthians. The Church at Corinth gave Paul a good deal of concern and heartache because of its low spirituality.

CLAUDIA

Scripture Reference — II Timothy 4:21
Name Meaning — Lame

Tradition has more to say about this Roman Christian worker than the Bible. She can be included among the chief and honorable women of Gentile origin who heard and believed the Gospel. Doubtless she was a member of one of the great old houses in Rome. We find her associated with Paul and the other members of her church in sending Timothy Christian greetings. Several scholars suggest that Claudia was the wife of Pudens, with whom she is mentioned, and that Linus, who became bishop of Rome was their son. There is no warrant, however, for the assumption that Claudia might possibly have been Pilate's wife, who was traditionally known as Claudia.

There is an interesting legend that affirms Claudia, as a British lady of high birth — the daughter of the British king, Cogidubnus. She was put under the patronage of Pomponia, wife of Aulus Plautius, conqueror of Britain and from this Christian learned the truths of the Gospel. Tacitus the Roman historian speaks of an inscription found in Chichester, England, declaring Claudia to be of British stock. All the Bible tells us of her is that she was among the devout women who greatly encouraged the Apostle Paul in his arduous labors for the Master he dearly loved.

COZBI

Scripture Reference — Numbers 25:6-18
Name Meaning — Deceiver, deception

This Midianitish woman, daughter of Zur, head of a chief house in Midia, had a pure Hebrew name the meaning of which corresponding to her character, for Cozbi is derived from the verb *cazab*, meaning, "deceiver" or "deception." Given by her parents the name may have expressed their disappointment over the birth of a daughter instead of an expected son. But, says Wilkinson in *Personal Names*, "It is conceivable that this name may have been given from the observation of proneness to falsehood and deceit in early childhood." In the degraded moral condition of the Midianites of the time, craftiness and deceit were common.

Although a princess, her influence among leaders was evil. She was among those who effected the moral and religious corruption of the Israelites. She cast a spell over Zimri, son of Salu, prince among the Simeonites. This temptress was slain by Phinehas, son of Eleazar and grandson of Aaron (see Psalm 106:30, 31). It would seem as if the javelin "thrust through her belly" stayed the plague overtaking Israel for its whoredom and idolatry. What a sad day that was when thousands of Israelites perished! (Numbers 25:9; I Corinthians 10:8.)

DAMARIS

Scripture Reference — Acts 17:34
Name Meaning — A heifer

This female convert of Paul's witness at Mars Hill (Acts 17:34), must have been a well-known Athenian. Her name is from the form of *Damalis,* meaning a "heifer," and in use signified a young girl. Singled out with Dionysius the Areopagite, one of the court judges, indicates personal or social distinction (Acts 17:12). There is no evidence that she was the wife of Dionysius, as some writers affirm. When Paul was mocked at Athens, Damaris along with Dionysius clave unto the Apostle and believed. How their conversion must have cheered his heart! What a precious touch the chapter ends with "and others with them." Although their names are not given they are recorded in the illustrious Lamb's Book of Life.

Among the female characters in Scripture biography are two with the name of Deborah — the one was the wet-nurse who served with her bosom's milk in Jacob's patriarchal family; and the other was the prophetess and the only female judge in the era when Israel was ruled by judges or saviours whom the Lord raised up.

DEBORAH No. 1

THE WOMAN WHO SPENT HER LIFE AS A NURSEMAID

Scripture References — Genesis 24:59; 35:8
Name Meaning — Deborah means a "bee,"

and is emblematic of industry, patience, sagacity and usefulness — a beautifully appropriate name for a maidservant or nursemaid. Deborah's conduct throughout her long life fulfilled the expectation, or hope, expressed by her name. As a bee symbolizes constant activity, industrious diligence and care, the God of grace enabled Deborah to live her life as a devoted, quiet and faithful nurse.

Family Connections — We know nothing of Deborah's background. She was probably born in servitude, yet her parentage was commendable enough to warrant the domestic office of great trust in the patriarchal household of Nahor.

As Rebekah's nurse she accompanied her mistress to her new home after her marriage to Isaac. When Jacob and Esau were born into the home we can imagine how lovingly Deborah would care for them. Then when Jacob married, and his family increased rapidly, it is probable that Rebekah and Isaac gave Deborah to nurse them. When Rebekah had no further use for her nurse, she did not dismiss her. Deborah remained in the family and was held in great reverence. She became an indispensable treasure in that ancient patriarchal circle. When she died at an advanced age — almost 100 years according to some writers — she was lamented for as one of the family, and great honor was paid to her at her death. Her name and the place of her burial are immortalized in the words, "Deborah, Rebekah's nurse, died, and she was buried beneath Bethel under an oak tree whose name Jacob called Allon-bachuth (which means, *Oak of Weeping*)." The entire family was touched by her passing, and all who had been the recipients of Deborah's faithful devotion wept for her as for one of their own. Through her faith to God, she had transformed the bonds of servitude into those of love, and earned the devotion and gratitude of those whom she had so long and loyally served. Deborah brought the glory of God into the most commonplace duties of Jacob's home. No wonder all eyes were wet with tears as they buried her aged, bent body under that oak tree. Famous men, like Earl Shaftesbury and Robert L. Stevenson, have testified to the debt they owe to devoted nurses who were so kind and devoted to them in their earlier years, and who greatly influenced their lives, even more so than their own parents.

DEBORAH No. 2
THE WOMAN WHO WAS A FEARLESS PATRIOT

Scripture References — Judges 4 and 5; Hebrews 11:32-34

Name Meaning — Although we know nothing of the early history of this prophetess-judge, it may be that her parents with a knowledge of the unselfish and untiring service of Deborah the nurse, gave their baby girl the same name which, as already indicated, means "a bee." This we do know that the practical qualities symbolized by the busy bee were as necessary to Deborah as they were to the right performance of the less conspicuous and humbler duties of the former nurse Deborah. While Deborah the patriot gathered honey for her friends, like a bee she had a fatal sting for her enemies as the Canaanites came to experience. "Science confirms the ancient belief that, of all the animal kingdom, the bee ranks among the highest in intelligence" says Mary Hallet. "So Deborah stands out as among the wisest of all the Old Testament women."

Family Connections — We have no genealogy of this female warrior and writer. The only personal touch we have is that she was "the wife of Lapidoth" (Judges 4:4), whose name is the only thing the Bible gives us. Their home was between Bethel and Ramah in the hill country of Ephraim. The palm tree under which Deborah ruled and possibly lived was a land mark, as palms were then rare in Palestine. In honor of her works, it became known as "The Palm of Deborah" (Judges 4:5). Although referred to as a "mother in Israel," we have no record of Deborah being a mother of natural children by Lapidoth.

Occasionally, a strong-minded and unique woman breaks in upon human history and by her exploits leaves the impact of her personality upon events and secures for herself an imperishable honor. England, for instance, will never forget the bolds deeds of Margaret of Anjou, who at the head of her northern forces swept over the country like a cyclone, destroying armies and tearing down thrones. In France, Joan of Arc, the patron saint of her country, professed to have divine visions as to her destiny to restore peace to her distracted nation by the crowning of Charles. From school days we have known how she led 10,000 troops against the English at Orleans, and compelled them to retreat, and of how other victories followed as her consecrated banner struck terror into the hearts of her enemies. Ultimately, she was burned at the the stake as "a martyr to her religion, her country and her king." Her ashes, thrown into the Seine, were carried to the sea, and the sea, taking them around the world became emblematic of her universal fame.

Similarly gifted with superior spiritual, mental and physical powers to leave her mark upon the annals of time was Deborah whom God raised up and endowed with a remarkable personality and varied gifts for the deliverance of His distressed and defeated people. A woman of unusual attainments, Deborah carved out an enviable niche for herself. With characteristic resoluteness she occupied several positions.

She Was a Wife

While nothing is said of her husband and home life, there is no reason to affirm, as some writers do, that being born to rule, Deborah was master in her own home. Some writers feel that since Lapidoth was the husband of a prominent woman, that he was "hen-pecked" or that Deborah "wore the trousers." Wharton in *Famous Women* suggests that Lapidoth was a weak man married to a strong-willed and a strong-bodied woman. "His very name is in the original Hebrew put not in the masculine, but in the feminine gender. I have no doubt that while by no means so great, he was yet 'as meek as Moses.'" Although meek, Moses was by no means weak.

We prefer to believe that Lapidoth admired the ability and influence of his more conspicuous wife. His name means, "torches" or "lightning flashes," and we can well imagine how in his quieter way he was the encourager of Deborah in all her activities. Although not so forceful and capable as his wife, yet he was illuminative in his own way and behind the scenes was as good and conspicuous in faith as the woman he loved, and in whose glory he was content to bask. Many of the notable men of the world have testified to the succor and inspiration they received from their wives who walked with them in full agreement as they climbed the heights. Perhaps the shoe was on the other foot in that God-fearing home. Deborah would never have become the dazzling figure she did, had she not had the love, sympathy, advice and encouragement of a husband who was happy to ride in the second chariot.

She Was a Prophetess

Deborah is one of several females in Scripture distinguished as being endowed with the prophetic gift, which means the ability to discern the mind and purpose of God and declare it to others. In the days of the Old Testament, prophets and prophetesses were the media between God and His people Israel, and their gift to perceive and proclaim divine truth stamped them as being divinely inspired. Such an office, whether held by a male or female, was a high one and corresponds to the ministry of the Word today. Can you not picture how hungry-minded Israelites found their way to that conspicuous palm tree beneath which Deborah sat, stately in person with her dark, penetrating, prophetic eyes, and poured out wisdom and instruction as she declared the whole counsel of God? As a woman, she had intuition as well as inspiration, which is always better than a man's cold reasoning. Had Pontius Pilate taken the advice of his wife he would not have signed the death warrant of Jesus Christ.

She Was an Agitator

As one meaning of "agitation" is to stir up or excite public discussion with the view of producing a change, then Deborah was an effective agitator who stirred up Israel's concern about its low spiritual condition. The land was debauched and well-nigh ruined, and under the rule of the Canaanites liberty had been lost. The people were dejected and afraid, for their spirits had been broken and all hope of deliverance had vanished. But Deborah did more than prophesy; she aroused the nation from its lethargy and despair. Hers was a fearless and unsolicited devotion to the emancipation of God's people, and she awoke in them a determination to free themselves from their wretched bondage and degradation. Out went her call and challenge to the help of the Lord against the enemy. Day after day, she excited those who gathered to hear her words of divine wisdom with the certainty of deliverance from a heathen foe if only they would bestir themselves from their folly and fear and go out and fight.

She Was a Ruler

Deborah was the fifth of the leaders or "Judges" of Israel raised up by God to deliver His people from the bondage their idolatry had caused, and instant both in word and deed she fulfilled her role as "Judge," at a time when men tried to do right in the sight of their own eyes. As the position of woman in those days was of a distinctly subordinate character, Deborah's prominence as a ruler is somewhat remarkable. All Israel was under her jurisdiction, and from the palm tree bearing her name, and elsewhere, called "the sanctuary of the palm," she dispensed righteousness, justice and mercy. After the victory over the nation's foes, she ruled with equity a land that had rest from war and captivity for forty years.

She Was a Warrior

Having fought with words she went forth to throw off the oppressor's yoke with swords, and what a fighter this patriotic and inspired heroine proved to be. Deborah sent for Barak, the son of Abinoam of Naphtali, and told him that it was God's will that he should lead her forces and deliver the country. Long slavery and repeated failures made Barak hesitate, but ultimately he decided to lead the army provided Deborah, the brave-hearted and dauntless ruler, went with him. Barak felt he could face the foe if his ruler were at hand, and out they went to meet Sisera, a mighty man of war, who had terrorized Israel for many years. Great were the odds against Deborah and Barak, for their army consisted of some 10,000 men. Sisera commanded 100,000 fighters, and had 900 iron chariots. When the eventful moment of combat came, the dauntless spirit of Deborah did not quail. True, tremendous odds were against them, but Deborah had God as her Ally and "the stars in their courses fought against Sisera." A fearful hailstorm overtook the land, and the Canaanites were almost blinded by the rain, and were ultimately overwhelmed in the swollen river of Kishon. Sisera escaped but was killed by Jael while asleep in her tent. (See JAEL.) Thus Deborah gained undying fame as the female warrior who rescued her people from their cruel foes.

She Was a Poetess

The prose and poem of Judges 4 and 5 are associated with the same historic event, and reveal that Deborah could not only prophecy, arouse, rule and fight, but also write. It was said of Julius Caesar that, "he wrote with the same ability with which he fought." This observation can also be true of Deborah, who, after her victory over the Canaanites, composed a song which is regarded as one of the finest specimens of ancient Hebrew poetry, being superior to the celebrated song of Miriam (see MIRIAM). This song of praise, found in Judges 5, magnifies the Lord as being the One who enabled Israel's leaders to conquer their enemies. Out of the contest and conquest came the moral purification of the nation, and the inspiring genius of it was a woman daring and dynamic in the leadership of her nation. No character in the Old Testament stands out in bolder relief than Deborah — prophetess, ruler, warrior and poetess. Her song is immortal because her life was dedicated to God and her deeds heroic and sublime.

She Was a Maternal Figure

The last glimpse we have of Deborah is as "a mother in Israel" (5:7). Commenting upon our Lord's action in taking up little children into His arms and blessing them as being a father's act in Hebrew custom, Bengel says, "Jesus had no children that He might adopt all children." Perhaps it was so with Deborah who, as far as we know, had never experienced actual motherhood, but yet became as a mother to all in Israel, and the source of this spiritual motherhood was her piety. Above all of her remarkable

gifts was her trust in God which is ever the source of any woman's highest adornment. As she sat under her palm tree to rule in righteousness and translate the revelation of God, her heart was filled with that "grace divine which. diffused itself like a sweet-smelling savor over the whole land." Hers was a brilliant career because of a heart that was fixed in God. Meroz failed God, and under a curse, vanished, but Deborah is immortal because she served God to the limit of her ability and capacity. She was indeed the female Oliver Cromwell of ancient Israel who went out to fight the Lord's battles with a psalm on her lips and a sword in her hand.

DELILAH
THE WOMAN WHO BETRAYED HER HUSBAND FOR SILVER

Scripture References — Judges 16:4-21 (Read Proverbs 5)

Name Meaning — Delilah is a sweet-sounding name which any vain woman would covet, for it means "delicate" or "dainty one." Because of the foul deed of which Delilah was guilty, no other female in Scripture appears with such a tarnished name. In fact, it is rare indeed to find a woman bearing this name.

Family Connections — The Bible gives us no knowledge of her parentage and background save that she came from the valley of Sorek which extended from near Jerusalem to the Mediterranean, and which entrance was beautiful with rare flowers perfuming the air with sweet odors.

The record of Delilah, the heartless wrecker of a mighty man, is given in eighteen verses; and the description of Samson's betrayal, fall, bondage and death is one of the most graphic in the Bible. We cannot, of course, write of Delilah without mentioning Samson. What a contrast they present, and how symbolic they are of characters in the world today! Samson was physically strong but morally weak. Although able to rend a lion, he could not fight his lusts. He could break his bonds, but not his habits. He could conquer Philistines but not his passions. Delilah was a woman who used her personal charm to lure a man to his spiritual and physical destruction, and she stands out as one of the lowest, meanest women of the Bible — the female Judas of the Old Testament.

This Philistine courtesan was a woman of unholy persistence and devilish deceit, who had personal charm, mental ability, self-command, and nerve, but who used all her qualities for one purpose — *money*. She and womanly honor and love had never met, for behind her beautiful face was a heart as dark as hell, and full of viperous treachery. "Her supreme wickedness lay not in betraying Samson to his enemies but in causing him to break faith with his ideals." Shakespeare might well have had Delilah in mind when he wrote —

O Nature! What hadst thou to do in Hell,
When thou didst bower the spirit of a fiend
In mortal Paradise of such sweet flesh.

Deluding Samson into believing she really loved him, Delilah sold him to blindness, bondage and death. The ease with which she betrayed her husband revealed that she belonged to the enemies of God's people, the people of whom Samson was the recognized leader at that time. The Philistines did not like Samson around because he was the champion of Israel and as such interfered with their practices. Therefore he must be got rid of, and in Delilah, the Philistine prostitute, the Philistines had one who was willing to be bribed to act as their agent. She had one purpose and that was to secure money, and had no qualms of conscience to trifle with love for the sake of wealth. Thus, as Kuyper expresses it, "All the while she kept a police force quartered in her rooms and awaited the moment in which she could surrender her lover into his enemies' hands."

Samson became a traitor to himself because he could not resist a woman's charm. First one woman and then another took advantage of this deep-seated weakness and basic sin of his, and Delilah was the most effective in destroying him. She remains as a warning to all men to beware of the charm and wiles of a wicked, scheming woman. As one unknown writer puts it —

The women of the Bible pass before the imagination in the vision of antiquity, like pure and radiant stars, their frailties scarcely more than the wing of a transparent cloud upon these beautiful spheres. Delilah rises suddenly from darkness, as a glorious meteor, describes an arc of romantic and fatal light, and goes down in a horizon of awful gloom.

The lords of the Philistines offered an enormous sum as a bribe, namely, 1,100 pieces of silver. Jesus was sold by Judas for only 30 pieces of silver. Such a fortune was no small temptation to Delilah, and sharing her tempters' passion for revenge, she set about, in a subtle way, to earn the price of blood. She tried four times in her cunning, evil way to get Samson to reveal the secret of his supernatural power. The first three times Samson humorously lied in answering Delilah's question by enumerating the green withs or twigs, the new ropes, and the weaving of the hair. Thrice deceived, Delilah the enchantress employed her final weapon — *tears*. Sobbing, she said, "How canst thou say I love thee, when thine heart is not with me? Thou hast mocked me these three times, and hast not told me wherein thy great strength lieth."

Samson was conquered. A weeping woman melted his heart, and he confessed the truth of his Nazarite vow, and how, if shorn of his long hair, his strength would depart and he would become like any other normal man. Recognizing that the truth had been told, Delilah lulled Samson to sleep. As he slept, the waiting Philistines destroyed the sign of the vow, and when Samson awoke, although he tried to exert his power as before, he found it had deserted him. The rest of the tragic story belongs to Samson. His foes gouged out his eyes, bound him in fetters and in Gaza, where his God-given strength was manifested, he was made to grind corn. The spiritual Hercules had been reduced to the very depth of degradation. Samson knew that his bitter servitude was the result of his sin and could confess—

Myself my sepulchre, a moving grave.
    Prison within prison,
    Inseparably dark!
Nothing of all these evils hath befall'n me
But justly; I myself have brought them,
Sole author I, sole cause. If aught seems vile,
As vile hath been my folly.

But out of the depths Samson cried unto the Lord, and, as we read, his hair began to grow. Forsaken by all, there was One near at hand, and the God of grace restored unto His sinning and now repentant servant, the power he had lost. Samson's extremity became God's opportunity. While Samson was in prison, in the palace, three thousand Philistines gathered to honor their god Dagon for victory over their feared enemy. As hearts beat high and warm, with banquet wine and dance, the cry goes up to have blind Samson brought in to be made the butt of their jests and ridicule. A lad brings the giant in and places him between the pillars of the heathen temple where all eyes could see him. The mockery of the drunken crowd begins. They ask for a riddle and Samson acted one they did not expect. With his arms around the pillars, and deeply penitent for his sins, he prayed, "O Lord, remember me and give me strength only this once."

Then shaking himself as of old, he threw his arms around the pillars, the massive temple tottered and the 3,000 Philistines, including the treacherous Delilah perished. It was a victory that cost Samson his own life, and we find that he slew more at his death than he had in the heyday of his power.

There is no evidence for John Milton's idea that Delilah was deeply repentant for her crime against Samson, and visited him in prison imploring his forgiveness, or of his stern reply —

> Out! out! hyena, these are thy wonted arts,
> And arts of every woman false like thee;
> To break all faith, all vows, deceive, betray.
> Then as repentant, to submit, beseech
> And reconcilement move with feigned remorse.

In his drama, *Samson Agonistes*, Milton goes on to describe Delilah's further efforts to secure forgiveness and at last throws herself upon her reserved resource and pleads her love of country and the grateful esteem in which she will be held by her posterity. But a woman like Delilah did not know how to repent; and as Judas went out and hanged himself, so it would seem as if Delilah, gloating over the price received for Samson's betrayal, died a terrible death when buried beneath the frightful ruins of the temple her husband's restored, divine strength had caused.

What are the lessons to be gathered from Samson and Delilah, whose record Hollywood could not resist turning into a sexy movie with box-office appeal? The ques-

tion may be asked, How can we learn any lesson from such an unpleasant story? Why is this sordid record to the last degree in the Bible? The reading of the man under a vow to God and of great physical strength and mental agility choosing a woman of no morals may be deemed unfit for inclusion in Holy Writ. Yet *all* Scripture is given by inspiration of God, and the writer of the Book of Judges was guided by the Spirit to set forth the details of the amorous life of Samson. Our answer is that the Bible would not be true to life and to its mission in the world if it did not hold up the mirror and reveal to us, in restrained language, workings of evil, and the boundless love and grace of God toward those whose lives are so bankrupt of virtues pleasing to Him. As the biography of humanity, the Bible is most up-to-date for us, as H. V. Morton reminds us —

> The police courts are always telling the old story of Samson and Delilah. It comes up in a number of ingenious disguises, a theme capable of infinite variation, but the main motif throughout is that of a man who plunges deeper and deeper into his own lack of self-control until the moment arrives when, trapped and shorn of his strength he is blinded and branded.

This same writer goes on to say that Delilah vanished, as such women do, when her task was completed and she received a reward. Morton then relates a conversation he had with a criminal lawyer about the prosecution in a recent case when certain charges were brought against a man who ruined him. "It is simple," said the lawyer. "A girl pretended to be in love with him and gave him away."

"You mean his enemies bribed her?"

"Of course," he said.

This incident, like the story of Delilah, needs no moralizing. The record is sufficient in itself. Delilah was not concerned about the weakness of Samson, but his strength. Once a man betrays his strength, he has no reserve, and courts disaster. A further lesson to be learned from the story before us is that true feminine charm and the appeal of love are gifts received from the Creator, and that when these fairest and most effective of gifts are misused or deliberately trifled with, divine retribution overtakes those who prostitute such gifts.

Another lesson to be gleaned from the ancient record before us is that of the folly of being unequally yoked. Samson married outside his own country, people and religion. Had Samson, hero of Israel, married an Israelitish maiden, the tragedy overtaking him would never have happened. But he took to wife a devotee of a heathen god which, for a judge of Israel, was against the divine decree, and he paid the fatal price of his action.

DINAH
The Woman Whose Sightseeing Had Fatal Results

Scripture Reference — Genesis 34

Name Meaning — Dinah means "justice" or "one who judges," and was doubtless given her as a token of her parents' belief in divine justice.

Family Connections — She was a daughter of Jacob and Leah, and as a member of a family under covenant blessing should have been more careful regarding her personal obligation in maintaining the honor of her home and nation.

Dinah's love for sight-seeing set off a train of tragic consequences. Young and daring, and curious to know something of the world outside, she stole away one day from the drab tents of her father, to see how the girls in their gorgeous Oriental trappings fared in nearby Shechem. Roaming around, the eyes of Prince Shechem, son of Hamor lighted upon her. He *saw her* means he lusted after her (see Job 31:1), and then as the record puts it, "he took her, lay with her, and defiled her" (Genesis 34:2). Although Dinah's vanity was flattered at Shechem's attention so that she went to his palace, she never meant to go so far. *Took her* implies he forced her, and although she may have resisted his advances, resistance was futile and she was seduced.

Had Dinah been content to remain a "keeper at home" (Titus 2:5), a terrible massacre would have been averted, but her desire for novelty and forbidden company spelled disaster. Josephus tells us that Dinah went to the Canaanite annual festival of nature worship (Numbers 25:2) — a forbidden association for an Israelite. Sin, shame and death came to Dinah and Shechem through the windows of their eyes

and ears (see Genesis 39:7). The young prince offered the usual reparation for his seduction of Dinah — marriage and a payment to her father which was sufficient according to Hebrew law (Deuteronomy 22: 28, 29). Evidently there was more than lustful desire on the part of Shechem, for we read — "His soul clave unto Dinah the daughter of Jacob, and he loved the damsel, and spake kindly unto her." When Hamor went to Jacob and his sons to discuss the matter of marriage between his son and Dinah, he said, "The soul of my son Shechem longeth for your daughter. I pray you give her him to wife."

The sons of Jacob, angry over the shame brought to their sister and nation, said that such a thing "ought not to be done." By what Dinah had become — a seduced woman — she caused her father to be a "stink among the inhabitants of the land."

Seeming to acquiesce in Hamor's suggestion that his son and Dinah should marry and that there should be established a friendlier association between the Israelites and Shechemites, the sons of Jacob, particularly Simeon and Levi, said that they would agree to Hamor's proposition on one condition. The condition was that all the male Shechemites submit to the rite of circumcision — an act of priestly consecration. When the pain of the operation was at its height and movement was difficult, on the third day, Simeon and Levi attacked and slew all the males in the city, including young Shechem himself. For centuries, among the Arabs, seduction was punishable by death, the judgment being generally inflicted by the brothers of the one seduced. For their crime, Simeon and Levi received a curse instead of a blessing from Jacob their father, as he came to die.

One salutary effect of this tragedy was the reconsecration of Jacob who had lapsed somewhat as the result of his settlement near Shechem (Genesis 33:17-20). Remembering his vow to make an altar at Bethel to God who had appeared to him while fleeing from Esau years before, his family surrendered their strange gods and purified themselves, and at Bethel the forgotten covenant was fulfilled. In this way God overruled evil for good (Genesis 35:1-5).

How many young Dinahs there are today

captivated by the glitter and glamor of the world, and, tired of life at home, leave without warning, and become lost in the whirl of a large city. There is an alarming increase in the numbers of girls who, anxious for change and wanting to see something of the world, turn aside from the shelter of a good home and are never heard of again. Many of them end up in sin, crime and degradation. May we never cease to pray for those who try to seek out and restore the lost, young womanhood of our day!

DORCAS
THE WOMAN WHOSE DRESSMAKING MADE HER FAMOUS

Scripture Reference — Acts 9:36-43

Name Meaning — Dorcas implies "the female of a roebuck," "a gazelle" — an emblem of beauty. Dorcas is the first Greek name of a female in the New Testament, its Hebrew equivalent being *Tabitha* which is the Syro-Chaldaic form of the Hebrew *Zibiah,* or *Tsibiah,* the name of a princess of Judah, the mother of King Joash. Wilkinson says that "the Greek equivalent for her Syriac name may be accounted for by her residence at Joppa, a seaport much frequented, and no doubt partially inhabited by foreigners speaking chiefly the Greek language.

Family Connections — The Bible is silent concerning the parentage and genealogy of Dorcas. In the seaport town of Joppa she became known for her acts of charity and is the namesake for a charitable group named the Dorcas Society. Here was a woman "who with her needle embroidered her name ineffaceably into the beneficence of the world." Where did she learn to sew, make garments for the poor and become notable for her charitable works? It could possibly have been in a godly home that she was taught how to use her fingers and her funds for the comfort and relief of the needy. Dorcas must have been a woman of means to serve humanity as freely as she did. We have five glimpses of her witness and work in the historical account Luke gives us.

She Was a Christian

She is called, "a certain disciple," and is thus included among the numerous disciples mentioned in the New Testament. Through the Spirit-empowered ministry of Philip the evangelist, a Christian Church was established at Joppa — now known as Jaffa — and from an early date the church was not only a center of fervent evangelism but also of a well-organized social service. Possibly Dorcas came to know Christ as her Saviour in this church, and there caught the vision of how she could serve Christ with her money and her needle. Dorcas knew what it was to have a regenerated heart and this was the source of her unselfish life and charitable acts. Behind her sewing of garments was a saved soul. Giving of alms, and the making of garments in themselves gain no merit with God who, first of all, claims our hearts before our talents. It was only when Mary Magdalene was recovered from her stained past, that Christ accepted her desire to minister to His wants.

In our churches and also in commendable societies there are many public-spirited women who, with humanitarian ideals, are engaged in various relief activities, and whose sole object is to do good. But they are not actuated by Christ. Trying to emulate Dorcas, they lack her Christian discipleship, forgetting that caring for widows and others in need springs from "pure religion" which also reveals itself in keeping oneself unspotted from the world (James 1:26, 27). When Luke says that Dorcas was *full* of good works, he meant the word "full" to refer primarily to her inward grace, which prompted the outward deeds. "Good works are only genuine and Christian when the soul of the performer is imbued with them." The cup of cold water to be acceptable must be given in His name. With Dorcas, then, *being* good meant *doing* good. Her manifold good works flowed from a heart grateful to God for His saving grace.

Lange the commentator says that "The gazelle is distinguished for its slender and beautiful form, its graceful movements and its soft but brilliant eyes; it is frequently introduced by the Hebrews and other Oriental nations as an image of female loveliness, and the name was often employed as a proper name, in the case of females." Whether Dorcas, whose name means "gazelle," was a beautiful woman or not we are not told. She certainly lived a lovely life, and had eyes reflecting the compassion of the Master whom she so faithfully served. All whom she influenced and helped saw in her the beauty of Jesus. As a disciple she certainly had faith in the One who had called her, but she came to see that faith without works is dead. She also knew that works without faith gained no merit with God, and so the hands that dispensed alms and made garments were inwardly inspired by Him whose hands were nailed to a tree.

She Was a Philanthropist

Dorcas the believer was likewise Dorcas the benefactress. "This woman was full of good works and almsdeeds *which she did.*" How significant are these last three words! Too many well-meaning people sit around and talk about charitable works they never do. Sometimes they propose these works and leave others to execute them. Dorcas not only thought up ways of relieving the needy, but she also carried out her plans. *Which she did!* She knew what she could do, and did it. Studying the female characters of Scripture it is interesting to discover how several of them are conspicuous for one grace or work of mercy, or for another.

Rizpah we remember because of her loving care of the dead.

The widow of Zarephath for giving bread to the hungry.

Anna the prophetess for her fastings and prayers day and night.

Martha, as the queen of gracious hospitality.

Mary for her box of fragrant ointment.

Joanna, and her ministering unto Jesus.

Dorcas, for her care of widows and clothing the poor.

Further, a few Bible characters have inspired profitable institutions for the welfare of human society —

Mary Magdalene — home for wayward and lost girls.

Lazarus — whose name has been given to hospitals caring for the sick and poor.

Dorcas — source and inspiration of Dorcas Societies all over the world.

Among her good works was that of fashioning coats and garments for widows and the needy of her church and community with her own loving hands. The practical, unselfish service of this Christian philanthropist has filled the world with fragrance, for there flowed out of that little city of Joppa a multitude of benevolent and charitable organizations in which women have been prominent. The question came to Dorcas as it did to Moses when he felt he was not the man to deliver Israel from Egyptian bondage, "What is that in thine hand?" And Moses answered, "A rod" (Exodus 4:2). And that rod became the symbol of delegated divine power. "What is that in thine hand?" the Lord asked Dorcas. She said, "A needle," and He took what she had and she stitched for Christ's sake. All praise, then, to the needle that represented practical benevolence among the needy. The garments Dorcas cut out and sewed represented Christian faith in action. "I was naked and ye clothed me," said Jesus of those who clothed His poor and destitute children.

She Was Mourned and Missed

It was a sad day for the church at Joppa when one of its most beloved and devoted members died in the midst of her works of charity. "Death loves a shining mark, a signal blow," and death certainly found such a mark in the bountiful Dorcas whose passing was a blow to the community. The vessel containing the costly ointment was broken, and the odor filled the house as never before. Kind hands washed the corpse and placed it in the upper chamber, with feelings expressed by the poet —

> Sister, thou wast mild and lovely,
> Gentle as the summer breeze,
> Pleasant as the air of morning
> When it floats among the trees.

While Dorcas doubtless owned her home, she seemed to have no relatives to mourn her going. The widows she had clothed and to whom she had been a friend laid her out; and great grief prevailed. Although so diligent on behalf of others, Dorcas died in the midst of a useful life. The writer had a preacher-friend who always said that he would like to die with his boots on — and he did, one Sunday morning, while preaching the Gospel. Is it possible that Dorcas had a sudden call with her needle in hand? What a grand way to go!

She Was Raised From the Dead

Her fellow disciples at the church where she had worshiped, learning that Peter was nearby, sent two members to beseech the apostle to visit the grief-stricken company. They knew that he had exercised supernatural power, and doubtless entertained the hope that their greatly-loved benefactress might live again. Like the faithful minister that he was, Peter did not delay in accompanying the two men to the death chamber at Joppa where the weeping widows were assembled. The apostle must have been moved as they reverently exhibited the coats and garments Dorcas had made for them. Then after Christ's example at the raising of Jairus' daughter, "Peter put them all forth, and kneeled down, and prayed" (see John 11:41, 42). When he felt his request had been received, Peter spake the word of power and authority, "Tabitha, arise," and life returned. Dorcas sat up, and Peter presented her alive to the saints and widows (compare Matthew 9:25; Mark 5:40, 41).

What a moving scene that must have been! What joy must have prevailed among her fellow-saints and the widows, now that their much-loved Dorcas was alive again, and in her resurrected life, with fuller dedication to the service of the Master, was willing to take up her needle again. Her return from death must have been a great gain to her church. Her only pang was that she would have to sicken again and for the second time enter the gates of death.

She Was the Cause of Revival

The resurrection of Dorcas had a twofold effect. First of all, the miracle comforted the mourners for she had returned to her life of good works and almsdeeds. This miracle was thus like our Lord's miracles — one of mercy. The second effect was to convince all of the truth of the Christian faith attested as it was by miraculous power. Throughout Joppa the message rang, "Dorcas is alive again," and "many believed in the Lord." The miracle in that upper chamber, then, was not a miracle for the sake of a miracle. Dorcas raised from physical death became the cause of the resurrection of many from their graves of sin and unbelief. How the church at Joppa must have

increased its membership through the many who were saved as the result of the return of Dorcas from the realm of death. After the resurrection of Lazarus we read that many of the Jews believed on Jesus. Is not the same true in a spiritual resurrection? A transformed life attracts others to the Saviour. We read that after the miracle, Peter stayed in Joppa for many days, and we can assume that his ministry greatly helped the church there in the establishment of the new converts. Peter stayed with Simon the tanner, a saint who prepared skins for leather to the glory of God, just as Dorcas made up her garments with consecrated hands.

A lesson to bear in mind as we part with our saintly benefactress is that she was unconscious of the magnificent work she was doing and of its far-reaching consequences. Dorcas did not aspire to be a leader, but was content to stay in her own home and try to do all she could in all the ways she could. Thus, in spite of herself, she became a great leader in an almost universal philanthropic cause, just as "The Lady of the Lamp," Florence Nightingale, did when she went to Crimea to care for the wounded, dying soldiers on the field of battle. May grace be ours to do whatever our hands find to do, as unto the Lord!

DRUSILLA

THE WOMAN WHO WAS LOVELY BUT LOOSE

Scripture Reference — Acts 24:10-27

Name Meaning — "Drusilla" is a diminutive formed from Drusis, a notable name among the Romans and means "watered by the dew." What a different record Drusilla would have left behind if only her heart had been refreshed by the dew of heaven, and her life made as "a watered garden full of fragrance rare."

Family Connections — She was a granddaughter of Herod the Great, and the youngest daughter of Herod Agrippa I, "the first royal persecutor of the Church" whose other two daughters were Mariamne, not mentioned in Scripture, and Bernice (see BERNICE). These three girls were nieces of Herod Antipas who beheaded John the Baptist. At about the age of 15, Drusilla married King Aziz of Emesa on his becoming a Jew. She proved to be unfaithful to her husband whom she left. She illegitimately married the Roman governor, Felix, who, enamored of her Oriental beauty, abducted her through the subtlety of Simon, a Jewish necromancer. Her marriage to Felix was sinful in that as a Jewess she married a heathen who did not confess the faith of her fathers. It was also sinful because she married Felix illegally, seeing her first husband from whom she had not been divorced, was still alive. Her only child, born to Felix, was Agrippa.

Drusilla was more beautiful than her sisters, and between her and Bernice there was great hatred. Also, both of them were shameless. Drusilla is first mentioned in connection with Paul's second appearance before Felix, and she would be about 20 years of age at this time. Felix, whose name means, "fortunate," was chosen by the dictator Sylla, and the choice was certainly justified by his extraordinary fortune. Beginning life as a slave he ended up as a ruler of a Roman province. But as Tacitus says, "There was a slave's heart all the time under Felix's royal robes." Savage, treacherous and steeped in blood he had every reason to tremble as Paul preached.

As a Jewess, a wicked one at that, Drusilla had a guilty conscience about Paul in his prison cell awaiting judgment at the judgment seat of Felix, and doubtless urged Felix to bring him forth again that she might hear what he had to say concerning his faith in Christ. Both Drusilla and Felix heard a message they did not expect. As Paul "reasoned of righteousness, temperance or self-control, and judgment to come" Felix trembled or became afraid — and no wonder! What Paul said of "righteousness" convicted Felix of his unrighteous, illegal act in abducting Drusilla. The emphasis on "temperance" or strict self-control of passions and lusts hit hard at his loose living. "Judgment to come" would remind Felix of the certainty of eternity and of the harvest he would reap for his sins. It also would remind him of the fact that he was judging a man who was innocent and had no right to be in the position he was in, but that for Felix himself there was a justifiable

assize awaiting him. So, as Alexander Whyte expresses it —

> Felix sat in transfixed silence while Paul stood up before him, and plunged the two-edged sword of God's holy law into his guilt conscience, till the hardened reprobate could not command himself. A greater seal was never set to the power of Paul's preaching than when Felix shook and could not sit still under the Apostle's words.

So greatly was Felix moved and disturbed that he dismissed Paul, saying that a convenient season he would hear him again. Although he communed often with Paul after that, the apostle refused to pay a bribe for his release. What about Drusilla? How did she react to the faithful preaching of Paul? Alexander Whyte says that he has a suspicion that because her conscience was greatly disturbed by Paul's convicting truth, that it was she who cut short the discourse and had the apostle sent back to prison.

> My belief about the royal pair is, that had Drusilla not sat beside Felix that day, Felix would have been baptized, and Paul would have been set free, before the sun had gone down. But Drusilla and her sisters have cast into their graves many wounded. Many strong men have been slain to death by them. Their house is the way to hell, and their steps go down to the chambers of death.

Had Drusilla trembled and repented, and as a Jewess, a daughter of Abraham, intreated Paul to pray for her that she might be saved, what a trophy of grace she would have become. But the earnest look and manner of Paul, and the power with which he preached, filling the palace as it did with the light and awe of the Great White Throne itself, failed to bring the lustful Drusilla to her knees. She saw in Paul the enemy of all she represented and hated him for his exposure of her private sins.

After the trial Felix and Drusilla disappear from the pages of sacred history. What became of them? In respect to Drusilla, Josephus the historian, who lived about the same time, relates that about 20 years after Paul's transfer from Felix to Festus, the terrible eruption of Vesuvius occurred when prosperous Pompeii and Herculaneum were buried under the burning lava. Many fled to escape the catastrophe but Drusilla, endeavoring to escape with her child, Agrippa, was too late to evade disaster. Underestimating her danger, she left the retreat too late, and with her son was buried beneath the lava. At last, judgment overtook her, and she realized too late what it was to fall into the hands of the living God.

EGLAH

Scripture References — II Samuel 3:5; I Chronicles 3:3

Name Meaning — Heifer *or* Chariot

Eglah was one of the eight wives of King David of whom so little is known. She became the mother of David's sixth son Ithream. Unsuccessful efforts have been made to identify Eglah as another name for Michal, Saul's daughter, and David's first wife.

ELISABETH

The Woman Who Bore a Son in Her Old Age

Scripture Reference — Luke 1:5-80

Name Meaning — Elisabeth means "God is my oath" that is, "a worshiper of God." In his hymn of praise, uttered soon after the birth of his son John, Zacharias alludes to the significance of his wife's name when he said, "the oath which God swore to Abraham." The son was called John by divine command, and means "the mercy or favor of God."

Family Connections — Luke describes Elisabeth as "one of the daughters of Aaron" which means she came of an honored priestly line (Exodus 6:23). She was the wife of a priest, Zacharias, of the course of Abia, that is one of the sets of priests who ministered in the Temple from Sabbath to Sabbath (I Chronicles 24:10). There was thus a priestly descent on both sides. Priests were allowed to marry pious women (Leviticus 21:7). Elisabeth became the mother of John the Baptist, the forerunner of Jesus Christ. Assessing the life and character of Elisabeth we know that she was prominent as —

A Godly Woman

It is said of both Elisabeth and Zacharias that they were "righteous before God, walking in all the commandments of the Lord blameless." What a coveted commendation! The priestly wife was a woman of unusual piety, strong faith and spiritual gifts. All through her life she preserved the blessed traditions of Aaron and his descendants.

A Childless Woman

Righteous toward God and most faithful to her husband we yet have five words containing a world of heartbreak and disappointment, "And they had no child." For years they had both prayed and longed for a child; now they were both well-stricken in years and the prospect of natural childbearing was past. A childless state, more so for the daughter of a priest and the wife of a priest, was humiliating, for in Israel it was the dream of every woman that it might be her privilege to be the mother of the Messiah, promised to Eve, earth's first mother.

A Privileged Woman

For this beloved wife with a pious heart and cultivated intellect, God performed a miracle, as He did for Mary her cousin. "She conceived a son in her old age." It was while Zacharias was exercising his holy office in the sanctuary that the angelic messenger appeared and said, "Thy prayer is heard; and thy wife Elisabeth shall bear thee a son, and thou shalt call his name John." Although beyond the age when the birth of a child was possible, did Zacharias and his wife believe that God was able to do the impossible, and even at their advanced age remove their "reproach among men"? Well, the miracle happened. God gave Elisabeth conception, and after six months of her pregnancy, another miracle happened when without cohabitation Mary conceived by the Holy Spirit.

Zacharias, who had been struck dumb as a sign that God would fulfill His word and grant him a son, had his speech restored when John was born. He hailed John's birth with a God-glorifying song in which he said of the God-given child, "Thou shalt be called the prophet of the highest." This famous son, who came to prepare the way of the Lord, was privileged to have such godly parents to teach him ineffaceable lessons. But John was also directly nurtured by God in the deserts where he lived "till the day of his shewing unto Israel." Thus, as Donald Davidson reminds us in *Mothers of the Bible* —

It was not at his mother's knee that John learned the mysteries of the Kingdom of Heaven, but out on the lonely desert where in the silence and the solitude he found close fellowship with God, and came to know the secrets of His will.

Because of their old age when their son was born, we can assume that Zacharias and Elisabeth both died years before their godly son was cruelly murdered by Herod.

But Elisabeth was a privileged woman in another way in that she was the first woman to confess Jesus in the flesh. When she was six months with child she was visited by her cousin Mary and as soon as the Virgin entered the home, the babe leaped in Elisabeth's womb, as if to welcome the One whom Mary was to bear. Both mother and child were affected by the Holy Spirit, and Elisabeth gave Mary the most honorable of names, "The mother of my Lord." Elisabeth knew the Messiah was come and she prayed to Him and confessed Him. All Messianic hopes were about to be fulfilled for, "There, beneath that woman's clothes, my Saviour is concealed." It was her Spirit-filled greeting which prompted Mary to reply in a song called, *The Magnificat* (Luke 1:46-56; compare I Samuel 2:1-10).

For queens and females of all walks of life Elisabeth has been a favorite name, evidenced by the fact that in America alone there are almost two million females bearing such an honored name. If only all who bear this name would be "righteous before God" and blameless in character, what a mighty spiritual force they would be in the life of the nation of which they are a part. The present sovereign of Great Britain is Queen Elizabeth II, who seeks to live a life beyond reproach, and who manifests deep interest in Dr. Billy Graham's work.

ELISHEBA

Scripture Reference — Exodus 6:23
Name Meaning — God's oath *or* God is her oath

This name is the Hebrew form of Elisabeth and may be an allusion to the great promise to Abraham confirmed by the oath of God. Wilkinson remarks that, "Perhaps the name was an appeal to that oath in the extremity of national depression and distress; for she must have been born towards the close of the bondage in Egypt, and about the time during which the cruel edict of Pharaoh for the destruction of male children was in operation."

Elisheba was the daughter of Amminadab, and sister of Naashon, captain in Judah's army. She became the wife of Aaron, the high priest and brother of Moses, and marrying thus she connected the royal and priestly tribes. To Aaron and Elisheba were born Nadab, Abihu, Eleazar and Ithamar (Exodus 6:23). Thus Elisheba became the foundress of the entire Levitical priesthood. Isaac Williams in his *Female Characters of Scripture* has this most interesting comparison —

It is not only in the New Testament that Elisabeth and the Holy Mary are those associated together: their types in the Old Testament are in like manner combined, for there is a remarkable circumstance which sets forth beforehand what was now taking place, and there we find them brought into a like connection. Elisabeth herself was, it is said by Luke, of the daughter of Aaron, but it is mentioned in the Book of Exodus that Aaron's own wife was named Elisheba, that is Elisabeth (6:23); again, we find in Luke, that the Virgin Mary was the cousin of Elisabeth, so in the former instance the sister of Aaron was named Miriam, that is, Mary, for it is the same name; Miriam or Mary, the virgin prophetess, who took the lead of all the other women in singing the song of thanksgiving for the miraculous deliverance of Israel (15:20). Thus even now the Blessed Mary is followed by all other women in singing her Magnificat; the virgin and the prophetess, she leads the sacred company in the Church unto this day.

EPHAH

Scripture Reference — I Chronicles 2:46
Name Meaning — darkness

Ephah was the name of Caleb's concubine, prince in Judah, who was alloted Hebron as an inheritance. She bore Caleb three children, namely Haran, Moza and Gazez. Ephah was also the name of two males (Genesis 25:4; I Chronicles 2:47).

EPHRATH

Scripture References — I Chronicles 2:19, 50; 4:4; see Genesis 35:16
Name Meaning — Fruitland land

Ephrath is a shortened form of Ephratah, and Ephrathah. As Bethlehem means, "house of bread" so the above terms imply fruitfulness because the region of Ephrathah abounded in corn (Psalm 132:6). *Cruden's Concordance* has the note, "It is believed that the city *Ephrath* otherwise called *Beth-lehem*, took its name from Ephrath, Caleb's wife." She was his second wife and became the mother of Hur, and the grandmother of Caleb the spy. After her husband's death she cohabited with his son, and a son was born of the illicit union who became the father of Tekoa.

ESTHER
The Woman Who Saved Her Nation From Genocide

Scripture Reference — The Book of Esther

Name Meaning — Esther was the Persian name of this descendant of Benjamin and is from "aster" meaning "a star" and implies, like Venus, that of "good fortune." We refer to "the star of hope" — "the star of joy" — "the star of superiority," and Esther was all these to her people for in "the splendid galaxy of Hebrew women of the olden time, no name stands more prominent or shines with a richer lustre." Rabbi Jehudah affirms that Esther is "sether," meaning "to hide," because she was hidden in her guardian's home and because her nationality was concealed (2:7). Mordecai had made the girl promise that she would not reveal her nationality to the king — which she did not until the opportune moment came. Hadassah, signifying "myrtle" was Esther's original name. The change of name from Hadassah to Esther may indicate the style of beauty for which this once captive, now a Persian queen, was famous for. She is revealed as "a woman of clear judgment, of magnificent self-control and capable of the noblest self-sacrifice." The lines of Byron can be fittingly applied to Esther—

> She walks in beauty, like the night
> Of cloudless climes and starry skies;
> And all that's best of dark and bright
> Meet in her aspect and her eyes.

Family Connections — This last woman of the Old Testament of whom we intimately know nothing, was related to a family carried away captive with Jeremiah, about 600 B.C. and was born of this family preferring to remain in the land of captivity rather than return to Jerusalem. Esther was the daughter of Abihail who lived at Shushan, the Persian royal city. When her parents died she came under the guardian care of Mordecai, a palace official, to whom she was related by marriage. Mordecai had a deep affection for her and reared her as his own daughter. Esther was always obedient to her uncle and even when she became queen, sought his practical advice. She trusted this gentle Jew as her father. As Alexander Whyte expresses it, "Mordecai brought Esther up, and his one love in his whole life, after his love for Israel and for the God of Israel, was his love for his little adopted daughter. . . . He stood by and watched his sister's child lifted up in a moment from her exile and poverty, and actually made the queen of the greatest empire then standing on the face of the earth."

The story of Esther as we have it in the book bearing her name is a romance of captivity in Persia, for a king set at nought Persian law and prejudice to make her his queen. The marriage of Ahasuerus to Esther, a Jewess, was against Persian law which held that one of the royal line must marry a wife belonging to the seven great Persian families. What Esther did and how she did it is described in ten intensely vivid chapters, and her story is one of great dramatic power in which "incident after incident is related until the climax of difficulty is reached and the knot is so tied that it seems impossible to escape. Then it is untied with wonderful dexterity."

A peculiar feature of the Book of Esther is that, with the Song of Solomon, it shares the distinction of not mentioning God or any divine name once throughout its pages. Yet the fast-moving action in this drama is eloquent with the overruling providence of God in bringing Esther to the throne for such a time. At times, God may appear as if He is hiding Himself, but seen or unseen He ever accomplishes that which is according to His will. Because of her beauty Esther became an inmate of the palace, and when courageous Queen Vashti was deposed, Esther was chosen to succeed her. The combined wisdom of Mordecai and Esther's courage became the means of lightening the load of the Jews under Persian rule.

With Mordecai, Esther shared faith in the high destiny of Israel as a nation.

Haman, the chief court favorite, was the Jews' enemy — the Old Testament Adolph Hitler — and conceived a plan to massacre the Jews *en bloc*. Exhorted by Mordecai, Esther revealed her Jewish nationality to the king, and this courageous action brought about a complete reversal of the decree. Haman was executed, Mordecai was honored by the king, and Esther's position as Queen was considerably strengthened. It is because she saved the Jews from destruction that the Book of Esther is read every year by Jews at the Feast of Purim, held on the 14th day of Adar. We cannot but agree with the summary of Esther, as one of the most attractive women in the Old Testament that —

> As an historical character, Esther is the supreme heroine who delivers her nation from disaster: as a woman, she is that rare individual, a mixture of charm, strength and guile: a human being whose character is secure from the rot of wealth, prosperity and power.

That Esther had great personal beauty goes without saying. Her dark, exotic features marked her out, and she was thus chosen as a candidate for the king's favor who, when he saw her for the first time must have been captivated by her physical charms. But through her beauty there shone a radiance of personality and character which enhanced her beauty and gave it distinction in the eyes of Ahasuerus who chose her as his queen. Kuyper, who does not have anything good to say about Esther's character when he deals with her in his *Women of the Old Testament*, confesses that Ahasuerus reckoned her to be the most beautiful of the maidens presented to him when seeking a successor to Vashti. The one thing about Esther we cannot understand was the way she exhibited the vindictiveness of the age and the country in her request that Haman's ten sons should be hanged, and a day set apart when the Jews could take vengeance on the enemies who had sought to kill them. She had not learned to love her enemies. She lived on the other side of the cross and therefore was ignorant of its cry for the forgiveness of enemies.

What are some of the lessons to be gleaned from the fascinating story of Esther? First of all, her record abides because she was one who kept her pledge. May such allegiance be ours! She dutifully obeyed her foster father. Having no natural father or mother to honor, she loved and was loyal to her guardian parent. How commendable it is when young people revere their parents and obey them in the Lord! Further, Esther loved and clung to (although she concealed) her despised but honorable descent. She was a true patriot and in the hour of crisis was not ashamed to own her race. The lesson to learn from the dramatic moment when she revealed her identity as a Jewess has been applied by H. V. Morton in this way —

> When a person has gone up in the world and has achieved a position of power and eminence, it requires strength and beauty of character for that person still to love and remember the simple people from whom he, or she, sprang. Humble girls have often married rich men and have forgotten their origin. They have, in fact, been ashamed of anything that might remind them of it.

Witnessing to the rock from which she had been hewn, Esther dared to risk death for her people and so escaped dying with them. By her patriotism she won for her nation a great deliverance and God used her as an instrument of His providence for the working out of a glorious purpose. There had been preparations of humiliation and prayer and when the king held out his scepter and she approached to make her plea the cry was in her heart, "How can I endure to see the evil that shall come unto my people? or how can I endure to see the destruction of my kindred?" How national life sorely needs godly patriots after this order? You may be tempted to sigh and say, "If only I were like Esther with great opportunities what would I not do to glorify God." Realize that all around you, no matter how mean your environment may be, there are magnificent and unparalleled opportunities of serving God and a needy world that angels envy. Serve the Master to the limit of your ability where in His Providence He has placed you, and thus prepare yourself for a larger circle of service if such be His will.

Leaders of women's groups could elaborate on the following points while dealing

with the story of Esther, the strong-minded
woman of ancient history —

From her character we learn —

1. To seek divine guidance in times of
   difficulty (4:15-17).
2. To obtain a knowledge of human nature, so that we may know how to
   take advantage of any circumstances
   which may favor our cause if it be a
   proper one.
3. When there is a necessity, to be ready
   to renounce self and exert ourselves
   for the good of others.
4. To value and seek the cooperation of
   fellow-believers.

Dealing with the ultimate safety of the Jews
which Esther secured, we learn —

1. To have unbounded confidence in
   God's Providence—not to undervalue
   small things.
2. To acknowledge God as the Author
   of all mercies.

Thinking of the reversal of fortune of Haman, which Esther brought about, we further learn —

1. There is such a thing as righteous retribution. Haman himself received
   what he had proposed for others. He
   was paid back in his own coin.
2. The transitory nature of earthly grandeur and the end of all ill-gotten
   earthly power and possessions.

EUNICE

THE WOMAN WHOSE SON BECAME A FAMOUS EVANGELIST

Scripture References — Acts 16:1-3; II Timothy 1:5; 3:14, 15; 4:5

Name meaning — Eunice implies "conquering well," and was a name expressive of
a good or happy victory, and in its origin doubtless commemorated some such
event. *Nice* or "nike" was a favorite ending of female names in the Macedonian
age. Eunice lived up to her name for she
conquered in the effort to bring up her
son in the nurture and admonition of the
Lord.

Family Connections — Eunice was the
daughter of Lois whose name is of Greek
origin. Scripture is silent as to the identity of her father. A Jewess, Eunice married a Gentile, and as nothing is said of

him it can be assumed that he was dead
by the time Paul contacted the family.

The commanding feature of the Scriptural record of Eunice and her mother is their
religious influence upon Timothy who, from
childhood days had known the Scriptures
(II Timothy 3:14, 15). These two godly
women had trained him up in the way he
should go (Proverbs 22:6). How gratified
they must have been when Timothy set out
to do the work of an evangelist! (II Timothy
4:5). His name, Timothy, means "one who
fears God," and must have been chosen by
his Jewish mother, and not by his Gentile
father who probably had little leaning Godward. Evidence seems to point to the contention that Lois, Eunice and Timothy were
won to Christ by Paul on an earlier visit to
Lystra where the family lived (Acts 14:
6, 7). Although Lois and her daughter were
Jewesses and well-versed in Old Testament
Scriptures, and taught the child Timothy
the same, it was Paul who brought them to
see that the One who died upon the cross
to save sinners was the long-promised Messiah. That the Apostle led Timothy to Christ
is proven by the way Paul speaks of him
as his "beloved son" and his "son in the
faith." How grateful to God Eunice must
have been when Paul chose her much-loved
son to be his companion in his evangelistic
work! How she would appreciate the word
of Solomon, "She that bare thee shall rejoice" (Proverbs 23:25).

Hereditary piety and personal faith are
implied in Paul's reference to the unfeigned
faith which first dwelt in Timothy's grandmother, Lois, then in his mother, Eunice,
and then in himself also. While one parent's
faith can sanctify a child (I Corinthians 7:
14), it is a personal faith in Christ that saves
the soul. Notice is taken of the faith of
Timothy's mother, but not of his father.
After Paul's reference to Lois and Eunice
in his second epistle to Timothy, they are
not mentioned again. There may be a veiled
reference to them, however, in what Paul
had to say about widows and the children
of widows (I Timothy 5:4, 5).

The important feature we glean from the
record of Timothy is that of the value of
a positive Christian training in the home.
Paul seems to be saying to Timothy in effect, "That you have always been schooled

in the Scriptures represents an inestimable grace, for which you ought always to thank your God." We can be sure that Timothy constantly praised God for a home wherein His honor dwelt. Augustine always confessed the debt he owed to his saintly mother, Monica. Not all children have godly parents and the safeguard of a Christian home, but those born into a home where Christ is its Head are privileged and grow up to bless God for their spiritual heritage. Alas, the heartache of godly parents is to have a child or children who, as they come to the age of accountability, spurn the Christian influences of the home created for them!

EUODIAS

THE WOMAN WHO FELL OUT WITH HER FRIEND

Scripture References — Philippians 4:2 (see Acts 16:13-15; 17:12)

Name Meaning — Euodias is actually a man's name. Euodia is its right form here (Philippians 4:2, R.V.). Euodias means "prosperous journey"—Euodia, "fragrant." Wilkinson has the note, "Euodia is 'a good journey,' and was used in the colloquial Attic Greek as the French use the expression *bon voyage*." Euodia is coupled with another female, Syntyche, and both may have been among the women who resorted to prayer at the river bank (Acts 16:13-15), and among the honorable women who believed (Acts 17:12). Scripture is silent on the genealogy and family association of these two women who, after their conversion became colaborers with Paul in the Gospel (Philippians 4:3). Belonging to a class bespeaking prosperity they doubtless ministered unto Paul of their substances.

At Philippi women were the first hearers of the Gospel and Lydia the first convert. If Euodias and Syntyche were also brought to the Lord there, they naturally took a leading part in teaching the Gospel to other women in a private sphere of labor once the Church had been formed there (I Timothy 2:11, 12).

When Paul exhorted these two prominent workers to "be of the same mind in the Lord," he implied that they had been previously at variance. What caused the breach between these two deaconesses in the Philippian Church we are not told. Perhaps one had a more dominant personality than the other and received more attention. Whatever the dispute was, it became serious and hindered the work of the Lord, so Paul besought the two women to give up their differences and live at peace in the Lord. The lack of harmony between Euodias and Syntyche disturbed the Apostle, so he urged a reconciliation, for as those professing to be redeemed their whole life should be lived in peace and in an endeavor to please Him who had saved them.

A humorist has suggested that because of the strife between these sisters in Christ they should have been called *Odious* and *Soon-touchy*. It was sad that there was this difference of opinion, and more tragic still that divisions have kept Christians apart all down the ages. "How can two walk together except they be agreed?" is an old adage we have lost sight of. We like to believe that Paul did not plead in vain, and that Euodias and Syntyche were completely reconciled and went on unitedly to serve the God of peace. Is there any need of such a reconciliation in your life as a Christian? If so, for the sake of your own peace of heart and your influence in the world, go out and put wrong things right.

EVE

THE WOMAN OF UNIQUE DISTINCTION

Scripture References — Genesis 2 and 3; II Corinthians 11:3; I Timothy 2:13

Name Meaning — There are three names applied to Adam's wife. She is called "Woman, because she was taken out of Man" (Genesis 2:23). "Woman" is more of a generic designation than a name, and is associated with Eve's relation to Adam, a relation she was created to fulfill. Literally "woman" means "man-ess." Then both Eve and her husband are called "Adam." "Male and female created he them . . . and called their name Adam" (Genesis 5:2). This inclusive name implies that the divine ideal for man and wife is not merely that of association but an indissoluble unity. God made them "one flesh" and gave them one name. Eve, the name given her after the transgression and its prophesied results, was the choice of Adam "who called his wife's name Eve; because she was the mother of all living" (3:16, 20). This was the name describing her function and destiny in spiritual history of which she was the beginning. Eve means "life" or "life-giving," or "mother of all who have life," and her life is in us all. In Bible days great significance was attached to a change of name. Why then did Adam change his wife's name — which was his own, Adam, to Eve? Donald Davidson says that, "In view of the awful judgment pronounced upon them, the man might have been pardoned if he had reproached her as 'death,' for it was her sin that brought death into our world and all our woe. But Adam gives her a name which is expressive of the prophetic life bound up in her. For through the seed of the woman, sin would one day be vanquished, and death would be swallowed up in victory."

We have given our cameo of Eve the caption "The Woman of Unique Distinction" because she is distinct, in so many ways, from all other women who have ever lived. There are a good many "Firsts" to her credit.

Eve Was the First Woman to Live Upon the Earth

The product of a divine creation, Eve appeared as a complete, perfect woman. She was never a child, or a daughter or a maiden. The first female born into the world was Eve's first daughter (Genesis 5:4). How many daughters were born to Adam and Eve we are not told. If Eve lived as long as her husband — 930 years (Genesis 5:5)— there would likely be many sons and daughters in earth's first family. Eve, then, was not born. She was created out of Adam. Having existed in God's thought, she appeared upon the earth.

Modernists, evolutionists, and secular writers may mock that "rib of Adam" out of which Eve was made. Adam was directly created by God out of the dust of the earth, but Eve was fashioned out of a bone taken from Adam's side. George Herbert comments, "The man was dust refined, but the woman was dust double refined." Says Secker, "The rib was taken from under his arm. As the use of the arm is to keep off

blows from the body, so the office of the husband is to ward off blows from his wife."

There is a spiritual application of the bride God created for Adam. It speaks of the sacred mystery, the bride of the Lamb, who owes her existence to His wounded side (John 19:36), and who, even more than Eve, has a place near to the Bridegroom's heart (Jeremiah 31:3), and who is destined to enjoy His companionship in a sinless paradise (Revelation 2:7; 21:9). The marriage of the Lamb, like that of Eve's, is made in heaven.

Eve Was the First Woman to Be Called a Wife

Fashioned out of man, she became man's counterpart and companion. God saw that although Adam was in a state of perfect innocency, it was not good for him to be alone. It would be good for him, spiritually, intellectually and socially to have a wife. He needed someone to love and bear his children since the command had gone forth "to multiply and replenish the earth." And so with Adam —

> The world was sad, the garden was a wild,
> And man the hermit sighed till woman smiled.

God spoke of the woman He was to provide for Adam as his "helpmeet" — a help meet or adapted to him — a term giving woman her true position in the world. It is only where the Bible exists and Christianity is practiced that she attains to such a position as the helper, or equal of man. In lands where darkness reigns, woman is the slave, the chattel of man. Thus Eve was given to Adam and their two hearts beat as one in love for each other and for God. Eve was formed while Adam slept. He knew no pain during the operation for as yet there was no sin in the world. How true it is that God is continually working while men sleep! He often imparts real blessings to His own as they sleep (Psalm 127:2).

> When I wake from sleep,
> Despair has fled, and hope is near;
> The sky seems blue, and visions clear
> Have banished all my dread and fear.

Eve Was the Most Beautiful Woman the World Has Known

Century after century women have appeared renowned for their beauty of face and form but Eve excelled them all. Created by a perfect God, Eve reflected the divine perfection. Hers was no artificial beauty. Face, features and form were the loveliest women have ever had. While the Bible has no description of Eve's physical appearance, Adam's first reaction as he saw the lovely figure before him was to give voice to earth's first poem —

> This, then, at last is bone of my bones,
> and flesh of my own flesh:
> This shall be called Wo-man
> For from man was she taken.

While we have Biblical warrant for the beauty of Sarah, the Talmudist says —

> All women in comparison with Sarah are like monkeys in respect to men. But Sarah can no more be compared to Eve than can monkey be compared with man.

John Milton expresses a similar commendation in one of his most daring idioms —

> Adam the goodliest man since born
> His sons; the fairest of her daughters Eve.

The blind poet goes on to say of the loveliness Adam saw —

> So absolute she seems
> And is herself complete.

The Venus of Milo, in marble, or the *Venus of Titian* in oil, only convey a faint idea of what Eve must have looked like as she came from the creative hand of God. No wonder she has been described as

> Heaven's best, last gift.

To quote from Milton's *Eve* again —

> O fairest of creation, last and best
> Of all God's works, creature in whom excelled
> Whatever can to sight or thought be formed,
> Holy, Divine, Good, Amiable or Sweet.

Yet again Eve's original beauty is expressed in these lines —

> That what seemed fair in all the world seemed now
> Mean, or in her contained or in her looks;
> Grace was in all her steps, Heaven in her eye,
> In every gesture dignity and love.

Eve Was the First and Only Woman Born Without Sin

Being the first woman Eve had no inherited sin. Coming from the hand of God, Eve had an advantage no other woman has ever had — she was pure and holy, with the divine image unimpaired. Created sinless, she yet became the world's first sinner, and introduced sin to her offspring, and thus, all since her were "born in sin and shapen in iniquity." The best and holiest born into the race have natures that are prone to evil (Romans 7:21). Fashioned with "innocence and sinless perfection and endowed to all fullness with gifts of body and mind, and rich in external blessing without spot or alloy she yet transgressed in the sin with which she caused Adam to sin." Fresh from the hand of God with unmatchable grace and beauty of body and mind, sin and ruin followed, and paradise was surrendered for a world of thorns, thistles and tears.

Eve Was the First on Earth to Be Assailed by Satan

Before her creation, Satan, who like Eve had been created a holy being, led a rebellion against the Creator and was cast from his high estate. Now he begins his rebellion on earth and beings with one who is fascinated by his approach. Thus we have the Fall and the source of original sin. There was no great daring to sin for the first time on Eve's part. As sin was unknown to both Adam and Eve when created by God, Eve saw no wrong in the masterpiece of satanic subtle suggestion. Satan did not tell her to sin, but insinuated in the cleverest way that there was nothing to worry about in eating forbidden fruit. As George Matheson puts it, "The temptation was not in itself the wish to transgress, but the will to possess; the transgression is merely a means. . . . If the tempter had said, 'Steal,' he would not have been listened to for a moment. But he did not say, 'Steal!'; he says, 'Speculate!' . . . Temptation since the days of Eden has never ceased to clothe itself in a seemly garment."

Satan succeeded in painting the downward way as leading to an upward path issuing in God-likeness or a fall upwards, "Ye shall be as gods, knowing good and evil." Eve succumbed to the wiles of Satan and the steps leading to her surrender are illuminating — she saw, she coveted, she took, etc. "The tree was good for food" — bodily appetite was tempted. It was "a delight to the eyes"—her sensuous nature was tempted. Then, "the tree was to be desired to make one wise" — the most powerful temptation of all, namely, "the spiritual temptation to transcend the normal experience of men and to taste of the wisdom that belongs only to God."

What about her husband? Well, Adam made no effort to restrain Eve from eating of the fruit although the divine prohibition was addressed to him as well as to Eve. If he was not the first to pluck the fruit, he must have been standing under the tree, and when he saw that it was safe to eat, then he took his share of the forbidden fruit. When God faced Adam with that first act of sin, he not only blamed Eve, but God Himself — "The woman *Thou* gavest me" — as if to say, "If You knew that Eve would have tempted me, why did You create her for me?" H. V. Morton says that "the words of the first Adam are like the words of a rather sneaky little boy caught out by the headmaster and blames another — *She* gave me of the tree and I did eat." But thereafter, in Scripture, Adam, the federal head of the human race, is made responsible for adamic sin. ("In Adam we die"; "By one man's sin"; Roman 5:12; Job 31:33.) What followed the disobedience of the world's first sinners is only too well-known — pain in childbearing, the introduction of sin and servitude into the world, the earth cursed, expulsion from paradise, and the introduction of disease and death.

Eve Was the World's First Dressmaker

If Adam was earth's first gardener, Eve was the first to fashion garments out of leaves. "They sewed fig leaves together and made themselves aprons" (Genesis 3:7). Andrew Johnson, who became president of the U.S.A. after the murder of Abraham Lincoln, once was a tailor in Greenville, Tennessee, where he had a shop. In a speech made at Gallatin in 1874 he said —

> Adam, our great father and head, the lord of the world, was a tailor by trade. Adam and Eve "sewed fig leaves together, and made them aprons." That is the first we ever heard of tailors, and I do not see that — without intending to be personal — anyone need be ashamed to be called a tailor, nor any young lady need be ashamed to be a seamstress, for her mother Eve, it seems, handled a needle with some skill.

Clothing is a reminder of sin, for in their innocency our first parents had no sense of shame because they had no sense of sin. "They were both naked . . . and were not ashamed" (Genesis 2:25). Says Matthew Henry, "They need have no shame in their faces, though they had no clothes to their backs." But after they sinned their eyes were opened, and they *knew* that they were naked. Although shame may have a fairer and a gentler face than sin, it is still its twin sister. Shame can be an expression of regret for sin, or the protest of consience against it. When Ezra blushed and was ashamed to look up, the pardoning mercy of God came out to meet him (Ezra 9:6).

Conscious of their nakedness, why did Adam and Eve seek a covering? Not only because they knew they were without clothing but also because they were exposed to the gaze of Him against whom they had sinned. However the fig leaves they made into a garment were not sufficient to hide them from God's piercing eyes, so they hid among the trees. Even there they were under His gaze and discovered, and they tried to cover themselves with vain excuses (3: 7, 8, 11, 13). Those who try to cover their sin never prosper (Proverbs 28:13, see Job 31:33). God rejected the covering the first sinners on the earth made because it represented their own effort. So God provided them with "coats of skins" (3:21), and placed them on the guilty ones. The wonderful invention of fastening animal pelts together was ascribed by the ancient Hebrews to God. Skins speak of sacrifice. Animals have to be slain ere man can be covered with clothes or shoes. Surely the divine provision of those sacrificial skins foreshadowed Calvary, where Jesus through the sacrifice of Himself provided a spotless robe of righteousness for all who repent and believe.

Naked, come to Thee for dress.

Eve Was the First Mother to Have a Son Who Was a Murderer

What a trail of sorrow and anguish followed her transgression! When Cain, her first born, came into her life and home how Eve must have loved him. She named him Cain, meaning "to get" or "to possess" or, "acquisition." He became a tiller of the ground. Her second son was Abel, a name implying, "that which ascends" or "a vapor"

—something doomed to fade. The latter was a spiritual man and sacrificed the firstlings of his flocks unto the Lord. The former son brought of the fruit of the ground, that is, that which he had produced, and presented it to the Lord who rejected it and accepted Abel's offering because of its sacrificial content. Cain lost his temper over this act of divine acceptance and rejection, and slew his brother Abel. Thus Eve's favorite first born was branded with shame, and spiritual Abel became a martyr. Behind Cain's slaughter of his brother was the serpent who had made their mother the world's first sinner. Jesus said that he was a murderer from the beginning (John 8:44). After the crime and banishment of her first son, and the burial of her second one, God gave her another whom she called Seth. "For God," she said, "hath appointed me another seed instead of Abel, for Cain slew him." In naming her third son thus she voiced her faith in God's love, mercy and provision. It was through Seth that the spiritual lineage was maintained and it was after his birth that Eve's name disappears from the pages of the Old Testament, although it is mentioned twice in the New Testament. While Eve doubtless shared the length of Adam's life — 930 years — and bore an indefinite number of sons and daughters, we have no record of her maternity apart from the three named sons.

Eve Was the First to Receive the Divine Prophecy of the Cross

Eve was the first sinner and saw the fruit of her sin as she stood at the world's first grave and buried her dead. After confessing her sin she heard the Lord say to that old serpent, the devil, "I will put enmity between thee and the woman, and between thy seed and her seed; it shall bruise thy head, and thou shalt bruise his heel" (Genesis 3:15). With this first promise of the Redeemer there began the scarlet highway ending at the cross where Christ, born of a woman, provided a glorious victory over sin and Satan. Through a woman, God's fair universe was blighted and became "a world of sinners lost, and ruined by the fall." Now, through a woman, a perfect salvation has been provided for a sinning race. Through Eve's sin, death entered the world, but at the cross both sin and death were conquered, for by "dying, death He slew." When Jesus cried, "It is finished," He meant that the serpent's head, representing power and authority, had been bruised. He laid hold of all satanic principalities and powers that Eve's transgression brought into the world, and put them under His feet. Hallelujah! What a Saviour!

As we leave our reflection upon the world's first woman, first wife, first sinner, and first mourner, there are one or two lessons to be gleaned from her record. For instance, "many daughters of Eve have discovered that the serpent is never more dangerous than when he professes to be the earnest well-wisher interested in nothing but her advancement and welfare." What a subtle, cruel deceiver Satan is. How ignorant so many are of his devices! Further, temptation is a universal experience, and each of us should learn from the first person on earth to be tempted, its manner of approach and successive steps, and safeguard ourselves from a fall through the appropriation of Christ's own victory over the enemy. There is no sin in being tempted. We only sin when we yield to temptation. Refusing to yield to the enticement of sin, our Garden of Eden remains inviolate. At the heart of Eve's pathetic story, however, is the moral lesson that a woman has the power for bane or blessing over a man's life. If she falls, man falls with her. How expressive are the verses John White Chadwick quotes in his chapter on Eve in *Women of the Bible* —

> Ah, wasteful woman, that she may
>   On her sweet self set her own price.
> Knowing we cannot choose but pay,
>   How has she cheapened Paradise;
>
> How given for naught her priceless gift,
>   How spoil'd the bread and spill'd the wine
> Which, spent with due respective thrift,
>   Had made men brutes and men divine.
>
> O Queen, awake to thy renown,
>   Require what 'tis our wealth to give,
> And comprehend and wear the crown
>   Of thy despised prerogative.

It will be noticed that we have said nothing about whether the story of Creation, and of the appearance of Adam and Eve should be taken literally and historically, or treated as an allegory of sacred symbolism.

We firmly reject the unproven, anti-Christian theory of evolution, just as we protest that the account of the creation of Adam and Eve, and the temptations of the serpent is ancient myth or folklore conveying withal a pertinent truth or message. It is becoming more common for modernistic preachers and writers to speak of the beautiful fables and myths of the Bible. We believe the first three chapters of Genesis contain historic realities. If Adam is a myth, so is Christ. Luke reminds us that Adam was a son of God (3:23-28), and the first man from whom Christ was descended. How could a mythical son become one of the ancestors of the actual Christ? The whole of Luke's genealogy of Jesus is based upon the assumption that Adam was an actual person. Further, in discussing Adam and Christ as the two federal heads of the human race, Paul said, "in Adam we die — in Christ we are made alive." You cannot die in a myth. By deduction, if Adam is a mythical figure, so is Christ.

Then Eve and her association with the serpent is likewise treated as a myth. Paul says that the serpent beguiled Eve (II Corinthians 11:3). Paul regarded the tempter of Eve not as a myth, but as a stern and powerful reality. If there has never been a personal devil, then we would like to know who is doing the work that only a denizen of hell could do. In urging loyalty to Christ, Paul uses Eve to illustrate the ease with which one is corrupted, and to him she was a historical figure whose record should be taken literally (see I Timothy 2: 12-14). The mythical treatment of Old Testament historical figures and events is an evidence of the appalling apostasy of our age.

GOMER

THE WOMAN INFAMOUS FOR HER HARLOTRY

Scripture References — Hosea 1:1-11; 3:1-5
Name Meaning — Gomer means "completion," that is, the filling up of the measure of idolatry, or ripeness of consummate wickedness. Her name was indicative of the wholesale adultery and idolatry of the kingdom she represented. As "a wife of whoredoms," this woman of the Northern Kingdom, regarded as an idolatress, became a symbol of her people.

Family Connections — Gomer was the daughter of Diblaim, whose name signifying "double layers of grapecake," speaks of one completely given up to sensuality. With such a father we can understand why Gomer became such a woman of sensual pleasure. She became the wife of Hosea, the godly prophet, and symbolized God's grace in taking out of "a world which had whorishly departed from Him a Church to be sanctified by communion with Himself in Christ, as Gomer was sanctified by communion with the prophet (I Corinthians 7:14). The Saviour unites to Himself the unholy, to make it holy."

To Hosea and Gomer were born three children whose names are meaningless if the record of Gomer is to be treated as mere allegory as some critics do. The marital experience of Hosea was an acted parable for the whole nation to see, and the poetic description of a figure so ugly would have been unnnatural in such a writer if he had not had a bitter experience of all the figure represented. "Only the real pain of that experience could have made the man brave enough to use it as a figure of God's treatment of Israel." The symbolic names Hosea and Gomer gave their children indicate divine displeasure with Israel for her whoredoms. Some writers suggest that the three children were not Hosea's but those of his wife's paramours during her period of unfaithfulness, hence the term "the children of harlotry" (1:2). But the names themselves discount such an idea.

Jezreel, the first born means, "God sowed," which is susceptible of two senses — "God scattereth" or "God planteth" (1:4). Calvin, commenting on this typical name represents God as saying, "Ye are not *Israel,* but *izrahel,* a people whom God will scatter and cast away." Later, the same name appears in connection with the promise of restoration to divine favor, "Great shall be the day of Jezreel." "They shall hear Jezreel, and I will *sow* her in the earth" (1:11; 2:22, 23). *Israel,* once called *izrahel* as "the dispersed of God," shall not be called *izrahel,* as "the sown of the Lord" (Isaiah 60:21). At the birth of his first son, Hosea was not aware of his wife's whoredom.

Lo-ruhamah signifies "She will not be

shown compassion." This girl's name, meaning "unfitted," speaks of God's rejection of the house of Israel because of its iniquity. He was more pitiful toward the house of Judah (1:6, 7).

Lo-ammi. This name of the third child meaning, "Not my people or kinsman," extends the judgment on the nation expressed in the first two names. Gomer and her children, then, give us a clear picture of wayward Israel in its relationship with God. Yet, as we shall see, the story ends with the wonderful love and faithfulness of God.

We are not to assume that at the time of Hosea's marriage to Gomer she was depraved. Because of her ancestry the evil taint was in her veins, and having inherited immoral tendencies they manifested themselves. Thus, as the unfaithful wife of the prophet, she went deeper into sin, left Hosea and became the slave of one of her paramours (3:1). Commanded by God, Hosea bought her back, paying the price of an ordinary slave for her. What the prophet experienced in his own life was typical of Israel's unfaithfulness, and of her exile, but also of God's willingness to take her back. The love of Hosea for his wayward wife was not quenched by her betrayal of love and faithfulness. "Go yet, love a woman, beloved of her friend (Hosea himself), *yet* an adultress." Thus out of his anguish Hosea rises to a deeper understanding of the forgiving love of God. As Dean Farrar expresses it, "If the love of man can be so deep, how unfathomable must be the love of God." If Hosea's love enabled him to take back his poor misguided, repentant wife, how much more will the love of God receive as graciously and love us freely.

Dr. G. Campbell Morgan in *The Minor Prophets,* gives us the following excellent summary of the significance of Hosea's anguish —

Out of his own heart agony Hosea learned the nature of the sin of his people. They were playing the harlot, spending God's gifts in lewd traffic with other lovers. Out of that agony he has learned how God suffers over the sin of His people, because of His undying love. Out of God's love Hosea's new care for Gomer was born, and in the method God ordained for him with her, he discovered God's method with Israel. Out of all this process of pain, there came full confidence in the ulti-

mate victory of love. Thus equipped he delivers his messages and all through them will sound those deep notes of Sin, Love, Hope.

HADASSAH

This is the Jewish name for Esther (see ESTHER). In Jewry this revered name is recognized in Hadassah Societies which exist for beneficent purposes.

HAGAR

THE WOMAN WHO LOST A BOTTLE BUT FOUND A WELL

Scripture References — Genesis 16; 21:9-17; 25:12; Galatians 4:24, 25

Name Meaning — Hagar, an Egyptian name, closely resembles the root of the Arabic, *flight,* familiar to us as the history of Mohammed, descendant of Hagar. It may be taken as an adaptation of her original name to the principal circumstances of her life, and understood to mean, *fugitive* or *immigrant,* which Hagar became.

Family Connections — While the Bible gives us no record of Hagar's genealogy, legend has supplied her pedigree, as being the daughter of Pharaoh, the king of Egypt, the same who coveted the possession of Sarah in vain. This legendary source affirms that the Egyptian princess became so attached to Sarah that she told her royal father that she would accompany her when she returned to Abraham.

"What!" cried the king, "thou wilt be no more than a handmaid to her!"

"Better to be a handmaid in the tents of Abraham than a princess in this palace," the daughter replied.

Hagar would not stay behind and join again in the idolatrous rites of her home, so when Abraham and Sarah moved on, she went with them. Sarah was an active missionary of the faith of Jehovah among women, as Abraham was among men, and so Hagar became a convert to the worship of the true God. While this is a pleasing tradition, the likelihood is that Hagar was an Egyptian girl-slave whom Sarah secured for her household while she and Abraham were in Egypt. Hagar bore Abraham his first son, Ishmael, and thus became the foundress of the Ishmaelites and Arab peoples from whom came Mohammed, the founder of Islam.

If Hagar was a slave girl then her mistress was legally entitled to do as she pleased with her. Knowing that it was humanly impossible for her to have children by Abraham, she gave her handmaid to him, that she might have children by her — a custom consistent with moral standards prevailing at that time. Abraham reminded Sarah that her word was law to her own slave and that he had no choice in the matter. Under Sumero-Babylonian law there is this clause in Hammurabi's Code —

> If she has given a maid to her husband and she has borne children and afterwards that maid has made herself equal with her mistress, because she has borne children her mistress shall not sell her for money, she shall reduce her to bondage and count her among the female slaves.

But Sarah ran ahead of God in giving a Gentile idolater from a pagan country to Abraham to bear the promised seed. Poor Hagar — she became the helpless victim of Sarah's scheming! The whole affair was a sin before God — a sin all three were guilty of. Sarah distrusted God when she resorted to such a wicked expedient. As a child of faith, did she not know that God was able to raise up children out of stones unto Abraham? As for this "friend of God," in spite of current custom, he should have stoutly refused Sarah's scheme and obeyed the law of God, and believed the divine promise made to him. The attempt to secure the Child of Promise by Hagar was the result of a lack of faith in God's omnipotence. Then, Hagar, although the least free and the least responsible, should not have yielded to such an unholy alliance merely to gratify any ambition she may have had. What sorrow, anguish and loneliness Hagar reaped for her compliance in such a plan to forestall God's promise of an heir for Abraham (Genesis 15:4, 5).

Although the chapter recording the unworthy method of trying to fulfill a divine purpose is only a short one, yet like the shortest verse in the Bible, it is saturated with tears. Genesis 16 is made up of only sixteen verses and with such we have these three features —

The Folly of Sarah

We have already seen that Sarah's folly had its root in unbelief. She was impatient, and wanted the promised child without delay. Her unbelief became contagious for "Abraham hearkened unto her voice." The pious phrases she uttered were worthless. "The Lord judge" (16:5). She should have appealed for judgment to the Lord before she took the wrong step. She was a godly woman (Hebrews 11:11), but fell into the meshes of unbelief. With distrust there came dishonor. She confessed "my wrong," but Hagar was the real sufferer, and Sarah's sin bore bitter fruit, for when she gave Hagar to Abraham, she originated a rivalry which has run in the keenest animosity through the ages, and which oceans of blood have not quenched.

The Flight of Hagar

Strife quickly followed the human arrangement which Sarah had made. Having conceived by Abraham, Hagar chides the childless Sarah, and the jealousy begotten between these two women was transplanted to their maternal hearts and penetrated even their children. Ishmael came to tease and vex Isaac, and discord arose between Abraham and Sarah. The ill treatment accorded to Hagar by Sarah was not only cruel, but also irrational. Had Sarah not instigated the wrongdoing that was the cause of her jealousy? Therefore it was unreasonable for her to lay the blame upon another. As things were, mistress and maid could scarcely dwell together, so Hagar fled. Better a flight than a fight! Being compelled to flee was a thing forbidden to a bondwoman.

Far from home in "the way to Shur," the appearance of a calm and gracious angelic messenger from God must have been a relief to the poor, pregnant fugitive. As Hagar traveled further from her jealous mistress the Lord was at her heels, and said to her in her distress, "Return to thy mistress." Hagar had left her position as handmaid without notice and without permission, so she must return. Sarah had wronged her, but she was not permitted to retaliate by doing wrong herself. Two wrongs do not make a right. It was no easy matter for Hagar to return and submit herself to Sarah, but it was the only right course, and a divine revelation helped her to pursue it.

At that renowned well Hagar met God, and in awe cried, "Thou God seest me." He had given her counsel, and although not pleasing to flesh and blood, Hagar took it and went back to Sarah. Had she persisted in remaining in the desert she might have died in it. God gave her a promise that although the wrongdoing of her master and mistress had led her into a false position, yet His favor would rest upon her and she would have a son who would be the progenitor of a great multitude. The soothing promise of God was a balm for the wounded spirit of the poor and lowly handmaid. Though Ishmael, the name God gave Hagar for her coming son, might not be the Child of Promise as Isaac would be, yet he would be the child of a promise made to her.

Is it to be wondered at that she called the well where God spoke to her and revealed the future of her son "Beth-lahai-roi," meaning, "The well of Him that liveth and seeth me"? It was there that the veil fell from Hagar's eyes, and she received the assurance that she was the object of God's special care. Dr. Alexander Whyte extols Hagar for her submission to God in this glowing fashion —

> Hagar, by reason of the extremity of her sorrow; by reason of the utter desolateness and brokenness of her heart; and by reason of the sovereign grace and abounding mercy of God — Hagar, I say, stands out before us in the very foremost rank of faith, and trust, and experience, and assurance. Hagar, to me, stands out among God's very electest saints. Hagar has only one or two who can stand beside her in her discovery of God, in her nearness to God, in her face-to-face fellowship with God, in the instructiveness, in the comfort, and in the hopefulness of her so close communion with God. . . . The best and the most blessed of them all was not more or better blessed than was Hagar the polluted outcast on her weeping way to Shur. The pure in heart shall see God.

The Forecast Concerning Ishmael

In the strength of the revelation of God received in the desert, Hagar returned to her mistress and bore Abraham his child. Abraham was 86 years of age (Genesis 16:16) and then, when he reached his 100th year (Genesis 21:5), Sarah bore him Isaac.

This means that for over 14 years Hagar and her son lived in the patriarch's home with all the tension and feeling there must have been as Sarah daily looked upon the son of her husband by another woman. After Isaac was born Hagar and Ishmael began to manifest their jealousy, and when Ishmael began to maltreat Isaac, Sarah could stand it no longer, and compelled Abraham to cast out the bondwoman and her child. As Bible names often set forth some feature of the character or history of those who bore them, so Ishmael meaning "God shall hear," was fully understood by Hagar when in the wilderness (Genesis 21:9-21) God heard the moaning of her broken heart.

How painters and poets have seized upon this pathetic incident of the poor woman and her boy in the wilderness, thirst-ridden and ready to die! One of the finest masterpieces adorning the Dresden Gallery is the painting called *Hagar in the Wilderness* — and cold is the heart that can gaze upon it without deep emotion. The boy is pictured on his back, dying with thirst, while his poor but beautiful mother in an agonizing prayer, "lifted up her voice and wept," saying, "Let me not see the death of the child." Could anything be more poignant? True, Hagar had "despised Sarah" and "mocked Isaac," but surely she had not deserved such cruel treatment as this — death from hunger and thirst in a barren land!

But how Hagar's extremity became God's opportunity. When the last drop of water had gone, and Hagar tenderly places her almost dead boy under the shrubs, God heard the dying cry of the lad, and also the wail of Hagar's broken heart, for out of heaven came His voice, "What aileth thee, Hagar? Fear not." Then God opened her eyes and she saw a well of water, and both she and her boy were saved from death. Abraham had given Hagar a bottle, but it was soon empty. God gave her a well, and the lad drank and God was with him, and he grew and became an archer in the wilderness. The last glimpse we have of Hagar is of her securing a wife for her son, out of the land of Egypt, her own land (Genesis 21:21) — the land of idols and worldliness. Untaught by the piety and instruction of Abraham, and by God's mercy to herself, Hagar failed Him in the choice of such a wife for the boy whom He had blessed.

The practical lessons to be learned from the history of Hagar have been fittingly summarized by Dr. James Crichton in his article on Hagar in *The International Standard Bible Encyclopedia* —

> The life and experience of Hagar teach, among other truths, the temptations incident to a new position; the foolishness of hasty action in times of trial and difficulty; the care exercised over the lonely by the all-seeing God; the Divine purpose in the life of everyone, however obscure and friendless; how God works out His gracious purposes by seemingly harsh methods; and the strength, comfort and encouragement that ever accompany the hardest experiences of His children.

It only remains to be said that Paul uses the story of Hagar as an allegory to distinguish law from grace (Galatians 4:21-31). Hagar the bondwoman is contrasted with Sarah the freewoman, and Ishmael "born after the flesh" with Isaac "born through promise"; thence freedom and grace appear as the characteristic qualities of Christianity. Hagar represents the Old Covenant and Sarah the New Covenant which is superior to the Old with its ordinances. Under grace all within the household of faith live by faith, and Sarah represents "the Jerusalem that is above" — "our mother" (R.V.), which is the free spiritual city to which all children of the promise even now belong (Philippians 3:21).

HAGGITH

Scripture References — II Samuel 3:4, 5; I Kings 1:5, 11; 2:13; I Chronicles 3:2
Name Meaning — Festival *or* dancer

This female character was the fifth wife of David, and the mother of his fourth son, Adonijah. In all references to her she carries the label, "the mother of Adonijah." He was born in Hebron while David had his capital there.

HAMMOLEKETH, HAMMOLECHETH

Scripture Reference — I Chronicles 7:17, 18
Name Meaning — The Queen *or* the Regent

This long name, found in the genealogy of Manasseh, suggests the characteristics of eminence. Tradition has it that she reigned over part of Gilead. She was the daughter of Machir, sister of Gilead, the granddaughter of Manasseh and the mother of Ishdod, and Abiezer, from whose line sprang the mighty Gideon, and Mahalah.

HAMUTAL

Scripture References — Jeremiah 52:1, 2; II Kings 23:31; 24:18
Name Meaning — Kinsman of the dew *or* father-in-law of dew

This wife of a king and the mother of two sons who became kings had a most interesting name. She was the daughter of Jeremiah of Libnah and mother of the ungodly sons, Jehoahaz and Mattaniah, or Zedekiah whom Jeremiah denounced for his wickedness.

Whenever the phrase "his mother's name was" — "her mother's name was" — occurs, the characteristics of the child or children whether good or bad suggest the potential influence of the mother. It did not seem as if the two sons followed the example of their father who, when he was yet young, "began to seek after the God of David his father," and who in life, "declined neither to the right hand nor to the left."

HANNAH
THE WOMAN WHO PERSONIFIES IDEAL MOTHERHOOD

Scripture References — I Samuel 1; 2:1, 21
Name Meaning — The Hebrew setting of Hannah has the beautiful and attractive meaning of "gracious" or "graciousness" or "favor" and by a slight change becomes the smoother Ann, Anne, or Anna — the latter form touching the classic world with keen interest. Anna was the name given by Virgil to the twin-souled sister of the lovelorn Queen Dido.

> And now Aurora from the heavens had rent the mist apart,
> Sick-souled her sister (Anna) she bespeaks, the sharer of her heart.

Family Connections — Hannah was the favorite wife of Elkanah, a Levite of Ramathaim Zophim who belonged to one of the most honorable families of that priestly portion of Jacob's progeny — the Kohathites. Although a godly man he followed the common custom of polygamy in those days when "every man did that which was right in the sight of his own eyes." As it was the burning desire of every Hebrew parent to have a son, Hannah who was barren, may have urged her husband to take another wife, as Sarah arranged with Abraham to do, so that Elkanah's name might be perpetuated. The second wife was Peninnah, of whom we know nothing save that she bore Elkanah several children, and grieved Hannah with her cruel and scurrilous tongue. "The sacred writer does not keep us long in Peninnah's company," says Alexander Whyte, "he hastens past Peninnah to tell us about Hannah, that sorely-fretted and sequestered woman, who waters her couch with her tears." The curse accompanying polygamy shows up in Elkanah's home life. Hannah became the mother of the renowned Samuel, and also bore Elkanah three other sons and two daughters none of whom are mentioned by name (I Samuel 2:21)

The Bible has been called "The World's Gallery of Lasting Fame," and in this gallery the portrait of Hannah occupies a conspicuous place. All that is recorded of this mother, who was one of the most noble Hebrews who ever lived, is an inspiration and a benediction. Whether she was as beautiful as Sarah we are not told, but because of her inner serenity she must have had "a very sensitive face, in which her moods were reflected like sunshine and shadow on a quiet lake." The story we have of her is "a harp-note of the immortal triumph of patience." Hannah is a beautiful example of how the most unpleasant and untoward circumstances can produce a character blessing the world. "The outline touches of her life," says John F. Jurst, "sombre and mournful at first, but radiant with faith and hope at last, form the fitting introduction to the narrative of the career of her great son Samuel in his combined character of Judge and Prophet of Israel." Perhaps we can best summarize Hannah's career in the following fivefold way —

Her Sanctity

From the record we have of Hannah she appears to have been a woman with an unblemished character. Piety reigned in her heart, and she maintained constant communion with the religious ordinances of her nation. Pious Hannah was separated unto the Lord, and amidst trying domestic relationships knew how to have recourse to Him for all necessary grace to bear her troubles. She cried day and night unto the Lord, and was heard in that she feared Him whom her soul loved. Because of her godliness, devotion, trust, patience and self-sacrifice, she came to be signally blessed of the Lord, and, in turn, communicated to her renowned son Samuel something of her saintliness of life and character. It was no easy task to live for years with a nasty woman like Peninnah, but Hannah retained her serenity of soul and was a veritable lily among thorns.

Her Sorrow

While Hannah had a house she did not have a home. The ideal of every Jewess was to be "head of the home," but she had no child, no family. True, she had a devout husband who loved her, and bestowed richer gifts upon her than he did upon his other wife, but she was childless. Comforting her yearning heart Elkanah said, "Am I not better to thee than ten sons?" Hannah, however, longed for a son out of her own womb to love and fondle. As the years went by her agony became more intense, and her barrenness was a greater burden because of the jealousy and heartlessness of her rival, Peninnah, who frequently tantalized Hannah for being childless. But true to her name, she manifested the grace of self-control amid the cruel chidings and reproaches of Peninnah, "her adversary who provoked her sore, and made her to fret." Can we wonder that Hannah referred to herself as, "a woman of a sorrowful spirit"? Jealousy, "the green-eyed monster that mocks the meat it feeds on," had taken possession of Peninnah, but not of Hannah. Although the Lord had "shut up her womb" her heart was still open toward Him. Made to sorrow by those nearest to her, Hannah was never guilty of any unwomanly, retaliatory conduct. Whenever her husband tried to comfort her stricken heart, her adversary was provoked to fresh insults and taunts. The fact that Elkanah loved Hannah and bestowed a double portion upon her only added more fuel to the fire of contempt in Peninnah's heart.

Her Supplication

Childless, Hannah was not prayerless. Barren, she still believed, and her pain found a refuge in prayer. In God's house, she besought the Creator "to raise her into the empire of motherhood," and to interfere with the law of nature on her behalf. How moving is the episode of Hannah pouring out her soul before God in His house and vowing that if He would give her a son, then she would give him back to God for His exclusive use! She bargained with God, and kept her bargain. She took her particular sorrow to God, and prayed, not that Peninnah's joy might be less, but that He would take away the cause of her own anguish. She gave herself to prayer, and in the presence of God her sorrow burst its bonds. Yet even in God's house at Shiloh she did not find at first the sympathy and understanding she sought. Think, for a moment, about some of the features of her heartfelt cry!

First of all, her prayer was of a peculiar kind. It was a supplication without external speech. Her lips moved but there was no sound. Her prayer was internal, and as she spoke thus to herself she created the impression that she was drunk with wine. She had learned that prayer is the Christian's native breath, "unuttered or expressed." While she never said a prayer, "she breathed a wish in her soul and sent it up unspoken right to the throne of God. It is a unique experience for the age of the Judges; the piety of Hannah is a ripe flower in an almost sterile field." The old priest Eli, not meaning to be unkind when he saw Hannah's lips moving and her whole being caught up in the fervency of her supplication and yet heard no words being expressed, somewhat felt that Hannah was drunk and upbraided her for coming into God's house in such a condition. How his hasty, ill-founded conclusions added gall to the sorrow of her heart.

Hannah protested her innocence and declared that she had never taken strong drink, and then poured out her soul to Eli who, discerning that her desire for a child was intense and her spirit, sacrificial, for she wanted nothing for herself alone, assured her that her inarticulate prayer had been

heard. "Go in peace, and the God of Israel grant thee thy petition that thou hast asked of him." Down she went to her house content for *she believed*. She was no longer forlorn, sorrowful, heart-hungry, but joyous and buoyant. God granted her wish, and the yearned-for child arrived and she called his name Samuel, which means, "asked of the Lord."

Her Song

Hannah's Psalm of Thanksgiving marks her out as a poetess and prophetess of no mean order. With her desire fulfilled she bursts into song and pours forth her gratitude to God for His goodness, and her Magnificat became the basis of the one the blessed Virgin Mary was to offer to the same covenant-keeping God. The reader will find a strong resemblance between Hannah's song and that of Mary's (Luke 1: 46-55). The spiritual lyric of Hannah is equal to any of the Psalms and is eloquent with the divine attributes of power, holiness, knowledge, majesty and grace. Such an elevated poetic utterance elicited by God's answer to her prayer, has stirred the hearts of saints all down the centuries. The following parallel arrangement brings out the points of resemblance between Hannah's song and that of Mary's —

Mary's Song and	Hannah's Song
My soul doth magnify the Lord	My heart rejoiceth in the Lord,
And my spirit hath rejoiced in God my Saviour.	Mine horn is exalted in the Lord;
He hath shewed strength with his arm;	The bows of the mighty men are broken
He hath scattered the proud in the imagination of their hearts.	And they that stumbled are girded with strength.
He hath put down the mighty from their seats,	The Lord killeth, and maketh alive: He bringeth down to the grave and bringeth up;
And exalted them of low degree.	They that were full have hired out themselves for bread;
He hath filled the hungry with good things;	And they that were hungry ceased.
And the rich he hath sent empty away.	

Her Sacrifice

Hannah prayed and promised, and when her prayer was answered she quietly redeemed her promise. More than anything in the world she wanted a son, and when

God gave her one, she gave him back to the Lord. Although Samuel was not born to the priesthood, his mother had sacredly pledged him to the Lord; and that pledge must be kept no matter what it might cost her in loneliness. So when weaned, Samuel was taken to the house of the Lord, "there to abide forever." Once a year she visited him and what a human touch we have in that she made a little coat for him to wear. Her saintliness and sacrifice were rewarded for she bore Elkanah five more children. As for Samuel, he grew up to reflect his revered mother's godliness. True to the meaning of his own name, and in likeness to his mother's prevailing intercession, he became a man of prayer and intercession all his days — and beyond all men had power with, and from, God. How appropriate are the lines of Tennyson as we think of Samuel and his saintly mother, Hannah —

> Happy he
> With such a mother! Faith in womankind
> Beats with his blood, and trust in all things high
> Comes easy to him, and tho' he trip and fall
> He shall not blind his soul with clay.

The lessons to be gathered from the fascinating story of Hannah are clearly evident. First of all, as we think of all Samuel became we realize how the excellencies of many men have usually been foreshadowed, if not exemplified, in the characters of their mothers. "The genius and intellectual sweep of Goethe were foretokened in the many-sided brilliancy of Frau Rath." The mother of John Wesley was remarkable for her intelligence, godliness and executive ability earning her the title of "The Mother of Methodism." As no one in all the bleak world is more fitted to guide little feet Godward, may heaven grant us more mothers like godly Hannah.

From Peninnah's harsh treatment of Hannah we discover how a thoughtless, unloving word of ours can give sorrow to others. How necessary it is to guard our tongues! (James 3:9, 10). From Hannah's conduct under much provocation we first of all learn that the heart of God is a comforting retreat for a sorrowful soul. Whatever our particular sorrow may be, the Man of Sorrows waits to undertake. Hannah carried her trial and yearning to God in prayer and she teaches us something about the necessity for form and the spirit of intercession. Compare her silent heart-prayer with Psalm 19:14. From Eli who misjudged Hannah we learn not to be too hasty in our conclusions. Too often we wrong others by misinterpreting their motives. In Hannah's mild and dignified defense of her character we learn how to defend our rights in all humility (see John 8:48, 49; Acts 26:24-26).

HAZELELPONI, ZELELPONI

Scripture Reference – I Chronicles 4:3
Name Meaning – Deliver me, O God who regardest me, *or* the deliverance of the God who regardeth me

This word with its somewhat strange and uncouth sound for a female name includes the sacred name El, meaning "God" as one of its medial syllables. Zelel or Tselel means "a shade or shadow," which occurs in the formative of such proper names as Bezaleel, Zilthai or Zillethai, and implies "the shade turned towards me," and doubtless suggests a sense, or acknowledgment, or hope of divine protection, and embodying the idea conveyed by the assurance, "The Lord is thy shade upon thy right hand." Tzelphoni is the name of a daughter of Etam, and she was the sister of Jezreel, Ishma and Idbush appearing in the genealogy of Judah.

HELAH

Scripture Reference – I Chronicles 4:5, 7
Name Meaning – Sick

Many names in the various lists of pedigrees found in the Old Testament are derived from the sorrows, dangers, and other circumstances of the natal hour. Mahli, meaning "sick," and Mahlal, "sickness," are understood to allude to the precarious state of the mother at the time of birth. Mahalath has a similar meaning, so has Helah who was one of the wives of Ashur, the posthumous son of Hazon, and the father of Tekoa. Ashur was the head of a family of the tribe of Judah, and Helah bore him three sons, Zereth, Jezoar and Ethnan.

HEPHZIBAH

Scripture References—II Kings 21:1; Isaiah 62:4
Name Meaning – My delight is in her

This musical, symbolic name was borne by the wife of godly King Hezekiah, who became the mother of his son, Manasseh. Manasseh, who reigned over Judah for 55 years, a longer period than any other king, was as ungodly as his father was godly. He was the exact opposite of his father both in life and in the leadership of the nation.

Hephzibah is Jehovah's symbolical name of Zion when restored to His favor —

"Thou shalt be called by a new name. . . .Thou shalt be no more termed *Forsaken* (Agubah, the name of the mother of Jehoshaphat), neither shall thy land any more be termed *Desolate* (Shemamah), but thou shalt be called *Hephzibah* (my delight is in her) and thy land *Beulah*" (married). The words "desolate," "forsaken" and "married" also appear in a similar promise (Isaiah 54:1, 6).

Having lived and prophesied in the days of good King Hezekiah, it was appropriate for Israel to employ the use of symbolical names in the writing of his prophecies. Hezekiah's marriage to Hephzibah naturally suggested Beulah, meaning "married," and also the implication of the queen's name, "My delight is in her." These names are likewise symbolic of the church. Paul speaks of her as being married to Christ whose delight is in her.

HERODIAS
The Woman Responsible for the Murder of a Preacher

Scripture References — Matthew 14:3-12; Mark 6:14-24; Luke 3:19, 20

Name Meaning — As a member of the Herodian dynasty, perhaps the most despicable dynasty history has known, the name Herodias is but the female form of Herod, the royal name for the political rulers during the time of Christ and the apostles. It was under the vile and cruel orders of the Herods that Jesus and His followers were often persecuted and punished. Herod means "heroic" — not very applicable to the Herodian family, the majority of whom, particularly Herodias, were more hellish than heroic.

Family Connections — Herodias was the daughter of Aristobulus, son of Herod the Great and Mariamne, daughter of Hyrcanus. Her first husband was Philip I, son of Herod the Great and Mariamne,

so she married her own uncle, by whom she had a daughter, Salome, whom her mother used to destroy John the Baptist. When Herod Antipas visited Rome, he was entertained by Philip and Herodias. Herod abducted his royal brother's wife. His own wife, an Arabian princess, was an obstacle to an illicit marriage, so he divorced her, and Herodias became queen in her stead, and with her daughter was installed in the palace. "The corroding immorality of Herod's race shows itself in his marriage with Herodias his brother's wife and the wanton offense thereby given to Jewish sensibilities."

Among the female characters in God's portrait gallery there are many wicked women as we are discovering, but surely Herodias stands out among them as one of the most vile and vicious. Amid the putrefying influence of the palace, however, there was one man who knew no fear, John the Baptist. Herod "feared" him and regarded him as "a just man" and whom "he heard gladly." Herod found music in the preacher's message until he sternly rebuked the king by saying of Herodias, "It is not lawful for thee to have her." But such a warning bell was to toll the Baptist's doom. For his faithful rebuke of Herod's sin, John was cast into prison, and the evil, scheming mind of Herodias began to work. She was stung by the arrow from the preacher's quiver and hated him for exposing her shame. "For Herodias' sake," he was imprisoned and thus the greatest of the prophets was sacrificed for this lewd and vicious woman. But the hatred of such a vile creature was more to be desired than her affection (Matthew 10:23; Luke 6:26). Herodias, with her conscience in turmoil because of her accuser, planned to silence him. She did not want Herod to listen too closely and constantly to John's forceful preaching. She feared her illegal husband — for her first husband was still alive — might repent, and her position as queen, imperiled.

Herodias knew Herod only too well. He easily succumbed to sensual excitement, and as his birthday drew near her foul design was hatched. On the day when drink freely flowed, Herodias used her own daughter to inflame Herod's passions. She was willing to sacrifice her child's modesty in order to bend Herod to her will. Herod was overcome by Salome's form seen through the flowing flimsy garment she wore, and influenced by the act of the dancing girl took a rash and foolish oath to give her whatever she asked, even to half of his kingdom. Approaching her mother, Salome said, "What shall I ask?" Without hesitation Herodias, the female hyena, replied, "Ask for the head of John the Baptist." Returning to Herod she presented her demand, and Herod was extremely sorry at such a request. Yet, because of his oath's sake, he sacrificed the preacher whom he regarded as just and holy, and all because of his guilty love for a vile woman. No wonder he was smitten with fear when he heard of the fame of Jesus, thinking it was John the Baptist risen from the dead to torment his conscience further. One wonders how Salome felt when the gory dish of the preacher's head was handed to her? (See SALOME.)

Herodias' Old Testament counterpart was Jezebel. What Herodias was to Herod, Jezebel was to Ahab. Both Ahab and Herod were wicked, and in both cases the woman was more wicked. Both Jezebel and Herodias fostered hate that became deadly against a prophet of God. Jezebel hated Elijah and sought to kill him — Herodias hated John the Baptist, the New Testament Elijah, and succeeded in his murder. What was the end of Herodias? Since she was the source of Herod's sin, Herodias also became the source of his shame. According to Josephus, Herodias' ambition was the ruin of Herod. Jealous of the power of Agrippa her brother, she prodded Herod to demand of Caligula, the emperor, the title of king. Agrippa saw to it that this demand was refused, and Herod was banished and ended his days in shame and exile. The pride of Herodias forced her to be faithful to her husband in the disgrace and misfortune she herself had caused.

HODESH

Scripture Reference — I Chronicles 8:8, 9
Name Meaning — New moon

This is the name of one of the wives of Shaharaim. The other wife of the Benjamite was Hushim. It will be noticed that in the pedigree of the family of Benjamin the wives of Shaharaim are said to have been Hushim and Baara; but, when the children of each of his wives are enumerated, the name of Hodesh appears instead of that of Baara. The explanation of these two names on the one person is given thus by Wilkinson — "The word Baara is derivable from baar, 'to burn,' and may thus mean 'a burning,' 'a kindling,' which is the sense of beera in Exodus 22:6; whence some suppose that it designates the same person called Hodesh, by allusion to the kindling of fires as beacons, by which it was customary among the Israelites in very ancient times, to announce the appearance of the *new moon.*"

HODIAH

Scripture References — I Chronicles 4:18, 19; Nehemiah 10:18
Name Meaning — The Splendor of Jehovah

Evidently there is some confusion over whether this is the name of a male or a female. It is identified by various scholars with Hodijah, a Levite (Nehemiah 10:18). The AV says that Hodiah was the wife, one of Mered's two wives (I Chronicles 4: 18, 19) but the RV shows that Hodiah was a man who married the sister of Nahum, who was reckoned in the tribe of Judah. If by Hodiah is meant Jehudijah, then she was the mother of the three sons Jered, Heber and Jekuthiel.

HOGLAH

Scripture References — Numbers 26:33; 27: 1-11; 36:1-12; Joshua 17:3
Name Meaning — A partridge *or* a boxer

This is the name of the third daughter of the five girls born to Zelophehad, a Manassite. Banded together these daughters fought for and declared their rights to their deceased father's property and won a decision upheld by legal courts in law to this day. Their right of inheritance was decided in their favor because there were no male joint-heirs, and on the condition that they marry men within their own tribe.

HULDAH

THE WOMAN WHO UNVEILED THE FUTURE OF A NATION

Scripture References — II Kings 22:14-20; II Chronicles 34:22-33
Name Meaning — Huldah, signifying "wea-

sel" is supposed to have been an old totem clan name.

Family Connections — All we know of her, apart from her ministry is that she was the wife of Shallum, the keeper of the royal wardrobe. As a prophetess in the reign of King Josiah, she could be found sitting in the central part of the city ready to receive and counsel any who wished to inquire of Jehovah.

Ranking with Deborah and Hannah among the rare women of the Old Testament, Huldah's standing and reputation are attested to in that she was consulted, rather than Jeremiah, when the lost book of the law was found, and that her word was accepted by all as a divinely revealed one. When Hilkiah the priest found the book in the Temple, Josiah sent immediately for Huldah and, attesting to the genuineness of the scroll, she prophesied national ruin because of disobedience to the commands of God. Her prophetic message and the public reading of the law brought about a revival resulting in the reforms carried out by Josiah. With a renewed spiritual life king and people vowed to follow the God of their fathers more faithfully. When men recover the lost truths of Scripture, and apply them to life and morals, what great and mighty changes take place!

HUSHIM

Scripture References — I Chronicles 8:8, 11, see Numbers 26:42; I Chronicles 7:12

Name Meaning — To hasten

This name is from Hush (*chush*), and is supposed to denote a hasty or a premature birth. Hushim, a Moabitess, was one of the two wives of Shaharaim, a Benjamite who went to live in Moab, and the mother of his two sons, Abitub and Elpaal. Hushim is also the name of two males.

ISCAH

Scripture Reference — Genesis 11:29

Name Meaning — She will look out

Here we have the interesting name of the daughter of Haran, Abraham's younger brother. It is to be hoped that she shared her uncle's forward look of a city without foundations (Hebrews 11:10). Josephus identifies this sister of Lot and Mileal as Sarah, Abraham's wife. There is not suf-

ficient proof, however, for the historian's contention.

JAEL
THE WOMAN WHO KILLED A MAN WHILE HE SLEPT

Scripture References — Judges 4:17-22; 5: 6, 24-27

Name Meaning—Jael means "wild or mountain goat" or "gazelle," and as Dean Stanley expresses it, "a fit name for a Bedouin's wife—especially for one whose family had come from the rocks of Engedi, the spring of the wild goat or chamois."

Family Connections — The only association given of this woman who sprang from obscurity by a single deed which, because of its nature, hardly deserved fame, is that she was the wife of Heber, the Kenite. In those days everything connected with a tent was a woman's job and the women became expert in all the phases of making, pitching and striking tents. This was why Jael was able to turn her skill to good account, as with a tent pin in one hand and with a maul in the other, she drove the pin home through the skull of Sisera as he slept — a deed not allotted to divine leading although the victory over Sisera was (Judges 5:10).

How can we explain or justify such an act deemed treacherous according to the morals of Jael's own time? "Hospitality was one of the most strictly adhered to, of all desert obligations, and was a matter of honor among the Hebrews," says Mary Hallet. "In betraying Sisera, Jael broke this code of hers; but to us that is more easily understood than the revolting cruelty of her method of murder!" "So Sisera died" — and Jael's treachery was forgotten in the more important fact of her courage. The circumstances occasioning such a revolting act have already been touched upon (see DEBORAH). Israel chafed under the severe rule of Jabin, king of the Canaanites, and Deborah arose and with Barak went out against the armed force of Jabin. God intervened, and unleashing the powers of nature completely disorganized Jabin's army. Sisera, captain of the host, and Israel's cruel oppressor escaped and fell into the hands of a woman (4:9).

Sisera fled to the tent of Heber the Kenite, whose wife Jael met Sisera and urged him not to be afraid but to turn in and rest. Seeing how worn and weary Sisera was, Jael covered him with a mantle, and when he asked for water to slake his thirst she opened a bottle of milk for him to drink. Then, assuring him that she would shield him from any searchers, she watched him as he fell asleep. Going softly to his side, Jael drove the tent nail through his head and pinned it to the ground. Shakespeare says of woman that "she can smile and smile and be a villain." Jael was not a crude or coarse woman, or a tiger of a woman. Lacking courage, she dare not attack Sisera fairly. She resorted to trickery, for although she met Sisera with a beaming face, there was murder in her heart, and she killed him by foul and reprehensible means. Had Sisera attempted to rape Jael, and in defense of her honor she had killed him, that would have been another matter, but to kill him as an assassin kills a victim was something different. Her murder of Sisera reminds us of Judith of Behulia, who drove a sword through Olopernes' throat as he slept.

Jael did not kill Sisera as David did Goliath, a champion of the Lord bent on destroying His arch-enemies. While divine judgment fell upon Sisera, Jael erred in that she did not allow God to designate the means of punishment. Perhaps she felt an irresistible impulse to slay the persistent enemy of God's people, but she remains forever censurable for the cruel way she killed Sisera, even though Deborah gloated over the act and praised it in poetic form. When Deborah said, "Blessed above women shall be Jael," perhaps she was only praising her faith and not her treachery. Any woman killing the country's enemy must be the friend of Israel, and so the method of Sisera's death mattered little to Deborah who doubtless thought that all was fair in time of war. What atrocious crimes have been committed in the name of patriotism! Jael had no conception that she was the one person at the opportune moment to render "stern justice on an enemy of God." Knowing that the tide of battle had turned against the Canaanites she realized that Sisera would be captured and killed, therefore she acted as the executioner herself, thereby cementing a friendship with Deborah, the conqueror, who thought Jael worthy of praise because of her love for Israel.

JECHOLIAH, JECOLIAH (RV)

Scripture References — II Kings 15:2; II Chronicles 26:3
Name Meaning — Is powerful

The only record we have of this female character is that of her name and the fact that her "son did that which was right in the sight of God," and that "he prospered so long as he sought the Lord" — a sure evidence of her good influence over her child. Jecholiah was the wife of Amaziah, king of Judah, and mother of Azariah, or Uzziah, king of Judah whose death was deeply mourned by the prophet Isaiah (Isaiah 6: 1-3). As to the meaning of her name, Wilkinson remarks upon the names of Uzziah's parents being similar in such to his own and to each other, though in them the name of Jah is compounded with different words. In Amaziah, his father's name, the word Amaz or Amatz signifies "is strong" or "hath strength," and in Jecoliah, his mother's name, Jecol signifies "is powerful," or "hath prevailed."

JEDIDAH, JEDIDA

Scripture Reference — II Kings 22:1, 2
Name Meaning — Darling of Jehovah

This sacramental name must not be confused with Solomon's birth name, Jedidiah, signifying "beloved of Jehovah" (II Samuel 12:24, 25) even though it is similar to it. Jedidah was the daughter of Adaiah of Boscath, or Bozhath, and the wife of Amon, the wicked king who was murdered by his own servants. Jedidah became the mother of Josiah, who succeeded his slain father when he was only eight years old, and reigned most prosperously for 31 years. While Josiah had a wicked father, his mother Jedidah must have been a godly woman who greatly influenced her son, for after his name we have the suggestive phrase, "And he did that which was right in the sight of the Lord."

JEHOADDAN

Scripture References — II Kings 14:2; II Chronicles 25:1
Name Meaning — Jehovah is her ornament

The stepdaughter of Athaliah, Jehoaddan

became the wife of Joash, who was rescued when he was but six years of age by Jehosheba. Her diseased husband was slain in bed after a reign of some 27 years. Jehoaddan was the mother of Amaziah who succeeded his murdered father. Although he started out to rule the nation in righteousness, he reintroduced idolatry into the land. Like his father, Amaziah was murdered.

JEHOSHEBA, JEHOSHABEATH

Scripture References — II Kings 11:2; II Chronicles 22:11

Name Meaning — Jehovah is her oath

Here we have another divine name — a name referring to some solemn promise of God, or representing Him as the Being to whom vows are to be offered, or to whom alone appeals are to be made, as in the frequent phrase, "Swear by His Name." Jehosheba was the daughter of King Jehoram, or Joram, by his secondary wife, half-sister of King Ahaziah. She became the wife of the high priest, Jehoiada, and is the only instance of a princess marrying a high priest. She was also the courageous woman who stole her nephew, Joash, from among the corpses of the king's sons and hid him for six years from the murderous Athaliah. Thus to Jehosheba goes the credit of preserving "The Seed Royal," for had Joash also perished the line of Judah would have been extinct.

JEHODIJAH (see also HODIAH)

Scripture Reference — I Chronicles 4:18

She is referred to as the Jewish wife of Mered as distinguishable from his Egyptian wife, Bithiah.

JEMIMA

Scripture Reference — Job 42:14

Name Meaning — A little dove

Several commentators refer to Job's three daughters as those who were born to him after the return to his prosperity. The same is said of the seven sons born to him following his restoration to peace after severe trials, but are not the three daughters, "the three sisters" (1:4) who are assumed to have been destroyed when a hurricane destroyed their home? Although the sons and daughters were eating and drinking together before the storm struck (1:18), when it did fall upon the house we read that it "fell upon *the young men*, and they are dead" (1:19). There is no mention, however, of their "sisters" being killed with these young men. Are we justified in affirming that "the young men" who perished, were Job's sons? Then, seeing 1:2 is identical with 42:13 are we not right in affirming that the more Job had at his latter end refers only to the material blessings of sheep, camels, oxen and asses (42:12), and not to added children? If children were included in the statement "The Lord gave Job twice as much as he had before" (42:10), and his original seven sons and three daughters (1:2) were all killed by the hurricane that destroyed his house, livestock and servants, then we should read after his restoration to health and prosperity when his latter end was blessed more than his beginning — "He had also fourteen sons and six daughters." But the verse said, "He *had* (past tense) seven sons and three daughters." If *all* these whom the Lord gave were taken away, then it would be a most remarkable coincidence indeed if He gave Job at the end of his trials exactly the same number of children again. Certainly Job was blessed in this area also seeing he lived to love four generations springing from his original seven sons and three daughters. The writer adds to the original mention of three daughters, their names and facts about their beauty and inheritance. The sons' names are not mentioned.

Jemima, the name of the eldest daughter, is reckoned to have an Arabic association meaning "a little dove." Says Wilkinson, "the name, like those of her two sisters, is apparently due to some trivial occurrence, or experience, connected with early infancy. . . ." The Septuagint renders Jemima as derived from the Hebrew word for "day," so that her name could mean "bright or beautiful as day." The three daughters were unsurpassed in their beauty in all the land (42:15). Jemama, a central province of Arabia, was so named by the Arabs, tradition says, in honor of Job's first daughter.

JERIOTH

Scripture Reference — I Chronicles 2:18

Name Meaning — Tent curtains

This name is given as belonging to the wife of Caleb, son of Hezron. Some writers regard Jerioth as another name for Azubuh.

JERUSHA, JERUSHAH

Scripture References — II Kings 15:33; I Chronicles 6:12; II Chronicles 27:1-6
Name Meaning — Taken possession of *or* married

This name belonged to the daughter of Zadok, a priest during David's reign. She became the wife of King Uzziah who died a leper, and whose death was deeply mourned by Isaiah (6:1). Jerusha bore Uzziah a son, Jotham, who became king of Israel. The household must have been a godly one for we read that Jotham "did that which was right in the sight of the Lord" and that he "became mighty, because he prepared his ways before the Lord."

JEZEBEL No. 1

THE WOMAN WHO WAS A SHE-DEVIL

Scripture References — I Kings 16:31; 18: 4-19; 19:1, 2; 21:5-25; II Kings 9
Name Meaning—This heartless woman with a bloody history belied the name she bore, for Jezebel means, "chaste, free from carnal connection"; but by nature she was a most licentious woman. She was a voluptuary, with all the tawdry arts of a wanton woman. Thus no name could have been more inappropriate for such a despised female.
Family Connections—She was the daughter of Ethbaal, king of the Zidonians, and both king and priest of Baal worshipers. The Phoenicians were a remarkable race, and outstanding as the great maritime peoples of the ancient world, but they were idolaters who regarded Jehovah as only a local deity, "the god of the land." Their gods were Baal and Ashtaroth or Astarte, with their innumerable number of priests, 450 of whom Ahab installed in the magnificent temple to the Sun-god he had built in Samaria. Another 400 priests were housed in a sanctuary Jezebel erected for them, and which she fed at her own table. Cruel and licentious rites were associated with the worship of Baal. Jezebel sprang from an idolatrous stock, the same source which afterward produced the greatest soldier of antiquity,

Hannibal, whose temper was not more daring and unforgiving than hers.

It was this heathen woman who married Ahab, king of Northern Israel, and who in so doing was guilty of a rash and impious act which resulted in evil consequences. As a Jew, Ahab sinned against his Hebrew faith in taking as his wife the daughter of a man whose very name, Ethbaal, meant, "A Man of Baal." How or where the strong-minded idolatrous woman and the weak and spineless king met we are not told. Doubtless seeing her, Ahab was fascinated by her beauty and forcefulness of character and fell for her, and Jezebel, ambitious and proud, eagerly seized the opportunity of sharing the throne of a king. Any man, able to resist the wiles of a beautiful but wicked woman possesses true heroism. Joseph succeeded against the lovely yet lustful wife of Potiphar, but Caesar and Antony after conquering almost the whole world, were conquered by the fair but foul Cleopatra.

> Let conquerors boast
> Their fields of fame. He who in virtue arms
> A young, warm spirit, against beauty's charms,
> Who feels her brightness, yet defies her thrall,
> Is the best, bravest conqueror of them all.

Ahab, captivated by Jezebel, "took her to wife, and went and served Baal and worshipped him." All the other sins of Ahab were light compared with his marriage with Jezebel and the serving of Baal that followed (I Kings 16:31, see Micah 6:16). For over 60 years idolatry had made terrible inroads upon the life and ways of the Hebrews and meant more to them than the breaking of the first two commandments of the law; it produced spiritual and moral disintegration which was accentuated by Jezebel's determined effort to destroy the worship of Jehovah. Let us try to delineate the character of Jezebel — a name which has come to mean in all ages a striking proverb for seductive power, worldly subtlety and wickedness of the worst type.

She Possessed an Extraordinary Force of Character

Jezebel was no ordinary woman. Such was her demeanor that she attracted immediate attention. Edward B. Coe wrote of her as "the Clytemnestra, the Lady Macbeth of Hebrew history. Though by no means an attractive personage, she was invested by her extraordinary force of character and her appalling fate with a tragic grandeur which belongs to no other woman of the Bible." While the Bible does not analyze or even portray her character, but simply sets forth the events in which she bore so prominent a part, yet as we read between the lines we cannot fail to see her as a woman of prodigious force of intellect and will. The sacred narrative does not record that she possessed any of the finer, nobler feminine qualities. She knew nothing of the restraint of higher principles. Savage and relentless, this proud and strong-minded woman carried out her foul schemes. A gifted woman, she prostituted all her gifts for the furtherance of evil, and her misdirected talents became a curse. Persuasive, her influence was wrongly directed. Resolute above other women, she used her strength of character to destroy a king and her own offspring, as well as pollute the life of a nation.

She Was an Ardent Idolater

Baal had no more dedicated devoteé than Jezebel. None could match her zeal for the worship of Ashtaroth the famous goddess of the Zidonians, as zealous and liberal maintenance of hundreds of idolatrous priests clearly proves. Not content with establishing the idol worship of her own country in her husband's court, she sought to convert Israel to Baal worship. Two heathen sanctuaries were built, one at Samaria with its 450 priests, and the other at Jezreel with its 400 priests. In a most relentless fashion Jezebel tried to drive out the true prophets of Jehovah from the land, and thus became the first religious female persecutor in history. From her idolatrous father, a high priest of Ashtaroth, she inherited her fanatical religious enthusiasm which inspired her to exterminate the worship of the true and living God, and almost succeeded in the attempt.

The flooding of the nation with all the immoralities and cruel superstitions of such a demoralizing cult as Baalism, brought upon the scene the chief of the true prophets, Elijah. He appeared suddenly before Ahab, predicted three years of drought, and at the end of the period unexpectedly appeared again and challenged the 850 prophets of Baal to a supreme test of power on the top of Mount Carmel. "In language of unparalleled audacity Elijah taunted them with the impotence of their boasted deities, and the strange contest ended in the triumphant vindication of Jehovah." The people seized the priests of Baal and massacred them and Ahab was completely frightened.

The triumphant Elijah had yet to reckon with Jezebel, however, who, when she heard from Ahab about the slaughter of all her well-fed priests, swore a terrible oath to destroy Elijah and his partners "by tomorrow this time." But Elijah, although he had defied the king and stood out alone against the multitude of the priests and worshipers of Baal, felt that the fury of a murderous woman was more than he could face, and fled for his life across the kingdom of Judah, leaving the haughty queen, for the time being, in undisputed possession of the stage.

She Was a Dominating Wife

Ahab was like a puppet in the hands of his overpowering wife. Because he was pliant and weak, Jezebel found it easy to achieve her murderous designs. How could worthless and spineless Ahab resist the evil scheming of his unscrupulous partner? With Lady Macbeth, Jezebel was the evil genius of the man, and a frightful crime ensued. It was Jezebel who became the feared commander in Israel and not the cowardly husband she could wrap around her thumb. It may be that Ahab was more luxury-loving and sensual than cruel, but under the complete domination of a ruthless woman he was forced to act against his finer feelings. "His culpability in this hideous drama lies chiefly in his using his personal power as a means to Jezebel's wicked ends," says Mary Hallet. "For without Ahab's authority, Jezebel would have been a serpent without fangs." In this marriage, Ahab was the weaker vessel with a wife who mocked at his conscientious scruples and bound him in all wickedness as with strong chains.

She Was a Corrupt Tree

Our Lord used a striking figure to illustrate the continuing influence of evil, emanating from a life destitute of godly principles —

> Do men gather grapes of thorns, or figs of thistles? . . . a corrupt tree bringeth forth evil fruit. . . . a corrupt tree cannot bring forth good fruit (Matthew 7:16-20).

Jezebel was rotten root and branch, and thus everything connected with her was contaminated. How appropriate are the lines of Shakespeare as we think of Jezebel who, in her strength of character, lust for power, remorseless rejection of godliness, and unshrinking and resolute activity to abolish all that interferes with the fulfillment of her wicked designs, was a veritable prototype of Catherine de Medici —

> A strong adversary, an inhuman wretch, incapable of pity, void and empty from every drachm of pity.

Her offspring imbibed and continued the wickedness they grew up in. Jezebel's evil influence was revived in her daughter Athaliah of Judea (see ATHALIAH). Her malign character reappears in her eldest son, Ahaziah, who, like his idolatrous mother, was a devout worshiper of Baal. Her second son, Jehoram or Joram, was another image of his mother — further corrupt fruit from a corrupt tree. It was Jehoram, who heard from the lips of Jehu who had been raised up to obliterate the Ahab dynasty, that there would be no peace in Israel, "so long as the whoredoms of thy mother Jezebel and her witchcrafts are so many" (II Kings 9: 22). Is it to be wondered at that Jehoram suffered a similiar fate to that of his mother's at the hands of Jehu?

She Was a Treacherous Schemer

The tragedy of Naboth and his vineyard reveals how despicable a woman Jezebel was. Life was cheap to such a female who had murder in her veins. Her father, Ethbaal, murdered his predecessor, Phelles. Brought up in such a home of intrigue and massacre what else could we expect but a she-devil as Jezebel became? Clarence E. Macartney in his volume on *Bible Characters* in dealing with Naboth says —

> His refusal was the introduction to one of the strangest, most powerful, and most terrible dramas of the Bible; a drama, on the one side, of innocence, courage, independence, and the

fear of God, and, on the other side, of covetousness, avarice, cruelty, perjury, death and terrible retribution. Outside of the Bible itself, it would take a Shakespeare or one of the Greek tragic poets to do justice to it.

As a typical Oriental despot, Jezebel was prepared to murder in her stride toward the desired objective, as the incident of Naboth's vineyard reveals. King Ahab happened to see this fruitful vineyard and inquired as to its owner. Learning it belonged to Naboth, Ahab called him to the palace and offered to buy the vineyard. But it was not for sale. It had belonged to his forefathers and had become precious to Naboth, and as an Israelite Ahab understood his desire to retain it. Thwarted in what he coveted, Ahab took to his bed and refused food.

Then Jezebel came upon the scene. Learning what had happened, and, as a foreigner from a country where the wishes of a king were never questioned, she revealed herself as a woman of accumulated authority when she consoled Ahab by saying —

> Arise and eat bread, and let thine heart be merry. *I will give thee* the vineyard of Naboth the Jezreelite.

Jezebel ordered, by letter, stamped with the royal seal, a public feast. She also instituted an assembly of the people of Jezreel to try the pious Naboth for blasphemies against God and the king. Naboth was arrested, tried and condemned on the false witnesses secured by Jezebel. She found these witnesses in order to appear within the bounds of the law. Found guilty, Naboth was stoned until his innocent life was beaten out of him, and Ahab took possession of the much-coveted vineyard. But the blood of godly Naboth did not cry out in vain. God called Elijah out of his retirement to go to Ahab and pronounce the fearful doom awaiting the murderous pair and their unholy seed. The prophet told the king of his fate —

> In the place where the dogs licked the blood of Naboth, shall dogs lick thy blood, even thine.

This prophecy was fulfilled shortly after its pronouncement for war broke out between the Israelites and the Syrians, and Ahab, while riding in his chariot, received his death wound. The blood-soaked chariot was taken to the spring which ran through Naboth's vineyard, and the dogs came and licked up the bloody water. Concerning Jezebel, Elijah said, "The dogs shall eat Jezebel by the wall of Jezreel," and shortly we shall see how this prophecy was also fulfilled to the very letter.

She Loved Personal Adornment

The death of the one whom Jezebel had "stirred up to work wickedness in the sight of the Lord" revealed her to be as incapable of remorse as of fear. There was no sign of repentance in her, as she went out proudly to meet her prophesied doom. Jehu had been appointed and anointed as the avenger of Jehovah, and he set about his grim task of meting out justice to those who had polluted the land. Jezebel's son and grandson met Jehu in the blood-stained vineyard Naboth had once possessed. Jehu slew Jezebel's son, the king of Israel, and her grandson was overtaken in flight and was slain. The still proud, defiant queen-mother knew her last hour was not far away, and great-grandmother though she was, she took time to arrange her hair and paint her face, and looked out at a window to greet Jehu as he passed by. Perhaps as Morton suggests, "Jezebel did not paint her face from any motive of coquetry or vanity. She knew that death was ready to take her. Therefore, she determined to die like a queen. . . . As Cleopatra, when about to die, robed herself in festal garments, so Jezebel painted her eyes with antimony and placed her jewelled crown upon her head; then, mounting to the palace tower, she watched the thundering advance of Jehu's chariot."

This one touch of grandeur in her foul life gave rise to the bitter taunt, "a painted Jezebel," which came into vogue in England during the sixteenth century when, as Edith Deen reminds us, "painting the face was accepted as *prima-facie* evidence that a woman had loose morals. Certainly no woman's name in history has become so commonly accepted as a synonym for wickedness."

She Died a Horrible Death

The climax came as Jehu entered the city gate. Reaching the palace, he looked up to the window from which came the taunting voice of Jezebel: "Is it peace, thou Zimri, thou murderer of thy master?" Such a taunt maddened her victorious enemy, and seeing the two eunuchs standing at the window with the defiant queen he shouted up to them, "Who is on my side? Who? Throw her down!"

They obeyed and threw her out of the window, and as she fell the walls were sprinkled with her blood. Below her were the soldiers with their spears, the horses to tread her underfoot and the hungry dogs waiting for her flesh. The triumphant Jehu entered the palace over Jezebel's dead body. As he ate and drank, he remembered that the one who had just died as prophesied had been a queen and a mother of kings, so he ordered —

Go, see now this cursed woman, and bury her. And they went to bury her, but they found no more of her than the skull, and the feet, and the palms of her hands.

So died Jezebel, the idolater, the tyrant, the murderess. She had sown to the wind, and reaped the whirlwind. Many of the godly in Israel must have felt that while Jezebel held evil sway over the land, the mills of God seemed to grind slowly. They came to realize, however, that they grind exceedingly sure and small. Thus Jezebel encountered a "mysterious, terrible and divine retribution."

Ere we turn from our portrait of one of the most wicked women who ever breathed, there are one or two lessons to glean from her deeply stained record. No matter from what angle we approach the life of Jezebel she stands out as a beacon to both nations and individuals that the wages of sin is death. Further, from this great tragic figure of literature and of history we learn how important it is for the influence of a wife and mother to be on the side of all that is good and noble. As Ahab's evil genius, Jezebel was the absolute negation of all God meant woman to be, namely, a true help-meet of man. Ahab, we read, was "stirred up" by Jezebel but stirred up in the wrong direction. When a man marries a woman because of her beauty or forceful personality, or marries a wicked woman or one opposed to his religion, he usually courts sorrow, heartache and disappointment. Jezebel retained her obstinate, unbending character to the very end. The death of the man whose life she polluted brought no repentance. What a difference story would have been written if only she had learned how to stir up her husband and children to love God and follow good works (II Timothy 1:6; II Peter 1:13). Her misdirected talents, however, brought upon her a curse. The evil she perpetrated was donè under the guise of religion, just as the cruelties of the Inquisition and the tortures of Smithfield were.

Finally, evil and craft and godlessness bring their own reward, and the wicked reap what they sow. Retribution overtook Jezebel when her body was thrown out of the window to be torn and mangled, and then eaten by dogs. As a daughter of the devil, she suffers a worse retribution in the realms of the doomed. Milton wrote of the God-rejector as —

Him the Almighty Father hurled headlong flaming with hideous ruin and combustion down to bottomless perdition, there to dwell in adamantive chains and penal fires, who durst defy the Omnipotent to arms.

There are those who reject such a lurid description of the fate of the wicked who, like Jezebel, defy and deny God, but the divine Word still stands, that Christ is to be revealed from heaven to take vengeance on those who spurn God and who reject the saving Gospel of His beloved Son (II Thessalonians 1:5-10).

JEZEBEL No. 2
THE WOMAN WHO SEDUCED GOD'S SERVANTS

Scripture Reference — Revelation 2:18-29

In His message to the church at Thyatira, Christ, whose eyes are as a flame of fire, searches out the character of another Jezebel, the New Testament counterpart of Jezebel we have just considered. The question arises, was the Jezebel whom John mentions a real person, or are we to think of her in a symbolic sense? Walter Scott in his renowned exposition of the Book of Revelation suggests that Jezebel represents the rise and power of papacy through the centuries.

Jezebel (O.T.) was a woman, a queen, an idolator, a persecutor, and the virtual ruler and director of the government of Israel. Ahab was a puppet in her hands (I Kings 18 - 21). All this and more is Jezebel of the Apocalypse. Combining in herself these and other features of the Popish system (Revelation 17:18), she arrogantly assumes the title "prophetess." She professes to teach with authority. Combined with teaching she can employ all the arts and seductions of minds specially trained to effect her full purpose. "Hear Mother Church" is the cry of every Romanist.

Scott goes on to enlarge his contention that the Roman Church is still the Jezebel of modern times. It is evident that in the church at Thyatira there arose a group guilty of a sinful mixture of Christian confessions with idolatrous necromancy, and that this section of the church became antagonistic to the spiritual integrity of the true Christian faith. With a sentimental fanaticism indulgence in terrible wantonness and positive fornication grew, and the name Jezebel is given to this unworthy element in the church because of the resemblance between its perversion of truth and the idolatrous wife of Ahab. "Prophetess" can mean "a set of false prophets — the Hebrew feminine expresses collectively a *multitude* — as closely attached to the Thyatira church as a *wife* is to be to a husband, and as powerfully influenced that church for evil as Jezebel did her husband."

It is more than likely that there was a forceful, influential woman in the church who held sway over those who prided themselves upon an enlightened liberalism (2:24), and whose sorceries, prognostications and lax morals exercised a dangerous influence upon weaker Christians in the community. It is interesting to observe how many false religious systems began with a misguided woman. Because of this strongminded woman's prominence at Thyatira she earned the name synonymous with idolatry and wickedness, but in a broader sense the name covers the cult she founded. We rest the case with Ellicott's comment —

It seems best to view the name as symbolical, always remembering that the Jezebel spirit of proud, self-constituted authority, vaunting claims of superior holiness, or higher knowledge, linked with a disregard of—and perhaps a proud contempt for — "legalism," and followed by open immorality, has again and again run riot in the churches of God.

JOANNA
THE WOMAN WHO, HEALED BY CHRIST, HONORED HIM

Scripture References — Luke 8:1-3; 23:55; 24:10

Name Meaning — The Hebrew name of this woman who was numbered among Christ's disciples is the same with Joannes, Johanan, or John, and means, "Jehovah hath shown favor" or, "The Lord is grace" or, "The Lord give graciously." It was because the Saviour showed favor unto Joanna that she rose up and followed Him.

Family Connections — All we know of Joanna's history is that she was the wife of Chuza, the house-steward of Herod the Tetrarch—whom some writers identify as the Nobleman of John 4:46-54. Joanna was also the name of a male, the son of Rhesa (Luke 3:27), an ancestor of Christ who lived about 500 B.C.

As we read between the lines in the short account Luke gives us in his sacred narrative of the female Joanna, we see her a devoted disciple of the One to whom she owed so much. There is as much difference between her and the monstrous Jezebel we have just considered as there is between light and darkness. We breathe a purer air while in Joanna's company whose life and labors are set forth in a fivefold way —

A Sick Woman Healed by Christ

Joanna, along with Mary Magdalene and Susanna were among the "certain women who had been healed of evil spirits and infirmities" (8:2). Whether Joanna had been demon-possessed or suffered from some mental or physical disability we are not told. It is evident that this female of the upper class, restored to normal health by Christ, gave her life to Him. She is here seen as one of the traveling company who went before Christ and the Twelve to arrange for their hospitable reception. Out of her own resources many expenses were met, and in this way she ministered *unto Him* of her substance. Having freely received His healing touch, she freely gave of herself and of her means for His welfare.

A Loyal Witness in an Unusual Sphere

Chuza, the husband of Joanna, was the "steward" of Herod, which is the same word given as "tutor" (Matthew 20:8) or "guardian" (Galatians 4:2). Chuza must have been a man of intelligence and ability in order to hold the position he did as manager of Herod's income expenditure. Both Chuza and Joanna were likely among the servants to whom Herod imparted his belief, when he heard of the fame of Jesus, that it was John the Baptist, whom he had murdered, now risen from the dead. As Joanna was known as one of the Lord's disciples, naturally she would speak of Him among Herod's servants (Matthew 14:2), and Herod would often speak concerning the Master, for his foster brother, Manaen, was a teacher in the church (Acts 13:1). The office of Chuza gave Joanna an excellent opportunity of witnessing in the palace, and we can imagine how she took full advantage of it. As a child of the heavenly King she felt that she must speak her joy abroad. Often through divine grace, Christians find themselves in most unlikely places, wherein they can witness a good confession for Christ. Paul, a prisoner in Rome, persecuted by Nero, the worst ruler who ever lived, was able to write of the saints in Caesar's household. Tradition has it that Chuza lost his position in Herod's palace because of his wife's conversion to Christianity and her courageous testimony among Herod's servants. If this really happened we know that both of them were sheltered by the Lord.

A Generous Supporter of Christ

Healed and saved, Joanna gave thanks. Christ had ministered to her physical restoration and salvation and in turn she ministered to Him. By "substance" we are to understand material possessions, such as money and property, and Joanna honored the Lord with these. Knowing that He and the disciples accompanying Him had very little to support them, Joanna, out of her plenty, gave liberally to their needs and thus exemplified the grace of giving. It is said that Cato, the philosopher, at the close of his honored life, told his friends that the greatest comfort of his old age was that "that which gave him the highest satisfaction, was the pleasing remembrance of the many benefits and friendly offices he had done to others." We can imagine what joy filled the liberal heart of Joanna as she recalled how she had ministered unto the Lord who had done so much for her, and helped to meet His material needs.

A Sorrowful Mourner at the Grave of Christ

Among the women at the cross, the heart of Joanna must have been rent with anguish as she saw her beloved Lord dying in agony and shame. Was she not among the number of the consecrated women who had followed Him from Galilee, and who, after His brutal death, prepared spices and ointments for His body (Luke 23:55, 56)? The One who had cured her body and her soul had become precious to Joanna, and, having ministered to Him while He was alive, she continues her ministry of love as His body is still and cold in death. Too many save their flowers for the grave. Joanna gave hers to Jesus when He was alive and could appreciate them, as well as produce them at the tomb in honor of Him. Her "last respects" were the outward token of the inner reverence in which she had ever held the Saviour.

A Joyful Herald of Her Lord's Resurrection

Joanna was among the sorrow-stricken women who early on that first memorable Lord's Day gathered at the sepulcher to linger in the presence of the dead. But to their amazement the tomb was empty, for the living Lord was no longer among the dead. Perplexed over the vacant grave, they beheld the angelic guardians and heard them say, "He is not here, but is risen: remember how he spake unto you when he was yet in Galilee." How could they forget His words! Recalling all He had said of His sufferings, death and Resurrection, Mary Magdalene, Joanna, and Mary the mother of James, became the first human heralds of the Resurrection. With all haste they went to the apostles and told them the good news, but for awhile their words seemed as idle tales until Peter saw for himself the graveclothes but no dead Master (Luke 24:1-12). He then believed the women's declaration of the Lord who was alive forevermore. Joanna, then, was among the last at

the cross, and among the first to witness the empty tomb and likewise among the first to proclaim that the Lord whom she had so dearly loved was risen indeed. How much the cause of Christ owes to its consecrated Joannas!

JOCHEBED

THE WOMAN WHOSE CHILDREN BECAME GREAT

Scripture References—Exodus 1; 2:1-11; 6:20; Numbers 26:59; Hebrews 11:23

Name Meaning—Jochebed implies, "glory of Jehovah" or, "Jehovah (is her or our) glory." It is plain from this name of the mother of Moses, that the announcement of Jehovah, as the name of God, was not made for the first time when God revealed Himself in a special manner under that title to Moses in the burning bush. Jochebed is the first person in Scripture to have a name compounded with Jah — or Jehovah. One cannot but be fascinated with Alexander Whyte's suggestive comment on her name —

It is very tantalizing to be told her remarkable name and to be told no more. Was *God-thy-glory* the remarkable name that Moses gave to his mother as often as he looked back at all that he owed to her, and as often as he rose up and called her blessed? Or was her very remarkable name her own invention? Was her striking name her own seal that she had set to her own vow which she made to her own God after some great grace and goodness of her own God? Or, again did the angel of the Lord visit that daughter of the house of Levi or some Jabbok-like or Annunciation-night, and so name her as the sun rose upon her prayer?

Family Connections — Jochebed is spoken of as a daughter of Levi who married a man of the house of Levi (Exodus 2:1; Numbers 26:59), whose name was Amram. Strange though it may seem, she married her nephew, and was thus both the wife and aunt of Amram, seeing his wife was his father's sister (Exodus 6:20). Marriages with aunts and nieces were not unlawful before the giving of the law by Moses. They were very common throughout the East.

To Amram and Jochebed were born three children each of whom became renowned in their own sphere (Numbers 26:59). She bore and suckled all three on the same strong milk, till she weaned them from milk and put them on the marrow of lions. The oak has its roots around the rock, and the children of Jochebed had their roots around their godly mother.

There was Moses, who became one of the greatest national leaders and legislators the world has ever known.

There was Aaron, who became Israel's first high priest and the founder of the Aaronic priesthood.

There was Miriam, the gifted poetess and musician, who was intimately associated with her two brothers in the history of Israel.

Jochebed's prominent place in the divine gallery is secure, then, and the aspect of her career especially emphasized in Scripture is that of her clever design to preserve the life of her baby boy. It was for her courage and trust in such an act that had far-reaching consequences for the nation that she is placed among the heroines of faith in Hebrews 11:23. Let us recall the circumstances of the preservation of Moses which caused his mother to be included among that "great cloud of witnesses" whose lives and labors testified of their faith in God's providential care and goodness.

At the time of Pharaoh, the Hebrews had multiplied so greatly as to cause the monarch to fear lest they should outnumber the Egyptians and take over the nation. Thus he commanded that all newly-born Hebrew boys be thrown into the Nile — a most dastardly edict! Jochebed was heavy with child. Already there were Miriam, about ten years of age at the time, and Aaron, possibly about three, in the home. Now another child was on the way. Knowing of Pharaoh's command and that, as a rigid executive, he closely checked up on all male births, Jochebed must have had intense suspense as she awaited her third child. Would it be a boy that would be wrenched from her and thrown into the Nile? What were her feelings when the child was born and the midwife told her it was a boy? What maternal grief must have been hers!

But the horror of that crocodile-infested Nile transforms Jochebed into a heroine and the preserver of a boy who became one of the world's greatest figures. The moment she saw her baby, she was determined to fight for his life. Three times over we read that "she saw that he was a goodly child" (Exodus 2:2; Acts 7:20; Hebrews 11:23). This means that Moses was not only a lovely child to look at, but also, as the margin explains, he was "fair to God," implying that there was something other-worldly or angelic about his features. As the little one lay in her lap, Jochebed felt that he had been sent from God, and that He, along with her mingled faith and love, would somehow preserve the child.

How Jochebed managed to hide her baby, who doubtless cried as lustily as other babies, in some secret place where he could not be seen or heard, is a mystery! When she was unable to conceal him any longer, "God through the intensity of her faith caused her to inherit a vision of what He had appointed for Moses." She made a little cradle of plaited reeds which were believed to be protection against crocodiles, then placed the cradle with its treasure secretly among the rushes at the river's bank, and told Miriam her young daughter to stand near to watch over the small craft. The brief but vivid account of what happened is given by the historian, even by Moses himself who, in his latter years, by divine inspiration, wrote the first five books of the Bible.

At her usual time Pharaoh's daughter came to the feathery greenness edging the ancient Nile to wash herself, and her maidens walking by the river side saw the cradle among the rushes. When the royal lady saw the beautiful baby and heard his cry she had compassion on him. A Hebrew woman must be found to nurse the child. Jochebed was fearfully watching the fate of that precious child she had borne and the rough cradle she had fashioned. Young Miriam was also near at hand, and quite naively said to Pharaoh's daughter, "Shall I go and call to thee a nurse of the Hebrew women, that she may nurse the child for thee?"

Pharaoh's daughter said, "Go!" Miriam was not long in calling her mother and presenting her as a nurse. Pharaoh's daughter asked her to nurse the child for her at a given wage. Thus Jochebed's baby was not only saved, but Jochebed was paid to care for him until he was weaned. Pharaoh's daughter must have loved the child for she brought him up as her son. However, Moses later refused to be called the son of Pharaoh's daughter, even though she had given him her name, Moses, which means "drawn out of the water" (Exodus 2:10). If Jochebed was guided by God to make that small cradle and place her three-month old baby in it, and hide him among the rushes, surely the steps of Pharaoh's daughter were ordered by the same God, even though she was an idolater. It was to her that Jochebed owed the saving of her son, as well as the royal protection and all the advantages of Pharaoh's palace as his home for the first forty years of his life.

How long Jochebed lived after her delivered child no longer required her nursing, we are not told. Doubtless she was dead by the time Moses fled into the wilderness when he was forty years of age. Although she did not live to see how famous her children became, dead, she yet spake again in their utter devotion to God. She had lived her life as unto Him, and her sons and daughter lit their torches at her flame. Jochebed was the chief influence unto God in their preparation for the great tasks they were to accomplish in leading His people out of Egyptian bondage. It was Jochebed's love, faith and courage that saved her child from a cruel death and preserved him to bless the world. A mother who loves the Saviour, and who has a more severe anguish when she knows that, not the life of her child is at stake, but its soul, can rest in the assurance that Jochebed's God still lives, and is able to save her dear one from eternal death.

JUDAH
Jeremiah 3:7, 8, 10
(See chapter on SYMBOLIC BIBLE WOMEN)

JUDITH

Scripture Reference – Genesis 26:34
Name Meaning – The praised one

This daughter of Beeri the Hittite and one of the wives of Esau whom he married when he was forty years old, was a Hittite with a Semitic name. Esau was exactly the same age when he violated the Abrahamic principle of marrying an idolater (Genesis 24:3), as his father Isaac was, when sixty

years before, he married Rebekah. By his act in taking both Judith and Bashemath, who were Hittites, as his wives, Esau caused his parents much bitterness of spirit or mingled anger and sorrow (Genesis 26:34; 36:2), and also forfeited his birthright. Judith is the feminine form of Judah. Wilkinson observes that "Judith as a pure Hebrew name is a feminine form of Jehudie, which as a proper name has the same sense as Judah, 'praise' or 'one who is praised.'" Unsuccessful efforts have been made to identify Judith with Aholibamah spoken of as a wife of Esau (Genesis 36:2, 24, 25). As a female name Judith has ever been a popular one. There are over 250,000 girls and women in America alone who are known by this name. Judith is the heroine in the apocryphal book bearing her name.

JULIA

Scripture Reference – Romans 16:15
Name Meaning – Having curly hair

By birth a member of one of the great old homes in Rome, Julia was doubtless a member of the imperial court and therefore among the saints to be found in Caesar's household. Perhaps she was the wife or sister of Philologus with whose name she is coupled. She is named among those to whom Paul sent a warm salutation. The extension of her name, Julius, implies, "curlyheaded" (Acts 27:1, 3).

KEREN-HAPPUCH

Scripture References – Job 1:2; 42:14
*Name Meaning–*Beautifier *or* horn of paint

This was the name of the last of Job's three daughters, and she shared with her two sisters the paternal inheritance (see JEMIMA). Her name speaks of "box of paint" which was a vessel containing liquids frequently made of horn, and called "horns." Such a name is indicative of beautiful eyes made so from the dye used to tinge the eyelashes and make the eyes more lustrous (II Kings 9:30; Jeremiah 4:30).

KETURAH

Scripture References – Genesis 25:1-6; I Chronicles 1:32, 33
Name Meaning – Incense

After the death of his beloved Sarah, Abraham took as his third wife, if we count

Hagar as a wife, Keturah, a young woman. When Sarah died, and Isaac his son married, doubtless Abraham now an old man was very lonely and remarried for the sake of companionship. Keturah is called a concubine (I Chronicles 1:32). Her name is like Kezia, a perfume name. She became the mother of Abraham's six sons: Zimran, Jokshan, Medan, Midian, Ishbak and Shuah who became the progenitors of six Arabian tribes of Southern and Eastern Palestine. Ancient Israelites regarded the Arabs as distant relatives. It was through Keturah's offspring that Abraham became "the father of many nations." The patriarch in his declining years was surrounded by a woman's care and love, and a circle of dear children. Kuyper, writing of the relationships between Abraham and Keturah, says that we cannot think of it as being romantic. It was a marriage in which a less passionately vehement love attains high ethical qualities.

> Keturah is not depicted as a young wife who has come to an independent position in a tent of her own. She appears as a wife who nurses and provides for the aged. Such an attitude also implies a devotion but it is a devotion which combines the love of a wife with that of a daughter.

Although Abraham's wife, Keturah, sustained and cared for him as the eldest daughter of a family would support her father, she therefore has something to say to any unmarried woman who marries a far older man with previous marital experience. "There must be sincere devotion and the consecration of that higher quality in which love combines with a sacred urge to be a helpmeet to the desolate and forsaken."

KEZIA

Scripture Reference — Job 42:14
Name Meaning — Cassia

This second daughter of Job has a perfume name speaking of an aromatic herb (Psalm 45:8), and was expressive of her beauty. (See JEMIMA.)

LEAH

THE WOMAN LACKING LOVELINESS
WAS YET LOYAL

Scripture References—Genesis 29; 30; 49:31; Ruth 4:11
Name Meaning — Leah as a name has been explained in many ways. "Wearied" or

"Faint from Sickness" with a possible reference to her precarious condition at the time of birth, is Wilkinson's suggestion. Others say the name means "married" or "mistress." The narrative tells us that she was "tender eyed" (Genesis 29:17), which can mean that her sight was weak or that her eyes lacked that luster reckoned a conspicuous part of female beauty which Rachel her sister "beautiful and well-favoured" evidently had.

Family Connections — Because Jacob was Rebekah's son he was related to Leah by marriage. Leah was the elder daughter of Laban who, by deception, married her to Jacob, to whom she bore six sons and a daughter. By her maid, Zilpah, Leah added two more sons to her family.

The romantic story of Jacob and his two wives never loses its appeal. After fleeing from and meeting God at Bethel, Jacob reached Haran and at Laban's well he met his cousin Rachel drawing water for the sheep. It was love at first sight for Jacob, and his love remained firm until Rachel's death in giving birth to her second child. Going to work for his Uncle Laban, Jacob was offered wages in return for service rendered, but he agreed to serve Laban for seven years on the condition that at the end of the period Rachel should be his wife. Because of his love for Rachel those years seemed but a few days.

At the end of the specified period however, Jacob was cruelly deceived by his uncle. As it was a custom of the time to conduct the bride to the bedchamber of her husband in silence and darkness, it was only with the morning light that Jacob discovered that he had been deceived by Laban as he saw Leah and not Rachel at his side. Laban condoned his unrighteous act by saying that the younger girl could not be given in marriage before the first-born, and Jacob covenanted to serve another seven years for Rachel, his true love inspiring him to be patient and persevering. Perhaps Jacob treated the deception as a retributive providence, for he had previously deceived his blind and dying father.

Whether Leah participated in the deceit to win Jacob from her more beautiful sister we do not know. The moral tone of the home was low, and Leah may have been a child of environment. This much is evident, that although she knew that the love of her husband's heart was not for her but for Rachel, Leah genuinely loved Jacob and was true to him until he buried her in the cave of Machpelah. While Jacob was infatuated with Rachel's beauty, and loved her, there is no indication that she loved him in the same way. "Rachel remains one of those women with nothing to recommend her but beauty," says H. V. Morton. "She is bitter, envious, quarrelsome and petulant. The full force of her hatred is directed against her sister, Leah."

The names Leah gave her children testified to the miraculous faith God had planted in her heart. Somewhat despised by Jacob, she was yet remembered by the Lord. In spite of the polygamous marriage, she became the mother of six sons who were to become the representatives of six of the twelve tribes of Israel. The names Leah chose revealed her piety and sense of obligation to the Lord.

Reuben, her first-born, means "Behold a son," and Leah praised God for looking favorably upon her. Thus, divine compassion was carefully treasured in such a name which also the holder tarnished.

Simeon, the second son, means "Hearing," so given by Leah since God had heard her cry because of Rachel's hatred. Such a name as Simeon is a lasting monument of answered prayer.

Levi, the next to be born implies, "Joined" and Leah rejoices feeling that her husband would now love her, and that through Levi's birth she would be more closely united to her husband.

Judah was the fourth son to be born to Leah, and she gave him a name meaning "Praise." Perhaps by now Jacob had become a little more affectionate. Certainly the Lord had been good to both Leah and Jacob, and with the selfishness in her heart defeated, Leah utters a sincere *Soli Deo Gloria* — "I will praise the Lord." Leah had two other sons named Issachar and Zebulun, and a daughter, Dinah. Leah was uncomely when compared to her lovely sister, but what she lacked in beauty she made up for in loyalty to Jacob as a wife, and as a

good mother to his children. "It seems that homely Leah was a person of deep-rooted piety and therefore better suited to become instrumental in carrying out the plans of Jehovah than her handsome, but worldly-minded, sister, Rachel."

One evident lesson we can learn from the triangle of love in that ancient Israelite home is that solemn choices should not be based upon mere external appearances. Rachel was beautiful, and as soon as Jacob saw her he fell for her. But it was Leah, not Rachel, who bore Judah through whose line the Saviour came. The unattractive Leah might have repelled others, but God was attracted toward her because of an inner beauty which the lovely Rachel lacked. "There are two kinds of beauty," Kuyper reminds us. "There is a beauty which God gives at birth, and which withers as a flower. And there is a beauty which God grants when by His grace men are born again. That kind of beauty never vanishes but blooms eternally." Behind many a plain or ugly face there is a most lovely disposition. Also God does not look upon the outward appearance, but upon the heart.

LOIS

Scripture Reference — II Timothy 1:5
Name Meaning — Agreeable *or* desirable

While there are numerous grandmothers mentioned in the Bible, as these cameos show, the term "grandmother" itself is only used once in the Bible, and that is in connection with Lois, the mother of Eunice, and grandmother of Timothy (see EUNICE). Lois preserves in her name an old Greek word and corresponds to Naamah and Naomi, both of which carry a similar significance. We can imagine how the nature of Lois corresponded to the implication of her name.

Lois was a devout Jewess who had instructed her beloved daughter and grandson in Old Testament Scriptures. The family lived at Lystra, and it is possible that Paul, during his visit there, had the joy of leading Lois, Eunice, and Timothy to Christ (Acts 14:6, 7; 16:1), and then wrote of the "unfeigned faith" that dwelt in all three. We have no record of Timothy's father apart from the fact that he was a Gentile. Fausset observes, "One godly parent may counteract the bad influence of the ungodly, and win the child to Christ" (I Corinthians 7: 14; II Timothy 3:15). Paul dwells upon the faith of *the mother and grandmother alone* in the spiritual instruction of Timothy who became his son in the faith.

LO-RUHAMAH

Scripture References — Hosea 1:6, 8

Name Meaning — Not pitied *or* not have mercy

Nothing beyond the name of the bearer is known. She was the daughter of Hosea and Gomer and her symbolic name was applied to Israel from whom God had withdrawn His loving compassion because of the nation's spiritual whoredoms (Hosea 2: 1, 23; Romans 9:25).

LYDIA

The Woman Who Was Diligent in Business

Scripture References — Acts 16:12-15, 40; Philippians 1:1-10

Name Meaning—Lydia, who was an Asiatic, derived her name from the country on the borders of which her native city, Thyatira, was situated. It was not an original Greek name, but probably Phoenician, and a common name meaning "bending." Readers of Horace will be familiar with Lydia as a popular name for women. There are those writers who think that it means "The Lydian," seeing Thyatira was a city of Lydia, and that her personal name is unknown.

Family Connections — Scripture does not supply us with any information regarding Lydia's background apart from the fact that she lived in Thyatira which was one of the Macedonian colonies. From names discovered on monuments it is evident that the city was the melting pot of many nations, and that the chief object of worship was Apollo, who was worshiped as the sun-god under the name of Tyrinnus. There was also a strong Jewish element in the city maintaining faith in Jehovah. Lydia, one of the prominent women of Thyatira, is presented to us in various ways, namely —

As a Business Woman

Thyatira was conspicuous for its many guilds which were united by common pursuits and religious rites. One of these guilds was that of *dyers*. The water of the area was so well-adapted for dyeing, that no other place could produce the scarlet cloth out of which fezzes were so brilliantly and so permanently dyed. This unique purple dye brought the city universal renown. Lydia was a well-known seller of this product (Acts 16:14), and typifies a successful business woman in a prosperous city. Ability, enthusiasm, singleness of purpose and mental acumen were hers, and she prospered greatly in an honorable and extensive calling of "selling purple." Lydia was an example of the comparatively independent position some women attained to in Asia Minor. That she became prosperous in business is seen in that she owned a spacious home, and had servants to care for her.

As a Devout Woman

While it is not certain whether Lydia was of Jewish descent it is evident that she was a Jewish proselyte. "She worshipped God," we are told. Often business people are so engrossed in their affairs as to have no time for religion. But Lydia, in spite of all her secular obligations, found time to worship according to the Jewish faith. Daily she made her way to the riverside where prayer was wont to be made. She knew that in order to successfuly meet the stiff competition of the Philippian traders, she needed grace as well as knowledge. At that riverside prayer meeting perhaps she met other Jewish dyers, and with them eagerly waited upon the ministry of Paul and his companions.

As a Seeking Woman

Although sincerely religious, Lydia was not a Christian. She did, however, have a hunger for a deeper spiritual experience. The mind is closed against the full truth either from ignorance or prejudice and cannot discern it, or from pride and perversity and will not admit it. Ignorance was responsible for Lydia's closed mind, but as she attended to the truth of Christ which Paul spoke of in conversational style in that small seated Jewish gathering, the light dawned, and her heart opened to receive that Christ as her Saviour. As Chrysostom puts it, "To open is the part of God, and to pay attention that of the woman." Her faith was born through hearing the Word of God (Psalm 119:18, 130; Luke 24:45).

As a Christian Woman

As an evidence of her surrender to the claims of Christ she was baptized, "the waters of Europe then first being sacramentally used to seal her faith and God's forgiveness in Christ." Her conversion was declared by a public confession, and such was her enthusiasm that she immediately told her household what had happened, and all within it likewise believed and were baptized as disciples of the same Saviour. Thus Lydia had the honor of being Paul's first European convert — the forerunner of a mighty host to honor the Lord. Becoming a Christian did not make her less of a successful business woman. Now she had Christ as her Senior Partner and with Him we can imagine that trade remained good and that much of her profit was used to assist His servants in the work of the Gospel.

As a Hospitable Woman

Lydia's transformation of life was evidenced by her eagerness to give missionaries the hospitality of her fine home. Truth in her heart was manifested in kindness to each other — as they ought to be! "Be ye kind one to another." First came Lydia's faith, then the winning of her servants to Christ, then her love in gracious hospitality, and finally her reception of Paul and Silas into her home after their discharge from prison, bruised and battered though they were. She was not ashamed of the Lord's prisoners (see I Timothy 5:10; Hebrews 13:2; I Peter 4:9). While benefiting from Lydia's generous hospitality Paul warned all present of the terrible trials before them, and then parting from godly Lydia, praised God for all she had meant to him and his companions.

As a Consecrated Woman

Lydia always had "open house" for the saints of God and her home became a cen-

ter of Christian fellowship in Philippi with perhaps the first Christian church being formed therein. When Paul came to write his letter to the Philippians, we can rest assured that Lydia was included in all the saints at Philippi to whom he sent his salutations (Philippians 1:1-7); and was also in his mind as one of those women who labored with him in the Gospel (Philippians 4:3). William Ramsay thinks that Lydia may have been either Euodia or Syntyche (Philippians 4:2).

When Paul penned the triple exhortation — "Not slothful in business, fervent in spirit, serving the Lord" (Romans 12:11), we do not know whether he had his hospitable convert, Lydia, in mind. She certainly exemplified these three virtues, and grace can be ours to emulate them.

"Not slothful in business"

If our business is honorable and we are diligent in it, and if we are the Lord's, we have the assurance that if we honor Him in all transactions, He will honor us. He places no premium upon idleness or indolence. Did not Paul say that if we are not willing to work we have no right to eat?

"Fervent in spirit"

Moffatt's translation is suggestive here. He expresses it, "Maintain the spiritual glow," which, by God's grace Lydia was able to do as she cared for her business interests and pursuits which were no bar to her spirituality. Too often, we allow the secular to rob us of our glow. Our affection becomes too set on things below.

"Serving the Lord"

Lydia not only sold her dyes — she served her Saviour. She stayed in business that she might have the money to help God's servants in their ministry. How her generous care of Paul and Silas, and of many others, must have cheered their hearts. Lydia was, first of all, a consecrated Christian, then a conscientious business woman who continued to sell her purple dyes for the glory of God. When we reach heaven, we shall find this "seller of purple" wearing more superior garments, robes not stained even with the notable dye of Thyatira, but "washed and made white in the blood of the Lamb."

MAACHAH

Name Meaning — Oppression *or* depression

Scripture employs this name in three different ways. It is given as the designation of a city in Syria (II Samuel 10:8; I Chronicles 19:6, 7); of three or four males (II Samuel 10:6; I Kings 2:39; I Chronicles 11:43; 27:16); and of several females distinguished thus —

1. Maachah, the son of Nahor by his concubine, Reumah (Genesis 22:24).

2. Maachah, the concubine of Caleb, son of Hezron (I Chronicles 2:48).

3. Maachah, a woman of Benjamin, the wife of Machir the Manassite who was the father or founder of Gilead. This Maachah was the daughter-in-law of Manasseh, son of Joseph and mother of Peresh and Sheresh (I Chronicles 7:12, 15, 16).

4. Maachah, the wife of Jehiel, father or founder of Gibeon, and ancestress of King Saul (I Chronicles 8:29; 9:35).

5. Maachah, the daughter of Talmai, king of Geshur, and therefore a woman of royal rank. Taken in battle by David, she became one of his eight wives and mother of Absalom (I Chronicles 3:2; II Samuel 3:3).

6. Maachah, daughter or granddaughter of Absalom. According to common oriental usage, "daughter" must be understood as "granddaughter." Absalom had only one real daughter, Tamar, who, if she married Uriel of Gibeah, had Maachah or Maacah as her daughter (II Chronicles 13:2). The Maachah before us became the favorite wife of King Rehoboam and mother of King Abijah of Judah (I Kings 15:1, 2; II Chronicles 11:20-22). Although a woman of strong character, her influence was on the side of idolatry. She maintained her position in the palace until the reign of her grandson, Asa, who finally degraded her for an act of peculiar infamy (I Kings 15:13; II Chronicles 15:16).

7. Maachah, the daughter of Abishalom, mother of Asa, king of Judah, who followed his forbear David in doing that which was right in the sight of the Lord (I Kings 15:10; II Chronicles 15:16).

MAHALAH, MAHLAH

Name Meaning — Sickness *or* disease

This name found in several lists of pedigrees is a birth name and may have been related to the sorrows, dangers and other circumstances of the natal hour, personal either to the mother or the child. Thus, used as a title for Psalms 53 and 88, its significance is apropos seeing that in these Psalms the writer is dwelling upon the subject of man's spiritual sickness.

1. Mahalah, the sister of Machir, and daughter of Hammoleketh, and identified as the granddaughter of Manasseh, Joseph's first-born son (I Chronicles 7:18).

2. Mahalath, the daughter of Ishmael, son of Hagar, sister of Nebaioth, and the woman Esau took as his third wife (Genesis 28:9).

3. Mahalath, the first of the eighteen wives of King Rehoboam who had sixty concubines. She was David's granddaughter (II Chronicles 11:18).

4. Mahlah, one of the daughters of Zelophehad (Numbers 26:33; 27:1; 36:11; Joshua 17:3. See Hoglah.).

MARA

Scripture Reference — Ruth 1:20
Name Meaning — Bitter

Returning from Moab, Naomi chose this name for herself. She felt it to be appropriate to her pitiable plight (see Naomi).

MARTHA

The Woman Who Was More Practical
Than Spiritual

Scripture References — Luke 10:38-41; John 11; 12:1-3

Name Meaning — As a Chaldee or Syriac word, Martha is the feminine of *moro* or *more*, meaning "lord," "master." We find this in the form *maran* in the well-known phrase Maran-atha, "The Lord cometh" (I Corinthians 16:22). There are those who think that *Kyria*, translated "lady" in II John, verse 1, is a proper name, the Greek equivalent of this word. Carpzov supposes that this *Kyria* was the same person as Martha of Bethany.

Family Connections — Of the history of Martha, the Bible tells us nothing save that she was the sister of Mary and Lazarus, and lived with them at Bethany. Some early writers have made Martha, the daughter, wife, or widow of Simon the Leper, and that on his death the house became hers, hence the reference to the house when the resurrection of Lazarus was celebrated (Matthew 26:6; Mark 14:3). Others think that Martha may have been a near relative of Simon for whom she acted as hostess. But the narrative seems to suggest the home belonged to Martha and being older than Mary and Lazarus, she carried the responsibility of all connected with household affairs in a home where "Jesus found the curse of the sojourner lifted from Him, and, in reversal of His own description of His loneliness and penury, found where to lay His head." What strikes us forcibly is that after Jesus left His natural home at the age of thirty to enter upon His public ministry we do not read of Him returning to it for rest and relaxation. It was to the warm, hospitable home at Bethany to which He retired, for He loved the three who lived in it, Martha, Mary and Lazarus — in this order — which is something we do not read concerning His own brothers and sisters according to the flesh.

Martha and Mary seem to belong together in God's portrait gallery, just as Cain and Abel, Jacob and Esau do. Expositors also bracket the two sisters together, comparing and contrasting their respective traits. Martha, busy with household chores — Mary, preferring to sit before Jesus for spiritual instruction. Martha, ever active and impulsive — Mary, meditative and reticent. Truly drawn are the characters of these two sisters, Martha usually busy supervising the hospitality of the home, Mary somewhat indifferent to house work, anxious only to seek that which was spiritual. But we have no Scriptural warrant for affirming that the difference between the quiet, pious Mary and her industrious sister is that of the opposite of light to darkness. In the church there are vessels of gold and others of silver, but we are not justified in saying that the character of Mary is worked in gold and that of Martha in silver. These two sisters in that Bethany family had their respective, appropriate talents, and each of them served the Master accordingly.

George Matheson deprecates the effort to always bracket Mary and Martha together. Each figure stands for itself alone. These sisters have "both suffered from being uniformly viewed in combination, and the bracketing has been more injurious to Mary than to Martha. To say that Mary stands in contrast to Martha is true, but it is inadequate." Too often "Martha has been held up to fine scorn as a worldly-minded and jealous creature, and Mary exalted for an indifference to the duties of hospitality, concerning which, for aught that we know, she may at various times have been quite as zealous as Martha." Let us, therefore, take these female characters separately, and beginning with Martha note how she nobly fulfilled her mission in life.

The majority of the women of the Bible are revealed to us in passing hints. None of them are as fully pictured as we would like. But when we look at Martha it does seem as if her character is more fully revealed than that of many other females. Luke gives us our first glimpse of her in "a piece of writing which is one of the marvels of literature," as H. V. Morton expresses it. "There is not one word we could do without, yet the picture is complete, and framed, as it were, by a kitchen door. Luke tells it in ninety-eight words" (10:38-42). We have scattered evidence as to Martha's ability to care for Jesus and the saints in the practical ways she did. Her home at Bethany was one of the few of social standing and substance with whom Jesus was on friendly terms. The hospitality afforded Him, the supper of some pretensions Martha provided for invited guests, the number and quality of friends who gathered around the sisters in the hour of their deep grief, and the wealth displayed in the anointing of Jesus, all alike bespeak of affluence. When Bethany is referred to as "the village of Mary and her sister, Martha," the implication is that they were important figures in the community and that their home was the chief one in the village.

What, then, are the characteristics of Martha, the only Bible woman to have her name repeated, as Jesus did, when affectionately He said, "Martha! Martha!"?

She Was Most Hospitable

The first glimpse we have of Martha is that of one "given to hospitality," for we read she "received Jesus into her house"— *her house,* suggesting she was its owner. Then, when Jesus was sent for to hurry to the aid of her sick brother, Lazarus, we read that when Martha heard that Jesus was coming "she met Him," and bade Him welcome (John 11:20, 30). And the provision of that home meant much to Jesus. One day we have Him saying, "The Son of man hath not where to lay his head," but the next day, "He came to Bethany . . . and Martha made him a supper." His lonely heart found in that loving, hospitable home a woman waiting to minister to His weariness and exhaustion, and from the swift-handed care of gentle womanhood Jesus received the physical refreshment He needed. Even when there was death in the home, the energetic and practical Martha dried her tears and went out to meet the Lord of life, leaving the mystical Mary sitting in the house still weeping. What a superb life-like touch that is! "Martha went and met Him: but Mary sat still in the house."

Knowing Martha as we do, we can be assured of this fact, that whenever Jesus visited Martha's home she never had any need to apologize for untidy rooms, a neglected household, or lack of necessary provisions. To her, home responsibilities were never a drudgery. Martha loved her home, was house-proud, kept it "spick and span," and was ever ready to entertain her divine Guest or others seeking a refuge beneath her hospitable roof. Eugenia Price expresses this aspect of Martha's character when she says —

> The superb hospitality He found in Martha's home was extremely important to Him. No one enjoyed her cooking more than He enjoyed it. No one found her spacious home more beautiful, more inviting. But always He had the real issues in full view. He could not be distracted from them, even by His tired body and His human need of Martha's services.

She Was Meditative

We do not read the record of Martha and Mary aright if we think that the former did all the serving, and the latter all the sitting. Too often, we think of Mary as the meditative one, and Martha as the practical one. But the next glimpse we have of Martha shows us that she was found at Jesus' feet— "which *also* sat at Jesus' feet, and heard His word." So both sisters studied in the College of the Feet. Conversely the phrase,

"she has *left* me to serve alone," suggests that Mary joined her sister in the reception of Jesus, and worked with her for a while but betook herself to her place at Jesus' feet. We must not for a moment feel that Mary thought serving beneath her, or that Martha had the idea that sitting was beyond her spiritual capacity. Both sat before the Master, but while Mary thought that listening was better, Martha felt that feeding Jesus was just as necessary as waiting upon His word. Martha's practical service on His behalf was inspired by what she had heard from His lips and came of her love for Him. As George Matheson puts it —

> Every article on Martha's table was constructed out of sympathy, built of the fibres of her heart. The feast which she devised was the fruit of solicitude for Jesus and would have had no existence apart from that solicitude.

She Was Guilty of Complaint

Luke, who must have gone with Jesus to the house, noticed that "Martha was cumbered about much serving." The word "cumbered" means "distracted." It is God's will "that we attend upon the Lord without distraction" (I Corinthians 7:35). But being the one who managed the household and served, Martha found herself drawn hither and thither by conflicting cares. She loved Jesus and wanted all in the house to do their best for Him. So we have her double complaint, with the first part of it directed to Jesus Himself, "Dost thou not care that my sister hath left me to serve alone?" The next half of the complaint was a command, "Bid her therefore that she help me." This means that if Jesus were still speaking to Mary sitting at His feet, her somewhat vehement complaint must have interrupted our Lord's calm demeanor while conversing with Mary. It irritated Martha to see Mary, cool and idle, while she was busy getting the meal ready for the visitors, and most likely their accommodation for a night or so.

It may have been that Martha was "secretly vexed with herself as much as with Mary, that the latter enjoyed the privilege of hearing Jesus' word seated at His feet, while she could not persuade herself to do the same for fear that a varied enough repast should not be served up to Him." It was as if Martha had said to Jesus, "Lord, here am I with everything to do, and this sister of mine will not lay her hand to anything; thus I miss something from Thy lips, and Thou from our hands — bid her, therefore, that she help me."

Martha would not presume to call her sister away from Jesus to help. In her vexed state of mind she included Jesus in her rebuke, and asked Him to release Mary from the season of meditation to help out with practical duties.

She Was Rebuked by Jesus

In our Lord's answer to Martha's complaint there was no condemnation of her activity, for He must have appreciated her warmhearted, practical management of the household. He knew that she was seeking to entertain Him with her best, and so lovingly warned her of the danger of forgetting amid her many cares the one thing needful. In the repetition of her name, Martha! Martha! there is an affectionate reproof. The only other example of a twofold utterance of a name during our Lord's ministry was when He said, Simon! Simon! (Luke 22: 31). From glory He said Saul! Saul! (Acts 9:4). Following His repetition in which there was a gracious blending of kindness, sadness and surprise Jesus went on to remind Martha that she was careful and troubled about many things but that one thing was needful—the good part Mary had chosen and which He would not take away from her.

Jesus did not tell Martha that she had neither part nor lot in Him, or that she was allowing the cares of this life to choke the seed. He recognized that she was working for Him, but reminded her that she was permitting her outward activities to hinder her spiritually. Because of wrong emphasis regarding her necessary labor, her inner communion with her Lord was being hindered. In her restless activity Martha felt that her sister carried "her quiet, peaceful, faith-engendered mysticism" too far. H. V. Morton says that in our Lord's reply to Martha's complaint there can be traced a play of ideas, and that His words can be interpreted —

> Martha, Martha, you are busy with many courses when one dish would be quite sufficient. Mary has chosen the best dish, which shall not be taken away from her.

The term "careful" refers to inward worrying anxiety. Martha was mentally solicitous, anxious with a divided mind which is forbidden (Matthew 6:22-31; I Corinthians 7: 32). "Troubled," means disturbed, distracted outwardly about many things or dishes. Fausset comments that "Much serving has its right place and time (I Thessalonians 4: 11; II Thessalonians 3:12; I Timothy 5:14), but ought to give place to hearing when Jesus speaks, for faith whereby the good and abiding portion is gained, cometh by hearing" (Romans 10:17). The "good part" Mary chose was bias in the direction of that which is spiritual.

She Was Loved of the Lord

In a marvelous way John takes up where Luke leaves off, and with his skillful brush fills in the details of the character study of Martha the "practical." First of all, the "apostle of love" tells us that "Jesus loved Martha, Mary and Lazarus." How different were their personalities and temperaments, yet Jesus loved each of them with an equal love! He had a human heart enabling Him to love those who loved and cared for Him. So all three in that Bethany home had a place in His heart, and were embraced in His holy kindness. Such a love must have knit those sisters and their brother more closely and tenderly together than did even the bond of natural affection. Knowing all about Martha, Jesus loved her, and she in turn ardently loved Him and shared His confidence and became the recipient of a sublime revelation of her Lord.

She Was a Woman of Deep Sorrow

Sickness and death shadowed that loving, hospitable Bethany home. Lazarus fell sick, and his sister sent word to Jesus, "Behold, he whom Thou lovest is sick." Jesus did not hurry to Bethany but abode where He was, and by the time He reached Bethany Lazarus had been in his grave four days. Was He indifferent to the call and grief of Martha and Mary? Loving them, how could He be? He wanted them to learn that His delays are not denials; that He knows the exact moment to display His power. He knew that this was a death that would result in Him being glorified as the Son of Man (11:4).

While many of the Jewish friends came to comfort grief-stricken Martha and Mary, they eagerly awaited the coming of the divine Comforter Himself and as soon as they heard He was on the way, Martha dried her tears and went out to meet Him, leaving Mary sitting disconsolate in the house. As soon as Martha met Jesus she uttered a rebuke in her usual blunt fashion, "Lord, if thou hadst been here, my brother had not died." Then uncovering the real depths of her soul she hurried on to say, "But I know, that even now [with my dear brother in the grave] whatsoever thou wilt ask of God, God will give it thee."

What unbounded faith and confidence in her Lord's omnipotence she had! A most remarkable conversation on the Resurrection followed between the Master and Martha. Immediately Jesus healed her broken heart by assuring her that her brother would rise again. No explanation of His delayed arrival was given. Jesus began right away to unfold the truth He meant both His delay and the death of Lazarus to convey.

A desolate heart now, in the presence of the Prince of Life, expressed its faith in a resurrection of the dead in "the jubilee of the ages," as Martha knew the ancient Hebrew Scriptures taught. What she was not prepared for was the revelation that the One before her was the Resurrection and the Life. Jesus sought to lead the thoughts of Martha away from her dead brother to Himself, the One in whom the yonder becomes the here. Martha thought of the resurrection of her much-loved brother as a far-off event, but Jesus asserts His claim to be in Himself the power by which the dead are raised. Martha's reply provided the Master an occasion to present one of the most outstanding statements in the Bible as to His deity, power and authority — "I am the resurrection and the life." How astounded Martha must have been as she listened in awe to the tremendous truths flowing from the lips of Jesus. When He challenged her with "Believest thou this?" she uttered a remarkable confession of faith

which some professed Christians today, alas, cannot subscribe to —

"Yea, Lord: I believe that Thou art
   The Christ,
   The Son of God,
   which should come into the world."

Although Martha could not fathom the depths of the Master's revelation of Himself, she believed and implied three well-known titles to Him who loved her —

The Christ — The One of whom glorious things had been predicted as the anointed prophet, priest and king.

The Son of God — A confession of His deity, for this is a title pertaining not to His office or position, but to His nature and Person as the Only Begotten of the Father.

He that should come into the world — This was a common description among the Jews of Him who was at once the heart of prophecy, the object of the aspirations of all illuminated and reborn souls, and the desire of all nations (Haggai 2:7; Matthew 11:3).

With her heart stilled by the mighty and mysterious message of the Master, and yet more by the calm majesty of His presence, Martha confessed her faith, and while she did not fully understand the depth of her own words, the Lord's Resurrection from the dead enabled her to understand in some measure why He came into the world. Leaving Him after such an overwhelming experience, Martha went back to the home and called her sister "secretly," perhaps for fear of the Jews. This precious touch reveals how concerned Martha was for the safety and cause of Him who had done so much for her. Mary was told that the Master asked for her, and rose up "hastily" and went to Him.

'Tis love that makes our willing feet
   In swift obedience move.

Meeting Jesus, she fell down at the feet she had loved to sit at, and between her sobs repeated the complaint of Martha, "Lord, if thou hadst been here my brother had not died." Mary was in no way behind her sister in her love for her departed brother (11:19), her faith in the Lord Jesus (11:21), and in her belief in the final resurrection. The tears of Mary and of the mourning Jews moved the sympathetic spirit of Jesus, and affected by such sorrow He groaned in His spirit (11:33, 38). The groaning here was possibly an innner indignant feeling over the mockery of sorrow of the Jews whom He knew would try to kill Lazarus after his resurrection (11:47; 12:10), as well as kill Jesus also (11:53). It was this hypocrisy that stirred His spirit to anger so intense that it caused nerve and muscle and limb to tremble beneath its force. Then came the spectacle of "A God in Tears," for we come to the shortest verse in the Bible, "Jesus wept!"

How true it is that in every pang that rends the heart, the Man of Sorrows shares a part! Here was the evidence of His humanity.

At the grave Martha gives vent to her feelings again, and implied by her statement that as her dead brother's body had passed to corruption, it would be terrible to see him thus. But the miracle happened and the glory of God was manifested. Jesus uttered the all-commanding word, and Lazarus came forth, with a body fresher than it had been for years. Thus Jesus justified His claim to Martha of being "The Resurrection," not merely able to raise the dead, but also the Life-Power conquering the death-power in its own domain. The great I Am is the Resurrection for in Himself He has the keys of death. Then when He spoke of Himself as "The Life," He gave utterance to one of the most profound expressions in the Gospel (John 14:6). He *is* Life — the primal, all-originating, all-comprehending, everlasting life. It is in Him we live.

She Was a Joyful Woman

What tears of joy both Martha and Mary must have shed as they embraced their brother risen from the dead! That physical miracle resulted in spiritual miracles, for many believed on Jesus. The last mention of Martha was at the supper in her home to celebrate the resurrection of Lazarus, and as usual she was active and served. While the guests were seated at her hospitable table, Mary anointed the feet of Jesus with costly spikenard, but Martha raised no objection. She acquiesced in her sister's preparatory act associated with Christ's own burial. For all that we know Martha may have had a large share in the purchase of

the precious ointment, which Judas Iscariot thought was being wasted. While the service of Martha was the same, her spirit was blessedly changed. She was no longer "distracted" over her tasks, nor mentally anxious and outwardly bustling, but calm, trustful and in full agreement with her sister's act of love and devotion to the Master. At last Martha, too, has chosen that good part which could not be taken from her. It is more than likely that Martha was present with the two Marys and other devout women at the cross and then at the empty tomb of the Saviour, and joined them as a herald to the disciples that Christ was risen indeed (Matthew 28:1-11).

What are some of the lessons to glean as we think of the life and character of Martha? One of her noblest acts was to open her home to Jesus and entertain Him. She little knew at the beginning of His visits that He was the Son of God with power, and when we receive Him into our hearts as Saviour we do not know all there is to know of His majesty and power. Eternity alone will bring us the full revelation of why and what He is.

Further, Martha represents those dear religious women who allow themselves to be distracted overmuch with their home cares and obligations. Some are all Martha, and no Mary. Others are all Mary and no Martha. The happy combination is that of Martha and Mary, the practical and the spiritual making possible the glory of the commonplace. The church requires both the Marys and the Marthas for both are necessary to complete the Christian character (I Timothy 4:13-16; James 1:25-27). From the records we have considered we surely learn, do we not? —

1. To sit at the feet of Jesus and learn of Him.

2. To keep so-called secular service in its right place, conscious that both *serving* and *learning* are duties, and *in* both we should honor God.

3. To trust the Lord with our cares, responsibilities and sorrows knowing that He is able to undertake for us. If His help appears to be delayed we must remember that He is never before His time, and that He never lags behind.

4. To offer our best to Him who broke

the alabaster box of His own body that heavenly forgiveness and fragrance might be ours.

MARY

The Woman Honored Above All Women

Scripture References—Matthew 1; 2; 12:46; Luke 1; 2; John 2:1-11; 19:25; Acts 1:14

Name Meaning — No female has been honored as has Mary by millions of peoples in all the world who have named their daughters Mary. This Hebrew name has ever been popular in all countries of the Western world, and has altogether some twenty variations, the most conspicuous being Maria, Marie, Miriam and Miriamme. Mary is about the only feminine name that has pronounced masculine forms such as Mario, Marion and Maria. Elsden C. Smith says that Mary heads the list of female names in America, the estimated number some ten years ago being 3,720,000 — Marie, 645,000 — Marion, 440,000 — Marian, 226,000. "The name of Mary has been given at least 70 different interpretations in a frantic effort to get away from the Biblical significance of bitterness." Today the most common name for girls is the Biblical Mary, just as the Biblical John is for boys. In Christian lands the name of Mary is first.

The name Mary occurs 51 times in the New Testament, and its prevalence there has been attributed to the popularity of Miriamne, the last representative of the Hasmonean family, who was the second wife of Herod I. As a name Mary is related to the Old Testament Miriam, to Mara, the name Naomi used to describe her affliction (see NAOMI), and to Marah, the name of the bitter water reached by the Israelites in their wilderness journeys. The original and pervading sense of these root-forms is that of "bitterness," derived from the notion of "trouble, sorrow, disobedience, rebellion." Cruden gives "their rebellion" as the name-meaning of Miriam. Mary the virgin, whom we are now considering, certainly had many "bitter" experiences, as we shall see.

Family Connections — According to the sacred record, Mary was a humble village woman who lived in a small town, a place so insignificant as to lead Nathanael to say, "Can there any good thing come out of Nazareth?" (John 1:46), but out of it, and from the womb of the peasant woman came the greatest Man the world has ever known. Mary was of the tribe of Judah, and the line of David. In the royal genealogy of Matthew and the human genealogy of Luke, Mary is only mentioned in the former, but her immediate forebears are not mentioned. She became the wife of Joseph, the son of Heli (Luke 3:23). Apart from Jesus, called her "firstborn," a term implying that other children followed after the order of natural generation (Luke 2:7). As a virgin, Mary bore Christ in a miraculous way, and Elisabeth most spontaneously and unaffectedly gave her the most honorable of titles, "Mother of the Lord" and praised her unstintedly as one, "Blessed among women." Later Mary was married to Joseph the carpenter and she bore him four sons and several daughters, the former being named — James, Joses, Judas and Simon, and the daughters unnamed (Matthew 13:55, 56; Mark 6:3). During His ministry, none of His brothers believed in Him. In fact, they sneered at Him, and once concluded that He was mad, and wished to arrest Him and take Him away from Capernaum (Mark 3:21, 31; John 7:3-5). But as the result of His death and Resurrection, His brothers became believers, and were among the number gathered in the Upper Room before Pentecost. None of His brothers was an apostle during His lifetime (Acts 1:13, 14).

The Roman Catholic Church, in its effort to support its erroneous dogma of Mary's perpetual virginity, produces two theories as to "the brethren of the Lord." First, they were sons of Joseph by a former marriage, having thus no blood relationship with Mary or Jesus. Second, they were Christ's cousins, sons of Mary, the wife of Alphaeus (Matthew 27:56; Mark 15:40). The term "brother" only implies mere kinship, just as Laban called Jacob, his sister's son, his "brother" (Genesis 29:15). We reject, however, all theories of Rome, preferring to take the Scriptures at its face value. Mark says, "His brothers and sisters," and we believe these to have been the natural children of Joseph and Mary, after the birth of Jesus by the Spirit's power. Coming to the events of Mary's life, as well as the excellencies of her character, perhaps we can group them around the following key heads —

Her Super-eminence

Mary, as the mother of Jesus, is better known than any other female character in the Bible, and has been the best-known woman in the world since those days of the manger in Bethlehem. After the centuries, the statement still stands, "Blessed art thou among women" (Luke 1:28). While we have no word as to her beauty or pedigree, we know that she was poor. Yet in the Bible and outside of it she came to occupy the highest place among women. Madonnas abound in which eminent artists have vied in trying to imagine what she looked like. What she did possess was beauty of character. In spite of the fact that he was a Roman Cardinal, Gibbons rightly says —

> The word is governed more by *ideals* than by *ideas;* it is influenced more by living, concrete models than by abstract principles of virtue. The model held up to Christian women is not the Amazon, glorying in her martial deeds and prowess; it is not the Spartan women who made female perfection consist in the development of physical strength at the expense of feminine decorum and modesty; it is not the goddess of impure love, like Venus, whose votaries regards beauty of form and personal charms as the highest type of female excellence; nor is it the goddess of imperial will like Juno. No; the model held up to women from the very dawn of Christianity is the peerless Mother of our Blessed Redeemer. She is the pattern of virtue alike to maiden, wife and mother. She exhibits virginal modesty becoming the maid, the conjugal fidelity and loyalty of the spouse, and the untiring devotedness of the mother. . . . The influence of Mary, therefore, in the moral elevation of women can hardly be over estimated.

Although the Roman Catholic dogmatic and sentimental exaggeration of Mary's eminence has removed her from the clear and vivid picture we have of her in the gospels, we cannot fail to be impressed with her character even though we are not told more than we have in sacred history. "Highly favoured of the Lord" and having "found favour with him" (Luke 1:28, 30) surely gives her a pedestal all her own. Mary belongs to those grand majestic females inspired with the spirit of prophecy, who is capable of influencing those who become rulers of men and also the destiny of nations.

Her Selection

Among all the godly Jewish maidens of that time in Palestine why did God select such a humble peasant young woman as Mary? Her choice by God to be the mother of the Incarnate Son is as mysterious as her conception of Him within her virgin womb. When the fullness of time had come for Jesus to be manifested He did not go to a city, but to a remote and inconsiderate town — not to a palace but a poor dwelling — not to the great and learned but to lowly partisans — for a woman to bring the Saviour into a lost world. The gentle and lowly Mary of Nazareth was the Father's choice as the mother of His beloved Son, and that she herself was overwhelmed at God's condescending grace in choosing her is evident from her song of praise in which she magnified Him for regarding her lowly estate, and in exalting her.

Mary, then, was selected by divine wisdom from among the humblest and it was in such an environment that the Father prepared His Son to labor among the common people who heard Him gladly. The one of whom He was born, the place where he was born were arranged beforehand by the determinate counsel and foreknowledge of God. Centuries before Mary became the mother of the Saviour of mankind, it was prophesied that it would be so (Isaiah 7:14-16; 9:6, 7; Micah 5:2, 3). Born of a peasant maiden, and having a foster-father who eeked out a frugal living as a carpenter, Jesus was best able to sympathize with man as man, and be regarded by all men as the common property of all.

Her Sanctity

Because Mary's divine Child was to be "holy, harmless, undefiled and separate from sinners," she herself had to be holy unto the Lord. When Gabriel announced to the virgin whose name was Mary that she was to bring forth a Son to be called Jesus, he recognized her spiritual fitness for such an honor when he said, "The Lord is with thee" (Luke 1:28). The woman who was to give Him birth, whose breast would be His pillow and who would nurse and care for Him in infancy, who would guide His steps through boyhood years, and surround Him with true motherly attention until His manhood, had to be a sanctified vessel and meet for the Master's use. That Mary excelled in the necessary, spiritual qualities for her sacred task is evident from the record we have of her character. Augustine says that, "Mary first conceived Christ in her heart by faith, before she conceived in the womb," and the testimony of Elisabeth expresses and stamps the whole character of the Virgin, "Blessed is she that believeth," implying that she wore the crown of faith above all others.

Mary exhibited a true and genuine piety, as well as a profound humility — the accompaniment of holiness. As we read the narrative given by Luke, to whom, as a physician, Mary could speak intimately of her profound experience, we are impressed with her quietness of spirit, meditative inwardness of disposition, admirable self-control, devout and gracious gift of sacred silence, and a mind saturated with the spirit and promises of the Old Testament. All who reverence Mary for her true and womanly character are pained by the way in which some of the early Church fathers treated her. Origen, for instance, wrote that "the sword which should pierce through her heart was unbelief." Chrysostom did not control his "golden mouth" when he accused Mary of "excessive ambition, foolish arrogance, and vainglory," during her Son's public ministry.

Advanced as she was to the highest honor that could be granted to a woman, Mary yet retained a deep sense of personal unworthiness. She would have been the last to claim perfection for herself. Born like the rest of women in sin and shaped in iniquity, she had her human faults and needed a Saviour as others did — "My spirit hath rejoiced in God my Saviour" — but the witness of Scripture is that in circumstances of unparalleled responsibility she was a true and godly character, and in spite of any female weaknesses she may have had, she was "the most pure and tender and faithful, the most humble and patient and loving, of all who have ever borne the honored name of Mary."

Her Submission

What amazes one about the Annunciation is the way Mary received it. She was in no way credulous or skeptical. Certainly she asked intelligent questions of Gabriel as to how she could become the mother of Jesus, seeing she was a pure virgin. Following a full explanation of how the miracle would happen, she, with a tremendous feat of faith, replied, "Be it unto me according to thy word." In these days when reason is seeking to dethrone revelation, and the Virgin Birth of Christ is rejected as a fundamental fact and treated in a mythical way, we affirm our faith in this initial miracle of Christianity. We accept by faith the Biblical statement that Jesus was conceived by the Holy Spirit as He overshadowed the virgin. Thus, as Fausset states it —

> Christ was made of the substance of the Virgin, not of the substance of the Holy Spirit, whose substance cannot be made. No more is attributed to the Spirit than what was necessary to cause the Virgin to perform the actions of a mother.

When Mary willingly yielded her body to the Lord saying, "Behold the handmaid of the Lord, be it unto me according to thy word," the Holy Spirit, by His gentle operation, took Deity and humanity and fused them together and formed the love-knot between our Lord's two natures within Mary's being. Therefore, when Jesus came forth it was as the God-Man, "God manifest in flesh," or "that holy thing which shall be born of thee shall be called the Son of God." *Son of Mary*—humanity! *Son of God*—Deity. We may not understand the mystery of what happened when Mary yielded up her body that Christ should be formed within it, but believing that with God nothing is impossible we accept what Scripture says as to the birth of Christ. Further, there is the unanswerable argument Donald Davidson reminds us of, namely, "that Jesus Christ Himself is such a miracle that it is no straining of faith to believe that His birth was also a miracle." We cannot account for His perfect holiness apart from His Virgin Birth. Born of a woman, He was yet clean.

Her Salutation

Taking the Lord at His word, Mary praised Him as if what He had declared had been fully accomplished. What a marvelous song of rejoicing the Magnificat is! It reveals poetic and prophetic genius of the highest order, and takes its place among the finest productions of the world. This extemporaneous ode expressing Mary's joy is indeed one of the choicest gems of Hebrew poetry. As given by Luke (1:46-55) this lyric expresses Mary's inward and deeply personal sacred and unselfish joy, and likewise her faith in Messianic fulfillment. It is also eloquent with her reverential spirit. Her worship was for her Son, for her spirit rejoiced in Him as her own Saviour.

Her "hymn" also spoke of her humility, for she was mindful of the fact that she was but a humble village maiden whose "low estate" the Lord regarded. Mary's "firstborn" Child was to say of Himself, "I am meek and lowly in heart," and such poverty of spirit is the first beatitude and the very threshold of the kingdom of heaven. By her "low estate" Mary not only had in mind the material poverty she was accustomed to, but also the sharpest of all poverty, the low estate of one of Royal birth. Mary never claimed anything for herself, but Christendom wrongly selected her as the object of worship and one entitled to a consideration above her Son.

Her Service

What must not be forgotten is the fact that Mary not only bore Jesus, but also mothered Him for the thirty years He tarried in the poor Nazareth home. Thus from childhood to manhood she did everything a devoted mother could do for the Son whom she knew was no ordinary Man. "Hers was the face that unto Christ had most resemblance." While Mary did not neglect her motherly duties to the sons and daughters she bore Joseph, because of all she knew Jesus to be she surrounded His early years with character-forming influences. From the divine side we know that as Jesus grew "he waxed strong in spirit, filled with wisdom, and the grace of God was upon him," and that He "increased in stature and in favour with God and man."

But from the human side Jesus was subject to the home control of Joseph and Mary.

There were some things Mary was not able to give her Son. She could not surround Him with wealth. When she presented the divine Infant in the Temple all she could offer as a gift was a pair of pigeons — the offering of the very poor. But little is much if God is in it! Then she could not introduce Jesus to the culture of the age. Being poor, and enduring an enforced exile in Egypt, she had little of the acquired education of one like Luke who recorded her story. But she gave her Saviour-Son gifts of infinitely more value than secular and material advantages. What did she give Him?

First of all, from the human angle, she gave Him life, and He became bone of her bone, flesh of her flesh, and, until He was weaned, her warm milk nourished Him.

Then, along with Joseph, she gave Jesus a home, which although it was most unpretentious, was yet the only home He knew in the days of His flesh. Because of the character of Mary, we feel that her home was permeated with mutual trust and love and sympathetic understanding.

Purity of heart was among the flowers of character Mary cultivated in the home in which Jesus — and the other children — grew up. Can it be that when Jesus left home to become a preacher, He had His pious mother in mind when He said, "Blessed are the pure in heart, for they shall see God"? Christ's holiness was a part of His divine nature, but it was also a part of His humanity received from His mother who thought of herself as "the handmaid of the Lord."

Another quality Jesus grew to appreciate in His mother was the sense of the presence of God. Gabriel said to Mary, "The Lord is with thee" and this divine awareness surrounded the holy Child Jesus. To Mary, God was not a being afar off, uninterested in her life or in the world. He had created but One who was so near and real. Why, because her Son was "very God of very God," Mary was ever in the divine presence, and must have realized it.

Obedience, a trait prominent in Mary's own life, was another quality in which she trained her Son. There is an old saying to the effect that a child who is not taught to obey his parents will not obey God. Mary submitted to the Father's will as the channel of the Incarnation, and her holy Child grew up not only obedient to Mary and Joseph but also to His heavenly Father whose will was His delight.

Further, the one book in that Nazareth home was the Old Testament. That Mary's mind was saturated with its promises and prophecies is evident from her song of praise. Like Timothy, Jesus, from a child, was familiar with the Holy Scriptures (II Timothy 3:15). As His mother read to Him the records of the saints and prophets, how interested He must have been. Then there came the time when He knew that the Scripture testified of Him; that He came to be the Living Word.

Her Sorrow

When Mary brought her infant Son to be dedicated in the Temple, the aged, godly Simeon, taking the Babe in his arms and blessing Him, said to His mother, "A sword shall pierce through thy own soul also." Mary was to experience darkness, as well as delight, as her "first-born" went out to fulfill His mission in the world. She would see Him as the "sign spoken against." Manifold sword piercings were to be hers as the mother of the Lord. We cannot imagine the bitter trials of the years of her Son's sojourn on the earth, particularly His last three and a half years ending in His death. Mary had listened to those angel voices rending the air as they hailed her new-born Baby as the Saviour of mankind, and heard the shepherds as they recounted the vision they had seen. She had witnessed the worship and homage of the wise men when, guided by a star, they came to the feet of her Child; and "she kept all these in her heart." Whether she recounted these things to her growing Child we are not told. Personally, we believe that born the Son of God, Jesus had an inner awareness of who He was, from whence He came, and what His mission in the world was to be, from His earliest conscious years. During the years that Jesus was at home, Mary must have had many an inner pang, but by divine grace both then and after, she remained silently submissive, patient and trustful, knowing that the sword, piercing her heart

from time to time, was in her heavenly Father's hand.

Following the records of the gospels concerning the conversations between and about Jesus and Mary, the first event we notice took place in Jerusalem where Mary and her husband, Joseph, and Jesus had gone for the annual Feast of Passover. When the ceremonies were over Joseph and Mary, with their relatives, left for home, lost in animated gossip about each other's affairs. Mary suddenly realized that Jesus, now twelve years of age, was not near her, and searching for Him among her kinsfolk and acquaintances could not find Him. Retracing her steps to the Temple she found Jesus where He had been left, and came upon Him in conversation with the fathers of the sanctuary. Remonstrating with her Son, Mary said, "Thy *father* and I have sought thee."

Christ's reply was like a sword piercing her heart: "Wist *ye* not that I must be about *my Father's business?*" He had no earthly father for He came as the only babe to enter the world without any earthly father. He was born of a woman, but not of a woman *and* a man. Young though He was, He knew of His divine parentage that separated Him from others, and He expected His mother to realize what such a gulf meant. Perhaps now, for the first time, Mary understood that her Son knew God to be, in a special sense, His *only* Father. There in the Temple, Nazareth faded from the mind of Jesus and earthy ties receded into the distance. He felt only one presence — the Father above in whose bosom He had dwelt from the dateless past. Mary had left her Son behind — behind with God. Her divine, "lost" Boy was to be God's only hope for a "lost" world.

The mixed feelings in the mother's heart, and her almost reproachful language as she sought to charge Jesus with having disregarded His mother's natural feelings, must have been checked by a sort of awe as she looked at Him in the Temple with rapt countenance and then heard Him say that His place was in His Father's house. Thus the narrative develops so naturally, tenderly, and in a most human way.

Being only twelve years of age, Jesus knew that every Jewish son must be subject to his parents. He indicated this in His reply to Mary, for He "went down with them, and came to Nazareth, and was sub-ject unto them." For the next eighteen years He yielded to His home authority. It is felt that during this period Mary lost the protection of her husband, for if he had been alive he would have been certainly mentioned in succeeding events (Mark 3:31; John 2:1; 19:25). Joseph had been a carpenter, and on his death Jesus took over the village business. In that carpenter's shop we have "the toil of divinity revealing the divinity of toil." "Is not this the Carpenter?" Then Joseph's place in the home would be filled in measure by Jesus the first-born, who would care for His mother and give her years of peace.

We now come to recorded incidents causing Mary to realize that Jesus had severed Himself once and for all from her control. There were to be further sword-thrusts as she understood that her illustrious Son was absolutely independent of her authority and of human relationships. For thirty years Mary had carried in her heart the secret of His birth and the prophecy of His Messianic mission. Now the moment of parting comes when Jesus leaves the home that has sheltered Him for so long. And the striking thing is that we do not read of Jesus ever returning to it. In the home Mary had made for her Son, God had been preparing Him (for thirty years) for a brief but dynamic ministry lasting just over three years. As Jesus began His public life, His first miracle gave Him the occasion for impressing His mother with the fact that she must no longer impose her will and wishes upon Him (John 2). There must have been a pang in Mary's heart the day Jesus left her home for good, and another heart-wound as she encountered the lack of official recognition as His mother. Whenever He met her it seemed as if He repelled her.

At the marriage feast in Cana of Galilee, at which Jesus and Mary were guests, a predicament arose when the stock of wine failed, and Mary, who failed to see that the youth had become a man, sought to order her Son to meet the crisis. His mother, conscious of the supernatural power Jesus was to manifest, approached Jesus and said suggestively, "They have no wine."

Jesus replied abruptly: "Woman, what have I to do with thee? mine hour is not yet come." He was not disrespectful when He used the term "woman," for such was the common mode of respectful address among the Hebrews. Thus, in the original the words addressed by Jesus to His mother are free from any element of disrespect or of hardness. Mary said to the servants: "Whatsoever he saith unto you do it," and a short time later Jesus performed His first miracle. His purpose in speaking to His mother as He did was to check any undue interference on her part of His mediatorial work. As Augustine put it —

He does not acknowledge a human womb when about to work Divine works.

Although blessed among women, Mary was to learn that she must not be permitted to control the operations of the One sent of the Father. As the Son of Mary, Jesus was willingly subject to her, but now as the Son of God, Mary must endeavor to be subject to Him. The very fact that He addressed her as *woman* and not as *mother* must have had but one meaning for her, namely, that from now on the direction of His course had entered into His Father's hands. Fausset's comment is —

The Christian's allegiance is solely to Him, not to her also: a prescient forewarning of the Holy Ghost against mediaeval and modern mariolatry.

After a double circuit of Galilee during which crowds gathered around Jesus for teaching and healing, so much so that He had little time, "to eat bread," His mother and brothers came to remonstrate with Him to take care. Had not the men of Nazareth sought to throw Him over the brow of the hill (Luke 4:29)? Now, anxious for His safety and fearing He would destroy Himself by His constant work and lack of food and rest, Mary and her sons "sought to speak with him, and to lay hold on him, for they said, He is beside himself" (Mark 3:21, 31-35). It was natural for a mother to be concerned about her Son wearing Himself out. He might fall exhausted under His load of work and perhaps sink into an untimely grave.

Thinking, perhaps, that she might save Jesus from the effects of an imprudent enthusiasm, Mary receives another mild rebuke in which He hinted that the blessedness of Mary consisted not in being His mother, but in believing in Him and in His God-given mission, and in obedience to His words. Jesus again denies any authority of earthly relatives, or any privilege from human relationships. "My mother! Who is My mother and My brothers?" Then pointing to those sitting around Him who had believed His word and followed Him, He said, "Behold my mother and my brethren! For whosoever shall do the will of my Father which is in heaven, the same is my brother, and sister, and mother" (Matthew 12:46-50; Luke 11:28). In effect Jesus said, "I, in working out the world's redemption, can acknowledge only spiritual relationships." So the distance between Mary and her Son widens, and the piercings of the sword, which old Simeon had prophesied, were keenly felt. Although all generations were to call Mary blessed, yet privileged and highly favored beyond all members of the human family, here was a bitter cup of sorrow she was compelled to drink.

Mary's deepest sword piercing came when in agony she stood beneath that old rugged cross and witnessed the degradation, desolation and death of the One whom she had brought into the world and intensely loved. She heard the blasphemies and revilings of the priests and the people, and saw the lights go out — but her faith did not die. If Calvary was our Lord's crown of sorrow, it was likewise Mary's, yet how courageous she was. Others might *sit* and watch the suffering Christ, or smite their breasts and cry, but "Mary *stood* by the cross." Should she not have been spared the agony of seeing the Son of her womb die such a despicable death? No! It was in the divine order of things that she should be found beneath that cross to receive the parting benediction of her Son and Saviour, and His committal of her to the affectionate care of the disciple whom He loved.

> At the cross her station keeping
> Stood the mournful mother weeping,
> Close to Jesus to the last.
>
> Through her heart His sorrow sharing,
> All His bitter anguish bearing,
> Now at length the sword has passed.

At previous meetings with Christ, Mary expressed her feelings. Now, as He dies, she stands in silence. Those around her had no conception of her inner grief as she stood where her Son could see her. No Spartan mother ever displayed such fortitude as Mary manifested at the cross. How impressed we are with the valor of Mary, as the sword pierces her heart again "now that which she brought forth was dying"! Before He died Jesus recognized His human relationship to Mary, which He had during His ministry put in the background, that His higher relationship must stand out more prominently. Commending Mary to John, Jesus did not address her by name, or as His mother, but as "Woman." To John He said, "Thy mother" (John 19:26, 27). But even then she did not desert her Son. Some of His disciples forsook Him and fled, but her love never surrendered, even though her Son was dying as a criminal between two thieves.

To John, His much-loved disciple, Jesus left His mother as a legacy. In the last moments of His life, and in the crisis of His deepest sorrow, His thought was of the future of His brokenhearted mother whom John took to his own home. Thus, as Augustine expresses it, "He needed no helper in redeeming all; He gave human affection to His mother, but sought no help of man." The transference of the bond of motherhood from Himself to John raises the question, "Why did He not entrust Mary to one of her older sons or daughters?" Evidently she was a widow, otherwise Jesus would not have called upon His beloved disciple to perform the duties of an elder brother. But why not commit Mary to His own brother who would 'become the elder in that Nazareth home? Perhaps in John's home Jesus knew that Mary would find the spiritual atmosphere more suited to her thirst for God, and that in John Mary would find a soul on fire similar to His own zeal for God.

We may feel, that because of the steadfast tie of tender love and mutual understanding between Jesus and Mary, Jesus should have used a softer word and said, "Behold My mother!" and not "thy mother." Was this the final sword thrust Simeon had predicted some thirty-three years before?

No! He knew that Mary would be a true mother in Israel to John, and that he, in turn, would care for the blessed among women in her declining years. Further, as Donald Davidson reminds us, "In that moment the tremendous truth must at last have dawned upon Mary, that He who hung upon the cross was not her son; that before the world was He was; that so far from being His mother, she was herself His child." On the morning of His Resurrection Jesus did not appear first to Mary His mother, but to Mary Magdalene — surely an evidence of His matchless grace.

The last glimpse we have of Mary is a heartwarming one. We find her among the group of believers gathered together in the upper chamber. She is mentioned, not first in the list, before the apostles, where the Roman Catholic Church places her, but *last*, as if she were of less significance than they (Acts 1:12-14). Her Son is alive forevermore, and life has changed for her. So she takes her place among those awaiting the coming of the Spirit to equip them for the beginning of the Christian community. Mary was present in that upper room not as an object of worship, not as the directress of the infant church, but as a humble suppliant along with the rest, including her sons, who, by this time, were believers. So the last mention of Mary is a happy one. We see her praying, along with her sons whom she had possibly led into a full-orbed faith, as well as the other disciples who had met to pray and await the gift of Pentecost.

This is the last glimpse we have of Mary. Her name is not mentioned again in the rest of the New Testament after the upper room appearance, which plainly teaches that she did not have the superhuman powers the Roman Catholic Church has assigned to her. With the gradual development of Roman Catholicism from the third or fourth century, there emerged the Mariolatry so foreign to the Scriptural presentation of Mary as the most tender and lovable of women, yet a woman still. If Rome had only observed the reticence of the New Testament concerning Mary, it would not have been guilty of blinding the eyes of multitudes to the ineffable glory of the One who, though the Son of Mary, came as the express image of the Father and the only Mediator between God and men.

Mary does not stand apart from the rest of the sinful human race, born immaculate and remaining sinless throughout her life. As a member of a fallen race she recognized her need of deliverance from sin and guilt when she sang, "My spirit hath rejoiced in God *my* Saviour." The "culture" of Mary does not have its origin in the Bible for "there is not a word there from which it could be inferred; not in the Creeds, nor in the fathers of the first five centuries." Titles such as *The Tower of David; The Arch of Holy Alliance; The Door of Heaven; The Queen of the Apostles, Confessors and Martyrs; The Co-adjustrix with God in the work of salvation,* as applied to Mary, are the invention of Rome. Mary never magnified herself — only her Lord. Her glorification as the object of worship, her function as an intercessor through whom prayers must be addressed to Christ, her perpetual care of Christ and her present influence over Him, are the false creations of Rome. Therefore, "Mariolatry belongs, historically, to unauthorized speculation; and psychologically, to the natural history of asceticism and clerical celibacy." The elevation and worship of Mary is most unscriptural and idolatrous. The Bible portrays her as a woman "blessed among women," but only as a mere faithful, humble, godly woman. Rome's exaltation of Mary consists largely of fictitious and unreliable legends and dogmas. The true Christian portrayal of the mother of Jesus is that to be found only in the gospels in which the Master taught that man has access to God *only* through His all-sufficient mediatorial work (John 14:6).

MARY MAGDALENE
THE WOMAN WHO HAD SEVEN DEVILS

Scripture References — Matthew 27:56, 61; 28:1; Mark 15:40, 47; 16:1-19; Luke 8:2; 24:10; John 19:25; 20:1-18.

Name Meaning — For significance of Mary see the previous study. The present Mary is distinguished from all others of the same name as "The Magdalene," which identifies her with her place of birth, just as Jesus was called "The Nazarene" because of His association with Nazareth. Magdala means "tower" or "castle," and

in the time of Christ was a thriving, populous town on the coast of Galilee about
three miles from Capernaum. Dye works
and primitive textile factories added to
the wealth of the community. It may be
that "The Magdalene" was connected
with the industry of the town for it would
seem as if she was not without means, enabling her to serve the Lord with her
substance.

Family Connections — We have no record
of Mary's parentage, her marital status or
her age. That she was free to follow Jesus
in His journeyings would suggest that she
had no home obligations.

Before we outline Mary's life and character, we deem it necessary to disassociate
ourselves from those who connect her with
the unnamed woman "which was a sinner."
Luke, who knew her, wrote about this
woman (Luke 7:37). The Jewish *Talmud*
affirms that Magdala had an unsavory reputation, and because of the harlotry practiced
there was destroyed. Doubtless it was from
this tradition, and from the fact that Luke's
first reference to her follows the story of the
sinful woman, that the idea developed that
Mary was a prostitute, but there is not an
iota of genuine evidence to suggest such a
bad reputation. Those theologians who describe her as a profligate do her an injustice,
just as calling institutions for the care of
fallen women "Magdalen Homes" does. One
writer defines Magdalen as "the inmate of a
female penitentiary," but the Bible depicts
Mary as a pure, though deeply afflicted
woman before she met Jesus. To suggest
that she was dissolute because she was possessed by seven devils, is to affirm that
every insane person is depraved. There is
no word whatever in the writings of the
Christian Fathers, whose authority stands
next to the apostles, as to Mary having a
foul reputation.

The Roman Catholic Church was guilty
of fastening this slander upon Mary Magdalene when at Naples, in 1324, it established its first "Magdalen House" for the
rescue and maintenance of fallen women.
Great masters, taken up with the idea that
Mary was formerly a courtesan, have provided art galleries with paintings of her as
a voluptuous female. The name of the
woman taken in adultery was graciously

withheld, but with every reference to "The
Magdalen" her name is given, and after her
liberation from demonic influence appears
as one of the most faithful and beautiful
characters of the Bible. The wide acceptance of the tradition that she was a reformed prostitute is utterly baseless. Mary
was only a sinner in the sense that we all
are, having been born in sin and shapen in
iniquity. "All have sinned and come short
of the glory of God." Having sought to relieve Mary's name of the foul stigma attached to it, let us now outline her career.

She is mentioned fourteen times in the
gospels, and from references to her we can
see clearly what she did and how she did it.
A striking feature in eight of the fourteen
passages is that Mary is named in connection with other women, but she always
heads the list, implying that she occupied
the place at the front in service rendered
by godly females. In the five times where
she is mentioned alone, the connection is
with the death and Resurrection of Christ
(Mark 16:9; John 20:1, 11, 16, 18). In one
instance her name comes after that of the
mother and the aunt of Jesus. She stood
close by the cross with these women, but
because of their relation to Jesus it would
not have been fitting to put her name before
theirs (John 19:25). No woman, however,
superseded Mary in her utter devotion to
the Master.

In Demonic Bondage

Although Mary was a woman of high
standing and comfortable circumstances,
she suffered from the malady of periodic
insanity. For "the seven devils" we should
read seven *demons*. There is only one devil
— and one is more than enough — but there
are legions of demons, or roaming fallen
angels, who possessed men and women —
and still do! Seven is a mystic number suggesting "completeness," implying that when
the evil spirits dominated Mary the suffering was extremely severe. Afflicted with
nervousness, she may have been the victim
of violent epilepsy, and when Jesus saw her
with her peace of mind and control of will
destroyed she must have been a revolting
object to look at with her disheveled hair,
glaring eyes and sunken cheeks. Her demonic possession did not affect her morals,

only her mind. Badness of character did not ensue, only the derangement of her mental faculties. Sometimes "love — misplaced and guilty love — has destroyed many women, first leading to insanity, and then to suicide. . . . Sometimes, too, women become victims of insanity by inheritance." What weakness Mary may have had, making it easy for demons to enter her, we are not told. This we do know, they met their Master in Him who came to destroy the works of the devil.

A Liberated Soul

Luke links Mary with Joanna and Susanna and "many others" as those healed of evil spirits and infirmities by Jesus. As Mary is referred to as having "seven demons" her condition must have been worse than the rest. But the moment Jesus' compassionate eyes saw the wild-eyed and cringing woman of Magdala, He saw in her the ministering angel who would be a blessing to His own heart and to others. In His authoritative voice He commanded the tormenting demons to come out — and stay out — of her. "Back! back! to your native hell, ye foul spirits of the pit," and the miracle happened. Her deranged and nerve-racked mind became as tranquil as the troubled lake Jesus calmed. Sanity returned, the rosy tint was restored to her cheeks, and she was made whole. Now, "clothed and in her right mind," she was ready to become one of the most devoted woman disciples of Him to whom she owed so much. That she was deeply grateful for physical and mental healing is shown by what she endeavored to do for her Deliverer and His cause. Saved from the terrible power of hell, she gave of her best to Him who had fully emancipated her from demonic possession. When Christ saved her, He liberated the highest virtues of sacrifice, fortitude and courage.

In Journeyings Oft

Delivered, Mary became a disciple. Freed from satanic bondage she became harnessed to the chariot of the Lord, and her personal ministrations, along with those of other women who had been healed, greatly aided Jesus in His missionary activities as He went from place to place preaching and teaching His message. Grateful, these women became generous, ministering unto Him of

their substance. Mary left her home in Magdala to follow Jesus. Constantly on the move as Jesus and His disciples were, there were many details in connection with their personal comfort and well-being requiring attention to which these women could see. Quietly and effectively Mary would do what she knew needed to be done. Further, money was necessary for the Master's campaign work. We never read of Him or His disciples asking for money, yet funds were necessary. Much of it came from Mary and other women like her who had been so richly blessed of the Lord. Alas, not all who have benefited are grateful! Christ once healed ten lepers, but only one came back to thank Him for His grace and power. Emancipated, Mary helped Jesus to evangelize as she willing gave of her substance to help meet His needs. How much her personal presence and service must have meant to Jesus.

At the Cross

Mary went with her Lord into the shadows, and is thus represented as being among those who followed Jesus on His last sad journey from Galilee to Jerusalem. And as they followed, they still "ministered unto Him." Mary was present with the other holy women at the mock trial of Jesus. No longer is He on the road with crowds gathering and hanging on His words. Fearless in His declaration and denunciations, He is arrested and tried for His life. Some of His intimate friends had deserted Him, but Mary and her band did not forsake Him. The poet reminds us —

Not she with traitorous kiss her Master stung,
Not she denied Him with unfaithful tongue;
She, when Apostles fled, could dangers brave,
Last at the Cross, and earliest at the grave.

Mary was present in Pilate's Hall and saw and heard the religious leaders clamoring for the blood of Him who was so precious to her heart. She listened as Pontius Pilate pronounced His death sentence of crucifixion although he had found no fault in Him. She witnessed and wept as Jesus left the hall to be spat upon and ill-treated by the crowd thirsting for His blood. Then she saw Him led out to Calvary's fatal mount to be nailed to a tree.

Mary was one of the sorrowing group

of holy women who stood as near as they could to comfort Jesus by their presence in the closing agonies of the crucifixion (Luke 23:49). Mary listened with a broken heart to His bitter cries and watched through those dread hours until at last the Roman soldier thrust his spear into the Saviour's side and declared Him dead. In the renowned picture gallery in the Louvre, there is a painting of desolation, despair and love. The artist has depicted the night of the crucifixion. "The world is wrapped in shadow; the stars are dead; and yet in the darkness is seen a kneeling form. It is Mary Magdalene with loving lips and hands pressing against the bleeding feet of Christ." Yes, she was there when they crucified her Lord.

No sooner had Jesus dismissed His spirit than the question arose among the Marys at the cross, "How could they secure that blood-stained body, and prepare it for burial?" Joseph of Arimathaea and Nicodemus, to the relief of the sorrowful mourners, had come for that very purpose. The artist Rubens, in his masterpiece, *The Descent of the Cross* represents Mary Magdalene, and Mary the wife of Cleophas, assisting Joseph and Nicodemus in receiving the battered body from the tree, preparing it for burial, then placing the precious remains in the new tomb in the garden. Mary Magdalene remained "sitting over against the sepulchre" and "beholding" until Joseph had laid the Lord's body away (Matthew 27:61; Mark 15:47; Luke 23:55).

In the Garden

Last at the cross, where Jesus died as the Lamb of God, Mary Magdalene was also the first at the garden tomb to witness the most important event in world history and the pivotal truth of Christianity, namely the Resurrection of Jesus Christ. What a great honor God conferred upon the faithful Mary Magdalene in permitting her to be the first witness of that Resurrection! She was at the tomb early on that first Easter morning, and as the light of earliest day filtered across Jerusalem, she peered into the cave. Seeing it was empty, she wept. Then John, the inspired genius who wrote in unusually terse Greek, describes what happened in a way unparalleled in narra-

tive literature. Finding the grave empty Mary rushed to Peter and John, and most excitedly said, "They have taken away the Lord out of the sepulchre and we know not where they have laid him." These disciples returned with Mary Magdalene to the tomb and found that what she had told them was true, then departed "to their own homes." But not Mary! She stood at the door of the sepulcher weeping, and as she wept two angels appeared, one at the head and the other at the feet, where the body of Jesus had lain. Seeing her distressed and afraid, they tenderly asked, "Woman, why weepest thou?" Tremblingly she replied, "Because they have taken away my Lord, and I know not where they have laid him."

What pathos is in the word *"my* Lord" — my very own Lord, the One who did so much for me, and whom I loved to serve. Turning away she saw a figure, and thinking He was the gardener answered in reply to the question: "Woman, why weepest thou? Whom seekest thou?" — in words most courageous — "Sir, if thou have borne him hence, tell me where thou hast laid him, and *I will take him away.*"

Mary, so full of her Lord, felt that all others must know Him whose body was missing from the tomb. "She never stopped to think of her own weakness as a woman: love nerves had to take it for granted she is able for the blessed task of taking the sacred body away." Then one word from the Voice she now recognized uttered her name, "Mary"! That old familiar tone gripped her heart, and instantly she cried "Rabboni!" which was her strongest expression of reverent love. Casting herself before the risen Lord, she would have clasped His feet, but He said, "Touch me not!" Thrilled at having Jesus alive again, Mary's love was of a nature which leaned upon the human presence of Jesus. Along with the other disciples, Mary, too, had to learn how "to rise to a higher and at the same time a nearer, but spiritual communion with Him. . . . Her earthly affection needed to be elevated into a heavenly love" (John 20: 25-29).

Then Jesus commissioned Mary to become the first herald of His Resurrection. She had to go and announce the greatest good news ever proclaimed, "Go to my brethren, and say unto them, I ascend unto my Father, and your Father; and to my God and your God." We can imagine with what speed Mary ran back through the gates of Jerusalem to tell the disciples that their Lord who had died was alive forevermore. Mary had stayed near to Christ in His journeyings, and had cared for many of His human needs until His corpse was laid in the tomb. He now rewarded her with a closer knowledge of things divine, and she was given an honor that cannot be taken away from her, namely, that of being the first among men or women to see the Risen Lord, and to receive the first message from His lips (John 20:18). Although this is the last glimpse we have of Mary Magdalene, we have no hesitation in assuming that she was present with the women (Acts 1:14) who assembled with the apostles in the upper chamber for prayer and supplication, and to await the coming of the promised Spirit. Upon that historic day, Pentecost, when a bequeathed Guide and Comforter came, Mary must have been caught up by His power and made an effective witness of her risen and now ascended Lord.

There are one or two important lessons we can learn from Mary of Magdala. First of all, in her we see what Christ is able to do for a woman. When He first met her she was an afflicted, tormented soul, but Jesus healed her of her insanity and also of the maladies of her soul, and made her His loyal and sacrificial follower. Have we been cleansed of demon-like sins? This is the application Alexander Whyte makes in his study of this Mary: "We do not know just what Mary Magdalene's seven scars were. But for our learning, Dante's own seven scars are written all over his superb autobiographical book —

> Seven times
> The letter that denotes the inward stain,
> He on my forehead, with the truthful point
> Of his drawn sword inscribed. And "Look,"
> he cried,
> When enter'd, "that thou wash these scars away."

John Bunyan has the same number at the end of his *Grace Abounding* —

> I find to this day these seven abominations in my heart. Pride, envy, anger, intemperance, lasciviousness, covetousness, spiritual sloth — these were Dante's seven scars on his sancti-

fied head. . . . It is better to enter into Heaven with seven devils excavated out of our hearts as with a knife, than to have them gnawing in our hearts to all Eternity.

A further lesson is that of what a woman can do for the One who has done so much for her. Once Mary was healed and saved, she practiced her faith in following Jesus and ministering to Him and His disciples of her substance and witnessing to His death and Resurrection to others. Are there not a thousand ways in which converted and consecrated women can serve the Master acceptably. Mary's gratitude and love manifested itself in devotion to Christ. She owed much, gave much, loved much, served much. Has He expelled Satan from our lives? If so, are we loving and serving Him to the limit of our capacity, daily witnessing to the power of His Resurrection?

MARY OF BETHANY
The Woman Everlastingly Remembered

Scripture References—Given under MARTHA
Name Meaning — See material under MARY
Family Connections—Given under MARTHA

Comparisons and contrasts between the two sisters have already been noticed. Both loved the Master and were loved by Him. Martha sat at His feet but "her love and piety alike found adequate and satisfying expression at all times in the ordinary kindly offices of hospitality and domestic service." Mary also sat at Jesus' feet and was content to linger there because her disposition and inward, silent brooding made it hard for her to be at home in the world of affairs. Bustling around a house was not native to her deep emotion. In this cameo of her, then, let us try to sketch her as she was, as an individualist.

At the outset we affirm our disagreement with those expositors who connect Mary of Bethany with the woman who was a sinner (Luke 7:36-50 with John 11:2; 12:1-8). Certainly both anointed the feet of Jesus, but the language used to describe the sinful woman is utterly out of harmony with what we know of the commendable character of Mary. The former's anointing expressed the gratitude of a forgiven and cleansed penitent — the latter's anointing was an act of gratitude for a much-loved brother brought back from the dead. Although the two anointings had the same outward form, they were not duplicates. (See further the chapter on NAMELESS WOMEN.) We likewise dissociate Mary of Bethany from Mary Magdalene. There are those writers who suggest that these two Marys are the same — that once the Magdalene was fully emancipated from demonic possession which drove her from home, she returned and became the Mary who loved to sit at the feet of Jesus. But we hold that Mary of Bethany cannot be identified with any other New Testament woman of the same name. Among the women mentioned in the gospels she occupies a prominent position, for she it was who won the golden commendation from the Lord she dearly loved when He said, "She hath done what she could" (Mark 14:8).

There are four profiles of Mary who occupied her own peculiar place among the inner groups of Christ's friends. She was a woman who cultivated deep, spiritual inner thoughts, and who was busier internally than she was externally. This inner world charmed her more than it did her sister Martha, as the particulars we have of her testify. She was —

A Spiritual Scholar

More than anything else she loved to sit quietly and peacefully at Christ's sacred feet, and become lost in His unfolding of the truth. Mary, more than any other individual in the New Testament, was associated with His feet, betokening her humility, reverence and hunger for spiritual knowledge. She sat at His feet as a disciple, eager to learn of His will and word; fell at His feet in worship and grief; anointed His feet with precious ointment and wiped His feet with her lovely long hair — all of which is in keeping with her spiritual character.

Believing Jesus to be the Prophet, she drank of the teachings He alone could impart as "the Truth." Paul wrote about being "brought up at the feet of Gamaliel" (Acts 22:3). Like his Master before Him, the apostle sat in the midst of learned men, learning and answering questions (Luke 2:46). David sat before the Lord, and listened for His voice (I Chronicles 17:16). Usually the rabbis, or teachers, sat on a high chair, and their scholars on the ground,

and so they were literally at their master's feet. Probably this was Mary's position as with all teachableness she hearkened unto the Lord. George Matheson says, "We see Martha preparing the feast; we see Mary sitting quiescent at the Master's feet and listening to His words, and we say, 'The one is an outward worker and the other an internal mystic whose sympathies are all beyound the veil.' Mary's sympathies are nothing of the kind. Both sisters made their contribution to the Master." But the "good part" Mary chose was that of a fuller appreciation of the necessity of mystic communion with her Lord. It was this glimpse of Mary that Charles Wesley had in mind when he wrote —

> Oh, that I could forever sit,
> Like Mary, at the Master's feet:
>   Be this my happy choice:
> My only care, delight and bliss,
> My joy, my Heaven on earth be this,
>   To hear the Bridegroom's voice.

A Sorrowful Sister

Without doubt, both Martha and Mary loved their brother Lazarus, but we do not read of Martha weeping when death claimed him. We have mention only of Mary's tears. Yet we cannot but believe that Martha's grief was as deep and poignant as that of her sister. When word came that Jesus was on His way to their shadowed home, Martha arose and quickly ran to meet Him, but Mary sat at home nursing her sorrow. Yet when Martha had met Jesus, she came to Mary and told her of the desire of Jesus to see her. Mary arose and went out with the same haste to meet Him, and when she saw Him she threw herself at His feet and wept, and repeated the complaint of Martha, "Lord, if thou hadst been here, my brother had not died." Jesus, deeply moved by the tears of Mary, mingled His warm tears with hers. Why did Jesus groan in spirit at the weeping of Mary? The term "groaning in himself," actually means, "He breathed indignation." What was He indignant about? Could it have been the fact that death was a blot upon creation, and that in Lazarus death had claimed one whom He loved? How privileged Mary was to witness His sense that death ought not to be (John 11: 28-37), even though at the time she did not understand why Jesus had allowed her brother to die!

An Effective Evangelist

We are apt to forget the mighty effect of the resurrection of the dead upon the unconverted Jews who knew the Bethany family. The record says, "Then many of the Jews which came to Mary, and had seen the things which Jesus did, believed on him" (John 11:45; 12:9-11).

It would have been a wonder that any should not have believed after such a display of miraculous power. These Jews who came to Mary were those who had come to comfort Mary and Martha at the burial of Lazarus. They had remained with Mary after Martha had left the house to meet Jesus, and they followed Mary when she herself went to see Him. Whether or not she witnessed to these Jews of the glorious truths she had heard from the lips of Jesus we do not know. What is evident is that her brother was alive again, and such a miracle convicted their hearts of their need of a spiritual resurrection from the grave of sin. So "they believed on him."

A Grateful Giver

To honor Christ for the return of Lazarus from the grave a feast was prepared for the rejoicing friends in the house of Simon — a common name at that time. He had been a leper, but had been healed and converted as the result of his contact with the wonder-working Christ (Matthew 26:6-13; Mark 14:3-9; John 11:1; 12:1-11). The marginal note in the Scofield Reference Bible reads —

> As Martha stands for service, and Lazarus for communion, so Mary shows us the worship of a grateful heart. Others before her had come to His feet to have their need met; she came to give Him His due. Though two of the evangelists record her act, John alone gives her name.

What impresses us about the record of that feast of gratitude is the absence of any conversation. Mary said nothing! While the others sat at the table, Mary was at her accustomed place at the feet of Jesus. "In Martha's house Mary listens, and is silent; at her brother's grave she weeps and is silent; in the house of Simon she works and

is silent." In fact, the only time Mary is found saying anything at all, was when she repeated the complaint of Martha (11:32). Silent love can be a mighty force. The greatest work in the world is not accomplished by the best talkers. As to the nature of her offering —

It Was Costly

Mary had been the recipient of priceless truth from the lips of Jesus, now she is lavishly communicative. The box of spikenard, treasured up for such an occasion (John 12:7), was worth 300 pence, a great sum in those days. "A penny a day" wage (Matthew 20:2), means that 300 pennies would cover her wages for almost a year. Mary made that supper a sacrament as "she mingled divine poetry with the prose of the situation by anointing Jesus with a bottle of expensive spikenard." When Mary sat at His feet and heard His word she recognized Him as the *Prophet;* when in her grief she fell at His feet she knew Him to be the sympathizing *High Priest;* now as she anoints His feet she knows Him to be the *King* at whose girdle could be found the keys of death and Hades. Had He not triumphed over death and raised her beloved brother? No wonder the house was filled with the odor of the ointment. The odor of Mary's loving service has filled the whole world.

It Was Criticized

While the odor of the spikenard was sweet to many, it smelled of waste to others. Judas with his calculating mind quickly figured up the cost of it and called it wasted on Jesus. Its price would have fed many poor people. The word Judas used for waste actually means "perdition." A "fit question," says Bengel, "on the lips of the son of perdition" (John 17:12). Sordid Judas thought only of the money aspect of Mary's expensive gift, because he kept his heart in the money bag he carried which "by office he bare, and by theft left bare."

It Was Commended

As our Lord quickly replied to the pious talk of Judas, He replied also to the reflection upon Mary by declaring that she had done a good work. Here was the charm of her service — she poured out the costly ointment for the sake of her Lord. "She hath wrought a good work on *me*" (Mark 14:6). Had she had more spikenard she would have given it, but she gave to the fullest extent of her ability — "what she could" (Mark 14:8).

> Selfishness seeks a gift,
> Love loves to give;
> Love gives itself away
> Love loves to live.
>
> Love's grand munificence
> Counts not the cost;
> Feeling, tho' nought is left,
> Nothing is lost.

It Was Commemorative

Mary had often heard Jesus speak of His coming death and burial, and her alabaster box of precious ointment had been treasured up for the anointing of His body. But now she brings it out and uses it to dedicate the Lamb of God to the sacrifice He was about to make. "Against the day of my burying hath she kept this" — and Jesus appreciated the fragrance of that ointment while He was alive. Its perfume would have been lost upon His corpse. The grateful Christ went further and said, "Wheresoever this gospel shall be preached in the whole world, then this also that she hath done shall be told for a memorial of her." He erected a memorial to Mary who gave all she could, more enduring than many of the proud monuments that have perished with time. Mary's love and unselfish goodness have been immortalized.

What are some of the lessons to be gleaned from the life and character of Mary of Bethany? She was a woman of vision but was by no means a visionary. She not only sat at the feet of Jesus, but also anointed them with the best she had and wiped them with her hair. She was practical as well as spiritual. If we have learned that "our higher place is lying low at our Redeemer's feet," then like Mary, our vision will become a vocation. Moses wrote of the fourfold privilege of all the saints —

> He loved the people;
> All His saints are in His hand:
> They sat down at His feet;
> Every one shall receive of Thy
>   words (Deuteronomy 33:3).

Mary gave to the limit of her love and ointment. Will the Lord say of us when we see Him face to face — You have done what you could? Do we constantly anoint Him as the Chosen of our hearts? Are His feet perfumed with our richest gifts? The world may count a life wholly consecrated to Him as a life wasted, but only the life abandoned to His sway is the one richly reproductive in the saint's own life and also in the sinful world in which he lives.

MARY, THE MOTHER OF JAMES AND JOSES

We are told practically nothing about this particular Mary, save that she was the mother of two children one of whom Jesus chose as an apostle, namely, James (Matthew 27:55-61; Mark 15:40, 47; 16:1; Luke 24:10, see Luke 23:49-56). Some writers identify her as "the other Mary" (Matthew 27:61), or as the wife of Cleopas or Alphaeus (Matthew 10:3; Luke 24:18), or as a sister of Mary, the mother of Jesus. We do know that she was one of the women who followed Jesus and, having sufficient wealth, ministered unto Him and His disciples in material things thereby assisting them in their work (Luke 8:2, 3). The narrative suggests that her two fine sons likewise followed her from Galilee to Jerusalem. "It is interesting to note that two mothers with their sons joined the company of the disciples and that three out of the four became members of the apostolic group." We feel that Mary's sons were older than Jesus else they probably would not have dared to interfere with Him by force (Mark 3:21). These facts are evident —

Mary was among the women from Galilee who followed Jesus to Jerusalem there to witness His death on the cross (Matthew 27:56; Mark 15:40).

She was likewise a spectator at the tomb and fled when told by the angels that Jesus was not there (Mark 16:8).

She was among the first to bear spices to anoint the dear dead body of her Lord, and with joy went forth to declare that He was alive forevermore.

She was the mother of a son who became an apostle, known as "James the Less," or James the Little to distinguish him from the more conspicuous apostle of the same name.

She thus sacrificed both her sustenance and her son for the service of the Master. Motivated by the inner urge of gratitude to Him for all He had done for her, she became generous, faithful, loving and true. Hers was a simple faith and a trusting love. Thousands of Christian women down the ages have been likened to her because she loved her Lord and served Him unobtrusively. Kuyper, comparing this Mary with Mary Magdalene by an analogy of our two types of letters, calls Mary Magdalene "a vowel" and Mary, the mother of the apostle, "a consonant."

> The same analogy holds if we compare Peter with James the Less. We should then name Peter, who always took the initiative, the vowel, and James, who always remained in the background, the consonant. This Mary and those other quiet women were very much like James. They were consonants, they harmoniously joined in with the song of love that was sung for Jesus, but they were not originally creative.

Then applying this analogy and pointing out that the world generally deems quiet, unobtrusive and ordinary service somewhat tame and unambitious, Kuyper goes on to remark —

> But God's scale of values weighs differently than ours does. In our alphabet, God gave us five vowels and twenty-one consonants. And He has given the human race very few people to assume the solo parts. To the many others He has granted only the capacity to harmonize when others lead in creation's hymn of love and praise. That situation is quite appropriate. Only in that way can a supreme harmony be attained. A company of successive soloists would be repulsive to our aesthetic taste.

The question is, Am I content to be a *consonant?*

MARY, MOTHER OF JOHN MARK

Among the Marys mentioned in the New Testament, Mary, the mother of Mark who wrote the second gospel, is spoken of but once (Acts 12:12 — read 12:1-19), yet this brief description of her is suggestive of her life and labors. She was probably the aunt or sister of Barnabas, the one-time companion of Paul (Colossians 4:10), and such a relationship accounts for Barnabas' choice of Mark as his companion — a selection over which Paul and Barnabas parted. Further,

being related to Mary would account for the leadership among the saints gathering in her spacious home. Evidently the family belonged to Cyprus, hence the choice of such by Barnabas as the first station in his journeyings (Acts 4:36; 13:4). Sir William Ramsay holds that the narrative of Mary in the Acts was by Mark, which would account for the details of his mother's large house becoming a well-known center of Christian life and worship. There is a legend to the effect that this same house was the scene of a still more sacred gathering when, in its upper room, Jesus observed the Lord's Supper on the night of His betrayal.

It was to Mary's home that Peter found his way after his miraculous escape, for he knew that a company of believers had gathered there to pray for his release. Peter had a peculiar affection for the godly home. He called Mark, "his son" (I Peter 5:13) — a spiritual son, having led him to yield his life to the Saviour. The way in which the saints met in Mary's home bespeaks her tried steadfastness and the bond of intimacy that existed between them. That Rhoda was one of the maids indicates that the household was considerably large, implying that Mary was a widow with means to maintain such a commodious home. As Barnabas her relative gave up his land for Christ, Mary gave up her Jerusalem home to be used as an infant church.

Mary was a woman of sterling qualities and was loyal to her Christian ideals. At that time Christians were a persecuted sect, yet she faced the consequences of yielding up her home as a center of spiritual power and influence, and was self-sacrificing in time, effort and money to serve the Lord. It has been suggested that young Rhoda who went to open the door for Peter was hesitant thinking perhaps it was the soldiers of Herod who had come to arrest some of the homeless Christian friends whose benefactress and patron Mary had become.

As for Mark the evangelist, her son, he was deeply attached to his mother which was probably one reason why he returned to Jerusalem from Perga (Acts 13:13). He wanted to be nearer the one who had meant so much in his life. Doubtless he derived something of Mary's straightforward and decided character so prominent in the gospel he wrote portraying Jesus as the lowly servant of God.

MARY OF ROME

In Paul's portrait gallery of those saints in the church at Rome, to whom he was deeply indebted and to whom he sent warm greetings, another Mary has honorable mention. All we know about her is in Paul's personal salutation, "Greet Mary, who bestowed much labour upon us" (Romans 16: 6). Among the twenty saints Paul designated by name, Mary is the only one with a Jewish name. It is quite likely that this Roman lady adopted this name, with its hallowed associations, at her conversion and baptism, and such a combination exemplifies how Christianity binds all in one bond of fellowship. If she was a Jewess she yet labored for the uplift of Rome — Judah's oppressor.

How Mary labored energetically for Paul and his co-workers we are not told. Evidently she had a capacity peculiar to herself for lightening the apostle's heavy load, and furthered thereby the cause of the Lord. As another Roman female, Persis, is mentioned in the list as having "laboured much in the Lord" (16:12), Kuyper was led to suggest that Mary and Persis were evangelists who were employed in making the gospel known in the same way as the Salvation Army uses women today. These godly women exerted their influence in every possible way to aid Paul in making Christ known. Whatever personal gifts, or means, they possessed were dedicated to the Lord whose saving grace they had experienced. Paul thus commends them for their sacrificial and unstinted service.

MATRED

Scripture References — Genesis 36:39;
I Chronicles 1:50
Name Meaning — Thrusting forward *or* expulsive

This name belonged to the mother of Mehetabel, who, through her daughter's marriage to Hadad or Hadar became the mother-in-law of the last of Edom's kings. The LXX Version designates Matred as a male — a son, not daughter of Mezahab.

MEHETABEL

Scripture References — Genesis 36:39;
I Chronicles 1:50
Name Meaning — Whom God makes happy *or* benefited of God

The daughter of Matred, Mehetabel became the wife of Hadar or Hadad who was apparently the last of the ancient kings of Edom. A male in the time of Nehemiah bore this same name (6:10-13).

MERAB

Scripture References — I Samuel 14:49; 18: 17, 19
Name Meaning — Increase *or* multiplication

This is the name of King Saul's eldest daughter. In II Samuel 21:8 *Michal* should read *Merab*, as the context shows. Merab was promised by her father Saul to David for his victory over Goliath, but was finally given to Adriel, the Meholathite (II Samuel 21:8) by whom she had five sons, all of whom were subsequently hanged by the Gibeonites as a revenge for Saul's bloodthirsty zeal against them (II Samuel 21:9). Thus Saul's sin recoiled on himself and his children (Exodus 34:7). Commentators suggest that possibly Merab died comparatively young and that her children were given over to her sister Michal who, being childless, cared for them as if they were her own (II Samuel 6:20-23; 21:8).

MESHULLEMETH

Scripture Reference — II Kings 21:19
Name Meaning — Those who repay *or* retribution

This is the name given to the daughter of Harez of Jotbah — the earliest instance of adding the birthplace of a queen-mother. Meshullemeth became the wife of Manasseh, son of Hezekiah, and mother of Amon, who succeeded his father Manasseh as king of Judah. After her name we read that her son, "did that which was evil in the sight of the Lord." How much, we wonder, did his mother's influence contribute to his departure from the Lord and his disobedience to His commands?

MICHAIAH

Scripture Reference — II Chronicles 13:2
Name Meaning — Who is like Jehovah?

The various spellings of the name are

Micah, Micaiah, Maachah, the full form being Micaiahu. The name occurs at least 12 times in the Old Testament and occurs as the name of males as well as females. Michaiah, or Maachah was the daughter of Uriel of Gibeah, and married Jeroboam (see MAACHAH No. 3).

MICHAL
THE WOMAN WHO TRICKED HER FATHER

Scripture References — I Samuel 14:49; 18: 20-28; 19:11-17; 25:44; II Samuel 3:13,14; 6:16-23; 21:8; I Chronicles 15:29

Name Meaning — This name is allied to the previous name, Michaiah, and also to Michael, and mean the same — "Who is like Jehovah?" Michal, along with its cognates, illustrates the comparatively small class of proper names composed of more than two words. It is a name describing an admiring acknowledgment of the transcendant unapproachable majesty of the divine nature.

Family Connections — Michal was the younger daughter of Saul, Israel's first king. Her mother was Ahinoam. She became David's first wife, was given to Phalti the son of Laish, of Gallim for a-while, but was recovered by David. As the aunt of her sister Merab's five sons, Michal cared for them after the somewhat premature death of her sister.

Michal, although a princess, does not appear to have had a very commendable character. Desire for prestige, fervor of infatuation, indifference to holiness, and idolatry mark out this Jewess who knew the covenant God yet persevered in idolatrous practices. Closely associated with David, her career can be broken up thus —

She Loved David

What young woman would not be attracted by such a strong, athletic young man, who was "ruddy, and withal of a beautiful countenance, and goodly to look to"? Further, David was the young shepherd who defied and killed the giant Goliath who had terrified Michal's father and his people. Thus Michal grew passionately fond of David, and made no effort to conceal her love for this much-lauded champion of Israel. While there may not be very much to admire in Michal, we cannot but express

sympathy for her experiences in an age when women were treated as chattels, being thrown from one husband to another. But while "Michal, Saul's daughter, loved David," she did not love the Lord as David did. What a different story might have been written of her if she had been a woman after God's own heart!

She Married David

Saul had vowed that the man who killed Goliath would become his son-in-law, and Merab, Saul's first daughter should have been given to David, but Saul, regretting his promise, gave her to another man. David was now a veritable hero among the people, and Saul's jealousy prompted him to devise means whereby David would be slain by the Philistines. Learning of Michal's love for David, Saul asked as a dowry, usually paid to a father according to Eastern custom, the foreskins of 100 Philistines. David slew 200 Philistines, and Saul was forced to give his daughter to wife to the man whose death he had planned. As David had been victorious, Saul dared not go back upon his word. How Saul illustrates the adage that "Jealousy is as cruel as the grave"!

She Delivered David

Still bent on destroying David, Saul had David's house surrounded. In a frenzy of envy Saul had messengers "watch David to slay him in the morning." But Michal's love smelled danger and, discovering her father's intention, "let David down through a window; and he fled and escaped." Then, as a truehearted wife she tricked her father and his emissaries. With her husband safely out of the way, Michal put a hair-covered image in David's bed, and when the men burst into the supposedly sickroom, they found that they had been cleverly tricked. When Saul heard he had been outwitted, he accused his daughter of disloyalty to her father, and was most bitter in his reproach. Michal, however, pretended that David had threatened to kill her if she did not help him to escape.

She Forsook David

After this incident, Michal's love for David waned. Where was the pleasure in being the wife of a man forced to spend his days a fugitive, hunted like a wild animal in the wilderness? Phalti of Gallem was a better catch, she thought, seeing he was on his way to royalty which she was eager to secure and hold. So Michal became the wife of Phalti. This was an illegitimate union seeing David was alive and was in no way lawfully separated from Michal as her husband. That Phalti cared for Michal is proven by the way he followed her, weeping, when she decided to leave him for her former husband.

She Was Restored to David

With Saul's death, circumstances changed for David whom God had already chosen to be king over His people. Michal and her husband Phalti were living to the east of Jordan during the short rule of Ishbosheth. Abner made an arrangement to assist David to take over the kingship of the nation, and David made the restoration of Michal the one condition of the league. So despite Phalti's sorrowful protest, Michal was forcibly restored to David as he returned from his wanderings as king. Evidently his ardor for Michal was the same as at the first, and his desire to claim her proves how he wanted her as queen in Hebron.

How pathetic it is to read of Phalti with whom Michal had lived for some considerable time. We see his sorrow as he went with her in tears, only to be rudely sent back by Abner! We do not read of Michal weeping as she left the man who had showered so much affection upon her. It did not require much force to make her leave Phalti. Her pride and love for prestige left little room for weeping and although she knew she could never become David's ideal love, seeing she had been the possession of another man, yet as his first wife Michal thought of the position that would be hers at court.

She Despised David

The closing scene between Michal and David is most moving, for what love Michal might have had for David turned to scorn and disdain. After making Jerusalem his capital, David brought the sacred Ark of the covenant, the ancient symbol of Jehovah's presence, to Moriah. On the day of

the Ark's return David was so joyful that, stripping himself of his royal robes, he "danced before the Lord with all his might." Michal watched from a window and seeing David—the king—leaping and dancing before the Lord, she "despised him in her heart." Although she had loved him, risked her life for his safety, she now abhors him for his loss of royal dignity. Her haughtiness was shocked by David's participation in such an excitable demonstration.

Nursing her contempt Michal waited until David returned to his household. When they met, she with a biting sarcasm, revealing "her self-pride, and lack of sensitiveness to her husband's magnificent simplicity," sneeringly said, "How glorious was the king of Israel to day, who uncovered himself to day in the eyes of the handmaids of his servants, as one of the vain fellows shamelessly uncovereth himself!" For her there were no pious and affectionate feelings at the return of the Ark to Zion. Like her father, Saul, she had no regard for the Ark of God (I Chronicles 13:3). But David, mortified by Michal's pride as a king's daughter, was curt in his reply. Resenting her reproach, he made it clear in no uncertain terms that he was not ashamed of what he had done "before the Lord" who had chosen him rather than any of Saul's family to reign as king. Michal had missed the essential significance of David's career, that in spite of his failures he was a man after God's own heart. As Alexander Whyte put it, "What was David's meat was Michal's poison. What was sweeter than honey to David was gall and wormwood to Michal. . . . At the despicable sight [of David dancing] she spat at him, and sank back in her seat with all hell in her heart. . . . Michal is a divine looking-glass for all angry and outspoken wives."

She Lost David

After such an outburst of reproach we read that "Michal the daughter of Saul had no child unto the day of her death," and such a final flat statement practically means that she lived apart from David, more or less divorced (II Samuel 6:16). The estrangement between them likely became more acute because of the other wives now sharing David's prosperity. Childless till her death was a punishment appropriate to her transgression. David was given many sons and daughters, and her sister Merab bore five sons, but Michal never achieved the great attainment of being a mother. She ended her days without the love and companionship of a husband, caring for her dead sister's five children, all of whom were ultimately beheaded.

What can we learn from this story of Michal and David? Misunderstanding arose in their relationship because of a clash of temperament, outlook and purpose. Had Michal shared David's faith in God how different life would have been for both of them. But Michal made no effort to understand her husband's Godward desires and so passed a wrong judgment upon him. How certain we should be of a person's motive for his acts or attitudes before we condemn him. Further, had Michal loved David enough, she should have sought his forgiveness after he had explained his demeanor before the Lord. "She worshipped him when he was poor and unknown and now that he is King 'she despised him in her heart' . . . David realized they could never love the same God. Therefore he cut her from his heart." But being eaten up with pride there was no tolerance in her heart and so harmony was impossible. Love brings harmony and understanding into every human relationship. A fellow-minister confided in Alexander Whyte that he preached and prayed best when his wife stayed at home. This was something of the gulf between David and Michal. How different it is when husbands truly love their wives and wives sincerely reverence their husbands!

MILCAH No. 1

Scripture References — Genesis 11:29; 22: 20, 23; 24:15, 24, 47

Name Meaning — Queen *or* counsel

Nothing is recorded of the life and character of this daughter of Haran, who became the wife of her Uncle Nahor, the eldest brother of Abraham. She bore Nahor eight sons, the youngest being Bethuel who became the father of Rebekah and Laban. Thus Milcah was the grandmother of them both.

MILCAH No. 2

Scripture References — Numbers 26:33; 27: 1; 36:11; Joshua 17:3

This female bearing the same name was one of the five daughters of Zelophehad, and co-heiress of his inheritance. See HOGLAH.) Some authorities affirm that Milcah is an abbreviation of Bethmilcah, and is a geographical rather than a personal name.

MIRIAM No. 1
THE WOMAN WHOSE JEALOUSY BROUGHT JUDGMENT

Scripture References — Exodus 15:20, 21; Numbers 12:1-15; 20:1; 26:59; Deuteronomy 24:9; Micah 6:4

Name Meaning — As a name Miriam belongs to a family of words having different root-form, all of which suggest "bitterness," Mary, Maria, Mariamne. (See under *Name Meaning*, MARY.) Miriam, then, the same as Mary, meaning "bitterness," "rebellion" was apropos, for because of her jealousy, Miriam's fate was one of extreme bitterness

Family Connections—Miriam was the eldest child of Amram and Jochebed, and the sister of Aaron and Moses. Says Bulwer, "I honour birth and ancestry when they are regarded as incentives to exertion, not title deeds to sloth." Miriam owed much to her ancestry. She was the daughter of godly parents and the sister of two of Israel's greatest figures. Josephus in his *Antiquities* informs us that Miriam became the wife of another well-known leader in Israel namely, Hur, one of the judges of the people when Moses was on Mount Sinai (Exodus 24:14). This would make Miriam to be the grandmother of Bezaleel, the famous artist in the construction of the Tabernacle (Exodus 31: 2). The Biblical narrative, however, suggests that Miriam remained in single blessedness all her days. "Miriam stands before us in an absolutely unsexual relation," says George Matheson: "there is neither marriage nor courtship. Her interests are not matrimonial! they are national. Her mission is not domestic, it is patriotic. . . . Miriam the unmarried is a heroine in an age when female celibacy was not a consecrated thing, in a Book where the nuptial tie is counted the glory of womanhood."

Some of the grandest women to benefit mankind were content to remain unmarried. Was there ever such a ministering angel in human form as Florence Nightingale, "The Lady of the Lamp," whose sacrificial work among the suffering soldiers during the Crimean War laid the foundation for the great reformation that took place in the hospitals of the world? Many noble women do not marry from sheer choice, as the biographies of some female missionaries and nurses testify. We see Miriam —

As a Clever Girl on the Banks of the River Nile

In dealing with Miriam's mother, Jochebed (which see), we saw how Pharaoh had commanded all the male babies of the Israelites to be drowned in the Nile and how Jochebed took every possible precaution for her beautiful baby's safety. Out of the common reeds grown along the banks of the river she fashioned a small basket-boat, and making it watertight by an inside covering of clay and an outside protection of bitumen, laid the baby in its boat by the edge of the stream which she knew was frequented by the princess and her female court.

The anxious mother took the wise precaution of leaving the baby's sister, Miriam, nearby to mount guard over his safety (Exodus 2:4). Whether Pharaoh's daughter came down to bathe in the stream or wash her clothes in it, we are not told. Among the reeds the little boat with its precious cargo was spotted and brought to the princess who, seeing the child, loved him. As he was lifted up, he cried. He wanted feeding. But who was to nurse the mite? Then came young Miriam's opportunity. Out of the shadows she stepped forth so innocently, and appearing to be curious at the screaming baby and puzzled princess, ask if she would like her to try and find a Hebrew nurse. Miriam kept her silence and did not reveal her relation to the baby and the nurse she secured. Thus the ready wit of Miriam, a girl of ten to twelve years old, saved her brother whom the Princess called *Moses*. When he became the great hero, how Miriam must have been grateful for her share in preserving her baby brother from the cruel fate of other Hebrew infants.

As a Gifted Poetess and Prophetess at the Red Sea

Miriam appears for the first time by name when she is called a "prophetess," and is identified as the sister of Aaron. Both her words and work were full of the inspiration of God and she is brought as a leader and pattern to the women of Israel. Prophets and prophetesses are those raised up by God and inspired by His Spirit to proclaim the will and purpose of God. It is at the Red Sea that we see Miriam standing out so prominently, proclaiming and singing the power and faithfulness of God. She, it was, who led the Israelite women in dancing and instrumental accompaniment as she sang the ode of praise and victory (Exodus 15: 20, 21). By this time Miriam was well past middle life. If she was about 12 years of age when Moses was born, and he spent 40 years in Egypt, then another 40 in the land of Midian before the dramatic episode of the Red Sea, then Miriam was an aging woman in that time when longevity was normal.

After the plague that fell upon Egypt, Pharaoh let God's people go. Moses, leader of the almost two million people, with his brother Aaron as high priest, and his sister Miriam as his chief singer, set out for the land of promise. God caused the waters to roll back and the Israelites passed through on dry ground, but as soon as they were through the waters rushed back and drowned the pursuing Egyptians. Miriam, the first poetess in the Bible, led the joyous acclamations of the multitude, and using her timbrel, sang, "Sing ye to the Lord, for he hath triumphed gloriously: the horse and his rider hath he thrown into the sea." The Song of Moses and Miriam has been referred to as one of the oldest and most splendid natural anthems in the world. Whether Miriam composed the poem or not, we cannot tell. What we do know is that she wove the matchless, mighty ode of victory into the conscious life of the people.

Henry Van Dyke reminds us that, "The spirit and movement of the song are well expressed in the English verse of Thomas Moore's paraphrase:"

Sound the loud timbrel o'er Egypt's dark sea!
Jehovah has triumphed, — His people are free!
Sing — for the pride of the tyrant is broken;
    His chariots, his horsemen, all splendid and
        brave,—
How vain was their boasting! the Lord hath but
        spoken,
And chariots and horsemen are sunk in the wave.
Sound the loud timbrel o'er Egypt's dark sea!
Jehovah has triumphed, — His people are free!

Praise to the Conqueror, praise to the Lord!
His word was our arrow, His breath was our sword.
Who shall return to tell Egypt the story
    Of those she sent forth in the shew of her pride?
For the Lord hath looked out from His pillar of
        glory,
And all her brave thousands are dashed in the
        tide.
Sound the loud timbrel o'er Egypt's dark sea!
Jehovah has triumphed — His people are free!

This is a powerful verse. But there is
even greater majesty and force in the form
of the ode as it stands in the Book of Exodus. How grandly the antiphonal ascrip-
tions of praise to Jehovah come into the description of the overthrow of Egypt's pride
and power!

> Jehovah is a man of war:
> Jehovah is his name!
>
> Thou didst blow with thy wind:
> The sea covered them:
> They sank as lead in the mighty waters.
> Who is like unto thee among the gods,
>   Jehovah?
> Who is like unto thee?
> Glorious in holiness!
> Fearful in praises!
> Doing wonders!

As the first of the sweet singers of Israel,
Miriam sang for God, using her gift for the
elevation of human souls into a higher life.
A dreary wilderness faced the children of
Israel, and Miriam knew that they would
march better if they sang. So her song was
one of cheer and full of the memory of all
God had accomplished for His people. "The
greatest stimulus for the crossing of Jordan
is the fact that we have already crossed the
Red Sea," wrote George Matheson. "It was
wise in Miriam to begin with that Sea and
over its prostrate waves to sound her first
timbrel."

A Jealous Sister in the Wilderness

What a faithful mirror the Bible is of the
characters it portrays! Blemishes, as well
as beauties, are revealed. It tells the naked

truth of those it describes. There is a blot
upon almost all its portraits, and "its blots
are as much a bit of the art as its beauties."
A double feature of the failure of the Bible's
heroes and heroines is that they are usually
associated with middle life after the morning inspired with hope and courage unbounded is past, as in the case of Miriam.
Further, such failures come where we
should not expect them to overtake the
otherwise true and noble. Miriam, for instance, rebelled against the mission of her
life, namely, to protect and labor in partnership with Moses whom she had been the
means of saving for his country. Miriam
was, above all things, a faithful patriot, with
a love for her country greater than the love
for her renowned brother. It was because
he was the chosen emissary of God to lead
Israel out of bondage into freedom that she
rebelled against him in a twofold way. Jealousy led Miriam to reject both the position
of Moses as the leader of the host, and his
partner in the wife he took unto himself.
She found the management and marriage of
Moses most irksome.

In the first place, Miriam rebelled against
the bride of Moses whose first wife, Zipporah, was a Midianite or Gentile (Exodus
2:21). The second wife was an Ethiopian,
a Cushite, a dark-skinned beauty from the
African country south of the Nile cataracts.
By this time Miriam was an old woman
and possibly resented the presence of a
younger and more attractive woman so
close to her brother. Miriam despised the
bride of Moses not because of her color,
but because she was a foreigner. Race-
pride made the Ethiopian woman objec-
tionable. It was not so much feminine
jealousy on Miriam's part as patriotic jealousy. She was a confirmed member of the
Hebrew race, and dead set against any
foreign alliance. Because the blood of a
mean ancestry was in the veins of the Ethiopian whose people hated the worship of
the true God, Miriam feared the influence
of the new wife upon Moses.

But Miriam's greatest offense was her
sarcastic rejection of the leadership of
Moses. Hitherto, she had been a symbol of
unity as she shared in the triumphs and
hopes of Israel. Now, unfortunately, she is
prominent as a leader of discord, division

and discontent. It will be noted that Aaron is paired with his sister in the outburst against the acquisition and the authority of Moses. But by the order of the names it is evident that Miriam was the instigator and the spokeswoman in the revolt. "Miriam and Aaron spake against Moses" (Numbers 12:1). This is understandable because of the close bond of friendship between two who had never been parted. After Miriam as a young girl saved Moses' life, she scarcely saw him for almost 80 years, but with Aaron she had lived quietly at home. Now she takes the initiative in opposition against the younger brother, and uses his Ethiopian wife as a pretext to rebel against the superior authority of Moses. Her jealous heart led her to reject God's discrimination in favor of Moses against her and Aaron.

Thus personal jealousy and fear of their own respective leadership are mingled in their question, "Hath God indeed spoken only by Moses? Hath he not spoken also by us?" Miriam and Aaron aspired to a joint partnership in state power and in the government of Israel, and they failed. If Moses had erred in marrying his dark bride, it was a personal mistake and not a public crime. Miriam's chief error consisted in her effort to break down the God-given authority of Moses, and thereby imperil the unity and hope of the nation. Her fault then was greater than that of Moses, because it was an offense against the commonwealth.

It is true that Miriam had functioned as a prophetess and used Aaron as a prophet, but God had distinctly said, "My servant Moses is not so. With him will I speak mouth to mouth, even apparently and not in dark speeches." Such was God's elective sovereignty, and Miriam's sin was grievous in that she rebelled against what God had spoken. That such a sister should be jealous of her brother is beyond conception, but human nature even at it best is very frail. How true it is that "jealousy is the apprehension of superiority and the towering character of Moses doubtless disturbed the peace of Miriam." George Eliot has the phrase, "One of the torments of jealousy is that it can never turn away its eyes from the thing that pains it." Paul places "evil speaking" among the cardinal sins.

Moses, meekest of all men, acted as a deaf man who heard not, and as a dumb man who opened not his mouth. God had heard the complaints Miriam had voiced and He called the trio of leaders to meet Him at the tabernacle of the congregation. Taking up the defense of Moses, God spoke directly to Miriam and Aaron in no uncertain terms that they had not only hurt Moses but that they had failed in their duty toward Him. Moses received divine vindication as God's servant who had been faithful, and as the one whom He had chosen as the medium of a divine revelation. Then the rebellious sister and brother were reprimanded by God for speaking against His honored servant. How silenced the three must have been when, standing at the door of the tabernacle, they were silenced by the austerity and authority of the divine voice! In righteous wrath God withdrew from the holy place.

A Repentant Leper Outside the Camp

As the divine cloud left the tabernacle, the eyes of Aaron sought his beloved and forceful sister, and to his horror she had been smitten with leprosy—the foul disease that made the victim look like death, white as snow, a living corpse (Numbers 12:12). The proud, jealous prophetess was condemned to endure the most humiliating of diseases. While Aaron was united with Miriam in rebellion against Moses, judgment only fell upon Miriam which indicated that she had been the instigator, and had influenced her pliable brother. "Look at her in her rapture, like one out of the body with the joy of the Lord, at the Red Sea," says Alexander Whyte, "and now see to what her wicked heart and her wicked tongue have brought her. Look at her with her hand upon her throat, and with a linen cloth upon her lip, and with her hoarse, sepulchral noisome voice wandering far from the camp, and compelled to cry Unclean! Unclean! when any one came in sight."

How humiliating it must have been for Miriam to see people fleeing from her — the one who had before led them so triumphantly. Her judgment was swift and signal, even though hers was a temporary disgrace. Aaron and Moses, overcome with pity for their condemned sister and filled with brotherly love, prayed for Miriam that the punishment might pass from her. Prayer was heard on her behalf, and after her separation from the camp for seven days, she was healed of her leprosy. Evidently Miriam had the sympathy of the whole nation during her week of purification. Although she held up the progress of the host for those seven days, such was her popularity that "the people journeyed not [from Hazeroth] till Miriam was brought in again." When Moses came to write out the law in respect to leprosy, he mentioned his sister Miriam as an example (Deuteronomy 24:9). Thus her presumptuous effort to change the leadership of Israel ended in her humiliation and in the divine vindication of Moses as the undisputed leader of the people.

What happened to Miriam during her seven days without the camp as she bore the sorrow of seeing Israel's march to the Promised Land arrested because of her jealousy we are not told. Doubtless she was repentant, but her strength was broken and the gift of prophecy had left her. One also wonders what the thoughts of Moses' wife were during that lonely week as she thought of her sister-in-law punished and excluded because she condemned Moses for making her his wife. Further, had the confidence of Moses in Aaron and Miriam been so shaken as to make him walk alone? Restored to divine favor we would fain believe Miriam was noble and submissive through the rest of her days, even though we do not hear again of her until her death.

A Dying Saint at Kadesh

Alexander Whyte reckons that Miriam did not live long after that dread week, that she died not because of her old age, or the dregs of the leprosy, but of a broken heart. The Bible is silent as to any further service she rendered once the camp moved on. Had her sorrow crushed her song, and her presumption silenced her prophetic voice? This we do know, that as Moses was not permitted to enter the Land of Promise because "he spoke unadvisedly with his lips" at the rock, so Miriam because of her sin died before the entrance to Canaan, and was buried at Kadesh-barnea, where Israel mourned for her. She passed away at the eleventh hour of the completion of Israel's journey of forty years (Numbers 20:1). Tradition has it that she was given a costly funeral and buried on the mountain of Zin, and mourned for some 30 days. But her last resting place, like that of her great brother, Moses, is one of the secrets of God. As an epitaph for her grave, wherever she sleeps, we can inscribe "She sang the song of Moses: but it was also the song of the Lamb."

What are some of the lessons to be learned from the feminine jealousy and ambition which were the drawbacks in Miriam's otherwise commanding character? First of all, we should learn to avoid the temptation to wield power at the expense of losing influence. Miriam had great influence in her sphere as prophetess and leader of the praises of Israel, but she was not content. She coveted equal power with Moses. Then is it not folly in trying to add to our prestige and dictating to others, as Miriam and Aaron when they gave vent to their feelings against Moses? The most impressive lesson to learn from Miriam is that it is injurious to our character to be discontented with our own distinction, and to jealously desire the higher place of honor which another holds. My soul, never forget that it was envy that crucified the Lord who personified humility!

MIRIAM No. 2

Scripture Reference — I Chronicles 4:17

While listed as a daughter of Ezra of the tribe of Judah, scholars are not certain whether a man or woman is meant.

NAAMAH No. 1

Scripture Reference — Genesis 4:22
Name Meaning — Pleasant *or* sweetness

This heathen name is of the same derivation with Naomi and Naaman. It is one of the earliest female names recorded in Scripture. Naamah is the feminine form of Naam, son of Caleb (I Chronicles 4:15); and is also the name of a town in the low country of Judah mentioned by Joshua (15:41). Our first Naamah was the daughter of Lamech and Zillah and brother of Tubal-cain, the first worker in brass and iron. The refinement and luxury of Cain's descendants appear in the names of their wives and daughters (see ADAH and ZILLAH).

NAAMAH No. 2

Scripture References — I Kings 14:21, 31;
    II Chronicles 12:13

This was also the name of one of Solomon's numerous wives. She was from the royal line of Israel's inveterate enemies, the Ammonites, and her evil influence was abhorrent to the people of Israel as they witnessed her leading Solomon into her idolatrous ways. Since she was chief lady, the king erected a high place for her god, Moloch. Naamah became the mother of Rehoboam, who succeeded Solomon, and who was the last king of the united Kingdom of Israel. Rehoboam lived and died a monument of his evil mother's hatred of the true God.

NAARAH

Scripture Reference — I Chronicles 4:5, 6
Name Meaning — Girl *or* Child of the Lord

Naarah was one of the two wives of Ashur, the father of Tekoa. It is also the name of a town on the border of Ephraim (Joshua 16:7), which was also known as Naaran (I Chronicles 7:28).

NAOMI
THE WOMAN WHO TASTED THE CUP
OF BITTERNESS

Scripture Reference — The Book of Ruth
Name Meaning — As indicated under Naamah No. 1 (which see) Naomi means "my joy," "my bliss," or "pleasantness of Jehovah," and is a name suggestive of all that is charming, agreeable, attractive. Until deep sorrow overshadowed her, we can understand Naomi having a nature corresponding to her name. Although her character came to be purged and enhanced by her suffering, Naomi had an innate nobility that gave her personality an irresistible charm.

Family Connections — While both Naomi and Elimelech were staunch members of the Hebrew race, we are told nothing of their genealogy. Elimelech, who married Naomi, is thought to have belonged to one of the outstanding families in Israel, being a brother of Salmon, prince

of Judah, who married Rahab. If this was so, then Naomi began her married life in comfortable circumstances. Naomi and Elimelech belonged to Bethlehem-Judah where two sons were born to them, namely, Mahlon and Chilion.

The Book of Ruth, which is one of the most lovely idylls in literature, and has enchanted every age, presents us with two women who are among the best-loved in history and whose story still captivates the world because of their unique devotion. Naomi and Ruth, her daughter-in-law, afford a relief after characters like Tamar, Delilah and Jezebel. In this sketch let us try to delineate the life and experience of Naomi who knew a great deal about "the ringing groove of change," to use Tennyson's phrase. Because of her manifold changes in life, Naomi came to fear God in a deeper way (Psalm 55:19).

Her Change of Country

During the rule of the Judges, Israel suffered a serious famine which was deemed to be one of the punishments visited upon the people when they had sinned (Leviticus 26: 14, 16). Driven to consternation, Elimelech the Ephrathite of Bethlehem decided to emigrate with his family to another land where food was more plentiful, and so traveled from Judah and settled in the highlands of Moab. For Naomi such an uprooting from her native home must have constituted a real sacrifice. Sincere in her faith, she loved the people of God and was strongly attached to the wonderful traditions of her race.

In taking the initiative to go to Moab — a foreign country — from Bethlehem, Naomi's husband stepped out of the will of God. If the famine was a judgment upon the nation, Elimelech should have repented, tried to have helped his fellow countrymen back to God, and prayed for the removal of the scourge (Psalm 34:9, 10, 17). One may argue that Elimelech was wise in taking Naomi and their two sons out of a famine-stricken area to another land where there was sufficient food. But Elimelech was a Hebrew, and as such had the promise, "In the days of famine, thou shalt be satisfied." Elimelech means, "My God is King." Had he truly believed God was his King, he would have stayed in Bethlehem, knowing that need could not throttle God who is able to furnish a table in the desert. But Elimelech belied the name he bore when he left Bethlehem — "the house of bread"— for Moab, meaning "waste" or "nothingness." With his family he went from a place where God was honored to another land so heathen in its ways.

Although the land of Moab may sound remote it was only some 30 miles from Bethlehem-Judah — a long enough journey in those far-off days when they had no transportation. The distance, however, was not one of *miles*, but of *mind*. As H. V. Morton puts it, "Distances in the Bible are not measured from one place to another, but from God. Naomi and her husband felt they were going into a far country because Moab was a land of foreign worship." Thus Bethlehem to Moab measured the distance from God to the alien worship of an alien country. What disturbed feelings Naomi must have had as, with her family, she found herself in a strange land, unknown, and with all the problems of establishing a home in repellant surroundings.

Her Change of Connections

It was not long before Naomi discovered the error in leaving Bethlehem for in the new and heathen land nothing but misfortune dogged her footsteps. Her two sons married women of Moab. Instead of helping to support their mother they took wives of the alien country they were in. The Jewish law forbade marriage outside of the nation. Naomi's husband, Elimelech, died. He had fled to Moab to escape a possible death from famine, and died in the midst of plenty leaving his wife a widow in a land of idolaters. Bereft of her husband, Naomi loses all heart to live on in a land of foreigners.

> When the stem dies, the leaf that grew
> Out of its heart must perish too.

Naomi became one of the widows whom Paul describes as being "desolate." To add to her desolation and grief, she also lost both of her sons and so Naomi "was left of her two sons and husband." By this time she was old and helpless with her widowed daughters-in-law, Ruth and Orpah, to shelter. As they were not of her people, nor of her faith in God, Moab true to its name, must have been empty, desolate and inhospitable to Naomi's grief-stricken, aching heart. Doubtless, Ruth and Orpah, whose hearts too had been emptied, were a source of comfort to Naomi, even though they knew that their marriage to Mahlon and Chilion was against her religious principles. So, as George Matheson fittingly expresses it —

> To all appearance Naomi was desolate. Husband and children were gone — the place of sojourn was a land of strangers — the voices of the old sanctuary were silent. Her heart and spirit were broken, her conscience was up in arms. The God of her fathers, she felt, had deserted her for her desertion of Him. She must retrieve the past — she must go back — back to the old soil, back to the favour of her God.

Bethlehem was Naomi's native land, and all her relatives and friends were there. Thus she left for Bethlehem, not so much because of her cup of sorrow in Moab, but because she had heard that "the Lord had visited his people in giving them bread."

Her Change of Character

Naomi was determined to return to Bethlehem alone, but her daughters-in-law left with her, possibly excited about a new start in a new land. But on the journey back, Naomi paused and pleaded with Ruth and Orpah to return to Moab. She knew what it would mean for them as Moabites to cross the boundary line, stressing the point that in Canaan there would be very little prospect of their finding husbands. What a moment that must have been as those three widows stood there at the parting of the ways. Orpah, without much ado, kissed Naomi, and then went back to her own idolatrous people, but Ruth clave unto Naomi and begged her to take her to Bethlehem (see RUTH).

As Naomi and Ruth entered the city together the thoughts of each must have been different. To Naomi there came flashing back thoughts of a happy youth and of a life at peace with God — thoughts which tended to aggravate her desolation. But for Ruth, there was the novelty and strangeness of a foreign people, a speech not fully understood, and youth's quest for new adventure. Naomi's arrival in the old community created a sensation. Quickly it passed from lip to lip that the well-known, beautiful and pleasant woman who had left ten years before was back, and as all the city met her they cried, "Is this Naomi?" Why the question form of their welcome? Did they detect a radical change in her appearance and demeanor? The repetition of her significant name irritated her as she cried —

> Call me not *Naomi* [pleasant, winsome, agreeable], call me *Mara* [bitter]: for the Almighty hath dealt very bitterly with me. I went out full, and the LORD hath brought me home again empty: why then call ye me Naomi, seeing the LORD hath testified against me, and the Almighty hath afflicted me?

Naomi could not bear the contradiction between the name she bore, and the person she was. Ten years in Moab with all its anguish, and also the loss of fellowship with God and His people had dried up her finer feelings. Once so sweet, Naomi was now sour, and blamed God for the poverty and desolation she had endured. But why chide God? Was not her cup of bitterness the result of the act of disobedience when, with her husband, she left Bethlehem for Moab? Had she stayed in her own land and maintained her trust in God, in spite of the famine, He would have undertaken for her and her family and brought them through. But the journey to Moab was a journey from God, and consequently her bitterness was the fruit of such an act of disobedience.

Her Change of Circumstances

Naomi was back in Bethlehem as a "returned empty." She went away to Moab with plenty but retraced her steps in poverty. How descriptive of her adverse circumstances is her lament! "I went out full, and the Lord hath brought me home again empty." Naomi and Ruth, then, clinging to each other, plunge into the poverty and solitariness facing them — but with a different outlook. Both women were widows and sufferers, but suffering old age often yields to hopelessness and despair, whereas suffering youth rebounds and seeks to be responsive to the life that is around. Thus Ruth felt the stir of excitement in her new surroundings. Naomi and she must eat, and knowing that her mother-in-law, whom Ruth surrounded with loving care, was too old to bend her back to work in the fields, Ruth goes out and secures work as a gleaner in the fields of Boaz. Under Jewish law the poor were allowed to glean in any harvest field, and Ruth qualified for the weary, humble task of following the reapers and gathering up the gleanings for Naomi and herself.

What romance followed is more fully told in our study on RUTH (which see). Boaz, related to Naomi's husband, was therefore connected by marriage to Ruth, and by Jewish custom, Boaz, as next of kin, could be regarded as Ruth's rightful betrothed. Naomi, with her bitterness now subdued and her former pleasant disposition restored, took a lively interest in the kindness of Boaz to Ruth, and advised her in the steps leading to her marriage to Boaz. The idyllic conclusion was reached as Naomi, through her tender boldness, saw Ruth lifted out of obscurity and poverty into marriage with a godly man, as well as a mighty man of wealth. For Naomi, the winter of desolation was past, and the time of the singing of birds had come. Although her natural hopes had perished, Naomi lived again in the life of her dear, sacrificial daughter-in-law, and there were loud rejoicings when Ruth's firstborn, Obed, was carried to Grandma Naomi. Now her daughter-in-law who loved her was better to Naomi "than seven sons." How lovingly she would nurse Ruth's child and bless God because, as Professor R. G. Moulton expressed it —

> The family she thought she had seen perish has been restored to the genealogies of Israel; for baby Obed lives to become the father of Jesse, and Jesse is father of the great King David. And in the genealogical tables of Matthew, the Moabitess who left her people for love of Naomi is duly named as an ancestress of the Messiah Himself.

NEHUSHTA

Scripture Reference — II Kings 24:8
Name Meaning — A piece of brass

Nehushta is allied to Nehushtan (II Kings 18:4). She was the daughter of Elnathan, a well-known Jerusalem man, and became the wife of the ungodly Jehoiakim, Josiah's eldest son (Jeremiah 26:22). When King Nebuchadnezzar subdued Jehoiakim's kingdom, his mother, Nehushta, followed him in captivity at Babylon. Nothing is said of the queen-mother's character. As her son emulated the evil ways of his father, it is assumed that the mother's influence was likewise corrupt.

NOADIAH

Scripture Reference — Nehemiah 6:14
Name Meaning — One to whom the Lord revealed Himself

Here we have a female character who contradicted the name she bore. She was a false prophetess, and stands over against Hulda who was a divinely inspired, true prophetess. Noadiah was an exceptional woman but most dangerous in her influence. She substituted the pseudo-ecstasy of her own feelings for the Spirit's direction through the Word of God. Noadiah is conspicuous as a companion, and possibly inspirer, of Sanballat and Tobiah in their opposition to Nehemiah whom they tried to terrorize. But the reformer never tried to debate and argue with the satanically-inspired woman and her evil-minded friends. He simply prayed, "My God, think thou upon Tobiah and Sanballat . . . and on the prophetess Noadiah . . . who would put me in fear." Prayer was answered. Noadiah's wiles were thwarted and Nehemiah finished the work of restoration.

Noadiah is also the name of a Levite in the time of Ezra (8:33).

NOAH

Scripture References—Numbers 26:33; 27:1
Name Meaning — Rest *or* comfort

Here we have another of the five daughters of Zelophehad. (See HOGLAH.) Noah is likewise the name of the son of Lamech, preacher of righteousness among the antediluvians who with his family escaped the Flood (Genesis 6).

OHOLIBAMAH (see AHOLIBAMAH)

ORPAH

THE WOMAN WHO REJECTED HER CHANCE

Scripture Reference — Ruth 1
Name Meaning — Various interpretations have been given of Orpah. Wilkinson says that by a not unusual change of letters it can be identified with Ophrah meaning, "a fawn, or young doe" and so is the feminine of Ephron, a Canaanitish

name, signifying a "roebuck or stag." Orpah is also said to mean "double-minded" which means to describe her dilemma when the crisis on that road to Bethlehem-Judah demanded a decision. Should she, like Ruth, go on to Bethlehem with Naomi, or return alone to Moab. James reminds us that a double-minded person is unstable in all his ways (1:8; 4:8). Other scholars assert that Orpah is derived from a Hebrew word for "neck" and so means "stiff-necked" or "stubborn" because of her turning back from following the other two widows (Ruth 1:4-14; 4:9, 10).

Family Connections — Of her pedigree we know nothing save that she married Chilion, the son of Elimelech and Naomi after they took up their abode in Moab. Because Ruth married the other son, Mahlon, Orpah became her sister-in-law. After Naomi lost her husband and two sons it is quite possible that both Orpah and Ruth lived in Naomi's home, but what a difference there was in the two young women of Moab, hence the personal decision of each when Naomi, going back to her own country, urged Orpah and Ruth to return to theirs.

Both had been brought into contact with the truth of Jehovah because of their relation by marriage to the sons of Elimelech and Naomi. But while Ruth opened her heart to the revelation of the true God, and was ready to say to Naomi, as she urged the two widowed maidens to return home, "Thy God shall be my God — thy people my people"; Orpah continued to embrace Moloch, the heathen god of Moab as the object of her worship. Kuyper suggests —

Naomi had often studied Orpah, and had frequently observed that beneath her apparent piety there lurked the unmistakable influence of her former, heathen tendencies.

Naomi was determined to put Orpah to conclusive test. But when that test came, Orpah failed. She looked at the aged, childless and embittered Naomi of whom she no doubt thought highly. She also saw Ruth determined to go all the way with Naomi into an uncertain future, and felt that a bird in the hand was worth two in the bush. So she made her choice in favor of the rich and prosperous Moab she knew. She was likewise aware that the Jews hated the Moabites and she preferred to be with her own kin and kind. Ruth said to Naomi, "Thy *God* shall be my *God*," but Orpah wanted nothing of Jehovah. She had left Moab along with Naomi and Ruth, but Moab was very much in her heart and so, after embracing Naomi, Orpah went back to her own people and to her own gods. After the farewell kiss, Orpah separated herself not only from Naomi and Ruth, but from the only true God. Back to Moab and Moloch Orpah went, and also into obscurity. She also vanished from the pages of sacred history. Calvary was enacted on that Bethlehem-Judah road. From the side of Naomi one woman went out into an abundant life, and the other retreated into darkness and despair. From the riven side of Jesus, one thief went to paradise, the other to perdition. (See RUTH and NAOMI.)

PENINNAH

Scripture References — I Samuel 1:2, 6
Name Meaning — Coral

By taking Peninnah as his second wife, Elkanah brought much sorrow to his first godly wife, Hannah. Peninnah has no record apart from the fact that she lived in Ramah, was the wife of Elkanah and the mother of his children. Because of her initial barrenness, Hannah became the target of Peninnah's jealousy, and her life was a constant fret through her rival's tantalizing. If ever there was a heartless woman it was Peninnah. Her provocation became intensified because of Elkanah's love and tenderness toward Hannah whose heart often smarted from Peninnah's jealous thrusts. But Hannah's patience, self-control and intercession prevailed and she became the mother of Samuel who was "more than a prophet" (compare HANNAH).

PERSIS

Scripture Reference — Romans 16:12
Name Meaning — One who takes by storm

Here we have an illustration of a name taken from a country for the Greek significance of Persis is "Persian" although there is no evidence that this Christian female worker in the Early Church at Rome was a Persian. Her name is apropos to her per-

son, and because of her intense labors in the Lord, she must have seized many opportunities of witness. Regardless of hindrances and difficulties, she fought the good fight of faith. Herbert F. Stevenson points out "a delicacy indicative of profound Christian courtesy" is seen in that "the Apostle adapts the phrase from 'my beloved' when dealing with two brethren to 'the beloved' when writing of Persis, 'which laboured much in the Lord.'" What a model of Christian conduct was the Apostle! (See MARY OF ROME.)

PHANUEL

Scripture Reference — Luke 2:36
Name Meaning — The face or vision or appearance of God

It is not certain whether Phanuel was the name of the father or the mother of Anna the prophetess who was the first to proclaim Jesus to be the Messiah. The name is identical with Penuel, the name Jacob gave to the place where he wrestled with the angel.

PHEBE, PHOEBE
THE WOMAN WHO WORE THE BADGE OF KINDNESS

Scripture Reference — Romans 16:1, 2
Name Meaning — Pure *or* radiant as the moon

We know nothing of this pious female who delivered Paul's "inestimable packet"— The Epistle to the Romans — to Rome. We just have the brief mention of her name and service. Phoebe, a devout Christian, bore without change and without reproach the name of the Moon-Goddess of the Greeks. The goddess Artemis, known by the common epithet "Phoebe," was supposed to have been identified with the light of the moon. But the Phoebe whom Paul so highly commended shone as a light for Jesus, the "Light of the World." That she must have been a woman of some consequence appears from the fact that she planned a long journey to Rome on business of her own, and offered to convey to the saints there Paul's letter — "an inspired masterpiece of logic which struck the keynote of orthodoxy for the universal Church through all the succeeding ages."

In some fifty words Paul gives us a beautiful cameo of this saintly servant of Christ for whom he urged the saints at Rome to do their utmost. The importance of her visit is indicated by the appeal of Paul to the Romans to "assist her in whatever matter she had need of." Phoebe was —

A Sister

As used by Paul, this designation implies a spiritual relationship. He calls the believing husband and wife, "the brother and the sister" (I Corinthians 7:15; 9:5). Young Timothy was his "son in the faith." Phoebe, then, was a member of a spiritual family in which the relationship is based upon the redemption of Christ and the regenerating work of the Holy Spirit (Galatians 4:4-7). Apart from natural relationships, no woman is my "sister" unless she shares my experience of God's saving grace through which alone we are made members of His redeemed family. How or when Phoebe became a Christian and a sister in the Lord, we are not told. What is evident is the manifestation of her sisterly love and labors among her sisters and brothers in Christ. "Our sister" is a term indicating her Christian status.

A Servant of the Church

Phoebe was not only a member of a spiritual family, but likewise a member of the visible church at Cenchrea when Paul arrived there on his third journey and from where he wrote Romans. Phoebe was not merely a confessing and active believer, she was also "a ministrant of *the Church*." The word for "servant" is *diakonos*, from which we have "deacon" or "deaconess." It is not certain whether such an official female Order as "Deaconess" was in vogue at that time. Phoebe, however, occupied such a position in the church, and as such could be a teacher of all female inquirers of the faith, and be active in the relief of the temporal needs of the poor among the flock. We can safely assume that Phoebe was one of the first, if not the first, of the noble band of deaconesses in the Christian Church. If hers was not an official ministry, it was certainly a most gracious and effective one, and she was indeed one of the forerunners of the vast army of women who have rendered such loyal service to Christ and His Church.

A Succourer of Many, and of Myself Also

The word Paul used for "succourer" — *prostatis* — is a most expressive one. It literally means "one who stands by in case of need." It is classical Greek describing a trainer in the Olympic games, who stood by the athletes to see that they were properly trained and not over-trained and rightly girded when they lined up for the signal. Moule translates the phrase, "She on her part has proved a stand-by (almost a *champion*, one who stands up for others) of many, aye, and of me among them." Phoebe was the unselfish, liberal helper or patroness of the saints, conspicuous for her works of charity and also hospitality. To quote Moule again —

> She had been a devoted and it would seem particularly *a brave* friend of converts in trouble, and of Paul himself. Perhaps in the course of her visits to the desolate she had fought difficult battles of protest, where she found harshness and oppression. Perhaps she had pleaded the forgotten cause of the poor, with a woman's courage, before some neglectful richer "brother."

As for the personal touch "a succourer . . . of *myself also*," it has been suggested that Paul had in mind the visit he paid to Cenchrea and, shaving his head took a Jewish vow (Acts 18:18). "The vow seems to point to a deliverance from danger to sickness in which Phoebe may have attended him." Because of her saintliness and practical works, Paul urged the believers in Rome to "receive her in the Lord, as becometh *saints*." All in the Lord are saints but some are more saintly than others. Godly Phoebe is witness to what Christ can accomplish through consecrated spinsterhood.

PRISCA (See PRISCILLA)

PRISCILLA
THE WOMAN WHO WAS FOREMOST IN SERVICE

Scripture References — Acts 18:2, 18, 26; Romans 16:3; I Corinthians 16:19; II Timothy 4:19

Name Meaning — Priscilla is the diminutive of Prisca, feminine of Prisca meaning "primitive," hence, "worthy, or venerable," as belonging to the good old time. This name is also found as a family name in the earliest Roman annals, and appears in the form "Prisca" in Paul's Second Epistle to Timothy (4:19). Cruden says Priscilla means "ancient, old-fashioned simplicity." It is also interesting to note that Aquila, Priscilla's husband, had the family name of the commander of a legion, for it means "eagle" — emblem of the Roman army. Both names are Roman. From the prominence given in Roman inscriptions and legends to the name Prisca it is concluded that she belonged to a distinguished Roman family.

Family Connections — Of Priscilla's background and parentage Scripture is silent. Doubtless, like her husband, she was born in Pontus. Both were Jews of Asia-Minor, and as such were expelled by Claudius from Rome, and in Corinth, Priscilla and Aquila became the honored and much-loved friends of Paul. In fact, they were the most distinguished among his fellow-helpers in the cause of Christ.

As Priscilla is always paired with her husband, Aquila, it is difficult to separate her and place her on a pedestal of her own. Their two hearts beat as one. Harmoniously, they labored together in the service of the church. They walked as one for they had mutually agreed to put Christ first. In the six references where both are mentioned, the name of Priscilla comes first in three instances, and Aquila first in the other three. They are never mentioned apart. Is there any significance attached to the fact that Aquila is not named first every time, but equally shares mention with his wife? A number of conjectures have been put forth why Priscilla comes first at all in the references to them both. Some writers suggest that she was the more energetic of the two, and perhaps had the stronger character. Dinsdale Young thinks that Priscilla may have been a believer before her husband, and that she won him for the Lord by her "chaste conversation," or that perhaps hers was a primacy of character and service, or a more conspicuous intellectual ability, or that she may have been of nobler birth and social quality than Aquila.

Personally, we see no reason at all for Priscilla's name coming first in half of the Scripture references to her, even though she may recall the wonderful prominence of women in early Christianity, and in martyrdom and service for Christ. If, in any way, Priscilla outshone Aquila, he must have praised God for such a precious gifted wife. Charles Kingsley makes one of his characters in *Westward Ho!* say, "In her he had found a treasure and knew what he had found." This must have been Aquila's sentiment also. Let us now look at the many fascinating facets of the union existing between these two old-time saints.

They Were One in Marital Bliss

What romance, love and blending of personalities are associated with such an ordinary phrase as "Aquila . . . with his wife Priscilla." How interesting it would be to know where and how they met, fell in love with each other and married! As nothing is said about any children that through the years came to grace their lovely home, we can take it that Priscilla was childless. From the record we have of Aquila and Priscilla their story is a beautiful idyll of home life. Together from the time of their marriage they are always named together, and were inseparable. What a pleasant picture of wedded love they present! To these two, wedlock was a divine ordinance and indissoluble union, and one which halved their sorrows and doubled their joys. They were not unequally yoked together but joined in the Lord.

In the truest sense, Aquila and Priscilla were "no more twain but one flesh," and all that they covenanted to accomplish together from the hour of their marriage vows was realized as the result of the perfect unity of the spiritual, nature of purpose, and of aim. As twin stars, Aquila and Priscilla were "bright with borrowed rays divine." They moved in one orbit and were united in all their labors as well as in their love. With Nabal and Abigail we have a sad illustration of husband and wife who had nothing in common, who were diametrically opposed to each other in character, and in whom sordidness and sublimity were associated. But with Aquila and Priscilla it was so different, for like Zacharias and Elisabeth they, too, were "both righteous" and like them, manifested a union, idyllic in its full-orbed loveliness and charm. Because the Bible is everybody's Book, it is the married people's Book revealing how the Aquilas and Priscillas can live happily together.

They Were One in the Lord

Further, this Christian couple were one in their experience of God's saving power, and so became one in their holy zeal for the Saviour, and in their service for His church. They were partners in faithful endeavors, not only to present Christ by lip, but also in the excellency of their walk and conversation. The supreme need of our critical time is not for more preachers, but for more lay workers like Aquila and Priscilla ready to exemplify Christ in the common round of life. Paul first discovered this godly pair when he came to Corinth from Athens where they had been driven by the edict of Claudius against the Jews. What an arrestive phrase that is, "Paul *found* a certain Jew named Aquila . . . with his wife Priscilla" (Acts 18:2). What a find that was! Fewer, grander discoveries have ever been made. "Paul was a wonderful discoverer. He was always finding, now a truth, now a grace, now a personality. He was ever finding because he was ever seeking." How many have we found for the Lord?

Just when Aquila and Priscilla became the Lord's, Scripture does not say. Had they been unconverted when Paul found them it would have been impossible for them to remain so, with Paul living in their home for eighteen months, and their contact with the Apostle's constant teaching of the Word of God in the nearby synagogue. The inference is that when Paul met them they were firmly established in the Christian faith, and that in them he found two saintly souls after his own heart. Both Aquila and Priscilla as Hebrews were drenched in Old Testament Scriptures and had found in the promised Messiah, their Saviour and Lord, and were thus able to enter into Paul's remarkable ministry during his stay in Corinth. With honored Paul as their guest, what times the three of them must have had together in prayer and meditation upon the Word. What spiritual knowledge Aquila and Priscilla must have acquired from the Early Church's greatest Bible teacher. Theirs must have been a thorough theological course.

They Were One in Secular Occupation

Luke informs us that "by their occupation they were tentmakers" (Acts 18:3). This must have added to Paul's delight in living with Aquila and Priscilla for he was of the same craft, and at times supported himself in this way (Acts 20:34; I Thessalonians 2:9; II Thessalonians 3:8). When not preaching and teaching we can imagine Paul, Aquila and Priscilla sitting together in Aquila's shop as they plied their needles and fashioned or repaired tents. Aquila and Priscilla shared the duties of their workshop. They were not ashamed of manual toil. Proud of their craft, we can believe that the product of their joint labors was known for its excellent quality. The tents from their establishment made of honest goat's hair, sewn with honest thread, seamed and disposed of at an honest price, gave Aquila and Priscilla a wide reputation. They were in the tent business first of all, for the glory of God.

As Jews, Paul, Aquila and Priscilla were taught the tent trade when they were young, for the teaching of rabbis was that the father who failed to teach his son a trade educated him to be a thief. Jesus Himself was taught a trade and was thus known not only as "the carpenter's son" but also as, "the Carpenter." We are thus shown the dignity of labor. The craft of Aquila and Priscilla may have been a common one, but it was approached in an uncommon spirit. Their toil was honorable and they honored God in their toil, even as Jesus did when for long years He worked at the bench. Do we turn our particular craft to good account for the Lord? "A particular craft will throw one into association with a particular class of persons, and if one is alert and always about the Master's business, he may find in his particular calling a special opportunity for testimony from which others, not of the same craft, are circumstantially excluded."

They Were One in Their Friendship for Paul

As we read the references to Aquila and Priscilla we cannot fail to be impressed with the affection they had for Paul, and of the way he held them in high esteem. Of all the Apostle's co-workers none were to prove themselves as loyal and helpful as these two. As a lonely man, and in constant need of friendship and comfort, none cared for Paul as that home-making couple provided for him. Their oneness in spiritual things made Aquila and Priscilla so precious to the heart of Paul who designated them "my fellow-workers in Christ Jesus" (Romans 16:3, ASV). They were *workers* not *shirkers* in the divine vineyard, and their labors with and for the Apostle were not in vain, seeing they wrought "in Christ Jesus." They shared Paul's itinerant ministry. They went to Ephesus and to Rome assisting their friend in every way. As missionaries they scattered the good seed of the Gospel wherever they went (Acts 18:18; Romans 16:3; II Timothy 4:19).

This is why Paul was generous in his recognition and acknowledgment of indebtedness to these godly souls, who, for love of Christ labored with him so devotedly in the Gospel. When Paul left Corinth after a residence of a year and a half in the home of Priscilla and Aquila, they left with him for Ephesus. After some time he "left them there," and sailed to Jerusalem. Being "left there" was in the providence of God as we shall see when we come to their contact with Apollos there. In the furtherance of the Gospel Paul tells us that Priscilla and Aquila laid down their own necks for his sake, earning thereby not only his heartfelt gratitude, but also that of all the Gentile churches which Paul had founded. Moule translates this passage, "For my life's sake submitted their own throats to the knife" (Romans 16:3, 4)—referring to some stern crisis otherwise utterly unknown to us but well-known in heaven. In some way or another, possibly during the great Ephesian riots, they had saved the man whom the Lord consecrated to the service of the Gentile world.

The way Paul describes their readiness to sacrifice themselves on his behalf conveys the thought that they had been exposed to martyrdom for his sake. He never forgot the self-sacrifice of Priscilla and Aquila who, for the most part of their lives worked at their trade as tentmakers but who were capable of noble deeds equal to the occasion. In perilous circumstances they exhibited a martyr-like self-sacrifice, and thereby emulated the example of the Master whom they so faithfully served. Can we say that we are ready to lay down our necks for apostolic causes? Must we not confess with shame our effort to save our necks as much as possible.

While the last mention of Aquila and Priscilla is to be found in Paul's Second Epistle to Timothy where they were back at Ephesus about the year A.D. 66 (II Timothy 4:19), there is a tradition to the effect that they ultimately laid down their lives for Christ's sake. The 8th of July is the day set apart for them in the martyrology of the Roman Church when it is said the faithful couple were led out beyond the walls and beheaded. If this is so it is not difficult to fill in the details of the pathetic picture. Aquila and Priscilla had loved each other through the years, and together had served the Lord so loyally. Now with eyes so full of unfading love, as if to say to each other "Farewell, fear not!" they were ready for the flash of the blade that sent them home to God, and to eternal fellowship with Paul, Apollos, and others they had so signally helped.

They Were One in Their Profound Knowledge of Scripture

One of the most impressive aspects of the spiritual influence of Priscilla and Aquila was the way in which these two simple souls with a deep knowledge of Christian truth were used to open the eyes of a great Alexandrian divine to the reality of the Gospel. The eloquent and fervent Apollos with all his brilliance and power suffered a sorry limitation as a preacher. He knew only "the baptism of John" (Acts 18:25, 26). He knew nothing of salvation through the cross and the accompaniments of salvation. The larger truths of the Gospel of Redemption were as yet unknown to him. Priscilla and Aquila followed the crowds who went to hear this most popular and persuasive preacher.

As they listened, Priscilla and her husband detected the negative defects of the preaching of Apollos. He taught no positive error, denied no essential of the faith. What he preached was true as far as it went. Apollos knew the truth, but not all the truth, and so in the quiet way, with all humility, Priscilla and Aquila set about correcting the apparent deficiency of Apollos. Inviting him to their home they passed no word of criticism on what they had heard him preach but with consummate tact instructed him Biblically in the truth of the crucified, risen and glorified Saviour. "They expounded unto him the way of God more carefully" (ASV).

What was the result of that Bible course which Apollos received from those two godly, Spirit-enlightened believers? Why, Apollos became so mighty in the Gospel that he was called an apostle. In fact, he became so effective as a true gospel preacher that some of the Corinthians put him before Peter and Paul. But all that Apollos became he owed, under God, to the quiet instruction of Priscilla and Aquila. In Apollos, Christ gained a preacher whose spiritual influence was second only to Paul himself. Says Alexander Whyte in his chapter dealing with Aquila, Priscilla and Apollos—

> I admire all the three so much, that I really do not know which to admire the most; Aquila and Priscilla in their quite extraordinary wisdom and tact and courage, and especially love; or Apollos in his still more extraordinary humility, modesty, and mind of Christ.

If we cannot be great, by God's grace we may be the means of making others great. Quiet, unobtrusive Andrew little knew when he brought his brother Peter to Christ that he would become the mighty Apostle to the Jews. As husband and wife, and humble tentmakers, Aquila and Priscilla greatly enriched the ministries of Paul and Apollos whom God, in turn, used to establish churches.

They Were One in the Service of the Church

Paul gives us a still fuller insight into the passionate desire of Aquila and Priscilla to bind the saints together in fellowship. To the Corinthians he wrote, "Aquila and Priscilla salute you much in the Lord, *with*

the church in their house." In Romans, the Apostle sent his greetings to them and to "the church that is in their house." At stated times they gathered the followers of Christ for worship, meditation and remembrance at the Family Altar, and thereby invested "the domestic circle with a peculiar sanctity as the germ of that great organism which we call the Church of God."

In those apostolic days, poverty and persecution made separate buildings for worship almost impracticable, and so private, sanctified homes became the house of God. Aquila and Priscilla consecrated their home to God, as a gathering place for the saints. Because of this they became doubly sanctified by the Word of God and prayer. If such a dedicated home is "the masterpiece of the applied Gospel," should we not be careful that nothing enters our home to "unchurch" it? Perhaps the church of God could become a mightier spiritual force in the world if she could return to upper chambers and churches in the home.

As we take farewell of Aquila and Priscilla we remind ourselves that in the history of Christianity the truly great characters have always been simple and humble men and women. The God who made the mountains also made the valleys, and both are needed. Paul, ever conscious of his indebtedness to inconspicuous persons, paid just tribute to Aquila and Priscilla. Whether we are prominent or otherwise, may we be found serving God to the limit of our ability. How much we owe to the quiet and useful lives of the world's Aquilas and Priscillas, as well as its more conspicuous saints we shall never know this side of heaven! The humble tentmakers we have thought of are, "a bracing and cheering study for Christians of every type and condition. They are especially a pertinent ensample for Christian husbands and wives. It will be a true loss if we neglect to contemplate this spiritually-minded pair who walked in all the commandments and ordinances of the Lord, blameless."

PUAH

Scripture Reference — Exodus 1:15
Name Meaning — Child bearing *or* joy of parents

Alarmed over the rapid increase of the

population of Israelites in Egypt, Pharaoh ordered two Egyptian midwives to destroy all male children as soon as they were born (Exodus 1:15-20). He would never have employed Hebrew women to destroy the males of their own nation. The answer of the two named midwives, Puah and Shiprah, to Pharaoh's anger when he discovered that his cruel edict was not being carried out, implies that they were used to wait upon Egyptian women who only employed them in difficulty at childbirth (Exodus 1:19). Hebrew women seldom employed midwives for they were more "lively," or had far easier births than the Egyptians.

Puah and Shiprah are Egyptian names. Aben Ezra, the ancient Jewish historian, says that these two women "were chiefs over all the midwives, who were more than 500." As superintendents of such a large staff to which they had been appointed by the Egyptian government, Pharaoh ordered them to carry out his terrible command just as he would give orders to any other of his officials. As it is likely that only the chief Hebrews could afford the service of midwives, probably the order of Pharaoh only applied to them. Although Egyptians by birth, it would seem as if they had embraced the Hebrew faith, for we are told that Puah and Shiprah "feared God" (Exodus 1:21).

Receiving the royal command to commit murder, these two loyal, vigorous, middle-aged women were caught between two fires. Whom should they obey? The God of the Hebrews in whom they had come to believe, or the tyrannical king of Egypt? True to their conscience and honored calling they knew it would conflict with the divine command to kill, and so "saved the men children alive." Thus, they obeyed God rather than man, and in so doing brought upon their heads the rage of Pharaoh. Confronting his anger, Puah and Shiprah took refuge in a partial truth. They said that because Jewish women had easy deliveries, their children were born before they could reach them and assist the mothers in labor. Cognizant as He was of the partial truth the two midwives told, God knew all about the crisis behind it, and commended Puah and Shiprah for their courage of faith. They had risked their lives for many Jewish

infants. Such an act was meritorious in the eyes of the Lord, and He honorably rewarded them by building them houses. Fausset suggests that the nature of such a reward consisted in the two midwives marrying Hebrews and becoming mothers in Israel (II Samuel 7:11, 27). Puah and Shiprah are striking witnesses against the scandalous practice of abortion, which several nations have legalized.

RACHEL
THE WOMAN IN WHOM ROMANCE AND TRAGEDY WERE BLENDED

Scripture References — Genesis 29; 30; 31; 33:1, 2, 7; 35:16-26; 46:19, 22, 25; 48:7; Ruth 4:11; I Samuel 10:2; Jeremiah 31:15; Matthew 2:18

Name Meaning — Rachel was the first person in the Bible to have a proper name derived from the brute creation. Wilkinson remarks, "that, for the most part, the formation of a human name from that of an animal is traceable to some peculiarity either observed or desired in an individual, which would thus be most intelligently expressed in a rude and simple age." Rachel, the name of Jacob's beloved wife means "ewe," employed more or less as a title of endearment, just as the word "lamb" is among ourselves. Laban, accustomed to tenderly nursing the weak ewes as they were born, thought "ewe" to be a fitting name for his second daughter.

Family Connections — Rachel was the daughter of Laban, the son of Bethuel and Rebekah's brother. Rachel became the second wife of her cousin Jacob and the mother of his two sons, Joseph and Benjamin. (Compare material under LEAH.)

As we have already shown, the characteristic feature of the Bible in pairing certain individuals, compelling us to compare and contrast the lives they lived together, makes it difficult to separate any couple and deal exclusively with one or the other. Invariably, as in the instance of Leah and Rachel, their lives were lived out in close association. Yet we must try and isolate Rachel from her sister, for the galaxy of the Bible's famous women would be incomplete without such a star. Surely, the much-loved wife of Jacob, and mother of Joseph, Israel's saviour, and also Benjamin, could not have been an ordinary woman even though she shone with reflected glory. From the many references to Rachel we have the following facets of her life and character —

She Was Naturally Beautiful

It would seem as if Rachel had all the loveliness of her aunt, Rebekah. The sacred record speaks of her as "beautiful and well favoured" (attractive). Her sister Leah was "tender-eyed," meaning some form of eye blemish making her less appealing than Rachel who prepossessed Jacob physically. Seeing her in all her natural charm and beauty, Jacob loved her. Although beauty may be only skin deep, it nevertheless wins admiration. The Hebrew form of Rachel's description (Genesis 29:17) suggests that she was "beautiful in form and beautiful in look." That God does not look upon the outward appearance merely is evidenced by the fact, of which Ellicott reminds us, that "it was not Rachel, with her fair face and well-proportioned figure, and her husband's lasting love, that was the mother of the progenitor of the Messiah, but the weary-eyed Leah."

She Was Divinely Guided

While, as the younger daughter, it was Rachel's task to go to the well and draw water for her father's sheep, it was no mere coincidence that she went that day when Jacob arrived. She might have been sick or indisposed, and if Leah had had to go for the water *that* day, what a different story might have been written of Jacob, as well as of the history of Israel. Fleeing from his home to Haran, Jacob met God at Bethel and left it "lifting up his feet" (Genesis 29:1, margin), implying a lighthearted alacrity as he continued his journey with the divine promise in his heart, "I am with thee, and will keep thee in all places whither thou goest" (Genesis 28:15). Thus, with the assurance of the divine presence and guidance as a guarantee of favor and safety he met the shepherds who told Jacob of Rachel (Genesis 29:6) — the name that was to charm his heart the rest of his life. That meeting between Jacob and Rachel

was of God, and it was His providence that ordered the first glimpse of each other at the well. We are apt to forget that often the most seemingly ordinary incidents in life are as much of the divine plan as the smallest parts of a watch, and upon these smallest parts of the plan all the others depend. Our steps, when ordered by the Lord, lead to great issue.

As far as Jacob and Rachel were concerned that meeting was unforeseen and unpremeditated. "A divinely directed life is often shaped by circumstances that human prescience could not have foreseen." As soon as they met it was love at first sight, at least with Jacob. The first sight of his cousin's beautiful face and figure cast a spell over him and he "kissed Rachel, and lifted up his voice, and wept." As she was his cousin, Jacob was not prevented from kissing Rachel by the etiquette of the East, which was the home of warm feelings and demonstrative actions. Probably the tears Jacob shed were those of gratitude to God in bringing him to his mother's relatives, and also tears of joy because he knew instinctively that the lovely maiden he kissed would be his wife. Jacob removed the stone from the mouth of the well, helped Rachel water the flock, acquainted her with his story, and was taken home by an excited Rachel where he was hospitably welcomed.

George Matheson draws our attention to the interesting fact that the meeting of Jacob and Rachel is "the first courtship in the Bible growing out of a cousinly relationship—in other words, as having its roots in a previous friendship." Jacob, a poet by nature, dazzled by Rachel's beauty, broke out into a deep love *before* marriage — a thought to ponder in these days when young people are being told that pre-marital experiences are quite in order, to test whether they are suited for each other. Jacob was to prove that the typical trial of love is waiting, and he had to wait many a year before the one whom he loved, as soon as he saw her, became his wife.

She Was Deeply Loved

We are distinctly told that "Jacob loved Rachel," and that the seven years he served Laban for his daughter, "seemed to him but a few days, because of the love he had for her" (Genesis 29:18, 20). Even after Jacob found that he had been deceived by Laban and had been given Leah instead, he served and waited for Rachel another seven years because "he loved her more than Leah" (29:30). From the first moment Jacob saw Rachel he loved her, and she became his choice as a wife. But while she alone was in the heart of her lover, "the real choice was not Jacob's but God's, and for the first place God had chosen Leah." In his second marriage, Rachel only received half of Jacob, the other half had been given to her rival sister.

While Leah might have had "the keys of Jacob's house, Rachel had the keys of his heart. Leah seems to have influenced his judgment: Rachel never ceased to hold his love. Leah bore Jacob six stalwart sons, Rachel was the mother of only two: but the sons of Rachel were dearer to him than the sons of Leah." Jacob is outstanding among male lovers in the Bible for the true, romantic, abiding love he bore for Rachel. Whether such a deep and ardent love was reciprocated we are not told. The Bible has no reference to Rachel's love for Jacob. She appears as a somewhat placid character. We have no record of any grief she felt, or protest she made when she discovered how Leah had taken the first place in Jacob's life. We would like to believe that Rachel's love for Jacob was as romantic as his was for her, and that also the years she had to wait for him seemed but a few days because of her heart's affection for Jacob.

She Was Cruelly Deceived

The deceit perpetrated by Laban upon Jacob, Leah and Rachel, adds color to the record. Laban cunningly beguiled Jacob into marriage with Rachel's elder sister and less beautiful sister. Jacob had accepted Laban's terms to take no wages for his labor in his fields, and at the end of the seven years' waiting expected to receive Rachel. In the gloom the bride appears closely veiled, according to custom. The ceremony is performed and the wedded pair return to their bridal chamber. But in the light of early morning Jacob discovers Laban's duplicity — a duplicity in which Leah must have had a part. How shocked Jacob must have been to behold the plain-looking, undesired Leah instead of the face of his dearest Rachel.

Leah, by her father's deceit, had stolen her sister's blessing. Isaac had blessed Jacob, believing him to be Esau, and now Jacob marries Leah believing her to be Rachel. In the moment of his surprised discovery did Jacob remember how he had stolen his brother's birthright by covering himself with a hairy skin and venison-smell, and making himself appear as Esau? Was this a retributive providence for his own deception of his blind and dying father?

Laban condoned his unrighteous act by declaring that in those times the younger daughter should not be given in marriage before the first-born. He should have told Jacob this when he covenanted to serve the first seven years for Rachel, or before the marriage anyhow. Jacob then became involved in two marriages, which were not deemed unfitting in an age when polygamy was tolerated even by godly men. For another seven years Jacob toiled bravely on, true love enabling him to persevere until Rachel was his. What interests us is the absence of any recorded protest on Rachel's part against her father's deception! Why did she not cry out when she saw that Leah, instead of herself, was being given to Jacob? If Rachel had resentment at the hour of marital vows between Jacob and Leah, she must have suppressed it. Why was she so placid amid such a calamity, at least for the man who loved her so deeply? Unmurmuringly, she goes on waiting for another seven years, ere she is able to share Jacob with the woman who by that time had borne him many children. Perhaps the deep, unchanging love Jacob had for Rachel found little echo from her own heart.

She Was Lamentably but Not Finally Barren

Once Rachel became Jacob's second wife, her continued barrenness created an unreasonable and impatient fretfulness within her soul. Seeing Leah's many happy children made her jealous. What anguish is wrapped up in the phrase, "But Rachel was barren" (Genesis 29:31). Says Donald Davidson, "Rachel would taunt Leah on not having the love of her husband, while

Leah would find revenge in the childlessness of her rival." Rachel's whole being was bound up in the desire to become a mother, so she cried to Jacob, "Give me children, or else I die" (30:1). Rachel should have cried to God instead of Jacob whose anger was kindled against her for her impossible request. Certainly he loved Rachel with a true and tender love, and indignation because of her, must have been a source of bitterness. He should have thought of the bitterness of Rachel's disappointment, and quietly pointed out to her the withholdings of Providence.

Poor, childless Rachel was not forgotten by the Lord for He remembered her and opened her womb (30:22-24). She gave birth to a son, and thereby took away her reproach. The grateful mother became a prophetess for she called her baby Joseph, which means, "The Lord shall add to me another son" — which was not merely the language of desire but the prediction of a seer. Of all the children of Jacob, Joseph became the godliest and greatest. Renowned as the saviour of Israel he stands out as the most perfect type in the Bible of Him who was born of woman to become the Saviour of the world.

She Was Secretly Idolatrous

The time had come for Laban and Jacob to part. While Laban had learned by experience that he had been blessed for Jacob's sake the patriarch likewise had been blessed, and with his wives, children and rich possessions found he could no longer live at Haran. So he set out for his old home, and took with him all that God had given him. Laban was loathe to lose the diligent partner who had worked with him so faithfully for twenty years. While Laban was absent for a few days caring for his many sheep, Jacob gathered all his family, cattle and possessions and secretly left. Returning home and finding Jacob gone, Laban set out to overtake the travelers. Catching up with them Laban took Jacob to task not only for leaving so secretly but also for stealing some of his household goods and gods.

It was this accusation that revealed Rachel, lovely as she was, in an unlovely light. Although the wife of the heir to God's promises, she evidently was a secret believer in old heathen superstitions. She stole the household gods, and when Laban sought for them among the goods of Jacob, she had them hid beneath her person. In her cunning in hiding the small images in human form used for divination and which had a religious significance (Judges 17:5; 18:14, 17, 18, 20, etc.), Rachel manifested something of her father's duplicity. It was not until Jacob reached memorable Bethel that he buried those strange idols under the oak at Shechem. Those lifeless deities, the size of a miniature doll, were regarded as "indispensable evidence as to the rights and privileges of family ownership. Hence, Laban's query, 'Wherefore hast thou stolen my gods?'" (31:30). Because of his superstitious beliefs, Rachel likely stole the gods to insure a prosperous journey. Such relics from the old home would guarantee all continuance of the old good fortune. Jacob's trust was in the great God at the top of a ladder with its ascending and descending angels, but Rachel wanted humbler gods that she could see. Further, those household divinities suggest the laxity of true worship in the home.

Thus, although living in a polygamous state, maritally, Rachel was also guilty of religious polygamy. There was a professed relationship to the God of Israel, yet at the same time she was married to idols (30:23, 24). Rachel had no right to carry away what was not her own. Had she known that those stolen images would become a terrible snare in Jacob's family, perhaps she would not have taken them (35:1-5). Images and relics have always been dangerous elements in connection with true religious worship. How prone the human heart is to forsake the spiritual for the material, the Unseen for the seen and temporal! May ours be the constant desire to obey the apostolic injunction to keep ourselves from idols! (I John 5:21).

She Was Tragically Taken

We now come to a feature peculiar of Rachel as a mother. Hers is the first recorded instance in the Bible of death in childbirth and her sepulchral pillar is the first on record in the Bible. It would seem as if Rachel had surrendered her idolatry before the death stroke fell on her. The hallowing influences of divine blessing on her husband and his seed as the result of Bethel, begot within her a sense of divine awareness. Young Joseph's great reverence for God bespeaks of Rachel's godly training in his boyhood years. Jacob's love for her and his stronger faith (35:2-4) helped to purify her character and she lived on long after her death in the life of her noble son.

While Jacob and his host were on the way from Bethel to Ephrath, tragedy overtook Jacob when Rachel died in giving birth to her second son, Benjamin (35:16). She had named her first son Joseph, meaning, "The Lord shall add to me another son," which prediction was fulfilled when Benjamin was born. How often the brightest anticipations of life are clouded by the gloom of the grave! Rachel prayed for children, but the beginning of her second son's life was the ending of her own. What travail and anguish are resident in the phrase, "Rachel travailed, and she had hard labour . . . she died" (Genesis 35:16, 18). Facing death she called her son, Benoni, meaning "son of sorrow." Suffering had brought her to the gates of death and the gift she coveted proved to be a crushing burden under which she sank. But Jacob chose another name for their child and called him Benjamin, signifying, "the son of the right hand," and showered much affection upon the motherless child.

The last cry Rachel uttered as she died was "Benoni" — son of sorrow — and it is in the spirit of this Benoni that the Bible portrays Rachel. When Jacob came to die in extreme old age, he spoke sorrowfully of the early loss of his beloved Rachel who through her years had been caught in a web of much sorrow and unhappiness. He had loved her at first and ever afterward. Brokenhearted, Jacob buried Rachel on the way to Bethlehem, and set up a pillar over her grave. In "his heart that grave remained ever green, and he never ceased in fancy to deck it with flowers." In a previous grave at Shechem he had buried Rachel's idols, and with them her superstitious beliefs. Now he stands at the grave containing the dust of his beloved one and the pillar he placed over it was a sad memento of a broken heart. In later days Rachel's tomb

became a conspicuous landmark (I Samuel 10:2). With Leah, Rachel had helped to build the house of Israel (Ruth 4:11). One day Rachel's precious dust will be reanimated and she will sit down with the glorified with "Jacob in the kingdom of heaven."

She Was Symbolically Recalled

Rachel's cry for children was prophetic of the slaughter of the innocents when Christ was born (Matthew 2:16-18). Jeremiah pictures Rachel as rising from the grave to weep over the children being carried away to Babylon, never to return (Jeremiah 31:15). Thus the "Benoni" of Rachel's heart as she died has been re-echoed throughout the entire history of Israel. Often it does seem as if tragedy triumphs, but the key to the mystery of sorrow can be found in the words of the church which for centuries has been singing for Rachel whom Jacob loved—

Sad-eyed Rachel, do not weep,
  Your children die as martyrs go;
They are the first-born of the seed
  Which from your blood began to grow;
In spite of tyranny's dread days
  They bloom in glory to God's praise.

RAHAB

The Woman God Took From the Dunghill

Scripture References — Joshua 2:1, 3; 6:17-25; Matthew 1:5; Hebrews 11:31; James 2:25

Name Meaning — The first part of Rahab— "Ra," was the name of an Egyptian god. As an Amorite, Rahab belonged to an idolatrous people, and had a name meaning "insolence," "fierceness," or "broad," "spaciousness."

Family Connections — While Rahab's parents, brothers and sisters were alive at the time of her association with the spies Joshua sent out, we are not given any of their names (2:13). Some of the ancient Jewish fathers who held her in high reputation reckoned that she was the wife of Joshua himself, but in the royal genealogy of Jesus, Rahab is referred to as being the wife of Salmon, one of the two spies she sheltered. In turn, she became the mother of Boaz, who married Ruth from whose son, Obed, Jesse the father of

David came, through whose line Jesus was born (Matthew 1:5, where the ASV reads, "Salmon begat Boaz of Rahab" — not Rachab). Salmon was a prince of the house of Judah, and thus, Rahab, the one time heathen harlot, married into one of the leading families of Israel and became an ancestress of our Lord, the other foreign ancestresses being Tamar, Ruth and Bathsheba. The gratitude Salmon felt for Rahab ripened into love, and when grace erased her former life of shame he made her his wife. Jerome's comment of the inclusion of the four foreign women in Matthew's genealogy is suggestive —

> In it none of the holy women are included, only those whom the Scriptures blame, in order that He who came in behalf of sinners, Himself being born of sinners, might destroy the sins of all.

Both Jewish and Christian writers have tried to prove that Rahab was a different woman from the one whom the Bible always speaks of as a "harlot." To them it was abhorrent that such a disreputable person should be included in our Lord's genealogy and by Paul, as a woman of faith, and so her story has been distorted in order to further a scheme of salvation based upon human goodness. Although man's sense of refinement may be shocked, the fact remains that Rahab, Tamar and Bathsheba were sinful women who were purged by God, and had their share in the royal line from which Jesus sprang.

It has been suggested that the word "harlot" can be translated "innkeeper," thus making Rahab the landlady of a wayside tavern. Guesses have been made that she had been a concubine, such as Hagar and Zilpah had been, but that in Jericho she was a reputable woman identified with a respectable business. The Bible, however, makes no attempt to smooth over the unpleasant fact that Rahab had been a harlot. Endeavoring to understand her character, we have —

Her Sin

Three times over Rahab is referred to as "the harlot," and the Hebrew term *zoonah* and the Greek word *porne* have at no time meant anything else but "harlot"—a woman who yields herself indiscriminately to every man approaching her. Rahab indulged in venal wantonness as traveling merchants came her way and were housed in her ill-famed abode. Evidently Rahab had her own house and lived apart from her parents and family. Although she never lost her concern for her dear ones, perhaps she was treated as a moral leper. We are told that prostitution was not regarded with the same horror then, as now, but the Bible with one voice speaks of harlotry with moral revulsion and social ostracism.

Rahab's house was built against the town wall with the roof almost level with the ramparts, and with a stairway leading up to a flat roof that appears to be a continuation of the wall. Thus, the people of Jericho knew all about the men who entered and left such a disreputable house. While her name came to be sanctified and ennobled, both Paul and James affix the label to her name, *Rahab the harlot*. She still carried the evil, distinguishing name, thus declaring the peculiar grace of the transforming power of God. How Rahab came to forsake her evil career we are not told! Like many a young girl today perhaps she found the restrictions of her respectable home too irksome. She wanted a freer life, a life of thrill and excitement, away from the drab monotony of the home giving her birth and protection. So, high-spirited and independent she left her parents, set up her own apartment with dire consequences. Frequently women like Rahab are more often sinned against than sinners. Man's lust for the unlawful is responsible for harlotry.

Her Scheme

It was from some of the travelers Rahab entertained and sinned with, that she came to learn the facts of the Exodus of Israel, the miracle of the Red Sea, and the overthrow of Sihon and Og. So, when the two spies from Joshua sought cover in her house, she knew that sooner or later the king of Jericho would get to know of the accommodation she gave them. Here were two men, different from other men who came seeking her favors. These were men of God, not idolaters, bent on one mission, namely, the overthrow of the enemies of His people, and brilliantly she planned their protection and escape. The flax that she spread on her roof and the scarlet cord she used as a sign indicated that Rahab manufactured linen and also dyed it. If only, like Lydia, she had kept to such an honorable occupation, what a different story would have been hers.

Rahab's skillful scheme succeeded. The two Jewish spies were in desperate straits, seeing the Amorite pursuers were hot on their trail, but Rahab, although her safety and patriotism as an Amorite would be assured if she informed against the spies, decided to hide and preserve them. Seeing their hunted and dreaded look, Rahab assuredly said, "Fear not, I will not betray you nor your leader. Follow me," and tak-. ing them up to the flat roof of her house, bade the men cover themselves completely with a pile of flax lying there to dry. Shortly after, when the pursuers had tracked the two spies to Rahab's house, she met them with a plausible excuse that they were there but had left by way of the Eastern Gate. If they doubted her word, they could come in and search her house. But off the pursuers went to catch up with their prey, not knowing that the spies were being befriended by Rahab. As soon as the way was clear, under cover of night, she let the spies down from the window in the wall and, knowing the country, guided the spies in the best way to escape capture.

There are one or two features associated with this clever plan of Rahab which are worthy of notice. First of all, idolater though she had been, with a phase of immorality associated with her idolatrous life, she witnessed to a remarkable understanding of the sovereignty of the true God for she said to the spies —

> I know that the LORD hath given you the land, and that your terror is fallen upon us. . . . The LORD, your God he is God in heaven above, and in earth beneath (Joshua 2:9-11).

Harlot though Rahab had been, intuition from above had been given her that the spies were men of God, the forerunners of His people who were to execute His will, and that to take sides with them was to take sides with God Himself.

Further, there was in Rahab's mind, no matter how faintly understood, a distinct call from God, that she was being singled out from her own idolatrous people to aid the God she had a growing conception of. Her faith of this God who worked great wonders was altogether marvelous and singular. It was such a call that made her willing to sacrifice her own nation — an act which would have been otherwise treasonable. Does not her confession of God's power and purpose, and her service for the spies indicate that she knew the race of which she was part was accursed of God for its crimes and idolatry, and that she wished to be separated from such a doomed people, and identified with the people of God? The declaration of faith given by this Canaanite woman places her in a unique position among the women of the Bible.

Her Sacrifice

When Rahab hid the spies, put those who sought them on a false trail and helped the spies to escape and melt away into the shadows of night, and lay concealed until they could reach Joshua with their report, she took her life in her own hands. We cannot but admire her courage and willingness to risk her own neck. Had those spies been discovered hiding in her house, she would have died at the hands of the king of Jericho. Yet with a calm demeanor, and without the slightest trace of inner agitation, she met the searchers and succeeded in setting them out on a false trail. By her act Rahab was actually betraying her own country, and for such treason certain death would have been hers had she been found out. To hide spies was a crime punishable with death. Seeing the faces of the spies filled with fear, Rahab assured their hearts that she was on their side, and in spite of the sacrifice involved said, "I will not betray you. Follow me!" By military law the spies were likewise liable to instant death because of the threat of war, and Rahab, willing to do all in her power to protect her nation's enemies, faced a like terrible end. How gloriously daring was her faith, and how richly rewarded she was for her willingness to sacrifice her life in a cause she knew to be of God!

Her Sign

As Rahab offered to shelter the spies and aid them in their escape, she received from them the promise that when they returned to her country, along with Joshua and his army, that she and her family would be spared alive. While her sin had possibly estranged her from her loved ones, she was concerned about their safety as well as her own. Rahab wanted the kindness she was showing the spies to be reciprocated, and they assured her that she would be dealt with "kindly and truly." The spies said, "Our life for yours if ye utter not this our business." Then the sign of the scarlet rope — their means of escape — was arranged. "According unto thy words, so be it," said Rahab as she let the spies down, and making fast the scarlet rope, she awaited her own deliverance. That red token at the window was likewise a signal to the outside world that Rahab believed in the ultimate triumph of Jehovah.

Much has been said of Rahab's deceit when confronted by the king of Jericho. She told a lie and Scripture forbids a lie or any "evil doing, that good may come of it" (Romans 3:7, 8). But under the rules of war, Rahab is not to be blamed for her protection of those righteous forces set against the forces of evil. What the Bible commends is not her deception, but the faith which was the mainspring of her conduct. The characteristic feature of the scarlet rope was that it had to be placed outside the window for Joshua and his men to see. Those inside did not see the token of security. As that scarlet line, because of its color and sign of safety, speaks of the sacrificial work of Christ (Hebrews 9:19, 22), the ground of our assurance of salvation is not experience or feelings within, but the token without. Like the Israelites, Rahab and her relatives might not have felt safe within the house, but the same promise prevailed, "When I see the blood, I will pass over you" (Exodus 12:13).

Her Salvation

Jericho was the worst of the cities of the Amorites, thus God commanded Joshua to destroy both the city and the inhabitants. By divine decree, it was to be given over to a perpetual desolation. When Joshua entered the city he set about the execution of the divine command, but respected the promise made to Rahab by the spies. Under

the protection of the scarlet line, Rahab and all her kindred were brought out of the house. The spies came to her house, not to indulge in sin with Rahab, but to prepare the way for Joshua to take Jericho. She saved the spies not out of human pity, or because of expediency, but because she knew that they were servants of the Lord. In turn, she was saved. The spies she had hid brought her, and her father, her mother, her brothers, and all that she had out of her doomed house, and made them secure without the camp of Israel (Joshua 6:17-25). Brought out of an accursed city, and from her own sins which were as scarlet, Rahab is a fitting illustration of another miracle of divine grace, namely, the calling forth of His church out of a godless, Gentile world.

Her Status

The threefold reference to Rahab in the New Testament reveals how she became a faithful follower of the Lord. She had been taken from the dunghill and placed among the saints in the genealogy of the Saviour (Matthew 1:5 where Rachab [KJV] and Rahab [ASV], are to be identified as the same person). Her remarkable faith was a sanctifying faith leading her to a pure life and honorable career. As the result of her marriage to Salmon, one of the two spies whom she had saved, who "paid back the life he owed her by a love that was honourable and true," Rahab became an ancestress in the royal line from which Jesus came as the Saviour of lost souls. "Poor Rahab, the muddy, the defiled, became the fountainhead of the River of the Water of Life which floweth out of the throne of God and of the Lamb." Her name became sanctified and ennobled, and is worthy of inclusion among many saints.

Paul highly commends Rahab for her energetic faith and gives her a place on the illustrious roll of the Old Testament of those who triumphed by faith. "By faith the harlot Rahab perished not with them that believed not, when she received the spies with peace" (Hebrews 11:31). What a suggestive touch that is, "with peace." There was not only faith in her heart that God would be victorious, but also an assured peace when she hid the spies that her deliverance from destruction would be taken care of. She knew the *rest* of faith. In fact, Rahab is the only woman besides Sarah who is designated as an example of faith in the great cloud of witnesses. What a manifestation of divine grace it is to find the one-time harlot ranked along with saints like Enoch, Noah, Abraham, Joseph, Moses and David!

The Apostle James adds to Paul's record about Rahab being justified by faith by saying that she was likewise justified by works (2:25), and there is no contradiction between these two aspects for Rahab's courageous deed was but faith in practice. Faith had wrought in her a change of heart and life, and it likewise enabled her to shield the spies as she did in the confidence God would triumph over His enemies. She exemplified her faith by her brave act, and so James quotes Rahab as exemplifying justification by *works evidentially.* As Fausset puts it —

Paul's justification by faith alone means a faith, not *dead* but working by love (Galatians 5:6). Again, Rahab's act cannot prove justification by works as such, for she was a woman of *bad* character. But as an example of *grace*, justifying through an *operative* as opposed to mere verbal *faith*, none could be more suitable than the saved "harlot." She believed, so as to act on her belief, what her countrymen disbelieved; and this in the face of every improbability that an unwarlike force would conquer a well armed one, far more numerous. She believed with the heart (Romans 10:9, 10), confessed with the mouth, and acted on her profession at the risk of her life.

In conclusion, what are the lessons to be gathered from the harlot whom God used to fulfill His purpose? First of all, we are reminded by Rahab's change of heart and life, that "His blood can make the vilest clean," and that "His blood avails for me." Was it not a wonderful condescension on the part of the Redeemer when He became manifest in the flesh to take hold of a root so humble in type as poor, despised Rahab to magnify His abounding grace for all sinners? Rahab was well worth saving from her evil life both for her own sake and for the place she had in God's plan. Other women in Jericho saw no beauty in Rahab that they should desire her company, but through faith she became one of God's heroines, and is included among the harlots

entering the kingdom of God before the self-righteous. Rahab's sins had been scarlet, but the scarlet line freeing the spies, and remaining as a token of her safety, typified the red blood of Jesus whereby the worst of sinners can be saved from sin and hell (Matthew 21:31, 32). While the door of mercy stands ajar, the vilest sinner can return and know what it is to be saved and safe.

A further lesson to be gleaned from Rahab the harlot is that of deep concern for the salvation of others. With the shadow of death and destruction over Jericho, Rahab extracted a promise from Joshua's spies not only to spare her, but also all those bound to her by human ties. While her life of sin and shame had estranged her from her family, self was not her sole consideration in her request for safety. She desired all her loved ones to share in the preservation. What a vein of gold that was in such a despised character! When the mighty change took place in Rahab's life, and she was transformed from a whore into a worshiper of Jehovah, we are not told. As she received and hid the spies, her tribute to God's omnipotence and sure triumph over His foes reveals a spiritual insight God grants to all who believe. And restored to honor and holiness, the redeemed harlot pleads for her parents, and brothers, and sisters. Do we make Rahab's prayer for the salvation of her family, the cry for our own homes? Is ours the same passionate supplication for all of our dear ones that when death strikes they may be found sheltered by the atoning blood of the Redeemer? When at evening the sun goeth down, will our loved ones be as stars in our crown?

Rahab is likewise a poetic and symbolic name for Egypt (Psalms 87:4; 89:10; Isaiah 51:9. See SYMBOLIC WOMEN).

REBEKAH, REBECCA

THE WOMAN WHOSE FAVORITISM BROUGHT SORROW

Scripture References — Genesis 22:23; 24; 25:20-28; 26:6-35; 27; 28:5; 29:12; 35:8; 49:31; Romans 9:6-16

Name Meaning — Rebekah is another name with an animal connection. Although not belonging to any animal in particular, it has reference to animals of a limited class and in a peculiar condition. The name means a "tie rope for animals" or "a noose" in such a rope. Its root is found in a noun meaning a "hitching place" or "stall" and is connected with a "tied-up calf or lamb," a young animal peculiarly choice and fat. Applied to a female, the figure suggests her beauty by means of which men are snared or bound. Thus another meaning of Rebekah is that of "captivating." If, then, Rebekah means "a noosed cord," the loop was firmly around Isaac's neck. When Isaac took her as his bride he forgot his grief for his dead mother, and lived happily with his wife for twenty years during which time they had no children.

Family Connections — Rebekah is first mentioned in the genealogy of the descendants of Nahor, Abraham's brother (Genesis 22:20-24). When the pilgrims set out from the Ur of the Chaldees, Nahor was one of the party, and settled down at Charran where Terah, his father, died. Among Nahor's sons was Bethuel who, by an unknown wife, became the father of Rebekah, the sister of Laban. Rebekah married Isaac the son of Abraham, by whom she had two sons, Esau and Jacob.

The story of Isaac and Rebekah as a love lyric full of romance and tender beauty has been retold times without number, and is a charming record that never loses its appeal. Such an idyllic narrative is almost too familiar to need rehearsal, and too simple to require comment, yet because it constitutes one of the most romantic scenes in the Bible, its "moving scenes, so fresh and artless in their old world simplicity" have a pertinent appeal for present-day society. Ancient Bible histories with their arrestive characters and remarkable sequence of events and fortunes never fail to leave an indelible imprint on our hearts. The chapter recording how a wife was found for Isaac (Genesis 24) presents a link in the chain of events leading up to —

> That far-off Divine event
> To which the whole creation moves.

Through the marriage of Isaac and Rebekah, Abraham saw that day of Christ in which the church should become the Bride of Christ.

Almost two millenniums after the days of the patriarch whom God spoke of as His "friend," there were those who considered it a privilege to belong to the race having Abraham as its fountainhead. To be "a son of Abraham" or a lineal descendant of such a grand, great old divine was an honor, but Isaac enjoyed a still greater advantage for Abraham was his own natural father. What a rich dowry of blessing must have been Isaac's because of such a close relationship. He had the inspiration of his father's godliness, and the benefit of his prayers and wise counsels — even in the matter of securing the right kind of wife.

Abraham's opposition to idolatry is seen in his request that the partner for his son, Isaac, must not be "of the daughters of the Canaanites" (24:3). As he had refused a grave for his wife, Sarah, amongst the sepulchers of the Hittites (Genesis 23), so a wife for their son must not be sought among their daughters. Thus it came about that Abraham's trusted, godly servant, Eliezer, was divinely guided to Haran where Nahor, Abraham's brother settled. Too feeble to make the journey himself, Abraham gave his servant the most careful instructions, and impressed upon him the solemn significance of his mission. Confident as to the result of the search for a suitable wife for Isaac, Abraham assured the earthly seeker that he would be guided by God's angel. Eliezer, the intelligent, prudent, obedient and praying servant went forth. Seeking a sign of divine guidance, not to prove God's faithfulness, but for his own direction in the choice of a woman of character as a wife for his master's son, the servant came to Nahor's well at Nahor, and saw in Rebekah who had come to draw water the answer to his prayer and quest.

Eliezer lost no time in telling Rebekah who he was, and from whom he had come, and the purpose of his search. He revealed his tact in the way he wooed and won the heart of Rebekah. The gifts he bestowed upon her and the good things he said of his master, secured the favor of Rebekah's family who gave its consent to the proposed marriage. Faced with instant departure from her dear ones, Rebekah is given her choice — "Wilt thou go with this man?"

Without hesitation, feeling that she, too, was following the leading of God, as Eliezer had, Rebekah replied in a firm voice, "I will go."

The caravan set out for Abraham's home, and now we come to a superb touch in the romantic story. Isaac was out in the fields at eventide for his usual period of meditation. He saw the approaching camels and sensed the success of Eliezer in the choice of a wife. Reaching Isaac, Rebekah, according to custom, veiled her face, and the end of this exquisite poem of the meeting of bride and bridegroom is stated in most expressive terms — "Isaac brought her into his mother Sarah's tent, and took Rebekah, and she became his wife; and he loved her."

Marrying "sight unseen" is a most dangerous venture, but in this case it was successful because "the angel of the Lord" had directed the events leading up to the union. When Rebekah saw the handsome, mild-mannered and meditative Isaac, her heart went out to him. As for Isaac, a man of forty, and some twenty years older than Rebekah, he instantly loved the most beautiful woman he beheld, and she remained his only love. Some matrimonial matches have been described as "Lucifer Matches," because of clash of temperament and temper, but the marriage of Isaac and Rebekah was certainly one "made in heaven." There would be fewer broken homes if only young people looking for partners would seek the guidance of God as the servant of Abraham did. We agree with Alexander Whyte when he says of the ancient record of the circumstances leading to the securing of a wife for Isaac —

> A sweeter chapter was never written than the twenty-fourth of Genesis. . . . The picture of aged Abraham swearing his most trusty servant about a bride for his son Isaac; that servant's journey to Padan-aram in the far east; Rebekah, first at the well, and then in her mother's house; and then her first sight of her future husband — that long chapter is a perfect gem of ancient authorship.

As with other pairs in the Bible, it is hardly possible to separate Isaac from Rebekah whose lives were so closely knit together. Yet let us see if we can sketch a portrait of Rebekah herself.

Her Character

As a damsel, that is, a maiden around twenty years of age, Rebekah was "fair to look upon," meaning that she had an unaffected Oriental beauty. She was a virgin, and had a childlike simplicity. There was no trace of wantonness in her. As with her mother-in-law, Sarah, beauty carried its dangers. During his sojourn in Gerar, Isaac feared lest the physical charms of his wife might excite the desire of the king of Gerar and so he lied. Thus Isaac passed Rebekah off as his sister — a course of action which might have had dire consequences (Genesis 26:6-16). He fell into the same error as his father before him (see SARAH). Andrew Fuller says, "The falls of those that have gone before us are like so many rocks on which others have been split; and the recording of them is like placing buoys over them for the security of future mariners." But in the story of Isaac the buoy served no beneficial purpose.

Beautiful Rebekah had been taken by Abimelech, but one day as he looked out of the window he saw Isaac caressing Rebekah, and he knew that he had been deceived. Isaac's untruthfulness was discovered, and the heir of God's promises was rebuked by a heathen king for his lying and deception. In the providence of God, Abimelech, an idolater, was made the protector of the child of promise (see Psalm 17:13). As "an amiable and lovely girl," as her name suggests, she was industrious, for although she was a member of a family of standing she was not afraid to soil her hands. The hard work of drawing and carrying water, the provision she made for Eliezer's camels, and the meal she prepared, speak of Rebekah as one who did not shun domestic duties. That she was a woman of faith is evident from what Paul says of her as being the recipient of a direct revelation from the Lord regarding universal blessing through her favorite Jacob (Romans 9:12).

Rebekah's best qualities come out in the simple yet heartwarming narrative describing her response to Eliezer's approach, in her service to him, and in her willingness to believe and act upon all he had told her. In his remarkable cameo of Rebekah, George Matheson uses the following terms or expressions — "a fine manner" — "remarkable tact" — "a sunbeam to her household"—"a very beautiful young woman, with the gift of physical charm which was apt to produce self-consciousness"—"the gift of intellectual sympathy" — "Rebekah's morning ray is a ray of sympathetic insight."

Modest and meek, frank and open, ready kindness, great energy and faith, graciousness matching her physical charm, describe Rebekah. When she became a mother she revealed how masterful and clever she could be — a direct contrast to Isaac who was probably more simple, slow of wit, and mild of manner than his wife. The lines of Wordsworth can express Isaac's feelings when for the first time he gazed upon the lovely Rebekah and came to experience her comforting love as she filled the empty place in his heart because of his mother's death.

> She was a phantom of delight
> When first she gleamed upon my sight;
> A lovely apparition, sent
> To be a moment's ornament;
> Her eyes as stars of twilight fair,
> Like twilight's, too, her dusky hair.
> But all things else about her drawn
> From May-time and the cheerful dawn.
> A dancing shape, an image gay,
> To haunt, to startle, and waylay.
> I saw her upon nearer view,
> A spirit, yet a woman too!

Her Children

Motherhood came to Rebekah somewhat late in life when Isaac was an aging man. For twenty years she had been childless, and conscious of God's promise that the Abrahamic Covenant could not be broken, Isaac entreated God that his long barren wife might conceive. He graciously answered his earnest intercession (Genesis 25: 19-34). As his prayer was in the line of God's purpose, it was sure of an answer (I John 5:14). The years of waiting on the part of Isaac and Rebekah show that God has His own time for the fulfillment of His purpose.

> Like coral strands beneath the sea,
> So strongly built and chaste,
> The plans of God, unfolding, show
> No signs of human haste.

In an age of almost universal polygamy, Isaac took no handmaid, concubine, or second wife. Rebekah and he were bound together by the bonds of a mutual affection, and although childless, yet became the parents of two sons who were destined to be the progenitors of different nations. But when Rebekah became the mother of twins —the first of two Bible women mentioned as giving birth to twins — the other was Tamar (Genesis 38:27)—somehow she changed and was a different character from the young bride who rode south so gaily to meet her lover in Canaan, as our next glimpse of her will show.

The opposite characters of Rebekah's twins, Esau and Jacob, brought into sharp focus the dark side of their mother. As Esau was the first to emerge from her womb he had the precedence and was thus the heir of two things, namely "the sovereignty and the priesthood, of the clan — the birthright and the blessing. The birthright was the right of succession. . . . The blessing was something to be given during the lifetime of the father." We learn that as the boys grew, "Esau was a cunning (skillful) hunter, a man of the field; and Jacob was a plain man, dwelling in tents." At the time of their birth, Jacob seized his brother's heel — an incident prophetic of the day when he would supplant Esau. Often in children there are characteristics predictive of the manner of adults they will be.

The divergence of Rebekah's twins in temperament, inclination, occupation, and religious aspirations is most apparent. Esau was wrapped in a raiment of hair, a rough man of the wilderness, a clever hunter with something of the wild daring spirit of the modern Bedouin. Jacob was the opposite of his brother. He preferred a fixed abode, to dwell in his tent rather than roam the desert. Esau was probably more brilliant, attractive, forceful, daring than his twin brother. Jacob, in spite of his weaknesses and mistakes was the finer character, and on the whole truer to the Lord and more fitted to possess the blessing of the birthright. Further, there was the difference of regard on the part of Isaac and Rebekah toward their two sons that resulted in sorrow and separation.

Isaac loved Esau, but the love was somewhat sensual. He loved his son "because he did eat of his venison." Such love is of a carnal nature, for love in its highest sense has regard not so much to what the loved one *gives* as to what he or she *is*.

Rebekah loved Jacob, not because he was more of a "homebody" than his brother, or possessed a more loving nature than he, but because Jacob was the Lord's preference (Romans 9:13). Esau thought so lightly of the birthright that he was willing to sell it for a mess of pottage, and be guilty, thereby, of the sin of profanity (Hebrews 12:16). Jacob, however, recognized the solemnity of the birthright and wished to possess it. Esau thought of it as of no more value than a mouthful of food, but Jacob knew something of the sacred significance of the birthright and was therefore a more fit channel through which the blessing of God could flow to the seed of Abraham.

As Rebekah is often blamed for the partiality or favoritism she manifested for Jacob, it may be profitable to consider the matter of preference in family life. When parents single out one of their children as a favorite and shower more love and attention upon that one than the rest, such an unwise and unnatural course inevitably results in jealousy and strife. Although Isaac found "in Esau that strong practical nature, and energetic character which distinguished the woman he so dearly loved; and Rebekah saw in the gentle Jacob a replica of the father who had so strangely attracted her that first day when she met him meditating in the fields at evening," the partiality was absolutely indefensible and led to lying and deception on Rebekah's part.

What else can be expected but confusion and trouble when there is a crossing of purposes between parents concerning their children? Was the root-cause of Rebekah's unnatural and unmotherly preference of Jacob over Esau and her treatment of Esau as though he was not, the lack of deep love for her husband, and that union of moral and spiritual ideas and ideals characteristic of every true marriage? We are certainly told that Isaac loved Rebekah, but not that she loved Isaac. Somehow we feel that if husband and wife had been *one* in all things in that ancient home, Rebekah would have been more concerned about Jacob's character than his prosperity. But Isaac was partial to Esau and Rebekah partial to Jacob—

which favoritism resulted in Esau leaving home, and Jacob fleeing from it. Rebekah's record therefore shows that while Isaac was faithful to her, she was unfaithful to Isaac in a twofold way. First, she cheated Esau, her oldest son, and Isaac's pet out of his birthright. Then she cheated Esau out of his father's blessing, which prerogative had the effect of a testamentary bequest.

Comparing the chapter of the romantic meeting of Isaac and Rebekah (Genesis 24) with its perfection of writing, and the dark chapter of Rebekah's deception (Genesis 28), Alexander Whyte says, "That the ship was launched on such a golden morning only the more darkens the surrounding gloom when she goes to the bottom." Then dealing with the secret alienation that developed between Isaac and Rebekah, the same renowned expositor adds —

When the two twin-brothers were brought up day after day and hour after hour in an atmosphere of favouritism, and partiality, and indulgence, and injustice, no father, no mother, can surely need to have it pointed out to them what present misery, and what future wages of such sin, is all to be seen and to be expected in that evil house.

One result of Rebekah's preference for Jacob was the spite and the sight of Esau going out and grieving his parents by marrying two ungodly women. Esau was forty years old when he did this — the same age at which Isaac married Rebekah. His parents must have seen in the foreign wives he brought home the firstfruits of the devil's garden they had sowed for themselves. "Their great grief would seem to have been almost the only thing the two old people were at one about by that time." Esau had seen little in his mother to admire and respect; therefore he was never in any mood to please her. What a different story would have been written if Esau's home had been "without partiality"!

Her Chicanery

Chicanery is described as the act of one who deliberately deceives, and this was Rebekah's sin. The destiny of her favorite son, Jacob, was strongly influenced by his mother's strong-mindedness, and thus she became the authoress of the treacherous plan to deprive Esau of his father's blessing. Isaac is old, feeble and blind, and informs the members of his household that the time has come to give Esau, officially, what was left to him after selling his birthright, namely, the blessing which carried with it the recognition of his headship, the ratification of the birthright. So Isaac told his favorite son to take his bow and arrow and go into the fields, hunt for his much-liked venison, and make a savory meal. At that time, and for centuries in the Orient, a meal taken together was a common symbol of a saved pledge when father and son partook together. In such an hour of sacred fellowship the father bestowed upon the elder son his rank and place.

Rebekah overheard, and her deceitful heart was stirred to action. She set about to thwart her husband's purpose. Her favorite son must not be displaced, and her hopes for him dashed to the ground, by the impetuous hunter whom Isaac loved. Cunningly she devised the plan of impersonation. While Esau was out in the fields hunting, Rebekah told Jacob to go to a flock nearby and bring two kids for her to dress and cook and pass off as venison. While cautious about his mother's duplicity, he had no conscience against it. What made Jacob hesitant was the fact that his brother was a hairy man, while his own skin was smooth, and that if his father felt him and sensed the deception, he would not bless him, but curse him.

Rebekah, however, was equal to this fear of Jacob, and he followed the counsels of his treacherous mother. He put the skin of the kids upon his hands and upon his neck, thus making himself feel and smell like Esau, and so deceived his aged, blind father. Doubtless Rebekah stood nearby in convenient concealment to see how her ill-conceived ruse would succeed. Smelling Esau's clothes, and feeling the false hairy hands, Isaac was a little doubtful and said, "The voice is the voice of Jacob, but the hands are the hands of Esau." But reassured by the repeated lies of Jacob, the deceived father bestowed the unalterable blessing upon his son, and Jacob, by fraud, became the father of Israel's race. To his discredit, he played the role successfully which his mother had drilled into him with masterly skill. Covetous of the sacred, patriarchal blessing for her favorite son, Rebekah felt she had to resort to duplicity to gain her ends, and in doing so she prostituted parental authority. "My son obey my voice" (Genesis 27:8), and Jacob the misguided son obeyed, and in his subsequent career bore the bitter fruit of his conduct when Laban deceived him regarding Rachel.

> A deceiver Jacob was
> Full of craft and guile;
> Thro' long years he bore his guilt,
> Unrepentant all the while.

Samuel Morely once said, "I am much what my mother has made me." It was so in a wrong sense in the life of Jacob, for as in the case of Athaliah, "his mother was his counsellor to do wickedly" (II Chronicles 22:3). The thoroughness with which Jacob carried out his mother's plan of deception is surely one of the worse features of the narrative. Fearful of the failure of his mother's plot, Jacob said, "I will bring a curse upon me and not a blessing." But Rebekah replied, "Upon me be thy curse, my son, only obey my voice." The future scheming life of Jacob, however, was but the extension of the deceitful qualities of his mother, and both suffered as the result of adopting false methods to accomplish right ends.

When Esau found that he had been robbed of his blessing through the cunning scheme of his mother, he became a remorseless avenger and swore the death of his brother who was forced to flee for his life to Haran, some 500 miles away. Rebekah never saw the face of her much-loved son again. To add to her reproach she had to endure the grief of seeing her other son marry heathen women. Esau's heathen wives caused Rebekah to be weary of her life (Genesis 27:46). Esau received a promise from his father that he would be the progenitor of a great nation — the Edomites — and much misery accrued to Israel because of Edom. The wrath of Esau's enraged blood boiled in the blood of Herod the Idumean on the day he reviled the Man of Sorrows.

There are some writers who try to justify the actions of Rebekah by saying that she was prompted to take the course she did concerning Jacob because of the prediction that, "the elder shall serve the younger," but God had no need of trickery and deceit to fulfill His promise. Ambitious for her son, Rebekah sacrificed the love of her husband, the loss of the esteem of her elder son, and the peace of her soul, for the idolized son whose face she never saw again. Without doubt, Jacob was the divinely-appointed heir of Abraham (Genesis 25:23), and Rebekah seeking to overrule the purpose of Isaac in his blessing of Esau, resorted to deceit to accomplish the will of God. Her guiding principle was, "Let us do evil that good may come" (Romans 3:8), but wrong is never right (James 1:20). Esau had sold his birthright for a mess of pottage, and Rebekah catered to Isaac's carnal appetite in order to accomplish a divine purpose. Had she laid aside "all guile, and hypocrisies" (I Peter 2:1), and reasoned with her husband about the solemn issue at stake she would have been saved from the disgrace which her worldly policy brought upon her own head and from the sorrow others had to endure.

Almost the last picture we have of Rebekah is when she tearfully witnessed the hasty departure of her favorite son. "A strong-minded, decisive girl had grown into an autocratic matriarch," and ends her days a brokenhearted woman. When she died we are not told. Isaac, although much older than Rebekah, was still living when Jacob returned to Canaan over 20 years later. It is assumed that she died during Jacob's long absence, and was buried in the cave of Machpelah near Hebron (Genesis 49:31). A fitting epitaph for her grave would have been, "Died of a broken heart." The only monument Rebekah has is to be found in the Anglican marriage service of *The Book of Common Prayer* where we read —

That as Isaac and Rebekah lived faithfully together, so these persons may surely perform and keep the vow and covenant betwixt them.

While she may have been faithful during the first 20 years of marriage while she was childless, Rebekah, by her unjustifiable treacherous and wholly inexplicable intervention for her favorite son, stained her solemn marriage.

Reviewing Rebekah's life and character what are some of the warnings to heed? Are we not forcibly reminded that love which seeks success at the cost of truth and right-

eousness is of the earth, earthy? The devil's maxim is, "Nothing succeeds like success." But from God's standpoint nothing succeeds which does not follow the way of truth and honesty. Then, while she had physical beauty, her domination of Jacob and her scheme to deceive her husband revealed the lack of the beauty of a godly character. Further, Rebekah is a warning to all parents that there should be no favorites in the family; that all alike should be dear to them. If there is partiality for any in a family, it should only be for those who are weak and helpless.

Another warning bell is that when a wife conspires against her husband, or vice versa, they are guilty of a baseness which language cannot describe. When one partner finds that he has been betrayed by the other, the world becomes a blank.

> The mind has a thousand eyes
> The heart but one,
> But the light of a whole life dies
> When love is done.

There is one beneficial application we can make of Rebekah's prompt decision to follow Eliezer to meet her future bridegroom, Isaac — *I will go!* In connection with the higher betrothal of the soul to the heavenly Bridegroom, He comes to the sinner saying as Eliezer did to Rebekah, "Will you go with Me? Will you follow Me into that country where saints immortal reign?" When hearts respond to such an appeal, "Yea, Lord I will go. I will follow Thee, whithersoever Thou goest!" they are twice blessed.

REUMAH

Scripture Reference — Genesis 22:24
Name Meaning — Exalted

The first female in the Bible to be named a "concubine" is Reumah. Nothing, however, of an exalted nature is recorded of this secondary wife of Nahor, Abraham's brother, who became the mother of four children, Tebah, Gaham, Thahash and Maachah.

RHODA

THE WOMAN WHO WAS CALLED MAD

Scripture Reference — Acts 12:1-19
Name Meaning — Foreign born, this domestic servant of Mary the mother of Mark had a Greek name meaning "rose."

Wilkinson remarks that as "Barnabas, Mary's brother, was of the country of Cyprus, it is a very reasonable supposition that the family had been resident there, and brought thence this maiden, who, like so many of her nation born in foreign parts, had received a Greek name." Although she carried one of the most beautiful names she was called by another not so pleasant. The saints in Mary's home called her *Manias* meaning, "a mad woman."

In the human episode in which Rhoda is the prominent character, nothing is said of pedigree. As a slave-maid she did not merit any genealogy. As a servant, she had no hours. The fact that it was long past midnight when Peter reached Mary's house, and that Rhoda the portress answered the door, indicates that she was willing to serve long and late. Mary, her mistress, also found in Rhoda a spiritual help. Doubtless she, too, was on her knees with the others praying for Peter, and hearing his knock went to the door. Perhaps we can break up the narrative in this threefold way. Peter knocked — Rhoda was shocked — The saints mocked.

Peter Knocked

The background of the record which Rhoda shares can be briefly cited. Mary of Jerusalem, a rich widow and mother of Mark the evangelist, owned a large and conspicuous house in the city which she placed at the service of the Lord. During the days of terrible persecution the saints in Jerusalem gathered regularly in her lovely home not only for the reading and exposition of the Word, but also to pray for afflicted saints. On the night in question the saints concentrated on the deliverance of a precious life, namely, Peter their leader. Herod's sword of persecution had fallen heavily upon the church in Jerusalem. James the Greater had already drunk the cup of martyrdom prophesied for him by his Lord, and the gathered intercessors had learned that Peter, imprisoned by Herod, was the next to be led forth to die. If their shepherd was smitten what could the sheep do. Such a crisis brought Peter's fellow believers to their knees in night-long intercession.

As the church in the house earnestly petitioned the Lord, their prayers were heard. In the prison the Lord, by means of an angel, miraculously freed Peter. Peter sped past guards and through opened doors, and came to the closed door of a house where he knew the saints were gathered together praying. Peter knocked at the door, but because of Rhoda's excitement, she failed to open the door. Peter continued knocking until the door was opened, not by angelic hands, as at the prison he had left, but by unbelieving human hands. Such a delay might have been dangerous, if the guards, discovering their prisoner had escaped, had tracked him down and found him standing at the closed gate of Mary's ancient house.

Rhoda Was Shocked

Peter not only knocked but also spoke, for we read that she knew his voice — the dear voice she had listened to so often expounding the sacred truths of the Word. But she was so stunned and overwhelmed at the answer to those midnight prayers standing there, that she failed to draw the bolts and admit Peter. "She opened not the gate for gladness." Such gladness would have been changed to sadness had Herod's soldiers appeared at that moment and taken Peter back to prison. We can understand Rhoda not opening the gate as soon as she heard the knock. "Never open a door in the dark until you know who is behind it." In those days when the saints were not sure who would be the next to join the noble army of martyrs, great caution was necessary. That knock might have been the summons of cruel Herod, making a fresh inroad on the little flock. But when Rhoda asked, "Who is knocking?" and received the muffled reply, "It is Peter, open quickly," she should have opened the gate before opening her mouth to others in the house about Peter standing outside. Knowing that for certain it was Peter, it was her duty as the maid to open the door. But stunned by the glad tidings she was momentarily thoughtless.

There are some characteristics of this maidservant who only has this one notice in Scripture, which are attractive. First, unbounded joy was hers. Luke, the beloved physician, who wrote the Acts, analyzes

Rhoda's state of consciousness when the good news of answered prayer on Peter's behalf overpowered her presence of mind. She forgot herself — and her duty — and *ran in* to tell the intercessors to pray no more for Peter was at the gate. We can imagine how excitedly she shouted, "Peter is free! Peter is knocking at the door!" A spontaneous child of nature, she manifested her exuberance. Had hers been a calmer, less passionate nature, she would have opened the door when she knew it was Peter, and then gone in to tell the praying band that Peter was safe and free.

Further, when her good, glad information was scorned by the saints whose prayers for Peter had been interrupted by Rhoda's joyous outburst, "she constantly affirmed that it was even so." Her young heart believed in God and in the power of prayer, and knowing definitely that prayer had been answered, she would not suffer the praying band in the house of her mistress to browbeat her into silence. Although only the maid, she was not to be subdued by the sarcastic criticism of the large congregation present. She knew it was Peter, and nothing could move her from that belief. Rhoda wore the red rose of courage so beautifully as she persisted against opposition to constantly affirm the truth.

The Saints Mocked

How revealing was the reaction of those gathered together to Rhoda's excited announcement. First of all, they told the glad maid that she was *mad*. They accused her of insanity! But Rhoda was in good company because it had been said of the Saviour whom she had come to know and love, "He is beside Himself." Then, when Paul's eye kindled with the glory of his message, just as the face of Rhoda glowed as she told of answered prayer, Festus said of the Apostle, "Thou art beside thyself, much learning doth make thee mad." The prophet speaks about the spiritual man being mad (Hosea 9:7). Have we ever been thought mad for Christ, or fools for His sake? We are in the best of company if others sneer at us as we declare and live the message of God's power through Christ. But being told she had lost her senses did not deter

Rhoda from the repetition of what she knew to be true.

Departing from their accusation, the band said, "It is his angel." Failing to move Rhoda from her persistent testimony, the saints treated her message as coming from the dead. It was a common Jewish belief that every true Israelite had a guardian angel especially assigned to him, who, when he appeared in human form, assumed the likeness of the man whom he protected. The continued knocking of Peter, however, stifled that interpretation of Rhoda's testimony because guardian angels are not prevented from carrying out their mission by closed doors. So, feeling that there was something insistently human about that constant knocking "they opened the door, saw Peter, and were astonished."

Astonished! How this description of their feelings revealed their unbelief! They had been praying for hours for Peter, yet when Peter stood at the door they did not believe it. Lack of faith was mingled with their intercessions, and so they were surprised at the miracle God had performed in Peter's escape from prison. Our Lord instructed His disciples to pray believingly. "When ye ask, believe that ye receive." Spurgeon once said, "If the Lord wants to surprise His people, He has only at once to give them an answer. No sooner do they receive an answer than they say, 'Who would have thought it?'" Mary of Jerusalem came to value her godly maid, Rhoda, more than ever because of the great assistance she had rendered that memorable day. And once in the house, Peter must have commended her for her persistence.

RIZPAH
THE WOMAN WHO GUARDED HER DEAD

Scripture References — II Samuel 3:7; 21: 8-14

Name Meaning — "A hot, or baking stone." Rizpah certainly exhibited a white-heat passion in the protection of her murdered sons.

Family Connections — She was a daughter of Aiah, or Ajah, the Horite (Genesis 36: 24; I Chronicles 1:40; II Samuel 3:7). Saul took her as a concubine and she bore him, Armoni and Mephibosheth. Ishbosheth, another son of Saul by a different woman, accused Abner, a cousin, of incest with Rizpah, and enraged by such an accusation Abner transferred his allegiance from Saul to David (II Samuel 3:7-21).

Among all the heart-moving episodes in the Bible, none is so compelling and touching as the story of Rizpah and her care of the dead. This narrative is probably responsible for the great poem of Tennyson, *Rizpah*, a verse of which reads —

> Flesh of my flesh was gone,
> But bone of my bone was left —
> I stole them all from the lawyer —
> and will you call it a theft?
> My baby, my bones, that had sucked me,
> the bones that had laughed and had cried
> Theirs? O no! they are mine —
> not theirs — they had moved in my side.

Donald Davidson reminds us that, "Beauty is often to be found in the most unexpected places, and here we find the blackness of that pre-Christian night pierced by a pure white shaft of sacrifice and love." It may prove profitable to present a threefold portrait of this most courageous woman.

She Was a Victim of Vengeance

Like millions of women through the centuries, Rizpah, caught up in the holocaust of national strife and war, found herself bereft of husband and children and was left to fight a battle against loneliness and poverty. The background of Rizpah's empty heart and home is plainly stated. Saul, who became conspicuous for his pride and self-will, broke an oath that had been made with the Gibeonites by Joshua. Although the idolatrous Gibeonites had deceived Joshua, yet the treaty with them had been made, and an oath not to destroy them by the sword was sealed in the Lord's name. But when Saul came to power he set about the obliteration of Israel's enemies, and treating the Gibeonites as a heathen settlement in a holy land, endeavored to annihilate them. As soon as Saul met his death on Mount Gilboa, the Gibeonites sought for redress for the profanation of the oath given by Joshua.

A severe famine lasting for three years overtook the land of Israel, and David was divinely informed that the famine was in consequence of Saul's slaughter of the oath-protected Gibeonites. They demanded by way of compensation that the seven sons of Saul should be hung up "before the Lord" in expiation for what had been done there. It thus came about that innocent children had to bear heavy punishment for the sin of their father. The five sons of Saul by Merab, who were cared for by Michal after her sister's death (see MICHAL), and Saul's two sons by Rizpah were taken and hanged upon a hilltop for all to see. Thus vengeance, a divine prerogative (Romans 3:5; 12:19), was taken out of God's hands, and executed by revengeful men in God's name upon seven innocent men. They were cruelly slaughtered, not to appease divine wrath, but to satisfy a human thirst for vengeance. History affirms that innocent people suffer for the sins of their rulers.

She Was a Defender of the Dead

The next glimpse of Rizpah offers a sharp contrast to the brutal revenge and slaughter that broke her motherly heart. What an effective illustration she gave of a mother's love being as strong as death! What a ghastly scene that must have been during barley harvest with those seven blood-covered bodies hanging on the respective trees, and noble Rizpah protecting them from the vultures waiting to gorge themselves on the corpses! Through the days and weeks she watched those broken bodies gradually blacken, decay and wither, and never relaxed her vigil. She had no power to prevent the gruesome murder of her two sons, but none could stay her from the act of mercy in caring for their mangled bodies on the gallows-tree. Leaving those bodies to hang unburied testified to the vengeance being of man and not of God, for the law demanded that anyone hanged on a tree must be buried before sunset of the same day.

Rizpah continued watching the mouldering bodies of the dead standing out stark against the sky. Her beautiful, sacrificial motherhood wrestled through anxious days and more anxious nights with the foul stench of those rotting corpses filling her nostrils. Here is an episode unmatched in literature. As a widow who feared God, perhaps her tender care of the dead implied an instinctive sense of resurrection.

Rizpah spread sackcloth on the rock. Sackcloth is not only associated with mourning for the dead (Genesis 37:34; II Samuel 3:31), but also with the public expression of humiliation and penitence in view of some misfortune, present or impending (I Kings 21:27; Nehemiah 9:1, etc.). Was Rizpah's use of the sackcloth a sign that the land had repented of its sin? At any rate, she defended the dead till the rain came — a token that Gód had withdrawn His judgment. Water out of the heavens, reviving the famine-stricken land, was recognized as the sign of God's mercy, and that the painful watch in sackcloth on the dead was over. "Refrain thine eyes from tears — thy work shall be rewarded — they shall come again from the land of the enemy."

Rizpah's long vigil was over. She had clung at all costs with desperate, sacrificial tenacity to guard the lifeless remains of Saul's seven sons (Song of Solomon 8:6; Isaiah 49:15), now she was at liberty to bury their withered corpses. David heard of her motherly devotion and long vigil. Remembering that the uncared-for bones of Saul and Jonathan were still exposed in the streets of Beth-shan he commanded that they should be recovered and mingled with the precious bones which Rizpah had guarded, and buried in the family grave at Zelah. "God was intreated for the land," and Rizpah's desire for proper respect for her dead was fulfilled.

She Typified the Gloom of Golgotha

Different writers have drawn attention to the similarities between Rizpah as she stood by those seven trees on the hillside, and Mary who stood by the tree on which her Son was hanged. In that "hill before the LORD" (II Samuel 21:9), we have a shadow of Golgotha. Seven innocent men were hanged, or as the Latin Version puts it, *crucified*, to make atonement for the sin of others. They bore the curse of a broken oath, for "cursed is every one that hangeth on a tree," and those trees on that hill of Gibeah were the shadow of the one bearing the one great expiatory Sacrifice. By His death upon the tree, God's Son satisfied His Father's justice and righteousness, and provided a perfect salvation for a sinning race.

There is a striking way in which Rizpah the mother of two sons, and Mary Magdalene, the devoted follower of Christ, resemble each other. Rizpah could not forget the sons of her love, and in her sacrificial vigil of her dead expressed the secret instinct of faith in the hope of resurrection. In like manner, Mary sat over against the sepulcher watching the place where her dear Lord was buried. While not mindful of His predicted Resurrection (Psalm 16:9, 10), she was at His grave early the next morning to embalm His body, and would have been prepared to guard it as Rizpah had defended her dead, but that body was no longer in the tomb. Christ was alive forevermore, and Mary was privileged to become the first witness to this cardinal truth of Christianity. Rizpah saw her dead buried out of her sight (Genesis 23:4), as we have, but the Crucified One, "dead and buried" did not remain out of sight. He rose again, and provided, for all those redeemed by His blood, a glorious resurrection.

RUTH

THE WOMAN WHO ROSE FROM OBSCURITY TO RICHES

Scripture References — The Book of Ruth, Matthew 1:5

Name Meaning — Since the Ruth of ancient Bible times, her name has ever been a most popular one for girls. Elsdon C. Smith, in his compilation of the first hundred female names in America, places Ruth seventh in the list, with an estimated number of almost one and a half million bearing the name. The author's only daughter bears this honored name. As to its significance, we cannot do better than the interpretation Wilkinson gives us in his *Personal Names of the Bible*, in the chapter on "Heathen Names" —

The most distinguished person of the Moabitish race is Ruth, who became the wife of Boaz, and ancestress of David. Her name is a contraction of *reuth*, which may either be the word for "the act of seeing," "sight" and hence, as in English, objectively "a sight," "something worth seeing" — or the word for "friendship" or "a female friend," like *reu* in Reuel, "friend of God." If the former etymology be adopted, we must ascribe the name to the early beauty of the child; if the latter, it may be due to the exhibition in infancy of that amiable and affectionate disposition which was so characteristic of the woman.

Both meanings of the name were true of Ruth, for as a beautiful girl from Moab she was certainly a sight worth seeing, and her character revealed her to be a woman capable of rare friendship.

It took the grace of God to befriend a bitter woman as Naomi became, but Ruth was bound to her mother-in-law by the cords of love, and literature has no exhibition of friendship comparable to that dramatic episode on the way to Bethlehem (Ruth 1:16, 17). Not wanting to go back to Moab, as Orpah did, Ruth, cleaving to Naomi said with passion in her voice—

Intreat me not to leave thee, or to return from following after thee: for whither thou goest, I will go; and where thou lodgest, I will lodge: thy people shall be my people, and thy God my God:

Where thou diest, will I die, and there will I be buried: the LORD do so to me, and more also, if ought but death part thee and me.

What an appealing and stirring demonstration of undying friendship that was, and Ruth meant it, and through it changed Naomi's sourness into sweetness! We have dear friends like Ruth who cling to us, and others like Orpah whose friendship is only veneer and who quickly leave us (see NAOMI and ORPAH). Scripture gives us a fivefold profile of this famous Moabitess —

A Young Widow

The first glimpse we have of Ruth is as a young wife robbed by death of her husband. In our previous cameos of Naomi and Orpah we have already seen how Elimelech and his wife, along with their two sons Mahlon and Chilion, in order to escape prevailing famine in Bethlehem, emigrated to the neighboring country of Moab, the inhabitants of which were idolaters. After a while Elimelech died, and the two fatherless sons married women of Moab. Mahlon took Ruth to wife, and Chilion, Orpah. After some ten years' sojourn in Moab, Mahlon and Chilion died leaving their wives childless. In marrying women of Moab those two Hebrew men sinned against the Mosaic Law which prohibted any association with the idolatrous Moabites (Deuteronomy 7:3; 23:3).

Mahlon means "the sickly one," or "invalid"; Chilion, "the pining one," or "wasting away" — names probably associated with their natal frailty. They may have been twins, and from their birth Naomi had to surround them with great care and attention. This is evident that life in Moab, with all its food and comfort, hastened their end. Like their father, Elimelech, they found graves in foreign soil, and the desolation of widowhood came upon both Ruth and Orpah, who became sharers of Naomi's desolation. Ten years of widowhood brought the two younger women to a mature age. How far they had been influenced Godward by their marriage into a Hebrew family, with its recognition of God, and not their idols, as the only true object of worship, we are not told. As Ruth's husband, Mahlon, was the first-born of Elimelech and Naomi, we can imagine how he would strive through their years together to draw her from her heathen ways. With all we know of Ruth's honest nature, it is quite possible that she warmly received all her husband told her of the mighty Jehovah.

Bereft of her husband, Ruth, as well as Orpah, would be left without material resources of support, and would face the hard and bitter lot of a biting poverty, as many widows do when the breadwinner is taken. But if Ruth shed any tears over her sorry plight as she faced a gloomy future without her husband, there is no record of them. She did not seek for self-pity neither did she manifest the bitterness that had gripped the heart of Naomi because of her sad lot. Amid the shadows, Ruth maintained a poise and a serenity which even her mother-in-law must have coveted. When happy homes are ravaged by death, it requires grace to say, "The Lord gave, the Lord hath taken away. Blessed be the name of the Lord." Naomi's self-confessed bitterness over the loss of husband and sons spoke of her lack of faith in God's good providence. But Ruth, heathen though she may have been, seems to have calmly acquiesced in the divine will.

A Faithful Daughter-in-Law

Bound together by a bond of common grief, the three widows found consolation in each other's company. "Fellow-feeling, makes us wondrous kind." The widowed

Naomi, now bereft of her two sons who died childless, had no links with Moab. As famine had passed in Bethlehem, the decision was made to pull up stakes and return to her own country and people, perhaps with a faint hope that God would prove Himself to be the Guardian of widows. "Let thy widows trust in me." What about Ruth and Orpah? Deeply attached to their mother-in-law, who had become a second mother to them, and to whom they clung as their friend and counselor, they decided to accompany the pilgrim on her way. Naomi used no persuasion, but left the two young widows to make their own choice. Therefore all three left Moab together, but on the way they stopped and Naomi urged them to return to their own country, marry again and settle down. She did not want them to face uncertainty in a strange land. With poor Orpah, ties of kindred and her own idolatrous practices won out. Her heart failed, and kissing her mother-in-law she went back to her people and to her gods. It is possible that when among her heathen friends again, her conscience often whispered to her of the wrong course taken.

As for Ruth, the choice was different. She loved Naomi and was willing to leave her own land and share the unknown future with the aging woman in whom her life was bound up. In her happier days with Mahlon, and then in her desolation and bereavement, Ruth found in Naomi a home for her heart. Orpah manifested a show of passionate affection as she kissed her mother-in-law good-by! But Ruth, as always, revealed a quiet fidelity so characteristic of her association with the embittered woman now returning to Bethlehem. We agree with the sentiment of Alexander Whyte that there is not a love story comparable to the love of the Moabite daughter-in-law for her Hebrew mother-in-law.

Ruth's love for her dead husband's aged mother is as pure as gold and as strong as death. Many waters cannot quench Ruth's love. And her confession of her love, when she is constrained to confess it, is the most beautiful confession of love in all the world.

Ruth's declaration of love and loyalty for Naomi marks it out as being the purest and most unselfish form of devotion, especially when we remember that Naomi was more than twice the age of Ruth, and that, proverbially, it is not easy to live with a mother-in-law. Here we have a strong contradiction to modern flippancy — the passionate affection of a young widow for her widowed mother-in-law. History and literature cannot provide a more exquisite expression of love and loyalty as that to be found in the lovely idyll bearing the name of the lover herself. The matchless beauty of the character of Ruth appeared when she cried, "Intreat me not to leave thee." As A. S. Geden puts it, "The piety and fidelity of Ruth are early exhibited in the course of the narrative, in that she refused to abandon her mother-in-law, although thrice exhorted to do so by Naomi herself, on account of her own great age, and the better prospects for Ruth in her own country." In an age like ours with its ever growing number of strained relationships, broken homes and loveless lives it is most refreshing to go back to the charming picture of loyalty found in a short yet sublime book in which every prospect pleases.

A Determined Convert

In spite of her heathen background and association with the degenerated tribe of Moab, Ruth became a devout worshiper of the true God. Just when she cast off her idolatry with its folly of bowing down to gods of wood and stone, and turned to the beauty and blessedness of true religion we are not told. Perhaps in her somewhat short married life, her heart was stirred by what her husband told her of the greatness of Jehovah. Then she must have seen that Naomi's God was totally different from the lifeless deity she worshiped. This much is evident, that her outburst of song of life devotion on the road from Moab to Bethlehem was the birth-strain of a new life. From henceforth the Hebrews would be her people, and Naomi's God her God. Her new-found faith constrained her to say, "The Lord do so to me, and more also, if aught but death part thee and me."

Had Ruth accompanied Orpah to Moab and to obscurity, she would have returned to the altars of Baal. But now with God in her heart, she longed to live with those people "whose God is the Lord." Faith burst forth into the light of day, took the form of quiet, humble service, and remained untainted by any trace of pride or of spiritual haughtiness, as Kuyper expresses it. To which we can add the sentiment of Fausset that, "Ruth is an instance of natural affection made instrumental in leading to true religion. A blossom of heathendom stretching its flower cup desiringly towards the light of revelation in Israel."

The firm decision of Ruth to follow Jehovah, and to completely identify herself with His people, brought her a rich reward when she became the ancestress of the Saviour who came into the world to save idolaters and sinners of every race. With her surrender to the claims of God, Ruth's "beauty of heart, generosity of soul, firm sense of duty and meekness" were sanctified, and were used to place her winsome portrait among the immortals. There are thousands of Christian parents whose heavy load would be lifted if only their unsaved children would come home one day confessing, "Thy God shall be my God, thy people my people." The miracle happened in the heathen heart of Ruth, and God is still the same today as when He won the young widow of Moab for Himself.

A Humble Gleaner

Back in Bethlehem, Naomi was reminded of how her afflictions had changed her. Friends found it hard to believe that this was the beautiful woman who had left them ten years before. At that time she was clothed so well, but now she is clad in a poor and sorrowful dress. Her brow was wrinkled and her back bent, but by her side was the "foreigner," to share her sorrow, and to taste any joys that might come to her. At first it seemed as if they were to remain desolate and uncared for, but fortunately it was harvest time, and the golden sheaves were being gathered in. Naomi and Ruth must live, and Ruth, with her characteristic thoughtfulness, knew that her aged mother-in-law was not able to work. Thus she went out and was directed to join the poor gleaners in the fields of the rich, godly landowner, Boaz.

We find ourselves in disagreement with those who try to portray Ruth as a lonely girl overcome with homesickness for her old Moabite friends as she bent her back to glean in an unfamiliar field. In his *Ode to a Nightingale*, Keats sought to immortalize such a feeling in the arrestive lines —

Perhaps the self-same song that found a path
Thro' the sad heart of Ruth, when, sick for home,
She stood in tears amid the alien corn.

There is no trace whatever of such a doleful note in the record of Ruth. Having deliberately severed all association with Moab, she found joy among the strange people whom she had made her people, and when she went forth that bright morning to follow the reapers, it was with joy and confidence that the God under whose wings she had come to trust would undertake for her. Thus we much prefer the beautiful tribute Thomas Hood gives us in his poem on *Ruth*.

She stood breast-high amid the corn,
Clasped by the golden light of morn,
Like the sweetheart of the sun,
Who many a glowing kiss had won.

On her cheek an autumn flush,
Deeply ripened — such a blush
In the midst of Brown was born,
Like red poppies grown with corn.

Round her eyes her tresses fell,
Which were blackest none could tell,
But long lashes veiled a light,
That had else been all too bright.

And her hat, with shady brim,
Made her tressy forehead dim —
Thus she stood amid the stooks,
Praising God with sweetest looks.

"Sure," I said, "Heav'n did not mean,
Where I reap thou should'st but glean;
Lay thy sheaf adown and come,
Share my harvest and my home."

Ruth was not ashamed of the low order of her work as she took her place as a gleaner with the poor and outcast. The sacred historian tells us that as Ruth went out to secure food for Naomi and herself that it was "her *hap* to light on a part of the field belonging unto Boaz, who was of the kindred of Elimelech." But her entrance into the field of Boaz, and not into another man's field, did not just happen. Under Jewish law Ruth had the right to glean in any harvest field. It was no mere chance, then, that brought Boaz and Ruth together, for even the steps of God's children are directed by Him. In His plan for His own there is no such a thing as *luck*. Determined not to eat the bread of idleness, industrious Ruth walked right into the arms of divine providence. Little did she dream that she would become the much-loved wife of the master of the field in which the reapers had given her a friendly welcome (Ruth 2:12; Psalms 17:8; 36:7).

Being one who feared God, and one who cared for the poor, Boaz went among his reapers, spoke kindly to them, and earned their benediction. Coming upon Ruth he was arrested by her staid and modest look. Although poorly clad there was a dignity in her mien, a refinement giving her distinction, and Boaz is arrested by her beauty and personality. Making inquiries about her, Boaz learns of her sacrifice for Naomi, and of her conversion to the worship of Jehovah (2:6, 7), and commands the reapers to purposely drop extra sheaves for Ruth's benefit. Boaz also bade Ruth to glean only in his field, and to stand fast by his female workers. He wanted to preserve her from coarse contact with men who might take advantage of such a poor woman, who was in his admiring eyes a superior one. She was not to eat with others but present herself at his feasts.

As for Ruth, her heart was full because kindness had been shown her by a stranger in the solitude of a strange land. How excited she must have been when she reached home and told Naomi all about her good fortune, and showed her all the parched corn she had gathered. Was there a lyric note in Ruth's story of that first day? Had she sensed that somehow Boaz had been strangely attracted to her, hence his generosity in spite of the alien blood in her veins? As for Naomi, when Ruth came to mention the name of her benefactor, Boaz, she recalls the name as that of a kinsman of her deceased husband, Elimelech. It may be that in the mind of Naomi there entered a feeling that perhaps a brighter future may be hers and Ruth's.

An Honored Mother

We all know how matters between Boaz and Ruth developed which caused Goethe to say of the Book of Ruth that "we have nothing so lovely in the whole range of epic and idyllic poetry." The name of Boaz became immortalized because of his loving-kindness toward Ruth, the poor Moabitess, while the kinsman who would not mar his own inheritance is unknown. It turned out that Boaz was one of Naomi's nearest relatives and one of the few remaining kinsmen of her husband's family. Therefore he was able to befriend the widow of Mahlon, Elimelech's son, according to the deep principle pervading the law of Israel regarding the preservation of families. This Levirate Law stated that where a husband died without issue, the nearest brother-in-law (levir) might be called upon by the widow to perform for her all the duties of a husband, and raise up seed for the deceased.

In the case of Ruth, however, no brother-in-law was available seeing the only sons Elimelech had were dead. Consequently, the nearest of kin could be called upon to act as "redeemer" (goel) for the unfortunate, relieving them thereby of their distress. The nearest relative to Ruth by marriage was unable to function as her goel, and being the next relative, Boaz did not shirk his responsibility toward the lovely woman who had won his heart. Before the council of ten men at the city gate he announced before witnesses his decision to buy Ruth's inheritance and marry her. Although bachelor Boaz was advanced in years, he was determined to play his part and as Naomi said, "The man will not rest, until he has finished the thing this day" — and finish it he did! So the idyllic conclusion was reached, with Ruth being lifted out of obscurity into a happy union with Boaz, the mighty man of wealth. This story provides us with one of the first records in world history of a rise from rags to riches, from poverty to plenty.

God smiled upon the marriage of honorable Boaz and virtuous Ruth, and blessed them with a son whom they named Obed which means "a servant who worships." As Ruth was the servant who came to worship Jehovah, we can imagine her son's name as being expressive of her own conversion from idolatry. Through the birth of Obed, who became the father of Jesse, who, in turn was the father of King David, Ruth found herself numbered among the elect, and God wove the thread of her life most intricately into the web of the history of His people, both before and after Christ.

A Gentile by birth, Ruth yet became the chosen line through which later the Saviour of the world appeared. As He came to redeem both Jew and Gentile alike, it was fitting that the blood of both should mingle in His veins. "A good name," says Solomon, "is rather to be chosen than riches, and loving favour than silver and gold." Ruth found it so, and thus her good name found a place in the royal genealogy of Jesus (Matthew 1:5). As George Matheson so beautifully puts it, "In the soul of Jesus the wedding bells of Ruth and Boaz are rung once more. Here again Moab and Israel meet together. In the heart of the Son of Man the Gentile stands side by side with the Jew as the recipient of a common divine fatherhood."

Those of us who are Christians praise God for Ruth's inclusion in His portrait-gallery, for she was the ancestress of Him who, by His death, brought us nigh to God. It was from Boaz, an Israelite without guile, and from Ruth, who became an "Israelite not in race, but in mind; not in blood but faith; not by tribe but by virtue and goodness," that Jesus came as the most perfect expression of all graces.

One could say much of the merits and message of the book to which Ruth gave her name, as well as of the many lessons to be gathered from it. Benjamin Franklin, who was ridiculed at one time in Paris for his defense of the Bible, was determined to find out how much of it his scoffers had read. He informed one of the learned societies that he had come across a story of pastoral life in ancient times that seemed to him very beautiful but he would like the opinion of the society. A night was arranged for Franklin to read to the assembly of scholars a lyric which impressed him. The Bible lover read the Book of Ruth, and when he had finished the scholars were in ecstasies and begged Franklin to print it. "It is already in print," said Franklin. "It is a part of the Bible you ridicule."

There is nothing in the entire range of biography sacred or profane, comparable to the idyllic simplicity, tenderness and beauty of the story of Ruth, the young widow of Moab. There are only two books out of the sixty-six forming the Bible that are named after women. Ruth is one, and the other is Esther — and both books have enchanted succeeding ages. The Jews have a peculiar regard for both books. At their Feast of Purim they read Esther, and at the Feast of Pentecost, the scroll of Ruth. Among the many typical features in the latter, the most outstanding is that of the composition of the true church of Jesus Christ. Ruth was a Gentile, Boaz a Hebrew. Boaz redeemed Ruth's possession and then became her husband. All have sinned, both Jews and Gentiles, but Jesus died for all, and His church is composed of regenerated Jews and Gentiles whom He calls His Bride. Thus "the marriage-bells of Ruth at Bethlehem were the same bells which sounded at the marriage-supper of the Lamb."

From Ruth's outstanding qualities of unselfishness and loyalty we learn that such virtues are the only foundation upon which true happiness can be built. Without them, abiding friendship is impossible, home ties are loose, and the social structure weak. Ruth also teaches us that attractive graciousness is worth cultivating; and that racial hatred and religious bigotry can be solved by a right relationship to Him who made of one blood all nations. Further, the rare literary gem of the Book of Ruth, which takes one some fifteen minutes to read, shows us how our industrial and labor problems can be solved. Boaz was a wealthy farmer, yet he maintained a delightful relation to those who worked for him in a dark, chaotic period of Israelitish history. As he walked through his fields, meeting his servants he would say, "The Lord be with thee," and such was the harmony that prevailed that they would reply, "The Lord bless thee." In our time, the strained relationship between masters and employees would be quickly solved by the application of the good will manifested in those ancient days. Combining as it does all the traits of human life and character, Ruth is a book all can read with both pleasure and profit.

SALOME No. 1
THE WOMAN WHOSE DANCING MEANT DEATH

Scripture References — Matthew 14:6-11; Mark 6:22-28

Name Meaning — Salome is the feminine form of Solomon, and according to Wilkinson, is the Greek form in *shalom* meaning "peace." Cruden, however, says that Salome implies, "very shady," which is truer of the debased character of the daughter of Herodias—which was indeed shady, morally. The New Testament does not name her. It is Josephus the Jewish historian who identifies her as Salome.

Family Connections — She was the daughter of Herodias by her first husband, Herod Philip, a son of Herod the Great. Josephus tells us that Salome was married first to Philip the tetrarch, and afterward to Aristobulus, king of Chalcis, the grandson of Herod, and brother of Agrippa.

Mention has already been made of the part Salome played at the birthday of Herod, and how through her sensual dancing John the Baptist was beheaded, and Herod lost his kingdom (see HERODIAS). Kitto, the eminent expositor tells us that, "In the age of Herod, dancing was exceedingly rare and almost unheard of, and therefore the condescension of Salome, who volunteered to honour that monarch's birthday by exhibiting her handsome person as she led the mazy dance in the saloons of Machaerus, felt it to be a compliment that merited the highest reward." It was more at the instigation of her evil-minded mother, however, than her own initiative that Salome took part in her dance of death.

What must be borne in mind in our modern times with its evils of mixed dancing is that the Bible nowhere speaks of the mixing of the sexes in the dance. The only social dancing for mere amusement was engaged in by men void of shame whom Michal alluded to when she rebuked her husband for dancing alone *before the Lord;* the godless families described by Job, which produced increased impiety, and ended in destruction; and that of Salome which terminated in Herod's rash vow and in the murder of John the Baptist, our Lord's forerunner. As almost all forms of mixed dancing are taught and practiced in schools and colleges, and alas, countenanced by some churches, Christian parents are deeply concerned about the moral effect of dancing on the lives of their children. If they refuse permission for their children to dance, parents are daubed as being too tight-laced, old-fashioned, or out of fashion. Well, Noah was certainly out of fashion, but with

his family was saved from the terrible deluge, while the giddy and corrupt world around perished. As the fashion of this world is to pass away, why should Christians shrink from non-participation in it? Moses, we are told, chose "affliction" rather than "enjoy the pleasures of sin for a season" (Hebrews 11:25). The evil heart of Herodias planned the evil act of Salome's dance, and God's greatest prophet died. Surely such a tragedy is sufficient to condemn dancing as we know it?

SALOME No. 2

THE WOMAN WHO WANTED THE BEST FOR HER SONS

Scripture References — Matthew 20:20-24; 27:56; Mark 10:35-40; 15:40, 41; 16:1, 2

Name Meaning — See SALOME, No. 1. Mark alone gives her name. Matthew designates her as "the mother of Zebedee's children."

Family Connections — Legendary attempts had been made to connect Salome with Joseph by a previous marriage, and therefore link her up with the family of Mary; or to make her a daughter of Zacharias. Inadequate attempts have sought to identify her as the sister of Mary, the mother of Jesus, using John 19:25 as the basis of association. Scripture is silent as to her genealogy. All we know is that she was the wife of Zebedee, the prosperous fisherman who had hired servants. The only glimpse we have of him is in his boat, mending his nets when Jesus came upon him and called his two sons to follow Him. That Zebedee shared his wife's devotion to Jesus is evidenced by the fact that there was no action on his part to detain his sons from leaving his fishing business to accompany Jesus. Reading between the lines, it is not difficult to detect the harmony in that Capernaum family, concerning the call and claims of Jesus (Matthew 4:21; Mark 1:19, 20).

Her Devotion

Salome, one of the saintly women who followed Jesus in Galilee and ministered unto Him, appears to have been one of His disciples from the outset of His public ministry (Mark 15:40, 41; Matthew 20:20-28). She had no doubt whatever as to His Messiahship, and faced no difficulty in persuading her sons, James and John, to accompany her in obedience to the Master's word. Both Zebedee and Salome by their life and teaching prepared their children to follow Jesus. That they never forgot their home influence and instruction is seen in the depth of devotion, wide range of vision and a godly joyousness the writings of James and John, who became apostles, clearly reveal. Salome remained a faithful disciple of Jesus up to the very end. She was present at the crucifixion, beholding that grim scene afar off, even when her two sons had withdrawn.

Salome, along with the other women "stood afar off," probably because of the malicious crowd, the rough soldiers, and the horrors of the cross, all of which was sufficient to make them timid. They were full of love and sympathy, even though they stood afar off. With tear-filled eyes with which they had shown their devotion on the way to the cross (Luke 23:28), they still beheld Him as He hung there in death. Salome was also with the women who came to anoint the body of Jesus, and shared in the glorious news of His Resurrection (Luke 24:10). They hastened to perform their last service for their Lord, but were not at the tomb soon enough to perfume His body with spices. Their devotion was rewarded by the revelation of the angel that He whom they loved and mourned was alive forevermore. They went forth to proclaim the blessed truth of the Resurrection — a miracle which Salome's son, John, was to give emphasis to as he came to write the last book of the Bible (Revelation 1:17, 18).

Her Demand

Salome was ambitious for her sons, and ambition is commendable when it is in full agreement with the mind and purpose of God. Ambition, when divinely directed, can lead to the heights of honor but when selfishly pursued can cast one down to the depths of degradation. Salome knew she was an honored mother because her two sons, James and John, were two of Christ's best-loved disciples and along with Peter formed the inner circle among the Twelve. On different occasions, Peter, James and John are grouped together. Salome knew that Christ was the Messiah, but as a mil-

lennialist could not separate Him from Israel's temporal glory. Feeling that the kingdom would soon be established, she requested that her sons be placed one on Christ's right hand and the other on His left when He inaugurated His kingdom. Although such a demand arose from maternal pride and jealousy, it did not arise from true faith. She knew not what she asked (Matthew 20:20-24; Mark 10:35-40) when seeking seats of honor for her sons.

In His rebuke of Salome for her misguided ambition Christ did not reject the request of the mother for her children, but corrected it, and accepted it in a way mother and sons did not anticipate. To be intimately near Him on His throne meant fellowship with Him in His sufferings. Our Lord did not treat Salome's ambition as if it were sinful but he was compassionate because of the ignorance behind the request. Salome did not know "what manner of spirit" she was of (Luke 9:55). In effect, Jesus asked if her sons were prepared to drink the cup of martyrdom, and implied that James and John would share His throne of suffering. This they did, for James was the first apostolical martyr and John, the last. Salome's dreams of the kingship of Christ with her sons sharing His rule were rudely shattered as she saw her much-loved Messiah dying as a felon on a wooden gibbet. Along with others she thought that it would have been "He who would have redeemed Israel," but there He is, hanging on a cross in agony and shame. Salome came to learn that the only way to sovereignty is through sacrificial service. "Whosoever will be chief among you, let him be your servant" (Matthew 20:26, 27). The mother sought earthly crowns for her sons, but through losing their lives for Christ's sake, they gained greater honor in heaven.

As we leave "the mother of Zebedee's children," it is with the realization of the influence of a godly mother in, and over, the lives of her children. So often it is from a mother's tender affection that her child imbibes the love of God, so that it becomes almost part of the child's nature. Further, there is no more potent antidote against sin within or without than faith in God generated by the holy life and teaching of godly parents. Salome and Zebedee were the

Lord's and both of their sons became His followers and died for His cause. Happy and grateful are those Christian parents who live to see their offspring wholly dedicated to the service of the Lord.

SAPPHIRA
The Woman Who Dropped Dead

Scripture Reference — Acts 5:1-11
Name Meaning — A Hebrew name, Sapphira means the jewel, "sapphire" — a precious gem of deep blue, and probably is given in allusion to the color of the eyes. The name is from a Hebrew word signifying "beautiful" or "pleasant." The sapphire represents the blue veins of a beautiful person (Ezekiel 28:13). The Bible gives us no record of Sapphira, nor of her husband with whom she sinned and died. Although we do not know their genealogy we are given an insight into their greed and deceit. It is not easy to separate these two who were partners in falsehood. Our cameo of Sapphira therefore is likewise that of her husband.

The satanically inspired deception of these two who agreed together to lie against God in the Spirit, was the first gross act of disobedience within the newly formed Christian church, hence, the justification of the severe punishment inflicted. As Meyer puts it, this was "the first open venture of deliberate wickedness" and the punishment was "an awe-inspiring act of Divine church-discipline." As Satan sought to ruin God's original creation through the disobedience of earth's first pair, Adam and Eve, so here he is active again seeking to destroy the testimony of God's new creation, His blood-bought church, through another pair, Ananias and Sapphira. "She is His new creation" we sing of the church, and its early members realized the necessity of being one in Christ Jesus, but Satan strikes at such a spiritual unity not from without, but within by two of its members who might have wrecked the church.

It has been suggested by some writers that Sapphira was the instigator of the deceptive transaction, costing the life of Ananias and herself. As Eve tempted Adam into sin, and Jezebel caused Ahab to perpetrate his terrible crimes against ancient Israel, so Sapphira tempted her weak husband to sin to his ruin. The narrative says that they "agreed together" to lie, and that both were equally guilty, for whatever Ananias proposed, his wife was "also privy to it."

Discipleship

A tragic aspect of the agreed decision of Ananias and Sapphira is that both of them were professed Christians who had turned from Judaism and had associated themselves with the newly-formed Christian community. Faith and zeal of some sort had led them to declare themselves as believers. Whatever they did, they accomplished together, and some time after Pentecost they unitedly became part of "the multitude of them that believed" (Acts 4:32). It was, therefore, their professed discipleship that aggravated their sin. Deceit and lying are to be deplored in the lives of those who are not the Lord's. Lacking the ethical standard of Christianity they so act, but for two of Christ's own followers to try and deceive the Omniscient Spirit was indeed a sin unto death. To the best of saints there comes the exhortation, "Take heed lest thou fall."

Disposal

In order to fully understand the record of Ananias and Sapphira we must read it in the light of what goes before. The days in which they lived were days of a voluntary Christian communism in the primitive church, when there was no compulsory abandonment of property, or absolute community of goods. The godless Communism of today in which there is an enforced equal distribution of property, and human rights are denied is totally different from the willing surrender of possessions for the sake of all which the apostolic age experienced. Then, "all that *believed* were together, and had all things common; and sold their possessions and goods, and parted them to all men as every man had need." Such a voluntary forsaking of property for the sake of the cause of Christ was characteristic of the members of the church at Jerusalem, after the descent of the Holy Spirit at Pentecost. This compact on the part of the believers to sell what they had and place the proceeds of the sale in one common fund for the benefit of the needy, was a remarkable demonstration of their willingness to follow the Master's call to forsake all and follow Him. There has never been, in the long history of the church, such an exhibition of Christian stewardship and a sense of individual responsibility in the sight of God.

Conspicuous among those who had surrendered was Barnabas, who had gained praise and power because of his self-sacrifice. He had sold all his land and surrendered all the money it brought, to Peter, the representative and spokesman of the Twelve and leader in the Early Church. Then we come to the "melancholy *but*," as Matthew Henry describes the opening of the fifth chapter of the Acts. "But a certain man named Ananias, with Sapphira his wife, sold a possession." The action of Barnabas to sell all was inspired by the Holy Spirit. Now two other believers are actuated by the spirit of evil to pretend a similar surrender. Seeing the gladness and enthusiasm of others who had become generous benefactors, and of the way they were praisingly spoken of because of their sacrifice, Ananias and Sapphira did not want to be thought selfish in retaining what they had. They wanted to be included among those who, from the highest motives, denied themselves of their earthly possessions, and so tried to ape the intense brotherliness which other believers had manifested. But the sincerity and spontaneity of the surrender of others only set forth in dark contrast the calculated deceit Ananias and his wife were to practice.

Deceit

Acting together, Ananias and Sapphira sold the plot of land they had owned, and brought only "a certain part" to Peter. They were not bound by any rule of the church to sell their land and make a gift of any size. Had they brought nothing to Peter there would not have been any blame. Their sin consisted in surrendering a part as if it had been the whole, and keeping back the other part for themselves. They wanted to give the impression that their all was on the altar, when it was not, and thus they became guilty of sacrilege in the attempt to obtain the reputation of saintliness with the reality of sacrifice. It was an effort to serve God *and* mammon. Theirs was "the double

mind"—the heart divided between the world and God which James describes (1:8; 4:8). Their money was their own to keep, or give in part or wholly. "Whiles it remained, was it not thine own?" Their deceit came in trying to represent themselves as completely sacrificial as Barnabas, but in the attempt they acted a lie. The part was offered as if it were the entire proceeds of the sale of land. The phrase "*keep back* part of the price" is rendered "purloining" by Titus, and conveys the idea of stealthy and dishonest appropriation (2:10), and is used of the sin of covetousness by Achan (Joshua 7:1).

Twice over the unworthy action of these two believers is referred to as "lying." "Lie to the Holy Spirit" — "Thou hast not lied unto men but unto God" (5:3, 4). The margin gives "deceive" for "lie." If there is any difference between these terms, deceiving is the end, and lying the means of its accomplishment. There was the attempt to cheat or deceive the Holy Spirit. Ananias and Sapphira felt that no one knew how much money their land brought, and dishonesty became a deliberate lie. Alas, they were not spiritually motivated as Barnabas had been when he sold and gave all, and so in their resemblance of a full surrender, Ananias and Sapphira were most dishonest. They fell into temptation and a snare, and their avarice resulted in a fraud. Peter, who knew by experience the machinations of Satan, told the fraudulent couple that they had allowed Satan to possess their hearts, even as the same enemy moved Judas to sell his Lord for money. But falsehood and hypocrisy rather than greed were the sins which Ananias and Sapphira were so severely punished for.

Peter did not shrink from exalting the Holy Spirit as *God* (compare the phrases "lie to the Holy Spirit" — "lie unto God"). Here the personality and deity of the Spirit are emphasized. We cannot lie against a mere influence. Ananias and Sapphira tempted the Omniscient Spirit, by agreeing to practice a deception on men in whom He manifestly dwelt in an extraordinary manner, and through whom He now spoke and acted, as He did through Peter, the ruler and guardian of the Spirit's infant church. How deceived by Satan they were into believing that they could sin in the dark without the divine Searcher of the secrets of all hearts — even their own — knowing of their pretension!

Death

Judgment, swift and severe, overtook the two conspirators whose sudden death was a signal proof of God's anger on their Judas-like hypocrisy. Had it not been for the exposure of the false, dishonest action of Ananias and Sapphira, the church at Jerusalem would have continued thinking of them as pious people who, like Barnabas and others, had sacrificed their possessions for the benefit of the flock. But Peter, reflecting the righteous indignation of the Lord over the deceit of Sapphira and her husband, "ripped the texture which had been woven out of the threads of pious appearances and greediness to shreds."

Ananias was the first to suffer for the sin against the Holy Spirit. When he brought the "certain part" of the sale of his land to Peter, the Apostle immediately charged him with keeping back part of the price. Whether Peter had heard from others what the full price was, or had the amount been revealed to him by the all-knowing Spirit we do not know. All Peter did was to press home the intensity of the guilt of Ananias and immediately he was struck dead. Peter did not announce any sentence of death upon him. Because the Church had just been established as a divine institution which its Founder was to use for the extension of His cause in the world, it was necessary to condemn on its first appearance by a visible, divine judgment, the particular form of evil Ananias had committed. This was, namely, the worst corruption of the best — the effort to gain "the reputation of a saint, without the reality of holiness." While the shame and agony of detection, the horror of conscience not yet dead, paralyzed the powers of life and resulted in a quick death, behind any natural cause there was a visitation of God. The burial of Ananias followed immediately, in the burial place of the infant church. Ellicott asks whether the cemetery which the saints had free access to was the potter's field that had been bought to bury strangers in and was Ananias buried near

to Judas in the same grounds? (Matthew 27:7, 8).

Fortunately, Sapphira was not present during the three hours when her husband was brought face to face with his sin of deception, dropped dead and wrapped up in his winding-sheet and buried. Returning home, she expected to join her husband in receiving high honor for their pretended sacrifice, but in meeting Peter she continued the lie of Ananias. The Apostle's question, "Tell me whether ye sold the land for so much?" that is, the amount given to Peter and which they represented as the full price they had received for the sale, gave Sapphira an opportunity of telling the truth and repenting of her share in the deceit. Unknown to her, it was too late to warn Ananias, but she had it in her power to clear her own conscience by a frank confession, and thereby save herself from death. The lie agreed upon, however, came glibly from her lips, and the solemn word of judgment was pronounced. Sapphira heard of the doom of her husband and that having shared in his crime, she must now share in his condemnation. Sudden death overtook her, and her warm body was carried to the grave to rest with that of her husband.

A word is necessary as to Peter's ministry in this tragic episode of exposing the ugly secret of two hearts. Through the coming of the Spirit at Pentecost, Peter received a prophetic insight enabling him to read the thoughts and intents of Ananias and Sapphira, and to trace their evil to its fountainhead, namely, Satan, who had previously sifted Peter himself. Infidels have charged Peter with cruelty in bringing destruction upon these persons, but he did not decree or will their death. He only declared the penalty which was carried out by the Spirit of God on whom the horrible deception had been attempted. Further, Ananias and Sapphira did not die from apoplexy caused by the shock of a sudden disgrace, but died miraculously through a divine stroke. Peter's exposure of their sin was the occasion of their death.

Remembering that Sapphira and her husband were Christians, how did their swift judgment affect their relationship Godward? Jeremy Taylor reminds us that God sometimes accepts a temporal death in place of an eternal death, and that a sudden death stands instead of a long and an explicit repentance. Augustine and others affirm that the two who were suddenly destroyed come under the category of those church members delivered unto Satan for the destruction of the flesh so that the spirit may be saved in the day of the Lord Jesus (I Corinthians 5:5; I Peter 4:6). Alexander Whyte expresses the trembling hope that "they were struck down in sanctifying discipline, rather than in an everlasting condemnation. And that they so died that we might learn of them so to live as not to die. Let us hope that both husband and wife had the roots of the matter in them at the time; and that we shall see them also saved in that day, in spite of Satan and all his fatal entrances into their hearts. The Lord rebuke thee, O Satan, is not this a brand plucked out of the fire?"

The effect of this horrible experience in the early days of the church was immediate. A sense of awe and dread came upon the community of believers. When Ananias dropped dead, "great fear came upon all them that heard these things," and when it came to the turn of Sapphira to follow her husband in a sudden exit we read that "great fear came upon all the church." The assembly, purged of its deceivers, went forward to experience a succession of miraculous performances. Those saints stood in awe of sin, as the result of the exposure of the lying of two of its members, and the terrible judgment that overtook them. We, too, in this far-off day can be warned by the subtle sin to which Ananias and Sapphira succumbed. Avarice, fraud, deceit, lying, false pretensions, must be guarded against. Honor in the church cannot be bought by money. How we sin when we sing, "My all is on the altar," yet do not bring all the tithes into the storehouse! If God dealt with His erring saints today as He did with those two long ago when they lied to the Spirit, there would be scores of vacant seats in our churches and assemblies because of removals by sudden death. Because all things are seen by His all-searching eye, may we be found living and walking in the light having, thereby, lives that are clear and transparent.

SARAH, SARAI, SARA
THE WOMAN WHO BECAME MOTHER OF NATIONS

Scripture References—Genesis 11:29-31; 12:5-17; 16:1-8; 17:15-21; 18; 20:2-18; 21:1-12; 23:1-19; 24:36, 37; 25:10, 12; 49:31; Isaiah 51:2; Romans 4:19; 9:9; Hebrews 11:11; I Peter 3:6

Name Meaning — Among the classified names of the Bible are those known as sacramental names, and are so-called because they were names given by God Himself, or under His inspiration in association with a particular promise, covenant or declaration of His, as to the character, destiny or mission of those distinctly named. Thus a sacramental name became a sign and seal of an established covenant between God and the recipient of such a name. Two Bible characters bearing sacramental names are Abraham and Sarah, both of which signify the gracious purposes and promises of God.

The wife of the patriarch was originally known as Sarai, meaning "princely" or "a princess." Elsdon C. Smith suggests it may signify "contentious" or "quarrelsome," but was changed, not accidentally, or by the whim of the bearer, but by God Himself that it might be a sign of His purpose, into Sarah, implying the princess, a princess or princesses, the source of nations and kings. Sarah or "chieftainness," the feminine of Sar, meaning a "captain" or "commander" is repeatedly used in this sense as a common noun as, for instance, by Isaiah who renders it "queen" (49:23). It has been observed that among ancient Jews there was a sort of a cabalistic translation that "the Hebrew letter *yod* signifies the creative power of God in nature, while the letter *hay* symbolizes the state of grace — that state into which Sarah had entered after receiving the covenanted promises." The promise of ancestorship of many nations came with the change of the name of *Sarai to Sarah*. "I will bless her and she shall become nations." She was thus associated with her husband in the great blessing of the covenant whose name was also changed from *Abram to Abraham*. The former, original name means a "high, or honored father," the latter, "a father of many nations." The Apocrypha speaks of Abraham as "a great father of a multitude of nations" (Ecclesiasticus 44:20).

The root idea of Sarah means "to rule," and fits the personality of the bearer. It was a name intended as a seal of the promise given to Abraham, "kings of peoples shall be of her." Paul has an allegorical reference to Sarah as one who typified the gospel dispensation, "Jerusalem which is above . . . which is the mother of us all' (Galatians 4:26). Thus, Sarah was to be *the* princess, not only "because she was to be the ancestress of a great nation *literally*, of many nations *spiritually*, but also because the rank and power were to be possessed by her descendants, or rather because the people descended from her were to be ruled over by a regal dynasty, by a succession of kings of their own race and lineage, is derived from her." In the genealogy of the descendants of Esau, Sarah's grandson we read, "These are the kings that reigned in the land of Edom before there reigned any king over the children of Israel." The line of kings descended from Sarah terminated in God's Anointed One, the Messiah, whose "kingdom is not of this world." The sacramental name of Sarah, therefore, also symbolizes the spiritual seed, the whole multitude of believers of all nations who are "kings and priests unto God."

Then the personal application of the changed name must not be forgotten. Called *Sarah* by God and the Angels (Genesis 17:15; 18:9), she exhibited the traits of a princess, "wielding a sceptre by the magic of which she could lord it over men's hearts after her own will, even bring kings to her feet. If she came into the world with a will of her own as her dowry, nature further assisted her in developing it by the great beauty of her face and the grace of her stature. By these gifts she made her wish a command and disarmed opposition." Both in bearing and character she illustrated the significance of her name. Through the long, long years of the quiet and stedfast devotion of Abraham to Sarah, peace reigned in the matrimonial tent more be-

cause of Abraham's gentleness, kindness and forbearance, even though he lived so long with the more expressive and possessive ways of Sarah. Twice over in the KJV of the New Testament she is referred to as *Sara*, but the ASV uniformly gives us *Sarah* (Hebrews 11:11; I Peter 3:6).

Family Connections — Sarah came from Ur of the Chaldees, Babylonia, and her former name Sarai, "princely," identifies her as coming from an honored family. She was the daughter of Terah and was therefore half-sister to Abram, her senior by ten years (Genesis 17:17), whom she married in the Ur of the Chaldees. While Abram and Sarai had the same father, they had different mothers (Genesis 20:12). Marriages between near relatives were countenanced in those days and were sometimes common for religious reasons (Genesis 24:3, 4; 28:1, 2), but not marriages between those actually by the same mother. Sarai was well past middle life and childless when with Abram she left her own country and with him went out "not knowing whither they went" (Genesis 11:29, 30).

There are various ways of looking at this remarkable woman who through a long span of life was the faithful wife of a prophet known as "The Friend of God."

Her Uniqueness

Strange though it may sound and seem, the first Jew was a Gentile, for Abraham who came from beyond the Euphrates was the first man to be called a *Hebrew*, "Abram the Hebrew" (Genesis 14:13). The word Hebrew itself means, "the immigrant," and was no doubt the usual designation among the Canaanites. As his wife, Sarah was the first Hebrewess — the joint fountainhead of the great Jewish race (Genesis 11:29-31; Isaiah 51:2). Abraham has been fitly called, "The fountainhead of the Hebrew hero life," and Sarah is the heroine of such life. She remains the first unquestionably historical woman of the Hebrews, and their first mother. She is, therefore, one of the most important female figures in the world's history, as the natural source of the Jewish people, through whom the nations of the earth were to be blessed. Only two women are named in the illustrious roll of those conspicuous for their faith; Sarah is the first, and Rahab the second (Hebrews 11:11, 31), both of whom lived by faith and died in faith (Hebrews 11:13). Sarah or Sara have always been popular female names both among Jews and Gentiles.

Her Beauty

The testimony of the Bible is that Sarah was unusually beautiful (Genesis 12:11, 14). The lines of Keats were true of her —

> A thing of beauty is a joy for ever:
> Its loveliness increases; it will never
> Pass into nothingness; but still will keep
> A bower quiet for us, and a sleep
> Full of sweet dreams . . .

Hebrew folklore has kept alive stories of her remarkable beauty and ranks her next to the most perfect woman the world has known, Eve, "the mother of all living." Sarah seems to have had beauty that grew more attractive with the passing years. "Of the things that are unfavourable to the preservation of beauty, the Orientals count travel as one that is most baneful, even fatal to it," says Gustav Gottheil. "Yet when Sarah arrived, after a long journey through dusty deserts and under a scorching sun, at the frontiers of Egypt, she was more beautiful than ever, and this explains the curious speech of Abraham to his wife at that juncture: 'Now I know that thou art a woman beautiful to look at.' Did he not know that before? Not so convincingly, explains the rabbi, as after he had seen that even travel had left no touch on her countenance."

Isaiah says that, "Beauty is a fading flower" (28:1), and a song of old has the stanza—

> Beauty is but skin deep,
> And ugly to the bone.
> Beauty soon fades away,
> But ugly holds its own.

But with Sarah it was different, for even when she was 90 years of age she was so lovely that Abraham feared that kings would fall in love with her bewitching beauty — which Pharaoh and Abimelech did, as our next glimpse of her proves. As one of the most beautful women who ever lived we can imagine that wherever she journeyed the admiring eyes of all were cast upon her. "Grave is all beauty," and Sarah's renowned loveliness certainly brought its trouble.

Her Peril

When famine drove Abraham and Sarah into the land of Egypt, and they felt that hostile kings might take them prisoners, Abraham came up with the abject, base proposal that if taken prisoners then his wife should represent herself as his sister. Fear of death unmanned him and led him to risk the dishonor of his wife and thereby save his own neck. She dearly loved her husband, and his life was too precious to her to make her think of the shame she might incur. Sarah was utterly wrong in yielding to her husband's plot. How nobler she would have been had she stoutly refused Abraham saying, "How can I do this great wickedness and sin against God?" But she called her husband "lord," and evidently he was lord of her conscience.

Abraham felt that if oriental despots knew that Sarah and he were married they would slay him and add the lovely woman to their harem. Married to a conspicuous beauty caused Abraham to be afraid, and he resorted to a falsehood to save his life. If taken, Sarah was not to say that she was his wife but his sister. This pretense was not an outright lie, but a half-truth, seeing that she was his half-sister. They were children of the same father, but not the same mother. It seems hard to believe that such a good man could deliver his lovely wife over to a heathen monarch, but he did, and Sarah entered Pharaoh's harem. But God protected her by sending plagues upon the monarch. Pharaoh sent her back to her own husband, untouched. The same unworthy plan was carried out when Abimelech, king of the Philistines, admiring her bewitching beauty had her taken to his harem. But again God interfered and commanded the king to restore Sarah to Abraham, seeing she was his wife. Threatened with violent death, Abimelech obeyed, but severely rebuked Abraham for his deceit (Genesis 12:10-20; 20). Years later Isaac, the son of Abraham and Sarah, used this same form of deception (Genesis 26:6-13, see REBEKAH).

God expressed His displeasure with Abraham and his wife because of their ill-conceived plot. As the Righteous One, He could not condone such trickery. Had He not called them out from their country for a specific mission? And was He not able to protect and preserve them from harm and danger in a strange land? Was not the half-lie told on two occasions an indication of the lack of faith in God's overshadowing care and power to fulfill His promise? Abraham's lofty soul suffered an eclipse of the virtue of faith for which he was renowned when he adopted such a plan of deception, exposing his wife to great peril, and also thwarting of the divine plan for and through Sarah. (Compare HAGAR.) Abraham's deception was followed by an attempt to ease an offense, and the patriarch was more blameworthy than Sarah who should have resisted the dangerous plan of exposing herself for the sexual gratification of other men.

> A lie that is half a truth
> Is ever the worst of lies.

A half-truth is always a lie. While it was true that Sarah was Abraham's sister, the assertion was in reality a falsehood. After the severe rebuke from Pharaoh for their deception, they should have learned their lesson, but to commit the same sin again a few years later, and further imperil God's plan to make of them a great nation, leaves Abraham and Sarah without excuse. How slow we are to learn from our past failures?

Her Sorrow

The one great grief of Abraham and Sarah was that through their long life together they had no children. To a Hebrew woman, barrenness was looked upon as a gnawing grief, and sometimes regarded as a sign of divine disfavor. Childless, even when back in Babylonia (Genesis 11:30; 16:1-8), Sarah remained so until at 90 years of age God miraculously fulfilled His promise and made her the mother of the son of promise. Through the long years, "side by side with the prosperity, beat for beat with the pulse of Abraham's joy, there throbs in Sarah's heart a pulse of pain . . . There is as yet no heir." The constant grief of barrenness caused Sarah to become "The Woman Who Made a Great Mistake." In spite of the fact that, along with her husband, she had received the divine promise, that from her nations would spring, the possibility of

ever becoming a mother died in her heart. Such a cross as barrenness inflamed and intensified her pride, and forced her to find a way out of this embarrassment to her husband. "Sarah sacrificed herself on the cruelest altar on which any woman ever laid herself down; but the cords of the sacrifice were all the time the cords of a suicidal pride: till the sacrifice was both a great sin in the sight of God, a fatal injury to herself, to her husband, and to innocent generations yet unborn."

Sarah revealed the sad defect of her qualities when she said to Abraham, "Take Hagar my maid, and let not the promises of God fail through me. Through her I can continue your hereditary line." But all poor Hagar could do was to produce an Ishmael. It was only through Sarah that the promised seed could come. Although it might have been a custom of the time for a man with a barren wife to take a concubine in order that he might have an heir, Abraham, as a God-fearing man, should have stoutly refused to go along with the unworthy scheme, which in the end produced jealousy and tragedy. "Abram hearkened to the voice of Sarai," but the voice was the fatal siren of Satan who sought to destroy the royal, promised seed (Genesis 3:15). As one modern writer expresses it —

> Little did Sarai think when she persuaded Abram to take Hagar, that she was originating a rivalry which has run in the keenest animosity through the ages, and which oceans of blood have not quenched.

In our cameo of Hagar (which see) we sought to show all that followed the blunder of Sarah, when she intervened in God's plan and chose her way to continue her husband's posterity.

Her Joy

In His forgiving love and mercy God appeared to Abram when he was 99 years old, and assured him that his long barren wife, although now 90 years old, would conceive. To confirm His promise God changed the name of Abram to Abraham, and of Sarai to Sarah (Genesis 17; 18). At such a revelation of God's purpose, "Abraham fell upon his face and laughed." Although he marveled at the performance of the naturally impossible, Abraham yet believed, and his laughter was the joy of a man of faith. Laughter is sometimes mad (Ecclesiastes 2:2) but that of Abraham was highly rational. He rejoiced in the thought that Isaac should be born, and perhaps at that time he had a vision of the Messiah. Jesus said, "Your father Abraham rejoiced to see my day" (John 8:56). As for Sarah, what was her reaction when she overheard the Lord say to her husband, "Sarah thy wife shall have a son"?

The record says, "Sarah laughed within herself," but hers was the laugh of doubt. Yet when her son was born he was named Isaac, which means "laughter"—a memorial of her sin (Genesis 18:13), and of her husband's joy (17:17). Sarah's joy knew no bounds, "God hath made me to laugh" (21:6; 24:36). She had laughter before, but God was not the author of her laugh of doubt. The joy of Sarah in the birth of Isaac reminds us of "the great joy" proclaimed by the angels who made known to the shepherds the birth of Christ who came of the line of Isaac (Luke 2:10; Romans 4:18-21). Paul reminds us that it was by faith that Sarah conceived beyond nature (Hebrews 11:11). It was not only in itself a miracle wrought by faith, but also in earnest of something far greater, even the Incarnation of Jesus Christ.

Her Longevity

Sarah is the only woman whose specific age is stated in Scripture. A girl's approximate age is given us in the gospels. The only daughter of Jairus whom Jesus raised from the dead was "about 12 years of age" (Luke 8:42). Sarah called herself old when she was 87 (Genesis 18:12), but she was 127 years of age when she died. Abraham had reached the patriarchal age of 175 when God called him home. Godliness has always been favorable to longevity. The "good old age" (Genesis 15:15) was a signal proof of the faithfulness of the Lord. When the Countess of Huntingdon came to die she said, "My work is done, and I have nothing to do but to go to my Father." Surely the same contentment was experienced both by Sarah and Abraham who were not satiated with life, but satisfied with it. Abraham lived for another 38 years

after Sarah's death before his God-given task was completed.

The day came, then, for Sarah to leave the world in which she had sojourned so long, and hers is the first grave to be mentioned in Scripture. Although Abraham and Sarah were nomads living in their tent in a desert land, the aged patriarch wanted a more permanent resting place for his beloved wife than the shifting sand of the desert. Here vultures and beasts of prey would wait to gorge themselves off the dead, leaving behind nothing but white bones. Breaking with the ancient custom of the desert burial, Abraham purchased a cave at Machpelah as a sepulcher for his dear Sarah, and when Abraham himself came to die his sons "buried him beside Sarah." Thus, in death, symbolically, they were unseparated as they had been through their long and eventful life together. When Cornelia, the mother of Caius and Tiberius Gracchus, whom she called her "jewels" died, on her monument was inscribed, "Cornelia, the mother of Gracchi." Had a monument been erected for the noble woman we have been considering, the simple inscription in enduring marble would have been sufficient —

Here lies
SARAH,
the devoted wife of Abraham
and
mother of Isaac.

There is a legend that Sarah died of a broken heart as she learned of God's command to Abraham to offer their son Isaac as a sacrifice on Mount Moriah. The sword pierced her heart, as it did Mary's when she witnessed the slaying of her illustrious Son at Calvary. When Sarah saw her husband and son leaving the tent, taking with them wood and a large knife she became terrified with shock and died. When Abraham and Isaac returned — Isaac brought back from the dead as it were — it was only to mourn and weep for Sarah. Had she lived she might have received her dead son back from the hands of God, and heard from her husband how his hand had been restrained by the angel, "Lay not thine hand upon the lad, neither do thou anything unto him: for now I know that thou fearest God, seeing thou hast not withheld thy son, thine only son, from me." But in the legend it goes on to tell us, eye and ear of the devoted wife and mother were closed to earthly things, and her heart stilled forever beyond the reach of the terrors, to which human flesh, and especially mothers' hearts, are heirs.

Her Example

When Paul came to emphasize that law and grace cannot exist together (Galatians 4:19-31), and uses the two sons of Abraham to illustrate the contrast, he mentions Hagar by name, but not Sarah. The Apostle called her "the freewoman" and "mother of us all." In Hebrews, however, which we believe to be Pauline, the Apostle mentioned Sarah as being one of the cloud of faithful witnesses (Hebrews 11:11, 12). The reason she received strength to bear Isaac when she was so old was because she came to believe in the faithfulness of God. If Abraham is "the father of all them that believe" (Romans 4:11; Galatians 3:7), surely Sarah is their mother. "Sarah speaks of that which is in faith, and by promise, and is free—and therefore is carried on in those who live on God's promises by faith in Christ, and have that perfect freedom which is alone found in His service, and thus belong to the Heavenly Jerusalem."

Then Peter takes his brush and adds another touch to the portrait of Sarah (I Peter 3:5-7), where she is especially distinguished for obedience to her husband, becoming thereby a model of wives in subjection to their husbands. Beautiful, strong-willed and determined, Sarah, although on two occasions she lost her temper, never disobeyed her husband. From the moment she left Ur of the Chaldees with her husband, she became the obedient wife. Martin Luther once declared that if he wanted an obedient wife he would have to carve her out of marble. But Peter, exhorting wives to obedience, holds up Sarah as their model. She called Abraham "my lord" (Genesis 18:12), still her declaration of her husband's lordship suggested incredulity rather than the obedience of faith. Yet Peter was right because all through her wanderings in desert places, and her occasional waywardness there ran the golden thread of a beautiful and loving submission to her husband's interests, and in this respect is a pattern for

"holy women" to copy. Sarah and Abraham were "two lives fused into one," with Sarah conspicuous in sacrificial submission. How apropos are the lines of Longfellow as we think of her —

> As unto the bow the cord is,
> So unto the man is the woman.
> Though she bends him, she obeys him,
> Though she draws him, yet she follows,
> Useless each without the other!

With peculiar force Peter describes Christian wives who manifest conjugal obedience, as daughters of Sarah, as long as they do well and are unafraid (I Peter 3:6). By her faith and obedience, a Sarai became a princess among women, and she teaches us the lesson that if "Man proposes: God disposes." It was only after much suffering and sorrow that grace was hers to look up into the face of God and say, "Thy will, not mine, be done!" Applying the life of Sarah with Abraham, Mary Hallet draws attention to Sarah's weaknesses of jealousy and selfishness as being akin to ourselves, but by sharp contrast her fine qualities point to us an ideal of perfection. Her remarkable physical beauty may be regarded as indicative of inner grace.

We cannot doubt that, living with Abraham in an atmosphere of reverence and worship, Sarah developed a spiritual loveliness. Perhaps this can serve as a suggestion to girls of a modern day to take time for communion with God. For only in quietude, only as we listen, can we hear His unmistakable Voice.

SERAH

Scripture References — Genesis 46:17; I Chronicles 7:30

Name Meaning — Abundance

Serah, a daughter of Asher, was a granddaughter of Jacob by his wife Leah's handmaid Zilpah. In the KJV of Numbers 26:46 she is called Sarah, but the ASV cites her as Serah.

SHELOMITH

Many of the Hebrew proper names are grouped as Miscellaneous, seeing they represent individuals less important than others. Further, there are names of men with a feminine termination, and names of women with a masculine ending. In cases where two forms of a word exist — a masculine and a feminine — the feminine is repeatedly found in use as the name of a man. A case in point is the miscellaneous name before us. *Shelomi* ("my peace," or "peaceable," Numbers 34:27), an Asherite; and *Shelomoth* ("God is peace," I Chronicles 24:22), a descendant of Izhar; and *Shelumiel* ("God is peace," Numbers 1:6; 7:36), chief Simeonite who was census officer in the time of Moses, are masculine forms and masculine names of *Shelomith*, which is in the feminine form and which is the name of several men and several women. It occurs seven times in the Bible, but only in two cases can the individuals be positively identified as women.

SHELOMITH No. 1

Scripture Reference — Leviticus 24:10-13
Name Meaning — Peaceful

This was the name of the daughter of Dibri of the tribes of Dan in the time of Moses, who married an unnamed Egyptian — an association unfavorable to piety (II Corinthians 6:14, 15). She became the mother of the half-bred son who was stoned to death for blaspheming "the Name." Angered because he was by divine law excluded from camping with his Israelitish mother, he cursed God who gave the law, and reviled the judges who pronounced sentence against him. Tradition has it that the Egyptian father of this blasphemer was the taskmaster under whom Shelomith's husband worked in Egypt, that he had injured Shelomith and then killed her husband. It also says that this was the Egyptian whom Moses slew (Exodus 2:11) for the injuries inflicted both upon the Hebrew and his wife, and that the culprit before us is the issue of the outraged Shelomith by the slain Egyptian. The ancient Chaldee version, agreeing with this legend says —

> A wicked man, a rebel against the God of Heaven, had come out of Egypt, the son of the Egyptian who slew an Israelite in Egypt, and outraged his wife, who conceived and brought forth this son among the children of Israel.

SHELOMITH No. 2

Scripture Reference — I Chronicles 3:19

This further bearer of the name was the daughter of Zerubbabel, not the great Zerubbabel who led back the Jews at the behest of Cyrus, but his cousin of the same name. She was the sister of Meshullam and Hananiah (see Matthew 1:12; Luke 3:27).

SHELOMITH No. 3

Scripture Reference — II Chronicles 11:20

It is not certain whether the son or the daughter of Maachah and King Rehoboam is meant by the historian. If a daughter then she was the sister of King Abijah of Judah.

SHERAH, SHEERAH

Scripture Reference — I Chronicles 7:24
Name Meaning—A female relation by blood

This further miscellaneous name belonged to a daughter of Ephraim who must have been a woman of physical power for she built or fortified three villages which she probably received as an inheritance and enlarged for family reasons (II Chronicles 8:5).

SHIMEATH

Scripture References — II Kings 12:21; II Chronicles 24:26
Name Meaning — Fame

The bearer of this interesting name was the mother of Jazachar, or Zabad who was one of the servants who conspired against the ailing King Joash of Judah and slew him in his bed. As an Ammonite, her evil influence appeared in her son.

SHIMRITH (Compare SHOMER)

SHIPHRAH

Scripture Reference — Exodus 1:15
Name Meaning — Prolific *or* to procreate

Under PUAH (which see), we drew attention to this midwife who with her companion risked her life in saving the male babies born to Israelite mothers. Shiphrah with Puah were the forerunners of a multitude of noble women to help to bring children into the world and bestow such loving care upon them in the first days of infancy.

SHOMER

Scripture Reference — II Kings 12:21
Name Meaning — Keeper *or* guarded of the Lord

Shomer is a masculine name. She was the Moabite mother of Jehozabad who along with Shimeath slew King Joash as he lay in bed. She is also named Shimrith (II Chronicles 24:26).

SHUA

Scripture References — Genesis 38:1, 2
I Chronicles 7:32
Name Meaning—Rich *or* prosperity *or* noble

Here is another name used of both sexes. Among the males cited in Scripture is Shua, the Canaanite whose daughter became Judah's wife. Shua, or Shuah was a Canaanitish name, and designates the daughter of Heber, the grandson of Asher. She was also the sister of Japhlet, Shomer and Hotham. No other facts of her are mentioned.

SUSANNA

Scripture Reference — Luke 8:2, 3
Name Meaning — A white lily

Along with Shushan, Susanna is from the root *shush*. Susanna was one of those women whom Christ healed both physically and spiritually, and who revealed their gratitude by following Him and ministering unto Him and His disciples of their substance. Susanna was the name of the mother of John and Charles Wesley, and along with its shortened form, Susan, has ever been a popular name for females. In apocryphal literature it is also the name of the heroine in *The History of Susanna*.

SYNTYCHE

Scripture Reference — Philippians 4:2
Name Meaning — Fortunate

What we indicated in our sketch of Eu-odias (which compare) applies here. A working member of the Early Church at Philippi, Syntyche doubtless became more so in her relationship with Euodias after Paul's admonition.

TABITHA (See Dorcas)

TAHPENES

Scripture Reference — I Kings 11:19, 20
Name Meaning — The head of the age

Among the heathen names of Scripture we have Tahpenes or Taph-hanes. This name in a variated form describes an Egyptian city, but in its original form was the name of the queen of a king of Egypt in Solomon's time, whose sister was the wife of Hadad an Edomite king. When this sis-ter, whose name is not given, died, probably in childbirth, Tahpenes became the foster-mother of her only son, Genubath, and brought him up as her own child.

TAMAR

A few of the proper names in the Bible are associated with trees and flowers (Susanna — "white lily"), and it would prove a profitable exercise to group these names together. Tamar, used of three females, which means, "a palm tree," is one such name. Abiathar, a compound of Tamar, signifies "a palm-island" or "like a palm." As the palm tree is the most valuable of Eastern trees, the ideas of beauty and wealth are combined in such names. It is very rare, however, to come across a modern female with the name of Tamar, in spite of its rich significance.

TAMAR No. 1
The Woman With a Pathetic History

Scripture References — Genesis 38:6-30;
Ruth 4:12; I Chronicles 2:4; Matthew 1:3
Family Connections — The Bible is silent as to her genealogy. All we know is that she was a Canaanite as her heathen name suggests, and that when widowed the second time, she returned to her father's home, but who he was and where he lived we are not told. What we do know is that when she married into the family of Judah, heartache and tragedy were her lot.

First of all, Tamar married Er, the oldest son of Judah and Shuah — who, like Tamar, was also a Canaanite. What Er did to displease God we are not told. Whatever it was, it was sinful enough for God to slay him. The wickedness of Er is declared but not described. There are no sins He cannot see, and there are sins He alone can see. The Bible provides us with many instances of the personal intervention of God for the purpose of punishing the sins of individuals and of communities by death. But Tamar did not remain a widow long, for in accordance with Hebrew law, she married the next son in the family so that he could raise up seed for his deceased brother.

Onan was Tamar's second husband, but he failed to fulfill his responsibilities to his dead brother's memory and posterity. Unwilling to do his duty according to the law of the Levirate marriage, and knowing that any offspring would not be his, Onan spilled his semen on the ground, and for this act of faithlessness to the dead, God slew him also. Widowed again, in the ordinary course of events, the next son of Judah, Shelah, should have become the third husband of Tamar as the tribe-law required (Deuteronomy 25:5; Matthew 22:24). Judah promised to give his third son to the childless widow, but when Shelah became of age, his father broke his promise. Perhaps Judah feared that the fate that had overtaken his other two sons might also be the fate of Shelah, and the refusal of Judah to give Tamar his son Shelah in marriage led to far-reaching results.

Although we have no evidence of Tamar's faith in Jehovah, she must have had some conception of the important Messianic significance of the line of Judah,- for denied Shelah, she was determined, though in an incestuous way, to save from extinction the family and tribe from which the Messiah was to spring. Tamar may have thought that if she could not marry Shelah, then according to the law of the country his father should marry her. So she resorted to a method we cannot condone for the purpose of securing her desired end. Thus it came about that she laid a trap for Judah, and consequently she and her sons found a place in the greatest of all genealogies.

After the death of his wife, Shuah, Judah was stricken with grief. Bereft of his two wicked sons, and now of his wife who, in spite of her idolatrous nationality, has nothing against her character, Judah went to his friend Hirah the Adullamite. Tamar, hearing of this, set her trap to reach the ideal which three times had been denied her. Disguising herself to look like a harlot, she sat in an open place where she could be approached. Not knowing Tamar's true identity, Judah bargained for her favors and secured them. His desire for intercourse with a harlot is reported without any moral judgment, seeing "there was little or no prejudice against purely secular prostitution in Israel."

Learning that Tamar had been playing the harlot, he commanded, "Bring her forth and let her be burnt." But when he learned that he was the cause of her guilt, Judah was compelled to vindicate Tamar and was forced to admit that she had been more righteous. Judah was motivated in his despicable conduct by sensual lust alone, but Tamar by nobler motives, namely, to become the mother of Judah's tribal representative. Twin sons were born of that incestuous union, Pharez, or Perez, and Zerah. Through Pharez Judah and Tamar became ancestors of Jesus (Matthew 1:3).

Shocked as we are by the incestuous way Tamar sought to aid the perpetuation of Judah's line, a fruitful race followed, "God not sanctioning but over-riding evil to His own good purpose" (Ruth 4:12, 18; Romans 3:5-8). It shocks our inner, finer feelings to see Christ's lineage interwoven with such abhorrent degradation as we have in this chapter (Genesis 38). We cannot but wonder how Judah and Tamar have the distinction of mention in that sacred genealogy of Jesus Christ, but as Bishop Hall expressed it, "God's election is only by Grace, for otherwise Judah would never have been chosen." Judah was a Jew; Tamar, a Gentile, and thus their parentage of Pharez (Matthew 1:3) can be looked upon as a foreshadowing of the fact that both Jews and Gentiles were to share in the blessings of the Gospel.

TAMAR No. 2
THE WOMAN WHO WAS SEDUCED BY HER OWN BROTHER

Scripture References — II Samuel 13; I Chronicles 3:9

Family Connections — This second Tamar was the beautiful daughter of David and Maacah, and the sister of Absalom, and half-sister of Amnon, David's son by another of his wives, Ahinoam. Amnon, inflamed with passion as he gazed upon the beauty of Tamar, listened to the abominable suggestion of his bad friend, Jonadab, that he should seduce Tamar. What a snare physical beauty is unless grace accompanies and guards it! (Proverbs 31:30). Amnon invited Tamar to his quarters, and knowing what an excellent baker she was, feigned sickness and sought her care and attention.

Tamar tried to resist the incest but Amnon forced her, and after his sinful act turned with hatred upon Tamar and drove her from his apartment. Humiliated, she fled to her brother Absalom's house, because David failed to punish his son Amnon for his crime. It is to David's discredit that he failed to enforce the law of God against incest (Leviticus 18:9, 11). Even Absalom seemed to think the sin against his sister was not too heinous for, in trying to comfort her, he said, "Hold your peace, my sister; he is your brother; do not take this to heart" — a sidelight on the low moral standard of David's home because of its polygamy. But in his heart Absalom hated Amnon for forcing his full sister, Tamar. Her rape rankled in his heart for two years when he arranged the murder of his half-brother for his violation of Tamar (II Samuel 13: 10, 22, 32). How dreadful sin is — one step leads to another and we never realize what the end will be.

TAMAR No. 3

Scripture Reference — II Samuel 14:27

Probably out of regard for his own sister, Tamar, Absalom called his sole surviving beautiful daughter by the same name. Like a palm tree, she might have been tall, attractive, even as her father was. She seems to have been a moral improvement on the other Tamars. She married Uriel of Gibeah, and bore Maachah, the wife of Rehoboam, king of Judah (I Kings 15:2; II Chronicles 11:20-22; 13:2), and became the mother of Abijah.

Tamar is also the name given by Ezekiel to the territory of the future Holy Land to be occupied by Israel (47:19; 48:28. See also I Kings 9:18; II Chronicles 20:2).

TAPHATH

Scripture Reference — I Kings 4:11
Name Meaning — A drop of myrrh or stacti

Among Bible names are a few associated with perfume of some sort, such as the one before us. The only female with this name was one of the daughters of Solomon who married a son of Ben-abinadab who was Solomon's commissariat officer in Dor.

THAMAR (See TAMAR)

TIMNA

Scripture References — Genesis 36:12, 22; I Chronicles 1:39
Name Meaning — Restraint

Two women bear this name. First, there was the concubine of Eliphaz, a son of Esau, who became the mother of Amalek. It is most likely that she was taken as a slave during the war between the Edomites and Horites. She is referred to as a sister of Lotan. The other female with the same name, but sometimes given as Timnah, was probably the daughter of the previous Timna.

TIRZAH

Scripture Reference — Numbers 26:33
Name Meaning — Pleasantness

This was the name of one of the five daughters of Zelophehad (see HOGLAH). Tirzah is also the name of a city captured by Joshua (12:24).

TRYPHENA and TRYPHOSA

Scripture Reference — Romans 16:12
Name Meaning — Delicate or dainty one

As Paul links these two Christian ladies together, we shall think of them as one — which they were in many ways. Probably they were twin sisters in the flesh, as well as in Christ, or very near relatives, and belonged to the same noble Roman family. They must have been conspicuous in the service of the church at Rome — perhaps deaconesses — otherwise Paul would not have singled them out for his expression of gratitude for their devoted labor in the Lord.

Their names, characteristically pagan, are in contrast to their significance. Having a similar resemblance in appearance and constitution, if twins, they were given names having a like meaning. Being of noble birth they "lived delicately," that is, in plenty and pleasure and luxury. Lightfoot says that, "It was usual to designate members of the same family by derivatives of the same root." "Delicate" may, of course, refer to physical weakness, and as tender and delicate women, Tryphena and Tryphosa stand out as early examples of incessant and arduous labors in the service of the church. Whether of gentle and refined manners, or delicate in health, or both, these active workers carved a niche for themselves in Paul's portrait gallery of saints. Early Christian inscriptions in cemeteries used chiefly for the servants of the emperor contain both of these female names, and so can be identified as being among "the saints of Caesar's household" (Philippians 4:22). How we bless God for the record of those early "honourable women which were Greeks" (Acts 17:12) who became humble followers of the Lamb!

VASHTI
THE WOMAN WHO EXALTED MODESTY

Scripture References — Esther 1; 2:1; 4:17

Name Meaning — Vashti corresponded to the significance of her name, "beautiful woman." She must have been one of the loveliest women in the realm of King Ahasuerus who thought so much of his wife's physical charms that at a drinking debauchery he wanted to exhibit her beauty for she "was fair to look upon."

Family Connections — Bullinger identifies this Persian beauty as the daughter of Alyattes, King of Lydia, but the only authentic record of Vashti is what we have in her brief appearance in Scripture as the queen of the court of Ahasuerus, or Artaxerxes. It would be interesting to know what became of the noble wife after her disgrace and divorce by her unworthy, wine-soaked husband.

While the Book of Esther holds a high place in the sacred literature of the Jews, it yet has no mention of God or of the Holy Land, and contains no definite religious teaching. Martin Luther is said to have tossed the book into the river Elbe, saying that he wished it did not exist for "it has too much of Judaism and a great deal of heathenish imagination." The book contains a genuine strain of human interest, but it is also heavy with the air of divine providence (compare ESTHER). Although the story of Vashti only covers a few paragraphs in the book, yet in the setting of oriental grandeur we have the elements of imperishable drama. While the bulk of the book revolves around Esther, from our point of view the shining character in the story is the queenly Vashti, who was driven out because she refused to display her lovely face and figure before the lustful eyes of a drunken court.

By birth Vashti was a Persian princess, possessing along with her regal bearing, an extraordinary, fragile beauty. Although her husband was a king "who reigned from India even unto Ethiopia, over an hundred and seven and twenty provinces," her self-respect and high character meant more to her than her husband's vast realm. Rather than cater to the vanity and sensuality of drunkards, she courageously sacrificed a kingdom. Rather than lower the white banner of womanly modesty, Vashti accepted disgrace and dismissal. The only true ruler in that drunken court was the woman who refused to exhibit herself, even at the king's command.

The Demand

An impressive banquet was to be held in Susa the capital of Persia, lasting for seven days, with the king and his dignitaries joining with hundreds of invited guests in an unceasing whirl of festivities during which wine flowed freely. Both great and small were to be found "in the court of the garden of the palace." Then came the crowning touch of a drunken tyrant's caprice. When "the heart of the king was merry with wine" he commanded that Vashti, his royal consort, appear before the guests. For a week, inflamed with wine and adulation, he had displayed the magnificent wealth and power of his kingdom and the princes had poured flattery upon him. Now for the climax! Let all the half-drunken guests see his most lovely possession, Queen Vashti, who was probably the most beautiful woman in his kingdom. He wanted the intoxicated jubilant lords to feast their eyes on her. The Bible plainly declares that Ahasuerus summoned his wife to the feast simply "to show her beauty."

Had the king been sober he would not have considered such a breach of custom, for he knew that Eastern women lived in seclusion and that such a request as he made in his drunken condition amounted to a gross insult. "For Vashti to appear in the banquet hall, though dressed in her royal robes and crowned, would be almost as degrading as for a modern woman of our modern world to go naked into a man's party." What Ahasuerus demanded was a surrender of womanly honor, and Vashti, who was neither vain nor wanton, was unwilling to comply. Plutarch reminds us that it was the habit of a Persian king to have his queen beside him at a banquet, but when he wished to riot and drink, he sent his queen away and called in the wives of inferior rank—his concubines. Perhaps that is the historic clue to Vashti's indignant refusal for she knew only too well that Persian custom dictated that a queen be secluded during the feasts where rare wines flowed freely.

The Disobedience

To Vashti, the command of the king — her husband, who alone had the right to gaze upon her beautiful form — was most revolting to her sense of propriety, and knowing what the consequences of her refusal to appear before the half-drunken company would entail, refused in no uncertain terms to comply with the king's demand. She stood strong in womanly self-respect and "refused to come at the king's commandment." Her noble scorn at her threatened indignity deserves finer recognition. What the king sought would have infringed upon her noble, feminine modesty, therefore she had every right to disobey her wine-soaked husband. A wife need not and may not obey her husband in what opposes God's laws and the laws of feminine honor and decency. All praise to the heroic Vashti for her decent disobedience.

The Deposition

Vashti's disobedience excited the king to madness. No one, especially a woman, had ever dared to humiliate such a despot whose word was law in all his realm. Such a slight had but one issue, for forth went the decree, "that Vashti come no more before King Ahasuerus." This degradation also meant divorce, not only from her husband, but also from the life and luxury she had been used to. Thus amid the tragic darkness Queen Vashti — never more queenly than in her refusal — disappears like a shining shadow. The wise men, court astrologers and princes agreed with the king that banishment from the palace was the only fit punishment for

such a crime. They knew that Vashti's bold stand might incite other Persian ladies to disobey their liege lords, and so the warrant, silly as it was royal, was enacted that "Every man be master in his own house, and that all the wives shall give to their husbands honour, both to great and small!"

As a Persian law once made could never be revoked, Ahasuerus, now sober, and likely regretful of his impulsive anger could not reinstate Vashti, thus Esther was chosen to succeed her as queen. It is quite probable that "Vashti continued to live in the royal household, stripped of the insignia of royalty, but with her own integrity clothed in purple." Surrendering the diadem of Persia, Vashti put on a crown which was beyond the power of a despot king to give or take away, namely, the crown of exalted womanhood. How apropos are the lines of Tennyson as we think of the fine character of Vashti, the pagan Persian —

> Self-reverence, self-knowledge, self-control,
> These three alone lead life to sovereign power.
> Yet not for power (power by herself
> Would come uncalled for), but to live by law,
> Acting the law we live without fear;
> And, because right is right, to follow right
> Were wisdom in the scorn of consequence.

Vashti chose deposition rather than dishonor with a mortifying refusal to obey. Her refusal to exhibit herself was visited with "a punishment severe enough to reestablish the supremacy which it threatened to overthrow," but to Vashti, conscience and personal dignity occupied a higher supremacy and for this ideal she was dethroned. Allied to her beauty and regal charm were courage and heroism, securing her character from the rot of power. Vashti had a soul of her own, and preserved its integrity; and if women today fail to honor their life they will never win the best God has for them. It is to be regretted that in our modern world many women are not as careful as Vashti the pagan was in guarding the dignity of the body. Fashion and popularity are a poor price to pay for the loss of one's self-respect. Christian ideals in womanhood may be deemed old-fashioned and in conflict with the trend of the times, but divine favor rests upon those who have courage to be ridiculed for such high ideals. Any woman is one after God's own heart when, as Mary Hallet puts it, she determines by His grace —

> To remain refined in speech and action, when it is the style to appear "hard-boiled"—
> To be dignified when everyone else pretends to be "wild"—
> To maintain a true perspective, a real sense of values, in an irresponsible age.

ZEBUDAH, ZEBIDAH

Scripture Reference — II Kings 23:36
Name Meaning — Bestowal *or* a gift

Often some of the names of God are compounded with other words to form proper names and are found in those exalting God as the Giver, such as Zabad, meaning, "He hath given" of which Zebudah is the feminine form. Zebadiah—New Testament, Zebedee, implies "Jehovah hath given."

Zebudah was the daughter of Pedaiah of Rumah, and became the wife of King Josiah, and the mother of their sons, Jehoiakim and Jehoahaz. Of Jehoiakim, who succeeded his father as king at the age of 25 and reigned for 11 years in Jerusalem, we read that "He did that which was evil in the sight of the Lord, according to all that his fathers had done." Can it be that his godless life was the fruit of his mother's unwholesome influence, in and over his early days?

ZERESH

Scripture References—Esther 5:10, 14; 6:13
Name Meaning — Star of adoration *or* gold

What a tragic experience it must have been for this wife and mother to see her husband and sons hanged on gallows! Here we have the Persian name of Haman's wife. Haman the Agagite, and cruel enemy of the Jews, was prime minister under King Ahasuerus and the monarch's favorite vizier. When Zeresh his wife learned that Mordecai whom Haman despised was a Jew, she predicted her husband's downfall (see Isaiah 54:17). The irony of the story is that Haman was hanged on the very gallows he had built for Mordecai (compare ESTHER).

ZERUAH

Scripture Reference — I Kings 11:26-40
Name Meaning — Leprous

The significance of this name of the mother of Jeroboam who became king of the Ten Tribes who revolted against Solomon's son, and successor, Rehoboam, is somewhat uncertain. She married Nebat of Zereda, who was a servant in Solomon's employ. As she is spoken of as a "widow woman," her husband was dead when their son lifted up his hand against the king.

ZERUIAH

Scripture References — II Samuel 17:25; I Chronicles 2:16
Name Meaning — Balsam from Jehovah

The name of this desired and welcomed daughter expresssed a similar sentiment of one or other of the parents. Zeruiah, a sister of David, became the mother of Abishai, Joab and Asahel who are always referred to as "the sons of Zeruiah." Edith Deen remarks, "The fact that her name appears 25 times besides that of her sons is sufficient proof that she was a mother of distinction who had a marked influence over the lives of her sons." Two reasons are advanced for the absence of their father's name. He may have died early, or Zeruiah may have been a most remarkable woman, with a more impressive personality, or we have in the omission a survival of the ancient custom of tracing kinship through the female line. Zeruiah's sons were conspicuous in Israelite history during David's reign.

ZIBIAH (TSIBIAH)

Scripture References — II Kings 12:1; II Chronicles 24:1
Name Meaning — A female gazelle

The name of this princess of Judah carries the ideas of grace, agility and beauty. A woman of Beersheba, Zibiah became the wife of King Ahaziah and the mother of Jehoash, or Joash, who was saved from murder in childhood and lived to become king of Judah and reigned for 40 years. All we know about Zibiah is her name, but the fact that her noble son is spoken of as one who did "that which was right in the sight of the Lord all his days wherein Jehoiada the priest instructed him," indicates something of her care to bring up her son in the fear of the Lord, and also of his willingness to follow the godly advice of his appointed representative, Jehoiada. How grateful we should be for the spiritual instruction of those who themselves are taught of the Lord!

ZILLAH

Scripture Reference — Genesis 4:19-23
Name Meaning — Shadow of darkness *or* protection

Lamech had two wives, Zillah and Adah (which compare). Zillah was the mother of Naamah (which see), the first named daughter in the Bible whose name indicates "loveliness." Zillah was also the mother of Tubal-cain, who became the founder of the ancient crafts of metalsmiths and ironmakers. There is nothing suggestive of God or His service in the record of Lamech and his family. The names his wife and he gave their children "mark the growing voluptuousness and luxury of the Cainites. It was the period of transition to art and refinement; attended with the evils which often accompany such times."

ZILPAH

Scripture References — Genesis 29:24; 30: 9, 10; 35:26; 37:2; 46:18
Name Meaning — Meaning uncertain

The slave girl Laban gave to his daughter Leah as a handmaid came to have a definite share in the development of Israel as a nation. When, for a time, Leah ceased to bear children, she gave Zilpah to Jacob that she might enlarge her brood by the handmaid, thus Zilpah became the mother of two sons, Gad and Asher. They became the progenitors of two of the tribes of Israel (see LEAH).

ZIPPORAH

THE WOMAN WHO WRONGLY OPPOSED HER HUSBAND

Scripture References — Exodus 2:21, 22; 4: 24, 25; 18:1-6
Name Meaning—A Midian name, Zipporah means "a little bird," "a sparrow." Wilkinson observes that "the feminine termination *ah* added to the common word Zippor, which is also the father of Balak, king' of Moab. Such a name like "dove" or "lamb" would originally be a term of endearment, and thus the word *passer* — "a sparrow"—is used by the Roman poets. Passer is also being found as a Roman

family name. The root of this word is an Arabic verb, signifying "to chirp."
Family Connections — Zipporah was one of the seven daughters of Jethro who is also called Reuel and Raguel (Exodus 2:18; 4:24, 25; 18:1-6; Numbers 10:29). It was to the home of this shepherd-priest in Midian that Moses came when at forty years of age he fled from Egypt, and meeting the seven girls drawing water Moses assisted them. Arriving home earlier than usual they told how the Egyptian had helped them. Brought up as a son of Pharaoh, Moses must have looked every inch a cultured Egyptian. Invited home, Moses was content to live with Jethro's family, and married Zipporah, eldest of the seven daughters. Two sons were born of the union, Gershom and Eliezer. Some writers affirm, without adequate support, that the dark-skinned Ethiopian, "the Cushite woman" whom Miriam and Aaron were jealous over, is merely a description of Zipporah, and that therefore Moses was only married once. But the statement "He had married an Ethiopian woman" implies a recent occurrence, and that Zipporah, whom Moses had married 40 years previously, was dead. It is most unlikely that Miriam and Aaron would have waited all those years to murmur against Moses if Zipporah and the Ethiopian had been one and the same woman.

Zipporah, as a woman of Midian, did not share the spiritual values of her notable husband who found himself acting against the sacred tradition of Israel. This may be one reason why he named his second son Eliezer, meaning "The Lord of my father was my help." To keep the peace, Moses compromised with his unbelieving wife and withheld circumcision, the sign of God's covenant, from Eliezer. The Lord intervened, and as a sign of divine displeasure, Moses is stricken with a mortal disease. Both Zipporah and Moses became conscience-stricken over the profanation of God's covenant, and Zipporah yields. Moses is too prostrate to take a knife and circumcize the child, so his wife severed the boy's foreskin and, throwing it down before Moses said, "Surely a bloody husband art thou to me."

When Moses was restored to health relations in the home were not congenial, for he went on alone to Egypt, and Zipporah and the two sons went back to her home in Midian. Of this unhappy incident Alexander Whyte says, "There are three most obscure and most mysterious verses in Moses' history that mean, if they mean anything at all to us, just such an explosion of ill-temper as must have left its mark till death on the heart of Moses and Zipporah. The best of wives; his help meet given him of God; the most self-effacing of women; the wife who holds her husband in her heart as the wisest and best of men — under sufficient trial and provocation and exasperation, even she will turn and will strike with just one word; just once in her whole married lifetime."

When Moses became the mighty leader and law-giver of Israel, there was the episode when Jethro, his father-in-law came out to the wilderness to see Moses and brought with him Zipporah and the two sons. The union was devoid of any restraint for Moses graciously received them and neither disowned nor ignored his wife and sons. But after this visit during which Jethro gave his over-burdened son-in-law some very practical advice, nothing more is said of Zipporah. She disappears without comment from the history of the Jewish people in which her husband figured so prominently. "Neither as the wife of her husband nor as the mother of her children did she leave behind her a legacy of spiritual riches." How different it would have been if only she had fully shared her husband's unusual meekness and godliness and, like him, left behind footprints in the sands of time!

Zipporah is far from being an inspiring character with which to end our alphabetical coverage of all the *named* women of the Bible. One could have wished for a nobler and more godly example of female biography as a fitting conclusion to this section of our study. Looking back over the large number of women whose names are recorded in Holy Writ we realize that taken together they represent all aspects of human nature — good, bad and indifferent. For the majority, they lived their lives as they passed through this short scene of trial into eternity, leaving little trace behind them. But as we have seen, others, by their character and history, have left their names engraved in the impregnable Rock of Holy Scripture, with their records serving as either warning signals where they were conspicuous for evil, or as shining examples of high endeavor, where their lives were lived as unto Him who created both male and female for His glory.

Whatever was thus written in former days was written for our instruction, that by [our steadfast and patient] endurance and the encouragement [drawn] from the Scriptures we might hold fast *and* cherish hope (Romans 15:4, *Amplified Bible*).

3

Nameless Bible Women

While there is a good deal of fascination in an understanding of the majority of *named* women of the Bible, its *nameless* women, many of whom hold a conspicuous place in sacred history, are often neglected by many writers of female biography. A somewhat baffling question is: "Why are these women associated with well-known men, and with outstanding events not named? What is the reason behind their anonymity? For instance, we have the names of the sons of Noah, but not those of his wife and daughters-in-law. We have a full portrait of "righteous Lot," but silence prevails as to the names of his wife and two daughters. The three daughters of Job are named but we have no clue as to the identity of his wife or sons. Scripture gives us the name of the natural brothers of Jesus, but not His sisters. The two sisters at Bethany whom Jesus loved, have well-known names, but of His own sisters silence reigns as to how they were known. Peter "the big fisherman," occupies a large niche in the portrait gallery of the New Testament, but all that is said of his dear partner is that she was his wife. Do you never wonder what her name was, and also that of her mother? Because of the close fellowship existing between Christ and the Twelve, the wives of the latter, if they were all married, must have been known both to the Master and to a large circle of disciples, yet the Bible is silent as to their existence and to the names they bore. Why did Paul not give us the given name of his own sister according to the flesh?

There is no satisfactory answer to the silence of Scripture regarding the identity of its nameless women. George Eliot once remarked that, "The happiest women, like the happiest nations, have no history." But many of the happy — and unhappy — unknown Bible women left their impact upon history. They played their part in important events, but their signatures are not attached to their service. Surely, it was not the oversight of Bible writers to omit the names of those in female biography whose deeds are published. What many of them did is history, but history without a title page. Could it be that they willed the reticence as to who they were? Certainly, many of these unnamed female characters were far from being righteous, such as the sensual, faithless wife of Potiphar, and of the woman of Samaria. The historians may have felt that they were unworthy of being named. In other cases, perhaps the male members of a family are mentioned because of what they became and achieved, while the female members are not designated by name seeing they accomplished nothing of any merit warranting the use of their names. The brothers and sisters of Jesus did not believe in His divine mission, but as the result of the cross His brothers came to accept Him as Messiah, and two of them are numbered among the apostles (Matthew 13:55, 56; Galatians 1: 19; Jude 1). Nothing is said of the surrender of His sisters to His claims.

In the Bible, humanity's intensely biographical volume, we have vivid sketches of a goodly company of saintly women who are "only remembered by what they have done." Their deeds are undying, and their characters glow in the sacred page, but the recording angel above alone knows who they were. Sir John Suckling gave us the lines —

Like the Milky Way is the sky,
A meeting of gentle lights without a name.

As we are to see in the chapter before us, there are many "gentle lights without a name" in the Bible, as, of course, there are in world history. The Scripture gallery of unlabelled portraits well repays repeated visits, for these unknown ones have, like beauty, their own excuse for being. Although for some inscrutable reason the names of so many noble women have been withheld from us, yet they themselves have something of the immortality Rupert Hughes most impressively wrote about —

Sometimes at night within a wooded park,
Like an ocean cavern, fathoms deep in gloom,
Sweets scents, like hymns, from hidden flowers fume,
And make the wanderer happy; though the dark
Obscure their tint, *their name*, their shapely bloom.

So in the thick-set chronicles of fame,
There hover deathless feats of souls unknown;
They linger as the fragrant smoke-wreaths blown
From liberal sacrifices. Gone face and *name!*
The deeds like homeless ghosts, live on alone.

Plutarch, the ancient Greek biographer, once said that he "would not write the lives of bad men," but the divine Author of the Bible saw fit to delineate, not only good men and good women, but likewise the bad and corrupt. If we want to know what human nature actually is in the ungodly or godly, all we have to do is to study the biographies the Bible revolves around. This is why we have endeavored to set forth *all* the anonymous women so that we can learn lessons from the vices of the bad, as well as the virtues of the righteous. As can be seen, we have dealt with these nameless women in chronological order. We believe that in such a way they can be easily traced, and likewise found to be wonderfully woven into the texture of a divine and progressive revelation — which the Bible is! Edgar Allan Poe has the lines —

Sorrow for the lost Lenore —
For the rare and beautiful maiden,
Whom the angels name Lenore —
Nameless here for evermore.

Whatever names the unidentified godly women of the Bible may have in heaven, they must remain "Nameless here for evermore."

CAIN'S WIFE
Genesis 4:17

An "old chestnut" of a question, and one which agnostics and hecklers are fond of hurling at defenders of the authority of the Bible is, "Where did Cain get his wife?" To many who are not enemies of the Faith, such a question may cause an unnecessary anxiety. As Adam and Eve were the first human pair on earth, and by natural generation had three sons who are named — Cain, Abel, Seth — and there is no mention of any named daughters — it does seem as if there is a problem in knowing where the female came from whom Cain made his wife. In the genealogy of Adam, as the natural head of the human race, we are told that "Adam begat sons and daughters" (Genesis 5:4). How many sons there were, apart from the three named ones, and how many daughters were born to Eve we are not told. Thus, because they lived long before the Sinaitic Laws were given, there was no moral difficulty involved in the marriage of near relatives. With Cain, the course was obviously a necessary one as it was with his brothers — they married their sisters. As we have already seen, Abraham married his own half-sister, Sarah.

After the birth of Seth, Adam lived for another 800 years, and died at the age of 930. When Eve died we are not told, but if she lived as long as her husband, and she was able to continue procreation through the centuries, then the family of earth's first pair must have been large indeed. The register of births and deaths in Genesis 5 is an instructive record of remarkable longevity. The name of the earliest patriarchs are given, and the long years each of them lived upon the earth. If you add together the years that each one lived, you will find that their united lives cover a long period indeed. Enoch lived for the shortest period, 365 years — a year for every day of our normal year; while Methuselah lived the longest period of any known man, namely 969 years — 31 years short of a millennium. Adam lived for over one hundred years after the birth of Methuselah, and the latter would have been over 300 years old when his grandson, Noah, was born. There is little room for doubt that Enoch, the seventh from Adam, had the privilege of conversing with earth's first man. By the end of the first two millenniums the population of the earth through direct intermarriage must have been enormous.

As there may have been a lapse of

many, many years before Cain's marriage, during such a period — 130 years between the birth of Cain and Seth, the substitute for slain Abel — some of the unnamed sons and daughters of Adam and Eve were likely born. As there were no other humans on earth apart from their descendants, Cain, attracted to one of his sisters, took her to wife. Whoever the sister was who chose to go into banishment with her branded brother, she deserves credit for her willingness to share Cain's curse and wanderings. It is significant that they called their first child Enoch, which means "dedicated," and may suggest a change in Cain's character. The word is akin to "train" as found in the phrase, "Train up a child" (Proverbs 22:6), and is also used in the dedication of a new house (Deuteronomy 20:5). Cain called the city he built after the name of his son "Enoch," or "dedicated," and, as Ellicott comments —

> In old times the ideas of training and dedication were closely allied, because teaching generally took the forms of initiation into sacred rites, and one so initiated was regarded as a consecrated person. Though, then, the [Cain's] wife may have had most to do with giving the name, yet we see in it a purpose that the child should be a trained and consecrated man; and Cain must now have put off those fierce and violent habits which had led him into so terrible a crime. We may add that this prepares our minds for the rapid advance of the Cainites in the arts of civilization, for the very remarkable step next taken by Cain — a fit spot where his offspring should dwell together in some *dedicated* common abode.

SETH'S DAUGHTERS
Genesis 5:6-8

Like his father, Adam, Seth had many daughters who are unidentified. Cain's wife is not named, and the wife of Seth, who likely lived as long as her husband (912), is not even mentioned. There were wives aplenty for the numerous sons born to those early patriarchs. Many of the daughters of these men, however, were among those caught up in the Flood because of their unholy alliance with fallen angels (Genesis 6:12).

ENOS'S DAUGHTERS
Genesis 5:9-11

Hebrew genealogies omit the names of many sons, as well as daughters. Where they are named, the sons predominate because, as civilization expanded, daughters did not have the same value as sons. Sometimes a father sold his daughter as a bondwoman (Exodus 21:7), but only within Israel (21:8).

CAINAN'S DAUGHTERS
Genesis 5:12-14

Cainan lived for 910 years, and must have experienced much pleasure in his family of sons and daughters. How much more fascinating these antediluvian genealogies would have been if only they had been replete with the names, marriages and incidents in the lives of their anonymous females!

MAHALEEL'S DAUGHTERS
Genesis 5:15-17

In this sixth generation since Adam we have the repeated phrase "begat sons and daughters," but without their number and names.

JARED'S DAUGHTERS
Genesis 5:18-20

It will be observed that after the wives of Lamech, who are both named (4:19-23), the wives of succeeding patriarchs down to Noah are not even mentioned. They shared the same anonymity as their daughters and some of their sons. Among Jared's sons and daughters, was one son who, because of his spiritual excellencies, is referred to as "the seventh from Adam," and as a prophet (Jude 14). Seven is the number of perfection, thus Enoch attained the highest rank among the patriarchs. Jared lived for 800 years after the birth of his godly son, and one wonders how far Jared influenced Enoch, and what his sisters and brothers thought of his unique life and of his translation, at 365 years of age, into heaven without tasting death.

ENOCH'S DAUGHTERS
Genesis 5:21-24

The only named son of Enoch, Methuselah, was to be a man of distinction in that his is the longest known age in human history. He died at 969 years of age. Significantly we read that it was after Methuselah was born that "Enoch walked with God," for "three hundred years, and begat sons and daughters." During those 300 years spent in the immediate presence of and in constant communion with God, we can imagine what a godly home Enoch must have had, with his wife sharing his high ideals, and all his sons and daughters endeavoring to please God. The mournful refrain in these genealogies, *and he died,* is not attached to Enoch for God translated him that he should not taste death. In comparison with the longevity of those who died, Enoch's pilgrimage before God took him was of short duration — 365 years! Do you not try to imagine what the feelings of Enoch's wife, sons and daughters were like when one day God took His companion to be with Himself? It is to be hoped that all within the family followed Enoch in a steady continuance in well-doing and that his daughters were as "corner stones polished after the similitude of a palace" (Psalm 144:12), and his dear wife for so many decades was as a fruitful vine by the sides of his house (Psalm 128:3).

METHUSELAH'S DAUGHTERS
Genesis 5:25-27

Enoch gave his son a prophetic name for Methuselah means, "when he is dead it shall be sent," that is, the Flood with its terrible destruction. Having lived for almost a millennium, Methuselah and his wife must have had numerous offspring, what with their own sons and daughters, and the children's children. Who would not like to have had some indication of the kind of daughters the man who lived so long had? We can but hope that like their grandfather, Enoch, they too, walked with God.

LAMECH'S DAUGHTERS
Genesis 5:28-31

Lamech named his first child Noah which means "rest" or "comfort." This is "the first recorded instance, since the days of Eve, of a child being named at his birth, and in both cases the name ended in disappointment. Noah brought no 'rest' but in his days came the Flood to punish human sin." The longing of Lamech for comfort, however, is in strong contrast with the arrogance of his namesake of the race of Cain (4:18). After the birth of Noah "sons and daugh-

ters" were born to Lamech and his unknown wife. Evidently these other children did not share the faith of their notable brother, and perished in the Flood, from which Noah, his wife, three sons and their wives were preserved.

DAUGHTERS OF MEN
Genesis 6:1-8

This remarkable portion of Scripture has been variously interpreted. First, who were the anonymous "daughters of men" thrice mentioned? They were the offspring of men who began to multiply on the face of the earth, and thus include some of the daughters already considered. There are those expositors who suggest that these "daughters" with their cultivated beauty and yet corrupt ways were Cainites. They were descendants of the Cain who was the founder of civil institutions and social life, and that "the sons of God" were "Sethites," pious men of noble rank. But there is no Scriptural evidence that either Seth or his descendants were conspicuous for their moral goodness, apart from Enoch. In our Lord's human genealogy Adam is called "The son of God" (Luke 3:38). So the usual interpretation is that the pious descendants of Seth entered into alliances with the women of the corrupt race of Cain.

But no such marriages between humans— pious men and inferior women could have produced "giants," "mighty men," "men of renown" (6:4). Dealing with the Flood that overtook the world of the ungodly, Peter speaks of the angels that sinned and were cast out of heaven (II Peter 2:4, 5), and Jude refers to these angelic beings as those who kept not their first, or original, estate but left their own habitation, and of those who went after "strange flesh" (Jude 6, 7). It is our conviction that the abnormal men who appeared were the fruit of the corrupt union of fallen angels and godless women, and that it was this terrible phase of wickedness which precipitated the Flood that destroyed all save Noah and his family. It is true that angels, all the while they remain unsinning angels, "neither marry nor are given in marriage." But when they leave that blissful, original estate, and go after "strange flesh" — strange to them — unique creatures emerge as the result of such an illicit union. This necessitated a Flood to cleanse the earth of such pollution. In Spiritism there are spiritual marriages, contracted between female mediums and spirits of the unseen world.

In his *Lectures on the Pentateuch*, Wm. Kelly, dealing with Genesis 6:2 says that, "The sons of God, in my judgment mean the same beings in *Genesis* as they do in *Job* (1:6; 2:1). This point will suffice to indicate their chief guilt in the traversing the boundaries which God appointed for His creatures. No wonder that total ruin speedily ensued." Further, this record of unnatural union became the basis of fact for some of the tales of mythology in which gods and women intermarried and produced great heroes. Bishop E. H. Bickersteth in his remarkable poem, *Yesterday, Today, Forever*, describes the descent of the malign fallen spirits and singles two out as being guilty of the violence and corruption it would take a total Flood to erase from the earth —

> Of whom
> Were Uziel and Samihasai his mate,
> By birthright sons of God, now sons of wrath,
> Who prompted by the boast of Lucifer,
> Mankind should be his bride, and stung with lust,
> Mix'd with the daughters of unhappy Eve,
> Heir of her beauty, not her penitence,
> In wedlock. Fatal leaguel whence soon arose
> The monstrous brood of giants, ruthless race,
> Offspring of human and angelic kind,
> Who now confusion more confused, and stain'd
> The fairest homes with violence and blood
> Rapine ran riot on the earth.

As the shadows of judgment gather around a guilty world, "seducing spirits" are becoming increasingly active, and the coming "Great Tribulation" may provide the earth with a repeat of the appalling conditions resulting in the waters of divine wrath. Things were as rotten as they could be in the days of Noah, but grace was his to walk with God, and to live as perfectly as a human being could in a generation that was so vile and evil continually. Thus he was saved out of judgment.

NOAH'S WIFE, SONS' WIVES
Genesis 6:18; 7:1, 7, 13; 8:16, 18

While nothing is said of the uprightness of Noah's wife, whose name we do not know, his three sons whose names are given,

and their wives who are unnamed, all of them must have shared the righteousness God commended in Noah (7:1), otherwise they would not have been saved by water (I Peter 3:20). They were among the uncorrupted flesh and were included in the divine invitation, "Come thou and all thy house into the ark." As Noah was 600 years old when the Flood came (7:6), he had had a long life walking with God. He had endured much scorn from the ungodly as he went on building the ark, and preaching righteousness, calling on the ungodly to repent before judgment fell. During all those trying years, and in the tremendous venture of going into the ark with all its living cargo, Noah's wife must have been a source of great encouragement to him. In his sons and their wives he found those in full sympathy with his faith and witness, and thus became the source of a new race on a purified earth. All the nations of the earth sprang from the children of the nameless wives of Shem, Ham and Japheth, who bore their children after they settled again upon the earth (Genesis 9:8, 9).

SHEM'S DAUGHTERS
Genesis 11:10-32

While the genealogies of Ham and Japheth have fragment references to sons born to them, and to their successors, we have no mention of daughters although there must have been many of them (Genesis 10). When we come to Shem and his successors, Salah, Eber, Peleg, Reu, Serug and Nahor we have the repeated phrase, "begat sons and *daughters*." When Shem was 100 years of age, he, two years after the Flood, begat his first-born, Arphaxad, and then lived for another 500 years, during which his offspring must have been numerous. The Flood was universal, and Noah and his family were the only persons on the earth, once the waters subsided. In order to replenish the earth, it was necessary, as at the beginning with Adam and Eve, for brothers to marry sisters. Thus, the children and grandchildren of Shem, Ham and Japheth intermarried, and laid the foundation of the nations divided on the earth after the Flood.

LOT'S WIFE
Genesis 19:15-26; Luke 17:29-33

When Abraham heard that his nephew, Lot, had been taken captive by the kings of Sodom and Gomorrah, he pursued the enemies and freed Lot, and "the women, and the people." Who the women were, Scripture does not say. They may have been Lot's wife and daughters, or Sodomite female servants. The first direct reference we have of Lot's unnamed wife is when the angels came to hasten the family out of doomed Sodom (Genesis 19:15). Who she was, of what race and family, of what life and character, by what name she was known, the Bible is silent. All the information we have about her is packed into one short verse, "His wife looked back from behind him, and she became a pillar of salt." Yet we must give attention to her for it is written in burning words by the finger of God —

"Remember Lot's wife."

Some dozen words in the Old Testament, and three words in the New Testament, then, are all we have of this female character.

When, because of strife, Abraham and his nephew, Lot, came to part, Abraham gave Lot the pick of the land before them. Lot selfishly chose the best stretch of the country, "well watered everywhere . . . even as the garden of the Lord" (13:10). But such a greedy choice had dire consequences. Lot pitched his tent *toward* Sodom, and before long was in Sodom where its inhabitants "were wicked and sinners before the Lord exceedingly" (13:13). Lot became a citizen of Sodom, sat at its gate as the city's mayor, and was treated with honor and reverence as a relative of the mighty Abraham who had delivered Sodom from the Elamite invasion. While Peter speaks of Lot as being just and of having a righteous soul vexed with the filthy lives of the Sodomites (II Peter 2:7-9), he yet somehow closed his eyes to the wickedness of the people, married a woman of Sodom and consented for his two daughters born in Sodom to marry Sodomites.

Sodom was such a cesspool of iniquity that God said He would destroy it. But because of Lot's presence in the city Abraham interceded for its preservation. If only there had been ten righteous people in it God said the city would be spared. The only apparent righteous person in it—whose righteousness had been made ineffective through compromise — was Lot. So the two angels came to deliver Lot and his family from the terrible judgment about to fall on Sodom. They were entertained overnight, and Lot's wife doubtless shared in the hospitality shown. Early the next morning the angels sought to hasten Lot and his family out of the city, but they lingered. They were loathe to leave the luxury, pleasure, and sin of Sodom, so the angelic deliverers had to remove them forcibly from the city and compel them to escape for their life.

The account of the tragedy is briefly related. As fire and brimstone out of heaven fell upon Sodom, Lot's wife looked back from behind her husband. In oriental countries it was the rule for the wife to walk some distance behind her husband, but as Lot's wife lingered and looked back she was overtaken by sulphurous vapors, and, encrusted with salt, perished where she stood. Entombed as a pillar, she became "as a monument of an unbelieving soul" in a desolate region, "of whose wickedness even to this day the waste land that smoketh is a testimony" (Wisdom 10:7). The wife of Lot looked back upon her own city with regrets at having to part with its sinful pleasures. She had been compelled to leave Sodom as a city, but all that Sodom represented was very much in her heart.

All the while Lot's wife was in Sodom, its "filthy communications" soaked into her soul, so much so that when the angel of mercy sought to save her from the angel of judgment, she could not be saved. In the look back to Sodom was regret for all she was leaving for an unknown life before her, and as she sighed the salt air whitened her body into marble, and "nature made for her at once a grave and a monument." "She became a pillar of salt," and in that word we have a symbol of *character* as well as a monument of *destiny*. A pillar of salt is the picture of many a society woman today. All the sweet blood of a true woman's heart has become brackish by the life she leads. Instead of a woman, you have only *a pillar of salt*. In Sodom, Lot's wife lived in pleasure but was dead as she lived. As the wife of a righteous man, she had a name to live, but the gay life of Sodom asphyxiated her soul. Thus when the warning voice of God sounded in her ear, she may have heard it but did not heed it. Sodom with its society and sin had been her whole life.

When dealing with the truth of His Second Advent, our Lord used the overthrow of Sodom and Gomorrah and Lot's deliverance from their destruction as an illustration of His emancipation of His own from the catastrophe to overtake a godless world, and warns believers to remember Lot's wife and not linger, look, and be lost. As those who wait His coming we are not to look back nor draw back, but *look up* for our redemption draweth nigh. How arrestive is Christ's exhortation! "Remember Lot's wife." Mary's one act of piety in breaking her alabaster box of precious spikenard brought her a perpetual memorial, and in like manner the one tragic act of Lot's wife brought her a different kind of remembrance. For all who preach the Gospel what an appeal for immediate decision there is in the urgent summons of the angels to Lot and his family, "Escape for thy life, look not behind thee . . . lest thou be consumed." That stirring evangelistic hymn has led many a sinner to escape to the arms of the Saviour —

> The Gospel bells give warning,
> As they sound from day to day,
> Of the fate which doth await them
> Who forever will delay —
> Escape thou for thy life;
> Tarry not in all the plain.
> Nor behind thee look, oh, never,
> Lest thou be consumed in pain.

LOT'S DAUGHTERS
Genesis 19:12-17, 30-38

The two daughters born to Lot in Sodom were as shameless as they are nameless. Their father, righteous though he may have been in contrast to the godlessness around him, exercised no influence over them. In fact when Lot came to warn them and their husbands to leave Sodom because of its impending doom he seemed as one that mocked them, or as one that was joking, and so not in earnest. To his own, the warning of Lot was utter nonsense. Had he not made his home in Sodom, married one

of its women, and "lingered" in the place of his choice, and become identified with its life and luxury? Further, had not Lot, when the men of Sodom sought to commit sodomy (which we now have legalized and call homosexuality), offered to give his virgin daughters to the Sodomites to rape (19: 7, 8)? No wonder the girls had no respect for their father! Added to this, there was the evil influence of their socialite mother who was so much a part of life in Sodom.

The lack of any true morality whatever in Lot's daughters is evident by what happened in that cave once all three were clear of the smoking Sodom. There is no mention of any remorse on their part over the sin occasioning the destruction of the city, and the tragic death of their mother. Their utter degradation ending in Lot's intense shame is the most dreadful part of his story. How revolting was the conduct of the daughters when they made their father drunk in order to make him the unwilling father of their children, Moab and Ben-ammi who were begotten in shame and had a shameful history! (Deuteronomy 29:19; Psalm 83:8). The family of Lot was a bad group, and have disgrace, disaster and death written in their epitaph. They remain for all time a solemn reminder of the truth that "God is not mocked: for whatsoever a man soweth, that shall he also reap" (Galatians 6:7).

POTIPHAR'S WIFE
Genesis 39

H. V. Morton in his sketch of Potiphar's wife says that "she occupies a prominent place as the first sensualist in the gallery of Scriptural women. The sins against morality committed by women up to this point in the Bible story were committed for dynastic reasons, or were due to the customs of the times." The immortal story of this ruler's wife's lust for Joseph is "a picture of a woman, spoilt, rich and beautiful, the product of a luxurious and licentious civilization," coveting one of the holiest and most attractive men in Egypt. Joseph enjoyed the favor of God who prospered him in his service in the house of Potiphar, the chief of Pharaoh's bodyguard. That he had the confidence of his master is seen in that he "found grace in his sight, and the Lord blessed the Egyptian's house for Joseph's sake." If there had been ten like him in Sodom it would have been spared.

But temporal prosperity was not an unmixed blessing for Joseph. He was "a goodly person, and well favoured," and his form and face were to bring him days of trial. His master had a godless wife whose character is revealed in her brief biography. If a wholly bad woman is Satan's masterpiece, then Potiphar's nameless wife takes the prize for diabolical cunning and dastardly wickedness. Joseph was a young man with natural instincts, but divine grace kept him from following youthful lusts, enabling him to resist the advances of the faithless wife of Potiphar to share her bed. She was persistent in her endeavor to have Joseph "to lie by her." This female wretch tempted him to commit adultery "day by day" (39: 10). The more she persisted, the easier Joseph found it to say, No! Each victory helped him the battle to win. On one of the days of the severe conflict we read, "There was none of the men of the house there within." Secrecy often provides the facility for sinning, but Joseph knew what it was to be much alone with God, therefore his isolation with his temptress did not disturb him.

Amid all the fierce testing, Joseph acted magnificently. He had a deep respect for the husband of the lustful wife and could not sin against Potiphar who trusted Joseph with all he had and raised him to a position of influence and authority. Never for one moment had he the shadow of doubt as to Joseph's integrity. That was the human side — the resolute determination not to betray his master who relied on him so fully. Then there was Joseph's estimation of what Potiphar's wife constantly tempted him to do. He called the suggested adultery, "great wickedness." In his old Hebrew home he had been taught that it was a grievous sin to disregard the sanctity of the marriage law, and so power was Joseph's to honor the claims of chastity. But above and beyond all reasons why he should not sin in the way he was urged to, was the recognition of the claims of God, "How can I do this great wickedness, and *sin against God?*" Joseph

knew God to be the antagonist of all evil, and so sided with Him.

The last day of Joseph's period of temptation was the most fatal. Coming into the house on business, Joseph saw that he and the she-devil were alone and with one passionate outburst she cried as she laid hold of his clothes, "Lie with me!" Disentangling himself from her grasp, Joseph fled, leaving some of his torn clothing in her hands. But Joseph little knew that in fleeing from a woman's passion, he was fleeing into prison. The shreds of Joseph's garment in the woman's hand gave her a diabolical idea. Her desire for Joseph turned to hate, lust turned to lying and adultery to accusation. Calling in the servants, she showed them the remnants of Joseph's garment, and with this piece of circumstantial evidence of his effort to force her to share her bed with him. Joseph's quick flight from Potiphar's wife underlines the strength of a character without flaw, but the woman's slander cast a reflection upon his piety. Contemptuously, she called Joseph a "Hebrew" which her husband had brought into the house to mock its inhabitants. She may have been the first woman, but she was certainly not the last "to exhibit the classic retaliation of the woman scorned."

When Potiphar returned, his wife displayed the pieces of Joseph's garment which she had torn from him, and with added color repeated her slanderous lie. How deeply the holy heart of Joseph must have felt the foul accusation, as the master he respected charged him with a sin he abhorred and never committed! Potiphar's wrath, fed by the jealousy and falsehood of his wife, was kindled, and Joseph suffered the unjust punishment of imprisonment. But even in prison Joseph knew that it was better to rot there with an unsullied conscience than to prosper in a palace, if prosperity meant degradation. Yet in the prison the Lord was with Joseph, for He was the gracious Keeper of the pure prisoner. Others had wrongly blamed Joseph, but he had the approval of his own conscience and the confidence that the God he refused to sin against, would vindicate him, as He did. We can imagine how Potiphar's wife had many a sleepless night as she thought of Joseph in his narrow cell all because of her passion and perjury. But to Joseph's credit, we have no recorded word he uttered in his own defense, or against the evil woman responsible for his degradation. Thus —

This stirring old-time story of a soul
That dared to do the right,
Is ripe with helpful inspirations still
That move toward the light.

SHAUL'S MOTHER
Genesis 46:10; Exodus 6:15

An Israelite was forbidden to take a Canaanite to wife (Genesis 24:3). Ellicott comments, "Jewish tradition represents Shaul as being really the son of Dinah by a Canaanite father, Shechem, but as adopted by Simeon to save his sister's honour, yet with a note that he was of half Canaanitish blood."

PHARAOH'S DAUGHTER
The Woman Who Adopted a Baby
Exodus 2:5-10; Acts 7:21; Hebrews 11:24

Although we have already briefly considered this royal, unidentified female (compare JOCHEBED), a closer view of the only mother Moses really knew may be profitable. Who, exactly, was the new king over Egypt at the time of the birth of Moses we do not know. Conjectures have him as Aahames I or Rameses II, or Seti I. In like manner, what the name of his daughter was no one knows. This princess credited with a royal deed, without leaving her signature, has been made out to be Thermuthis, or Myrrina, or Mercis. Whatever name legend may give her, the Bible preserves her anonymity even though "she stands to the fortunes and fate of the Israelite nation, as its instrumental providence and contributory saviour." Described as "the daughter of Pharaoh" suggests that she was the Egyptian ruler's only daughter. Our first impression of the princess is the contrast her character affords to the portrait of another Egyptian female we have just written about. Potiphar's wife manifests, "the undisciplined forces of womanhood in their most violent form — Pharaoh's daughter blots out that dark portrait and gives us one of a woman — kind, tender and compassionate."

She Was a Heathen Woman

Destined to be the woman who should save a baby from a terrible death, care for him although he was a Hebrew, and lay the foundation of his great work for God, Pharaoh's daughter was an Egyptian, an idolater who worshiped the sun. Yet in the motherhood of the child whom she delivered from the Nile and named Moses, she revealed that she was above the pagan plane — even above the cruelty of her pagan parent. At the risk of jeopardizing her favor with her father who had decreed the drowning of all male Hebrew babies, she felt it too cruel to murder the precious bundle of humanity found in the bulrushes.

She Had a Human Heart

As an Egyptian woman, the princess enjoyed great liberty. Along with her female attendants, she came to a reserved part of the Nile to wash seeing its waters were considered to be healthy and fructifying. Seeing the small basket, Pharaoh's daughter sent one of her maidens to fetch it. As soon as she opened it and saw the lovely child, she had compassion on him in spite of the fact that he was one of the Hebrew's children, whom her despot father had ordered to be killed. The babe wept, and his tears opened a well of compassion in the heathen heart of the princess, and she exhibited a tender affection for children. With her love she mingled concern for the baby's welfare, and, as we have seen, his own mother was secured as his nurse until he was weaned (compare MIRIAM). Pharaoh's daughter did not look upon little Moses as a delightful plaything for the palace, but as the foundling for whom she had risked her own life.

She Became the Female Saviour of Israel

Think of what would have happened if Pharaoh's daughter had not come down to the waters at the hour she did. The babe might have been destroyed in some way. But as God called a heathen ruler, Cyrus, "His servant," so He used the pagan princess to deliver the child who was to become one of God's greatest heroes. For 40 years Moses was cared for and educated as the son of Pharaoh's daughter, having all the privileges of a son of the royal court. Stephen declared that "Moses was learned in all the wisdom of the Egyptians, and was mighty in words and in deeds" (Acts 7:22). Surrounded with all the wealth and luxury of Pharaoh's court, Moses was taught to speak and write the Egyptian language correctly. Attention would be given to the grace of style which was later to guide Moses as the writer of the first five books of the Bible. His education would also include arithmetic and geometry, something in which the Egyptians even in that far-off age were most proficient. Moses also acquired a knowledge of Egyptian law, which he put to good use when he came to write the Mosaic law. From the priests of religion, he learned much about religious morality. Thus, in the education the princess gave her adopted son, we have an evidence of God's overruling providence in the shaping of the future of Israel's great leader. Theron Brown reminds us that —

> The Hebrew nation — the whole world, proud of the sublime man Moses came to be, is indebted to her for his life, his education, and his name. . . . She alone stood effectually between him and death. . . . The tomb and fillet of this interesting woman have not been found. If ever her unperished form is brought to light, clad in the enduring cerements that wrap the dead of her kingly family, we shall know her name. But it would be dearer to know that her living soul dwells not far from the son she adopted and loved, the grandest man of sacred history, who but for her would never have been.

Moses never forgot that he was a Hebrew, and through many years of his sojourn in Egypt he had to endure the ceaseless and implacable envy and hostility of the officers of the royal court. But Pharaoh's daughter never lost faith in her gifted son. One wonders whether Moses brought her to know Jehovah as God over all! It must have been a heartache for this foster mother when she could no longer protect her son. In a fit of indignation Moses killed an Egyptian taskmaster for savagely flogging a Hebrew, and fearing the vengeance of Pharaoh, Moses hid the body in the sand. But someone witnessed the deed, and Moses fled for his life from the stately lady who, for forty years, had lavished care and attention upon him, making life tolerable for him in a land of bondage. Did she ever see him again? Was she alive when, 40 years

later, he returned to Egypt as the mighty deliverer of the Israelite nation from cruel bondage? We do not know. We think of her as the Bible pictures her—a kindhearted Egyptian princess, a noble and tender woman who lived in a cruel time. Through divine providence she was the instrument of saving the babe from death, who became "Moses, the Servant of God."

DAUGHTERS OF REUEL
Exodus 2:15-22

When Moses fled from Pharaoh, he came to the land of Midian and, while sitting at a well, the seven daughters of Reuel, the priest, or prince of Midian, came to draw water for their father's flocks. The virgins, pestered by the shepherds, were afraid, but Moses—very much Egyptian-looking—came to their aid, and assisted them in the watering of the flock. The daughters invited Moses home, and he was glad and grateful for the hospitality offered. Reuel, impressed with the manner and appearance of Moses, invited him to share his abode which he did for almost 40 years. He married Zipporah (which see), one of the daughters, and she bore Moses two sons, Gershom and Eliezer. When faced with the necessity of observing the rite of circumcision, Zipporah, petulant and reproachful, regarded such a blood-drawing rite of her husband's religion as cruel and barbarous. She failed to understand the significance of the divine visitation upon Moses because of his negligence in not circumcising their newborn son. Often our obedience to God is not understood by those nearest us. Not being one with us in our desire to honor the Lord, close friends think our devotion to Him somewhat strange.

DAUGHTERS OF PUTIEL
Exodus 6:25

In the genealogies of Moses and Aaron, given in this chapter, Eleazar the priest, Aaron's son, is mentioned as having married one of the daughters of Putiel. Who Putiel was, how many daughters he had, and what was the given name of the daughter Eleazar took to wife and bore him Phinehas, we are not told. The zeal of Phinehas for the cause of the Lord was possibly the fruit of his wholesome home influence.

WISEHEARTED WOMEN
Exodus 35:22-29

The Tabernacle and all its services form God's picture book of redemption. They were figures of a more glorious, eternal sanctuary (Hebrews 9). All the gold, silver and materials necessary for the Tabernacle had been received as presents from the Egyptians, ere the Israelites left Egypt (Exodus 3:22; 11:1-3), and these, along with the personal adornments of men and women alike, made possible the earthly Tabernacle in which God was pleased to dwell. Men, like wisehearted Bezaleel and Aholiab were empowered by God to fashion the furniture of the Tabernacle, and the women also played their part (35:22-29; 36:1-3). Here is the record of their share in the holy project —

All the women that were wise hearted did spin with their hands, and brought that which they had spun, both of blue, and of purple, and of scarlet, and of fine linen. And all the women whose hearts stirred them up in wisdom spun goats' hair (35:25, 26).

These skillful women of the wheel and the spindle, with willing hearts labored as unto the Lord. They gave their treasures, time and talents ungrudgingly for the completion of the Tabernacle which God commanded Moses to erect for His worship and service in the wilderness. We have a touch of their prodigality in donating all that was required in the arrestive lines —

The men and women were restrained from bringing. For the stuff they had was sufficient for all the work to make it, and *too much*.

How the church of today could do with a revival of such consecrated giving and working! Dorcas (which see) must have been a descendant of those wisehearted women of old who served God with their needles and thread. As women predominate in present day church attendance and activity, it would seem as if they are more willing-hearted than its men. So many necessities for the mission field are made possible by Christian women who spin with their hands.

TABERNACLE WOMEN
Exodus 38:8

The margin mentions that these worshiping women "assembled by troops" at the door of the Tabernacle. What greatly impressed Moses was the surrender on the part of these women of their most highly prized of their possessions, namely, the beautiful, perfectly polished brass mirrors, wonderful specimens of Egyptian handicraft, which these women of Israel had brought with them from Egypt. As a mark of his approval of the devotion of the women, Moses melted down the mirrors and fashioned the laver, and recorded the fact to the women's credit. Renouncing the articles associated with personal vanity, for the higher beauties of holiness, those anonymous women made possible a utensil of great service for the priests. After offering sacrifices upon the brazen altar, they had to tarry at the laver and wash their blood-stained hands and their soiled feet before going into the Holy Place to serve and worship the Lord. Hands represent work and feet represent walk, and both had to be clean in the priestly service of the Tabernacle. What a lesson there is for all women —and men—in the joyful sacrifice of valued treasures to the Lord for the needs of those whom He calls to serve Him!

PRIESTLY DAUGHTERS
Leviticus 21:9

The Levitical law has much to say about the treatment of, and also the types of women. Whores, wizards, adulteresses, and the defiled are all dealt with in a way eloquent of God's holiness (Leviticus 19:20). Because of their sacred office, priests were to receive reverence, and their daughters, if guilty of violating the holy law of God, received greater punishment than those of the ordinary men who sinned. The daughter of an Israelite going astray was punished with death by strangling (Leviticus 20:10; Deuteronomy 22:23, 24), but the disgraced daughter of a priest endured the severer death by burning. By her whoremongering she had "profaned her father," brought shame upon his witness and office. It is to be feared that not all the children of Christian ministers realize their solemn obligation to live lives in keeping with the profession and position of their fathers, called of God to care for the souls of men.

ETHIOPIAN WIFE OF MOSES
Numbers 12:1

We know the name of the first wife of Moses, and the names of his children (see ZIPPORAH and MIRIAM), but his second wife whom he took after Zipporah's death is an unnamed Cushite. Many Cushites followed Israel out of Egypt, and marriage with them was not forbidden by the Law (Exodus 34:16). This second marriage caused a rift between Moses and his sister and brother. Not all second marriages turn out happy.

MIDIAN WOMEN
Numbers 31:9

Having made Midian his home for 40 years, Moses must have found it hard to war against the Midianites and slay their kings and rulers as well as people. The women of Midian along with their children were taken captive, and one can imagine the anguish of those women bereft of husband, uprooted from their homes, and robbed of their possessions. But many of these women, through Balaam, had been the cause of the apostasy of Israel, and were consequently punished for their seduction. As the result of this tragic episode, the law concerning marriage with captives was enacted (Deuteronomy 21:10-14). Does not James remind us that wars and fightings come because of lusts (4:1, 2)?

SISERA'S MOTHER
Judges 5:28-31

If Deborah had any tenderness in her heart as "the Mother of Israel," she must have found it hard writing about "the mother of Sisera," waiting so anxiously for the return of her son, whom Deborah knew had been slain. What a pathetic scene it is of the mother sitting at the window and with a wail of impatience passing into deep concern asks, "Why is his chariot so long in coming? Why tarry the wheels of his chariot?" What pathos there was in such a cry, and what a broken heart there must have been when the terrible truth was known! Deborah, prophetess and poetess, in a few broad sketches sets before us the last scene in the conquest of Israel's foes.

The mother of Sisera and her attendant princesses had looked for the triumph and return of the host as confidently as the ladies of Spain expected the return of the Armada, or the ladies of Aberdeen sat "with their fans in their hands" looking out for the sails of Sir Patrick Spens.

But Sisera did not return to the mother who loved him. Another woman's hand had killed him (see JAEL). In any war women are always the worst sufferers. The longing, yet fear and dread of Sisera's mother has been multiplied millions of times in the wars of history.

GIDEON'S WIVES
Judges 8:29-31

Honorable in many ways, Gideon revealed the worst side of his character in the polygamous practice he emulated (Judges 10:4; 12:9). He had forgotten the Mosaic law concerning the marital life of a king or ruler: "Neither shall he multiply wives to himself . . . neither shall he greatly multiply to himself silver and gold" (Deuteronomy 17:17).

Gideon had many wives, how many and who they were are not known. From these unknown wives there came 70 sons, all of whom were slain by another son (9:56). In keeping with oriental fashion nothing is said of his daughters. Gideon's concubine, contemptuously called his "maidservant" (9:18), comes in for special mention as the mother of Abimelech, who became a bad reproduction of his father whose courage and energy he possessed but very few of his virtues. While the Bible leaves the mother of Abimelech unidentified, Josephus gives her the name of Drumah. While Gideon died in peace, and in a good old age, the evil seed he had sown bore bitter fruit in the next generation (Judges 9).

WOMAN OF THEBEZ
Judges 9:50-57; II Samuel 11:21

Abimelech met his death at the hands of his armorbearer (9:54). The constant mention of towers and strongholds in a time when men did what was right in the sight of their own eyes reveals the disturbed state of the country, and the Thebez tower to which all the people fled for safety as bloodthirsty Abimelech approached, speaks of the panic that prevailed. Fired with ambition for power, and scorning the decree of his father, "Neither shall my son rule over you. The Lord shall rule over you," Abimelech was determined to be king. In order to make sure of his reign he murdered all rivals, including his 70 brothers — all except young Jotham who escaped. After the destruction of his own city, Shechem, flushed with victory, Abimelech attacked another revolted city, Thebez, but here he was to experience divine vengeance for his lust for blood and power.

Standing on the roof of the tower was an obscure daughter of Israel, who was to become the instrument of heaven to punish a sinner too bold and wicked to live. As a true patriot, this unknown heroine of Thebez saw her opportunity as Abimelech rushed against the tower to burn it and its terror-stricken occupants with fire. Seizing a large piece of millstone on the battlement she hurled it with all her strength upon Abimelech as he came near the tower door. As God was behind the aim of young David when with his sling and stone he killed the giant, Goliath, so He directed the fall of the millstone. It fell upon Abimelech's head and broke his skull. As his armorbearer dragged him out of the perilous range of more millstones, Abimelech, recovering his senses for a moment, commanded his armorbearer to kill him off lest it should be said that a mere unknown woman killed him. He did not, however, escape the taunt (II Samuel 11:21).

At a critical moment in her nation's history this "certain woman" delivered her people of a cruel monster, and made possible forty five years of national peace. Alas, there was no one to record the name and sing the praise of this heroine who must have received the gratitude of the now liberated people of the city! The fate of Abimelech at the hands of a woman is but another instance of God's frequent method of justice — choosing the weak to destroy the strong. The battle is not always to the strong. The concluding verses of this dark chapter were doubtless added to prove that "God punishes both individual and national sin, and that men's pleasant vices are made the instruments to scourge them. The murderer of his brothers 'upon one stone' (9:5), is slain by a stone flung on his head, and

the treacherous idolaters are treacherously burnt in the temple of their idol."

GILEAD'S WIFE
Judges 11:1-3

Two women are to be distinguished in the life of Gilead, the grandson of Manasseh. First of all, there is the unnamed harlot who bore him Jephthah the Gileadite, who became a judge of Israel. Then there is Gilead's anonymous wife who bore her husband many sons who rose up and drove Jephthah from their father's house because he was the son of a harlot. Such an action was in perfect accordance with the law, and with family rules and traditions (Genesis 21:10; 25:6; Deuteronomy 23:2, 3). Expulsion was hard on Jephthah who could not help his illegitimacy. We speak wrongly of a child as being illegitimate. The shame is on the parents who conceived him in an illegitimate way.

JEPHTHAH'S DAUGHTER
THE WOMAN WHO WAS SACRIFICED FOR AN OATH
Judges 11:30-39

After he was expelled from Gilead's home, Jephthah, who made a name for himself as a fearless, brave and successful chief of robbers, was recalled by the elders of Gilead to lead them in war against the Ammonites who had made war with Israel. Jephthah offered to fight on condition that if victorious over Ammon, he should be recognized as their head. In spite of his half-heathen origin, Jephthah seemed to have had a Godward inclination, for we are told that he "uttered all his words before the Lord." "The Spirit of the Lord came upon Jephthah," "He vowed a vow unto the Lord," "I have opened my mouth unto the Lord," and his name is enrolled among those who were conspicuous for their faith (Hebrews 11:32), displayed at memorable crises in national history.

While we have no mention whatever of Jephthah's wife — she may have died in childbirth — he is memorable because of his affection for his daughter, and of the vow he made concerning her. The full pathos of the story is the peculiarly tender language used. The nameless girl was "his only child," and, "beside her he had neither son nor daughter." His precious child was ever beside him. He made a rash vow that if God delivered Ammon into his hands he would sacrifice unto Him whatever came out of the door of his house to meet him on his victorious return. Leaving God to choose the victim, Jephthah likely thought one of the slaves would come out to greet him and be the burnt offering. God took Jephthah at his word, but he was stunned when he saw his precious daughter crossing the threshold to greet him. God answered his prayer and punished him through its answer. Shakespeare, when he selected an example of paternal tenderness, seized upon Jephthah in the scene between Hamlet and Polonius —

HAMLET: O Jephthah, judge of Israel what a treasure hadst thou!
POLONIUS: What a treasure had he, my Lord?
HAMLET: One fair daughter and no more, The which he loved passing well.

But when Jephthah felt the loving arms of his fair daughter thrown around him, he cried, "Alas, my daughter! crushing, thou hast crushed me: for I have opened my mouth unto the LORD and I cannot go back." What was her reaction as she saw the agony in her dear father's eyes, and heard his much-loved voice pronounce her doom? What did she think of her father's anguish and of the sudden realization of her own fate?

Her Response

Her answer was most heroic. There were no resentful or rebellious tones in it. She shed no tears, nor shook with despair after her father with a crushed heart spoke of his vow. There was the quiet acceptance of the tragic fact that she was to be the burnt offering her father had promised. Only known by the simple title of "Jephthah's daughter," this most commendable maiden may not have had the gifts and talents of some other women of the Bible, but she will ever remain as the incarnation of willing sacrifice. "My father, if thou hast made this promise to the Lord, do to me according to the promise." If there is a quality for which a woman is supreme, it is sacrifice, and in this virtue the obedient daughter of Jephthah gave what was nobler than gifts— she offered *herself*. Her father said, "I can-

not go back," and she did not go back. She did not run away from her father, but with true devotion accepted his will and acquiesced in his grim behest. She felt that her blood would be a good price to pay for divine vengeance over the enemies of Israel. Known only as the daughter of a famous father, this lovely girl by her noble consent revealed a nobility of character which quickens our imagination and stirs our sympathy.

Ellicott comments, "We may well rejoice in the gleam of sunlight which is flung upon the sacred page by his [Jephthah's] faithfulness in not going back from his vow, though it were to his own hurt (Psalm 15: 4), and in the beautiful devotion of his daughter, cheerfully acquiescing in her own sacrifice for the good of her country." History records similar sacrifices as when Marius offered his daughter for victory over the Cimbri. Tennyson caught the willing spirit of the daughter's submission to her father's vow when he wrote —

When the next moon was rolled into the sky,
    Strength came to me that equall'd my desire.
How beautiful a thing it was to die
For God and for my sire!

Her Request

To a Hebrew maiden the bitterest pang was to die unwedded and childless, and so Jephthah's daughter asks for a delay of two months that she might bewail her virginity. "Let me alone," indicated a postponement of the vow for a definite purpose (see Deuteronomy 9:14; I Samuel 11:3). To the desolate mountains she went to bewail the destruction of her hopes as a Hebrew maid of ever fulfilling the dream of motherhood. The heartbroken father willingly granted his noble daughter's request, doubtless with the secret hope that somehow she might never return, and he be spared the terrible sight of seeing his daughter, his only daughter, sacrificed upon the altar. How apropos are the lines of Tennyson as we think of the crushing of all aspiration of bearing a child that might be in the Messianic line!—

My God, my land, my father — these did move
    Me from my bliss of life, that nature gave,
Lowered softly with a threefold cord of love
Down to a silent grave.

And I went mourning, "No fair Hebrew boy
  Shall smile away my maiden blame among
The Hebrew mothers" — emptied of all joy,
  Leaving the dance and song,

Leaving the olive gardens far below,
  Leaving the promise of my bridal bower
The valleys of grape-loaded vines that glow
  Beneath the battled tower.

Her Renunciation

True to her promise, the sorrowing maiden returned from her weeping place upon the mountains. She was a woman of her word, and came back for the execution of her father's vow, "who did with her according to his vow which he had vowed." Doubtless among the mountains her heart gathered strength and courage for her sacrifice in the valleys. Says Ruskin, "All great inspiration comes from the hills" (Psalms 121:1, 2; 123:1).

> Up to the hills
> Where the torrent fills
> With storms of the Winter's brewing,
> Close in the clasp,
> Of Nature's grasp,
> There tell thy heart's undoing.

The great question is, What did Jephthah actually do to his daughter on her return? The fulfillment of his vow could only mean one thing, namely, the offering up of his precious child as a burnt offering (11:31). But Bible scholars disagree over what is precisely meant by this "burnt offering." According to one interpretation the vow of Jephthah consisted of two parts —

1. What *person* soever met him should be the Lord's, or dedicated to His service forever.

2. What *beast* soever met him should be offered as a burnt offering, like the Tabernacle lambs, upon an altar.

Based upon this view, it is affirmed that Jephthah kept his daughter in sacred celibacy for the rest of her life; that what she and her female companions bewailed was not the prospect of coming sacrifice but her *virginity*. "She knew no man." So the phrase "he did with her according to his vow" is made to signify the exclusion of his daughter as a kind of Old Testament nun, surrendered to live a secluded life in the service of the Tabernacle — a vestal virgin. Thus the shuddering thought of a terrible

human sacrifice is softened down in this way —

> It was not a human sacrifice in the gross sense of the word, not a slaughter of an unwilling victim, but the offering of a devoted heart, to free, as she supposed, her father and her country from a terrible obligation. . . . The heroism of the father and daughter are to be admired and loved in the midst of the fierce superstition round which it plays like a sunbeam on a stormy sea.

That Jephthah could not have sacrificed his daughter as an actual burnt offering is argued against in this way —

1. The sacrifice of children to Moloch was an abomination prohibited by an express law, and not an instance occurred of a human sacrifice to God.

2. The case of Abraham offering Isaac is not in point, as Isaac was not sacrificed. The command was given only to try Abraham's faith.

3. No father could put even a criminal child to death without the consent of the magistrates.

4. The traditional laws of the Jews say: "If a Jew should devote his son or his daughter, his man servant or maid servant who are Hebrews, the devotement should be void."

But in spite of the reasons advanced against a human sacrifice, the Scripture is heavily on the side of Jephthah's vow being fulfilled as it was made. Martin Luther wrote, "Some affirm that he did not sacrifice her; but the text is clear enough." The ancient Jews who had an intimate knowledge of the customs of their race and a unique meaning of their own language, have always understood that the daughter of Jephthah was a literal burnt offering. *The Targum* of Jonathan has the explanation —

> It was a custom in Israel in order that no one should make his son or his daughter a burnt-offering, as Jephthah did, and did not consult Phinehas the priest. Had he done so, he would have redeemed her with money.

While the Levitical law forbade human sacrifices, the time of the Judges was a period when "every man did that which was right in the sight of his own eyes," and consequently it was a period of ignorance and barbarity when the sacrifice of human life was common. They were the times of appalling ignorance which "God winked at." Certainly we deplore Jephthah's rash vow and terrible mistake in making such a useless sacrifice, but he fulfilled his vow; he did not set aside his daughter to perpetual virginity such as a girl does when she enters a convent to become "a bride of Christ." He did not dedicate her thus, and then offer a burnt offering of an animal to seal his pledge. The heroic virgin became the burnt offering, and the giving of her life transfigured the wicked vow of her father. Her sacrificial love turned the blackest deed in Israel's early history into a theme for "the songs of the daughters of Israel."

Ancient writers wove into history, drama and poetry the tragic theme of such propitiatory sacrifice. Virginian submitted to be stabbed to the heart by her father, Virginius, rather than fall into the hands of the enemies of her country. The Spartan mothers told their sons to come back victors or be borne back dead on their shields. The sacrifice of Jephthah's daughter was a perfect one because it was actuated by a twofold love — love for her father and love for her country. Mackintosh Mackay reminds us that this is the view Tennyson takes of her in his beautiful picture of her in the *Dream of Fair Women* —

In this splendid pageant of the illustrious women of history, the most lovely picture of all is this humble Jewish girl. Upon her breast the poet still sees the mark of the spear-wound; upon her face the gaze of tragic sorrow. Yet, when he would commiserate her, she refuses the proffered pity:
"Heaven heads the count of crimes
With that wild oath."
She neither wished or needs pity. What matter her poor life be sacrificed if her country be free.

Then Tennyson goes on to give us this beautiful picture of one infusing her sacrifice with the spirit of perfect love, which makes all things beautiful —

It comforts me in this one thought to dwell,
That I subdued me to my father's will;
Because the kiss he gave me, ere I fell,
Sweetens the spirit still.

Moreover it is written that my race
Hew'd Ammon, hip and thigh, from Aroer
On Arnon unto Mianeth. Here her face
Glow'd, as I look'd at her.

She lock'd her lips: she left me where I stood;
"Glory to God," she sang, and past afar,
Thridding the sombre boskage of the wood,
Toward the morning-star.

Her Remembrance

Is it any wonder that the daughters of Israel remembered and honored the sacrifice of Jephthah's daughter with a four days' festival during each year? Although this was probably a local custom only, it was a gracious gesture not to "lament" her, but "to praise" or "celebrate," as the word can imply. The feelings of those Jewish maidens toward their departed companion were akin to those of the Romans toward Claelia, the virgin martyr of A.D. 280, and of other national heroines whose self-sacrifice helped their nations to victory. Byron expressed this sentiment in his lines —

Though the virgins of Salem lament,
Be the judge and the hero unbent;
I have won the great battle for thee,
And my father and country are free.

IBZAN'S DAUGHTERS
Judges 12:8, 9

The period covered by the Judges was a time of moral degeneracy which always brings with it national weakness. The reins were given over to the passions of men, and as wealth accumulated, polygamy became rife, as already seen in Gideon (8:30). In the narrative before us we have the record of Abdon with his forty sons and thirty "nephews" (12:14, ASV), and also of Ibzan with his thirty sons and thirty daughters, and another thirty daughters from abroad he took as wives for his sons. The history of polygamy is stained with jealousy, hatred, intrigue, fatal favoritism and death.

MANOAH'S WIFE
THE WOMAN WHO MOTHERED EARTH'S STRONGEST MAN
Judges 13; 14:2-5; Hebrews 11:32

It would have added greater interest to the story of Samson if we had had the name of his mother. It must have been a sweet and suggestive one for she was such a good woman. But while her husband's name is preserved, she herself is nameless although the Talmud says that she bore the name of Hazelelponi or Zelelponi (see I Chronicles 4:3), and that she was of the tribe of Judah. Zelelponi means "the shadow falls on me," and Manoah's wife was certainly one who dwelt under the shadow of the Almighty and became the mother of the strongest man who ever lived.

She Was a Disappointed Woman

Once again we have the poignant phrase "She was barren," with the redundant expression common in ancient literature, "and bare not." "Sarai was barren: she had no child." "Thou shalt live and not die," etc. As we have already seen, God made many barren wives to rejoice over the birth of children (see SARAH, REBEKAH, HANNAH, ELISABETH). These godly women who felt the intense sorrow and disappointment of a childless home received divine announcement and accomplishment of maternal joy. Manoah's wife was a God-fearing Israelite whose faith taught her that heaven knew all about the maternity she cherished, and of the vain waiting that saddened her life. Evidently Manoah and his wife had all necessary material benefits. They seemed to have been fairly prosperous, but their greatest joy had been denied their home. Their child-longing and child-loving hearts had never been satisfied. Swinburne expressed the sentiment —

Where children are not, Heaven is not.

She Was a Privileged Woman

The wife of Manoah of Zorah was greatly honored in that she experienced a pre-incarnate appearance of the Messiah. By "the angel of the Lord" who visited her with the happy message that her barrenness would pass, and she would become the mother of a most unusual son, we are to understand not any human messenger, but a supernatural being. The phrase constantly used in Judges implies, "The angel of His presence," and is equivalent to earlier references (Genesis 16:7; 22:11; Exodus 2:2, 6, 14, etc.). Speaking in the first person, the august visitor who came to Manoah's wife was "the captain of the LORD's host" (Joshua 5: 13-15). Heavenly beings brought revelations to individuals, but the prophets were the media of revelation to nations. The announcer of the good news, "thou shalt conceive and bear a son," assumed a human

form, for reporting his appearance to her husband, she spoke of him as, "A man of God . . . his countenance was like the countenance of an angel of God, very terrible."

Later on, when the heavenly visitant appeared to both Manoah and his wife and repeated his message that their prayer and desire for a child would be answered, again his name was asked for. "Neither told me his name" (13:6). "What is thy name?" (13:17). But the angel answered, "Why askest thou thus after my name, seeing it is *secret*," or "wonderful," as the margin expresses it, where the same term is used of the promised Messiah. "His name shall be called Wonderful" (Isaiah 9:6). The same word is used in the phrase, "the angel did *wonderously*" (13:19). As angels do not receive worship, the supernatural person the over-awed couple saw was no ordinary angel, for they fell on their faces and said, "We shall surely die, because we have seen *God*" (Exodus 33:20). It is clearly evident, therefore, that Manoah and his wife had witnessed one of those Old Testament theophanic appearances of Christ.

She Was a Godly Woman

Both of those humble Israelites must have walked with God to have been counted worthy to receive such a marvelous interview with the heaven-sent messenger. Barren though the nameless wife was, she was yet believing. We have no record of complaint or impatience over her childless state as we have in the case of Hannah. Constantly, she prayed for a child, and her prayer lightened the burden of her loneliness and sustained her patience. As a God-fearing Israelite, she had faith that He would answer her prayer.

Further, the fact that her promised son was to be separated unto God from the womb to the day of his death, marks her out as the sanctified vessel.

The cause of God is holy,
And useth holy things.

This faithful, self-sacrificing, holy woman then, must have had a life corresponding to the separated character of the son she was to bear, and grace was hers to dedicate him to the Lord before his birth. That she was likewise a woman of sanctified common sense is seen in her reply to her husband's cry, "We shall surely die, because we have seen God." Calmly and sensibly, she said, "If the LORD were pleased to kill us, he would not have received a burnt-offering and a meat offering at our hands, neither would he have shewed us all these things, nor would as at this time have told us such things as these." This woman of godly intuition knew that having seen God she was to live as never before. A divinely promised son would come to brighten the home.

She Was a Happy Woman

At last the prayers of Manoah's wife were answered, and she became a joyous mother. "The woman bare a son, and called his name Samson." How grateful to God she must have been as the promised son was now a reality and nestling on her breast! She understood God's overruling throughout her barren years, and rejoiced in the knowledge that her long-awaited child would be the saviour of Israel. We note, in the first place, the significance of the name she gave him — Samson. His father's name, Manoah, meant "rest" or "consolation" while his son's name implied "strength of the sun" —prophetic of his prowess as a Hebrew Hercules. The association of the sun with strength was most natural (Judges 5:31; Psalm 19:5, 6). Ancient Jewish fathers said that "Samson was named after the name of God, who is called sun and shield of Israel" (Psalm 84:11). Another scholar affirms that the name the mother gave her son is from an Egyptian root, and means "the servant of God," in reference to Samson's Nazarite vow. But the name itself is a Hebrew one, and meant to Manoah and his wife that the glory of their family would be sustained through the champion who would be without a rival in Israel.

The second thought is that the son God gave to wreak vengeance upon the enemies of His people was to be a Nazarite from his birth, and the angelic announcer gave to Manoah and his wife explicit instructions as to how they should live and rear their mighty son who was to "judge Israel twenty years." The mother herself, while pregnant, was under a dedicatory vow not to drink wine, or eat anything of an unclean nature, thus the son she conceived was in blood

and bone a Nazarite. For Samson, his uncut hair was to be the sign that he was separated unto God (Numbers 6). In spite of his moral lapses, he never broke the sacred vow until a seductive woman discovered the secret of his power, and left him the helpless victim of carnal passions.

She Was a Sorrowful Woman

Granted the blessing of motherhood, Manoah's wife must have wondered why such a turbulent son had been given her as a gift of heaven. It was true that Samson loved Israel and smote those who were his country's oppressors. How the Philistines feared this giant of a man who knew no fear, and how unceasing they were in their efforts to destroy him. As his mother saw how he triumphed over Israel's foes, she doubtless blessed God for creating him as the answer to her prayer, for the removal of her barrenness, fashioning her son like an Atlas and giving him sinews of steel. But some of his unruly traits must have cast a shadow over her heart. Although his name carried the idea of "splendor," or "sun-like," some of his desires lacked the splendor of his name.

Appearing as the avowed enemy of the Philistine, Samson went to Timnath, and coveted the daughter of an "uncircumcised Philistine," which on the lips of a Jew was a term of peculiar hatred (I Samuel 17:36). Samson urged his parents to secure the woman as his wife seeing it was the custom for parents to make arrangements for a marriage and pay the dowry (Genesis 34: 4-12). How such a marriage must have been repugnant to Manoah and his wife, and what sorrow must have been theirs when Samson came back after one of his conquests and found his Philistine wife taken from him and given to another man! Then there came his association with the harlot Delilah (see DELILAH) which brought about his tragic end. After Samson's marriage to the Philistine woman of Timnath we do not read of his parents again. It is to be hoped that they had died and were thus spared the tragedy of seeing their son, craftily seduced, robbed of his mighty strength, blinded and made as a slave at Gaza. What a different end Samson would have had, if only he had chosen a wife after the lovely character of the mother who bore him!

MICAH'S MOTHER
Judges 17:1-7

The name of the Ephraimite, Micah, is suggestive. It means, "Who is like Jehovah?" and was doubtless given him by pious parents. His nameless mother, however, sinned against the second commandment in making a graven image to worship. Micah first stole 1,100 shekels from his mother, then restored them. Because of his penitence and confession of the theft, she forgave him and said, "Blessed be thou of the LORD, my son." But, taking the restored silver, aided by her son, she used it to establish an idolatrous form of worship. She spoke of wholly dedicating "the silver unto the LORD," but how could He receive that which was employed to set up a house of gods? Perhaps Micah and his mother did not altogether abandon the worship of Jehovah, but in trying to co-ordinate such worship with that of idolatrous symbols they sinned against the Lord. Like others they tried to serve Him yet bow to idols of their own creation. Was it not to God's own redeemed children that John wrote "Keep yourselves from idols"?

LEVITE'S CONCUBINE
Judges 19:1-10, 20-30

The somewhat sordid narrative takes us back to wild times when a man was a law unto himself, and when his passions expressed themselves in turbulent and fierce ways. Here we have a chapter revealing "the unutterable depth of profligacy and shamelessness into which some of the Israelites had sunk. At the same time, we see that the moral sense of the nation was still sufficiently keen to be aroused by the glare of unnatural illumination thus flung upon their consciences." The unnamed Levite, because of his sacred associations, should have manifested a more commendable life. Residing in Ephraim, he took a concubine out of Bethlehem-Judah. As he is spoken of as "her husband," this unfaithful woman was actually a wife with inferior rights. While the Levite was away for four months his wife played the whore against him. When he returned, he sought out his prof-

ligate wife, and spoke to her heart about a reconciliation.

A terrible tragedy overtook this woman as the result of the infamous conduct of the inhabitants of Gibeah who raped her "all the night until the morning." Such a repulsive episode is made more repugnant when we realize that the Levite sacrificed his defenseless wife for such a night of sin and brutality. Stumbling home as morning dawned, the wretched woman fell down and died on the threshold, and her husband dismembered her polluted body into twelve pieces, a piece for each tribe of Israel, and roused the hearts of all throughout Palestine to seek retribution upon the guilty inhabitants of Gibeah (Judges 20:1-48). The whole of Israel felt the stain and shame of that dark night (see Hosea 9:9; 10:9). A similar method of arousing a nation for action can be found in the reign of Saul when he sent around pieces of a slain ox (I Samuel 11:7). How our hearts are moved as we try to picture the outraged woman spreading out her hands upon the threshold after the night of shocking abuse as if she were stretching them out in one last agony of appeal. John Milton describes the corruption of Gibeah that fearful night —

> When night
> Darkens the streets, then wander forth the sons
> Of Belial, flown with insolence and wine.
> Witness the streets of Sodom, and that night
> In Gibeah, when the hospitable door
> Exposed a matron to avoid worse rape.

FOUR HUNDRED VIRGINS OF JABESH-GILEAD
Judges 21

Eleven tribes of Israel judged that the tribe of Benjamin had permitted the atrocity in the matter of the Levite's concubine which was inconsistent with the moral stature of Israel as a whole, and asked that those who had committed such an outrage be handed over to them for punishment. But the men of Benjamin refused this request and set out to defend themselves against the attack of the other tribes with the result that 18,000 valiant Benjamites were killed. Some 600 escaped and found refuge in the rock of Rimmon. As almost all the tribe of Benjamin had been destroyed the question was what to do to save the tribe from complete extinction. The other tribes had vowed that none of their daughters should marry Benjamites. How, then, could the tribe be preserved? It was found that 400 virgins remained after the battle at Jabesh-Gilead and these were given as wives to 400 of the scattered Benjamites, and from the daughters of Shiloh 200 more were gathered as wives for the remaining 200 men. With their wives, all the men returned home and rebuilt their cities destroyed by war.

DAUGHTERS OF ELKANAH
I Samuel 1:4; 2:21

How many sons and daughters Peninnah bore Elkanah we are not told. None of them are mentioned by name. We do know that Hannah, his other wife, had six children by him, but only one is named, Samuel. The rest are unidentified (see PENINNAH and HANNAH).

TABERNACLE WOMEN
I Samuel 2:22-25

Old and weak, Eli the priest, guilty of indulgence for his wicked sons, brought discredit upon the national sanctuary he had loved and served most faithfully through many years. The shameful, adulterous conduct of his sons, Hophni and Phinehas on the very threshold of the tabernacle resulted in a terrible death for them and their families. The women they abused were in some way connected with the service of the tabernacle, perhaps in the liturgical side of the sanctuary worship. By their immoral act, the sons of Eli not only sinned against the women in question but also "against the Lord," and against their godly father whose voice of rebuke they scorned. With hardening hearts they were suddenly destroyed. Their terrible transgression seemed to be beyond the limit of divine forgiveness.

ICHABOD'S MOTHER
I Samuel 4:19-22

Scripture does not give us the name of the wife of Phinehas, who, with his brother, died at the hand of the Lord. All we are told of her is her anguish in travail and the striking name she gave her son whom his father never saw. There is a remarkable resemblance between this unnamed wife and Rachel, both of whom died in childbirth — were comforted by friends — and in death's agony gave their sons impressive names. Perhaps Ichabod's mother's story is more touching than that of Rachel's, for in spite of her husband's immorality and godlessness, she died a martyr to her firm faith in Jehovah. Premature labor pains seized her as she heard that the ark of the Lord had been lost, yet she believed.

The fatal death of her husband, and also the death of her father-in-law, Eli, did not affect her so intensely as did the taking of the ark, and when her son was born she did not give him a family name but called him Ichabod meaning, "The glory is departed," a fact she confirmed by repeating the lament, "The glory is departed from Israel for the ark of God is taken." Ellicott says the name can be translated, "Alas! the glory." She knew that the holiness and honor of God had been profaned and that divine judgment was just. "The wife of this deeply corrupt man," wrote Von Gerlach, "shows how penetrated the whole people then was with the sense of the value of its covenant with God." We cannot think of the tragic death of this anonymous wife and mother, perhaps one of the most pathetic deathbeds in the Bible, without saying that she represents many a God-fearing woman who, in spite of a shameless and godless partner, remains true to divine realities. Disappointed and crushed though she was, because God's honor was her honor, no word against her worthless husband left her lips, nor did she utter any complaint against God for the death of her dissolute priestly husband.

I-chabod, "where is the glory," is a sad yet suggestive name, and can be written over many a church and life in which God was honored and glorified. There are religious areas, as well as professing Christians who were once most outstanding in their allegiance to God and to His Word. What spiritual influence they exerted, but their glory has departed. They may still have a name that they live, but are spiritually dead. Modernism, popularity, worldly compromise robbed them of their one-time power for God in a world of need. Profession remains, but it is the same as a kernel without a nut. Previous joy and fruit-fulness in service have gone, and life is destitute of its former zeal for God. The Ark, symbol of God's presence and favor, has been taken away by the Philistines. But the Ark was returned, and with it the fresh manifestation of the glory of the Lord — once the people returned to the Lord with all their hearts (I Samuel 7).

FEMALE WATER-DRAWERS
I Samuel 9:11-14

What a captivating account that is of Saul's early life as a choice young man deeply concerned over his father's lost asses! While searching for them Saul and his servant remembered that there was a man of God near at hand who, they thought, might be able to direct them in their search. As they came near to the city they met young maidens drawing water — a recognized female occupation of those times — and one that afforded occasion for family gossip. Accosting the maidens of Ramah, Saul asked if the prophet they sought had been seen. In common with all the people of Ramah, the maidens knew all about Samuel and his comings and goings. "Yes, this very day he came from his house unto the town. It is a festival day — you will find him presiding up here," the young females said, as they pointed to the high place where sacrifices were offered. Following the instruction of the water carriers, Saul and his servant found Samuel to whom the Lord had revealed the previous day the quest of Saul and His choice of him as Israel's first king. Little did those girls know of the momentous consequences of their information about the whereabouts of Samuel. Often the most insignificant details have their share in great events.

MUSICAL WOMEN
I Samuel 18:6 9

The joy of the singing and dancing women at the triumph of David over Goliath begat jealousy in the heart of Saul. Their song, "Saul hath slain his thousands, and David his ten thousands," irked Saul and begat in him a determination to kill his rival. Music and song were closely related to dancing (Exodus 15:20, 21; II Samuel 6:14-16),

and these happy women of Israel met to-gether to laud young David for his defeat of the dreaded Philistine champion. There is alway the outburst of song on the part of those victorious in war, but, alas! only tears for the conquered.

ABIGAIL'S FIVE DAMSELS
I Samuel 25:42

After the death of Nabal, his wife Abigail gathered her possessions together, and after the set time of mourning became the wife of David. Abigail took with her five damsels, probably her devoted female attendants. Who they were and what part they had in the court of David we are not told. Doubt-less they continued to care for Abigail and her son, Chileab (II Samuel 3:3).

WITCH OF ENDOR
I Samuel 28

Without doubt, this is one of the most mysterious and difficult chapters in the Bible to deal with. Samuel was dead and buried (I Samuel 28:3), yet he reappeared to seal Saul's doom. Here is a startling rec-ord unparalleled in the creations of the greatest masters of fiction. Lord Byron said of the narrative of the Witch of Endor —

> I have always thought this the finest and most finished witch scene that ever was written or conceived, and you will be of my opinion if you consider all the circumstances of the ac-tors of the case, together with the gravity, sim-plicity and density of the language. It beats all the ghost scenes I have ever read.

The actors of the cast are Saul the king, the witch, and Samuel the prophet — surely a most unusual trio! Saul about to join the dead; the Witch and her traffic with the dead; Samuel, brought back from the dead.

Saul — About to Join the Dead

In God's portrait gallery there is no more tragic figure than Saul, the son of Kish who, in his early days was "the glory of Israel." What physique and personality were his! Physically and morally he was head and shoulders above his fellowmen, and when anointed by Samuel as the first king of Is-rael, the people had high hopes of his pros-perous reign. But corrupted by power, sin and murder and jealousy reduced this won-derful specimen of a man to a physical and spiritual wreck. At last, facing the hosts of Philistines, Israel's ancient foes, Saul was scared and felt that his hour of retribution was near and that unless help came from God he must perish. But he cried to heaven in vain for God would not answer the doomed ruler "by Urim, by prophets, or by dreams." Driven by despair, Saul sought the ghost of the prophet who by his prudence and piety had prevented the ruin of Israel during Saul's reign.

Like a drowning man trying to clutch a straw, Saul came to countenance what he had so strongly condemned. He had issued orders that all who seek to traffic with the dead should be destroyed. "Saul had put away those that had familiar spirits, and the wizards, òut of the land." But what fearful pathos there is about Saul driven by despair, hastening to consult "the crooked crone who peeped and muttered in the caves on the height of Endor." As he looked at the huge camp of the Philistines "he was afraid, and his heart trembled greatly," and his fear was a premonition of his approaching doom. Although full of dread, there was no sign of repentance in Saul and thus when he cried to the Lord, "the Lord answered him not." By his dark sins he had severed himself from all divine influences, and as a last desperate resort disguised himself in the garb of a common soldier. He then leaves God to consult a witch for any ray of hope she may be able to bring about by producing the departed spirit of Samuel whose past counsel Saul had spurned.

The Witch — Traffic With the Dead

Jewish tradition affirms that the nameless spiritualist medium was the mother of the great Abner. Whether this is true or not, certainly this witch of Endor has a distinction all her own in that she had a king of Israel for a consulter, and a prophet of God for an apparition. This well-known female at Endor, introduced to Saul by his servants, had a "familiar spirit," that is, the supposed possession of a gift to induce or compel a departed spirit to revisit the world and submit to questioning. This aspect of the "black arts" was one of the things the Israelites copied from the original inhabitants of Canaan but the Mosaic command respecting those who practiced these arts is clear and decisive: "Thou shalt not suffer a witch to live" (Exodus 22:18; Leviticus 20:27).

The manifold shapes of witchcraft had prevailed among the people and is given under a variety of names as "enchantments," "sorceries," "familiar spirit," "wizard," "observer of times," "dreamer of dreams," diviners," "charmers," "necromancers," or "consulters of the dead." The New Testament speaks of "seducers," "seducing spirits," "unclean spirits, working miracles," all of which are associated with arts of the devil. Those having intercourse with the unseen world were put to death, and all who sought the offices of such people were defiled (Leviticus 19:31). Idle curiosity and concern in the unseen world leading to a sinful interest in trifling with matters so awful was strictly forbidden (Deuteronomy 12:30-32). The Witch of Endor knew that the practice of dark arts was a capital offense still punishable by death. Thus she told Saul — although her professed power to contact the other world did not include the ability to recognize Saul in his disguise — that a snare was being laid to expose and kill her as the law demanded. But assured by Saul's oath that nothing would happen to her, she asked him whom he wanted to have reappear from the dead.

Although this woman was a witch — the equivalent to a female medium in present day Spiritism or Spiritualism — yet the Bible does not depict her as a despicable character. Hers was not the gamut of illusions and tricks often practiced in séances. She actually indulged in forbidden communication with the unseen world of spirits. No obvious deceit was hers, and natural, feminine virtues were still prominent, for when she discovered Saul's identity and heard Samuel pronounce his doom, she tried to assist and comfort the distracted king prostrate on the ground before her after hearing of his fate. She demonstrated her sympathy for Saul by having his servants lay him on her own bed, and insisting that he eat, prepared an abundant meal for him and his servants. Yet in spite of her good points, she had sold herself to Satan. One wonders what level of spiritual achievement she might have attained had she wholly followed the Lord instead of her black art.

Samuel — Back From the Dead

How those with spiritualistic tendencies take shelter in this episode of the apparent recall of Samuel from the dead! It is advanced as Biblical proof for the clairvoyance. But modern Spiritualism, which is merely a rehash of the Israelitish abomination, is spiritually and morally wrong, and still under divine condemnation seeing the Mosaic law against it has never been abrogated — even though witches are no longer burned. The question we now face is, Did God work through a spiritualistic medium, and through a witch satisfy Saul's request? Was it actually Samuel who appeared? Having sternly forbidden any traffic with witches, did God deign to use what He had condemned?

On the genuine appearance of the departed Samuel there has always been a great diversity of opinion. Some commentators believe that his supposed appearance was a deception practiced by the witch and was most effective with Saul because of his distraught, nervous and excited condition. Others say that it was an evil spirit who impersonated Samuel, or that it was a phantasm or semblance of the prophet that appeared, even as the figure of a man we have known may appear to us in a dream or vision, and not the man himself. Satan and his ministers are able to transform themselves into the appearance of angels of light, and they may also have represented the saintly prophet. But what are the actual facts of the case?

Saul said to the witch, "Bring me up Samuel," and the issue is plainly stated, "The woman saw Samuel." "Then said Samuel," and "Saul was sore afraid, because of the words of Samuel." The woman described the God-like, majestic and mantled form she saw, and Saul perceived that it was Samuel. Thus by some "hidden dispensation of the divine will, the prophet allowed himself to be thus made use of," says St. Augustine, "even as our Lord Himself in the days of His humiliation submitted to be taken by Satan, and set by him on the pinnacle of the Temple." It has been suggested that Samuel was sent by God to the consternation of the witch herself as she was about to have recourse to her usual arts;

thus God Himself intervened to answer Saul by the prophet Samuel.

Further, the overpowering effect the apparition had upon Saul, the rebuke he received, and the prophecy of his death and of his sons the next day, all imply the reality and genuineness of Samuel's appearance. Evil spirits are not permitted to forestall God's decrees, thus no witch was able to make the prediction Samuel did. We therefore believe that as God allowed Moses and Elias to return to comfort Christ in view of His cross (Matthew 17), so He allowed Samuel to return to warn Saul of his doom. Bishop Wordsworth explains what happened in that cave at Endor in this way —

> God designed that the spirit of Samuel should be recognized by human eyes and how could this have been done but by means of such objects as are visible to human sense? Our Lord speaks of the *tongue* of the disembodied spirit of Dives in order to give us an idea of his suffering; and at the Transfiguration He presented the form of Moses in such a garb to the three disciples as might enable them to recognize him as Moses.

As Samuel appeared, Saul told his woeful tale, but was reminded that God could do nothing for him because of his blatant sins. The prophet reminded the king of his past wickedness and its effects upon the nation, and then heard the solemn announcement: "Tomorrow shalt thou and thy sons be with me," and this sentence of death was executed on Mount Gilboa. Yet it would seem as if mercy rejoiced over divine judgment for note well what Samuel said, "Tomorrow shalt thou . . . be *with me*." Where was Samuel in the unseen world? Not in the realms of eternal woe that is sure. As the Saviour said to the dying thief, "To day shalt thou be *with me in paradise*," so to the stricken, and it may be, now fully repentant Saul there came the message, "Thou and thy sons shall be with me." Tomorrow with Samuel in the abode of bliss! What a comforting thought that must have been for Saul's troubled heart! Charles Wesley asked —

> What do these solemn words portend?
> A ray of hope when life shall end.
> Thou and thy sons, though slain, shall be
> Tomorrow in repose with me.
> Not in a state of hellish pain,

If Saul with Samuel do remain.
Not in a state of damned despair,
If loving Jonathan be there.

Our God is One who delights in mercy, and the gospel hymn states it —

Whilst the lamp holds out to burn
The vilest sinner may return.

Hardened, reprobate, and self-condemned as Saul was, if on that dark night in the witch's cave he heard God's voice as Samuel spoke, and on that last day of his life flung himself upon divine mercy, then his end was not one of unrelieved gloom. We would like to believe that ere Saul went out to be slain in battle, he set the house of his heart in order. Augustine wrote that Samuel's word "Shalt thou be with me" does not refer to an equality in bliss, but to a like condition of death. Samuel himself was very much alive, although his body was in the graveyard at Ramah. If Samuel had said to Saul, "Tomorrow thou shalt be among the damned," that would have crushed him completely, and likely hardened him to his impenitence. By using the gentler expression, *with me*, Samuel mildly exhorted Saul to repentance even at the end of a somewhat tragic life.

DAUGHTERS OF THE PHILISTINES
II Samuel 1:20; Ezekiel 16:27, 57, etc.

We have frequent references in the Bible to the custom of women joining together to celebrate national deliverances and victories (Exodus 15:21; I Samuel 18:6). David did not want the daughters of the uncircumcised Philistines to rejoice over the death of Saul and Jonathan and so urges "the daughters of Israel" to weep for the slain king who had brought them so much prosperity in past campaigns. In any war, however, women of the conquerors, and also of the conquered, are those who cry more than rejoice.

MEPHIBOSHETH'S NURSE
II Samuel 4:4

Mephibosheth was the son of Jonathan. He had been lame in both feet since he was a child, five years old, and was thus physically incapacitated for the throne. Because of this, the house of Saul became practically extinct with the death of Ish-bosheth. The portrait of the unknown nurse who inadvertently was responsible for Mephibosheth's crippled condition is given with one bold stroke, "His nurse took him up, and fled; and it came to pass, as she made haste to flee, that he fell, and became lame." Tidings of war between the tribes and the murder of Ish-bosheth constrained the devoted nurse to preserve the child, but as she fled he dropped from her arms and became a cripple for life. Perhaps she made more haste than good speed, and fell with the child. She may have forever regretted the sight of him growing up and not being able to walk properly.

WOMAN OF TEKOAH
THE WOMAN WHO WAS A GOOD ACTRESS
II Samuel 14:1-20

Theron Brown, whose work, *The Nameless Women of the Bible*, was published over 60 years ago, in which he deals with only sixteen of these unidentified females, tells us why he did not report on *all* the anonymous women of the Bible. His purpose was not to write about every unnamed individual of the female sex mentioned in the Bible, as we have endeavored to do, but rather to call attention to a few among the number "who by act or influence illustrated some virtue or pointed some useful lesson." This is why Brown in his Preface dismisses the wise woman of Tekoah with the paragraph —

Whose shrewd parable reconciled a father to his son, becomes an unprofitable example to discuss when the son happens to be Absalom. The question whether he was not a safer foe, or at least a better-behaved subject, in exile than he could be in the heart of the capital did not appear to be worth debating.

We beg to differ on this point, however, and agree with Clarence Macartney in his study on *The Woman of Tekoah* that the one sentence from her eloquent speech has made her immortal — "Yet doth he devise means, that his banished be not expelled from him" (II Samuel 14:14). As a whole the speech of this female orator is one of the great speeches of the Bible, so full of beautiful metaphors and of language of pathos. It is comparable to the eloquent pleas of Judah to Joseph to let Benjamin go home to Jacob with the other brothers; and also of Abigail's speech to David to stay his hand when he was determined to slay Nabal and all his house.

Kuyper profitably compares and contrasts the character we have just considered, the Witch of Endor, with the Woman of Tekoah. "Both stepped out of the occupational spheres common to women. She of Tekoah chose that of intriguing and acting. The Witch of Endor identified herself with secret and mysterious powers. Thus both made their living and gained an influence in their community by resorting to unusual spheres of activity. The woman of Tekoah created her own art, planned her own intrigues, and relied upon her own skill at dramatization and speech. The woman of Endor employed quite different means. She was not a particularly striking personality. She was hardly an artist; she said nothing extraordinarily significant. She borrowed her resources not from herself, nor from the Lord her God, but from demons and from the mysterious forces of nature."

The Occasion of the Parable

It was Joab who saw how King David yearned to see his rebel son, Absalom, and who conceived the artifice to bring him home. Living near Tekoah, Joab probably knew all about the reputable wise woman living there. She was no witch or a female with a disreputable character, but she was *wise*. Hers was not the spiritual wisdom springing from the fear of the Lord, but a sagacity and common sense coupled with the ability to make her sponsorship of any matter clear and effective. She was worldly-wise and able and willing to play any assigned role without readiness. When Joab gave this capable woman the gist of the parable which he knew would impress David, the woman in her eloquent way dressed Joab's idea up and put it across with charm and heart-moving appeal. She took the bones of the idea Joab had given her, and clothed them with beautiful flesh. While Joab is said to "put the words in her mouth," she certainly used her oratorical skill in expanding the appeal of those words.

Joab, the capable and loyal aide of David, knew more than any man, the longing the king had to see his son. Absalom had been in exile three years for the murder of his brother Amnon, who had ravished his sister, Tamar (which see). Joab could see how grief was eating at the heart of David, unfitting him for his kingly duties. "In David's breast there was a conflict between David the king, the administrator of justice, and David the father," says Macartney. David the king, the upholder of the law, is saying: "Absalom, you are a murderer. You treacherously slew your brother. You dipped your hand in the blood of Amnon. You have broken the law of God and the law of man. Absalom, remain in exile. Never see my face again."

But David the father speaks in a far different manner saying: "Absalom come home. Without thee the feast is tasteless; without thee my heart is tuneless; without thee the palace halls are cheerless; without thee the pomp and circumstance of war is but an empty show. Thou hast slain thy brother; yet with all your faults I love thee still. Absalom, my son, my son, Absalom, come home!"

Thus for three long, dreary years "the soul of King David longed to go forth unto Absalom," and Joab sought the help of the woman of Tekoah who had a reputation for wisdom, tact and eloquence to assist him in a scheme to bring the banished son home again.

The Oratory of the Parable

The woman Joab solicited was well-able to dress up for, and act the part of, a widow, heartbroken over the threatened death of her remaining son. She attired herself in garments of sorrow and affliction, and in every detail looked the part of a mournful widow and distressed mother. Extending the outline of the speech Joab had given her, the woman of Tekoah, in a most eloquent fashion, used heart-moving metaphors to illustrate her appeal such as the one, "Shall quench my coal which is left," which was a covert and crafty allusion to Absalom as heir to David. What pathos and poetry are packed in this moving metaphor — "My coal which is left — her last lump of coal glowing with affection for her bereaved soul and glowing with the light of hope for her lonely heart.

With consummate ease and poise she

stood in the presence of the king, after making obeisance as she came before him. She masterfully executed her role, watching all the while the effect of her story as the widow with two sons who had quarreled, come to blows, with one being killed and an avenger pursuing the murderer. If her only son was taken and killed what could she as a poor, desolate, defenseless and childless widow do? So would the gracious king intervene in her favor, and protect her remaining son. David was moved and told the woman to go home assured that he would take care of the matter. But the woman wanted more definite assurance, and as an accomplished actress, prolonged the interview in order to lead the king to commit himself more completely, which he did, affirming that not one hair of her son would fall to the earth. Skillfully, the woman adapted her approaches to David's emotional responses to her carefully prepared story. Having led him on to bind himself with the solemnity of an oath, the woman with incomparable grace, tact and humility came to the heart of her plea.

"Let thine handmaid, I pray thee, speak one word unto my lord the king." Fascinated by the demeanor, charm and eloquence of this woman of Tekoah, David replied, "Say on," little expecting the direct appeal to his heart regarding the necessity of fetching his son home lest he die in banishment. In effect, her eloquent plea centered upon David's action to do for his own son, Absalom, what he had promised to do for her supposed son. The force of her argument was irresistible. One of the king's sons, Amnon, was dead, and it was useless to grieve over him; God does not respect persons. Absalom must die too, and so must David himself. Therefore, he must improve the time and the blessings yet left while there was opportunity to temper judgment with mercy.

The Outcome of the Parable

Deeply moved by the words, gestures, intonations and personality of the woman, David came to feel that she was acting her role for another, and penetrating her disguise asked if "the wily and politic and unscrupulous" Joab was behind her act. The

woman confessed it was his scheme, and sought to absolve herself of all responsibility in her presence before the king. She had not been motivated by her own feelings regarding the exiled prince, but had simply professionally complied with Joab's request. The woman's clever presentation of Joab's strategem worked, and David sent for his aide and commanded him to bring young Absalom back to Jerusalem. The banished son came home but not to full fellowship. Absalom did not see his father's face for two years. He forced the issue, however, by burning Joab's crops, and compelling him to affect a full reconciliation with his father. "The king kissed Absalom." But what followed the reconciliation makes sorrowful reading. How different is our Heavenly Father's ministry of reconciliation when His banished ones return! At Calvary, through the death of His own beloved Son, He devised means whereby His banished sons should be no longer expelled from Him, and when Jesus cried, "It is finished," a full and perfect reconciliation was procured for a sinful, exiled race. What a glorious Gospel this is to proclaim that God waits to welcome penitent sinners home to His loving heart.

TEN CONCUBINES OF DAVID
II Samuel 15:16; 16:22; 20:3

What sorrow, shame and degradation polygamy heaps upon women! When David fled from his rebellious son, Absalom, he left ten of his concubines behind to keep his house, but when Absalom came to the forsaken, royal court he followed the counsel of Ahithophel to rape these women, who were unable to resist or flee. In a tent on the top of the house, and in sight of all Israel, Absalom satisfied his lustful revenge on the ten helpless women. The prophet Nathan had foretold that the nature of David's punishment would correspond to the character of his secret crime in his adulterous act with Bathsheba, and in the planned murder of her husband Uriah. Ellicott observes that —

The fact that this punishment takes place on the very roof where David had first yielded to his guilty passion makes it particularly striking.

When David returned home after the tragic death of his rebel son, he took the ten concubines Absalom had outraged and kept them in pleasant captivity as "widows" or in "the widowhood of life," having no further sexual contact with them. What a boon Christianity brought womanhood! Through grace, woman is elevated to her God-given position as man's companion — not chattel.

WENCH OF EN-ROGEL
II Samuel 17:17-19

This is the only time in the Bible where the word "wench," a once good English term for a young female, is used. Wycliffe's rendering of Matthew 9:24 reads, "Go ye away, for the wenche is not dead but slepith." In the Midland counties of England when a peasant spoke of his wife as "my wench," he expressed endearment. The Biblical reference probably indicates a well-known maid of the high priest who, although she saved the secret messengers, her deed, good in itself, only covered a risk that seems to have been needless, and her words to the pursuing party invite the casuists to explain "justifiable lying." The wench from Bahurim was devoted to David's cause with her whole heart and soul, and when Jonathan and Ahimaaz found an empty well in a garden, to escape their pursuers they jumped into the pit, and the wench looking out of a window took in the situation. Seizing a cloth, she dashed out and covered the mouth of the well, then spread corn over the cloth to make it appear as if it was a heap of corn drying in the sun. When the pursuers arrived she directed them in a wrong direction, and David's life was saved.

It is most likely that David had never heard of, nor had seen, this inconspicuous, nameless, faithful follower, yet she was chosen by God to induce Absalom's runners to follow a blind trail, and thereby thwart his strategy against his father. Often in great movements the strength of a conqueror is not always found among his conspicuous friends and allies. The anonymous woman from En-rogel was used in a crucial moment to save the cause of David, and likewise the cause of the kingdom.

WISE WOMAN OF ABEL
II Samuel 20:16-22

The city of Abel had become proverbial for its wisdom. The Jewish *Targum* with Deuteronomy 20:10 in mind reads, "Remember now that which is written in the book of the Law to ask a city concerning peace at the first? Hast thou done so, to ask of Abel if they will make peace?" (II Samuel 20:18). It was from this reputed center of wisdom that a woman who spoke of herself as one of "the peaceable and faithful in Israel" and as "a mother in Israel" went out to tell the people out of her wisdom, and aroused them to destroy the rebel Sheba. This unknown woman manifested commanding courage to act as the voice and champion of "the weaker side before an enraged soldiery in an age when all ethics of war made little scruple of sex." Her influence with the people, and her skillful diplomacy mark her out as a lady of consequence. Joab was taken aback by her rebuke, but he assured this patriotic female that he did not want to slaughter indiscriminately. All he wanted was the man responsible for revolt among the tribes. When the woman found that the one sought was Sheba, who had entrenched himself among her people, she told them all about the crime of this traitor. The wrathful citizens then beheaded Sheba, delivered the head to Joab, and the city of Abel was saved. By her stern action this unknown heroine delivered up one guilty life and saved, thereby, thousands of innocent lives, and also secured peace in the kingdom of David. History, sacred and secular, is replete with records of women who, by their wit and courage in a time of crisis, brought deliverance and hope to their nation.

SOLOMON'S WIVES AND CONCUBINES
I Kings 11:1-8; Song of Solomon 6:8

In the law regulating the life and reign of a king, it was distinctly laid down that he must not multiply wives who would turn his heart away from God (Deuteronomy 17:17). Solomon, above all other kings in Israel, sinned against this decree with disastrous consequences. The nameless daughter of Pharaoh whom he married started him out on the downward course of idolatry (I Kings 3:1-3; 7:8). He loved many "strange women," that is, women of different nationalities, apart from Israel, and he had 700 wives, princesses, and 300 concubines. His wives turned his heart toward other gods, and because of his idolatry accruing from such a strong female influence, God said that at his death He would rend Solomon's magnificent kingdom in two. While Solomon had built a magnificent temple for God, he likewise built heathen shrines for his idolatrous wives. "No man can serve two masters," said the Master Himself. "Ye cannot serve God and the idols of the world." May we keep our heart perfect toward God, and not be guilty of seeking to worship and serve Him, yet at the same time have a forbidden shrine housing an idol!

TWO HARLOT MOTHERS
I Kings 3

The notable wisdom and intuitive sagacity of Solomon is revealed in his appeal to the maternal instinct of these two harlots who lived together, both of whom gave birth to children within three days of each other. One woman's child died during the night from accidental smothering. In the morning, discovering that her child was dead, she accused her fellow-harlot of having substituted the dead, illegitimate child for the living one. It was a shameful assertion, and one wonders why the woman whose child died was anxious for a living one. Seeing that the child was the evidence of her prostitution one would have thought that she would be relieved over her baby's death, seeing it was the fruit of a life of abandonment to sin. Seized with fear, perhaps she felt she would be held responsible for its death. The mother of the living child protested her innocence. As Israelites, withal degraded specimens, there was one way to settle the matter. Solomon, their king, was the wisest of men, and he would be able to decide which of the two was the mother of the living illegitimate child.

These female plaintiffs at court presented Solomon the royal judge with a problem. It was a difficult situation for him to solve. The only evidence he had to go on was

that of the social outcasts themselves. There had been no witnesses of the asserted swap of babies, and because of the low character of the mothers the word of one was as good as the other. Which of the two was trying to save her own skin? As they argued back and forth, Solomon had a flash of genius. He asked an officer to bring him a sword, and silence fell upon the courtroom. As the officer came in with the sword, Solomon ordered him to cut the living child in two, and give a half to one mother and a half to the other. A heart-rending cry broke the silence, and the real mother of the living child, in spite of her sinful character, manifested true maternal affection. Rather than see her child killed, she was prepared to surrender it to her callous companion. Flinging herself before the king she begged him to spare the child — "O my lord, give her the living child, and in no wise slay it." As for the other woman, her response betrayed her lying accusation, and appearing to be on the side of Solomon's judicial action she said, "Yes, divide it: neither of us shall have it!" That settled it. Commanding the officer to put up his sword, Solomon, pointing to the prostrate woman willing to give up her child said, "Give her the living child . . . she is the mother thereof." The judgment of Solomon in this case greatly enhanced his reputation, for when the people of his kingdom heard of what had happened, "they saw that the wisdom of God was in him, to do judgment."

The record is a most revolting one and emphasizes the shame and sorrow of the illicit practice of prostitution. Yet a gem in the frail rubbish heap of humanity represented by these two harlots is the noble maternal affection displayed by the true mother. Wicked though she was, she retained a remnant of genuine worth. Unlike her baser companion, she was prepared for self-sacrifice and reminds us that down in the most sinful heart, feelings lie buried that grace can restore. It would be interesting to have the next chapter in the story of those two harlots. Did they part, and did the more noble of the two reform her ways? Did she seek to bring her son, without a father's name, up in the fear of the Lord?

MOTHER OF HIRAM
I Kings 7:13-45; II Chronicles 2:13, 14;
4:11-16

Here is another instance of a renowned man whose name is known but whose parents are not mentioned by name in Scripture. This remarkably skilled craftsman who bore the same name as the king of Tyre, is also spoken of as Huram (II Chronicles 4:11-16). We do know that Hiram who was "filled with wisdom, and understanding, and cunning to work all works in brass," had a widowed mother who was of the tribe of Naphtali, and that his late father was "a man of Tyre, a worker in brass." But their names and genealogy are not given. Having a mixed parentage — Jewish mother, Tyrian father — enabled clever Hiram to enter into the spirit of Israelite worship, for which Solomon prepared the gorgeous Temple. Hiram brought to the Temple all the practical skill of a Tyrian artificer. Doubtless he received much of his skill in metal work from his unidentified father. While we have no record of any religious home life Hiram may have had, he must have heard from his mother all about David's dream to build a house for the Lord, and of Solomon's determination to fulfill his father's dream. Because of the magnificent work he produced for the Temple, it would seem as if the Spirit of God augmented Hiram's skill as He did in the labor of Bezaleel.

QUEEN OF SHEBA
THE WOMAN WHO LOVED WISDOM
I Kings 10:1-13; II Chronicles 9:1-12;
Matthew 12:42

Among all the queens of the Bible none is so fascinating as the one who came from somewhere on the Persian Gulf to Jerusalem to prove for herself the profound wisdom of Solomon. (Consult the writer's volume on *All the Kings and Queens of the Bible*.) What she heard from the king's lips and saw of his wealth and power astounded her. We know nothing of her beauty, but it is certain she was all that could be desired in this respect. As we are discovering, the names of some of the most remarkable women of the Bible have been omitted. While this queen's name is not given in the Bible, Arab writers call her Balkis, and Ethiopian writers name her Makeda. In fact, the Abyssinians not only claim her as their ancient queen, but trace the descent of their present king from a son who, these traditions say, was born to her by Solomon. But such a contention is without any Biblical foundation. After her royal visit to Solomon we read that she returned to "her own country."

What She Came For

What was the quest of this queen of the South? She did not take her long journey from vanity nor out of any feminine curiosity because she had heard of the much heralded greatness of Solomon. Hers was not a State visit to make a new treaty of some sort nor to behold the magnificence of the court of Solomon. No, she was a seeker after wisdom and so made the tedious journey from her own palace to that of Solomon's to increase her knowledge. She was inspired to make the visit because the fame of Solomon as the wisest man in the East had reached her. The Bible distinctly says that "she came to prove Solomon with hard, or perplexing questions," and her questions were both numerous and varied. This nameless queen had heard that Solomon knew all about "the name of the Lord," and it was this particular aspect of his wisdom that attracted her to Jerusalem. She had not come to see the king's material possessions and trappings of wealth, for as a queen of considerable importance she had plenty of these herself. She came to see and hear "the Wisdom of Solomon," as Christ said of her. As, centuries later, wise men came from the East to Bethlehem to worship Him who appeared as, "the Wisdom of God," so Sheba's queen came to the Holy City in search of higher knowledge. She was not only a woman of enterprise and affluence but also of a penetrating mind. Cultured, she had a thirst for wider intellectual pursuits, and therefore represented the desire in the hearts of all princely characters for a deeper understanding of the true knowledge.

Josephus the Jewish historian says of the queen that "she was inquisitive into philosophy and on that and on other accounts also was to be admired." Word had reached her that it was Solomon's God who had made him so remarkably wise, and as a worshiper of other gods she wanted to know about this Jehovah who had favored the king in an outstanding way. Thus, there was no mere sensation seeking in her visit. The renown of such unparalleled wisdom drew her to Solomon and in going to him she revealed how wise she was. Possibly she had read some of Solomon's great proverbs, and the one affirming that "the fear of the Lord is the beginning of wisdom" gripped her and prompted her to seek out the king occupying the throne of Israel. She was seeking for a deeper knowledge of his God. While she gave utterance to religious expression such as "Blessed be the Lord thy God, which delighted in thee, and set thee on the throne of Israel: because the Lord loved Israel for ever, therefore made thee king to do judgment and justice," we have no Bible evidence that she was converted from her heathen gods to worship the God of Solomon. Her acknowledgment of God does not imply the acceptance of Him. "It expresses the belief that He, as the tutelary God of Israel, is to be held in reverence, proportionate to the extraordinary glory which He has given to His nation." We can but trust that the spiritual truths Solomon enunciated found a lodgment in the queen's heart and bore much fruit in her life after she returned to her own country.

What She Heard

Accustomed to gorgeous finery, the queen of Sheba was an eager student of a more coveted adornment — truth for the mind. What the true nature of her "hard questions" was we are not told. What the narrative does say is that "Solomon told [or answered] all her questions, there was not anything hid from the king, which he told her not." What did he tell? Did he recite the facts of creation of the earth and man, the Fall, the promise of the Redeemer, the significance of the law and the sacrifices, and of how the glorious "house of the Lord" she saw was designed to honor God? Did he unfold the significance of Israel's choice and destiny and how she herself was connected with his God-honored nation? How is a descendant of Sheba, the son of Abraham by Keturah had wandered off and

settled in the country bearing her name and from which she had come?

The queen "communed with Solomon of all that was in her heart." *Her heart!* All the deepest questions within had been answered. Learned herself, she found Solomon's knowledge supreme. How she would listen as the king opened his lips and gave utterance to truths that left her speechless! How the minds of these two royal persons must "have struck sparks in each other, their mutual attraction a leaping flame between them"! The lines of Addison are appropriate as we think of this king and queen, desiring above all else, wisdom and understanding —

> Great souls by instinct to each other turn,
> Demand alliance, and in friendship burn.

By instinct the Queen of Sheba was drawn to Israel's wise king, and we can imagine how, after they had parted, any further questions the queen had received a ready answer from Solomon.

What She Saw and Said

Not only did Solomon's "wisdom excell the wisdom of the children of the east country." God also added to his wisdom, countless precious possessions. Although accustomed to grandeur herself, the magnificence which the queen gazed upon in Jerusalem was beyond her conception. What she *saw* was almost as remarkable as what she had heard — Solomon's gorgeous palace with its retinue of servants, ministers and cupbearers with their conspicuous apparel and also the most beautiful house of the Lord, in which gold was everywhere. Such external wealth and prosperity overwhelmed her until "there was no more spirit in her," implying an almost speechless condition because of all the wonders she had seen. Her highest expectation had been outstripped by the abundant rich stateliness she had witnessed. Seeing Solomon in all his glory enraptured the queen's senses, and so overcome she confessed to the king —

> Howbeit I believed not the words, until I came, and mine eyes had seen it; and, behold, the half was not told me: thy wisdom and prosperity exceedeth the fame which I heard. Happy are thy men, happy are these thy servants, which stand continually before thee, and that hear thy wisdom.

Ellicott says of these sincere sentiments, "They breathe at once the spirit of Oriental compliment, and a certain seriousness of tone, as of a mind stirred by unusual wonder and admiration."

What She Gave

After expressing her heartfelt gratitude for all she had seen and heard, she bestowed upon Solomon rare and costly gifts. The queen was accompanied by "a very great train" or numerous attendants and servants to care for all the camels bearing her gifts to Solomon — not that he needed any of them. "She gave the king an hundred and twenty talents of gold, and of spices very great store, and precious stones: there came no more such abundance of spices as these which the Queen of Sheba gave to King Solomon." The price represented by spices and stones must have been fabulous. As for the 120 talents of gold, the same was equivalent to a gift of about $3,500,000 from the opulent queen.

What She Received

The queen's gifts doubtless seemed lavish — and they were — yet they were in the nature of tribute for what her ears had heard, and her eyes seen. When Solomon loaded her with gifts he gave "of his royal bounty." We read that he gave the queen "all her desire, whatsoever she asked." Doubtless they were many wonderful creations of Solomon which she praised and coveted, and all she said she would like to have in her own royal court, the king gave her. In addition, what he willingly gave her out of his enormous bounty must have been fabulous. But the greatest treasure she took back with her was the spiritual and moral wisdom God had put into the heart of Solomon.

What Christ Said of Her

As the Queen of Sheba returns to her own country, the curtain falls, and we do not know how she acted upon the knowledge of God received from Solomon, or when she died. We hear no more of her until the Lord Jesus Christ came into the world, and when, exercising His public ministry He said to a crowd gathered around Him —

The queen of the south shall rise up in the judgment with this generation, and shall condemn it: for she came from the uttermost parts of the earth to hear the wisdom of Solomon; and, behold, a greater than Solomon is here.

The Queen of Sheba was superior to the generation Jesus wrestled with in that she journeyed some 1,200 miles to hear and see Solomon, yet a greater than Solomon was in their midst and they would not listen to His God-given truths. They failed to appreciate Christ as Wisdom incarnate. "A greater than Solomon is *here*." How blind were the religious enemies of Christ to the fact that the manifold wisdom of God, some of which Solomon had been made the recipient of, was before them personified in Him who was made unto us Wisdom! So, the illustrious Queen of Sheba "rises up in judgment," and is poised in mid-air for all to see. She does not say a word, but Jesus voices her appreciation and appropriation of the divine wisdom to which Solomon gave utterance. The Queen of Sheba will not rise in judgment to condemn any of us, if only in our hearts there reigns the One who is, in every way, greater than Solomon. She sought the wisest and most wonderful teacher she knew of. Loving wealth and wonders, she loved wisdom more, and made the long and patient journey to the throne-city of the king. Is it not the height of folly to despise all which the King of kings, who is closer to us than breathing, so freely offers us out of His royal bounty?

WIFE OF HADAD
I Kings 11:19, 20

Hadad, a prince of the royal house of Edom, escaped from Joab's massacre, and fled to Egypt where he was graciously treated by Pharaoh. The female relative whom Pharaoh gave to Hadad to wife is unidentified. She was the sister of Queen Tahpenes, the wife of the Pharaoh who governed Egypt toward the end of David's reign, and bore Hadad a son named Genubath, which means "theft."

WIFE OF JEROBOAM
I Kings 14:1-17

Because of the new idolatry Jeroboam I introduced at Bethel, it is always described as pre-eminently "the sin of Jeroboam who made Israel to sin." But away from God, the gross idolater seeks guidance from God through the medium of Ahijah the prophet. Abijah, Jeroboam's son, fell sick and he instructed his nameless wife to journey to the prophet, disguised as an ordinary woman. She feigned herself to be another woman, that is, different looking from the wife of a king. Ahijah may have been old and blind but his sixth sense told him that the sound of the feet he heard belonged to the distracted wife of Jeroboam. "Why feignest thyself to be another?" It is quite probable that God who gave Ahijah the heavy, or hard and tragic sayings to deliver to Jeroboam, also revealed to him the identity of the female visitor, who soon had her answer as to whether her sick son would live. The prophet not only told her that Abijah would die, but that the idolatrous house of Jeroboam I would be utterly destroyed, with the king himself having a contemptuous end. As soon as Jeroboam's wife returned, crossing the threshold of her home, the boy died according to the word of the prophet. It was a mercy that the child did die before being contaminated by his father's iniquitous ways, and caught up in his deserved destruction for casting God behind his back. We learn, do we not, from the tragic episode that God is never fooled by our disguises?

WIDOW OF ZAREPHATH
The Woman Who Shared Her Last Morsel

I Kings 17:8-24; Luke 4:25, 26

What deeper interest we would have in some of the conspicuous characters of the Bible if only we knew their names and their significance! The renowned widow of Zarephath, or Sarepta, so sympathetic, kind and self-sacrificial, must have had a lovely name. Yet both her own name and that of her boy are not given. The prophet Elijah who lived with them for so long must have come to know them well, but he has left us with no clue as to their identity. Even the Lord, who has our names engraven upon the palms of His hands, does not lift the curtain of anonymity, but simply refers to this commendable female, as "a woman that was a widow." Evidently, attention is focused on what she did, rather than on who she was.

Her Position

She lived in Sarepta which belonged to Zidon — a fact marking the striking providence of God. When the land of Israel was apostate and unsafe, Elijah found a welcome refuge in a heathen country, which was, moreover, the native place of his deadliest enemy, Jezebel, daughter of King Eth-Baal of the Zidonians. Although brought up among worshipers of strange gods, it would seem as if she had come to know about the faith of the Hebrews before Elijah the prophet came her way. She came to accept it more fully as the result of what she saw and heard due to Elijah's sojourn in her poor home.

Of an alien race, she was likewise a widow with a child to keep. Half-way between Tyre and Sidon, she had the humble home her husband had left her, and from a few olive trees and a small barley field she was able to eke out a frugal living for herself and her growing boy. When seasons were favorable what she was able to gather sufficed for her modest needs, but when a terrible drought killed the growing harvest then her poverty was most acute. What struggles some women have after they become widows. Straitened circumstances and oppressive cares make life difficult. With the able breadwinner taken, widows frequently have more cares than they can cope with. Yet godly widows have the promise of divine provision and protection, as this widow of Sarepta came to experience. When famine struck she did not know where the next meal could come from to keep the two of them alive.

Her Provider

Little did the distressed widow realize that deliverance was at hand — that never again would she and her son suffer the pangs of hunger — that the rough-looking stranger who appeared at her door one day was to be her provider for many a day. Elijah was a hunted man on the run, for the godless Queen Jezebel had set a price upon his head, and the sleuths of the wicked queen hunted in vain for the prophet who had pronounced the doom of Jezebel and her equally godless husband, Ahab. They never thought of looking for Elijah in the poor home of a starving widow. Yet she was the one whom God had singled out to shelter the prophet for some two years. She fed him, as a heaven-protected guest, with fearless faith. When Elijah met the widow she was gathering sticks to make a final scanty meal out of the last cakes and oil she had. What pathos was in the woman's reply to Elijah's request for a drink of water and a morsel of bread. She said —

> As the LORD thy God liveth, I have not a cake but an handful of meal in a barrel, and a little oil in a cruse: and, behold, I am gathering two sticks, that I may go in and dress it for me and my son, that we may eat it, *and die.*

Famine in the land had emaciated the widow and her boy, now they have come to their last meal. Once this was eaten there would be nothing to do but throw their haggard, fleshless bodies on the bed and await their release from suffering — the terrible death of starvation. But she was to be the widow whom God would command to sustain Elijah. His commands were to be His enablings, as she was to daily prove. Hereafter she and her son were to live from hand to mouth, but it would be from God's ever open hand to their mouths — and the prophet's as well!

Although she came to speak of Elijah as the "man of God," and saw in him the prophet as he performed the miracle of multiplication, there is no evidence that she recognized in him, as he came to her as a stranger in a crucial moment asking for water, that he was indeed God's honored servant. While God had marked her out as the widow to sustain Elijah, she had not received any advance word that the beggar coming to her would be the prophet. She did not know beforehand of God's purpose for she was preparing to die. Further, lacking any intuition that the one asking for water would miraculously preserve her and her son from death by starvation, as soon as Elijah told her to go on with the preparation of what the widow felt would be her last meal, and share her penury with the prophet, she mechanically obeyed, believing what he had said about her meal never wasting and the cruse of oil not failing until

the famine was past. "She went and did according to the saying of Elijah."

This woman of true hospitality who, in her willingness to share her only mouthful of food with a stranger whose face indicated a weariness born of fatigue and thirst, and exhaustion due to long travel, knew not that she was to entertain an angel unawares. She yet took the stranger in, and proved herself to be a noble type of Christian hospitality in that it was exercised out of the depth of her poverty. She might have protested when the beggar asked for food by saying, "Have a heart, sir! Do not mock me, a destitute widow who, with a dying son, has only one scanty meal left." Had this nameless woman met the request of Elijah with bitter scorn, asking him what he expected to find in a famine-stricken house, and also what kind of a man was he to take the last morsel of food out of her mouth, we would have understood her refusal. But no, she did none of these things. It may be that her kind heart said, "I'll share these last cakes with him, for death will soon end our hunger." Although she felt sharing the final meal would hurt both herself and her boy, she ventured out to give the hungry man who had come her way a portion of it, not realizing that her venture was to be one of faith, and would become the evidence of things not seen.

The widow of Sarepta, then, went ahead with her baking and used up her last handful of meal. She served the stranger *first* for this was what he had said, "Make me a little cake first, and bring it unto me, and after make for thee and for thy son." The astonished woman had little to say for the bold prediction and the manner of its announcement gave the man's message a commanding solemnity and convinced her that this man was no ordinary beggar. Hastening to do what her innate love of hospitality prompted her to do, she came to prove that "little is much if God is in it." Can you not imagine her after that first meal together— which she thought would be the last — was over, how anxiously she would steal away to the empty meal tub and examine her oil cruse to see if the prediction of the stranger had been fulfilled. How hope must have leaped in her heart as she fingered fresh meal and saw the empty cruse refilled. Truly the guest with whom she was willing to share, was a prophet! The widow was to experience a continuing miracle for until the rains came and famine was past —

> The barrel of meal wasted not, neither did the cruse of oil fail, according to the word of the LORD, which he spake by Elijah.

Daily, the widow of Sarepta proved that sharing what she had with another needy one did not impoverish her life, but greatly enriched it, just as the heavenly Stranger does when we open the door for Him to come in and sup with us. Yes, God multiplied her handful of meal and cruse of oil as Jesus multiplied the five loaves and the two fishes to feed the hungry crowd following Him. How expressive are the stanzas an American poet has given us —

> Is thy cruse of comfort failing?
> Rise and share it with another:
> And through all the years of famine
> It shall serve thee and thy brother.
>
> Love divine will fill the storehouse,
> And thy handful still renew;
> Scanty fare for one will often
> Make a royal feast for two.
>
> For the heart grows rich in giving;
> All its wealth is golden grain:
> Seeds, which mildew in the garner,
> Scattered, fill with gold the plain.
>
> Is thy burden hard and heavy?
> Do thy steps drag wearily?
> Help to bear thy brother's burden —
> God will bear both it and thee.

Her Perplexity

What a difference the God-sent prophet had made to the home of the widow! All trial was past and daily their need was met by Him who opens His hand and supplies what His own require. Before this the widow had come to know that her guest was a prophet and what blessed truths she must have received from his lips. As the weeks and months rolled by Elijah became part of the home, and without exposing himself unnecessarily must have helped in gathering sticks and helping in other ways when manual labor was required. Then there was the widow's young son, who, like the rest of his kind, must have been inquisitive and full of questions as to the lodger's name and experiences. The rugged personality of Elijah must have had an impact on the mind of that boy, whose coming had saved him from death by starvation.

As time rolled by the widow must have grown to feel as calmly secure as Elijah himself who knew that whomever the Lord hides is safe. But one day the peace and contentment of the home miraculously sustained were disturbed for the widow's son was suddenly seized with illness and finally died. Once again the widow knew despair. Before Elijah came to the home, she feared the death of her boy because of the famine. Now he is actually dead and her mother-heart is perplexed and torn with unspeakable anguish. Why was her child rescued from death the first time, if only to die now? In her grief her conscience seems to trouble her. She feels that the boy's death was a form of divine judgment because of sin and she said to Elijah —

> What have I to do with thee, O thou man of God? art thou come unto me to call my sin to remembrance, and to slay my son?

The presence of the prophet in her home must have impressed her with the reality of God, resulting in a deeper sense of sin within herself, and thus she connected Elijah, whom she had come to regard, with this terrible calamity. She felt that this man of God had looked into her heart and had detected that it was sinful, and that divine vengeance had fallen upon her. But Elijah knew the bereaved mother was beside herself, and had committed no evil meriting the death of her son. This anguish was to be another trial of her faith.

Her Praise

Somewhat bitter, the Sarepta widow was not permitted to reproach Elijah who did not rebuke her nor answer her question, but simply said, "Give me thy son." The dead form she was clasping was placed in the prophet's arms, who took the lifeless body up to his chamber and asked God why He had allowed such a grief to overtake the widow who had been so kind to him. Three times he stretched himself upon the child and prayed most earnestly that the child might live again. For the mother downstairs it must have been an agonizing wait, but she was to be the witness to another miracle. The Lord heard Elijah's prayer, the child's soul came into him again, and, hastening down the stairs, the prophet handed over the precious burden saying, "See, thy son liveth." The faith of the mother returned with a fervent vigor, and her sorrow turned to song as she praised God and exclaimed —

Now by this I know that thou art a man of God, and that the word of the LORD in thy mouth is truth.

In such a declaration we have the final victory of faith brought out by the crowning mercy of her child's resurrection. The widow's growing apprehension of God is seen in her concept of Him. As a heathen woman speaking of Jehovah from without, she said, "The LORD thy God" (I Kings 17: 12). Not *her* God but Elijah's — *thy* God, and as "the LORD God of Israel." Now she believes as never before that Elijah, God's servant, is indeed "a man of God" and in accepting "the word of the Lord" from his lips as "the truth" seems undoubtedly to express the widow's full surrender to Him whose miraculous power on her behalf had been manifested through His servant whom she had befriended.

Her Prominence

It must have been a sad day when God called Elijah to leave the shelter and love of the widow's home and go to show himself to Ahab and pronounce the end of the three and a half years drought. While, possibly, Elijah never lost contact with the Sarepta widow who had become such a part of his life, the Bible does not tell us anything further about her and her son whom God raised from the dead. Yet because of our Lord's reference to her, she is held in everlasting remembrance. While in the synagogue at Nazareth He selected this incident from the Old Testament and said that although there were "many widows in Israel in the days of Elijah," unto none of them was the prophet sent save unto the widow of Sarepta (Luke 4:26). As the heathen woman was visited of God, so Christ had come to gather Gentiles, as well as Jews, unto Himself. Jesus immortalized that lowly woman who was so hospitable, to emphasize the immortal truth that in this dispensation of divine grace God is no re-

specter of persons. No favored nation, nor exclusive privilege enters into His scheme of salvation. God's favor becomes the portion of those who repent of their sin and accept His Son as their Saviour and Lord.

MOTHER OF ELISHA
I Kings 19:20

Whoever this nameless mother was she must have been a holy woman to have had such a godly son who came to perform twice as many miracles as Elijah. Evidently it was a home where there was deep affection between its members for when the call came to follow Elijah, Elisha said, "Let me, I pray thee, kiss my father and my mother, and then I will follow thee." In Elijah's reply, "Go back again: for what have I done to thee," we have a reminder of a similar request made to our Lord by the young man who had declared his willingness to follow Him but wanted time to bid farewell to those at home (Luke 9:61, 62). Says Ellicott in his comment on Elijah's words —

The comparison suggests that the answer of Elijah is one of half-ironical rebuke of what seemed hesitation — "Go back, if thou wilt; what have I done to restrain thee?" In both cases we have the stern but necessary rejection of half-hearted service, even if the heart be distracted by the most natural and sacred love. But Elijah sees that Elisha means simply farewell, and he apparently waits till it is over.

WIDOW AND HER POT OF OIL
THE WOMAN WHO WAS DEEP IN DEBT

II Kings 4:1-7

Evidently this bereaved woman was the widow of one of Elisha's pupils who, left with two sons, faced the anguish of seeing her sons taken as slaves in payment of the debts facing her. She confessed to Elisha that her dead husband was a man who "feared the Lord," even though he was not able to make adequate provision for her and their children. As a prophet, his calling prevented him from making money. Here was another widow who was to prove what God was able to accomplish. Because of the interest Elisha had in all of his students, the penniless widow of one of them approached the prophet for advice and help in her predicament. Those "sons of the prophets" were not young unmarried men living in a monastic life under the supervision of their chief, but were heads of families having their own separate houses, with Elisha taking a deep interest in their welfare.

"Heaven helps those who help themselves," the axiom has it, but how could this debt-ridden woman help herself? Elijah said to her, "What hast thou in the house?" She replied, "Not anything, save a pot of oil," and like the Sarepta widow, and the lad with his loaves and fishes, the young student-prophet's widow was to prove how God is able to multiply what we surrender.

Elisha is conspicuous in Bible history as a miracle worker. For a full coverage of all the miracles he performed the reader is referred to the author's volume on *All the Miracles of the Bible*. The miracle of the pot of oil is most instructive. First of all, it reminds us of the Levitical law concerning children exchanged for debt (Leviticus 25: 39), who continued in servitude until the year of Jubilee. Under the ancient and more severe Roman law, no provision was made for the future release of an unhappy debtor (see Matthew 18:26). Then, as to the miracle itself, we note the combination of faith and action for the young widow, believing that the prophet would find a way out of her problem, obeyed his command to borrow all possible vessels from her neighbors. The one small pot the widow possessed did not hold sufficient oil to sell and pay off her husband's debts which were not due to any profligate living on his part. The vessels borrowed had to be empty ones. Often we pray for the infilling of the Divine Oil, but we are not empty enough for Him to fill. "Emptied! that Thou mayest fill me."

A further feature of the miracle is that when all the vessels had been gathered, the widow and her sons had to shut the door and follow the instructions of Elisha in private. Curiosity and disturbance from without had to be avoided because widespread publicity would be undesirable in such a miracle. Jesus imposed a similar injunction of secrecy on those whom He healed (Luke 8:51, 54). Spiritual miracles are entirely contingent upon the closed door.

Pray to thy Father in secret: and thy Father which seeth in secret shall reward thee openly.

Empty vessels are of little use if there is no closed door. With the door shut the widow took her own pot of oil and started to fill the empty pots, and as she measured out the oil it miraculously multiplied, as did the water turned to wine (John 2:1-12). When all the borrowed vessels were filled, the excited yet grateful widow said to her eldest son, "Bring me yet a vessel," but sorrowfully he replied, "There is not a vessel more." Then comes the suggestive phrase, *And the oil stayed*. God never allows His provision to run to waste.

The conclusion of the miracle is likewise suggestive. The delighted widow went and told Elisha of the wonderful amount of oil which her own meager supply had produced, and he told her to sell the abundance of oil she had and pay her creditor, and with her children *live on the rest* of the money secured for the oil. Over and above what was necessary for the debts the widow inherited, there was sufficient for the family to live on without any further shadow of debt. How like God it is to give us more than we could possibly ask or think! What a prodigality characterizes His giving! With divine benevolence there is never any niggardliness. After the miracle of the loaves and fishes, the disciples gathered up twelve full baskets of fragments. The pattern of divine bounty was set forth by Jesus in His Sermon on the Mount, "Good measure, pressed down, and shaken together, and running over" (Luke 6:28-46).

GREAT WOMAN OF SHUNEM
THE WOMAN WHO WAS BOTH GREAT AND GRACIOUS
II Kings 4:8-37; 8:1-6

Although Rabbinic tradition identifies this woman with Abishag the Shunammite (I Kings 1:3), the Bible clothes her with anonymity. Great though she was in her own city, that is, a female of high rank and riches (see I Samuel 25:2; II Samuel 19:33), conspicuous and well-known as she was, she is yet nameless in Scripture. It would have added greater interest to her record of hospitality and benevolence if Elisha had given us the name of this noble woman who had been so kind to him, and for whom he had done so much. All that we know of this lady of social distinction is narrated in the chapter before us.

Her Persuasion

It is evident that she and her husband were of the Jewish persuasion and that although theirs was a social distinction they were yet humble and devout worshipers of Jehovah. As a true daughter of Issachar, she was faithful to the motto of her tribe, "Ready for the Burden." Doubtless this childless pair who did not permit their domestic disappointment to embitter them, determined to use their lovely home in the beautiful city of Shunem on the Jezreel plain for the entertainment of God's people who passed that way. Before any traveler was invited as a guest the wife consulted with her husband as to the invitation. Dutiful, she never acted on her own initiative. Her husband and she were one, thus with her it was always, "Let us" (II Kings 4:10). Elisha came to experience the delightful harmony that prevailed in their home, and how husband and wife never faltered in their task of happiness which was their way of serving the Lord. It would seem as if the "great woman" was much younger than her God-fearing husband. "She hath no child and her husband is *old*." The Shunammite could have made her own way in the world, but as a worshiper of Jehovah she took a partner older in years and experience than herself, and thus prepared to care for the aged Elisha when he came her way.

Her Perception

From the window of their large house the Shunammite and her husband had a commanding view of the well-traveled road from Samaria or Carmel to Shunem and watched the travelers, remarking on those who appeared to be different from others. Such a passer-by was a man of grave and masterful countenance, wearing a pastoral mantle and having a long staff in his hand. Although they may not have known who he was, his whole demeanor attracted attention, and marked him out as "an holy man of God." Her perceptive ability told her that this man who often passed their way was no ordinary man, and she decided to invite him into thē house to rest whenever his mission brought him her way. Perceptiveness is indeed a useful gift and in this case resulted in true considerateness for

a weary prophet in need of gracious hospitality. More of us ought to try and cultivate this spirit of perceptive helpfulness so that as tired and needy people pass our windows, we may have the joy of building for them a little chamber on the wall.

When Elisha was a younger man he could make the journey from his home in Carmel to Jezreel in a single day and not feel at all fatigued, but as he grew older his pace slackened and his periodic visits became more tiring and wearisome. As he passed the house of Shunem's most prominent woman, she noticed how the step of this frequent passer-by lagged, and with her husband she decided to have this man of God, whose fame was in all Israel, to share the rest and refreshment of their spacious home. They felt that this man, looking like a prophet, must be a holy man going about doing good continually. So one day she went out and met Elisha as they noticed his approach and extended to him the generous hospitality of their home.

Her Provision

The decision to invite the prophet in and to make full provision of a guest room for him was taken before they accosted Elisha. On the roof of their house was a small chamber walled on each side against the weather which the Shunammite and her husband felt would secure the prophet from interruption or intrusion on his journey, and they fitted it out with the essentials in oriental furnishing — a bed, a table, a stool and a candlestick or lampstand. We can imagine what pleasure the wealthy woman had in preparing a chamber for a poor prophet. When it was all ready she likely said to her husband, "There, now, when that weary traveler passes this way again, we will ask him to turn in hither, and tell him it is for his use as often and as long as he needs it." What a sanctum of health and peace to the weary man of God that prophet's chamber proved to be!

One day as Elisha journeyed along that highway he knew so well, he received the invitation to pause and rest himself. Readily he responded to the kindness extended, and must have been grateful for the provision made for his comfort and needs. Doubtless he spent many happy hours with that godly pair. "Many a night, if not many a day," says Theron Brown, "Elisha enjoyed that pleasant chamber as his regular way-station, going and coming probably no less than four years. Did he ever look through his windows down the next twenty-eight centuries, and contemplate what multiplicities of comfort to 'prophets' yet unborn would during that time develop from his aboriginal bed, table, stool and candlestick?" Throughout the Bible there are many accounts of women in all the circumstances of domestic or public life — wives, mothers, queens, prophetesses—brought into contact with prophets and apostles, even with Jesus Himself and greatly helped them by ministering unto God's servants of their substance. Prominent among these female benefactresses is the great and good woman of Shunem.

Her Perquisite

Because of her affluent position the Shunammite needed no remuneration for the food and shelter she afforded Elisha. Noblehearted as she was, as one of God's own had she been as poor as the woman with her pot of oil, she would have still given of her best for the relief of the prophet. Deeply appreciating all she had done for him, Elisha felt that the Shunammite should have some return for her kindness. Thus one day he sent his servant, Gehazi, with a message that he wanted to reward her for her most gracious and frequent hospitality. Would she like the prophet to further her interests by securing a position for her husband at the court, or in the army, seeing he had influence both with the king and the captain of the host? Her reply was characteristic of the humility of her nobility. "I dwell among mine own people," or "in the midst of my people I am dwelling far from the court and courtly interests. My husband and I are humble commoners, quietly living in the country, and do not seek the company of exalted personages."

When Gehazi reported the refusal of the woman to accept any perquisite for service rendered, Elisha said, "What then is to be done for her?" He felt that he was deeply in her debt and must somehow repay her. Gehazi said to the prophet, "Verily, she hath no child and. her husband is old." Imme-

diately Elisha said to his servant, "Call her." We must pause here and draw attention to Elisha's manner in dealing with the Shunammite. As a servant of the Most High there was no undue familiarity or worldly courtesy. Elisha approached her through his servant Gehazi. When she did come before the prophet "she stood at the door," and heard him pronounce the end of her misfortune and reproach. Her barrenness was to end. "Thou shalt embrace a son." Overcome with emotion she said, "Nay, my lord, thou man of God, do not lie unto thine handmaid," meaning that she did not want the prophet to raise any delusive hopes (see Isaiah 58:11). Perhaps she remembered the credulity of Sarah when she received the promise of motherhood (Genesis 18:12, 13). The miracle happened, and the glad day the woman of Shunem thought could or would not come dawned, and she nestled her promised baby to her breast. What greater reward could God have given her and her husband for their kind treatment of His servant!

Her Pang

The grateful Shunammite had three or four years of happy motherhood. What a difference her son made in the home! Would you not like to know what she and her husband named him? How eagerly they watched the boy grow up and trot with his daddy to the fields. Alas, however, human hopes are often uncertain, and are sometimes crushed! One day the little boy, with uncovered head, went out by himself to the fields and stayed too long, and under the blazing sun of the hot climate was stricken with sunstroke and could only cry as he held his burning brow, "My head, my head." The father carried him back to his pang-stricken mother who had bestowed so much care upon the boy, and she nursed him until he died. Up the stairs she went carrying the little corpse. She placed it tenderly on the bed of the man of God, and shut the door. Ellicott comments —

She wished to keep the death secret, and the corpse inviolate, during her intended absence.

As experiences often sanctify places, that precious prophet's chamber in which Elisha had spent so many hours in prayer and meditation was held in reverence. What better place, therefore, was there in the home for the lifeless form of the child with whom the prophet was the means of delighting the home. As a godly woman, the brokenhearted mother knew that her child was safe in the arms of the Lord, and doubtless felt —

> I thought him lovely when he came,
> But he is saintly now;
> Around his pure angelic brow
> I see a slender ring of flame.

Her Pilgrimage

In her great grief the Shunammite thinks only of God and of the man of God through whose instrumentality the blessing of motherhood came to her. So she determined to journey to Elisha with the hope in her heart that he might be able to restore her treasure. Seeking the co-operation of her likewise distressed husband, she set out on an ass, accompanied by one of the male servants, and promised to return as soon as possible. The servant was urged to ride without restraint for such was the bereaved mother's eagerness to tell Elisha what had happened. As she sped along her heart nursed the hope that the wonder-working power of the prophet would reverse the terrible blow that had made her childless. Ultimately Carmel was reached and never had a burdened beast traveled those thirty miles from Shunem so quickly before.

Recognizing the woman in the distance and sensing some calamity had overtaken her, and seeing her visit was unusual, Elisha sent his servant, Gehazi, to inquire if all was well with her and her husband and child. To Gehazi she replied: "It is well." Then, because she had come to see Elisha and not his servant, the desperate woman fell as a humble and urgent suppliant before the feet of Elisha. Gehazi, thinking her passionate outburst was a trespass upon his master's dignity, made to thrust her aside (see Matthew 19:13; John 4:27). Elisha intervened and said, "Let her alone; for her soul is vexed [bitter] within her: and the LORD hath hid it from me, and hath not told me." The latter part of the prophet's reply reveals that supernatural knowledge of *every* event was not a characteristic of the gift of prophecy (see II Samuel 7:3). The Shunammite's question to Elisha was the spontaneous outflow of a mother's poignant sorrow: "Did I desire a son of my lord? did I not say, Do not deceive me?" In effect she meant, It would have been better to have had no son, than to have one and then lose him. From the few words she uttered Elisha discerned that something was wrong with the boy, and surmising that he had fallen into a death-like lethargy, or swoon, sent Gehazi to the home and bade him lay the prophet's staff across the child's face.

But a dead stick was of little use in the raising of a dead child, and the grief-stricken mother herself felt that what Elisha had arranged was a cheap substitute, and vowed she would not leave Carmel until the prophet accompanied her. Convinced of the fearful need that compelled the Shunammite not to return to the shadowed home without the prophet, he set out with her, and outside the gate of Shunem, Elisha met the returning Gehazi who confessed that the child was dead and that the prophet's staff was of no avail to revive him. "The reaper whose name is *death*," had visited the hospitable house of the godly parents. Hurriedly, Elisha went up to the room preserved as his chamber, and there on the bed where he had often refreshed his weary frame, was laid out the corpse of the child. Closing the door, and left alone with the dead, Elisha prayed unto the Lord beseeching Him to bring back the departed spirit of the lad.

Earnest intercession was accompanied by vigorous action for Elisha gathered the lifeless form to his bosom and pressed its face to his, as if to impart the magnetism of his own strong vitality, and warm the still, little heart into motion again. In that caress and kiss of life, all the energy of the prophet's love and faith were focused, and so "the flesh of the child waxed warm" — the life of the divine Spirit, the Giver of life, was miraculously imparted by contact with that still, cold form. "All the force and virtue of Elisha's inspired will pleaded in that contact with the tender clay for the return of its absent soul." Exhausted, the prophet left the bed and paced the floor, then returned to the child, picked him up and repeated the same embrace, still praying for another's life as he would never have prayed for his own. Then, what relief, a feeble gasp shook the child's frame, and he sneezed seven times, the repeated sneezing being a sign of restored respiration, and the boy opened his eyes and with delight saw the saintly face of the prophet.

Exhausted with the stress of trial, Elisha called his servant and told him to bring up the Shunammite who, weak from hours of sleepless exertion and solitude, dragged herself up the stairs. But all pain, strain and despair quickly vanished as she came into "the little chamber" and saw her boy alive, and heard Elisha say, "Take up thy son." Agony gave way to joy, for the funeral had been turned into a feast. With her mother's heart overflowing with worshiping gratitude she sank at her benefactor's feet in deep veneration for his miraculous ministry as a servant of Jehovah.

> The man of God came forth and led the child
> Unto his mother, and went on his way
> And he was there — her beautiful — her own —
> Living and smiling on her — with his arms
> Folded about her neck, and his warm breath
> Breathing upon her lips, and in her ear
> The music of his gentle voice once more.

The dark shadow had lifted from that loving home, and once again the laughter of the lad brought joy to his loving parents. Doubtless Elisha continued to visit the home, and enjoyed its ungrudging hospitality. He praised God for His life-giving power as the happy boy "climbed the prophet's knee the envied kiss to share."

Her Penury

Alas, our last glimpse of the Shunammite is not a pleasant one! It had been revealed to Elisha that a seven year's famine would overtake the land as divine judgment upon its idolatry. Because of his long association with the pious Shunammite, Elisha advised her to leave her cherished home and inheritance in Shunem and with her son escape the horrors of the famine by seeking exile on the south seaboard. Because of her faith in and reverence for the prophet she left home and "sojourned in the land of the Philistines." As her husband is not mentioned again he probably died just before or during the famine. Through all those years of the long and terrible drought the woman must have often thought of her old home and the desolated fields.

Her son, now a strong, fine youth must have been a consolation to her during that trying period: and when, at the end of the famine, she entered her appeal for the restoration of her abandoned possessions, the thought of what her grown son would be able to do, filled her with hope. King Joram asked Gehazi for a recital of the miracles Elisha had performed, and came to the raising of the Shunammite's son from the dead. The woman herself with her son appeared, and the king asked the woman to verify the story, which she did with a conviction that must have impressed the king for he commanded that all that was hers should be restored unto her. Although she returned to the old home husbandless, she had her son, the image of his father, to comfort and care for her in her old age. Thus her story has a happy ending and with Theron Brown we agree that —

> None of all the more glorious females on the roll of ancient Hebrew wifehood, motherhood and queenhood ever more justly earned a place for her picture in the sacred cabinet of nobility and virtue than this highminded daughter of Issachar; and none of all the nameless more richly deserve a name. Were we to invent one for her it would be *Asherel* —"Blessed of God."

Among the lessons to be gleaned from the story of the Shunammite there are two we can single out and emphasize. First of all, we have in her the personification of the hospitality the New Testament exhorts us to manifest. Spoken of as a "great woman," one phase of her greatness came out in her kindness toward God's servant, Elisha, for whom she provided the best. How lovingly hospitable she was! Hospitality is defined as "the practice of entertaining strangers gratuitously — kindness to strangers," and the woman of Shunem excelled in such an art. The original word from which hospitality is derived — *hospes* — means a guest, and also a host, one who entertains a guest. From this word names have come describing institutions, like hospital, for the sick, and hospice, an inn for the benefit of travelers. Hotel is likewise related to *hospes*. "Use hospitality one to another without grudging," was a guiding principle of the Early Church (I Peter 4:9).

The other precious lesson is to be found in the Shunammite's reply to Gehazi's question, "Is it well with the child?" Although he had just died, she said, "It is well." While she may have spoken thus to avoid any further answers, being desirous to tell her grief in Elisha's ear, and to no other, yet her answer expressed an unfaltering faith in God's overruling providence and in immortality. With her darling child dead, she was able to say, "It is well." When death robs our home of a treasure do we share the Shunammite's secret and confess, "All, all is well"?

WIFE OF NAAMAN
II Kings 5:2-4

While the captain of the host of the king of Syria who was honorable, had great influence with the king, and was a mighty man of valor is named — Naaman — his wife is unidentified. Naaman had been stricken with leprosy although the case was not so severe as to incapacitate him for his conspicuous military service. Such a condition must have caused his nameless wife much concern, and when her maid told her of the wonder-working prophet in Samaria who could cure her husband of his loathsome malady, eager to try anything that would relieve him she told him of what her maid had said. Evidently the testimony of the little Jewess sounded convincing, for when Naaman's wife repeated it, and the king of Syria came to know of it, action was taken to contact Elisha. How fortunate a wife is when she has a faithful maid as Naaman's wife had!

MAID OF NAAMAN'S WIFE
The Woman Who Shared Her Faith

II Kings 5:1-19

The whole of Naaman's fascinating story revolves around the nameless, captive little maid who belonged to Israel. Do you never wonder why this maid's name is not given, while another maid's is — Rhoda? Some twenty words cover all we know of this Jewish female slave whose record consists of only one remark, which is often sufficient to describe a character as it does in the story of this nameless heroine. Mary Hallet reminds us that "one of the most amazing things about Bible stories is their sheer restraint. With one or two deft strokes a scene is painted, a character is sketched, or an incident described. . . . There is, I say, something astonishing in the terse poetry of the Bible." How true this observation is in the three brief paragraphs in which principal characters are portrayed, the scene laid, and the play presented. From what is recorded of the captive maid we gather that —

She Was a Believer

The home from which she was forcibly taken was a godly Hebrew one in which God was honored, and His servant, Elisha, was revered. Young though the maid was, she feared the Lord and her incorrigible faith was a flame lighting the spirit of every other person in the drama. Naaman and his wife, the Syrian king, the servants who quickened Naaman's spirit, and the prophet Elisha himself, all felt the impact of a little maid who was wholly the Lord's and believed implicitly in His power. Brought to live among idolaters, she clung to her own faith in the living God and sought to share her knowledge of Him with others. Hers was a strong, contagious faith, enabling her to live without any feeling of homesickness in an alien land, and any resentment against her captors. Her love for God inspired her to love her masters and to win her way into their affection and confidence. She never hid her light under a bushel. Although only a maid, this godly girl did not feel she was too unimportant to influence others.

She Was a Slave

Think of the tears and tragedy wrapped up in the phrase, "Brought away captive out of the land of Israel." Nothing but a slave, the Hebrew girl was counted among "the spoils of war." During one of the Syrian incursions or flying raids, she was stolen and taken across the border. Perhaps the raid occurred at night and she was aroused by the groans of those who were being slaughtered, among them those of her own father. All at once she felt the grasp of a cruel raider, and was wrenched from all that was dear to her heart. That tragic night she lost all that made life precious — all her dear ones, and even liberty itself—and was taken to the slave market of Damascus where Naaman secured her as a servant for his wife. Can you not imagine how bewildered, frightened and tearful this lone and sorrowful figure must have been when Naaman secured her? Heaven has seen oceans of tears shed by slaves, and heard their groans of anguish, and God-fearing men like Shaftesbury and Lincoln have arisen to loose the captive's chains. How the dear girl dragged away by the Syrians must have turned her heart heavenward for the protecting care of the Jehovah who had promised to be as a covert from the tempest!

She Was a Maid

Among the girls taken as slaves, some were used to labor in the fields and stables of their chaptors, others had a higher rank in the social life of Naaman's day and became house servants and were given as maids-in-waiting to the mistress of a home. It was in this capacity that the Jewish girl whom Naaman had appropriated, served his wife. While such a lowly station was inferior to the position she occupied at home before it was plundered by the Syrians, she yet became attached to her master whom she admired as a "mighty man of valour," and to her mistress to whom she was most loyal and whose confidence she held. While Naaman's wife was not a follower of Jehovah, she must have respected the religious faith of her maid who doubtless expressed it on more than one occasion, and who certainly lived it in her captured home. Reading between the lines we somehow feel that the Syrian lady was kind to the lonely slave, and treated her more as a confidant. The possibilities and environment of the maid were limited but she had a strong faith and a loving heart, and although humble, was true to her God in a moment of need. Thus she is remembered throughout succeeding generations. Does not her fascinating story, brief though it is, teach us the far-reaching influence of the humblest and most insignificant in God's service? Godly maids and nurses, with an appropriate sense of their responsibility, wield a tremendous influence over their fellow-servants, and also over children and parents in a home. It was thus with the nursemaid in the home of the Earl of Shaftesbury to whom that great reformer

said he owed his soul. His parents had little interest in his well-being but his pious nurse loved him, filled his young days with joy, and led him to the Saviour. Shaftesbury owed much to that nursemaid, and he never forgot her. Those in lowly spheres of labor should ever remember that their opportunities of service for the Lord are not as restricted as they think.

She Was a Herald

As she dutifully waited upon Naaman's wife, the captive maid came to know about the great soldier's disease, and how concerned her mistress was over his condition. Perhaps one day while the maid was waiting upon her she expressed the feeling, "If only something could be done for my husband's leprosy, how relieved I would be. While it is not a severe type of the disease, I wish some means of curing him could be found." The maid might have noticed how the incurable disease was preying upon the mind and body of her kind master. This shadow over the household gave the maid her opportunity, and having learned to sing the song of the Lord in a strange land, she was ready to tell her distressed mistress that her husband could be cured. Listen to the cry that forced itself from the heart of this young Hebrew herald! —

> Would God my Lord were with the prophet that is in Samaria! for he would recover him of his leprosy.

Because of her concern, Naaman's wife was willing to welcome any sympathy and snatch at any hint of relief for her husband. The pity and yet faith in the face of her maid did not escape her, and she immediately told the leprous man of the good news her maid had so positively declared.

Naaman believed what the captive maid had said, took her word to his ruler who, impressed with the testimony of the girl, sent an embassy to the king of Israel asking that Elisha might be allowed to cure his brilliant but diseased commander. While it might have been the diplomatic thing to do on the part of King Benhadad in his letter to King Joram, and Naaman arrived in great pomp at the house of the prophet Elisha, his pride received a blow when he was met by Gehazi, Elisha's servant who conveyed to Naaman the message that if he desired to be cured of his leprosy he must bathe himself seven times in the muddy water of Jordan. At first, Naaman was enraged and humiliated, but with a temper somewhat cooled by his servants, and remembering the maid's convincing testimony as to Elisha's power as a miracle-worker, Naaman carried out the prophet's instructions and came out of the river after the seventh bathing completely healed of his leprosy. He went home to Syria not only with a body thoroughly healed but also with a cleansed soul. No longer a worshiper of idols, he became an avowed worshiper of Jehovah, and received Elisha's benediction on his confession of faith.

How the little maid must have felt rewarded for her loyalty to God for her part in the entire episode. Wordsworth wrote of her as "one in whom persuasion and belief had ripened into faith, and faith became a passionate intention." Had she not expressed her faith as her mistress expressed her anxiety over her husband's leprosy, the narrative before us would never have been written, and we should have "missed one of the finest bits of literary perfection and of religious inspiration in the Scriptures." Mackintosh Mackay wrote of the little captive maid as, "The First Girl Guide" because, "in the first place she was a guide to Naaman, a guide to him to those waters of blessing in which alone he could find healing. And in the second place, she evidently belonged in spirit to that sisterhood who believe in doing a kind action every day."

We have no doubt whatever that the maid's mistress came to share her husband's newly-found faith in God, and their home became thoroughly transformed. A star can be placed upon the Jewish girl's head as the one who had brought such relief and blessing to it. Because of her acceptance of her lowly lot, and her simple faith and sweet intercession, that despised captive, too obscure to be called by any name, will be held in everlasting remembrance. As a true daughter of Abraham she was true to God in an idolatrous family. While we have no further word about the maid after her faithful testimony, we would believe that Naaman did not forget his young benefactress, as the chief butler forgot his friend, Joseph.

The valiant soldier had a generous heart, and wanted to reward Elisha with a gift as a token of his gratitude for the gift of healing, but the prophet refused any gift. Gehazi had different thoughts, however, and the liberal way Naaman treated Gehazi revealed how generous he was. We wonder how the restored mighty man of valor treated the captive maid after his return. Did he reward her for all she had meant to him with her freedom, sending her home to surviving relatives with rich gifts to establish herself among her own? Whatever recompense Naaman gave his wife's wonderful maid we know that it was an expression of his grateful heart and noble character.

MOTHERS WHO ATE THEIR SONS
II Kings 6:26-30

When King Benhadad of Syria besieged Samaria severe famine overtook those within the city, and as Israel's king, Jehoram, went around the defenses encouraging his garrison, a woman seeing him appealed to him for justice against her neighbor. The two women, driven to despair by the terrible scarcity of food, entered into a pact to eat their sons. One day the two women ate one of the boys, but the next day the mother whose son was still alive hid him and refused to deliver him up for human consumption. When the king heard this appalling story from the woman whose son had been eaten, he dressed himself in sackcloth, a sign of his desire to appease the wrath of Jehovah who permitted the dire famine because of the nation's departure from Him. Jehoram, holding Elisha responsible for the famine, threatened to kill him, but heard from the prophet the prediction of the days of plenty. The hideous recourse of eating human flesh in time of siege is referred to elsewhere (Deuteronomy 28:55; Ezekiel 5:10).

SHESHAN'S DAUGHTER
I Chronicles 2:34, 35

Listed in the posterity of Jerahmeel is Sheshan who had daughters but no sons; and to his Egyptian servant, Jarha, he gave one of his unnamed daughters to wife and she bore him Attai.

JABEZ'S MOTHER
I Chronicles 4:9, 10

When this anonymous woman gave birth to her child she named him Jabez meaning "sorrowful," because as she said, she bore him with sorrow or with much pain. In his prayer Jabez prayed to be saved from sorrow or pain. Behind his faith in God and his desire to be blessed of Him, and also because he was more honorable than his brethren one can detect the influences of his nameless yet good mother.

SHIMEI'S DAUGHTERS
I Chronicles 4:27

None of the sixteen sons or six daughters of Shimei are mentioned by name in the genealogy of the tribe of Simeon which tribe increased greatly, but not as much as the prolific tribe of Judah.

MACHIR'S WIFE
I Chronicles 7:14, 15

It is not easy to explain the curious tribal record in parts of this chapter. The woman Machir took to wife was a sister of Maachah, but she herself is not identified. For mention of the daughters of Zelophehad in this portion see HOCLAH.

HEMAN'S DAUGHTERS
I Chronicles 25:5, 6

To Heman, the celebrated musician, God gave fourteen sons and three daughters all of whom assisted their father in the sanctuary praises. None of the children are named, and the mention of "the three daughters" in connection with the service of song bears out David's description of the worship of God in His sanctuary. Among the singers and players on instruments "were damsels playing with timbrels" (Psalm 68:25). In our day, women play a large part in leading church congregations in thanksgiving and praise (see Nehemiah 7:67).

ARTAXERXES' QUEEN
Nehemiah 2:6

It was not at a public feast that Nehemiah revealed his heart's desire to the king. Usually a queen was not present at public feasts (Esther 1:9-12). Here, Artaxerxes and his nameless queen were wining and dining in private and Nehemiah as the cupbearer was serving them. The word for "queen" used here is *Shegal* found again in Psalm 45:9. "Upon thy right hand did stand the queen in gold of Ophir." Who the legitimate queen — wife of Artaxerxes — was we are not told. Tradition identifies her as Damaspia.

SHALLUM'S DAUGHTERS
Nehemiah 3:12

Evidently Shallum, governor of the second half-district around Jerusalem, had no sons to assist him in the repair of the city's walls. But he had daughters. How many, we are not informed, and these nameless females voluntarily helped in the work of restoration. They were thus the forerunners of those good women who labored with Paul in the Gospel (Philippians 4:3).

BARZILLAI'S DAUGHTERS
Nehemiah 7:63, 64

Barzillai was so named because he married one of the daughters of the noted Barzillai the Gileadite. The daughter's name, like those of her sisters, is not given. Perhaps their names were among the registration of names that had been lost.

WOMEN OF MIXED MARRIAGES
Nehemiah 13:23-29

Jewish men in marrying women who were not of Israel sinned against the Covenant (Ezra 9:12, 14; Nehemiah 10:30). Ezra, who labored with Nehemiah in the restoration of Israel after the captivity, is most explicit regarding the unraveling of mixed marriages, or the affinity of Jewish males with women of nations apart from Israel. Because Israel was a "holy nation" — "peculiar people" — "holy seed," affiliation with foreign female idolaters was a desecration (Exodus 19:6; Ezra 9:1, 2, 12-15; Deuteronomy 7:3; Isaiah 6:13). Nehemiah found that children born of the women of Ashdod, of Ammon, and of Joab, whom the Jews married had a kind of mongrel language. Brought up by their mothers, the speech of the children betrayed them. They found it difficult to pick up the Hebrew of their fathers. Therefore as Jews must speak the

Jews' language, Nehemiah set about correcting such a corruption of the national tongue.

JOB'S WIFE
THE WOMAN WHO URGED HER HUSBAND TO COMMIT SUICIDE
Job 2:9, 10; 19:17; 31:10

Strange, is it not, that while we have the names of Job's three daughters (42:14, 15), we do not have the name of his wife who remained at his side all through his trials and tribulations? She is identified by only ten words which she uttered to her husband as she saw him suffering from so much bodily pain and discomfort. "Dost thou still retain thine integrity? Curse God, and die," or "Curse God and die by your own hand. End your suffering by taking your own life." She urged him to commit suicide and thus relieve himself of further anguish. There was also the diabolical suggestion that he should relinquish his faith in God, seeing He was permitting him to endure such terrible physical torment and material loss. It is because she allowed Satan to use her as an instrument to grieve rather than comfort her husband, that commentators have spoken ill of her character. Augustine referred to her as "The Devil's Accomplice," and Calvin wrote of her as "An Instrument of Satan" and as a "Diabolical Fury." The little she said to her husband whose heart was at breaking point was enough to crush him altogether. The one closer to him than all others should have encouraged him and offered him human sympathy. Job's wife, however, was the female foe in his household and reminds us that "the worst trial of all is when those nearest us, instead of strengthening our hand in God and confirming our faith, conspire to destroy it" (Micah 7:6; Matthew 10:36).

Job's triumphant faith is seen in his most appropriate answer to his wife: "What, emancipate myself from God, and take my own life?" Sitting on his ash-heap he replied: "Thou speakest as one of the foolish women speaketh." He was not biting, bitter or condemnatory in his rebuke but gave vent to a question that multitudes of perplexed hearts, all down the ages, have found consolation in: "What? shall we receive good at the hand of God, and shall we not receive evil?"

Job was determined not to sin with his lips as his thoughtless wife had done. What a sublime contrast there is between the testing of Job and that of Jesus! (Matthew 26:39-42; Hebrews 5:8). Because God has given woman an affectionate heart, and a large capacity for sympathy and compassion, it is incumbent upon women who profess faith in Christ, to bind their husbands closer to Christ and persist in encouraging them in times of great trial and tragedy. It is only thus that a woman functions as God meant her to, as an "helpmeet."

LEMUEL'S MOTHER
Proverbs 31:1

Unsuccessful efforts have been made to make Lemuel another designation for Solomon, but who he actually was is not revealed. The opening statement reads, "The words of king Lemuel, the prophecy that his mother taught him." As mothers, especially queen mothers, were looked upon with great veneration, and treated with marked respect in the East, this mother expected her royal son to give heed to what she said regarding the vices of women to shun, and also of female virtues to look for in one whom he would select as his partner in life (see IDEAL BIBLE WOMAN).

ZION'S DAUGHTERS
Isaiah 3:16-26

In this sad chapter, Isaiah describes the desolation of Jerusalem, with its tyranny, anarchy, oppression of the poor, and luxurious living on the part of few. In this portion the prophet turns from the princes who had caused the people to err, to their wives, sisters and concubines who had manifested themselves as degenerate daughters of godly Sarah and Rebekah (see also 32:9-12). It would be interesting to know how far Isaiah's godlike outlook influenced his denunciation of the gross extravagance of Zion's daughters. The minuteness of detail given of dress and ornaments would indicate that Isaiah's wife told him of all that could be found in the boudoir of one of the female leaders of fashion in Jerusalem. Altogether, 21 distinct articles, the majority of which had a foreign association, are mentioned. The downfall of Zion's daughters who put fashion before faith is predicted by the prophet. How Christian women delight in giving heed to what Peter has to say about outward adorning and inward adornment (I Peter 3:1-7). Males, as well as females, need to possess the ornament of a meek and quiet spirit.

VIRGINS OF HONOR
Isaiah 7:14-16

The somewhat mysterious prophecy which the Lord gave to Ahaz concerning the virgin and her conspicuous son has been interpreted in different ways. There are those writers who see in this portion a sign Isaiah gave the faithless king, of a young virgin or bride who would bear a son whose name would be a rebuke to the faithlessness of Ahaz. Immanuel, meaning, "God with us," would witness to God's living and abiding presence among His people. The land of Israel was peculiarly the land of Immanuel (Isaiah 8:8), and that in spite of the sin of its inhabitants. God was still in their midst to restore unto them the years the locusts had eaten.

The generally accepted view of the virgin and her child is that they are prophetic of the Messiah, the Son born of the virgin mother and his name was called Immanuel (Matthew 1:23). The prophet Isaiah, borne along by the Spirit, declared the truth of the coming Christ. In the virgin mother he spoke to Ahaz about, Isaiah had a vision of the far-off event of the Incarnation. The direct and present application of Isaiah's prophecy was the natural birth of a child whose mother would name him Immanuel. He would be a pledge and earnest of the abiding presence of God with His people during the prophet's generation, because prophecy has its "springing and germinant accomplishments." The prophecy of Isaiah also takes a forward leap to the appearing of Jesus, the ultimate and true Immanuel. What comfort we can continually derive from the name the virgin gave her son—Immanuel, "God with us"! God's beloved Son is very near, and has promised to be with us always even unto the end of the age.

ISAIAH'S WIFE
Isaiah 8:1-4

Apart from the fact that Isaiah, the evangelical prophet, was the son of Amoz, we know almost nothing about his background. His name meaning, "Help of God" or "God helps" was doubtless given him by parents who had experienced divine assistance in their lives. Isaiah himself certainly knew God as his unfailing Helper. We know that his wife was a prophetess and that there were two sons who were given as signs (8:18). As a prophetess, the prophet's wife, like Deborah, and Huldah (which see under respective names), possessed prophetic gifts to be used in the service of God. Isaiah and his nameless wife were one in the understanding of God's thoughts and counsels. Their united life was so different from the celibate life of Jeremiah (16:2), the miseries of Hosea's home life (1:2), and the tragic loss Ezekiel had (24:16-18). The first of their two sons was Shear-jashub, who was old enough to be taken to meet Ahaz (7:3), and whose name means, "The remnant return" and was prophetic of the literal and spiritual return of Israel. As Isaiah and his wife had the gift of prophecy they gave their son a name that was so hopefully significant.

The second son had an extended, mystic name, Maher-shalal-hash-baz, meaning, "haste, spoil, speed, prey," and implies "They—the Assyrians—hasten to the spoil—the taking of Syria and Samaria—they speed to the prey." Such a name, prophetic of the desperate flight of Syrian and Samaritan armies before their conquerors, was thought of as an enigma in Jerusalem. The prophecy was fulfilled in 732 B.C. when Tiglath-pileser III captured Damascus. How grateful the godly prophet must have been for a wife who shared his prophetic insight!

JEREMIAH'S MOTHER
Jeremiah 15:10

Jeremiah, the "prophet of tears," gives us his father's name, Hilkiah, possibly the high priest of that name (1:1; II Kings 22:4; 23:4), but leaves his mother unnamed. Anonymous, she was yet godly, for Jeremiah came out of her womb sanctified and destined to be a prophet to the nations (1:5). Called while quite a young man to the extraordinary office of a prophet, he exercised his great ministry for at least 40 years. His name, meaning, "elevated or exalted of the Lord," given him by God-honoring parents, expressed their desire to have their son set apart for the Lord from his birth to magnify and extol Him as he did. But what intense grief was Jeremiah's as he earnestly and constantly called the people of God to repentance. His reproofs and threatenings for their sins were saturated with his tears. Imprisoned because of his faithful ministry, he yet lived to see his people return from captivity.

In the remarkable mural to be seen in the Sistine Chapel, Rome, Michaelangelo depicted Jeremiah with brooding, downcast eyes, and in sorrowful meditation which fittingly describes the weeping prophet's character and life. Of all the Old Testament prophets, Jeremiah seems to have had the hardest lot of suffering. Was there "sorrow like unto his sorrow" (Lamentations 1:12; 3:1)? He seemed to protest fruitlessly against the sins of his time. In the portion where he addresses his mother in tones of pathetic tenderness, it would seem as if she were still living and that the thought of her suffering because of her son's grief only added to his burden. The sword of anguish of the nation's sins pierced her soul also (Luke 2:35). What heartbreak is behind his cry, "Woe is me my mother, that thou hast borne a man of strife and a man of contention to the whole earth!" In previous verses Jeremiah speaks of widows being increased above the sand of the seas, and doubtless his dear mother was one of them. As he addresses her, he wants her to understand "the awfulness of his calling as a vessel of God's truth," and that he had found that he had been raised up "not to send peace on earth, but a sword," like the Greater Prophet after him (Matthew 10:34). All the while Jeremiah's mother was alive she must have consoled her son's sorrowing heart, seeing he was divinely forbidden to take a wife to weep with him as he wept (16:2). For vividness of imagery, pathos and passionate intensity the Book of Jeremiah is unsurpassed.

ZEDEKIAH'S DAUGHTERS
Jeremiah 41:10

What a terrible spoiler war is! How it breaks up and destroys the home life of many caught in the holocaust of plunder and slaughter! The sons of King Zedekiah were slain before his eyes, then his own eyes were put out. Bound with fetters he was taken to Babylon, and his royal house was consumed by fire. Now Zedekiah's daughters suffer the horrors of war. Fortunately their lives were spared, but they were consigned as captives to the protection of Gedaliah. Doubtless these princesses and survivors of Zedekiah's harem were among the women who were liberated after the death of Gedaliah (41:16).

WICKED HEBREW WIVES
Jeremiah 44:7-10, 15-30

The wickedness of these females, as well as the males, condemned by the prophet, consisted of participation in idolatrous practices which the Israelites as exiles in Egypt came to adopt. Women were responsible for introducing Solomon, as well as some of his successors, to gross idolatry (I Kings 11:4; 15:13; II Chronicles 22:2). The particular form of idolatry countenanced by the wives, and acquiesced in by their husbands was the burning of incense to an imaginary goddess, the queen of heaven, which consisted of offerings of crescent-shaped cakes, and the pouring out of drink offerings. While the husbands tried to excuse themselves as they came under the solemn warning of Jeremiah, the women were convicted by his exposure of their idolatrous practices, but sought to disclaim any sole responsibility for such forbidden worship. Had not their husbands turned a blind eye and likewise paid homage to the goddess? As Israelites they were doubly guilty for they had the Law: "Thou shalt have no other gods before me."

WOMEN WHO WEPT FOR TAMMUZ
Ezekiel 8:13-15

Tammuz, nowhere else mentioned in Scripture, is identified by ancient tradition with the Babylonian god recognized as the king of the underworld, and who gave his name to the fourth month of the Jews. This

Adonis was supposed to have died and then returned to life, and at an annual feast accompanied by terrible abominations and licentiousness the women engaged in the service of idolatry near the Temple, indulged in the wickedness Jeremiah exposed and condemned as being corrupt and debasing (II Kings 23:7; Jeremiah 7:18).

EZEKIEL'S WIFE
Ezekiel 24:15-27

To our finite minds, many of God's actions are hard to understand. "Now we see through a glass darkly." Ezekiel's wife was deeply loved, "the desire of his eyes," yet with one fell stroke God removed her from the husband whom she had loved. To add to the poignancy of such a tragic separation, Ezekiel was not to weep for her, not engage in the accustomed period of mourning, but to work away as if nothing had happened. Did the wife deserve no tears? Was she a depraved, prodigal woman and worthy of departing without being desired? No, Ezekiel's wife was the best of women with a lovely face and a still lovelier soul, and a woman who was a true comforter of her prophet-husband in his hard and sorrowful task. Yet Ezekiel was forbidden a dying farewell of his beloved one.

The reason given for this terrible experience is that Ezekiel in his loss was to be a sign of what God would strip His people of because of their departure from Him. As the lines of an anonymous Scotch poetess expresses it —

> He needed me,
> To be a sign for Him; my death to stand
> A figure to my people of the things
> Which He will do to them, except they turn
> And seek His face. I am so content
> To die for this. I could not speak for God
> As thou hast done so well; but I can be
> To God and for my people, and for thee
> To aid in thy great work — a sign.

Die as a sign she did, and the morning after her death the prophet with grief buried in his heart sternly fulfilled the divine command. When chided by those who knew how he and his wife loved each other, he told them that the sorrowful experience was but a sign of the greater grief they were to endure, and that when such overwhelmed them they must "bear themselves bravely like men, not sink with despair, but by courage and repentance prepare the way for a national resurrection in the distant future." The prominent truth for our hearts in the surrender Ezekiel was called to make is that "there are times in life when love and duty should always be paramount." Our natural love and desires must be subject to a higher love.

> I could not love thee, dear, so much,
> Loved I not honour more.

BELSHAZZAR'S MOTHER
Daniel 5:10-12

None of the names of the king's wives or concubines are mentioned (Daniel 5:2), neither is the name of his mother — the queen mother — given. Herodotus, known as "The Father of History," would have us believe that this queen is not without a name. He recognizes her as Queen Nitocris who did so much to beautify fabulous Babylon. But in Daniel's record of her "she appears and disappears, like a face at the window, with not even a pseudonym to tell us who she was. She rightly belongs, therefore, in our Bible cluster of un-indexed luminaries." She is conspicuous in the narrative because of her short and single speech to her frightened son.

After Belshazzar succeeded his illustrious father, Nebuchadnezzar, he gave himself over to his vicious pleasures. During his periods of dissipation, it is more than likely that his strong and wise mother, practiced in administration, took over some of the affairs of State as Queen Regent. Thus, when during the extravagant feast when Belshazzar profaned the consecrated cups of God's Temple by using them in their debauchery of what followed, the shape of a naked hand moved along the wall. Its fingers wrote three mysterious words, and a sobering fright gripped the drunken crowd. The terror-stricken king called for his wise men, the Babylon magicians who professed to have power to interpret signs. But they were all baffled by the mystic handwriting on the wall. It was then that the stately queen entered the banquet hall, and, as mistress of the situation, said to her son, "O King, live forever," a formula to be quickly shattered.

Although an idolater, the queen had an

intuition as to Daniel's superiority to all the wise men of Babylon. She told how the divinely inspired prophet had interpreted the dreams of Belshazzar's father, and because the wisdom of the gods was in him would be able to read out the significance of the writing on the wall. The king following the command of his mother, "Let Daniel be called!" sent for him to interpret the words, which he did to the consternation of Belshazzar who heard Daniel pronounce his doom. One wonders what the thoughts of his mother were like as she heard the crushing sentence, which the great Hebrew prophet whom she had come to revere, pronounced. Theron Brown concedes her a place among the queens of the world. It was she who produced the prophet as the interpreter of the heavenly message, even though she had a fear of its tragic import. As Brown expresses it —

We picture her facing with heroic fortitude the decree of Heaven that made her city the stranger's prey, and herself the consort of a crownless captive and mother of a crownless son. She stands the grandest figure, next to Daniel, in one of the most dramatic of the world's events. The Hebrew interpreter and seer was there by her own instructions, and vouched for by her own testimony, and her noble candour would not gainsay his words. She knew at last that Divine vengeance must smite the throne of Babylon, and no descendant of hers would ever ascend it again. . . . Her plume of honour was her friendship for the great Hebrew Prophet who foretold the coming of Christ.

SOUTHERN KING'S DAUGHTER
Daniel 11:6-9, 17

Whatever futurist application there may be in Daniel's prophecy of this southern princess, her historical reality must not be lost sight of. There are those expositors who affirm that the language used here is very general and that the "daughter" refers to the Southern Kingdom itself rather than to a princess out of it. The generally accepted historical interpretation is after this order. The king's daughter from the South refers to Berenice, daughter of Ptolemy Philadelphus of Egypt. In order to end his war with Antiochus Theus, "King of the North," or Syria, Ptolemy gave Berenice to Antiochus, who thereupon divorced his former wife, Loadice, and disinherited her son, Seleneus

Callinicus. But Berenice was not able to effect the purpose of the alliance, namely, that she should be the mainstay of peace. When Ptolemy died, Antiochus took back Laodice who poisoned him and caused Berenice and her son to be put to death, and raised her son, Seleneus Nicator, to the throne. The intrigues following this abortive plan are related to the disasters overtaking Egypt.

As for the reference, "He shall give him the daughter of women, corrupting her: but she shall not stand on his side, neither be for him" (11:17), the same is the wily purpose of Antiochus who, instead of immediately invading Ptolemy's country with his "whole strength," devised the plan of giving to Ptolemy Epiphanes his daughter, Cleopatra, in marriage promising Coelo-Syria and Judea as a dowry, thereby securing his neutrality in the war with Rome. He hoped through his daughter to obtain Syria, Cilicia and Lycia, and even Egypt itself at last. But the scheme failed because Cleopatra favored her husband rather than her father. For the prophetic significance of the rulers of the South the reader is referred to the same exposition to be found in *The Climax of the Ages*, by Dr. F. A. Tatford. Through history women have often been used as pawns in international and national politics, sometimes beneficially, but often with tragic results.

As we approach the nameless women of the New Testament, the majority of whom are mentioned in the four gospels, it is a most profitable avenue of study to find out what our Lord's attitude was toward women. Luke, the beloved physician, whose gospel depicts Him as "the Man," has a good deal to say about His treatment of the women who crossed His pathway. Condescending to be born of a woman, Christ exalted the female sex, and in all generations countless numbers have risen to call the mother of the Redeemer blessed (Luke 1:48). As we think of Jesus among women we note the following ways He dealt with them.

He Elevated Woman

Jesus raised her social position, and wherever Christianity travels and is accepted woman is emancipated from inferiority, and gains equal respect with men. Think of the five widows Luke mentions, and see how Jesus gives them prominence—Hannah (2: 36), Sarepta widow (4:25), Nain widow (7:11), distressed widow (18:3), widow in the treasury (21:1-4). Woman's elevation is likewise seen in the place given her in the Christian Church. They were present in the upper chamber praying and awaiting Pentecost (Acts 1:14) "With the women." "Both of men and women" (Acts 5:14). This fact is all the more impressive seeing that at that time participation in the worship of and work for God was mainly for men. It was somewhat new for women to gather with men in a religious assembly. Women owe more than they realize to the example and teachings of Jesus who lived with His mother for thirty years.

He Knew and Fulfilled Woman's Longings

When John said that Christ knew what was in man, the generic term for man includes woman. He knew all about the woman of Samaria, as we shall presently see, and met her instinct for worship which is more strongly marked in a woman than in a man (John 4). It was the instinct for deep meditation that Jesus responded to in Mary of Bethany (Luke 10:39). Martha, her sister, was more concerned about serving Jesus, and He appreciated such service. Then, mark how He dealt with Salome's ideal for her two sons.

He Ennobled the Marital Relationship

Jesus set His seal upon monogamy, which means God's original purpose in the creation of the first pair, one man—one wife. Behind His teaching on marriage there is the thought that such a union means the devotion of a whole person to another whole person. That Christianity enhances the relationship of the woman to her husband is proven by its use as a symbol of the indissoluble union of Christ and His Church (Ephesians 5:23-33). The home where He is the Head is protected against the disintegrating influences of the outer world. The observation of the sacred relationship of marriage in the humble Nazareth home in which He lived for so long, colored Christ's teaching on marital affairs, and fostered

sympathy for motherly cares and griefs seen in His compassion for the widow of Nain burying her only son (Luke 7:13).

He Relieved the Bodily Sicknesses of Women

Both named and unnamed women came under Christ's healing power as He responded to their faith and cry. Whatever the nature of their physical infirmity or disease He quickened their mortal body, and, as in the case of Jairus' daughter, raised the dead (Luke 8:43, 47, 49; 13:11). Many of the women He healed served Him with their treasures and time, and He condescended to accept and honor what they gave. How He extolled the sacrificial mind of the poor widow who gave her all! (21: 1-4).

He Accepted the Service of Women

Luke begins his gospel with a number of songs of praise, in which women play a prominent role: Hannah, Elisabeth and Mary (1:42-55; 2:36-38). Christ sang the praises of Mary when she anointed His feet and earned the testimony, "She has done what she could." He was grateful to the women who followed Him in His itinerary missions, and cared for His material needs, and whom He rewarded by making them the witnesses and heralds of His Resurrection. Then His apostles also recognized the part women can play in the tasks of His cause. Think of Dorcas, Phoebe, Euodias, Syntyche and Priscilla, and others who labored with Paul in the Gospel. (See under these named women.) All through the ages, the practical life of Christian women has been a living demonstration of their gratitude to Christ for all He has meant — and means — to the women of the world.

We now come to the unidentified women of the New Testament in which the writers, recording the unknown females, have obscured "their tent, their name, their shapely bloom." While it may be true that "written lives that answer to no proper noun are unique in the interest that keep both the narrator and reading wishing for the missing name," it would be more fascinating to have the names and background of many of the females more or less prominent in their chronological order in the gospels.

PETER'S WIFE
Matthew 8:14-18; Mark 1:29-34; Luke 4:38-41

In the references to Peter's nameless wife attention is focused upon her equally nameless mother. Although the Roman Catholic Church, falsely claiming Peter as its first pope, would like to discredit the fact that the Apostle had a wife, the Scripture is emphatic in its assertion that he had both a wife and that his wife's mother, living with them, was healed by Jesus. From Paul we learn that Peter's wife accompanied her husband on some of his missionary journeys, caring for his many needs (I Corinthians 9:5). We do not know why the name of this noble woman who was a faithful partner of Peter during the days he fished for a living, and then during the long years of his apostleship, is hidden from us. Peter's writings in the New Testament were written after his surrender to the claims of Christ, but behind him, as behind many men attaining eminence, is a sympathetic, discreet and understanding woman.

Naturally, Peter was an impulsive man, and had a tendency to quit when things went against him. Coming home in such a mood we can imagine how his wife would reason with him, caution him to go slowly, and encourage him to rise above trials and disappointments. In sickness she would be his comfort, as she was when her mother was stricken with fever. We are not told whether there were any children in their Capernaum home. If there were we are sure that Peter's wife was the best of mothers. When the Apostle came to write his two epistles, and described in them ideal womanhood and wifehood, did he have before him the example of his wife, as one who was equal to, subject to, her husband, and worthy of all honor as the weaker vessel (I Peter 3:1-12)? Did she inspire Peter's description of a modestly dressed woman who thought more of the ornament of a meek and quiet spirit than gaudy apparel? We feel that she was a most worthy wife who was willing to be hidden in order that the cause of the Master to whom Peter and she were dedicated, might be advanced and adorned.

Tradition has it that Peter's wife was the daughter of Aristobulus, so that while Mark is described as "sister's son to Barnabas" he was also brother-in-law to Peter. There is also a touching legend concerning Christians in Rome who ceased not to urge Peter to escape when seized and cast into prison so that he might continue to be of service to the church at large. The Apostle yielded to their entreaties and somehow escaped, but when free on the open road he was arrested by a vision of Christ, and he asked Him, "Whither art Thou going?" The glorified One replied, "I am come to Rome to be crucified a second time." Peter, humiliated, turned back to prison. When death came, his wife was martyr first, and as she was led out to die, Peter comforted her with the words, "Remember the Lord." When Peter's turn came he begged his crucifiers to crucify him head downward, feeling he was unworthy to die in exactly the same way as his Lord. In heaven, Peter and his loyal wife shine together as stars for having turned many to righteousness.

PETER'S MOTHER-IN-LAW
(References above)

The gospels do not say whether Andrew, Peter's brother was married, but evidently the brothers had a house in Bethsaida or Capernaum, probably their father's legacy, and that this was the home the mother of Peter's wife shared after the death of her husband. Mothers-in-law have been made the objects of ridicule, but in that ancient home there was a happy domestic relationship in which Peter loved his mother-in-law as well as he did her daughter. It was because of this fervent filial love permeating the families of Israel that all the relatives were concerned when fever brought Peter's mother-in-law down to the door of death. Anxious about her, Peter told Jesus of her condition, and He went immediately to the house and, stretching out His hand, touched her and she was healed. The healing was by personal contact for Jesus took her by the hand — it was a rapid healing because she rose immediately — the reality of the healing was manifested in that she ministered unto all who were present as soon as she was healed. What she did as soon as she was cured suggests her love of hospitality and her habit of usefulness. Fully healed she went immediately to the kitchen and prepared a meal for her Healer and for all who had witnessed the miracle. Serving was such an essential part of her make-up that even in the thrilling, excited moment of her recovery she could not refrain from doing menial yet necessary tasks. This grateful mother-in-law loved and was loved, and found delight in caring for those who loved her — a fact the evangelists notice. "Anon they tell Him of her." How foolish we are not to seek Jesus in hours of need! All He has for sorrow and suffering that may arise is ours for the asking.

WOMAN WITH ISSUE OF BLOOD
The Woman Who Was Healed by a Touch

Matthew 9:20-22; Mark 5:25-34;
Luke 8:43-48

This sick, anonymous woman must have been emaciated after a hemorrhage lasting for twelve years, which rendered her legally unclean. She could not throw herself, therefore, at the feet of Christ and state her complaint. Her modesty, humility, uncleanness and pressure of the crowd made close contact well-nigh impossible, hence her eagerness to touch in some unnoticed way the hem of His garment. Who was this woman of faith? The primitive church, feeling she was entitled to a name, called her Veronica, who lived in Caesarea Philippi, but in the gospels she is enrolled in the list of anonymous female divines. There are several aspects of her cure worthy of note —

She Was Cured After Many Failures

What this poor woman really endured at the hands of the medical men of the time is left to the imagination. What a touch of reality is given to her story by the knowledge that she had suffered many things of many physicians and was no better but rather "grew worse." Where men failed, Christ succeeded. Down the ages men and women which no agency could reclaim have been restored by Christ. What is not possible with men is blessedly possible with God. Her disease was of long standing yet she was swiftly healed, for as soon as she touched the hem of His garment, "straightway the fountain of her blood was dried up." If a person suffers for a while from a complaint and seeks no medical advice, but in the end goes to the doctor, he invariably says, "You should have come to me sooner." But it is the glory of Christ that He can heal those who come late to Him.

She Was Cured With the Utmost Rapidity

Mark's favorite word, "straightway," which he uses 27 times in his gospel, is in most cases related to Christ's rapid cures. How swift He was in His relief for the suffering! As at creation, so in His miracles of healing, "He spake and it was done." Spiritual parallels of His instantaneous power can be seen in the conversions of Matthew, Paul and the dying thief. Many of us, too, can testify to the fact that He can transform character in a moment of time. The term Jesus used in addressing the nameless sufferer suggests that she was still young, though wasted and faded by her malady which made her look older than she was. But the nature of her disease and the age of the one afflicted made no difference to Him in healing the sick and saving the lost. As Jesus passed by the withered fingers of the woman brushed the border of Christ's sacred dress, and all at once her thin body felt the painless health of her girlhood return. A strength she had not known for 12 years renewed her being, and she knew that Christ had made her whole.

She Acknowledged Receipt of the Benefit Bestowed

As soon as the woman touched Christ's garment, He felt that "virtue had gone out of Him," and turned about and said, "Who touched me?" The disciples mildly rebuked Jesus by saying, "Thou seest the multitude thronging thee, and sayest thou, Who touched me?" Perhaps her touch had been unnoticed by the eyes of those around, and she must have been one of many who touched the Master that day as he proceeded on His errand of love, but a *touch of faith* could not be hidden from Him. Quickly the Physician saw the patient, and trembling with self-consciousness but too glad and grateful to falter, she confessed to her touch of His robe. "She told him all the truth." She experienced that open confession is good for the soul. What a glow of gratitude her countenance must have had, as she publicly stated that her burden for twelve years had rolled away!

She Was Commended for Her Faith

The crowd who listened to her confession also heard the Saviour's benediction, "Daughter, be of good comfort; thy faith hath saved thee; go in peace." As a true daughter of Abraham (Luke 13:16), her faith is crowned by the Master. Hers was not faith without a touch, or a touch without faith. Believing, she appropriated and was healed. "Daughter," was an endearing term for Jesus to use. Some tender insight of His own must have prompted Him to use it. As Theron Brown puts it so beautifully—

> The restored sufferer would never forget the friendly benignity that assailed her with one indulgent epithet or the sympathy in that endearing term by which the Messiah of Israel recognized her as His own. . . . She cherished her debt to the Man of Galilee.

She Has a Place in Legend

It is said that this woman who was healed of her plague walked with Jesus as He went to His cross, and that seeing His blood and sweat, she drew out her handkerchief and wiped His brow. Later on, as she reverently caressed the piece of linen, she found the image of the blood-stained face of Jesus imprinted on it. Face cloths for the Roman catacombs alleged to hold the impress of His features were called Veronicas. About A.D. 320, Eusebius, Bishop of Caesarea and a dependable historian records that when he visited Caesarea Philippi, he heard that the woman healed of her issue of blood out of gratitude for her cure had erected two brazen figures at the gate of her house, one representing a woman bending on her knee in supplication — the other, fashioned in the likeness of Jesus, holding out His hand to help her. The figure had a double cloak of brass. Eusebius adds this explicit statement as to these figures, "They were in existence even in our day and we saw them with our own eyes when we stayed in the city." The well-known Sankey gospel hymn recalls and applies the story of the nameless woman whom Jesus healed —

> She only touched the hem of His garment,
>   As to His side she stole,
> Amid the crowd that gathered around Him,
> And straightway she was whole.

It is encouraging to know that His saving power this very hour can give new life to all who by faith take hold of His skirt (Zechariah 8:23).

JAIRUS' DAUGHTER
THE CHILD — WOMAN JESUS RAISED FROM THE DEAD
Matthew 9:18-25; Mark 5:21-43; Luke 8:41-56

Actually, the miracle previously considered was "a miracle within a miracle," for Jesus was "on the wing," as it were, during His journey through a busy city street to the house of Jairus to heal his young daughter. Thus the healing of the woman with an issue of blood was a story folded in a story and vividly illustrates the swift and strenuous ministry of Jesus while in Galilee. The wayside incident of the sick woman and her sudden care as she touched Jesus was an interruption in His walk in response to the call of Jairus. But what a miracle He performed during that interruption. Often when extremely busy we resent any interruption, but Jesus turned interruptions to good account.

The subject of this cameo comes before us nameless in her girlhood, just as her mother who shared the deep anxiety of Jairus over their child, is also nameless. Unlike many other unidentified feminine lives and characters, the part of this girl of twelve summers is a passive, not an active one in the Bible record. The woman Jesus healed on the way to her, suffered for twelve years — the girl herself was twelve years of age. What a blow it is to a family where love reigns, when one of its members is taken in life's fair morning. The miracle Jesus performed in raising Jairus' daughter from the dead marked the beginning of the end for Jesus, who was being closely watched by the Sanhedrin whose members hated Him and sought His death. There were not many happy days left to Him in Galilee, and "when He raised up the little maid of Israel it was as if, by a sweet domestic deed of love, He sought to leave in His cherished city one young life to shed its gratitude on His path of pain, and assure one welcome if ever again He came to His own and His own received Him not. He had saved perhaps, a future Christian mother." We would like to believe that when the resurrected Jewish maid grew up that she was numbered among the saints who loved and worshiped the Redeemer, and who held communion with His risen life. For those wishing to develop a message on the petition of Jairus and the raising of his daughter from the dead, the following outline might help—

His Position

Jairus was "a ruler of the synagogue," and was presumably a man of no small worldly means with an inherited distinction, as well as a personal one. Yet with all his pedigree position and possessions he was unable to do anything for his dear daughter's relief. His coming to Christ proves how He reached out to all classes, lowly and great, just as the sun shines on a hovel as well as a palace. The religious rulers of which Jairus was one, were, as a body, adverse to the claims of Christ (Isaiah 53:3; Matthew 11:19; John 10:20). The appearance and social position of Jesus, poorly clad and poor did not mark Him out as the expected Messiah. But one of these rulers had the moral courage to manifest his faith in Christ's authority, and the homage he paid Him is a miniature anticipation of the universal adulation He will yet receive (Romans 14:11).

His Prayer

Falling at the feet of Jesus, Jairus presented his request, "My little daughter is at the point of death." Trouble, a common heritage, attracted him to the Man of Sorrows, acquainted with human grief, and in a greater Ruler he found relief.

> Trials give new life to prayer;
> Trials bring me to His feet,
> Lay me low and keep me there.

His Perception

This ruler with his most urgent mission was delayed by the interruption of the healing of the woman with the issue of blood. Every moment counted if the life of his daughter was to be saved. Yet the healing "on the wing" as Jesus was making His way to the home of Jairus was an encouragement to his faith. He believed that once the hand of Jesus was laid upon the fatally sick girl that she would live, but his faith was tried when word reached him as he was soliciting Christ's aid that his daughter had died. However, such an announcement made more room for trust in Christ's power. While the sad news added the last pang to his sorrow, his faith did not weaken. Had not he sought the aid of One who had raised the widow's son at Nain?

His Promise

The grief-stricken father had the best of promises whispered by Jesus, "Fear not, only believe." What a staff to lean upon that was in the shadow of death! How faith receives strength from the divine promises! (II Peter 1:4; 3:13). At last Jesus reached the death-stricken home and the ruler's faith was honored when his child was raised to life. The hired mourners attracted attention by their "weeping" and "laughing" (Mark 5:39, 40). With authority He rebuked the unseemly noise of those whose presence in the death chamber was an impertinence. Those professional mourners mocked Jesus when He said, "The little girl is not dead, but asleep" — sleep, referring to the body (see John 11:11-13; 12:1).

His Praise

What praise and adoration must have filled the heart of Jairus as he witnessed Christ's power as "The Resurrection and the Life." With the weeping mother and sorrowful father, along with Peter, James and John, Jesus went into the room where the young girl was lying in a dreamless world. Already she had heard the heavenly voice saying, "Come up hither!" Now she was to hear the majestic voice of One who could command both worlds.

Standing by the little bed, Jesus took one of the girl's cold hands in His and tenderly said in her own Aramaic tongue, "Rise up, little maid!" No lengthened process was necessary once His divine hand had been put forth. Quickened by His word and touch, the dead girl revived, saw the Saviour and got out of bed and walked. In his description of the miracle, Luke the physician says, "her spirit came again . . . her parents were astonished." The command of Jesus that the grateful parents should not publicize the miracle was meant to guard them against the temptation to talk unnecessarily about the wonderful event, and thereby lose the full benefit of the blessing they had received. Then when Jesus further requested that food be given to the resurrected girl, He revealed how practical He was, and how He fully recognized and honored natural laws. Yet in spite of the silence imposed on Jairus and his nameless wife whose praise for Jesus knew no bounds, the two miracles of that brief period caused His fame to spread "abroad through all the land." Thus a woman with her helpless disease of twelve years charmed away in a moment, and the extinguished life of a girl twelve years of age lit again, to burn in gratitude, both lived to glorify the Lord and Giver of life. How Jairus, his wife and restored daughter must have become bound to Jesus in loyal faith, and consoled His lonely heart when friends who misunderstood His mission "walked no more with him."

JESUS' SISTERS
Matthew 13:55, 56; Mark 6:3

While we have the names of the natural brothers of Jesus, we know nothing of the number, names, history, belief or unbelief of His sisters. When Jesus declared who His spiritual relatives were He said, "Whosoever shall do the will of my Father which is in heaven, the same is my brother, and sister, and mother." It would seem, as Ellicott suggests, that the special mention of the sister implies the thought that those who bore that name had joined their brothers in the attempt to interrupt His work. Mother, sons, and daughters were offended at Him (Mark 6:4). Among His foes were those of His own household. Can it be that those privileged sisters of Jesus came to recognize in Him the Saviour of the world, and experience that in Him they had a Friend, sticking closer than a brother?

HERODIAS' DAUGHTER
(See Salome)

SYRO-PHOENICIAN WOMAN
The Woman Who Begged as a Dog
Matthew 15:21-28; Mark 7:24-30

This remarkable female in Bible biography is called by Matthew, "a woman of Canaan," and by Mark, "a Greek." There is no contradiction here because the term

Greek was commonly used to distinguish Gentiles from Jews. She was a heathen woman of Gentile stock who came to earn a rare commendation from Jesus even though she was a descendant of the old Canaanite worshipers of Baal. Her name, and that of her husband and also of her daughter are not known. She is presented as a mother suffering unspeakable grief because of the incurable demoniac affliction of her daughter. We likewise have her portrayed as a woman of resolute determination as she sought to get relief for her child from the great Israelite Healer of whose fame she had heard.

Her Region

This unhappy woman of heathen surroundings belonged to the coasts of Tyre and Sidon whose inhabitants had been despoiled by the children of Israel, and who were given over to idolatry (Ezekiel 28:22-26). No love was lost between the Jews and the Phoenicians, but the One who went through Samaria where the Jews had no dealings with the Samaritans and left a blessing behind Him, here visits the Gentile district of Northern Galilee to reach some of "the lost sheep of the house of Israel," mixed up Gentiles in the district. As the Shepherd, He went out after the sheep (Luke 15:4), and brought His salvation to Jew and Gentile alike (Luke 10:9; 19:10). It may be that one object of Christ's unusual trip to the coasts of Tyre and Sidon was to seek rest and have closer fellowship with His apostolic band, seeing that Capernaum had ceased to be a home of peace for Him. But He could not be hid. His fame followed Him and news of this miracle-worker reached the ears of this poor Canaanite mother, whose excitement would not let her wait until Jesus arrived. Out she ran as if to be the first to meet Him with a cherished hope that He could relieve her daughter. Coming before Him she immediately told Him her sad story, and besought His mercy.

Her Request

Briefly, yet explicitly, the Canaanite woman presented her plea which contained three appealing elements —
1. Her Petition: "Have mercy upon me."

In dire need we are so dependent upon the unfailing mercy of Him who is full of compassion.

2. Her Recognition: "O Lord, Thou Son of God." Heathen though she was, this grief-stricken mother yet recognized the authority and deity of Him whose name was great in Israel and also among the Gentiles (Psalm 76:1; Malachi 1:11). In the royal title she used she implied that Jesus alone was able to cast out the devil from her daughter.

3. Her Statement: "My daughter is grievously vexed with a devil." Mark says she had an "unclean spirit." This mother never wasted words as she stated the terrible trial shadowing her home. Eloquent language is not necessary when we present our needs to Him who knows all about them before we state them.

Her Repulse

The pitying Saviour, who refused no call for mercy, was silent to the pleader's pointed prayer. "He answered her not a word." Weary with the pressure of His long and arduous ministry in Galilee, He retired into a friendly, hospitable house nearby, and left the seeking mother outside. Why did our Lord appear to turn a deaf ear to the pitiful cry for the relief of her afflicted daughter? Usually He responded immediately for the exercise of His power, but at this time He was silent, and His disciples as bigoted Jews who were deeply nationalistic and despised all Gentiles, shared the Master's silence. Why should their Lord bestow a favor upon a Gentile?

Artists never depict Christ with His back turned. He stood with His face to blind Bartimaeus, to the foaming demoniac, to the limping paralytic, to the turbulent sea which He hushed, to the dead whom He raised, but here He turned His back on the suffering woman, throwing positive discouragement upon her petition: "Lord, spare the life of my demon-possessed daughter; it will not cost You anything." Because of all we know of Christ's love and compassion, we cannot believe that He meant to ignore altogether her cry for help. Often the problem of unanswered prayer is acute, but He who ever hears the pleas of those who seek Him always answers prayer in His own best way. Perhaps with this Gentile mother, His repulse was meant to try her faith, which proved to be a faith accepting no rebuff.

Her Resoluteness

Driven by a pressing need, this woman of Canaan was determined not to take, No! as an answer. She knew Christ was able to cure her daughter and was determined that the assistance she sought would be granted. So she pestered the disciples for another audience with Christ whose expression of His mission might have discouraged her Gentile heart, "I am not sent but to the lost sheep of the house of Israel." He rallied to the woman's earnestness, however, and to make His mercy more conspicuous, met her persistence by saying, "It is not meet to take the children's bread [that is, salvation appointed for the Jews] and cast it to dogs" (or the Gentiles which was the ordinary parlance of the Jews in regard to Gentiles). The gentle, gentlemanly, and loving Jesus never meant to characterize the woman as a dog.

Even this further rebuff did not deter her from falling at the feet of the great Galilean Teacher and sobbing, "Lord, help me!" Although a wild Gentile she begged grace of the Shepherd of Judah. In the passion of her sorrow and resolve she would not let Him go until He blessed her. Even when He further denied her in the words, "Let the children first be fed. It is not fitting to take the children's bread, and cast it to dogs." Such a sentence might have crushed her, but inspired humility enabled her to quickly reply with all meekness, "Truth, Lord, yet dogs [tame, house, pet dogs] eat of the crumbs that fall from the master's table."

Behind Christ's seeming frowning countenance there was the smile of love. Although He had addressed the helpless woman in a somewhat austere, traditional way, His coolness made the final favor sweeter. The stranger had not asked for a whole loaf of bread or even for a large slice — only for the crumbs falling to the floor. The Master felt the wit and the earnestness and the stratagem and the faith of this determined woman who dared to persist in her desperate petition, and the expression of His heart revealed Him in His true mission — the Saviour of mankind.

Her Reward

"The aptness and the subdued beauty of her patient reply had charmed Jesus," and she heard Him say, "O woman, great is thy faith; be it unto thee even as thou wilt." It was as if He had meant, "You have conquered Me. Your daughter is well now. Go home, mother; but before you get there she will come down, skipping to meet you. The devil has left her." Her conquering faith exhibited the three ascending degrees of all true faith. The trial of her faith consisted of silence (15:23), refusal (15:24), and reproach 15:26), all of which were intended by Christ for a beneficent, loving purpose. The trial resulted in triumph, for the woman had turned a seeming rebuff into an argument in her favor, and her faith resulted in definite and practical results. Blind Bartimaeus broke through hindrances cast up by his fellow men, but this woman broke through apparent hindrance even from Christ Himself.

Reaching home the poor Canaanite mother found her darling girl in her right mind, calm and smiling, and how her relieved heart must have praised the Man of Galilee. Her faith had prevailed, and Christ's disciples began to learn that divine pity was larger than racial boundaries and that their Master's salvation was a fountain for all. A peculiar feature of Christ's miracle on behalf of the Canaanite woman is that it was accomplished by remote control. He did not go to the home of need as in the case of Jairus, but stayed where He was, and the moment He uttered the word of healing, the demon-possessed girl was made whole. It was one of His "absent cures." Distance makes no difference to Omnipotence. "He spake and it was done."

WIFE SOLD FOR DEBT
Matthew 18:25; Luke 17:3, 4

In His law of forgiveness which Christ propounded to Peter, Jesus drew attention to the lord who commanded one of his servants deep in his debt to sell wife, children, and all that he had to meet the debt. Many a righteous woman was sold for silver, and a poor one for a pair of shoes

(Amos 2:6; 8:6; Nehemiah 5:4, 5). The law was strained to allow an insolvent debtor to sell himself and his family into bondage to redeem a debt (Leviticus 25:39; II Kings 4:1). In this far-off enlightened age, there are still parts of the world where women and children are bartered with.

MAIDS AT PETER'S DENIAL
Matthew 26:69-71; Mark 14:66-69; Luke 22:56-59; John 18:16, 17

In the High Priest's palace the damsels employed there asked questions of Peter, causing him to deny the Master he had vowed to be true to until the end. His first denial came in the courtyard of the palace as he answered the question of the female slave who kept the door (John 18:17). The second denial came as the result of another statement by a second maid who possibly tended the fire (Matthew 26:69). About an hour later, after Peter left the fire at which he warmed himself, he answered the maid who had spoken to him before (Mark 14:69; Matthew 26:71). These nameless maid servants in the employ of Caiaphas did not imitate each other in their conversation with Peter. Both of them knew that Jesus who was being tried was no ordinary prisoner, and that He faced the death penalty. With womanly intuition, the maids also detected Peter's reticence and that he tried to hide himself. Teasing him about concealing who he was, they uttered words that tore at his heart like the thrust of a dagger. Heartless girls, they entertained themselves at the cost of Peter's embarrassment, and caused him to curse his Lord. How smugly they would laugh as they saw Peter weeping bitterly in deep remorse over the way he had failed his Master in such a grim hour. From those gossipy maids we learn that superficial prattle can prove disastrous — that unnecessary talk can inflict grievous wounds. How we need to be saved from the sin of unguarded lips!

PILATE'S WIFE
Matthew 27:19

While the Bible does not tell us who the wife of Pilate the governor was, the Apocryphal book, *The Gospel of Nicodemus,* identifies her as Claudia Procula, and a granddaughter of the Emperor Augustus. The book also says that she was a proselyte to Judaism, being among the women of higher classes over whom the Jewish religion exercised considerable influence. Her appearance is brief and all we know about her and what caused her to be included among the nameless in God's portrait gallery, is told in thirty-eight words. As Jesus was being tried by Pilate in the Praetorium, a messenger hurried to him with a brief but urgent note from his wife. In the moment of crisis she had had a dream and begged her husband not to condemn the Prisoner before him.

> When he was set down on the judgment seat, his wife sent unto him, saying, Have thou nothing to do with that just man: for I have suffered many things this day in a dream because of him.

Because of her interest in the Jew's religion she must have discussed Jesus with Pilate, and the urgency of her petition revealed a sharp appreciation of the tragedy facing Him. Calling Jesus the "just man" testifies to the impression He had made on her mind in contrast to the religious leaders seeking to destroy Jesus because of His claims. We can appreciate why the Greeks and Abyssinians made a saint of her, and legend says that she became a Christian, and may have been the Claudia mentioned by Paul (see CLAUDIA).

Various interpretations of the dream, convincing this wife that Jesus was an innocent Man, and that if her husband condemned Him he would certainly invite disaster, have been given. The safest understanding of her dream is that it was the reflection of her day thoughts as a sensitive and devout woman of One who was holy, just and innocent. God directed that dream in order to add a striking testimony to the sinlessness of the One being tried for the truth He declared. Pilate's wife sensed her solemn responsibility and made her plea, even though her husband who was also convinced of Christ's innocence, ultimately delivered Him to be crucified.

WOMEN AT CALVARY
Matthew 27:55

Distinct from "the daughters of Jerusalem" (Luke 23:28), this group of women is identical with the certain women who followed Jesus, and ministered unto Him (Luke 8:2, 3). Who all the "many women" beholding the final agonies of the cross were we have no means of knowing. Two or three of them are mentioned, namely, the Marys, but for the rest they are the nameless lovers of the Lord who remained near Him until the bitter end. Of this we can be certain, that their names are inscribed on the illustrious Lamb's Book of Life.

WIDOW WITH TWO MITES
THE WOMAN WHO GAVE HER ALL
Mark 12:41-44; Luke 21:1-4

Of all the nameless women in female biography, this most sacrificial widow is one whose name and background we would dearly love to know about. As we read the gospels her devotion always touches our hearts, and we are grateful that Jesus noticed her sacrifice and has preserved her story in the safekeeping of His praise and Word.

The Occasion

During Paschal Week women from all over poured into their court in the Temple with their offerings for its manifold services. Along the walls of the court there were receptacles into which the people dropped their gifts. Many who were rich cast in much and probably took no pains to conceal what they gave. The Scribes who devoured widows' houses, getting all they could, doubtless paraded their giving, but here was a widow intent on a far nobler purpose, namely, to give all she could. The Scribes were rich, but selfish — the widow, poor, but sacrificial (Mark 10:24; James 2:5). Among the crowds this poor anonymous widow was unnoticed by those around her as she dropped into one of the chests her two tiny copper coins. Making her offering, she passed along unaware that any one but herself knew the measure of her gift and what it cost. When we speak about "the widow's mite" we have in mind a small offering, but to this nameless widow her mite represented *all* she had. If the rich had given proportionately that Holy Week, what a tremendous offering the Temple would have had. Among all the money gathered that day none had the stain of blood on it apart from those two mites. With true Israelite devotion she gave all she had earned, and then went on her way to earn a little more to care for her frugal needs, and for those of any children she might have had.

The Omniscience

As an Israelite the widow would have a knowledge of Hagar of old and of how she called Jehovah by the distinguished and comforting name, "Thou God seest me" (Genesis 16:13). She surrendered her all that day feeling that God's eyes alone would know of her offering. Little did she know that the One sitting near the treasury was God manifest in flesh, and that because of His omniscience He knew all about her and also the amount of her sacrificial gift. Whether Jesus may have learned of this godly widow on one of His previous visits to Jerusalem, we do not know. The narrative seems to suggest His divine insight into the lives and characters of people as in the cases of Nathanael (John 1:47, 48) and of the woman of Samaria (John 4:18).

Because of her penury, the widow would come and go unobserved in the presence of the crowd for she had none of the ostentation of the Pharisees in dress and disposal of gifts. But an All-Seeing eye saw her and knew all about her secret and took an exact inventory of the comparatively small gift she had dropped into the treasury box. The Bible does not tell us whether Jesus spoke to her and thanked her for her offering. It is probable that she was not conscious of what omniscient eyes had seen, and how her minute offering among so many gifts that day had gladdened the sorrowful soul of Him who was on His way to give His all at Calvary and also provided Him with a text for an everlasting lesson on what sacrificial giving really is.

Her Offering

What a rebuke Jesus delivered to the rich Scribes and Pharisees who cast large gifts into the treasury-boxes! But what they gave was insignificant, proportionally, alongside what the widow gave, and her slender gift brought forth from the greatest Giver of all a message that lifted the poor to their rightful fraternity of service with the godly rich in the kingdom of God: "Of a truth . . . this poor widow hath cast in more than they all: [With this sentence Jesus must have waved His hand in the direction of those who loved the praise of men and not of God.] For all these have of their abundance cast in unto the offerings of God: but she of her penury hath cast in all the living that she had."

Over against the show of easy service, Jesus placed the piety of self-denial. The widow's two mites represented her two hands that had earned the mites, and which would earn more for another sacred fraction for the God she worshiped. Paul commended the churches of Macedonia because their deep poverty had abounded unto the riches of their liberality (II Corinthians 8: 1, 2). As it is "by him actions are weighed" (I Samuel 2:3), in His balances the loving act of the poor widow outweighed the munificence of the rich Pharisees. It is not *what* we give but *how* we give that counts with Him who gave Himself for a lost world. The widow gave all she had at the time, and surrendered it gladly. May we ever remember that our giving must be inspired by what we owe Him who redeemed us at such cost, and also placed over against what is left after we give! How apropos are the words of Solomon as we think of the poor, unnoticed widow whom Jesus rewarded with everlasting remembrance: "The eyes of the LORD are in every place, beholding the evil and the good" (Proverbs 15:3).

WIDOW OF NAIN

THE WOMAN WHOSE DEAD SON CAME BACK FROM THE GRAVE

Luke 7:11-18

Among the many widows who were in Israel (Luke 4:25), quite a few of them crossed the pathway of Jesus in the days of His flesh. He seemed to have a special, tender care for these women whom death had impoverished, and who often became the particular prey of the unscrupulous, and victims of the fraudulent. Already in this volume we have written of the significance of Bible widows, who were not to be afflicted, and whose cry heaven always heard

(Exodus 22:22; Jeremiah 7:6; Matthew 23:14). The accounts of widows deserving of honor and care are both instructive and interesting for our guidance in church life today (I Timothy 5:3; James 1:27). Before us is another widow whom Jesus helped in her affliction. Like other widows, this grief-stricken one of Nain received a special dispensation from heavenly hands, and is an example of "millions of bereaved mothers whose sorrows have been sweetened by some revelation of divine love and pity."

The Mourner

Luke alone records the breaking up of the funeral procession Jesus met on the way to the cemetery. The city of Nain was approached by a steep ascent, with burial caves on each side of the road. The day after Jesus had healed the centurion's servant, He set out with His disciples on a missionary tour around the Lake of Galilee, and as He journeyed, the size of His followers increased. As they reached the rock-hewn tombs, they met a humble train made up of one weeping mourner and a few sympathizing neighbors. They learned quickly of the widow's loss of her only son and child, and of the two facts enhancing the bitterness of her sorrow. She was a widow, bereft of her beloved partner for many years, and now was motherless seeing that the one prop of her life, her hope and stay in widowhood, had been taken from her. The young man doubtless worked and kept the home together. Now he is dead and the widow's future must have seemed so bleak.

The Master

A peculiar feature of our Lord's miracle on the widow's behalf was the fact that this was the first manifestation of His power to raise the dead. The resurrection of Jairus' daughter and of Lazarus followed. Prophets of old, like Elijah and Elisha, had raised the dead, and when Jesus raised the dead youth, the people knew that He was a prophet of the same order. We further notice that the heartbroken widow did not seek Jesus, but that He came to where she was. The moment He saw her drooping figure alongside the hand-borne bier with its lifeless form, He had compassion on her. The miracle that followed was not only an unmistakable credential of His diety and mission, but also the spontaneous outflow of His infinite sympathy with human suffering.

Note His fourfold action —

"He said unto her, Weep not." What authority and consolation were wrapped up in that tender exhortation! As God incarnate, He was able to dry the widow's tears.

"He touched the bier." On the open stretcher lay the corpse wrapped in a winding sheet with a handkerchief over the face, and as Jesus touched the bier, its bearers stood still. All around knew that He was a Teacher and that most rabbis would not touch the dead for fear of pollution. But here was One who came into contact with the dead, and that cortége, stopped in its progress, came to experience that His touch had still its ancient power.

"He said, Young man, I say unto thee, Arise! And he that was dead sat up, and began to speak." How awe-stricken the onlookers must have been as in a moment of time, at the mighty command of Jesus reaching the abode of the dead, the spirit of the widow's only child returned! As the mother had no idea of what would happen as she left her humble home for the grave, what a shock of joy must have been hers when her son sat up, and tearing away the cerement of death around his face, "began to speak." How fascinating it would have been if Luke had set on record what the youth's first words were when brought back from the dead by Jesus!

"He delivered him to his mother." What a lovely touch this is! It literally means, "He gave him to his mother." At birth he came as God's gift to the home; now that he is risen from the dead, he was God-given in a higher sense. As the Lord of life came to die He manifested the same care of His own widowed mother, Mary. Thinking of her uncertain future, Jesus said to John, the disciple whom He loved, "Behold thy mother," and from that hour the Apostle took her home and protected and provided for her through the rest of her days.

The Multitude

The fame of this miracle quickly spread. The people of the city of Nain who accompanied the widow, and those who had followed Christ were overwhelmed at His first resurrection miracle, and great fear came upon them all. They glorified God, for in the One who had brought life and immortality to light God had visited His people. The grateful company saw in Jesus the Great Prophet raised up by God and was indeed —

> Creator from the wreck of things;
> Death is but hope with folded wings.
> When light from His strong spirit streams
> And stirs cold dust to breathing dreams.

What was the reaction of that widowed mother as she returned home with her restored son? We can imagine how both of them expressed their thanks to Jesus, and set about knowing more of Him and the gracious truths He taught. Blessing Him for His ineffable goodness in giving back her boy, the attitude of this poor Galilean Jewess must have been —

> Her eyes are homes of silent prayer;
> No other thought her mind admits,
> But "he was dead"—and there he sits.

WOMAN WHO WAS A SINNER
The Woman Who Sinned Yet Loved Much
Luke 7:36-50

All women since Eve, the world's first sinner, were born in sin and sinners by birth became more or less sinners by practice. But this woman whom Jesus met in the house of Simon has the distinguishable labels, "Which was a sinner," "She is a sinner," "Her sins which were many." Her doom seemed to be sealed in that word "sinner." The simple but moving record of this disreputable woman that Luke alone gives us, compells us to say that no human imagination invented it. As Mackintosh Mackay says, "The story bears stamped on its very face the impress of Him who spake as never man spake."

A striking aspect of the episode before us is the willingness of Jesus to fellowship with the sinful or the sole purpose of reaching their hearts with the truth. While He never sought such feasts, as the one to which Simon the Pharisee invited Jesus, He never refused them but deemed them openings for doing His Father's work. While He never ate with sinners for any personal gratification, He was careful not to adopt a holier-than-thou attitude toward

them. Separate from sinners, in respect to their original and practiced sin, He yet was willing to contact them in order to transform their lives. Thus, when invited by Simon to a dinner, Jesus graciously accepted in order to instruct him, as He did. And when a notorious female sinner tried to reach Him at the dinner, He did not refuse her admission to His presence, but graciously received tokens of her penitence and love, and commended her for her faith. If we would rescue the perishing we must be willing to go where they are.

Her Past

The word used for "sinner" in connection with this city woman suggests the special sin of unchastity and that she was known among the people in her community for her sensual and hateful calling — a woman of the streets. Jesus evidently knew that "her sins were many," implying that her prostitution was habitual, and that her illicit practices were continuous. All in Nain knew her as a woman who had rejected her virtues and her honor. She had sacrificed the white flower of a blameless life for monetary gain. Harold Begbie, in one of his volumes describing miracles of grace experienced in Salvation Army activities, tells of a prostitute who was saved from her life of sin by the gift of a flower from a female Salvationist on a London street. As the biographer puts it —

> The flower was white. The idea of this whiteness pervaded her consciousness. She made a contrast of the whiteness of that flower and the spreading darkness of her own soul. She said to herself, "I was once white like this flower." She looked at the white flower through a mist of pain and said to herself, "I wish I could be pure." She covered her eyes with her hands, moved her face to the pillow, and wept.

As that white flower unlocked the cabinet of memory and began a spiritual process resulting in the transformation of her character, it was thus with the woman who was a sinner. She saw her degraded life in the white light of divine holiness personified in Jesus, and as she wept her tears brought her triumph over a shameful past. Coming to Simon's house in all her guilt, afraid and ashamed to mingle with the invited guests, she flung herself at the foot of Him who said that Publicans and harlots would go into His kingdom before the self-righteous Pharisees.

There is no Biblical evidence whatever for identifying this sinful woman with Mary Magdalene or with Mary of Bethany as some commentators have done. While the first Mary is spoken of as having "seven devils," there is no evidence that she was immoral when under demoniac influence. The conduct of the sinful woman in Simon's house was totally different from the wild frenzy of a demoniac. As for Mary, sister of Martha, what is said of her devout spirit is strikingly adverse to that of a harlot of the streets. While "the woman which was a sinner" was probably known to the women Jesus healed of their infirmities (Luke 8:1-3), reticence as to her name both on their part and that of Luke was at once natural and considerate. That she was a woman deep-dyed in her particular kind of sin and yet found deliverance from her shameful past, confirms the truth that His blood can make the vilest clean.

Her Penitence

Those tears of hers, evidence of her sorrow for her many sins, cleansed her vision and gave her a sight of Him who came to save sinners. Guilt produced grief. Evidently she knew all about Jesus and followed His movements. It is most likely that she had heard of His compassion for the sorrowing widow of Nain, and had listened to His parable on the prodigal son. As a prodigal daughter of Israel, drawn by the ineffable pity and tenderness of His words and looks, she, like the prodigal son said, "I will arise and go to my Father." Brought back to God and purity, she found her way to Simon's house where her gift and her tears revealed how much she owed the Saviour and how greatly she loved Him.

The grateful woman brought with her an alabaster box of ointment and anointed the feet of Jesus, who did not refuse such a token of her love. While it does not say that the aromatic ointment was as costly as that with which Mary anointed Jesus, we can assume that it relatively was as precious. "The lavish and luxurious use of perfumes characterized the unhappy class to which the woman belonged." Now she

brings the store she had saved to seduce men, and with it anoints Him, the purest of men. He accepted the gift and transfigured it into the devotion of a saint, thereby making the instrument of sin a symbol of penitence and she surrendered to the claims of Jesus.

Further, this transformed sinner not only anointed the feet of Jesus with ointment, but also washed them with her tears and wiped them with the flowing locks of her hair. She could not manifest stronger tokens of her sorrow for sin and of her faith in Jesus. She was looking upon the compassionate face of Him who was about to be pierced and mourned for her sin (Zechariah 12:10). As Jesus reclined on a couch, the woman, modestly, and without attracting the notice of assembled guests, recognized by her tears and perfume the august character of the One who had raised her from the dunghill. Those sobs and the deed at Jesus' feet revealed the woman as having a sympathetic and fervent character. She was not too hardened in her sin as to be incapable of tears. In this she was so different from the cold, calculated attitude of the unsympathetic Simon who witnessed the woman's expression of gratitude and devotion. The different emotions of shame, penitence, joy, praise, love, found natural relief in her tears, ointment and kiss.

Her Provoker

What a study of contrasts we have in the attitude of the sinful woman and Simon the Pharisee! How incensed Simon was over the way Jesus allowed such extravagant attention from such a woman of ill-repute! Expressing his irritation and disapproval over the Saviour's countenance of the woman's gift of tears and perfume, he received his just rebuke for his lack of a sympathetic understanding of the situation. Because of the Pharisee's cold, austere, loveless manner, the woman knew she could not approach him for he would despise and dismiss her. But with a revelation of the Saviour's condescension and compassion, she believed He would mercifully receive her and so she cast herself upon His mercy.

We are told that what Simon had witnessed at the feet of Jesus had aroused thoughts of protest and provocation in his heart. He spake within himself about the action of one who professed to be a Prophet receiving homage of such a shameful woman. Was this not inconsistent with His character as the Prophet? He never voiced his irritation over the recognition on the part of Jesus of the woman's approach, but He who could read the secrets of the heart, answered the unspoken thoughts of the Pharisee (I Corinthians 15:24, 25). Then in masterly manner, without directly reproving Simon for his pharisaical thoughts, told the story of the two debtors which is similar to another parable of His (Matthew 18:25).

What a moving and thrilling climax Luke gives! In a quiet authoritative tone Jesus said, "Simon, I have somewhat to say unto thee," and recognizing Him as a Teacher come from God, Simon replied, "Master, say on." Then came a question "in the form of a kind of ethical proposition sum of the debtors that owed, the one five hundred pence, and the other fifty pence — a question that needs no answer."

Whatever hope either debtor had lay in the fact that pardon was offered to both as a matter of free gift and bounty, and driving home His point that the creditor had freely and frankly cancelled the sums owed him, Jesus asked Simon the pointed question, "Tell me which of them will love him most?" He answered somewhat indifferently, not fully understanding the drift of Christ's parable, "I suppose that he to whom he forgave most." This was the answer needed to rebuke Simon, and so with dramatic swiftness He turned to the half-concealed, worshiping woman, and in a tone vibrating with authority, indignation and condemnation said —

> I entered into thine house, thou gavest me no water for my feet: but she hath washed my feet with tears . . . Thou gavest me no kiss: but this woman hath not ceased to kiss my feet. My head with oil thou didst not anoint: but this woman hath anointed my feet with ointment.

The contrasts which Christ used are impressive. Simon gave no *oil* — the woman anointed His feet with costly ointment. Simon gave nothing for the *head* of Jesus — the woman lavished her love upon His *feet*. How Simon reacted to Christ's message on forgiveness and love we are not told! His cold, unloving, and unforgiving heart must have been smitten as Jesus revealed the depths of love in the woman's contrite heart, in the words, "Her sins, which are many, are forgiven; for she loved much; but to whom little is forgiven, the same loveth little."

Her Pardon

Turning from Simon to the female sinner who must have been overawed by Christ's parabolic defense of her tears and gift, He uttered the assuring word, "Thy sins have been forgiven." Any lingering fear in her penitent heart as to divine acceptance was banished and assurance became hers. The guests at the feast, seeing and hearing all that had taken place, ask the question, "Who is this that forgiveth sins also?" This was an echo of the Scribes who said that Jesus was a blasphemer because He forgave the sins of the man sick of the palsy (Matthew 9:3). Who can forgive sins but God only, and in Simon's house God was present in the person of His Son? Because He was God manifest in flesh He accepted the woman's sobs and perfume as the pledge of a past forgiveness and the promise of a life to be lived for His glory.

Christ's final word to the saved sinner was, "Thy faith hath saved thee, go in peace." Twice He uttered the joyful tidings that her sins had been pardoned and her soul saved. What He emphasizes in His confirmation of deliverance from her sin was that it was by her *faith* that she had been saved. When He said to Simon, "Her sins are forgiven, for she loved much," attention must be given to the single word "for." The phrase does not mean that Christ forgave because of her overflowing love; that because she was a soft and loving woman Christ forgave her faults so natural to her past life. He did not mean, "Forgive her, she has a kind and tender heart, and was more sinned against than sinning." It was not her *love* but her *faith* that brought about her forgiveness, for a sinful soul can only be saved by grace through faith in Christ. Forgiven on the basis of her penitence and faith, pardon expressed itself in the tokens of her love. "Go in peace" was the last word the transformed harlot heard. It actually means, "Go *into* peace." Peace was to be the new home in which she was to live, even the perfect peace Paul wrote about in his letter to the Philippians —

God's peace [be yours, that tranquil state of a soul assured of its salvation through Christ, and so fearing nothing from God and content with its earthly lot of whatever sort that is, that peace] which transcends all understanding, shall garrison *and* mount guard over your heart and minds in Christ Jesus (Philippians 4:7, *Amplified Bible*).

A CERTAIN WOMAN'S MESSAGE
Luke 11:27, 28

Bursting with enthusiasm over Christ's healing of the blind and dumb demoniac and His answer to His enemies about being in league with hell, a nameless woman in the crowd exclaimed, "Blessed is the womb that bare thee, and the paps which thou hast sucked." This charming little incident and profoundly instructive record is only given by Luke who had an eye for details. With true womanly feeling, this unidentified female envied the mother of such a wonderful Teacher. Our Lord did not condemn the woman for her saying but held it up and replied, "Blessed rather are the hearers and keepers of God's word" (Luke 11:28). Spiritual relationship, which acceptance of His saving truth makes possible, is higher than any natural or family relationship. Any woman wholly given to Christ is as His mother (Matthew 12:47).

AFFLICTED DAUGHTER OF ABRAHAM
The Woman Who Was Made Straight
Luke 13:11-13

The miracle of the infirm woman recorded by Luke the historian, is not only the report of a trained observer, but because of medical terms used, reveals Luke as the beloved, gifted physician, who alone cites the incident that took place on a Sabbath Day in a synagogue. Unbelievable as it may seem, it was on this day when religious leaders went the round of their prayers that they closely watched Christ in the hope of trapping Him in the breaking of some law concerning the Sabbath. Our Lord consecrated such a sacred day to the purposes of His Gospel, and performed many of His miracles on it. What

blind leaders of the blind those leaders were! They failed to see Him as One greater than the Sabbath. They thought more of the day than its Designer. This Sabbath miracle can be summarized thus—

The Daughter Suffering the Malady

Christ spoke of this crippled woman as "a daughter of Abraham," and was therefore more precious in His eyes than the ox or ass about which He chided the Pharisees. This title by which He called her suggests that she was one of the inner circle of pious Israelites like Simeon and Zacchaeus (Luke 2:25; 19:9). Being a descendant of Abraham, this female was possessed of his faith, and because of it, was in the Lord's house on the Lord's Day. As an inheritress of Abraham she was in the right place to be healed. Although a firm believer in Jehovah she yet was afflicted for a long time. However her painful malady did not keep her from attendance at the synagogue. Walking must have been difficult for her, but her seat was never vacant when the Sabbath came around. Think of what she would have missed if she had absented herself from God's house that Sabbath when Jesus visited it! What encouragement this faithful daughter of Abraham brings to all godly women, who, in spite of bodily infirmities, household cares and chores, find their way to the sanctuary where the Lord is ever present to undertake for true worshipers.

The Description of Her Malady

The phrases Luke employs reveal his professional touch. First of all the woman had "a spirit of infirmity" which does not mean that she had a weak and infirm spirit, but a mysterious derangement of her nervous system. She was "bowed together, and could in no wise lift up herself" — language implying a physical curvature of the back, a condition producing mental obliquity. She was "bowed together," a phrase not found elsewhere in the Bible and indicating dislocation of the vertebrae. Jesus said that she had been bound by Satan — that her disorder had been inflicted on her by Satan, just as he had smitten Job with sore boils. Her deformity must have made her a pitiable sight and caused her a good deal of mental despair, but she was to experience the power of One who had come to destroy the works of the devil and was able to relieve both mind and body of affliction.

The Duration of Her Malady

For eighteen long years the woman suffered, and eighteen years is a large slice out of one's life. Her trouble was long-standing and hopeless, and as the years dragged by we can imagine how she, as "a daughter of Abraham" resigned herself to the divine will although she did not understand why she had been afflicted thus through all those years. Many a saint is destined to suffer a lifetime, but he acquiesces in the will of God believing that as the Potter, He knows best how to shape the clay. Thus as Professor Laidlaw expresses it —

Her bent form and furrowed face were to Him as a book in which He read the story of her eighteen years' bondage and patient struggle to sustain her infirmity. Her faithful attendance at divine worship, and perhaps other features to which we have no clue, showed Him genuine religious and spiritual character.

It made no difference to the divine miracle-worker how long a person had suffered, or how deep-seated their disease or malady. A word from Him was sufficient to heal the worst.

The Deliverer of Her Malady

It is most profitable to study our Lord's varied methods in healing the sick. He did not cure in the same way all who came to Him. No standard rule was followed in His miracles. In the display of His power before us, note these actions: He saw — He called — He laid His hands on her. Nobody and nothing escaped the look of Jesus. There in the synagogue, at her habitual devotion, His eye singled out her crippled form as a special object of His mercy. Then with that compassionate voice of His, He called the woman to His side and said to her, "Thou art loosed from thine infirmity." There was no approach by the woman for relief. Christ took the initiative, and unsolicited, uttered the all-commanding authoritative word of healing. His eye saw her, His voice called her — now His hand touched her and conveyed an instantaneous

cure. Neither length of time nor inveteracy of her disorder could in any way obstruct the combined action of His eye, lips and hands.

"Thou art loosed from thine infirmity." "Immediately she was made straight." These two phrases reveal the knowledge of Luke as a physician. "Thou art loosed," the only passage where this phrase is used of a disease, is a term which medical writers use to describe release from disease, relaxing tensions, and taking off of bandages. Through Christ's word and touch a current of new life entered the deformed body of the woman, and her bonds were loosened.

"She was made straight." After eighteen years of such apparent physical deformity immediate erectness became hers. Contracted muscles were relaxed, the curvature of the spine vanished, and all at once she stood erect — a lovely specimen of a woman. What He did in the physical realm for this woman He is able to accomplish spiritually in our lives in which there are so many crooked things needing to be made straight (Isaiah 42:16). Such a miracle resulted in opposite effects —

The woman herself glorified God. The unasked-for, immediate manifestation of divine power was followed by immediate gratitude. Although she was so badly deformed, she was constant in her attendance at the synagogue to worship and praise God, but this momentous day resulted in the pouring forth of her thankfulness in a continuous strain of praise. Now, with the restored use of physical powers she would be able to serve the Lord, as she had not been able to through those long, hard and weary eighteen years of infirmity.

The people rejoiced. All her friends, fellow-worshipers in the house of God, who knew of her piety and sweet resignation under severe trial, likewise "rejoiced for all the glorious things that were done by Him." Surely this benediction must have gladdened the Healer's heart. Alas, too often He looks in vain for gratitude from those He blesses! (Psalm 107:8).

The ruler of the synagogue answered with indignation. What an opposite effect the miracle had on this religious leader who should have been the first to lead the praises of the assembled congregation for the Mas-

ter's mercy in healing the needy woman!
But no, while the crowd acclaimed Christ,
His adversaries accused Him. At the back
of the ruler's adverse criticism of Christ's
miracle was not so much the performance
of it on the Sabbath Day, but that his feelings were hurt over the popularity of the
Master. His pride of position was hurt as
he saw the crowds applauding Christ as He
confirmed His divine mission by such displays of power. The ruler's professed regard for strict Sabbath observance was a
thin veil, hiding a heart destitute of any
compassion for the suffering.

In His reply to the ruler's indignant rebuke, Christ vindicated His act of mercy
in a most unanswerable manner, by tacitly
acknowledging the necessity of sanctifying
the Sabbath, and that there was no better
way of honoring it than by caring for the
needy. His convincing argument was that
if the rigid Sabbath-keepers considered
themselves at liberty to loose an ox or an
ass from the stall in order to meet its material needs, surely the effort to loose the
grievous bonds of a rational being was more
justifiable, particularly when the bound one
was a daughter of Abraham. Was it not a
true Sabbath deed to heal a woman who
had suffered much through eighteen years?
So apparent was our Lord's argument, that
His adversaries were put to shame and silenced, and His character as the Messiah
rose in the estimation of the friends of the
healed woman, for whom that Sabbath Day
was a memorable one indeed.

What a comfort we can gather from this
miracle! In all our troubles Jesus is at hand,
and whether our disorders are spiritual or
bodily, the word of His mouth and the
touch of His hand are ours. If we are
"bowed down greatly," the Son of God with
power is near to "heal that which is sick,
and to raise up them that are bowed down"
(Psalms 38:6; 146:8; Isaiah 61:1). All that
concerns His own is of deep concern to
Him.

DAUGHTERS OF JERUSALEM
Luke 23:28

After Pilate had passed sentence of death
upon Jesus, whom he knew to be innocent
of the trumped-up charge of the Jewish
rulers, He was taken out to die upon the
cross which He was compelled to carry and
a great company of people followed Him.
Making up the crowd were "the daughters
of Jerusalem who bewailed and lamented
him." Who were these women whose wailing was loud and bitter as they looked upon
Him who was despised and rejected of
men? Deutsch, the commentator, suggests
that they may have formed one of the sister-
hoods resident in Jerusalem for mitigating
the sufferings of condemned criminals by
narcotic drinks. Among those weeping
women were those women from Galilee including Mary and Martha who had followed Jesus for many a day (23:49). He
had always been most gentle to their sex,
and women saw in Him their emancipator.
Now they express their deep sorrow with
their tears.

But comforted though Jesus must have
been by the sympathy of those women, He
said, "Weep not for me." To the outward
eye Jesus was in a most woeful plight seeing
He was being led to Calvary to die as a
felon on a wooden gibbet, but He wanted
them to see Him with the eye of faith as
One going forth to His coronation. How
amazed those loving women must have
been when on His Via Dolorosa He said to
them "Weep not for me"! Some there are
who have never wept for Him. As they
pass by, all His suffering on their behalf is
nothing to them.

> Have we no tears to weep for Him,
> While foes revile and men deride?

Jesus accepted those tears of womanly grief,
but implied that they would soon be dried
because His thorn-crowned brow would
soon be diademed with glory. They must
save their tears for themselves and for their
children and shed them when the dark days
of judgment will overtake their city rejecting Him. Under Titus in A.D. 70, women
remembered His word about the barren being blessed when they saw babies delivered
up to the knife. So Jesus urged those
women not to weep for Him, but to weep
over the sin taking Him to His cross, and
over the coming national disaster such sin
would occasion. Alive for evermore, and
Prince of the kings of earth, Christ does not
need our tears. But our gross sin against
Him, whether personal or national, should
result in deep contrition of soul.

WOMAN OF SAMARIA
The Woman Who Left Her Waterpot
John 4

The pregnant phrase to underline in the incident at Sychar's well which is so rich in spiritual instruction, is the announcement John gives at the beginning of the chapter, namely, "He must needs go through Samaria." Why the necessity? While this was the shortest and most usual road for a traveler going from Galilee to Jerusalem (Luke 9:52), the Pharisees avoided this customary route, and took a longer, round-about one through Peraea. They did this in order to avoid any contact with the Samaritans with whom, as Jews, they had no dealings. While the Jews and the Samaritans were physically alike in many ways, requiring the same food, following the same occupations, having the same hopes and ambitions, and suffering the same diseases, yet there was a racial hatred that kept them apart. The origin of this hostility between these two peoples may be traced back to the Assyrian colonization of the land of Israel (II Kings 17:21). From this followed the antagonism of the Samaritans to the Jews at the return from captivity (Ezra 4; Nehemiah 4), which led to the erection of rival temples on Mount Gerizim. This was in the mind of the woman at the well when she said, "Our fathers worshipped in this mountain" (4:20). From that time the spirit of religious bitterness lingered, and this accounts for the Jewish reproach.

"He who eats the bread of a Samaritan is as he who eats swine's flesh."

"No Samaritan shall be made a proselyte."

"They have no share in the resurrection of the dead."

Jesus spoke of a Samaritan as an alien (Luke 10:33; 17:16, 18), and in turn was accused by the Jews of being a Samaritan Himself and possessed by a demon (John 8:48). While the Jews had no dealings with the Samaritans, Jesus had. He spoke well of them, healed one of them of leprosy, and rebuked two of His disciples for wishing to destroy some of their number with fire from heaven (Luke 9:55, 56; 10:30-37). As the omniscient Lord, He knew all about the woman in Samaria and went there to show

and teach that He was above all religious and racial prejudices and that true worship consisted of worshiping God in spirit and in truth.

Thus necessity brought Jesus to the place where the Samaritan woman lived, and reaching Jacob's well, being wearied because of the long noontide journey, He sat by the well while His disciples went into the city to buy food. The reality of our Lord's fatigue testifies to the reality of His humanity. As the Man, He was weary and required food and drink, but as the God He could tell the woman who met Him at the well all about her guilty past and her soul's deepest need. Jesus was often weary *in* His work, but never weary *of* it. As Man, He knows all about our human and spiritual needs, and as God, He can meet every one of them. So about noon that day, Christ, a Jew, and the God-Man, met a Samaritan who was a woman, whose life was to be transformed as the result of that contact.

Her Individuality

Twice over this nameless female is referred to as "a woman of Samaria" (4:7, 9). Prominent in this phrase is her religious and national position. She was not only an alien as far as the Jews were concerned, but was also poor, for women of affluence did not draw water in those times. The Samaritan woman differs from many of the other women who came before Christ in His itinerant work. Some of them pressed into the kingdom or took it by violence with their earnest prayers. We think of Anna who spent her nights and days in fastings and prayers — of the sinful woman of Canaan who washed His feet with her tears — of the widow of Nain who moved His heart by her silent weeping in her great loss, but for the woman before us no petition was granted, no miracle was wrought except her spiritual transformation. Yet she was a privileged woman in that Christ confessed to her that He was indeed the Messiah which He did not usually confess even to His disciples, leaving them to discern for themselves the truth of His Godhead from His mighty works and miracles of mercy. Thus this woman has an individual prominence in that she was among the number who sought Him not (Isaiah 65:1). Further, He did not usually offer His gifts unasked, but waited until they were sought or importuned. Here He offered the woman the unspeakable gift of Himself. First of all, He asked relief of the woman, then He offered her relief, not common water to slake her thirst, but Himself, the Well of Everlasting Life.

Her Iniquity

What kind of a woman, morally, was this Samaritan water-carrier? When the disciples returned from their shopping errand they "marvelled that Jesus talked with the woman." Perhaps they were surprised to see Him talking in public with a woman, which was directly contrary to the Rabbinic precepts affirming that a man should not speak in public to his own wife, and that the words of the Law should be burned rather than taught publicly to a woman. Probably there were three reasons why the disciples marveled at the sight of Jesus and the Samaritan woman in earnest conversation. First, they wondered that He, as a Rabbi or Teacher sent from God, talked with her because she was only a woman. Second, because she was a Samaritan woman with whom no Jew should have dealings. Third, because she was a sinner. Some versions speak of her as *the* woman of Samaria," and she was likely well-known because of her association with men.

As a Samaritan, this woman had and knew the Pentateuchal law against adultery. When Jesus found her she was living with a man who was not her husband, but He did not expose her sin to others. He wanted her to feel the sense of sin herself. So when she asked Jesus for the living water of which He spoke, He replied: "Go, call thy husband." Her life had to be a clean receptacle to hold the living spring, so Jesus revealed the foulness that had to be destroyed, and His thrust left its mark. Her past and present life had been laid bare by the omniscient Lord who said, "Thou hast had five husbands; and he whom thou now hast is not thy husband." If death had invaded her home upon five occasions, and the five men she had lived with in succession were actual husbands, she certainly did not gather praise for her five marriages. But to bury her fifth husband and go and live with a man who was not a husband, re-

vealed how she had fallen into the depths of sin. We can imagine how the people of her locality avoided her because of her lack of feminine modesty and purity.

Behind the questions, "What seekest thou?" "Why talked thou with *her*?"—such a woman — is the thought that whatever His talk with such a woman, whose reputation the disciples may have heard about in the city, it must have been of the highest nature and was related to her spiritual welfare. Because those disciples believed that Jesus was perfect, and knew no sin, ulterior motives could not be ascribed to such a Holy One, as He talked with one whose sin became apparent in the white light of His holiness.

Her Ignorance

It is inferred that the woman complied immediately with the thirsty Man's request for a drink of refreshing water, even though she could see by His features and dress that He belonged to the nation who hated her people. As she drew water from the well she asked Him, "How is it that thou, being a *Jew*, asketh drink of *me*, which am a woman of Samaria?" Little did she realize that in her willingness to give the Jew a drink she was fulfilling the Christian law toward Him, "If he thirst — even if he is thine enemy — give him drink," and that cup of water she gave Him did not lose its reward (Matthew 10:42). Jesus answered the woman's question by bringing home to her mind her ignorance of the greatness of the One sitting at the well.

If thou knewest the gift of God, and who it is that saith to thee, Give me to drink; thou wouldest have asked of him, and he would have given thee living water.

What the Samaritan woman was so ignorant of was the fact that she had been coming daily to a deep well of water that had been God's gift of refreshment to man and beast since Jacob's time, yet there was a deeper well of spiritual truth so necessary for man's hidden needs, of which she was unconscious. She was a traveler in the journey of life, travel-stained by her sins, but had not discovered as yet the fountain opened for uncleanness. Instead of Christ begging her for a refreshing draught of water, she should have been beseeching Him for the unfailing supply of spiritual water from the eternal well.

From her ungracious manner and slur at Christ's people, she answered His comment in a tone of respect. There was something about His voice and manner that gripped her heart, and while she did not understand His message, she was conscious of its latent force, and felt that this traveler was no ordinary man. He seemed to speak with authority, and so passes in her address to Him from, "Thou, being a Jew" — the last word uttered in the tone of contempt — to the reverential, "Sir," Having had five husbands she was not easily worsted in conversation and wanted to know where was the better well than Jacob's from which the "living water" could be secured, and her ignorance begins to vanish as she asks Him, "Art thou greater than Jacob, our ancestor?"

Her Instruction

As the woman spoke of the deep well before her, and of Christ having no bucket to secure more vitalizing water from the depths of the well, Jesus, pointing to the ancient well, said, "Anyone who drinks of this water will be thirsty again, but anyone who drinks of the water I shall give him will never thirst any more; the water I shall give him will turn into a spring of water, welling up to eternal life."

What Jesus supplied was not external water to satisfy the recurring physical need, but an internal and eternal source of unfailing spiritual, life-giving water. Such living water was a divine gift (Isaiah 55:1), was Christ Himself (4:10), easily reached— the woman walked far to reach Jacob's well, but the spiritual well is ever at hand — and a satisfying, unfailing gift for "whosoever drinketh" (Revelation 22:17). As light broke in upon her darkened mind, the woman replied to Christ's teaching, "Sir, give me this water, that I thirst not, neither come hither to draw."

But a full understanding of His words was not yet hers. Still thinking of them in their physical sense, she thinks of toilsome hours and weary journeys that could be saved if only she knew the marvelous well the Stranger was speaking about. Jesus an-

swered her request, and cut short her argument with a command that went straight to her heart: "Go, call thy husband and come hither." Our Lord wanted to turn her from a proud argumentative frame of mind to the humility of confession. Here was a sinful creature worth saving, but she must be made conscious of her sin, and when she humbly said, "I have no husband," she became a different woman.

Proceeding gently, Jesus replied, and revealed His omniscience as He unmasked her secret: "Thou hast well said . . . For thou hast had five husbands, and he whom thou now hast is not thy husband."

The very wounds her shame would hide were seen by His all-searching eye, and her ignorance gives way to spiritual insight as she reverently confesses the prophetic gift of the One who knew all about her past and present life and asks Him to solve the problem of the right place of worship for both Jew and Samaritan. The woman was taken up with the *place* of worship, but Jesus sought to teach her that the *spirit* of worship is more important than the place. Alas, on any Lord's Day there are thousands in the place of worship as they gather in churches, but they are strangers to the spirit of worship which is related to the worship of God in spirit and in truth — worship inspired by the Holy Spirit in conformity to the truth of the Word.

It was to this woman that Jesus revealed the only basis of acceptable worship, and also the truth of His Messiahship. Perceiving that Jesus was a Prophet, the woman felt He knew the nature of true worship, namely, the spiritual worship of a spiritual Being not only at Jerusalem or Gerizim, but wherever there is a heart seeking Him. With her mind opening to Christ's instruction about spiritual worship, the Samaritan woman confessed the power of the coming Messiah to reveal all things, and perhaps now sensed that because the Jew before her had told her all things about her life, He must be the Messiah. Then came the dramatic word of Christ's claim, "I that speak unto thee am the Messiah." How privileged this sinful woman was to hear from the lips of Jesus Himself the divine secret of His Messiahship!

Her Influence

By the Spirit, the woman acknowledged the truth of Christ's Messiahship and Omniscience, and immediately became a powerful witness to her remarkable discovery. With her mind full of the new truth she had learned, she left her water-pot and, full of her great discovery, hurried back to the city. In her enthusiasm she left her waterpot behind as a pledge of her return, not only for natural water, but also for a further spiritual draught from the living well she had found in Christ. Reaching the city, she met the men who knew her only too well, and declared the truth she had learned of Christ's Messiahship. Because He had unveiled her past life, He must be the Christ for whom both Jew and Samaritan were looking.

Her ignorant mind had grasped the secret of true worship and of Christ's mission, and her instinct for telling news became apparent as with the passion of an evangelist she said, "Come, see a man, which told me all things that ever I did: is not this the Christ?" He had awakened her to a new and better life and such was the effect of her earnest witness that many of those Samaritans went out and came to Jesus at the well. For two days they listened to His teaching, and came to believe in Him, and accept Him as the Christ, the Saviour of the world. This was not only because of what His first native woman evangelist in Samaria had said of Him, but also because they had heard Him for themselves, and hearing, believed. In the glow of her newborn faith, the woman had to tell others and share with them all she had heard and experienced. Some four years later, when Philip the Evangelist came to preach "in many villages of the Samaritans," he doubtless met "the woman of Samaria" and realized how wonderfully the Holy Spirit had used her life and witness as well as the testimony of the Samaritans she had been the means of leading to Christ, to prepare the way for his miraculous ministry in Samaria. When the disciples returned from the city and saw Jesus talking with the woman, they knew what He meant by telling them that the fields were white already unto harvest. Because of the seed sown by the woman who, when she found the well, left her

water-pot, Philip experienced a great ingathering of souls in Samaria, so much so that there was great joy in that city. The most joyful inhabitant was the woman who from her heart confessed, "Come see a man, who told me all things that ever I did; is not this the Christ?" (Acts 8:5-25). She had laid the foundation of that Samaritan Pentecost. At Jacob's well she saw Jacob's Star (Numbers 24:17), and ascending Jacob's Ladder (John 1:51) became the means of others climbing to God.

WOMAN TAKEN IN ADULTERY
THE WOMAN CHRIST SAVED FROM DEATH BY STONING
John 8:1-11; Deuteronomy 17:5, 6

Having come to seek and save the lost, Jesus never shrank from close association with sinners. He ate and drank with them, in order to win them to Himself. In His journeys He conversed with at least three women who had been guilty of adultery — the Woman of Samaria, the Woman who came to Him in the house of Simon, and now the woman of the narrative before us, and His loving-kindness and tender mercy characterized His dealings with each of them. It is interesting to observe the circumstances leading up the exposure of the woman taken in adultery. After spending a night on the Mount of Olives, Jesus, rising early the next morning made His way to the Temple where a large company of people soon gathered to hear about His Messianic work. But as He fearlessly witnessed, danger hovered around Him, for members of the Sanhedrin were seeking to kill Him, and the Scribes and Pharisees were in sympathy with such a wicked design. While He was seated in the Temple instructing the people, a number of the Scribes and Pharisees arrived bringing with them a woman who had been caught committing a most degrading and serious offense.

The Accusers

The religious leaders who brought the woman to Christ, preferring a charge against her, and trying to trap Him by asking what should be done to her, belonged to a class most eager to deal with harlots. They regarded themselves as custodians of public morality and woe be to those who came under the observation of these self-appointed inspectors of moral nuisances. Knowing all about the requirements and punishment of the Mosaic Law, and their own traditions surrounding it, they treated sinners with sanctimonious contempt. To them, it was sinful to be touched by a woman like the one they brought to Jesus, but as we shall see, their zeal against the sins of others was only a cloak to cover their own vileness.

How partial those accusers were! They brought the woman taken in the very act of adultery, but where was the man, the chief offender? Why was he not brought? Was he a Pharisee belonging to our Lord's enemies, and one whom policy demanded should be allowed to escape? The law and justice demanded that the adulterer and the adulteress should be brought together and be put to death (Leviticus 20:10), but true to the way of the world those foes of Christ made the woman bear the severity of her offense. Divine justice, however, is "without partiality" (James 3:17).

The Adulteress

The woman presented to Christ by her accusers was without doubt guilty of the sinful conduct with which she was charged, and He in no way condoned her serious offense. Doubtless He pitied the woman's weakness and made full allowance for the force of temptation compelling her to sin. But He regarded her conduct as being a manifestation of wickedness evidenced by His command that she sin no more. Adultery takes its place in the front rank of "the works of the flesh" (Galatians 5:19), and is ever against the Creator's just and holy law regarding the welfare of the race (Exodus 20:14). But could anything have been more cruel or harsh than that of setting this sinful woman "in the midst" of the Temple, exposing her to the gaze of the multitude? The conduct of those Scribes and Pharisees "showed on their parts a cold, hard cynicism, a graceless, pitiless, barbarous brutality of heart and conscience." It was bad enough for the woman to be conscious of the guilt of her sin, but to parade her before others was a cruel act and destitute of the love eager to hide a multitude of sins (I

Peter 4:8). While Jesus never excused sin in those who came His way, He was ever tender and gracious in His treatment of them.

The Advocate

As a Jew, and as the Messiah, Jesus was under solemn obligation of respecting the law of Moses (Deuteronomy 31:9; Matthew 5:17), and in His life on earth fulfilled the law (Matthew 5:18). Therefore when the Pharisees quoted the law about an adulteress being stoned to death, they appealed to a standard which He regarded and honored (Psalm 40:8), even though the great prevalence of adultery had made punishment of being stoned to death obsolete. Our Lord told the Pharisees that Moses was their accuser (John 5:40), and is it not strange that in their accusation of the woman they should appeal to Moses? Their question, "What sayest thou?" did not imply that they respected His teaching about the law. All they hoped to do was to snare Jesus into making an answer contrary to the law. If He had said, "Let her be stoned," His tenderness and kindness in dealing with the sinful and degraded would have been shown as being false. Had He said, "Let her go," there might have been a revolt among those who, although they were favorable to Him were yet staunch defenders of what Moses taught.

The cunning of the old serpent, the devil, was behind the effort of the Pharisees to tempt and accuse Christ and He needed wisdom to deal with such a situation. But able to read the hearts of men He knew how to answer their question, which He successfully did — by silence. He stooped and wrote in the dust around His feet, "*as though he heard them not.*" We pause here to ask two questions, namely, Why did He look down? What did He write with His finger on the ground?

Why did He look down?

It may have been out of consideration for the feelings of the guilty woman, that Jesus fixed His gaze on the ground and not on her. Men of corrupt hearts Peter speaks of as "having eyes full of adultery" (II Peter 2:14), might stare at the exposed woman, but as the Holy One having a compassionate heart He looked away from the frightened female dragged into His presence. She was humiliated by so many eyes fastened upon her, but here was the Friend of sinners, not guilty of any morbid curiosity, bowing His head and looking downward.

Another reason for His action might have indicated the lack of relish for what had been thrust upon Him. He always looked upward to heaven and spoke to His Father (Matthew 14:19), and directly at Peter and others whom He sought to restore to His favor (Luke 22:16), but when asked to pronounce judgment upon a guilty soul, more sinned against than sinning, His whole being shrinks from such a task (John 3:17; Luke 9:56; 12:14). As He came to fulfill the law, He cannot evade it now and thereby shield a manifest sinner from her sin which the law justly condemned.

What did He write on the ground?

It has been suggested that this was a common method of signifying intentional disregard. Jesus certainly acted as if He had not heard the woman's accusers. What His finger actually wrote we are not told. It was the divine finger that wrote the law (Exodus 31:18), and perhaps Jesus reflected upon this fact as He wrote on the ground. As He stooped in the Temple that He might write, our Lord may have remembered how He had stooped from heaven that the broken law might be rewritten in the temple of man's being. The woman had broken the law, but He would honor it. Incensed at the evident unconcern of Christ, the Pharisees, discerning the symbolism of His writing, kept up their demand for an answer to their question. That solemn silence was more than they could stand, for it spoke in a power greater than His words. He was slow to anger, even with the most obdurate.

When He did look up and speak, the judicial decision was not forthcoming, but what the Pharisees did hear stunned them. "He that is without sin among you — that is, the type of sin men engaged in with such a woman, the particular sin the Pharisees had condemned her with — let him cast the first stone." The only One present that day without sin of any kind, was the sinless Lord Himself, but He would not cast a stone nor pass judgment as to what should be done with the woman in the role of a civil or ecclesiastical judge. Delaying any

word for the woman, He again stooped down and wrote on the ground, the repeated action expressing His determination to avoid the office of a judge. What He wrote this second time must have been seen by His accusers, and they slunk away, lest He reveal their further guilt. One ancient translation adds to the repeated verse (8:8), the words, "Wrote on the ground the sin of each of them."

Whatever that writing was, the Pharisees were convicted by their own conscience, and beginning with the eldest, all of them left Jesus and the woman alone. Says Matthew Henry, "They that are convicted by their conscience will be condemned by their Judge if they are not requited by their Redeemer." How the hypocrisy of these accusers, both of Christ and of the woman, was exposed! Here they were condemned as being guilty of the very sin they cast against the woman. Not one of them was innocent of the sin of adultery they brought against the woman, even the eldest man among them.

The Acquittal

The second time Jesus looked up from the ground, He saw none but the woman. She might have fled as the convicted Pharisees left the Temple in shame, but somehow she was constrained to remain with the One who had become her Advocate and Deliverer. Now, facing her, Jesus asked, "Where are those thine accusers? hath no man condemned thee?" The woman simply answered, "No man, Lord." She recognized that He was the only One who had the right to pass sentence on her. But there was no attempt at defense or excuse on her part, no plea for divine mercy and forgiveness. He knew all about her, and thus she reverently called Him "Lord."

Then came the word her heart longed to hear, "Neither do I condemn thee: go, and sin no more." The accusers who had just left could not condemn her, neither would Jesus. "Go, sin no more," or "Be no longer a sinner," was an utterance in harmony with His purpose of saving sinners from their sin. While there was no expression of forgiveness or peace as in the case of others (Matthew 9:2; Luke 7:48), we believe that she went forth, and in obedience to Christ's command, entered a new life of pardon, peace and purity. The old adulterous life passed away, and she became a new creation. It would be most interesting to have more history of this nameless female. Our obligation is to glean these lessons so patent from the episode, namely, be slow to condemn every human judgment of another's sin; to condemn every sin in our own lives; to declare to every sinner God's forgiveness.

HEBREW WIDOWS
Acts 6:1-4

Evidently some of the widows and children of many Jews had been neglected. The chief objects of relief from a common fund, somehow their daily needs had been overlooked, and so seven men of honest report, full of the Holy Ghost and wisdom, among whom was Stephen, were appointed to care for these women as Scripture directed (I Timothy 5:3-16). Being particularly helpless, widows were reckoned to be the special care of God, because few others troubled, and to show them kindness was to qualify for God's approval and blessing (Job 29:13; Psalms 68:5; 146:9; Isaiah 1:17; Jeremiah 7:6; see further under WIDOWS in Index).

THE WOMEN OF ANTIOCH
(Acts 13:50)

Luke mentions that these women were the proselytes converted from heathenism to Judaism who gave absolute submission of conscience to the Rabbis and Jewish Elders. These women had a real hunger for a higher and purer life than they could find in the infinite debasement of Greek and Roman society. "Satisfaction and grace in the life are the fruit of Grace."

But when Paul and Barnabas came upon the scene proclaiming salvation and eternal life these "devout and honorable women," meaning, they were worshiping females of high rank and station, the Jewish leaders strove to influence them against the effective ministry of the apostles. As for the "chief men of the city," these may have been the husbands of these women of renowned social position who evidently acquiesced in their wives' conversion to Judaism. "The potent influence of the female character

both for and against the truth is seen in every age of the church's history."

DEMON-POSSESSED DAMSEL
THE WOMAN WHO WAS DELIVERED FROM DIVINATION
Acts 16:16-24

It was after the conversion of Lydia and her household that Paul and Silas after a period of gracious hospitality in Lydia's spacious home, left for a season of prayer on the following Sabbath — not by the riverside (16:13), but in a sanctuary where prayer was wont to be made. On the way, people gathered about the apostles, whose mission produced friends — and foes — and excitement was evident as they continued their journey, especially when one like the demon-possessed girl cried after them, and sought from them the way of salvation.

Her Divination

What exactly was "the spirit of divination" which possessed this slave girl and made her soothsaying so lucrative to the masters who owned her? The margin gives us the rendering, "a spirit of Python," or as some MSS give it, "a Python spirit." In Greek mythology Python was the name of a serpent which guarded an oracle on Mount Parnassus and was slain by Apollo, thence called Pythius, as being himself the god of divination. This girl was not a mere ventriloquist or sheer imposter, nor a somnambulist or lunatic as some have supposed. She was a demoniac who, when she was possessed by the evil spirit, was looked upon as having power to divine and predict. When caught up by the demon, the girl's wild cries were received as oracles, and her masters or joint-owners who usually had partnership in valuable slaves, traded on her supposed inspiration and made her answer those who sought for oracular guidance in the problems and perplexities of their lives. Luke, who in his gospel describes "soothsaying" as coming from evil or unclean spirits, here, in his record of the demon-possessed girl, recognized in her phenomena that which was identical with those of the priestesses of Delphi — the wild distortions, the shrill cries, the madness of evil inspiration. How ignorant we seem to be of the reality of the power of Satan's emissaries, especially in these last days when their influence is more apparent than ever!

Her Declaration

If the girl was under the spell of a demon, how can we account for the content of the continued cry, "These men are the servants of the most high God, which shew—declare or proclaim—unto us the way of salvation"? This was indeed a true description of Paul and his companions in their itinerant ministry. Was the demon using the girl to mock the apostolic witness to Christ in order to thwart their work? Were the expressions "servants of the most high God," and "the way of salvation" among those the girl had heard Paul use beforehand? Did she now repeat them under demoniac influence not knowing what they meant, and which demons Jesus had dispossessed (Luke 4:34; 8:28) now used in scornful irony, or as an involuntary testimony to the truth that Paul declared? Did the declaration indicate any particular motive on her part to conciliate Paul, or to increase the profits of those who owned her by acting as a prophetess? Or can it be that the unfortunate girl was impelled by a desire for emancipation from her demoniac influence to cry forth the message she did? Had she listened to Paul and Silas at the riverside to which many had resorted, not only to pray, but also to hear the apostles preach, and felt that these men were able to deliver her, and were as unlike as possible to the masters who traded on her maddened misery? The fact remains that she came to experience that Paul was a servant of the most high God with power to make her whole.

Her Deliverance

We read that the girl followed Paul and his co-workers for many days and that Paul became worn out, wearied, impatient over her constant repetition of cries, which impeded the apostolic task of speaking to inquirers. Perhaps Paul was grieved or sorry by her constant cries, not in any sense of being offended, but because she was demonpossessed and therefore not responsible for her utterances and actions. It will be noted that Paul in no way reproved the girl herself, but, facing her, spoke to the evil spirit

possessing her: "I command thee in the name of Jesus Christ to come out of her." As the authoritative representative of Christ, Paul ordered the demon to vacate his abode in the girl. Command means to order peremptorily, as an officer his soldiers, and at the name of Jesus the demon was subject unto Paul and withdrew his control of the girl.

Two aspects of her restoration to her true self are conspicuous. First, it was instantaneous, "he came out the same hour," or "that instant." Immediately, the miracle took place, and the girl was wonderfully emancipated from her degradation. Second, her deliverance was complete for "her masters saw that the hope of their gains was gone." All their present and future profit from the girl's demoniac gift had gone. There she was silent and subdued, clothed in her right mind, no longer a slave, but a transformed girl. When "the spirit of divination" went, with it vanished the lucrative business of her owners. Angry at Paul and Silas over their obliteration of financial gain, they seized the apostles and brought them before the magistrates who found them guilty of the trumped-up charge of the slave owners, and cast them into prison. Rough treatment was given the apostles for the saving work God enabled them to accomplish, but triumph was also theirs, for they were able to pray and sing praises even at the midnight hour in their prison cell. Also, witness again God's miraculous power both in the earthquake and the salvation of the jailer and his household.

What of the girl herself whose history ends with the expulsion of the demon and his evil influence? We cannot believe that she was left to drift back into ignorance, unbelief and demoniac possession. Lydia and the other noble women would know all about the girl, laboring with the Apostle as they did (Philippians 4:3), and likely afforded the transformed girl all necessary shelter, comfort and guidance. As for the girl herself, did she show her gratitude to Paul for the miracle performed in her life, by including her gift with the gifts sent to the Apostle to assist in his work of salvation? (Philippians 4:15). Now, saved herself, did she confess out of a delivered and cleansed heart, "Paul is indeed a servant of the Most High God, for he showed unto me the way of salvation"?

DAUGHTERS OF PHILIP
Acts 21:8, 9

Philip the evangelist was one of the seven disciples set apart as a distinct body for the exercise of a particular ministry in the church (Acts 6:3). While blessed with four commendable daughters, whose names, along with the name of their mother, are not given, nothing is said of any sons that Philip might have had. Absence of any mention of Philip's wife may imply that he was a widower, and that his four daughters cared for him and the home. We are safe in assuming that his wife had been a devout wife and mother, and that she had had a formative influence over the lives of her four daughters who became a remarkable quartet of gospel women who lived out their lives among heathen neighbors.

The Four Daughters Are Nameless

It would have been interesting to have had their names, as we have those of Job's three daughters, but they would have been non-existent in Bible history were it not for the one single verse telling us that they actually lived and occupied so important a place in the primitive fellowship of the church. Reticence as to their identity we accept as one of the wise silences of the Bible. Their names are inscribed upon the roll of the redeemed in heaven. "Not every flower that blooms on earth, and not every star that moves in Heaven has a name in human syllables; but all the same they smile and shine; and Philip's four anonymous daughters represent countless numbers of the faithful, serving a generation who knows them not."

They Were Virgins

We think of these four daughters as being beyond the period of youth, women in the full ripeness of godly experience and exercising rare spiritual gifts, who had chosen a celibate life deeming such preferable for women called or specially qualified to be God's interpreters, like Miriam of old. Roman Catholic writers regard them as the first nuns of the Christian Church. J. D.

Alexander suggests that their virginity is probably mentioned, "only as a reason for their still being at home, and not as having any necessary connection with their inspiration." Paul sanctioned the unmarried life as presenting a higher standard of excellence than the duties of domestic life (I Corinthians 7:8-34).

They Prophesied

Joel had prophesied extraordinary spiritual gifts to be bestowed upon both sexes, and to daughters as well as sons. At Pentecost Peter, inspired by this prediction said, "Your sons and daughters shall prophesy." It may be that Philip and his four daughters were present on that historic day, shared in that marvelous outpouring of the Holy Spirit, and became by that divine unction, Christian exhorters. How those four handmaids of Christ "Who kept their maiden record white," must have been blessed and used as they declared a God-given message, giving not only predictions of the future, but also expounding the Word for the enlightenment and edification of those who heard them. Because of the teaching of Paul regarding the silence of women as preachers in churches (I Corinthians 14:34; I Timothy 2:12), it is possible that Philip's daughters confined their ministry to their own sex. If, and when, they accompanied their father in his missionary journeys, opportunities would come their way of preaching to women, both among Jews and Gentiles, and of assisting in the baptism of female converts. Their utter devotion to the Lord must have constantly cheered the heart of their father whose faith they followed. The church will never know how much it owes to its unknown, consecrated women.

PAUL'S SISTER
Acts 23:16-22

Like Zinzendorf, Paul had one passion, namely, Christ, and thus the passage before us is the only reference we have to any of the Apostle's natural relatives — his sister and her son — both of whom are unnamed. Whether his sister and his nephew were Christians, we are not told. The latter's eagerness to save his uncle from imminent danger suggests he had a deep regard for him. How could mother and son be so closely related to the mighty Apostle, and not share his devotion for Christ! If mother and son were among his kinsmen at Rome whom Paul mentions (Romans 16:7, 11), then they might have come up to Jerusalem to keep the Feast. While there the son heard of the plot to kill his notable uncle, and thus became the means of his escape from death. Ever grateful for the assistance of those who loved him in the Lord, Paul must have been thankful for the nephew who came to him as soon as he heard of the intention of the Apostle's foes to get rid of him. Here, again, we wonder at the silence of Scripture as to the identity of many it mentions! Why does Paul give us the names of other women and their sons, yet withhold the names of his own dear sister to whom he must have been attached in childhood, now, probably, a widow, and her son?

RUFUS' MOTHER
Romans 16:13

There may be those who dismiss the last chapter of Romans as being just a catalog of names. In many respects, however, it is a most impressive chapter seeing it contains twenty-six personalities, all of whom are named with some of their relatives who also are nameless as in the case of the mother of Rufus. About most of the personalities we know almost nothing. That they had their joys and sorrows, burdens and cares, hopes and disappointments, trials and triumphs, can be assumed, seeing we all drink of the cup of human experience. What is evident is the fact that all whom Paul mentions as being his friends in this most personal chapter were all followers of the Lamb, and had in some way served the Apostle, and who now receive his gratitude, greetings and salutations. A few of them may have been near relatives, his kinsmen. Handley G. Moule's comment on the chapter is worth quoting —

> We watch this unknown yet well-beloved company, with a sense of fellowship and expectation impossible out of Christ. This page is no mere relic of the past; it is a list of friendship to be made hereafter, and to be possessed for ever, in the endless life where personalities indeed shall be eternal, but where also the union of personalities, in Christ, shall be beyond our utmost thought.

Who, exactly, was Rufus, whose mother Paul wished to be remembered to? Mark speaks of Simon of Cyrene as "the father of Alexander and Rufus" (15:21), and there is a substantial tradition that the Rufus of whom Paul speaks was Simon's son. As Mark wrote primarily for Roman readers the family was well-known to him, and so Paul, writing to the Romans, mentions the son of the cross-carrying Simon with whom he was so friendly. Paul speaks of Rufus as a chosen man in the Lord, "a saint of the *élite*" as Moule calls him, or "that choice Christian," as Dr. James Denny wrote of him. Doubtless Rufus was conspicuous in the service of the church. As a youth he may have seen his father shouldering the Saviour's cross to Calvary, and witnessed His death there, and from then on became His bond-slave.

Further, what are we to understand by the inclusion of the phrase in Paul's greeting to Rufus — "and his mother and mine"? Did he have two mothers in mind, Rufus' and his own mother? Above all unknown mothers in the Bible, Paul's mother is the one whose biography we wish we could have had. Brought up a Pharisee of the Pharisees, Paul's parents must have been thoroughly Jewish and antagonistic to the claims of Christ when He appeared as the Messiah. Did a sword pierce the heart of Paul's mother when she learned that her brilliant son had forsaken the Jews' religion and had become a Christian, or was she brought to experience His saving grace and power? Was she alive when Paul wrote his epistle to the Romans, as some writers seem to suggest, seeing that he mentions a few of his relatives in this epic chapter, who, with his mother, had found their way from Tarsus to Rome? The more general acceptance, however, of Paul's salutation — his mother and mine — is that Rufus' mother had been so kind to him on different occasions, mothering him in days of sickness and strain, and is remembered by the Apostle for all her loving attention. Says Herbert F. Stevenson in his *Galaxy of Saints* —

> Through an overflowing of "motherly" love and care for the Apostle, a tender relationship had been established. The most sturdy self-reliant and ruggedly resourceful still need oc-

casional "mothering"; and in this gracious tribute, Paul pays the mother of Rufus the highest compliment which even an apostle could confer.

Although the nameless mother of Rufus had played a mother's part to the probable motherless apostle in his hours of need, her name, along with her loving-kindness stands recorded now: "In either Book of Life, here and above."

NEREUS' SISTER
Romans 16:15

Doubtless there were other godly women among "all the saints" whom Paul includes in his greeting to Nereus and his sister. The Apostle must have known the name of this woman as well as that of her brother, yet for some reason he left her nameless. We have glimpses of information about some

in this roll of names, but total ignorance regarding others, save that they were in Christ. Seeing that Nereus and his sister are grouped together would seem to suggest that they were unmarried and remained as the only members of the family and that they cared for each other, Nereus experiencing, in the words of Christina G. Rossetti that —

There is not friend like a sister
In calm or stormy weather;
To cheer one on the tedious way,
To fetch or if one goes astray,
To lift one if one totters down,
To strengthen whilst one stands.

We have thus reached the end of the list of the actual, yet anonymous women of the Bible, thick-set in chronicles of saints and sinners. Although unknown, they live on in their deeds whether good or bad.

4

Symbolic and Representative Bible Women

Both animate and inanimate objects are used in the Bible to illustrate and enforce various aspects of truth, and women form a large part of animate beings employed to typify different vocations, vices and virtues. Even in our time female names are attached to certain phenomena, such as wind storms in America, where the last was known as Hurricane Betsy.

Capable of angel heights, or devil depths, the female sex has ever been employed to symbolize the vices or virtues of the human race. The ancient nation of Israel was pictured as God's adulterous wife; the coming federation of apostate religions is as "the great whore"; while the true church is figured as the Bride of the Lamb. Familiar and indispensable objects such as "ships" are often given female names and referred to in a feminine way as, for instance, "*She* is a sea-worthy vessel." Think of the applications of the precious term "mother" that we have. A true patriot speaks of the land of his birth affording him privileges and protection, as his "Motherland" —

> Land of our birth, our faith, our pride,
> For whose dear sake our kinsfolk died,
> O Motherland, we pledge to thee,
> Head, heart and hand through years to be.

It is because so many necessary blessings spring from the great world upon which both man and beast are dependent, that we speak of it as "mother earth." Further, the first thing we learn to do after our birth is to speak, and so the language we learned from our parents and were brought to use is our own tongue, our "mother tongue." Because Jerusalem gave us the Christian faith it is spoken of as "The Mother of Our Religion," and the church which Jesus founded as "The Mother Church." Thus, the aspect of Bible female biography which we are now to consider is the way femininity is used in a symbolic and a representative fashion. In the interpretation and application of any Bible symbol or metaphor we must guard against extreme and unwarranted handling. Often we are tempted to read into symbols what their authors never intended. As the reader can see, we have followed the chronological sequence of these particular women in the Bible.

SEED OF WOMAN
Genesis 3:15; 9:9, etc.

Metaphorically, seed represents offspring, race, family. All descended from Abraham are spoken of as "The seed of Abraham" (Genesis 13:15; 17:8; Galatians 3:7, 29). When John wrote of the "seed" within the believer, he had in mind vital energy, or indwelling principle of the divine life by which the child of God is kept from known sin. After our first parents sinned, the one responsible for their sin received the first promise and prophecy of deliverance from sin. It was Satan who heard the initial message of the cross, "I will put enmity between thee and the woman and between *thy seed* and *her seed.*" At His incarnation, Christ came as "the seed of the woman," to fulfill the predicted truth which Satan received after his deception of Eve. Born of a woman, Christ, by His death and resurrection, made possible freedom from Satan's thraldom. Between "his seed" and all born of God through Christ by the Spirit, there is constant enmity. There are other legitimate applications one could make of Christ as the Seed.

PAGAN GODDESSES
I Kings 11:5, 33; II Kings 21:3; 23:6

Among the host of heaven worshiped by pagans, and, alas, by the Israelites through their contact with idolatrous nations, were female deities existing only in the imagination of those who worshiped them. Prominent among Canaanite gods we have —

Asherah

Worshiped as the goddess of fertility, Asherah was represented by a wooden pole bearing her name and planted in the ground (Judges 6:24; I Kings 14:22; 18:18; II Chronicles 15:16). Sacrificial vessels were used in her worship, which she shared with Baal (II Kings 23:4). Her sacred tree was spoken of as "an abominable image" and "a graven image" (II Kings 21:7). It was the image of Asherah which Manasseh set up in the Temple, and which was destroyed by Josiah (II Kings 21:7; 23:6). Priests of this goddess were slain after Elijah's challenge on Carmel (I Kings 16:33). Asherah, which is the Hebrew form of Ashirtu, stood in Canaanite places of worship, and was periodically decorated by woven hangings by her female votaries (II Kings 23:7). The totem poles of Indians carried a corresponding symbolical significance.

Ashtaroth

This plural form of Ashtoreth was the general name of the goddesses of the Canaanites, whose center of worship was the ancient Bashan (Deuteronomy 1:4; Joshua 9:10). Ashtoreth, parallel to Astarte, has been identified with Venus or Aphrodite, goddess of love. She also appears as goddess of war, and was worshiped in Sidon. Gross sexual orgies were associated with the worship of Ashtoreth (I Samuel 31:10; I Kings 11:5,33; II Kings 23:13). The Queen of Heaven, to whom Jeremiah refers, was probably this same Phoenician goddess (Jeremiah 7:18; 44:15-30). The Roman Catholics erroneously worship the Mother of our Lord as "Universal Queen of Heaven and Earth."

PASSING THE LOVE OF WOMEN
II Samuel 1:17-27

There is no pathetic and expressive eulogy comparable in the realm of literature to this one that came from David's lips when he heard of the death of Saul and Jonathan upon Mount Gilboa. Between David and Jonathan there existed a remarkable affection in spite of the most untoward circumstances, and when David compared his friend's deep love as being beyond the love of a faithful wife for her husband, he expressed an affection that could only exist between two such noble natures united as they were in the fear of God. David's intense personal sorrow over his friend's death is felt in his praise of him, "Thy love to me was wonderful, passing the love of women." David had every reason to speak thus of Jonathan, particularly when the latter knew that the one he loved was to take the crown over his head, and yet to remain so loyal and loving to his rival.

KING'S DAUGHTER — HONORABLE AND GLORIOUS
Psalm 45

In this great psalm of the king, we have references to his queen and daughters. As one of the prophetic psalms, it looks forward to Christ's coming reign (Hebrews 1: 8, 9). The queen is symbolic of church, the queen consort, whom, by an everlasting covenant Christ had betrothed unto Himself (Revelation 19:7-9). The daughters can be looked upon as individual believers, born from above, all glorious within. Theirs is an inherent beauty and holiness, and not merely an outward professed relationship with the King. What joy will be theirs when together they are brought into the palace of the King whose worship of Him shall be eternal!

RAHAB CUT IN PIECES
Psalm 89:10

Rahab was not only the name of an actual female character (see RAHAB), but was also a poetical name for Egypt, conveying the idea of haughty and inflated arrogance. "Rahab sitting still'" was a political caricature, but she was cut in pieces (Psalm 87: 4). Rahab was most likely a Coptic name for a large sea or river monster, symbolic of Egypt (see Job 9:13, 26, 27), which God conquered and crushed (Isaiah 30:1-7).

DAUGHTERS AS CORNER STONES
Psalm 144:12

What a beautiful simile this is of the daughters of those happy parents whose God is the Lord! (Psalm 144:15). The phrase "corner stones" only occurs once again in the Old Testament, namely, in Zechariah 9:15, where it is used of the corners of the altar. Hewn and polished (Isaiah 51:1), these stones have the resemblance of a stately palace, an image suggestive of the wall of which Solomon speaks (Song of Solomon 8:9) and implying unassailable chastity and virtue. Such daughters are "women of strength or of a strong fortification." Matthew Henry's comment on the symbolism used here is suggestive —

> By daughters families are united and connected, to their mutual strength, as the parts of a building are by the cornerstones; and when they are graceful and beautiful both in body and mind they are then polished after the similitude of a nice structure. When we see our daughters well-established and stayed with wsidom and discretion — when we see them by faith united to Christ — when we see them purified and consecrated to God as living temples, we think ourselves happy in them.

In these over-sexed days, when so many girls are growing up with warped morals, how grateful godly parents are when they see their daughters as "daughters of the King," whose inner beauty He greatly desires.

MOTHERS LIKE MERCHANT SHIPS
Proverbs 31:14

Because of his prolific practice of polygamy, King Solomon knew more about women than any other man of his time. He certainly had ample opportunity to study them from every angle even though they resulted in his loss of the smile and favor of God. This may be one reason why he had much to say about women, especially in Proverbs in which the advice about women that he gave, but did not follow, is prominent. In Chapter Five, under "The Ideal Among Bible Women," we have summarized what Solomon wrote about their vices and virtues in this "book of wisdom." At this point we draw attention to one of the many ways by which he symbolizes the work and worth of a virtuous woman—"She is like the merchants' ships; she bringeth her food from afar" — which metaphor implies that she is ever on the lookout for opportunities of buying cheaply at a distance from home, instead of paying a larger price on the spot. This striking simile of "the

merchant ship" describes the mother "whose price is above rubies," and was analyzed in this sevenfold way by Dr. Fred John Meldau in a "Mother's Day" article in his commendable *Christian Victory* magazine.

1. Merchant Ships Must Have a Pilot — A true Christian mother has Jesus Christ as the Pilot of her heart and home.
2. Merchant Ships Are Guided by a Compass and the North Star — True Christian mothers guide their lives and homes by the Word of God.
3. Merchant Ships Bring Precious Cargo From Distant Lands — True mothers transfer the blessings of heaven to the lives around them.
4. Merchant Ships Endure Storms at Sea — True mothers have divine protection when moral and spiritual storms threaten the welfare of her children.
5. Merchant Ships Are Ever Active, and Well-Stocked for Long Journeys — True mothers are always on duty to cheer and comfort, exhort and encourage.
6. Merchant Ships Head for a Harbour to Unload Their Cargo — True mothers seek to bring those around them into the harbour of safety and security in Christ. They want their children to be prepared for the high seas of life.
7. Merchant Ships Keep Nothing for Themselves. What they carry is for others. Reaching their destination, their goods are unloaded for the benefit of others — True mothers are unselfish and sacrificial, whose lives are spent for the enrichment of others, and who never fail to deliver the best of goods to those around them. Home, is ever a "sweet home" to its inmates when amid all harassing circumstances, when its queen is a woman after God's own heart.

> There are in this loud stunning tide
> Of human care and crime,
> With whom the melodies abide
> Of the everlasting chime.
> Who carry music in their heart
> Through dusky lane and wrangling mart,
> Plying their daily task with busier feet
> Because their secret souls a holy strain repeat.

May God grant us more homes where mothers drink daily of the well of spiritual water, and who, by their devotion to Him bring a serenity into the home safeguarding it thereby from breakdown amid the heat and strain of modern life!

FEMALES AS SNARES AND NETS
Ecclesiastes 7:26

Solomon experienced that none of his sinful follies had been so ruinous as snares in seducing him from God as idolatrous women (I Kings 11:3, 4; Proverbs 5:3, 4; 22:14). He knew that "God's favor is better than life," and that the women who had enticed him from God were "more bitter than death." Solomon used "snares" to describe the trapping of birds, and of those who lay siege to a city (Ecclesiastes 9:12, 14). As for the "nets" which ungodly women employ to catch their fish, the same describe the fisherman's craft (Ezekiel 26:5; Habakkuk 1:15). "Bands" represent a fettered condition (Judges 15:14). This disparaging estimate of the female sex Solomon cites, and the condition of life in countries where polygamy is practiced. Evidently with all the women in his harem, the king could not find a good one among them. He yet recognized the wholesome influence of a woman whose life was lived unto God and not unto the lusts of men (Proverbs 18:22; 19:14; 31:10).

THE SHULAMITE
Song of Solomon

Although Solomon composed 1,005 songs (I Kings 4:32), the one before us from his gifted pen was in a class by itself, which he named, "The Song of Songs," meaning a very excellent song, or the most surpassing of his Songs. Because of the sexual atmosphere of this song, or poem, there have been those writers who have protested against its inclusion in Holy Writ, not only because of its love content, but also because it is destitute of any declared divine name or truth. Solomon's "Song" is not simply an oriental love poem, full of exquisite beauty and charm, set amid beautiful pastoral scenes. It is also the portrayal of a lovely yet lowly maiden from her northern home who could not be swayed by the wealth and splendor of a gorgeous court life. She loved her beloved for what he was, not had, and gave him all her love, and was adverse to his sharing his love with any other woman.

Immersed in polygamy as Solomon was, and which in his heart, he knew to be against God's law, it may be that he wrote this Song as a protest against an almost universal practice, and as a portrayal of the purity and constancy of a pure woman's love and of the ideal relationship God ordained for a man and a woman. Today,

human society is saturated, to its detriment, with lower ideals of free love, loose practices and easy divorces. The attractive Shulamite impressed upon the ladies (?) of the court her love and loyalty to the one man who had wooed and won her heart. That she triumphed can be gathered from her confident confession, "I am my beloved's, and his desire is towards me," and many waters could not quench such singular love. Spiritual minds all down the ages have seen in this remarkable Song a symbol of the new union and communion existing between Christ and His true church — His Bride.

CARELESS WOMEN
Isaiah 32:9-20

It would seem as if the prophet is here describing the sinful and selfish indulgences of the harem, somewhat unaffected by the reformation under King Hezekiah. "Women at ease," "careless daughters" were exhorted to repent before desolation overtook the country. They must cast away their sloth and careless living, strip themselves of their costly finery and clothe themselves in sackcloth — the outward symbol of inner repentance (Jonah 3:3-5). In the unabated luxury of these easy-living women of Jerusalem, Isaiah saw the precursor of the riches the city would be stripped of when the palaces would be forsaken as the result of divine judgment. One ancient writer understood by the careless women who cared little about the political signs of the times, the cities and villages of Judea (Ezekiel 16; Amos 6). In our affluent society, people have more leisure than ever. At ease and careless, they kill so many precious hours that could be used for the service of God in a world of sin and need. Alas, too many professing Christians are at ease in Zion and live carelessly! (Isaiah 47:8).

THE LADY OF KINGDOMS
Isaiah 47:1-15

Here is an instance of a nation being personified as a woman. "The virgin daughter of Babylon," "Daughter of the Chaldeans," "The Lady of Kingdoms," "A Lady for ever," all describe Babylon itself, unconquered for so long but about to be dethroned and made to sit in the dust as a menial slave. Stripped of its boasted possessions, Babylon would be as a widow bereft of husband and children, experiencing the full bitterness of widowhood. When Isaiah depicted Babylon as "a lady for ever," he caricatured Babylon with all its pride and snobbishness and self-importance. But pride of possession became Babylon's shame and ruin. Mackintosh Mackay, dealing with the denunciation of Isaiah, says that there are three types of woman's pride Babylon manifested — Pride of Rank, Pride of Wealth, Pride of Intellect — and gives us these three Bible illustrations of them —

Michal — the wife of David, who loved *pride of rank.*

Salome — the mother of Zebedee's children, who represents *pride of wealth.*

Miriam — the sister of Moses, who typifies *pride of intellect.*

Babylon was mistress of the world (Isaiah 13:19), "a lady of the kingdoms," puffed up with pride of rank, wealth and intellect, but her utter humiliation was depicted and was experienced when her king was slain and she sat as a widow and childless because its inhabitants were to be carried away as captives (Isaiah 23:4; 54:1-5). Judgment overtook the lady of the kingdoms suddenly, "in a moment." This was realized when in a single night Babylon was taken, unexpectedly, by Cyrus, the heathen king, whom God called His servant.

WOMAN WHO FORGETS HER CHILD
Isaiah 49:13-16

Describing the preservation and restoration of Israel, God reminded His people that even in those dark days when it seemed as if He had been indifferent regarding their trials, that they were ever before Him, graven upon the palms of His hands. Although it is unthinkable that any mother could act in such an unnatural, cruel way toward a child of her womb and forget him, yet the fact remains that some mothers have this feeling toward unwanted children. But God assured Israel — and our own hearts — that His own are precious in His sight and are ever remembered by Him. Too often He is the One who is forgotten. In this same chapter, when Isaiah comes to

predict judgment upon the foes of His never-forgotten children, he asserts that God will make "kings their nursing fathers and their *queens* their nursing mothers" (49:23).

Can a woman's tender care
Cease towards the child she bare?
Yes, she may forgetful be
Yet will I remember thee.

MOTHERS WHO COMFORT
Isaiah 66:13

Because God created both man and woman, father and mother, He combines in His own nature the highest and noblest attributes or virtues of the male and female part of His creation. It is thus that He manifests a fatherly pity toward His children (Psalm 103:13), and in the tender simile before us, the comfort of a mother for her dear ones. "Like as a mother comforteth her children." How does a mother exhibit her comfort when her child is in trouble or pain? Is it not by her love, sympathy, consoling words, and willingness to go to the limit in helping her needy offspring? What consolation the loving heart and warm breast of a good mother affords her troubled child! As God is the God of *all* comfort, the Source of all effective consolation, there is no comfort comparable to that which He offers His grief-stricken children (II Corinthians 1:3-7).

QUEEN OF HEAVEN
Jeremiah 7:18; 44:17-19

Attention has been drawn to this heathen goddess (see ASHERAH). We pause here to show how Assyrian cult practices invaded God's own precincts and by Jeremiah's time became a flood. Even within the temple area the worship of heavenly bodies — sun, moon, planets and constellations—had been established. Ishtar, the planet Venus, appeared as the queen of heaven, who as morning star was goddess of war and as evening star was goddess of love and harlotry. This supposed queen was worshiped on the housetops of the city, and the whole family in every household was employed in the ritual of her worship—children would gather fuel, fathers would kindle the fires, and the women would knead the dough and make cakes to her honor. How deeply rooted this system of false worship was can be gathered from what the exiled Judeans in Egypt said to the prophet: "When we worshiped the queen of heaven we were prosperous, and when we turned to Jehovah he destroyed our nation, henceforth the good old queen for us!" How explicit is the second commandment, "Thou shalt have no other gods before me"! (Exodus 20:4, 5).

> Is there a thing beneath the sun
>   That strives with Thee my heart to share?
> Ah, tear it thence and reign alone,
>   The Lord of every motion there:
> Then shall my heart from earth be free,
> When it hath found repose in Thee.

WOMEN THAT SEW PILLOWS
Ezekiel 13:17, 18

The prophet was commanded to expose and testify against the women of his nation who were false prophetesses who made cushions to recline on assuming, thereby, the semblance of perfect serenity as they foretold to the people consulting them, their pretended inspired utterances. The pillows and magic wrist bands they made and sold were supposed to give the users a sense of security. These women who prophesied out of their own mouths and deceived people by the charms they fashioned and traded with, were threatened with deserved judgment. Akin to this supposed transference of protection and peace by means of handkerchiefs is the deceptive practice by some religious healers in their prayed-over and offered for sale, linen cloths. What days of religious deception these are!

CORRUPTED DAUGHTER OF WOMEN
Daniel 11:17

The language Daniel uses here, and also in a previous passage, in which he speaks of the king's daughter (11:6), must be taken in a symbolic and general sense. While efforts have been made to identify "the daughter" as a historical female, the context in both cases seem to suggest that by "her" the southern kingdom is meant. Does not God liken the city of Zion unto a daughter (Jeremiah 6:2)? (See NAMELESS WOMEN.)

WOMAN AND HER MEAL
Matthew 13:33; Luke 13:21

For a full treatment of this parable of the housewife using her leaven and meal in baking, as well as an exposition of the symbolism of all Bible parables, the reader is referred to the author's work on *All the Parables of the Bible*. Briefly stated, the Parable of the Leaven represents degeneracy in power, a breaking in upon divinely ordered fellowship, and the corrupting influence of apostasy. Many women, like Mary Baker Eddy, founderess of Christian Science, were guilty of mixing leaven, which in the Bible symbolizes evil, with the meal.

WOMAN WITH SEVEN HUSBANDS
Matthew 22:25-32; Luke 20:27-38

The Sadducees, who consisted largely of the upper class of the Priesthood (Acts 5:17), were dead set against the doctrine of resurrection, arguing that it was not mentioned in the law — their only rule of faith. When they stated their case to Jesus it is most improbable that they knew of an actual female who had buried seven husbands, but thought up such an absurd illustration to press home their point. "Stress is laid on the childlessness of the woman in all seven marriages," comments Ellicott, "in order to guard against the possible answer that she would be counted in the resurrection as the wife of him to whom she had borne issue."

In His stern reproof of these rejectors of the Resurrection our Lord exposed the cause of their error. First, they had an imperfect knowledge of the Old Testament Scriptures in which they professed to believe. They were blind to its advocacy of the future state. Second, they had an imperfect conception of divine attributes, and so were ignorant of the limit of God's power before which a thousand difficulties disappear (Mark 12:24). Marriage was ordained to perpetuate the human family on earth, but in heaven this ordinance ceases and the redeemed are like unto angels in respect of the immortality of their nature. They are called "the children of God," not only because of their character but also because of their nature, seeing that they share the Father's immortality (I Timothy

6:16). As "the children of the resurrection" theirs is an undecaying existence (Romans 8:21-23).

WOMEN AT THE MILL
Matthew 24:41

In this solemn message of His Second Coming in glory and judgment, our Lord not only describes the diversity of character existing in the midst of the closest relationship of life, but also the inevitable separation experienced when He returns. Using a scene He had often witnessed of two women engaged in the lowest form of female labor at that time, Jesus enforces His warning of separation based on character. Here were two poor peasant women grinding corn with their small hand-mill with its upper and lower stones. Week after week, year after year, these two females continued their monotonous routine of hard and irksome labor. They looked alike and worked alike but what opposite characters they were. One saw nothing but a grindstone, while the other had an inner hope enabling her to see beyond her treadmill existence to the glory beyond. Hers was a noble soul, and by grace she saw the mill transfigured as she sought to do her menial task as unto the Lord. When He returns, the woman whose drudgery imprisoned her, and made her insensible to eternal things is left behind to judgment, but the other woman who, although she endured the same prison-like experience yet could "soar like a bird into the blue of heaven's thoughts," was taken to be with the Lord forever. Relationship to Christ is not only a great determining factor of human life, it is also the guarantee of translation into His presence at His return.

THE TEN VIRGINS
Matthew 25:1-7

Introducing his chapter on this portion, Alexander Whyte says, "Everything that our Lord saw on the earth immediately made Him think of the kingdom of heaven." He had known of an actual marriage to which prepared bridesmaids were ready to participate on such a joyous occasion, and other bridesmaids who, although invited, failed to join in the marriage because of their thoughtless neglect, and used such an incident to typify what will happen when He returns. With this parable, as with all others, we must try not to spiritualize every detail given, but discover the true key of the parable and be satisfied with it. Broadly speaking, this Parable of the Ten Virgins teaches the necessity of readiness for the coming of Christ as the Bridegroom, and also the *inclusion* and *exclusion* that glad hour will manifest. (See page 237, *All the Parables of the Bible*.) What remorse will be for those who find a shut door and hear the dread word, "Ye cannot enter now!"

SPIRITUAL MOTHERHOOD
Matthew 12:46-50; Mark 3:31-35; Luke 8:19-21

Our Lord's natural mother and brothers, concerned about the antagonism He was facing and of the efforts to take His life, came to advise Him to control and check His public ministry. In His somewhat stern reply, Jesus, who always acknowledged the duties of natural relationships, revealed that spiritual relationship supersedes them; that devotion to God and the fulfillment of His will comes before the wishes of those nearest to Him. All who know and obey the will of God are bound by spiritual ties to Jesus — who delighted to do that will — as His brothers, sisters and mother. These are the members of a family transcending and surviving an earthly family and represent the indissoluble bond of union between Christ and those related to Him by grace.

WOMAN WHO LOST HER SILVER COIN
Luke 15:8-10

The key to the three incomparable parables Jesus tells in this chapter is to be found hanging on the door: "This man receiveth sinners, and eateth with them" (15:2). While the characters He portrayed are representative as well as figurative, He doubtless recalled, as He told these parables, actual cases He came to know of as He lived out His life for thirty years in His Nazareth home. Many a time He had seen a tired yet happy shepherd returning from his search, carrying the lost sheep on his shoulder. Perhaps He remembered the day His own poor mother had lost a precious silver piece in the house, and how relieved she was to recover it. Then there was that fast, gay young fellow who wanted to see life, and whose prodigal ways were well-known in the town. Thus, from actual life, Jesus took these three figures and clothed them in appealing parabolic form.

Common to each parable is the thought of something or someone lost but whose recovery brought much rejoicing. How the women who were among our Lord's listeners must have appreciated this parable of one of their sex who, having to live frugally and eke out her housekeeping money, was so concerned about finding the lost coin! They would also understand her emotions when discovering the piece of silver she called in her friends to rejoice with her; and likewise understand our Lord's application of the story that He had every right to ask us to rejoice with Him and with the angels over lost souls repenting of their sin and being reconciled to God.

Unlike the shepherd and the prodigal, what the woman lost, was lost at home. Are there not many, living in Christian homes, or who seek to worship and serve in a Christian church who are lost? Those nearest to us have hearts destitute of grace. They may not be as conspicuously sinful and degraded as the prodigal son, yet they are just as lost and need to be recovered by the same Saviour who came to seek and to save the lost. Further, the woman found her coin, and how God is pleased to use consecrated women for the rescue of those around them who are perishing in their sin.

IMPORTUNATE WIDOW
Luke 18:1-8

In this parable in which Jesus teaches us that we ought always to pray and not give up, He vividly portrays a determined widow who brought an ungodly and unjust judge to his senses. The three figures Jesus sketches so admirably are the Importunate Widow, the Unjust Judge, the Divine and Righteous Judge. The object of the parable was to teach patience and perseverance in prayer. There may come occasions when it seems as if God disregards our petitions. We pray, and pray, but the heavens seem as brass. But we must pray *always*, that

is, continually, just as the widow did not give up asking. "Ask, and ye shall receive." Ask is in the continuous tense, "keep on asking." We must pray always with all prayer and supplication in the Spirit (Ephesians 6:18). Further, we are "not to faint." Sometimes delay produces discouragement. If prayer is not answered we have the tendency to lose heart, and hope sinks. But all prayer which the Spirit inspires must be answered in the Lord's own way and time. He is not like the reluctant judge, unwilling to help the widow, but He is ever ready to hear and answer our petitions if they are in accordance with His will (I John 5:14, 15).

DAUGHTER OF SION
John 12:15; Matthew 21:5

Here our Lord uses "daughter" in a representative sense, and quoted from memory the prophecy of Zechariah, "Rejoice greatly, O daughter of Zion; shout, O daughter of Jerusalem" (9:9). Daughter implies parents who brought her into being, and surrounded her with loving care and provision. God brought Jerusalem and her inhabitants into being, and blessed them with His favor, and raised them up a king, even His own Son, who will yet exercise a wider dominion than David or Solomon had (Zechariah 9:10). With Jerusalem as His seat of government, He will reign, "where'er the sun doth its successive journeys run."

WOMAN IN TRAVAIL
John 16:20, 21

The figure of a woman in birth pangs is frequently used in the Bible to express divine truth (Isaiah 23:4; 54:1; 66:7, 8; Galatians 4:19, 27; Revelation 12:2, etc.). In our Lord's use of this delicate simile, He explains that the sorrow of the disciples over His departure from them would result in the birth pangs of joy. For as with a mother, the joy of maternity swallows up the pangs of childbirth. The pangs cease, but the joy continues. She forgets the one in the fullness of the other. The cross was at hand with its travail pangs, both for the Saviour and His disciples, but they would pass away and fullness of joy would come in the realization of the abiding presence of their

Lord. Anguish over His being taken from them would only be temporary. When risen from the dead, their joy of His constant nearness would know no bounds. Many mystical expositors have interpreted our Lord's use of the woman in travail as signifying His death as the birth pang of a perfect humanity. Paul's use of the illustration indicates his heart pang for the sanctification of those Galatian believers (Galatians 4:19).

UNBELIEVING WIFE
I Corinthians 7:10-14

Among his various admonitions to the married, Paul has explicit instructions as to the matter of the unbelieving wives of Christian husbands, and vice versa. How is the unbelieving, non-Christian wife sanctified by her Christian husband? The sanctification or holiness Paul speaks of here is not that inward sanctification springing from the action of the Holy Spirit in the individual heart of the believer, but the consecration which arises from being in the body of Christ — the true church (Romans 11:6). Jamieson explains Paul's considered advice to imply that —

Those inseparably connected with the people of God are *hallowed* thereby, so that the latter may retain the connection without impairing their own sanctity (I Timothy 4:5); nay, rather imparting to the former externally some degree of their own hallowed character, and so preparing the way for the unbeliever becoming at last sanctified inwardly by faith.

DIANA OF THE EPHESIANS
Acts 19:24-41

This heathen goddess is not merely referred to as "great" because of the praise and admiration she received. The same was a standing epithet, a proper name, distinguishing her from other inferior deities bearing the same name of Diana or Artemis. The great goddess Diana resembled the attributes of Ashtoreth (which see). She symbolized the generative and nutritive powers of nature, and so was represented with many breasts. Her original temple was founded 580 B.C., and burned by Erostratus in 356 B.C. The second temple, built in the reign of Alexander the Great in Ephesus, the capital of Asia, became a renowned

center of the worship of Diana and was the idol "whom all Asia and the world worshipped." A lucrative trade was developed by the silversmiths in silver replicas of Diana. As the result of Paul's powerful ministry in Ephesus, not only were curious arts and books of divination burned, but the silver shrine of Diana trade also received its death blow. Through the intervention of the town clerk of Ephesus, Paul was saved from rough handling by the enraged silversmiths.

WOMEN SILENT IN CHURCHES
I Corinthians 14:33-35

There are differing and confusing interpretations of Paul's rules regulating the exercise of spiritual gifts. What the Apostle emphasized was that as God is the God of peace, and not of confusion, order must reign in the church (I Corinthians 11:1-22). Regarding the women keeping silence in churches, their ministry in public would be an act of independence, as if they were not subject to their husbands (I Corinthians 11:2-6; Ephesians 5:21-26; I Timothy 2:11, 12; Titus 2:5; I Peter 3:1). Wives were subject or "under obedience" to their husbands, and it was to them they must look for knowledge. They might have argued that if they did not understand some spoken message why could they not ask a question publicly so as to learn. Paul said "No! If you want information, ask not in public, addressing your questions to any enlightened brother, but ask their own particular husbands at home." What must not be forgotten about the imposition of female silence in the church is that the whole context is taken up with speaking and prophesying in tongues, and of questions being asked to the interpretation of same. The church owes a great deal to the effective public ministry of consecrated women.

WOMEN PROFESSING GODLINESS
I Timothy 2:9-15

Professed godliness had to be practiced godliness. Inner belief must express itself in outward behavior. When attending the church, the women, as worshipers, had to be "adorned with neatness of apparel and modesty of demeanour, and the holy reputation of kind deeds." They had to avoid anything that would attract attention, such as showy ornaments or conspicuous dress or an unusual hair-do. As devout Christian women, they had to practice sobriety and shy away from anything unbecoming about their apparel which would distract the thoughts of the assembled worshipers. Their dress and demeanor had to be in the Spirit. In this modern age when in our affluent society we seem to be fashion-crazy, we certainly have need to think anew about this question of seemly, quiet apparel, in our gatherings for divine worship.

IDLE WOMEN
I Timothy 5:11-13

Dealing with dangers and faults to be guarded against in the church, Paul has some pertinent things to say about young widows who after their grief become restive, and lose their love for Him who promised to be as a Husband to the widow, and expose themselves to God's corrective judgment for casting off their vows to Him.

> As they go about from house to house they learn to be idlers, and not only idlers but gossips and busybodies, saying what they should not say *and* talking of things they should not mention (*Amplified Bible*).

Instead of using their widowhood for the highest purpose, and as "widows indeed" visiting needy homes, with their object of consoling the sorrowful and instructing those who desire a fuller knowledge of the truth, these backsliding young widows wasted their precious hours in indulging in frivolous and harmful conversation. Paul did not want these widows to withdraw from public service and live an ascetic life. Rather than waste their time and influence wandering from house to house, it would be better for them to remarry and have a home life glorifying to Christ. Remarriage is recommended as an antidote to idleness and to other evils (I Timothy 5:11-13).

SILLY WOMEN
II Timothy 3:6

In his exposure of the evil purposes of false teachers, Paul speaks of the stealthy way they worm their way into homes where weak women with consciences burdened with sin, are a ready prey to those who promise ease of conscience if they will but follow their erroneous teachings. These hypocritical professors of the Christian faith must have been numerous in the Apostle's day and renowned for the power they acquired over some of the women in the church at Ephesus. As these women lived in a state of comparative exclusion, fraud and deceit were necessary for the false teachers to enter their apartments. The term Paul used to describe these women whose good home life was often disrupted by the crafty teachers is one expressing contempt. "Silly" has come to mean lacking in sense, stupid, weakness of mind. It was employed contemptuously by the Apostle to describe the spiritual immaturity of those women who in name were Christians, but who were impulsive and emotional, and lacking depth of character, became an easy prey to the lying doctrines and the false peace offered by those who had a form of godliness but who were destitute of its power. Christian women today have need to constantly pray for spiritual intuition enabling them to turn immediately from voices alien to the clearly revealed Word of truth.

AGED AND YOUNG WOMEN
Titus 2:3-5

Among the charges to both sexes which Paul sent to Titus for him to deliver to the church at Crete, were those for aged women and the younger women in the Christian community there. The aged women received both positive and negative exhortations. Positively, their behavior had to be holy, and they had to be teachers of good things among young women. Negatively, they were not to be false accusers, and not given to much wine. Those elderly women of the flock, as with the aged men, must understand their grave responsibility and live as unto Christ. The word for "behavior" included an outward deportment arising from an internal relationship to a thrice holy God. In dress, appearance, conversation and manner, those aged women were urged to manifest the inner beauty of Jesus. In all things they had to foster a sacred demeanor. In their old age they must not be guilty of slander and backbiting, or of interference, but be examples to their younger sisters in the faith of truth, faith, sobriety and love.

As spiritual instructresses they had to teach the young women in the following ways —

To be sober, that meant, to practice self-discipline and control.

To love their husbands, and *love their children.* As women of Christ their first duty was to make their home life beautiful by the sacrificial love resulting in the forgetfulness of self.

To be discreet. Prudence and discretion were the jewels they should wear. What treasured virtues they are!

To be chaste. Although young, they must be modest, immaculate, pure from carnality.

To be keepers at home, or workers at home. They must not be gadabouts, but look upon their home duties, cares and sacrifices as God's will for their lives.

To be good. Because the God whom they served is good, then, like Him, they must be gracious, kind, considerate of others.

To be obedient to their husbands. Loving Christ their Master, they must recognize the law of subordination to the rightful head of the family. If all of these exhortations were carried out then the word of God would not be blasphemed. There would be nothing about their personal and home life to contradict their testimony, or bring shame upon the name of Christ. By their good life and corresponding good deeds they would so shine in their home as to bring glory to the Father in heaven whom they professed to serve. Never forgetting they were Christians, their lives would reflect the beauty of the Lord.

We can couple with Paul's charges to Titus what Peter had to say about the true marks of *holy women* who trust in God (I Peter 3:1-7). Along with decorum, as against personal adornment, we have a further reference to the subjection of wives to their husbands. As to this obedience, Leighton says —

The Christian wife hath love to God though her husband be not so comely, or wise, or any way so amiable, as many other, yet because

he is her *own husband,* and because of the Lord's command in the general, and His providence in the particular disposal of His own, therefore she loves and obeys.

ELECT LADY

THE WOMAN WHO WAS AN ELECT LADY
II John 1-13

The reality and names of the two women John mentions in his brief epistle — "The elect lady" (verse 1), and "thy elect sister" (verse 13), have given rise to endless discussion. Did he write to a particular, prominent woman in the local church or was his precious letter addressed to the church itself that John represented as a lady? As the Bible was written by plain men for plain people, that they might understand it in the most common-sense way, the explicit language John uses implies that the woman he addressed was prominent in the vicinity of Ephesus, and being of a most worthy Christian character, she was worthy to receive an exhortatory epistle from him. We concur with the statement of Dean Farrar in his commentary —

I take the letter in its natural sense, as having been addressed to a Christian lady and her children. Some of the children the Apostle seems to have met in one of his visits of supervision of the churches of Asia. They may have been on a visit to some of their cousins in a neighbouring city.

There are several features of this Christian woman, who was well known, and well-loved in the local church.

She Was a Lady

This is by no means an unscriptural term. It occurs four times (Isaiah 47:5, 7; II John 1, 5), and the plural, "ladies" appears twice (Judges 5:29; Esther 1:18); and is a word implying a higher grade of a woman — one possessing more dignity than others. Ladies means "princesses." A bad woman is one having proprietary rights, rule or authority — the feminine correlative of "lord." This is why the Roman Catholic Church refers to the Virgin Mary as "Our Lady." In Britain, a lady is the wife of one who has received a title or honor from the Crown, or a woman of social distinction or position — the correlative of gentleman. The word John uses for "lady" is *kuria,* and as Bengel the commentator expresses it, "A title so lofty as *kuria* was rarely used even to queens." The margin of the RV turns *Kuria* into a proper name, "Kyria" or "Cyria," in use in John's day.

As to the explicit absence of the matron's real name, Ellicott observes that "it is not absurd to suppose that the dangers of the times, or family persecutions, may have made it advisable that both her name and that of the writer should be withheld."

She Was an Elect Lady

Paul uses "elect" in the same' way when he speaks of Rufus, "chosen in the Lord" (Romans 16:13. See I Peter 1:1, 2). Not only was the lady elect in the sense of being of excellent character, but also as being with her children and her sister elect or chosen of God according to His eternal purpose, to the inheritance, incorruptible and undefiled that fadeth not away. Probably this elect lady was a convert of John's ministry and through him had come to know what it was to repose by faith in the bosom of the Father, and in this epistle standing "as a tall, white, graceful monument, erected to her memory, John extols her for her devotion to the One in whom she was safe and secure."

She Was a Hospitable Lady

It is evident that she was well-known to the Apostle John, who most likely had been graciously entertained in her spacious home. As no husband is mentioned she was probably a rich widow with ample means to care for the saints of God who came her way. All around her, those who knew the truth (verse 1) shared John's expressed hope that he might have the joy of visiting the lady's home again to share with her the glorious truths he had discovered. It was because she was given to hospitality that John forewarned her about welcoming false teachers.

She Was an Exemplary Lady

Milton wrote of "Ladies whose bright eyes rain influence." The elect lady, bearing her divine commission in her looks, not only had a countenance radiating an inner peace as one in Christ, but also a sweet influence upon those around. Her children, following her faith, walked in the truth, and because of pious witness and their god-ly conversation, were praised by John for their walk in love, walk circumspectly and worthily of their vocation. The Apostle knew that the correct Christian walk and witness came as the result of early training in truth and in love. No wonder John warmly congratulated the godly mother for having children proving their adherence to the Word of God by their daily conduct. They not only believed the truth but also *walked* in it.

She Was a Privileged Lady

Further, this elect lady was highly privileged to have the veteran apostle, who called himself, "the elder" or "aged man" as her guide in spiritual matters, not only instructing her in the many facets of truth but also warning her against the nature and evil work of false prophets in sheep's clothing. Safeguarding her against the peril of these deceivers who were guilty of deception, both of heart and life, John did not mince his words. These commissaries of an anti-christ were not only guilty of intellectual errors, but also of leading people astray in conduct. Their wrong thinking resulted in wrong living, and thus their whole influence was anti-christian (I John 2:26).

Their manifest error was related to the fact and reality of Christ's Incarnation. They denied that Christ had come as God manifest in flesh — which truth is the heart of Christianity. Of all errors Satan is responsible for, this is the most destructive. The crucial test of the orthodoxy of any person is the place he or she gives to Jesus Christ in the economy of God. So John urged the lady and her children not to be led away but, to guard themselves in a twofold way. First, by taking care not to lose what they already possessed; second, by the shunning of error have the satisfaction of a full reward. Because of their stability and firmness in the truth there was the present reward of an inner peace passing all understanding, and beyond the witness on earth, the overcomer's reward (Revelation 2:7, 11, 17).

In somewhat harsh language for John, the Apostle of Love, to use, he told the lady that as a sincere Christian she must not stretch out the hand of fellowship to deceivers, or entertain them in her home. Their presence would be dangerous in the family circle (II Timothy 3:6). The Roman Church, regarding herself as the "lady," seized upon this passage about the exclusion of those notable for their evil doctrine and deeds, to pronounce their anathemas, excommunications, and cruel inquisitions. "Receive him not into your house" may sound unchristian, but as Ellicott puts it —

> These are no terms of ordinary politeness, which the Apostle does not forbid, but terms of close Christian intimacy and spiritual communion, the deliberate cultivation of personal acquaintance, fraternal intercourse. The highest sort of Christian brotherly love — love, that is, in its fulness and truth — can only find reciprocity in the same atmosphere of Christ, on the same basis, and in the same characteristics (II Corinthians 6:16).

To accommodate those who deprave the doctrine of Christ injures our own orthodox witness. To bid them Godspeed is to be a partaker of their corrupt deeds. Thus, John warns the matron that the only safeguard against terror is the ever-expanding knowledge of the truth, and obedience to it. The ground of the Apostle's love for the lady and her family was that they cleave to the truth. "Truth" occurs 5 times; "Commandment," 4 times; and "Doctrine," three, and so making the whole truth of God as our home (verse 9) "abideth in the doctrine" is the adequate provision against all error.

We have every confidence that the elect lady valued the spiritual advice of her aged friend and teacher and followed his practical counsel of keeping close to Christ by keeping close to His truth. How appropriate and necessary is the apostolic exhortation for the saints in our own apostate age! Alone on the Patmos isle, John, the old man, thinks of his dear friend at Ephesus, and thinks of all the blessed seasons of fellowship he had had in her lovely Christian home, and taking his pen sent the elect lady an expression so full of tenderness: "I trust to come unto you, and speak face to face, that our joy may be full." John's heart was full of things to write about, but he hopes for a time of unlimited conversation, and to experience the deep satisfaction of the interchange of spiritual thoughts and aspirations and experiences, writing materials were not able to supply. Living near the elect lady's sister, John would tell her of his letter, and so includes her family's best wishes, just as we express our love and greetings when we send a letter to a loved one away from us. Thus, "in transmitting this familiar message, John had a most instructive finish to what is throughout a beautiful picture."

WOMEN IN THE APOCALYPSE

The last book of the Bible, being highly symbolic, perplexes a good many people. When they reach the Revelation in their Bible reading they skip it, and go back to other portions which they can more readily understand. But this should not be our attitude for the Book of Revelation is not wrapped in mystery but is a *Revelation* as it declares itself to be. We thoroughly disagree with Edith Deen in her most excellent work, *All the Women of the Bible*, that "the key has been lost to its apocalyptic symbolism." Surely the opening verse is explicit enough —

> The Revelation of Jesus, which God gave unto him, to shew unto his servants things which must shortly come to pass; and he sent and signified (or sign-ified) it by his angel unto his servant John.

As the book, then, is the unveiling of Jesus Christ in respect to:

Time — past, present and future (1:4);

Relationship—to the churches (1:9–3:22), to tribulation (4–19), to the kingdom 20–22);

Offices—High Priest (8:3-6), Bridegroom (19:7-9), King-Judge (20:1-15) —

He is the key or central theme of this dramatic book in which all events move toward a sublime consummation, "The world kingdom of our Lord and His Christ has come."

We recognize how varied symbols crowd the pages of this book, which is a prophecy (1:3). But a simple guide to help us in an understanding of Revelation is the fact that whatever symbol you come across is explained for you in some other part of the Bible — which is its own interpreter. Thus, all you need is a good, serviceable Bible Concordance so that when you come to a symbol you can trace its usage throughout Scripture and thereby discover what truth the symbol or metaphor clothes. Gerhardt says that John, the writer, clothed his thoughts "in reverential and only suitable drapery of ancient sacred language and symbolism, in the conviction that the reader would penetrate the veil and reach the sense." Concluding this section of our study let us consider the symbolic and representative women in the book which was not written without tears, and without tears cannot be fully understood.

JEZEBEL
Revelation 2:20-23

As we have already dealt with this woman in the portion dealing with named women of the Bible (see JEZEBEL 2), all we need to do at this point is to briefly remind the reader of the way this sinister female is dealt with. Some writers adopt the reading, "thy wife Jezebel" and so regard her as an actual person, a false prophetess who sought to seduce the saints in the church in Thyatira. Other commentators regard the name Jezebel not as one belonging to an individual, but one representative of an apostate faction in the church. "It seems best to view the name as symbolical," says Ellicott, "always remembering that the Jezebel spirit of proud, self-constituted authority, vaunting claims of superior holiness, or higher knowledge, linked with a disregard of — and perhaps a proud contempt for — 'legalism,' and followed by open immorality, has again and again run riot in the churches of God."

In this longest of the letters to the seven churches, Christ utters a solemn warning to those who persistently indulge in spiritual harlotry. If they refuse to repent, then they must share the condemnation of Jezebel. How gracious the Lord is, even to the worst of evil-doers — "I gave her space to repent."

To those in Thyatira who had not been influenced by Jezebel and her fornications and demoniac depths (verse 24) there was promised a share in the rule of Christ (verse 26). Works based on love play a prominent part in this letter (2:19, 26). Deeds and depths belong to Satan (2:22, 24). The Morning Star is Christ and all overcomers are fully to possess Him. What a future awaits all those who shun Jezebel and her

evil ways and who have Christ in the heart as the Harbinger of the coming glorious day!

THE WOMAN CLOTHED WITH THE SUN
Revelation 12:1-17

Evidently there are those who have difficulty in identifying "the woman clothed with the sun." The Roman Catholic Church says it is the Virgin Mary. Christian Scientists make the woman out to be Mary Baker Eddy, founder of this false cult. There are conservative expositors who identify the sun-clothed woman as the church, the Mother of us all. But the woman, we hold, is Israel. It is true that both Israel and the church stand closely related to Christ — Israel as the mother, the church as the wife. It was Israel, however, who became the mother of the Messiah (Isaiah 9:6; Micah 5:2; Romans 9:5, etc.). A passage like Isaiah 54:1 is very expressive, "Sing, O barren, thou that didst not bear; break forth into singing, and cry aloud, thou that didst not travail with child: for more are the children of the desolate than the children of the married wife, saith the LORD."

Clothed With the Sun!

Here Israel is represented as the bearer of divine, supernatural light. She has supreme authority. Or the Sun can stand for Christ whom Israel will yet recognize as the Sun of Righteousness and who will surround her with glory.

The Moon Under Her Feet!

As the moon is subordinate to the sun and derives its light from the sun, all Israel's glory and influence are derived from the One who brought her into being. The moon shines at night and Israel is to give a light, a bright witness, amid the world's gathering darkness.

A Crown of Twelve Stars on Her Head

By the twelve stars we understand the twelve tribes of Israel. In Joseph's dream (Genesis 37:9) the future glory of these tribes is symbolized in the same way. Israel's future glory and rule, therefore, are here portrayed. She is yet to be invested with the splendor and fullness of governmental authority on earth. Twelve, as we know, is the governmental number.

She Travailed in Pain!

The metaphor of childbirth is common enough in Scripture (John 16:21; Galatians 4:19). With a passage like Isaiah 66:7 before us, we have difficulty in reconciling maternal anguish as applicable to Israel. "The travailing and pain refer to Israel's coming hour of trial," says Walter Scott. "But *before* the Great Tribulation the Messiah, the Man-Child, is born. The prophet Micah confirms this in a clear and unmistakable passage. After referring to the birth of the Messiah (5:2) he adds, 'Therefore will he give them up, until the time that she which travaileth hath brought forth; then the remnant of his brethren shall return unto the children of Israel' (verse 3). The travail of the woman is at least 2,000 years subsequent to the birth of the Messiah and refers to her sorrow in the coming Tribulation. Before she travailed, she brought forth; before her pain came she was delivered of a Man-Child."

It only remains to inquire: Why then is the travail of the woman put in juxtaposition to the birth of the Messiah?

First, notice that the present lengthened period of Israel's rejection, coming in as it does between the birth and the travail, is passed over in silence in the chapter before us; it is a parenthesis, the history of which is not given in prophecy but found elsewhere, of course.

Second, it shows the deep interest the Messiah takes in His people. He thought of the tribulation, and made certain a conditional provision as to lightening it many centuries ago (Matthew 24:15-28).

Third, at the time in which our chapter has its place, the nation is about to pass into its awful sorrow, and the object of going back in this history to the birth of Christ is to connect Him with them in it.

The travail, then, indicates Israel's sufferings during the Tribulation. At present the Jews are being persecuted, but still darker days are ahead for God's chosen people. The last half of the Tribulation is referred to as "the time of Jacob's trouble."

The Red Dragon (12:3, 4)

Another tableau follows upon the first and is inseparable from it. We now witness the remarkable sign of "a great, red dragon." Without doubt this is a presentation of Satan in his worst character. John expressly identified the devil as the dragon in 20:2. Both Pharaoh and Nebuchadnezzar are spoken of as great dragons because of their cruelty and haughty independence (Ezekiel 29:3, 6; Jeremiah 51:34). It may be that the Old Testament crocodile or leviathan is the reptile depicted. The term is used of Satan only, in the Revelation, and suggests the hideousness and horror of his rule (verse 9).

Red, being a blood color, indicates the devil's murderous nature, who has been a murderer from the beginning (John 8:44). Once the most beautiful of angelic beings, Satan is now and always will be the object of abhorrence.

As the ape of Christ, who, as the Conqueror, will wear many diadems, Satan is adorned with his crown of diadems. The seven crowned heads signify the cruel and despotic exercise of earthly power and authority, while the ten uncrowned horns stand for the future limits of the empire as distributed into ten kingdoms, and the rule of Satan is a ten-kingdom form. Satan delegates power and authority to the first beast who is similarly described in 13:1.

The tail, representing the most dangerous part of a dragon, is like a great comet in this monster (Daniel 8:10). As a lying prophet is likened unto a tail by Isaiah (9:15), Satan's malignant influence as a liar and deceiver is herewith described.

The terrible spectacle of the dragon standing before the woman waiting to devour her newborn child is easily interpreted. It was not the woman but *her seed* the monster wanted to destroy, just as Pharaoh tried to devour all the male children of Israel (Exodus 1:15-22).

The Man Child (12:5, 6)

The man child or "male child," a son, a male, as the original expresses it, surely represents Christ who was born to rule (Genesis 3:15; Psalm 2:9 with Revelation 12:5; Psalm 110:1, 5; Daniel 4:26). Yet there are teachers who see in the man child a group out of Israel. The 144,000, for example, are identified with Christ in a special way and because of their relation to persecution, may well be treated as the child here. But the following prophecy of universal rule nullifies such an interpretation.

It was the Virgin Mary who brought forth the promised man child (Galatians 4:4, 5), and whom Herod tried to kill while He was under two years of age. Born as a king, Christ came into the world having universal dominion which He will yet exercise (Psalm 8).

The iron rule of the nations will be broken by Him who comes to shepherd them with an iron rod. Here the world "rule" means to "tend as a shepherd," and in this role Christ will break up the consolidated powers of the earth gathered against Himself and His people. With irresistible might He will mete out judgment to guilty kings and peoples in the West (Revelation 19), and then deal with those of the North and East (Isaiah 10). Further, this ruling with a rod for long-continued obstinacy until submission results in obedience, reveals the nature of His reign. The revolt at the end of the Millennium reveals what forced submission characterized the peoples of the earth.

The Ascension of Christ is before us in "her child was caught up unto God, and to his throne" (Mark 16:19; Luke 24:50, 51; Acts 1:9; 7:56). Nothing is here said of the death of the man child, seeing that He is connected with Israel and the rule of all nations, both of which are dependent upon His birth and Ascension to His throne. And yet, in that shepherd-hand grasping the rod will be the marks of the nails. In passing, we discredit altogether the interpretation that we here have the rapture of those who are sufficiently holy when Jesus comes. Those who hold the "partial rapture" theory sometimes employ the last part of this fifth verse to enforce the erroneous doctrine of a selected rapture. All who are Christ's, irrespective of their state, will be caught up to meet the Lord. If unfit, they will suffer in respect to their reward.

Between verses 5 and 6 we have the entire stretch of history from Christ's Ascension to the Tribulation or the time of Jacob's trouble.

By the determined counsel and foreknowledge of God, a place of safety and sustenance is provided for the remnant. The rapid flight and journey of the persecuted woman is likewise aided by God. Between the interrupted statement of verse 6 and the resumption of it in verse 14 we have the episode of the war in heaven and the rejoicing consequent upon its success. The careful numbering of days, 1,260 in all, testifies to the Lord's tender interest in His afflicted people. This last half of Israel's week of prophetic sorrow will elicit constant care and provision on the Lord's part.

The wilderness, of course, is sometimes used as a condition destitute of natural resources, a place of isolation. In Ezekiel 20:35, 36, we find the wilderness used, not literally and locally, but spiritually, as a state of discipline and trial among the Gentile peoples.

MICHAEL AND HIS ANGELS (12:7-12)

After the complete picture of the first six verses given under the two "signs," we come to the climax of age-long antagonisms. The Book of Revelation is a book of wars, and here in the war in heaven we have one of the most dramatic battles. At last the prophetic word of Isaiah is about to be fulfilled. "And it shall come to pass in that day, that the LORD shall punish the host of the high ones that are on high, and the kings of the earth upon the earth" (24:21). The most significant of battles in all history is now to be staged. What a spectacle! Forces heavenly and hellish are to clash. In World War II we had the Allies and the Axis. Opposing ideologies are grouped together in this twofold way. Well, John represents the Allies — Michael and his angels; the foes — Satan and his angels! Of the issue there is no doubt. The declaration of final victory against Satan was given by Christ in Luke 10:18 and John 12:31. Surely such a hope should nerve us to soul-saving activity.

THE WOMAN AND HER SEED (12:13-17)

Fiercely persecuted, the woman is forced to flee (verses 6 and 14), and is wonderfully assisted in her flight. She receives "*the* two wings of *the* great eagle." We cannot agree with those who interpret these eagle wings as world powers of Babylon and Egypt

(Ezekiel 17:3, 7). The eagle symbolizes God's protection of His own. His past care and deliverance from impending danger are indicated in this way in Exodus 19:4 and Deuteronomy 32:11, 12: "Ye have seen what I did unto the Egyptians, and how I bare you on eagles' wings, and brought you unto myself." "As an eagle stirreth up her nest, fluttereth over her young, spreadeth abroad her wings, taketh them, beareth them on her wings; So the LORD alone did lead him, and there was no strange god with him."

Fleeing from "the face of the serpent" (verse 14) offers a strong contrast to earth and heaven fleeing from the face of Him sitting on the Great White Throne (20:11). The crafty nature of Satan is emphasized in the effort of the serpent to destroy the woman by a flood. Earth swallowing the flood may represent those friendly nations willing to befriend the Jew, neutralizing and circumventing Satan's wily method to energize other nations against the Jew. Such overruling providential frustrations will raise the ire of the dragon, causing him in his baffled rage to make war with the godly remnant in Palestine. Keeping the commandments of God and having the testimony of Jesus Christ always "excites the wrath" of the devil. "To make war" can imply every form of attack upon the saints, whether by persecution or war. Physical harm and evil of every kind of which the devil is capable is referred to under this technical expression (11:7; 16:14; 17:14; 19:19). But both the man child and God-fearing Jews are delivered from the murderous hate of the devil. What a chapter! No wonder Walter Scott concludes with these words: "In it are grouped perhaps the greatest events in this marvellous book. It is a chapter second to none in its range of subjects, and goes further back in its historical grasp than any other portion of the book. Who but God could have furnished such a connected grouping of events?"

THE MOTHER OF HARLOTS
Revelation 17:1-24

Chapters 17 through 20 are highly dramatic. In this section Christ, as the Conqueror, moves swiftly in the subjugation of all His foes. What fast moving action these chapters present! How majestic is the scene of the Omnipotent Lord taking unto Himself His power and reigning supreme! Once He rises to deal with all antagonistic elements, none can withstand His might. With a rod of iron, He breaks the strongest. Proud, arrogant rulers, both hellish and human, are dashed to pieces as a potter's vessel. Whether it be systems, cities, or citizens, everything and everyone contrary to His will and rule fall before His withering look and lash.

In this fascinating yet fearful portion we have the following sevenfold doom:

The Doom of Mystical Babylon —
Chapter 17
The Doom of Material Babylon —
Chapter 18–19:19
The Doom of the Beast — Chapter 19:20
The Doom of the False Prophet —
Chapter 19:20
The Doom of the Nations —
Chapter 19:21–20:9
The Doom of Satan — Chapter 20:1-3, 10
The Doom of the Lost—Chapter 20:11-15

An introductory word on the close relationship existing between chapters 17 and 18 is necessary, seeing that both deal with Babylon, withal from different angles. Scant notices of Babylon's destruction are given in 14:8 and 16:19. What we have in Chapters 17 to 19 fills in all the details on God's judgment upon a guilty system. It is essential to take all these passages together, and read them as one, since they synchronize.

In Chapter 17 we have:	In Chapter 18 we have:
Mystical Babylon	Material Babylon
A Corrupt System	A Doomed City
Judgment on Papacy	Judgment on Paganism
Apostate Christendom	Godless Commercialism
The Whore and Beast	God and Babylon
Religious Pretension	Worldly Pride
Delight of the kings of the earth over the drunken harlot, mystery Babylon.	Rulers of the earth will wail and lament over the destruction of actual Babylon.

Other opposites can be traced by comparing these two chapters.

The twofold development of the chapter before us is clearly evident:

The Great Whore Dominates the Beast (1-6)
The Beast Destroys the Great Whore (7-18)

I. THE GREAT WHORE DOMINATES THE BEAST (1-6)

As a woman and a city are both used as symbols of the church (I Corinthians 11:12; Revelation 21:9, 10), so both figures are before us in this descriptive portion of apostate Christendom. In verse 18 the woman is identified as the city: "And the woman which thou sawest is that great city, which reigneth over the kings of the earth."

The scarlet woman, one of the profound marvels of Scripture, is Satan's masterpiece of counterfeiting. What a travesty the mother of harlots is of the true church! The dream of some religious leaders, presently laboring for church unity, will be realized in the coming universal church controlled by the Papacy.

Believing as we do, that the chapter before us sets forth Romanism in its most powerful and pernicious form, the dominant force in apostate Christendom, let us seek to classify our material under convenient sections.

Her Domination

Pictured as "sitting," we note the woman's seat. She "sitteth upon many waters" (17:1); "I saw a woman sit upon a scarlet coloured beast" (verse 3); "Seven mountains, on which the woman sitteth" (verse 9). "Sitting upon many waters" receives the following exposition by John in verse 15: "And he saith unto me, "The waters which thou sawest, where the whore sitteth, are peoples, and multitudes, and nations, and tongues." The "many waters" therefore typify the vast multitudes of the human race over whom the woman had cast her spell. Ancient Babylon got its wealth by means of the Euphrates and its numerous canals for irrigation. And the Roman Church fattens on the nations she governs. "Sitting upon the waters" (Jeremiah 51:13), indicates that the great whore rules and dominates the nations religiously, just as the Beast does politically. Representing a vast religious system, the woman's following is a universal one. And that the Roman Catholic Church is on the road to world-wide supremacy is a fact that none can at present gainsay.

"Sitting upon the beast" means that the harlot sits astride the Beast. She not only exercises religious dominion over the multitudes, but is also able to manage and guide the Beast. All vassal kings and human rulers, especially within the revived Roman Empire, are under her sway. Civil and political power are subservient to her rule and supremacy. And such thorough and complete subjugation over the vast imperial and apostate power headed up in the Beast is already in the making. Two distinct ideas are represented by the woman and the Beast. We can express the opposites thus —

The woman personifies corruption of truth,
The Beast personifies open defiance of God;
The woman embodies all that is licentious,
The Beast embodies all that is cruel and ruthless.

Thus corruption and violence, which brought about the Flood (Genesis 6:11), are to reach their climax in the woman and the Beast. Seated on the back of the Beast, is a prophecy that the apostate church will be carried and supported by the nations, and will rule and reign with temporal power. As we shall see more fully when we come to the portion on "Romanism," as a religious and political dictator, Rome's influence will extend far and wide. Already Rome is working for that hour, when once more seated on the back of human government, she will seek to rule the earth.

"Seven mountains, on which the woman sitteth." This third aspect of the woman's posture is capable of a twofold interpretation, which "the mind which hath wisdom" will recognize.

First of all, the seven heads represent seven mountains or hills. Both Christian and pagan refer to literal Rome as the "seven-hilled city." It is this fact that identifies the city and the woman as Rome. "The woman which thou sawest is that great city" (verse 18). Rome alone was the ruling power in John's day. Therefore, the present tense "*hath* a kingdom" must signify Rome. Rome is fast becoming the seat and center of universal authority and influence, as is evidenced by the visit of the pope to the UNO, and by the fraternal meetings between the pope and the Archbishop of Canterbury which envisages a united church with the pope as its head.

In the next place, the seven mountains are the seven kings or successive forms of political government. Of seven Roman emperors, five "fell," which can mean death by violent means, before John's day. The five are listed as Julius Caesar, Tiberius, Caligula, Claudius and Nero. The sixth, who reigned as John wrote the Revelation, was blasphemous Domitian, who also was assassinated. He can be looked upon as the "one is." The other, who had not yet come in John's day, will be the seventh Roman head. The Beast will be the eighth, out of the seventh. While the Beast is distinctive in character and work, yet he continues the form of autocratic rule of the seventh head. And it is the woman who dominates this last sovereign expression of every anti-Christian movement and sect then in evidence, consolidated and controlled by Satan. The following contrasts might prove helpful:

The True Church	The Mother of Harlots
Chaste Virgin	Great Whore
Subject to Christ	Subject to Satan
Out of Heaven	Out of the Earth
God adorned (19:8)	Satan adorned (17:4)
Preserved by Christ	Destroyed by the Beast
Eternal glory ahead	Eternal ruin
True Bride	Counterfeit Church
Has heavenly calling	Covets earthly possessions
Christ's Masterpiece	Satan's masterpiece
Indwelt by Holy Spirit	Possessed by evil spirit
Mystery hid from ages	Mystery of Iniquity
Caught up in the air	Cast down to perdition
Exercises spiritual power	Seeks secular power
Exhibits glory of Christ	Glories in sensuous things
Comes out of the Cross	Bows before a Crucifix
Believes in direct access	Stresses human priesthood
A called-out body	Apostate Christendom

As "the great whore," Romanism represents a frightful system, hypocrisy and lust over the souls and bodies of men. It is also a term unfolding the licentious character of the apostate church in her last days.

"Mystery"

Such a word implies a spiritual fact hitherto hidden and incapable of discovery by mere reason, but now revealed. The union between Christ and His church is a mystery. Likewise the union between the apostate church and the world will be the mystery of iniquity.

"Babylon the Great"

This appellation of the woman suggests a widespread system of spiritual evil, which represents the culmination of all evils operating against the true church while it was on the earth. What we have before us in this seventeenth chapter is mystic Babylon. The next chapter presents us with commercial Babylon. In the seventeenth chapter the word "Babylon" is used for "Rome," while in the eighteenth chapter we have actual Babylon. And that there is nothing forced or unusual in such a transfer of names is evident from Chapter 11, verse 9, where Sodom and Egypt are given as equivalents for Jerusalem.

"The Mother of Harlots and Abominations of the Earth"

The harlot's name on her forehead is another sample of Satan's mimicry. Rome is the mother of harlotry and of the world's idolatries. The offspring of this mother of harlots will be numerous. Apostate Christendom will be the parent of all kinds of religions, idolatries and arts used by Satan to turn men from God. Under the figure of the mother of harlots we have religion at its worst and the source of all that is morally loathesome.

Her Fornication

Two phrases describe the abominable nature of "the great whore," namely "the wine of her fornication," and "the filthiness of her fornication" (verses 2, 4). Fornication is illicit intercourse, and spiritual fornication is tantamount to idolatry. "With their idols have they committed adultery" (Ezekiel 23:37).

Her Ornamentation

In the description John gives us of the luxurious attire of the harlot, Dr. A. T. Robertson says that the Apostle applies the finery of the temple prostitutes in Asia Minor. As the distinctive color of the woman is scarlet, it is not hard to identify the Roman Catholic Church whose official and distinguishing color is scarlet. Scarlet is everywhere in this scarlet-colored church — scarlet bands, scarlet cardinal hats, scarlet robes for pontiff and priests. Altogether Rome has five different articles of dress of scarlet colors.

Her Persecution

A bloody as well as a morally licentious system is indicated by the phrase, "I saw the woman drunken with the blood of the saints, and with the blood of the martyrs (or witnesses) of Jesus" (verse 6). What caused John to wonder was not the Beast's cruelty (13:7), but that the woman inspired such diabolical persecution. That papal Rome has far exceeded pagan Rome in bloodshed and the killing of saints is a fact that cannot be disputed. It was secular power in the hands of the Romish Church that devised the unspeakable, hellish cruelties of the Middle Ages.

II. THE BEAST DESTROYS THE GREAT WHORE (7-18)

The "I will show thee" now passes to "I will tell thee" (verses 1, 7). Explanation is now offered of the Revelation. John is given the divine interpretation of the mystery of the woman and of the Beast carrying her. The Apostle had wondered with the amazement of a horrible surprise. Now the earth is to wonder and admire outpoured judgment upon the woman and the Beast (verse 8).

A double mystery is revealed:

The Mystery of the Beast (7-14)
The Mystery of the Whore (15-18)

a travesty of the New Testament mystery "concerning Christ *and* the Church."

The Mystery of the Beast (7-14)

The woman and the Beast are treated separately, seeing they are distinct, although companions in wickedness and apostasy. With the woman we have ecclesiastical power. The Beast personifies civil power. Four phases of the Beast's history are explained to John. In four, brief, crisp sentences John learns of the course and consummation of the greatest empire of the world:

"Was"
"Is not"
"Out of the abyss"
"Go into perdition"

The Mystery of the Whore (15-18)

In the waters on which the whore sitteth there may be an impious parody of Jehovah sitting upon the flood. The waters which the Seer saw (verse 1) are explained as typifying "peoples and multitudes, and nations, and tongues." Here we have the immense moral influence of Romanism over vast masses of mankind.

"These shall hate the whore." What abject desolation awaits the Romish Church! Determined to rid himself and his empire of the subtle and impoverishing influences of the harlot, the Beast turns and dismounts her from her exalted seat. The rulers of the federated empire strip the harlot of all her seductive, gaudy ornaments. The combined nations with their masterful head combine in hatred of the whore. The downfall of the great whore comes because of a sudden change in subject peoples. "Rome's greatest danger lay in the multitudes which were under her sway." And as it was when Rome fell, so will it be when Rome is revived! Not only is there loathing and disquiet for the harlot, and plunder of all her wealth and finery, but also her flesh is eaten. Flesh here is in the plural, and signifies masses of flesh, earthly possessions, the fullness of carnality. But the Beast and the ten kings, once the harlot's admirers and slaves, are now her bitterest foes, and gorge themselves on her gathered possessions.

Further, she is burned with fire. In this step of graduated punishment there may be a reference to the legal punishment of abominable fornication. Harlots were sometimes burned.

Who or what the woman is, is revealed in the last verse of this chapter. The unfolding of the mystery of the great whore is given to John: "The woman which thou sawest is that great city which *hath a kingdom* over the kings of the earth" (RV).

Within recent years the Vatican and its area have been proclaimed a kingdom, and the pope is a ruler as well as the titular head of a religious system. Like surrounding kingdoms, Rome has her court to which nations send their ambassadors and envoys. Papacy and Rome cannot be separated. Rome will ever remain the seat and center of the scarlet woman's authority. Strange, is it not, that in those days of terrible destruction from the air, during World War II, sacred shrines in many national centers were destroyed? St. Paul's in London was bombed and partially destroyed, but all during the late war, the Vatican in Rome was carefully preserved. But Rome's day will come, and such a delegate of Satan in religious corruption (16:19), will be forced to endure the hatred of God and man. Thus, the mystic Babylon of chapter 17 is Rome. And that Rome is before us is proved by the mention of the scarlet, color of imperial and papal Rome — by the topographical situation of the seven hills — by the reference to a golden cup, which is traced on medals with the self-condemning inscription — *Sedet super universum** — by the fact that when John wrote, Rome was the mistress of the world — by the fact that the false and corrupt system of Romanism has its capital in Rome.

BABYLON THE QUEEN
Revelation 18:7, 8

In chapters 17 and 18 John reveals the character of Babylon, her relation to the Beast, and to the kings of earth in general, with details of her judgment. In chapter 17, the Seer is awed by the contemplation of Babylon's splendor and guilt. Here, the harlot is Babylon the great. But in chapter 18 she is Babylon the queen — a combination of worldly pride and religious pretension, and in her union with a world at enmity with God, is guilty of whoredom. The language describing the lamentation of the world over her gate is of unparalleled sublimity and pathos. Pride came before destruction for in the midst of her plagues she said, "I sit a queen, and I am no widow" (see Isaiah 47:7, 8). "Degraded from her exalted position by the kings of the Roman world," says Walter Scott, "she yet maintains her pride. Her spirit is unbroken. Her haughtiness is asserted in spite of the fact that she sits in the dust of her former grandeur, and that her final end is at hand." She

* He sits above the universe.

still boasts, "I sit a queen," and with the vain hope that her queenly state and fortunes may be retrieved she exclaims, *I am not a widow*.

THE BRIDE, THE LAMB'S WIFE
Revelation 19:7, 8; 21:2, 9; 22:17

In present day Christian circles much confusion exists as to who or what constitutes the Bride. A year or so ago the writer heard a fundamental believer boast that he would give a thousand dollars to the person proving from Scripture that the church is ever identified as the Bride of Christ. This friend claimed that Israel was the Bride. The church, he argued, could not be the Body and the Bride at the same time.

There are still others, orthodox Christians, who believe that only those in their denomination are the Bride, and that all believers not in their close communion are simply friends of the Bridegroom. Evidently theirs is a spiritual aristocracy none can share unless they are prepared to enter their exclusive entrance into the privileged intimacy such as exists between a bride and her groom.

Israel was certainly espoused to God (note, *God*) and became His wife. Because of her rejection of His Word and will, Israel was abandoned as an *adulterous* wife. Later on she will become Jehovah's restored wife (Isaiah 54:6, 7; 62:4, 5). Those who advocate that Israel is the Bride erroneously teach that "wife" is her earthly title and "bride" her heavenly designation. But a study of the following Scriptures proves that God cast Israel off as a wife, and that it is impossible for Him to marry her as a "virgin" (Jeremiah 3:1-18; Ezekiel 16; Hosea 2; 3:1-5). Jamieson, Fausset and Brown, in their renowned commentary, remark, "On the emblem of the heavenly Bridegroom and Bride cf. Matthew 22:2; 25:6, 10; II Corinthians 11:2. Perfect union with Him personally and participation in His holiness, joy, glory and kingdom are included in this symbol of 'marriage'; cf. Song of Solomon everywhere. Besides the *heavenly* Bride, the transfigured, translated, and risen Church, reigning *over* the earth with Christ, there is also the *earthly* bride, Israel, in the flesh, never yet *divorced*, though for a time separated, from her divine husband, who shall then be reunited to the Lord and be mother Church of the millennial earth, Christianized through her. Note, we ought, as Scripture does, restrict the language drawn from marriage — love to *the Bride*, the Church *as a whole;* not use it as *individuals* in our relation to Christ, as Rome does in the case of her nuns."

The Church as the Bride

The portion in Revelation 19:7-10 describing the marriage scene in which the Bridegroom makes His Bride His wife, is worthy of full consideration. A woman, of course, only becomes a wife on the completion of her marriage to the man to whom she has been engaged or espoused. In this age of Grace, the church is the *affianced Bride* of Christ. At the marriage of the Lamb, she becomes His wedded *wife* (Ephesians 5:22, 23; II Corinthians 11:2).

The joy over such a blessed union will be mutual. It will be Christ's highest occasion of joy when His redeemed church, complete, is by His side forever. Then the completion of this union will also be the source of rejoicing and unending joy.

Evidently the church has to be made ready for this occasion. Now the earthly part of her is not ready. The militant church on earth is not without spot or blemish. But the Judgment Seat of Christ will bring about all necessary readiness, for there all adjustments and rectifications will be executed. Then she can don her beautiful wedding garments, described by John in no uncertain terms — fine linen, bright and pure.

This adornment is described as ,"being given unto her" (19:8). All we have comes from God (see 13:5). But the arraying is a double process. God donates the garments and the Bride must wear them. Fine linen implies that there is no mixture of human merit. The bridal array is white, emblematic of holiness. It is pure, that is, free from all earthly impurity. This adornment is also referred to as "the righteousness of the saints," or, as the RV expresses it, the "righteous acts of the saints." Thus it is clear that we have here, not Christ's imputed and imparted righteousness, which must be ours if we are to be included in the

Bride, but the righteous acts, or works, of the saints themselves (Zechariah 3:4; Luke 15:22). Each saint must have righteousness, not merely be justified, as if he belonged to the Church in the aggregate. The saints together have righteousness. Christ is accounted "The Lord our Righteousness" to each believing one, the robe being made white in the blood of the Lamb. The righteousness of the saint is not inherent but "imputed."

The Church as a City

Among the many marvelous scenes John witnessed was that of "the holy city, new Jerusalem, coming down from God out of heaven, prepared as a bride adorned for her husband" (Revelation 21:2). In verse 9 this glorious city is identified as the Bride, the wife of the Lamb. The glorified church, then, is both a *city* and a *bride*. She is "the city of God" in that she represents the sum of perfected individuals. In her love and unity she is the "Bride."

The Bride and the city are identical, thus the New Jerusalem is to be the home and residence of the Bride. She is to be the prominent center of the city and saved nations are to partake of her blessedness (verse 24). Her brightness is to supply the light they will walk in. Indwelt by her Lord, she will be the medium of blessings to the new earth (see Luke 19:17, 19). The church is to stand out as the most magnificent of all created works.

In the description John gives us of perfect unity, the church's governmental relationship to the Lamb is noted. God's eternal home is to be in the capital city of the new creation. Here is the center of divine presence and the government of all in the universe of God and the Lamb. With each view of the city the Lamb is named and the sevenfold reference (21:9, 14, 22, 23, 27; 22: 1-3) indicates that although Christ delivers up the kingdom of God, He yet shares it with the redeemed.

The Spirit and the Bride

A brief word is all that is necessary on this last glimpse of the church in Holy Writ. "The Spirit and the bride say, Come" or "Come Thou" (Revelation 22:17). The combined call is addressed to Christ to come for His church, not for Israel, although she also will participate in the blessings of His return.

After granting John a panorama of coming events, Christ returns to His church with a final exhortation. "I Jesus have sent mine angel to testify unto you these things in the *churches*" (22:16). But in how many churches is the Book of Revelation testified to? Generally speaking, they are guilty of sinful silence when it comes to this closing book of the Bible.

The church collectively is before us in the "Bride." Then the individual's yearning for Christ's appearing is expressed in the second "Come." "Let him that heareth say, Come." The appeal for the sinner to partake of the water of life is based upon the return of Christ (22:17). Three times over in the chapter we have the promise of Christ to come again, and so the Holy Spirit and all true believers in the church call upon the Lord to fulfill His promise to return. John's reply to Christ expresses the desire of the Bride all down the ages, "Even so, come, Lord Jesus."

Among the similes used of the church we have these three—*The Bride*, in which there is the thought of loving union; *The Body* (Ephesians 1:23; 4:4, 12, 16) implying the idea of a living organism; *The Building* (II Corinthians 6:16; Ephesians 2:21, 22) or *City* (Revelation 21:2; Philippians 3:20, RV) conveying the truth of an ordered unity.

Long ago John Milton, the blind poet, wrote, "Come forth out of Thy royal chamber, O Prince of all the kings of the earth, put on the visible robes of Thy imperial majesty; take up that unlimited sceptre which Thy Almighty Father hath bequeathed Thee. For now the voice of Thy bride calls Thee, and all creation's sight be renewed." It is to be hoped that this meditation has intensified your longing to see the blessed face of the Bridegroom, who, at His coming, will transform all His own into His likeness.

> The Bride eyes not her garment,
>   But her dear Bridegroom's face;
> I will not gaze at glory,
>   But on my King of Grace:
> Not at the crown He giveth,
>   But on His piercèd hand;
> The Lamb is all the glory
>   Of Immanuel's land.

5

The Ideal Woman Among Bible Women

Among the many women whose imperishable records the Bible possesses there are a few who are conspicuous for their chaste and commendable characters. They are examples of womanhood at its best, and as nothing is said of any failure they might have had, it would seem as if theirs was "the white flower of a blameless life." In fact, by way of comparison, the women of the Bible come out better than its men. It is satisfying to find very few despicable female characters portrayed in the pages of Holy Writ. In the last days and death of the Saviour, not one woman among those mentioned, acted in any harsh way, hurtful to Him who was born of a woman. Accustomed as they were to pain and sorrow they wept for Him.

In the "Foreword" of his *Studies of Famous Women*, H. T. Sell remarks that —

The *best* Bible women are well worth the most careful study as they are the acknowledged trail-blazers for the larger freedom of thought and action.

Then in his study of 21 of the most typical women, Dr. Sell considers aspects of their lives and careers which bring out in clear light their important contributions to the present high status, destined to go higher, of womanhood. Of the *worst* Bible women the same writer says that "human nature does not change — save to mark the dangerous shoals, quicksands and rocks of life, where their lives are wrecked, and which still exist as death traps."

No man has ever lived who has had as much experience with women as King Solomon, who "loved many strange women." Having 700 wives, princesses, and 300 concubines, all of whom it would seem were idolaters, we can readily understand how they turned away his heart from God (I Kings 11:1-8). It was because of Solomon's gross adultery and idolatry that the kingdom he had raised to illustrious heights was so tragically rent in twain. Cleaving unto his hundreds of heathen wives in love (none of whom are named, apart from Naamah, mother of Rehoboam), Solomon could be expected to say something about the vices and virtues of women, as he does, particularly in the Book of Proverbs.

The strange women Solomon loved were "foreign" women, or women who were not Israelites. When men of Israel took wives out of lands not their own, they trespassed against the Lord. In Proverbs, however, the strange women Solomon writes about were actually harlots. "The son of a strange [RV 'another'] woman" (Judges 11:1, 12) is parallel to "the son of a harlot." In no other book in the Bible do we find so many references to loose women and grim warnings against any association with them, as in Proverbs (2:16; 5:3, 5, 20; 7:5; 20:16; 23: 27, 33). Solomon knew to his own cost that "the lips of a strange woman drop as an honeycomb, and her mouth is smoother than oil."

Cognizant that woman was bone of Adam's bone and flesh of his flesh (Genesis 2:23), Israel's spiritual leaders always advocated respect for women, and were ready to praise their diligence, piety and qualities, which they valued more highly than their beauty. It is to be regretted that a notorious polygamist like Solomon did not illustrate his own proverb in his own life that, "He who finds a wife, finds a good thing and obtains favour from the Lord" (Proverbs 18:22). Had he found a godly wife out of Israel, and remained the husband of one wife, he would have been more signally favored of the Lord. But because of the multiplicity of wives, his reign ended in tragedy and the forfeiture of divine favor. What a mightier spiritual force Solomon would have been had he had one prudent wife from the Lord! (Proverbs 19:14). It is interesting to trace Solomon's references to women in Proverbs. Having hundreds of women around him he learned a great deal about their influence for good or evil.

A man should always rejoice in the wife of his youth (5:18).

A man should not be enticed by an evil woman's beauty (6:25).

A man should never tamper with his neighbor's wife (6:29).

A man should never waste his substance on a harlot (7:10, 11, 12; 29:3. See Luke 15:30).

Clamorous, foolish women are empty-headed (9:13).

Gracious women retain their honor (11:16).

Lovely women without discretion are like jewels in a swine's snout (11:22).

Wise women build substantial homes (14:1).

Foolish women destroy a home (14:1).

Contentious women are like a continual dropping on a rainy day (19:13; 27:15).

Brawling women are not easy to live with (21:9; 25:24).

Angry women are never good company (21:19).

Adulterous women can be self-righteous (30:20).

Odious women ruin the peace of a home (30:21, 23).

Loose women are like snares and nets (Ecclesiastes 7:26; Proverbs 7:10).

A virtuous woman is a crown to her husband (12:4).

The chapter on a virtuous woman (Proverbs 31) whose price is far above rubies, is a eulogy unsurpassed in classical or religious literature. In the original form it appears in acrostic form to render the portion more easy for committal to memory. Such a method is characteristic of some of the Psalms didactic in character (25; 36; 37; 119). Mystical interpretations of the virtuous woman have been made to signify the law, the church, the Holy Spirit. Here is Dr. Richard Moulton's arrangement of the delineation which Lemuel, king of Massa, gives us of a good wife —

The Virtuous Woman: An Anonymous Acrostic

A. A virtuous woman who can find?
   For her price is above rubies.

B. The heart of her husband trusteth in her.
   And he shall have no lack of gain.

C. She doeth him good and not evil,
   All the days of her life.

D. She seeketh wool and flax,
   And worketh willingly with her hands.

E. She is like the merchant-ship,
   She bringeth her food from afar.

F. She riseth also while it is yet night,
   And giveth meat to her household,
   And their tasks to her maidens.

G. She considereth a field and buyeth it:
   With the fruit of her hands she planteth a vineyard.

H. She girdeth her loins with strength,
   And maketh strong her arms.

I. She perceiveth that her merchandise is profitable;
   Her lamp goeth not out by night.

K. She layeth her hands to the distaff,
   And her hands hold the spindle.

L. She spreadeth out her hand to the poor:
   Yea, she reacheth forth her hands to the needy.

M. She is not afraid of the snow for her household;
   For all her household are clothed with scarlet.

N. She maketh for herself carpets of tapestry;
   Her clothing is fine linen and purple.

O. Her husband is known in the gates,
   When he sitteth among the elders of the land.

P. She maketh linen garments, and selleth them,
   And delivereth girdles unto the merchant.

R. Strength and dignity are her clothing;
   And she laugheth at the time to come.

S. She openeth her mouth with wisdom;
   And the law of kindness is on her tongue.

T. She looketh well to the ways of her household,
   And eateth not the bread of idleness.

U. Her children rise up, and call her blessed;
   Her husband also, and he praiseth her.

W. Many daughters have done virtuously,
   But thou excellest them all.

Y. Favour is deceitful, and beauty is vain:
But a woman that feareth the Lord, she
shall be praised.

Z. Give her of the fruit of her hands;
And let her works praise her in the gates.
— Proverbs 31:10-30

From the above picture of a queen
among women these prominent features of
her character are noticeable and could be
expanded by the preacher or teacher.

1. She is a commendable wife and mother.
2. She lives for her home and family.
3. She is constantly industrious.
4. She is self-disciplined and orderly.
5. She is a sharp business woman.
6. She has good, refined tastes.
7. She manifests the grace of hospitality.
8. She is charitable in time of need.
9. She is virtuous because she is spiritually-
minded.

Some time ago the following excellent
paraphrase of this portion in Proverbs by
William J. Krutza was used in *The Sunday
Times.* We acknowledge our indebtedness
to such a strong, evangelical weekly for the
reappearance of Krutza's most unique treatment.

They Call Her MOTHER

Who can find a virtuous woman? for the
value of her life is beyond monetary calcula-
tions. Her husband has absolute trust in her
so that he has no need of satisfaction from
other women. She will do him good and not
evil all the days of her life.

She keeps his clothing up-to-date, clean and
tidy. She willingly works around the house.
She provides variety at mealtime by wise selection and nutritious and delicious foods. She
gets up early each morning to make his break-
fast and sees that her children also eat properly.

She knows a bargain when she sees one and
is always concerned about the future stability
and supply of her home. The strength of her
character is shown in her attitude toward her
household tasks. She takes pride in a job well
done even if she must work late hours to accomplish it.

She knows how to use a sewing machine
and needle. She has a compassionate heart
and hand toward those who have great needs.
Those in her home especially benefit from her
domestic talents. Her own clothing shows
good taste and modesty. Even her husband is
known by her concern for his wearing apparel.
She often uses her household talents to provide extra income for her family.

She is known as a woman of honorable

character. The humble expression of this character gives her an inner joy.

She is wise in her speech and especially
knows how to say kind words. She is concerned about the interests and problems of all
in her house. She is not a gossip or kaffee-
klatscher. Her children are happy to talk about
her to their friends. Her husband also praises
her to others.

Other women have done great deeds, but
this type of a mother and wife ranks highest.

Popularity is deceitful and glamor is shallow, but a woman who has personal contact
with the holy God, she shall be praised. She
shall receive great satisfaction from her labors
and others shall talk about her good deeds
wherever they go.

Matthew Henry in his comments on Proverbs 31:10-31 says that "this description of
the *virtuous woman* is designed to show
what wives the women should make and
what wives the men should choose. . . . We
have the abridgement of it in the New Testament (I Timothy 2:9, 10; I Peter 3:1-6),
where the duty prescribed to wives agrees
with this description of a good wife." We
heartily agree with Dwight M. Pratt in his
article on "Women" in the *International
Standard Bible Encyclopaedia* that, "Literature contains no finer tribute to the domestic virtues and spiritual qualities of
women than in the beautiful poem dedicated to the gifted mother by King Lem-
muel," who some writers affirm is but another name for King Solomon.

The *Apocrypha* at greater length praises
feminine virtues and beauty as the writer
of Proverbs does.

Happy is the husband of a virtuous wife,
The number of his days is doubled.
A worthy wife is the joy of her husband,
And he passes his years in peace.
The virtuous wife is a good gift;
She shall be given to those who fear the Lord.
Rich or poor, her husband has a joyful heart
And gaiety shines from his face at all times.
Ecclesiasticus 26:1-4

And again from Ecclesiasticus —

Happy is the husband of a virtuous wife,
And her understanding fatteneth his bones.
A silent woman is a gift from the Lord
And a well instructed woman is above worth.
Grace upon grace is a modest wife
And there is no price of a chaste woman.
— 26:17-19

The inner and outer beauty of a good woman is praised thus —

As the sun arising in the highest places of the
    heavens,
So the beauty of a good wife shines in her well-
    ordered home;
As the lamp shining on the holy candlestick,
So is the beauty of a face on a stately figure.
Like golden pillars upon silver bases,
So are elegant feet upon firm heels.
                   — 26:20-22

From the Jewish *Mishnah* we have similar
tributes —

A man owes great respect to his wife, for it
is only through his wife that prosperity comes
to a man.

The death of a good wife is for him who loves
her a misfortune as great as the rain of Jerusalem.

A man should love his wife as himself and
honor her more than himself.

J. R. Green, in his *History of the English
People*, in the section dealing with "The
Puritans" speaks of how the meanest peasant felt himself ennobled as a child of God.
Green cites the portrait of a John Walling-
ton, a turner of Eastcheap, who has left us
this comment of his mother, a London
housewife around A.D. 1600.

She was very loving and obedient to her parents, loving and kind to her husband, very
tender-hearted to her children, loving all that
were godly, much misliking the wicked and
profane. She was a pattern of sobriety unto
many, very seldom seen abroad except at
church; when others recreated themselves at
holidays and others times, she would take her
needle-work, and say, "Here is my recreation."
. . . God had given her a pregnant wit and
an excellent memory. She was very ripe and
perfect in all the stories of the Bible, likewise
in all the stories of the Martyrs, and could
easily turn to them; she was also perfect and
well seen in the English Chronicles and de-
scents of the Kings of England. She lived in
holy wedlock with her husband twenty years,
wanting but four days.

Much as the Puritanism of the sixteenth
century is scorned by many in our age of
loose morals, society today could do worse
than return to some of the Puritan principles, the adoption of which would make
for a better world.

Praising as it does the value and virtues
of noble womanhood, the Bible is not silent
as to its condemnation of a debased womanhood. Judgment against unworthy women
is most severe because of the influence they

exert. Thus: *Amos* vigorously attacks the
dissolute women of Samaria (4:1); *Isaiah*
mocks and threatens the coquettes of Jerusalem (3:16); *Ecclesiasticus* strongly condemns wicked women —

There is no poison worse than the poison of a
    snake,
And there is no wrath greater than the wrath
    of a woman.
I would rather dwell with a lion and a dragon,
Than keep house with a wicked woman . . .
Grief of heart and sorrow is a jealous wife,
And the whip of tongue that tells its grief to
    all the world.
An evil wife is like a yoke of oxen in disaccord;
He that takes hold of her has seized a scorpion.
          — 25:15, 16; 26:6, 7

In this sex-mad twentieth century, when
women, generally, are sacrificing their characteristic femininity and nobility and are
as nicotine-doped as men, it is encouraging
to know that there are those Christian
women—spinsters, wives and mothers—who
strive to keep themselves unspotted from
the world. Books are not written about their
true love, loyalty, sacrifice and uncomplain-
ing days. These precious women are writing their history in the lives of those around
them whom they love and serve. Although
often weary *in* their task — for theirs is no
forty-hour week job — they are never weary
of their task. They spend their lives unknown by the world in the narrow circle of
their home within which they labor unceasingly for God and others, but they will
not lose their reward. God's eye is upon
them as they live out their lives in the orbit
of His will amid all the cares, trials and
sorrows of the home. One day, when the
books are opened, their devotion will be
commended by Him who sees and knows
all. We can apply to them the expressive
verses of Alfred Tennyson on Mary of Bethany in *In Memoriam* —

Her eyes are homes of silent prayer,
    Nor other thought her mind admits
    But, he was dead, and there he sits,
And he that brought him back is there.

Then one deep love doth supersede
    All other, when her ardent gaze
    Roves from the living brother's face
And rests upon the Life indeed.

All subtle thought, all curious fears,
    Borne down by gladness so complete,
    She bows, she bathes the Saviour's feet
With costly spikenard and with tears.

Thrice blest whose lives are faithful prayers,
Whose loves in higher love endure;
What souls possess themselves so pure,
Or is there blessedness like theirs?

In keeping with all we have said regarding the characteristics of "The Ideal Woman," how apropos are the verses of Wordsworth on —

A Perfect Woman

I saw her upon nearer view,
A spirit, yet a woman too!
Her household motions light and free,
And step of virgin liberty;
A countenance in which did meet

Sweet records, promises as sweet;
A creature not too bright or good
For human nature's daily food,
For transient sorrows, simple wiles,
Praise, blame, love, kisses, tears and smiles.

And now I see with eyes serene
The very pulse of the machine;
A being breathing thoughtful breath,
A traveller 'twixt life and death;
The reason firm, the temperate will,
Endurance, foresight, strength and skill;
A perfect woman, nobly planned,
To warn, to comfort and command;
And yet a spirit still, and bright
With something of angelic light.

6

Aids for Women's Groups and Meetings

The design of this chapter is to assist leaders and speakers of women's groups and meetings to make Bible and Christian female characters applicable to women of today. To these weekly gatherings of women come wives, mothers and widows whose lives are shadowed with grief and for whom life has many cares, problems and heartaches. Many among them do not know the Saviour who, as He died, was solicitous about the future welfare of His own mother. For all such, the devotional, fellowship hour spent with kindred spirits is an oasis in the desert. It is also a season presenting the consecrated leader or speaker with magnificent opportunity of imparting spiritual uplift for many a trouble-laden woman.

Because of the heavy responsibilities of home life, and the influence of a woman's influence therein, gatherings for women should be of a bright and inspiring character and calculated to send them back home to live for God amid all their trials and tasks so that they can experience the sentiment expressed by Alfred Tennyson that —

> The path of duty was the way to glory:
> He that ever following her commands,
> On with toil of heart and knees and hands,
> Through the long gorge to the far light has won
> His path upward, and prevailed,
> Shall find the toppling crags of Duty scaled
> Are close upon the shining table-lands
> To which our God Himself is moon and sun!

Most suitable and suggestive literature for leaders of women's groups and mother's meetings has been prepared by the Zondervan Publishing House, Grand Rapids, Michigan. First of all there are the volumes by Al Bryant under the title of *Encyclopedia of Devotional Programs for Women's Groups.* Volume One, for instance, contains completely planned programs on a variety of themes. Then there are the three volumes by Lora Lee Parrot on *Programs for*

Women's Groups and her companion volume on *Missionary Devotional Programs for Women's Groups* containing eighteen programs with the missionary slant. All of these most commendable aids follow a similar pattern of

> Hymns to Sing,
> Scripture to Read,
> Meditation to Preach,
> Prayer to Offer.

With the publishers' gracious permission we herewith include a sample from each of the above programs.

From Al Bryant's most helpful collection we cite the following program for a Thanksgiving Day women's meeting —

GRATITUDE

Preparatory note: When planning this devotional period, prepare slips of paper with the following Biblical quotations. These should be distributed to be read at given intervals: Psalm 92:1; Daniel 6:10; Matthew 26:27; Mark 8:6; John 11:41; I Thessalonians 1:2; Philippians 4:6; II Corinthians 9:15; Colossians 4:2.

Song: "May Jesus Christ Be Praised"

Prayer: We thank Thee for bringing us here to praise Thee, O Father, for Thou art worthy above all others to be praised. Thou hast made us, O God, and hast given us a home on the earth. Thou hast given each one of us a work to do. Thou hast restored us in Thy fellowship and hast given us the blessed privilege of being co-workers with Thee. Instruct us in the art of gratitude. In Jesus' name we pray. Amen.

Scripture: Luke 17:11-18

Devotional Talk: *The Art of Gratitude*

At the time of Jesus' ministry on earth, leper colonies as we know them today were unheard of. Unfortunates suffering from that dread disease dwelt in caves or huts outside the walls of city or village, usually in squalor and misery. Even their shadow must not cross a wayfarer, and the cry that branded them was the one terrifying word, "Unclean!"

One day Jesus and His disciples were on their way to Jerusalem and were traversing the road which was the shortest route from Galilee. It led them through Samaritan territory. Prejudiced Jews often preferred the longer, Trans-Jordan route rather than have any dealings with the Samaritans. But Jesus very often travelled the shorter route. This day as He and His disciples no doubt conversed together while they walked, they were conscious of the hush of the great out-of-doors, with only perhaps the soft pad-pad of passing mules or camels, or perhaps the far-off cry of an eagle. Then suddenly as they neared a Samaritan village a piercing cry rent the air as ten lepers emerged in the distance and the pleading wail met their ears: "Jesus, Master, have mercy on us." It may be that someone had told them that Jesus was coming that way. If only they could reach the road as He passed they might feel the power of His healing. Jesus never refused a plea. When Jesus met them, He gave them a first lesson in faith in the form of an act of obedience: "Go into the village and show yourselves to the priest," was His command. And as they went, the surge of healing within them quickened their pace. The nine sped on to health and liberty; the one, a Samaritan, halted to praise, and with the praise came the desire to retrace his steps to say thank you.

It took time to come back. It always takes time to be grateful. But gratitude is a virtue, for it helps the one who is thanked, and sends unconscious rays of healing into the mind and heart of the one who gives it.

Let us now search God's Word, and in it we will find that here is much to be said about gratitude, and that it is usually linked with petition and praise.

(Ask for the reading of Psalm 92:1.)

The Psalmist knew the value of gratitude and calls it good.

(Ask for the reading of Daniel 6:10.)

It was a trying time for the statesman Daniel. Jealous nobles had formed a conspiracy against him which ended in a decree going out from King Darius that any person in the kingdom who made petition to any god or man save the King would be cast into a den of lions. All eyes were on Daniel, but "when Daniel knew that the writing was signed, he went into his house . . . and prayed, and gave thanks before his God." His petition linked with gratitude proved his key to protection, freedom and honor.

Not only the Old Testament, but the New Testament as well is full of testimonies to the value of gratitude. Let us hear some of them.

(Ask for the reading of Matthew 26:27.)
(Ask for the reading of Mark 8:6.)
(Ask for the reading of John 11:41.)

The whole life of Jesus showed forth gratitude. A thank you to God seemed the natural preliminary to every act. And it was the same grateful spirit that dominated the lives of His followers. Let us hear their testimonies.

(Ask for the reading of I Thessalonians 1:2.)
(Ask for the reading of Philippians 4:6.)
(Ask for the reading of II Corinthians 9:15.)
(Ask for the reading of Colossians 4:2.)

It was once said of an old saint that thanksgiving was the aria which interpreted the harmony of his whole life.

The return of the one grateful leper must have warmed the heart of Jesus, for by his gratitude the leper glorified God the Father. Moreover, the leper's gratitude brought upon himself further blessing when Jesus remarked, "Thy faith hath made thee whole."

Song: "Oh, It Is Wonderful!"

Prayer: Dear Heavenly Father, we pause today in the midst of our busy lives to look up with heartfelt praise and deep gratitude for Thy manifold love toward us. We thank Thee for the wonderful universe in which we live, for life itself with the opportunities it affords. We thank Thee for Thyself -- our Father, for Jesus Thy dear Son who died for us, and for Thy Holy Spirit who guides us. We petition Thee on behalf of those whose hearts are too deep in sorrow, or darkened by sin to be able to praise. May the reflection of Thy love through our lives bring hope and comfort to them, that they too might know the joy of praising Thee. Amen.

—RUBY I. KINGSWOOD

Then from the most popular *Devotional Programs for Women's Groups* we have selected this one on

UNCONSCIOUS RADIATION

Suggested Music:
"Holy Ghost With Light Divine" (Reed)
"Yield Not to Temptation" (Palmer)

Scripture:
Psalm 131

Text:
"Moses wist not that the skin of his face shone as he talked with him" (Exodus 34:29).

Meditation:
The American Medical Association recently gave advice for people caught in an atomic raid. If you see an unusual brilliant flash of light in the sky, you are to immediately fall flat on your face and count slowly to five. If you are able to count to five, you may consider yourself safe from the radiation of an atomic bomb. Radiation can be lethal; but it also can be a blessing Let me explain:

Moses had been on Mount Sinai in conference with God. A great cloud separated him from his waiting people below. Finally as Moses came down the mountain to speak to his followers, they looked upon him and immediately saw a most unusual glow on his countenance. Moses did not realize it for the Scripture says, "Moses wist not that the skin of his face shone as he talked with him" (Exodus 34:29).

Whether we realize it or not, there is a definite radiation through our personalities. We cannot hide a display of the spirit which we have within our hearts.

Abraham Lincoln said that he would hire a man simply on his looks. Someone told Mr. Lincoln that this was not fair since a man was not accountable for his face. However, Lincoln answered, "Any man forty years of age is the maker of his own face." Your face may radiate the goodness, kindness and gentleness within your soul; or it can radiate the hard lines of a soul marred by evil thoughts and acts.

Let me illustrate. Outside Stephen's Gate in the City of Jerusalem, down the hillside only a few yards is a stony area where we are told that Stephen knelt while he was made the first Christian martyr. The mob pelted him with stones until his poor body was black and blue. There were gushes of blood and groans that came forth. While they were stoning this man Stephen, nearby stood a young Hebrew man who held the coats of those who did this awful thing. Everyone of those new groans or new gushes of blood brought joy to this young persecutor, known as Saul of Tarsus. Saul was enthusiastic in persecuting the Christians.

Soon after, he received letters of authority that he might go to Jerusalem and other places to further the acts of persecution. But as Saul was on his way to Damascus he kept thinking about the face of Stephen. Stephen's face shone like that of an angel. Even in his dying moments, he lifted up his face and prayed, "Lay not this sin to their charge" (Acts 7:60). Even though Saul of Tarsus was unmoved by the sermon which Stephen had preached, he could never forget that face which radiated love: Stephen never realized that his face was radiant, that there was an unconscious influence about him that shone out on Saul.

And so we must remember that each of us has a radiation through our personality. If we are filled with the love of Christ and have His spirit in us, it can shine through our lives. What you are is more important than what you do or what you say. For what you are radiates through your eyes and the lines of your face; it cannot be hid.

By discipline we may adhere to the Ten Commandments. However, radiation of a Christlike spirit is not governed by law. It cannot be put on. It comes only when a heart is filled with the love of Christ. It is the greatest single testimony we have, so we must guard it carefully.

Unfortunately, this Christian radiation can be dissolved. You can even lose it and not know it. The Scripture says, "And [Samson] wist not that the Lord was departed from him" (Judges 16:20). Samson was a handsome man who radiated faith and power everywhere he went. But he lost his power when he fell into the ruthless hands of a young temptress. We pick up the story in Judges 16:16, "And it came to pass, when she pressed him daily with her words, and urged him, so that his soul was vexed unto death; That he told her all his heart, and said unto her, There hath not come a razor upon mine head . . . if I be shaven, then my strength will go from me, and I shall become weak, and be like other men.

"And when Delilah saw that he had told her all his heart, she sent for the lords of the Philistines saying, Come up this once, for he hath showed me all his heart. . . . And she made him sleep upon her knees; and she called for a man, and she caused him to shave off the seven locks of his head; and she began to afflict him, and his strength went from him. . . . And he awoke out of his sleep, and said, I will go out as other times before and shake myself. And he wist not that the Lord had departed from him."

The cruel Philistines bound Samson and took him off to Gaza where they gouged out his eyes and made him a slave. He ground the corn and furnished the power in the prison mills.

Many a person who one day had the power of Christ radiating through his personality is today grinding in the mill of Satan because he has allowed the Spirit of Christ to go from him.

Prayer:

We pray, our Heavenly Father, that we may realize the importance of our unconscious influence. Help us to realize our personality radiates what we are inside. May we never, Lord, be filled with bitterness or resentment which would reflect itself in our expressions to others, but keep us filled always with Thy divine love. In Thy Name we pray. Amen.

As a guide to an impressive missionary service for women we have chosen the following from Lora Lee Parrott's book on *Missionary Programs for Women's Groups—*

GOD'S WILL AND OURS

Suggested Music:

"Where Cross the Crowded Ways of Life" (*By Frank Mason North*)

"Work, for the Night Is Coming" (*By Annie L. Coghill*)

Scripture:

"Wherefore seeing we also are compassed about with so great a cloud of witnesses, let us lay aside every weight, and the sin which doth so easily beset us, and let us run with patience the race that is set before us, Looking unto Jesus the author and finisher of our faith; who for the joy that was set before him endured the cross, despising the shame, and is set down at the right hand of the throne of God (Hebrews 12:1, 2).

Poem:

Thy Will

To know Thy will, Lord of the seeking mind,
To learn Thy way for me, Thy purpose kind,
Thy path to follow and Thy guide find —
    For this I pray.

To do Thy will, Lord of the eager soul,
To bring my restlessness 'neath Thy control,
To give Thee, not a part, but all — the whole —
    For this I pray.

To love Thy will, Lord of the ardent heart,
To bid all selfishness, all sloth depart,
To share with gladness all Thou dost and art—
    For this I pray.

          —ALICE M. KYLE

Meditation:

When David Livingstone was 16 years of age, he became obsessed with the dream of being a medical missionary to China. Through his long years of study which prepared him for the practice of medicine, he never forgot that vision.

But after David Livingstone had finished all his preparations and was ready to begin active service abroad, God stepped in to take a hand in weaving his destiny. An opium war had broken out in China which dissolved every dream of working in that land. During the dark days which followed the shattering of this dream for entering China, David Livingstone went to hear Robert Moffat, missionary to Kuraman in

Africa. At a great London church Livingstone heard Moffat tell of seeing the smoke from a thousand villages where missionaries or white men had never been. In one evening a new dream was born in the heart of David Livingstone. He now dreamed of those whiffs of smoke which streaked Africa's jungle skyline, and a passion came over Livingstone to invest his life in that dark land.

In private conversation, Robert Moffat told young David Livingstone, "Do not sit down in lazy contentment. Do not choose an old station. Push on to the vast unoccupied and unknown district to the north. In that direction, on a clear morning I have seen the smoke of a thousand villages. There no missionary has ever been. There, sir, is your field."

Knowing God's will for our lives is an important part of Christian living for each of us. Certainly this story from the experience of David Livingstone should give us new insight into the ways which God uses to direct our paths. Often what seems to be our shattered dream is actually the closed door which God uses to direct our feet in other paths. The Scripture says, "The steps of a good man are ordered by the Lord" (Psalm 37:23).

But knowing God's will is not the problem for missionaries alone. Each of us faces this problem every time a new decision must be made. It is comforting to know that God's Word says, "If any of you lack wisdom, let him ask of God, that giveth to all men liberally . . ." (James 1:5). Besides the reliability of the Scriptures there are three ways in which we may assist ourselves in learning God's will for our lives:

1. We must learn to rely on our best spiritually illuminated judgment, and all the common sense we can muster. Thoughtless decisions and blind stabs in the dark are frustrating but spiritual common sense is like eyesight. The Scripture says, "Wherefore be ye not unwise, but, understanding what the will of the Lord is" (Ephesians 5:17). Also, ". . . for the children of this world are in their generation wiser than the children of light" (Luke 16:8). In seeking God's will for our lives on major decisions, every Christian should learn the significance of seeking counsel from godly pastors, elderly Christians who have proved themselves by their own successful living, and other sources of help which illuminate our own best judgment.

2. We must learn to recognize providential circumstances as coming from God. Although it is difficult, we should learn the lesson that a closed door may be God's will for us as definitely as an open door. Paul had this experience at Troas when it seemed every door which he himself had planned to open was abruptly closed by the inner check of the Holy Spirit. But God had purpose in closing these doors to Paul for in a vision the missionary heard the voice out of Macedonia which eventually took him across the Aegean Sea to be the first preacher of the Gospel in Europe.

3. We often learn God's will by an inner compulsion of His Spirit. Someone suggested that when a thing is right there seems to be a ring from within. Perhaps all of us have experienced times when the checks of the Spirit have directed us away from a dangerous path. If we are going to be directed by this inner compulsion, we must will to do His will. The Scripture says, "Not with eye service as menpleasers; but as the servants of Christ, doing the will of God from the heart" (Ephesians 6:6).

One final consolation is this — that even when we miss God's best will in our lives, He does not forsake us. If God only loved us in times when we were at our best, certainly He would not have sent His Son to die on Calvary nor have planned the free gift of salvation, not conditioned by works. God's plan is one of co-operation between ourselves and Him. And this spirit manifested within ourselves day in and day out is the greatest assurance we can have for trusting God's purposes.

Prayer:

Our Father in Heaven, we pray that Thou wilt help us in all instances to overcome any tendencies to self-pity because of injustice which we have suffered. May we always remember that there shall be no temptation but such as is common to man and that Thou art able to deliver us from every trial and tribulation. Let us not take our blessings for granted and may we always be sympathetic toward those who are less fortunate than ourselves. In Thy Holy name we pray. Amen.

Following a similar plan of service, much of the material we have given in the volume before you can be adapted for women's meetings. Let us cite an example or two from the Bible's world of women. For instance, the story of Ruth could be used under the caption —

RUTH THE GLEANER

Opening Hymn: "O Worship the King"

Invocation: Gracious Father, we praise Thee for another opportunity of gathering ourselves together in the name and merits of Thy beloved Son our Saviour. Prepare our hearts for the further and fuller revelation of Thyself through Thy Word. Because Thou knowest all about our sins, sorrows and circumstances may this hour bring to us the succor and support, the grace and guidance we need. For Jesus' sake. Amen! (The Lord's Prayer could follow with all participating.)

Reading: Ruth 2:1-12

Hymn: "Simply Trusting Every Day"

Message: Use material found under the cameo of RUTH.

Hymn: "Loved With Everlasting Love"

Prayer: Heavenly Father, we do thank Thee because in Thy portrait gallery of women there is one like Ruth who shone only by heart, and who, although she was poor, was yet conspicuous for her domestic affection. May grace be ours to serve Thee devotedly as Ruth came to do! If there be any among us who know Thee not, may the decision Ruth made be theirs — "Thy God shall be my God." Enable us to emulate her noble example in coming to trust under Thy wings. May her God be our God forever and ever! Bless us in the name above every name, even in the peerless name of Jesus. Amen!

HANNAH THE PRAYERFUL

Hymn: "Sweet the Moments, Rich in Blessing"

Invocation: "Heavenly Father, we do thank Thee for Thy goodness in sparing us to meet together again in the name of Thy dear Son, the Lord Jesus Christ. Enable us for the brief hour we have together for mutual worship and fellowship, to remember that Thou art in our midst. We commend to Thee our sisters who are not able to be with us. Break unto them the portion of the children's bread, and bless them as Thou art to bless us. For Christ's sake. Amen!

(Repeat the Lord's Prayer if desired.)

Reading: I Samuel 1:9-19

Message: Use material found under HANNAH.

Hymn: "Father Before Thy Throne, My Soul Would Bow"

Prayer: We thank Thee, O Lord, for revealing Thyself as the God who hears and answers prayer. We have been meditating upon Hannah who waited upon Thee, and who did not wait in vain. By the aid of the Spirit enable us to reflect her reverence and manifest her utter dependence upon Thee. As Thou didst hear her heart's cry and answer her prayer, so bow Thine ear and listen to the desires and longings of each heart before Thee. Teach us how to persist in prayer, and praise Thee. Thou dost grant those petitions in accordance with Thy will. For the sake of Him whose prayers were heard because He feared Thee. Overshadow us as we part and go our separate ways. Amen!

THE GLORY OF MOTHERHOOD
(Mother's Day)

Hymn: "O God Our Help in Ages Past"

Invocation: Gracious Lord, we magnify Thee for all that Thou hast been to Thy saints through succeeding ages. How unfailing Thou hast proved Thyself to be in the lives and experiences of those who trusted in Thee. Today as we think of those to whom we owe our life, and all that we have come to know through their faith and example, especially the love, devotion and sacrifice of our mothers, may our remembrance result in praise and gratitude for all that our mothers have meant to us. Make us conscious of Thy presence as we tarry together, and think not only of the glory and influence of godly motherhood, but also of Thyself who didst create the world's first woman, and who didst give to the world a Saviour who was born of a woman. In His name. Amen!

(If suitable, use "The Lord's Prayer" known as "The Family Prayer.")

Reading: Proverbs 31:10-31

Hymn: "Tell Mother, I'll Be There"

Message: Choose any of the outlines or messages given in Chapter 8 of this volume.

Hymn: "I've Found a Friend, Oh, Such a Friend"

Prayer: We thank Thee, Heavenly Father, because the perfection of noble fatherhood and sacrificial motherhood is found in Thee. Hast Thou not said that as a father pities his children, so Thou dost pity us; and that like as a mother comforts her children, so Thou dost comfort our hearts? We thank Thee for our mothers who, as daughters of the King, were the means of bringing many of us into His palace of Grace. For those of us who have mothers in heaven, prepare us for the glorious reunion above. But for the mothers still with us, may we ever remember our duty toward them. For those who are aged and infirm may there be increasing light for them in the eventide of their life. May Thy favor continue to rest upon them — and upon our hearts! The grace of the Lord Jesus Christ, the love of God, and the fellowship of the Holy Spirit be with you all. Amen!

We trust these guideposts may prove helpful. For speakers who may prefer to work out their own form of message on a Bible character for use in women's groups or meetings, the hints given in Chapter 7 on "How to Prepare a Biographical Study" may be of assistance.

Advantage should also be taken to adapt and apply the lessons women can learn from the faith and witness of noble-hearted and courageous women through the centuries. What a wealth of material in the numerous biographies of female saints and martyrs is at hand for a leader of women to use! A fascinating volume of this order published by Nelson and Sons, in 1882, but long out of print, is *Stories of the Lives of Noble Women.* The object of the eleven biographical sketches making up this book was "to fix upon women who have not been less distinguished by their domestic than by their public virtues; upon women who have been Christians 'faithful to the end,' and patriots firm in their loyalty to their country, as well as upon women illustrious as wives, mothers, daughters or sisters. . . . It is well that these examples should be kept before the eyes of the younger female members of our families; and that they should be encouraged to aspire to a high standard of duty, while not forgetting that their true happiness will always lie with the home circle." W. H. Davenport Adams, author of these stories uses as a preface, the lines of Tennyson —

The woman's cause is man's: they rise or sink
Together, dwarfed or godlike, bond or free;
For she that out of Lethe scales with man
The shining steps of Nature, shares with man
His nights, his days, moves with him to one goal,
Stays all the fair your planet in her hands.
. . . O we will walk this world,
Yoked in all exercise of noble end.

1. *The Steadfastness of Truth* — Story of Anne Askew.

In his *History of England From the Fall of Wolsey,* Froude says of Anne Askew that her name is written among those who serve heaven in their deaths rather than their lives. Perhaps it would have been truer to say that she was faithful in her brutal death at the earthly age of 28 because she strove to be faithful to heaven in life. With thousands of other martyrs the subject of this sketch is numbered among those who —

Have made an offering of their days,
For truth, for heaven, for freedom's sake,
Resigned the bitter cup to take,
And silently, in fearless faith,
Bowing their noble souls to death.

Born in 1520, at Kelsey, Lincolnshire, the second daughter of Sir William Askew, Anne became a young lady of great beauty, gentle manners, warm imagination and poetical ability. While particulars of her early life, education and history have not been preserved, we do know that an unhappy marriage forced upon her by a stern father, resulted in a loveless, cold and dreary home.

During 1525-26, a copy of Tyndale's translation into English, which had just been completed, fell into the hands of Anne, and such was her thirst for the Word that she quickly discerned the falsehood of the doctrines of the Romish Church of which she had been a devout member. Conscious of what would happen if she renounced the creed of papacy, she took the step and identified herself with the Wycliffites. She separated from her ungodly husband, dropped his name of Kyme, and resumed her original name of Anne Askew.

When the day of her martyrdom came the shocking conditions of imprisonment and constant torture had so exhausted her that her foes were compelled to carry her to the place of execution, where Anne was burned to death along with three noble male martyrs. As these burnings drew large crowds, an excited multitude rolled to and fro, like a wind-driven sea to witness a frail, pain-ridden saint die well. Just as the fire was about to be kindled, a pardon from King Henry VIII was handed her, but she refused it, saying: "I came not hither to deny my Lord and Master." The fagots were set ablaze, and Anne Askew, with "an angel's countenance and a smiling face," became another noble martyr to seal her testimony with her life's blood. Before she perished, like the Master she dearly loved, she prayed for her enemies —

Lord, I heartily desire of Thee that Thou wilt of Thy most goodness forgive them that violence which they do, and have done unto me. Open Thou also their blind hearts, that they may hereafter do that thing in Thy sight which is only acceptable before Thee, and to set forth Thy verity aright, without any fantasy of sinful men. So be it, Lord, so be it.

While languishing in the most horrible and dreary solitude of Newgate Prison, she wrote the following poem, so expressive of her faith and hope in God in spite of all she was being made to suffer —

Anne Askew's Prison Song

Like as the armed knight,
  Appointed to the field,
With this world will I fight,
  And faith shall be my shield.

Faith is that weapon strong
  Which will not fail at need:
My foes, therefore, among,
  Therewith will I proceed.

As it is had in strength
  And force of Christ's own way,
It will prevail at length
  Though all the devils say nay.

Faith in the fathers old
  Obtainèd righteousness;
Which make me very bold
  To fear no world's distress.

I now rejoice in heart,
  And hope bids me do so;
For Christ will take my part,
  And ease me of my woe.

Thou say'st, Lord, whoso knock
  To them wilt Thou attend;
Undo, therefore, the lock,
  And Thy strong power send.

More enemies now I have
  Than hairs upon my head;
Let them not me deprave,
  But fight Thou in my stead.

On Thee my care I cast,
  For all their cruel spite;
I set not by their haste,
  For Thou art my delight.

I am not she that list
  My anchor to let fall,
For every drizzling mist,
  My ship substantial.

Not oft use I to write
  In prose, nor yet in rhyme;
Yet I will show one sight
  That I saw in my time.

I saw a royal throne,
  Where Justice should have sit,
But in her stead was one
  Of moody, cruel wit.

Absorbed was righteousness,
  As of the raging flood;
Satan, in his excess,
  Sucked up the guiltless blood.

Then thought I, Jesus, Lord,
  When thou shalt judge us all,
Hard is it to record
  On these men what will fall;

Yet, Lord, I Thee desire
  For that they do to me,
Let them not taste the hire
  Of their iniquity.

In 1539 parliament agreed on six fundamental tenets, papal in character, to be used in the English Church. Failure to comply with these tenets meant death by burning. This Act of Six Articles became known as "the whip with the six strings; a whip which, wherever it fell, drew blood." Anne Askew was one of those who refused to recognize the Articles and became a heretic in the eyes of popery. A clerk from the Court of Chancery, Wadloe by name, and a Roman Catholic, was sent to spy on Anne so that there would be sufficient evidence to imprison her. But Wadloe returned to his superiors with the testimony that she was the most devout woman he had ever known. "At midnight," said he, "she begins to pray, and ceases not for hours, when I and others are addressing ourselves to sleep or to work."

Ultimately, however, through the determined hostility of her own Catholic, estranged husband and the Romish priests, Anne Askew was arrested for having publicly said that she would rather read five lines of the Bible than hear five masses in the chapel. There followed examinations and persecutions as Davenport Adams fully records in his *Story of Anne Askew*. Opportunities to recant and save her life were scorned. Extreme torture was inflicted in order to change her faith, and reveal the names of others like herself whose only crime was to serve and obey God. In an age of horrors, the terrible cruelty she endured upon the rack was deemed unusual. But in spite of brutal inhumanity she steadfastly refused to renounce her faith. To her callous-hearted tormentor she said, "My Lord God, I thank His everlasting goodness, will give me grace to persevere, and I will do so, to the very end."

2. *Hospitality* — The Story of Lady Alicia Lisle.

Here is the record of another admirable lady who was burned to ashes, not because she defied popish doctrines, although she was a pronounced Protestant, but because of her untiring benevolence and generous charity. To be in need was the only passport required to the sympathetic heart of Alicia Lisle, who was born Alicia Beconsaw. The daughter of Sir White Beconsaw, a knight of illustrious lineage and unblemished character, Alicia married the son of Sir William Lisle, of the Isle of Wight. John Lisle was a man of outstanding courage, clear intellect and ambition. He became one of the judges of the High Court of Justice which condemned Charles I. Knighted, it fell to his lot as the President of the Court to sentence royal conspirators. After the restoration of Charles, Sir John Lisle fled to the continent. His home estates were confiscated, and he himself was shot to death on August 21, 1664 as he was entering the Protestant Church at Lausanne. His murder was at the instigation of Henrietta, Duchess of Orleans, daughter of Charles I, in revenge of her father's death.

Left a widow, Lady Alicia Lisle, with her three children, retired to Hampshire, and living in seclusion, devoted herself to acts of charity and munificence. Esteemed even by the Royalists of her country, she had a large heart, protecting Royalists and Cavaliers alike when in distress. When James II, with great cruelty, hunted down the rebels to his reign, two of these unfortunate men, John Hicks, a Protestant minister, and Richard Melthorpe, a lawyer, knowing of Lady Lisle's reputation for hospitality, sought refuge in her ever open home. Had she known that her guests had been connected with the insurrection she would have been guilty of a capital crime. It is questionable, however, whether she knew that the needy men she sheltered were rebels. But the savage and implacable James II had no qualms of conscience about consenting to the cruel and shameful death of such a benevolent lady for so venial and amiable a transgression. When the soldiers broke into her home and condemned her for harboring the king's enemies, Lady Lisle's reply was, "I know nothing of them. I am a stranger to it, that is to the report which you make of them." Searching the house, the soldiers found Melthorpe concealed in a chimney. Lady Lisle was arrested on August 27, 1685 and had the misfortune to be arraigned before that callous monster in British history, the infamous Judge Jeffreys, whose name became the synonym for brutal cruelty and lust of blood.

In spite of her age and infirmities, no respect was shown Lady Lisle by Jeffreys, the cruel-hearted judge, at the tribunal. The jury felt that the noble woman was innocent of the charges leveled against her, and told Jeffreys so. With wrath that became uncontrollable he threatened the jury with dire consequences if they did not bring in a verdict of "guilty." Menaced and brow-beaten, the jury at length, with evident reluctance, yielded to his threats and returned the verdict Jeffreys wanted. Throughout her severe trial Lady Lisle exhibited the courage and composure of a Christian martyr. Her only crime was her fulfillment of the apostolic exhortation about being "given to hospitality." On the day she was sentenced to be burned alive, she remained calm, and on September 2, 1685 met her terrible fate with resignation in the city marketplace at Winchester. Thus was completed the most barbarous murder of a barbarous age at the instigation of one of the most barbarous judges England has ever known. As Lady Lisle was about to die she handed the sheriff a parchment containing her innocence of the crime laid against her, and also of her eternal hope. Sentences from her long statement read —

> My parents instructed me in the fear of God, and I now die of the reformed Protestant religion; that if ever popery should return into this nation it would be a very great and severe judgment; that I die in the expectation of all the pardon of all my sins, and of acceptance with God the Father, by the imputed righteousness of Jesus Christ, He being the end of the law for righteousness to every one that believes. . . . I forgive all the world, and therein all those that have done me wrong.

When Melthorpe came to be executed, he completely cleared Lady Lisle from the crime of which she had been falsely accused, and when William III came to the throne in 1689, he reversed the charge against her. Thus not a shadow rested upon the fair fame of a noble, generous and Christian lady whose remains lie buried in Ellingham Churchyard, Ringwood, Hampshire. Of Lady Alicia Lisle the lines of Donne were so expressively true —

> Courage was cast about her like a dress
> Of solemn comeliness;
> A gathered mind and an untroubled face
> Did give her dangers grace.

3. *The Patience of Genius* — The Story of Charlotte Brontë.

Author Evans opens his last chapter with the paragraph, "Among the women of letters who lend so much lustre to the records of English literature, a foremost place will always be alloted to Charlotte Brontë, the author of *Jane Eyre*. As her life and works have been written about so often, and the latter popularized by stage plays and films, it is not necessary to linger long over Charlotte's story. Her father was the Rev. Patrick Brontë from the County of Down, Ireland; and her mother, Maria, a woman of considerable mental power and much gentleness of disposition. Two daughters, Maria and Elisabeth died in childhood. Charlotte, her brother Patrick, and her sisters Emily and Anne were born in the vicarage at Thornton. Charlotte was only five years old when her mother died in 1821.

Left alone with his family, the bereaved husband, a godly minister, surrounded the motherless children with deep affection, all of whom became bound together with more than average love. They lived within themselves, and for one another. Endowed with more than average ability, the children grew up to appreciate the arts. They read all the books they could procure and between them would try to write plays, poems and romances. Charlotte became conspicuous as the guide, philosopher and friend to the rest. In spite of the frugal life and monotony of Haworth parsonage, Charlotte read widely and cultivated that faculty of close, keen observation and criticism, to which her brilliant novels owe so much of their power. All lovers of the gifted Brontë family are familiar with the many hardships Charlotte and her two sisters, Emily and Anne, endured not only at home but when away from the parsonage earning a meager livelihood as governesses and teachers.

It was the publication of *Jane Eyre*, one of the most powerful works of fiction given to the world, that brought Charlotte universal fame, and because of this great literary achievement and her works that followed, her name will endure as long as English literature itself endures. The death of her revered father, then her brother and sisters left its mark upon Charlotte whose cup of bitterness was full to the brim. Those who knew her as she passed through the furnace of affliction, admired her self-restraint, sublime patience and sweet resignation to the will of God. To look at her calm, intelligent face indicating the control and firmness of a lofty nature and deep faith, the fine description of Wordsworth came to mind of —

> A being breathing thoughtful breath,
> A traveller betwixt life and death;
> The reason firm, the temperate will,
> Endurance, foresight, strength and skill,
> A perfect woman, nobly planned,
> To warn, to comfort, and command;
> And yet a spirit still, and bright,
> With something of angelic light.

It was in the spring of 1853 that Charlotte was united in marriage to a curate at Haworth, the Rev. Nicholls, and after a honeymoon in Ireland returned to Haworth to the quiet of a home life that was unspeakably happy while it lasted. Toward the end of the year Charlotte caught a severe cold which lingered through the winter, and the decline of physical strength alarmed her seeing there was the prospect of coming motherhood. In March, 1854, her end drew near, and she whispered in her husband's ear, "Oh, I am not going to die, am I? God will not separate us, we have been so happy." But, alas, the separation came speedily on Saturday morning, March 31st, and the solemn chime of the bell of Haworth announced that Charlotte Brontë, endowed with "the deep intuitions of a gifted woman, the strength of a man, the patience of a hero, and the conscientiousness of a saint," had entered the realms of eternal bliss. Dead, however, she still speaks through her inspiring and admirable works. The story of her life enables all women who learn the lesson of duty and the nobility of self-sacrifice.

The other *Noble Lives of Women* which Davenport Adams deals with in an absorbing manner are —

The Story of Lady Vere — *Matronly Excellence*

The Story of Elizabeth Gaunt — *The Charity That Endures*

The Story of Elizabeth Inchbald — *Mental Energy and Self-Reliance*

The Story of Lady Arabella Stuart — *Faithful to the End*

The Story of Lady Jane Grey — *Womanly Virtues in an Exalted Position*

The Story of Mary, Countess of Pembroke — *A Noble English Mother*

The Story of Queen Jeanne D'Albert — *A Heroic Life*

The Story of Madame Roland — *Woman the Enthusiast*

While not exactly Biblical studies, the lives of these famous women exhibit many Christian virtues, and their stories can be used with great effect in speaking to women. It will not be found hard to accompany any of these historical sketches, as well as the records of early female martyrs and also ladies among the Scottish Covenanters, with appropriate Scriptures, hymns and prayers.

7

Biographical Study of a Bible Woman

That Scripture female biography ever proves a fascinating and fruitful aspect of meditation, is evident from the fact that books on the women of the Bible abound, as can be seen in the exhaustive Index which Edith Deen cites at the end of her own volume on all the named and nameless women of the Bible. A perusal of some 30 volumes which the writer possesses on such a theme, revealed that the majority of authors deal with 25 to 50 characters at the most, and in the majority of cases, the same women. But as we have already indicated, there are almost 200 named women in the Bible, and almost the same number who are unnamed. Thus the preacher or teacher has a wide field to work when it comes to biographical material.

The Bible revolves around personalities, and is the biography of humanity. Sometimes the biographies of men and women outside the Bible leave us cold. The characters portrayed seem to be too ideal. Theirs are heights we cannot reach. Nothing is said about their faults, weaknesses and sins. But with the Bible it is different for here are men and women of like passions as ourselves; and as Augustine expressed it, "The Sacred Record, like a faithful mirror, has no flattery in its portraits." In an arrestive chapter in his volume on *The Joy of Bible Study,* dealing with "Composite Portraits," Dr. Harrington Lees reminds us that —

> The lives of men and women who speak to us from the pages of Scripture may be a veritable gold-mine of experience to us if we can remember the fact that they lived similar lives, and triumphed by faith, as the writer to the Hebrews reminds us — or, if they entered not into their land of promise, failed through disobedience or unbelief. All good biography is fruitful, but Scripture biography is singularly so.

Endeavoring to deal with any Bible character in a biographical way there are several principles to bear in mind.

First of all, it is essential to gather together all references to the person studied. This can be easily done with the aid of a Bible concordance. For instance, if Eve is taken, the Scriptures in which she is mentioned are Genesis 3: 20; 4:1; II Corinthians 11:3; I Timothy 2:13. If these are written out in full on a slip of paper, and carefully scanned, all pertinent facts concerning the world's first woman can be noted.

Secondly, with all listed passages before you, check elements of power or weakness, success or failure, privileges or limited advantages and disadvantages; mistakes made and perils to be avoided, as well as help and pardon obtained from God. It will be found that the lights and shadows stand out in bold relief. Character and conduct are set forth in no uncertain terms. Angel heights and devil depths are displayed causing one to confess with Carlyle that, "Biography is the only true history."

Thirdly, the gaps must be covered as well as the wealth of detail given. It will be seen that some lives are more fully described than others. Where facts are meager, imagination or history of the times can provide expansion. Not much is said of Lot's wife, but a knowledge of Sodom enables us to understand why she was destroyed as she looked back to Sodom as the family fled from it. She left Sodom as a place, but Sodom was ever in her heart and she was loathe to leave it.

Fourthly, characters may be studied in a variety of ways. One can follow them consecutively, marking how strong yet vulnerable they were. Causes of success and failure can also be traced. Persons can be treated in a typical fashion as Jezebel is when John does so in connection with the church at Thyatira (Revelation 2:20). What one must guard against is the tendency to over-spiritualize a Bible character. As Harrington Lees says in this connection, "It may be overdone, but sanity and spirituality taken for granted, it cannot well be denied that both our Lord and His apostles read the Old Testament, to some extent, in this way. The lives of individuals may be outlined and filled in by holy meditation and wise inference." As demonstration is worth more than description, let us take one or two illustrations of female biography.

Mary of Bethany, who is among the most renowned in God's portrait gallery, comes before us in Mark 14:3-9; Luke 10:39, 42; John 11:1-45; 12:3, all of which references must be carefully examined for a complete cameo of one of the best among Bible women. She belonged to Bethany, a favorite haunt of our Lord. She was a member of a close-knit family, and along with her sister and brother, was loved of the Lord. She was of a deep, meditative frame of mind — devoutly religious with an intuitive insight into the mission of her Lord. She was extravagant in her preparation of Jesus for His death. Dealing with these and other traits in her character, the teacher could use Tennyson's poem which we have quoted at the end of Chapter 5. A dual keynote can be stressed. On the human side Mary was misunderstood, but on the divine side she was at the place of blessing when sitting at the feet of Jesus. Here is an outline combining this double trait —

1. Her misunderstood *stillness*—Luke 10:40 — understanding at Christ's feet — Luke 10:39, 42; Isaiah 60:13.
2. Her misunderstood *search* — John 11:31, 32 — understanding at Christ's feet — John 11:31.
3. Her misunderstood *service* — John 12:2-8 — understanding at Christ's feet — John 12:3, 7, 8.

For a perfect example of how to deal with a female character, we go to *Biblical Character Sketches*, published by James Nisbet and Co., London, in 1896. This rare volume, long out of print, is made up of 13 male characters and 7 female characters of the Bible. Among the latter is a contribution from Dr. F. B. Meyer on Mary Magdalene, which one feels should be recovered for the benefit of Bible lovers today. Here it is in full —

"There is nothing to attract the modern traveller to the site of Magdala save the fragrance of this woman's name. A squalid Arab village looks out from the south of the plain of Gennesaret on the same sapphire lake, with its encircling hills, but the joyous stir of life, the gleam of thickly-populated cities, familiar to her girlish eyes, are gone. How marvellous is the interest with which a human life can invest scenes in which it was nurtured!

"Thither, probably, the Saviour came, in the course of His itineracy of Galilee, and there expelled from her the seven devils, who had held her nature as a gang of pirates might seize a man and employ a vessel which they had torn from its legitimate use. Her case was one of those many unrecorded miracles which are concealed beneath the general statements of the Gospels, as when we are told, 'They brought unto Him all that were sick, and holden with divers diseases and torments, and *possessed with devils*, and He healed them.' The miracles of the Gospels are but a fraction of those which He wrought, as He went about doing good and healing those oppressed with the devil.

"Tradition has been more than usually busy with her name, and has woven many a legend into the simple statements of the Gospels. With the majority of these we have nothing now to do; most of them were dictated by the desire of the enemies of Christ to load His name with contempt.

"There is that, however, which identifies her with Mary of Bethany, the sister of Martha and Lazarus, whom, we are told, Jesus loved. But this is surely in direct collision with the Lord's own statement that she came beforehand to anoint Him for His burying. This interpretation, placed by Jesus on her act of love, indicates that she had a closer sympathy with His intentions, and a deeper insight into his predictions concerning Himself, than any other human being. She probably realized all the tragedy of His death and burial as no one else of the little band which surrounded Him, and she would not have been likely to overlook His express anticipation of resurrection.

"The only other legend to which we need refer is one which has obtained great currency in the Western Church, and has discerned Mary of Magdala in the unnamed woman who anointed Jesus in the earlier days of His ministry at the house of Simon the Pharisee, who wet His feet with her tears and wiped them with her hair. Some color is given to this tradition by the statement that out of Mary Magdalene Christ cast seven demons. Whatever that expression may mean — and there is no reason to dispute its literal accuracy—there had been, not improbably, some collusion between her and those foul spirits, both in disposition and habit, before they had been able to make her nature their home. Such are the barriers that the Creator has reared between us and the evil spirits which haunt even the heavenly places, that they cannot enter us unless we unbar the door and open it from within. And thus we infer from the possession of Mary Magdalene by so foul a crew that she had yielded to the solicitation of sense, had allowed her nature to be swept to unlawful indulgence before the current of unrestrained and unholy passion, and that on the wings of this wild hurricane the spirits of evil had entered her.

"Beneath the influence of Jesus these unhallowed passions had been succeeded by holy love. 'She loved much.' Her tears, her tender ministry to the beloved feet, the shattered box of ointment, all attested the strength and earnestness of her devotion. But, after all, there was a good deal of the merely human element in this. She ministered to His physical needs, waited by His cross keeping watch with Him till He expired, and hurried to anoint the cold, stiffened body with all a woman's tenderness to a reverend and beloved teacher. And Christ sought to lift this love to a higher level, from the human to the divine, from sense to spirit, from earth to heaven. 'Touch me not, for I am not yet ascended.'

"What a gracious development of character awaited that warm-hearted woman, who was destined to pass from passionate gratitude for deliverance, to the 'Rabboni' of the Easter morning, and finally to the reception of the Holy Ghost on the Day of Pentecost! 'These all with one accord continued stedfastly in prayer, *with the women . . .*' 'And they were all filled with the Holy Spirit.'

"There were, therefore, three stages in the development of her character. In the first place, *passion was replaced by love.* These two are too often confused in thought and ordinary talk; but they are essentially distinct — as distinct as the orgies of the groves of Astarte and the shrine of Aphrodite from the courtship of Miles Standish. Passion is always selfish, and brooks no obstacle in the way of personal gratification. It will tear up the very planks out of its home to feed its fires. Love, on the other hand, is full of reverence and respect and consideration. It will suffer the uttermost of pain rather than seek its own at the expense of another. It looks not on its own, but on the interests of the beloved objects of its solicitude. It is strong and self-restrained, and lives with the girded loin.

"Thus these two are mutually destructive. Let passion have its way, and love shows signs of consumption. It pines and withers. It cannot live in the poisonous air, like that which lurks in the tropic jungle or beside the fatal Congo.

"Jesus Christ comes to extinguish the lurid glow of passion. But His work does not stay with this, great and blessed as it is. A mere negation will not save. It is not enough to extinguish the unhallowed fires of passion from the altar by emptying on it barrels of water: a fire is still needed for the sacrifice. And the true Prophet of Heaven must furnish the latter as well as accomplish the former, or He will fail to meet man's most urgent need. Thus the glory of our Master lies in this — He replaces the fires of hell by live coals from heaven's altar. He readjusts us with human relationships. He drives out the pirate crew, and fills the vessel with a heavenly one. Mary not only is delivered from the frenzy of wild passion, but clad in the white robes of stainless purity. 'She loved much.'

"But, in addition to this, *human love was lifted to the divine.* The love of Mary Magdalene to Jesus exhibits all those traits which we are accustomed to associate with woman's love when it reaches its ideal.

"It was so faithful. Men dread to fail in

life, not for themselves so much as for the anguish which it will bring on those that love them. Often a man reasons with himself that to fail will alienate from him precious friends. This is true of some. They are hollow and superficial. Like the nautilus, they swim on the surface in all their glory and beauty in fair weather, but disappear at the first overcasting of the sun. But no man ever lost a true woman's love when he failed. Failure and loss and trouble only bring out a woman's noblest traits, and principally her tenacity of affection, which strong waters cannot drown. So Mary clung to the cross, the grave, the mangled body. 'There was standing by the cross of Jesus . . . Mary Magdalene.' 'Mary Magdalene was there, sitting over against the sepulchre.'

"A woman's love must always find something to do for its beloved. As long as a woman can nurse or minister, or get ointments ready, or come to anoint, she can endure her sorrow. She will put away the thought of what may come afterwards of blankness and despair by her occupation in doing something practical in the present. This saves her from entire collapse. It was this that made Mary so eager to anoint the dear body, and so agonized when it was not where she had left it. To her, that ministry was more than she realized, as a salvation from heart-break.

"And how brave it made her! She was indifferent to the perils of an Eastern city, not a fit place for defenseless woman while it was yet dark. She beheld with steadfast gaze the glorious forms of the angels, that else had filled her with panic. She did not hesitate to assure the gardener that she, lonely and weak, would carry off the body unaided, if only he would show her where it was. Ah, woman's love, what will it not dare and do? The mother for her babe! The wife for the husband! The girl for her lover!

"Of course there was mistake — gross and palpable mistake — mistake that was almost culpable, for He had so often tired to explain each of these scenes, that His friends might not be surprised when they arrived! And yet through all there shines that blessed love, which, like the river in the prophet's vision, has done so much to sweeten the marshes and dead seas of our world.

"Ah, sisters, compete with us if you will in literature and science and business, but never let anything rob you of this marvellous faculty of holy love, the divinest gift of any that lingers amid the wreck and ruin of our fall — like the Virgin's Well amid the ruins of the Roman Forum, as old as Rome, but fresh and beautiful today.

"But this love could not satisfy. It clung to the Man, the Brother, the Flesh, rather than to the Word who had assumed it. Christ loved her too well to be willing to pass over this incompleteness. He is the true Gardener of souls, and when He finds a plant capable of the best He will not let it come short. If the highest ideal can only be realized through the use of the knife, He will not scruple to employ it. And so the sepulchre was vacated, the body was gone; those loving hands must not ever touch Him. Thwarted, frustrated, deprived of its object, the Magdalene's love was first stunned, benumbed, struck dumb with grief, then suddenly it saw

'Gleaming on high, diviner things.'

She reached up towards the risen Christ; addressed Him in her mother-tongue, 'Rabboni'; realized that though He were essentially unchanged, yet she must no longer know Him after the flesh, but enter into a spiritual relationship, which would give her deeper draughts of throne-water higher up the stream, satisfying divine capacities with the divine.

"So still does the Gardener of souls deal with us. He will not let His white flowers trail on the earth, lest they become soiled. He lifts them sunwards on trelliswork, but the process is sorely painful and against nature. The earthly objects to which we had clung are taken away. We cry out. We think we must die. We ask what there is to live for. Then He speaks about His ascension to the Father. Slowly we take in His meaning. We too begin to ascend. We set our affections on things above. We seek the things where He sits at the right hand of God. As time goes slowly, very slowly by, we find that we have gained, not lost. The mould is destroyed, but the casting is left; the scaffolding is taken down, but the house is finished; the earthly and human are gone, but the heavenly and divine are ours for ever. All our love is permitted to entwine around some human object then all suddenly it is removed; but the wrenched tendrils are taken by a man's hand and gently taught to grasp the unseen and eternal. The sap ebbs for a moment, and then begins to return, and pulse and throb with an intenser energy than ever. Such things worketh God oftentimes with men and women.

"But when the training is complete, the gains are great. Mary Magdalene came to anoint the dead; she found the living already anointed of the Holy Ghost. All His garments smelt of aloes and cassia, the perfumes of heaven, with which His Father had made Him glad.

"She came to a Victim; but lo, a Priest, who was on the point of entering the presence of God for her, and all mankind.

"She came to the Vanquished; but a Victor over the principalities and powers of hell stood radiant there, the keys of Hades and the grave hanging at His girdle, the devil bruised beneath His feet.

"She thought she had come to put the final touch to a life of sad and irremediable failure; but she discovered that on that morning a life had been inaugurated which was destined to be endless and incorruptible.

"With what better response could she greet her risen Lord than by the cry, 'Rabboni,' He is Brother, but He is also King? Through the door of service we enter the temple of fellowship. The slaves of Jesus

alone become nobles and friends. To obey is to be His mother, sister, and brother. Then we consort with His brethren and disciples, and wait in prayer and supplication, and tarry expectant in the upper room, until the heavens open, the coronet of flame encircles our brow, we are baptized in the fire of celestial love, whilst the power of the Holy Ghost enters to fill and flood the inner shrine of the spirit.

"When souls are thus baptized, they are proud to become the patron-saints and beacon-lights for other souls as low down as they once were. Do you not think that even if Mary Magdalene never fell so low as the fallen of our streets, that she is proud to be identified with efforts for their deliverance? This is the only light in which we can find comfort from our past sins, that by them we have learned the stepping-stones across the Stygian log, and have learned to point the way for those who are almost in despair."

Biographical study convinces one that Scripture was not given merely to satisfy the intellect, but to enrich one's own life, to quicken the conscience, correct judgment, reinforce the will and direct the feet. Allowing for differences of time and place, the temptations and possibilities coming to Bible women meet the daughters of Eve today. Their God is the God of modern women, who have a spiritual armory Bible saints did not possess. Women on this side of the cross and of Pentecost need not know shame and defeat in life. Christianity has supplied women with a full emancipation.

8

Messages for Mother's Day

An annual celebration of the work and worth of mothers has become both a religious observance and a most profitable commercial occasion particularly in America where this day originated. As it approaches, the stores will be filled with eager shoppers, striving to find something unique, or accustomed gifts and cards and flowers, to bring a quick smile of appreciation to old lips, to light up old eyes. Gifts will be sent to mothers in distant parts.

While we can justify the observance of a Mother's Day on the grounds that the Bible is so full of admonitions regarding motherhood, and of the influence of godly mothers as they endeavor to bring up their children in the fear of the Lord, thereby making a wholesome and substantial contribution to human society, we must guard against the sickly sentimentalism and shallow eulogism and emotionalism frequently characterizing such a day. As the one great commission of the church is the glorification of God and the proclamation of His Word for the salvation and sanctification of souls, the mere eulogy of pure human virtues is outside her message. Extolling human qualities, as humanism does, is to contradict the teaching of the Word regarding the glorification of the flesh.

The aspect that must be stressed on Mother's Day is that God created woman to "multiply and replenish the earth." To mothers, then, is "the privilege of populating God's perfect creation with beings whose hearts were to be in full harmony with the thoughts of God who would in all their activities reflect the glory of their Creator, and who would in perfect bliss and holiness live on forever." Alas, when the first mother yielded to the seductive voice of Satan, motherhood came under the blight of God's curse! Yet immediately after the fall of Eve, there came the first prophecy

and promise of an event which would again hallow motherhood. Through grace, every woman bearing a child can rejoice in the fact that the babe of her heart is a manifestation of divine mercy and privilege. As the result of Calvary, motherhood has been sanctified and through the acceptances of the merits of Christ, the Son of Mary, women can bring into the world those over whom God has yearned from all eternity, and whose salvation He planned.

Further, mothers do not exist solely to satisfy maternal instincts and to have children they can nurse and fondle, but the bringing into the world of eternal entities—males and females — which are to live on for weal or for woe forever and ever.

One of the most magnificent features of God's work of Creation was the power He gave to all creatures and plants to reproduce after their own kind, a fact adverse to the theory of evolution. It was so with our first parents, Adam and Eve, to whom God gave the command, "Be fruitful, and multiply and replenish the earth" (Genesis 1: 28). Parenthood, then, is God's plan for a constantly growing and developing world, and every time a new life is brought into being, God as the Creator, is magnified. In Bible times barrenness was the saddest plight of women, particularly in Old Testament days when any given Jewish woman nursed the hope that she might become the mother of Israel's Messiah. Today an alarming number of marriages are childless both through natural and unnatural reasons. Manufacturers of contraceptive materials, and traders in illegal abortion, are growing rich over the desire of women to remain childless. Yet, it is still true that children are a gracious gift from God, as the psalmist reminds us —

Lo, children are an heritage of the LORD: and the fruit of the womb is his reward. As arrows

291

are in the hand of a mighty man; so are children of the youth. Happy is the man that hath his quiver full of them (Psalm 127:3-5).

True, God uses mothers for the establishment and maintenance of human institutions in government and state, but primarily Christian mothers are for the purpose of sending forth into a sinful world those who will become the salt of the earth and permeate the world with Christian idealism. Mothers are, or were meant to be, the chief soul-molders, character-constructors, God's recruiting agents for the eternal realms of heaven. Both mothers and fathers are richly blessed of the Lord when they can approach the throne of grace praying in true sincerity —

> With joy we bring them, Lord,
> Devoting them to Thee,
> Imploring, that, as we are Thine,
> Thine may our offspring be.

A store, providing suitable gifts for those who love the best, put out this acrostic of Mother —

M is for the million things she gave you.
  (Today's your chance to give something to her.)

O is only that she's growing old.
  (That's what happens to Mother. One never notices it until one day, she's a little old lady.)

T is for the tears she shed to save you.
  (Many's the tear. Don't make her cry today.)

H is for her heart of purest gold.
  (That heart has ever been filled with love for you.)

E is for her eyes, with love-light burning.
  (Have you ever seen them when deep down inside you, they weren't filled with love for you?)

R is right — and right she'll always be.
  (Who dares to say differently?)

For those who do not know the story behind the origin of Mother's Day, now observed by all English speaking peoples, we retell its humble beginning —

That fame often is fleeting—and the memories of most men and women short — has been brought home once more by the pathetic story of Anna M. Jarvis, who is the founder of Mother's Day.

If it hadn't been for the philanthropic spirit of a few Philadelphians who came to her rescue recently, the blind and penniless 83-year old woman would have been doomed to spend the last months of her life alone in a charity hospital.

It was over 60 years ago that Miss Jarvis got the idea of having a day set aside when men and women throughout the nation would pay special honors to their mothers.

Anna Jarvis' own mother, Mrs. Ann Reeves Jarvis, had died on the second Sunday in May, 1905, and that is why this particular Sunday has been designated as Mother's Day. It was first celebrated in a tiny church in Grafton, West Virginia, the town where Anna was born.

Anna Jarvis was 10 at the time and attended the church with her parents and brothers and sisters. At the age of 20 she was graduated from Augusta Female Seminary at Staunton, Virginia, and returned home to teach in the public schools.

She also taught with her mother in the Sunday school of Andrews Methodist Church. During that time her mother laid plans to set aside a day in honor of the mothers of the world but never lived to see her work completed.

Move to Philadelphia

On December 31, 1902, the father died and Mrs. Jarvis and her children moved to Philadelphia to live with a son, Claude. Three years later on May 9, 1905, Mrs. Jarvis died.

In 1907, Miss Jarvis invited some friends to her home in Philadelphia to commemorate the anniversary of her mother's death and announced plans to make Mother's Day a national observance on the second Sunday in May.

Next, Miss Jarvis wrote L. L. Lear, superintendent of Andrews Sunday school, with the suggestion the church celebrate a Mother's Day in honor of her mother.

On Sunday, May 10, 1908, the first Mother's Day church service was held at Andrews Church. Two years later, Governor William E. Glasscock of West Virginia officially proclaimed the first Mother's Day.

Although a sincere devotion and a deep realization of her loss undoubtedly were behind the movement, the real beginning of Mother's Day might be said to go back to the time just after the Civil War when Anna's own mother organized the Union and Confederate mothers of her little community in an effort to get the boys in blue and the boys in gray to be friends again.

Anna carried this memory on.

In those early days in Philadelphia, Anna Jarvis paid out of her own pocket to have carriages take old people and those who were invalids to church on Mother's Day. She bought and gave away hundreds of carnations — the emblem she herself had designated.

There were expensive trips abroad to spread the custom of Mother's Day in Europe. Anna wrote personally to editors, ministers, presidents and even to kings.

Gradually, as she got more and more wrapped up in the thing she'd created she lost contact with most of her friends and her only close companion was Elsa, the blind sister with whom she lived alone in a rambling Philadelphia house. There the two aging women kept the furnishings as they had been during their mother's lifetime.

The years went by and Anna's money dwindled. It was all spent on the cause that seemed to have become her one interest in life.

Claude Jarvis, a bachelor brother and a shrewd business man, thought that he had left both of his sisters well provided for in his will when he died in 1926. But as a result of various legal and technical complications, the Jarvis sisters failed to receive the inheritance the brother had intended for them.

They struggled along as best they could until the day when Anna Jarvis' eyes began to get dim. Finally she was nearly as sightless as her sister. By this time few people remembered that this shriveling little old lady once had been an internationally known figure.

No one paid any heed to the comings or goings of the woman anymore. But the doctor she finally consulted about her eyes was worried after he'd sent her home without hope of ever regaining the full use of her sight.

He asked a welfare worker to go around to find out if Miss Jarvis was getting proper care — not realizing that it was her responsi-

bility to do the caring for someone who was worse off than herself.

There, in a big, chilly house the investigator found a true case of the blind leading the blind. And the two invalid sisters were near starvation when found. Anna Jarvis, the spinster who founded Mother's Day over 60 years ago, seemed doomed to a lonely and penniless old age.

Miss Anna had suffered a nervous collapse and was sent to the city hospital. Elsa was cared for by social service until her death in 1941.

And there the story might have ended with the woman who had devoted so many years of her life to honoring the world's mothers eventually dying alone and friendless.

But word of Miss Jarvis' unhappy situation finally came to a lawyer who had known her from the time when he was a little boy.

He called together the few men and women who still felt a friendly regard for the now helpless old lady and digging down into their own pockets they built up a fund large enough to move her to a luxurious private room in a sanitarium where her every whim would be provided for for the rest of her days.

When word got around about the way these sons and daughters of Philadelphia had rallied to help the founder of Mother's Day other people started sending contributions for her welfare.

Florists from every state in the nation, and from Hawaii, made voluntary gifts of money.

The makers of Mother's Day cards also contributed to the cause.

Some of the money donated was used to erect a memorial to Mother's Day and its founder. So widespread became the observance of Mother's Day that in 1934 the government issued a stamp bearing Whistler's portrait of his mother.

It is indeed appropriate to have a day set aside as one on which we can pay tributes of love and reverence to the mother who brought us into the world and nursed us through childhood and who loves us even unto old age. Mothers are honored because their children are their first thought and care. They are the ones to cheer us in our successes and console us in our defeats. We think of millions of mothers who saw their sons march out to war, many of whom never came back — others returned maimed for life. True, the sacrifice of the boys was great; equally so were the sacrifices, heartaches and tears of mothers left at home to pray and wait. Who can measure the pain of the mother's anxiety as she awaits news of a son or husband when war engulfs the world?

The observer of this day who has a living mother to honor is truly fortunate, for the opportunity still remains to him to speak the word of endearment and appreciation and pride which is the only thing she covets.

The observer of this day who has only the memory of a mother can know the richness and beauty and comfort of it by calling back the memory and cherishing it, which fulfills the faith of the one who gave him life.

Let Mother's Day bring happiness where it can, and let it turn the key of loving remembrance upon the cherished days of the past where that is our only recourse, and we will have observed the day in keeping with its high and lovely purpose.

Yes, we welcome the institution of Mother's Day, but is it not more commendable to remember our mothers every day, and not reserve our roses, gifts and candies for one day in the year? There are many lonely, almost forgotten mothers, finding it hard to make ends meet, whose long days would be considerably brightened if only thoughtless, ungrateful children would remember their obligations to those who gave them life.

As pastors and leaders of women's groups are ever on the lookout for suitable material for messages and programs, we include a few appropriate poems we have gathered by the way. On May 11, 1946, Harry H. Schlacht wrote the following unique poem for *The New York Journal American* entitled "Mother's Day — Honor Her." The last part of Schlacht's moving lyric awaits fulfillment.

MOTHER'S DAY — HONOR HER

Mother.
> It is the sweetest word in the language.
> It is the first word that springs from the heart.
> It is the first word we learn to lisp as we begin life.
> It is the last word we gasp as we depart from life.
> It is the golden cord which binds the earth to heaven.
> It is the love that changes the poorest cottage into a paradise.
> It is the greatest of all loves.
> It is the eternal love.

O wondrous word mother.
> We bow our heads at your shrine.
> We kneel at the altar of sacred memories.
> We venerate your sacred name.
> We are transported upon the wings of imagination back to the scenes of our childhood.
> We recall your tender caresses, your loving embrace, and your sweet lullaby at twilight.
> We hear again your soft voice which once made our infant hearts rejoice.

The songs and poems inspired by the love we hear, the touching eulogies delivered, the flowers we wear in her honor, the trees we plant in her memory, all these are tributes to her sublime influence.
The story is told of an angel that was sent from heaven to return with the three most beautiful things on earth.
As he pursued his mission, he beheld a beautiful rose, that, he thought, he would bring back.

He then saw a baby's smile; that, too, he must bring back.

He looked and looked until he finally saw the sacrifice a mother's love was making for her son, and that, he concluded, was the third.

He proceeded back to heaven, and when he returned, the rose had withered away, the baby's smile had been gone, and nothing remained but a mother's love.

Her love is the nearest approach to divine love that God grants to man.

She walks unafraid into the valley of the shadow and emerges forth with new life.

She showers her tenderest devotion on that bud of life.

She is the keystone to the home.

She is the guiding star of man.

She is the fountain of inspiration that thrills the hearts of men.

She is the true heroine of the war.

Ere the fragile threads which sustain her part, while she can still hear words of honor and praise, and feel the warm embrace of your love, take her to your heart and give her your devotion.

Blessed are the children that can still have the benediction of her fading eyes and the caress of her trembling lips.

For many of us she is a hallowed memory.

Her hands touch us only in our dreams.

There has never been an act of heroism that could compare with the life's work of the humblest mother.

To the soldier who falls on the battlefield, we give bronze and tablet.

But to the MOTHER *it is a battle without glory.*

She wears no medals of a nation.

Her badge is the furrowed lines upon her face.

No bugle sounds taps over her — only the purling of the placid streams, the birds in the air.

Remember mothers.

We will see that never again shall the forces of evil sacrifice your handiwork upon the field of war.

We will see that mothers of every race and clime shall witness their children born in freedom, reared in peace, matured in homes that shall be free.

We shall see America, historic mother of the world's oppressed, lead the way.

We shall see mother's love find its full expression in the world of tomorrow.

We build monuments to generals, admirals and statesmen.

LET US BUILD A MEMORIAL TO MOTHERHOOD IN WASHINGTON — FOR THE GREATEST SOLDIER OF THEM ALL.

Let us dedicate it to:

The uprooting of all causes of war.

The ending of prejudice of race and nation.

The strengthening of all peacemakers.

THAT IS WHAT EVERY MOTHER SEEKS,

THAT IS WHAT EVERY MOTHER SHALL HAVE.

For we know:

"Behind the dim unknown

Standeth God, within the shadows,

Keeping watch over His own."

THE MOTHER

A book unheeded in her lap, she sits with dreaming eyes
And looks from out the window at the distant hills that rise —
Yet soon she crosses all the hills and finds a pathway straight
To where the children clamber on the fence beside the gate;
To where the children hail her with their shouts of wondrous glee,
Yet still the book, unheeded, lies half-open on her knee.

And far from out the window bends the sky in hazy blue,
And she fares forth upon a road that leads the meadows through,
That hurries down the city streets until she finds a door
Which opens to her gentle knock; and then, as oft of yore,
She hears the laughter of her boy, she sorrows when he grieves.
Yet still the book is lying with her hand between the leaves.

And now she goes another way, where mountains touch the sky;
She threads the forest fastness until she draws anigh
The little cottage where her girl has helped to make a home,
Where, in the distance on the sea, are gleams of upflung foam;
And for a while they speak of all the joys that used to be —
Yet still the book, unheeded, lies half-open on her knee.

And so she fares till sunset, she goes far and far away,
But always finds her haven at the ending of the day;
And takes her book and idly at the opened pages peers
With eyes that have the softness that is caused by unshed tears,
And sometimes she will murmur low, and sometimes she will smile,
For out and over all the land her heart has been the while.

— *Wilbur D. Nesbit*

THE WATCHER — MOTHER

She always leaned to watch for us,
  Anxious if we were late,
In winter by the window,
  In summer by the gate.
And though we mocked her tenderly,
  Who had such foolish care,
The long way home would seem more safe
  Because she waited there.

Her thoughts were all so full of us —
  She never could forget!
And so I think that where she is
  She must be watching yet.
Waiting till we come home to her,
  Anxious if we are late —
Watching from heaven's window,
  Leaning from heaven's gate.

— *Margaret Widdemer*

MOTHER FOREVER

If I could live ten thousand years,
  I still would think of Mother,
Remembering her smiles and tears,
  And how we loved each other.

Years cannot dim that vision bright,
  I count my dearest treasure;
They only seem to shed more light
  Upon her worth and measure.

The Christian faith that through her shone
  Is still my inspiration;
The wisdom of her ways I own
  With more appreciation.

If I could live ten thousand years,
  How think you, friend and brother,
Could I forget that dream that cheers
  And oft brings back my Mother?

Beaver, W. Va.   —*Ralph T. Nordlund*

A TRIBUTE TO MOTHERHOOD

God made the streams that gurgle down the purple mountain-side —
He made the gorgeous coloring with which the sunset's dyed.
He made the hills and covered them with glory; and He made
The sparkle on the dewdrop and the flecks of light and shade;
Then knowing all earth needed was a climax for her charms,
He made a little woman with a baby in her arms.
He made the arching rainbow that is thrown across the sky,
He made the blessed flowers that nod and smile as we pass by;
He made the gladsome beauty as she bows with queenly grace,
But sweetest of them all, He made the love light in the face
That bends above a baby, warding off the world's alarms —
That dainty little woman with a baby in her arms.
A soft pink wrap embellished with a vine in silken thread —
A flimsy, snow-white cap upon a downy little head —
A dress 'twould make the winter drift look dusty by its side —
Two cheeks with pure rose-petal tint, two blue eyes wonder wide,
And bending o'er — the mother face imbued with heaven's own charms,
God bless the little woman with a baby in her arms.

— *Author Unknown*

A CHRISTIAN BECAUSE OF MOTHER

Because someone prayed, and to be sure it was Mother.

For I remember in the evening when the fire was burning bright she would call me to her side and say, "Be brave, my boy, and faithful; and never be ashamed of the teaching that you learned in your dear Mother's name."

Though years have gone I can't forget, those words of love I hear them yet,
I see her by the old arm chair, my Mother dear in humble prayer.

But one day the scene changed, and how sad and how strange, too,
Now over there's the old fireplace, and the old arm chair, and there lies Mother's dear little sun bonnet she used to wear.

There's the pictures on the wall and the vases on the mantel, I am sure can see,
That in sweet remembrance Mother gave them to me.

There's the candles and the old lamp, and the rag carpet on the floor,
And over there sits Mother's dear little soft slippers, her tender feet will wear no more.

There's the old spinning wheel, and the balls of yarn you can see,
And Mother's dear old tear-stained Bible that she read so much to me.

It was there we bowed our heads together, as Mother began to call on heaven;
My heart was young, and tender, and true, as the Lord well knew and Mother too.

And as Mother prayed both night and day, those golden threads were mixed with gray,
Then Providence came our way one day that made me sad and sad to say.

I'm standing by your grave, Mother, and the winds are soaring high as the winter stars look dimly down upon your orphan child.

Dark clouds, they wreath along the skies as many a time before, and the moon-
light on the frosty grass looks very pale and cold.

We had a happy home with Mother upon the mountain side,
And the summer birds sang all day long before dear Father died.

And Mother dear, her cheeks grew pale and paler every day
Until at last the angels came and bore her, too, away.

I had a gentle sister then; she is not with me now, but the gloomy shadow of her
     grave lay on my baby brow.
And strangers gather around the old fireplace, upon the old hearth stone.
Oh, Mother, in this cold wide world I'm all alone, alone.

I'm kneeling by your grave, Mother; no human form is near
And the pitiful murmuring of the wind is the only sound I hear.
And I tremble when the old tree sways its branches to and fro,
As I close my eyes and say my prayers you taught my baby lips long ago.

Now I lay me down to sleep, I pray the Lord my soul to keep,
And if I should die before I wake, I pray the Lord my soul to take.

Then Mother would say, as she placed her hand upon my brow,
I thank You, Lord, and good-night, Dear.

— Composed and arranged by the Rev. G. W. Hartman

THE MOTHERS

So linked are all the mothers of the earth,
Though white or black or yellow they may
     be,
Not only through the suffering of birth,
But through the sterner, graver agony
Of world-wide need, of hunger of the soul
And of the body in this crucial hour;
The need of Christ to make a sick world
     whole;
The desperate need of His sustaining power.

O Mothers, on your knees! Prevailing prayer
Is often wrought by women as they pray
For their own sons — it reaches out to share
With other mothers' sons along the way.
Women of earth, within your lifted hands
May lie the sure salvation of all lands.

— Grace Noll Crowell

SO LITTLE AND SO MUCH

Mother, Mother! You remember the
     lunch I took today?
Five little loaves and two dried fish?
     I gave it *all* away!
They gave me back some bread He blessed,
     and some, too, of the fish.
Mother, Mother, all five thousand
     ate all they could wish.

Yes, and there were little children
     and their mothers, too.
Oh, but they had all they wanted,
     I brought some back to you.
No, no, Mother — I'm not crazy,
     they had naught to eat;
One called Andrew told the Master,
     "Here are bread and meat."

In His strong, firm hands He took them,
     (How His face did shine!)
Blessed and broke, and fed them all
     with MY food, Mother, MINE!
I was frightened — all those people!
     Such a little bit!
Mother, Mother, just suppose
     I HAD NOT GIVEN IT!

— Mrs. S. May Wyburn

THE CHRISTIAN HOME
(For Family Week)

The most sacred place on earth
Originated, ordained, and blessed of God
The world's first institution
The cradle of civilization
The child's first university
The most influential of all institutions
Typical of all that is best and most endur-
     ing in civilization

The greatest teachers of all ages have
   sought to magnify it
Men have sacrificed and died for it
Women have toiled and suffered for it
Now the world's greatest need.

Planners of devotional programs for
women's groups may find in the cameos of
the women of the Word we have given,
material that can be profitably used in a
series of messages on female characters. For
the required message for a Mother's Day
program choice can be made from the following which we have taken from our personal file.

GOD AND OUR MOTHERS

Christianity is adverse to the exaltation
of a mere mortal. Extolling purely human
virtues or qualities is contrary to the clear
revelation of Scripture. God alone must
be glorified.

The observance of Mother's Day, however, has Biblical warrant, seeing that the
Bible is full of exhortations regarding the
rightful honor of parents. It is for this
reason that the church does not sanction
"the sickly sentimentalism and shallow emotionalism which so frequently characterizes"
Mother's Day.

Christian mothers are the world's greatest asset. The greatest human influence,
and the most wholesome and substantial
contribution to human society, comes from
our mothers. Joaquin Miller has expressed
it —

   The bravest battle that ever was fought;
   Shall I tell you where and when?
   On the maps of the world you will not find it,
   It was fought by the mothers of men.

Much has been written as to how God
uses mothers physiologically. The marvelous mystery of human propagation causes
us to reverence motherhood. It was God's
purpose to use woman for the populating
of his perfect creation with beings who
would live in full harmony with himself,
but the first mother of the world wrecked
the holy plan of God. Thus, under the
blight of sin's curse, motherhood became
a calamity. In grace, however, God came
to the help of condemned motherhood. At
Calvary, the Son of a mother took upon

Himself the curse pronounced upon woman,
making possible thereby God's original intention of hallowed motherhood.

God's Purpose in Motherhood

God uses mothers for the development of
the soul-life of their children. What a different generation of children we would
have if only all mothers, as they fondle their
babies, could realize that they have brought
into existence "not sublimated animals, not
mere physical organisms which live and
breathe for awhile then pass away, but
through the power of God . . . immortality."
Any child resting on a mother's breast is
"an eternal entity, something that shall
never cease to exist, but live on for weal or
for woe forever and ever."

The influence of mothers is without comparison or competition. The church, nations, governments, society depend upon
our mothers for their stability. Within the
home, mother is the reigning queen. Thus,
when home life is decadent, every phase of
life lacks wholesomeness. D'Aubigne, the
historian, claims that the Reformation was
born in the early years of Martin Luther's
childhood. Behind the monk who shook the
world was the influence of a mother.

   Faith of our mothers, Christian faith,
   In truth beyond our stumbling creeds,
   Still serve the home and save the church,
   And breathe thy spirit through our deeds:
   Faith of our mothers, Christian faith,
   We will be true to thee 'til death.

Yes, we do well to honor mothers, who
are the prime kingdom-builders, chief soul-
moulders, conspicuous character-constructors, and the foremost recruiting agents for
the eternal realms above.

As Mother's Day comes around, it is fitting to express our gratitude and honorable
esteem to the one who gave us birth and
through whose sacrificial love we owe our
place in the world. She it was who cheered
us in our successes and consoled us in our
defeats. Mother is a sacred name, and
children who fail to pay their tribute of
love and reverence to their mother are unworthy of a mother's love.

Perhaps one of the sweetest sentiments
concerning motherhood is the sentence of
Henry W. Longfellow: "Even as Christ died
for us upon the cross, in the last hour in the

unutterable agony of death, he was mindful of his mother, as if to teach us that this holy love should be our last worldly thought."

God offers to comfort us as a divine, eternal mother. Tenderly He draws near and gathers us to His bosom.

> The watchful mother tarries nigh
> Though sleep has closed her infant's eye;
> For should he wake and find her gone,
> She knows she could not bear his moan;
> But I am weaker than a child,
> And Thou art more than mother dear,
> Without Thee, heaven were but a wild,
> Without Thee, earth a desert drear.

THE HOLIEST THING ALIVE

Mother's Day is nationally observed during the month of May. The inspiration and influence of "motherhood" is world-wide. For us sons and daughters it is worthwhile to think for a moment or two about what this means to us. Here, then, is a fresh appreciation of a mother's value.

Although scores of mothers are grateful for the remembrance of their love and sacrifice Mother's Day brings with it, doubtless they would like to have a little more thoughtfulness shown them on the other days of the year. A bouquet of flowers is certainly pleasing when sent to mother, as the nation seeks to remember its mothers, but it may be that the rest of the year witnesses a heartless forgetfulness of the kindly thought mother ought to have.

Volumes could be compiled of all the beautiful things said and written concerning mothers. A loving mother is God's tenderest image in humanity. As Coleridge expressed it,

> A mother is a mother still
> The holiest thing alive.

Washington Irving wrote, "The love of a mother is never exhausted. It never changes — it never tires — it endures through all, in good repute, in bad repute, in the face of the world's condemnation, a mother's love still lives on."

Of the virtue of a good mother, Lowell says,

> Blessing she is, God made her so
> And deeds of weekly holiness
> Fall from her noiseless as the snow.

Amid multitudinous friends a man has only one mother, who in the majority of cases can never be replaced.

Maurice Maeterlinck would have us know that "all mothers are rich when they love their own. There are no poor mothers, no ugly ones, no old ones. Their love is always the most beautiful of the joys. And when they seem most sad it needs but a kiss which they receive or give to turn all their tears into stars in the depth of their eyes."

N. P. Willis has reminded us that "one lamp, thy mother's love, amid the stars shall lift its pure flame, changeless and before the throne of God burn through eternity."

And that mothers are moulders of character is evidenced from the testimony of those who attribute their greatness to a mother's patience, training and love.

Emerson once remarked that "men are what their mothers make them." Phillips Brooks, the renowned preacher, confessed that "the happiest part of my happy life has been my mother and, with God's help, she will be more than ever." John Quincy Adams adds his tribute of praise in the phrase, "All that I am my mother made me."

Charles Lamb believed that at the Judgment Day the Recording Angel will forgive much to him who can say, "I never knew my mother." Blessed is the man whose mother is his first heroine.

What unsung heroism is behind the stories of mothers like Jochebed, the mother of Moses; Hannah, the mother of Samuel; the Shunammite mother; Eunice, the mother of Timothy; Mary, the mother of our Lord; Susannah, the mother of John and Charles Wesley. The great work of D. L. Moody was ushered into being by the prayers of a woman. Almost every notable achievement has come through a woman's fervent prayers.

Once in North Africa there was a mother named Monica who had prayed through the years for her wayward son. Before her son left for Italy she prayed through the night that he might not go, but with the light of morning the ship sailed. Later on the son wrote: "That night I stole away and she was left behind in weeping and prayer. And what, O Lord, was she with so many tears asking of Thee but that Thou wouldst not suffer me to sail? But Thou, in the depth of Thy counsels, knowing the main point of her desire, regardest not what she then asked that Thou mightest accomplish the greater thing for which she was ever imploring Thee." Yet, though long delayed, the mother's prayers were answered. And her boy became Saint Augustine.

Further, what fuller or more charming revelation of God's nature can we find than the description in which God likens Himself to a devoted mother? "As one whom his mother comforteth, so will I comfort you" (Isaiah 66:13). A mother is a ministering angel in times of pain and sorrow. She has the art to comfort better than a man. And this mother love, inexpressibly beautiful and tender, is planted in her breast by the mother heart of God. The mother love of earth, however, is but a pale reflection of the feeling within the heart of God as with unfailing tenderness He comforts the weary, wounded spirit of His child.

What can surpass the love of a noble woman, especially the love of a devoted wife or the self-sacrificing love of a mother! What a power a mother has to live in others, which power is "her gracious prerogative and happiest attribute" and yet her keenest agony! It is the woman who suffers most, and who can hide her feelings more effectively than a man. She it is who struggles against much heartache, bleeding sorrow and even sin, and who in the hour of approaching death strives to arrest the inevitable demon creeping over some loved treasure. And how like God this is! How silently He suffers! How He strives in a thousand ways to avert the eternal doom facing souls, and win them to Himself! The woman may forget her child, but God's promise is that He will never forget His own (Isaiah 49:15, 16).

God offers Himself as a divine, eternal Mother. Tenderly He draws near and gathers us in His bosom and by His very nearness consoles and comforts us. "I will not leave thee comfortless, I will come to thee."

The truth, then, regarding the mother love of God, is that He strives to soothe, relieve, cleanse, emancipate. And what fools we are to cut ourselves adrift from the God who made all mothers and who waits to do far more for us than the best and holiest mother is capable of doing!

THE MOTHERHOOD OF GOD

As one whom his mother comforteth, so will I comfort you (Isaiah 66:13).

In these homely words we have one of the sweetest and tenderest pictures of the character of God. And that revelation is not in the New Testament, but in the Old! In the New Testament, Jesus teaches us to think of God as our Father. But here in the Old Testament, God is likened unto a comforting mother.

The Jews have a sweet saying to the effect that "God could not be everywhere, so He made mothers." And this is true, for a loving mother is God's tenderest image in humanity.

> A mother is a mother still,
> The holiest thing alive.

Mother love on earth, however, is but a pale reflection of the feeling within the heart of God, as with unfailing tenderness He comforts the weary, wounded spirit of His child.

God combines in Himself all the virtues of a perfect character. The best are usually lacking in one or more graces. God possesses them all. Manly virtues and womanly graces meet in Him. All that is best, holiest, sweetest, and most gracious in a noble man, and also in purehearted women, can be found in the Lord, who is the source of all. Male and female created He them, and the characteristic feature of both are resident in His loving heart. He fuses together in His own adorable Person the strong, protective love of the man, and the patient, tender, brooding, comforting, sacrificial love of the woman. John Oxenham expresses this beautifully in his *The Father-Motherhood*:

> Father and mother, Thou
> In Thy full being art —
> Justice with mercy intertwined,
> Judgment exact with love combined,
> Neither complete apart.
> And so we know that when
> Our service is weak and vain,
> The Father-justice would condemn,
> The Mother-love Thy wrath will stem
> And our reprieval gain.

It is the woman who suffers most and who can hide her feelings more effectively than a man. She it is who struggles against much heartache, bleeding sorrow, and even sin, and who in the hour of approaching death strives to arrest the inevitable doom creeping over some loved treasure. And how like God this is who created true motherhood! How silently He suffers, bearing the pain of rejection and desertion! How He strives in a thousand ways to avert the eternal doom facing souls and win them to Himself! Truly, His is a love that will not let us go. Later in this same prophecy, Isaiah again speaks of the manner in which the love of God transcends all human love: "Can a woman forget her sucking child? . . . Yea, they may forget, yet will I not forget thee" (Isaiah 49:15). Doubtless it was this tender verse Robert Burns had in mind as he closed his lament for James, Earl of Glencairn:

> The bridegroom may forget his bride
>   Who made his wedded life yestreen;
> The monarch may forget his crown
>   That on his head an hour has been;
> The mother may forget the child
>   That smiles sae sweetly on her knee,
> But I'll remember thee, Glencairn,
>   And a' that thou has done for me!

A Mother's Presence

Mother is the queen of her home. The house is dull and cold when she is absent. Her presence therein means comfort, joy, help and love. It is worse still to have a heart and home without God. And yet this "God of all comfort" (II Corinthians 1:3, 4) is not so very far away from any one of us. Ever near to soothe and to sympathize, He lifts His troubled child into His everlasting arms, and silently folds around him the deep sense of Himself, and so the heart is comforted.

Of course, this aspect of God's character bids us remember that the very grace we seek from Him depends upon our thoughts of Him and of His care. So many treat Him as a kind of convenience. He is a tower they run to for safety when the storms of life appear. The tragedy is, however, that as soon as the storms blow by, many depart from the tower, and forget God until the storms break afresh.

How different in turning to God as our Mother! And mark, the prophet is not thinking of a little child, but of a grown man heartsore and broken, fleeing back for the comfort of his mother's presence. "As a man whom his mother comforteth, so will I comfort you." Many a man weary and broken by a pitiless world, with things against him, and fortunes ruined, or with dear ones gone, or faith almost giving way, or entangled in the net of sin, has retreated in such dark, lone hours to the mother who gave him being. Many a man has crept back home like a wounded animal and has cast himself upon the mother love that warmed his heart in childhood days.

And here is God, the source of our being, the ancient home to which all belong, offering Himself to us as the divine, eternal Mother.

> The watchful mother tarries nigh
> Though sleep has closed her infant's eye;
> For should he wake, and find her gone,
> She knows she could not bear his moan.
> But I am weaker than a child,
> And Thou art more than mother dear;
> Without Thee, heaven were but a wild;
> Without Thee, earth a desert drear.

A Mother's Counsel

The child's first teacher is his mother. From her lips he receives his earliest and most sacred lessons of God and life and duty. When discouraged, mother's words comfort and inspire. When disobedient, her remonstrance brings penitence. When in doubt, her counsel leads to firm resolve. Think of the young men who, amid the strong temptations of city life, have been encouraged to keep straight by the remembrance of prayers and words they learned at mother's knee!

Yes, and is it not true that to a mother's heart her child never seems to grow up? To her, he is always the child who nestled near to her side. He may pass out into the world and meet honor or disgrace, but in her imagination he is always the little form that clung to her knee and ran to her for comfort, and whose little aches and pains she soothed away.

The grown man, broken in the battle of life or by his own sin, may return to his mother, but it is not the grown man she sees, only her child! Thus it is with God. To Him, we can never be anything else but children — weak, foolish, inexperienced and erring. God comforts as a mother by His gracious words. He utters "comfortable words." He exercises a mother's pity over our sin and folly, makes every allowance for our circumstances, and then, with His own heart, pleads for us. What a pathetic scene that was when, as Jesus watched the retreating forms of those who were unwilling to face the cost of discipleship, He said to His own, "Will ye also go away?" How touching was the reply: "To whom shall we go? Thou hast the words of eternal life."

A Mother's Silence

When in trouble, the mother receives her child without asking many questions. A mother's intuition tells her what is wrong. It is enough for her to know that her child is in distress. She may guess much, and fear more, but comfort is her first consideration. Explanations can wait.

How like the motherhood of God! God does not probe the wound when there is power to heal. How beautifully tender is the mother comfort of God! He asks no questions, utters no reproach, demands no explanation. He has not the scrutiny of a detective, but the sympathy of a devoted parent.

One phase of this silent comfort is what Dr. Carroll calls the mother's "inarticulation." When a child flees to his mother for consolation, with what or how does mother comfort her distressed one? Not with many words which often increase the child's grief. Mother is wiser, and catching up the child bends over him and smothers him with kisses of love. And in the silence, his poignant pain is healed. Silent sympathy is a soothing balm. It was not anything mother said, but simply her own soothing touch and presence that brought relief.

Thus it is with God who with a strange, inarticulate comfort calms the troubled breast. He asks no question, strikes no wounds. We carry to Him our torturing doubt, worldly loss, stab of heart, deep gashes of disappointment, ruin of sin within the soul, and He comforts us with His forgiving presence. What we weep over may remain, yet, in carrying all to the mother-heart of God, we are comforted. We kneel before Him but we cannot see His radiant form; we speak to Him but receive no articulate answer. Yet we leave His presence calmed and consoled as a child folded within the breast in the silence of love.

A Mother's Sympathy

A wise child speaks out all his joys, sorrows and burdens without reserve into that most sacred confessional box, his mother's ear. And the need of a confidant is not only characteristic of childhood: it belongs to us all. This is why those heartbroken men came back from the grave and "went and told Jesus."

But to return to the child. Think of him as he scampers home from school and places his books in mother's hands, finding the chief award for his diligence in mother's approving smile! And, further, it is because of her gift of sympathy that he turns to her in pain and sorrow.

And God offers us the same motherly tenderness and sympathy. He heals, gladdens, sympathizes, loves, cares as no mother could. Does He not give Himself the attractive name of Comforter? Yet is it not strange to think that men will seek for comfort almost anywhere else than in the love of God? Can we not detect the sob of unwanted love in the lament over Jerusalem, where the sympathizing Jesus uses the figure of the mother bird? "O Jerusalem, Jerusalem, . . . how often would I have gathered thy children together, as a hen doth gather her brood under her wings, and ye would not!"

Men try to escape from sorrow by drowning it in drink, in seeking a change of circumstances or surroundings, in harder work, in eager pursuits, in the distractions of sin and pleasure. And all the while God stands open to every sufferer. This truth regarding His motherhood means that He strives to soothe, relieve, cleanse, emancipate. What fools we are to cut ourselves adrift from the God who made all mothers, and who waits to do far more for us than the best and holiest mother is capable of doing!

A Mother's Discipline

When we come to manhood and womanhood, and, it may be, have children of our own, how often we have cause to remember what mother said to us: "But mother *must* punish you"! That surely is the sorest test of mother love. Above everything else, she wants her children to be good men and women when they grow up; and, though it causes her a sore heart, she will not shrink from correcting the willfulness and disobedience of those she loves so dearly. When Moses tried to interpret to the children of Israel the meaning of their trials and wanderings "through that great and terrible wilderness," this is what he said: "Thou shalt also consider in thine heart, that, as a man chasteneth his son, so the LORD thy God chasteneth thee" (Deuteronomy 8:5).

This "chastisement" is not necessarily punishment; at least, it is, as we are learning to say today, "corrective punishment." "My son," says the writer to the Hebrews, in the language of the King James Version, "despise not thou the chastening of the Lord, nor faint when thou art rebuked of him, for whom the Lord loveth he chasteneth. . . . If ye endure chastening, God dealeth with you as with sons" (Hebrews 12: 5-7).

This makes sense of life, for character, life's choicest gift, is not to be won any other way. "We glory in tribulations also," says Paul the Apostle, "knowing that tribulation worketh patience; And patience, experience; and experience, hope; and hope maketh not ashamed; because the love of God is shed abroad in our hearts" (Romans 5:3-5). That is Christian character.

In a troubled chapter in England's checkered history, Samuel Rutherford learned that secret, and Mrs. Cousin captured it in her immortal hymn, *The Sands of Time.*

> With mercy and with judgment
> My web of time He wove,
> And aye the dews of sorrow
> Were lustered by His love;
> I'll bless the hand that guided,
> I'll bless the heart that planned,
> When throned where glory dwelleth
> In Immanuel's land.

SWEET MINISTRY OF MOTHERHOOD

As the month of May brings us our national Mother's Day, it is but fitting that we should pay tribute to our dear mothers who nourished us at their breasts and hushed us to sleep in warm security of their arms.

Many there are, who, as they remember the mothers who gave them birth, have a Mother's Day every day. Tireless love, uttered and voiceless prayers, agony which followed them through their sins and won them back, and the Christlike power of sacrifice are never forgotten. And in honoring their mothers they are giving honor whenever it is due.

The eloquence of saintly motherhood is beautifully expressed in the following unidentified lines —

> Her love outlasts all human love,
> Her faith endures the conquest's hardest test;
> Her grace and patience through a lifetime prove,
> That she's a friend, the noblest and best.

There are two ways in which we can honor our mothers to whom we owe our homes, and whose mother love gave us a glimpse into the heart of God. First of all, we can express our love and gratitude in some tangible way. While, of course, we can never repay mother for her love, sacrifice, tears and patience, we can certainly use an occasion like Mother's Day for cheering her heart. May God have mercy upon you if you have a forgotten mother somewhere in the world!

In the next place, we can resolve to be the men and women our mothers want us to be. Are you a child of many prayers? Has a mother yearned over you and striven to lead you to the feet of the crucified Saviour? As yet, however, her prayers and pleadings have been in vain. What a load it would lift from her loving heart if only you would turn to the Master she dearly loves!

If your beloved mother has journeyed beyond the shadows of earth, rest assured that even in the glory land her heart can be made to rejoice over the tidings of your salvation, carried to her by divine messengers.

> Oh, Mother, when I think of thee,
> 'Tis but a step to Calvary!
> Thy gentle hand upon my brow
> Is leading me to Jesus now.

LEGEND FOR MOTHER'S DAY

Once long ago, so legend tells, there was a mother in a faraway land who had a son in whom, as mothers ever have and ever will, she centered all her dreams and ambitions. Early she determined that this her lad should become a great and splendid person, that he should be successful, that when he became a man his fellow men should look upon him and say, "This was a goodly lad, and now he is a man. How well he has grown and prospered, and what a credit he is to his mother."

But, as some sons ever have and ever will, the boy did not grow as his mother willed he should. True, he was an obedient son, and never did he bring dishonor or shame or reproach upon his mother. He listened quietly but without much enthusiasm to her dreams so lavishly poured out for him and his inspiration, and agreed that he would do his best to justify her faith in him and efforts for him to become the great and successful man she desired. Many a glowing tale did he hear of how such a one had achieved success and grown to greatness because of a mother's will and his own efforts. And he would smile quietly and agree.

And so the boy grew and approached manhood. But often in his growing his mother was assailed by doubts as to how deeply this puzzling son of hers was affected by her ambitions for him. True, he was not a failure, nor would he likely be. But neither was he a glowing success. Quietly smiling and undisturbed, he observed men about him growing in possessions and in stature in the eyes of their fellowmen. Undismayed, he saw his mother's version of success passing him by for lesser men.

Then, because this mother had somewhere in her more wisdom than many mothers, she began slowly to realize that her son might have chosen the better part. Dimly at first, she began to understand that his serenity, his quietness, his way of looking at himself and his fellow men calmly and without envy — that these things might be of more true value than the tangible successes she had so desperately desired for him. Bit by bit there came to her the knowledge that from some unknown, inner source her son had been drawing deepening assurance that the only realities were those that could not be seen, that life was a river and not a pool.

Slow was this realization in coming to her, and difficult to accept. This man her son had become — this quiet, calm being who looked upon the world so clearly — this was not the son she had willed. But because she had in her somewhere more wisdom than many mothers, finally she understood and accepted the truth that her son was doing what all men must do if they are to remain men — fulfilling his own destiny after his own fashion. With this understanding came ultimately the assurance that his success was deeper and higher than any she had ever dreamed for him.

Further suggestive sermonic aids on Bible mothers can be gathered from Chapter 2 of this volume. See under these named mothers: Eve, Sarah, Rebekah, Rachel, Leah, Jochebed, Ruth, Hannah, Bath-sheba, Mary, Elisabeth, Salome, Eunice, Lois. Reference can also be made to mothers in the section on unnamed women.

Our painstaking, yet pleasurable task is completed, and as one bids adieu! to all the women found in God's ancient portrait gallery, it is with a sense of gratitude to Him for giving us so many who shine as bright illustrations of all that is so noble in woman. A goodly company of them "look like a queen in a book." My own life has been enriched through a closer acquaintance with them. Alas, there are those like Delilah the destroyer, and Jezebel the murderess we shall not meet in heaven unless in their last moments they lifted up their hearts in penitence to Him who said, "Whosoever calleth upon the name of the Lord shall be saved."

But what rapture will thrill our soul when in a fairer paradise we gaze upon —

The glorified body of *Eve,* the first woman who ever cast her smile over the lonely path of man.

Sarah, "the mother of the faithful," the central jewel in Abraham's glorified bosom.

Rebekah, crowned with celestial beauty.

Rachel, no longer weeping over her children, but rejoicing in their eternal bliss.

Ruth, her arms full of golden sheaves.

Deborah, standing under the celestial palm-tree.

Jephthah's Daughter, enshrined in glory for her willing sacrifice.

Hannah, bowing before the eternal throne with her famous son, Samuel.

Abigail, the noble-hearted in queenly robes.

The Woman of Shunem, rejoicing in the hospitality of her heavenly mansion.

Esther, bending before the golden rod of the Almighty.

Elisabeth and Mary, blessed above women, engaged in sweet and holy conversation and worshiping Him to whom they were related on earth.

Mary of Bethany, scattering the perfume of love and adoration.

The Elect Lady, with her children around her, lost in wonder as they constantly look upon Him who came as "The Truth."

Bible female saints, and women of all ages who loved the Saviour and ministered unto Him of their substance, will form a large part of the ever-expanding circle of the redeemed and join in the song which the angels cannot sing —

Unto him that loved us and washed us from our sins in his own blood, and hath made us kings and priests unto God and his Father, to him be glory and dominion for ever and ever. Amen!

Bibliography

Adams, W. Davenport, *The Lives of Noble Women* (Nelson and Sons, New York, 1882)

Bailey, Albert E., *Daily Life in Bible Times* (Charles Scribner's Sons, New York, 1943)

Barnes, Albert, *Barnes New Testament Notes* (Kregel Publications, Grand Rapids, 1962)

Batten, J. Rowena, *Women Alive* (Marshall, Morgan & Scott, London, 1965)

Besse, H. T., *God's Heroes and Heroines* (Wesleyan Publishing Association, 1909)

Bowman, W. D., *What Is Your Name?* (Faber and Faber, London, 1932)

Brown, Theron, *Nameless Women of the Bible* (American Tract Society, New York, 1921)

Bullinger, E., *The Companion Bible* (Oxford University Press, New York, n.d.)

Bunyan, John, *Grace Abounding* (Dutton, New York, n.d.)

Burrell, David J., *Paul's Companions* (American Tract Society, New York, 1921)

Chadwick, John White, *Women of the Bible*

Cook, Vallance C., *Queens of the Bible* (Charles H. Kelly, London, 1908)

Corswant, W., *A Dictionary of Bible Life and Times* (Oxford University Press, New York, 1960)

Cruden, Alexander, *Cruden's Complete Concordance* (Zondervan Publishing House, Grand Rapids, 1949)

Davidson, Donald, *It Happened to Them* (Marshall, Morgan & Scott, London, 1965)

Deen, Edith, *All the Women of the Bible* (Harper, New York, 1955)

Ellicott, Charles, *Ellicott's Bible Commentary* (Zondervan Publishing House, Grand Rapids, 1954)

Fairbairn, Patrick, *Fairbairn's Bible Encyclopedia* (Zondervan Publishing House, Grand Rapids, 1957)

Fausset, A. R., *Bible Dictionary* (Zondervan Publishing House, Grand Rapids, 1966)

Green, J. R., *History of the English People* (Harper and Row, New York, 1884)

Hallet, Mary, *Their Names Remain* (Abingdon Press, New York, 1938)

Hasting, James (ed.), *The Dictionary of the Bible* (T. and T. Clark, Edinburgh, 1909)

Henry, Matthew, *Commentary in One Volume* (Zondervan Publishing House, Grand Rapids, 1963)

Jamieson, Fausset and Brown, *Commentary on the Whole Bible* (Zondervan Publishing House, Grand Rapids, 1966)

Kuyper, Abraham, *Women of the Old Testament* (Zondervan Publishing House, Grand Rapids, 1934)

————, *Women of the New Testament* (Zondervan Publishing House, Grand Rapids, 1934)

Lockyer, Herbert, *All the Kings and Queens of the Bible* (Zondervan Publishing House, Grand Rapids, 1961)

————, *The Man Who Changed the World* (Zondervan Publishing House, Grand Rapids, 1966)

Lundholm, Algot Theodore, *Women of the Bible* (Augusta Book Concern Rock Island, Illinois, 1923)

Luther, Martin, *Table Talk* (World Publishing Co., n.d.)

Macartney, Clarence E., *The Woman of Tekoah* (Abingdon Press, New York, n.d.)

Mackay, W. Mackintosh, *Bible Types of Modern Women* (George H. Doran Co., New York, 1920)

Matheson, George, *Representative Women of the Bible* (Hodder & Stoughton, London, 1906)

Moody, D. L. and T. D. Talmage, *Bible Characters* (Zondervan Publishing House, Grand Rapids, n.d.)

Morgan, G. Campbell, *The Minor Prophets* (Revell, Westwood, New Jersey, 1960)

Morton, H. V., *Women of the Bible* (Methuen and Co., London, 1940)

Orr, James (ed.), *The International Standard Bible Encyclopedia* (Eerdman's, Grand Rapids, 1957)

Oxenden, Ashton, *Portraits of the Bible* (Hatchards, London, 1870)

Pfeiffer and Harrison, *The Wycliffe Bible Commentary* (Moody Press, Chicago, 1962)

Price, Eugenia, *God Speaks to Women Today* (Zondervan Publishing House, Grand Rapids, 1964)

Robinson, Thomas, *Scripture Characters* (Longmans, London, 1824)

Scott, Walter, *Exposition of the Revelation of Jesus Christ* (Revell, Westwood, New Jersey, n.d.)

Sell, Henry T., *Studies of Famous Bible Women* (Revell, Westwood, New Jersey, 1925)

Smith, Elsdon E., *The Story of Our Names* (Harper, New York, 1950)

Stevenson, Herbert F., *A Galaxy of Saints* (Marshall, Morgan & Scott, London, 1957)

Tatford, F. A., *The Climax of the Ages*

Tenney, Merrill C., *Zondervan's Pictorial Bible Dictionary* (Zondervan Publishing House, Grand Rapids, 1963)

Van Deursen, A., *Illustrated Dictionary of Bible Manners and Customs* (Marshall, Morgan & Scott, London, 1958)

Wharton, Morton Byran, *Famous Women of the Bible* (W. Blessing Co., Chicago, 1889)

Whyte, Alexander, *Bible Characters* (Zondervan Publishing House, Grand Rapids, 1952)

Wilkinson, W. F., *Personal Names of the Bible* (Alexander Straham, New York, 1866)

Williams, Isaac, *Female Characters of Holy Scriptures* (Rivingtons, London, 1859)

Young, Dinsdale T., *Neglected People of the Bible* (Hodder & Stoughton, London, 1901)

Young, *Young's Analytical Concordance* (Religious Tract Society, London, n.d.)

Topical Index

A

Aahames I, 178
Aaron, 39, 50, 51, 80, 111, 112, 114, 115, 168, 179
Abdon, 185
Abel, 58, 59, 87, 171, 172
Abi, 22
Abia (Abiah), 22, 23
Abiathar, 162
Abiezer, 64
Abigail, 23-25, 26, 29, 190, 194, 306
Abigail's Five Damsels, 190
Abihail, 26, 53
Abijah, 22, 26, 86, 161, 164, 201
Abimelech, 136, 157, 181, 182
Abinoam, 41
Abishag, 26, 36, 205
Abishai, 167
Abishalom, 86
Abishur, 26
Abital, 26, 27
Abitub, 70
Abner, 110, 143, 191
Abraham, 61-65, 70, 81, 82, 134-136, 138, 140, 155-160, 171, 175, 184, 199, 212, 222, 233, 235, 247
Abraham, Afflicted Daughter of, 233-235
Absalom, 29, 86, 163, 164, 194-196
Achan, 153
Achsah, 27
Adah, 15, 27, 28, 34, 116, 168
Adaiah, 28, 71
Adam, 13, 15, 28, 55-60, 152, 171-174, 270, 291
Adams, John Quincy, 300
Adams, W. H. Davenport, 281, 283, 285
Addison, Joseph, 199
Adonijah, 26, 36, 64
Adriel, 108
Aged and Young Women, 256, 257
Agrippa, 37, 49, 69, 150
Agubah, 68
Ahab, 32, 33, 69, 73-77, 152, 204
Ahasuerus, 52, 53, 165-167
Ahaz, 22, 215
Ahaziah, 32, 33, 72, 75, 167
Ahijah, 201
Ahimaaz, 28, 34, 196
Ahinoam, 28, 29, 109, 163
Ahithophel, 34, 195
Ahlai, 29
Ahola, 29
Aholibah (Aholiab), 29, 180
Aholibamah, 29, 81

Aiah (Ajah), 142
Aids for Women's Groups and Meetings, 275-285
Alexander, 245
Alexander, J. D., 244
Alexander the Great, 36, 37, 255
All the Kings and Queens of the Bible, 199
All the Men of the Bible, 7
All the Miracles of the Bible, 205
All the Parables of the Bible, 252, 253
All the Women of the Bible, 7, 259
Alphabetical Exposition of Named Bible Women, 21-169
Alphaeus, 92
Alyattes, 165
Amalek, 164
Amasa, 26
Amaziah, 71, 72
Ammiah, 34
Ammiel, 34
Amminadab, 51
Ammon, 183
Amnon, 29, 163, 164, 194, 195
Amon, 71, 108
Amos, 273
Amoz, 215
Amram, 78, 111
Anah, 29
Ananias, 152-155
Andrew, 125, 220
Anna, 14, 29-31, 47, 120
Anne Askew's Prison Song, 282
Antigonus, 37
Antiochus Theus, 218
Antiquities, 111
Antony, Mark, 73
Apollos, 124, 125
Apphia, 31
Aquila, 122-125
Archippus, 31
Ardon, 34
Aristobulus, 68, 150, 220
Armoni, 142
Arphaxad, 174
Artaxerxes, 165, 213
Artaxerxes' Queen, 213
Artemis, 255
Asa, 34, 86
Asahel, 167
Asenath, 31, 32
Asher, 30, 31, 160, 162, 168
Asherah, 248, 251
Ashtaroth, 248, 255
Ashur, 22, 67, 116
Askew, Anne, 281-283
Askew, Sir William, 281-283

Atarah, 32
Athaliah, 32, 33, 71, 75, 139
Attai, 29, 212
Augustine, St., 55, 94, 97, 98, 155, 192, 193, 214, 301
Augustus, Emperor, 227
Aulus, Plautius, 38
Azariah, 71
Aziz, King, 48
Azubah, 33, 34, 72

B

Baara, 34, 69
Bailey, Albert E., 18
Balaam, 181
Balak, 168
Balkis, 198
Barak, 29, 41, 70
Barnabas, 107, 153, 154, 220
Bartimaeus, 225, 226
Barzillai, 213
Barzillai's Daughters, 213
Bashemath (Basemeth, Basmath), 28, 34, 81
Bathsheba, 26, 34-36, 131, 195, 305
Bath Shua, 34
Beconsaw, Alicia, 283
Beconsaw, Sir White, 283
Beeri, 29, 81
Begbie, Harold, 230
Belshazzar, 217, 218
Belshazzar's Mother, 217, 218
Ben-abinadab, 164
Benaiah, 26
Ben-ammi, 176
Bengel, 42, 105, 257
Benhadad, 211, 212
Benjamin, 69, 86, 126, 127, 130, 193
Benoni, 130
Berenice, 218
Bernice, 36, 37, 48, 49
Beth-laharoi, 63
Bethuel, 111, 126, 135
Bezaleel, 67, 180, 198
Bible Characters, 75
Bible Types of Modern Women, 7, 22
Biblical Character Sketches, 287
Bickersteth, E. H., 174
Bilhah, 37
Biographical Study of a Bible Woman, 286-290
Bithiah, 37, 38, 72
Blunt, A. W. F., 37
Boaz, 118, 130, 147-149
Book of Common Prayer, The, 140
Bronte, Anne, 284
Bronte, Charlotte, 284, 285

Bronte, Emily, 284
Bronte, Rev. Patrick, 284
Brooks, Phillips, 300
Brown, Theron, 179, 193, 206, 209, 218, 222
Browning, Elizabeth Barrett, 25
Bryant, Al, 275
Bullinger, Dr. E., 28, 165
Bulwer, 111
Bunyan, John, 103
Burns, Robert, 302
Byron, Lord, 52, 185, 190

C

Caesar, Julius, 73, 265
Caiaphas, 226
Cain, 15, 28, 58, 59, 87, 115, 171-173
Cain's Wife, 171, 172
Cainan, 172
Cainan's Daughters, 172
Caius, 159
Cairo Museum, 18
Caleb, 27, 34, 51, 52, 73, 86, 115
Caligula, 69, 264
Calvin, John, 60, 214
Camden, William, 21
Candace, 38
Canterbury, Archbishop of, 264
Careless Women, 250
Carlyle, Thomas, 286
Carroll, Dr., 303
Cato, 78
Certain Woman's Message, A, 233
Chadwick, John White, 59
Charles I, 283
Chaucer, Geoffrey, 20
Claudius, 264
Chileab, 25, 190
Chilion, 116, 117, 119, 145
Chloe, 38
Christian Because of Mother, A, 297, 298
Christian Home, The, 298, 299
Christian Victory, 249
Chrysostom, 85, 94
Chuza, 78
Claelia, 185
Claudia, 38, 227
Claudia Procula, 226, 227
Claudius, 122, 123
Cleopatra, 14, 73, 76, 218
Cleophas, 102
Climax of the Ages, The, 218
Coe, Edward B., 73
Coghill, Annie L., 278
Cogidubnus, 38
Coleridge, Samuel, 300
Cornelia, 159
Corrupted Daughter of Women, 252
Countess of Huntingdon, 159
Cousin, Anne Ross, 304
Cowper, William, 20

Cozbi, 38, 39
Crichton, Dr. James, 64
Cromwell, Oliver, 42
Crowell, Grace Noll, 298
Cruden's Concordance, 29, 52, 92, 122, 150
Cyrus, 161, 178, 251

D

Daily Life in Bible Times, 18
D'Albert, Queen Jeanne, 285
Damaris, 39
Damaspia, 213
Dan, 37, 161
Daniel, 217, 218, 252, 276
Dante, Alighieri, 103
Darius, King, 276
D'Aubigne, 299
Daughter of Sion, 254
Daughters as Corner Stones, 248, 249
Daughters of Jerusalem, 235
Daughters of Men, 173, 174
Daughters of the Philistines, 193
David, King, 8, 15, 23-29, 34-36, 50, 64, 71, 73, 86, 92, 104, 108-111, 130, 134, 143, 144, 148, 163, 164, 167, 182, 190, 194-198, 213, 248, 251, 254
David, Ten Concubines of, 195, 196
Davidson, Donald, 50, 56, 94, 99, 128, 143
Deborah, 13, 14, 39-42, 70, 71, 181, 215, 305
Deen, Edith, 7, 33, 76, 167, 259, 286
Delilah, 22, 42-45, 116, 187, 305
de Medici, Catherine, 75
Demetrius, 255
Demon-Possessed Damsel, 242-244
Denny, James, 245
Descent of the Cross, The, 102
Deutsch, 235
Diana of the Ephesians, 255
Diblaim, 60
Dibri, 161
Dido, Queen, 29, 64
Dinah, 45, 46, 83, 178
Dionysius, 39
Domitian, 264
Donne, John, 284
Dorcas, 46-48, 180, 219
Dreams of Fair Women, 185
Drumah, 181
Drusilla, 37, 48-50

E

Eber, 174
Eddy, Mary Baker, 252, 260
Edna, 14
Eglah, 50

Eleazar, 39, 51, 179
Elect Lady, 257-259, 306
Eli, 66, 67, 189
Eliab, 26
Eliam, 34
Eliezer, 135, 136, 140, 168, 179
Elihu, 19
Elijah, 69, 74-76, 192, 201-204, 229, 248
Elimelech, 116, 119, 145, 147, 148
Eliot, George, 114, 170
Eliphaz, 28, 164
Elisabeth, 50, 51, 92, 94, 122, 186, 219, 305, 306
Elisha, 204-210, 229
Elisha, Mother of, 204
Elisheba, 51
Elizabeth II, Queen, 51
Elkanah, 15, 64-67, 120, 189
Elkanah, Daughters of, 189
Ellicott, Charles J., 23, 24, 77, 127, 154, 172, 178, 189, 195, 200, 204, 207, 224, 252, 258, 259, 260
Elnathan, 118
Elon, 28, 29, 34
Elpaal, 70
Emerson, Ralph Waldo, 300
Encyclopedia of Devotional Programs for Women's Groups, 275, 277
Enoch, 134, 171, 172, 173
Enoch's Daughters, 172, 173
Enos's Daughters, 172
Ephah, 51
Ephraim, 32, 161
Ephrath, 51, 52
Ephron, 119
Er, 162
Erostratus, 255
Esau, 28, 29, 34, 39, 81, 86, 87, 128, 135, 137-140, 156, 164
Esther, 13, 14, 26, 52-54, 61, 165-167
Etam, 67
Ethbaal, 73, 75, 201
Ethiopian Wife of Moses, 181
Ethnan, 67
Eunice, 36, 54, 55, 83, 300, 305
Euodia(s), 55, 85, 162, 219
Eusebius, Bishop, 222
Eve, 13, 15, 18, 22, 28, 55-60, 152, 157, 171, 172, 174, 230, 286, 291, 305
Eve, 51
Ezekiel, 18, 164, 215, 217
Ezekiel's Mother, 217
Ezra, 58, 115, 119, 213
Ezra, Aben, 126

F

Famous Women of the Bible, 40
Farrar, Dean, 61, 257
Father-Motherhood, The, 301

Scriptural Index

ZONDERVAN®